Handbook of Stemmatology

History, Methodology, Digital Approaches

Edited by
Philipp Roelli

DE GRUYTER

Publiziert mit Unterstützung des Schweizerischen Nationalfonds zur Förderung
der wissenschaftlichen Forschung

ISBN 978-3-11-155143-2
ISBN 978-3-11-067417-0 (Hardcover)
e-ISBN (PDF) 978-3-11-068438-4
e-ISBN (EPUB) 978-3-11-068439-1
https://doi.org/10.1515/9783110684384

This work is licensed under the Creative Commons Attribution 4.0 International Licence (CC BY 4.0).
For details go to https://creativecommons.org/licenses/by/4.0/

Library of Congress Control Number: 2020939075

Bibliographic information published by the Deutsche Nationalbibliothek
The Deutsche Nationalbibliothek lists this publication in the Deutsche Nationalbibliografie; detailed bibliographic data are available on the Internet at http://dnb.dnb.de.

© 2024 Philipp Roelli, published by Walter de Gruyter GmbH, Berlin/Boston
Cover: The graphic on the cover is a stylometric plot of the contributions in this book, illustrating the vocabulary and style used by its authors. The groupings hint at the extent to which the topics in the book are shared between the authors across their respective fields. The plot was generated by the editor of the book with the R package *stylo* (cf. *The R Journal* 2016, vol. 8:1) using the distribution of the 500 most common words in the book. The resulting tree (Cosine Delta distance) was subsequently retouched with FigTree and Inkscape, thereby assigning one colour per chapter.

This volume is text- and page-identical with the hardback published in 2020.

Typesetting: Meta Systems Publishing & Printservices GmbH, Wustermark
Printing and Binding: CPI books GmbH, Leck

www.degruyter.com

Contents

Introduction (Philipp Roelli) —— 1

1 **Textual traditions** —— 9
Elisabet Göransson (Ed.)
   1.1   Literacy and literature since Antiquity (Gerd V. M. Haverling) —— 11
   1.2   Transmission of texts (Sinéad O'Sullivan) —— 15
   1.3   Book production and collection (Outi Merisalo) —— 24
   1.4   Textual traditions and early prints (Iolanda Ventura) —— 32
   1.5   Palaeography, codicology, and stemmatology (Peter A. Stokes) —— 46

2 **The genealogical method** —— 57
Odd Einar Haugen (Ed.)
   2.1   Background and early developments (Gerd V. M. Haverling) —— 59
   2.2   Principles and practice (Paolo Chiesa) —— 74
   2.3   Criticism and controversy (Giovanni Palumbo) —— 88
   2.4   Neo-Lachmannism: A new synthesis? (Paolo Trovato) —— 109

3 **Towards the construction of a stemma** —— 139
Marina Buzzoni (Ed.)
   3.1   Heuristics of witnesses (Gabriel Viehhauser) —— 140
   3.2   Indirect tradition (Caroline Macé) —— 148
   3.3   Transcription and collation (Tara Andrews) —— 160
   3.4   Data representation (Joris van Zundert) —— 175

4 **The stemma** —— 208
Tara Andrews (Ed.)
   4.1   Definition of stemma and archetype (Philipp Roelli) —— 209
   4.2   The stemma as a computational model (Armin Hoenen) —— 226
   4.3   A typology of variation and error (Aidan Conti) —— 242
   4.4   Dealing with open textual traditions (Tuomas Heikkilä) —— 254
   4.5   The stemma as a historical tool (Caroline Macé) —— 272

5 **Computational methods and tools** —— 292
Joris van Zundert (Ed.)
   5.1   History of computer-assisted stemmatology (Armin Hoenen) —— 294
   5.2   Terminology and methods (Sara Manafzadeh, Yannick M. Staedler) —— 303
   5.3   Computational construction of trees (Teemu Roos) —— 315

         5.4   Software tools (Armin Hoenen) —— 327
         5.5   Criticisms of digital methods (Jean-Baptiste Guillaumin) —— 339

6   Editions —— 357
     Aidan Conti (Ed.)
         6.1   Types of editions (Odd Einar Haugen) —— 359
         6.2   Text-critical analysis (Marina Buzzoni) —— 380
         6.3   Representing the critical text (Franz Fischer) —— 405
         6.4   Publication of digitally prepared editions (Tara Andrews) —— 427

7   Philological practices —— 437
     Caroline Macé (Ed.)
         7.1   The New Testament (Christian-Bernard Amphoux) —— 440
         7.2   Classical Greek (Heinz-Günther Nesselrath) —— 451
         7.3   Mediaeval Romance Philology (Frédéric Duval) —— 456
         7.4   Mediaeval German (Ralf Plate) —— 466
         7.5   Ethiopic (Alessandro Bausi) —— 479
         7.6   Hebrew (Chaim Milikowsky) —— 493
         7.7   Chinese (Christopher Nugent) —— 501
         7.8   Early modern printed texts (Iolanda Ventura) —— 512
         7.9   Genetic maps in modern philology (Dirk van Hulle) —— 524

8   Evolutionary models in other disciplines —— 534
     Armin Hoenen (Ed.)
         8.1   Phylogenetics (Heather Windram, Christopher Howe) —— 537
         8.2   Linguistics (Dieter Bachmann) —— 548
         8.3   Anthropology (Jamshid Tehrani) —— 568
         8.4   Musicology (Cristina Urchueguía) —— 576

Terminology in other languages —— 587

References —— 597

General Index —— 667

Index of Manuscripts —— 683

List of authors —— 685

Handbook of Stemmatology

Introduction

This volume provides an interdisciplinary introduction to stemmatology as a branch of textual criticism that studies textual genealogy. The point of departure which finally led to this book were a number of workshops, the "Studia stemmatologica", organised by Tuomas Heikkilä, Teemu Roos, and Petri Myllimäki, beginning in Helsinki in January 2010. After a couple of meetings, some of the participants decided, again in Helsinki two years later, to set up an online lexicon of terminology used in stemmatology, the *Parvum lexicon stemmatologicum* (*PLS*), housed first at the University of Bergen and then (and still now) at the University of Helsinki (wiki.helsinki.fi/display/stemmatology). This project was initially edited by Odd Einar Haugen (from 2012 to 2015), then taken over by Caroline Macé and me, and reached a first final version in November 2015. A fixed PDF copy of this lexicon briefly covering some 250 terms can be freely downloaded at zora.uzh.ch/id/eprint/121539. In 2015, the main contributors to this online lexicon decided that a fuller and stricter treatment of the different fields involved in stemmatology would be useful, and I volunteered to become the editor-in-chief. We decided to cover the topic in eight chapters, each with its own chapter editor: Elisabet Göransson (Lund), Odd Einar Haugen (Bergen), Marina Buzzoni (Venice), Tara Andrews (Vienna), Aidan Conti (Bergen), Joris van Zundert (Amsterdam), Caroline Macé (Göttingen), and Armin Hoenen (Frankfurt am Main). In contrast to the *PLS*, this book offers longer essays covering the process of determining the genealogical relationship between witnesses of a text and editing it. It also adds a historical dimension covering the development and use of traditional and computerised genealogical methods, and considers various aspects of the approaches involved further, including how they differ between fields. Essays about the current approaches in nine philological fields in chapter 7, written by specialists in those fields, also give it a wider and more practical scope. The book can still serve as a lexicon to a certain extent: definitions of important terms can be found via the general index and are highlighted in the text.

In the field of what may be called "stemmatology", many very different branches of scholarship and science come together, and it is quite impossible for one individual to keep track of all of them today. This book tries to remedy this situation by providing an introduction to this vast field written by specialists in many different branches, from philologists and linguists to biologists and computer scientists. The computerised methods in the field of textual criticism come from other fields that share a common problem: understanding descent with modification. In the case of stemmatology, the objects copied with modification are linguistic expressions, in particular written texts. In some cases, the changes texts have undergone due to repeated copying over long periods of time can be reconstructed very well and, among other things, this can help to reconstruct a text closer to the original than any of the surviving witnesses (the critical edition). Other fields study similar situations, albeit not in relation to texts but, for instance, concerning living beings (see chapter 8). Mathematical and software solutions from one evolutionary field may be useful in others (as discussed in chapter 5).

The book's contributions are written for a general academic audience; care has been taken to ensure that the texts are also understandable to non-specialists: terminology has been defined and explained, and examples and illustrations provided to make the content more easily accessible. Although the book's structure is progressive, thus inviting readers to peruse the volume from beginning to end, single chapters and sections of the book can be read independently as well. To facilitate this, there are cross-references within the book, as well as indexes at its end, which provide quick access to topics treated in the book (sometimes by different authors in different sections and contexts). The reader will quickly realise that the authors come from different fields and schools. Even so, differences in terminology and opinion are surprisingly insignificant, thanks to the fruitful discussions that have taken place between the authors and editors over the past three years.

As for the terminology used in the field of textual criticism, several aids already exist. There is a neo-Latin dictionary of terminology in the field (Springhetti 1962), and several introductions to editing methodology and terminology have been published over the past twenty years: for methodology, Greetham (1995) in general and, focusing on oriental philology, Bausi et al. (2015) in English; for terminology, G. L. Beccaria (2004) and Gomez Gane (2013) in Italian, and Duval (2015) in French. In contrast to these works, the present book has a wider scope. It includes both the traditional and computerised new approaches to this topic, and tries to cover the topic both theoretically and practically. For broader and more general accessibility, we decided to follow the trend in the natural sciences and to write the entire book in English only, but the book is full of quotations in other languages: they are given in their original form and complemented with an English translation. Despite being written fully in English, a glance at the list of contributors at the end of the book shows how many linguistic and methodological backgrounds the authors hail from. Indeed, one of the primary goals of this book is to present the approaches of various schools and fields which are still too often confined to their own linguistic contexts. Of course, different scholarly fields must have their own specific approaches for their specific problems, but we believe that there is a large enough common basis for all approaches dealing with the genealogical relations between textual witnesses to allow the description of a common framework in what, it seems, could well be treated as a single field.

The general, historical development of these schools may be summarised very briefly as follows (for more detail, see chapter 2). In the nineteenth century, the German and French schools of Karl Lachmann (1793–1851) and Gaston Paris (1839–1903) respectively may be seen as foundational for the genealogical method, but radical dissent on the part of Paris's pupil Joseph Bédier (1864–1913) rapidly ensued; he is still influential among many French philologists (see 2.3). On the other hand, Paul Maas (1880–1964), who wrote a very influential, almost algorithmic manifesto of Lachmann's method in 1927, can be seen as a champion of a German approach. Less well known outside its own country, the twentieth-century Italian school of textual editing contributed crucial improvements to the original method. Both theoretical and practical studies by scholars such as Giorgio Pasquali (1885–1952), Gianfranco Contini (1912–1990), Sebastiano Timpanaro (1923–2000), or Cesare Segre (1928–2014) have deepened our understanding of the genealogy of texts significantly and shown that matters are much more complex and cases much more varied than they seem when reading Lachmann or Maas, but also that there are solutions to the problems uncovered by Bédier (see 2.4 below). Indeed, many of the desiderata of the New Philology (another more recent Anglo-French school dating back to 1990) had been answered by Italian scholars half a century before they were raised. The recent publication of Gomez Gane's (2013) and Duval's (2015) lexicons may show a growing awareness of the problem of differences in terminology between the main languages used in this field. In this vein, the present book adds a comparative table of important terminology in the four most important languages in the field – English, French, German, and Italian – at the end. Besides these differences between what might be called German, French, and Italian schools, there are of course also significant differences between the various fields dealing with historically transmitted texts. Traditionally, classical philology, Romance scholarship, and biblical scholarship can be seen as the three most distinct and influential such fields. They roughly correspond to the textual transmission of authoritative texts, of more fluid ones, and of overabundant traditions. This fact alone can already account for much of the methodological divergence between these three fields. Over the past few decades, methods making use of phylogenetic computerised approaches have also been applied to textual traditions – again, of course, with their own vocabularies. The present book was written by specialists from all of these fields, though the same depth could not, of course, be reached in all cases. For instance, biblical philology is treated somewhat marginally (primarily in 2.3.5, about Quentin, and in 7.1, discussing the Greek New Testament). In general, our focus is more on literary works, while practical or legal documents or charters are only covered in passing. The crucial difference is that the former are "works" of a fixed extension with an (at least) putative author and were perceived as such by most scribes and editors copying or editing them. Such works are abstract entities embodied by single manifestations (textual witnesses) which can, therefore, have their own textual genealogy for study by stemmatology. Less well fixed, growing "works", such as florilegia, glosses, or commentaries, can still be studied with similar methods (see 3.2), but they are not central to this book.

What is stemmatology?

The parts of textual criticism dealing with the genealogical dependencies between witnesses of texts can be termed "stemmatology" or "stemmatics". It is the genealogical tree of the transmission of a text, the *stemma codicum* (see 4.1), which provides the name. The term "stemmatology" is usually used as synonymous with "stemmatics" (e.g. by the *OED*). As with many other fields, the endings "-ology" (from λόγος, "word, meaningful or scientific utterance") and "-ic(s)" (the adjective-forming suffix -ική, feminine because the feminine noun τέχνη, "art, field of study", is implied) tend to be used for the same purpose, namely to label a "scientific field about *X*". If a difference between the two terms is perceived, "stemmatology" tends to be the wider term, whereas "stemmatics" may be confined to the method of genealogical reconstruction often named after Karl Lachmann (Duval 2015, 241–242, mentions both possibilities for the corresponding French terms).

The number of schools and a p p r o a c h e s dealing with such textual reconstruction and the tools available for it have multiplied ever more quickly over the past century. Computer tools have made many steps in editing a text easier and faster; moreover, computer simulations now also allow scholars to study the behaviour of large amounts of textual data used as models, which opens up new possibilities for understanding the processes of textual transmission (see 5.1). Stemmatology as described above is a branch of textual criticism. Textual criticism may be seen as the scientific study of the origins and development of texts in general (hence its Russian name, *tekstologia*, "textology", with the "-ology" suffix). In contrast, stemmatology is more restricted in scope: its focus lies on the genealogy of textual traditions. This can be studied practically, with the goal of untangling a concrete case of a textual tradition, or *in abstracto*, seeking to understand in general how textual traditions tend to behave. In the former case, an edition of the text in question is often the main goal. In either case, the strongest tool for the endeavour are shared indicative errors (see 2.2). The question of what exactly qualifies as such is an important question that this field studies (see 6.2.2).

Although the process of finding the stemma of a text's transmission can be described in very mathematical terms (as Maas did), on a closer look it becomes clear that there are crucial parts in the process that stubbornly refuse to yield to algorithmic description. This has led some extreme contemporary currents (see 2.3) to dismiss reconstructive textual criticism as a scholarly or scientific discipline, likening the method of common errors to something that does not work and rejecting the ensuing editions as composite and unreal, the whole endeavour as not worthwhile. The often heated debates about the possibilities of scientific methodology in the study of texts are, unfortunately, too often pursued by people who have never edited a text themselves. Those who have know that it is indeed often difficult to find shared indicative errors and to determine which reading is the primary and which the secondary one (the latter alone can define families of witnesses). Indeed, it often takes a long time of familiarising oneself with a text and its contexts to understand its transmission. Our discipline is to such an extent a practical art (*ars*) that it can hardly be grasped without getting one's hands dirty by trying for oneself. Everyone who has tried to edit a historically transmitted text with at least a moderately complicated transmission – of (say) half a dozen witnesses – knows that the process of finding the correct genealogical tree is an iterative process, to some extent even a circular activity, typical of what is called the "hermeneutic circle" among German philosophers. This is so because we usually start the process knowing very little about the original text or, often, about its author, his habits of writing, and the environment in which the text was written, possibly not even the century it was written in or whether it grew considerably over time. But in order to determine the direction of copying between witnesses (what is called "polarising the tree"; see 4.3.1), one cannot do without such information. As one continues studying the extant witnesses in more detail, things that were initially unclear become clearer: phrases that one may have taken as "obviously" original, for instance, turn out to be later additions. Thus, the textual critic goes through non-linear stages, approaching an ever-better understanding of the tradition under scrutiny. This process is, indeed, not so much circular as comparable to a spiral. Although one seems to move in circles in two dimensions, one's understanding does improve in a third, metaphorical dimension. This same process can be observed at a much lower level of complexity when transcribing a difficult manuscript, one in hardly legible handwriting or badly damaged by time. With every new pass through the text, one understands more and sees more. Although such a process can clearly go wrong and a palaeographer or a textual editor may become convinced of things that are unfounded, in both these disciplines a strong consensus is usually reached among experts about the point up to which things can safely be said and the point from which they become mere speculation or even plain wrong. In short, this circularity does not imply that the process is unscientific; but it does imply that it is hard to program it in full. The book will show that computers facilitate much in this field but that we are nowhere near having computer tools that can algorithmically produce a stemma and a critical text from a bundle of scanned manuscripts.

The same is, of course, true in other fields. So the often-heard question of whether textual scholarship is a mere "art" or actually a "science" finds an easy answer: it is both. As an art, it produces a work (as *artes* in Latin usually did and do), in this case an edition of a text following the best available methods – a text that is the best hypothesis of how the text was at some point in time that can be reached with the available information. But, as the general search for a general understanding of how texts are handed down in time, it is as much a scientific discipline as the English language permits for fields in the humanities (it may be noted in passing that, in contrast to English, most other European languages subsume much more than the natural and mathematical sciences under *science*, *Wissenschaft*, *scienza*, *nauka*, ἐπιστήμη). Detractors of the claim that textual criticism is scientific may mention errors and the difficulties of proving, for instance, that one stemma is the true one while another is wrong; but every science works on hypotheses and they are often hard to test. Often they cannot be confirmed at all, and merely cannot be refuted, as Karl Popper (1965) would demand in general for science. Wrong stemmata can certainly be refuted, though there may remain unclear cases (as in any other science). It may be added that claiming that the genealogical method does not work is an easy way out for some scholars today who would rather not spend much time and effort learning it and thus seek "short cuts" when editing a text.

Structure of the book

This book consists of eight chapters organised in forty sections of some five to thirty pages each, written by a total of thirty-eight authors. Each chapter has been taken care of by a chapter editor who has also provided a brief introduction to his or her chapter stating its main goals. Information about the authors and editors can be found at the back of the volume. In keeping with the process just described of arriving at the best possible understanding of a textual tradition, the structure of the book is not fully linear either: important points are sometimes taken up again in different contexts.

The book begins with a description of the material commonly used in our field in chapter 1, edited by Elisabet Göransson: what kind of transmissions are usual, what material carrying the texts is to be expected, what auxiliary disciplines study these material contexts and how? The focus here is on the Graeco-Roman and then European tradition, which is the basis of most modern approaches to the study of texts. It is instructive to see differences in other cultures, so chapter 7, which provides case studies of the usual approaches in a number of fields, includes some that have been more or less isolated from the European approach: philology in China (7.7) or Ethiopia (7.5). Then, some historical background and the basic concepts of the genealogical, reconstructive method of textual criticism are provided in chapter 2, edited by Odd Einar Haugen: from its roots in Greek Antiquity (Alexandria) to its scholarly formulation among mostly German nineteenth-century philologists and to the debates about and improvements of the method in the twentieth and early twenty-first centuries. Then, the necessary first steps towards inferring the genealogy of a textual tradition are discussed in chapter 3, edited by Marina Buzzoni: how are witnesses found, what sources of information besides witnesses bearing the full text can be used, how is their information about the text gathered and worked with? These steps will, in many cases, lead to the proposal of a stemma. The stemma, important elements in it such as the archetype, and common problems such as contamination are therefore considered in greater detail and more formally in chapter 4, edited by Tara Andrews. So far, the book has dealt mostly with traditional textual criticism; chapter 5, edited by Joris van Zundert, then goes into some depth introducing computational aspects, studying how the information from various witnesses can be dealt with computationally. Some necessary mathematical background in graph theory is provided. Informatics tools are also presented and the relationship between computational and traditional philologists explored, including criticism of the new methods. Chapter 6, edited by Aidan Conti, reunites the different threads into a bigger picture: what kinds of edition are possible, and which ones are preferable under certain circumstances? How should the insight gained into the tradition be presented in an edition? For the traditional print edition, there are standards and established approaches. For the relatively young digital medium, these are still more fluid and evolving.

The remaining two chapters go further afield: as already mentioned, chapter 7, edited by Caroline Macé, presents short case studies in order to provide more concrete material on how textual critics work, giving a sample of nine different fields. Both similarities and differences become clear, as does the fact that methods are exchanged between fields and discussed, sometimes harmoniously, sometimes controversially. The last chapter – chapter 8, edited by Armin Hoenen – provides overviews of other fields that use evolutionary models. Techniques and approaches can be taken from these fields or offered to them. In general, it would seem that the evolutionary ideas of the nineteenth century produced new and unexpected insights into many parts of science and of life in general. This movement is often associated with the name of Charles Darwin (1809–1882), who used the expression "descent with modification" frequently in *The Origin of Species* (Darwin 1859), but it would seem that this new way of thinking about change was already in the air: from the geologist James Hutton (1726–1797) and the demographer Thomas Robert Malthus (1766–1834) around the turn of the nineteenth century, to naturalists such as Alfred Russel Wallace (1823–1913) or Darwin himself around the middle of the nineteenth century in biology. Similar evolutionary ideas were being voiced by linguists such as August Schleicher in the early 1850s (see 8.2), but textual critics such as Lachmann were already very much into studying descent with modification in the 1830s, two decades before Darwin's pivotal publication. At any rate, this new approach in science brought new insights not only into the evolution of living beings but also in very different fields, such as that of textual criticism.

Acknowledgements

This book was written over a long time with the help and collaboration of many people. A closed wiki environment was used to pen and subsequently discuss the contributions between 2015 and 2019; this facilitated discussions among authors and editors and made it easier to arrive at a harmonious global presentation. We thank De Gruyter for accepting our book, and especially Dr Alastair Matthews for copy-editing the entire text very accurately, as well as the Schweizerische Nationalfonds (SNF) for financing digital open access for the book. Care has been taken to acknowledge all image reproduction rights (indicated in the caption of images that are neither our own nor in the public domain); please contact the editor if we have missed anything. Our special thanks go to the very attentive anonymous external peer-reviewer who evaluated the book for the SNF and who helped to improve it significantly, as well as to a number of anonymous internal and external peer-reviewers who helped the editors beforehand.

Practicalities

The book is made more accessible by a general index covering persons, authors, works, and technical terms, as well as a special one of cited manuscripts. There is one common bibliography for all contributions. The back matter also includes a list of terminology as used in the most important languages in the field (English, French, German, Italian) and brief information about the volume's authors.

In general, we have tried to keep the technical knowledge necessary to read this book to a minimum. Examples are always also translated into English, and scripts other than the Latin and Greek ones are transliterated. To this end, the ISO 259 transliteration system for Hebrew, *Hanyu pinyin* without tone marks but accompanied by Chinese characters for Chinese, and the International Alphabet of Sanskrit Transliteration for Sanskrit are used. Edited historical texts are usually quoted by the name of the editor; the editions are included in the general bibliography.

Vosa, Switzerland
Pentecost 2019

Philipp Roelli

1 Textual traditions

Introductory remarks by the chapter editor, Elisabet Göransson

Textual criticism and the study of the transmission of texts is by and large dependent on writing and written sources. The development of literacy, from the oral transmission of texts to the development of written records, was a long process indeed, and it took place in various parts of the world. The earliest stages of writing were pictograms, used by the Sumerians, Egyptians, and Chinese, from which ideographic or logographic writing, which expressed abstractions, was developed. Phonetic writing, in which symbols, phonograms, represent sounds rather than concepts, was then developed into syllabic and later into alphabetic writing. Early Sumerian literature and Egyptian literature, both extant from the late fourth millennium BC onwards, constitute the oldest literatures we know of. A wide range of literary texts – letters, hymns, and poems, but also autobiographical texts – were written in Egyptian hieroglyphs. A narrative Egyptian literature became common from the twenty-first century BC onwards (during the Middle Kingdom). The cursive shorthand known as the hieratic script gradually became more widely used, both for record-keeping and for correspondence. Later on, the demotic script was developed from the late Egyptian hieratic script for the same day-to-day uses, and finally the Egyptians settled on a revised form of the Greek alphabet, the Coptic alphabet, which simplified writing most decidedly. Similarly, cuneiform literature from the ancient Near East, preserved on mostly fragmentary clay tablets, consists of a large corpus of narrative and laudatory poetry, hymns, laments and prayers, fables, didactic and debate poems, proverbs, and songs (T. L. Holm 2005).

Even though writing and literature thus existed for a long time before classical Antiquity, for the study of textual criticism and stemmatology – i.e. the relations between the textual witnesses of a textual tradition – approaches to studying the transmission of Greek and Latin texts have been the main points of departure. The basic concepts, methodology, and terminology used by scholars within the field of stemmatology draw exclusively on the literary development and the copying of texts in ancient Greek and Latin. Hence, the perspective in this book and in this introductory chapter is based on the background of the ancient Graeco-Roman world. An overview of other types of literary cultures, specific textual traditions, and editorial approaches used for manuscript traditions in other parts of the world can be found in chapter 7 of the present book (on early Ethiopian, Hebrew, and Chinese literary cultures). For more case studies of oriental manuscript traditions, the reader is referred to the *Comparative Oriental Manuscript Studies* handbook (Bausi et al. 2015, 363–462).

The textual traditions and transmission of the literary texts we study and analyse depend on many different circumstances. The nature of the preserved manuscripts, their material transmission, authorship, genre, the complexity of the textual tradition, and so on constitute specific challenges for the editor when deciding upon the method(s) to use for analysis and the form of presentation of the text. These circumstances all define the specific editorial situation in a process that can be described as more hermeneutic than strictly linear, so there is no simple recipe applicable to all cases (Göransson 2016, 401). What types of structural and textual variation are there in a specific textual tradition? Sometimes, it is possible to trace the development of a text that underwent changes; in other cases, the evidence may be lacking. Sometimes, the differences in the tradition can be described without the intention of tracing the actual origin of the textual tradition. It all depends on the unique editorial situation, on how the texts have been transmitted, what evidence of the transmission we can find. Still, there are general rules and tools, applicable to these many varying cases, with which the present book is concerned. In this introductory chapter, different perspectives on transmitted texts witnessed primarily in manuscripts, but also in early prints, will be presented to give a historical and methodological perspective on the field.

Gerd Haverling starts by providing an introduction to aspects of literacy and the development of literature in ancient Greek and Latin in section 1.1. Sinéad O'Sullivan, in section 1.2, explains the basic terms used when discussing the transmission of texts, the media transmitting them, and the copying of them. Next, book production and libraries from Graeco-Roman Antiquity onwards, including the paradigm shifts from written to printed books, as well as from printed to digital, are presented in section 1.3, by Outi Merisalo. The ancient libraries of handwritten books, private and public, were replaced by other types of libraries as a result of the renaissance of book production in Carolingian times (ninth century) as well as in the late Middle Ages and the early modern period. Merisalo also gives a broad introduction to the history of our modern-period libraries and their collections, while closing with some perspectives on the digital turn and on the effects of current digitisation processes in libraries and other institutions holding historical heritage.

After this historical background and introduction to the basic terminology used, Iolanda Ventura and Peter Stokes provide a context for the study of stemmatology from two different perspectives. In section 1.4, Iolanda Ventura discusses earlier textual scholarship with specific reference to the role of philological practices when literature was first presented in print. The reception of older texts as witnessed in early prints has often been neglected in modern critical editions, despite the fact that the prints not only witness the reception of those texts but are sometimes apographs of lost manuscript witnesses. The humanists, who were the first to make classical, patristic, and mediaeval literature available in print, had various approaches: their editions are not a homogeneous group, for the early prints were established on quite different principles that are far from transparent since they were often not described at all. Nevertheless, this reception also deserves to be studied: early prints sometimes contribute to the establishment of a critical text. Examples are given both for classical and patristic texts.

Palaeography and codicology, which study the material forms that texts have been transmitted in, are vital for stemmatology. They illuminate other aspects of the transmission and reception of the texts, and inform the discussion of the relevant methods to use when editing them. In section 1.5, Peter Stokes addresses this by giving some definitions and a historical introduction to the development of palaeography and codicology; moreover, he illustrates with examples how editing is intimately intertwined with a deep understanding of palaeography and codicology. Finally, the question of collaboration and multidisciplinarity/interdisciplinarity as a prerequisite for successful scholarship in the field of stemmatology in the digital age is raised and discussed.

1.1 Literacy and literature since Antiquity

Gerd V. M. Haverling

Literacy was no doubt a very rare thing following its introduction, and it was not always used for literature. However, from the classical period in Greece (ca. 480–323 BC) onwards, we witness a growing importance of writing and books. In the Roman world, literacy seems to have been more common than during the first centuries of the Middle Ages; only in the later Middle Ages did the use of writing and books increase again.

1.1.1 Orality and literacy in Antiquity

The earliest texts in Greek date from the latter part of the second millennium BC. The Mycenaean civilisation flourished on mainland Greece and the surrounding islands ca. 1600–1100 BC. Its syllabic script (linear B) was used for administrative purposes and not for literature; with the end of the Mycenaean culture in the twelfth century BC, it was lost. Around 800 BC, the Greeks adopted the Phoenician writing system and created their alphabet, for the first time including vowels. The new Greek script arrived in Italy as early as the first part of the eighth century BC, when the various peoples on the peninsula started to use it for their own languages. The Romans obtained it from the Etruscans; both the earliest known Etruscan and Latin inscriptions date from the seventh century BC (see e.g. Harris 1989, vii, 45, 149; Mallory and Adams 2006, 27–28; M. Weiss 2009, 23–30).

Before literacy became an important factor, there was a tradition of transmitting long stretches of texts orally. The Vedic texts, the oldest part of Sanskrit literature, were transmitted orally for centuries before they were finally written down (see e.g. Mallory and Adams 2006, 33). There are traces of similar traditions among the ancient Greeks and Romans, too.

The extent of the use of writing for literary works among the Greeks in the archaic period (eighth century to ca. 480 BC) is a much-discussed topic. Before they were written down, the Homeric poems were recited orally from memory by specially trained rhapsodes. The *Iliad* and the *Odyssey* contain formulae, stock epithets, and phrases which reflect such oral habits: it therefore seems likely that the poems were not the work of one individual but the product of a "long series of compositions and re-compositions" (Graziosi 2002, 15). Some scholars have followed the traditional account, according to which the Homeric poems were first written down in the middle of the sixth century in Athens during the reign of Pisistratus (thus e.g. Skafte Jensen 1980, 9–10, 128; cf. also e.g. Hinge 2006, 304–306). Others believe, however, that the poets who first wrote down the Homeric poems lived earlier and that Hesiod, the first Greek poet known to us as an individual, already used writing when he composed his poems around 700 BC (thus e.g. West 1978, 41–59; cf. also Reynolds and Wilson 2013, 1; Pöhlmann 1994, 11–12). The first literary works were thus poetry, but from the sixth century we hear of works composed in prose on history and philosophy. In the classical period (ca. 480–ca. 323 BC), a growing number of genres in prose as well as poetry are cultivated (see e.g. Lesky 1996, 216–223, 241–641; see also Pöhlmann 1994).

There are also some traces of a pre-literary form of poetry among the Romans: religious songs such as the *Carmen Saliare* and the *Carmen Arvale* seem to have such a background, and had become virtually incomprehensible to Romans in the later Roman Empire (see e.g. Poccetti and Santini 1999, 204–208; Clackson and Horrocks 2007, 160–163; Conte 1994, 19–22; see also G. Williams 1982). In the middle of the fifth century, the laws that were to apply in Rome were – after a political fight between patricians and plebeians – written down on twelve bronze tablets (*Leges XII tabularum*). The tablets are not preserved, but we know of their content from quotations in later texts (see e.g. Poccetti and Santini 1999, 197–204; Conte 1994, 16–17). The Latin texts preserved from the first centuries of Roman literacy are mostly short inscriptions, and it is not until the second part of the third century BC that Roman literature as we know it starts; the earliest preserved literary texts date from around 200 BC and from the second century BC. These first literary works in Latin are poetry and drama, but soon the Romans started to compose prose works as well. Knowledge of Greek language and literature was of great importance for an educated Roman from the third century BC until the last centuries of Antiquity (see e.g. Conte 1994, 16, 81–82, 715–717; Reynolds and Wilson 2013, 19; see also Marrou 1948, 29–61).

1.1.2 Literary norms

Literary norms were created for both Greek and Latin, and for both prose and poetry, in the respective classical periods (fourth century BC for the Greeks and first century BC for the Romans). These norms, which were based on a canon for the various kinds of literature and were taught in schools, were followed to a considerable extent by the literary elite until the end of Antiquity and were of importance for literary works in Greek and Latin even after that. As the difference between the literary norms and the forms of Greek and Latin as actually spoken grew, an increasing number of less literary texts which reflect some of the ongoing changes appear. In particular, some Christian authors in late Antiquity were inclined to accept some of the changes in the spoken languages, as this would facilitate comprehension of the teachings of the learned clergy among the unlearned congregations (see e.g. Clackson and Horrocks 2007, 183–228, 236–264; Poli 1999, 410–417; Horrocks 2014, 43–78, 210, 213–214; see also Haverling 2014).

The extent of literacy in the Graeco-Roman world is controversial, but it is clear that the ability to read was much more common than the ability to write correctly. In the Hellenistic period (after 323 BC), new literary genres such as the novel suggest that the ability to read was relatively common (see Hägg 1983, 81 ff., 87 ff.). In the Roman world, some regard literacy as already "quite extensive" around 200 BC (thus e.g. Conte 1994, 15), while others have estimated that less than 10 % of the population could read or write (e.g. Baldi 2002, 227); for an overview of the discussion, see Harris (1989, 3–42), who estimates (e.g. 22 ff., 331) that a relatively small part of the population could read and that an even smaller number could write during the Roman Empire. Pointing to the evidence provided by, among other things, the Vindolanda tablets from a Roman military post on Hadrian's Wall, Bowman (1991; 2003, 79–96) makes somewhat more optimistic assumptions in this respect (for further discussion, see Beard et al. 1991). We have private letters from the Roman Empire which were dictated to scribes, thus indicating lacking or partly lacking literacy, and we have private letters written in good Latin by the private persons themselves, which seem to imply a somewhat higher degree of literacy. Although it seems unlikely that mass literacy was achieved in the ancient world, by the time of the Roman Empire, a culture "characterised by the written word" had been established (Harris 1989, 196; for further discussion, see also e.g. Beard et al. 1991; Bowman and Woolf 1994; Johnson and Parker 2009). The habit of reading epic poetry and other literary works in silence instead of hearing it recited will not have been created overnight and ancient Greek and Roman literature would retain a strong oral – and aural – character for many centuries. Those who could afford it had servants reading aloud to them – not because they were not able to read themselves, but because it was more pleasant to have someone read the text aloud. In the late Roman Republic and in the early Empire, literary works were still supposed to be heard and not read silently. In imperial Rome, literary works were often "published" by public recitations (see e.g. Reynolds and Wilson 2013, 1; Salles 2010, 97–116).

1.1.3 Developments in the Middle Ages

Towards the end of Antiquity – in the sixth and seventh centuries – there were some serious changes in the formerly Graeco-Roman world. These changes were the result of political circumstances, such as the split between the Western and the Eastern Empires, the growing estrangement between the Greek-speaking and the Latin-speaking worlds, the barbarian invasions, and the collapse of the Western Empire towards the end of the fifth century AD, but also of natural disasters, such as the so-called Justinian plague, which from its outbreak around AD 540 seems to have reduced the population dramatically in certain areas. Finally, there were also cultural changes, such as the new perspective originating from the Christian faith (see e.g. Ward-Perkins 2005; Little 2007).

As a result of these changes, there was a sharp decrease in literacy and in interest in the classical literary texts for several generations. The reading, writing, and copying of books became a matter mainly dealt with in the monasteries; this activity was to some extent initiated by Cassiodorus Senator (ca. 485–585), who strongly recommended such activity to the monks in his monastery, the Vivarium in Calabria, in the late sixth century AD. The language used in texts written during the seventh and early eighth centuries often deviates considerably from the classical standards, and there was, especially in the West, little interest in the great pagan classics of Graeco-Roman Antiquity (see e.g. R. Wright 2002, 9–10; Reynolds and Wilson 2013, 53–55, 64, 80–87; Horrocks 2014, 211, 223–224). Even a few texts from the Roman period which had certainly been written in very good Latin were affected by the lack of familiarity with the classical norm when they were copied during this period: there are, for instance, traces of "Merovingian spellings" in some manuscripts of Caesar's *De bello Gallico* (vulgarisation). Some of the texts from the last centuries of Antiquity are therefore problematic in this respect. A frequently discussed example is the *Decem libri historiarum* by Gregory of Tours (ca. 538–594): the Latin is rather literary in several respects, and some very important contemporary features are lacking, but in some of the manuscripts the orthography is very unorthodox (see e.g. Buchner 1955, xxxvi–xliii; Haverling 2008; Hilchenbach 2009, 85–90).

However, around AD 800, there is a renewal in interest in classical literature in both the East (sometimes called the "Photian Renaissance") and the West. In the West, this is connected to Charlemagne's school policies and the so-called Carolingian Renewal or Renaissance. This resulted in the realisation that there was such a difference between the current form of spoken proto-Romance languages in the Carolingian empire (*rustica Romana lingua*, "rustic Roman language") and the literary Latin of the Roman classics that they were actually different languages (see e.g. R. Wright 2002, 14–17). The knowledge of Latin grammar was now greatly improved, and as a result there is a growing tendency from the ninth century onwards to "improve" the Latin of certain texts from late Antiquity and the early Middle Ages and render it more in accordance with the standards of the literary language of the classical period (normalisation; see e.g. Coleman 1999; Haverling 2003, 2008). In both the West and the East, the renewed interest in the classical texts resulted in the production of many new manuscripts containing such texts – very often, the oldest preserved manuscripts containing such texts are from the ninth or tenth centuries, and in other cases the preserved manuscript tradition can be traced back to a lost manuscript from this period (see e.g. Reynolds and Wilson 2013, 58–66, 91–93, 96–103; Gastgeber 2003, 28–29).

After a certain decrease in the cultural level of the Latin world in the tenth century, there was a new cultural renaissance around 1100, when the earliest universities were founded and a considerable amount of important Greek philosophical and technical texts were translated into Latin from Greek and Arabic. The scholastic movement, newly arisen in the universities, was focused on theological, philosophical, and logical problems, but not on classical literary culture (see e.g. Reynolds and Wilson 2013, 107–122). In the late Middle Ages, this new culture was challenged by a new cultural outlook inspired by a renewed interest in the pagan classics: this is the Italian Renaissance, which starts in the fourteenth century and gains full force in the fifteenth, and which leads to a renewed interest in the classical texts in both Greek and Latin as well as in the literary Latin of the classical period, which was now regarded by some as the model to follow. The new interest in Greek language and literature received further impetus when learned Greek refugees arrived in Italy with their books at the time of the fall of Constantinople in 1453. Another change in connection with the late Middle Ages and the Renaissance is the growing number of educated private persons – already in the twelfth century, there had been a marked increase in lay literacy, and this tendency grew stronger. As a result, literature and learning were no longer a matter almost exclusively dealt with by the Church (see e.g. Reynolds and Wilson 2013, 112, 123–155; Gastgeber 2003, 36–37). The influence of the printing press is considered below (1.4).

1.2 Transmission of texts
Sinéad O'Sullivan

This section focuses primarily on the transmission of written texts: the types of media in which texts circulated, the complex nature of manuscript culture, and the process of copying texts, as well as some of the basic terminology associated with the practices of copying.

1.2.1 Oral and written transmission

The heading "transmission of texts" points towards a first subsection on oral vs written transmission. Already noted (see 1.1) have been both the oral transmission of the Homeric poems, which contain stock phrases underscoring their oral-formulaic composition (Parry 1930, 73–148; Lord 1960; Skafte Jensen 1980, 9–10), and the aural character of Graeco-Roman literature, which accords with the role of oral culture in Antiquity, evident not only in the archaic and classical periods, but also in imperial Rome, where public recitations of literary works, the dictation of letters and other kinds of texts, and the use of readers demonstrate that the Greek and Roman elites "retained a strong element of orality in their lives" (Harris 1989, 36). More recently, scholars have foregrounded the variety of ancient literary practices and have seriously questioned the assumption that orality was the dominant form of reading practice (Johnson and Parker 2009; Johnson 2010). Interestingly, the oral-aural character of textual transmission finds a reflex in the mediaeval world, where, for instance, certain kinds of texts were rooted in "a 'monastic present' in which the correct oral performance of liturgical and other texts was a crucial component of everyday life" (Grotans 2010, 63).

With regard to the preservation and circulation of texts, written transmission was vital. Key developments were the transition from roll to codex; the promotion of the written word through the foundation and expansion of libraries (e.g. under the Ptolemies in Alexandria and the early Empire); and the standardisation of texts by the Alexandrian scholars, for instance by Zenodotus of Ephesus (ca. 325–ca. 270 BC) and Aristophanes of Byzantium (ca. 257–ca. 180 BC; Dickey 2007, 5). The text-critical efforts of the Alexandrine grammarians were important for establishing canonical written texts (see 2.1.2). Also significant for the transmission and reception of texts were the production of extensive commentaries, especially in the late antique period, and their reuse and appropriation in the Carolingian age (Zetzel 1975, 336; Werner 1998, 172). These commentaries often transmitted excerpts from earlier works. Their importance is, for instance, strikingly evident in early mediaeval glossed Virgil manuscripts, where compilers extracted information from the major commentaries available on the poet. Above all, as we shall see, the written transmission of texts was far from straightforward, subject as it was to the additions, revisions, and transformations of contemporary and later scribes and editors, as well as to the relatively fluid nature of textual transmission in a manuscript book culture. The material aspects of written transmission, discussed below, are thus essential for understanding the dynamics of textual transmission in Antiquity and the mediaeval world.

1.2.2 Media transmitting texts

Over the centuries, many different kinds of media have been used to transmit texts, ranging from tablets to scrolls and codices. As for the writing materials, stone, slate, birch bark, papyrus, parchment, and paper have all been deployed (Bischoff 1990, 13–16). For example, wax tablets made of wood and covered with wax were used in Antiquity and the Middle Ages. Two of the most important media transmitting texts were the *volumen* and the *codex*. The former denotes a book in roll format that was made from papyrus, leather, parchment, or paper. The scroll is unrolled to reveal one page at a time and was the standard form of transmitting texts in Antiquity. In the early centuries of Christianity, the scroll was replaced by the codex, a development of enormous consequence for the history of the book. Less fragile than the papyrus scroll, the *codex* or *caudex*, meaning "trunk or stem of a tree", denotes a book made from sheets of papyrus, parchment, or paper. It evolved from Roman wooden writing tablets. In a codex, folios were gathered together and formed into g a t h e r i n g s or q u i r e s comprising two double folios (binio), three double folios (ternio), four double folios (quaternio), and so on. These quires were often bound between wooden boards. The term "codex" is generally used for manuscripts, that is, for handwritten books produced before the invention of the printing press. Derived from the Latin words *manus*, "hand", and *scribere*, "to write", manuscripts were written on p a p y r u s (made from the papyrus plant and commonly used in Antiquity), p a r c h m e n t or v e l l u m (made from animal skin and widely used from the third century onwards), and p a p e r (a Chinese invention attested in the Latin West by the eleventh century). Manuscripts could be in different formats (scroll or codex) and transmitted all kinds of material, ranging from written texts to illustrations, diagrams, notes, colophons, and marginalia. Premodern texts circulated primarily in manuscript witnesses, examination of which is central to the study of the reception of an author or text. The term "manuscript" is also applied to the final version of a modern text before it has been printed.

Parchment was extremely expensive and manuscripts were, therefore, sometimes reused, as in the case of p a l i m p s e s t s. The word "palimpsest" derives from the Greek πάλιν ψάω, "to smooth over again". It denotes a manuscript page from which the original text has been effaced, that is, the writing surface has been scraped or the text washed off in order to prepare it to be reused for another work which is superimposed on the earlier text. Usually, the economic value of parchment was a primary motive for the reuse of writing material made from animal hides. Modern decipherment of the original text generally relies on ultraviolet light and photography rather than on chemicals, which can be quite damaging to the parchment. A famous example of a palimpsest manuscript is the *Codex Nitriensis* (cf. fig. 1.2-1), written on palimpsest leaves taken from manuscripts of the *Iliad* and the Gospel of Luke and from a seventh- or eighth-century manuscript of Euclid (London, British Library, Add. 17210 and 17211).

Mediaeval manuscripts were sometimes composite entities, comprising different c o d i c o l o g i c a l u n i t s. They could transmit contemporary and homogeneous elements, or comprise heterogeneous sections, sometimes dating from the same or different periods (Andrist, Canart, and Maniaci 2013). Composite manuscripts are the result of many factors. For instance, the interests of an owner or the content of a manuscript could dictate what was added to a manuscript. Equally, replacement of a lost part of a codex sometimes resulted in the inclusion of a fascicle for a missing section. By way of illustration, we may note two examples. The first is a ninth-century manuscript, London, British Library, Harley 2782, comprising two codicological units, which together provide commentaries on all of the major works of Virgil (O'Sullivan

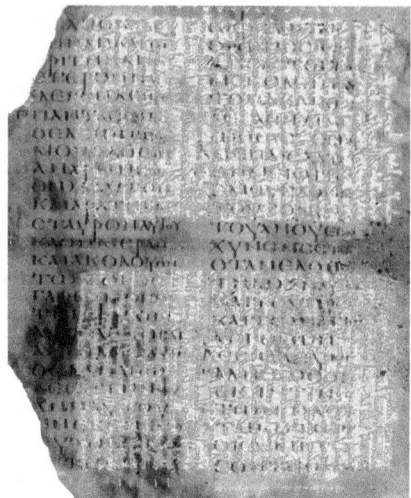

Fig. 1.2-1: *Codex Nitriensis*, f. 20r, showing the upper Syriac text and the effaced Greek text of the Gospel of Luke under ultraviolet light. Source: commons.wikimedia.org/w/index.php?title=File:Codex_Nitriensis,_f.20r_(Luke_9,22-33).jpg&oldid=129699031.

2016). The second is another ninth-century manuscript, Paris, Bibliothèque nationale de France, lat. 10307 + Città del Vaticano, Biblioteca Apostolica Vaticana, Reg. lat. 1625 (III), which consists of two contemporary and homogeneous elements that transmit Christian and pagan works (Munk Olsen 1985, 764–765; Bischoff 1998–2017, no. 4627, 3:160–161). The first element (f. 1–43) transmits Caelius Sedulius' *Carmen Paschale* flanked by Juvencus' *Evangeliorum libri quattuor*, the second (f. 44–245) the works of Virgil surrounded by the commentary of Servius. Many factors suggest that the different sections of the manuscript were part of the same enterprise (format, ruling, script, decoration). All kinds of material are found in the manuscript, which contains classical, late antique, and mediaeval texts, commentaries, and excerpts (e.g. from Homer, Ennius, Sallust, Virgil, Pseudo-Ovid, Servius, Pseudo-Dares Phrygius, Priscian, Caelius Sedulius, Juvencus, Alcuin, and John Scottus Eriugena). Interestingly, the pagan material sits comfortably alongside the Christian.

Occasionally, only a part or parts of a manuscript survive (Brownrigg and Smith 2000). Manuscript f r a g m e n t s can vary in size. In some instances, a single leaf or a strip of parchment is all that remains. Fragments of mediaeval manuscripts may be dispersed across several libraries. There are many reasons, material and historical, that result in a manuscript becoming fragmentary or being taken apart. These include lack of interest in a work and material damage. The latter may have happened in the mediaeval, early modern, or modern periods, as illustrated by the Cotton Library fire (1731) and the bombardments of World War II. Some fragments only survive because of their reuse as binding material. In other cases, the interests of collectors resulted in fragments of a manuscript being divorced from its original setting. An example is that of the German scholar Karl Bernhard Stark (1824–1879), in whose collection we find a fragment of a ninth-century glossed Virgil manuscript (Ottaviano 2013, 222–223). Given Stark's interest in Roman antiquities, it is no surprise that he should have included this fragment in his collection (München, Archäologische Staatssammlung, Bernhard Starks Collectaneen, his. Ver. 18, VIII, f. 693–694). Fragments might seem less useful than complete codices because they contain less text, but this is not the case. In fact, fragments sometimes provide clues as to the circulation of a work. They can also help in dating a work extant only in later codices, as illustrated by the Lorsch fragment of the *Waltharius*, the oldest witness of the Latin poem (Bischoff 1998–2017, no. 1491, 1:311; Turcan-Verkerk 2016; see also fig. 1.2-2 below). And, of course, fragments may be the only witnesses of otherwise lost readings in a text.

Additionally, manuscripts can be lacunose. The Latin word *l a c u n a*, meaning "pit, hollow, gap", denotes a gap in a manuscript. Lacunose manuscripts usually have missing sections of text or commentary. The causes are many. As physical objects, manuscripts frequently suffer all kinds of accidents and material damage. Consequently, there may be loss or damage to the content of manuscripts. Material damage, for instance, may be the result of fire, fungi, insects, rodents, or water. Furthermore, quires may be misplaced or lost because of bad binding or accidents. A fascinating example, and one that has produced irretrievable loss, is the case of the *Cantar de mio Cid*, extant in a lacunose *codex unicus* (Madrid, Biblioteca Nacional, Ms. Sig. v. 7–17; Montaner 2018).

Clues as to the production and material history of a manuscript may be furnished by a c o l o p h o n, that is, the inscription or short account at the end of a

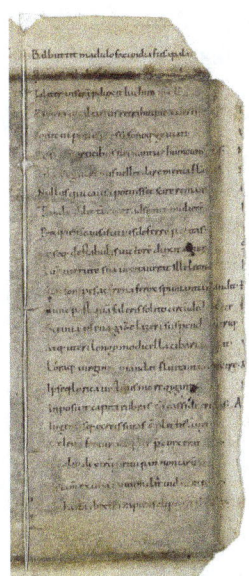

Fig. 1.2-2: One of the *Waltharius* fragments from Lorsch (Hamburg, Staats- und Universitätsbibliothek, Cod. 17 in scrin.).
Source: bibliotheca-laureshamensis-digital.de/view/subhh_codscrin17_fragm1/0003). Image: CC-BY-NC-ND.

manuscript or book. An invaluable and extensive collection of occidental colophons is that published by the Benedictines of Bouveret (1965–1982). The colophon may provide information about the scribe, the printer, or the person who commissioned, bought, or sold the manuscript or book. As such, it is often a source of historico-geographical and cultural information. For instance, in a humanistic manuscript there appears the colophon of a scribe named Statilius Maximus, whose identification is debated and who is generally seen as operating in the second century CE. The colophon, found in Poggio's manuscript (Città del Vaticano, Biblioteca Apostolica Vaticana, Vat. Lat. 11458), furnishes information about the scribe's correction of Cicero's *De lege agraria* and his use of various revisions (Schiegg 2016, 131). Moreover, in the famous Lindisfarne Gospels, an Old English colophon lists those involved in the manuscript's production (Schiegg 2016, 132). In some instances, colophons provide clues as to the existence of ancient but otherwise largely unknown authorities (Cadili 2008, 204; Herren 1999, 55–61, 67; Miles 2011, 32).

1.2.3 The manifold elements in mediaeval manuscripts

As material objects and text-carriers, manuscripts housed all kinds of elements, providing different types and layers of information (Géhin 2005). For instance, in the "long twelfth century", texts in the following fields circulated widely: liturgy, theology, classics, medicine, law, and the sciences (Kwakkel and Thomson 2018, 4). Texts often attracted accompanying material: commentaries, glosses, diagrams, illustrations, decoration, musical notation, scholarly and personal notes, codes, signs, symbols, captions, headings, titles, subtitles, syntactic markers, and corrections (Kwakkel 2018; Steinova 2013). Two examples should illustrate this phenomenon. The first is the emergence of the sequence c o m m e n t a r y in the twelfth and thirteenth centuries (Kihlman 2006). Mediaeval commentaries on sequence texts, that is, chants sung before the recitation of the Gospel during the Eucharist, represent a new genre that is found in both monasteries and cathedral chapters. Such expositions often incorporate a whole range of different kinds of text: the introductory section or prologue, the sequence, the commentary text, and even, at times, interlinear annotations. Sequence commentaries sometimes quote the incipit of the strophe or strophes they are elucidating; at other times, they include the sequence text itself, either as a complete text or broken up or intertwined with the commentary. The sequence text may precede the commentary or be found alongside it on the same page. As for the nature of sequence commentaries, their character is diverse in scope, ranging from philosophy and theology to grammar and vocabulary. The second example consists of g l o s s e s, which sometimes circulated as textual traditions. A gloss may be in a classical language, in the vernacular, or even in Tironian notes, an ancient form of stenography. The functions of glosses range from grammatical and explanatory elucidation to the provision of encyclopedic and allegorical interpretation (Wieland 1983; Teeuwen 2010; O'Sullivan 2017a, 2017b). Glossators often assembled informa-

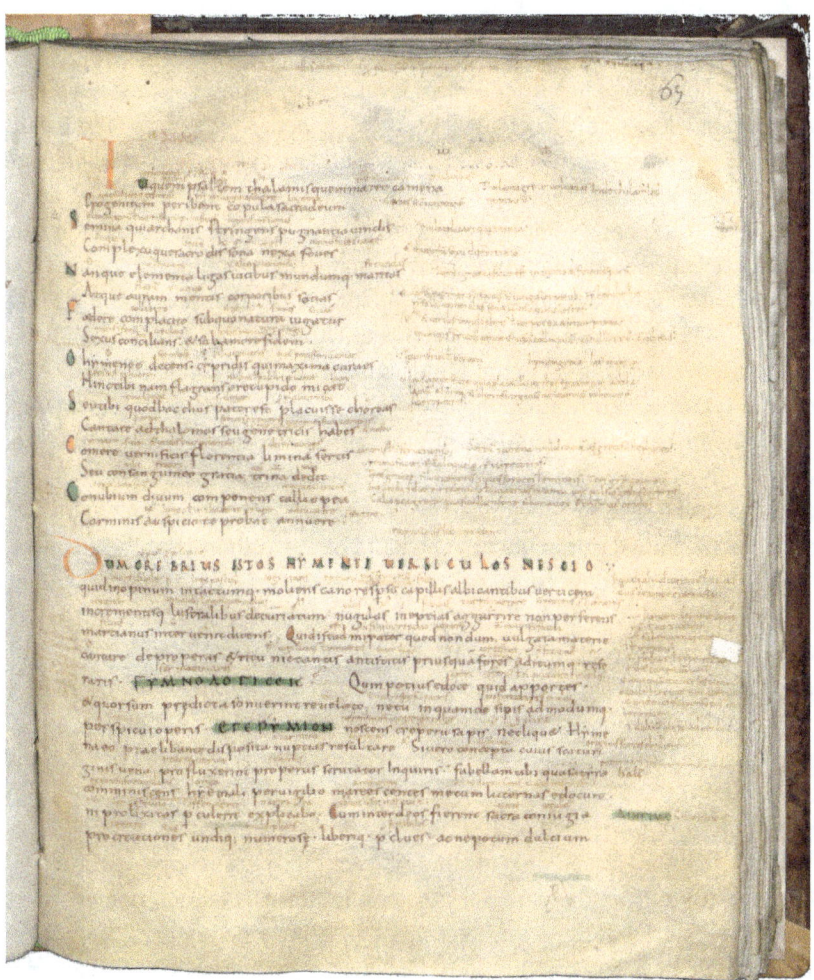

Fig. 1.3-3: A glossed manuscript page with marginal and interlinear annotations (Trier, Bibliothek des Priesterseminars, Ms. 100, f. 67r). The manuscript is a parchment manuscript dating to the ninth and tenth centuries and transmitting glosses from the oldest gloss tradition on Martianus Capella. Image: CC-BY-NC.

tion. They not only gathered materials but also collated, paraphrased, condensed, and cross-referenced sources. At times, glosses exhibit the vitality of the encyclopedic tradition with its age-old antiquarian priorities of excerpting, summarising, synthesising, and citing authorities. Glosses often circulated in major centres of learning, were used by prominent scholars, and were quarried for compendia of all kinds. In the case of a ninth-century glossed Virgil manuscript, Montpellier, Bibliothèque interuniversitaire, Section Médecine, H 253, a number of glosses show overlap with various mediaeval compilations such as the *Liber glossarum* and the mythographic collection by the author known as the First Vatican Mythographer (Ottaviano 2013).

1.2.4 The copying of texts

The practices deployed by ancient and mediaeval scribes when copying texts provide insight into how the tradition of a text was established. At the heart of transmitting texts was the copyist, also known as the scribe. While all copyists were scribes, not all scribes were copyists (a scribe could also be the author of a document). Scribes in the early Middle Ages were primarily to be found in monastic or ecclesiastical centres. The identity of most remains uncertain. Palaeographical clues, however, can provide insight into the home of a scribe. For example, in a fragmentary Virgil manuscript from St. Emmeram, the principal gloss hand has been characterised as writing a "Celtic minuscule". Bernhard Bischoff (1960, 219–220) suggested Wales or Cornwall as the home of the scribe. Noteworthy is the fact that the same hand has been identified in other ninth-century manuscripts either linked with St. Emmeram or originating at the abbey. In some instances, we know the name of the scribe who may be the author of the text. The term "autograph" is used to denote a manuscript written by the hand of the author. Usually, however, authors did not write down or copy their own work themselves. More commonly, works were written down under the supervision of the author. For ancient and mediaeval works, then, autographs are a rarity. An interesting example is furnished by John Scottus Eriugena's *Periphyseon* in Reims, Bibliothèque municipale, 875. Believed, in part, to be the autograph of Eriugena, the manuscript, written by several hands, is perhaps most illuminating for the insight it furnishes into the practices of revision (L. Smith 1992, 55).

An important term associated with scribal activity is the all-encompassing word *documentum* (*doceo* + *-mentum*), meaning "teaching, instruction, or an example". The term derives from the verb *doceo*, "to tell, inform, instruct, demonstrate, show, teach". It primarily designates something that is inscribed or written. A document transmits evidence, information, or a text such as a charter, treatise, inscription, or official paper. A document can also be the instrument on which information is recorded. In the course of transmitting written documents, witnesses were produced, and these too are documents. The term "documentary" also occurs in an important distinction made by palaeographers, namely between "book hands" and "documentary hands". The former denotes the plethora of formal handwriting scripts circulating in the ancient and mediaeval worlds, the latter the array of cursive scripts written with a running hand.

Texts generally survive in manuscript witnesses. A distinction is made between direct witnesses, that is, copies or prints of a work, and indirect witnesses, which may be paraphrases, summaries, translations, or simply references to a work (see 4.5.1). An indirect witness (see 3.2) can consist of quotations or portions of a work in later texts, as in the case of Rabanus Maurus' *De rerum naturis*, which includes much of Isidore's *Etymologiae*. Texts are usually extant in copies. Here, the terms "apograph" and *codex descriptus* are important ones. The first derives from the Greek ἀπόγραφον, meaning "transcript", and denotes any copy of an exemplar (which may also be lost); the second refers to a copy derived from another extant manuscript (see 4.3.3). Crucially, texts were regularly transcribed in manuscript copies that frequently served as e x e m p l a r s for further copies. Various methods were deployed by scribes to copy texts. Ancient and mediaeval texts were sometimes copied by dictation, that is, a copyist or copyists wrote down that which was read aloud or dictated to them. More commonly, scribes copied texts visually from an exemplar or exemplars, that is, from an older manuscript or manuscripts. The term "exemplar" denotes a text that has been copied or transcribed into a new manuscript witness. A copy, in turn, can serve as the exemplar for another copy (for an example of a series of exemplars and copies whose existence can be inferred, see 1.4.2 below on the transmission of Lucretius). The term "e x e m p l a r s h i f t" denotes the practice of shifting between exemplars, that is, the use of several exemplars for different sections of a text (see 4.4.4.2). In textual scholarship, exemplar shift is one form of c o n t a m i n a t i o n. The term "contamination" denotes the combination of readings from more than one exemplar. In the field of textual criticism, contamination presents real challenges for the modern editor (see further 4.4).

In the process of copying texts in the ancient and mediaeval worlds, errors and misreadings of all sorts emerged. For a typology of all errors, Louis Havet's classification (1911) is seminal. A few examples should illustrate the problems that often emerged in the process of copying texts. For instance, there was omission of text due to haplography and the addition of text due to dittography, that is, when a copyist repeated a letter, word, or phrase. In the case of haplography, a scribe omitted a section of text by inadvertently skipping from a word/words in the text to a similar word/words further on in the text (details in 4.3). Later copyists sometimes sought to correct such errors and establish the integrity of the text. For example, they corrected the errors of earlier scribes by filling in lacunae, that is, by supplying the omitted words either in the interlinear or marginal spaces.

1.2.5 Types of text transmission and editorial choices

Modern editors regularly confront the many difficulties presented by the transmission and circulation of ancient and mediaeval texts. Working with all kinds of works (e.g. multilayered texts, texts that can be classed as fluid, non-authored texts, glosses, lemmatised commentaries, and works that are the result of collective authorship), they endeavour to produce editions that sometimes present an earliest form, sometimes underscore an ongoing process, and sometimes seek to capture an entire tradition (Iversen, in Göransson et al. 2016, x; Göransson 2016, 405). For a discussion of some of the principle types of editions, see section 6.1. Challenges, however, are continually posed by the various forms in which ancient and mediaeval texts survive, as well as by the practices of ancient and mediaeval scribes. This has led to scholarly debate on how best to edit all kinds of texts, especially ones that defy the traditional method of Lachmannian genealogical *recensio* (see 6.2). Interesting solutions have been suggested. For instance, Alexander Andrée proposes an expanded single-manuscript edition of the *Glossa ordinaria* on the Gospel of John, Barbara Crostini an electronic edition of the interrelated visual and textual material in a Greek catena on the psalter extant in a single manuscript witness, Greti Dinkova-Bruun an edition of the original text and later versions of a section of Peter Riga's commentary on the Bible surviving in several hundred manuscripts, and Andrew Hicks a synoptic edition of the anonymous late mediaeval commentary tradition on Martianus Capella (Göransson et al. 2016). The obstacles are manifold, requiring all kinds of possible solutions to underscore the creative and dynamic nature of textual transmission in a manuscript culture.

1.3 Book production and collection
Outi Merisalo

The impact of the modalities of book production on the transmission of texts is still often ignored by editors of texts with little interest in book history, including palaeography, codicology, and library history. The subsequent media revolutions (passage from the rotulus to the codex form, introduction of the Carolingian minuscule, invention of the art of printing, and so on) have, however, deeply influenced what was transmitted and in what form. This chapter will outline the development of book production and collection from Antiquity to the modern period.

1.3.1 Book production and libraries in Antiquity

The earliest information on mechanisms of book production in ancient Greece comes from fifth-century BC Athens. Normally, the author would be responsible for having the work both copied and distributed, but there is already evidence of commercial booksellers. Book production is evidently connected to the intense debate about the general desirability of books, which pitted the Sophists, who are in favour of the written word, against figures such as Plato and Aristophanes, convinced of the deleterious effect of written transmission on how individuals analyse, internalise, and interpret ideas. According to the latter, written culture encourages superficiality as memorising is no longer necessary.

From the seventh century BC onwards, the book form of the Greek world had been the papyrus rotulus. Since the material was exclusively produced in Egypt, its availability in other regions was, of course, subject to fluctuations in imports connected to war and so on. The earliest evidence for book collections in the Greek world goes back to the sixth century BC (Nielsen 2006). In late fifth-century Athens, such figures as the politician Euclides (archon, 403–402 BC; König, Oikonomopoulou, and Woolf 2013, 87) were known to have a private library. In the fourth century, private collections increased in number and size, for example Aristotle's considerable library in the Lyceum grove in Athens (Vössing 2006). In the same period, commercial book trading covered not only mainland Greece but also southern Italy (*Magna Graecia*) and Sicily in the west, as well as Asia Minor as far as the Greek cities of the Black Sea in the east.

With the fragmentation of the short-lived empire created by Alexander the Great (356–323 BC), the successor states ruled by dynasties established by his generals, such as Seleucus, Antiochus, and Ptolemy, consolidated a new political, cultural, and linguistic reality characterised by the status of Greek as a new all-round language of communication in the Middle East. The libraries established by Hellenistic rulers were prevalently public in nature (Vössing 2006). From the point of view of book collections, the establishment of the Mouseion (Μουσεῖον) research centre and library by Ptolemy I Soter and Ptolemy II Philadelphus in Alexandria at the beginning of the third century took library collections to a new level. Despite the traditional name associated with the cult of the Muses, there is no obvious model for this research centre with a well-appointed library. Ptolemy I, appreciative of learning just like Alexander, who had been taught by Aristotle himself, recruited the Peripatetic philosopher Demetrius of Phaleron, another disciple of the Stagirite, as administrative counsellor. The research centre, organised as a cult association with a priest as head and scholars as members, was financed by the state. In addition to the library, the Mouseion housed an observatory as well as zoological and botanical collections. The scope of the library was to make available the knowledge of the whole world, οἰκουμένη, in Greek and, when necessary, in translation (e.g. the Septuagint, the Greek translation of the Old Testament; Glock 2006). Both editorial techniques (philology; Zenodotus of Ephesus, ca. 325–260 BC) and scholarly bibliography were developed, especially by Demetrius of Phaleron. The collections were accessible to rulers and members of the Mouseion. Contrary to what has been believed (e.g. Plutarch *Caesar* 49), the Mouseion library was not burnt down during the civil war between Caesar and Pompey. The fire in Alexandria's harbour only destroyed a book depository, not the entire library, in 47 BC (Vössing 2006). From Augustus onwards, the Mouseion was subsidised by the emperors and pursued its original mission well into the third century AD (Glock 2006). The collection survived virtually unscathed until the rebellion of Zenobia, queen of Palmyra, in ca. AD 270, when the palace quarter was destroyed (Glock 2006). Ptolemy III had established another library in Alexandria, the Serapeum, for religious, non-Greek texts; it is probable that this library assumed most of the functions of the Mouseion after AD 270. It was closed down by Emperor Theodosius in 391 (Glock 2006). The last known scholar of the Mouseion was the mathematician and astronomer Theon at the end of the fourth century.

Ptolemy III and Berenice II established the Ptolemaeum, a gymnasium with a library, in Athens in the third century BC, and Attalus I an institution specialising in bibliography and bibliophily, evidently modelled on the Mouseion, in Pergamon in ca. 200 BC (Clayman 2014, 140; Vössing 2006).

While the Latin language was committed to writing as early as the seventh century BC, book culture seems to have spread but slowly outside official circles and the upper echelons of society (Petrucci 1992, 35–36; see also 1.1.1 above). The situation radically changes in the second century BC, when, through conquest, the Romans come into direct contact with the Hellenistic culture described above. On the Italian peninsula, even the prosperous upper classes of the towns become increasingly literate. Important libraries of the East are brought to Rome as booty, such as that of Perseus, king of Macedonia, by L. Aemilius Paullus after the battle of Pydna in 168 BC, and that of the philosopher Apellicon, who acquired parts of the libraries of Aristotle and Theophrastus, appropriated by Sulla during the conquest of Athens in 86 BC.

In the first century BC, there is ample evidence for both private and public libraries. While volumes of early Latin-language literature, such as the translation of the *Odyssey* by Livius Andronicus (ca. 284–ca. 205 BC) and the epic poetry of Quintus Ennius (239–169 BC), seem to have been difficult to find, knowledge of Greek language and culture, as well as owning books, seems to have become an essential element of the education of middle- and upper-class Romans. Furthermore, in the first century, with formal schools becoming increasingly common, the need for books increased. Private libraries, such as those of Cicero (106–43 BC), who had Greek- and Latin-language collections not only in his city residence on the Palatine Hill but also in his houses in Tusculum, Cumae, and Antium, are well documented (Vössing 2006). From the early imperial age onwards, there is ample evidence (e.g. Petronius, Seneca, Pliny the Younger, Juvenal, and Martial) for different phases of publishing: first, both private and public readings of work in progress, then copies made for friends, and finally commercial publishing. The copies were produced either through dictation or visual copying, or a combination of both methods. Commercial publishers employed a large number of scribes producing copies contemporaneously. A corrector controlled the quality of the output, though complaints about the bad textual quality of Latin books abound (e.g. Cicero *Epistolae ad Quintum* 2.5.6; Martial *Epigrammata* 2.8.1). By the end of the first century AD, a good distribution network covering all of the Empire catered for the needs of customers.

While the constant increase in private libraries (Persius, Martial, Silius Italicus, and Pliny the Younger, among others, in the first century AD) testifies to the appreciation of book culture among the upper classes, from the first century BC books also became increasingly accessible through the establishment of public libraries, the first of which were those of the politician and historian C. Asinius Pollio in the Atrium Libertatis near the Capitoline Hill in 39 BC, with Greek- and Latin-language sections (P. L. Schmidt 2006; Förtsch 2006; Nielsen 2006), and, even more importantly, of his friend Octavian, soon to become Augustus, near the temple of Apollo on the Palatine in 28 BC (Nielsen 2006). At the beginning of the second century AD,

Emperor Trajan placed two libraries on his Forum, one for Greek- and the other for Latin-language books. By the mid-fourth century AD, there were twenty-eight or twenty-nine public libraries in the city of Rome (Nordh 1949, § 97.9; Brodersen 2006; but see Vössing 2006 on doubts regarding the number).

1.3.2 Libraries and archives in late Antiquity and the Middle Ages

Book production radically changes from the fourth to the sixth century AD with the legalisation and triumph of Christianity after the Edict of Milan (AD 313). Whereas commercial editing houses at first compete successfully with well-established Christian structures based on parish and diocesan writing centres, by the sixth century the latter prevail even in the Eastern Empire. Until the end of the Byzantine Empire (1453), the state maintains the imperial library, whereas the political complexity of the former Western Roman Empire after AD 476 is reflected in the book production carried out by the monastic scriptorium (Binder 2006; for the development of the scriptorium throughout the Middle Ages, see Gamper et al. 2015).

Thanks to the triumph of the Benedictine Rule (sixth century; for St Benedict, see Böckmann 2006), which incorporates the copying of books into the monastic way of life as part of bodily work, and the authoritative defence of ancient non-Christian literature as part of Christian culture by a series of important ecclesiastics such as Cassiodorus (sixth century), monastic communities form important book collections of both ancient and contemporary works. These collections, which ensure the transmission of ancient texts that had survived the book-format revolution (see 1.2.2), are continuously enriched and renewed, facing new challenges such as the next media revolution: the adoption of the Carolingian minuscule in the late eighth and early ninth centuries, an essential instrument of the reforms carried out by Charlemagne (r. 768–814) in his new Roman Empire of the West (Bischoff 2009, 179 ff.). In fact, the vast majority of manuscript volumes preserved until modern times date from the period after the eighth century (Bozzolo and Ornato 1980, 84). In the Carolingian Empire, subsequently divided into three parts at Verdun in 843, the thriving monasteries, such as Corbie, Fleury, Tours, and St Gall, among others, are an essential part of the economic, cultural, and religious structures of society, with their scriptoria disseminating texts deemed important in the new script (Bischoff 1961–1981; Pellegrin 1988). Charlemagne's court library, no doubt modelled on the Byzantine imperial one, is part of the network of libraries ensuring the dissemination of texts in the new medium. The texts not considered worth recopying have a high probability of disappearing in the subsequent centuries, when Carolingian minuscule, a kind of trademark of the Western Church and western feudal society, spreads even in newly (re)conquered areas such as the Iberian peninsula from the year 1000 onwards, and in the territories acquired by the Church of Rome in eastern and northern Europe.

Fig. 1.3-1: Duke Humfrey's library in the Bodleian Library, Oxford, dating from the late fifteenth century. Source: commons.wikimedia.org/w/index.php?title=File:Duke_Humfrey%27s_Library_Interior_6,_Bodleian_Library,_Oxford,_UK_-_Diliff.jpg&oldid=269845871.

It is only with the establishment of the universities as ecclesiastical institutions in the twelfth and thirteenth centuries that the position of the scriptorium changes. Some monastic scriptoria successfully compete for the book market with new secular ateliers. The latter abound not only in university cities, such as Paris, Oxford, Cambridge, Bologna, and Padua, where secular scribes reproduce university texts through a highly efficient system of multiple copying based on the rental of *peciae* (each containing a relatively short segment of text; see Murano 2005), but also elsewhere, to address the needs of the new, dynamic bourgeoisie gaining access to literacy. Universities, such as the Collège de Sorbonne or Balliol College in Oxford, actively develop book collections both through acquisition and through donation (Delisle 1868, 180–182; Nebbiai, Angotti, and Fournier 2017; Mynors 1963, 247; Merisalo 2012, 108). These collections are accessible to members of the community but in many cases also to outsiders. From the thirteenth century onwards, princely, royal, and imperial courts, and indeed the papal Curia (Manfredi 2010), develop increasingly important book collections, seen as an essential element of the prestige of the ruler. Cases in point are, for example, the libraries of the kings of France and England, several times dispersed and reconstituted in the last centuries of the Middle Ages, those of the dukes of Burgundy in the fifteenth century, and the Vatican

Library, also incorporating remnants from earlier papal libraries, officially established as a public library in 1475 by Sixtus IV (Manfredi 2010, 199–225). In Florence, in addition to the private library of the Medici, the library of the humanist luminary Niccolò Niccoli (d. 1437) is opened as a public library thanks to the financial input of Cosimo de' Medici the Elder (Ullman and Stadter 1972). Even north of the Alps, important private libraries are assembled, such as that of Hartmann Schedel (d. 1514), a Padua-educated humanist physician and author of a Latin *Cronica* and its German version, the *Weltchronik* (1493), who seems to have allowed other scholars to use his collection (Stauber 1908; Wagner 2014; Merisalo 2016, 830).

1.3.3 Libraries and archives in the modern period

With the advent of printing in the second half of the fifteenth century, both book production and book collections enter another period of revolutionary change. The new *ars artificialiter scribendi*, incomparably cheaper than handwriting due to the elimination of the salary of the scribe, supersedes the traditional modes of production by the end of the century. As regards transmission of texts, this media revolution constitutes another bottleneck: the texts not deemed interesting are not transferred into the new medium and risk disappearing. Libraries react to the media revolution by actively purchasing printed books: for example, the library of the Collège de Sorbonne establishes, in addition to the manuscript collections, a special section of printed volumes that will continue until the seventeenth century (Delisle 1868, 200). The Reformation, with the abolition of monasteries, sets the old monastic collections in flux, with handwritten books either wandering into other libraries or being recycled in, for instance, bindings (e.g. in the kingdoms of Denmark and Sweden: approximately 50,000 manuscript fragments; see Ommundsen and Heikkilä 2017). Texts only preserved in old handwritten books constitute objects of interest for historians for centuries to come, such as Jacques Bongars (1554–1612), whose manuscripts went to the Burgerbibliothek in Berne (see burgerbib.ch/en/the-holdings/bongarsiana-codices), and philologists, such as Pierre Daniel (1531–1604). Luxury manuscripts, still produced in the sixteenth century, have an aesthetic, representative, and financial value for their owners. Indeed, a well-appointed book collection housed in representative buildings, on a par with *Wunderkammern*, that develop into fully-fledged museums, is consolidated as a set part of the self-representation of political leadership, whether of kings, emperors, popes, or a republic. The old and new libraries are made more accessible through systematic cataloguing, especially from the sixteenth century onwards (e.g. the Vatican Library; Montuschi 2014, 243–543). Donations and acquisitions of entire collections make important developments possible, for example in the case of the library of the dukes, later electors, and finally kings of Bavaria (Stauber 1908). The dispersal of library holdings is also intensified by military operations. During the Thirty Years War (1618–1648), entire collections of handwritten and printed books are transferred as highly appreciated booty to the libraries of victorious powers, for example in the acquisition of important private and public libraries by Sweden (Walde 1916–1920) and the transfer of a large part of the Palatine Library from Heidelberg to Rome (Montuschi 2014, 279–336). In the seventeenth and eighteenth centuries, accessibility of collections is enhanced on the one hand by detailed printed catalogues, for example Bandini's catalogue of the Laurentian Library in Florence (Bandini 1774–1777, 1778; see also Siponta De Salvia 1986), and such monumental overviews of European library collections as Montfaucon's *Bibliotheca bibliothecarum* (Montfaucon 1739) on the other. The decades of the French Revolution and the Napoleonic era (1790s–1815) witness the transfer of ecclesiastical collections into central repositories (most systematically in France) or simply onto the book market, where they are acquired by such collectors as the Venetian Jesuit Matteo Luigi Canonici (1727–1805) or Giacomo Morelli (1745–1819), librarian of the Biblioteca Marciana (Valentinelli 1868, 136 ff.; Zorzi 1980, 235 ff.).

The nineteenth century is a period of consolidation of important state-run and institutional collections of a public nature, such as the Bibliothèque royale/de la Nation (1790)/impériale (1804–1815)/royale (1815–1849)/nationale (1849–1851)/impériale (1851–1871), and again nationale (1871–) of France, often considerably enriched through the turbulent book market of the Napoleonic era, as well as the formation of large private libraries made possible by large fortunes generated by industrialisation, such as that of Sir Thomas Phillipps (1792–1872), dispersed between the last decades of the nineteenth century and 2006 (see Munby 1951–1960; Bell 2009). In the United States, Congress establishes a library in 1800, which develops into the most important collection in the country and the national library (Cole 2018). Cataloguing and recataloguing projects (e.g. Italy: Mazzatinti 1890–2013; France: Libri et al. 1849–) enhance the accessibility of these collections, and the historicising and contextualising approach to the study of writing and book production represented by such scholars as Léopold Delisle (1826–1910; see Vielliard and Gosset 2004), Wilhelm Wattenbach (1819–1879), and, last but not least, Ludwig Traube (1861–1907; see Merisalo 2017) throws light on the formation and development of collections. Such a work as Delisle's *Le Cabinet des manuscrits de la Bibliothèque Impériale/Nationale* (Delisle 1868) is still the basis of any research on the manuscripts of the Bibliothèque nationale de France. The development of reproduction techniques, for example heliography and photography, also contributes to the accessibility of collections. Such an epochal political event as the unification of Italy (1861, 1870) forcefully impacts the book market, with the confiscation of the libraries of ecclesiastical institutions and their incorporation into state-run libraries, such as the Biblioteca nazionale of Rome, that of Florence (see Fava 1939), and the Biblioteca Marciana in Venice. Some libraries, such as the Königliche Bibliothek in Berlin, proceed to undertake vigorous acquisition campaigns, such as that of five hundred manuscripts of the Phillipps collection in 1889 (see staatsbibliothek-berlin.de/die-staatsbibliothek/abteilungen/handschriften/abendlaendische-handschriften/sammlungen/mss-phill/), among others.

1.3.4 Media revolution: Digitisation

Most of the state collections consolidated in the nineteenth century continue to exist and enrich their collections in the twentieth despite the two World Wars and political upheavals. During World War I, some important collections are destroyed, such as (in 1914) the library of the Catholic University of Leuven, established in 1834, which was reconstituted with international donations only to be destroyed again in 1940 (see Coppens, Derez, and Roegiers 2005). The states emerging from the demise of such political entities as the Austro-Hungarian Empire transform previous state libraries such as the Öffentliche k. k. Universitätsbibliothek (C.k. Veřejná a univerzitní knihovna) of Prague (for the history of the older collections, see Truhlář 1905, iii–xvi) into national libraries (Národní a univerzitní knihovna, 1935–1939/Zemská a univerzitní knihovna, 1939–1941/after incorporation of other Prague libraries, Národní knihovna, 1958–; see National Library of the Czech Republic 2012). In the Soviet Union, the Imperial Public Library, established in St Petersburg by Catherine II in 1795 and forcefully developed in the nineteenth century, survives the Russian Revolution as the Russian Public Library (1917–1925)/Official M. Saltykov-Shchedrin Library (1932–1992)/Russian National Library (1992–; see National Library of Russia 2018). From the early decades of the twentieth century, the accessibility of collections is enhanced by microfilming, which had been developed in the second half of the nineteenth century and was vigorously adopted for reproductions (e.g. the microfilming of millions of pages of British Library collections by the Library of Congress, 1927–1935). Both microfilms and microfiches are still in use in 2019, guaranteeing a lifespan of approximately five hundred years when stored properly (NEDCC 2007). In addition to microfilming campaigns of individual libraries, extensive microfilm collections are created, for example that at the University of Saint Louis, Missouri, which covers more than 37,000 manuscripts of the Vatican Library as well as 3,000 of other origins (slu.edu/library/special-collections/vatican-film-library), or that of the Institut de recherche et d'histoire des textes in Paris (IRHT; www.irht.cnrs.fr), currently containing microfilms of approximately 76,000 mediaeval manuscripts (medium-avance.irht.cnrs.fr). Accessibility is also enhanced through reproductions on paper, such as the volumes of the *Catalogue de manuscrits datés*, the oldest and still the most important project of the Comité international de paléographie latine, established in 1953, aiming at cataloguing, including reproductions, all manuscripts bearing the name of the scribe and/or date and/or place of copy (palaeographia.org/cipl/cipl.htm).

The great media revolution was, however, that of digitisation during the last decade of the twentieth century and in the early twenty-first century. Not only were library catalogues transferred from paper and microfilm/microfiche to online platforms in the 1990s, but intensive digitisation campaigns completely changed the accessibility of all types of formats. On the one hand, digital publications by commercial publishing houses transformed the printed collections of libraries; on the other, non-copyrighted older books and, in the 2010s, entire manuscripts became available free of charge through such databases as *Gallica* (gallica.fr; National Library of France), the digital library of the Münchener Digitalisierungszentrum (digitale-sammlungen.de; Bavarian State Library, Munich), the German database *Manuscripta mediaevalia* (manuscripta-mediaevalia.de), the Swiss database *e-codices* (e-codices.ch), the digitised manuscripts site of the Vatican Library (www.mss.vatlib.it/guii/scan/link.jsp), or the collaborative digitisation project of the Bodleian and Vatican Libraries funded by the Polonsky Foundation (bav.bodleian.ox.ac.uk, 2012–2017). The "Europeana Regia" project (europeanaregia.eu, 2010–2012, run by a consortium of five important research libraries) digitised some 1,000 manuscripts from Carolingian libraries (eighth to ninth centuries), Charles V and his family (fourteenth to fifteenth centuries), and the Aragonese kings of Naples (fifteenth century). Although reproductions, however good, will never supplant the original object, they make it easier to prepare for the indispensable work on originals. So far, digitisation has not induced most libraries to deny access to originals. On the contrary, a considerable increase in user-friendliness in the form of photography of original library holdings being allowed for personal research use, already common in Scandinavia, has occurred in the 2010s in such countries as France, the United Kingdom, Germany, and Italy. Thanks to these policies, library collections are today more universally accessible than ever.

Acknowledgements

The research for this article was carried out thanks to the Lamemoli project (Academy of Finland and University of Jyväskylä, no. 307635).

1.4 Textual traditions and early prints
Iolanda Ventura

In this section, I describe and discuss the philological practices developed by humanist and Renaissance scholars and philologists, as well as the role played by philology and textual criticism in the transition from manuscript to print. In order to do so, the focus will lie on selected examples from classical, patristic, and mediaeval literature. The way in which humanist and Renaissance scholars and philologists contributed to the transformation of culture, to the diffusion of literature through the printed editions that replaced manuscripts, and to the transition from manuscript to print – in short the transition from mediaeval to Renaissance culture – will be elucidated. Last but not least, practices and methodologies will be met which are still acknowledged or even imitated by textual scholars today.

1.4.1 The reception of a text as witnessed in print: Philological practices

For the history of texts and books, the fourteenth and the fifteenth centuries are a crucial time. The intellectual approach to the book and its content, as well as the structure and the characteristics of the contemporary reference libraries, were deeply changed, on the one hand by the rediscovery of classical texts and the new appreciation of classical literature, with a corresponding estrangement of the learned elite from mediaeval works, especially from theological and philosophical works; and, on the other hand, by the invention of the printing press and the subsequent changes in the book as an object – a product resulting from new technologies – and as a medium of transmission and communication of culture and literature (Pettegree 2011; Eisenstein 2000; Hellinga-Querido 2014, 2018; Barbier 2017; Nuovo 2013; Dondi 2016). This transition also radically influenced philological practices and methods of perceiving, evaluating, and editing texts. If the changes in the intellectual approach to the book and in the image of the ideal and real library can be gauged by the return to the literary milieu of classical works that had been either forgotten or more or less deliberately put aside because of their controversial content or difficult adaptability to Christian culture, the influence of philological practices can be easily seen in the various aspects of the humanistic engagement in bringing back to light, analysing both in content and form, and publishing classical and patristic texts. Examples include Lucretius (d. ca. 55–50 BC), Celsus (ca. 25 BC–AD 50), Aulus Gellius (125/130–after AD 170), or Caelius Aurelianus (early fifth century AD).

Philology, considered both as the desire to perform a critical examination of the text and the intention to improve its quality both in form and content, existed well before humanism and the Renaissance. Textual criticism was practised, for example, by learned scholars such as Lupus of Ferrières (abbot of Ferrières during the ninth century, d. ca. 862), who glossed manuscripts, recalling some variant readings from others or suggesting better readings, or Theodulf of Orléans (poet, philologian, and bishop of Orléans, d. 821), who contributed greatly to the establishment of a corrected text of the Bible compared to the corrupt one circulating before the cultural reform initiated by Charlemagne (on reading practices during Carolingian times, see Nebbiai 2013; O'Sullivan 2011, 2017). Glossing, commentating, and improving texts became a well-documented practice during the later Middle Ages, especially in the twelfth-century schools of grammar and philosophy. Nonetheless, the dimensions of philological engagement increased considerably during the fourteenth and the fifteenth centuries, when the activity of humanist scholars expanded the available classical library and the intellectual approach to it in several ways. First of all, they concentrated on a systematic search for manuscripts and texts in remote (especially monastic) libraries and on attempting to acquire new copies of old texts and/or to let them circulate among friends and fellow scholars. The most famous scholars engaging in such practices were Francesco Petrarca, Coluccio Salutati, and – above all – Poggio Bracciolini, who contributed to the rediscovery of Pliny the Younger, Cicero's *Epistolae*, and Lucretius (Sabbadini 1967). Second, they set upon tirelessly copying these texts and presenting them in a more appealing and comprehensible form, which led to the adoption of a new script, the humanistic script. They also undertook an in-depth examination of the preserved texts and a careful correction of them, as for instance in Ermolao Barbaro's *Castigationes Plinianae* or Angelo Poliziano's *Miscellanea* (Barbaro 1973–1979; Poliziano 1567), especially according to classical rules. Finally, after the invention of the printing press and the rise of the large printing enterprises, humanist scholars also acted as editors, correctors, and supervisors of the publication of printed editions. In this context, we may recall the cooperation of Marco Musuro, Andrea Navagero, or Giorgio Valla with Aldus Manutius, a printer with a strong classical background who endeavoured to print both graphically innovative and philologically correct editions (Reynolds and Wilson 2013, 123–164; Nuvoloni 2016, 80–86), or that of Erasmus of Rotterdam and Beatus Rhenanus with Froben's publishing house in Basle (Grafton 2011).

Despite all of these efforts, we cannot fail to note that the editorial work performed by humanists and the philological methodology employed by them at best consisted of (*i*) choosing the oldest and/or most authoritative manuscript (or group of manuscripts), and (*ii*) scattered or extensive corrections *ope ingenii*, mostly motivated by respect for the grammatical and syntactic rules of classical Latin (Timpanaro 2004, 15–27). Such an approach risked, for both classical and mediaeval texts, a dangerous distortion of the content through corrections not supported by a thorough and systematic collation of the entire manuscript tradition, and a transformation of the form based on personal or contemporary linguistic tastes. All of this lies at the roots of the later scepticism with which printed editions were met in modern philology and ecdotics. The editorial practices in the time of transition between manuscript and print have to be identified so that a modern editor can deal with the improvement or deterioration of the transmitted texts to be expected when preparing a critical edition. Therefore, we should ask ourselves not only how a text travelled through the age of handwritten manuscripts into that of printed copies; we should also identify the changes it experienced during that time, the places printed editions have in the stemma (the genealogical tree of the whole transmission; see 4.1), and what value scholars have assigned, or should assign, to the variant readings witnessed by printed editions.

I have chosen to provide some case studies as concrete examples of the way in which philologists and editors of texts have dealt with printed texts in the *recensio* of the witnesses of a text's diffusion, the establishment of a stemma, and the reconstruction of the correct and, if possible, original text. Before presenting them, it may be useful to briefly summarise our knowledge and basis for the interpretation of printed texts today. First of all, our knowledge of the extension of printing between the second half of the fifteenth century, that is, in the decades after the invention of the printing press and the first publication of the Gutenberg Bible, and the end of the eighteenth century has consistently improved. New attempts to catalogue incunabula (i.e. prints from before AD 1501) and early modern prints have considerably increased our knowledge of the number of printed texts of a classical, patristic, or mediaeval work. Examples include the *Gesamtkatalog der Wiegendrucke* (gesamt katalogderwiegendrucke.de), the *Incunabula Short Title Catalogue* (data.cerl.org/istc), the Italian *EDIT-16* database (edit16.iccu.sbn.it), the *Universal Short Title Catalogue* (ustc.ac.uk), or the *Medieval Evidence of Incunabula* database (data.cerl.org/mei/_search). Second, seminal research conducted, among others, by Andrew Pettegree, Lotte Hellinga, Anthony Grafton, and, more recently, Cristina Dondi and Angela Nuovo has shed more light on the history of the early modern printed book and the editorial and philological practices related to the preparation of a printed edition, its production, and its diffusion on the book market.

The way in which editors of classical, patristic, and mediaeval texts have dealt with prints cannot be called coherent. Depending upon (*i*) the number of manuscripts preserved, their quality, and their antiquity; (*ii*) the type and the quality of the printed texts, and their connection with one or more branches of the manuscript tradition; (*iii*) the connection between recent (read: fifteenth-century) manuscripts and first (read: incunabulum) printed editions; and (*iv*) the renown or obscurity of the learned scholar who edited the text, modern editors have made different choices: for example, when dealing with Beatus Rhenanus' editions, they have stressed the historical value of the edition in question but not necessarily the philological one. To my knowledge, there is neither a coherent approach nor a systematic discussion of the methodology to follow, one major exception being Alfredo Stussi's attention (and call for attention) to prints with special reference to vernacular or mediaeval "popular" texts, where the print is the last step in a long journey of a work from its origin to its first manuscript diffusion and later to its print reception (Stussi 2006, 37 ff., 88–95). More precisely, Stussi invites future editors of texts to look at both manuscripts and printed editions, since the latter may reproduce codices now lost or may offer better readings or interesting variant readings due to their particular history. This suggestion is undoubtedly important; but the editorial practice followed by editors is different and not homogeneous (on editions of printed texts, see 7.8). I will provide three examples of the state of the art – without any pretence of exhaustively dealing with the approaches – concerning a classical text (in this case, Lucretius), a patristic one (Tertullian), and a mediaeval one (Papias).

1.4.2 Classical literature: Lucretius

Lucretius' *De rerum natura*, edited, among others, by Martin (1963), by Ferguson Smith (1975), and by Ernout (1948–1955) can serve as an instructive example. Lucretius' *editio princeps* was published in Brescia in 1472/1473, edited by the humanist Tommaso Ferrando (on whom, see Baldacchini 1996; Beretta 2016). The long and well-studied textual tradition can be divided into two main eras, the Carolingian and the humanistic one. The tradition of Lucretius originates in a lost common an-

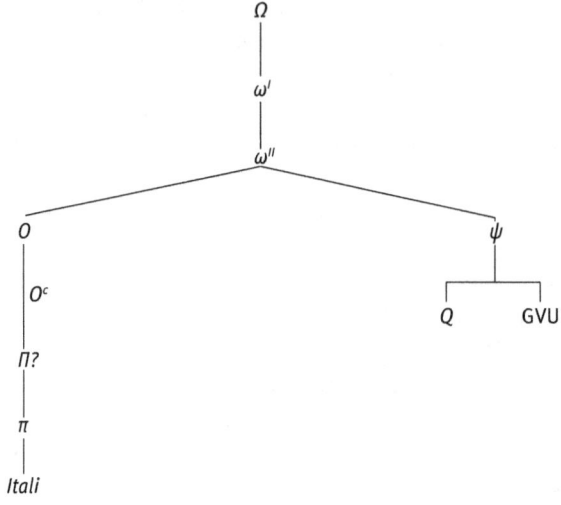

Fig. 1.4-1: Stemma of Lucretius' *De rerum natura*. Source: Reynolds (1983, 218).

cestor usually designated as ω^I and written, according to Karl Lachmann, in a pre-minuscule Caroline, whereas the pre-archetype (Ω) was produced in Gallia between the fourth and fifth centuries (Reynolds 1983; see also Butterfield 2013). This exemplar (ω^I) was affected by several accidents, causing mistakes in the sequence of the pages and errors in prosody in some verses. From its Carolingian copy, ω^{II}, which is the actual archetype (see 4.1.1) of all extant texts, the two main manuscript branches descend (see fig. 1.4-1), one represented by what is known as the *Codex oblongus* (O: Leiden, Universiteit Bibliotheek, Voss. Lat. F. 30), the other by the *Codex quadratus* (Q: Leiden, Universiteit Bibliotheek, Voss. Lat. Q. 94) and two fragmentary manuscripts, the *Schedae Gottorpienses* (G: København, Det kongelige Bibliotek, G. kgl. S. 211 2°) and the *Schedae Vindobonenses* (V and U: Wien, Österreichische Nationalbibliothek, 107, f. 1–6 and 7–10 respectively), all of which date back to Carolingian times. These codices sporadically resurfaced during the Middle Ages without giving the work any great renown or diffusion: Lucretius was rarely read during the Middle Ages. It was the discovery of an obscure, now-lost manuscript, ultimately derived from O and commonly designated as π, in a "locus satis longinquus" (quoted in Clark 1899, 125) [a rather remote place] by Poggio Bracciolini in 1417 that gave Lucretius' poem new popularity among the learned. Poggio entrusted his own copy of this manuscript (J) to Niccolò Niccoli and never received it back; it was subsequently lost. Niccoli's autograph copy is, however, preserved, and has been identified as the codex Firenze, Biblioteca Medicea Laurenziana, Plut. 35.30 (L). From this copy, albeit with some indirect connections to Poggio's and Niccoli's manuscript copies, a new tradition originated, the "Itali": twenty-three copied manuscripts in all, which help both in reconstructing Poggio's lost manuscript and in correcting the mistakes made by Niccoli while preparing his own copy. It is from this branch of the manuscript tradition that the first printed versions stem.

In the context of Lucretius' reception, the role played by the printed versions appears to be twofold. On the one hand, scholars dealing with cultural history have stressed the role played by the return of Lucretius' poem to the cultural scene where the development of scientific and philosophical culture during the Renaissance is concerned, a development reflected, above all, by the use of Lucretius as a source for the discussion of specific questions. But active philological interaction, for example annotations written in the margins of editions, was also not uncommon (see Beretta 2016; Norbrook, Harrison, and Hardie 2016; Passannante 2011; Palmer 2014; A. Brown 2010). On the other hand, philologists aiming to produce a reliable critical edition considered the "Itali" group only in terms of its connection to the older Carolingian codices, in order to establish that connection and the group's position in the *stemma codicum*, where it is now located at the end of a branch ultimately starting with the *Oblongus*. Thus, they concentrated their attention on the reconstruction of the origins of the tradition, without taking into account the characteristics of its later historical development. In this context, early printed editions cannot possibly play a relevant role for reconstructive philologists, neither as a source for emendation of the text nor as a conveyor of variant readings worth recording.

This clash between the "historical" and the "philological" approach becomes evident if we look at the three above-mentioned critical editions published during the twentieth century, namely by Martin (1963) in the Bibliotheca Teubneriana, by Ferguson Smith (1975) in the Loeb Classical Library, and by Ernout (1948–1955) in Belles Lettres. Browsing these editions, we notice that all "late" elements of the tradition are generally neglected, and the early printed editions are not used in a consistent way or even considered apart from some passing mentions. In this selective approach, not even the whole tradition of the "Itali" group is employed in the preparation of the critical edition and/or mentioned in the critical apparatus. Martin, for example, only quotes the manuscripts *A, B, C, F, L* from the "Itali" group, which he considers relevant to the reconstruction of Poggio's exemplar, and the lost manuscript *J*, and leaves aside the others. Besides, it is not easy to tell from the editors' methodologies what role the early printed editions played in the editions and apparatuses. For example, in the extensive commentary by Deufert (2017), variant readings from printed editions are mentioned, especially when they offer interesting conjectures produced *ope ingenii* and may be useful for an improvement of the text. Martin includes among his list of witnesses the *editio princeps*, the Aldina print from Venice (1500), and the Juntina print from Florence (1512), but I could not detect any relevant use or record of the readings featured in these printed versions in the critical apparatus, not even to show whether they feature *Binde-* or *Trennfehler* (see 4.3.1) that might connect them to early manuscripts and therefore elucidate their place in a stemma. The printed versions' existence is only acknowledged as a part of a large, multifarious group of later, indirect, and reception-related sources; these include authors from late Antiquity using or imitating Lucretius' syntagms, the early prints, and a long list of scholars and philologists who witnessed the use of a different text, emended it, and/or produced critical editions, such as Bentley, Diels, or Lachmann. The role these sources play is very limited. Ferguson Smith only refers to the prints in his bibliography (1975, lxv), but as a rule does not include them in the edition of the text. Perhaps he did not consider them relevant at all in an edition that aims to offer a reliable text rather than a large overview of variant readings, and where great attention was paid to the contribution of modern scholars to the improvement of the text. Even when he does occasionally include them, the result is hardly beneficial to the reader, for it lacks clarity and respect for the chronology of the scholarship. For instance, with reference to 1.306 (Ferguson Smith 1975, 26), he records that the variant reading "candenti" for "dispansae", witnessed by Nonius (as already pointed out by Martin), is a reading shared by Lindsay and adopted by "ed. Aldina, Pius, ed. Juntina, Pascal, Diels, Büchner". He thus merges indirect reception, printed editions, and earlier scholarship in one brief note. The third editor, Ernout, declares already in the introduction to his edition (1948–1955, 1:xix–xx) that, while facing such a clear, homogeneous textual tradition shown by the ninth-century manuscripts, he did not intend either to record errors witnessed by a single manuscript (!) or to overload the critical apparatus with "*variantes inutiles*". Although Ernout does not elaborate what a *variante inutile* is for him, and therefore makes his opinion on the matter difficult to judge, his statement could possibly be read as an attempt to respect a supposed "majority principle" aimed at avoiding any unnecessary overloading of the critical apparatus with variant readings featured in a single manuscript and clearly recognisable as errors (on what is to be included in a critical apparatus, see 6.3.1 below). But, as he provides no clear definition of what he classifies as *variante inutile*, we may well suspect that among them there are variant readings that could be of some interest for reconstructing the historical development of the text and/or textual innovations shown by humanist manuscripts and prints. This is not the place to discuss the editor's decision, merely to point out its consequences with regard to the later manuscripts and the printed editions, which may be summarised as follows: variant readings from humanist manuscripts (in fact only a selection of them) are mentioned "que là où elles apportent au texte une correction qui paraît sûre" (Ernout 1948–1955, 1:xix) [only when they offer a correction that appears to be sure], while printed editions are not considered at all.

The printed editions' low reputation is reflected both by their absence from the stemmata provided in the critical editions I was able to consult and by their scarce representation in the critical apparatus, and it appears to have affected the approach to the *editio princeps* as well. As noted by Beretta in the introduction to the facsimile published in 2016 (Beretta 2016, 45–47), the editorial work carried out by Ferrando (i.e. the editor of the 1472/1473 edition) has largely been either ignored or despised due to the fact that he relied on one single manuscript only, and his edition is considered as mediocre *tout court* (e.g. by Munro, who edited Lucretius in 1864). This is surprising because of the presence in it of several correct readings, and of its possible proximity to Niccoli's copy (as hypothesised by Reeve 1980, 33), which would grant the edition a place for itself and a certain independence within the "Itali" group.

1.4.3 Patristic literature

In Lucretius' case, late codices are considered *deteriores* from a philological point of view (possibly because of the enormous weight of the Carolingian tradition), despite the fact that they are seen as a decisive step in the historical reconstruction of the reception of the text and its role in the culture of the Renaissance and its philosophical predilections. The reason for this is clear: we have humanist manuscripts and, above all, early printed editions to thank for their decisive contribution towards the rediscovery of Lucretius and his subsequent renewed fame, but the reconstruction of the text is supposed to rely on the Carolingian tradition, namely on the codices believed to be closest to the archetype.

If we now turn our attention to philological practices used when editing patristic literature, the situation differs to some extent. It took some time for scholarship to acknowledge that humanism and the Renaissance were not classical-oriented times *tout court*, but that there was an interest, and consequently a market, for patristic authors and their works as well. As noted by Cesare Vasoli (1997), humanist culture was not just interested in literature, philology, and culture, but developed a critical conscience and a considerable interest in morals and ethics, and consequently became aware of the contemporary moral decadence and of the necessity of a spiritual instruction that only the Christian *patres* could offer, both the Latin and the Greek Church Fathers, some of whom had recently been rediscovered and whose return to western Europe en masse during the second half of the fifteenth century resulted in a large manuscript tradition and, later, in a blooming of printed editions. All in all, we can state that a "patristic humanism" emerged between the fourteenth and fifteenth centuries, characterised by a constant interest in Latin and Greek Christian literature and, like "classical humanism", by a certain fervour in discovering new texts as well as in examining and correcting them (overview in Gentile 1997).

The interest in patristic literature in the age of humanism has, at last, been thoroughly analysed during the past twenty years. Several anthologies have covered the philological and editorial practices devoted to the Fathers, the ways in which texts and authors were approached, studied, and edited (see, among others, Cortesi and Leonardi 2000; Cortesi 2002, 2004, 2006, 2010; Grane et al. 1993–1998; Colombi 2012; see also www-3.unipv.it/retrapa/). The mediaeval, humanist, and Renaissance transmission of the Latin and Greek Fathers has been thoroughly analysed with reference to selected examples, such as Jerome, Augustine, Tertullian, or Gregory of Nazianzus, as has the printed tradition of patristic texts. One volume has been devoted solely to *editiones principes* (Cortesi 2006). Finally, an anthology has been devoted to the transmission of patristic texts and the methodological issues it raises (Colombi 2012). At the centre of these studies, we find outstanding personalities, such as Ambrogio Traversari or Cardinal Bessarion, who played the same role for patristic literature as Petrarca, Salutati, or Poggio did for classical literature, as well as decisive historical circumstances, such as the Church councils that took place in Ferrara, Florence, and Constance. Editorial work performed by humanists in studying and editing patristic works, especially by leading figures such as Beatus Rhenanus or Erasmus of Rotterdam, has been taken into account as well. Finally, interest in *editiones principes* of patristic literature, both Latin and Greek, has strongly increased, in connection both with the history of print and the history of texts.

The reasons for this interest in *editiones principes* are numerous, but among them three stand out in importance. The first is the connection between the late branches of transmission of some works and the first printed editions, allowing philologists to identify, if not the exemplar used by the printers to prepare a print, then at least the branch of the manuscript tradition to which it belonged (Hellinga-Querido 2014, 37–66, 67–101, 156–167), and therefore to connect handwritten and printed transmission closely. The possibility of finding such a connection is particularly frequent for Greek texts, whose reception in Latin Renaissance culture finds its beginning with the arrival in Italy of Greek manuscripts during the second half of the fifteenth century, and with their use for the production of the first printed editions. The second reason for the renewed interest in *editiones principes* can be found in the significance of the commercial, cultural, religious, and sometimes even political circumstances forming the context in which a printed edition (or several printed editions issued in the same place and/or over a specific period of time) was produced. Obviously, this holds true for all prints, but the emergence of printed patristic editions during a period characterised by the need for religious and spiritual reform, and/or by contrasts between the ecclesiastical hierarchy and that need for reform, certainly means that the assessment of their meaning has facets that other editions lack. If we look, for example, at the Basle or Paris prints issued during the sixteenth century, that is, during the attempts to reform the Catholic Church and adapt it to the spiritual needs of contemporary Christians, or at the short "Golden Age" of the enterprise of printing patristic texts in Rome (see Dondi et al. 2016), we see that the significance of these editions and their study cannot be related only to the technical and commercial features characterising the history of print, but should also be linked with the intellectual, political, and spiritual history of the time. On the other hand, if we look at Erasmus of Rotterdam's activity as editor of Jerome's works, he did not act as a neutral learned scholar; instead, he considers the spiritual message delivered by the *pater ecclesiae* and does not hesitate to criticise it when he sees that it manipulates the truth of Scripture (see Pabel 2002, 2008). Third, there is a certain historical continuity linking the *editiones principes* first to their early modern reprints (e.g. the *Patrologia Latina* and the *Patrologia Graeca*) and then to the nineteenth- and twentieth-century projects of editions ultimately aiming at replacing them and at putting at scholars' disposal the pillars of patristic literature in a philologically improved form (e.g. the CSEL or CCSL/CCCM series). Therefore, a historical overview of the patristic printed editions and their analysis from a historical perspective cannot be split into separate periods, but must be considered as a whole divided into mutually dependent sections. In general, the philological enterprise cannot be separated from or carried out in the absence of a full historical examination that includes both manuscripts and prints.

A case in point may be the reconstruction of the history of Tertullian's corpus of writings, which Pierre Petitmengin (2004) has masterfully traced in a special study, and which I will attempt to summarise here. Quintus Septimius Florens Tertullianus (ca. AD 160–after AD 220) was one of the most outstanding early Christian theologians and a ferocious anti-pagan polemicist. The high mediaeval (before AD 1200) knowledge of Tertullian's numerous writings was conveyed in four collections, the most famous and relevant of which is the one put together in Cluny and handed down by the famous manuscript Firenze, Biblioteca Nazionale Centrale, Conv. Soppr. J.VI.9, used by Kroymann (1906) for his edition. From the Cluny corpus, a new collection originated in three stages, the Hirsau corpus, which was ultimately the basis for the edition supervised by Beatus Rhenanus and published in Basle in 1521. Only two treatises retained a certain independence from this corpus: *Adversus Iudaeos* and *Apologeticum*. The latter enjoyed success in its own right in the entire Middle Ages. During the thirteenth century, a new collection was formed, witnessed by the manuscript Città del Vaticano, Biblioteca Apostolica Vaticana, Ottob. Lat. 25; at the same time, the Cluny corpus continued to be copied, albeit in different arrangements. A "changement dramatique" (Petitmengin 2004, 76) [dramatic change] took place in Italy, or more precisely in Florence, during the fifteenth century, when the Hirsau corpus was brought there and a new phase of the manuscript diffusion and a new branch of the stemma originated. This corpus can be considered as the basis for the humanist and Renaissance reception of Tertullian, since it was diffused not only in Italy (and read, among others, by illustrious readers such as Poliziano) but also in France. Finally, as we have already seen, the same Hirsau corpus, in two manuscripts, was used by Beatus Rhenanus for the edition published in Basle in 1521 (one of the manuscripts is now lost; the other is preserved in the successor to Beatus' library, Sélestat, Bibliothèque humaniste, MS 88). Beatus Rhenanus' edition, although not the first of Tertullian's works, is particularly important for scholars, not only because it witnesses a late branch of the Hirsau corpus but also because of interest in its editor, an outstanding personality in the history of philology, textual criticism, and editorial work, as well as in the religious and spiritual debates of his time.

In the case of Tertullian, we notice how it is possible to reconstruct a more or less uniform path leading from the handwritten tradition to the printed editions, and to put together a history of the texts and of the types of corpora and miscellanies handing them down. The same can be said, of course, for other Fathers whose textual traditions are relatively limited, and therefore easy to map and to deal with. For the study of Tertullian, however, we must emphasise that we are reliant on a Renaissance editor (Beatus Rhenanus) whose contribution cannot be overlooked, and indeed has not been. Of course, we are not always so lucky. Sometimes, as in case of Augustine's *Confessiones*, the printed editions (in this case, the one published in Strasbourg around 1470; cf. *Gesamtkatalog der Wiegendrucke*, A02893) represent the last step of a long textual journey, or better, the last witnesses of a long and extremely rich manuscript tradition that includes hundreds of copies (see Simonetti 2012). When facing difficult choices in establishing a selection of manuscripts as the basis for an edition, the editor may tend to neglect printed versions, especially when a wide manuscript basis is available, which is what has happened in the case of Augustine.

It is often difficult to assess the role played by the philologists who produced the early printed editions. These editors (a good example is Beatus Rhenanus himself) were not just philologists or scholars, but learned men involved in religious discussions and polemics, and, even when dealing with a manuscript or a group of manuscripts they considered reliable, they could not refrain from correcting the text more for ideological than philological reasons, as in the case of the "Roman-" or "Protestant-oriented" editions (see Grafton 2011; see also Petitmengin 2006 on the main characteristics of the *editiones principes*). Thus, printed editions may include conscious manipulations of the texts. Such manipulations may have a historical value, for they bear witness to the intellectual and spiritual struggle of the sixteenth century; but do they have to be taken into account during the preparation of a critical edition? Evidently, the case is different here from a simple correction *ope ingenii* in the edition of, for example, a classical text, as that is meant only to improve the quality of the text, whereas the manipulations in early printed editions may heavily influence or manipulate the content and the intellectual background of a text. In most cases, it would not be easy to document all of this because of the overabundance of material, and for this reason the evidence of the reception of the patristic texts in early prints has generally not been taken into account. It seems that editors of patristic texts, especially of works characterised by remarkable length and by the availability of several manuscripts, have tried to reduce the amount of sources by selecting the most correct and reliable ones among the oldest codices, simply leaving the further development of the text aside. In this further development, the printed editions represent the final step because of their generally close connection with the most recent codices at the time.

We can summarise the scholarly attitude towards early printed editions and their historical and philological importance as follows. The textual variation in early printed editions in the case of Lucretius' *De rerum natura* has been recorded but has not been taken into account in the establishment of the text itself (perhaps unjustly). This might also be the case with other classical texts whose transmission relies on several copies and runs through the Middle Ages. The situation is, of course, different, in cases where we have only a printed edition at our disposal, as in the case of Caelius Aurelianus' *Tardae passiones*, of which only the printed edition published in Paris in 1533 by Johannes Günther von Andernach, and no manuscripts (except for a brief fragment), is preserved. On the other hand, when looking at scholarship devoted to patristic texts, we notice a growing interest in printed editions from a historical perspective, but these witnesses are nonetheless left aside when dealing with the *recensio codicum* and the constitution of the original text. They are therefore not used or represented, either in the establishment of the text or in the constitution of the critical apparatus. A rare, but important, exception is Tertullian himself: Heinrich Hoppe, in his edition of Tertullian's *Apologeticum* published in Prague in 1939, does devote a special paragraph (Hoppe 1939, xxix–xxxii) to the history of the printed editions and to the assessment of their value for the history of the text, tracing, for example, their inclusion in a specific branch of the tradition. Besides, in the case of the *Apologeticum*, a work that Rhenanus could not find in the manuscripts of the Hirsau corpus, Hoppe stresses Rhenanus' debt to the 1515 Aldina edition supervised by Iohannes Baptista Egnatius. Hoppe even incorporated their variant readings into the critical apparatus, especially – at least, this is my impression – when they turn against the vulgate version and bear witness to some alternative readings. The same positive attitude towards printed editions can be detected in cases in which philologists are forced to recognise the defective nature of the manuscript tradition. In these cases (e.g. Tertullian's *De pudicitia*), printed editions act as a necessary aid in establishing a better text (on this, see Micaeli 2014).

1.4.4. Mediaeval literature: The specific features of the edition of Papias' *Elementarium*

After dealing with examples derived from classical and patristic literature, it is now time to turn our attention to mediaeval Latin literature. The study of the transition from handwritten to printed form in the case of mediaeval Latin texts, and the assessment of the value that incunabula and sixteenth-century printed editions may have for accessing mediaeval Latin literature, is not highly developed, and is perhaps even tainted by some doubts and suspicions about the reliability of these sources. This somewhat negative attitude can be explained in terms of the following considerations. First of all, some works that we consider today to be excellent writings were never printed, whereas some minor, less original, compendium-like ones which had the function and the merit of being useful for spiritual and/or intellectual improvement found a market and a way into print. Works that were not printed and were left in manuscript form may afterwards have been lost (see Haye 2016, 191–

204). Two good examples of such a contrast between what we today consider literary masterpieces that were not printed and everyday compendia that were, are (*i*) the scarce *Fortleben* of Ratherius of Verona's (887–974) *Phrenesis*, one of the finest introspective autobiographies of the Middle Ages, which has been preserved in only one manuscript and was never printed in early modern times, and (*ii*) the fine performance on the book market of Guido de Monte Rocherii's (d. 1331) *Manipulus curatorum*, a manual for priests that enjoyed more than twenty-one editions in German territories alone between 1474 and 1500 (Aquilon 2013). Therefore, the study of mediaeval Latin literature had to build up (and indeed did build up) its own canon of representative texts that is not always congruent with their diffusion.

Mediaeval Latin philology is ultimately based on the principles of classical philology and textual criticism, although several scholars have tried to grant the analysis of mediaeval texts and the editorial techniques devoted to them a certain methodological independence and specificity (Orlandi 2008; Göransson et al. 2016; P. Chiesa 2016). We cannot deal with those attempts here; for our purposes, we simply recall that some edition projects have been started with the aim of replacing old – and flawed – early modern prints. Among these initiatives, the ongoing project of a critical edition of Albert the Great's *Opera omnia*, the *Editio Coloniensis*, can be mentioned; it has engaged the scholars of the Albertus Magnus Institute (albertus-magnus-institut.de) for several decades and aims at replacing the old editions printed during the seventeenth century by Petrus Jammy (1644–1651) and during the nineteenth by Emile Borgnet (1890–1899).

Could it possibly be a consequence of this mistrust of old prints and/or of the necessity of creating a specific philological method for editing mediaeval Latin texts that a discussion of the value of incunabula and early modern printed editions cannot be found in the manuals of mediaeval Latin philology (P. Chiesa 2002, 2016; Timpanaro 2004; Berté and Petoletti 2017), whose goal is to present problems and solutions when dealing with the manuscript tradition of mediaeval Latin texts? It is also rare, if not impossible, to find discussions of printed editions in the context of surveys of manuscript traditions. To give a single example: Barbara Fleith (1991) and Giovanni Paolo Maggioni (1995) are the most expert specialists involved in the study of the wide and complex tradition of Jacobus de Voragine's *Legenda aurea*, a collection of saints' lives written in several stages during the second half of the thirteenth century that enjoyed immense success both in manuscript and in print. Both scholars have worked extensively on determining the stemma and the accumulation of various redactions and versions; Maggioni has also studied the manuscript tradition in depth to distinguish the author's versions and establish how they evolved, and to classify manuscripts in the branches of the stemma. Astonishingly, neither Fleith nor Maggioni devoted even a single paragraph to printed editions, as if they were a disposable late by-product of the manuscript tradition and not witnesses of the development of the texts! Perhaps they made this choice because the search for an "original" or "author's" version was easier to perform with the help of codices alone, or because the richness and complexity of that same manuscript tradition made it necessary to untangle the manuscripts in order to select the ones an edition could be based on (see P. Chiesa 2016, 99–103).

An interesting exception to this selective editorial practice adopted by mediaeval Latin specialists, which ultimately results in a disregard for printed editions – which may be considered either too close to manuscripts, and consequently as belonging to the category of *descripti*, or not relevant in comparison with a large, rich, and complex manuscript tradition that becomes the ultimate "battlefield" of philological methodology – is represented by the critical edition of Papias' *Elementarium* initiated by the extensive work of Violetta de Angelis, whose published findings are still limited to a very small section of the work, namely the letter A (de Angelis 1974). Papias' *Elementarium*, one of the most successful Latin dictionaries of the Middle Ages, was written between 1041 and 1063, possibly by a member of the clergy whose biography is obscure. The dictionary enjoyed huge success during the Middle Ages (the *FAMA* database lists 146 manuscripts; see fama.irht.cnrs.fr/en/oeuvre/254652), and was printed in Milan in 1476 (printer: Domenico da Vespolate) and in Venice in 1485 (printer: Andrea de Bonetti), 1491 (printer: Teodoro de rogationibus de Aula), and 1496 (printer: Filippo Pinzi). Other editions followed afterwards, but de Angelis's attention was attracted by the presence in the three editions following the *princeps* (1485, 1491, and 1496) of several interpolations, omissions, and changes indicating a departure from the manuscript tradition. In her introduction (de Angelis 1974, xviii–xxi), she discusses the innovations shown by the first and the last of those prints, and explains them in terms of a contamination of the tradition and in terms of the work of the humanist in charge of the edition, Bonino Mombrizio (or Mombricius – see Spanò Martinelli 2001; de Angelis 2011). He concentrated his efforts mostly on the entries including Greek words, where he adds the correct Greek words after the usual Latin transliteration, and therefore introduces his own glosses. After this summary of the type of text and transmission de Angelis was confronted with, and having emphasised the attention she paid to the printed editions, which she did not simply dismiss as witnesses showing later interpolations, changes, and manipulations to be disparaged or left aside while longing for the purity of the "original text", it is now time to see how she made use of the readings and innovations provided by the two prints she mainly concentrated on (namely Milan, 1476, and Venice, 1496). Her method can be summarised as follows. Since she clearly acknowledges the impossibility of determining which family of manuscripts the original text rests on, and, on the other hand, which family already shows the interpolations that could lie behind the additions found in the prints, she adopts a threefold categorisation and treatment. All lemmata in the dictionary receive a number in the edition. Whereas interpolations shown by a whole family α and β are simply inserted into the body of the text with a running number "n" exactly like the entries represented in the entire manuscript tradition, the ones offered only by some codices are included in the main text but receive a number "n-bis". The same treatment and numbering as "n-bis" are reserved for the entries displayed by the prints that presuppose the contamination of the two families (in order to avoid confusion, she puts these in square brackets). Finally, the entries clearly interpolated by Mombricius are featured only in the critical apparatus (see de Angelis 1974, xlvi–xlix).

Clearly, the example provided by the critical edition of Papias' *Elementarium* cannot be considered the norm, for it represents a notable exception to the general lack of interest among philologists in prints and, above all, in their function as late witnesses of the dynamism of mediaeval Latin texts, especially as working tools or technical texts that could (and indeed do) show an internal instability per se, against which – or even adding to it – the humanist and Renaissance editors reacted or positioned themselves in their philological and editorial activity.

1.5 Palaeography, codicology, and stemmatology

Peter A. Stokes

As has been evident from the discussion so far, although there are printed books which are important or even central to textual transmission, the majority of texts which are addressed by stemmatology survive in manuscript books, and so the preparation of an edition will most often require working with manuscripts. This in turn means that an understanding of manuscripts as books and objects is essential for editors, and this in turn requires a good understanding of palaeography and codicology. At one level, this is obvious: editors need to be able to read the manuscript witnesses to their tradition, and this often requires familiarity with a relatively wide range of scripts and scribal practices. As well as simply reading the letters on the page, editors also need an understanding of abbreviations, likely scribal misreadings such as forms that may look like a certain letter in one script but a different letter in another script, and so on, as well as a broader understanding of the physical and cultural context of the text's transmission. This section will therefore commence with a brief historical introduction to the development and diffusion of the "auxiliary" disciplines; then, some examples of the significance of these to editing will be given; and finally the discussion will turn to some of the methodological implications of this section, particularly in today's digital context.

1.5.1 Definitions and historical introduction

In essence, palaeography means simply the study of "old" (παλαιός) writing, whereas codicology refers to the study of the *codex*, the physical book and its structure. In practice, however, the details of these definitions and their scope have evolved considerably over the centuries. Palaeography has long been seen as an "auxiliary" discipline, the goals of which still include being able first to read historical scripts and then to be able to determine the date and place of writing and to identify samples of writing that were likely to have been written by the same person. While these remain a core part of modern palaeography, the field also incorporates, and indeed often focuses on, broader questions such as the development of scripts, the cultural influences that lead to changes in scribal practice, and work on society and culture more broadly, such as what changes in script can tell us about the exchange and interaction of ideas and cultures, and about questions such as learning and education, authority and its perception, and so on. The chronological range of palaeography's remit is not clearly defined, but the inclusion in it of the (European) Middle Ages seems clear; the study of Renaissance and perhaps early modern script – but usually no later – is typically considered part of palaeography as well. Nevertheless, palaeographers certainly have worked on more recent writing (e.g. M. Smith 2008), and the methodological overlaps between palaeography and modern forensic document analysis have also been noticed (on which, see esp. Davis 2007). The study of pre-mediaeval handwriting is sometimes distinguished as part of papyrology, although palaeographers certainly work with material written on papyrus and so the distinction here is far from clear-cut. Much the same can be said for writing in inscriptions, which can be formally classified as epigraphy but which clearly has overlaps with palaeography as well. Codicology, on the other hand, broadly refers to the study of the physical object rather than the text or writing in it; it therefore includes aspects such as the written support (usually paper or parchment) and its preparation, the ways in which pages are formed and bound together, the structures of bindings, and the ways in which these can be interrogated to determine how the book was used and changed over time. This interrogation of layers in the physical object to determine the history around it has often led the field to be described as an "archaeology of the book" (e.g. CNRS 1987). Both palaeography and codicology can also extend into other related topics such as the ways in which books were transmitted, used, and gathered into collections or libraries, the book trade, and many other topics which are now often labelled under the broader heading of "book history".

Although an awareness of and, to some extent, study of scripts and handwriting is evident during the Renaissance, if not earlier, the beginning of palaeography as a discipline is normally associated with works such as Jean Mabillon's *De re diplomatica* (1681, 2nd ed. 1709), a study which included discussion, characterisation, and reproduction of different Latin scripts, as well as Bernard de Montfaucon's *Palaeographica Graeca* (1708) and Humfrey Wanley's *Librorum veterum septentrionalium catalogus* (1705), in which Wanley attempted to systematically catalogue many hundreds of manuscripts and documents, using dated documents as *comparanda* for undated scripts. As Mabillon's title suggests, much of the work at this time was aimed at establishing the authenticity or otherwise of charters and other documents, an emphasis continued in other important works such as

Scipione Maffei's *Istoria diplomatica* (1727) and the *Nouveau traité de diplomatique* by René Prosper Tassin and Charles François Toustain (1750–1765). Also significant during the Renaissance, but continuing at this time and indeed thereafter, was the search for and systematic cataloguing of manuscripts (a useful review of which has been produced by Touwaide 2010, 267–283; see also 1.4 above), often driven by the desire to find older and better exemplars of important texts. This emphasis on cataloguing and editing continued to develop throughout the eighteenth and nineteenth centuries, along with interest in the scripts and physical formats of manuscript books. Practices varied, particularly but by no means entirely according to country, with some institutions producing summary catalogues (such as those of the British, Bodleian, and Cambridge University Libraries) and others more detailed cataloguing. Similarly, some editors focused more than others on detailed studies of the known manuscripts in a given tradition: compare, for instance, the largely uncritical reprinting of older editions in the Greek and Latin *Patrologiae* of Jacques-Paul Migne with approximately contemporary works such as Emile Littré's edition of Hippocrates (1839–1861), in which he discusses how important it was for him to see and compare all the known manuscripts in libraries in Europe (Littré 1839–1861, 1:xviii–ix).

This emphasis on manuscript sources received further impetus in the later parts of the nineteenth century, in part connected to improved technologies such as photolithography that allowed cheaper and more accurate reproduction of images; a result of this was the increasing publication of albums and facsimiles such as those of the Palaeographical Society (E. M. Thompson, Warner, Kenyon, and Gilson 1903–1912; E. M. Thompson, Warner, Kenyon, Gilson, et al. 1913–1930). This increasing emphasis on scientific evidence can also be seen in developments such as the "New Palaeography", which was developed by students of Ludwig Traube such as Elias Avery Lowe and William Lindsay, both of whom worked to establish clear criteria for categorising and dating scripts, including a study with reproductions and descriptions of all known surviving literary manuscripts in Latin dating to before 800 (Lowe 1934–1971; see also Lindsay 1914 for further discussion of the "New Palaeography"). As well as making significant advances in method, the "New Palaeographers" (among others) served to increase the role of palaeography as a distinct discipline as opposed to a set of techniques and methods that formed part of diplomatics and textual criticism. Editors of texts also paid increasing attention to codicology, as demonstrated by works such as Jean Irigoin's *Histoire du text de Pindare* (1952). Indeed, both palaeography and the newly emerging discipline of codicology developed significantly during this time. Different approaches to, and indeed definitions of, palaeography continued to emerge, with some focusing more on the morphology or appearance of the script (Derolez 2003), some focusing more on writing as a dynamic process (such as Mallon 1952), and some looking more broadly at the social and cultural context of writing (an approach championed particularly by Armando Petrucci, among others); we might also mention the "integral" palaeography of Leonard Boyle (2001). The question of objectivity and clear criteria for dating, localising, and identifying hands continued to be discussed, and achieved prominence in a Latin context with work by Léon Gilissen (1977), who attempted to develop a purely quantitative method of scribal identification; although his work was not successful and was strongly criticised by his contemporaries, it is nevertheless still influential, particularly more recently with the application of computer vision and other related fields to this question. Another, much more nuanced attempt to find clear criteria for describing script is evident in the work of Collette Sirat, who worked principally on Hebrew palaeography and who drew on cognitive science and many other fields before finally concluding that no definitive, objective proof of scribal identification can be achieved (Sirat 2006, 310 and esp. 493). Indeed, the possibility or otherwise of using measurements and other quantitative methods in palaeography was the topic of fierce debate in the 1990s due largely to a series of articles that were published in *Scrittura e Civiltà* (Costamagna et al. 1995–1998). Technical developments also continued to be used here, such as the development of (relatively) accessible colour printing, which led to the publication of colour facsimiles from the 1970s. Codicology also progressed significantly in this period, with key works including those by Devreesse (1954), Gilissen (1977), Lemaire (1989), and Maniaci (2002); this list and substantial further bibliography has been given by Touwaide in his survey (2010, 307–309). Quantitative methods in codicology had considerably more success given that the material is much more suited to quantification and measurement, and also because the types of questions were different, focusing not on individual identification but rather on large-scale developments in book production, with perhaps the best-known work being Malachi Beit-Arié's *SfarData* database of mediaeval Hebrew manuscripts (sfardata.nli.org.il).

Moving into the present century, perhaps the biggest transformation in codicology and especially palaeography has been the advent of the so-called digital age, with near-universal access to personal computers among palaeographers, codicologists, and others working in related fields, along with increasing quantities of colour digital images of manuscript pages, catalogue descriptions, digital scholarly editions, and databases such as *SfarData*. Quantitative approaches to palaeography have taken on new life with the application of state-of-the-art techniques in machine vision and pattern recognition, and, at the time of writing, rapid progress is being made in the automatic treatment of handwritten text recognition, layout analysis, writer identification, and script classification (for one important discussion among many, see Kestemont, Christlein, and Stutzmann 2017). Access to images of manuscripts is also increasing enormously with the large-scale digitisation of entire repositories and with innovations such as the International Image Interoperability Framework (IIIF), meaning, on the one hand, that scholars now have images of handwriting of a scale and breadth that was never possible before, particularly for those based outside Europe, but also, on the other hand, that large-scale analyses of hundreds, thousands, or even millions of manuscripts, whether automatic, manual, or both, are now becoming feasible. Applications to codicology are less developed at this point, in part probably because existing technology is very advanced in the treatment of text and image but much less so for the intricate three-dimensional structures which form the basis of codicology, but nevertheless progress continues with codicological models, databases, and three-dimensional scanning and printing, including the increasing integration of codicological information into digital scholarly editions (a recent example being Stokes 2018b, esp. "Labs" > "Codicological Visualisation" and "Collation Visualisations"). As before, questions remain as to the nature of palaeography in particular and the degree to which these more "distant" approaches can or should respond to palaeographical questions, as well as where their limits might lie. Overall, however, quantitative and digital approaches are being increasingly accepted, as demonstrated by their presence in meetings such as those of the Comité international de paléographie latine; indeed, the view at the time of writing seems largely consistent with that expressed by J. Peter Gumbert some twenty years ago, namely that "palaeography *and codicology* are [...] *happily* [...] becoming *also* arts of measurement" (1998, 404; emphasis in original).

1.5.2 The relevance of codicology and palaeography: Some examples

Given this brief introduction to the background of palaeography and codicology, the question arises of how these relate to editing, textual criticism, and stemmatology. As has already been hinted, one aspect is the degree of overlap in some of the methodological and definitional debates in these "auxiliary" disciplines, including the question of being an "art" or a "science", which clearly applies across them. As Tanselle has observed, "the search for properly 'scientific' method has been perhaps the dominant thread running through the history of textual criticism" (1994, 18–19), with descriptions of editing as "scientific" and therefore "objective" extending at least back to Lachmann, and with Maas and others seeking at least in part to systematise the editorial process as much as possible. The pervasiveness of this dichotomy extends much further than this, however: the relationship between the "arts" and the "sciences" more generally has long been a fraught one, and, as Lorraine Daston and Peter Galison (2007) make clear in their five-hundred-page history of the concept of objectivity, many people have been seeking a resolution to this problem across different disciplines for centuries in ways that are very much tied up with different intellectual and even historical moments. It comes as no surprise, then, that more recent developments in computing and the digital humanities have been applied in no small measure to editing as well as to palaeography, with automated methods developed particularly for collation and stemmatics, as indeed they have also been for attempts at transcription (through optical character recognition) and even layout analysis (for further discussion, see esp. Pierazzo 2015, 109–117). Such work has raised real questions about the nature of editing just as it has for palaeography, as well as about the collaborative nature of the editorial project.

Furthermore, philology, and indeed most of the so-called "auxiliary sciences", deal to a greater or lesser extent with what can be claimed to be facts (if there is such a thing): a given text was written at some point, by someone, for instance. We may never know when, but there is presumably a "correct" answer in some sense, and it is very possible that the more technical sciences can help us find this "answer" in a way that is not at all possible with literature, for example, and perhaps even history (depending on one's point of view). However, the "answer" in this concrete sense is normally only a small part of what people in the humanities are typically interested in: knowing where and when something was written is normally the means, not the end. Furthermore, this notion of facts also has implications for editorial practice. It is sometimes argued that editors should distinguish between objective fact, "what is on the page", and editorial interpretation. A direct consequence of this is the idea of a library of digital texts which can be shared and used for different purposes since, if the "base" text is objective, then who (or what) transcribes it is irrelevant: by definition, the text will be the same, apart from any factual errors, and therefore it can be reused for any purpose (a discussion of such views is given in Pierazzo 2015, 92). However, as fig. 1.5-1 shows, context is essential in transcription: the only way we can resolve such ambiguities is by considering the linguistic context through the lens of our training and our understanding of the text. Simply deciding which letters are written on the page depends to a greater or lesser extent on the transcriber's understanding of the text and the physical object that carries it (Pierazzo 2015, esp. chap. 2).

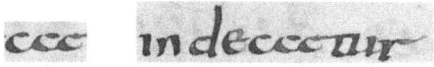

Fig. 1.5-1: St. Gallen, Stiftsbibliothek, Cod. Sang. 189, p. 76 line 5 (detail): *Eucherii instructiones, Isidori liber differentiarum, S. Hieronymus super Daniel*. Source: e-codices.ch/en/list/one/csg/0189. The example is taken from Pierazzo (2015, 87). The first image appears to read "ccc", but the context makes clear that the reading is in fact "ca". Image: CC-BY-NC.

In addition to these more theoretical considerations, examples also abound of very practical implications of palaeography and codicology for textual studies. One striking example of this among many, one which also illustrates problems in the subjectivity of transcription, emerged during the "LangScape" project, which ran at King's College London from 2006 to 2009 (langscape.ac.uk). One of the documents that was edited for this project was an English charter issued in 1061 which records the grant by King Edward of Ottery St Mary in Devon to St Mary's in Rouen (Sawyer 1968, no. 1033). The charter survives in seven manuscript copies, ranging in date from the thirteenth through to the seventeenth centuries. Like almost all charters from the period, the main text is in Latin, but a section, known as the "charter bounds", is normally written in Old English. However, a fourteenth-century enrolment of the charter is particularly unusual (London, National Archives, C 66/308 (*olim* PRO 4 Ric II pt 1), m 3). In place of the Old English bounds is an unintelligible text, beginning "Arcest opstruet sente ont celen porco þanon up ont celen [...]". The only way to understand this text is to think of it visually: to look at the letters as written in the cursive *anglicana* script of this fourteenth-century copy, and imagine which letters from the original eleventh-century script are closest in shape. Thus, eleventh-century æ looks somewhat like *anglicana ce*, eleventh-century g is close to round *s*, *f* is closest to *p*, *d* is similar to *io*, and so on. By making such comparisons, the project team was able to draw up a list of consistent misreadings, and, by more or less mechanically substituting these readings and adjusting the spacing where necessary, a very accurate Old English boundary clause emerged: "Ærest of stræt geate on tælen ford, þanon up on tælen [...]" [first from the street gate to the ford of the [River] Tale, then up into the Tale [...]]. Although this case is in many ways extreme, it illustrates the degree to which palaeography can impact on textual editing, and indeed any editor will necessarily make judgements of likely copying errors based on the scripts of the witness, exemplar, and any potential copies in between.

Although the importance of palaeography to editing is relatively well known, that of codicology is perhaps less often stressed. However, understanding codicology and the physical structure of the book in question can again have a significant impact on editing. This is discussed in some detail by Andrist, Canart, and Maniaci (2013), who give a detailed breakdown of the different ways in which codices can be rearranged, and what the implications are of these for the production and transmission of the book and its texts. They explain this in terms of "units of production" and "units of circulation" (*unités de production* and *unités de circulation*), and the "discontinuities" (*discontinuités*) which one may observe. For instance, a manuscript may have a series of quires or gatherings which are constructed in the same way, with the same type of parchment, the same number of lines per page, and so on, but the scribal hand might change at some point in the middle of a text and quire. In this case, the discontinuity in the scribe falls in the middle of units of production for the material, and so one can be certain that the second scribe was aware of the first scribe's work, and indeed it is likely that the first and second scribe were working together, probably from the same exemplar. In contrast, if the change of scribes coincides with the start of a new quire, with different rulings, parchment, and so on, then this coincidence of discontinuities suggests that the scribes were not working together, perhaps were entirely unaware of each other, and were likely working from different exemplars. These two cases have clear implications for editorial practice, as they tell us very different things about the state of the text and its position(s) in a stemma.

Concrete examples of this are numerous (for several, see Andrist, Canart, and Maniaci 2013, chap. 4), but one example of both palaeography and codicology impacting our understanding of a text is *The Vision of Leofric* (the following discussion is a summary of Stokes 2011). This text as it survives was written in Old English and narrates a series of near-miraculous visions experienced by Leofric, earl of Mercia

(d. 1057). Although brief and relatively little studied, this text has historical interest due to the person that it describes, as Leofric was one of the most important members of the lay nobility during the reign of Edward the Confessor (1042–1066; see further Baxter 2007). The *Vision* survives in only one known copy, which is written into a quire plus a bifolium added to the end of what is now Cambridge, Corpus Christi College, MS 367. Before the *Vision* in the quire is a *Vita brevior* of St Kenelm, namely a Latin text which gives an abbreviated life of a saint who was himself believed to have been Mercian royalty in the ninth century. Furthermore, the *Vita brevior* was copied by one of the few named scribes from Anglo-Saxon England, namely Hemming, who was a monk at Worcester (again in Mercia) and whose hand is found in several manuscripts, including *Hemming's Cartulary*, which is in turn an important historical document written at Worcester around the year 1096. The *Vision* falls between this text and a copy of a letter to the prior, cantor, and monks of Worcester, details which seem to place beyond reasonable doubt that this copy of the *Vision* was made at Worcester at the end of the eleventh century. This is a significant detail given that Leofric's sons, Edwin and Morcar, fared poorly after the Norman Conquest of 1066. However, the date and place of copying are not obvious from the text – indeed, the text itself suggests composition at Coventry – but its position codicologically in the same unit as the *Vita brevior* and the letter to Worcester makes its copying at Worcester almost certain. Furthermore, it is striking that the *Visio* and other texts survive in what is now a codicologically distinct unit comprising two quires, and we also have a slightly later Latin text which recounts that the bishop of Worcester had miracles associated with Leofric written down on a *schedula*. That the surviving text is that of the original *schedula* is probably stretching credulity too far, but it might suggest that the *Visio* was transmitted in such booklets, and so perhaps what we have now may always have been a single unit and perhaps never part of a larger manuscript.

A further and very prominent example of the importance of palaeography and codicology to textual studies is the second part of London, British Library, Cotton Vitellius A.xv, which among other things contains the only surviving copies of two important Old English poems, namely *Judith* and *Beowulf*, as well as three prose texts, again in Old English, known as *The Life of St Christopher*, *The Wonders of the East*, and *Alexander's Letter to Aristotle*. The received view of this part of the manuscript, often referred to as the *Nowell Codex*, is that it was written by two scribes in a single stage, both of whom were copying existing texts. However, Kevin Kiernan (1996, 120–139) has argued that the section of the manuscript containing *Beowulf* is codicologically distinct from those of the other texts, and therefore that this copy of *Beowulf* once existed in a separate codex, presumably a distinct manuscript book in its own right. He has gone on to draw several conclusions from this. One is that all of the scholarship arguing for (and against) the literary coherence of texts in the *Nowell Codex* is misguided, since the texts were not together at the time of writing and probably remained separate until the early modern period (Kiernan 1996, 139–

140). He has also argued that the section containing *Beowulf* was written not only at a different time but also "with a far different attitude on the part of the first scribe" than the prose texts, arguing in particular that the text of *Beowulf* was very carefully written and proofread (Kiernan 1996, 140 ff.). He has also used palaeographical and codicological evidence to argue that one folio of the manuscript was actively palimpsested and rewritten by the scribe. From these and other points, he has then argued that *Beowulf* in its current state is a product of the early eleventh century, rather than from several centuries earlier, and therefore (among other things) that editors should be much less invasive in their emendations of the text. These views have been extremely controversial, and different interpretations of the palaeography and codicology have also been proposed (e.g. Boyle 1981; Dumville 1988), but Kiernan's study has nevertheless demonstrated the importance of codicology and palaeography to textual studies and the way in which they can potentially overturn a century of editorial and text-critical practice.

1.5.3 Methodological implications: Collaboration and interdisciplinarity

In addition to the need to understand palaeography and codicology when editing texts, as demonstrated above, the discussion here has further methodological implications in editorial practice. One is the way in which palaeography in particular undermines the notion of a "factual" or "objective" transcription, or indeed the very idea that one possibly can record "everything that is on the page" (see 1.5.1 above; see also Pierazzo 2011). Furthermore, it seems clear from the discussion above that stemmatology and the other "auxiliary sciences" are fundamentally interdisciplinary, and this raises important methodological and practical implications. Although this has always been the case to some extent, it has also often been observed that digital methods have introduced a new degree of collaboration into humanities research in general, and probably into editing in particular. The traditional image here is of the "lone scholar", working hours, weeks, or years in solitude to produce the definitive edition of the text which then emerges as a printed volume. According to this model, the principal stages of the process are all conducted alone: the transcription, collation, and preparation of the critical text, and the preparation of the accompanying material such as the introduction, contextualisation, and so on (Pierazzo 2015). In contrast, newer digital approaches demand collaboration throughout: the editor's expertise, unsurprisingly, is typically in editing and not in software development, machine vision, deep learning, and so on. Instead, the editor must work closely with a team of experts all with different expertise: one or more analysts to help develop the software specifications and requirements; one or more developers to implement the software; and, potentially, experts in particular parts of the process such as machine vision, textual analysis, or even natural language processing or phylogeny (see 8.1).

The first point to note about this is that the "traditional" view of the lone editor is limited and somewhat romanticised, erasing as it does the significant input from librarians and archivists, conservators, series editors, subeditors, typesetters, proofreaders, sales and marketing staff, distributors of the printed text, and so on, not to mention often research assistants or students, and many others (on which, see McGann 1991, among others). Indeed, one might even go so far as to argue that the change with the digital is not so much that the work is more collaborative, but that the collaborative nature of the work is now brought more forcefully into view. Nevertheless, collaboration in a digital context seems more continuous and more dependent, insofar as the editor of a digital edition is often unable even to begin work on the edition without some initial contributions from an analyst and potentially a software developer, whereas an editor in a print context can generally produce the typescript of an edition without other help. Beyond this, however, are the assumptions and questions that arise when working in digital form. The types of collaboration in a digital context require effective communication across people trained in very different disciplines, and indeed the computer itself requires very explicit statements of knowledge and information that have typically been implicit in the past. Thus, questions such as "what is text?", or even "what is a letter?", become critically important (Caton 2013; Sperberg-McQueen and Huitfeldt 2018; Stokes 2018a). Indeed, the Text Encoding Initiative (tei-c.org) provides not only methods for encoding texts but also, as an inescapable part of these methods, a theory (or perhaps set of theories) of what texts are, "a tool for better understanding of texts and their features" (Pierazzo 2015, 118, citing Renear 2004 and Cummings 2008).

The challenge of being explicit and communicating across fields is well recognised; those taking it up often risk "becoming merely disciples" to a field that they do not fully understand, or, conversely, failing to see the complexities in a discipline and therefore seeing it as overly simplistic (Beer 2006). These challenges have also lain behind much of the difficulty that has been encountered in the application of digital methods to manuscript studies more generally. For example, in a meeting held at the Schloss Dagstuhl – Leibniz-Zentrum für Informatik, a group largely comprising computer scientists and palaeographers established a series of key challenges and questions for the application of digital methods and tools to palaeography (Hassner et al. 2012). The challenges, roughly paraphrased, included:

- how to optimise collaboration between experts in all the different domains;
- how to ensure that humanities researchers remain in control of their research, whilst taking advantage of the possibilities of computerised approaches;
- how to facilitate sharing, not only of data and results, but also of the methodologies involved more generally;
- how to use the outreach potential offered by computerised technologies to enrich humanities knowledge;
- how to obtain contextual knowledge and meaning from systematic analysis;
- how to gain and maintain access to data;

- how to maintain and support interdisciplinary approaches to research (in this context, but also more generally);
- how to avoid problems of communication and terminology; and
- related to all of this, the problem of the "black box" – namely a system (whether human expert or programmed computer) which takes input at one end and gives "answers" at the other, without allowing any understanding of what happens in between.

There is of course no simple solution to these challenges, but it can help in addressing them to consider the different roles that such interdisciplinary work can involve. Some of these are obvious: on the one hand the computer scientist, and on the other the philologist (or codicologist, or palaeographer), for instance. Here, there are some areas of overlap: both are in academic positions with similar (though different) requirements for progression, and so on. On the other hand, to a large extent, the principal interest of computer science is often in developing new methods and algorithms, and much less often in developing the robust, user-friendly software that is needed in the humanities, less in trying to understand what the algorithm or its results actually mean for the real-world questions. These questions, however, are precisely what typically interest those working in the humanities. Those in the humanities may therefore want or need to work with a software developer or engineer rather than an academic researcher. This is not to say that the developer does not need to have any interest in the material: as Choi and Pak (2006) and many others have noted, successful work across multiple disciplines requires all parties to be invested and interested, particularly given the very high salaries that such people can command in industry and which are normally beyond those in academic contexts. Another role that is relevant here is the analyst. This person may be the developer or one (or more) of the academic researchers, but another common possibility is a specialist analyst as a distinct role. This may well be someone with a higher degree in the humanities who has then acquired relatively advanced technical skills; the analyst is usually able to write software at a functional level but does not necessarily have any formal training in software development. Instead, the analyst acts as the "person in the middle" who understands both the humanities and computing elements and is able to translate from one to the other, who can model the domain in a way that the computer can analyse, can recognise and draw out the interest and potential on both sides, and so on. This person's interests are likely to include elements of both the developer and the academic. In short, the analyst may well be the person who brings the project from multidisciplinarity to interdisciplinarity, turning the work into a true collaboration rather than a simple and one-way application of digital methods to the benefit of humanities research.

2 The genealogical method
Introductory remarks by the chapter editor, Odd Einar Haugen

The genealogical method was developed during the nineteenth century, and by the second part of this century it had become a mature and broadly accepted method for the analysis of handwritten texts, primarily from the pre-Gutenberg era, although it had also been applied to printed texts. The genealogical method has often been associated with the German scholar Karl Lachmann (1873–1851), who was active in all major fields of editing – spanning works as diverse as the *Nibelungenlied*, Lucretius' *De rerum natura*, and the Greek New Testament. The title of the indispensable study by Sebastiano Timpanaro, *La genesi del metodo del Lachmann* (1961, rev. ed. 1981, repr. 2004, trans. Most 2005), leaves readers in no doubt about the founding father. However, while the contribution of Lachmann represents a turning point in editorial philology, the genealogical method was not fully developed during his lifetime. The emblematic stemma, part of almost any genealogical *recensio*, was developed from around 1830, but Lachmann never made one himself. As pointed out in section 2.3 below, it was rather Gaston Paris (with Léopold Pannier) who implemented the basic tenets of what we – in general terms – refer to as the genealogical method; they did this in an edition of the Old French *Alexis* legend, published at a time when France and Germany were not on particularly friendly terms (Paris and Pannier 1872). It is with this edition that the use of common errors as the major criterion for establishing the text was fully explored for the first time, as Michael D. Reeve reminds us (1998, 464), and it is from this time that we can fully describe the genealogical method as the method of shared errors, the *Methode der Fehlergemeinschaften*. The *Alexis* edition offers two fully developed stemmata, one drawn by Paris of the earliest version of the legend and one by Pannier of the latest version (Paris and Pannier 1872, 27, 344). Stemmata had indeed been drawn before the *Alexis* edition, such as the first modern-looking *schema cognationis* in the edition of the older *Västgötalagen* [Westrogothic Law] by Carl I. Schlyter and Hans S. Collin (1827), reproduced in section 4.1.1 below, or the stemmata of the Danish classical philologist Johan Nicolai Madvig (1804–1886), for instance the one he offered in his emendations to two speeches by Cicero, reproduced in section 6.1 below (Madvig 1833–1834, 1:9). While these tree models aimed at modelling the filiation process, they were not based on any strict genealogical analysis, and may therefore give a misleading impression of the development of the genealogical method. It is only with the 1872 edition of the *Alexis* legend, which dates back to work being done in the 1860s by Paris and other scholars such as Karl Bartsch, Gustav Gröber, and Paul Meyer, that the stemma actually becomes a model for the *recensio* of the manuscripts.

The first section of this chapter, 2.1 by Gerd Haverling, opens with the earliest traces of written literature. This is not to say that the filiation of oral literature falls outside the scope of the genealogical method; it is rather a reflection of the fact that the written text is a prerequisite for subsequent studies, millennia later, of a manuscript tradition. Considering the variety of literatures discussed in chapter 7, dealing only with Greek and Latin texts may look like a narrow approach to the discipline. However, textual criticism, at least in its Western manifestation, was developed in these fields. This tradition led to the professionalisation of the field in the nineteenth century, when the stemma became the supreme model. What Haverling shows in her chronological walk-through, starting with Alexandrian philology and ending two millennia later, is how text-critical concepts have grown over time, and that there was indeed a continuous development of the field that prepared the ground for the methodological advances of the nineteenth century.

In section 2.2, Paolo Chiesa offers a concise introduction to the method with a number of practical examples. Unlike the austere treatise by Paul Maas (1st ed. 1927, 4th ed. 1960), which remains an authoritative statement of the basic principles of the genealogical method, Chiesa takes a broader, at times metaphorical, approach to the subject, while he at the same time manages to present the method in a very precise manner. Looking at the length of Maas's treatise and Chiesa's section, one might wonder what all the fuss is about; if a method can be explained as succinctly as here, practising it should be straightforward. However, texts in all their variability can provide editors with seemingly contradictory combinations of readings. A large number of works contain readings which move from one branch to another in what Pasquali termed "horizontal transmission" and others "contamination" (to be treated in 4.4). As Maas famously observed, there is no remedy against contamination – "Gegen die Kontamination ist kein Kraut gewachsen" (Maas 1960, 30). While Chiesa is acutely aware of this problem, he underlines that contamination need not be the be-all and end-all of a *recensio* "if the genealogical pattern is used, more correctly, as a metaphor for the mechanisms of textual transmission" (2.2.7 below).

The genealogical method had become almost universal for the *recensio* of manuscripts in the decades following Gaston Paris's edition, but dissonance broke out during the early twentieth century. While many editors turned towards other editorial models (see 6.1 below) without excessive concern, Joseph Bédier became the leading opponent of Lachmann's method, or to be more precise, of the practice of his own mentor and predecessor, Gaston Paris. As described in section 2.3, by Giovanni Palumbo, Bédier had for a long time struggled with the complexities of the stemma, and, after having edited the vernacular text *Lai de l'ombre* in the footsteps of Paris (1st ed. 1890, 2nd ed. 1913), he threw in the towel in a groundbreaking article, "La Tradition manuscrite du Lai de l'Ombre" (Bédier 1928). He had come to the conclusion that too many stemmata seemed to be equally possible in a single tradition, even in a small one like that of the *Lai de l'ombre*, and that the stemmata published were almost always bipartite, that is, had two branches at the top level. This is the starting point for the discussion in section 2.3, which draws up a dichotomy between the criticisms levelled by Bédier and his contemporary Henri Quentin. While Bédier's and Quentin's contributions have been well covered in the historiography of textual criticism, Palumbo instructively uses their opposing strategies as a mirror for the critical debate up to the present time. Whereas some have seen the "New" (later often called "Material") Philology from around 1990 as a paradigm shift in editorial philology, to use the terminology of Thomas S. Kuhn (1962), Palumbo instead regards the New Philology in the light of the Bédier–Quentin schism, and as such as being less new than the name would indicate. In his view, the genealogical method is not without challenges, but it remains the most promising of those methods which so far have been tried – or, in a Churchillian understatement, "the worst method except all those others that have been tried" (Vàrvaro 2012, 87).

The New Philology saw itself as a break from the "old philology", moving the focus from the work and its witnesses to the document and its setting. Neo-Lachmannism, on the other hand, is not a break with Lachmannism but a continuous development of the genealogical method. This is an understanding that fits well with the philosophy of science of Karl R. Popper – the idea that there can be incremental development in a discipline (e.g. Popper 1965). Section 2.4, by Paolo Trovato, puts this into practice, tracing the development – or refinement – of the genealogical method step by step through the twentieth and early twenty-first centuries. This is not a story of a method in decline, but rather of a method which has been developed and supplied with new perspectives brought in from a number of textual fields, and often from unrelated ones as well. While chapter 2 opens in the tradition of editing classical – Greek and Latin – texts, section 2.4 demonstrates how the genealogical method has grown over the last two centuries and acquired a much wider potential.

2.1 Background and early developments
Gerd V. M. Haverling

"Philology" is originally a Greek word meaning "love of words", and textual criticism and editorial principles in the West in the Middle Ages and in the early modern age descend from Graeco-Roman Antiquity. The copying of a text tends to create mistakes: words are left out or written twice instead of once, synonyms replace the words actually used in the original text, and there may be changes in word order. This was known at a rather early stage in the history of Greek literature and philology. The people who assembled the great library at Alexandria preferred the original manuscripts they had borrowed from the cities (e.g. Athens or Sparta) that owned them, and returned new copies to those cities rather than the originals, which remained in Alexandria (see 2.1.2). A result of this insight was the birth of textual criticism and of editorial technique in the third and second centuries BC.

While the genealogical, stemmatological method was not developed as such until the early nineteenth century, the notions underlying that method gradually developed over more than two millennia. This development will be described in this section.

2.1.1 On writing, books, and editing in Antiquity and in the Middle Ages

In the earliest phases of a l p h a b e t i c w r i t i n g, there were only capital letters, which acquired their refined and elegant forms in inscriptions from the classical periods in Greece (fourth century BC) and Rome (first century BC). However, writing on different materials led to the development of various kinds of letters, and cursive writing systems were used for private purposes (figs 2.1-1–2.1-2). These systems influenced the letters used in books, which before late Antiquity always followed a m a - j u s c u l e system: in the second century AD, a new form of such a script, the uncial script, was introduced in both the Greek East and the Latin West (fig. 2.2-3). This form of script was used in books in the early Middle Ages as well. However, in late Antiquity and in the Middle Ages, new m i n u s c u l e scripts evolved. In the West, we find such scripts developing from the last centuries of Antiquity to the eighth and ninth centuries; the most famous and influential of these scripts was the Carolingian minuscule of Charlemagne's empire (fig. 2.2-4). In the East, a new Greek minuscule script was introduced in the production of books in the ninth century. In the West, the Carolingian minuscule was gradually replaced by the so-called Gothic script, beginning in the latter part of the twelfth century. In the late Middle Ages, the Italian Renaissance humanists preferred the Carolingian minuscule, which consequently served as the basis for the creation of the printed Latin alphabet in the

Fig. 2.1-1: Classical capital script on the Pantheon in Rome (27 BC): "M. Agrippa L. f. cos. tertium fecit" = "Marcus Agrippa Lucii filius consul tertium fecit" [Marcus Agrippa, son of Lucius, made this when he was consul for the third time]. Photograph: Philipp Roelli.

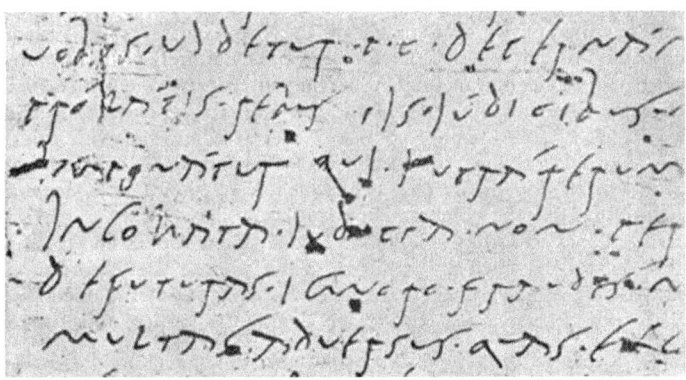

Fig. 2.1-2: Old Roman cursive, from a papyrus fragment in Berlin containing portions of speeches delivered in the Senate, ascribed to the reign of Claudius (r. AD 41–54). Source:commons.wikimedia.org/wiki/File:I_littera_in_manuscripto.jpg.

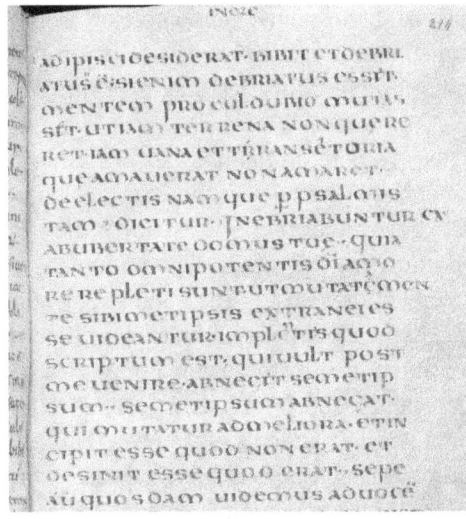

Fig. 2.1-3: Latin uncial from Einsiedeln, Stiftsbibliothek, Codex 157(372), p. 214. Source: e-codices.unifr.ch/en/sbe/0157/214. Image: CC-BY-NC.

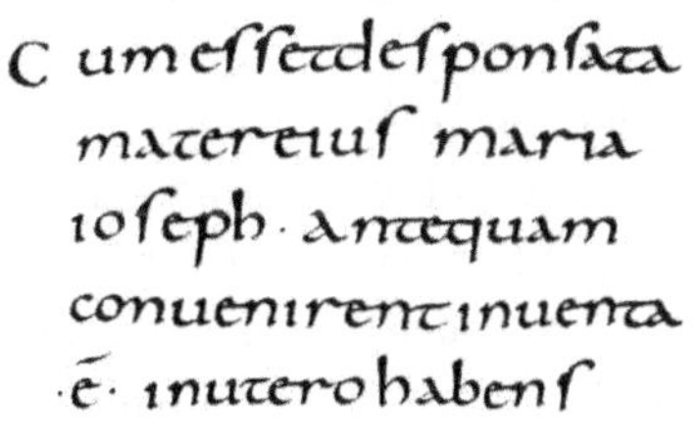

Cum esset desponsata
mater eius maria
ioseph. antequam
conuenirent inuenta
e. inutero habens

Fig. 2.1-4: Carolingian minuscule, Tours, ca. 850 (Paris, Bibliothèque nationale de France, MS. Lat. 266, f. 24v). Source: Gallica, Bibliothèque nationale de France, gallica.bnf.fr/ark:/12148/btv1b8451637v/f58.image. Image: CC-BY-NC.

fifteenth century (see e.g. Bischoff 2009, 76–201; Gastgeber 2003, 4–18; Reynolds and Wilson 2013, 59–61, 89–91, 95–96).

When a text written in one kind of script was rewritten in another script, e r r o r s were sometimes made by the scribes, who may have had difficulties reading the earlier script (on such errors of transliteration, see 4.3 and 1.2.3). This happened both in Antiquity and in the Middle Ages. Such mistakes were often also facilitated by the various abbreviations which were frequently used (this was, however, not so frequent in Greek uncial manuscripts; see also 1.5.2).

A particular difficulty consisted in what is known as *scriptio continua*, "continuous writing", in which there are no spaces or other marks to separate words and sentences. This was the practice in books until the end of Antiquity and sometimes even after that. In inscriptions, dividers are commonly found, often in the form of dots, but in books this was usually not the case (see e.g. West 1973, 25–28; see also Gastgeber 2003, 43–46). *Scriptio continua* seems to be a natural way of writing: there are examples from other languages, too. We often find it, for instance, in runic inscriptions in Nordic up to at least AD 1200, sometimes completely, sometimes in part, sometimes with dividers, sometimes not. It is, however, not attested in early Nordic manuscripts in the vernacular, where the earliest fragments are dated to around 1150 (see Haugen 2018a, 223–225).

Texts were copied by professional scribes working in the libraries or for booksellers, but sometimes also by private individuals who needed them for their own purposes. The copying could occur by d i c t a t i o n (i.e. somebody reading the text aloud to several scribes) or by visual inspection (i.e. the copyist had an original in front of him when writing down his new copy of the text). In the Middle Ages, the scribes often worked in *scriptoria* connected to the monasteries, but, as in Antiquity, the copyist was sometimes a person who wanted the text for his own purposes, for instance a professional who needed a technical handbook for his own work. In this later period, the professional scribes did not always understand the texts that they were copying very well. This is, however, more likely to have been the case if the copyist was copying for his own purposes, for instance a physician copying a medical treatise: such a person is more likely to introduce a synonym instead of the word used in the exemplar than a copyist who has a limited interest in and/or understanding of the text (see e.g. Pöhlmann 1994, 27–40, 47–52; Gastgeber 2003, 18–21; Klopsch 2003, 67–69, 91–92; Salles 2010, 170; see also Bayet 1961, lxxxvi).

A practice connected to the mediaeval universities is the *p e c i a* system. It was developed in the early thirteenth century at the Italian universities and spread from there to other universities. A manuscript was broken up into often rather short sections which were called *peciae*, "pieces": the size of such a section was often four folios. Students would rent them, section by section, in order to create their own copies of the text. In some cases, there may have been more than one approved exemplar divided into *peciae*, and in such cases contamination and exemplar shift may have occurred (see e.g. Siri 2013; 4.4 below).

Texts were published and handled in very diverse ways. Sometimes, there was an original version of a literary text which was relatively stable, but in other cases the picture was more complicated. We know that several classical Greek and Latin texts were revised after publication by their authors or were circulated before the text had been fully revised. In such cases, the various stages of elaboration may be represented by varying readings in the later transmission of the text. A famous example from the classical period is Ovid's work *Amores*, which, according to the first two lines of the prefatory epigram, was published twice by the poet himself, first in five volumes and then later in three; both editions seem to have been in circulation for some time (see e.g. Pasquali 1934, 18–19; 397–465; see also Booth 1991, 2–3). A mediaeval example of the same phenomenon seems to be the letter collection by the late-twelfth-century author Peter of Blois, which has come down to us in a great amount of manuscripts and in a rather bewildering state (see Wahlgren 1993).

In other cases, texts were altered in a later phase and new versions were created: this happened to many texts of a more technical nature, for example grammatical treatises or texts on medicine. In such cases, we sometimes find changes in the technical terminology or shorter as well as longer versions of the texts. In certain cases, literary texts too were changed in this way: a famous example is the *Alexander Romance*, of which we have several different versions. A particular kind of new version of a text is the e p i t o m e, which is a shortened version of an often much longer text (see e.g. West 1973, 16–18; Reynolds and Wilson 2013, 33–34, 235–238; see also Pasquali 1934, 118–121; Erbse 1961, 234–237; Büchner 1961, 344).

Sometimes, new editions were made because of a change in ideology or perspective. This happened to certain pagan texts which occur in both a "pagan" and a "Christian" edition: a famous example is the stoic philosopher Epictetus' *Enchiridion* from around AD 100 (see e.g. Gastgeber 2003, 25–26). The copyist may also unconsciously introduce mistakes facilitated by the intellectual or ideological context in which he is living. There are, for instance, some mistakes in the manuscripts of non-Christian texts which betray the influence of Christian thought, as when we read "Sathana" instead of "Athana" in a manuscript of Petronius' novel *Satyricon* from the first century AD (*Satyricon* 58.7; see West 1973, 18). An ideological change also affected the historiographical work of the sixth-century Gallo-Roman bishop and aristocrat Gregory of Tours, which was abbreviated and renamed the *Historia Francorum* [History of the Franks] a couple of generations after the author's death. The version of the text left behind by the author when he died in 594 consisted of ten books, and his own name for it was *Decem libri historiarum* [Ten Books on History]: it is a work on the history of the world from a Christian perspective, putting contemporary events in Gaul into the perspective of God's plan for the human race. The new, shorter version consists of a selection from the first six books, in which sections of less interest from the point of view of the history of the Franks have been left out. This new version is connected to later works on Merovingian history such as the *Chronicles* by someone who is conventionally called Fredegar (seventh century) and to the *Liber historiae Francorum* [Book on the History of the Franks] (eighth century), and reflects a change in perspective in a world in which the Gallo-Roman elite had merged with the Frankish one and a new common identity had been born (see Heinzelmann 2001, 94–115, 192–201; see also Haverling 2008).

Sometimes, an edition was made from a text which was not intended for publication in that form by the author. Some of Aristotle's transmitted works from the fourth century BC go back to lecture notes which seem to have been made by the author himself (see e.g. Howatson 1989, 57; Lesky 1996, 552–553; Erbse 1961, 230–231). The teachings of several mediaeval philosophers are known to us from such notes made by their students. In a mediaeval university lecture, the teacher read a text aloud to the students (cf. expressions like *lectio*, *lecture*, and *Vorlesung*): in the beginning, the intention was that they should learn the text by heart. However, when the matters taught gradually became more complex, it was clear that it was necessary to take notes during lectures. As a result, the *r e p o r t a t i o* arose – a collection of notes which the student could bring home and study. Sometimes, such annotations spread among the students and were copied among them (see e.g. Siri 2013). A famous modern example of a publication made on the basis of lecture notes made by others is Ferdinand de Saussure's *Cours de linguistique générale*. This fundamental work was published in 1916 (three years after the author's death) on the basis of annotations made by his students during lectures which he held between 1907 and 1911 (critical edition: de Saussure 1972).

A particular kind of edition is the anthology (*a n t h o l o g i a* or, in Latin, *f l o r i - l e g i u m*). In contrast to the epitome, which is a shortened version of a longer text, the anthology typically contains texts written by several different authors or a selection of texts written by the same author. In Antiquity, important anthologies containing the works of several different poets were thus created (reflected, for instance, by the *Anthologia Graeca* with Greek poems and the *Codex Salmasianus*, today Paris, Bibliothèque nationale de France, Lat. 10318, containing minor Latin poets). There were also anthologies produced for school purposes (see e.g. Lesky 1996, 741–743; Conte 1994, 609, 610–611; Erbse 1961, 227–230, 246). Anthologies remained important in the Middle Ages and were then made up of texts by both ancient and mediaeval authors: there were anthologies produced for school purposes but also anthologies of elegant l e t t e r s, which were to serve as models for those writing letters. Many mediaeval manuscripts contain collections of extracts from different authors and can therefore be regarded as a kind of anthologies (see e.g. Pöhlmann 1994, 95; Reynolds and Wilson 2013, 108, 114, 118; for a concrete example, see Nyström 2009).

2.1.2 On philology and textual criticism in Antiquity and in the Middle ages

Since various kinds of unintentional changes can be introduced when a text is copied (for example, something can be misinterpreted or left out, or mistakes can be induced by phonetic and orthographical changes; see, in more detail, 4.3), it soon became clear that no handwritten copy was entirely reliable. When the great library in Alexandria was founded in the early third century BC, as mentioned above, it was clear to those who acquired the books that the original was better than the copy, and therefore they did not hesitate to steal originals from the Greek cities that possessed them, replacing them only with new copies. It was in this environment that the philological practice of comparing several manuscripts in order to reconstruct a text was born. Important editions of pre-classical Greek poets, first Homer and then others, were created there (see e.g. Pöhlmann 1994, 26–40; Reynolds and Wilson 2013, 5–16).

The Alexandrian philologists were often able to take into consideration a rather large number of different manuscripts: this was the case when Aristarchus of Samothrace worked on Homer in Alexandria in the second century BC. It is, however, not likely that Aristarchus used all that material for a systematic study of the internal relationships between the manuscripts in a modern sense: he seems rather to have compared a version of the text which he considered particularly reliable to other versions, and thus produced a text which was free from obvious faults and which then replaced the multitude of earlier versions – this new version of the text was then copied and reproduced and the earlier versions were not. Various s i g n s to facilitate reading, such as the Greek accents invented at this time for this purpose, as well as others to draw attention to suspicious or problematic readings, were introduced (fig. 2.1-5). The Alexandrian practices of comparing manuscripts in order to produce a canonical version of a text, of drawing attention to problems in the text with the help of a number of signs, and of making editions of older texts were introduced to Rome in the second and first centuries BC (see e.g. Pöhlmann 1994, 26–40, 46–49, 61; Reynolds and Wilson 2013, 7–16, 21–22).

Discussion of difficult passages led to the production of more reliable texts, but also to c o m m e n t a r i e s in which such problems were discussed. The writing of such commentaries was introduced to Rome in the second and first centuries AD as well. These commentaries were initially separate texts, but they were later turned into s c h o l i a, which are a kind of commentary written around the text that is being studied. Some such scholia on papyrus scrolls from the Hellenistic period are extant, but they seem to have become more common in late Antiquity and in the Middle Ages, when parchment codices had replaced the papyrus scrolls of previous centuries. Sometimes, such scholia were later spelled out as commentaries again. Some commentaries on older texts are preserved (mostly from late Antiquity), and we have knowledge of numerous other such texts from quotations in later works on grammar and lexicography and from later commentaries on important literary works (see e.g. Pöhlmann 1994, 77, 79, 82; Reynolds and Wilson 2013, 10–11, 45, 52–53, 77; on scholia and commentaries, see also Dickey 2007; Zetzel 2018).

In the early Roman Empire, scholars were fully aware of several reasons why texts may become corrupt in the course of transmission. They discussed what kind

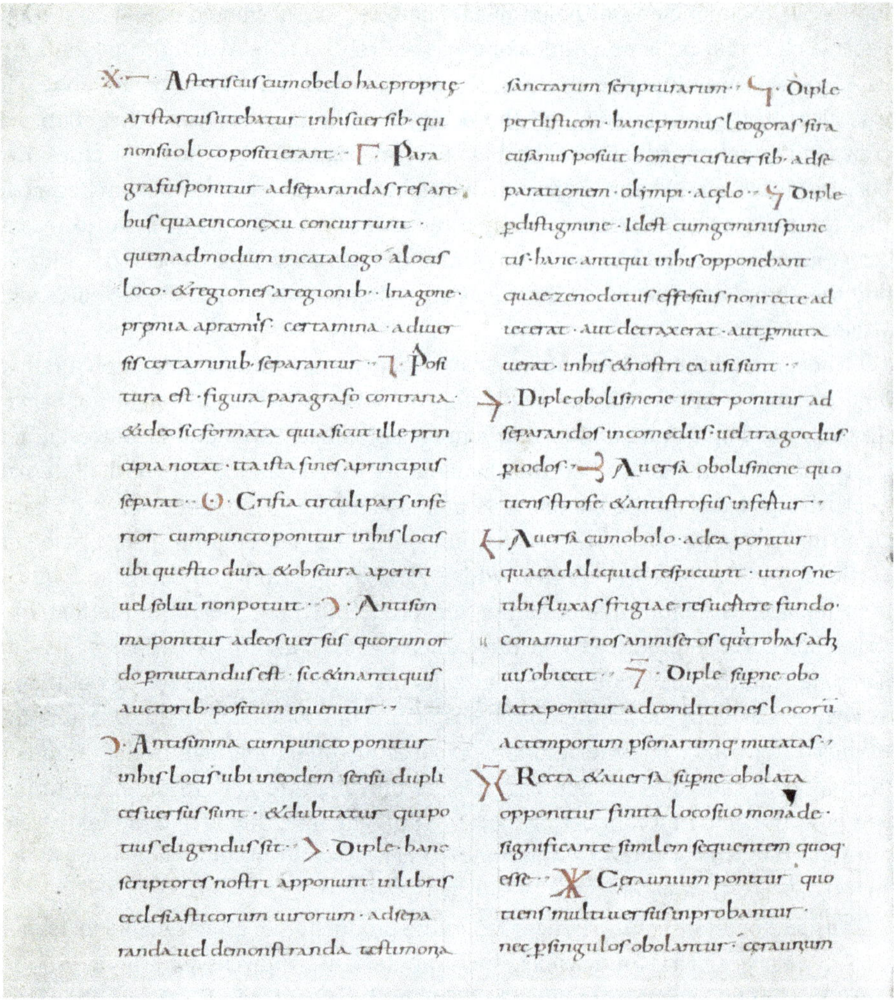

Fig. 2.1-5: A description of Alexandrian textual-criticism signs (in red) from Isidore of Seville *Etymologiae* 1.21 (St. Gallen, Stiftsbibliothek, Cod. Sang. 231, p. 36). Source: e-codices.unifr.ch/en/csg/0231/36 Image: CC-BY-NC.

of orthography might have been used in the old texts, and they were aware of the risk of unusual words getting distorted in favour of more common ones. The idea of the *lectio difficilior*, the more difficult but likely more correct reading, as the choice to be preferred by the editor was established in the first two centuries AD: in the first century, the grammarian Probus proposed such readings for Virgil's *Aeneid*, and in the second, the Greek physician Galen (129–200/216) considered older but more difficult readings more trustworthy. Therefore, scholars were not only comparing manuscripts when they tried to establish what might be the correct reading; they were also particularly interested in old manuscripts and the information they could furnish about the old texts (see e.g. Pöhlmann 1994, 61–78; Reynolds and Wilson 2013, 25–34).

The philological practice of comparing manuscripts (without necessarily trying to arrange them in a stemma) in order to produce a canonical version of a text was used when new editions of classical texts were produced in expensive parchment codices in late Antiquity. Sometimes, these new editions were sponsored by wealthy private persons: a famous example is the new edition of Livy's gigantic work on Roman history from the late first century BC and the early first century AD that was sponsored around AD 400 by two leading senatorial families who were also prominent in the pagan opposition to the Christianisation of the Roman Empire, the Symmachi and the Nicomachi. We are informed about this by certain colophons in the preserved manuscripts. This activity in late Antiquity is of fundamental importance not only for the survival of classical literature but also for the shape in which the classical literary texts have come down to us. In a few cases, late antique parchment codices of this kind have survived: there are some such manuscripts extant of, for instance, Virgil, Terence, and Livy. In many other cases, however, we can trace the preserved tradition back to such a manuscript in late Antiquity which has not survived (see e.g. Pöhlmann 1994, 82–86; Reynolds and Wilson 2013, 39–43; for Livy, see Bayet 1961, xvi–c).

These editorial principles were developed for and applied to canonical literary texts such as those of Homer and Virgil. They were not applied to the same extent to texts in which the original wording was considered to be of less importance, for instance to "technical" texts on medicine or grammar. In such cases, the copyists, who might be interested in using the texts for their own purposes, were more inclined to introduce changes intentionally: these changes could be changes in the technical vocabulary, but also involved rendering the text longer or shorter than the original. Certain texts which were to be used in schools were deliberately modified, too (see e.g. Pasquali 1934, 118–121; West 1973, 16–18; Reynolds and Wilson 2013, 235–238; for a concrete example, see Haverling 2003).

After the problematic period at the beginning of the Middle Ages sometimes referred to as the "Dark Ages", scholarly and philological activities were resumed. In the ninth century, texts were transcribed into the new minuscule scripts in both the Greek East and the Latin West. New commentaries on ancient texts were sometimes written, and old commentaries were studied and assembled. The value of different readings was discussed, and scholars compared different manuscripts with one another or suggested conjectures and emendations to improve the readability of the texts. Difficult words were commented on or explained in so-called glosses around the text. Scribes made annotations about such things: sometimes we can observe this in the form of various hands which have added such information in the margins or above the lines in the manuscripts. Sometimes, the mediaeval copyist used, with the intention of getting as accurate a text as possible, more than one manuscript when producing the new manuscript: to the modern scholar trying to figure out how the mediaeval manuscripts of a certain text relate to one another, this procedure poses a challenge known as contamination (see 4.4), but it is actually similar to the method used in Antiquity to produce readable texts (see e.g. West 1973, 12–14, 22–23; Reynolds and Wilson 2013, 59–60, 69–71, 78, 83, 99, 103–107; Pasquali 1934, 146–155, 491).

As examples of the use of such principles in the editing of texts during and shortly after the Carolingian Renewal, Theodulf of Orléans (ca. 750/760–821) and Lupus Servatus (ca. 805–ca. 862) may be mentioned. Theodulf of Orléans was a scholar of Visigothic descent who was named bishop of Orléans in 798 and who, in the early ninth century, produced an edition of parts of the Vulgate Bible in which he used sigla in the margin to indicate the sources of his variants. Lupus Servatus was a German who became abbot of Ferrières in France, and who eagerly tried to get hold of other manuscripts of texts which he already knew in order to compare them with the ones he had. He was also interested in points of grammar, prosody, and exegesis. His work is reflected in the manuscripts of several ancient texts which were copied in this period (see e.g. Reynolds and Wilson 2013, 105–106; Klopsch 2003, 79–80; Pasquali 1934, 155n2; see also 1.4.1 above).

This scholarly activity continued during the subsequent centuries, and important manuscripts of ancient texts were produced. Book collections were assembled, for example around the Ottonian court. Of great importance was the revival of the learned monastery of Monte Cassino in the eleventh century. The work to improve the text of the Bible was intensified, and in the twelfth century, the Roman monk Nicola Maniacutia produced a revised version of the psalter. The scholastic age (late twelfth–thirteenth centuries) was more focused on philosophy and science, due to the recent discoveries and translations of texts in those areas, but in the fourteenth century there was again a growing interest in the literary classics of the ancient world (see e.g. Reynolds and Wilson 2013, 107–135, 281; Peri 1967).

2.1.3 On philology and the editing of texts during the Renaissance

In the later Middle Ages and in the early Renaissance, literacy and learning had become more common outside the Church, and interest in classical literature grew stronger: as a result, there was a further increase in the search for and in the copying of such texts. There was now more contact with the Greek-speaking world, and Westerners, first Italians and then others, were learning Greek again. There was also an increasing production of new texts, in the classical as well as in the vernacular languages, which were copied and edited (see e.g. Reynolds and Wilson 2013, 123–141; Heldmann 2003, 97–102; see also 1.4 above).

It was in Italy that this new Renaissance movement started. One of its most significant traits was a renewed interest in Greek and in Greek literature. Greek was little known in the north of Italy, although it was still spoken in certain areas in the south, but in the fourteenth century there was an increasing demand for learning it, and from 1397 there were regular lectures on Greek in Florence. Some Italians travelled to the East to seek instruction in the language as well as to collect manuscripts. After the fall of Constantinople (1453), numerous Greek scholars fled to Italy, which considerably increased the number of available teachers of the language and of professional Greek copyists. The ties between the Greeks and the Italians were further strengthened by Cardinal Bessarion (1403–1472), a Greek orthodox bishop who had become a Roman catholic cardinal and who played a conspicuous role in the cultural life of Rome and Italy, for instance by collecting as many Greek books as he could and then offering them to the city of Venice to form the basis of a public library (see e.g. Reynolds and Wilson 2013, 147–155).

As a result of these changes, the conditions for working on and understanding the classical texts had greatly improved in the fifteenth century in Italy. In the first part of that century, Lorenzo Valla (ca. 1407–1457) made an important Latin translation of the Athenian historian Thucydides (ca. 460–ca. 400 BC), wrote a fundamental treatise on Latin style and grammar based on a close study of the classical texts, and published works on textual problems in the Roman historian Livy as well as in the Greek New Testament (see e.g. Reynolds and Wilson 2013, 141–144; Heldmann 2003, 128).

A generation later, Angelo Ambrogini, better known as Politianus (or, in English, Politian; 1454–1494), employed new and strikingly modern methods of dealing with textual problems. He emended a difficult passage in the Roman poet Catullus (84–54 BC) with the help of the Hellenistic poet Callimachus (ca. 310–240 BC), to whose *Coma Berenices* [Lock of Berenice] Catullus referred in poem 66: in Callimachus Fragment 35c, we read "Χαλύβων"; but, in the Catullus manuscripts, "Chalybum" or "Chalybon" (line 48), which Politian restored, had been changed to "celitum" (or "celerum"). When discussing the relationship between the manuscripts of Valerius Flaccus, a Roman poet from the first century AD, Politian observed that the later manuscripts were of less value since they were the copies of the older manuscripts, which means that he followed the principle of *eliminatio codicum descriptorum* (see 6.2). He generally preferred older manuscripts to more recent ones and employed the principle that conjectural emendation must start from the earliest recoverable stage of the tradition. Such ideas were to become common only in the nineteenth century and the age of Karl Lachmann. In his printed copies of classical texts, Politian frequently made annotations to readings found in manuscripts he had seen. Even if he thus paid much attention to the manuscripts, he did not hesitate to suggest conjectures when he found this appropriate; but, in contrast to some of his contemporaries, he honestly informed his readership when he proposed a conjecture and why he did so. He did not, as some of his contemporaries, try to hide himself behind some unspecified "good manuscripts" (see e.g. Heldmann 2003, 120–124; Reynolds and Wilson 2013, 144–147, 154–155).

When Politian was active as a classical scholar, printing technology had just been introduced. The Latin Bible was the first text to be printed, but soon it was followed by classical literary texts: by 1475, the most important Latin classics were already available in printed books, and the number of such texts which were printed was growing. The Greek texts which were available in print were, however, far less numerous. One problem was the designing of a suitable font, but another was the restricted number of potential buyers of Greek books in the West. However, in 1494, Aldus Manutius (ca. 1450–1515) set up a publishing house primarily for the printing of Greek texts. He did this in Venice, where he hoped to get access to the library of Greek texts that Cardinal Bessarion had donated to the city – which, however, he probably did not. Over a period of about twenty years, a great number of ancient Greek texts, especially classical and non-Christian ones, were printed (see Reynolds and Wilson 2013, 145–146, 155–160).

The early editions thus created were often based on only one manuscript (sometimes called monoptic editions; see 6.1), but often there were also attempts to compare different manuscripts with one another and to try to establish a better text in this way. The comparison of the manuscripts was, however, then often rather arbitrary, and it was frequently based on the probability of the various readings in mostly relatively recent manuscripts. A reason for preferring later manuscripts was probably the lack of sufficient palaeographical knowledge to deal with the older ones. Unfortunately, these early editors and printers did not always regard it necessary to keep the manuscripts they had used – nor did they necessarily indicate where they had introduced conjectures and emendations. Important information about the preceding manuscript traditions was therefore often lost (see e.g. Heldmann 2003, 108–112). One example of this is the first edition of Symmachus' *Relationes* (from AD 384), which was published in Basle in 1549 by Sigismundus Gelenius: this edition was based on a now-lost manuscript and evidently not on a comparison with the two eleventh-century manuscripts of the same text that have survived (see Seeck 1883, xix–xxii). These first prints were therefore often of a relatively poor quality.

The first print of the classical Greek poet Pindar (early fifth century BC) was published by Manutius in 1513. In contrast to the edition which, only two years later, in 1515, was presented in Rome by the Greek scholar Zacharias Kallierges (ca. 1473–after 1524), it was not of great importance. The Kallierges print was based on different manuscript material and also included the scholia; it has been – and still is – of fundamental value to scholars working on this fascinating but very difficult poet. There is, however, a problem connected to this edition: not all the copies of what appears to be the same edition are identical. Some pages at the beginning occur in two forms, each typeset differently: the printer had, in other words, changed the text before the printing of the book was finished. To throw away all the paper already printed was not something that a printer in the early sixteenth century could afford. The book was therefore published in what appears to be one edition but with these variations between the copies (see Fogelmark 2015, 1:3–4, 56–61).

The Dutch scholar Erasmus of Rotterdam (ca. 1469–1539) was a very famous Renaissance editor. Of particular importance is his edition of the Greek New Testament, which was published in Basle in 1516. This very first printed edition of this text in the original language was based on a few relatively recent manuscripts. Erasmus was aware of the likely value of old manuscripts, but he did not have sufficient palaeographical knowledge to consult them. When there were lacunae in the Greek manuscripts which he used, he consulted the Latin Vulgate translation and made his own Greek versions of them. There are thus some problems in the methods applied when this edition was made, but it was nevertheless of fundamental importance because it finally established the principle that texts should be studied in the original language and not in translation, and that the texts of the Christian Bible are to be dealt with in the same way as other ancient texts. This first edition would then be followed by several reprints and new editions, among them a fourth edition from 1527 for which further and better manuscripts, including the Spanish edition of the Greek Bible from 1522, had been consulted (see e.g. Heldmann 2003, 127–130; Reynolds and Wilson 2013, 160–164; see also 7.1.1.2 below).

Erasmus' edition of the New Testament was very successful, and it was reprinted in the sixteenth and seventeenth centuries. In one of these editions, the text edited by Erasmus is referred to as the *textus receptus*, "the accepted text", which was not supposed to be altered. Not only this edition but also editions of classical texts were sometimes treated in this way. Later Renaissance editors often chose to improve the first printed edition by conjecture (*ope ingenii*) or by consulting other manuscripts (*ope codicum*), without trying to make an entirely new edition based on an independent study of the preserved manuscripts (see e.g. Heldmann 2003, 130–134; Reynolds and Wilson 2013, 188, 210; Tarrant 2016, 65).

A quite different example of editorial approaches in the Renaissance should also be mentioned. It is found in the edition of a medical text, a commentary in Latin on a Latin translation of the Hippocratic *Aphorisms*, made by Johann Winter, a German scholar from Andernach (1505–1574; the full title of the edition, which was published in Venice in 1533 and in Basle in 1535, is *D. Oribasii Medici clarissimi commentaria in Aphorismos Hippocratis hactenus non visa, Ioannis Guinterij Adernaci Doctoris Medici industria, velut e profundissimis tenebris eruta, et nunc primum in Medicinae studiosorum utilitatem edita*). The translation commented on was probably made around AD 500, and the Latin in it is in several respects quite substandard, even more so than the Latin of the commentary, which was probably written around 600. Winter therefore chose to use a more elegant translation from around 1100, which is not combined with this commentary in the manuscripts, and he combined it with a relatively recent and polished version of the commentary which appears in some manuscripts from the eleventh century onwards (see Vázquez Buján 2010; see also Haverling 2003, 2019). In this case, the purpose was not to publish an admired classical text but to render an important medical text accessible to the physicians of the day.

The principles applied by the editors during the first century of the new printing technology often differed quite strongly from modern attitudes on such matters. However, at the same time, there was some awareness of the importance of older manuscripts and of the fact that the more difficult reading would often be the correct one. We also sometimes encounter the idea that the preserved manuscripts of a certain text probably descended from a common origin – what we now would refer to as an archetype – but the term *archetypus* was used in the Renaissance in a different sense, to refer to what we now call an autograph. This is confusing, since the modern use of the term is quite different (see Irigoin 1977; 4.1.2 below). Furthermore, there was also a growing awareness of the importance of taking the linguistic and stylistic habits of the author, as well as contextual information about, for instance, history or a Greek model, into account when choosing between variants in the manuscripts (see e.g. Heldmann 2003, 108–130). That there was a growing awareness of such things is shown by the fact that the first known treatises on textual criticism were the *De arte, sive ratione corrigendi antiquorum libros disputatio* and the *Thesaurus criticus*, first published in 1548 and in 1557 respectively, by the Italian scholar and skilled editor of Greek texts Francesco Robortello (1516–1567; see also Reynolds and Wilson 2013, 168). These same ideas, which can already be observed among some textual critics in Antiquity, will gain more importance in the following centuries.

2.1.4 On philology and the editing of texts from the late sixteenth to the end of the eighteenth century

The cultural climate changed drastically during the Reformation. In the Catholic countries in the south, there was now less tolerance for the critical spirit of the Renaissance and the Latin Vulgate translation of the Bible was again regarded as the correct version to adhere to (see e.g. Reynolds and Wilson 2013, 165–171). From the latter part of the sixteenth century, there is, however, increasing activity in the editing of classical texts north of the Alps. The Dutch scholar Justus Lipsius (1547–1606) made important contributions to the editing of several classical Latin texts, especially by the Roman historian Tacitus (ca. AD 100) and the Roman philosopher Seneca (first century AD). His contemporary, the very learned French scholar Joseph Justus Scaliger (1540–1609), reconstructed the chronological system of the ancient world and attempted to reconstruct the details of a lost archetype in his edition of the classical Roman poet Catullus (84–54 BC). Scaliger's younger friend Isaac Casaubon (1559–1614), born in Geneva as the son of French Huguenots, dedicated his vast erudition and energy to illuminating difficult but often widespread texts, and he commented on authors such as the Greek Diogenes Laertius, Strabo, and Athenaeus, but also on Roman poets such as Persius. There was now a stronger interest in the evidence of the manuscript traditions, and in an edition of Horace (65–8 BC) by Theodoor Poelman (1510–1607), sigla were for the first time used in a modern manner to denote the manuscripts. In an edition of Seneca's tragedies, Johann Friedrich Gronovius (1611–1671) used a manuscript which had been neglected since the Renaissance but whose importance was now firmly established. A general problem in philology much discussed at this time is the balance between emendation by conjecture (*ope ingenii*) and with the help of a close study of the manuscripts (*ope codicum*): Nicolaus Heinsius (1620–1681) managed to strike a reasonable balance in his editions of several Roman poets (see e.g. Reynolds and Wilson 2013, 171–185).

Scholars had known for centuries that older manuscripts can be of particular value for the editing of a text. Old manuscripts are, however, often written in old scripts which are not always easy to read, and sometimes the manuscripts themselves are badly preserved. Each change of script in Antiquity and in the Middle Ages therefore posed a problem. An important step towards the development of modern philology was the establishment of the study of manuscripts and of palaeography in the late seventeenth century (see e.g. Reynolds and Wilson 2013, 193–197; 1.5 above).

The idea that the first printed version – especially of the Greek New Testament, but of other ancient texts as well – had a particular status as the *textus receptus* prevailed for a long time. For a growing number of classical literary texts, this was gradually undermined by scholars who proved the importance of other textual witnesses than the ones used for the first printed versions of the texts and who proposed conjectures and emendations for those texts. Holy Scripture was, however, another matter. The Englishman Richard Bentley (1662–1742) had already contributed to the understanding of numerous classical texts with often brilliant conjectures when he started work on the manuscript tradition of the Greek New Testament in 1716 with the intention of publishing a new edition of the text; in this work, he broke with the tradition that treated Erasmus' version of the text as the *textus receptus*. Bentley never finished work on this edition, but he published a tiny pamphlet in which he announced that he would base his edition on the oldest textual witnesses and on the fourth-century Latin translation, the *Versio vulgata*. Similar views about what an edition of this text should be like were now proposed by others as well, and new editions following such principles were published. In 1734, the German theologian Johann Albrecht Bengel (1687–1752) published an edition of the Greek New Testament in which he discussed the internal relationship between the manuscripts. This methodological approach was soon adopted among scholars working on the classical texts in the latter part of the eighteenth century (see e.g. Heldmann 2003, 134–135; Pöhlmann 2003, 137–139; Reynolds and Wilson 2013, 185–190).

A new method based on a close study of the internal relationships between the manuscripts and the attempt to, if possible, establish an archetype was thus developing in the eighteenth century. This is the method later associated with the name of the nineteenth-century German scholar Karl Lachmann, which will be discussed in the following section.

2.2 Principles and practice
Paolo Chiesa

The genealogical method – also called, not quite appropriately, "Lachmann's method" (see 2.3) – played a pivotal role in developing a scientific approach to textual criticism, and it still remains an essential research tool. This section provides a short rationale of the method in its logical principles and practical application; its strengths and weaknesses are briefly discussed through examples, both real and invented.

2.2.1 A definition

The genealogical method meets the need, clearly felt at the historical moment in which it was developed, to limit the subjectivity (*iudicium*) of the critical editor in choosing between the readings (i.e. "what is read", the variants of the manuscripts) occurring in the tradition of a literary work. It attempts to replace, as far as possible, subjective criteria with objective ones. It advertises itself as a "scientific" method based on a set of predefined and encoded rules. The cultural climate in which the method developed was the eighteenth-century Enlightenment and nineteenth-century positivism; the "enemy" to overcome were the editions produced since the second half of the fifteenth century, which had generated a number of *textus recepti* (see 2.1.3) without philological value.

The genealogical method is also called "Lachmann's method", from the name of Karl Lachmann (1793–1851), a German classical scholar who was considered to be its creator or architect. In fact, this method was constructed over a rather long timespan (from the last decades of the eighteenth century to the early twentieth century) thanks to the contributions of many scholars, sometimes working in connection with one another, sometimes working autonomously. The predominance of Lachmann's name mainly arises from his famous edition of Lucretius' poem *De rerum natura*, in which he provided a spectacular reconstruction of the supposed earliest manuscript of the work, applying some principles of the method (the Lucretius transmission was discussed in 1.4.2). This demonstration and the long-standing fame of the scholar, kept alive by the academic circles of Berlin, produced an identification (largely undue) between his name and the method (see Timpanaro 1981, repr. 2004, trans. Most 2005; Fiesoli 2000, 359–461).

In the tradition of textual studies, the most consistent treatment of the genealogical method is considered to be that provided by the German scholar Paul Maas (1880–1964) in his *Textkritik* (Maas 1957, trans. Flower 1958); for a canonical description in English, see West (1973).

2.2.2 The genealogical metaphor

At the basis of the genealogical method lies the insight that a proper analysis of the tradition of a work is a powerful and indispensable tool for reconstructing the text. The tradition of a work consists of all the facts and objects that have transmitted the work through time, from its origin to us: primarily the preserved manuscripts, or even the lost manuscripts we are aware of (and secondarily the indirect tradition, i.e. quotations, extracts, paraphrases, imitations, and so on, which we do not discuss here; see instead 3.2). These objects are designated as witnesses of the work, using a judicial metaphor. In order to represent the tradition in its historical development, we can use another metaphor, representing every witness of the text as a member of a lineage. A lineage derives from a historical parent and materialises in individuals, children, grandchildren, and descendants, who in turn generate other children, grandchildren, and descendants. Similarly, the tradition of a literary work starts from a parent (the original, the text as conceived by the author) and proceeds through subsequent generations of handwritten copies that are produced by taking earlier manuscripts as models. As the development of a lineage is represented by a family tree, so too the tradition of a literary work can be represented by a similar diagram, a "family tree of manuscripts" (in Latin, *stemma codicum*), explaining historical relationships among witnesses; and the terminology of family relationships may be useful for representing relationships between manuscripts as well. Scholars say, for example, that a manuscript "descends" from another; that a manuscript is "ancestor", or "progenitor", or "sibling" of another; that two manuscripts are "twins"; that some manuscripts constitute a "family"; and so on. For a more theoretical view of the *stemma codicum*, see section 4.1.

2.2.3 Basic principles

The principles of the genealogical method are summarised as follows.

(*i*) The value of a reading depends on the value of the witness that reports it. The value of a single witness is measured in terms of its relationships of dependence or autonomy with the other witnesses.

(*ii*) Only when the relationships between the witnesses have been determined, can the text be reconstructed.

Thus, textual criticism based on the genealogical method clearly separates two phases of research which should be executed in succession: (*i*) reconstruction of the relationships between the witnesses (a step called *recensio*), and (*ii*) reconstruction of the text (a step called *constitutio textus*; see further 6.2).

2.2.4 What a *stemma codicum* is for

In order to illustrate how the genealogical method works, we start with a practical example. It is an (invented) case of an ancient or mediaeval work; no original manu-

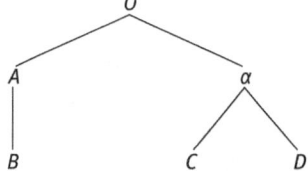

Fig. 2.2-1: Stemma (*i*).

script survives, but we have four later copies (witnesses *A B C D*). The relationships between the four witnesses could take many different shapes; at the beginning of the investigation, we do not know the correct one. For example, the witnesses might be related as shown in figure 2.2-1.

This is a *stemma codicum*, that is, a graphical representation of the relationships between the witnesses. In this stemma, we conventionally indicate the lost original with *O*, the surviving witnesses with Roman letters, and the lost witnesses whose existence has apparently been confirmed by research with Greek letters. In this stemma, the original, *O*, generated two copies, one still existent (*A*) and one lost (*α*); *A* generated another copy, still surviving (*B*); *α* generated two other copies, still surviving as well (*C* and *D*). Every stemma indicates derivation (in our case, of *B* from *A*), closeness (of *C* and *D*, descending from the same lost witness), and independence (e.g. of *A* from *α*). Every stemma is a diachronic schema, representing a historical sequence from the oldest object (the original, the starting point, the "parent") to the latest outcomes.

If scholars know that the relations between the witnesses are those outlined above, their work in reconstructing the original text becomes considerably easier and, above all, firmer. Since the goal is to rebuild *O*, *B* is useless as a witness, because it derives from *A*: we should consider every reading reported by *B* but not shared by *A* as an i n n o v a t i o n produced in the transition from *A* to *B*; such a reading is therefore "false" in terms of the goal of reconstructing the original. However, even a reading reported by *C* alone against the pair *A D* can be supposed to be "false": it was obviously generated in the transition from *α* to *C*, while the reading of *α* was the same of *A*, as demonstrated by its presence in *D*. The same holds for the readings reported by *D* alone. In this way, using the stemma, many variants found in the tradition are "automatically" or "mechanically" discarded: those reported by *D* alone, those reported by *C* alone, and all those reported by *B* (this witness may be excluded a priori from further consideration). When the reading of *A* coincides with the reading of *α*, it corresponds to the reading of the original, *O*. The only cases in which doubts still persist, and in which editors have to make a choice, are when the reading of *A* is opposed to the reading of *α*, that is, the common reading of *C D* – presumably, a small part of the total variants in the tradition; since the task was to reduce the editor's subjective choice, we gain a major advantage.

The relationship between the four witnesses, and their stemma, might be different, of course. Figure 2.2-2 offers another possibility.

2.2 Principles and practice — 77

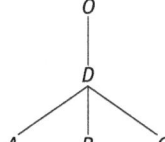

Fig. 2.2-2: Stemma (*ii*).

In this case, the reconstruction of the original, O, can proceed on the basis of a single witness (D), for the other three derive from the latter. This means a strong simplification in the work of any critical editor, and a stronger degree of certainty. Such certainty lies in the power to securely label as "false" each and every individual reading of the three manuscripts *A B C* (an operation scholars call *eliminatio lectionum singularium*). Actually, the single readings of *D* are not all necessarily "true" (i.e. corresponding to the original): in the transition from *O* to *D*, innovations may have been produced, which the editor needs to identify and eliminate. Nevertheless, the value of *D* as a witness is undoubtedly greater than the value of any of the other manuscripts.

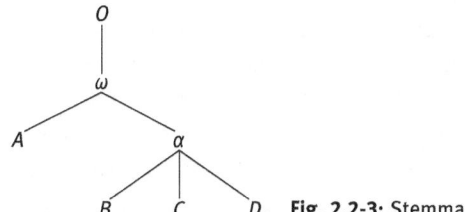

Fig. 2.2-3: Stemma (*iii*).

In this case (fig. 2.2-3), the tradition departs from a lost manuscript, ω, which contains some innovations compared to the original; in philological terms, such a manuscript is called an **archetype** (see 4.1.5). As a first step, the critical editor must recover the readings of ω. That can be done with certainty when *A* and α coincide, but requires a choice when they diverge. Once the readings of ω have been reconstructed, there is no guarantee that these readings correspond to the original, O: as with manuscript *D* in the previous case, some innovations might have been produced in the transition from O to ω, and they have to be detected and eliminated.

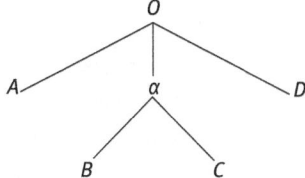

Fig. 2.2-4: Stemma (*iv*).

In this case (fig. 2.2-4), the tradition splits into three branches. Three witnesses, each independent of one another, are involved in the reconstruction of O: the surviving manuscripts A D, and the lost witness α, which can be reconstructed from B C. Here, we are able to reconstruct O – in principle, and with exceptions – mechanically: the agreement of two of the three witnesses A α D against the third, corresponds to the reading of O.

By now, the first principle of the stemmatic method is clear: the value of a reading depends on the value of the witness that reports it; this value is measured by that witness's relationships of dependence or autonomy with the other witnesses, and is represented by a *stemma codicum*. For example, in stemma (*i*), the value of a B-reading is zero (B is designated as a **codex descriptus**, that is, derived from another surviving manuscript); the value of an A-reading is very high, and equal to an α-reading; the value of a reading of C alone or of D alone is low, but if the same reading is present in both C and D, it reports a reading of α, whose value is equal to that of an A-reading.

Therefore, a genealogical representation of the relationships between witnesses provides a powerful guide for textual reconstruction. The subjectivity of the textual critic is strongly limited and replaced by mathematical criteria, apparently more "scientific" and "objective". The cases in which scholars are supposed to choose (by making recourse to their own *iudicium*) which variant to adopt, among all those attested in the tradition, are drastically reduced. If the stemma takes shape as (*i*) or (*iii*), the unclear cases are only those in which A is opposed to α. If the stemma takes shape as (*ii*), there is no doubt in choosing between the variants, because the D-reading is always the best (if its reading has to be changed, the scholar will do so without taking into account the variants of the other manuscripts, but on the basis of different arguments instead). If the stemma takes the shape of (*iv*), everything is resolved by applying a **majority principle**, except in the case (which will be rather rare) that each of the three witnesses A α D exhibits a different reading.

Among the advantages of the stemma is that it prevents the use of specious and in fact scientifically fallacious criteria, such as the following.

(*i*) A reading supported by the majority of manuscripts is not preferable for this reason alone. In the case of stemma (*iii*), when a common reading of the three manuscripts B C D is opposed to a reading of A alone, the theoretical probability of either of the two readings being original is equal. This is because B C D together represent the lost progenitor α, and this lost witness (and only this lost witness) is on the same level as A. The fact that B C D are three witnesses and A is a single witness does not confer priority on the former variant.

(*ii*) The reading attested in older manuscripts is not preferable for this reason alone. The stemmata above do not take into account the date of the witnesses. It is indeed true that an older manuscript is more likely to be "better" than a more recent one, because the greater the chronological gap, the longer the chain of copying (using manuscripts we are no longer able to see) is likely to be, and the longer the chain of copying, the more likely a modification of the text. This is, however, a mere statistical projection, not evidence at all. For example, in stemma (*iii*), the very valuable manuscript *A* might well be a recent copy of *ω*, while manuscripts *B C D* might even be earlier copies; what confers value on a witness is not so much its age, as its independence.

2.2.5 How to devise a *stemma codicum*

As can be seen, the usefulness of the *stemma codicum* for textual reconstruction is obvious. But how do we devise it? How can we know which of the theoretical configurations we have described above (and the many other possible ones) is historically correct?

The first phase of the genealogical method (*recensio*) deals with producing the *stemma codicum*. For this task, scholars use the **method of indicative (or significative) errors** (or, according to the German expression, *Leitfehler*, "leading errors"). This procedure was fully described in the second half of the nineteenth century by French scholars, albeit drawing on ideas and principles already introduced before (Reeve 1998, 450; Fiesoli 2000, 393). The method of indicative errors uses as its grouping criterion the innovations produced in the historical evolution of the text, that is, the divergences with respect to its original form. In current philological language, such innovations are often referred to as "mistakes" or "errors", in contrast to an original form considered to be "correct", regardless of whether these "mistakes" are involuntary errors (actually wrong) or intentional changes (which would hardly qualify as mistakes). The principle is that the "error", by creating a deviation from the original form, indisputably reveals a connection among the witnesses that report it; this does not happen for the "correct" reading. If several witnesses share the same mistake, they are supposed (with certain exceptions) to be connected: the "error" is supposed to have been generated in only one copy and transmitted to every descendant of this copy. The "correct" or original reading, on the contrary, is irrelevant for detecting relationships: many copyists may have accurately transcribed what their models reported, each independently of one another, and the fact that all their copies report the "correct" reading does not prove any connection. Turning back to the genealogical metaphor underlying the stemmatic method, we find here the principle – eugenic, in a way – of the "purity" of the lineage: it was "pure" in the parent, and progressively degenerated and polluted in the descendants. Every deviation is a hereditary taint, transmitted by the first carriers to their own children, and so on to all their descendants; by detecting the taint and its carriers, we can isolate a specific branch of the lineage.

The method of indicative errors is therefore the tool for drawing the stemma, but it is not an easy tool to use. Not every mistake is in fact an indicative error: the latter must fulfil certain requirements, that is, uniqueness and irreversibility. A mistake that is very easily committed (e.g. missing a name within a list of similar names) is not entitled to be evidence of relationship. Several copyists might have made this specific error independently of one another, so it is not a unique error (in philological terminology, m o n o g e n e t i c), and does not prove the existence of a single ancestor for all the manuscripts reporting it. Equally, a mistake that is very easy to correct (e.g. a manifest grammatical oversight) is not an indicative error: one or more copyists might have corrected it, and if we grouped a family of witnesses on the basis of this error, we would risk excluding indiscriminately some witnesses that are actually part of the family. This fact explains why scholars have devoted many studies to the analysis of errors, their typological classification, their genesis, and the possibility of correction by mediaeval copyists (for a summary and bibliography, see Trovato 2017, 52–58).

2.2.6 A real example

A non-invented example, which we choose here for its simplicity, is the *Apocolocyntosis*, the satire Seneca composed in contempt for the Roman Emperor Claudius, who had just died (AD 54). The work is preserved in three main manuscripts, written between the ninth and the twelfth centuries: St. Gallen, Stiftsbibliothek, Cod. Sang. 569 (*S*); London, British Library, Add. 11983 (*L*); and Valenciennes, Bibliothèque municipale, 411 (*V*; reference editions: Roncali 1990; Eden 1984; studies on the transmission: Russo 1942; Eden 1979). We begin by observing that *S*, the oldest manuscript of the three, has its own errors and therefore may not be ancestor of the other two. At the end of the *Apocolocyntosis*, for example, a court of gods condemns Claudius to play dice with a pierced box (*fritillus*). Seneca represents the scene with these verses: "Nam quotiens missurus erat resonante fritillo / utraque subducto fugiebat tessera fundo" [Every time he wanted to throw the two dice out of the resonant box, they both went out because of the missing bottom]. In *S*, the words "missurus erat resonante" are written in the form "missurus fratrae sonante", which does not make sense; the two manuscripts *V L* report the correct form, which they could not have done if they depended on *S*. Manuscript *V*, in turn, has its own errors, and may not be the ancestor of *L*; and obviously, *L*, which is the most recent, cannot be the ancestor of either of the other two. There is therefore no direct dependency between the three manuscripts.

The most interesting fact, however, is that the manuscripts *V L* are linked to each other by a genealogical relationship. The evidence is that they share some mistakes. In chapter 10, for example, Emperor Augustus – one of the characters who, in Seneca's story, is judging Claudius – is indignant about the many murders instigated by the recently deceased sovereign: "Sed quid ego de tot ac talibus viris dicam?" [What should I say of these murdered men, so many and so illustrious?], he says. Thus *S*; but in *V L*, instead of "ac talibus" we read a senseless "actibus".

This is obviously a reading or writing mistake. The fact that this mistake is the same in the two manuscripts proves that it took place in a previous manuscript, from which it was transmitted to these two; they are therefore genealogically connected. In chapter 9, Seneca makes the god Janus (another character) say: "Magna res erat deum fieri: iam Fabam mimum fecisti" [Once upon a time, becoming god was an important thing; now you have reduced it to the faba-mime]. In Seneca's Rome, *Faba mimum* – a theatre performance of the worst quality – was an idiomatic expression used to indicate something despicable, or of no importance. This jargon is supposed to have been incomprehensible to mediaeval copyists, and was hence subject to corruption. So, each of the three manuscripts reads, instead of "Fabam", a more trivial, and certainly erroneous, "famam" or "fama" [fame], a mistake made in a previous manuscript, that is, in a common ancestor of the three. In the same passage, the manuscripts *V L* share the variant "nimium" [a lot] instead of "mimum". In this case, an uncommon word, *mimum*, has been replaced by a very common but not quite meaningful one in the context; the error was very easy to make, and the copyists of *V L* may both have made it independently. It is not a unique or monogenetic error, and – on its own – it would not prove any relationship between them.

Using the method of indicative errors, we deduce two conclusions from this evidence: (*i*) all three manuscripts derive from a common lost ancestor (ω), where "fama(m)" was written instead of "Fabam"; and (*ii*) manuscripts *V L* belong to the same family, derived from an ancestor α, where "actibus" was written instead of "ac talibus" (and perhaps "nimium" instead of "mimum", but this case alone would be inconclusive). The *stemma codicum* of the *Apocolocyntosis* is therefore the one shown in figure 2.2-5.

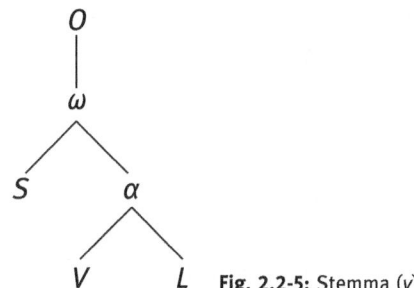

Fig. 2.2-5: Stemma (*v*).

This *stemma codicum* has several consequences for reconstructing the text:
(*i*)   readings occurring in *V* alone are supposed to be non-original;
(*ii*) readings occurring in *L* alone are supposed to be non-original;
(*iii*) readings occurring in *S* alone might be original, because they have the same value as those occurring in *V L* together (i.e. those occurring in α);
(*iv*) when the reading of *V* is the same as *L*, it corresponds to the reading of their lost ancestor α, and might be original;

(v) when the reading of V is different from L, and one of the two corresponds to the reading of S, the common reading of $S\,L$ or $S\,V$ reports the reading of α;
(vi) when the reading of S is the same as that of α, it corresponds to the reading of their lost ancestor ω;
(vii) when the reading of V is different from L, and neither of them corresponds to S, the reading of α is uncertain, and the critical editor will have to reconstruct it using other arguments; and
(viii) when the reading of S is different from α, the critical editor has to make a choice (*selectio*) on a different basis in order to recover the reading of ω.

Following these procedures, we are able to determine the text of ω; but this does not yet correspond to the original, for ω is an archetype, a copy we have above defined as depending on the original but also already affected by innovations or mistakes (as we have seen in the misinterpretation of "Fabam"). This lost manuscript is the highest point in the stemma we are able to reach by examining the surviving witnesses. In the passages where there is certainty, or at least a well-founded suspicion, that the text of the archetype does not correspond to the original, we can attempt to reconstruct the original by conjecture – an operation called *emendatio*, "correction". If it is not possible to do so – because the text of the archetype is too corrupt and resists any conjecturing – the critical editor will renounce the task of emendation; the failure of the attempt is usually indicated by inserting a cross (*obelus* or *crux*, †) in the passage. In the case of the *Apocolocyntosis*, for example, the story apparently lacks continuity between chapters 7 and 8 (as numbered in modern editions): a large part of the text seems to be missing, and the damage was already in the archetype, since the omission is in all the manuscripts of the work. We may have an approximate idea of the missing content, but we can never completely recover the text: therefore, we are forced to resign ourselves to the *crux*.

2.2.7 The limits of the genealogical method

The genealogical method apparently operates on a high scientific level, based as it is on logical rules and standardised procedures. A *stemma codicum* itself is a geometric diagram, built on mathematical principles, as a visual confirmation of the objectivity of the results. In addition to this, a stemma is a figure very effective in communication: scholars have, in its manuscript tradition, a clear and immediate view of the historical development of the literary work they are studying. Like any schema, however, this effectiveness of representation pays a price for simplification. The need to compress the tradition, as far as possible, into such a schema forces the critical editor to face and uniquely resolve every puzzling or problematic node – those nodes that in a discursive and non-schematic presentation might have been discussed in detail. "A stemma of the tradition must have historically existed" – a young philologist is likely to think – "and my task is to recreate it at any cost."

As we have said, the stemma figure is borrowed from the language of family descent, as are the metaphors indicating relationships in it. Historically, this borrowing took place from the very beginning of the method, in a fully conscious manner, as shown by the adoption of the key word, *stemma*, "family tree", which provided the name for the whole discipline. Yet: to what extent do the mechanisms of family descent really correspond to the mechanisms of textual transmission? How widely is the genealogical model legitimately applicable to a manuscript tradition?

The emergence of the genealogical model must be framed in the ideological climate of the time that first expressed it: an aristocratic world where the eugenic concept of "purity" of the lineage was significant. Therefore, in stemmatic descriptions, the "purity" of the text is often a key word: the editor's objective is to reconstruct the "pure" original text, eliminating the "impurities" that have progressively accumulated in it over the course of history. Such "impurities" that "pollute" the text are those produced in its historical evolution: changes made by the copyists – either mistakes or voluntary amendments – or material damage to manuscripts. Therefore, the genealogical model implies a degenerative process: the history of a family is the history of a progressive, inevitable, and regrettable departure from the "purity" of race. Applying this pattern to the tradition of the text, subsequent copies always involve a deplorable departure from the original "purity"; those who threaten and corrupt such "purity", the enemy to be fought, are the individual copyists. This eugenic vision, born in connection with the sole purpose of reconstructing the original text, classifies all copyists as ignorant vandals, and prevents the scholar from fully understanding the nature of what they did. In actual fact, the innovations introduced by the copyists are not always the effects of mistakes: they are often attempts to improve a text they considered – rightly or wrongly – incorrect, or to make it suitable for a different audience, that is, their contemporaries. In this fashion, the copyists engaged in the same tasks that face a scholar or critical editor nowadays, though they did so less consciously and with a less sophisticated method. In this view, textual transmission is not only a degenerative history, but may also be a history of recovering and attention.

There is more. There are, in fact, significant and crucial differences between the historical transmission of texts and the principles of family descent, though they have clear similarities in general patterns. The most important element of differentiation is the fact that, while in a family genealogy a child inevitably has only one mother, in the transmission of the texts nothing prevents a "child" from having more than one "mother". Outside the metaphor, a copyist might make his copy using more than one manuscript of the same work as models; in this case, his copy is treated as having more than one "mother". Such an event – always theoretically possible in the transmission of a text, albeit more or less probable depending on the nature of the work, the circles in which it was read, the uses it had – is one of the main obstacles to an "absolute" application of the stemmatic method (*strenge Stemmatik*, to use an expression of Maas). This case is called h o r i z o n t a l t r a n s - m i s s i o n (because convergent lines can appear in the stemma, unlike a family tree, which contains only divergent lines); using the eugenic paradigm, scholars speak of c o n t a m i n a t i o n (see 4.4 below) because the "purity" of the transmission model is spoiled here by the introduction of an external and non-relevant element. Figure 2.2-6 exemplifies the *stemma* of a contaminated tradition.

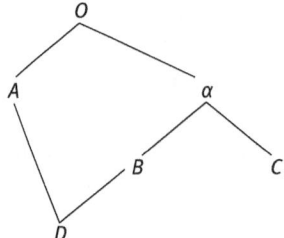

Fig. 2.2-6: Stemma (*vi*).

This stemma represents a situation where the copyist of D acquired his text from two different models, A and B. In this case, the critical editor detects contradictory evidence: witness D shares some errors with A, but not all the errors of A; witness D shares some errors with B, but not all the errors of B; witness D also shares other errors with both B and C, but not all the errors shared by B and C; witness B shares some errors with both D and C, but shares other errors only with D and other errors only with C; witness A shares some errors with D, but not all the errors of D; witness C shares some errors with both B and D, but other errors only with B. Another difficulty is the fact that, if the copyist of D was a clever scribe and was interested in the text he was copying (as is likely, since he is so careful that he uses more than one model for his work), he might have corrected the errors he found in his models: where A was wrong, the copyist of D would have written the reading of B; where B was wrong, he would have written the reading of A. As an ultimate consequence, witness D might be free of apparent errors, and it might seem to us the best of all the four; from the stemmatic point of view, however, it is the worst, but the derived nature of its text is no longer apparent to us because every indicative error – that is, the tool that would allow us to detect it – has disappeared. Faced in practice with a situation such as that in stemma (*vi*), therefore, the editor might be tempted to draw a stemma such as the one in figure 2.2-7.

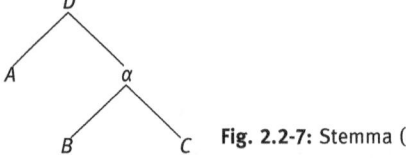

Fig. 2.2-7: Stemma (*vii*).

The problem is that, in principle, any tradition might be contaminated, and we have no way of knowing in advance whether it actually is. Therefore, contamination was traditionally considered an a priori obstacle to the application of the stemmatic method, an obstacle so strong that it was supposed to undermine its credibility. Maas considered contamination a disastrous circumstance and an insoluble problem; his sentence "Gegen die Kontamination ist kein Kraut gewachsen" (Maas 1957, 30) [No specific has yet been discovered against contamination] (trans. Flower 1958, 48; other renditions include "no medicinal herb has yet been grown", "there is no remedy") is one of the most famous aphorisms in the history of philology. Again: "im Bereich einer Kontamination versagt die strenge Stemmatik" [where contamination exists the science of stemmatics in the strict sense breaks down] (Maas 1957, 30; trans. Flower 1958, 49). In fact, the recourse by a copyist to more than one model is a historical possibility; as such, it has to be analysed without considering it problematic or disastrous, and it has to be faced using the proper tools of textual criticism. Simply put, such a circumstance is incompatible with the genealogical reference model if applied "absolutely"; but it becomes compatible if the genealogical pattern is used, more correctly, as a metaphor for the mechanisms of textual transmission, without expecting a total coincidence (for a discussion of contamination, with a deeper analysis and some "remedies", see Avalle 1961, 159–178; Segre 1961; Vàrvaro 2010; 4.4 below).

A second element of differentiation between a family tree and the real development of a manuscript tradition is the fact that the former implies uniqueness at the root, which is not necessarily the case for the latter. A family tree starts with a unique parent; a *stemma codicum* also departs from a unique original, and this unique original is the goal of reconstruction. When, therefore, in the tradition two variants differ, the scholar assumes that one of the two is "true" (i.e. corresponding to the original) and the other is "false" (i.e. not corresponding to the original); they might actually both be "false" (if each of them is the result of an independent innovation), but can never both be "true", because the original is unique. In historical reality, however, many works originally have more than one version, often made by the author himself over time. We are familiar with such cases from modern literatures, where the richness of documentation makes them readily demonstrable; nevertheless, similar events existed, without doubt in great number, even in ancient and mediaeval literatures. When this case pertains, the dichotomy between "false" readings and "true" readings fails: both of the opposing readings attested might be "true", and their duplicity might be explained by the succession of several editorial stages. Scholars, however, conditioned by the binary process imposed by the genealogical model, tend to classify every variant as "true" and "false"; thus, they first (in the *recensio*) draw the stemma on the basis of the readings categorised as certainly "false", and then eliminate (in the *constitutio textus*) the others categorised as likely "false". But, in the presence of **authorial variants**, such categorising is undue, because the tradition is not at all unique, and all readings might be "true".

2.2.8 The value of the genealogical method

As noted, the genealogical method originated from the need to base reconstruction on scientific and objective criteria, reducing as far as possible the subjectivity of the editors. In its golden age – namely in the second half of nineteenth century – this method was considered to be almost infallible due to the power ensured by the apparent rigour of the process. It was then restricted and even discredited, both because of its difficult application in certain circumstances (as we described above: contaminated traditions, traditions with authorial variants) and, above all, because of its nature as a reconstructive method, only capable of producing a text that is merely hypothetical. Maas's *Textkritik*, which, as we have said, is a systematic exposition of the subject, a kind of late manifesto, also met the need to dismantle criticism and to reiterate the validity of the method.

From a balanced perspective, the "scientific" aim of the method seems to have been achieved, and it does not seem to be greatly affected by the aforementioned limits. The genealogical method provided some key concepts for the analysis of the transmission of texts. Moreover, the method elaborated some principles and tools which have value in themselves and are applicable to a significant number of textual traditions, fully or in part. Indeed, the method has endowed textual studies with an essential diachronic perspective. It could not completely eliminate the editor's *iudicium* – nor was this possible – in choosing the variants; but it has provided editors with an indispensable guide in exercising their *iudicium*. Discovering some limits of the genealogical method and discussing them has produced greater self-awareness, and has given scholars a more mature and refined method. The objective limits we have recalled do not undermine the general validity of the system.

What is clear today is that the genealogical model, in its entirety, can be applied to specific textual traditions. Considered as a metaphor, however, the model does correctly explain many mechanisms and unravel many situations. The genealogical mechanism is the proposition of a basic principle which has an intrinsic and absolute value and corresponds to real phenomena, though it is rarely (or perhaps never) accomplished in a complete way. It describes the *in vitro* trend of textual transmission: the basic mechanism, the one that governs the process in an ideal situation. Real situations are obviously much more complex, but they can be interpreted only in the light of the idealised situation, the one where no accidental elements appear. If I am allowed to call into question a further pattern, the "absolute" stemmatic method "in a strict sense", (Maas's *strenge Textkritik*), might be likened to "uniform motion in a straight line", the rules of which constitute a basic lesson in kinematics: this kind of motion does not exist in nature (as movement is always influenced by other forces, such as friction or gravitation), but knowledge of the "ideal" law makes it possible to clarify every similar real motion.

The scarcity of stemmata in the introductions to today's editions of classical texts may seem surprising: this is generally due to the tradition of these works being too complex and having a much too irregular trend, far from a standard genealogical model, to be fully represented by a stemma. Yet the scholars who created these editions have almost always used the stemmatic method for analysing the tradition and for determining some important points in a text's history: for example, for the elimination of some *codices descripti* or for the identification of some families of witnesses. Going back to the example of the *Apocolocyntosis*, the stemmata we see in the current critical editions (Eden 1984, 25; Roncali 1990, x) actually reproduce the relationships between the three ancient manuscripts we quoted: the later tradition, consisting of about forty humanistic manuscripts, strongly interpolated and often contaminated, is not provided in detail and only partially appears in the stemmatic representation. The genealogical method served to disentangle some knots, and in this case the decisive knots; in the face of a more complex reality, it could not solve everything.

It is becoming rarer and rarer for today's editors – especially the editors of mediaeval texts, for which the scholarship is more recent and which have therefore benefited from a more refined genealogical method – to present vertical trees that only contain diverging branches, as is expected in a strictly genealogical pattern. Confirmed cases of horizontal transmission are becoming more and more frequent, not least because they are no longer exorcised as unmanageable anomalies; multi-root trees are also becoming more frequent. These representations continue to be called *stemmata*, following the traditional terminology, but are less and less similar to heraldic genealogies and are increasingly distant from Maas's *strenge Stemmatik*. Nevertheless, genealogical principles remain the only effective tool to work with.

Other metaphors and other patterns have been adopted over time: the judicial metaphor, which we have already mentioned (where the critical editor is a magistrate in search of a textual "truth", questioning the various "witnesses", ascertaining the credibility of the individuals, and exercising "judgement" in any doubtful cases); the medical metaphor (where the critical editor is supposed to "cure" a text afflicted by minor or serious degenerative diseases, investigating their causes and attempting to reduce their effects); or the chemical metaphor (where existing manuscripts are compared to streams emerging from an underground river whose original nature has to be discovered by removing impurities absorbed by the water on its journey; Maas 1957, 14–15, trans. Flower 1958, 20; Froger 1968, 268–271; Montanari 2003, 236–240). Other interpretative diagrams have also been proposed, linked to set theory (Froger 1968, 139–216) and, more recently, to cladistics (see 8.1.1.1) and rhizomorphic representation (Greetham 1996, 99–126; Sargent 2013, 247–251).

No one, however, has so far had the power to overthrow the genealogical model and stemmatic representation – and indeed, each enriches in its own way the descriptive spectrum of textual transmission – perhaps because genealogy is basically the machine language of textual transmission, the matrix which lies as a cornerstone of the real facts, and of our ability to understand them.

2.3 Criticism and controversy
Giovanni Palumbo

"Lachmann's method" and its applications have sparked methodological discussions since its first manifesto, Gaston Paris's introduction to his edition of *Saint Alexis*, published in 1872 (Paris and Pannier 1872). This section examines the main objections that were raised in the subsequent six decades up to 1934. From the point of view of the history of textual philology, this timespan appears to be coherent and of great importance in many respects. It is also a decisive period for many aspects of a debate between philologists and mediaevalists that extends into the present day, as we shall also adumbrate here. Thus, our presentation aims to be both historical and methodological.

2.3.1 Background

The genealogical method – also known as the scientific method, method of common errors, or "Lachmann's method" – was gradually developed during the nineteenth century, most decisively in the 1830s. It was fully formalised only in the first decades of the twentieth century, most notably in Paul Maas's *Textkritik* (1927). We now know that its attribution to the German scholar Karl Lachmann (1753–1851) is largely unfounded (see 2.2.1). This error (or rather, purposeful ambiguity) hails from Romance philology (Joseph Bédier) and biblical philology (Henri Quentin), and extended later to classical philology and finally to other philologies as well. In reality, Lachmann contributed little to the two main points of the method that would later bear his name: (*i*) the classification of witnesses on the basis of their genealogical relationship, and (*ii*) the mechanical application of the stemmatic majority in the preparation of the critical text, especially to guide the choices of the editor in all the cases in which the tradition has preserved two or more *varianti adiafore* (substantial readings – see 4.1.5 – between which an a priori choice cannot be made). On the contrary, Lachmann once termed the *stemma codicum* a mere *pons asinorum* (see Fiesoli 2000, 277, 407). The genealogical method is not, in fact, the fruit of a single scholar's invention but the result of a much more complex process based on collective reasoning initiated by scholars before Lachmann, extended by him and his contemporaries, and refined by later scholars (see 2.4). It is only out of convention that the term "Lachmann's method" persists today (in this volume and elsewhere) to refer to the method of classifying witnesses through common errors (on which, see 2.2).

2.3.2 The genealogical method according to Gaston Paris (1872)

The earliest explicit and mature theoretical approaches to the principles of the genealogical method go back to the second half of the nineteenth century, when the method began to be applied to vernacular texts. Within the span of a few years, Karl Bartsch's work on the *Nibelungenlied* (1866), Gustav Gröber's on the manuscript tradition of *Fierabras* (1869), the "Etudes sur la Chanson de Girart de Roussillon" by Paul Meyer (1870), and, above all, the edition of the *Vie de Saint Alexis* by Gaston Paris (1872) were all published. The latter had been initiated in 1869 but was interrupted by the Franco-Prussian War. In the introduction to this edition (Paris and Pannier 1872, 7–15), Paris sets out in detail the method he applied, including new developments that distinguish it from earlier editorial approaches that now came to be seen as inadequate due to new scholarly standards (see 7.3.1). Paris criticised editions that only reproduced (with minimal interventions) the text of the manuscript that the editor considered to be the best, as well as eclectic editions in which the editor favoured his own competence and taste when choosing among concurrent readings (for more on types of editions, see 6.1).

While describing the necessary steps to produce the critical text, Paris distinguishes two main stages which require distinct approaches: the constitution of the readings (c o n s t i t u t i o n   d e s   l e ç o n s) on the one hand and the constitution of the language (c o n s t i t u t i o n   d u   l a n g a g e) on the other. The former involves what are sometimes called s u b s t a n t i a l   r e a d i n g s in English, the latter a c c i d e n t a l ones. Regarding the former (the only one we are concerned with here), Paris highlights the following points (Paris and Pannier 1872, 10–14).

(*i*) For Paris, the aim of textual criticism applied to allographic traditions (i.e. in the absence of autographs) is that of reconstructing as much and as far as possible the form in which the work left the author's hand. Paris was, of course, fully aware of the fact that his aim can never be fully achieved: textual criticism can approach it to a greater or lesser degree, depending on the nature of the textual transmission (antiquity and completeness of the witnesses, the copyists' attitude towards their models, their provenance, and so on).

(*ii*) The most basic, but also fundamental, procedure in textual criticism is the systematic comparison of the readings of all extant witnesses. Its general postulate is that two different scribes copying the same text are unlikely to make the same errors or introduce the same innovations (this only happens when the tradition presents certain material and textual features). Comparison of the witnesses, when successful, allows the reconstruction of the text of the lost source from which they derive.

(*iii*) The goal of classifying the witnesses is to ascertain their reciprocal genetic relationships as well as their relationship with the original.

(*iv*) In order to classify the manuscripts, the editor must beforehand verify that each manuscript is not copied from another surviving manuscript (textual independence of the witness), as a direct or indirect copy of an extant witness (*codex descriptus*; see 2.2.4) has no authority in the reconstruction of the original.

(*v*) Given four witnesses $a\ b\ c\ d$, the editor has to test several genealogical hypotheses ($a + b + c + d$, $a + z\ (= b + c + d)$, $a + b + z\ (= c + d)$, $y\ (= a + b) + z\ (= c + d)$, and so on; see 2.2). If $a\ b\ c\ d$ are independent copies of the original, each will occasionally stand on its own, but no two will agree. If $a\ b$ on the one hand and $c\ d$ on the other frequently agree ("coïncidence habituelle"; Paris and Pannier 1872, 12), it has to be concluded that each pair derives from a lost copy ($y\ (= a + b) + z\ (= c + d)$) that contained all the shared (monogenetic) innovations and typical readings of each pair.

(*vi*) The classification of the witnesses can lead to more or less reliable results. The principal obstacles to a well-founded classification are the loss of many mediaeval manuscripts and the quality of what we have lost: in most cases, not only the autographs but also the earliest generations of copies are lost. Frequently, only a single witness survives for a given textual family, and everything that can be said about its lost models (generally, not very much) must come from its analysis.

(*vii*) If the classification brings to light or demonstrates the existence of three (or more) independent families, the critical text is likely to be established mechanically to a very large extent ("une opération pour ainsi dire mathématique"; Paris and Pannier 1872, 13 [a so to speak mathematical operation]), as long as there is a consensus of the majority, for example two families vs the third (*varianti adiafore* occur only when all the families independently diverge in the same *locus*). In contrast, when the classification establishes only two independent families, the editor may decide to give preference to one of them, or decide to employ *iudicium* (see 6.2.3), to resolve cases of such *varianti adiafore*. This part of textual criticism is the one in which the "savants vraiment supérieurs" (Paris and Pannier 1872, 13) [the truly great scholars] are revealed.

It has been rightly observed that Paris in 1872 "n'était pas ce qu'on appellera plus tard lachmannien" (L. Leonardi 2009a, 276) [was not what would later be called a Lachmannian]. His groundbreaking edition certainly affirms clearly, and probably for the first time, the basic principle according to which the genealogy of witnesses can only be established by the method of common errors (Reeve 1998, 450–465). However, his views are not exempt from oscillation and inconsistencies (relatively common at his time) on some key points of the method, which highlight a few fundamental problems:

(*a*) the limits to the applicability of the stemmatic method and the varying degree of reliability of the results it can attain, both in the classification of the witnesses and in the preparation of the critical text (points (*i*) and (*vii*) above);

(*b*) the possible relationship between shared errors (point (*i*)) and shared series of variant substantial readings (point (*v*); see also 2.3.4.4), that is, series of non-erroneous readings shared by two or more witnesses and not all the others, and their relevance for classification; and

(*c*) the tension between mechanical application of the stemma and recourse to the editor's competence (*iudicium*; point (*vii*)).

In the decades following the publication of Paris's *Saint Alexis*, after a period in which the method of common errors seemed to assert itself in an undisputed way,

the critical debate resumed in an especially fertile and animated manner. In this debate, the nature and the ultimate goal of textual criticism was dramatically challenged (point (i)). In just a few years, several seminal works had been published. These works have also had the merit of crossing frontiers between disciplines. We shall discuss the most important ones in chronological order:
- 1913, Joseph Bédier's second edition of the *Lai de l'ombre*;
- 1926, Henry Quentin's *Essais de critique textuelle*;
- 1927, Paul Maas's *Textkritik*;
- 1928, Joseph Bédier's "Réflexions sur l'art d'éditer les anciens textes"; and
- 1929, Giorgio Pasquali's review of the *Textkritik*, which would grow into the monumental volume *Storia della tradizione e critica del testo* (1934).

2.3.3 The method of common errors: Ineffective?

The first radical criticism of the method of common errors came from Joseph Bédier and Henri Quentin, two scholars from different fields – Old French and biblical philology respectively – both dealing with "living" textual traditions. They were engaged in an ongoing dialogue, both in private and in public (cf. Quentin 1926, 147–164; Bédier 1928), and found themselves agreeing on the defects of the method (some of them real, others just presumed by them), but they disagreed fundamentally about possible remedies.

Despite their fundamental criticism of it, each continued to remain (as we shall see) in the orbit of the genealogical method. Bédier drew attention to the weaknesses of the method of common errors and its dire consequences when wrongly applied. Quentin tried to modify the foundations of the method, radically changing the procedures of *recensio* and grounding them in a different set of principles. Each in his own way initiated significant lines of research which have subsequently led to profound transformations arising from their work.

2.3.4 Bédier's anti-Lachmannism

Although a disciple of Gaston Paris and later his successor at the Collège de France, Bédier would fight "la méthode usuelle [pour le classement des manuscrits], inventée, semble-t-il, par Karl Lachmann" (1913, xxiii) [the usual method [for the classification of manuscripts], apparently invented by Karl Lachmann] on the basis of his personal experience in the study of a short mediaeval French text, Jean Renart's *Lai de l'ombre* (for more on Bédier, see 7.3.2 below; Corbellari 1997; C. Baker et al. 2018). In 1890, Bédier first published this short poem, diligently applying the method of common errors and constructing a bipartite stemma. Paris reviewed (1890) the edition immediately and praised Bédier's instinct, which led him to nearly always choose the good reading in cases where the two families disagreed. Nevertheless, Paris proposed altering the bipartite stemma to make it tripartite (the first stemma is reproduced in fig. 4.1-6 below).

Two decades later, when he returned to the *Lai de l'ombre*, Bédier began ruminating on the teachings of his by then deceased master, Paris. In his second edition (1913) and in an article (1928), Bédier proposed a law whose main effect seems to have been to render the work of Lachmannian editors arbitrary in most cases, and to create general puzzlement among Lachmannians. The study of a textual tradition seemed to lead the editor always, or nearly always, to draw a bipartite (see 4.1.4) stemma: one in which exactly two surviving branches issue from the archetype. Having finished the editorial work, editors would thus (nearly) always find themselves in the situation of having to choose among differing variants by relying on taste or intuition – subjective criteria, precisely what the method of common errors endeavoured to eliminate. What Paris saw as one possibility among several, became an embarrassing norm in the eyes of Bédier. In the introduction to his 1913 edition, he described a marvellous forest of bipartite trees that grow in the introductions of critical editions. Bédier concluded this was a consequence of editors' unconscious desire to control their editions and to exercise their judgement in establishing the text. Editors, Bédier believed, aspire to be free from the "loi d'airain", or unyielding law (Bédier 1913, xxxi; 1928, 174–175), imposed by the tripartite stemma. In his 1928 article, he added interesting considerations about the binary logic ("good" vs "bad" readings) at the heart of the method of common errors.

At times, Bédier's scepticism seems to concern the stemmatic method as such. For him, very few stemmata are necessarily certain ("nécessairement vrai[s]"; Bédier 1913, xxxiv). A high degree of uncertainty in assigning witnesses to families seemed to him to be common, at least in vernacular textual traditions. The method of common errors allows the identification with a high degree of certainty of the principal groups of witnesses in the lower branches of the stemma, but fails to do this equally well for the relationships between those groups, that is, when trying to establish the stemma's upper branches. Ascending the stemma, the obvious errors become fewer and fewer, and the choice between competing readings becomes more delicate and subjective; readings that seem innovatory to one scholar might seem preferable or even original to another.

In some cases, an error that seems to define a group of witnesses may not be exclusive to that group: it could, for instance, go back to the archetype and have been corrected in the ancestors of the other groups. In other cases, it is possible that two conflicting readings are both original: the author himself may have revised his work. Bédier also observes that the absence of shared errors from two or more witnesses makes it impossible to prove their parentage, but at the same time does not guarantee their independence.

Bédier's arguments can be reduced to two major points: (*i*) a text should not be reconstructed with a stemma which is not the only one possible, and (*ii*) the stemma that allows one to ascertain the value of the readings rests on a *petitio principii*, that is, the discernment of "good" and "bad" readings (see Contini 1939b, 151 = 1946, 129). Therefore, Bédier judges the method of common errors to be ineffective and harmful. It is ineffective because it does not allow the reconstruction of the author's text with certainty. The harm comes from the editor being forced to mechanically combine readings from different witnesses under the rule of a stemma that cannot be certain; as such, the stemma could be replaced by others that are equally plausible and equally hypothetical, so that no reasoned choice is really possible. The method eventually produces composite critical texts that are highly arbitrary and that are based on no historical reality whatsoever. Put differently, for Bédier the method of common errors gives the editor the illusion of reconstructing the original text but in reality often just fabricates a new version of it. In contrast, "mediaeval editions" were at least prepared by the copyists to satisfy their audience. From this follows Bédier's editorial scepticism: cease reducing the variants *ad unum* in order to restore the original text. Instead, choose a good manuscript and keep to its readings as faithfully as possible, correcting only its most glaring errors. If a work is extant in various versions or traditions (recensions), prepare as many editions as there are recensions. In this case, according to Bédier, it is best to publish a good manuscript for each recension, possibly providing an apparatus of the variants from other witnesses containing the same recension.

Bédier thus tries to channel the editorial freedom he had gained from the "loi d'airain" imposed by incorrect or uncertain stemmata towards proper respect for a historical document (a "bon manuscrit"). At the same time, the scope of the edition changes: it is no longer the reconstruction of the authorial version but the publication of one or more scribal versions.

2.3.4.1 The genesis of Bédierism from musicology to textual criticism

Bédier's anti-Lachmann rebellion matured after Gaston Paris's death (1903), and belongs in the context of Bédier's general tendency to radically review his teacher's theses, not only in philological fields but also in historical and literary ones. M u s i c o l o g y played an important role in the genesis of Bédier's philological thought (Zinelli 2018). Before his second edition of the *Lai de l'ombre*, Bédier published a "Lachmannian" edition of the *Chansons de croisade* (1909) in collaboration with the musicologist Pierre Aubry, then a second, revised edition of Colin Muset's poems (1912), this time collaborating with the musicologist Jean Beck. In mediaeval music witnesses, the manuscripts of the same poem may be accompanied by different melodies. Bédier observed that musicologists do not reconstruct stemmata for the various melodies and their variants (for more on musicology, see 8.4). They do not combine elements from extant melodies in search of an "ur-composition" but instead classify these melodies as "versions", then publish them separately as if they were different originals. The affinities with Bédier's proposed editorial methodology of 1913 and 1928 are evident.

Bédier's musicological experience can help to understand the genesis of Bédierism; the gulf between Bédier and Paris can be gauged by the comparisons they drew with archaeological restoration. Paris writes in the introduction to the *Saint Alexis*: "J'ai essayé de faire ici pour la langue française ce que ferait un architecte qui voudrait reconstruire sur le papier Saint-Germain des Prés tel que l'admira le XIe siècle" (Paris and Pannier 1872, 136) [I have tried to do here for the French language what an architect who wants to reconstruct on paper Saint-Germain-des-Prés as it could be admired in the eleventh century would do]. Bédier responds implicitly to this assertion by including a quotation from the archaeologist Adolphe-Napoléon Didron in his edition: "Il faut conserver le plus possible, réparer le moins possible, ne restaurer à aucun prix" (Bédier 1913, xlv; 1927, ix–x) [One must conserve as much as possible, repair as little as possible, and never restore at all]. In this *dialogue à distance* between pupil and master, there is a clash between two approaches to restoration that are completely opposed in method and goal: restoration of the monument in the closest possible form to that of the original vs a conservative restoration of only one snapshot of the monument in time.

2.3.4.2 The shadow of Bédier and his complex legacy

The fertility of Bédier's warnings, but also their limitations, were quickly recognised and sparked a lively debate. There is no doubt that his contribution to challenging a primitive and overly simplistic version of the method of common errors (one that was seen as mechanically producing certainty) is to be counted among his merits. Such a simplistic version of the method was what the young Bédier subscribed to at the beginning of his career and what he characterised thus:

> Réunir tous les manuscrits discordants d'un même ouvrage; déterminer, par l'observation des fautes communes aux divers scribes, les rapports de dépendance qui groupent certains d'entre eux en familles; opposer ces familles; reconstituer, par la comparaison des leçons divergentes et selon des procédés presque mécaniques, le manuscrit original perdu; puis, quand on a retrouvé cet archétype, rechercher, grâce à l'examen des rimes, de la mesure du vers et des traits linguistiques, en quelle province, à quelle date, l'œuvre a été composée; restituer aux idées le tour qu'elles avaient dans l'esprit de l'auteur, aux mots la forme dialectale qu'ils prenaient sur ses lèvres; établir le texte *ne varietur*, à peu près tel qu'il serait, si le vieil écrivain avait connu l'imprimerie et s'il avait, de sa main, corrigé ses épreuves: c'est une tâche possible, voire facile. Elle requiert moins encore des dons d'esprit supérieurs que des qualités morales, la patience, la probité de l'esprit. (Bédier 1894, 912)

> [To collect all discordant manuscripts of a single work; to determine by the observation of errors common to different scribes the relationships of dependence that group some of them into families; to contrast these families; to reconstruct by a comparison of the divergent readings and according to nearly mechanical procedures the original lost manuscript; then, when one has retrieved this lost archetype, to study through the examination of rhymes, the measurement of verse and linguistic traits, where and when the work was composed; to reconstitute the ideas to what they were in the mind of the author, his words to the dialectal form they had on his lips; to establish the text *ne varietur*, more or less the way it would have been if

the ancient writer had known the printing press and if he had with his own hands corrected the proofs: this is a possible task, indeed an easy one. It requires even less the gifts of a superior spirit than moral qualities: patience, probity of the spirit.]

Once these excessive certainties were demolished, Bédier's main flaw was "di non accorgersi che un'edizione critica è, come ogni atto scientifico, una mera ipotesi di lavoro, la più soddisfacente (ossia la più economica) che colleghi in sistema i dati" (Contini 1939b, 151 = 1946, 129–130) [not realising that a critical edition, like every other scientific deed, is a mere working hypothesis: the most satisfactory one (that is, the most economic one) that connects the data into a system]. In other words, a critical edition represents not the ultimate truth about a text but the best possible solution that the editor was able to find for a textual problem. Where the uncertainties cannot be eliminated, it is the duty of the editor to look for what is most probable. But the probable must not be presented as certain. Rather, the status of things and the reasons for and against a given conclusion should be clearly expressed. What is subjective is not necessarily arbitrary. As in all science, a working hypothesis can be replaced by another more satisfactory one – this guarantees the progress of science.

Despite his vigorous anti-Lachmannism, Bédier's process of philological reflection did not develop in a linear, teleological manner (see Palumbo 2018). The programmatic declarations in his editions are not entirely consistent with their rather uneven implementations in his editorial practice. In the same years in which he heavily condemns the method of common errors and challenges the validity of two-branched stemmata (Bédier 1913, 1928), Bédier considers Theodor Müller's bifid stemma of the *Chanson de Roland* as "vrai" (Bédier 1921, vi) [true] and trustworthy. He uses it for his own edition of the poem (Bédier 1921, 1927). He also insists that it is essential to proceed to the classification of the versions of a text because otherwise "la notion de l'authentique et du primitif se brouille" (Bédier 1927, 83) [the notion of the authentic and of the primary becomes blurred]. In the 1928 article, Bédier reproaches Quentin for not having tried to "tracer les lignes de faîte du schéma, celles qui doivent relier les manuscrits réels à l'archétype" (Bédier 1928, 331) [trace the lines at the top of the schema, those that must connect the real manuscripts to the archetype], for not having taken care to "peser les variants" (Bédier 1928, 329) [weigh the variants] in order to constitute the subgroups, for not having applied the criterion of the "faute commune" [shared error] to group the manuscripts. Thus it becomes clear that, at least partly: "la polemica di Bédier si svolge all'interno, non, come parrebbe, all'esterno della prospettiva lachmanniana" (Segre 2001, 89) [Bédier's polemic develops within and not, as it might seem, outside the Lachmannian perspective]. Therefore, it is hardly surprising that his rich and fertile and partly contradictory legacy would be received in two radically different ways. Responses to his legacy have thus resulted in a fairly clear-cut philological geography (see Duval 2006).

On the one hand, Bédier's scepticism has been a stimulus to renewed reflection on the stemmatic method. His highlighting of the frequency of two-branched stemmata sparked a long-lasting and important discussion of the reasons why this is so, involving historical reasons, statistical ones, and ones linked to methods of study or to contamination (for bibliographical details, see 2.4.3 below; Haugen 2016). Moreover, Bédier was absolutely right in observing that ascertaining the stemma's lower branches is often easier while the connections between the highest branches are almost invariably less certain. He was also correct in warning against treating partially confirmed stemmata as if all their branches were equally secure. It is indeed possible that a tradition may not contain enough certain elements for a complete classification of all witnesses: the full solution of such problems depends not only on the scholar but also on the data he has at his disposal. Bédier was also right in recommending making several editions of different recensions, especially but not only when there is suspicion that they are authorial, or being content with the publication of one manuscript that enjoyed especial prestige if the data to reconstruct the original text is lacking. His suggestion of concentrating not only on the original text is also of importance: scribal versions (see 4.1.6 on vulgates) should instead be studied in their own right. In other words, his admonition to focus on understanding the copies themselves and changes in their own historical, cultural, and literary life, rather than seeing them merely as a means to reconstruct the original, is significant. An edition focused on a manuscript may be as justified as one focusing on the author; between the two, there are editions focusing on the textual tradition (see Altschul 2006; Beltrami 2010, 112–116, 121–150; Squillacioti 2011, 39; Palumbo and Rinoldi 2015, 70). All these admonitions have been assimilated by the stemmatic method: they have contributed greatly to making it more differentiated and more cautious in its application, and have enabled broader possibilities for editorial success (see 2.3.6 below, 2.4 below; Vàrvaro 1970).

On the other hand, Bédier's scepticism has frequently been oversimplified and erroneously interpreted as an editorial short cut that can be applied to all cases. This has produced a philological practice in which the systematic study of a textual tradition is no longer seen as essential for editing it consistently. This practice, with its apparent advantage of considerably simplifying the editor's work, has over time led to a separation of textual criticism and the study of the history of the text (see 4.5). According to this unsophisticated and comfortable Bédierism, it is sufficient to choose what seems (according to varying criteria) to be a "bon manuscrit" (see 7.3.2). This rather vague and problematic notion may mean a complete manuscript, or an old one, or one linguistically close to the author, or one with few dialectal features, or one that offers a possibly reworked text but that is in general correct, or one that contains errors that are easy to correct – sometimes it may even just be one that is easy to read, or easily accessible, or of artistic value. Thus, a "bon manuscrit" does not necessarily have to be the best manuscript, which would contain the text closest to the original, something that can only be determined after a thorough and complete study of the textual tradition. Instead, in this method, once the "bon manuscrit" is chosen, the editor has to reproduce its content scrupulously and to correct only the most obviously faulty readings in such a way that the resulting text is comprehensible.

2.3.4.3 Beyond Bédierism: Diachrony vs synchrony

This different receptions of Bédier's legacy have thus produced a deep chasm in the philological world. On the one hand, there are scholars who claim that the study of the textual tradition is still essential to preparing a critical edition, whatever the type. On the other, there are scholars who consider this an optional and accessory part of editorial work. A conception of philology as the diachronic study of a textual tradition is thus contrasted with manuscript philology concentrated on synchronous aspects of a single witness (cf. L. Leonardi 2011, 2014). This chasm is much more significant than the now rather superficial one that had long been the focus of discussion between "interventionist" or "reconstructive" editors (generally seen as followers of Lachmann) and "conservative" ones (generally seen as followers of Bédier). In the late 1980s, the so-called New Philology radicalised the synchronous approach.

2.3.4.4 Old philology vs New Philology

At the origin of the N e w P h i l o l o g y movement is Cerquiglini's *Eloge de la variante* (1989), inspired by two muses: French theory (Roland Barthes, Jacques Derrida, and others) and informatics (see 7.3.4). Cerquiglini claims that the nineteenth-century philological paradigm is inadequate for editing mediaeval texts and, more generally, for understanding mediaeval textual culture, because it is based on two anachronistic, modern notions: that of the author and that of the text as a definite and discrete entity (see, in contrast, Vàrvaro 1989). According to Cerquiglini, mediaeval literature is an "atelier d'écriture" [writing workshop]: "l'œuvre littéraire, au Moyen Âge, est une variable" (Cerquiglini 1989, 57) [a literary work in the Middle Ages is a variable]. Its primary characteristic is v a r i a n c e, on the basis of which Cerquiglini (1989, 111) intends to reconstruct historical and genetic development. Faced with two variant readings:

> Il ne convient pas de rechercher lequel [= énoncé] est le plus proche de l'"original" (réflexe du philologue), ou bien quel est le plus ancien (réflexe grammatical): il faut poser leur équivalence, et saisir la langue médiévale dans le balancement qui va de l'un à l'autre. (Cerquiglini 1989, 108)

> [It is not appropriate to seek which [= reading] is the closer to the original (the philologist's reflex), or which is oldest (the grammatical reflex): one must accept their equal value and grasp the mediaeval language in the swinging that goes from one to the other.]

From this point of view, clearly, none of the traditional editorial methods is able to adequately represent the textual flow of mediaeval works. For Cerquiglini, the solution is in an on-screen presentation: "l'ordinateur, par son écran dialogique et multidimensionnel, simule la mobilité incessante et joyeuse de l'écriture médiévale, comme il restitue la prodigieuse faculté de mémoire de son lecteur, mémoire qui définit sa réception esthétique" (1989, 115) [the computer, with its dialogic and multidimensional screen, simulates the incessant and joyous mobility of mediaeval writing, and it restores the prodigious faculty of memory of its reader, which defines its aesthetic reception].

The edition he envisages is

> une édition électronique fondée sur une numérisation scrupuleuse de ses objets, et sur leur commentaire infini: affichage syntagmatique des éléments signifiants internes au codex, liens paradigmatiques des éléments variants (autres versions), gloses interdisciplinaires diverses. (Cerquiglini 2007, 5)

> [an electronic edition founded upon a digitisation which is scrupulous with its objects and their infinite commentary: a syntagmatic display of the significant elements within the codex, the paradigmatic links between varying elements (other versions), diverse interdisciplinary glosses.]

American New Philology (Nichols 1990) shares, by and large, the paradigm proposed by Cerquiglini, which inspired it. This "renewal" of philology establishes two aims:

> On the one hand, it is a desire to return to the medieval origins of philology, to its roots in a manuscript culture, where, as Bernard Cerquiglini remarks, "medieval writing does not produce variants: it is variance". On the other hand, a rethinking of philology should seek to minimize the isolation between medieval studies and other contemporary movements in cognitive methodologies, such as linguistics, anthropology, modern history, cultural studies, and so on. (Nichols 1990, 1)

In other words, "the 'new' philology sets out to explore [manuscript culture] in a postmodern return to the origins of medieval studies" (Nichols 1990, 7). This approach kindled a heated debate that has demonstrated its merits but also its numerous limitations; it has also shown that it is not so novel after all (see Busby 1993; Glessgen and Lebsanft 1997). A few years later, the New Philology was relabelled as **Material Philology** (see Westra 2014), and began to emphasise and specify more strongly its interest in manuscripts:

> Material philology takes as its point of departure the premise that one should study or theorize medieval literature by reinserting it directly into the *vif* of its historical context by privileging the material artifact(s) that convey this literature to us: the manuscript. (Nichols 1997, 10–11)

From the editorial point of view, this postmodern return to manuscript culture has led to online libraries of digitised manuscripts (such as romandelarose.org) and/or to "imitative" transcriptions of single manuscripts (cf. e.g. Willingham 2007, 2012), preferably ones with miniatures or glosses, chosen as examples of "a collaborative effort bespeaking the social, commercial, and intellectual organization of a specific moment in time" (Nichols 1997, 12). The central figure – "hero" in Cerquiglini's words – of Material Philology is the s c r i b e, as opposed to the a u t h o r; but ignoring the diachronic perspective and not studying the textual tradition, sometimes aggravated by the editor's lack of the necessary linguistic and philological knowledge, opens the floodgates to complete relativism, favours misinterpretation, and thus is an obstacle to the appreciation of the specificity of the single witness (see L. Leonardi 2009b; Haugen 2010; L. Leonardi 2011, 2017). Indeed, we cannot understand a scribe's work without considering the sources he used, that is, the work of the preceding scribes. And we cannot understand the work of those previous scribes without considering the author's work.

2.3.5 Quentin's anti-Lachmannism

While Bédier exerted a profound influence on ecdotic practices, the same cannot be said of the Benedictine monk Henri Quentin (1872–1934), though his role as a precursor to computer-assisted approaches is generally recognised. He wrote a study called *Les Martyrologes historiques du moyen âge* (1908), and took part in the commission chosen by Pope Pius X to establish the critical text of the Vulgate Bible. The task was monumental. There were two principal obstacles, one qualitative, the other quantitative. The text of the Vulgate was continually revised, corrected, and modified by the scribes – one might speak of a "living" textual tradition; at the same time, the quantity of witnesses is enormous. Faced with such a complex textual tradition, earlier scholars judged a classification of the witnesses to be impossible and turned to the analysis of single variant readings for the reconstruction of the text (see Tov 1982). Assessment of the witnesses and their agreements was relegated to the background. For Quentin, however, the classification of witnesses was unavoidable and of great importance if textual criticism was to avoid becoming a purely subjective art exercised in a more or less virtuoso manner by the editor. But how could all these manuscripts be classified? Quentin agreed with much of Bédier's criticism of the method of common errors. He especially emphasised the vicious cycle of judging a reading "good" or "erroneous" based on the idea one has of the original text and of what the author might have written or not. But he disagreed completely in his approach to remedying the failures in Lachmann's method. He condemned absolutely an editorial practice that consists of adopting one manuscript chosen without fixed rules, to be corrected here and there when it seems necessary or opportune, according to the subjectivity of the editor. Quentin intended to revise the genealogical method, not to abandon it: a classification of the witnesses is necessary for a rigorous critical approach. While Bédier aimed to free editors from the fallacious "loi d'airain" of stemmata, Quentin believed, instead, that a new "r è g l e   d e   f e r", an iron rule, could make *recensio* fully objective.

2.3.5.1 Quentin's "règle de fer"

Quentin's innovative ideas were first set out in his *Mémoire sur l'établissement du texte de la Vulgate* (1922), then more succinctly, albeit with a greater variety of examples, in *Essais de critique textuelle* (1926). Quentin distinguishes two phases, each requiring its own procedures. First, the reconstruction of the text of the archetype, classically understood as the codex from which all extant witnesses descend (see 4.1.1). Once the archetype's text is established, one can approach the original's text, that is, the one written by the author. The study of the witnesses allows one, at best, to reach the archetype, which, however, may be full of errors of all kinds. This is why the distinction between "good" and "erroneous" readings is avoided in this phase of *recensio*, as it would make sense only with respect to the original, not the archetype. From the point of view of the archetype, two differing readings are neutral: whether "good" or "bad", they have the same probability of being in the archetype (the archetype might have had either a "good" or a "bad" text in this *locus*) or being innovations with regard to the archetype. In other words, a "good" reading is not necessarily an "authentic" reading, and vice versa. In the first phase of *recensio*, Quentin thus rejects the notion of "error" itself in the method of common errors. For him, two differing readings are merely two readings that define identities and similarities among and between witnesses. In order to establish the classification of the witnesses, Quentin proposed to collect all divergent readings in a list, then to study the data in the list and to thin out the useless cases using statistical procedures from the experimental sciences, and finally to analyse the results in order to group the witnesses into families. Only when one has thus arrived at families of witnesses, and by establishing the archetype on that basis, does it become possible to proceed to the reconstruction of the original. Only at this point does ecdotics turn into an art in which the editor can use textual criticism, taking care to mark his conjectural interventions typographically in the text.

2.3.5.2 *Orientation* and *enchaînement* of the stemma

Quentin's method was inspired by Ernst Bernheim's treatise called the *Lehrbuch der historischen Methode* (1889). Quentin identifies the witnesses that are most similar to one another by using tables, then compares them in groups of three, always looking for the intermediate one among the three. For instance, given three manuscripts *A B C*, the first goal of the editor is to find the intermediary one, the one that is in agreement sometimes with one, sometimes with the other, but which is never (or very rarely) isolated against the other two. If we find usually *AB* vs *C* and *AC* vs *B*, but (almost) never *A* vs *BC*, then the intermediate manuscript is *A*. In the table of correspondences, the relation *A* vs *BC* will thus receive a value of 0 (or nearly 0), in contrast to positive numbers for the agreements of *AB* vs *C* and *AC* vs *B*. Quentin speaks in the former case of a "zéro caractéristique": his "règle de fer" is based on the search for this value. Once the intermediate manuscript for a first series of three has been identified, the first ring in a genealogical chain has been established. The comparison can now be extended to a fourth manuscript, then a fifth, and so on, until, ring after ring in place, the entire chain has been established. Thus it is possible to establish the *enchaînement*, "linking", of manuscripts, but not their *orientation*, "rooting", or the direction of the chain. In other words, the method allows us to identify a set of relations between the witnesses, but not to interpret and hierarchise them. Returning to the example above, the statistics of the *enchaînement* leads to B – A – C (or, if one prefers, C – A – B). The analysis cannot inform us about the chain's *orientation*, which could equally well be any of the following (see fig. 2.3-1).

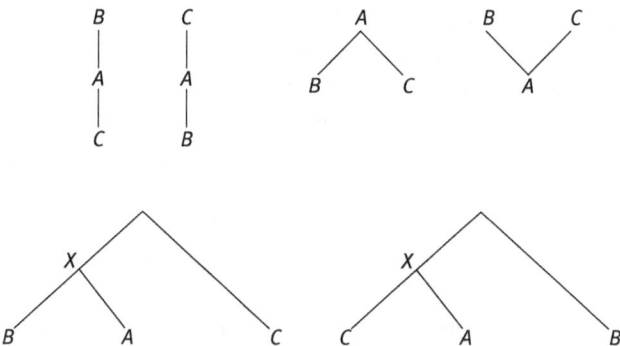

Fig. 2.3-1: Six alternative stemmata with intermediate manuscript A.

In order to orientate this chain and hierarchise the diagram (see 5.2.1) – that is, find the point of origin of the manuscripts' genealogy (the archetype, or root; see 4.1.5) – it is necessary to evaluate the readings in order to find what is earliest and what is latest. Set aside in the first phase of *recensio*, qualitative analysis and the notion of "error" have an essential role in the concluding phase of the task of classification, which is also a more delicate one.

2.3.5.3 Quentin's method as reviewed by Froger

Today, Quentin's method seems ingenious but also chaotic. Its most significant logical defect was pointed out in 1968 by another Benedictine, Jacques Froger. If Quentin had counted the disagreements between manuscripts instead of their agreements, his path would have been much more direct:

> Il est plus direct de mesurer la "distance", comme le nombre de kilomètres entre deux villes, que la "codistance", comme le nombre de kilomètres qu'il n'y a pas à parcourir, étant donné la longueur totale du réseau routier d'un pays, pour aller de telle ville à telle autre. (Froger 1968, 46–47)

> [It is more direct to measure "distance" as the number of kilometres between two cities than their "co-distance", the amount of kilometres that do not have to be covered to go from one city to another with regard to the length of the total road network of a country.]

In a manual full of good sense, based on both the logic of scholasticism and set theory, Froger radically revised Quentin's method. He substituted the uneconomical "comparaisons par trois" [comparison in groups of three] with the more efficient "méthode 'par les groupes'" (Froger 1968, 47) [grouping method], whose logical and operative steps he described with great clarity. Significant parts of the study are also devoted to anomalies in traditions, such as fragmentary manuscripts, errors corrected by conjecture, contamination, and so on, and he illustrated the limitations of quantitative analysis and the distortions they may produce. Thus, Froger's study also has the merit of allowing one to appreciate more clearly the methodological innovations introduced by Quentin. In particular, two points seem of paramount importance when comparing their method to that of common errors.

The first concerns the possibility of automating, at least in part, the editor's work by delegating quantitative analysis to a machine. In Froger's book, this is already mentioned in the title: *La Critique des textes et son automatisation*. The second part is, in fact, devoted entirely to a dialogue between the editor and the computer. This was highly innovative at the time, but it is also inevitably the part of the book that has aged most quickly. The obsolescence of this section has doubtlessly damaged the fortunes of the entire study, though there seems to be renewed interest in it (cf. Poirel 2016).

The second question is in several senses crucial and merits deeper consideration: how a dialectic between shared "errors" and shared series of non-erroneous readings can be achieved in the classification of witnesses.

2.3.5.4 Does congruity of readings imply identical origin? A controversial principle

Let us begin again with the basic principle of the method of common errors as formulated in Paris's *Saint Alexis* (see 2.3.2): two different scribes who copy the same text neither commit the same errors nor make the same changes unless there is common material or a textual factor that pushes them to intervene in the text in the same way (point (*ii*)). At the same time (point (*v*)), Paris asserts that if, among four manuscripts, two (*ab* vs *cd*) share a "coïncidence habituelle" in their readings, it must be concluded that they derive from two lost intermediaries (y (= $a + b$) + z (= $c + d$)). But this second assertion is not true, and partly contradicts the logic of the first. In Paris's fictitious example, the four manuscripts are classified into two groups according to shared readings, without making use of the concept of "error". However, the fact that the tradition attests two contrasting readings for a given passage does not imply the existence of two families, but only of one (the one with the innovative readings, A g r e e m e n t i n o r i g i n a l r e a d i n g s cannot serve to join manuscripts into a family, for their agreement is simply caused by a faithful transmission of the text of the original. Of course, the two pairs may both be families, but this can be demonstrated only if the scholar can show that both readings are innovations with respect to the original (which also means that none of the four copies preserve the text of the original), as Paris knew very well. In fact, this very situation is encountered when he presents the principles of the method's application (Paris and Pannier 1872, 21–22). The four manuscripts of *Saint Alexis* often form two contrasting groups: *LA* vs *PS*. As Paris explains, there are three possible forms of the stemma. If *L* and *A* only share "good" readings, their shared readings do not prove that they are a family, because they could have kept the original readings of the archetype independently. We would then get *L* vs *A* vs (*P* + *S*). If, on the contrary, *P* and *S* only agree on "good" readings, we would have (*L* + *A*) vs *P* vs *S*. Only if each group shares at least one erroneous (non-archetypal) reading, will there be two families: (*L* + *A*) vs (*P* + *S*).

Paris did rectify his methodological slip, but his apparent hesitation is certainly symptomatic. In his era, the reconstruction of the genealogy of the witnesses on the basis of common readings without considering whether the latter were correct (archetypal) ones or not, was widespread. Among the scholars who strongly affirmed that only shared errors (innovations) allow us to discern the filiation of the witnesses was the classical philologist Paul Lejay (1861–1920). He insisted several times that "les fautes seules permettent de discerner la filiation des textes" (Lejay 1899, 144) [only errors permit discerning the filiation of texts]. More precisely, he highlights that

> une famille de manuscrits est constituée par leurs fautes communes, ou, si l'on préfère ce terme plus exact, par leurs innovations communes. Ainsi, l'existence d'une série de leçons correctes et authentiques dans plusieurs manuscrits ne peut prouver que ces manuscrits dérivent d'une source commune. Les fautes seules sont probantes. (Lejay 1903, 171)

> [a manuscript family is defined by its common errors, or, if one prefers this more precise term, by its common innovations. Thus, a group of correct and authentic readings in several manuscripts cannot prove that these manuscripts derive from a common source. Only the errors are relevant.]

In 1927, Maas went further and affirmed that not all errors are equally significant. Only "indicative errors" can be used to draw the stemma (on the limitations of this definition, see 2.2.5 above, 2.4.3 below; Fernández-Ordóñez 2002).

This clarification was necessary to eradicate dubious philological practices. While he acknowledged the correctness of this methodology, Froger also pointed out its drawbacks. The main one is that the editor who applies the method of common errors

> ne peut plus raisonner sur toutes les leçons, mais seulement sur le petit nombre de celles que les critères conjecturaux permettent de regarder avec certitude comme des fautes [...]. On verra dès lors les critiques s'engager dans une voie dangereuse: établir la généalogie des manuscrits à l'aide d'un nombre de fautes ridiculement petit, dans le désir de ne retenir que celles qui sont probantes. (Froger 1968, 42)

> [can no longer consider all readings, but only the small number of those that the conjectural criteria allow with certainty to be regarded as errors [...]. Consequently, we will see philologists take a dangerous road: establishing the genealogy of manuscripts with the help of a ridiculously small number of errors, wishing to keep only those that have demonstrative force.]

The problem is real, especially for "living" textual traditions in which "indicative errors" are often very rare but variants are very numerous and their value is hard to judge. It is no accident that the best philologists or editors of texts have always used a series of substantial variants to confirm their classification or to double-check the degree of likelihood of their families in relation to possible alternative groupings (see 2.4.3). The exclusion of non-erroneous variants from stemmatic reasoning deprives the editor of a further means of control which can help to detect an erroneous assessment or perspective. Moreover, this also leads to only a partial view of the textual tradition, including the risk of overlooking relevant indicators. As an example, let us look at contamination by change of exemplar (see 1.2.3, 4.4.4.2), which is a more common and complex phenomenon than one would suspect. Let us say that manuscript B is grouped with A ($AB = x$) against CD ($= y$) on the basis of two "indicative errors", one at line 100, the other at line 1200. But imagine that B had changed its model for lines 600–900 to an exemplar from type y. If there is no "indicative error" linking BCD in this portion of the text, the contamination will easily go undetected in a classification based only on shared errors. In such a case, considering the series of shared variants would most likely flag up anomalies in the distribution of agreements (if it has shifted to the CD model, B possibly agrees less often with A and more often with CD) that would challenge the philologist to interpret them. In conclusion, a legitimate objection has been raised against a distorted use of the principle that identical readings imply identical origins, but this must not conceal the fact that the principle of carefully considering the distribution of variants while working on the classification is, in itself, valid if interpreted correctly (see Reeve 2011a, 59). The presence of series of shared readings in two or more witnesses is never without significance. The congruity of readings does imply a common origin, though it does not by itself tell us where to situate it. If a certain number of witnesses share innovative readings, they form a group and go back to the same ancestor, the one that introduced those innovations. If, on the other hand, they share readings that go back to the archetype or to the original, they do not form a group. This decisive piece of information (which of the variants is the archetypal/original one?) cannot come from quantitative analysis, only from qualitative analysis.

From this point of view, Quentin's merit, and even more so Froger's, lay not so much in proposing a method of classifying manuscripts that differed from that of common errors, but much more in consolidating and clarifying within the method of common errors the dialectic between analysis of variants and of errors. Thus, these two scholars awakened interest in contrasting "groupes variants" (witnesses sharing the same readings) with "groupes fautifs" (witnesses sharing the same errors), and they have shown the possible advantages of first reconstructing the *enchaînement* of the witnesses before tackling their *orientation*. Thanks to Froger, we have now a clear operational procedure, the application of which may be more or less advantageous and economical depending on the textual tradition in question.

It has to be judged in each particular case whether it is more advantageous and economical to use judgement right away or whether it is better to postpone it to a second stage of *recensio*.

2.3.5.5 The "Quentin line"

The Quentin–Froger method anticipates some of the most recent computerised methods of cladistics and phylogenetics applied to texts in that the study of variants can be automated, and also in its two steps in the construction of the stemma: *enchaînement* and *orientation*. It is no accident that Froger devoted the final pages of his study to the opportunity to confront philological procedures with the then new phylogenetic evolutionary approaches in biology (Froger 1968, 270–271). However, it must be noted that in most recent attempts to use computerised methods, and concepts and tools from phylogenetics, for the classification of witnesses, the computer is not only used to construct the *enchaînement* of the stemma but is also trusted to orientate the resulting tree, for instance by choosing between the various possibilities using the principles of parsimony (Roelli and Bachmann 2010 is an exception). Such experimental attempts bypass the notion of "error", which does not exist in phylogenetics (see Macé and Baret 2006, 102; 8.1 below). The difference is important: it is not at all clear that a correct inference of the stemma is possible without any qualitative analysis of errors within the *recensio*, and the efficacy and reliability of such methods is still to be confirmed. Such an assessment will be possible once these new approaches produce scholarly editions so that their results can be tested and confirmed or falsified, as the case may be. For this, the principles of the software involved must be understood in detail, but it must also be stated clearly what kind of input data was used, what information was excluded, and what criteria the software used to orientate the tree. In general, this topic is much too often swept under the rug. So far, editions based on computer-assisted stemmatics do not seem to be very promising (see Trovato 2017, 179–228).

2.3.6 How is the genealogical method used? Giorgio Pasquali's post-Lachmannism

Every *stemma codicum* has two immediate applications:
(*i*) a practical one, that of guiding the reconstruction of the critical text; and
(*ii*) a historical one enabling the reconstruction of the events in a textual tradition.

Maas's *Textkritik* (1927) expounded the first point very systematically. Pasquali's *Storia della tradizione e critica del testo* (1934), which grew out of a review of Maas's short treatise, may be the work that emphasises the second most significantly (see 4.5).

2.3.6.1 Textual criticism and the history of a textual tradition

When Paris formulated the genealogical method (see 2.3.1), he pointed out that the classification of manuscripts may yield more or less certain results depending on the circumstances. For him, the main obstacle was the great loss of witnesses in mediaeval textual traditions. He does not mention other factors that might disturb the vertical transmission of a text and thus the application of the method.

An early synthesis of some of these factors is offered in Louis Havet's *Manuel de critique verbale* (1911). But the core of this work is dedicated to the genesis of innovations, not the genealogy of witnesses. Still, some paragraphs (§ 1610–1617) of the last chapter (80, "La classification généalogique des manuscrits") are dedicated to a presentation of the genealogical method and then to the "pièges de la classification généalogique" [pitfalls of genealogical classification]. Havet lists four principal ones:

> 1° au lieu de diverger toujours, il arrive que les rameaux de l'arbre convergent; 2° dans un texte donné, certains morceaux, voire certains courts passages, parfois certains mots, peuvent avoir une généalogie particulière, autre que la généalogie de l'ensemble; 3° entre mss. comme entre personnes, il peut se produire des rencontres de ressemblance qui ne viennent pas d'héritage; 4° les surcharges comportent des interprétations multiples, dont le classement spécial peut contredire le classement généalogique. (Havet 1911, 418)

> [(*i*) Instead of always diverging, sometimes the branches of the tree converge; (*ii*) in a given text, certain pieces, that is, some short passages, sometimes some words, may have their own genealogy, different to that of the overall text; (*iii*) between manuscripts, just as between people, there may be resemblances that do not come from inheritance; (*iv*) additions may permit multiple interpretations, whose special classification may contradict the genealogical one.]

In other words, Havet lucidly points out four obstacles for the logical system on which the method of common errors is based: (*i*) contamination, (*ii*) selective collation, (*iii*) polygenesis, and (*iv*) corrections.

Pasquali's book returns to all these points with an in-depth and systematic approach including a vast array of examples. At the core of his work are different forms of non-mechanical traditions in which the text is not vertically transmitted from the archetype to the extant copies: cases in which there is more than one archetype at the top of the text's transmission, cases of conjecturing and contamination by scribes, of authorial variants in the tradition, and so on. But with regard to Havet and Maas the perspective is reversed: what appeared to be "pièges de la classification généalogique", pitfalls for the editor, are now studied as phenomena that are intrinsic in the life of texts. Pasquali's main purpose is to tightly connect *recensio* (*ex parte subiecti*, i.e. the philologist's method) to the history of textual traditions (*ex parte obiecti*, the textual phenomena). He intends to demonstrate that, in order to reconstruct the text of a work by *recensio*, that is, the comparison and evaluation of witnesses, it is essential to intimately know the vicissitudes the text has suffered from the moment of its composition down to the extant witnesses. Pasquali thus transcends the logico-mathematical approach of Maas's *Textkritik* by transforming the latter's set of abstract logical norms into a historical, applicable method. But he also reviews the approach to textual traditions that are no longer considered the result of a process of textual degeneration. The human activity of the scribes transcribing a text becomes the central focus: sometimes they reworked it unconsciously, but more often consciously, in order to achieve a version that seemed better to them.

The different assessments of contamination may help to gauge the difference in perspective. For Maas, contamination is a kind of virus, or even bug, in the system. In the case of contamination, the method of common errors may end up without defences and stop working, as the famous quotation shows: "Gegen die Kontamination ist kein Kraut gewachsen" (Maas 1957, 30) [No specific has yet been discovered against contamination] (trans. Flower 1958, 49; see 2.2.7 above). For Pasquali, in contrast, contamination is not an anomaly that provokes a crisis in the logical system and a "fatal system error", but rather a well-attested event in the text's transmission that sheds light on how scribes and early editors treated the text of their models and conceived the production of new copies. Pasquali does not neglect to present possible remedies against contamination, but focuses mainly on the questions of why, when, in what way, and where several exemplars of a text were compared by the scribes. One thus moves from a logical and formal point of view towards a historical one that focuses on concrete cases. Textual criticism and the history of the text are joined together indissolubly: it is no longer possible to engage in textual criticism without knowing the specific history of the text in question, that is, without knowing the culture and the *modus operandi* of the individuals and the groups who transmitted the text and who have left their imprints on it. From this follows Pasquali's conclusion: whenever the tradition of a text is not purely mechanical, whenever the scribes did not just passively reproduce their model, there is no general recipe for editing a text. The editor's work on a text is not mechanical; in order to reconstruct the original text as far as possible, it is necessary to employ judgement from the very beginning, which also leads to a reassessment of the value of internal criteria for evaluating readings with a stemmatic approach (*usus scribendi, lectio difficilior*).

The volume *Storia della tradizione e critica del testo* was published in 1934. One year later, 1935, Henri Quentin died. Three years later, in 1938, Joseph Bédier died. A crucial period in critical philology came to an end, and a new one began: one of continuity and renewal.

2.3.7 Conclusion: "The worst method except all those others that have been tried"

In the years between 1872 and 1934, from the edition of *Saint Alexis* to *Storia della tradizione e critica del testo*, the method of common errors underwent a healthy self-examination. Objections raised against it did not sweep it away, but rather made it more conscious of its own fragility and of its strong binding to the judgement of the editor. The task of the editor becomes more difficult but also more interesting: editors now have a better sense of the limitations and risks immanent to their method, and can better protect themselves from any sense of illusory certainty.

The principles on which the genealogical method is founded are still valid: if two witnesses contain one or more substantial errors in the same *loci*, they most likely descend from a common model, since it is unlikely that they acquired them independently. Once the genealogical tree of the extant witnesses has been traced, the agreement of two or more independent branches demonstrates the archetypal readings, because it is unlikely that they independently introduced the same substantial innovations. The new awareness comes from the knowledge of applying such principles correctly: "per essere oggi lachmanniani, [è] indispensabile aver attraversato un tirocinio antilachmanniano (cioè Bédier) e un'esperienza postlachmanniana (cioè se non altro, in filologia classica, Pasquali)" (Contini 1970, 344) [in order to be a Lachmannian today, it is necessary to have gone through an anti-Lachmannian (that is, Bédierist) apprenticeship and a post-Lachmannian experience (that is, at least in classical philology, Pasquali)].

From these presuppositions neo-Lachmannism is born, and it has produced some philological masterpieces such as d'Arco Silvio Avalle's edition of Peire Vidal's *Poesie* (Avalle 1960) or Cesare Segre's edition of the *Chanson de Roland* (Segre 1971; see 2.4 below). From the Bédierist school, Lachmann's method has, on the one hand, learnt prudence and definitively given up the practice of publishing mosaic-like critical texts, and on the other to draw attention to scribal versions that are of interest in themselves. From Quentin and his successors, the method has learnt to treasure the genealogical information provided by witnesses that agree in a series of non-erroneous variants, and to handle it carefully instead of ignoring it. Finally, from Pasquali, it has learnt the necessity of bringing the method down to earth from the heavens of logical principles with individual historical situations and individual textual phenomena, since textual criticism and the history of the text are bound together and inseparable. The marvellous forest of philological trees consists, in fact, not only of the bifid trees that preoccupied Bédier, but also and especially of trees whose ramifications cross and intertwine with one another in a great variety of ways. From here also follows the awareness that every text poses a specific problem that requires specific editorial solutions, and that different types of editions (see 6.1) can serve different aims (see Vàrvaro 1970). In spite of all possible objections to the genealogical method, we shall conclude with Alberto Vàrvaro's incisive wit:

> alla ricostruzione stemmatica della storia della tradizione manoscritta possiamo adattare quello che Winston Churchill disse della democrazia: la stemmatica è un sistema pessimo, ma è il migliore tra quelli che conosciamo. Bisogna accontentarsi e vedere cosa se ne può ricavare. (Vàrvaro 2012, 87)

> [we can adapt what Winston Churchill said about democracy to the stemmatic reconstruction of the history of manuscripts: stemmatics is the worst method except all those others that have been tried. We must make do with it and see what we can obtain from it.]

Acknowledgements

This section was translated from the Italian by Philipp Roelli. Giovanni Palumbo gratefully thanks Sarah Melker and Nicola Morato for their invaluable help.

2.4 Neo-Lachmannism: A new synthesis?
Paolo Trovato

This section addresses some of the most relevant improvements and refinements of the genealogical method following Joseph Bédier's sharp criticisms (see 2.3), that is, from 1929 to the present day. This complex, steadily improved set of procedures, scarcely known in most Western countries, where the method is often associated with its unrefined applications in the nineteenth and early twentieth centuries, deserves to be considered by any scholarly editor because of its effectiveness in treating even very complicated textual traditions, such as that of the Old French *Chanson de Roland*.

2.4.1 From Lachmann's method to neo-Lachmannism

Let us begin this overview with two important, though obvious, remarks ("important" and "obvious" are not necessarily at odds) by Karl R. Popper and G. Thomas Tanselle:

> The doctrine of [human] fallibility should not be regarded as part of a pessimistic epistemology. This doctrine implies that we may seek for truth, for objective truth, though more often than not we may miss it by a wide margin. And it implies that if we respect truth, we must search for it by persistently searching for our errors: by indefatigable rational criticism, and self-criticism. (Popper 1965, 16)

> Every statement about editing [...] reflects, directly or indirectly, an attitude toward certain fundamental questions, and various families of editorial approaches have grown up over the centuries because these questions have been answered in different ways. (Tanselle 1995, 9)

As can be gleaned from the studies of Timpanaro (1961, rev. ed. 1981, repr. 2004, trans. Most 2005), Kenney (1974), and Fiesoli (2000), the so-called Lachmannian or genealogical method, or method of common errors, "was constructed over a rather long timespan (from the last decades of the eighteenth century to the early twentieth century) thanks to the contributions of many scholars, sometimes working in connection with one another, sometimes working autonomously" (Paolo Chiesa in 2.2.1 above). Key aspects that are today considered fundamental were precisely formulated only several decades after the death of Lachmann, such as the criterion that only s h a r e d i n n o v a t i o n s can serve to prove the kinship between two or more witnesses (the oldest thorough formulation of this principle appears to be that of Lejay 1888; see Froger 1968, 41–42; Reeve 1998, 451–452 = 2011a, 57–58, with additions). Following the research of Reeve, one can also indicate a date for the birth of stemmatics based on shared errors that looks very reasonable, albeit conventional: 1872, that is, the year of the edition of the *Vie de Saint Alexis* published by Gaston Paris (1839–1903), the completion of which had been delayed by the Franco-Prussian War of 1870–1871. As Reeve puts it, no other editor "can challenge Gaston Paris for the title of the first scholar to have applied systematically the principle that only shared errors establish families of textual witnesses" (1998, 464 = 2011a, 68).

From then on, for nearly six decades, the method of shared errors spread and was applied – often in too naive and mechanical a way – in a variety of fields. Notwithstanding the appearance of the short but very dense treatise of Maas (1927), the party was ended rather brusquely in the second half of the 1920s when the Benedictine Henri Quentin (1922, 1926) and the most famous pupil of Paris, Joseph Bédier (1928), directed their critical blows against it (2.3 above). Even though many of their objections do not seem unassailable today, it happened, mostly thanks to the extraordinary argumentative skills of Bédier, that the relatively cohesive world of textual critics began to break up into several families. Classical philologists – who usually worked on texts from a millennium later than their lost originals, offering in many cases at least some easily identifiable common errors – remained in the Lachmannian orbit. North American Romance philologists did so too for several decades, and almost all Italian and several Spanish ones still do today (in Italy, the enormous prestige of Barbi, Pasquali, and Contini has been a decisive factor in this choice of method). In contrast, many biblical scholars (who have to work with overabundant traditions) were attracted by Quentin's theories, and many Romance philologists (both French and other) who dealt primarily with mediaeval French texts quickly sided with the Bédierist camp. They often had to deal with works which lack a strong authorial mark and present hard-to-track errors, and besides, the new method allowed them to produce an edition much more quickly (Foulet and Speer 1979; Reeve 1986 = 2011a, 28–44; Speer 1995; Trovato 2017, 77–108, 289–297; see also the important C. Baker et al. 2018).

The most unfortunate consequence of Bédier's "schism" was certainly the sometimes very heated conflict between the supporters of the different methodologies. Unfortunately, most members of many of these schools and traditions, which originated during the last century, are hardly even able to discuss their mutually incompatible methods with one another – even though textual scholars have become a much-reduced subset of that already small group that still does fundamental research in the humanities and they all basically address the same problems. Be that as it may, what is most important for this section is that Bédier's criticism became a very efficient stimulus for supporters of the genealogical method to reflect on its flaws and review their own positions:

> Sui principi di quello che fu chiamato lachmannismo [...] è seguitata a svolgersi nel secolo e mezzo successivo quell'opera di raffinamento, reazione e revisione per cui si può anche parlare di antilachmannismo (principalmente Joseph Bèdier e dom Quentin), postlachmannismo (così Giorgio Pasquali e in certo modo Michele Barbi) e, perché no?, neolachmannismo (parte della romanistica italiana). (Contini 1977, 995 = 2007, 1:6)
>
> [In the century and a half that followed [Lachmann's age], scholars were busy refining, reacting against, and revising [...] the principles of what was later called Lachmannism, so that we can also speak of anti-Lachmannism (first of all Joseph Bédier and Quentin), post-Lachmannism (Giorgio Pasquali and, to a certain degree, Michele Barbi) and – why not? – neo-Lachmannism (as part of the Italian school of Romance philology).]

As Paolo Chiesa puts this: "Discovering some limits of the genealogical method and discussing them has produced greater self-awareness, and has given scholars a more mature and refined method" (2.2.8 above). Even though, as far as I know, the term "neo-Lachmannism" (It. *neolachmannismo*) was coined by Gianfranco Contini in the 1970s in order to refer – by and large – to his own studies and to those of his pupils (cf. the above quotation), it seems nonetheless fully legitimate to employ the adjective "neo-Lachmannian" and the noun "neo-Lachmannism" in a wider sense to refer to all those who, from the 1930s onwards, have participated in the maturation and refinement of the method of common errors. Among others, Blecua (1995) did so in a substantial review of Spanish textual criticism, and Salemans – who occupies a unique position in what might be called the Dutch school – used the term in the very title of his noteworthy doctoral thesis (2000), "Building Stemmas with the Computer in a Cladistic, Neo-Lachmannian, Way: The Case of Fourteen Text Versions of *Lanseloet van Denemerken*".

In this larger sense, it can be argued that the refinements of Lachmannism triggered by Bédier's corrosive criticism constitute a new synthesis of theoretical positions that came into conflict in the third decade of the last century, and perhaps we can look at this as a new paradigm in a Kuhnian sense (Kuhn 1962).

2.4.2 The diffusion of neo-Lachmannism in the twentieth century

In central and southern Europe, methodological reflections followed almost immediately after Bédier's criticism in 1928, at least among the more attentive scholars. In order to suggest a list – albeit certainly incomplete – of the most timely and significant reactions, we may quote the studies of Rajna (1929), Pasquali (1934), Maas (1937), Barbi (1938), Fourquet (1946, 1948–1949), Castellani (1957), and Timpanaro (1961). Many of these scholars are Romance philologists, but the importance of the questions under debate did not escape classical scholars. Besides Maas, Pasquali, and Timpanaro, it will suffice to cite here the names of Kenney and Reeve (a very rich collection of Reeve's methodological papers is Reeve 2011a). Nevertheless, it seems that these discussions have remained almost unnoticed by the rest of the world.

As the fairly recent bibliography on textual criticism by William Baker and Kenneth Womack (2000, 75–131) evidently conforms to its own "Monroe Doctrine" and ignores any work not written in English, I suggest a simple experiment to estimate the diffusion of the neo-Lachmannian turn in twentieth-century North American textual studies. Let us take the important and popular book by Greetham (1995) entitled *Scholarly Editing: A Guide to Research*, which dedicates twenty-four chapters to the same number of research fields (from "The Hebrew Bible" to "Eighteenth-Century English Literature", and from "Russian Literature" to "Arabic Literature"), so that it may well be seen as a map of textual criticism at the end of the millennium from the American standpoint. On the basis of the invaluable "Name and Title Index" in Greetham's book, the following table (table 2.1-1) displays in chronological order the presence or absence of references to Lachmann, Maas (readable since 1958 in the English translation by Flower), the equally but differently anti-Lachmannian Bédier and Quentin, and well-known neo-Lachmannian scholars (Pasquali, Kenney, Reeve, and Timpanaro – the latter was not yet readable in the 2005 English translation by Most when Greetham's book was published, but had been translated into German by Irmer in 1971). The last column is for Tanselle, perhaps the leading American textual scholar of his generation. No references at all to these authors are found in the other twelve contributions in the collection, which are not listed here.

There is no need to emphasise both the knowledge mastered by Tanselle and his popularity among US textual scholars. On the other hand, we must note that, no differently from the Italianist Barbi or well-known neo-Lachmannian Romance scholars such as Avalle, Segre, Vàrvaro, and Contini himself, whose output is also very rich from the point of view of methodology, Kenney and Reeve are quoted mostly or exclusively within their own discipline, that is, classical Latin. Robert Huygens and Giovanni Orlandi, that is, two eminent and original textual critics in the field of mediaeval Latin, are never quoted. If we except Tanselle and Tarrant, the works of Bédier, Quentin, Maas, Pasquali, and Timpanaro are cited only by Romance scholars, and three out of four of those Romance scholars are Europeans or Latin Americans. Thus, the reader of this companion might be tempted to think that, in 1995, many North American textual scholars ignored or considered negligible not only the contribution of the Italians (for which a strong linguistic barrier may be to blame), but even that of two excellent British Latinists, Kenney and Reeve. Of course, this table might simply highlight the different relevance which the history of the discipline and discussions about methods have in North American textual criticism, but that does not substantially change its implications for methodological consciousness.

An analysis of the indexes of authors quoted in two important Dutch collections, both entitled *Studies in Stemmatology* (van Reenen and van Mulken 1996; van Reenen, den Hollander, and van Mulken 2004) would not yield all that different results. It is unnecessary to stress that a lack of interest in the history and methodological development of an academic discipline leads, very often, to the reinvention (sometimes in a wrong or imprecise way) of criteria and principles that have already been formulated perfectly well.

Tab. 2.4-1: Presence or absence of references to the lively European discussion on the genealogical method in the popular collection edited by Greetham (1995). A single plus sign (+) indicates 1 to 3 quotations, two signs (++) more than 3.

	Lachmann	Bédier	Quentin	Maas	Pasquali	Timpanaro	Kenney	Reeve	Tanselle
Tanselle: "The Varieties of Scholarly Editing"	++		+	+	+		+		+
Tarrant: "Classical Latin Literature"	+	+		++	++		++	++	
Edwards: "Middle English Literature"	+						+		
Speed Hill: "English Renaissance: Nondramatic Literature"	+			+					+
Howard-Hill: "English Renaissance: Non-Shakespearean Drama"	+								
Reiman: "Nineteenth-Century British Poetry and Prose"									++
Shillingsburg: "Nineteenth-Century British Fiction"									+
Myerson: "Colonial and Nineteenth-Century American Literature"									++
Speer: "Old French Literature"	+	++	+		+				
Campion: "Early Modern French Literature"		++	+	+	+	+			+
Cherchi: "Italian Literature"	++		+	+	+				
Blecua: "Medieval Castilian Texts and Their Editions"			+						
Orduna: "Hispanic Textual Criticism and the Stemmatic Value of the History of the Text"	+	+	+	++	++	+			
Plachta: "German Literature"		+			+				
Rocher: "Sanskrit Literature"				+					

2.4.3 Some neo-Lachmannian contributions to the improvement of the method: A provisional list

In 2014, I proposed and commented on a small list of Bédier's contributions to the improvement of the genealogical method (Trovato 2014; see also Trovato 2017, 82–94). Here, I take up that list again, updating it and opening it up to neo-Lachmannism in the broader sense. Even if a thematic arrangement might perhaps be more convenient (and certainly less dangerous for the present writer), I prefer to follow the chronological order in which these updates and refinements were proposed, and I offer only a few, essential bibliographical references (of course, since I am far from all-knowing and this is, to my knowledge, the first list of this kind, it is very likely that some achievements had been made earlier and should actually be credited to different authors). Note that I do not try to identify the first time that a specific criterion was used, but the first time that the advantage of a procedure was highlighted from a general, methodological point of view. For a more detailed and systematic treatment of the most relevant terms and notions touched on here from a diachronic perspective, see Trovato (2017) and chapter 4 below, which addresses some of them from different points of view.

Notwithstanding their different focus and size, the conceptual distance between my list from 2014 and the present one is not as great as one might think. Indeed, even when Bédier is not explicitly mentioned, the shadow of his sharp criticisms almost always seems palpable. The first group of entries mostly concerns developments which we must credit to Pasquali (1932, 1934) and to Maas (1937). As for the latter, it should be remembered that Maas (1937) was added afterwards as an appendix to the subsequent editions of his 1927 *Textkritik* (Maas 1950, 1957, 1960) and included in all the translations of it. Thus, when we use any recent edition or translation of Maas's substantial booklet, including the English translation by Barbara Flower from which I usually quote in these pages (Maas 1958), we must consider that the text was written in 1927, but Maas (1937) was added as an appendix to the treatise of 1950 and a second appendix ("Retrospect 1956") was added to the 1957 version, almost without any changes to the main text in each case. In other words, these three parts (pp. 1–41, 42–49, 50–54 in the English translation) mirror different phases and focuses in the research of this great scholar.

1929: Recognition of limitations of the method (Rajna)
A few months after Bédier's famous attack against "la méthode de Lachmann", Pio Rajna (1847–1930), one of the oldest and more authoritative Italian Romance philologists, wrote the following words, which did not go unheeded: "Troppo poco si è badato alle cause perturbatrici, tali in moltissimi casi da rendere inapplicabile il sistema; e si è commesso il grave errore di procedere allo stesso modo in condizioni assai diverse" (Rajna 1929, 50) [We have paid too little attention to disturbing factors, such that could make the system inapplicable in a great number of cases, and

we have made the serious mistake of proceeding in the same manner under very different conditions]. A few examples of cases and kinds of texts for which the method is inapplicable or requires adaptation (works transmitted by one or a few manuscripts; works that are too short, such as sonnets; popular genres such as *chansons de geste* or *cantari*, or mediaeval Latin hagiographical texts) are listed in Trovato (2017, 155–161), but we could also add encyclopedias, chronicles, collections of short, practical texts, and so on. Perhaps, among the top-notch Italian textual scholars, it was the late Alberto Vàrvaro (2004) who heeded Rajna's concerns the most.

1932: The method must not be used with different authorial versions (Pasquali)
From Bédier to the present day, many scholars have warned that a flaw of neo-Lachmannism is the possible existence of authorial variants. But the distinction between the treatment of scribal and authorial variants has been clearly presented since at least Pasquali (1932). Of course, whenever it is possible to distinguish two or more different authorial versions, approved by the author at different times (e.g. Ariosto's *Orlando Furioso* of 1516, 1521, and 1532; Chateaubriand's three versions of his *Atala*; Whitman's many versions of *Leaves of Grass*), scholars are not entitled to create a "texte unique et monstrueux" (Bédier 1913, xxxviii) by antihistorically merging variants belonging to the different versions. On the contrary, we must publish them separately or decide which version is more urgently to be made available to the community of readers. In fact, in the case of multiple authorial versions, it is not a matter of deciding which reading in every place of variation best represents the work of art, but of putting up for comparison two or more textual entities which, at different times, have reflected the author's intention. This will allow critics to compare these different works and contrast their features and evolution.

After a few but very clear hints by Pasquali (1932, 1934), Contini's seminal essay on Ariosto (1937), and the application of his "critica delle varianti" to Leopardi, Proust, and others, the treatment of authorial versions was addressed and refined by a scholar closely connected with Contini: Dante Isella. It must be emphasised that the Italian *critica delle varianti* is quite different from the French *critique génétique* (see Italia and Raboni 2010; Stussi 2015, chap. 5; 7.9 below).

1932–: Open vs closed recensions (Pasquali)
Nowadays, we frequently use the expressions "closed recension" and "open recension". It is often forgotten that the author of this common distinction was none other than Giorgio Pasquali (the distinction is already found in Pasquali 1932):

> Le riflessioni qui brevemente esposte [...] si applicano a ogni "recensione aperta", se mi sia lecito introdurre qui un termine nuovo, che mi pare indispensabile, vale a dire si applicano ogniqualvolta la lezione dell'archetipo non si può fissare meccanicamente, mediante la consta-

> tazione di coincidenze di lezione in certi apografi ("recensione chiusa"), ma si determina solo con il *iudicium*, scegliendo sul fondamento di criteri prevalentemente interni tra due (o più) lezioni nessuna delle quali è dimostrata secondaria dal criterio esterno, genealogico. (Pasquali 1934, 126)

> [The reflections briefly outlined here [...] apply to every "open recension", if I may introduce here a new term which seems to me indispensable, that is to say, they apply every time the reading of the archetype cannot be fixed mechanically through coincidences of readings in certain apographs ("closed recension") but is determined only through *iudicium*, choosing on the basis of predominantly internal criteria between two (or more) readings, none of which is demonstrated secondary by the external, genealogical criterion.]

Of course, the main cause of open recensions is the distribution of the variants in the stemma: if in a certain place of variation no reading appears in the majority of primary branches, we must use *iudicium*.

1934–: Extension of the field of philological studies to areas which Maas 1927 had excluded (Pasquali, Frank, and others)

Pasquali's crucial book (1934), which should be mandatory reading for everyone interested in textual criticism, was born as a review of Maas (1927). The best abstract of the book is found perhaps in Maas's preface to the second German edition of *Textkritik*:

> Die erste Auflage dieses Abrisses (erschienen 1927) wurde 1929 von G. Pasquali sehr eingehend und freundlich besprochen (Gnomon 5, 417 ff). Die anschließenden selbständigen Forschungen Pasqualis (Gnomon, 5, 498 ff. und Storia della tradizione e critica del testo (1934)) bewegen sich vorwiegend auf nahverwandten, aber von meiner Darstellung augeschlossenen Gebieten, dem *der speziellen Überlieferungsgeschichte und dem der kontaminierten, also nicht methodisch entwirrbaren, Überlieferung*. (Maas 1950, 3; my emphasis)

> [The first edition of this essay (published in 1927) was reviewed with great kindness and in great detail by G. Pasquali in 1929 (in *Gnomon*, V. 417 ff.), Pasquali's own investigations (in *Gnomon*, V, 498 ff. and in his *Storia della tradizione e critica del testo*, 1934) deal in the main with topics closely related to but excluded from my presentation, i.e. with *the history of transmission of the individual texts and "contaminated" traditions, which of course cannot be systematically disentangled*.] (trans. Flower 1958, n.p.; my emphasis)

Among other things, Pasquali also addresses authorial variants and explains with a wealth of erudition why scholars cannot dismiss recent witnesses (*r e c e n t i o r e s   n o n   d e t e r i o r e s*).

Frank pointed out that when we work with p o p u l a r g e n r e s such as mediaeval *chansonniers*, the conditions of the transmission are quite different from the ideal conditions in which the genealogical method can work at its best:

> La tradition que constituent les chansonniers lyriques du Moyen Âge apparaît, pour qui veut établir un stemma, comme grevée de tous les éléments de trouble: [1] original multiple (réel, virtuel ou possible), [2] variations et contaminations surgies de la transmission orale, [3] conta-

minations dues à l'utilisation par les copistes de plusieurs sources divergentes, [4] l'existence, enfin, dans les chansonniers mêmes, d'éditions résultant d'un travail réfléchi, usant de la conjecture. Que nous sommes loin de la transmission mécanique qui garantit l'efficacité du stemma! (Frank 1955, 472–473)

[The tradition constituted by the lyric *chansonniers* of the Middle Ages seems fraught with every sort of difficulty for the scholar who wishes to establish a stemma. (1) a multiple original (real, virtual, or possible); (2) variations and contaminations stemming from oral transmission; (3) contaminations due to the use of several divergent sources by the copyists; (4) and finally, the existence, in the *chansonniers* themselves, of editions resulting from thoughtful work, employing conjecture. How far we are from the mechanical transmission that guarantees the efficacy of the stemma!] (Frank 1976, 135)

In spite of this, some exemplary studies have shown that it is possible to approach the study of songbooks (*chansonniers, canzonieri*) in a rational way (e.g. Barbi 1915; Avalle 1985).

1934: Polygenetic vs monogenetic errors (Pasquali)

In order to single out significant tools for proving the relationship between copies (i.e. for inferring stemmata), it is important to distinguish between, on the one hand, unique innovations and, on the other hand, variants that copyists could produce independently of one another. The commonly used distinction between p o l y - g e n e t i c and m o n o g e n e t i c innovations goes back to Pasquali: "Corruttele comuni a tutta la tradizione [...] possono essersi prodotte indipendentemente anche in mss. indipendenti, per 'poligenesi'" (Pasquali 1934, 19) [Corruptions common to a whole tradition [...] may have occurred independently, even in independent manuscripts, by "polygenesis"]. Instead of "polygenesis", other scholars use the more opaque terms "parallelism", "coincident variation", "convergent variation", or "homoplasy". See also the next point.

1937: Indicative errors and formulation of the basic rules for determining the relationship between two witnesses (Maas)

In his paper "Leitfehler und stemmatische Typen" [Indicative Errors and Stemmatic Types], Maas (1937) introduces two fundamental distinctions. The first opposition involves i n d i c a t i v e vs n o n - i n d i c a t i v e e r r o r s, the former being useful, the latter of no use, for inferring a genealogical relationship even if errors of both types belong to the set of substantial errors (for more on significant errors, see 4.3.1 below). By the way, Maas only discusses the "logical" requirements of the indicative error, which must be "so beschaffen [...], dass aller Wahrscheinlichkeit nach B und C nicht unabhängig voneinander in diesen Fehler verfallen sein können" (Maas 1950, 27) [of such a nature that it is highly improbable that B and C committed it independently of each other] (trans. Flower 1958, 43). The first requirement for an indicative error is, in Pasquali's words, that of being monogenetic (see above). Second, the error must be really difficult to detect and correct.

The second opposition applies only to indicative errors and distinguishes between separative and conjunctive errors. The presence of a number of common errors (i.e. conjunctive errors) proves that two or more witnesses, *A B* ..., are part of the same group or family, while, say, indicative errors in witness *A* only (i.e. separative errors) show that *B*, which lacks them, cannot descend from *A*. Therefore, if two witnesses (say *A* and *B*) are connected by conjunctive errors, and both of them have separative errors, they must descend from a lost exemplar *y*. See Maas (1937) and subsequent editions, including Maas (trans. Flower 1958, 42–44).

As I have already noted, the wording of some sentences of Maas (e.g. the ones about conjunctive and separative errors) is very similar to that of Rajna (1907). Further research will show whether Maas (who indeed read a lot, even outside his own field of study, for example about Shakespeare or Bédier's theories) depends on Rajna or they both depend on a still unknown source. But all the "sources" of Maas's treatise, whether declared or implicit, deserve a specific study (Trovato 2017, 56). Conversely, the Maasian "rules" concerning the relationship among three witnesses (Maas, trans. Flower 1958, 44–49) do not hold water (Timpanaro 1981, 128–131 = 2004, 135–138 = trans. Most 2005, 162–166). See also "1937" and "2002" below.

1937: *Eliminatio codicum descriptorum* (Maas)

After the hints in Maas (1927, §8a), a rigorous set of logical rules for the individuation of copies of preserved copies (*codices descripti*), that is, genealogically useless witnesses, is found in Maas (1937, later included in Maas 1950, 1957, 1960). Between any two witnesses *A* and *B*, only three kinds of relationship can exist – types 1, 2, and 3 in figure 2.4-1 below.

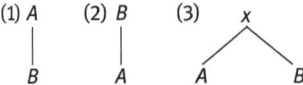

Fig. 2.4-1: The possible relationships between two witnesses *A* and *B*, according to Maas (1937).

There are two necessary conditions for type 1 (*B* derives from *A*) that must apply: *B* must contain all the significant errors of *A* and at least one that is not in *A* (obviously, a number of errors of the latter kind provide much more reliable proof than a single one). Likewise, for type 2 (*A* derives from *B*) to apply, *A* needs to contain all the errors of *B* plus at least one that is not in *B*. In both cases, we can distinguish between an exemplar, genealogically relevant, and a *codex descriptus*, genealogically of no use unless it preserves passages of the exemplar lost or destroyed after copying. See also "1958–" below.

1937–: First attempts to explain Bédier's so-called paradox (Maas and others)

The strongest argument against the genealogical method, known as Bédier's paradox, is the fact that, out of 110 stemmata of French manuscript traditions

Bédier examined, 105 were two-branched. According to Bédier, these figures were enough to prove that the method was inherently wrong. After Maas (1937) and Forquet (1946), other scholars also addressed the reasons why stemmata are so often bipartite in classical and Romance textual transmissions. Here, I mention at least Castellani (1957) and appendix C in Timpanaro (1961; appendix C is reprinted with updates in Timpanaro 1981; according to Reeve 1986, 69 = 2011a, 43, "there is no better warning against the pitfalls that may occur in classifying manuscripts"). More general and powerful explanations of the paradox were suggested later; see "1987–" below.

1938–: Recognition that, eventually, the method had been considerably updated and refined (Barbi)

Before presenting his brief criticism of Quentin's and Bédier's methods, Barbi notices:

> Tutti sentono che il puro metodo lachmanniano è insufficiente e in certi casi inapplicabile [...]. Che si sia da molti e per molto tempo creduto di poter risolvere, ricorrendo al metodo del Lachmann, speditamente e con sicurezza di risultati ogni problema, può essere; ma ormai quel metodo s'è sviluppato, arricchito, adattato variamente ai diversi casi, e resta fondamentale nella critica del testo; e anche l'aggiunta di altri mezzi è subordinata spesso al principio degli errori comuni. Condannarlo dunque senz'altro perché non risponde sufficientemente, o non risponde affatto, a certe particolari necessità, è privarsi di un mezzo che in qualche caso risponde benissimo anche da solo o è il solo sicuramente applicabile, e in ogni indagine dà aiuti dei quali sarebbe dannosissimo fare a meno. (Barbi 1938, xvi)

> [Everyone has the impression that the pure Lachmannian method is insufficient and in some cases inapplicable [...]. It is possible that many scholars for a long time believed they were able to solve quickly and with certain results every problem simply by applying Lachmann's method; but by now that method has been developed, enriched, adapted variously to different cases, and remains fundamental to textual criticism. Even the addition of other means is often subordinated to the rationale of common errors. Therefore, to condemn it because it does not respond sufficiently, or does not fit at all certain particular needs, means to deprive ourselves of a means that in some cases responds very well even on its own, or is the only safely applicable one, and in every investigation offers aids which it would be harmful to do without.]

1946–: *Stemma codicum* vs "real tree" (Fourquet and others)

While the *stemma codicum* consists only of survivors, that is, the extant witnesses, Forquet noted in 1946 that textual scholars should also consider, despite it being a merely theoretical entity, the "r e a l" or "c o m p l e t e   t r e e" (Fr. *arbre réel, arbre complet*), that is, "l'albero genealogico di tutti i manoscritti di un dato testo che sono realmente esistiti" (Timpanaro 1981, 129 = 2004, 136) [the genealogical tree of all the manuscripts of a given text that really existed] (trans. Most 2005, 164), lost witnesses included. For a long time even excellent scholars did not distinguish between the two notions; after Fourquet (1946) and Timpanaro (1961, appendix C), see Guidi and Trovato (2004) and Trovato (2005; 2017, 65, 81–93, 138–146). I can add now that, no differently from Bédier, Pasquali, and many others, Maas himself seems to confuse the real tree with the *stemma codicum*: "Ferner liegt es im Wesen der mittelalterlichen Überlieferung, dass bei wenig gelesenen Texten nur selten von demselben Archetypus drei Abschriften genommen wurden" (Maas 1937, 293 = 1950, 30) [It is in the very nature of the medieval tradition that in the case of little-read texts three copies were rarely taken from the same archetype] (trans. Flower 1958, 48). In reality, the fact that the stemma of a mediaeval work rarely has three or more branches does not mean that the shape of the real tree could not have had three or more branches stemming directly from the original.

1952: Recasting of the geographical criterion (Lachmann and others) as a criterion of peripheral areas (Pasquali)

Elaborating upon very recent developments in comparative linguistics (see 8.2) theorised by Matteo Giulio Bartoli, Pasquali formulated a criterion that can be particularly useful in the study of overabundant transmissions – see also the allusions in Pasquali (1932; 1934, 8, 160, 178 = 1952, 8, 160, 178):

> Come nella linguistica è ormai pacifico che gli stadi più antichi si conservano più a lungo in zone periferiche, e che quindi coincidenza di due zone periferiche lontane l'una dall'altra in un fonema, una forma, un vocabolo, un costrutto garantisce la loro antichità, così anche coincidenza di lezione in codici scritti in zone lontane dal centro della cultura e lontane tra loro costituisce una presunzione per la genuinità di questa lezione. Spesso di testi molto letti sia nell'antichità, sia nel Medioevo, si è formata una vulgata che, come suole la moda, progrediva da un centro verso la periferia, ma non sempre la raggiungeva. (Pasquali 1952, xvii–xviii)

> [Just as in linguistics it is universally agreed today that earlier stages are preserved for a longer time in peripheral areas, and that hence the occurrence of the same phoneme, form, term, or construction in two peripheral areas distant from one another guarantees their antiquity, so the agreement of codices written in areas far removed from the cultural centre and from one another constitutes an argument for the genuineness of a reading. Often texts that were much read, both in Antiquity and in the Middle Ages, form a vulgate text which spreads, as fashions are wont to do, from the centre towards the periphery, but does not always reach it.]

1955–: Diffraction (Contini)

The notion of **diffraction** is a refinement of the well-known criterion of *lectio difficilior* (see 6.2.3). It is a common experience that certain *places* of variation are surprisingly rich in readings. According to Contini, such richness often hinges on a particularly difficult or rare reading in the original, with which many scribes grappled and to which they reacted in different ways. The best criterion for addressing such richness is thus singling out the difficult variant that can best explain such a reaction by the copyists. This variant may still be preserved, but it may also no be longer present in the manuscript tradition. In Contini's words: "C'è una progressione dalla diffrazione in presenza, dove un testimone [...] ha serbato la voce o forma relativamente rara, a quella in assenza, dove essa è rimasta documentariamente stravolta" (1986, 102 = 2007, 2:989–890) [There is a progression from diffraction *in praesentia*, where a witness [...] has retained the relatively rare word or form, to diffraction *in absentia*, where this word or form has been lost in the transmission].

Nevertheless, diffraction "è sufficiente a legittimare una congettura *difficilior*" (Contini 1986, 102) [is sufficient to legitimate a *lectio difficilior* conjecture]. See also Contini (1955, 1977). Orduna (1995, 487) maintains that diffraction is "the most fertile development in the Lachmannian method since Pasquali". Buzzoni and Burgio add that "diffraction pushes the philologist's attention to focus less on the object (the identification/reconstruction of a 'good reading') than on the internal dynamism of the tradition, which is configured as a system of structures under tension" (2014, 174). A more detailed presentation of the concept of diffraction can be found in Trovato (2017, 117–124).

1961–: Research on contamination (Avalle, Segre, and Froger)

Maas's treatise warns the reader that the stemma can settle "das Abhängigkeitsverhältnis der Zeugen für jede Stelle des Textes" [the relationship of witnesses for every passage in the text] under examination only "wenn jungfräuliche Überlieferung vorliegt. Gegen die Kontamination ist kein Kraut gewachsen" (1950, 31) [if we have a virgin [i.e. uncontaminated] tradition. No specific has yet been discovered against contamination] (trans. Flower 1958, 49), that is, against copies which show shared innovations with exemplars from two or more different families. But, when a text from the past was important and thus repeatedly reproduced and widely circulating, its tradition almost invariably became contaminated. Thus, textual scholars have no choice but to address contamination. Among the works on this subject, I mention only Avalle (1961) and Segre (1961; see 4.4 below).

A useful criterion for deciding which is the main source of a contaminated witness out of two possible exemplars was suggested later by Froger:

> Le moyen de résoudre l'anomalie consiste à se fonder sur la fréquence relative [des accords] des groupes incompatibles, dont l'assemblage produit une irrégularité [...]. Pour choisir entre des groupes incompatibles, on accepte celui dont la fréquence est élevée, et l'on rejette celui dont la fréquence est faible; c'est-à-dire que l'on considère comme normal celui qui est engendré par une grosse collection de variantes et apparaît souvent, regardant comme anormal celui qui, engendré par une petite collection de variantes, n'apparaît que rarement. Ce faisant, on adopte l'interprétation la plus probable [...]. Étant donné par exemple les deux fréquences 15 et 1, on fait la somme 15 + 1 = 16; la probabilité en faveur du groupe dont la fréquence est 15 sera 15/16 = 0,9375, et celle du groupe dont la fréquence est un sera 1/16 = 0,0625, soit en chiffres arrondis, 94 % et 6 % respectivement. (Froger 1968, 112–113)

> [The way to solve this anomaly is to take as our foundation the relative frequency [of agreements] between the incompatible groups whose combination produces an irregularity [...]. To choose between incompatible groups, we accept the one whose frequency is high and reject the one whose frequency is low; that is to say, we regard as normal the one that is engendered by a large collection of variants and appears often, and regard as abnormal the one that is engendered by a small collection of variants and only appears rarely. By doing so, we are adopt-

ing the most probable interpretation [...]. Given, for example, the two frequencies 15 and 1, we sum them: 15 + 1 = 16. The probability in favour of the group whose frequency is 15 will be 15/16 = 0.9375, while that of the group whose frequency is 1 will be 1/16 = 0.0625, that is, in round percentage figures, 94% and 6% respectively.]

Segre (1961) also introduced a useful distinction between **contamination of readings** and **contamination of exemplars**. The former "è conseguenza di una collazione eseguita sull'ascendente di un codice" (Segre 1961, 64 = 1998, 71) [is a consequence of collation [i.e. of at least one collation] performed on the ancestor of a codex]. In contrast, the latter occurs as follows:

quando un copista, o per integrare un esemplare incompleto, o perché imbattutosi in un esemplare più leggibile o autorevole, trascrive alternativamente da due esemplari, la sua copia appartiene, alternativamente, a uno solo dei gruppi di provenienza dei due esemplari. (Segre 1961, 63–64 = 1998, 71)

[when, in order to fill in gaps in an incomplete exemplar, or because he has chanced upon a more legible or authoritative one, a copyist alternately transcribes from two exemplars, his copy belongs, in turn, to only one of the groups that the two exemplars belong to.]

Dutch stemmatologists use the term "**simultaneous contamination**" for the contamination of readings and the term "**successive contamination**" for contamination by juxtaposition of exemplars; this terminology is also used below (4.4). The problem was studied more deeply by Vàrvaro (2010). Tonello and Trovato (2011) showed that, in the case of a long and popular text such as Dante's *Commedia*, the replacement of one exemplar with another manuscript is a feature present in more than 15% of the manuscript transmission. A more detailed presentation of this issue is found in Trovato (2017, 128–134). It should be noted that, whenever we identify contaminated witnesses of this kind, it is convenient to use two or more slightly modified sigla in order to refer to the sections of the text that depend on different exemplars (e.g. A', A'', A'''): in this way, ambiguity and useless complications both in studying the genealogy and drawing the stemma can be avoided.

1961–: Application of the genealogical method to *cantari* and other popular genres, to theatre, and to opera librettos (De Robertis and others)

The genealogical method can also be applied, with some adaptations, to common portions of texts belonging to popular literary genres such as *cantari*, *chansons de geste*, and the like, which are often transmitted in versions of different length and content. As De Robertis points out:

La filologia redazionale [...] non è, per intenderci, la filologia del codex optimus; e naturalmente non prescinde dall'esperienza e dagli strumenti della più affinata tecnica ricostruttiva [sc. quella neolachmanniana]. Solo che quell'esperienza va trasferita entro una nuova realtà [...], questi strumenti hanno bisogno di essere riadattati ai nuovi oggetti e alle nuove esigenze. (De Robertis 1961, 124–125)

[Redactional philology [...] is not, to put it in plain terms, the philology of the *codex optimus*, and of course cannot do without the experience and tools of the more sophisticated reconstructive technique [i.e. the neo-Lachmannian method]. It is just that this experience needs to be transferred into a new reality [...], and these tools need to be readapted to new objects and new needs.]

For an example, consider the analysis of the transmission of Pucci's *Reina d'oriente* by Bettarini Bruni and Trovato (2009), summarised in Trovato (2017, 200–207). The method can be applied, with analogous adaptations, also to theatre plays (see Tissoni Benvenuti 1986; Riccò 1996). In order to allow a thorough study of the reception of *Il Turco in Italia* by Romani (libretto) and Rossini, the method was successfully applied also to around thirty librettos of the opera printed between 1814 and 1830 (Nicolodi and Trovato 2003).

1963: Extra-stemmatic (or extra-archetypal) contamination (Timpanaro)

There are cases where conjunctive errors indicate that a witness belongs to a clearly identifiable subset of manuscripts. However, some of its readings, although they cannot be found in the other manuscripts of the subset, or in any other area of the known tradition, have to be considered authentic – even after a careful examination. As Timpanaro observes:

> Vi sono lezioni giuste che nessun copista filologo medievale (in certi casi nemmeno il miglior filologo moderno) può raggiungere per congettura. Un pericolo più grave consiste nell'eventualità che un copista, per es., del ramo α [...] abbia risanato errori non per congettura e nemmeno attingendo a uno degli altri testimoni a noi giunti, ma collazionando un codice di un ramo o di una tradizione del tutto diversa, andato poi perduto. Casi in cui bisogna ricorrere a questa ipotesi sono citati in buon numero nel libro di Pasquali [...]. Nell'articolo in "Maia", XVII (1965), che ho già avuto occasione di citare, ho proposto (p. 397) di usare per questo fenomeno il termine di "contaminazione extrastemmatica" (cioè derivante da manoscritti che non fanno parte della tradizione a noi giunta più o meno integralmente). (Timpanaro 1981, 152–153)

> [There are correct readings at which no mediaeval copyist-philologist (in certain cases not even the best modern philologist) could arrive conjecturally. A more serious danger consists in the possibility that a copyist, for example, of the α branch [...] might have healed errors or filled lacunas not by conjecture and not even by checking one of the other witnesses that have survived to our day, but by collating a manuscript of a completely different branch or tradition which was later lost. In his book Pasquali cites many cases in which one must have recourse to this hypothesis [...]. At Timpanaro 1965: 397 I suggested designating this phenomenon by the term *extra-stemmatic contamination* (that is, contamination deriving from manuscripts that do not form part of the tradition that has survived more or less completely).] (trans. Most 2005, 179)

Other scholars have alternatively suggested designating this phenomenon as extra-archetypal contamination. See Trovato (2017, 134–138). Figure 4.1-6 in section 4.1 provides an example of the phenomenon.

1963–: Partial obscuring of a hyparchetype or the archetype (Timpanaro)

In some cases, a thorough review of the distribution of errors in the various families shows that some copies which offer some genuine or at least good readings belong to subfamilies full of innovations. In such cases, the good readings cannot go back to the archetype through the ancestors of a family: we are facing the **obscuring of a hyparchetype or the archetype**. This means that these copies owe their good or genuine reading(s) to conjectural emendation or to contamination with a lost witness (see "1963" above), and that our reconstruction of the relationships between the most important branches of the stemma, as well as the textual reconstruction, could become gravely biased unless we do not collate a very rich set of *loci*. While correct deductions about this bias can already be found in the seminal edition of Paris (1872), a recent presentation of the problem is found in Timpanaro (1981, 143–147 = 2004, 153–157 = trans. Most 2005, 179–184). The problem is also analysed in Trovato (2017, 147–154).

1970: Active manuscript traditions vs quiescent manuscript traditions (Vàrvaro)

In 1970, Vàrvaro published a brilliant article in which, starting from Fränkel (1964), he compared from many perspectives the practices of classical scholars and Romance philologists. Among other things, he distinguished between two different scribal attitudes, the one more respectful of the text and the other more prone to adaptations and modernisations:

> Quella di opere latine e greche è in genere una tradizione libraria poco folta nel settore fra archetipo e copie umanistiche [...]; è una tradizione di ambienti limitati, di professionisti (copisti o a volte studiosi) tendenzialmente rispettosi del testo tràdito: una tradizione che chiamerei *quiescente*. Le tradizioni di testi romanzi sono già a prima vista assai diverse per la minima distanza che intercorre tra autografo e archetipo (se pur questo esiste) e per quella assai ridotta fra questo e i testimoni conservati [...], la posizione del copista rispetto al testo è infine assai meno rispettosa: un tipo di tradizione che chiamerei *attiva*. (Vàrvaro 1970, 86 = 2004, 580; emphasis in original)

> [The manuscript tradition of Latin and Greek works is generally not very plentiful in the space between archetype and humanistic copies [...]; it is a tradition of very specific milieus, of professionals (copyists or sometimes scholars) that tend to be respectful of the written text: this is a kind of tradition that I would call *quiescent*. The traditions of Romance works are very different at first sight in the minimum distance between autograph and archetype (if one exists) and in the very small distance between this and the preserved witnesses [...]; the position of the copyist towards the text is, finally, much less respectful: it is a type of tradition that I would call *active*.]

Of course, it is obvious that, in the above contrast, "Romance works" can be substituted with "works written in vernacular languages in general". Nevertheless, as Vàrvaro adds further on, this is simply a polarised framework that does not exclude, in different times and environments, intermediary forms of both types, even in Latin or Greek.

1970–: The concept of confirmatory readings (Vàrvaro, Divizia, and others)

Indicative errors in the Maasian sense can be very difficult to find. Thus, some editors erroneously use lists of variants, which can by no means replace errors. Nonetheless, they can be useful for confirming textual relationships. In 1970, Vàrvaro noted:

> L'errore debolmente congiuntivo è intrinsecamente poligenetico, sicché in teoria sia la serie breve che quella ampia [di errori debolmente congiuntivi] potrebbero essere casuali, ma è evidente che ciò è tanto meno probabile quanto più la serie è lunga [...]. Questa labilità dell'errore, a sua volta, non è che una conseguenza dello stato "attivo" della tradizione [dei testi romanzi], che non tollera a lungo guasti senza tentare di ripararli in qualche modo, col risultato, spesso, di confondere la situazione testuale. (Vàrvaro 1970, 95 = 2004, 589–590).

> [The weakly conjunctive error is intrinsically polygenetic, so that in theory both the short and the long series [of weakly conjunctive errors] could be random, but it is evident that, the longer the series, the less likely this is [...]. This unreliability of the error, in its turn, is nothing but a consequence of the "active" state of the tradition [of Romance texts], which does not tolerate flaws for long without trying to repair them somehow, often with the result of confusing the textual situation.]

As pointed out above, it would be easy to object, with Maas or Luciano Canfora, that, if we do not have indicative errors, we cannot reconstruct a sound genealogy. But the question is quite different if at least a few indicative errors do exist. Paolo Divizia remarks:

> quanto più ci si allontana dai [...] punti in cui si riscontrano gli errori guida, tanto minore è la probabilità che i rapporti tra i testimoni rimangano gli stessi. Per questa ragione una serie identica di innovazioni poligenetiche di poco peso distribuite su tutta l'opera dà maggiori garanzie, nella costruzione di uno stemma codicum, rispetto a pochi errori monogenetici evidenti concentrati in una sola parte del testo. (Divizia 2009, 46–47)

> [the further one moves away from the [...] places where indicative errors are found, the lower the probability that the relationships between the witnesses remain the same. For this reason, an identical series of polygenetic innovations of little weight distributed over the whole work gives greater guarantees in the construction of a *stemma codicum*, than a few evident monogenetic errors concentrated in a single part of the text.]

Other scholars choose to connect these useful observations even more strictly to Maasian orthodoxy, maintaining that a series of weakly conjunctive errors added to a few indicative errors allows us to confirm that the relationship between the copies is the same in any passage of the work:

> Especially in areas [of the copies] that have few or no significant errors, it is best to supplement them with an adequate number of confirmatory readings as a control [...], which will serve the purpose of orienting judgment in the case of dense contamination. (Trovato 2017, 117)

See also Divizia (2011, esp. 63–71).

1976: The concept of diasystems (Segre)

Segre (1976) proposed applying to textual criticism the linguistic concept of the diasystem, which had been introduced by Weinreich in his classic work *Languages in Contact* to indicate a linguistic system which is a compromise between two systems that are in contact. As Segre underlines:

> Se è vero [...] che i concetti di variante, errore, lezione equipollente rientrano nei due insiemi complementari di lezioni conservate e lezioni innovate, l'individuazione del sistema stilistico proprio di ogni copista fornisce il filologo di un nuovo strumento di analisi. Non gli errori soltanto, infatti, permetteranno di cogliere l'affinità genetica tra due o più manoscritti, ma anche l'appartenenza di questi manoscritti a uno stesso sistema stilistico diverso da quello realizzato nell'opera [...]. Questo criterio diventa particolarmente fruttuoso se applicato a testi nei quali si incontrino, piuttosto che errori, vere e proprie rielaborazioni, come le *chansons de geste*. (Segre 1976, 283 = 1979, 59)

> [If it is true [...] that the concepts of variant, error, equally acceptable reading fall into the two complementary sets of preserved readings and innovations, the identification of the stylistic system of each copyist provides the philologist with a new analytical tool. Not only errors, in fact, will allow us to grasp the genetic affinity between two or more manuscripts, but also the belonging of these manuscripts to the same stylistic system different from that realised in the work [...]. This criterion becomes particularly fruitful if applied to texts like the *chansons de geste*, in which re-elaborations are encountered more frequently than errors.]

Perhaps we can recall here the lucid remark of Maas, who noted: "Den Kern fast jedes textkritischen Problems bildet eben ein stilistisches, und die Kategorien der Stilistik sind noch viel ungeklärter als die der Textkritik" (Mass 1950, 24–25) [The core of practically every problem in textual criticism is a problem of style, and the categories of stylistics are still far less settled than those of textual criticism] (trans. Flower 1958, 40–41). Nevertheless, the current growing availability of digitised texts and rich textual databases greatly facilitates stylistic analysis.

On a more general level, Paolo Divizia has kindly pointed out to me a paper by Segre (1978) which underlines, among other things, that neo-Lachmannism (though not mentioned as such) owes a lot of its refinements to key concepts of structural linguistics, such as the notions of the system and of paradigmatic and syntagmatic relations.

1981–: *Emendatio ex fontibus* (Orlandi, Brambilla Ageno, Maggioni, and Del Popolo)

Within some fields of research (mediaeval Latin, Old French, Nordic and Germanic philology), singling out indicative errors can be quite difficult due to a high degree of loss and fragmentation in the manuscript material, and the compilatory nature and anonymity of many works, that is to say, the lack of strong authorial marks more common in some other fields. In these very fields, the *Quellenforschung* of our positivist grandfathers can play an important role, offering precious clues for distinguishing between preserved readings and innovations:

Anche quando è possibile dimostrare obiettivamente, per via di varianti, che una famiglia sia migliore di un'altra, ossia contenga meno corruttele, ciò non ha pratica utilità a risolvere i problemi posti dal singolo passo in cui esse divergono. Qui possono valere soltanto i noti criteri interni; campo nel quale, quanto più dall'antichità ci si addentra nel medioevo, si ha a disposizione uno strumento di verifica che in generale il filologo classico non ha: le fonti dell'autore. Il caso più ovvio è rappresentato dalle traduzioni. In innumerevoli passi l'editore ha potuto decidere a favore dell'una o dell'altra classe di mss. della versione latina di Giuseppe Flavio [...] tenendo d'occhio l'originale greco [...]. *A fortiori* il criterio è valido per l'emendatio [...]. La scoperta di una fonte – specialmente di un modello d'imitazione letteraria, come ci ha insegnato in analoghi casi il Mariotti – serve proprio a correggere il testo. Cio è stato fatto da Dag Norberg per la *Vita ritmica* di s. Zeno, emendata appunto sulla base dell'opera prosastica di cui pare rielaborazione [...] e per talune poesie di Paolino di Aquileia, mediante il confronto con passi di poeti cristiani antichi cui il carolingio si era rifatto [...]. La ricerca delle fonti ha quindi fondamentale importanza anche per la critica testuale, e per tanti autori resta ancora in buona parte da fare. Talora, anzi, la lezione della fonte può funzionare come "terzo ramo" di uno stemma altrimenti bifido e "chiudere" una *recensio* per sé aperta. (Orlandi 1981, 336 = 2008, 7–8)

[Even when it is possible to demonstrate objectively, by means of readings, that one family is better than another, that is to say, contains fewer errors, this is not of practical use for solving the problems posed by a given passage in which they diverge. Only known internal criteria can apply here; this is a field in which, as one moves from Antiquity and enters the Middle Ages, one acquires a verification tool that, in general, the classical philologist does not have: the sources of the author. The most obvious case is represented by translations. In countless places, the editor was able to decide in favour of one or the other family of manuscripts of the Latin version of Josephus [...] by keeping an eye on the original Greek [...]. *A fortiori* the criterion is valid for *emendatio* [...]. The discovery of a source – especially of a model of literary imitation, as Mariotti has taught us in similar cases – serves precisely to correct the text. This has been done by Dag Norberg for the rhythmic life of St Zeno, corrected precisely on the basis of the prose work which seems to have been reworked [...], and for certain poems by Paulinus of Aquileia corrected by means of comparison with passages from ancient Christian poets whom the Carolingian poet had reworked [...]. The study of sources is therefore of fundamental importance also for textual criticism, and for many authors still remains to be done. Sometimes, the reading of the source can function also as the "third branch" of an otherwise two-branched stemma and "close" a *recensio* that appeared per se to be "open".]

See also Brambilla Ageno (1986), Maggioni (1994), Orlandi (1995, 4 = 2008, 100), and Del Popolo (2001). This method has been fruitfully applied to the edition of Old Norse sagas by Bullitta (2017), who systematically compared the witnesses of *Niðrstigningar saga* using the Latin source text underlying the work.

1982–: Deepening of the concept of the archetype (Weitzman, Reeve, Guidi and Trovato)

The genealogical concept of the a r c h e t y p e introduced and used by Lachmann and some of his contemporaries was, and still can be, rather difficult to handle because the new technical meaning of the term (a lost manuscript on which the extant transmission depends) overlaps with the classical and humanistic meaning of the word (an "official text" checked by the author and intended to be published afterwards in further copies), thus causing ambiguity or misconceptions. Reeve observes: "Since the Renaissance, when scholars at work on the text of Greek and Latin authors took it [*archetypus*] up, the classical term [...] has been used in so many senses that no-one today can safely use it without defining it" (1985, 193 = 2011a, 107).

Thus, even highly experienced scholars appear not to have broken completely free of the classical meaning of the term "archetype", failing to view the archetype as a manuscript whose existence is "by chance" detected by philologists within the stemma, and treating it instead as an especially authoritative exemplar or as the result of a sudden and inexplicable bottleneck in the ancient and mediaeval tradition whereby only one copy survived. To provide just one example of this line of reasoning, even the very competent Pasquali notes: "A chi ben consideri deve sembrare inverosimile che ogni volta di ciascun'opera tuttora superstite si fosse salvato nel Medioevo (occidentale e bizantino) un solo esemplare, mentre tutti gli altri erano andati a fondo con la caduta della civiltà antica" (Pasquali 1934, 15) [On careful consideration, it must appear unlikely that, each time, only one exemplar of each surviving work had been saved in the Middle Ages, whether Western or Byzantine, while all the others had perished with the fall of ancient civilisation].

The studies on two-branched stemmata and the loss of manuscripts by Weitzman (1982, 1987) and Guidi and Trovato (2004) allow us to explain the concept in a different and very simple way. As I have already pointed out,

> tracing a tradition back to an archetype dating, say, from the fourth century, does not at all mean that "in antiquity" (or in the Middle Ages, or in the early modern period) a single witness of our text was preserved, or a single copy that was authoritative for one reason or another. What it means is that the witnesses available today do not allow modern philologists to trace their way any further back than a given manuscript (usually lost), often far removed from the original, and sometimes datable with fairly reasonable approximation. [...] In Latin and Greek classics, the archetype is often from the age of Charlemagne, so what has disappeared is not just the first four or five generations of witnesses, but – with very rare exceptions – the whole manuscript tradition preceding the ninth or tenth century AD. (Trovato 2017, 66)

The following diagrams from Weitzman (1982) can help to explain how a copy can become the archetype, for they depict different phases of a simulated manuscript tradition. In Weitzman's own words:

> Omega represents the lost original. All manuscripts alive at the stated time are shown, without any ring, except that four codices descripti in the final population ("sons" of 61 and 95, another "son" of 95 and its own "son") are omitted. Manuscripts fully ringed are dead; many other dead manuscripts are omitted. A dotted ring indicates a dying manuscript. (Weitzman 1982, 59)

As noted above, the four diagrams in figure 2.4-2 depict four different phases of a manuscript tradition. It is easy to understand that, if today we could work with the witnesses extant in 1287, our knowledge of the archetype, that is "13", would be more sound than that obtained by working with the witnesses found in the final

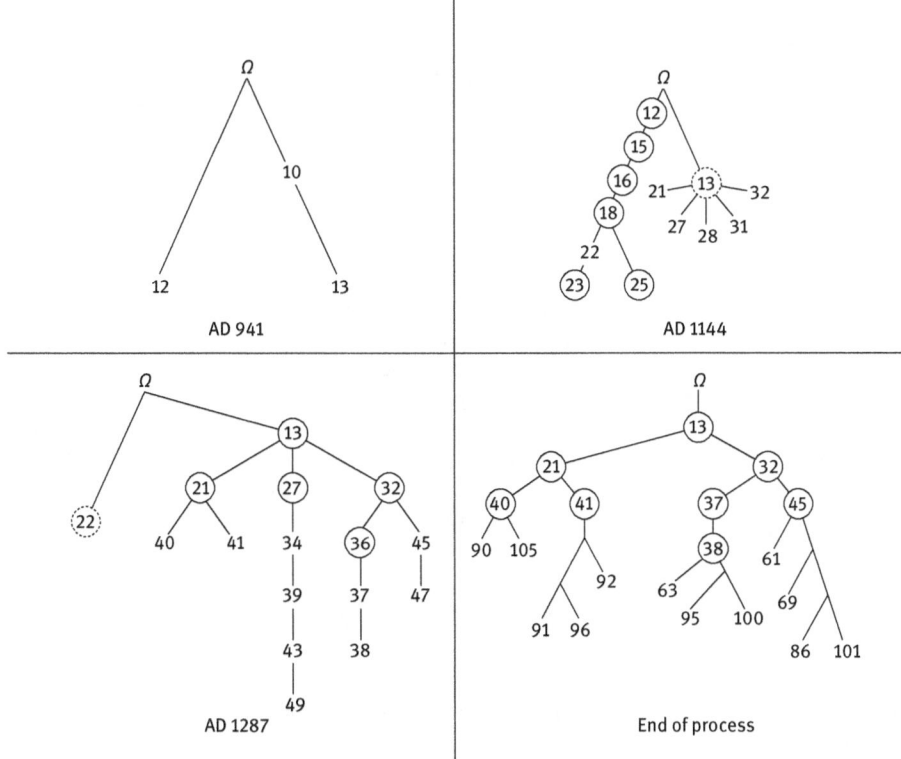

Fig. 2.4-2: Diagrams from Weitzman (1982, 59). The diagrams represent four phases of one of the artificial transmissions produced by means of software. I have corrected the last figure ("End of process") as per Weitzman (1987, 289).

diagram because we would still have three lines of descent from it. At the end of the process, in 1500, one of these lines is completely extinct, so we would be in trouble whenever the two surviving branches differ. What if we imagine that, both in 1287 and at the end of the process, due to a severe loss rate, only some copies that depend on "32" had survived? It is readily apparent that in this case the archetype that textual scholars could reconstruct would be "32" and not "13". Therefore,

> the archetype of the stemma has nothing to do with the history of the tradition (official copies, if any; copies commissioned for circulation by the author himself, etc.), but only with the ensemble of manuscripts that happen to be available today, used by the philologist in the stage of *recensio*. Textual critics should only use the word *archetype* to designate the point in the stemma beyond which the surviving tradition does not allow them to reach. (Trovato 2017, 66)

The concept of the archetype is further discussed in sections 4.1 and 4.2 below. In order to analyse in depth this recent process of clarification of the notion, the reader can consult Weitzman (1982), Reeve (1986), Weitzman (1987), Guidi and Trovato (2004), and Trovato (2005).

1985–: Additional criteria for *eliminatio codicum descriptorum* (Timpanaro, Reeve, and others)

In the wake of Maas (1927, § 8a) and Pasquali (1932; 1934, 30–34), Timpanaro, Reeve, and others maintain that physical evidence is an important clue for proving that a manuscript is a *codex descriptus*, and not simply a relative of another witness to which it is very close but in relation to which it cannot be definitively positioned. In the words of Reeve's most important work on this topic:

> Physical evidence is any peculiarity of a witness other than its reading that accounts for an innovation in another witness. The most familiar examples are physical changes, especially damage or misbinding: a tear in a Beneventan manuscript of Apuleius accounts for gaps in many later manuscripts, and Politian demonstrated in two traditions, those of Cicero's *Ad familiares* and Valerius Flaccus, that transpositions in the majority of manuscripts had their origin in extant manuscripts where leaves were misplaced. Perhaps the most familiar example of all is a physical accretion, the speck of straw in L of Euripides that the scribe of P reproduced as punctuation before it came away in 1960 under the heat of Zuntz's lamp and the finger of a librarian […]. A different form of physical evidence, not created by later accidents […], is peculiarities of layout. (Reeve 1989, 10–11, 13 = 2011a, 152, 155)

See also Timpanaro (1981) and Orlandi (1995 = 2008, 63–94).

1987–: New attempts to explain Bédier's so-called paradox (Weitzman and others)

In the wake of Weitzman (1987; see "1982–" above), Guidi and I addressed the problem of the modifications that a real, or complete, tree (see "1946–" above) may exhibit after more or less severe loss of witnesses. We used the stemma of a relatively rich printed tradition from the sixteenth century (Sannazaro's *Arcadia*) as the model for a real tree (see fig. 2.4-3).

Then, we decided to decimate this model tree between 10 % and 90 %. I quote here from my handbook the summary of the results of this experiment:

> Assuming a not too slender three-branched real tree, including some thirty witnesses, and – as is very often the case with the stemmata of the most diverse works – more or less markedly asymmetrical, low rates of decimation (from 10 to 30 %) do not result in very significant modifications. High decimation rates (70, 80, 90 %), however, result in:
> a') a clear-cut increase in the probability (varying from case to case, but not inferior to 60 % in the traditions Guidi and I studied) that the tree will lose some of its flimsier branches, turning into a two-branched stemma;
> b') a high probability (varying from case to case) that this two-branched stemma will be drawn up from what are actually descendants of a single branch (the more luxuriant one) of a multipartite real tree.
> The prevalence of two-branched stemmata thus depends on the intensity of decimation which in its turn depends on T, that is, as I said above, the time that elapsed between the early transmission of a given text and the genealogical classification of its surviving copies. (Trovato 2017, 92)

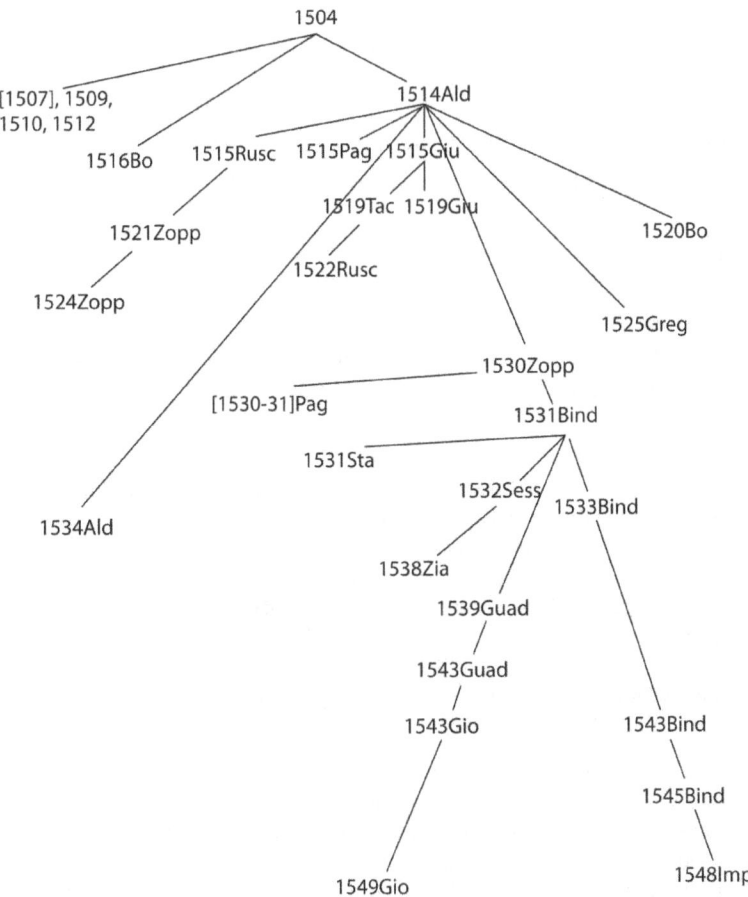

Fig. 2.4-3: The genealogical tree of a printed text (Sannazaro's *Arcadia*, second redaction), which is used as a model for a real tree and subjected to increasing decimation rates by Guidi and Trovato (2004, 23).

Several scholars (e.g. Divizia 2009, 42; L. Leonardi 2015) objected to our conclusions that a printed transmission is quite different from a manuscript tradition in many features. In my opinion, this point deserves close attention. Scientific modelling means generating a physical, conceptual, or mathematical representation of a real phenomenon that is difficult to observe directly. A theoretical model does not need to reproduce all the features of the phenomenon it intends to analyse. On the contrary: "Il problema fondamentale [nella scienza sperimentale] è stato quello di individuare per ogni fenomeno pochi dati giudicati rilevanti, decidendo di trascurare tutti gli altri" (Dalla Chiara and Toraldo di Francia 1999, 4) [The fundamental problem [in experimental science] has been to identify for each phenomenon the few data deemed relevant, deciding to neglect all the others]. For further details, I refer to Weitzman (1987) and Guidi and Trovato (2004), where the relationship between the loss of witnesses and the morphology of the stemma is studied in greater depth.

1995: *Interpretatio* vs *iudicium*: On the correct interpretation of Lachmann's "recensere sine interpretatione et possumus et debemus" and of the term *iudicium* (Orlandi)

Many scholars have criticised Lachmann's "recensere sine interpretatione et possumus et debemus" (1842–1850, 1:v) [we can and must undertake *recensio* without interpreting], often without even having read the context of the statement. In a lucid essay, Orlandi re-evaluated a good deal of Lachmann's bequest and analysed this well-known sentence in depth. After a close reading of Lachmann's words, he remarked:

> Dovrebbe essere chiaro [...] che il mantenersi al di qua dell'*interpretatio* non significa limitarsi a un lavoro meramente meccanico (quasi che la *recensio* e la conseguente *constitutio textus* non richiedessero scelte coscienti), bensì bandire, per quanto possibile, gli apprezzamenti personali sul pensiero dell'autore (o sulla sua poesia) per attenersi rigorosamente a ragioni oggettive: corruttele certe e indubitabili, lacune del testo, trasposizioni e così via. L'alternativa all'*interpretatio* è il *iudicium*: occorre rifuggire dalle scelte testuali fondate su preferenze individuali, e "giudicare" solo con l'ausilio dei fatti [...]. Perciò la polemica anti-lachmanniana, tante volte ripresa, a favore dell'interpretazione che tutto pervade, dipende in ultimo da un equivoco terminologico. (Orlandi 1995, 13 = 2008, 106)

> [It should be clear [...] that abstaining from *interpretatio* does not mean limiting oneself to a merely mechanical task (as if the *recensio* and the consequent *constitutio textus* did not require conscious choices), but banning, as far as possible, personal appreciation of the thought of the author (or his poetry) in order to strictly comply with objective reasons: certain and undoubted corruptions, lacunae of the text, transpositions, and so on. The alternative to *interpretatio* is *iudicium*: we must avoid textual choices based on individual preferences, and "judge" only with the help of the facts [...]. Therefore, the anti-Lachmannian controversy, claiming that interpretation is always present (so often repeated), is ultimately based on a terminological misunderstanding.]

2002–: Indicative errors again (Chiesa and Divizia)

Returning to Maas's contrast between separative and conjunctive errors, Chiesa noted:

> In pratica le innovazioni che effettivamente servono alla ricostruzione dello stemma sono quelle che identificano i gruppi in modo univoco. Quelle che possono essere poligenetiche non realizzano questa condizione perché la stessa innovazione può riferirsi a più di un gruppo; quelle che possono essere reversibili non la realizzano perché anche testimoni che non le riportano possono far parte del gruppo. (P. Chiesa 2002, 68)

> [In practice, the innovations that are actually needed to reconstruct the stemma are those that identify the groups in a unequivocal way: those that could be polygenetic do not satisfy this condition because the same innovation may refer to more than one group; those that could be

reversible do not satisfy it because even witnesses that do not contain them could be part of the group.]

Elaborating on the categories introduced by Chiesa, Divizia observes (the table in question is translated as table 2.4-2 below):

> I concetti di congiunzione e separazione stanno dunque su piani diversi e non contrastanti, così come le categorie di monogeneticità/poligeneticità e irreversibilità/reversibilità da cui dipendono, che possiamo rappresentare – secondo il loro combinarsi – nella seguente tabella: (Divizia 2011, 58–59)

> [The concepts of conjunction and separation are therefore on different and non-contrasting levels, as are the categories of monogeneticity/polygeneticity and irreversibility/reversibility on which they depend, which we can represent – according to their combination – as displayed in the following table.]

Tab. 2.4-2: A table recording the extreme poles of a continuum of the different kinds of innovation, translated from Divizia (2011, 59).

	irreversible innovations ("separative errors")	reversible innovations
monogenetic innovations ("conjunctive errors")	monogenetic irreversible (MI)	monogenetic reversible (MR)
polygenetic innovations	polygenetic irrreversible (PI)	polygenetic reversible (PR)

Divizia also adds:

> Da quanto si è detto, si può vedere che le opposizioni monogeneticità/poligeneticità, irreversibilità/reversibilità e evidenza/adiaforia, non sono opposizioni booleane, ma rappresentano piuttosto i poli estremi di un *continuum* che prevede una svariata gamma di sfumature intermedi. (Divizia 2011, 59–60; emphasis in original)

> [From what has been said, we can see that the oppositions between monogenetic and polygenetic innovations, irreversible and reversible innovations, inacceptable and equally acceptable innovations are not Boolean contraries, but rather represent the extreme poles of a *continuum* that provides a wide range of intermediate shades.]

2004: On the loss rate of mediaeval traditions (Guidi and Trovato)

"What fraction of the total number of manuscripts at one time in existence is represented by those that survive: is it 50 %, or 20 %, or less?" This quotation is from Reynolds (2000, 3). In 2004, I tried to address, at least partially, this crucial question by looking outside mediaeval manuscript traditions. I worked on the few printed books of the fifteenth and first half of the sixteenth century for which I could find the numbers of the initial prints, excepting booklets of a few folios (too thin to be easily preserved).

> Loss ranges from 73% for the parchment copies of the *Decretales* by Gregory IX and 76.9% for Poggio's *Historia* to 100% for some especially popular chivalric poems. Unsurprisingly, every edition has its own distinctive history. The only conclusion that can be drawn from these percentages is that, although the books in question were printed only a few decades before book-collecting spread amongst the European aristocracy and high bourgeoisie [...] and although an unknown but certainly significant number of early editions are still in private collections (but this is also true of manuscripts), natural calamities (including mice and bookworms), various ways of recycling parchment and paper, fires (including those started intentionally for ideological reasons, from Savonarola to the Inquisition, the Nazis, and Serbian nationalists), plundering, bombings, and mere use seem to have done away with the majority of early European printed production in the brief space of 500 years. I do not see valid reasons to imagine that the manuscripts of classical or medieval authors, which were exposed to the same agents for even longer periods, stood higher chances of survival. On the contrary, the fact that every printed book is produced in *n* copies, while manuscripts are unica, suggests that, with the increase of T [that is Time, Temporal distance], losses among handwritten texts were even more dramatic. (Trovato 2017, 108, based on Guidi and Trovato 2004, 27–29)

Loss rates are smaller in subsequent centuries. Thus:

> The probability that one of the many (and converging) factors in the possible destruction of a book, whether handwritten or printed (fires, floods, war, mold, use ...), will cause its loss increases proportionally to the temporal distance (T) between us and the early copies. (Trovato 2017, 135)

As a consequence of this very high loss rate, there is a high probability that surviving mediaeval textual traditions stem solely from witnesses belonging to some vulgate tradition (see Guidi and Trovato 2004; "1987–" above).

2009: Multi-text codices and cluster philology (Divizia)

The genealogical method, as is well known, does not work with very short texts (lyric poems, letters, and the like), which as a rule do not contain enough indicative errors to reconstruct a stemma. Elaborating upon studies by Barbi, De Robertis, Reeve, and others, Paolo Divizia theorised that not-obvious clusters of texts collated as a unique relatively long text could permit the determination of filiation. See Divizia (2009, 2017).

2019: Methods for studying scribal behaviour and scribal habits (Marchetti)

One of the aims of the so-called New Philology is the assessment of scribal behaviour, but the studies published so far do not provide relevant information. The Colwell method, named after Ernest C. Colwell (1901–1974), proposes, once a manuscript is chosen, attributing to the copyist all its *lectiones singulares* without attempting to make any distinction between group and individual innovations. Elaborating upon tenets of genealogical textual criticism such as *eliminatio codicum descriptorum* and combining the rationales of common errors and codicological evidence (see "1937" and "1985–" above), Marchetti studied in his PhD thesis five pairs of an exemplar and its copy (*exemplar* and *descriptus*) of Dante's *Commedia* belonging to different areas, years, and graphic models. The outcome is that, while innovations in the accidental readings are around 90 % of all variant readings, professional copyists, at least in fourteenth- and fifteenth-century Italy, have a dramatically low rate of significant innovations. Both if *exemplar* and *descriptus* are in a "bad" position in the genealogy (i.e. they share a number of common errors) and if they are in a prominent position (i.e. they exhibit only a few common errors), these copyists introduce new significant errors only once every eight hundred lines. There is no need to emphasise that the research of Marchetti – who is planning to verify his findings in other manuscript traditions – seems useful not only as a model for rigorously evaluating scribal behaviour but also as a diagnostic tool: whenever scholars face two or more copies which present (*i*) a high number of common errors and (*ii*) a dramatically low rate of *errores singulares*, they can suspect (even if codicological evidence is missing) that those copies could be in an *exemplar–descriptus* relation, or very close to this kind of relation.

My list, which is certainly, up to a point, personal and subjective and even partial, ends here. It can easily be enriched by readers, especially if they work in other research fields. Classical scholars will note, for example, the absence of references to the contributions of a master such as Jean Irigoin, but I preferred to work only on issues which I could master, at least to some extent. There is no need to underline that many of the additions and updates reviewed here are closely bound up with the starting assumptions of the founding fathers of the method. As Popper would put it, the theories of textual transmission on which the genealogical method was based were "passed on not as dogmas, but rather with the challenge to discuss them and improve upon them" (1965, 50). Therefore, they have become richer and more comprehensive. On the one hand, they are able to explain in a simple way intuitions of Lachmann's contemporaries which had not been adequately clarified (e.g. the very notion of "archetype"). On the other hand, they allow both predictions and diagnoses (e.g. that a two-branched stemma indicates, as a rule, that the witnesses suffered a high loss rate).

2.4.4 Neo-Lachmannism in the third millennium

As is naturally to be expected, as soon as cladistics and other forms of computer-assisted philology (the greatest novelty of the end of the last century) reached a certain maturity, their promises of amazing advances and their polemical stances against the method of common errors has diminished. The latter has more and more become recognised as a method "there is no need to defend" and whose "main elements [...] are simply self-evident" (I quote from an email by Odd Einar Haugen to the authors of this chapter). Even a champion of the "new digital frontiers" of textual criticism such as Peter Robinson could declare in 2013:

> There has been a great deal of rhetoric, some of it from myself, in the last decades about how scholarly editions and editing have been fundamentally changed by the digital turn. So let me say it plainly. *I don't think there has been any such change. A scholarly edition is still, as it has been for centuries, an argument about a text. The fundamental players in this argument are still documents, works, and the editor's interpretation of them.* The editor is the editor, and not a "facilitator". There are still many more readers than editors, and most readers do not want to be editors. (Robinson 2013b; my emphasis)

In this different context, in a situation of greater mutual respect between philologists who favour the new methods and "traditional" textual scholars, there are signals suggesting that a renewed interest in a refined kind of genealogical textual criticism is spreading even in fields and cultural traditions that have in the past shown little interest in what happens outside the confines of their own horizons. As many of the various traditions are studied in depth in chapter 7, I restrict myself to briefly commenting on a few examples.

In France, a country where scholars traditionally follow in the wake of the Bédierist (or maybe better neo-Bédierist) tradition, the few textual critics open to the genealogical method – who were until recently confined to the Ecole des chartes and the Institut de recherche et d'histoire des textes (IRHT) – are especially productive. I mention here only the non-Bédierist manual by Bourgain and Vielliard (2002), the interesting collection edited by Frédéric Duval (2006), and the latter's lexicon *Les Mots de l'édition de textes* (Duval 2015).

It becomes clear even from the terminology that Alberto Blecua uses in his survey – "Wagner confused polygenetic errors and modernizations with authentic common errors" (1995, 470), "the ten manuscripts [...] offer not varying versions, but, rather, scribal variants that had to be organized into a stemma" (472), "the criteria of *lectio difficilior* and diffraction" (473), and so on – that he has been spreading a very solid and up-to-date neo-Lachmannism in Spanish-speaking countries. He did the same also in his excellent manual (Blecua 1983) and his works of textual criticism (collected in Blecua 2012).

As has been noted, Russia

> did not develop its own tradition of stemmatics and the introduction of the printing press led to the search for a standard of uniformity, largely based on the ideological choices of church clerics, rather than to attention to text history. As a consequence Bédier's anti-stemmatic approach [...] was easily adopted and widely accepted during the Soviet period. (Bausi et al. 2015, 322)

Thus, and even though the Italian Angiolo Danti had tried to disseminate for many years the practices of neo-Lachmannism among Slavonic scholars (cf. the posthumously published collection Danti 1993), I consider it a very significant fact that both a partial Polish and a complete Russian translation of Maas (1960) have appeared since 1994 (trans. Sybilska 1994; trans. Toršilov 2011). For a reconsideration of Maas's fortunes as well as his importance, see now the introduction by Ziffer in Maas (2017).

In biblical studies, which for decades were quite isolated compared to other philologies, a desire to make contact with colleagues from other fields of textual criticism that seemed unimaginable a few years ago has developed. The discovery of and the research on the Qumran manuscripts certainly brought new life to the field. For instance, there is a very popular blog on Greek New Testament textual criticism, *Evangelical Textual Criticism*, with more than 4,700,000 page views as of September 22, 2018 (evangelicaltextualcriticism.blogspot.com), which publishes very interesting short contributions almost on a daily basis (I mention here only the one entitled "Top Ten Essential Works in New Testament Textual Criticism", which led to thirty-nine posts). The recent, very interesting book by Hendel (2016), called *Steps to a New Edition of the Hebrew Bible*, contains long quotations in English from works written in Italian by Pasquali, Contini, Segre, Chiesa, and the present writer.

In Sanskrit studies, besides Western textual scholars, there is a long tradition of Indian scholars educated abroad and knowledgeable about Western philological approaches (e.g. Sukthankar, Katre, De). In 1954, Katre published a revised edition of his *Introduction to Indian Textual Criticism*, in which, among other things, he offered "a glossary of some important terms used in textual criticism" and stated: "Textual criticism has come to India to stay" (quoted in Rocher 1995, 587). From the point of view of the present overview, it is worthwhile underlining, again, the interest in and comparison with European neo-Lachmannism evident in recent Indian publications (e.g. quotations from Barbi, Contini, Leonardi, Pasquali, Reeve, and Trovato in Adluri and Bagchee 2018).

A survey of Ethiopic editions can be found in Bausi 2016a (and 7.5 below). Moreover, we must remember the companion by Bausi et al. (2015), where the third chapter is dedicated to "textual criticism and text editing". This long chapter, authored by Caroline Macé et al. (pages 321–462), has a number of very detailed sections (e.g. "Textual Criticism and Oriental Languages", "Steps towards an Edition", "Heuristics of Manuscripts and Witnesses", "Witness Classification and History of the Text", "Apparatuses", "Philological Introduction, Translation, Commentary, Indexes and Appendices"), and offers a wealth of case studies. The chapter's introduction begins by referring to Lachmann's method, which

> can be very roughly summarized as follows: complete survey of all the direct and indirect witnesses of the work to be edited (manuscripts, printed editions, quotations, allusions, translations, etc.); defining mutual relationships between the witnesses; reconstruction of an archetypal text. Since the critical edition is a scientific hypothesis, it can be disputed and new hypotheses can be proposed or new evidence can be found, which is why some mediaeval texts are edited more than once. (Bausi et al. 2015, 321)

And further:

> In recent times, the opponents of the genealogical method of textual criticism and of the reconstructive method of text editing often associated with it are mustered under the flag of "new philology", a trend in scholarship which came about in the 1990s especially in the United

States (see Gleßgen – Lebsanft 1997), following the publication of Cerquiglini (1989), claiming that mediaeval literature being by nature variable, mediaeval works should not be reduced to an edited text, but all mediaeval manuscripts should be considered equally valuable [...]. *However attractive the "new philology" approach may be in the field of literary studies, it is nevertheless almost completely irrelevant for the purpose of this chapter, as it does not provide any method to edit texts with a more complex manuscript tradition.* (Bausi et al. 2015, 321; my emphasis)

To come to a close, one cannot but be impressed by the distance between these formulations and the attempt by Carter to justify objectively the impossibility of applying criteria of Western textual criticism to Arabic texts:

Both filiation and copy-text present themselves as different from the corresponding topics that have attracted so much attention in Western editing [...]. Knowledge is, after all, the common property of the community, administered and distributed by people of probity and recognized competence – for this reason there is probably a much lower proportion of truly anonymous works in Arabic than one finds in medieval European literature. *It is therefore unlikely that the indigenous Arabic manuscript tradition will reflect the principles and objectives of modern editing.* (Carter 1995, 556–557; my emphasis)

All in all, one gets the impression that this beginning of a new millennium may herald a vaster diffusion and a more conscious application of those most conspicuous refinements of the method of common errors which, not without hesitation, we have proposed calling the neo-Lachmannian method.

3 Towards the construction of a stemma

Introductory remarks by the chapter editor, Marina Buzzoni

The elaboration of a *stemma codicum*, representing the filiation between the witnesses that transmit a text whose original is lost, is the core of the genealogical method: on the one hand, only once these relationships have been determined can text restoration be tackled; on the other hand, the stemma may be the goal of the work of synthesising a certain textual tradition. In order to construct a stemma, some preliminary steps are needed; these steps are specifically treated in the sections of the present chapter.

The first step of the stemmatic workflow – namely, the identification of both direct and indirect witnesses (technically: heuristics) – is the subject of Gabriel Viehhauser's contribution (3.1). After sketching a brief history of the concept, he addresses the issue of how the heuristic process is carried out after the material turn in the twentieth century, providing useful information about both the traditional and the more recent tools that researchers have at their disposal. Particularly relevant is the advent of digital catalogues and digital facsimiles, which can offer easier and faster access to primary sources. This development has profound consequences for framing the history of transmission of a text, as shown in the critical review of various *Parzival* editorial projects based on different heuristic approaches.

Caroline Macé (3.2) deals with a frequently neglected aspect of editorial practice: the use of the indirect tradition of a given text (e.g. translations and rewritings, quotations, interpolations, glosses, and marginal notes) for stemmatological purposes. The conclusion reached, namely that "the main point of using indirect witnesses is that their text has been preserved 'outside' of the main tradition; they can therefore be used as an 'outgroup' [...] to orientate the stemma", is central from a methodological point of view. The indirect tradition can also be used to document the early history of textual traditions – especially when indirect witnesses are older than the oldest extant direct ones of a given work – as well as the appearance of (hyp)archetypes. Despite their relevance for stemmatic analysis, she warns us to use indirect witnesses with great caution due to the methodological difficulties inherent to them.

In her section (3.3), Tara Andrews addresses the problems of transcribing and then comparing (technically: collating) the different instances of a text preserved in several witnesses. In so doing, she presents both non-digital and digital ways of transcribing and collating witnesses, providing also some insights into the current theoretical debate on what these processes and the results they produce mean to different scholars and scholarly communities. She offers a definition of the central notion of a "variant location", which arises when different witnesses show different readings at a point that can be considered "the same place" in the text. The discovery of these places is key to the establishment of a stemma, as the set of variant locations is the information with which a stemmatic analysis is performed. In a traditional perspective, a distinction is primarily to be made between substantial readings and formal ones: usually, only the former are clues for determining the genealogical relationships between witnesses (see, among many others, Stussi 2006, 9–10). Andrews, however, discusses all variation (close to the traditional notion of *varia lectio*) – including, for example, spelling differences, abbreviation marks, and different letter forms – that may or may not later undergo a process of normalisation for the purposes of publication or for the purposes of stemmatic analysis, or both. The extent of normalisation, as well as the rules followed by the editors, depends on their judgement and the methods they adopt.

Once stemmatologically relevant data have been produced, they need to be represented, a need which is particularly acute when the editor chooses to take recourse to computational methods. Joris van Zundert's section (3.4) focuses mainly on the representation in various digital forms of both input and output information for computational stemmatological analysis. This is highly relevant, for the aim of data formats is not just to ensure the proper storage of data but also to favour its processing by algorithms specific to the data they represent. Besides, van Zundert turns his attention to two further key points: (*i*) whether the chosen format is best suited to the type of analysis the editor wants to perform, and (*ii*) interoperability, since "the scholar should also consider how other scholars and other software may want to reuse the data, and whether the chosen format supports such reuse well". Finally, he underlines that the choice of a specific data format may be influenced by considerations about the presentation of the data, either in separate form or within the broader context of a digital scholarly edition.

The four sections that make up this chapter demonstrate that even the steps that at first sight may appear merely descriptive or mechanical (e.g. the transcription of witnesses and their encoding using a given markup language) are actually always interpretative. In fact, they depend on the methods adopted for the analysis of the text and its witnesses, as well as ultimately on the very idea of textuality the editor embraces and intends to foster. The methods adopted may in turn be based on the type of textual tradition under inspection (e.g. an active tradition usually requires a different approach than a quiescent one; see "1970" in 2.4.3), as well as on the language of the text.

3.1 Heuristics of witnesses

Gabriel Viehhauser

In textual scholarship, heuristics is the identification and collection of direct and indirect witnesses (on the latter, see 3.2) of a text or a text corpus. Although often only discussed in the context of *recensio*, heuristics precedes *collatio*, *examinatio*, and *emendatio* in traditional outlines of textual criticism (see 6.2), and is commonly regarded as the first step of the editorial workflow.

Different philologies and disciplines arguably have specific perspectives on heuristics, mainly because of diverse research traditions but also because of the differences in the amount of extant witnesses that have to be dealt with (e.g. between Latin and vernacular traditions). This means that, although the following account aims at a comprehensive overview, it necessarily has to work with discipline-specific examples.

3.1.1 History

The idea of collecting witnesses to reconstruct a text can be traced back to the φιλόλογοι of the library of Alexandria, where, for instance, Callimachus of Cyrene (ca. 310–240 BC) compiled a catalogue of 120 volumes or Aristophanes of Byzantium (ca. 257–180 BC) established a bibliography of canonical Greek writers that had a decisive impact on their later transmission (Greetham 1994, 14–15). The library also collected different manuscripts of the same texts as a basis for the efforts of the φιλόλογοι (Greetham 1994, 15; on the case of Homer, see Plachta and van Vliet 2000, 15). However, a systematic concept of heuristics did not gain major importance until the emergence of critical philology in the nineteenth century (consider also the simultaneous development of the tripartite division between "heuristics", "source criticism", and "interpretation" in the "historical method" of the nineteenth century in historiography; Lorenz 2002, 139). In textual criticism, the insistence on a full survey of the extant transmission was based in particular on the rejection of the common practice of editing texts only on the basis of a single manuscript (especially the oldest manuscript or the vulgate version). According to Lachmann, an edition had to be built on a "hinreichende Menge an guten Handschriften" (Lachmann 1876, 1:82) [sufficient quantity of good manuscripts] (on Lachmann's predecessors in this respect, see Timpanaro 2005, 115), which served as the foundation for a critical examination of the transmission (*recensio*). Therefore, it was not enough to consult the witnesses only occasionally (for the correction of individual errors); this had to be done systematically in order to gain an overview of the genealogy of the manuscripts beforehand from which to build the basis for all future editorial decisions. Besides direct witnesses, this also includes indirect witnesses (translations or quotations of the text to be edited), fragments, and anthologies that contain the text (on which, see 3.2).

However, in Lachmann's conception, the manuscripts were of interest only insofar as they fostered the reconstruction of the archetype; Lachmann himself did not base all of his editions on the full range of known manuscripts because he did not see the need to go too far into the details of the transmission. Consequently, manuscripts were only relevant as witnesses of the text, but not in their importance as historical documents of their time, in other words in their m a t e r i a l i t y. This clearly changed with the material turn of philology in the twentieth century (see

Bein 2010). Against this backdrop, manuscript or print catalogues, which are of major importance as a tool for heuristics (see 3.1.3), obtain an interesting intermediate position between abstract indexes and detailed descriptions of the transmission, for they do not only register shelfmarks but also data about the provenance, language, layout, and material aspects of a manuscript. Thus, these traditional heuristic tools can also be useful for a kind of philology with a stronger orientation towards material aspects, one that is not only interested in the reconstruction of an archetype but also in the transmission history of a text. These two functions of a catalogue correspond to the distinction between the concepts of an enumerative vs an analytical bibliography: whereas the former confines itself to a list of sources, the latter also provides information with which to examine the sources as material artefacts (Greetham 1994, 7). The shift towards the materiality of texts is substantially helped by the advent of digital catalogues, which can be linked to digital facsimiles and therefore offer a more detailed picture of the manuscript cultures of the past. Thus, the same tendency that can be observed in the case of digital editions, namely the tendency towards a broadening of contexts (Sahle 2013, 2:168–172) fostered by the openness and the limitlessness of the digital medium, also holds true for digital catalogues: since catalogues do not have to be confined to printed book pages any longer, they can be enriched with various kinds of metadata and hyperlinks pointing to a huge amount of different online resources.

3.1.2 Implications of heuristics for building a stemma – an example

The different historical phases of attitudes towards heuristics, as outlined in section 3.1.1, have consequences for the devising of a stemma. In this respect, four phases may be discerned: (*i*) a pre-Lachmannian one, where the edition of a text did not necessarily imply a systematic pursuit of heuristics; (*ii*) an early phase of heuristics that meets Lachmann's stipulation to consider a sufficient basis of good manuscripts, but is as yet unable to draw on comprehensive catalogues of witnesses and on easily accessible sources; (*iii*) a phase where the heuristic work can rely on printed library catalogues and is thus based in principle on the whole transmission, but is sometimes still hampered by poor accessibility of the sources; and (*iv*) a phase that is shaped by the seemingly unlimited possibilities of the Internet and its digital resources. It may be added that the general approach, namely that of undertaking a study of the entire extant transmission, has, in theory, remained the same in phases (*ii*) to (*iv*).

Therefore, in the following, these four phases will each be characterised by a case study from the edition history of the Middle High German Grail romance *Parzival*, by Wolfram von Eschenbach, from the beginning of the thirteenth century. The text was one of the most successful German courtly romances, if its transmission is anything to go by. Today, sixteen complete manuscripts, one incunabulum from the year 1477, and around seventy fragments are known to be extant.

(*i*) The first modern print edition was established by Christoph Heinrich Myller, a student of the famous Swiss scholar Johann Jakob Bodmer, in 1784. The edition was based on a copy of St. Gallen, Stiftsbibliothek, Cod. Sang. 857 (the *St. Galler Epenhandschrift*) that Myller received from Bodmer. Bodmer himself knew two sources of the *Parzival* text: an exemplar of the incunabulum (which is now in the Zentralbibliothek Zürich, 2.103) and the St Gall codex. It is quite likely that Bodmer compared these two sources for his own works, which include modern adaptations of selected parts of *Parzival*, since it appears that the text of his adaptations is based on variant readings from both sources (Mertens 2011, 723). However, Myller, Bodmer's student, obviously did not strive to collect different exemplars for his edition, let alone to construct a stemma of the text, and only used Bodmer's modern copy of the St Gall manuscript.

(*ii*) Before Karl Lachmann, the first scholarly editor of *Parzival*, established his famous critical *Wolfram-Ausgabe* of 1833, he published an anthology of mediaeval texts which also included parts of Myller's edition, not without criticising the earlier editor for basing it solely on one manuscript (Lachmann 1820, viii; see Mertens 2011, 726). In order to prepare his own edition of 1833, Lachmann used two copies of Myller's edition, which he took with him on his travels to the libraries of St Gall, Heidelberg, and Munich. In order to collate the text, Lachmann inscribed the variant readings of the manuscripts into those copies (McCulloh 1983). Although Lachmann knew by this time of thirteen manuscripts as well as the incunabulum of *Parzival* (from a catalogue created by Friedrich Heinrich von der Hagen which was established in 1812), he himself did not use or even examine all of these sources for his edition, because he thought that, in the case of the *Parzival* transmission, three manuscripts were often reliable and representative enough to create his critical text (Schirok 1999, lix). Lachmann never devised a stemma of the *Parzival* tradition, but he claimed that the extant manuscripts can be grouped into two classes which are in principle "von gleichem werth" (Schirok 1999, xix) [of the same value]. These classes are known in *Parzival* philology as classes *D and *G. For the greater part of his text, he followed a representative of class *D, namely the St Gall codex which had already been the basis for Myller's edition. In fact, it appears that, because his workflow relied heavily on the two exemplars of Myller's edition, Lachmann's text even inherited some of the errors that Myller had made in the reproduction of the manuscript (McCulloh 1983; see also below 7.4.1).

(*iii*) Since Lachmann was only interested in the tradition insofar as it (according to him) justified the text of his edition, more precise research on the stemmatic relationships remained to be undertaken by later scholars. Eduard Hartl, who was responsible for the sixth and seventh editions of Lachmann's *Wolfram-Ausgabe*, was the first of Lachmann's successors to try to reconsider Lachmann's findings on the basis of the whole manuscript tradition (of which by then all sixteen manuscripts and a large amount of fragments were known). Although Hartl was only able to publish one volume of the comprehensive *Textgeschichte* he had in mind (Hartl

1928), he identified four manuscripts which constitute a stemmatic group of their own (in Hartl's terminology, class *W, now *T). Lachmann did not know, or did not take into account, any of the manuscripts of this group for his edition. Even if Hartl was not very clear about it, it seems that he considered this group *T to be a subgroup of *G, but thought that it was heavily contaminated with *D. The most striking evidence for this are twenty-two passages where *G lacks lines compared to *D (they are not necessary for the comprehension of the text and therefore cannot be considered *Bindefehler*). *T partly shares this loss of verses, but only in eight of the twenty-two passages. The far more obvious stemmatic explanation for this observation, namely that *G and *T are both descendants of a group *GT, was ruled out as unlikely by Gesa Bonath (1970). However, Bonath could base her judgement only on the variant readings of the first quarter of *Parzival* because she had to rely on Hartl's studies that remained incomplete (for details, see Chlench and Viehhauser 2014). Thus, it seems that there are mainly two reasons why the position of *T in the stemma of *Parzival* was obviously misjudged by Hartl and Bonath: first, the reductive approach of Lachmann fostered a canonical notion of the *Parzival* transmission as split into the two groups, *D and *G, which was hard to overcome; and second, despite knowing all the extant manuscripts, Hartl and Bonath obviously did not have the resources to consider the relatively wide manuscript tradition in its entirety. Even if in the times of Hartl and Bonath printed catalogues provided potential support for a heuristics that enabled scholars to find all the known manuscripts, those manuscripts could not always be easily accessed and considered in practice.

(iv) A thorough examination of the *Parzival* tradition has been made possible by the digital *Parzival* project (parzival.unibe.ch). The project aims at a digital edition of the text that considers all of the extant witnesses and provides digital transcriptions of them (Stolz 2002). In the project, digital phylogenetic methods have been used to visualise the stemmatic relations of the manuscripts (Stolz 2003). Along with the use of new methods, the project also offers a new attitude towards the transmission: instead of reconstructing an "original" text, it focuses on tracing the outlines of the three-centuries-long transmission history of *Parzival*. This also includes a new assessment of the classes of the text's witnesses. While Hartl and Bonath in principle considered *D, *G, and *T as subordinated groups of the archetype, the *Parzival* project is based on four versions which are treated as manifestations of the text in their own right (on *T, see esp. Schöller 2009). Besides *D, *G, and *T, it was possible to identify a further class, *m. While *m is mainly transmitted in three codices of the fifteenth century produced in the workshop of Diebold Lauber, and shares a single reading with a very short (and therefore not very indicative) fragment from the thirteenth century (F 6), the discovery of a longer fragment from the fourteenth century in 2006 (F 69; see Schneider 2006) corroborated the evidence that the group is not a late redaction from the workshop but dates back to earlier times. As this example demonstrates, not only the availability of comprehensive catalogues but also the accessibility of the sources is crucial for heuristics.

This exemplary review of the history of *Parzival* philology shows that the assessment of the stemmatic relationships of a text sometimes cannot be seen independently from the material basis that underlies the philological endeavour. Whereas Myller only had a very constrained knowledge of the transmission and used a modern copy of a manuscript text for his edition, Lachmann could in principle have drawn on catalogues for his heuristic work; however, since he did not yet have microfiche copies or facsimiles of the texts at hand, he had to undertake demanding journeys to see the manuscripts, which he then had to collate in a way that consumed as little time as possible. It seems that his lack of interest in the details of the transmission goes hand in hand with the need to employ a practical approach towards the collection of the witnesses. While Bonath and Hartl could rely on more modern tools for heuristics, they too did not have unlimited access to the transmission. It could be argued that the picture of *Parzival* transmission in the first one hundred years of editorial attention was strongly shaped by insufficient means to pursue the ideal of a complete heuristics of the whole textual transmission, which is most strikingly illustrated by the fact that printing errors in Myller's edition can be found even in the later revised editions of Lachmann's *Wolfram-Ausgabe*. In the case of *Parzival*, a comprehensive view of the transmission was only achieved using the possibilities of a digital edition that includes electronic facsimiles and transcriptions of the text.

Of course, a case study like this can only show tendencies and should not be overgeneralised. In contrast to *Parzival*, in many other traditions it was possible to establish reliable editions on the basis of complete heuristics of witnesses even before the advent of digital methods. Furthermore, the example of the newly found fragment of class *m shows that, even in digitally informed times, it is conceivable that the discovery of hitherto unknown witnesses can change the assessment of the transmission.

3.1.3 Old and new tools for heuristics

Since there is no single printed bibliography that can cover all existing books or manuscripts, and bibliographies therefore necessarily have to be selective (see Greetham 1994, 5), the heuristics of manuscript witnesses very often has to be based on a variety of sources. A first starting point is provided by libraries and their catalogues (see 1.3). In the modern period, libraries began systematically collecting books in the thirteenth century. Prominent early examples of catalogues that exceed the scope of individual libraries by uniting different collections are the *Registrum librorum Angliae* and the *Catalogus scriptorum ecclesiae* (Bischoff 1990, 203; Russell 2001, 27–28; Greetham 1994, 18). Besides the emerging public or semi-public libraries, private collections of the new humanist scholars provided valuable resources (Greetham 1994, 18), but according to Greetham it was not until 1627 and Gabriel Naudé's theoretical treatise *Avis pour dresser une bibliothèque* "that a true systematic enumera-

> 176   I CODICI DI MEDICINA DEL PERIODO PRESALERNITANO
>
> **39   Bibl. Nationale, Fonds latin cod. 13955:** membr., 218×190, cc. 169 num.   Minuscola della fine del secolo IX, a linee piene, senza elementi rubricati, fitta e sbiadita.   Nei margini si leggono alcune glosse e fra esse una altotedesca: (c. 142v) *artemisia*] *bibodis*, e un'altra francese: (c. 144v) *rubarba*, le quali sembrano porre il volume in un ambiente bilingue. Il Jones (*The scriptorium at Corbie*, 390) lo elenca fra i manoscritti presenti in quell'abbazia. A c. 1r, di mano settecentesca, sono la nota di provenienza: *S.ti Germani a Pratis*, e le segnature: *olim 544, n. 1094, 16* (cfr. OMONT, *Concordances*, 93); ma non è indicato nel catalogo del monastero del 1677.   Legatura in pergamena.
>
> Contiene una miscellanea per lo studio delle arti liberali e specialmente di quelle del quadrivio con aggiunte sull'agricoltura e sulla medicina ed appunti di teologia. Così dopo un gruppo di estratti da Columella seguono:
>
> 1. ⟨Antonio Musa, De herba vettonica liber⟩ (cc. 137v-138r). È soltanto il trattatello con i sinonimi, la descrizione e gli usi: Bettonica a grecis dicitur cestros — *I. Ad capitis fracturam et ossa extrahenda*. Herba bettonica tunsa et vulneribus capitis imposita — (*XLVI. Ad podagram*) ipsamque tritam et impositam dolorem lenire experti affirmant.
>
> 2. ⟨Apuleio Platonico, Herbarius, exc.⟩ (cc. 138r-145r): Plantago maior a romanis dicitur — estratti saltuari e alquanto rimaneggiati — (*XLVIII. Petroselinum*) nervorum dolores sedat.
>
> 3. Estratti dal Liber medicinae ex herbis feminis attribuito a Dioscoride, dai Dynamidia e da altre fonti (cc. 145r-146r): XLVIIII. Abrotanum vel aeraclion. Huius genera sunt duo — poi viola purpurea, elleborum nigrum, samsucus, yppericon, satureia, eruca, urtica, urtica cantirina, rubus, cicuta, fenum grecum — (*Verbena*) ad quartanas autem quattuor.
>
> 4. Ricette (cc. 146r-147v): Ut pili E N R — Apum percussus malvarum folia imposita continuo curant.
>
> DELISLE, *Inventaire des mss. de St. Germain des Prés*, 123: sec. X. G. SCHEPSS, *Zu Columella, Julius Victor, Macrobius-Plinius, Martianus Capella und PseudoApuleius* in *Blätter für das GymnasialSchulwesen* (Monaco), XXXII (1896), 407-08: sec. X. SANFORD, *The use of classical Latin authors in the Libri manuales*, 214, n° 187: sec. X. A. MUSAE *de herba vettonica*, PSEUDOAPULEI *herbarius* etc. ed. HOWALD e SIGERIST, XIV: sec. X.

Fig. 3.1-1: Page from a thematic manuscript catalogue (A. Beccaria 1956, 176) listing the content of a medical miscellany.

tive bibliography as related to the organization of book collections got under way" (Greetham 1994, 18). Catalogues may focus on manuscripts from single libraries or on specific languages (e.g. the catalogue of German manuscripts from the Universitätsbibliothek Heidelberg by M. Miller and Zimmermann 2007) as well as on specific temporal or thematic constellations (e.g. the catalogue of illuminated manuscripts of the thirteenth century from the Staatsbibliothek München by Klemm 1998, or A. Beccaria 1956 on pre-Salernitan Latin medical manuscripts; see fig. 3.1-1). Greetham (1994, 24–46), provides an extensive list of national and regional catalogues (especially for the United States, the United Kingdom, and France) and other bibliographical resources. An example of an important metacatalogue which assembles catalogues, inventories, and other resources for Latin manuscripts is Kristeller's *Latin Manuscript Books before 1600: A List of the Printed Catalogues and Unpublished Inventories of Extant Collections* (Kristeller and Krämer 1993; Krämer 2007).

In recent times, access to these catalogues and other resources on textual witnesses has been substantially facilitated by the retro-digitisation of catalogues and resources (e.g. the online version of Kristeller and Krämer 1993 and Krämer 2007 on mgh-bibliothek.de/kristeller, or the extensive list of retro-digitised catalogues on manuscripta-mediaevalia.de) and the advent of a vast amount of digital search tools on the Internet. The interlinking of different resources also opens up new possibilities for comprehensive research and the combination of hitherto separated knowledge bases. However, interoperability can only be achieved on the back of standardised metadata descriptions for entries (e.g. Dublin Core, dublincore.org; TEI, tei-c.org; OAI-PMH, openarchives.org/pmh/; see S. J. Miller 2011). Digital catalogues, therefore, have to be diligently built according to such standards to reach their full potential and to increase their chances of long-term sustainability. In particular, techniques related to the Semantic Web and linked data appear to be promising for this endeavour (Burrows 2010; Baierer et. al. 2016). Once these standards are met, more detailed analyses and visualisations of the material also become conceivable: provenances of manuscripts (for instance) could be geolocated on a map, which might also lead to new insights that can be used for the heuristics of witnesses.

Since the online resources for manuscript research are manifold, divergent in scope, quality, methods, and aspirations, and – due to the fluctuation of the Internet – also sometimes only short-lived (see e.g. the overview of German portals in Stäcker 2010), it is not feasible to give a comprehensive list of all digital catalogues for all traditions in this contribution. Instead, the potential of online resources will be illustrated by an example, namely handschriftencensus.de, which strives to list all German-language manuscripts and fragments from AD 750 to 1520 on a single website. The scope of the project hence encompasses approximately 26,000 witnesses that are held in over 1,500 libraries. The *Handschriftencensus* continues the efforts of the handwritten *Handschriftenarchiv* of the Berlin-Brandenburgische Akademie der Wissenschaften, which began a systematic list of German manuscripts in the early twentieth century (see Wolf 2007) and is now also available in a retro-digitised form (bbaw.de/forschung/dtm/HSA/hsa-index.html). Compared to the handwritten catalogue cards of the *Handschriftenarchiv*, a digital collection like the *Handschriftencensus* offers refined search functions (manuscripts can be listed by authors, works, or libraries) and the possibility of linking catalogue descriptions with digital facsimiles. The website also includes a list of manuscript catalogues and a bibliography that can – like all the resources of the website – be continually updated.

As an example, a search for manuscripts of the *Parzival* tradition in the *Handschriftencensus* will outline a possible workflow for heuristics in the digital age. On its starting page, the *Handschriftencensus* offers two of the above-mentioned possibilities for accessing the database of witnesses: either by sorting the manuscripts according to the libraries that hold them ("Verzeichnisse" > "Handschriften") or by searching for authors or works ("Verzeichnisse" > "Autoren/Werke"). With the latter approach, "Wolfram von Eschenbach" and "*Parzival*" can be searched for or

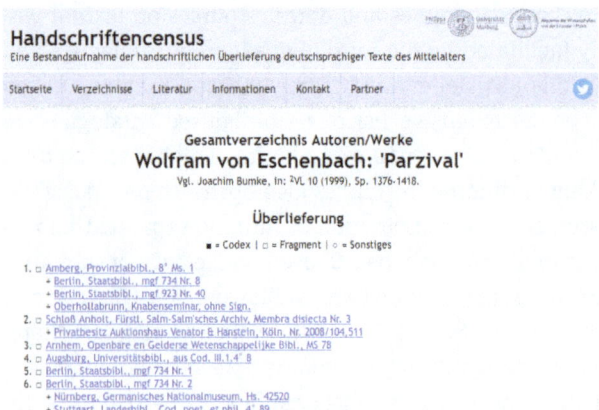

Fig. 3.1-2: The beginning of the list of *Parzival* manuscripts in the *Handschriftencensus* (handschriftencensus.de, accessed October 15, 2019).

selected from an alphabetical index. This search leads to a list of eighty-seven results that indicate the libraries and the shelfmarks of the known witnesses (fig. 3.1-2). Full codices are marked with a black square bullet point, fragments with a white one. Also, fragments that originally belonged to the same codex, but are now preserved in different libraries, are grouped together. By clicking on an entry, a full catalogue description of the witness can be obtained. It encompasses codicological details such as the number of folios, the size of the codex, a possible dating, and so on; the content (and context) of the codex; and finally a bibliography. If there are facsimiles (or parts of the bibliography) available online, the respective websites are linked. Due to the possibility of adding new entries to the list in the digital medium, the *Handschriftencensus* remains updated and also includes witnesses found only recently (e.g. the above-mentioned F 69, which plays an important role in the assessment of the **m* version).

3.2 Indirect tradition

Caroline Macé

Apart from direct witnesses containing a work (most usually manuscripts), the editor will be well advised to make an inventory of the indirect tradition, that is, of any other works or versions of a work that can bear witness to the history of the textual tradition in question, to the establishment of the stemma, and finally to the establishment of the text itself. This inventory is important for the history of the reception of the work, but may often yield some insights into the history of the tradition as well. Of course, these indirect witnesses are themselves generally preserved in manuscripts and have their own textual histories and editorial problems.

3.2.1 Types of indirect witnesses

The indirect tradition of a work may consist of
(i) ancient or mediaeval t r a n s l a t i o n s of that work into other languages;
(ii) q u o t a t i o n s of longer or shorter portions of the text, especially in florilegia or in commentaries;
(iii) i n t e r p o l a t i o n s into other works;
(iv) a d a p t a t i o n s of the text (epitomes, paraphrases, other recensions or redactions of the same work, and so on); and
(v) p a r a t e x t u a l elements (glosses, marginal notes, and so on).

In addition to this, direct witnesses preserved in o t h e r m e d i a than manuscripts (e.g. graffiti or papyri) or as underwriting in palimpsests may be considered similar to indirect witnesses since the text preserved in them may have followed different paths of transmission than the usual direct tradition.

The importance of indirect witnesses for the establishment of the stemma and of the edition will depend mostly on their antiquity and, more importantly, on their position in the stemma, on their fidelity to the original work (otherwise they may not be usable), and on the reliability of the editions through which they are accessible (or, failing that, of the witnesses transmitting them). In general, Dekkers and Hoste showed that, even in the case of well-preserved late antique works, the indirect tradition is crucial for establishing the text (*constitutio textus*; see 6.2 below): "Les citations anciennes sont une véritable pierre de touche pour distinguer les bons mss. des mss. corrompus" (Dekkers and Hoste 1980, 36) [Ancient citations are truly a touchstone for distinguishing the good manuscripts from the corrupted ones].

Some ancient and mediaeval works have an exclusively "indirect" existence, as all direct witnesses have disappeared and the work is known only through translations or citations. This is the case, for example, with three treatises on providence, free will, and evil by the Neo-Platonist Proclus Diadochus (fifth century CE; see 4.5.2), which are preserved in a thirteenth-century Latin translation and in citations (or plagiarism) by Isaac Komnenos the *sebastocrator* from the twelfth century (Isaac 1977, 22–25). See also the case discussed in section 4.5.4 below.

3.2.2 Translations

Late antique and mediaeval translations are potentially precious witnesses to the work from which they are translated, especially when they were made before the time of the oldest manuscripts of that work in its original language that are preserved. In the case of Greek and, to a lesser extent, Latin texts, manuscripts earlier than the beginning of the ninth century, that is, before the change from majuscule to minuscule, are relatively rare (see 1.2.3), and palimpsests or translations made before the ninth century are therefore very valuable.

When dealing with translations, scholars will face different types of problems. First, it is not so easy to find translations of a given work in languages with which the editor is not familiar. For Greek patristic works, the *Clavis Patrum Graecorum* (Geerard and Noret 1984–2018) often mentions translations into Latin (see also Siegmund 1949), the languages of the Christian Orient (Arabic, Armenian, Coptic, Ethiopic, Georgian, Syriac), and Old Slavonic. This is not done systematically, but it is nevertheless a valuable help. For several languages, scholars have provided lists and bibliographical tools, such as, for example, Graf (1944) for Arabic, Thomson (1995, 29–88) for Armenian, and the ongoing *Catalogus translationum et commentariorum* (Kristeller 1960–2003; Dinkova-Bruun 2014–2016) for Latin. Second, the translation might not be edited at all, as translations are often considered less important in the literary canon of a language, or edited in a way which does not meet modern standards (see Macé et al. 2015, 374, 435–439, on nineteenth-century editions of Armenian texts and editions of Syriac texts in the twentieth century respectively). An exemplary enterprise, but certainly not the only one, is represented by the critical editions of Arabic, Armenian, Georgian, and Syriac translations of Gregory of Nazianzus' homilies (fourth century CE) in the *Corpus Nazianzenum*, with a special apparatus highlighting the differences between the translations and the Greek originals (see e.g. Coulie 1994; fig. 3.2-1 below). One important methodological rule for editions of translations is that one should not correct the translator's mistakes, but only mistakes that may have appeared in the manuscript tradition of the translated text. In other words, the editor of a translation must attempt to reconstruct the text of the archetype of the tradition in the translation's language, using the text in the source language as a hint for orientating the stemma, but should resist the temptation of "correcting" the translator's text on the basis of that source. Moreover, the exact source used by the translator is often difficult to assess, and may not exist any longer.

Example 1

In figure 3.2-1, the difference between the edited Armenian text and the Greek original, as indicated in note 10, is most probably due to a confusion of two words which are graphically close in Greek, but not synonyms ("εὐσεβῶν" [pious] and "εὐσεβειῶν" [piety], both in the genitive plural), by the Armenian translator; the editor of the Armenian text kept the translator's mistake in the edited text. Divergences from the original can also point to original (primary) readings that have disappeared from the direct tradition, as with the reading given in note 8 in figure 3.2-1, reflecting the Greek "Βοσόρ", the name of a city in the Old Testament whose "garments" are "red" (Isaiah 63:1, Septuagint), that is, stained with wine or blood, and therefore impure. This reading, also present in the Latin translation, is not found in any of the Greek manuscripts, which all have "βόρβορον" [filth] instead, obviously a simplification (see Dubuisson and Macé 2003, 307–308). In this case, "correcting" the seemingly strange reading "Bosor" in the Armenian text, to make it conform to the Greek text as it exists today, would have made a likely primary reading disappear from the indirect witness, where that reading is preserved as a kind of fossil.

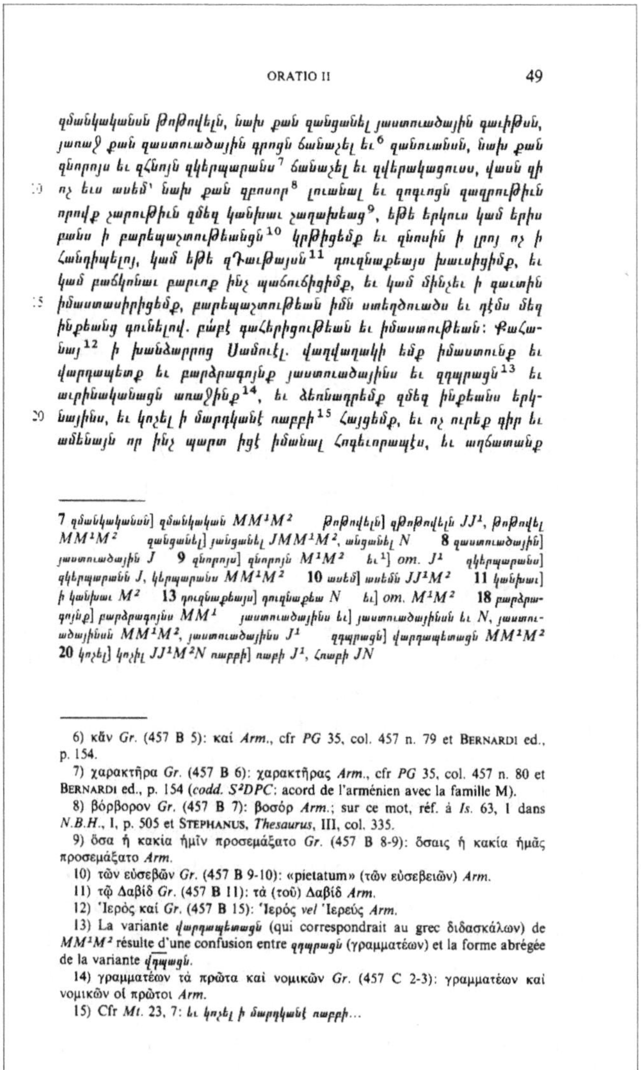

Fig. 3.2-1: Special apparatus comparing an Armenian translation with a Greek original (Coulie 1994, 49). © Brepols Publishers.

For the purpose of comparing them with the original works, translations can be divided into two types: *ad verbum* (according to the wording, i.e. literal) and *ad sensum* (according to the meaning, i.e. free; P. Chiesa 1987). The spectrum is continuous between extremely literal (to the point of becoming almost unintelligible; see Forrai 2012, 296) and extremely creative translations. There might be several translations of a given work even in the same language, or subsequent revisions of a given translation, or translations made not from the original directly but from another pre-existing translation (this is very common in Latin; see e.g. Dolbeau 1989).

Example 2
There are at least two different early Latin translations of the Greek *Physiologus* (an early Christian text moralising animal behaviour, edited by Sbordone 1936; see Pakis 2010 for an excellent *status quaestionis*). One of them (version C) exists only in two manuscripts (one of which is the famous *Physiologus Bernensis*; e-codices.unifr.ch/de/list/one/bbb/0318); the other (version y) was more widespread (Carmody 1941) and has an extremely large diffusion through adaptations in Latin and in vernacular languages (Henkel 1976; Orlandi 1985). An early mediaeval Armenian translation of the *Physiologus* exists as well, and was in turn translated into Georgian before the tenth century (Muradyan 2005, 5). In this case, the Georgian translation, being preserved in a much older manuscript than all extent Armenian ones, is an important indirect witness for the establishment of the Armenian text. In a review of Peeters (1898), Gottheil (1899, 120) drew a "pedigree of the Physiologus literature" (see fig. 3.2-2 below). Although outdated and now known to be wrong on several points, this diagram provides a good picture of the spreading of this work through many languages and over a large timespan. As defective as it may be, Gottheil's bird's-eye view of this tradition has not been replaced yet; research has made progress on some parts of the diagram, but not on all of them. Except for the Armenian translation mentioned above, the *status quaestionis* is no better today than in Gottheil's time for any of the "oriental" translations, and Carmody's edition (1941) of the Latin texts (of versions y and B, the latter probably derived from the former) did not really improve our knowledge of the early stages of the Latin tradition. Sbordone's edition of the Greek text (1936) took all known Greek manuscripts into account (and only a few more have been discovered since then), but neglected the ancient translations altogether in its stemma (see fig. 3.2-3) and critical text. Sbordone did, however, consider the Greek indirect tradition, especially a curious work attributed to Eustathius of Antioch (fifth century) and entitled *Commentary to the Hexaemeron* (the six days of creation), edited in a seventeenth-century edition (still the only one existing; *Patrologia Graeca*, 18:707–794). Even though this work is not an exegetical commentary, but probably part of a chronicle, and was not written by Eustathius of Antioch but dates from some time between the sixth and the eighth centuries, it is still valuable as an indirect witness because it quotes, more or less exactly, many passages from the *Physiologus* (see Macé forthcoming). Sbordone was able to locate the quotations from pseudo-Eustathius in his stemma (see fig. 3.2-3 below), but he gave too much credit to manuscript *M* (Milano, Biblioteca Ambrosiana, A 45 sup.), which he believed to be the oldest preserved Greek manuscript. In fact, earlier manuscripts exist (some known to Sbordone) but were at that time wrongly dated on palaeographical grounds; but this is not the real point. According to my own analysis of the tradition, *M* must actually be located rather "low" in the

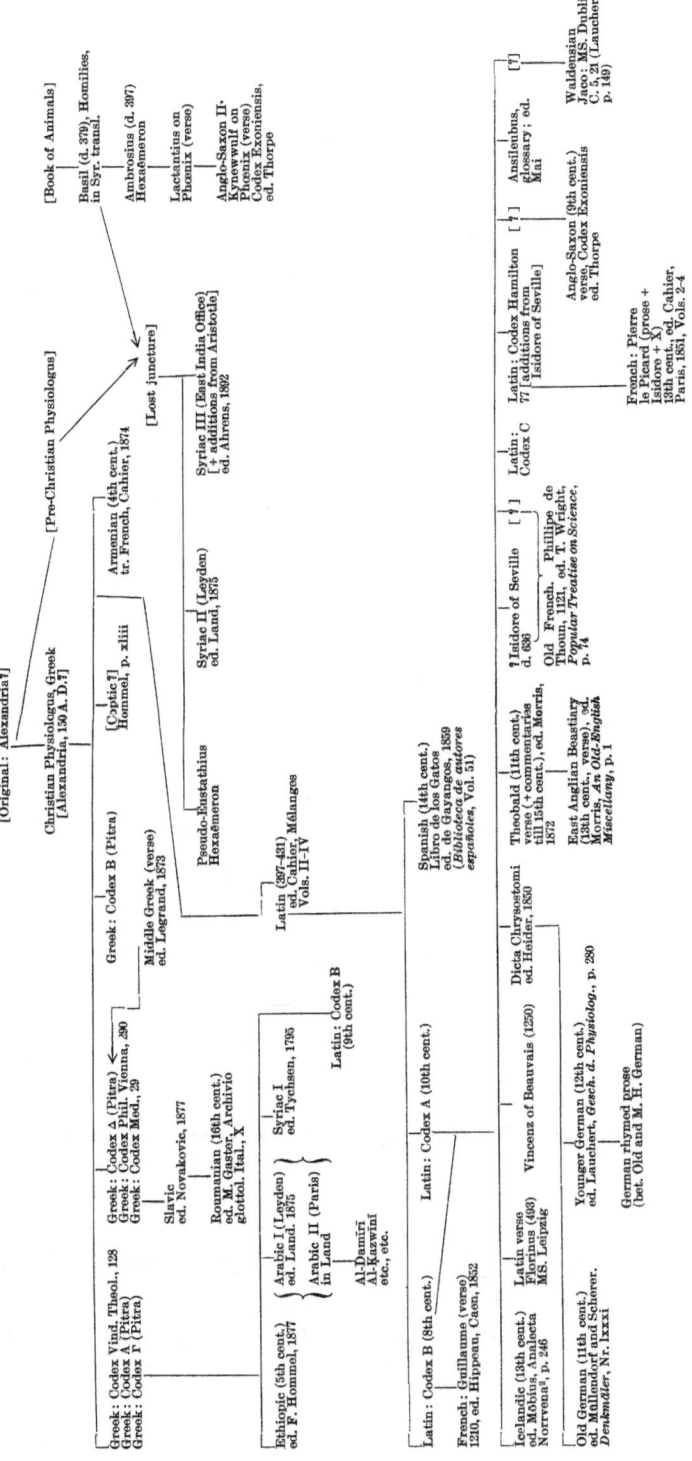

Fig. 3.2-2: Mediaeval translations and adaptations of the *Physiologus* (Gottheil 1899, 120).

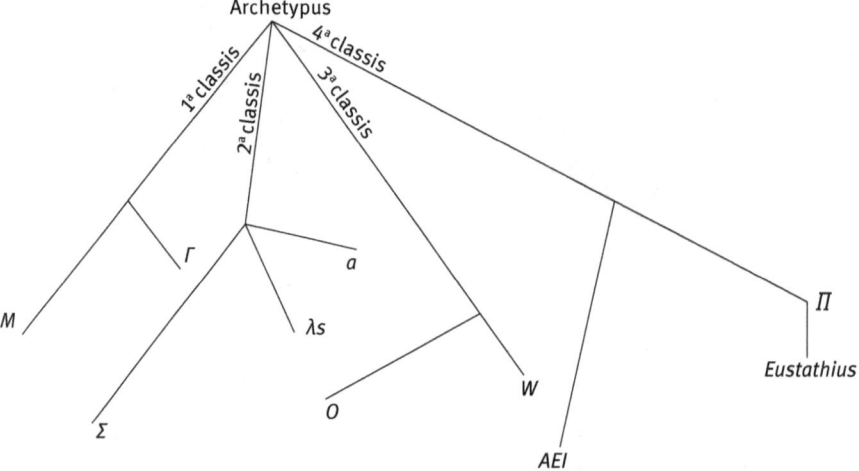

Fig. 3.2-3: Stemma of the manuscript tradition of the oldest recension of the Greek *Physiologus* (Sbordone 1936, lxxix, redrawn and simplified).

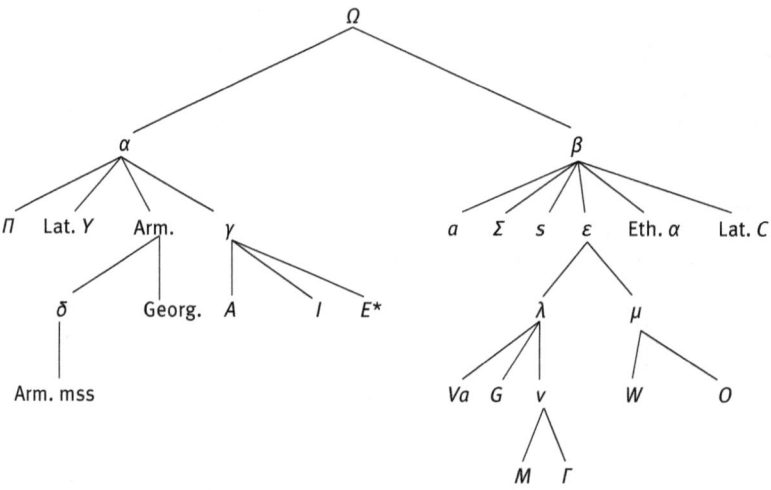

Fig. 3.2-4: My own stemma of the *Physiologus* tradition, taking the ancient translations into account (previously unpublished, the Greek letters in lower case represent postulated hyparchetypes).

stemma (see fig. 3.2-4). In critically evaluating this manuscript tradition, the ancient translations, which were made a few centuries earlier than the Greek manuscripts, prove to be crucial. The agreements between the Armenian and Latin *y* translations and the Greek manuscript *Π* (Moskva, Gosudarstvennyj Istoričeskij Muzej, Sinod. Gr., 467, dated to the eleventh century), as well as some more recent manuscripts, on the one hand, and the agreements between the Ethiopic and Latin *C* translations and the other Greek manuscripts on the other hand, are a very strong argument in favour of a split of the tradition between two main branches (and not four, as Sbordone thought). The differences between these two branches are such that they cannot be explained simply as copyists' mistakes or involuntary interventions; they are traces of the existence of two recensions or redactions (within the oldest recension singled out by Sbordone) very early in the history of the tradition (see fig. 3.2-4). Sbordone's second family ("2a classis" in fig. 3.2-3) cannot be confirmed on the basis of common mistakes, and therefore it cannot be a family at all. Two further manuscripts (*G* and *Va*) can be added to the branch formed by *M* and *Γ*; they are both older than *M* and both from southern Italy (like *M*), thus clearly showing that *M*, which contains many singular mistakes, is but a member of a family of manuscripts which is not situated very high in the stemma.

3.2.3 Quotations/(auto-)plagiarism

In Antiquity and the Middle Ages, texts were "recycled", often without explicitly crediting the original author, sometimes to such an extent that the new work does not contain anything (or not much) else than e x c e r p t s from one or more previous writers (see P. Chiesa 2012, 381: "gran parte di tale letteratura è compilativa" [a large part of such literature [of the early Middle Ages] is compilatory]). One out of very many examples would be the letters that the monk Jacob Kokkinobaphos addressed to the *sebastokratorissa* Irene around 1040 (edited by Jeffreys and Jeffreys 2009). These letters are actually a c e n t o, or a "tapestry of quotations" (Jeffreys 2012), taken from a large number of Greek Church Fathers. As Cassin (2018) has shown, those quotations are an important indirect witness, at least for the history of the reception, but also potentially for the history of the textual tradition, of Gregory of Nyssa's commentary on the Song of Songs. Compare also the case of pseudo-Eustathius quoting the *Physiologus*, as discussed above (3.2.2 – example 2). To provide another similar example from the Latin world, editors of Augustine of Hippo (354–430) are compelled to make use of Florus of Lyon's (first two thirds of the ninth century) compilations of extracts (Chambert-Protat 2014) because Florus had access to old manuscripts containing Augustine's works which are no longer extant. Yet another famous example is the citation of verses from the *Poetic Edda* in Snorri Sturluson's *Prose Edda* (beginning of the thirteenth century). Sometimes, these verses are preserved only there and not in the direct tradition, represented mainly by a thirteenth-century manuscript, the *Codex Regius* (*Konungsbók*) [Book of Kings], Reykjavík, Stofnun Árna Magnússonar í íslenskum fræðum, GKS 2365 4º.

An author may also reuse his own text in different places. For example, in the homilies of Gregory of Nazianzus, nine chapters are shared between homily 38 (on Christmas) and homily 45 (on Easter; Trisoglio 1965). For our purposes, it does not matter if Gregory himself did this or someone else interpolated the chapters of one homily into the other, because these chapters are present in both homilies in the whole tradition. At any event, the same text in one homily can be used as an indirect witness for the other homily (see Dubuisson and Macé 2003, 315–317).

Of a different kind are florilegia, in which longer or shorter excerpts of works are not reworked to form a new work but displayed as such, often with the name of their author, sometimes even with the name of the excerpted work. Those florilegia are organised thematically or alphabetically, and transmitted through a more or less broad manuscript tradition. In Greek patristics, one of the most important of these florilegia is the so-called *Sacra parallela* attributed to John of Damascus (Thum 2018), preserved in several recensions (one manuscript, Paris, Bibliothèque nationale de France, gr. 923, is illustrated). When editing such a florilegium, the danger is the same as when editing a translation: that the editor may hypercorrect the text on the basis of the source (De Vos et al. 2008, 179).

In mediaeval commentaries (see 1.2.1), smaller or larger portions of the commented text are quoted, either as a lemma or in the body of the commentary, which constitutes another type of indirect witness. The commentaries may be transmitted as works in themselves or as scholia accompanying the commented work (on mediaeval commentaries and glosses in general, see Copeland 2012). As an example, one can mention the lemmata of Proclus' commentary on Plato's *Parmenides*, which are one of the oldest witnesses, albeit an indirect one, to Plato's text (see 4.5.2). The ancient scholia (from the Alexandrian school or from late Antiquity; see 1.2.1) accompanying the text of Homer or of the Greek tragedies in papyri or in Byzantine manuscripts can help in restoring the oldest layer of those texts (see e.g. the project of an online edition of Euripides scholia: euripidesscholia.org). See also Browning (1960) for the importance of marginal variants and scholia to classical literature sometimes preserved in recent manuscripts.

3.2.4 Interpolations

The term "interpolation" is sometimes used to designate the process of reusing and reworking previous works in a new one, but for this we prefer the term "excerpting" (see 3.2.3). By interpolation we mean the introduction into a text of a portion of text foreign to it. This is different from gloss-incorporation (see 4.3.2), which is usually unintentional; interpolation normally happens intentionally.

One problem is that interpolations are normally removed from the edited text of a given work (see 6.2.3) as foreign to that work, and might not even be mentioned in the introduction to the edition, and so in this way they remain out of reach for scholars. If the interpolation is interesting, it may be edited for its own sake. For example, a passage present in some manuscripts of homily 38 by Gregory of Nazianzus, which was obviously introduced at some point in the transmission process, has been edited in an article; unfortunately, it was impossible to identify its author (Macé 2004). Some works considered "heretical" by the official Church were preserved only as interpolations in orthodox works (Tuilier 1987).

If the interpolated piece of text belongs to a known work, it can be considered an indirect witness to the corresponding part of that work because it was transmitted outside of it. Unfortunately, such cases are rarely documented. When collating the Armenian text of Pseudo-Dionysius' *Epistula de morte apostolorum Petri et Pauli* (see 4.5.4) in the manuscript Erevan, Matenadaran 993 (a hagiographical-homiletic collection copied in 1456), I discovered that the copyist (or his model) had interpolated into Dionysius' text a passage which belongs to the *Martyrium Pauli*, a second-century apocryphal text existing also in Armenian translation and transmitted in, among other manuscripts, Matenadaran 993. The text of the interpolation offers a variant reading (*ew asē pawłos c'neron* և ասէ պաւղոս ցներոն [and Paul speaks to Nero]) which is not found in the direct tradition of the *Martyrium*, where all manuscripts read "and he speaks to Caesar"; as a direct witness to the *Martyrium*, manuscript Matenadaran 993 presents a rather long omission including the passage in question (Calzolari 2017, 637).

3.2.5 Adaptations

Ancient and mediaeval texts were not only often reused; they were also often reworked: abridged (*recensio brevis* or *brevior*); summarised (epitome); expanded (*recensio fusior*); transposed into another genre, typically from poetry to prose or vice versa (paraphrase); rephrased (recension/redaction); and so on (on the Byzantine vocabulary and practice of rewriting, see Signes Codoñer 2014).

Depending on how deep the changes reach, another recension can or cannot be used as a direct or indirect witness to the transmission of the work. The Greek *Physiologus* (see 3.2.2), for example, is known in several recensions: three prose works in learned Greek, one verse adaptation, and one rewriting in "vulgar" mediaeval Greek (Sbordone 1936). Even in the prose adaptations, the text of the oldest recension was so much altered that the other two recensions cannot be used to establish the text of the first one. However, as far as the first recension is concerned, I was able to determine that the Greek tradition and the ancient translations are divided into two main branches, representing two different redactions of the same work. It is therefore possible to use the witnesses of one redaction to polarise some variant locations in the other redaction. For example, the adverb "καλῶς" [well] is present in manuscripts *a s Σ* of redaction *β* (see fig. 3.2-4), but omitted in *G M Γ O W*. In the corresponding passage of redaction *α*, the same adverb is present. Therefore (unless one supposes a contamination of one redaction by the other), the omission in *G M Γ O W* must be secondary, and if this is confirmed by other cases, it points to the existence of a hyparchetype common to these five manuscripts (*Va* is lacunary at this place). Similarly, Godfried Croenen has shown that it is possible to use one (authorial) recension of Jean Froissart's *Chronicles* (fourteenth century) to orientate the stemma of the manuscripts of the main recension (for a short methodological discussion, see Croenen 2010).

3.2.6 Paratextual elements

Marginal or interlinear corrections or indications of co-occurring variants in manuscripts can be the result either of philological emendation by mediaeval readers or of collation with other witnesses. In the latter case, these variants are sometimes accompanied in Greek manuscripts by γράφεται, "it is written [elsewhere]"; see fig. 3.2-5) or ἐν ἄλλῳ, "in another [witness]". For an example of a thorough collation of the text of a manuscript against another manuscript, lost in the meantime, see section 4.5.2 on Bessarion's (fifteenth-century) corrections to his exemplar of Proclus' commentary on Plato's *Parmenides*. In figure 3.2-6, the tenth-century copyist of the text (homily 38 by Gregory of Nazianzus, on Christmas) wrote in the margin next to the words "τὸ θεῖον" [the divine]: "ἐν ἄλλῳ τοὺς θεοὺς γραφὲν εὗρον" [in another [manuscript] I found "τοὺς θεοὺς" ["the gods"] written]. Interestingly, this variant is not found in the text of any still-extant manuscript, only in the margin of Paris, Bibliothèque nationale de France, gr. 515 and also in the margin of the codex Milano, Biblioteca Ambrosiana, E 50 inf., one of the two remaining illustrated uncial manuscripts of Gregory of Nazianzus' homilies.

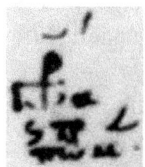

Fig. 3.2-5: Sinai, St Catherine's Monastery, gr. 399, f. 115r, marginal note: "γράφεται καὶ τραπῶμεν" [it is also written "τραπῶμεν"].

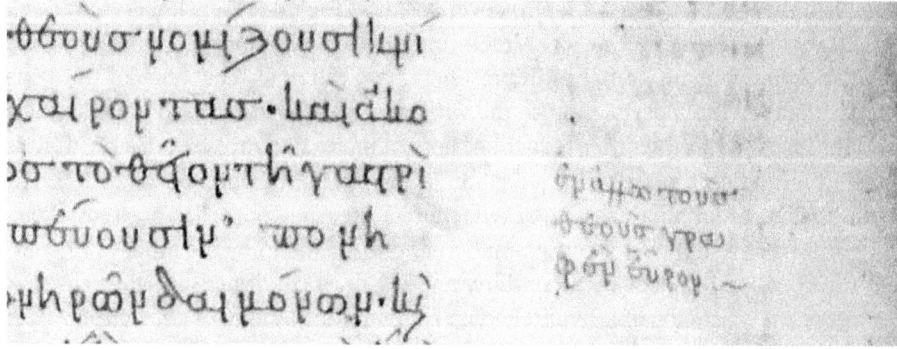

Fig. 3.2-6: Paris, Bibliothèque nationale de France, gr. 515, f. 124r, marginal note. Source: Gallica, Bibliothèque nationale de France, gallica.bnf.fr/ark:/12148/btv1b107215420/f128.image.r=grec%20515. Image: CC-BY-NC.

In the same way, glosses and other types of marginalia can be used as indirect witnesses: see Buzzoni (2011) for an example of the use of glosses in the study of the *Heliand* tradition.

3.2.7 Direct witnesses preserved in other media

Palimpsests (see 1.2.2) and papyri have often preserved works, especially from Greek and Latin literature from Antiquity, which would otherwise have been lost (Reynolds and Wilson 2013, 195–199). The text preserved on palimpsests or papyri is usually fragmentary because the material support may be heavily damaged and because the script has vanished (especially in the case of palimpsests) and may be hard to decipher. Because of this, the texts found in papyri and palimpsests are usually the object of a documentary edition and require a specific methodology (see Gippert 2015).

If they are not unique witnesses, palimpsests and papyri will usually be the oldest direct witnesses to works otherwise preserved. For example, the papyrus codex edited by Capron (2013) contains saints' lives of which there are also manuscripts and ancient translations – this allows a comparison between the fragments of the text preserved on the papyrus and the other witnesses. Because papyrus was a relatively cheaper material than parchment, papyri often preserve types of texts which may be characterised either as *Gebrauchsliteratur* or as documentary in nature (especially with commercial content), or sometimes as "school books" (see Turner 1968). For this reason, and not only because of their age, papyri are potentially very interesting witnesses, precisely because they did not necessarily follow the same "literary" path of transmission as manuscripts. There is an interesting methodological discussion about the place of papyri (the same could more or less be said about palimpsests as well) in a stemma. Collomp (1929) refutes the idea of the "eclecticism" of papyri (a theory according to which papyri would often contain readings from several families of mediaeval manuscripts), arguing that, because they are much older than the manuscripts, the variants they attest may often go back to the archetype or even predate it. The same line of argument was often taken by Irigoin (e.g. Irigoin 1968–1969, 138). In unpublished papers translated by Most, Timpanaro returns to this question as well (2005, 207–215).

Although they are much rarer, graffiti can also shed light on the history of a text otherwise transmitted in manuscripts. One famous example is the mediaeval (thirteenth- or fourteenth-century) graffito found in a cave near Vardzia (Georgia) containing two strophes from Shota Rustaveli's epos *The Knight in the Panther's Skin*, which is preserved in manuscripts, none of which are older than the sixteenth or seventeenth century (Gippert 2018, 157). Graffiti preserved in Pompeii also offer their share of literary verses and epigrams, for which they are amongst the oldest witnesses (see Milnor 2019).

Inscriptions can also serve as indirect tradition for literary works otherwise transmitted through manuscript tradition. For example, De Simini showed that extracts from two treatises written in Sanskrit (*Śivadharmaśāstra* and *Śivadharmottara*) and known through late manuscripts are quoted in mediaeval works and also known through inscriptions from as early as the eleventh century, much earlier than the manuscripts (De Simini 2016, esp. 237). Conversely, manuscripts can be used as an indirect tradition for existing but damaged or lost inscriptions: in his edition of Byzantine stone epigrams, for example, Rhoby (2014) more than once uses transcriptions of the inscriptions preserved in manuscripts.

3.2.8 Using indirect witnesses

In all the cases mentioned here, the main point of using indirect witnesses is that their text has been preserved "outside" the main tradition; they can therefore be used as an "outgroup" (see 5.2.1, 8.1.3.4) to orientate the stemma and document the early history of the textual tradition and the appearance of (hyp)archetypes. These witnesses should be used with great caution, however, and some of the methodological difficulties inherent to them have been highlighted above. Nevertheless, when they exist, indirect witnesses are indispensable for gaining access to the earliest stages of a tradition because direct witnesses to these earliest stages are usually missing. In this way, they often provide a clue for understanding how the tradition developed from the earliest stages on, and they will often help orientate the stemma, as illustrated in 3.2.2 (example 2 and fig. 3.2-4). Ancient translations are especially important in this respect because they have preserved larger portions of text than other types of indirect witnesses. Unfortunately, translations are not always considered in the process of editing, for reasons that have been explained above (3.2.2). It may indeed be perfectly justified not to make use of indirect translations; but, as a rule, one should never believe that direct witnesses alone are enough, because there is always much to be gained by looking at the indirect tradition of any work.

3.3 Transcription and collation
Tara Andrews

Once the manuscript witnesses to a text have been gathered and scrutinised for the clues they might give about the transmission history of a text, the individual text instances must be compared so that their similarities and differences may be analysed. This is the phase of textual criticism known as *collatio* (see 2.2, 6.2). In a digital environment, it is increasingly common to separate this phase into two distinct steps, transcription and collation. When the collation is made, a list of variant locations, or in certain cases *loci critici*, can be produced for further analysis. It should be noted that, although stemmatic analysis eventually requires the editor to distinguish significant from insignificant variation, this cannot be done before the texts are compared in the first place; the question of how to make that distinction will therefore not be treated in depth in this section.

3.3.1 Definition of terms

T r a n s c r i p t i o n is the act of transferring a text from one carrier to another. Normally, this refers to a transfer from one medium to another: for instance, the transcription of a recorded speech, or the transcription of a handwritten document into a corresponding digital form. The word may also refer to the textual version, or document, that results from this act. Transcription may also be said to happen in the process of collation if the editor chooses to collate texts without digital assistance (Nury 2018, 109–111). Such collations, however, are not normally considered "transcriptions" in the usual sense of the word.

C o l l a t i o n is the act of comparing different instances of a text; a collation is a document that contains the result of this comparison. A collation can take a number of different forms. Non-digital forms can include marginal notes on a physical version of a text, or a series of tabular records (fig. 3.3-1).

Digital forms of a collation can include a spreadsheet that mimics or extends the non-digital form of tabular collation (normally referred to as an a l i g n m e n t t a b l e), an XML document (Andrews 2009) or relational database (Robinson 1989) that stores a list of textual variants, or other less commonly used data structures such as the "multi-version document" advocated by Desmond Schmidt and Robert Colomb (2009). The advantage of a digitally stored collation is that, under most circumstances, it can be transformed more or less automatically into an apparatus of variants, an alignment table, or a variant graph (see 3.4) for display and examination. This is true no matter which format has been chosen to store the collation, although the particular mechanics of the transformation will vary.

A v a r i a n t l o c a t i o n arises when different manuscripts show different readings at a point that can be considered "the same place" in the text. Figures 3.3-2a–c show, in each of the various visualisations, an example of a variant location – the point in the collated text where "ἠκριβωκότων" (perfect passive participle of ἀκριβόω, "to make exact or accurate") appears in most manuscripts but an alternative, "ἠκριβηκότων", appears in manuscripts *P* and *S*. Variant locations are the units of change upon which almost all methods for stemma construction operate.

3.3.2 Transcription

One of the first decisions that must be made by the philologist who works with a particular text is to determine the extent to which transcription of that text is neces-

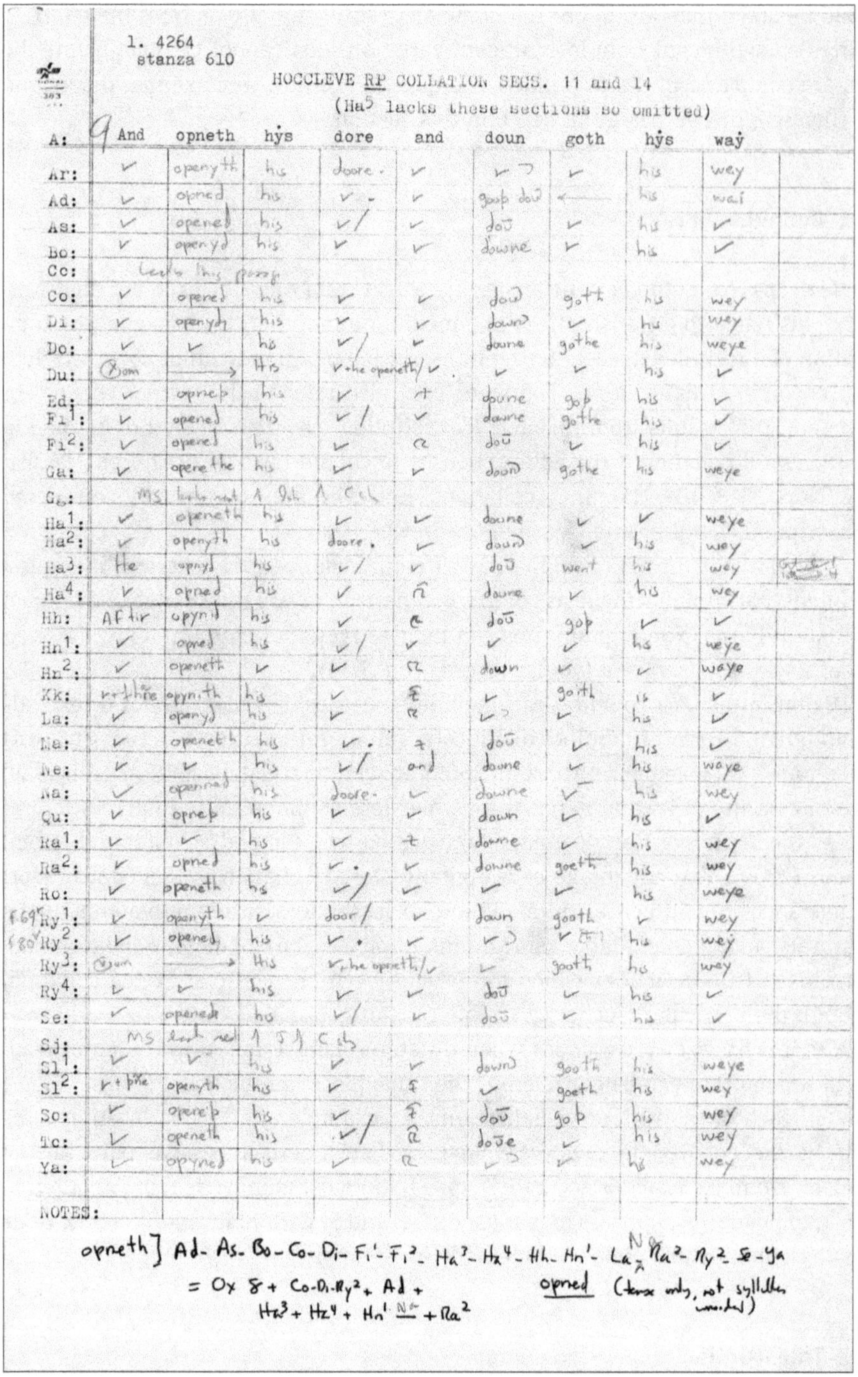

Fig. 3.3-1: Example of a tabular collation: Thomas Hoccleve's *Regiment of Princes*, line 4264. Hoccleve Archive, University of Texas Libraries. Image: CC-BY-NC-SA.

1.7 ἠκριβωκότων] ἠκριβηκότων PS 8 δι' ὧν…ἁμαρτημάτων] om. P 9 Ἐπειδή] γὰρ add. EKQ 11 μετανοήσῃ] μετανοήσει A 13–14 ὡς εἴρηται] om. DEFHKQ 14 ἐνταῦθα] om. T, post ἁμαρτήσας transp. Q   14–15   ἐνταῦθα…ἀδιαφόρως] om. P 14–15 ἁμαρτήσας…ἀγαθοεργήσας] ἀγαθοεργήσας … ἁμαρτήσας T17 ἔχομεν] ἔχωμεν A DF$^{a.c.}$, ἐχόμενα EKQ 20 τις] om. F21 κρίνετε] κρίνεται A T DH (sed ε H$^{s.l.}$) 22 κριθήσεσθε] κριθήσεσθαι A, κριθῆτε Q |κρίνῃ] κρίνει A T DEFHKQ$^{a.c.}$ 24 ἑαυτοῦ] om. PS26 οἰκονομῆται] οἰκονομεῖται S T DEFGH

Fig. 3.3-2a: A print-style apparatus of variants.

A	τοῦ πνεύματος	ἠκριβωκότων	τέσσαρας εἶναι τρόπους	δι ὧν συγχώρησις γίνεται ἁμαρτημάτων	δύο ἐνταῦθα καὶ δύο ἐν τῷ μέλλοντι Ἐπειδή
S	τοῦ πνεύματος	ἠκριβηκότων	τέσσαρας εἶναι τρόπους	δι ὧν συγχώρησις γίνεται ἁμαρτημάτων	δύο ἐνταῦθα καὶ δύο ἐν τῷ μέλλοντι Ἐπειδή
T	τοῦ πνεύματος	ἠκριβωκότων	τέσσαρας εἶναι τρόπους	δι ὧν συγχώρησις γίνεται ἁμαρτημάτων	δύο ἐνταῦθα καὶ δύο ἐν τῷ μέλλοντι Ἐπειδή
C	τοῦ πνεύματος	ἠκριβωκότων	τέσσαρας εἶναι τρόπους	δι ὧν συγχώρησις γίνεται ἁμαρτημάτων	δύο ἐνταῦθα καὶ δύο ἐν τῷ μέλλοντι Ἐπειδή
D	τοῦ πνεύματος	ἠκριβωκότων	τέσσαρας εἶναι τρόπους	δι ὧν συγχώρησις γίνεται ἁμαρτημάτων	δύο ἐνταῦθα καὶ δύο ἐν τῷ μέλλοντι Ἐπειδή
E	τοῦ πνεύματος	ἠκριβωκότων	τέσσαρας εἶναι τρόπους	δι ὧν συγχώρησις γίνεται ἁμαρτημάτων	δύο ἐνταῦθα καὶ δύο ἐν τῷ μέλλοντι Ἐπειδή
F	τοῦ πνεύματος	ἠκριβωκότων	τέσσαρας εἶναι τρόπους	δι ὧν συγχώρησις γίνεται ἁμαρτημάτων	δύο ἐνταῦθα καὶ δύο ἐν τῷ μέλλοντι Ἐπειδή
H	τοῦ πνεύματος	ἠκριβωκότων	τέσσαρας εἶναι τρόπους	δι ὧν συγχώρησις γίνεται ἁμαρτημάτων	δύο ἐνταῦθα καὶ δύο ἐν τῷ μέλλοντι Ἐπειδή
K	τοῦ πνεύματος	ἠκριβωκότων	τέσσαρας εἶναι τρόπους	δι ὧν συγχώρησις γίνεται ἁμαρτημάτων	δύο ἐνταῦθα καὶ δύο ἐν τῷ μέλλοντι Ἐπειδή
P	τοῦ πνεύματος	ἠκριβηκότων	τέσσαρας εἶναι τρόπους		δύο ἐνταῦθα καὶ δύο ἐν τῷ μέλλοντι Ἐπειδή
Q	τοῦ πνεύματος	ἠκριβωκότων	τέσσαρας εἶναι τρόπους	δι ὧν συγχώρησις γίνεται ἁμαρτημάτων	δύο ἐνταῦθα καὶ δύο ἐν τῷ μέλλοντι Ἐπειδή

Fig. 3.3-2b: An alignment table.

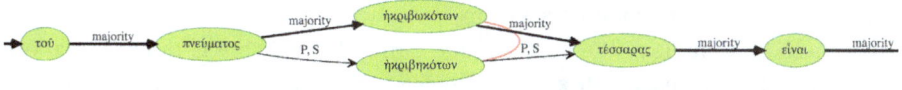

Fig. 3.3-2c: A variant graph. (The text for all visualisations is from De Vos et al. 2010.)

sary. This decision is usually made on a combination of scholarly-theoretical and practical grounds. As this is a handbook about stemmatology, we will deal here with the transcription of texts that exist in at least three instances, and quite often many more. (A *codex unicus*, or text surviving in only a single copy, cannot have a meaningful stemma; a text that has two instances can have a stemma drawn, but the stemma will not have any further use in the editorial process.) The decisions made about the methods and extent of transcription will, therefore, be a function of the editor's desire to represent and examine the minutiae of variation in each text, the overall length of the text, the number of manuscripts that would need to be transcribed, and the amount of time that is available for the work.

The first choice facing the scholarly editor is: should all texts be transcribed in full? If the use of computer-assisted collation tools is planned, then the answer must be "yes"; if the editors plan instead to collate the texts manually, then they may choose to transcribe only one text in full. This would then become the "b a s e t e x t", against which all other texts are compared. The relative trade-offs of computer-assisted vs manual collation will be discussed below, in section 3.3.3.

Digital transcription
Insofar as the vast majority of critical editions produced nowadays are done with the computer in some form, the focus here is on modes of digital transcription. There are several possibilities for how to transcribe a manuscript text; the editor's choice will depend on the later use to which the transcription will be put. Perhaps the simplest option is to make a plain text transcription; this entails typing the text of the manuscript into a text editor or word processor, and saving it in plain text format (see 3.4.5). The primary advantage of this approach is its simplicity. Many philologists, however, will quickly discover that the inability to use more than the most basic formatting becomes more of a hindrance than a help.

At this point, many philologists will be tempted to use the more advanced formatting features provided by word processing software – to change the font size, include footnotes, use colour or superscript formatting to represent additions or deletions, and so on. This must be avoided, unless the philologist intends that the transcription should never be imported into another tool! Hardly any word processor file formats can be read reliably by other programs; if the transcription is to be used further, it would need to be saved as plain text, and the formatting features in question would be lost.

Markup languages and markup schemes
To address this problem, the best solution currently available is to use a markup scheme. By far the most well known of these is the XML scheme provided by the TEI consortium and described in the TEI guidelines (tei-c.org/p5; see also 3.4 below). These guidelines provide a way to describe, in a form that is more or less machine-readable, the vast majority of textual and palaeographical phenomena that occur in manuscript texts. TEI XML has been the transcription format of choice for the vast majority of digital edition projects since the early 1990s, and has a large community behind its use. Users of TEI can also draw on a well-developed ecosystem of tools and programming libraries to parse XML documents, search and query them, and transform them into common online display formats such as HTML, EPUB, and PDF.

XML-based markup of text is justified by the OHCO model – the idea that text can be expressed as an "ordered hierarchy of content objects" (DeRose et al. 1990). The hierarchy imposed by XML syntax is a strict one: a text must be modelled, conceptually, as a branching (but never merging) tree (see figs 3.3-3a–b for an example). A text, for instance, can contain front matter, main body, and back matter; the main body can contain chapters, which contain paragraphs, which contain sentences, and so on.

```
<anthology>
  <poem>
    <heading>The SICK ROSE</heading>
    <stanza>
      <line>O Rose thou art sick.</line>
      <line>The invisible worm,</line>
      <line>That flies in the night</line>
      <line>In the howling storm:</line>
    </stanza>
    <stanza>
      <line>Has found out thy bed</line>
      <line>Of crimson joy:</line>
      <line>And his dark secret love</line>
      <line>Does thy life destroy.</line>
    </stanza>
  </poem>
  <!-- more poems go here -->
</anthology>
```

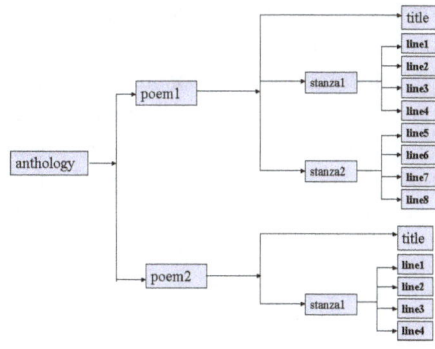

Fig. 3.3-3a: Example XML markup for a poem. Source: tei-c.org/release/doc/tei-p5-doc/en/html/SG.html.

Fig. 3.3-3b: Corresponding hierarchy model for the poem in fig. 3.3-3a. Source: tei-c.org/release/doc/tei-p5-doc/en/html/SG.html.

Alongside the increasingly widespread adoption of XML for text transcription came the realisation that the OHCO model is not always entirely adequate to describe a text (e.g. Renear, Mylonas, and Durand 1996). How, for instance, should the scholar deal with a quotation that begins in the middle of a paragraph and continues to the next paragraph? How should a manuscript text be made to fit into a strict hierarchy that its author, or its scribe, had no conception of when the text was written, and would therefore quite often violate? One can imagine, for example, an authorial rewrite of three and a half lines of text that cross a chapter boundary, or an annotation added to the margin of a manuscript that refers to a portion of the text not precisely defined.

These objections to the OHCO model have led some scholars to propose alternative schemes for text markup; perhaps the best known of these is LMNL (Piez 2014), which rejects the idea of a strict hierarchy, allowing arbitrary regions of the text to be annotated without regard to their place in the overall text structure. LMNL is not widely used, however, owing primarily to the lack of the technical infrastructure that makes XML so popular.

Normalisation for transcription
Alongside choosing a format, the next decision that a scholarly editor must make is the extent to which the transcription should be normalised for spelling, punctuation, layout, and so on. Here, the editor places the transcription on a continuum between the idea of a documentary transcription (Pierazzo 2011), in which every feature of the manuscript is represented as faithfully as possible in the chosen medium, and an interpretative transcription, in which the text of the manuscript is represented in a way that minimises the differences between versions.

There is no one "correct" level of normalisation to be observed in the transcription phase. The extent to which a text is normalised will greatly affect the possible results of collation and identification of variants, which will in turn have an impact on any stemmatic analysis to be done. If the editor chooses the more labour-intensive documentary approach at the transcription phase, there remains the opportunity to apply normalisation techniques in a later phase of text collation. If, on the other hand, the editor chooses at the outset to produce normalised transcriptions, the collation can never be made to reflect any manuscript variation that was omitted at the transcription stage. In making this decision, scholars should carefully consider their overall purpose in editing the text, as well as any material or time constraints on the project.

3.3.3 Collation

Although the acts of transcription and collation are often regarded as separate steps in digital workflows for critical editing, many textual scholars regard the collation as a distinct entity in its own right, comprising the text of the individual witnesses and the correspondence between them, inseparable from the acts that go into its creation. The collation is not only the centrepiece of a critical edition of a text, but also what makes any sort of analysis of the transmission of a text possible. Without a collation, there can be no stemma. We therefore need to understand what a collation is and how this might vary depending on context.

In recent decades, the concept of what a collation is has evolved, and varied, according to the aims of the editor whose definition is used and according to the capabilities of the time. Into and beyond the 1960s, one conceived of a collation as a process carried out with reference to a base text, usually some kind of norm such as a published edition (Colwell and Tune 1964, 253). By the early 1990s, perhaps spurred on by the adoption of computer technology, the relative ease of splitting text automatically into individual words based on the spaces between them, and the wide availability of algorithms for pairwise comparison, collation was described as the comparison of "two genetic states or two versions [...] of a text" (Grésillon 1994, 242) and something that was done "word for word" (Stussi 1994, 123), albeit still with respect to a reference text. Computational methods allowed this precision to be taken farther still, as is demonstrated by another definition of collation as an act that was carried out "character for character" (Shillingsburg 1996, 134). This definition is striking in another aspect: rather than referring to comparison with a base text, its author calls for the comparison of "all versions that could conceivably have been authoritatively revised or corrected". It is around this time that the notion of the base text ceases to be a central part of the definition of the collation. Later scholars define collation as an act whose purpose is to find agreements and divergences between witnesses (Plachta 1997, 137) or explicitly to track the descent of a text (Kline 1998, 270); they differentiate between collation as a process of comparison (carried out "word-for-word and comma-for-comma"; Eggert 2013, 103) and the result of comparison, which is known as the "historical collation" (Greetham 1994, 4); or they describe collation again as a process, whose result is described simply as lists of variant readings (Greetham 2013, 21).

From these descriptions, it is possible to detect a converging (though also evolving) definition of collation, and a distinction between the act and its result. Collation may be carried out against a reference text, pairwise, or as a many-to-many comparison. The comparison may be done at the word level, at the character level, or at another unspecified syntactic or semantic level, according to the sensibilities of the editor. The question of authority enters the picture with Shillingsburg's definition (1996); this arises more in modern genetic criticism than in classical or mediaeval textual criticism, but conveys the idea that some manuscripts may represent definite departures from the "original", "authorial", or "main" text and that these might therefore be left out of a collation. The purpose of collation is usually given as being the discovery of where witnesses to a text converge and diverge; one might also claim that its purpose is to track the descent or the genesis of a text.

The act of collation produces a result, also known as a collation. Although the term "collation" can be used for the set of data that results from the process in any of its forms (whether that be a spreadsheet based on a copy text, a list of variants keyed on an existing edition, or even a digital object such as a JSON-format alignment table produced by collation software programs), it usually has a more specific meaning. Eggert (2013, 103) uses for this the term "historical collation", by which he means "an extended report" on the substantive variants between the texts. It is important to note here that the historical collation is almost always a curated and pruned version of the results of comparison of the text, a fact to which Eggert also alludes when he writes that the historical collation "is often restricted to [...] 'substantives', leaving the now-orphaned commas and other 'accidentals' to look after themselves". In that sense, the collation, as many textual scholars understand it, is a document that reflects not only the "raw" results of comparing a text but also the scholarly work of interpreting these results into a particular argument about the constitution and history of that text.

Here, however, it would be useful to draw a distinction between the collation and the critical apparatus. These things can easily be conflated; for example, Greetham (1994, 4) refers to the *apparatus criticus* and historical collation as a representation of a "collation and the results of emendation". A reader might deduce from this that, for Greetham, a "historical collation" is the *apparatus criticus* of an edition minus any emendations. This is, however, almost certainly a misinterpretation of his words. Whereas a collation is a catalogue of variant readings in a text and may or may not be constructed with reference to a base text, an *apparatus criticus*, as its name implies, is a record of variants that takes the critically established text as its point of reference. In fact, the *apparatus criticus* may restrict itself to those variants judged to be genealogically revealing, that is, "significant errors". Maas (1960, 8) even goes so far to say that only the non-mechanically decidable readings of the archetype, which he calls "variant-carriers", deserve a place in the critical apparatus; in this case, even the substantive readings would be omitted if they were clearly secondary. Since a collation is a necessary prerequisite to the *constitutio textus*, and the *apparatus criticus* is a result of this process, it is clear that they cannot be the same thing. This distinction also serves to explain why, contrary to the expectations of many users of a critical edition, textual witnesses can almost never be reconstructed in full from the edited text and its apparatus.

Manual collation
A collation can, naturally, be made without the use of automated alignment tools. In this case, the scholar will follow the advice of West (1973, 66): write down the differences between each manuscript and a reference text. West recommends the use of a printed edition for this; if no edition is yet in print, the scholar can choose a manuscript copy of the text that seems well suited for the purpose. According to West, the collator should record even apparent trivialities in orthography, as they may be unexpectedly useful in constructing the stemma or otherwise understanding the relationship between manuscripts; this is, in essence, an argument for keeping normalisation to a minimum at the transcription phase. West also recommends including information in the collation about page divisions, scribal or second-hand corrections, and so on.

Automatic collation
In order to use any sort of automated collation software, every manuscript witness needs to be transcribed in full; the software operates on the basis of these transcriptions to identify and align the readings they contain. The author of one of the first well-known text-collation tools was initially taken with "the notion of feeding these manuscripts into one end of the computer, which would then extrude a critical apparatus on the other" (Robinson 1989, 99). His tool, COLLATE, was eventually designed to work interactively and closely with the editor. Robinson included the facility not only to align variant readings, but also to normalise selected readings and to choose the readings that should constitute the edited text, so that the result was not merely a collation but essentially a fully constituted text and its *apparatus criticus*.

The current generation of collation tools, on the other hand, limit themselves strictly to the act of comparison; the authors of the CollateX tool describe collation simply as text comparison and refer to it as a process (Haentjens Dekker et al. 2015, 453). The process of collation around which these tools are based, also known as the collation workflow, is known as the "Gothenburg model" after its definition there at a workshop in 2009. The workflow is composed of discrete steps – tokenisation, normalisation, alignment, analysis, and visualisation – which, taken together, form the process by which a scholarly collation artefact is generally produced.

Tokenisation refers to the subdivision of a text into discrete units suitable for comparison. Normally this is done word for word, but depending on the language, structure, or grammatical rules of a text, the units might comprise multiple words (e.g. "et cetera", "sine qua non") or, on the other hand, might split words apart (e.g. "filio-que").

Normalisation refers to the decision, for each token in the text, about whether to compare it to other tokens in its precise literal form, or whether to treat it as being a version of another known word for the sake of alignment. If spelling normalisation was not incorporated into a transcription process, it is often done here. Other examples of normalisation include the use of morphological analysis tools such as stemmers (which produce the root stem of a word, so that, for example, "give" and "given" are recognised as corresponding readings), the conversion of spelled-out numbers into their modern numerical equivalents (e.g. representing both "forty-two" and "XLII" as "42"), or the use of sound-value software such as SoundEx to account for shifts in spelling (as in Birnbaum 2014). It is important to realise that, in terms of automatic collation, the purpose of this normalisation is *not* to produce a canonical version of each reading, but merely to provide hints for a better alignment of the variant texts.

Alignment is the meat of an automatic collation process, whereby the (normalised) tokens of each text are compared with each other, and a proposal is produced for how they correspond to each other. The result of an alignment most often takes the form of a table, as described above; it may also take the form of a variant graph (see below).

Analysis and visualisation must follow any automatically produced text alignment. A good visualisation of results allows for a meaningful analysis, which is the scrutiny of a proposed alignment by the textual scholar. The purpose here is to evaluate the overall correctness of a given alignment. A scholar may choose to adjust the approach taken to tokenisation or normalisation until a satisfactory alignment is produced; alternatively, the scholar may wish to use the alignment as a starting point for producing a satisfactory collation without rerunning the automated steps.

Manual vs automatic collation

The choice of automatic or manual collation is a topic on which most scholars will eventually develop strong preferences, as well as strong opinions on which is faster or more efficient. In the case of automatic collation, the bulk of the work is in transcription of the source witnesses – a task that for some edition projects is too daunting to contemplate, but is perfectly feasible for others. Depending on how normalisation is handled during the transcription process, the collation workflow steps described above usually progress very rapidly once the transcriptions are finished. The use of automatic collation has two advantages: first, that the scholar emerges from the process with detailed transcriptions of each manuscript witness, and second, that there is no need to preselect a base text for comparison of witnesses. This allows for an easier and more flexible construction of an *apparatus criticus* in the final edition.

For manual collation, on the other hand, the bulk of the work is in the meticulous comparison and alignment of, and record-keeping about, a succession of witnesses. In practice, a manual collation must be done with reference to a base text chosen for the purpose at the outset. The scholar must therefore be very sure of the suitability of the chosen base text; once the collation has begun, a change of base can mean the repetition of an enormous amount of work. Moreover, with manual collation there can be an increased incentive for the scholar to speed up the process by disregarding the advice of West and omitting variation that is deemed to be trivial. This is particularly true for edition projects where full transcriptions were considered to be impractical, since a manual collation is essentially a codified form of normalised transcription. Insofar as a collation is meticulous and complete, it is possible in theory to reconstruct individual witness transcriptions from the collation itself; however, any variation omitted from the manually produced collation cannot be reconstructed at a later stage.

Where the text is unusually long and the number of its manuscripts is unusually large, as with, for instance the *Divina Commedia* of Dante (see the discussion of overabundant traditions in 6.2.2.1), an alternative to collating the full text is to select a certain number of *loci critici* (see 3.3.4 for a full definition) which are considered representative of the manuscript tradition and which will be used as the basis of comparison and stemma creation. In order to use this method successfully, the editor must be able to justify the selection of particular passages; for this, it is necessary to have a thorough and detailed grasp of the text, its manuscripts, and the sorts of variation they display.

3.3.4 Variant, variant location, and *locus criticus*

When a collation has been made, the scholar is left with information on where the witnesses to the text can be seen to differ, and what those differences are. A text, as carried in a particular witness, can be thought of as a series of r e a d i n g s – that is, a series of lexical units that are the reader's interpretation of the marks upon the page. An individual reading is often equivalent to a word, but in certain contexts might be multiple words (see the discussion of tokenisation above), or in other contexts might be suffixes (e.g. "-que"). Since each reading has its particular place in the text sequence in a given witness, each reading can be thought of as having a location.

To collate a text, then, is to align these sequences of readings. Once that is done, the collation (particularly in its form as an alignment table) contains an overall sequence of locations and, for each location, a set of readings that occur in that

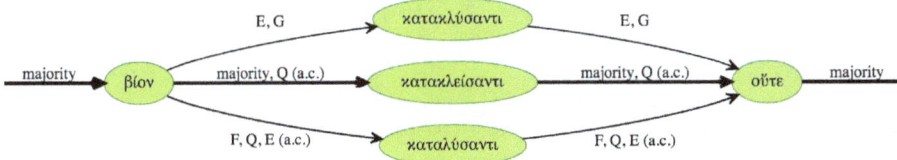

Fig. 3.3-4: A variant location as represented in a graph. This location includes corrections made by the scribe at the time of copying; the state of the text before these corrections has been denoted with the abbreviation "a.c." (*ante correctionem*). In this example, witness E has been corrected from "καταλύσαντι" to "κατακλύσαντι", and witness Q from "κατακλείσαντι" to "καταλύσαντι".

Referentie Variant (regel)	nr.	Griekse tekst	
		Basistekst	**Variant**
...	...	...	...
1.41.2.	38	κατακλείσαντι	κατακλύσαντι (1) καταλύσαντι (2)

Fig. 3.3-5a: A variant location with a lemma specified (here as "Basistekst").

location across the collated witnesses. When this set contains more than one reading, those readings are known as v a r i a n t s, and the place where they occur is their v a r i a n t   l o c a t i o n (see figs 3.3-4–3.3-5). The discovery and definition of these locations is key to the establishment of a stemma, no matter the method used for the stemma construction. The set of variant locations is the information, deriving from a collation, with which a stemmatic analysis is done.

Depending on the methods adopted for stemmatic analysis of the text, the editor may designate a subset of these variant locations to be *loci critici*: those places in the text where the variation is believed to betray information about the copying (i.e. text-genealogical) relationships between the manuscripts – that is to say, those places that show "significant" variation – and on which construction of the stemmatic tree should be based (see 2.2.5, 4.3.1). In some cases (see 3.3.3) the *loci critici* will be chosen prior to collation; they can also be chosen based on the results of collation, either of the whole text or of samples from it.

Whatever means is chosen to create the stemma, the editor will eventually use it to work through all variant locations in the text and make a choice about which (if any) of the extant readings should become part of the critical text (see 6.2 for a fuller description of this process). This reading will be designated as the l e m m a, and from that point on the term "variant" will refer specifically to the readings at the given location that differ from the lemma.

While most textual variation represented in a collation will concern the set of variants at a single location within the text, there are a few sorts of variation that comprise multiple locations. One common example of variation across locations is

1.27 ὡς...οἶδε] om. P^{a.c} (add. in mg. P ead. manu) 28 καθαίρει αὐτὸν] καθεαυτὸν S |εἰ] ἡ T, ὁ P 29 εὐχαριστία] εὐχαριστεία A PS G 31–32 ἀχαριστίας] ἀχαριστείας A P F 35 πολλὰς] πολλάκις CPS 37 εὖ ποιῶν] εὐποιῶν PS 37–38 ὑπεραπελογήσατο] ὑπεραπολογήσατο S 39 ἀπιστία] ἀπιστεία A T | ἑτέραν] om. PS 40 οὖν] om. EGK | τῷ] τῶν K | ἀπιστία] ἀπιστεία A P D 41 κατακλείσαντι] καταλύσαντι E^{a.c}FQ^{s.l.}, κατακλύσαντι E^{s.l.}G

Fig. 3.3-5b: The same variant location as represented in an *apparatus criticus* (highlighted).

textual repetition, for example when a scribe copies the same line of a manuscript twice in a row. As another example, when a reading has been moved in the text relative to other manuscripts, we speak of tr a n s p o s i t i o n. Some editors, however, refer to this as tr a n s l o c a t i o n; for them, transposition refers only to the situation where two readings have been swapped with each other. That is, given a base text that reads:

The **white** cat played with the dirty ball,

an example of translocation would be:

The cat played with the dirty **white** ball,

and an example of "true" transposition would be:

The dirty cat played with the **white** ball.

Editors may also speak of i n v e r s i o n, which is when the transposition involves two contiguous words, for example if one manuscript reads "ἑστῶσα βοτάνη" where the others read "βοτάνη ἑστῶσα" [grass standing].

The question of how to represent transposition (or translocation) adequately in a collation is a complex one. For the case where the transposition or translocation is not a simple inversion but is still relatively isolated (i.e. it comprises only one or a few contiguous readings), it usually suffices to add a row to the collation table (assuming one is collating manually). The collation software CollateX can also attempt to detect and mark translocations in its output, which works reasonably well for small and isolated cases. However the collation is rendered, the presence of a transposition will usually lead to overlapping entries in the resulting *apparatus criticus* in order to accommodate variation within the component readings as well as the transposition itself (see figs 3.3-6a–c).

In general, if the text to be collated includes substantial dislocation of text, the resulting collation – and the resulting apparatus – can quickly become very intricate and complex, especially if the editor also wishes to note variants of individual readings within the dislocated segment. One strategy is to collate these segments in a separate table and indicate in the main collation where this segment is located, in which witnesses, with reference to the rest of the text. If the editor is using auto-

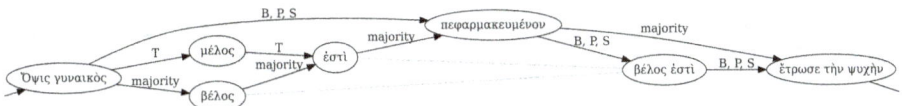

Fig. 3.3-6a: A transposition as rendered in a CollateX result graph. Note that the words "βέλος ἐστὶ" [is an arrow] appear twice.

Referentie Variant (regel)	nr.	Griekse tekst	
		Basistekst	Variant
9.1.1.	60	βέλος	μέλος
9.1.2.	61	βέλος ἐστὶ πεφαρμακευμένον	πεφαρμακευμένον βέλος ἐστὶ

Fig. 3.3-6b: The same transposition marked in a tabular collation. Note the need for the reading "βέλος" [arrow] to appear in both collation rows.

9.1 Ὄψις] ἡ praem. H | βέλος] μέλος T | βέλος ἐστὶ] post πεφαρμακευμένον transp. BPS 4 οὐ] οὔτε Q | πανδήμοις] δήμοις DEGHK, οὐκ ἐμφιλοχωρεῖ add. EGK | οὐδὲ] οὔτε Q 5 περιάγει] παραβάλλει Q 7 πάρεργον] παρανάλωμα H | τῶν ἐχθρῶν] τὸν ἐχθρόν A, τὸν ἐχθρῶν T^{a.c.} (τῶν T^{p.c.})8 μὴ δῷς] μηδαμῶς S | αὐταῖς] αὐτῆς P 12 λαλοῦσι] καὶ praem. Q 13 σεμνῶς] σεμναὶ P 13–14 ἀγνείας] ἀγνοίας P 15 ἀνένευσεν] ἀνάνευσον P

Fig. 3.3-6c: The same transposition represented in an *apparatus criticus*.

mated collation tools, it is often a good idea in any case to break the text into discrete logical segments, as the collation results improve markedly. If some of these segments are dislocated in some witnesses, a record will need to be kept of the respective order of collated segments across all witnesses.

Additions to, and omissions from, a text are also spoken of in reference to a variant location. These arise from the situation where, at a particular location, certain witnesses have no reading at all. In the absence of a base text and before the establishment of at least a preliminary stemma, it is impossible to label the missing readings as omissions, or conversely to label the readings that do exist at that location as additions. The terms a d d i t i o n and o m i s s i o n therefore gain their meaning only when a particular reading at the location (or, indeed, the absence of a reading there) is given some form of authority. Moreover, in the particular case of additions and omissions, the added or omitted text is usually considered a single reading, no matter its size (see fig. 3.3-7).

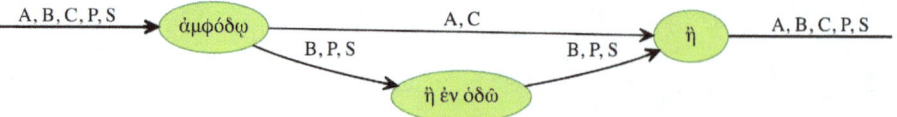

Fig. 3.3-7: An example of a reading that has been either added or omitted. The editors eventually chose to regard this as an addition (which is not expressed in the graph).

3.3.5 Normalisation for collation

Given the wide variety in ancient and mediaeval orthography, a full and exact collation of diplomatically transcribed witnesses will often show a great deal of variation that does not seem to impact the sense of the text; this may include spelling variants, abbreviation marks, accents, or variant letter forms. While in some cases, for instance in mediaeval works such as the *Hildebrandslied* (Baesecke 1945) where the dialect is itself an object of study, the editor may wish to retain every orthographical detail, in other cases the editor, or the reader, would prefer to reduce the amount of variation to be dealt with. In this case the editor will subject the text to a second process of n o r m a l i s a t i o n, which usually involves the substitution of a reading with a canonically written form of that reading. The obvious challenge, then, is to define what constitutes "canonical" in each particular situation. The particular conventions will depend as much on the text in question and the degree to which differences must be scrutinised as on the history and norms of the language and writing system that is employed in the text.

For the purposes of publication, the editor will usually choose a single set of orthographical conventions to use; each reading that is recognised as carrying the same text will then be written in the same manner. For example, the article written as "τον" in a manuscript may be given its usual accent and be rendered as "τὸν" in its normalised form; spelling will also be normalised. It follows naturally from this that the question of whether two readings carry the same text is in most cases up to the judgement of the editor. For example, if the two readings "κρίνεται" and "κρίνετε" are seen, which are both forms of the verb κρίνω, "to separate; to choose", the editor may choose to regard the second as a spelling variation of the first, given the context of the surrounding sentence and the fact that the pronunciation of αι and ε in Greek had already stopped being distinguishable in the classical period. On the other hand, it is also possible to conclude that, since these are two distinct recognisable conjugations of κρίνω (third-person present singular middle/passive indicative and second-person present plural active indicative, respectively), one should not be normalised to the other.

For the purposes of stemmatic analysis, entirely separate rules for normalisation may be needed. Here, we come back to the advice of West to note even apparent trivialities; it may be that a peculiar spelling or abbreviation of a word, or even a strange shape of a glyph, turns out to explain the emergence of an otherwise inexplicable copying error in the textual tradition and thereby shed light on the stemma, even if it is correctly interpreted in a different branch of the tradition. An example of sorts can be found in book 25 of the *Speculum historiale* of Vincent of Beauvais; the vulgate printing of 1624 (Vincentius Bellovacensis 1624) erroneously numbers as "Cap. CXIX" a chapter which is marked merely as "C.XIX" in its manuscript exemplars but is indicated more clearly as "Capitulum XIX" in other witnesses (e.g. Roma, Archivium Generale Ordinis Praedicatorum MS XIV.28b). It is, strictly speaking, debatable whether this error constitutes a significant one in the Lachmannian sense, and it concerns a reading that is almost paratextual in nature, which an editor may well be tempted to skip altogether in the collation; nevertheless, it does reveal some information concerning the textual transmission. Textual scholars will thus, in their analysis, often want to take into account variation, such as spelling, peculiar orthography, or even ink highlights, that is unlikely to be desired in a printed apparatus. To complicate the matter even further, some automated collation tools provide a string substitution feature so that a given string can be collated in place of the reading itself. This is also referred to as "normalisation". For example, given the two sentence fragments "the lazy dogs" and "the lazy sleeping dog", the user of a collation tool will want to ensure that "dog" aligns with "dogs", and may achieve this by normalising both words to "dog", "ANIMAL", or even "NOUN".

It is usually at the normalisation stage that editors must confront the question of how to handle punctuation within the text (see also 4.3.4). This first requires an answer to the question of whether punctuation marks should be regarded as readings in their own right, or simply as aids to the interpretation of the words and sentences they accompany. The latter point of view provides many editors with the justification necessary to discard entirely (or almost entirely) the punctuation of the manuscript witnesses once it has played its role in the interpretation of that witness's readings; punctuation is then reintroduced in the finished edition based on the conventions that modern readers expect (see 4.3.4). If, instead, punctuation is treated at the level of readings (either as independent reading tokens or combined with the readings it accompanies), then it too must at some stage undergo normalisation, and the considerations set out here concerning normalisation of readings in general also apply.

3.4 Data representation
Joris van Zundert

These days, as an editor, it may be hard to avoid the use of computers altogether. Even scholars aiming exclusively at a printed book edition will usually prepare such an edition using a computer. When inferring a stemma, the use of computers becomes even more likely. If a textual scholar opts to use digital tools for this, once direct (3.1) and indirect (3.2) witnesses have been found and collated (3.3), the resulting data needs to be represented and stored in a digital environment. Computational stemmatological analysis requires variant information as input and results in various kinds of output. Both input and output information can be represented in various digital forms. This section provides an introduction to the more technical sides of dealing with digital data representing texts available in different versions: the make-up and pros and cons of various digital data formats that scholarly editors may encounter when they start working with computational means and digital methods. The actual critical study of the textual variation, often leading to a critical edition, will follow in the next three chapters.

3.4.1 A tiny history of the genesis of storing text as digital data

As soon as digital computing became practicable for researchers in the 1950s and 1960s, textual scholars started to move text into the digital environment. Often, Father Roberto Busa is pointed to as a founding figure (Jones 2016), but many other examples of early work exist (Raben 1991; Nyhan and Flinn 2016, 2–4). In particular, tasks in concordancing and lexicography – tedious, repetitive, error-prone – lent themselves to the convenience of automation by computer. Another strand of work that applied computational means early on was stylometry. Stylometry is the study of quantitative aspects of style, mostly known for its frequent successes in authorship attribution – for example the identification of J. K. Rowling as the person behind the pseudonym Robert Galbraith (Juola 2013). Stylometry developed from earlier painstaking statistical work without the aid of computers. George Zipf, for instance, found in the 1930s that there is an inverse and roughly logarithmic relationship between a word's rank in a frequency table and the times it appears in a text (D. Holmes 1998, 112). That is, the most frequent word will occur almost twice as often as the second most frequent word, and three times as often as the third most frequent word, and so forth.

Computer-aided analysis of text required these early scholars to figure out how to actually record text in such a way that it could be both digitally stored and made processable for computers (i.e. made machine-readable). The first "digital" scholars therefore followed the computer engineers that were already familiar with storing text encoded as numbers. At a most basic level, the central processing units (CPUs) of computers process tiny voltage changes as discrete signals that represent binary states. In human terms, the central chip in a computer "listens" to voltage changes in the tiny electric currents that run through it. A higher voltage level is associated with a 1 or the logical value "true"; a lower voltage level is accepted as representing 0 or the logical value "false" (Crosley 2015). These bits, as atomic units of digital computing, can be used to encode higher-level representations. For instance, a set of 8 bits (a byte) can be used to represent numbers from 0 (all bits zero: 00000000), through 1 (one bit turns to 1: 00000001), to 255 (all bits 1: 11111111). Then, if we

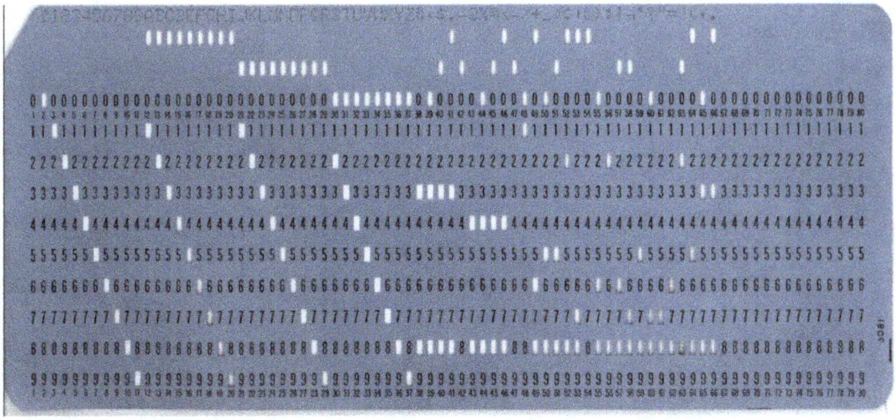

Fig. 3.4-1: Standard IBM punch card used commonly in the 1960s. Source: commons.wikimedia.org/w/index.php?title=File:Blue-punch-card-front-horiz.png&oldid=241324408.

agree on a certain translation table, it is possible to have specific numbers represent characters (Null and Lobur 2003, 62–76), as for example is depicted in table 1.

Table 1: Translation table encoding characters as (binary) numbers.

character	A	B	C	D	E	F	G	H	...
decimal	65	66	67	68	69	70	71	72	...
binary	1000001	1000010	1000011	1000100	1000101	1000110	1000111	1001000	...

In the early days of digital computing, such numerical values representing characters would be recorded on punched cards. Punch card systems to record information had been around for a long time. They were already used, for instance, in the first half of the nineteenth century to have Jaquard looms weave the same patterns into cloth (Ceruzzi 2012, 7–9) and to direct the play of pianolas (Petzold 2000, 239). Punch card systems similar to these were developed to feed numerical information into the early computers of the twentieth century via standardised punch cards (fig. 3.4-1). Meticulously standardised, precise places in the columns on a punch card corresponded to particular numerical values. Punched with a hole at those particular places, a column could thus represent or "hold" a numerical value; several such column values together would then, in turn, represent a character. Whole stacks of cards could, in this way, record a complete text.

Thus, the first ways of recording – and more importantly storing – digital data were very much through analogue carriers: straightforward tabular cards of sturdy paper. Since that time, the carriers have changed quite a bit. First, stiff paper punch cards were replaced by magnetic tape (which recorded magnetic "stripes" rather

text stream	meaning of control command
.ce	center next line
Introduction	
.ju	justify right margin
.ll 39	line length to 39 columns
.ss	use single spacing
The work of authors, publishers, and researchers involves, in varying degrees, three recognizable text	

Fig. 3.4-2: Example of typesetting commands inserted in a text stream (adapted from Goldfarb 1997, 659).

than punch holes). Tape cylinders were replaced by magnetic hard disks. Hard drives are still by far the most-used digital storage medium today, but they are finding "competition" in solid state disks (SSDs). SSDs are electronic chips recording digital bits in flash cells, microscopic containers that can hold electrons or not, each cell simply representing again a 1 or a 0.

3.4.2 From storing character streams to textual formats

It is a bit of a no-brainer for textual scholars that text is not just a linear and one-dimensional series of characters (see e.g. Buzzetti and McGann 2006; DeRose et al. 1990), but the first computers and computer languages offered few possibilities for capturing, expressing, and handling more elaborate text structures. The amount of information that could be handled was severely limited. Univac 9000 systems of the mid-1960s typically took up the space of a medium-sized conference room, and could store about 32 kilobytes of information. A typical modern smartphone may well boast 64 gigabytes of memory, which would be two million times more than such a Univac computer. The average novel contains 90,000 words, while the Univac could, with the best compression achievable, represent perhaps some 10,000 words. For early computational textual scholarship, cleverly encoding and storing information was an important challenge in itself, let alone representing complex text structures.

The practical need to meet the challenge of storing and representing more structure came from the publishing world. Typesetters had a very concrete need not just for electronically representing the characters of text in the right order, but also to know what needed to be in bold print or italics, where a page number went, and so forth. This was solved by inserting typesetting control codes into the linear character stream (Goldfarb 1997; see fig. 3.4-2 below).

More elaborate markup systems like SGML (Standard Generalised Markup Language) and XML (eXtensible Markup Language) were eventually developed from

```
<sentence>Many years later, as he faced the firing squad,
<protagonist><mil_rank>Colonel</mil_rank> <name>Aureliano
Buendía</name></protagonist> was to remember that distant
afternoon when his father took him to discover ice.</sentence>
```

Fig. 3.4-3: A gentle example of XML marked-up text with opening and closing tags, for instance "<name>" and "</name>".

these typesetting languages. These markup languages use a controlled vocabulary and grammar to express information about the text. Usually, angle-bracketed "tags" are then used to point out what part of the text that information pertains to (fig. 3.4-3).

3.4.3 What makes a good data format?

This tiny history serves to point to three foremost tenets of digital formats: formalisation, storage, and processing capabilities. As the roots of both *formal* and *format* suggest, formats are concerned with formalising the form in which we record information. It is only by conforming exactly to such an agreed-upon form that we can make information machine-readable. Computer programs are extremely bad at lenient interpretation. Consider the following markup examples: "My name is <name>Ismael</name>" and "My name is <name)Ismael</name>". A human reader would have little trouble inferring the intent of the markup, even with the "bracket typo" being present. Most computer programs developed to process XML markup, however, would simply choke on this typo, error out, and stop processing the data.

The exact formal structure of a data format is put into a written technical specification. In the case of XML, for instance, the W3C (World Wide Web Consortium) is the ruling body that has issued the precise specification for the data format or markup language (see w3.org/TR/xml). Anyone wanting to implement a computer tool that is going to process XML in some way should take these exact specifications into account. Technical specifications, however, are usually not the most gentle introduction to digital formats for users who are not highly specialised programmers. In the case of XML, a very successful and widely used data format, the last two decades have therefore seen a bewildering flood of handbooks and tutorials, from technical "bibles" such as *XML Unleashed* (Morrison 1999), geared towards professional programmers, to the proverbial *XML for Dummies* for a more general public (Dykes and Tittel 2005). Obviously, similar documentation on most of the other widely used data formats is available for the novice user.

Next to formalisation, the point of many data formats is simply to be able to store data for later use. When a computer program quits, it is removed from the memory of the computer, including any possible data that was associated with it. If such data were not stored safely somewhere, it would just evaporate. From the point of view of textual scholars, there is a point to be made that storing digital text should be done in a fashion that warrants some long-term sustainability. The mere

```
"Name","Sex","Age","Height(in)","Weight(lbs)"
"Alex","M",41,74,170
"Bert","M",42,68,166
"Carl","M",32,70,155
"Dave","M",39,72,167
```

Fig. 3.4-4: Example of CSV data (after Burkardt 2016).

formalisation of a data format according to a technical specification at least goes some way to guaranteeing this, but there are other aspects to consider. A rule of thumb is that, the simpler and the more open a format is, the more it will be resistant to changes in digital platforms, operating systems, programs, and so forth. A very complicated format requires equally complex programs to read the data and make it usable for a user/reader. An open format means a format of which the specification is shared publicly (such as with the XML standard of the W3C). This enables and allows any programmer to create software that will read the data format. In contrast to open standards, there are also closed or proprietary formats, whose internal structure is known only to the original creators and is legally protected. In the realm of textual studies, Adobe's PDF (Portable Document Format) and .doc (the Microsoft Word document format) used to be the best-known and most widely used closed proprietary formats. This meant that all works stored as such files could only be read via software originating from the vendors in question. Fortunately, nowadays it is pretty rare to come across digital text formats that are not open. Even PDF and .doc (supplanted mostly by the Office Open XML or .docx format) are now open formats. Obviously, non-open formats make it hard to recover data in the event that the original software developer is no longer able or willing to maintain the software. This should be reason enough for scholars to privilege open formats.

The aim of data formats is not just to ensure the proper storage and "memorisation" of data; usually, their structure is also geared towards ease of processing by algorithms specific to the data they represent. Thus, data for calculations usually takes a different form than data for text processing. Numerical and tabular data can, for instance, often be found stored as CSV (Comma Separated Values) files, of which an example is given in figure 3.4-4. Tabular formats are the bread and butter of spreadsheet programs and statistical computer languages such as R.

3.4.4 Structured and unstructured data

CSV data is what is known as structured data (data with a clear and predefined structure). Another such format is JSON (short for "JavaScript Object Notation"). JSON (see the example in fig. 3.4-5) is currently a rather popular format for storing structured (meta)data, though it should be pointed out that plenty of equally valid alternatives exist. A plain text file, in contrast, is an example of unstructured data (that is to say, there is no clear predefined formal structure to prose text). XML, especially TEI XML, of which more below, represents something of a compromise between structured and unstructured formats. It attempts to capture an interpreted structure of a text in a formal manner. Each in its own way, these formats capture different aspects of data, sometimes even of the same data, and make it easily processable for specific processing by computer algorithms. In the text-oriented domain of stemmatology, one is likely to encounter certain structured and semi-structured formats more than others. The most common ones are detailed below.

```
[{
    "Name": "Alex",
    "Sex": "M",
    "Age": "41",
    "Height(in)": "74",
    "Weight(lbs)": "170"
}, {
    "Name": "Bert",
    "Sex": "M",
    "Age": "42",
    "Height(in)": "68",
    "Weight(lbs)": "166"
}, {
    "Name": "Carl",
    "Sex": "M",
    "Age": "32",
    "Height(in)": "70",
    "Weight(lbs)": "155"
}]
```

Fig. 3.4-5: Example of JSON data (reworked from Burkardt 2016).

3.4.4.1 Plain text (.txt)

All the above suggests that the simplest possible open data format is a sensible choice for storing digital information. The simplest is known simply as plain text and is usually recognisable by the filename extension ".txt". Basically, .txt files only store unstructured data as the series of bytes that represent characters. Complicating matters is the fact that there are several possible encodings for how these bytes should get translated into characters. One of the earliest encoding standards was ASCII (American Standard Code for Information Interchange), the first version of which defined 127 characters (Mackenzie 1980). Obviously, this is far too few to represent, for instance, a Chinese character system with over 50,000 different characters. Therefore, several encoding standards have developed over time, with the

Unicode standard (unicode.org/standard/WhatIsUnicode.html) as the most comprehensive one, which even leaves room for a user's own encoding if needed. At present, the most widely used technical implementation of this standard is arguably UTF-8, which covers a large variety of character systems, including Latin, Greek, Cyrillic, historical scripts (runes, Ogham, polytonic Greek, and others), Asian scripts, mathematical symbols, and even emojis. Being sure of the long-term preservability of text thus means ensuring one uses an open and simple text format in the right encoding.

Ի սկզբանէ էր Բանն, և Բանն էր առ Աստուած, և Աստուած էր Բան   (Armenian)
အဓိက ဘွဲ့:ပါရှား: ခရီ:ေရာက်ါ ေမ:ပါရှား: စကား:ရှါ ပအိဒ်မငေန့ အသက်ရှည်ါ   (Burmese)
僕は大学教育の無意味さを悟るが、退屈さに耐える訓練期間として大学に通い続けた。   (Japanese)
Alea iacta est   (Latin)
Sîne klâwen durch die wolken sint geslagen   (Middle High German)
)┼ᚋᚋ/┈ᚋᚋᚋ⋅⋅ᚋᚋ/⋅ᚋᚋᚋ⋅┼ᚋᚋᚋᚋ⋅⋅⋅⋅ᚋ⋅ᚋᚋᚋᚋ⋅ᚋᚋᚋ⋅⋅ᚋᚋᚋᚋ⋅####⟨   (Ogham)
Πάτερ ἡμῶν ὁ ἐν τοῖς οὐρανοῖς· ἁγιασθήτω τὸ ὄνομά σου   (Polytonic Greek)
ᚺᛗᚱᚠᛗᚷᛏᚼᛒᛏᛁᛏᚾᚻᛗᛏᛞᚷᛇᛁᚿᛒᛗᚳᚻᚾ   (Runes)
ॐ अग्निमीळे पुरोहितं यज्ञस्य देवमृत्विजम् । होतारं रत्नधातमम् ॥१॥   (Sanskrit)

Fig. 3.4-6: Example of various scripts encoded in Unicode in a plain text file.

3.4.4.2 Text as structured data

The most widely advocated data format in textual scholarship today is without doubt TEI XML, the XML grammar developed by the Text Encoding Initiative (see 3.3.2). One way of describing TEI XML is to say it is a particular dialect of XML, one that is specifically aimed at describing the structure of texts and documents that can be of interest to scholarship (prose, verse, stage-play scripts, historical documents, charters, editions, letters, and so on). TEI XML has a defined grammar that describes what elements (tags) can be used and in what combinations. This grammar is maintained by the TEI Consortium, which publishes the guidelines containing the description and explanation of all TEI tags and attributes on its website (tei-c.org/index.xml). A brief example and its visualisation in a browser are shown in figures 3.4-7–8. TEI XML covers an extensive set of types and genres of text, but not all textual eventualities are accounted for. This is why TEI XML also allows the extension of the standard in both informal and formal ways. If a certain textual phenomenon requires some description for which there is no element to be found in the TEI grammar, an editor or scholar can choose to add an arbitrary tag. The TEI grammar is a community-maintained project, which means that tags that are not represented yet can become part of the officially accepted guidelines. The TEI Consortium boasts a number of special interest groups (SIGs), of which the Special Interest Group on Manuscripts will probably be of most interests to scholars and scholarly editors working on traditions and stemmata (tei-c.org/activities/sig/manuscript).

```
<?xml version="1.0"?>
<?xml-stylesheet type="text/xsl" href="#"?>

<xsl:stylesheet version="1.0"
                xmlns:xsl="http://www.w3.org/1999/XSL/Transform"
                xmlns:TEI="http://www.tei-c.org/ns/1.0">

  <!-- TEI-XML Document start -->
  <TEI:data>
    <text>
      <body>
        <pb/>
        <cb/>
        <head>Van den Vos Reynaerde</head>
        <l>Willem die
          <app>
            <rdg wit="#Co">Vele boucke</rdg>
            <rdg wit="#Dy">Madocke</rdg>
          </app>
          maecte</l>
        <l>daer hi dicken omme waecte,</l>
        <l>hem vernoyde so haerde</l>
        <l>dat die avonture van Reynaerde</l>
        <l n="5">in Dietsche onghemaket bleven</l>
        <l>- die Arnout niet hevet vulscreven -</l>
      </body>
    </text>
  </TEI:data>
  <!-- TEI-XML Document end -->

  <!-- XSLT Stylesheet templates start -->
  <xsl:template match="/xsl:stylesheet">
    <xsl:apply-templates select="TEI:data/*" />
  </xsl:template>

  <xsl:template match="text/body">
    <html>
      <head>
        <title>Example of HTML resulting from TEI-XML with an XSLT stylsheet transformation</title>
      </head>
      <body>
        <div style="font-size: 180%; margin-bottom: 12pt;"><xsl:value-of select="head" /></div>
        <xsl:apply-templates select="l" />
      </body>
    </html>
  </xsl:template>

  <xsl:template match="l">
    <div style="width: 28pt; float: left;"> <xsl:value-of select="@n" /></div>
    <div style=""><xsl:apply-templates/></div>
  </xsl:template>

  <xsl:template match="app">
    <xsl:apply-templates select="rdg[@wit='#Dy']"/>
  </xsl:template>

  <!-- XSLT Stylesheet templates end -->

</xsl:stylesheet>
```

Fig. 3.4-7: Example of a TEI XML document and an XSLT stylesheet combined in a single plain text file. TEI XML document above, stylesheet template specifications below.

Van den Vos Reynaerde

>Willem die Madocke maecte
>daer hi dicken omme waecte,
>hem vernoyde so haerde
>dat die avonture van Reynaerde
>5 in Dietsche onghemaket bleven
>– die Arnout niet hevet vulscreven –

Fig. 3.4-8: The resulting HTML file viewed in a Web browser after it has performed the XSLT stylesheet template transformations on the TEI document.

Most scholarly editors will take a special interest in chapter 12 of the guidelines, which describes the elements and procedures that pertain to the encoding of a critical apparatus for a (digital) scholarly edition. The markup devised by the TEI community for structuring the apparatus is founded on the idea that an edition takes the classic form of a base text with apparatus. The document model of TEI is thus conventional, and its concept of editions should hold few surprises for scholarly editors. The apparatus is obviously the place to account for different readings in various witnesses. TEI XML offers three ways of linking items in the apparatus to the actual text: the location reference method, double end-point attachment, and parallel segmentation. Location reference and double end-point attachment have the most resemblance to the conventional use of footnotes in editions of texts. They describe variants in separate blocks of the document and link them to either a specific point in the text or a specific part of the text (location reference and double end-point attachment, respectively). Parallel segmentation is different in that variants are coded inline (i.e. at the point in the text where they occur) and that all variants are considered as variants of one another, although a preferred or primary reading can still be indicated. From the point of view of automated stemma construction, parallel segmentation is the preferable choice as variants are unambiguously marked up and easier to parse from the XML source.

Although TEI XML is mostly accepted as a de facto standard for digital scholarly edition data, it has not been without its critics. On the theoretical level, TEI as a document model, and especially the strong hierarchical view of text inherent in XML in general, have drawn criticism. XML demands that all elements be neatly nested in other elements. This means that it is rather awkward and quirky, for example, to mark up the fact that a paragraph spans a page break. Paragraphs and pages are two different dimensions of the same text that do not mix neatly according to the hierarchical formalisation that XML demands; you can express either of them very well in a separate hierarchy of nested XML elements, but you cannot combine the two without violating XML's nesting rules. Because text is in fact multidimensional (think only of the lexical, syntactic, and semantic levels, and how they overlap, and of how material and typographical aspects can be intertwined, and how narrative structures can function on several interconnected levels), many text theo-

```
ad impossibilia nemo tenetur

ad impossibilia *nemo* tenetur

ad impossibilia <emph>nemo</emph> tenetur
```

Fig. 3.4-9: A single text in three different formats: as simple plain text, with boldface or emphasis according to Markdown/AsciiDoc markup, and as TEI XML.

rists have drawn attention to the rather limited conception of text that TEI offers (see e.g. Buzzetti and McGann 2006; Huitfeldt 1995). On a more practical level, these theoretical problems express themselves as the "problem of overlap" for which XML does not really offer an adequate solution. Several solutions for overlapping structures have been proposed (DeRose 2004), but none seem to have solved these problems satisfactorily in a fundamental way. Several scholars have therefore raised the question of whether the strongly document-oriented models of XML and TEI XML should be supplanted by more versatile digital models (e.g. Haentjens Dekker and Birnbaum 2017; van Zundert and Andrews 2017).

What can be gauged from the above is that there is no data format that "does it all". There is no format that will work for all purposes under all conditions, and choosing a proper format thus requires an understanding of the aims a scholar is pursuing and under what conditions he or she is pursuing them. A short description of various formats that a scholar may encounter while at work in the realm of digital text may serve to help facilitate such an understanding. What follows is categorised according to tasks scholars can reasonably expect to be executing in that realm, but note should be taken that a data format is rarely developed to address only one category. In practice, formats facilitate multiple tasks.

3.4.5 Transcribing and storing text digitally

One of the most basic tasks of any scholarly editor is transcribing the source (see 3.3.2). Even though this may look and feel a mundane and self-evident scholarly act, when a digital tool is used something quite exciting happens: for the first time, perhaps in centuries, the text is being made part of a new medium and becomes computer-processable. Scholarly editors may not always be as conscious as they could be about the fact that their digitally produced transcriptions are not only transcriptions but also imply a change of medium that creates new ways to use and experience the text (Karlsson and Malm 2004). As argued above, scholarship may be best served by keeping transcription formats as straightforward and open as possible. This favours the plain text format (.txt), as depicted in the first line of figure 3.4-9.

Plain text files can be created using editors purposefully tailored to that end, such as Notepad++ (notepad-plus-plus.org) for Windows or Atom (atom.io) on the Mac. One could even go as low-level as the command line and use a Unix tool like VIM (vim.org) or Emacs (gnu.org/software/emacs) to edit plain text files, though most editors will probably prefer some form of graphical interface. Many varieties of text editors exist, often also as open source and free alternatives to commercial tools. It does not really matter what editor is used for creating plain text files, as long as the editor checks that the actual file is a text file encoded in UTF-8. Most current text editors already store plain text files natively in that encoding. Many programs boast useful search and replace functions, scripting, and so forth.

One step up from plain text, a scholarly editor enters the domain of markup formats. As detailed above, XML is the most widely adopted form of markup in the scholarly editing landscape, but many forms of markup exist. For the initial transcription of the text, it may be useful to prefer a more lightweight markup language such as Markdown (Gruber 2004) or AsciiDoc (asciidoc.org). Such lightweight markup languages try to minimise the invasiveness of the markup, which may be less distracting when focusing on transcription: contrast lines 2 and 3 in figure 3.4-9, for example.

Other formats that may be considered when transcribing a text would be those known from word processing programs. Formats such as .doc (Microsoft Word document file), .docx (Office Open document format), .odt (Open Document Text, used e.g. by LibreOffice and OpenOffice), .rtf (Rich Text Format), and so on. Although often used, scholars and developers that have worked with digital text data mostly consider employing programs such as Microsoft Word, OpenOffice, Pages, Scrivener, and so on bad practice. Such word processors do a lot to facilitate the work of the writer, but they store all information in formats that are cumbersome to read and error-prone in processing by computer. From a point of view of information integrity, these programs are best avoided.

At some point, a scholarly editor will probably want to express or describe more of the structure of the text. This is the point where straightforward text will not suffice and some formalism will be needed to differentiate between source text and metadata. Those who want to rely on a digital formalisation that can count on some proven continuity may well opt for TEI XML. The Oxygen XML Editor, although not open and not free, is currently the go-to editor for many (oxygenxml.com/xml_editor.html). Some other text editing programs do have support for XML authoring and validating (e.g. Atom). The Text Encoding Consortium offers helpful information on how adjusting grammars and validation works in the case of TEI XML (tei-c.org/Support/Learn), and there are plenty of spaces on the Web that offer introductions to XML in general (e.g. w3schools.com/xml/default.asp).

As has been shown above, many alternatives to XML exist. It is doubtful if XML will be around for many more decades. It is more likely that it will be supplanted by some other markup language or an altogether different technology in a number of years. Much is expected from Semantic Web technologies such as RDF (w3.org/RDF) and HTML-RDFa (w3.org/TR/rdfa-lite, 2nd ed. 2015) as successors to XML. Although the latter are themselves XML-based, a transcription in RDF would look rather different from one in "plain" XML. It is unclear, however, how successful RDF and related technologies will be. XML has long been seen as the ultimate data exchange format, but JSON and other standards have found considerable success as well. Some scholars and technologists are looking into standoff markup, which is a technology that keeps the markup separated from the transcription text; by doing so, many problems associated with XML are resolved (Haentjens Dekker and Birnbaum 2017; Spadini, Turska, and Broughton 2015). These technologies, promising as they are, are still very immature. What is important to remember, however, is that if the formalisation used is open, strict, and consistent, all formats can be transformed into other formats. This may require particular software, but if a very successful new format should emerge, such "porting" software is very likely to come into existence as well.

TEI XML is not lightweight; it is rather aimed at very full and very detailed textual criticism. To illustrate this point, let us look at the very minimum that is required to encode the example from figure 3.4-9 in full so that it is a valid TEI XML document (see fig. 3.4-10). Normally, in the description there would also be detailed bibliographical descriptions of witnesses and other sources (in the h e a d e r), which have been omitted in the case of this one-line example. Obviously, the length of the header is a bit ridiculous for a one-sentence example. Most of an XML document is made up of metadata that will not be repeated, and when transcribing 13,000 lines rather than 1, the ratio between metadata overhead and text becomes rather more reasonable.

The salient point is that, due to its verbosity, TEI (and XML in general) may not be the most convenient format when transcription work and data for stemmatological analysis are still in a very volatile state. Although opinions among the technically informed may differ, TEI XML might best be regarded as a final format for digital publication, but transcriptions and data for stemmatological analysis may best be kept in more lightweight formats, such as plain text with a touch of idiosyncratic markup. Once all scholarly preparation is done, the text and its metadata can then be gathered and formed into a TEI XML online publication.

It may be less obvious that tabular data in CSV format may be of use to scholars and philologists as well. However, if fine-grained manual control and overview of word-based alignment, variant detection, and annotating is of the utmost importance, then the view of CSV data offered by s p r e a d s h e e t programs may be very helpful (see fig. 3.4-11). Spreadsheets safeguard openness and reasonable longevity of the data as long as files are stored in CSV format. Another advantage is that most analytical software packages are very well equipped to use CSV files as a data source.

The (collaborative) work of transcribing and annotating can easily involve maintaining multiple versions of a text in multiple stages of editing. It may be easy

```xml
<?xml version="1.0" encoding="UTF-8"?>
<TEI xmlns="http://www.tei-c.org/ns/1.0">
  <teiHeader>
    <fileDesc>
      <titleStmt>
        <title>Example of TEI-XML file</title>
        <author>Joris J. van Zundert</author>
      </titleStmt>
      <editionStmt>
        <edition>
           <date>Thursday 8 March 2018</date>
        </edition>
      </editionStmt>
      <publicationStmt>
        <distributor>The Huygens Institute for the History of the Netherlands</distributor>
        <address>
          <name type="institution">The Huygens Institute for the History of the Netherlands</name>
          <street>Oudezijds Achterburgwal 185</street>
          <postCode>1012 DK</postCode>
          <name type="city">Amsterdam</name>
          <name type="country">The Netherlands</name>
        </address>
        <availability>
          <p>CC BY-SA 3.0
            <ref target="https://creativecommons.org/licenses/by-sa/3.0/deed.en">
               (https://creativecommons.org/licenses/by-sa/3.0/deed.en)
            </ref>
          </p>
        </availability>
      </publicationStmt>
      <sourceDesc>
        <listWit>
        </listWit>
      </sourceDesc>
    </fileDesc>
    <encodingDesc>
      <variantEncoding method="parallel-segmentation" location="internal"/>
    </encodingDesc>
    <revisionDesc>
      <change when="2018-03-08" who="Joris J van Zundert">Transcribed</change>
    </revisionDesc>
  </teiHeader>
  <text>
   <body>
     <p>ad impossibilia <emph>nemo</emph> tenetur</p>
   </body>
  </text>
</TEI>
```

Fig. 3.4-10: The minimal TEI XML structure needed to describe our one-line example text.

to lose track of the status of transcription work, and of all the places that need to be checked, compared, and commented on. Apart from this, there is not enough commiseration in this world for all the times that months if not years of work have gone missing because of a careless click on a "delete" button, a failed hard drive, or a stolen laptop. This is therefore the place to point out the importance as well as convenience of backups and version management. When working with many (versions of) files, a convenient way of storing files safely is to use a code repository such as GitHub (github.com) or Sourceforge (sourceforge.net). Apart from guaran-

	A	B	C	D	E	F	G
1	Line	Position	Witn. A.	Witn. B.	Variant	Annotation	Type
2	1	1	1 χάρις	χάρις			
3	1	2	2 ὑμῖν	ὑμεῖν	y	substitution	
4	1	3	3 καὶ	καὶ			
5	1	4	4 εἰρήνη	εἰρήνη			
6	1	5	5 ἀπὸ	ἀπὸ			
7	1	6	6 θεοῦ	θεοῦ			
8	2	1	1 πατρὸς	πατρὸς			
9	2	2	2 ἡμῶν	καὶ	y	transposition (B) A.2.3-4,A.2.2	
10	2	3	3 καὶ	κυρίου	y		
11	2	4	4 κυρίου	ἡμῶν	y		
12	2	5	5 Ἰησοῦ	Ἰησοῦ			
13	2	6	6 Χριστοῦ	Χριστοῦ			

Fig. 3.4-11: Using LibreOffice to create transcriptions, alignment, and metadata as CSV files.

teeing a safe external backup location, such repositories tirelessly keep track of all changes and versions that happen to emerge during an edition project. If privacy is of importance, private repositories can be created online, or the software can be installed locally (e.g. in the digital infrastructure of an institution). Working with version management software and repositories does require an additional learning curve, but it protects the scholar from the dreaded prospect of errors that collating various versions by hand can present. The *Programming Historian* (van Strien 2016) has a helpful introduction to version management with GitHub, a must-read for any scholar wanting to avoid the mess of version confusion and lost files.

It is very possible for a scholarly edition project to end up with many files and many versions of files, certainly if one is working on larger traditions with many witnesses. In that case, it may become useful to keep track of all versions and text files with a database (e.g. mysql.com). A relational database can be used to keep track of the metadata of documents, files, texts, traditions, and so on, and how they relate to one another. How a database is designed is not covered here, as many useful resources exist. Stephen Ramsay (2004) offers a good introduction oriented towards humanities scholars and their work.

3.4.6 Representing variants

The transcription of different witnesses of the same work will generally lead to the identification of variant readings. In the above, we have already met some ways of representing these variants. When working with TEI XML files as a format for representing the text and apparatus, software engineers and scholars who need to parse text files to aggregate variants in order to compute a stemma will generally prefer parallel segmentation because of its unambiguous identification (oversights on the part of the editor aside) of variant readings. See figure 3.4-7 for an example of how parallel segmentation is used to express variant readings. However, it may very well be that a TEI XML file is not considered a suitable form of input for a stemmatic analysis. Automated stemmatic analysis requires only knowledge of the variant readings and does not (usually) take into account any other text. In fact, if one looks at an input file for PAUP* (one of the most-used programs for inferring phylogenetic trees), one might wonder if the data is related to text at all (see fig. 3.4-12).

Let us walk through the example in figure 3.4-12 to get a feel for the information that phylogenetic algorithms and software generally require, and to understand how this sort of file can be representative of texts and variant readings at all. First of all, all NEXUS files are simply plain text files. Although NEXUS files often have the file extension ".nex", PAUP* reads any file put to it as a plain text file and will error out if it does not recognise the formalities it expects. Internally, each NEXUS file starts with the marker "#nexus", which primarily just testifies to the human reader that it is meant to be a NEXUS file. Any information and comments that the author of the file wants to supply can be put anywhere in the file between square brackets, as shown in figure 3.4-12. PAUP* simply ignores anything between such brackets. All information really relevant to phylogenetic analysis and trees in NEXUS files is put in "blocks" that start with the word "start" and end with the word "end". The word after "start" identifies the type of block, that is, the type of information that is contained inside the block. Usually one will find here the definition of a matrix, specifying the number of rows (taxa, "ntax") and the number of columns ("nchar"). Thus, the line starting with "dimensions" just describes the length and width of the matrix that one finds further on after the command "matrix" and its closing semicolon. The next line describes how the information in the matrix is formatted. Many possibilities exist, but in the case of computing stemmata one usually only encounters a format described as "symbols="01"", which denotes that the values in the matrix should only be 1 or 0. In this case, the values for "missing"

```
#nexus
[Variant information (20160314): Maerlant Rhyme Bible, Book of Judith, Mss. Br1, Dh1, Dh2, Le1, Lo1.]
begin data;
    dimensions ntax=6 nchar=54;
    format symbols="01" missing=? gap=-;
    matrix
        Br1    110001101010101110001010001100111100010010000110100010
        Br2    110001101010101110101010001100011-00001001000011010001
        Dh1    110001101010101010001010001100011-00001001000011010001
        Dh2    110001101010101010001010001111110100011010000110100010
        Le1    110001101010101110001010001100110100011010000110100010
        Lo1    100001101010101010001010001111110100011010000110100010
    ;
end;
```

Fig. 3.4-12: Example of a NEXUS file used as input for PAUP*.

ms. A	ms. B	ms. C	ms. D	ms. F	ms. G	ms. E
Echt	Echt	ECht	Echt	Echt	echt	
daden	dadensi	daden	daden	deden	deden	
si		si	si	si	zi	
na	na	na	na	na	na	Doe
sanghers	sangers	SANGHERS	sangers	sanghers	sanghers	sanger
						die
						rechtre
						was
doot	doet	dod.	doet	doot	doet	doot
						Daden
						si
Dien	Die	Die	Dien	Die	die	dien
van	van	van	van	van	van	van
israel	israhel	YSRAHEL	israel	ysrahel	israhel	ysrahel
mesdaet	anxt	sonde	anxt	sonde	zonde	anxt
groot	groet	grod.	groet	groot	groet	groot

Fig. 3.4-13: Seven witnesses for a biblical verse in a Middle Dutch translation of Petrus Comestor's *Historia scholastica*.

and "gap" indicate that the symbols "?" and "–" may also occur in the matrix, identifying places where it is not known whether a 1 or 0 occurred ("?") or if there is just no value in that place in a certain row ("–").

But how do these rows of 0s and 1s represent witnesses? The truth is: they do not. They represent only very reduced information about variant readings in witnesses. To understand this, we need to look at how the matrix information can be derived from a representation of actual text. For this we need to take a look (again) at how different witnesses may be aligned using a spreadsheet or CSV file. Figure 3.4-13 lists a verse from the biblical tale of Deborah according to seven different witnesses from a Middle Dutch rhymed translation of Petrus Commestor's *Historia scholastica* (van Maerlant, 1858). The verse reads "Echt daden si na sanghers doot / Dien van israel mesdaet groot" [But after Shamgar's death the Israelites sinned greatly].

The tabulator format in fig. 3.4-13 is known as an **alignment table**, where all identical words of all witnesses are lined up in the same row (or column, if the text of witnesses is put in individual rows instead of, as in this case, columns). Let us consider first the witnesses that seem less problematic, those that are depicted in columns 1–6 (*A*, *B*, *C*, *D*, *F*, *G*). We can encode the variant readings of these witnesses by listing each different reading we find in another table, and we can then indicate column-wise whether a certain witness has that reading (1) or not (0). The results obtained by doing so for the table in figure 3.4-13 are depicted in figure 3.4-14. Manuscript *A* has the reading "daden si", as one can gauge from the first column in figure 3.4-14; therefore, in the row for that particular reading in the table in figure 3.4-15,

reading	ms. A	ms. B	ms. C	ms. D	ms. F	ms. G	ms. E
daden si	1	1	1	1	0	0	–
deden si	0	0	0	0	1	1	–
doe daden si	0	0	0	0	0	0	1
d[e|a]den si na	1	1	1	1	1	1	0
dien	1	0	0	1	0	0	1
die	0	1	1	0	1	1	0
mesdaet	1	0	0	0	0	0	0
anxt	0	1	0	1	0	0	1
sonde	0	0	1	0	1	1	0

Fig. 3.4-14: Encoding of readings for the same six witnesses as those in figure 3.4-13.

we find "1" in the column for that manuscript. Manuscript F, however, has a different reading, "deden si" (a linguistic variant of the Middle Dutch past tense of "to do"), so we find "0" in the relevant column in the same row. The reverse situation is found in the following row, which encodes whether a manuscript has the reading "deden si" or not.

As the reader will probably have noticed, there is more variation between the witnesses than there is encoded in the readings table of figure 3.4-14. This is a result of the particular choices an editor makes about which variants are to be encoded and which are not. In this instance, the editor decided that the spelling difference between "Echt", "ECht", and "echt" was not genealogically relevant, and thus that particular variant was not encoded. There is no absolute consensus between scholars on what type of variants reveal genealogical relationships and what types do not. Some hold that spelling variants are never interesting, some point out that spelling variation in vernacular manuscripts may well indicate geographical and, following from that, genealogical proximity. For a more thorough discussion of this issue, see sections 4.3 and 6.2.

Variant readings can become pretty complex. Let us now consider witness manuscript E in the last column of figure 3.4-13. In this case, witness E is still unmistakably a cousin of the original translation of Petrus Comestor's *Historia scholastica*, but because it was done from memory or by a very liberal copyist, witness E contains all kinds of wonderfully exotic readings. First of all, this makes alignment at various points a matter of debate and interpretation (in the example above, for instance, should "doot" be aligned with "doot", or rather "Daden si" with "daden si"? – one cannot have it both ways). Such variation also makes it a matter of interpretation how variants should be encoded. As can be inferred from figure 3.4-14, in this case the editor decided to treat the complicated variant as a transposition of "Doe [...] Daden si" [when [...] did they] in E with regard to the readings in the other manuscripts ("daden si na [...]" [did they after [...]]). Again, once it has been decided

```
#nexus
[Variant information (20160315): Maerlant Rhyme Bible, Judges: Deborah, mss. A, B, C, D, E, F, and G.]
begin data;
   dimensions ntax=7 nchar=54;
   format symbols="01" missing=? gap=-;
   matrix
      ms.A   100110100
      ms.B   100101010
      ms.C   100101001
      ms.D   100110010
      ms.F   010101001
      ms.G   010101001
      ms.E   --1010010
   ;
end;
```

Fig. 3.4-15: Example NEXUS file encoding for the variant readings from figure 3.4-14.

what the possible readings are, it merely remains to note down which manuscripts have which reading. Because *E* has neither the reading "daden si" nor "deden si", we find the gap indicator ("-") here.

The table that results from this process can subsequently be made into a NEXUS file by transposing it. A matrix transposition results in a new matrix whose rows are the columns of the original. After this operation, we end up with the representation in figure 3.4-15.

3.4.7 Representing alignment

We have already spoken (3.4.6) about aligning witnesses, which is the task of trying to line up the individual matching words in various witnesses. This work allows an editor to meticulously compare and examine variant readings. There are various ways in which this aligning can be achieved, and there is no "best" one because what works best is very much dependent on the context and preferences of the editor. There are, however, helpful tools and formats that facilitate the job. We have already seen above how CSV files, as simple text files, might be useful as a storage format for aligned texts. CSV files guarantee, most of the time, flawless processing and interchange between programs and tools. Typing and working in a CSV file via a plain text editor may turn out to be cumbersome, and most users will probably prefer to use a spreadsheet program that will provide convenient navigation, overviews, search and replace functions, and so forth. However, it should be noted that typographical information is never stored in CSV files, so it is not advisable to use elaborate typography or colour coding to encode any essential information about witnesses, because such information will evaporate when the content of a spreadsheet is stored as a CSV file. Here too, "less is more" counts.

Apart from CSV and spreadsheets, another possible way of denoting alignment is by way of a variant graph (see 3.3). This is a fairly new way of representing align-

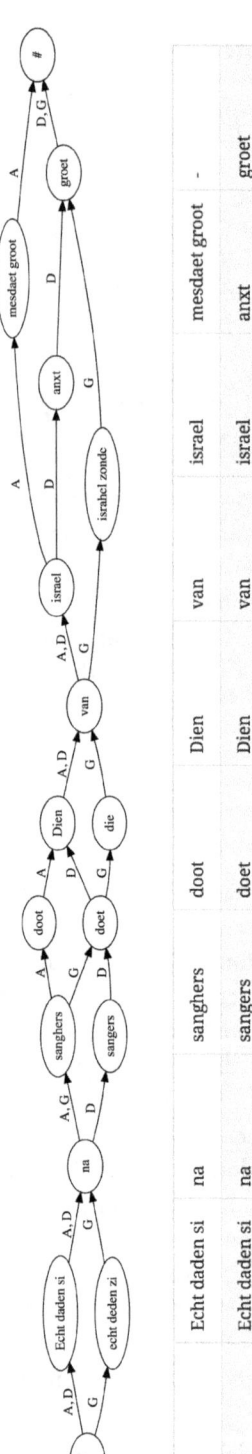

Fig. 3.4-16: A variant graph (top), reducing redundancy in an alignment table (bottom).

ment. An example is given in figure 3.4-16. Essentially, a variant graph collapses all redundant information from an alignment table or spreadsheet. If the columns of a table or spreadsheet represent the linear positions in witness texts, then wherever the same value (reading) is found in cells in the same column, those cells can be collapsed into a node of the graph.

3.4.8 Representing trees, networks, and graphs

The variant graph takes us into the realm of the representation of relational data (also called linked data or networked data). CSV files are very good at storing factual tabular data, but they do not store any information about the relations between values in particular rows, columns, or cells in a table or spreadsheet. Let us return to the example in figure 3.4-13. Some may argue that there is relational information in that table because it clearly depicts that manuscript A contains the reading "dien". However, this relation is not formally expressed at all in the CSV file. We can assume that the relation exists because we follow a convention for how rows and columns relate in a table and what their headers may mean, but all that information is in fact assumed by the reader/user; it is not formally noted in the CSV file. Thus, if we need to explicitly describe and sustain such relational information, we need to put more information into the file. Again, many plain text-based file formats, such as XML or JSON, would allow us to do this. For XML and JSON, some illustrations of expressing structures in and relations between data can be found in the examples above. Here, we limit ourselves to examples of file formats customarily used to describe trees, networks, and graphs, as these are the ones most often used to store variant graphs and stemmata of traditions (and possibly, related to them, correspondence networks and social networks, trees or networks of provenance, and so on).

A very basic yet powerful language for expressing graphs is DOT. Graphs consists of nodes connected by edges. Arguably the simplest graph consists, therefore, of two nodes and one edge between them. In the DOT language, this would be described as depicted in figure 3.4-17. This description corresponds to the graph in figure 3.4-18.

The graph in figure 3.4-18 is an undirected graph, which means the edges have no direction (in this case, node A does not "point to" node B, they "just relate"). However, edges can also have a direction, and both edges and nodes can have attributes,

```
graph SimplestGraph {
    a -- b;
}
```

Fig. 3.4-17: Description of a rudimentary graph in DOT.

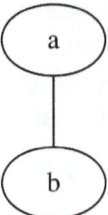

Fig. 3.4-18: The simplest graph.

```
digraph MoreComplexGraph {
        a [label="Node A",shape=box,width=0.75,height=0.75,fixedsize=true]
        c [fillcolor=green style=filled]
        a -> b;
        b -> c;
        b -> d;
        a -> d [label=" a-d    " ];
        d -> a [label=" back to a " color=green style=dotted];
        d -> c;
}
```

Fig. 3.4-19: A more complex graph description in DOT.

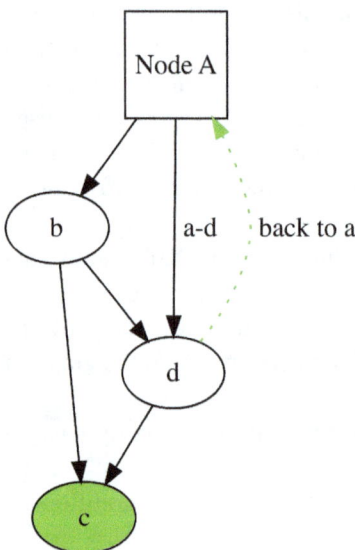

Fig. 3.4-20: The graph resulting from the formal description in figure 3.4-19.

```
digraph ReadingRelation {
    a [label="ms. A"]
    b [label="dien"]
    a -> b [label=" has reading"];
}
```

Fig. 3.4-21: Graph description in DOT of the relation between manuscript A and the reading "dien".

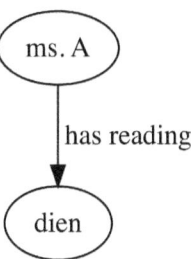

Fig. 3.4-22: Graph resulting from the description in figure 3.4-21.

which can all be described as text in the DOT language, leading to elaborate graphs. In figure 3.4-19, the DOT description of the graph in figure 3.4-20 is given. Note the notation for a directed graph ("digraph") and directed edges (e.g. "b → c"), and that properties of nodes and edges are added between square brackets. Using a relatively uncomplicated textual description, the DOT language thus offers a versatile way of describing very complex networks, graphs, and phylogenetic trees. A concise reference for the language is offered by Hayes-Sheen (2017); more comprehensive documentation is given by John Ellson et al. (graphviz.org).

Using DOT, we can formally capture the relation between pieces of data. Suppose we wanted to formally and explicitly express the relation between manuscript A and the reading "dien" in the table in figure 13. We could do so as in figure 3.4-21 (but note that there are also many other ways the relations could be expressed), with the resulting graph in figure 3.4-22.

The information in the table in figure 3.4-13 (excluding manuscript E) could then be captured in a DOT file as depicted in figures 3.4-23–24.

Of course, there is no reason why exactly the same information could not be expressed in other file formats. A graph can be described perfectly well in JSON, or in XML for that matter. In fact, there is a somewhat limited XML dialect especially geared towards describing graphs (graphml.graphdrawing.org/index.html). The benefit of using DOT is that it can be read by one of the most popular open source visualisation tools for graphs and networks, GraphViz (see graphviz.org). Downloading and installing GraphViz allows one to execute commands such as "dot -Tpng -Gdpi=600 graph.dot -o graph.png", which means that the program will take as input the file "graph.dot" (e.g. a text file like that in fig. 3.4-23), translate it into

```
digraph ReadingRelation {
    A [label="ms. A"]
    B [label="ms. B"]
    C [label="ms. C"]
    D [label="ms. D"]
    F [label="ms. F"]
    G [label="ms. G"]
    a [label="daden si"]
    b [label="deden si"]
    c [label="dien"]
    d [label="die"]
    e [label="mesdaet"]
    f [label="anxt"]
    g [label="sonde"]
    A -> a [relation="has reading"]
    A -> c [relation="has reading"]
    A -> e [relation="has reading"]
    B -> a [relation="has reading"]
    B -> d [relation="has reading"]
    B -> f [relation="has reading"]
    C -> a [relation="has reading"]
    C -> d [relation="has reading"]
    C -> g [relation="has reading"]
    D -> a [relation="has reading"]
    D -> c [relation="has reading"]
    D -> f [relation="has reading"]
    F -> b [relation="has reading"]
    F -> d [relation="has reading"]
    F -> g [relation="has reading"]
    G -> b [relation="has reading"]
    G -> d [relation="has reading"]
    G -> g [relation="has reading"]
}
```

Fig. 3.4-23: Full graph description in DOT of the information in figure 3.4-13.

the PNG graphics format with a resolution of 600 dots per inch, and store the resulting picture in a file named "graph.png".

It is likely that, for practical purposes, editors will prefer the CSV format for capturing variant readings, because writing a DOT or JSON file involves more and quite tedious work. The salient point in showing the capabilities of these formats is to demonstrate the various levels and differences of formal explicitness that can be

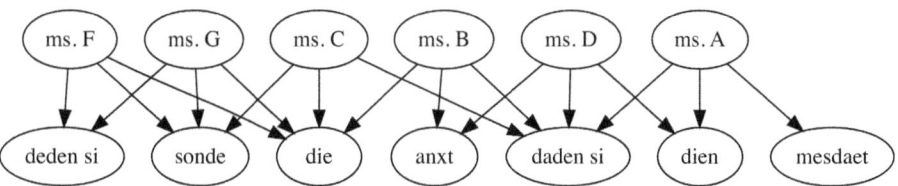

Fig. 3.4-24: Graph resulting from the description in figure 3.4-23.

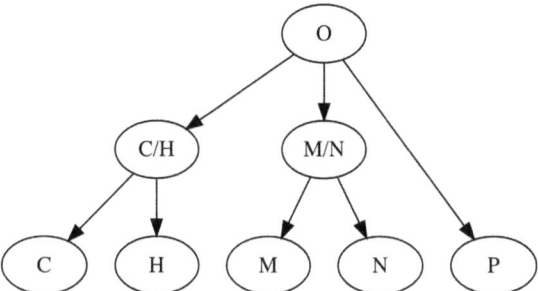

Fig. 3.4-25: Stemma of sources of the Middle Dutch *Reis van Sente Brandane*, adapted from Strijbosch (1995, 21).

achieved with them. However, one should bear in mind that a lot of the dullness of writing JSON, XML, or DOT files can be overcome by automating the boilerplate parts of the formatting.

When working with stemmata, it will be useful to express them in a machine-readable way; this is obviously a case where the application of a format such as DOT is warranted. For instance, a stemma inferred through conventional non-computational means for the sources of the Middle Dutch translation of the *Voyage of Saint Brendan* (in Middle Dutch, the *Reis van Sente Brandane*) could be captured as depicted in figure 3.4-25. The DOT description for this stemma is given in figure 3.4-26.

NEXUS files also support describing phylogenetic trees through the Newick format, which uses the nested parentheses approach to indicate branches (scikit-bio.org/docs/0.2.2/generated/skbio.io.newick.html). Those scholars with a linguistics background may be familiar with this format as it is similar to the labelled bracketing method of describing the linguistic tree structure assumed in sentences (see Kerstens, Ruys, and Zwarts 1996). The Newick expression describing the same stemma as that in figure 3.4-25 would be *((C,H)C/H,(M,N)M/N,P)O*. The NEXUS file format (see also above) just embeds this in some notation to indicate that it is indeed a tree (see fig. 3.4-27).

Another XML variant for describing cladistic trees that has been adopted by several popular phylogenetic tools and software libraries is PhyloXML (Han and Zmasek 2009; phyloxml.org). A file depicting the same tree as that given in figure 3.4-25 would look like figure 3.4-28.

```
diGraph StemmaBrandane {
    A [label="O"]
    B [label="C/H"]
    C [label="M/N"]
    D [label="C"]
    E [label="H"]
    F [label="M"]
    G [label="N"]
    H [label="P"]
    A -> B
    A -> C
    A -> H
    B -> D
    B -> E
    C -> F
    C -> G
    { rank="same"; D, E, F, G, H }
}
```

Fig. 3.4-26: DOT description of the stemma in figure 3.4-25.


```
#nexus
begin trees;
    Tree StemmaBrandane = ((C,H)C/H,(M,N)M/N,P)O;
end;
```

Fig. 3.4-27: NEXUS description of the stemma in figure 3.4-25.

The list of possible plain text-based formal description formats for graphs, trees, and stemmata is potentially much longer than the few formats shown here. The salient point to keep in mind, however, is that they are all able to express the same basic information about tree and network structures. Some support many custom attributes and visualisation properties (e.g. DOT), others solely capture the basic tree structure (e.g. Newick). One way or another, it is therefore possible to transform one format into another. Sometimes, tools for this even exist (see e.g. graphviz.org, s. v. "graphml2gv"), though the reader/user should be warned that support for migration can be dodgy or even completely lacking. Care should be taken, when migrating a graph description from one format to another, that all the properties available in one format also exist in another. If this is not the case, some information will get lost. A transformation of a file from DOT to Newick, for instance, would clearly not be without loss of information.

```xml
<?xml version="1.0" encoding="UTF-8"?>
<phy:Phyloxml xmlns:phy="http://www.phyloxml.org/1.10/phyloxml.xsd">
    <phy:phylogeny>
        <phy:name>StemmaBrandane</phy:name>
        <phy:clade>
            <phy:name>O</phy:name>
            <phy:branch_length>0</phy:branch_length>
            <phy:clade>
                <phy:name>P</phy:name>
                <phy:branch_length>10</phy:branch_length>
            </phy:clade>
            <phy:clade>
                <phy:name>M/N</phy:name>
                <phy:branch_length>5</phy:branch_length>
                <phy:clade>
                    <phy:name>N</phy:name>
                    <phy:branch_length>5</phy:branch_length>
                </phy:clade>
                <phy:clade>
                    <phy:name>M</phy:name>
                    <phy:branch_length>5</phy:branch_length>
                 </phy:clade>
            </phy:clade>
            <phy:clade>
                <phy:name>C/H</phy:name>
                <phy:branch_length>5</phy:branch_length>
                <phy:clade>
                    <phy:name>H</phy:name>
                    <phy:branch_length>5</phy:branch_length>
                </phy:clade>
                <phy:clade>
                    <phy:name>C</phy:name>
                    <phy:branch_length>5</phy:branch_length>
                </phy:clade>
            </phy:clade>
        </phy:clade>
    </phy:phylogeny>
</phy:Phyloxml>
```

Fig. 3.4-28: PhyloXML description of the stemma in figure 3.4-25.

3.4.9 Representing the edition

Stemmatology is usually undertaken as a subtask during research that should eventually lead to the publication of a scholarly edition or a work synthesising a certain textual tradition. Increasingly, we see such works also being published as digital works. In such cases, the issue of digital format obviously also applies to the eventual publication itself. More importantly, the digital medium allows us to model and produce anything we can think up as long as it can be depicted on a screen. With this r e - m e d i a t i o n, therefore, comes also a potential renegotiation of the digital scholarly edition and its related scholarly processes (see Bolter and Grusin 2000 on the topic of re-mediation). What constitutes an adequate digital scholarly edition is a much-debated issue (for more on this, see 6.3). Different scholars have arrived at different conclusions on this matter. Pierazzo (2015), for instance, seems to conclude that a digital scholarly edition should be a digitised form of an edition that is in all respects created the same as a printed edition, but with specific digital means and technologies. According to Bordalejo (2018), too, digital scholarship has in no sense changed the goals and methods of the scholarly editor. These attitudes could be called "mimetic", "conventional", or "conservative". Others hold that a medium shift also necessarily involves in part rethinking and reshaping the object that flows from one medium to another and is thus re-mediated. Sahle (2013) argues, for instance, that a digital scholarly edition is defined precisely by being inalienably digital. Thus, for Sahle, a digital scholarly edition is defined mostly by those aspects that would be lost if the edition were published as printed edition. More radical perspectives are offered by, for example, van Zundert and Andrews (2017), who argue that digital texts should indeed be regarded first and foremost as digital objects. A digital scholarly edition could thus, for instance, be equivalent to a database or graph model representing the text rather than to the visual, derived representation of them in a graphical user interface.

Databases and graphs, regarded as versatile modelling tools for text, certainly enrich the ability of scholars to express the multiple dimensions of a text and the different perspectives on it. Databases and graphs, understood in this way, do not merely provide a container for a collection of flat transcriptions and the additional information needed to create a critical edition. Beyond that, they allow the editor to augment such material with various interpretations, perspectives, and additional digital (or digitised) objects. Together with software to query and present the material thus stored in databases and graphs, these technologies allow for an unparalleled richness in representing editions. Not just the edition authorised by the editor can be visualised, but also other critical interpretations, as well as their constituent material. Specific dimensions or aspects that are of interest to a certain user or reader can be dynamically inferred and presented (e.g. social relations between persons or characters, a chronology of events, a histogram of topics related in a text, and so on). Creating such advanced digital scholarly editions requires assiduous effort by both scholar and programmer, for software and program code do not redefine the scholarly edition by themselves, nor do they create scholarly editions automatically – this all, obviously, remains human scholarly work. But, with the new possibilities they open up, digital scholarly editions do invite us to rethink what a scholarly edition could or should be. The volatility of the debate surrounding the digital scholarly edition may give scholars wanting to produce an edition cause to seek orientation about the various text-philosophical approaches towards digital textual scholarship. This specific debate is not covered in the present handbook, but good entry points into it may be Thaller (2004), Deegan and Sutherland (2008), Driscoll and Pierazzo (2016), Andrews (2013), Fischer (2013), and Robinson (2013a). Here, we limit ourselves to considering some of the formats that may be encountered when a scholar wishes to represent the results of editorial work (including stemmatology) digitally.

In a sense, any JSON, TEI XML, or DOT file can be made to contain the bare essential information that describes the results of scholarly work. Thus, when they represent all the information pertaining to a digital scholarly edition, such files can be said to represent that edition. The base data that CSV, JSON, XML, and other types of files contain is, however, usually only regarded as storage data. Additional processes are applied to derive visual representations of that data that cater to the user reading or viewing the edition. The data files, for instance, may be stored on the hard drive of a Web server where custom-made or out-of-the box Web software transforms it on request into files that are viewable by Web browsers. In other cases, formats will be derived that port the base data into file formats that are accessible via a tablet or e-reader. The most common file types for this visualisation are listed in what follows.

3.4.9.1 HTML

HTML is the first language that was used to create Web pages. It is a markup language that allows one to indicate how specific text should be visualised and how documents are linked. A comprehensive overview of its history and technology is offered by Shannon (2019). The Web itself offers many helpful introductions to crafting HTML and integrating related technologies for Web publishing (e.g. htmlprimer.com/htmlprimer/html-beginners; w3schools.com/html). An especially gentle entry-level introduction to HTML and related technologies for Web publishing is offered by Robert Mening (2018). HTML works in exactly the same way as XML and is thus again plain text interspersed with markup codes between angle brackets. In contrast to XML, HTML is concerned with layout and typography rather than with structure or content. HTML has meanwhile progressed to a fifth version (HTML5) that integrates support for many other types of output than text (audio, video, pictures, screen readers). HTML is still the basic fabric of most Web pages, but it is today often combined with many other technologies to provide elaborate styling (CSS, or Cascading Stylesheets; see Mills et al. n. d.), interaction and dynamic presentations (JavaScript; see javascript.info/intro), scalable graphics (for a comprehensive overview, see inkscape.org/develop/about-svg), fonts (e.g. Web fonts; see developer.mozilla.org/en-US/docs/Learn/CSS/Styling_text/Web_fonts), and so forth. The drawback of using ("stacking") many such technologies on top of base-data files to produce nice-looking visualisations is that the combined data and software that produce the digital edition may become hard to maintain and sustain over time. A responsible scholarly editor will therefore always make sure that the base data is also archived for perpetuity in some specialised institution, such as a digital library or an institutional data repository.

3.4.9.2 PDF
The Portable Document Format, developed by Adobe, is arguably the most commonly used file format for storing the visual representation of a document. PDF ensures that a document will look exactly the same whatever device is used to view it (w3.org/TR/WCAG-TECHS/pdf.html#pdf_notes). Most software that can be used to create texts and documents also supports exporting documents as PDF files. For scholarly editors wanting to produce a fully controlled document-style digital edition, PDFs can thus be a reliable solution. The downside of the PDF, however, is that it is a binary format: it stores all textual and layout information as a series of zeroes and ones, that is, it is not human-readable. This may be a hazard for long-term storage, as the format specification could change in future. Another drawback used to be that PDF was a proprietary format, that is, the specification and the related software technology were solely owned by the Adobe company. This made it difficult or impossible for software engineers other than those working for that company to do anything effectively with the format. These days, however, PDF is an open format and the specifications have been published for everyone to read and use. PDF is geared heavily to representing print-like documents. This means that interaction with a scholarly edition as a PDF will be limited almost completely to reading and searching. If more dynamic representation is required, editors would be better off looking into other formats and software.

3.4.9.3 EPUB
EPUB (idpf.org/epub) is a widely used format for publishing e-books that can be read both on computer and tablet screens. EPUB is basically a packaged form of HTML. Various HTML files are contained in a larger container file. A number of special files are used to describe indexes, chapter structure, front matter, and so on. As has already been said, under the hood EPUB is relatively "plain" HTML5 with the same possibilities for styling. EPUB should, in theory, also be able to support interaction and multimedia, but device support for this is sketchy at best. A common misconception is that HTML/EPUB does not support page numbers because of its responsive design (i.e. scaling fonts and reflowing text to fit different window and tablet sizes). It is certainly possible to anchor page numbers to the text, but publishers mostly choose not to do so because it is highly likely that page breaks due to reflowing content will not neatly coincide with the bottom of a reading frame. This choice makes reliable referencing inside an EPUB text a considerable pain, and an issue that is in urgent need of being solved by future technology.

3.4.9.4 LaTeX

LaTeX is a verbose document description language written by Leslie Lamport (for a history and technical details, consult latex-project.org). It runs atop a typesetting system called Tex developed largely by Donald Knuth (see tug.org/whatis.html). LaTeX and TeX have an important focus on publishing scientific papers containing complicated formulae. The LaTeX format has therefore found widespread adoption in academic publishing, both among researchers themselves as well as publishing houses. There are dedicated websites that support the authoring of LaTeX (e.g. overleaf.com). Like XML, LaTeX uses markup codes. These codes can indicate what a part of a text represents – a section called "Introduction" for instance: "\section{Introduction}". Such codes result in a fitting layout. Codes can also be more typographically specific, such as "{\large This Text Will Be Large }". Because LaTeX was one of the first general-purpose document typesetting languages, it has evolved considerably over time. It now supports various dialects, modules, and libraries, often offering multiple paths towards the same end. For this reason, LaTeX is generally seen as a powerful but not easy-to-use or intuitive solution to document production. This notwithstanding, it has found a very large community of users and support (e.g. tex.stackexchange.com; sharelatex.com/learn/latex/Main_Page), especially in the academic context.

3.4.9.5 XML and XSLT

If the base data of scholarly output is in the form of XML, scholars may choose to transform the XML into presentable HTML by using the specially designed templating language XSLT. XSLT is short for "eXstensible Stylesheet Language Transformations". XSLT is a standard technology for transforming XML documents into XML with a different structure, but also into different documents altogether. It is most often used to transform some XML as a data source into an HTML form to represent that data visually. A comprehensive example of this was given in figures 7–8.

The popularity of (TEI) XML, especially in the scholarly community, has given rise to a number of software applications that facilitate the publishing of XML data as HTML. Noteworthy are especially Edition Visualization Technology (EVT; evt.labcd.unipi.it) and the Versioning Machine (Schreibman 2016). In essence, these applications make the work of writing an XLST stylesheet less cumbersome through clear tutorials and examples, and by abstracting away a bit from the most basic level of angle brackets and code verbs.

3.4.9.6 On stacks, chains, pipelines, and sustainability

As mentioned, Web technologies are seldom used in isolation. Unless a scholar writes HTML directly, there will always be software, processes, templates, and transformations involved with publishing data in an electronic form. The full array of specific technologies that in a certain context is needed to produce a visualisation of some source of data on the Web is often called a stack, a technology chain, or a pipeline. Usually, a Web framework will also be part of such a stack, a Web framework itself being a combination of various Web-oriented languages and technologies for creating Web applications.

Consider the case where a scholar has produced an XML description of a certain physical manuscript. Although it is possible to place this XML file on a server and open it to the world, the viewing of the XML itself would probably not satisfy either scholar or reader. So, at the very least, the scholar will also compose an XSLT stylesheet to present the XML in some more conveniently readable form. This XML plus XSLT combination amounts to the minimum stack that is needed for Web publishing an edition. But with every further requirement (paginating, searching, comparing, annotating), more styling templates, software, and components will be needed. Digital scholarly editions can therefore grow into large, intricate software machinery that requires sophisticated software engineering knowledge, enduring maintenance, and careful balancing of all the integrated components. The more elaborate such structures are, the more questionable the longevity of the edition tends to become. Unless maintenance can be guaranteed institutionally for a very long period, it would seem that keeping things as lean and as simple as possible offers a scholar the best chances of seeing an edition survive the constantly changing turmoil of digital environments. A base format for the data (such as JSON) that is then transformed into a Web publication consisting of HTML, CSS, and JavaScript would arguably be a good, lean choice from the perspective of persistence.

3.4.10 Some concluding remarks

The key question with respect to data formats is how we store our data. How do we best inscribe in a digital medium textual data and the critical observations we have made about such textual data, and how do we ensure the longevity of the variants we have examined and identified; our alignments; the collations we have produced; and the stemmata and, possibly, other networks and graphs that are the results of our analyses? Scholars should want to know enough about how data is or can be stored to judge the adequacy of the storage in terms of precision, and indeed representing what was meant, and to judge the potential sustainability of the chosen technological solution(s). The potential for sustainability and preservation is probably key when it comes to which formats are chosen by a scholar. But, secondly, a scholar should always consider whether a format is suited to the type of analysis he or she wants to perform – in other words, does the format formalise the data adequately and does it enforce some consistency that will allow sufficient (computational) analysis? Third, it would be good to bring interoperability into the equation – that is, the scholar should also consider how other scholars and other software may want to reuse the data, and whether the chosen format supports such reuse well. Finally, the choice of format may be influenced by considerations about how an eventual presentation of the data or a digital scholarly edition as a whole might be published.

Unfortunately – or maybe not – there is no single format that does it all. A vast amount of work in the digital realm is to do with transforming data from one form to another to appropriate it for some other purpose, simply because not all formats are suited to all purposes. Some are better geared towards one function or another (Vitali 2016). The choice and use of a format should always be carefully evaluated, with respect both to the format's ability to store the information needed and to the ability of the format to be transformed (migrated) easily to other formats because of later and different requirements. In practice, different formats have different purposes and versatility, and turning one into another may affect readability or may lead to cumbersome and error-prone handling of information. For all of these reasons, good care should be taken when choosing formats, for these digital technologies do impact our ability to analyse historic texts, both in good and bad ways.

Finally, we may note that digital files require care to ensure their sustainability. Backups remain important, and any digital data or edition should be hosted on a server that is regularly maintained. Lastly, because digital data can still be vulnerable, and especially as institutional support can be fleeting, it may be sensible, while making a digital edition, to also provide for a print equivalent of some kind (e.g. PDF) to ensure longevity along both digital and analogue lines.

4 The stemma

Introductory remarks by the chapter editor, Tara Andrews

Thus far in this introduction to stemmatology, the reader has learned about the history of how literature was transmitted across the ages, the principles of text genealogy, and the preparatory work that needs to be done before attempting to reconstruct the genealogy, or transmission history, of a particular text. Now, at the centre of the book, we come to the centrepiece of stemmatology, which is the stemma itself. Where chapters 3 and 6 contain information on how an editor might approach the task of creating a stemma, this chapter is focused on the scholarly intellectual object that is the product of these procedures, what is signified by the parts as well as the whole, and how it relates to the history of the text as well as the editorial decisions that may need to be made in the process of (re-)constructing that text.

The first two sections define the stemma from, respectively, the viewpoints of traditional philology and of mathematical (computational) logic. Philipp Roelli begins in section 4.1 with a discursive definition not only of a stemma, but also of an archetype – the (real or putative) ancestor of all extant copies of a text. After giving a brief overview of the history of the use of stemmata in textual criticism, he moves on to venture a formal definition of the stemma as a hypothesis about the genealogical relationships between manuscript witnesses of a text, making reference to concepts defined elsewhere within the handbook. This is followed by a set of examples in which the reader can see how different sorts of hypotheses might be represented in different stemmata.

The traditional definition of the stemma is complemented in section 4.2 by Armin Hoenen, who approaches the concept from the perspective of constructing a formal model; the value of this is that the stemma then becomes subject to certain forms of computational analysis, and the consequences of the hypothesis that it expresses can also be followed in a formalised fashion. An understanding of the stemma as a computational model, and specifically the ability to differentiate what is implied by calling a structure a "stemma" as opposed to a "graph" or a "tree", is crucial for any editor working with digital tools that produce these structures. Hoenen sets out the general framework of graph theory and goes on to describe several versions of a stemma model that have been based on that framework. He touches briefly on related models from bioinformatics, which are also covered more thoroughly in chapter 8.

No matter the method chosen to construct a stemma, the vast majority of the steps we use revolve around variation among the text copies. Those who have prior exposure to the field of textual philology will have encountered a perhaps bewildering array of terms having to do with textual variation – "significant error", "conjunctive error", "separative error", "contamination", and so on – and their consequences for the construction of a stemma. Aidan Conti discusses in section 4.3 two different sorts of categorisation of variants. The first of these covers how a particular variant is to be understood in relation to constructing the stemma; the second categorisation addresses the different sorts of variation and their potential causes, relating them to Quintilian's four main categories of error (addition, omission, substitution, and transposition).

Although the text-genealogical principles behind stemmatology seem straightforward, even obvious, when they are first encountered, a philologist confronted with real historical texts will soon encounter complications. Foremost among these is the phenomenon of the so-called contaminated witness, which is to say, a text manuscript that was copied with reference to more than one exemplar. Tuomas Heikkilä treats this subject in section 4.4, where he demonstrates how contamination can lead to erroneous stemmata, describes the different modes in which a text might have been copied from multiple sources, and provides some guidelines for how an editor might deal with the situation, gaining insight into the transmission history of the text even if a complete and definitive stemma cannot be drawn.

The transmission history that is represented by a stemma is the subject of section 4.5, the last in this chapter, by Caroline Macé. Here, the reader is treated to a demonstration of the need to study the history of a text not only on the basis of its variant readings, but also in light of the paratextual and contextual knowledge that we have about the documents that carry the text. Macé presents three case studies, each of which shows in a different way the inadequacy of restricting oneself either to historical analysis or to stemmatic analysis. The third case study also discusses issues that arise when the text under examination exists only (or primarily) in translation, which may forestall the use of automated collation software but requires the editor nevertheless to find a way to carry out meaningful comparison of texts in different languages.

In sum, this chapter contains a great deal of information, sometimes presented in an unavoidably dense manner, about the form, function, and significance of what in many cases appears to be a simple diagram. Only with a full understanding of the concepts and complications covered in this chapter, however, can the reader avoid the pitfalls of a naive use of the computational methods that follow in chapter 5.

4.1 Definition of stemma and archetype
Philipp Roelli

This section considers the two key concepts for the genealogical reconstruction of texts, already mentioned in passing in previous chapters, in more depth: stemma and archetype. Their historical context, application, types, and definitions will be examined. The next section will then consider the stemma as a computational model.

4.1.1 Context

"Stemma" and "archetype" are probably the two most important terms in traditional genealogical textual philology. After some preliminary remarks, more formal definitions will be proposed. As a first approximation, one may imagine the stemma as the genealogical tree of all known, extant witnesses of a text and the archetype as their most recent common ancestor, usually lost. In practical terms, the archetype is the uppermost point in a stemma, on which all extant branches converge (on the relation between archetype and original, see 4.1.4), or, seen from the other end, the point beyond which *recensio* of the extant tradition of a text cannot reach (see Trovato 2005, 12). Originally, the main point of devising a stemma for a textual tradition was to reduce the amount of possible choice between variants for its editor: the stemma can in many cases show that a reading was innovated and could not have stood in the archetype (see 2.3.2 for Gaston Paris on this topic). Today, stemmata are also used in many other contexts when studying the transmission of a text. Often, editors who wish to edit a text as closely as possible to the original try to reconstruct the archetype's text as far as possible (see 2.2). But it is crucial to be aware that the archetype is usually not identical with the author's original text – in fact, many centuries may lie between these two texts. The archetype may be any witness that acquired this special and important function in the transmission of its text by historical chance; indeed, it may be a witness full of mistakes and deficiencies of all kinds. Faced with a faulty archetype of this kind, the editor will usually try to improve the archetypal text using external data or conjecture (see 6.2.3 on the delicate task of *emendatio*). If there are more than a very few witnesses, the reconstruction of a stemma is usually not a trivial task and is often disputed among editors of the same text. New insights into the text's transmission and significant changes in the stemma can necessitate an entirely new critical edition. As a rule of thumb, it may be said that, the more witnesses there are, the more difficult it becomes to figure out all relationships between them and to draw an adequate stemma; this problem is aggravated by the fact that the probability of contamination (see 4.4) increases as the number of witnesses does. In some cases, for instance if there are a great number of witnesses – there may be hundreds, occasionally even thousands – it may not be feasible to construct a stemma at all (see 7.1 for examples).

4.1.2 History of the terms

The Latin expression *stemma codicum*, or in short just *stemma* (plural *stemmata*), literally means "genealogical tree of the manuscripts". The word "stemma" ultimately derives from the Greek word στέμμα (pl. στέμματα), "wreath, garland",

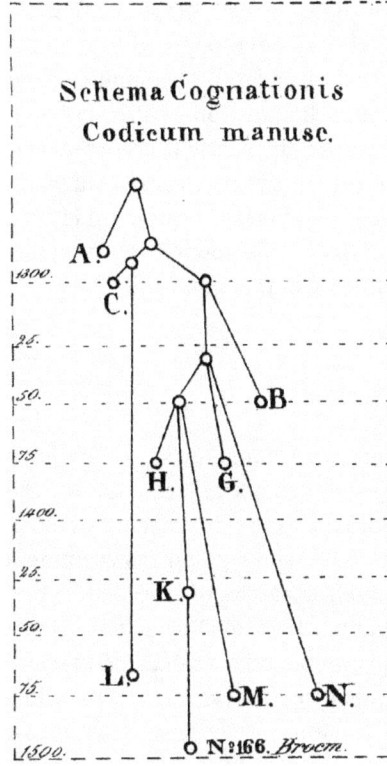

Fig. 4.1-1: Schlyter's *schema cognationis* for the *Västgötalagen* (Schlyter and Collin 1827, appendix), which may be the first printed stemma.

which is derived from the verb στέφω, "put/hang around". It is already used figuratively in Latin Antiquity to mean "genealogical tree" (e.g. in Suetonius *De vita caesarum*, Claudius 2). But what we today call a stemma in textual criticism is a recent acquisition: the idea was apparently proposed for the first time in the eighteenth century by Bengel in the context of a hypothetical genealogical tree of witnesses of the New Testament, although he did not use the name (he called it a "tabula quaedam quasi genealogica"; Bengel 1763, 20 [a certain, so to speak, genealogical table]). Apparently, it was only in the nineteenth century that such *tabulae* were first printed in editions; the first scholar to print a stemma may have been Carl Johan Schlyter in 1827 (Schlyter and Collin 1827, appendix; he called it a *schema cognationis codicum manuscriptorum* [diagram of relationship of the manuscripts], see fig. 4.1-1), whereas Carl Gottlob Zumpt (1831, xxxviii) may have been the first person to use the designation *stemma codicum manuscriptorum* in 1831 (see Timpanaro 1961, 61). Nevertheless, he still relegated the actual stemma to a footnote. The term becomes the accepted technical term in the wake of Paul Maas's *Textkritik* (1927). Some more details about the early history of scholarly stemmata can be found below in section 6.1.2. When prints, not manuscripts, are the witnesses to be discussed, the full Latin term *stemma editionum* is sometimes used (see examples in 7.8).

The word "a r c h e t y p e" is derived from the classical Greek compound ἀρχέτυ-πον, "archetype, pattern, model, exemplar", which was often opposed to ἀπόγρα-φον, "copy" (see 1.1.5). The compound itself consists of ἀρχή, "beginning", and τύπος, "the effect of a blow or of pressure" and thus "impression, seal, engraving, etc.". Renaissance scholarship (written in Latin) tended to use the word *archetypus* in the classical Latin sense as "autograph" (Irigoin 1977); this may cause confusion, as the modern scholarly meaning is rather different. In reality, the situation is even more complicated; Rizzo (1973, 308–318) differentiates at least four different Renaissance meanings of "archetype" and studies the history of the term further.

4.1.3 The *stemma codicum*

The basic, practical method of arriving at a stemma (*constitutio textus*), including a fictitious and a real example, has already been presented above (see 2.2.4–6). The general idea described there can be formalised into a d e f i n i t i o n such as the one we propose here: a *stemma (codicum)* is an oriented tree-like graph representing a hypothesis about genealogical relationships between witnesses of a text.

This definition uses the terms "tree-like", "graph", "'witness", and "text", some of which come from a traditional philological background, others from a mathematical one. The philological concept of a witness was discussed in section 2.2; while we refrain from attempting to define here the elusive term "text", some examples of the sometimes fluid boundaries of "texts" are provided in section 3.2. On the other hand, the terms "tree" and "graph" are mathematical ones. A purely computational approach to the concept of the stemma is presented in the next section (4.2). There, the Greg tree as a mathematically defined version of the traditional stemma without contamination (4.2.3.3) is introduced. Section 5.2 explains what "tree" and what the more general term "graph" mean in mathematics; the related terms "DAG" and "polytree" are also introduced there. The term "tree-like" is intentionally fuzzy: it is intended to hint at the fact that the graph can be turned into a tree by removing some edges, the ones accounting for contamination (see 4.4). The defining characteristic of a tree is that any two nodes are connected by exactly one path; this holds only in the traditional, uncontaminated situation in which all witnesses are copied from only one ancestor each. Put another way, if only the main line of descent for each witness is used, the stemma will become a tree. If all transmission of information between witnesses is included, and if there was contamination, the diagram will no longer be a tree. For example, if one witness, say C, is a copy of another witness, say A, then the graph depicting the two is oriented; in this case, the direction is from A to C. But if witness C was copied partly from A and partly from another witness, say B, then there will be two (or more) paths from the archetype to witness C (one through A and the other through B), and the stemma will no longer be a tree. In order to turn it back into a tree, either A or B would have to be regarded as the main line of descent, and the other path would have to be suppressed.

In order to arrive at the stemma most accurately depicting the historical transmission, a philologist will use all available information about the witnesses, including but not limited to the text-state they carry. There will be additional information about the witnesses as objects, such as palaeographical estimates of their age, the identification of different hands writing the text, or information gleaned from the page layout. And, with luck, additional information may also be contained in colophons (see 1.2.2) – scribes may explicitly state what their sources were, when and where they wrote, for instance. For editors, the stemma is crucial in that it helps them reconstruct the archetypal text within certain limits (as detailed in 2.2), but it also has other uses, such as displaying known information about the process of transmission of a text in a compact and formal way. In all of this, it is important not to forget that a stemma is always only a hypothesis, a map that must not be confounded with the mapped territory, as the above definition stresses.

Intermediate witnesses, that is, those that are lost and had exactly one descendant that is extant or gave rise to extant witnesses, cannot be depicted in a stemma unless their existence can be proven (which is rarely the case). Behind every line in a stemma, therefore, many lost intermediary witnesses may be hiding. Usually, one stemma is attempted for an entire text, but there can be cases where different stemmata for several parts of a text are necessary. In strongly contaminated transmissions, variant stemmata, that is, one stemma per *locus criticus* (see 3.3), are sometimes drawn (see 4.2.3.6). Any oriented tree has exactly one root (see 5.2), and the rest of the tradition represented by the tree descends from this root. This root is called the archetype in stemmatology. A stemma that is not a tree but only tree-like (and oriented) may have more than one root. In the case where parts of texts coalesced from various sources, the stemmata of the various components may grow into a "forest" of stemmata attached to one another with several roots. Moreover, indirect witnesses (discussed in 3.2) may provide evidence of texts that were the archetypes earlier in the textual history, before further loss of witnesses, but whose existence can now only be glimpsed in certain passages that happen to be transmitted indirectly. How to deal with such cases in a critical edition can be a difficult question, especially if the text changed significantly between earlier text-states only known incompletely from indirect witnesses and the archetype of the text as it now exists. This situation can arise, for example, in practical, fluid texts such as Latin medical texts of the Middle Ages. In general, it may be better to avoid "patchwork" editions if the text is of a rather fluid nature, and just to indicate the available older readings in an apparatus.

The stemma must not be confounded with what has, since Fourquet (1946, 5), been called the "real tree" or "complete tree" ("un arbre généalogique réel, complet"), by which is meant the (hypothetical) true genealogical tree of all witnesses of a text that have ever existed, including the lost ones (see Trovato 2017, 44–46). This entity is, of course, purely theoretical, as it would contain information that is no longer available (e.g. witnesses that are lost without a trace). In contrast, in a stemma, only known or traceable witnesses ("junctions" in the tree) can figure. These are often only a small minority, "rari nantes in gurgite vasto" [rare shipwrecks afloat in a raging surge], as Guidi and Trovato (2004, 11) nicely quote from Virgil (*Aeneis* 1.118). The designation "real tree" would seem doubly unfortunate, for this "real" object is completely hypothetical and, moreover, does not have to be a mathematical tree at all, as there may be cycles depicting contamination. This is a typical case of technical terminology from two fields being incompatible. The computer simulations by Weitzman (1982) show nicely how the position of the archetype shifts in the "real tree" as branches are made to die off probabilistically (see fig. 2.4-2 above). This concept will be studied from a modelling point of view below (4.2.3.4).

Examples
A few examples of increasing complexity will illustrate the kinds of stemmata one can expect to encounter in editions of texts. Figure 4.1-2 shows an old stemma (1881) that is completely binary. The archetype is called "Fort.", indicating the author's name and thus failing to differentiate between the original and the archetype. Figure 4.1-3 is another old stemma (1917) with two archetypes, or to be more precise, an original and a text reworked by the author that each led to further copies. Extant witnesses are shown by capital letters and numbers. Lost intermediaries are represented by lower-case letters, where today Greek lower-case letters would be more typical (at least in classical philology). This editor chose the manuscript sigla in a

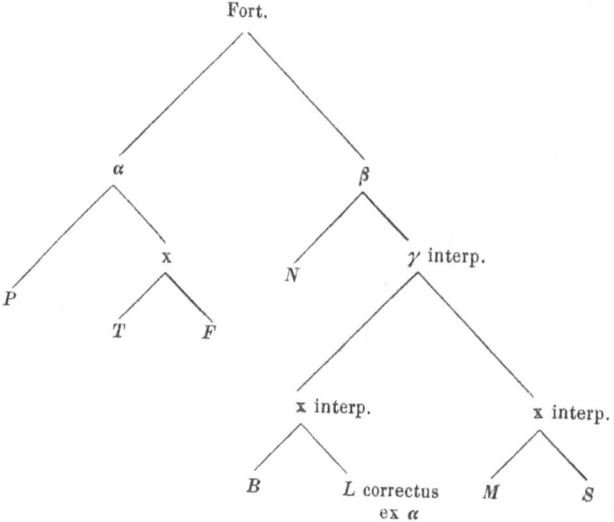

Fig. 4.1-2: Stemma for Venantius Fortunatus, *Opera poetica*, edited by Leo (1881, xxiii). Some lost intermediaries were "interpolated", that is, contaminated (see 4.4 below); manuscript *L* was corrected from a manuscript from family α and is thus also contaminated. Today, this would more usually be shown by a dotted line between α and *L*.

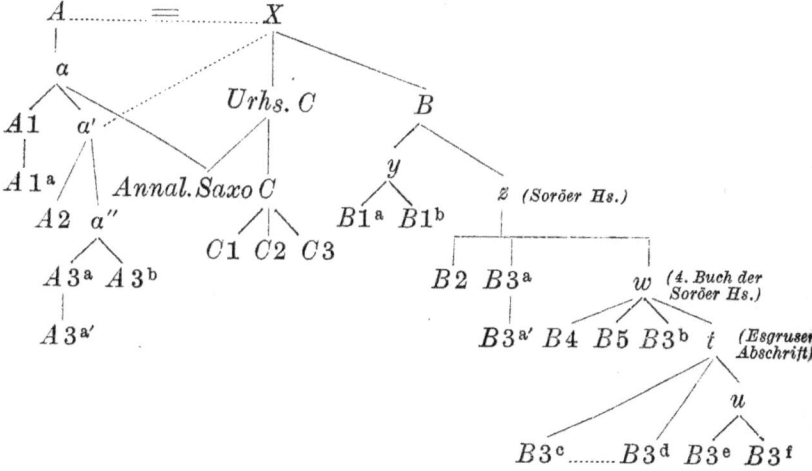

Fig. 4.1-3: Stemma of Adam of Bremen's *Gesta Hamaburgensis ecclesiae pontificum* by Schmeidler (1917, xxxiv). The author reworked his text (from A to X); α represents the archetype of the descendants of the first recension, A. Apparently, another author (Annalista Saxo) used both α and "Urhs. C" as sources for his own work.

way that fits their stemmatic relations (group A, group B, group C) in his stemma. The problem with this approach is that the sigla will have to be changed if his groups are proved wrong, thus causing confusion. Today, more neutral sigla, often indicating the present location of manuscripts – such as *V1*, *V2* for Vatican ones, or *P1*, *P2* for ones in Paris – are usual. The dotted line leading to *a'* indicates contamination, a convention that is still usual today.

A complicated modern stemma (2011) is depicted in figure 4.1-4. Lost intermediate witnesses are shown in lower-case Greek letters, extant manuscripts in upper-case Latin ones. Dashed lines represent contamination, except for the one between Ω^1 and Ω^2: Ω^1 represents the archetype, which was corrected after having been copied and gave rise to a Carolingian vulgate text (see 4.1.6), here named Ω^2. As the text became widely read in Carolingian times, this corrected, more intelligible vulgate text influenced nearly all extant manuscripts. Those older than Ω^2 were corrected ("pc" stands for *post correctionem*). Exceptions are only *A* and *W*. The estimated age of the witnesses is provided on the left-hand side.

Finally, figure 4.1-5 shows a stemma of a manuscript tradition with an extant autograph of the author (*R*; Reims, Bibliothèque municipale, 875). The original text was enlarged several times, producing extant manuscripts *B* and *P*. Sheldon-Williams believed both enlargements to be by the author and consequently based his edition on the most recent one, *P* ("Periphyseon C"); the most recent editor, Jeauneau (1996–2003), disagrees. Since the question is complex, Jeauneau decided to edit the three different versions in parallel, including his own edition in a fourth column.

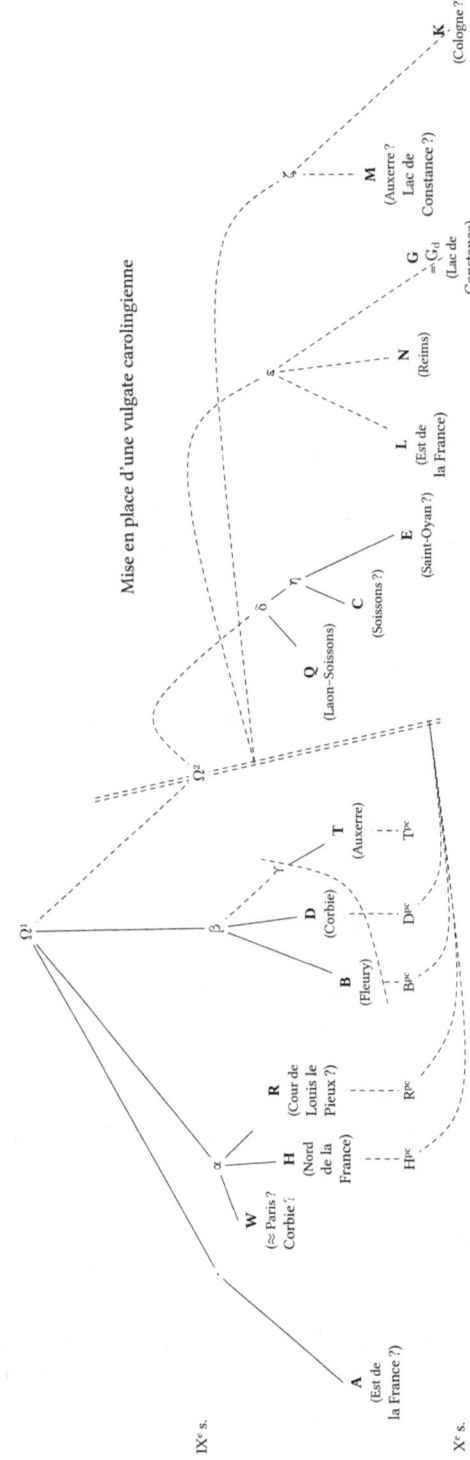

Fig. 4.1-4: Example of a complicated, modern stemma: Martianus Capella, *De nuptiis Philologiae et Mercurii*, proposed by Jean-Baptiste Guillaumin (Guillaumin 2011, cxv; slightly reworked by Guillaumin for this book).

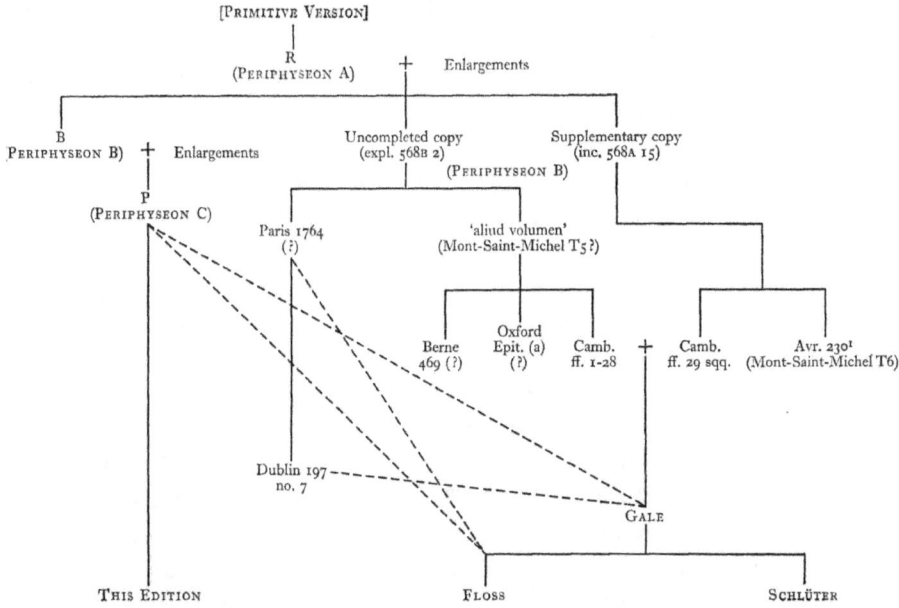

Fig. 4.1-5: Stemma of John Scottus Eriugena's *Periphyseon* by Sheldon-Williams (1968–, 1:29). The text was twice enlarged. Again, contamination is shown by dashed lines; printed editions are named in small capitals. The first print (by Gale) used a composite manuscript whose text source changed at folio 29. © Dublin Institute for Advanced Studies (DIAS).

4.1.4 Branching in stemmata

We have already mentioned above some of the possible types of stemmata one may encounter: there may or may not be contamination, and they may display one or more text-strata (as figs 4.1-3–5 above do). Others, such as variant stemmata (4.2.3.6) or the mathematical concept of the Greg tree (4.2.3.3), will be encountered in the next section. Here, however, we will address one classification scheme that has been the focus of debate for quite some time: the question of bifurcation in stemmata. In the wake of Bédier (e.g. 1928, 11), one often speaks of bifid, binary, bifurcating, or bipartite stemmata. All these adjectives derive from Latin, contain the prefix *bi-*, "two", and have related meanings. "Bifid" is derived from Latin *bifidus*, "divided into two parts"; *bipartitus* is a Latin synonym for *bifidus*; and *binarius* means anything "that contains or consists of two". "To bifurcate" stems from Latin *bifurcus*, "having two prongs or points" (all Latin meanings from Lewis and Short 1879).

A **bifid stemma** is a stemma in which the archetype produces exactly two branches, out of which the entire extant transmission derives. The term was first used by Bédier, who observed that, in the field of Old French manuscript traditions, almost all stemmata he encountered were bifid; this led him to question the validity of the Lachmannian approach (cf. Bédier 1913, 1928; see 2.3–4 above, 7.3 below). Bédier speaks of a "silva portentosa" [monstrous forest] of nearly exclusively bifid trees he had found. Several theories have been proposed to explain or rationalise this phenomenon (starting with Bédier himself); they are based partly on alleged forms of mediaeval text transmission, partly on statistics, partly on psychological grounds. In the latter case, it is argued that editors tend to continue trying to find conjunctive errors until they end up with only two families, in the process possibly mistaking some shared, but polygenetic innovations for conjunctive errors. This has the convenient side effect for the editor that he must (and therefore: may) choose between the two families' divergent readings, instead of following the criterion, which would be automatic in most cases, of choosing the reading of the majority of families. The psychological argument thus amounts to the idea that the editor wishes to have some freedom in determining his text. On the other hand, Guidi and Trovato (2004) have argued, based on computer simulations, that the higher the loss rate of witnesses, the more likely bifurcations become. They tried to estimate loss rates for some early prints of which the original number of copies is known. These tend to be very high (90–100 %). Weitzman (1987, 303) had already written, referring to his own simulations, that "the present model, for example, overturns Bédier's assertion that the majority of stemmata cannot be two-branched". Hoenen, Eger, and Gehrke (2017) put forward a mathematical argument that bifurcating stemmata are indeed the most common kind of stemmata. A further critical discussion of Bédier's points can be found in Reeve (1986).

A glance at the many (and often complicated) stemmata printed in volume 1 of the *Geschichte der Textüberlieferung* (Hunger et al. 1961–1964) seems to indicate that bifid stemmata are much less prevalent for classical (Greek and Latin) texts; this impression is confirmed when looking at some mediaeval Latin editions printed in the Corpus Christianorum continuatio mediaevalis collection. It would be interesting to examine whether these differences are due to the much more standardised classical languages, or different circumstances for the transmission of the texts, or even to different approaches by the editors. In a recent study of stemmata in Old Norse philology, Haugen (2016) arrived at figures for bifid stemmata that were very similar to those in the Old French tradition. The phenomenon needs to be studied further, especially taking into account different kinds of textual traditions (different languages, different witness survival rates, different timespans between original and archetype, and the like). For now, however, it seems safe to say that Bédier uncovered a real phenomenon and not, as he believed, an artefact of a method that does not work.

In contrast to a bifid stemma, a **binary stemma** or tree is one composed exclusively of nodes with either two children or none (not only, as in bifid stemmata, on the top level). Although real traditions of this kind of any magnitude are unlikely, one not infrequently encounters binary stemmata in editions (e.g. figs 4.1-2, 4.1-6; many examples are also printed in Bédier 1928), and many types of software (see 5.3)

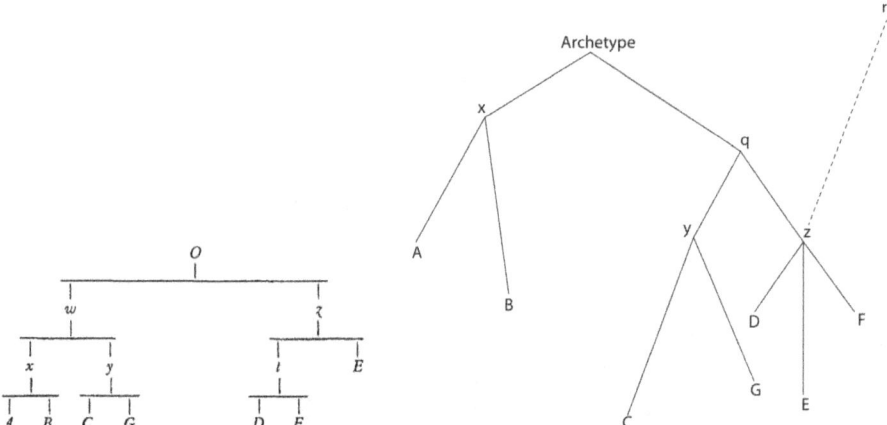

Fig. 4.1-6: (Left) the binary stemma initially proposed for the *Lai de l'ombre* by Bédier (1928; repr. 1970, 6). Bédier later accepted the criticism of Gaston Paris (1890) and modified the stemma to make it tripartite (by moving *E* directly below the archetype) before giving up on the stemmatic method. (Right) according to Trovato (2017, 294), the problem of a lacuna correctly filled in *z* can be solved by assuming extra-stemmatic contamination (see "1963" in 2.4.2). Of course, both *r* and the archetype go back to the original (not depicted).

can by design only produce binary trees, which, however, can easily be remedied by contracting nearby bifurcations into a single node (see 5.2 for more details). "Bifurcating" is a synonym for "binary" in manuscript studies, whereas "bipartite" may be used as a synonym for "bifid" or "binary". On the whole, the usage of these terms does not seem to be fully fixed yet.

There are, however, also many stemmata with a lot more than two branches issuing from the first node (the archetype). Figure 4.1-7 shows such a case: the stemma of Petrus Alfonsi's *Dialogus*, exhibiting eight branches directly from the archetype. This case, probably quite rare, of such a high initial filiation (the archetype is close in time to the original – indeed, the two may be identical in this case) is explained by the fact that the book immediately gained great popularity. It may be that the author, who was a travelling scholar, frequently left his abode, which will have made it likely that local disciples wanted to keep a copy (on this hypothesis, see Cardelle de Hartmann, Senekovic, and Ziegler forthcoming, chap. 1).

In graph theory, the term "bipartite" means something entirely different. There, a bipartite graph is a graph whose nodes can be arranged into two disjoint sets such that every edge connects a node in one of them to one in the other (i.e. in each of the two sets, there are no nodes that are connected with one another; Diestel 2005, 17). It can be proved by induction that every tree is a bipartite graph (in this mathematical sense). These two meanings of "bipartite" should not be confused.

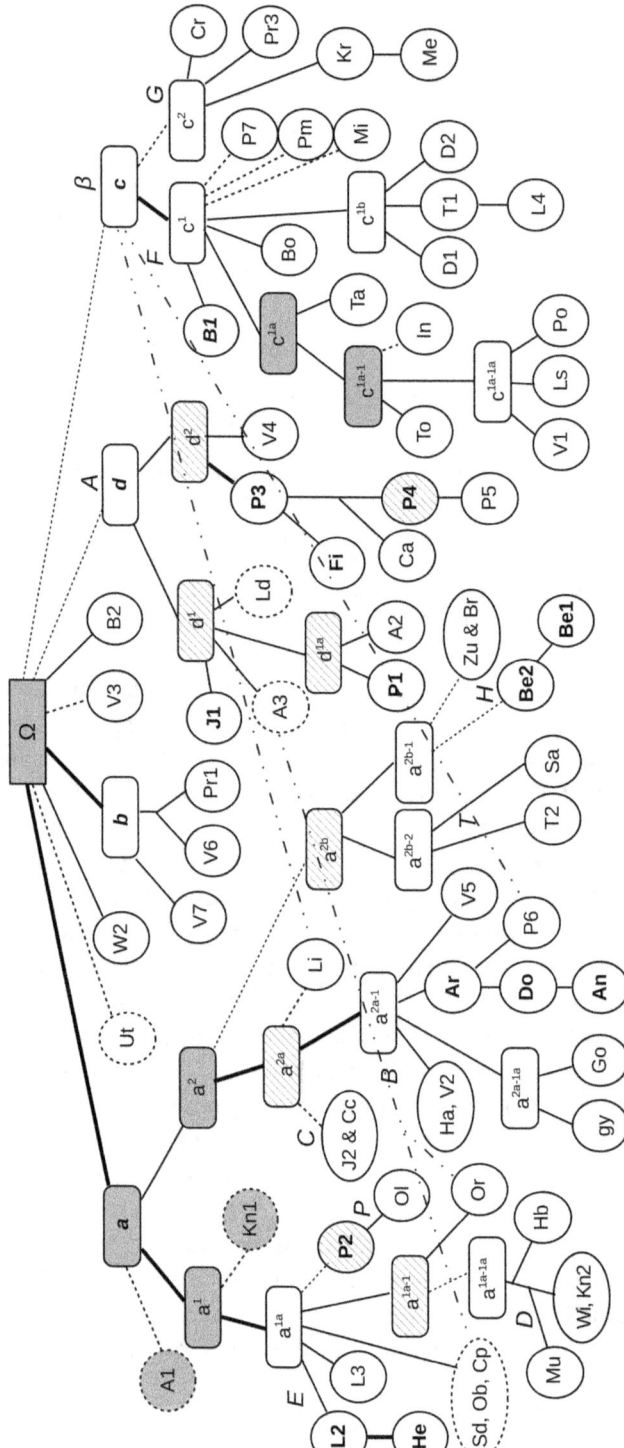

Fig. 4.1-7: A complicated stemma for Petrus Alfonsi's *Dialogus* with strong filiation from the archetype (from Roelli 2014, 55). Thick lines indicate few changes, dashed ones many. Dot-dash lines indicate contamination.

4.1.5 The archetype

Below, it will become clear that the term "archetype" is used in some slightly differing ways today. We would propose the following definition: the archetype is the most recent witness from which all extant witnesses of a text derive.

It follows from this definition that the archetype's text is as close to the original state of the text as the surviving witnesses can attest. According to this definition, the archetype may in some cases be identical with the original – if the original itself has survived, or if more than one copy of the original has produced extant offspring. For classical or early mediaeval texts, however, this is very rare. An example of a text from the ninth century that has come down to us in the original is the *Periphyseon* by John Scottus Eriugena (Jeauneau and Dutton 1996; see also 1.2.4, and fig. 4.1-5 above). At any rate, the concept of an original is stronger than that of an archetype; in other words, if an archetype of a text can be shown to have been the original, it is usually addressed as the "original" and treated accordingly. For texts from Antiquity or the Middle Ages, the low chances of having an extant archetype are still somewhat higher than those of having an extant original. If the archetype is not extant, one of the aims of *recensio* (see 6.2) is to reconstruct its text as far as possible. Insofar as it has become the archetype by means of historical accident, this witness may have borne a corrupt text and may have been written by an incompetent scribe; in order to arrive at a readable text, the editor may have to resort to *emendatio* (see 6.2.2.1). On the other hand, it may happen that an especially authoritative copy becomes the archetype because other less authoritative copies are discarded or not copied further (see 4.1.6). The quality of the archetype may be an important parameter for gauging the kind of *arbre réel* one has to expect for a textual tradition. For instance, for Varro's *De lingua Latina* we have an extant but very corrupt archetype from the eleventh century containing five of the original twenty-five books (Firenze, Biblioteca Medicea Laurenziana, li.10).

In a stemma, the archetype is placed immediately below the original (if the latter is depicted at all) and, especially in classical philology, it is often denoted by a Greek letter. Figure 4.1-8 shows the path between the original (X) and the archetype (a), which may have consisted of many and complex branches, all of which are completely lost, as a mere line. As we have seen above in figure 4.1-3, for some works, more than one version of the original may have to be reckoned with (e.g. if the text was reworked by the author); for similar reasons, more than one (state of the) archetype may exist (as in fig. 4.1-4). Several states of an archetype can arise if it was reworked and marginal or *supra lineam* variants were added to it. This will make the reconstruction of the stemma more difficult, as some copyists may simply have omitted these variants while others may have incorporated them (or some of them) into the text while omitting the original readings. In certain traditions (especially very contaminated or fragmentary ones), it may be impossible to arrive at an archetype.

A h y p a r c h e t y p e is a state of the text, often but not necessarily lost, which is situated directly below the archetype in the stemma. The word is derived from

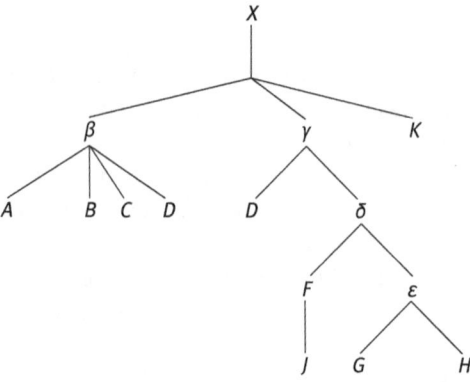

Fig. 4.1-8: Model stemma from Maas (1960, 7), redrawn and slightly simplified.

Greek ὑπό, "under, below", and ἀρχέτυπον (see above). Thus, in figure 4.1-8, β and γ are lost hyparchetypes, and K is an extant one. The term is also occasionally used more loosely for ancestors of families that do not go back directly to the archetype, such as δ in our example. Hyparchetypes are thus the ancestors of related families of preserved witnesses. Like the archetype, hyparchetypes are often denoted by Greek characters in the stemma, especially in classical philology. Paul Maas proposed using the term "hyparchetype" in a more exclusive sense to refer to reconstructed v a r i a n t - c a r r i e r s (1960, 8), that is, lost witnesses directly below the archetype. He considers as v a r i a n t only those readings directly below the archetype between which no mechanical choice is possible. The alternative form of the term, "subarchetype" – with *sub*, the Latin synonym for ὑπό – is not recommended, but is sometimes found in the literature.

There are many subtly different definitions of the key concept of the archetype in the literature. Reeve (1986) collected a list of about a dozen such definitions, some (but not all) of which are identical or equivalent to the above definition. In particular, there is contention about two points. First, it is disputed whether an e x t a n t a r c h e t y p e should still be called an archetype. It may be argued that in such a case all other witnesses can be eliminated (*eliminatio codicum descriptorum*; see 2.2.8) and – at least for the reconstruction of the primordial text – the situation becomes equivalent to that of a *codex unicus* (see 3.3.2) without an archetype. For instance, Montanari would in such a case speak of a "codex unicus secondario" (2003, 21). Other opinions differ; Pasquali, for example, was content to address an "archetipo conservato delle Metamorfosi di Apuleio" (1934, 33) [the extant archetype of the *Metamorphoses* by Apuleius], and we would prefer to speak at least of a t r i v i a l a r c h e t y p e in such cases. Second, in the cases where the same witness is both original and archetype, it will in most cases likewise make little sense to speak of the original as an archetype, and some authors would altogether avoid this. From a practical philological point of view, it is indeed preferable to avoid doing so, as the text has to be treated differently depending on whether it is sanctioned by the author (in the case of an original) or a product of historical chance (non-original archetype); but from a graph-theoretical point of view, both are MRCAs (most recent common ancestors) and stand in need of a common designation. The existence of an archetype different from the original can be proved by finding at least one error common to the entire tradition, one the author could not have written. One may, therefore, differentiate between a narrower concept of the archetype which excludes originals and extant archetypes and which is especially useful in the context of ecdotics, and a wider, purely positional one that equates "archetype" with "MRCA". Here, we follow the latter.

In graph-theoretical language, finding the archetype is equivalent to assigning a root in an unrooted tree (see further 4.2). In evolutionary biology, the term "most recent common ancestor" (MRCA) is used similarly to "archetype" in textual criticism. Here, however, the similarity to phylogenetics ends: the concept of an original makes little sense in biology, unless one chooses to go all the way back to the so-called LUCA (last universal common ancestor) of all living beings, to which, however, no urtext of all existing texts ever written can be compared.

No matter whether computerised or traditional approaches are used, deciding where in the tree the archetype is to be located is often the most difficult, but also the most crucial, task for a philologist studying a textual tradition with an interest in the original text. In the traditional method, the problem is usually less pronounced because good significant errors (see 2.2.5) can often be identified. They are, in Greg's terminology, "substantive variants" (also known as "substantial" ones), which he defined thus:

> we need to draw a distinction between the significant, or as I shall call them 'substantive', readings of the text, those namely that affect the author's meaning or the essence of his expression, and others, such in general as spelling, punctuation, word-division, and the like, affecting mainly its formal presentation, which may be regarded as the accidents, or as I shall call them 'accidentals', of the text. (Greg 1950–1951, 21)

A subclass of such substantive variants – those that cannot be undone by an intelligent scribe – can serve as significant errors. These tend to be directed; that is, the editor can determine which variant is original (or at least archetypal) and which one(s) are innovated. There are several aids at the philologist's disposal for this task: old ones such as *lectio difficilior* (see 4.3.2), as well as more recent ones such as diffraction (see "1955–" in 2.4.3). In order to do this correctly, knowledge about the text and its author, or the archetype and its scribe, must be inferred and used. Computerised approaches from biology are not usually helpful for this, as biologists tend to use an outgroup to root their trees. The outgroup, as will be explained more fully below (5.2.1), is an organism distantly related to the group of taxa being studied. The point where its branch exits the tree then corresponds to the MRCA of the studied group. As texts are written at some point in time *ex nihilo*, so to speak, this approach cannot usually be used for rooting the tree (see 3.2.8, 4.5.3 for exceptions). The example in figure 4.1-6 above shows how a stemma can change radically if another node in the tree is designated as the archetype. Such changes lead to a very

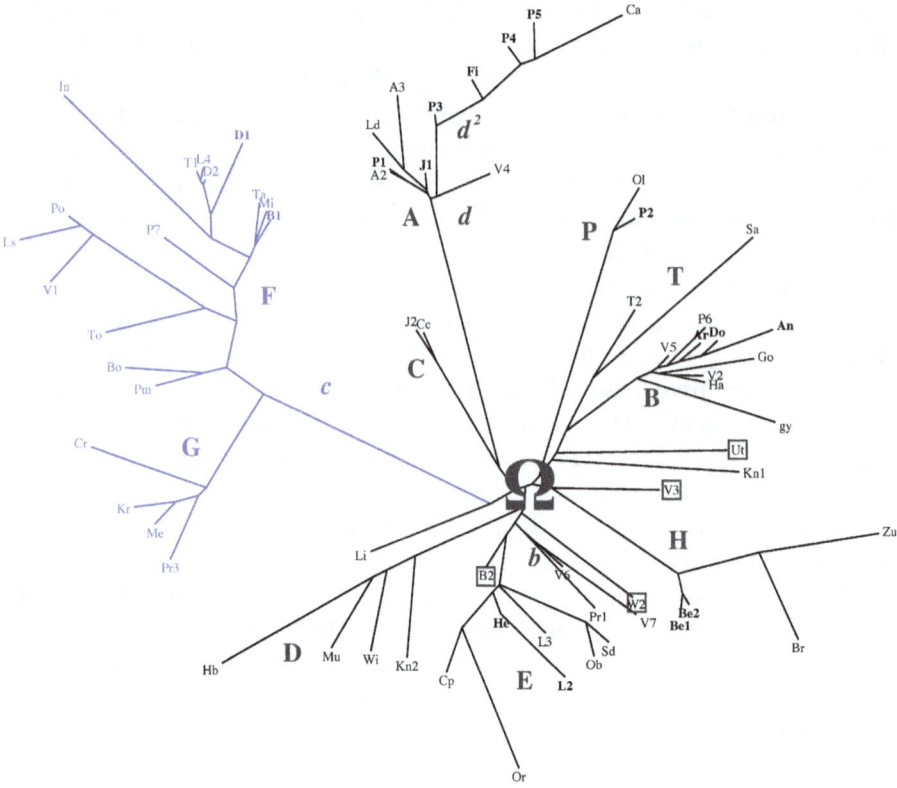

Fig. 4.1-9: How does one find the archetype in an unoriented tree? Example from Roelli (2014, 47) with added blue colour. The tree was drawn fully automatically; only the superimposed letters naming the families were added manually. The boxed witnesses are the oldest ones.

different influence of the witnesses on the reconstruction of the archetypal text. In Bédier's stemma, *E* is the most important witness (with a weighting of 25 %), whereas in Trovato's, *A* and *B* are (with a weighting of 25 % each). Once the philologist, perhaps using software, has arrived at an unrooted tree-graph of the relationships between all extant witnesses, direction in the tree must be provided by discerning for some variants which one is original or archetypal and which one(s) is (or are) innovated. A priori, the archetype may be hiding at any point in the tree, even perhaps on an edge between two nodes. An example from the recent edition of Petrus Alfonsi's *Dialogus* will illustrate the approach. "*Leitfehler*"-based software (as described in 5.3.7) produced the unrooted tree depicted in figure 4.1-9. In the following passage, the text marked "°...°" is missing in all witnesses of the *c* group (blue in fig. 4.1-9):

> Nunc cognoscere potes quia gradus signi qui est in oriente sole Aren ciuitati apparente °non est idem cum eo qui eadem hora alii ciuitati apparet. Similiter gradus qui est in occidente sole in Aren occumbente° non est idem cum eo qui eadem hora alii apparet ciuitati. (Cardelle de Hartmann, Senekovic, and Ziegler 2019, § 56)

Philological judgement is required to observe that the omission is best explained through eye-skip ("non est idem [...] non est idem"; see 4.3.2 for more on this phenomenon) and that, therefore, the *c* group has innovated by accidentally removing the words in question. It follows that the blue parts of the tree cannot contain the archetype. Similar arguments show that, in this case, the archetype is indeed in the middle of the plot (marked as Ω). If editors fail to conduct this step of determining the direction for some variants (the "significant errors" discussed in 2.2.5), it is likely that a wrong place in the tree will be chosen as the would-be archetype. This may be the most "neutral" text or the one most commonly read in some key period, possibly long after the archetype. This leads into the consideration of such textual vulgates.

4.1.6 Vulgates

To conclude this section, we look at a concept related to that of the archetype, that of a textual v u l g a t e. The word derives from the Latin *vulgata*, "spread among the multitude (*vulgus*)"; the feminine noun *editio*, "edition", is implied, so the form is feminine. The same term is more frequently met in biblical studies, but there it denotes something completely unrelated: St Jerome's Latin translation of the Bible, which became the most widely used one in the Middle Ages and beyond. In textual criticism, a vulgate text is the text form that reached the widest distribution at a time, possibly long after the archetype, when interest in the text experienced an upsurge for one reason or another and many copies were made. When interest in a text is high, it is also likely that some people will compare witnesses in order to arrive at a better text. This is, in fact, nearly the same thing that modern philologists using the genealogical method do, although before the nineteenth century the scientific tools for arriving as close to the archetypal text as possible were not yet in existence and the result depended a lot more on the editor's intuition. Vulgate texts are thus often a kind of early text edition or, to put it negatively, the product of heavy contamination. Their text may supplant all other text forms and thus eradicate them. Trovato (2017, 299–333) provides an example in his discussion of the transmission of Dante's *Divina Commedia*. A v u l g a t e r e a d i n g is a reading present in a vulgate; it can also refer simply to the most frequent reading, and often implies that this reading is not the original one.

If witnesses are grouped based on all undirected variants, instead of exclusively on directed common errors, as might be the case on the part of inexperienced textual editors using software methods, there is a great risk of arriving at a vulgate text instead of the archetype (see Trovato 2017, 138–144). In some cases, it will make sense to edit a vulgate text because it was the most frequently read one, but it is important to be aware of the difference between vulgate and archetypal texts.

4.2 The stemma as a computational model

Armin Hoenen

This section considers the stemma from a computational and mathematical point of view: as a model for the evolution of a text.

4.2.1 Modelling

Devising models is one of the typical activities in the digital domain, and – whether explicit or implicit – is one of the first activities in a computational project. The goal of modelling is to outline a basic, often formal concept of one's research object (in our case, the stemma) and the research process involved in attaining it, which can be used as a framework for implementations, operations, and exchange between scholars using the same model. It follows that, as a conceptual framework, a model is an abstract and structured representation of the research object and process that contains many definitions. However, there are different types of models, depending on how the scholar wants to conceptualise the object of study: for example, a model can be based on the entities involved in what is to be modelled and their relationships (entity-relationship models), or it can be based on the development over time of the object under study (process models). Models can be graphically presented and constructed with specialist software that employs a modelling language, such as the Unified Modelling Language. Furthermore, models differ in their level of abstraction (from conceptual to physical). Obviously, the kind of model which is needed depends strongly on the task at hand. The most basic kind of model to consider in our context is a purely conceptual model of a stemma. We have several cases in the computerised stemmatological literature that explicitly mention a model or are even focused on it (Najock and Heyde 1982; Spencer and Howe 2002; Andrews and Macé 2013). Andrews and Macé (2012), in particular, outline some models connected directly with stemmatology. For a more in-depth general discussion of modelling, see Minsky (1965); for modelling editions, see Vanhoutte (2010) and McCarty (2014).

In practice, since modelling – if undertaken seriously – is time-consuming and resource-intensive, many models are expressed simply as formal sketches using simple graphical elements (such as labelled circles, triangles, and so on) and idiosyncratic mappings of those shapes to entities in the context of the project at hand. Modelling can be a part of the good documentation practice that any project should engage in.

4.2.2 The stemma: A conceptual model

In order to work with a stemma, the general concepts behind what we mathematically intend to be a stemma should be formulated in clear mathematical terms in order to discuss implications, understand and develop extensions, and to reproduce and ultimately improve results. The process of formulating a concept using mathematical formulae is called formalisation, and the result can be a model. The computational aspects of a model can include, among other things, specifications of data structures saved to disk and the sequence and interaction of components, as well as other specifications at the interface of theoretical concepts and practical manifestation. Particularly in computational stemmatology, an explicit model is important as the model is the framework on the basis of which different approaches are evaluated: results may crucially depend on the underlying model. Metaphorically speaking, using different models is roughly comparable to belonging to different schools, for instance, in philosophy. Exchange between studies that use different models is not always possible and requires clearly defined abstractions. A model can be formalised in different ways adhering to different conventions. Van Zundert et al. (2012, 280) remark that a complete lack of formalisation has been blamed for failed attempts to apply computational approaches to questions in the humanities. Typical entities in the humanities tend to be complex in technical terms. The aforementioned lack of formalisation is in part due to this complexity when the object of study is described *expressis verbis* but not *expressis formulis* – in words rather than in formulae – and when those interested in the formulae tend not to be those interested in the words. The texts themselves are often written by philological experts for philological experts, which may create an invisible barrier for non-philologists when trying to formalise the concepts behind, for instance, stemmata and build algorithms on the basis of them. On top of that, van Zundert et al. (2012, 281) point out that different kinds of formalisation exist and that they are not universal across research domains. This explains why models based on formalisation apparatuses carried over from fields such as bioinformatics or mathematics may need some formal adaptation to cover certain aspects of textual criticism. Additionally, in this sense, the concrete meaning of the term "model" may slightly differ and depend on the approach to formalisation one chooses. Formalisation is not a trivial undertaking, but it helps clarify ambiguities and enables programmers to quickly implement approaches and mathematicians to outline general properties and limits within which a model operates. Some philologists have worked, or have tried to work, formally and will be considered in more detail. Some of them have explicitly used well-researched mathematical entities and terminology, while others have created their own notations for the formal representation of stemmatically relevant givens.

Finally, models are sometimes implicit and we have to deduce them from the way in which stemmata are displayed. For instance, one can often immediately see whether a stemma has a distinguished root node or whether it is unrooted, which easily translates into a mathematical property. Such implicit models are not problematic as long as no ambiguity arises concerning their interpretation; but an explicit formalisation could prevent such problems a priori. In other words, the model used is often retrievable from the text and the visualisations given in a study, although this may require some interpretation and profound knowledge of stemmatological phenomena and their implications. In this sense, translating or devising a computational model for stemmatology is an interdisciplinary and by no means trivial process.

It might be possible to develop a single model to represent all kinds of stemmata. However, such a model would have to be very general, so general that its concrete usefulness might become debatable. In the rest of this section, we present a theoretical modelling framework for stemmatology; look at the most explicit models which scholars have formulated in their publications, and then at implicit models and ways to deduce and formulate them; and finally summarise and conclude.

4.2.3 General frameworks: Graph theory

Most approaches to formalising stemmata rely on the basics of the mathematical framework of graph theory. In graph theory, we have two basic components: nodes and edges. Nodes represent entities, and edges represent relationships between them. Within graph theory, a stemma can be modelled in a number of different ways. Since section 5.2 introduces the basics of graph theory and gives more precise definitions of graphs and their components, we will only discuss here what kinds of graph-theoretical entities have been used as stemmatic models and how.

4.2.3.1 Graph-theoretical models for a stemma: The directed acyclic graph

A very commonly used entity to model a stemma is the DAG, which stands for "directed acyclic graph", that is, a directed graph whose paths never start and end at the same node (see further 5.2.1; it is also alluded to in the definition in 4.1.2). For instance, Andrews and Macé (2013, 509) explicitly use the DAG as a principal stemmatic model and elaborate on it at the level of variants. Often, when studies

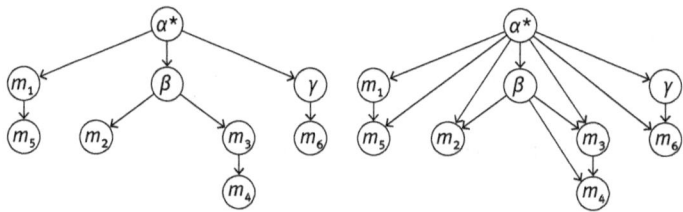

Fig. 4.2-1: (Left) a rooted tree, by necessity also a rooted DAG. Roots can be marked by asterisks, here within the node. The characteristics reflected in the term "rooted DAG" are the root, directed edges (copies from ancestor to descendant, here indicated by arrows), and the absence of cycles (explained in the main text). (Right) a rooted DAG that is not a tree: some nodes have more than one incoming edge, but there are no cycles, since paths can only be traversed in the direction of the edges.

do not explicitly mention their model, a DAG is a good first assumption. Moreover, for stemmata the DAG is often rooted (or oriented) with reference to a single root node. As Andrews and Macé (2012, 86) state, a rooted DAG can be used as a stemmatic model regardless of the amount of horizontal transmission (4.4) present. One can use the more restricted term "tree" (or, if rooted, "rooted tree") if no node has more than one parent (closed tradition; see 4.4.1). The more specific a model is, the more precise its implications are, but at the same time restrictions to its applicability arise. Thus, some scholars, although dealing in practice with trees, may prefer to model and refer to their stemmata as DAGs, since a tree is by definition a DAG but a DAG does not have to be a tree.

4.2.3.2 Graph-theoretical models for a stemma: Beyond the (usual) DAG

Stemmata may also be modelled with unrooted or undirected graphs, similar to the one depicted in figure 4.2-2 (see Quentin 1926 or Flight 1992, who at times in their work used non-DAG models, where direction comes into play at later stages). In summary, a conventional graph-theoretical stemmatic model can be outlined by more precisely specifying properties of the graph. Terms for such models can be constructed simply by concatenating terms referring to the properties, for instance an "unrooted undirected graph", a "labelled rooted graph", and so on. The most important properties commonly used are as follows.

– Rootedness. Possible standard configurations of a graph with respect to rootedness are rooted, unrooted (by default), or multiply rooted. "Rooted" simply means we mark one (or more) node(s) as root(s). In the case of a work with oral origins, for instance, a stemma could have multiple roots corresponding to the first dictations of different versions at different places (see Lord 1960).
– Cyclicity. Possible standard configurations of a graph with respect to cyclicity are cyclic or acyclic. It is usually clear a priori that cycles may exist in a graph, so one would usually not explicitly call a graph a "cyclic graph" in order to indicate that it has or can have cycles. The term "cyclic graph" can instead be

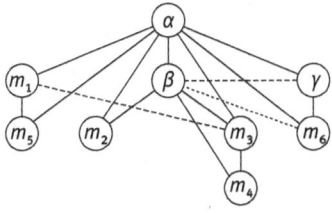

Fig. 4.2-2: A graph that is not a DAG – for instance, there is a path going from α to m_3 and from m_3 to β and then from there back to α since the edges are undirected. This is a cycle and makes the graph a non-DAG. There is no explicit root; the graphical layout suggests that α could be the root, but this is not made explicit, for instance by writing "α*". This particular graph has three textures (visual styles) of edges, which may correspond to different weights or types of edges.

used in special cases, such as when the entire graph constitutes a single circle. "Acyclic" means that there is no path (succession of adjacent edges) in the graph beginning in one node and ending in the same node. This interacts with the next property of direction insofar as an undirected graph can have cycles removed if direction is introduced. Finally, self-loops are allowed in some graphs; a self-loop is a single edge with the same starting and ending node. Corrections of later passages using earlier passages in the same manuscript may be modelled as self-loops.

- Direction. Possible standard configurations of a graph with respect to directedness are directed, undirected, or mixed. Being directed means that an edge does not connect two nodes equally but connects a source node to a target node. A directed edge can only be traversed in its direction; an undirected edge can be traversed in either direction. It is possible to have graphs with both directed and undirected edges, which are then called mixed graphs.
- Labelling. Possible standard configurations of a graph with respect to labelling are labelled, unlabelled, or mixed. Edges or nodes are either assigned a concrete name (labelled) or not (unlabelled). Again, partly labelled graphs are possible.

Graphs can have a number of other properties, such as multiple edges between the same two nodes, or indeed edges connecting more than two nodes. Also, nodes and/or edges can be weighted or have types assigned to them (e.g. edge-weighted graphs). This arsenal of additional properties can be exploited to generate more detailed models for stemmata.

Concerning terminology, certain combinations of properties are referred to by established names, as we have seen for "tree". However, for very specialised terms in particular, there are sometimes two or more empirically implied sets of properties with only subtle differences depending on the author, which is why, in addition to using a term such as "DAG", one should mention what exactly one means by it. In other words, the terms are not as important as the properties that are defined and used. Such a definition may include mathematical formulae. A brief formal mathematical definition of a graph is $G = \{V,E\}$. This means: a graph G is defined as a set (denoted by the curly brackets) of V and E. V is itself a set, the set of nodes, and E is the set of edges $e_i \in V \times V$. This latter definition says that an edge is a tuple (or set) of two elements of V, thus $\{v_i, v_j\}$, where $i \neq j$ (if self-loops are excluded). In a rooted graph, we simply add an element to our formal definition of G: $G = \{V,E,r\}$, where $r \in V$ (that is, r is an element in the set V). By formulating such definitions, we formalise the model we use.

4.2.3.3 Graph-theoretical models for a stemma: Greg trees and Greg graphs

Flight (1990) uses an important property of nodes for a stemmatic model: labelling. A label can be thought of as a distinct name which distinguishes a node from the

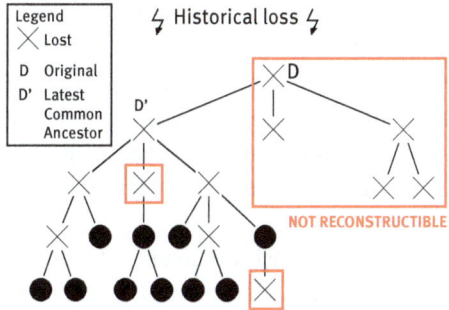

Fig. 4.2-3: The non-reconstructable portions of a tree depicting the complete transmission. Black nodes are the surviving manuscripts. Portions in red cannot be reconstructed according to the stemmatic models of Maas and Flight, which is why they will not appear in a stemma modelled accordingly.

other nodes in the graph. This property of distinction makes a label a very good means to represent the textual content of a textual witness. Conventionally, node labels in stemmata are used either to stand for the textual content or, less frequently, to denote the physical text carriers. The former case implies that we should assume that no two versions of a text (at least beyond a certain length) in a tradition are exactly the same. In model-theoretical terms, if two or more surviving texts are exactly the same, one may have to switch to the second convention: abandon the metaphor in which the label symbolises the witness texts, and instead use it to stand for the physical manuscripts. Such subtle differences can be decisively important from the point of view of a model – a model which has the property of labelled nodes standing for differing textual content is distinct from the one we would need for a tradition where the same text occurs in more than one surviving witness. They are mutually exclusive; that is, we can use either one convention or the other, but not both. In modelling, to a much greater extent than in prose description, one is forced to define precisely what is being talked about; this can compel the scholar to decide between modelling the "typical" case and excluding the exceptions, or modelling with a focus on the exceptions.

A node in a Greg tree may have a label but it may also be unlabelled, in which case it is indistinguishable from any other such unlabelled node. In this model, an unlabelled node represents a hypothetical text of a hypothetical ancestor. Flight (1990) introduces a Greg tree as a rooted directed graph with labelled and unlabelled nodes where an additional restriction applies for the unlabelled nodes: they must have at least two descendants. This property is derived from philological practice, where *codices interpositi* are not generally reconstructed (see Haugen 2016, 601) and lost leaves are omitted, but also concerns the entire portion above the most recent common ancestor (or archetype; see 4.1.4) of all labelled nodes (see fig. 4.2-3). One might go so far as to say that Flight formalises Maas.

Other scholars, such as Hering (1967), have implicitly worked with this model, especially in connection with the Bédier debate (see 2.3.4). Flight (1992) expands the Greg tree model to Greg graphs. Greg graphs are modelled on the basis of Greg trees, but allow cycles. Flight (1992, 1994) demonstrates how one can derive a Greg graph from a simple matrix of possible agreement between any pair of witnesses. Greg trees (and Greg graphs) represent stemmata as entities which can be reconstructed from surviving witnesses.

Two more types of trees remain to be discussed, which are again different in their model-theoretical features. These are not trees that a stemmatologist tries to reconstruct, which for convenience will be called here reconstructable stemmata, or simply stemmata; instead, they are closely related trees which have been used primarily to make theoretical points in the debates on the stemmatological method. These debates are where modelling and numerical reasoning are most firmly expressed within the field.

4.2.3.4 *Arbre réel*

Fourquet (1946) coined the term *arbre réel* for the entire tree of a tradition (see Trovato 2017, 44–46). This means that an *arbre réel* contains all witnesses that have ever existed in the tradition, including all that are irretrievably lost without a trace. The *arbre réel* was introduced as a purely hypothetical construct for an argument in the bifurcation debate initiated by Bédier. In fact, most publications using this term (which may bear other names) can be seen as part of this debate. But the *arbre réel* has gained new importance since the introduction of artificial benchmark datasets, or artificial traditions, by Lantin, Baret, and Macé (2004), Spencer, Mooney, et al. (2004), Roos and Heikkilä (2009), and Hoenen (2015a). These are texts given to volunteers to copy by hand while it is recorded who copied from which text. The *arbre réel* is, in this case, known to the person who organises the experimental copying, and it ceases to be a purely hypothetical entity. It may also be called a benchmark stemma, benchmark dataset, or simply a ground truth or gold standard under these circumstances.

Deriving a model for an *arbre réel* is in one respect easier than modelling a stemma: it is not necessary to model witness loss. In an *arbre réel*, the rooted labelled tree (as in Hoenen, Eger, and Gehrke 2017) can be used as a base model, since all nodes are distinguishable and present. If the artificial tradition included contamination, the *arbre réel* would instead be modelled as a rooted labelled DAG.

4.2.3.5 True stemma

While an *arbre réel* depicts the whole transmission, the one true stemma is that entity which a perfect philologist would ideally reconstruct. In other words, only one stemma is historically true for any tradition we try to make editions and stemmata for. This true stemma (or "stemma reale"; Timpanaro 2005, 137) is in principle just as hypothetical as the *arbre réel*, since for historical data we have no way to verify it in all its details. For the artificial datasets, however, we can draw the true stemma.

As we can see in figure 4.2-3, the true stemma is – if the conventions mentioned in section 4.2.3.3 are followed – not a substructure of the *arbre réel*, apart from having the distinction of labelled and unlabelled nodes which the *arbre réel* does not have. The deletion of *codices interpositi* is a non-trivial transformation: as nodes disappear, edges coalesce and change the general structure. In the underlying *arbre réel* in figure 4.2-3, there is no connection between D' and the descendant of its lost direct copy in the red box, whereas in the true stemma there must be. This aspect was one of the main points criticised by Fourquet (1946). In general, the same models as those for reconstructable stemmata – that is, DAGs, Greg trees, or Greg graphs – are applicable for the true stemma since it is, in theory, one of the possible reconstructable stemmata. However, a special way of modelling the true stemma on the basis of the *arbre réel* is as the result of a process of birth and death or something similar (see 4.2.3.7 below). In such a model, the *arbre réel* and true stemma are intertwined, with the latter as the ultimate stage of the former. The most sophisticated such model has been proposed by Weitzman (1982, 1985, 1987). He simulates true stemmata using a birth-death process (see below). Hoenen (2016), instead, first simulates complete *arbres réels* and then witness loss in different ways. The outcomes of both simulations are simulated true stemmata. Both are formalised in the respective publications.

4.2.3.6 Variant stemmata and variant graphs

While, so far, we have looked at models where the nodes of a graph stand for witnesses, the second entity they can stand for is the individual variant reading. V a r i a n t   s t e m m a t a as models are less complex than witness stemmata. Between two nodes of such a variant stemma stands a copying process: the source reading (e.g. "clash" on the left-hand side of fig. 4.2-4) is miscopied as the target reading (e.g.

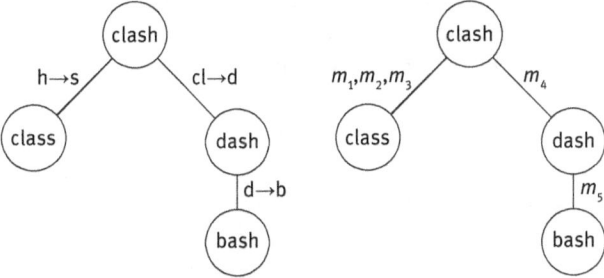

Fig. 4.2-4: (Left) a variant stemma with edges showing the shift events, simplified from Hoenen (2018). (Right) the same stemma, this time listing on the edges witnesses carrying the particular variant at the end of the edge.

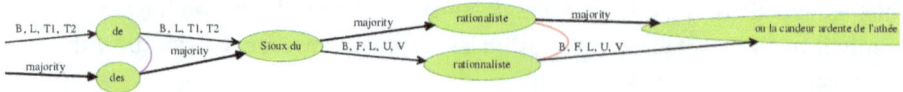

Fig. 4.2-5: Stemmatological variant graph; example from stemmaweb.net (see also 3.4.8 above).

"dash"), perhaps because of the visual similarity of "cl" and "d". Such a process is, in many cases, more straightforward than the hypothesis in a conventional stemma that witness v_i has been copied directly from witness v_j. Of course, variant stemmata are complicated in their own right and have their own set of problems in comparison to stemmatic trees. Various scholars have used stemmata for single variants; the closeness to historical linguistics and their sound-shift rules or grammatical changes (see 8.2.2) can also be noted. West (1973, 52) calls this kind of stemma a *stemma variantium* and gives some examples. Variant graphs display on the edges either those witnesses which adopt the variant or the particular shift which happened between the ancestor and the descendant. The implicitly underlying model for a variant stemma is almost always the rooted labelled DAG, or at least a labelled graph. Generally, variant stemmata often tend to be trees. It can be difficult to devise a model which combines variant stemmata and the overall *stemma codicum*. To this end, the Coherence-Based Genealogical Method has been designed by Mink (2004; see 4.4.8 below).

On the level between witness stemma and variant stemma lies an entity called the variant graph (fig. 4.2-5), introduced by Schmidt and Colomb (2009). Andrews and Macé (2012) elaborate on how this can be a model for a textual tradition. Their variant graph, in stemmatological fashion, displays the complete collation. The edges carry the names of the manuscripts which exhibit the variants in the following node.

4.2.3.7 Extensions to graph models

Depending on the focus of the task at hand, graph theory may not be the only ingredient of a stemma model. For example, Haigh (1970) models the genesis of a stemma using a Yule–Furry linear birth process in conjunction with graph theory. Except for artificial traditions, which always include a recorded *arbre réel*, the *arbre réel* will be an entity which did not really exist at any point in time, since there will be witnesses which are already lost when others are created. If this aspect of transmission is important to the scholar's model of an *arbre réel*, one option is to take a genetic approach where birth-death processes constitute the model-theoretical core of the endeavour. Weitzman (1987) and Haigh (1970) have used formulae defining birth (death) processes which they use to generate graphs (for an illustration from Weitzman, see fig. 2.4-2 above). All stages of the graph together may then be taken as the *arbre réel*. For illustration, we refer here to a specific model of an *arbre réel* as a Yule–Furry birth process outlined by Haigh (1970) and give his comment on the model-theoretical fit:

We consider a population which initially has one member, and which increases one individual at a time to a total size of N as follows. When k (>= 1) members are present, one of them is selected at random (i.e. each member has probability 1/k of being selected) to be the parent of the (k + 1)th member. [...] Clearly this model has many deficiencies: it allows no conflation of sources; missing manuscripts complicate matters enormously; the hypothesis of random selection before a copy is made can only be a crude approximation to the real method of selection. Nevertheless, even if these objections render the solution of the mathematical inference problem inappropriate for the manuscript problem, the mathematical problem does arise in other ways. (Haigh 1970, 79–80)

Thus Haigh (1970) also gives a rationale for using an imperfect model even when its imperfections are known. One might add that a best-approximation model can be useful as long as no better model exists. Kleinlogel (1968), Weitzman (1987), and Hoenen (2016) all define models where manuscript birth and loss are explicit. The model of Weitzman in particular (which is similar to Haigh's but more sophisticated) allows for a parametrisation to cover different types of transmission, which he uses to model transmission for different languages, Greek and Latin. Guidi and Trovato (2004) propose an analysis based on probabilities. They take existing stemmata of sixteenth-century printed books (where at least some copies have survived due to the larger overall numbers of copies) as *arbres réels* and consider the survival probabilities of each possible combination of surviving copies. Trovato (2017, 144–146) elaborates on the problem of the stemma vs the *arbre réel*. We have seen that modelling an *arbre réel* can be quite complex in dealing with witness birth and death. Consequently, the existing models are not easily comparable.

Another example of the use of probabilities in conjunction with graph theory is Gjessing and Pierce (1994). Consequently, for the stemma as a computational model, graph theory is not the only, but by far the most important, general framework we are dealing with. Historically, the emergence of graph theory as a discipline precedes the emergence of modern stemmatology. However, not all scholars have used its (formal) language for their stemmatic models. Merivuori and Roos (2009, 1) allude to other ways of conceptualising a stemma, not necessarily using graph theory, stating that such a stemma "corresponds to i) a clustering hierarchy, where joined subgroups make subtrees" and "iii) a network of information flow among the documents".

4.2.3.8 Criticism
Some explicit or implicit claims have been made that current models are insufficient for displaying some properties of actual stemmata. Irigoin (1954) already addressed a very important point which many models do not take into account – layers, most often encountered as redactions and/or corrections in the manuscript witnesses. He elaborates on an example where one witness was corrected at a certain point in its history, so that copies made before the correction and after it have been assigned misplaced affiliations. This circumstance should be expressed in a good stemmatic

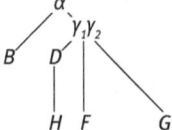

Fig. 4.2-6: Stemma with one node divided into two stages representing layers of the text in the manuscript, by Irigoin (1954, 214).

model, given the widespread occurrence of corrections in manuscripts. New and more holistic models may be required in order to model such phenomena (or, likewise, in the case of marginal notes).

Barabucci, Di Iorio, and Vitali (2014, 131) stated that no computational method of stemma generation has made use of XML-encoded (especially TEI-encoded) data. TEI does allow for the encoding of different strata (i.e. layers of correction) within a witness, but it is an open question in model theory how to reflect this in a stemma. (Identification of strata and hands is complicated in its own right, but an earliest and a latest layer can often be approximated.) Irigoin's graphical depiction shows a side-by-side representation of the labels y_1 and y_2 for the manuscript y and its stages (fig. 4.2-6), but a full formalisation remains to be done.

Yet another problem is text genesis (see also Hoenen and Brüning 2019). A text did not always begin its circulation as one single finalised entity; many different alternative versions or parts of the text may have existed side by side before it was released (see 7.9 for more discussion of such questions). Furthermore, if an author mentions parts of his text in, for example, letters to a fellow author (letters are, after all, as much written products in the age of handwriting as manuscripts, and the distinction drawn between these types of texts is certainly more debatable in that context) and the main text is altered as a result of this exchange, how much of this process should be reflected in a stemma? Can we draw a clear line between text genesis and text transmission, between oral and written transmission, between different strata of witnesses? This may be possible in some cases, but there seems to be no general solution. It would be necessary to formalise an appropriate model for each research question, in most cases the edition of a certain text, anew each time. Similarly, phenomena such as summaries or abbreviations of a text, partial transmission in compendia or florilegia, chapter sequence alternations, and so on are other critical features for much more complex models and still need future work (see 3.2). In this sense, the stemmatic models published to date may be characterised as often still lacking some detail.

4.2.4 Other formalisation frameworks: Stemmatic notation

Some scholars have engaged extensively in modelling by outlining complete frameworks or notations. One example will be briefly described as an approach to formali-

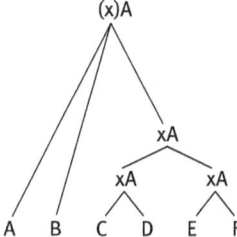

Fig. 4.2-7: A stemma which, in Greg's notation, can be described as *xA'* [A][B][(CD)(EF)]. *xA'* unambiguously stands for an unnamed (exclusive) ancestor, making such nodes equivalent to unlabelled nodes in a Greg tree (see 4.2.3.3). The apostrophe is used primarily as a visual separator in Greg's formulae.

sation that does not rely on existing mathematical frameworks: the s t e m m a t i c n o t a t i o n devised by Greg (1927). A notation is a vocabulary and rule inventory for formalisation, and in this sense can be used to describe properties of models. As Flight (1992, 39) put it, Greg "sought to construct a formalised notation which would satisfy all the needs of stemmatic analysis". Since this notation has subsequently been used only cursorily, and since it does not build on other formal mathematical approaches, we will provide here only a brief summary of it, omitting detail. The basis of the first part of Greg's notation is that witnesses are denoted by capital letters: *A, B, C,* and so on. Second, in order to express an ancestor of a group of witnesses, one uses *A'* in front of the grouping (read "A prime"): *A'AB*, for instance, for the ancestor of *A* and *B*. However, the presumably lost l a t e s t c o m m o n a n - c e s t o r of all witnesses in a group is expressed as *xA'*, in Greg's words the "exclusive" ancestor: *xA' ABC*. Now, round and square brackets can be used to add structure. The use of brackets represents an assertion that manuscripts within the same pair of brackets go back to an unnamed exclusive common ancestor (see fig. 4.2-7).

In this way, a formula can be expressed which corresponds to a tree: *(x)A'* [A][B][(CD)(EF)] (fig. 4.2-7). If the whole stemma is to be represented, the formula will begin with *(x)A'* instead of *xA'*, since there is a priori no other common ancestor. Note the parallels to graph representation formats such as Newick (evolution.genetics.washington.edu/phylip/newicktree.html; see 5.2.2 below, 3.4.9 above), where the ancestor can be written after the brackets and where only round brackets are used: for our example, one possible Newick rendering of the tree in figure 4.2-7 is $(A,B,((C,D)xA_3,(E,F)xA_2)xA_1)xA_0$, where the unnamed ancestors are distinguished by subscripts.

While his notation produces an exchange format for graphs, Greg also devised a formal language for talking about variants. An example might be *xyyx ABC: yxxy DEF* (Greg 1927, 14). This formula is used to show that the manuscripts *ABC* agree in the variants *xyyx* (each standing for one position) while *DEF* have in the same four positions *yxxy*, that is, different readings. This can be extended to any number of groups, for example: *xxyy AB: xyyx CD: xyxy EF*. In order to avoid enumerating all witnesses for large groups, Greg now (ab)uses the Σ (sigma) sign, which usually stands for a sum in mathematics, to stand for "all other" witnesses, for example: *xyyx Σ: yxxy F*. He extends this sigma notation by adding in subscript those manuscripts where the concurrent variants are omitted and in superscript those fragmentary manuscripts which are likely to be in the group. A special additional marker is assigned to printed editions, which are to be mentioned first and to be separated by a square bracket, for example: *xyyx] A: yxxy Σ*. Further, if it is known or asserted which variant is original, these can be connected by a > sign (Greg 1927, 42); for example, *X>Y>Z* means that *Y* was derived from *X* and *Z* from *Y*. Quentin (1926) described in similar terms groups of triples of manuscripts and how they can be connected with the goal of reaching an unrooted graph.

Neither the notation of Greg nor that of Quentin seems to have been applied extensively either in philology or in computational stemmatology, although Quentin's notation was taken up by Zarri (1973). There are many possible reasons for this. Such notations become useful if they facilitate understanding of otherwise complex arguments or if they allow inferences instead of being purely descriptive; otherwise, readers may prefer words or paragraphs that explain the actual argument rather than being made to decipher a shorthand which they would have to acquire (which can pose a difficulty similar to learning complex mathematical notation). Greg may not have been able to persuasively demonstrate the utility of his descriptive shorthand or to make it useful for drawing inferences. However, the author believes that at least one of the reasons Flight (1990) chose the term "Greg tree" was to honour this early attempt by a philologist to model stemmata rigorously with consistent results.

4.2.5 Implicit models

Philologists may not have rigorously formalised all the features of stemmata that make an appearance in their visualisations, but visualisations often strongly imply models, or at least impose model-theoretical limitations. A common visual language in philology has formed over time to a certain degree. In this implicit metamodel, contamination is a common feature (despite the oft-cited difficulty of dealing with it) and so are up to three (seldom more) edge depictions or textures, as well as node depictions that differentiate clearly between extant witnesses and hypothetical nodes (usually through different kinds of labels, such as Greek vs Latin letters for witness sigla). Multiple edges and roots are occasionally found. By implication, very many philological models refrain from requiring a strict tree when modelling stemmata, but rather use a DAG.

4.2.6 Bioinformatic models usable for stemmata

Phylogenetic trees display certain properties distinct from their underlying models. In almost all cases, they are exclusively bifurcating trees (unless some branches

Tab. 4.2-1: A fictitious symmetrical substitution matrix for DNA, which reflects the greater chemical similarity of A with G and C with T. The values are probabilities of substitution during a copying process.

	A	C	G	T
A	0.7	0.05	0.2	0.05
C		0.7	0.05	0.2
G			0.7	0.05
T				0.7

have been collapsed according to some criterion; see 4.1.4, 5.2) and the labelled nodes (this usually means extant species, or in our case extant witnesses) must be placed as leaves of their trees (that is, they have no children). This gives phylogenetic trees some mathematically interesting properties on which Felsenstein (2004) elaborates. These properties are also relevant for the design of heuristic algorithms and for the processing time such an algorithm can take in the worst case. (On the detailed properties of phylogenetic trees, see 8.1.) In order to see that the difference in the underlying entities can lead to complications in the transfer of models between fields and may require intervention, we will look at two basic incongruities between phylogenetic trees in biology and stemmatology.

The first difference with important mathematical implications is that the basic units of DNA are expressed as four letters (or, for proteins, twenty letters) but the number of possible readings per alignment position varies, and can be much larger. At first glance, this may seem negligible and require no intervention. However, some biological algorithms operate on **substitution matrices** between their basic units. If there are two possible ancestors of a variant, such a matrix facilitates the decision as to which of them is the more likely ancestor. Thus, where one sequence has an A (for adenine) and two possible ancestors have G (guanine) and T (thymine), we can look at the substitution matrix in table 4.2-1 and immediately understand that it is four times as likely that G is the ancestor than T. Certain algorithms can now use this information when building a tree; Bayesian computation, for instance, typically uses substitution probabilities. For variants in stemmata, we can imagine an analogous, similarly fictitious example in which we have the variant "arcus" and the possible ancestors "arctus" and "acus". The logical process may be similar: we look for some (empirical) clue that allows us to assign the probability of each of the variants being the ancestor, and create a similar matrix. However, if we look at this example in more detail, the analogy to the biological case begins to break down and another model (or model component) is needed. Whereas for DNA, a substitution matrix can easily list all possibilities (A, C, G, T) for mutation at any position in a DNA strand, in our philological example it cannot be ruled out that some lost manuscript had yet another variant besides "arctus", "arcus", or "acus". In order to be as comprehensive as biological substitution matrices, we would need a matrix of the complete vocabulary, considerably larger than even protein-based matrices. Reducing variants to pseudo-DNA, in which each variant location (see 3.3) is represented by one letter, may seem to be a remedy to the problem, but the letters in such manuscript pseudo-DNA do not have the same meaning across different variant locations. The question that arises from this, when using bioinformatic algorithms which do employ substitution matrices, is what we might usefully provide as a substitution matrix. A typical fallback is to use equiprobability, that is, to assume all substitutions as equally likely. This may be problematic insofar as we would forfeit a clear advantage that the substitution matrices provide in the biological case. Some variants clearly transform more easily into others, but with an assumption of equiprobability, we would lose this information. Another solution would be to provide empirically grounded stemmatological substitution matrices, but these would have to be very large in order to model the transition from every word to every other in an ancient language, including mistakes, pseudo-words, non-words, and so on.

Spencer and Howe (2002) have designed a model for scribal errors, not unlike a biological substitution matrix, which formalises the likelihood that one variant (word) was miscopied as another, but this has not been used to compute stemmata. To sum up, while in biology a substitution matrix can help elaborate the mechanisms for finding more reliable trees, such a device will require considerable work in modelling, algorithmic design, and implementation before it can be applied in stemmatology.

A second example is the strict bifurcation of biological trees. For stemmata, it is clearly desirable to have a model in which a node (witness) can have more than two direct descendants (copies). As Felsenstein (1978b, 31) shows, the tree space (that is, the number of possible trees) for a given set of witnesses grows enormously if one allows multifurcations (except for low numbers of witnesses). This is a problem which does not theoretically affect the modelling but which is a challenge for computation. Maximum parsimony, for instance, ideally scores each (!) possible tree and then chooses the best. Even with the tree space restricted to bifurcating trees, depending on the nature of the data, there are scenarios where the number of trees to score is so large that it cannot be computed in a feasible time. When this occurs, the maximum parsimony implementations resort to heuristic tree-space searches which, however, may not find the best tree but only a locally optimal one. The algorithmic design of many implementations is optimised with regard to bioinformatic data and the traversal of a tree space of bifurcating trees. Thus, while the first incongruity of the bioinformatic model with the stemmatological situation requires a complicated model-theoretical implementation of some form of substitution matrix, this second case would require some complex new algorithm design. To date, these issues have been a constant topic of discussion and further attempts at development.

There is one quite different model-theoretical method that was invented for the avoidance of systematic errors in phylogenetic tree construction from pairwise distance matrices (5.2.2) in biology: split decomposition (Bandelt and Dress 1992). Phylogenetic trees can misleadingly depict some of the relationships encoded in an underlying matrix. If we take two pairs of species, grouped respectively and connected by a phylogenetic relation, say group 1 (*A* and *B*) and group 2 (*C* and *D*), the sum of the distances *A* to *B* and *C* to *D* should be smaller than the sum of the distances *A* to *C* and *B* to *D*, but this is not always the case in the underlying distance matrix. This is the reason why split decomposition and phylogenetic networks (D. Bryant and Moulton 2004) have been developed – as a way to depict more than a simple binary tree derived from the distance matrix (see figs 5.5-9–10, 12 below). Alternatively, phylogenetic networks can be used to display multiple relationships. A fully connected graph showing all pairwise distances is another possible visualisation for a pairwise distance matrix, but it can become quite dense.

To summarise, while the scholarly models for biological gene transmission and philological text transmission may generally have a lot in common, models from other disciplines may not deliver (the best possible) solutions to all problems arising in stemmatology, and some adaptation of models, algorithms, or both will consequently be required.

4.2.7 Future challenges

In this section, we have outlined models which are used implicitly and explicitly for stemmata. We have found graph theory to be the predominant, though not the only framework on which formalisations of a model can be based. The DAG has been discussed as the most widely used model. We have outlined some criticisms of current models and have seen that modelling is by no means a trivial endeavour – many phenomena in stemmatology have yet to be modelled. These include indirect witnesses, translation, different types of contamination, oral transmission, gaps, and so forth. Thus, from a modelling perspective, there still remains a lot of work to be done in the field. Concepts such as hyperedges (edges connecting more than two nodes), for example, might be a good way to depict the individual influence of the copyists as authors (see *Il copista come autore*: Canfora 2002). Multiedges and multitrees (allowing more than one edge between the same two nodes) could be used to model different kinds of simultaneous contamination, while self-loops (edges with the same source and target node) can depict, for instance, a copy corrected using an earlier passage repeated in the same text (Andrews 2013), and forests (collections of trees) can depict translation (compare Hoenen 2019a). These properties of models are in some cases already used implicitly, as can be seen from published graphical representations of stemmata, but they are often not formally specified by philologists.

4.3 A typology of variation and error

Aidan Conti

As central concepts within stemmatological and related methods, an understanding of variation, error, and their typologies remains crucial for textual critics as well as those who use critical editions and commentaries. Efforts to understand changes in both the written and spoken transmission of texts have a long history; Quintilian's (ca. 35–ca. 100 CE) handbook on rhetoric, the *Institutio oratoria* (ca. 95 CE), mentions barbarisms in writing such as addition (*adiectio*), omission (*detractio*), substitution (*immutatio*), and transposition (*transmutatio*; Winterbottom 1970, 1:5–6). While premodern textual transmission recognised the importance of errors and variants for grouping textual traditions into families (see 2.1 and also 7.7), within the tradition of academic textual criticism we see a sustained interest in how errors arise in Jean Le Clerc's *Ars critica* (1730 [1697]; Timpanaro 2005, 61–63). Moreover, though error and variation have been important for grouping carriers within traditions (on the history of this, see 2.1–2), it is not until Louis Havet's *Manuel de critique verbale* (1911) that the genesis of errors during the course of transmission receives in-depth treatment. As this section will show, the genesis of variation during the course of transmission is of critical importance because this process helps us assess the likelihood or rarity of a particular reading or segment of text.

4.3.1 Usage and terminology

Differing approaches to textual reconstruction adopt and argue for different terminology, especially with respect to the distinction between variant and error. Critics working with non-normative linguistic traditions frequently prefer to refer to variation, and often employ methods that group variants rather than errors. For example, within a Middle English writing tradition known for its widespread spelling variation, the writing of "þourʒt" for the "thurhe" of an exemplar cannot be considered an error. Indeed, other types of variation, such as the use of alternative cases following particular prepositions, which would be regarded as errors within prescriptive linguistic textual traditions, may be acceptable within non-prescriptive traditions.

However, within many linguistic communities that do have prescriptive norms, contemporary critics assume that scribes, who are often educated within the linguistic norms of these same communities, endeavour to uphold the linguistic norms of their groups. In the case of Latin, which had a pronounced grammatical tradition buttressed by educational institutions, the writing of "amabit" [he or she will love] for "amavit" [he or she loved (or has loved)] is an error. The error is orthographical, and likely arises from a phonological development (/b/ > /v/). The effect is to change the grammar ("she will love the boy" to "she loved the boy"), and renders the overall sense of a passage incongruous or difficult to ascertain.

More serious lapses in transmission, however, can produce readings, or segments of text, that are difficult to construe due to syntax, meaning, or a number of other outcomes. For instance, if in the Middle English example above the phrase were "through the dark night", and the scribe wrote not "þourȝt" (a variant spelling of "through"), but rather "thouȝt" (a variant of "thought"), the subsequent "thought the dark night" would likely be nonsensical in the context of the passage. Within the stemmatological method, this type of variant or error is more important for the analysis of manuscript relations than most orthographical changes.

Given that "error" has been used with decidedly different meanings in a range of textual commentary and that the negative connotations associated with the term can attract criticism, there is good reason to consider the use of two alternative terms, namely "i n n o v a t i o n", any change introduced at some point in the textual tradition, and "s e c o n d a r y r e a d i n g", which similarly describes an alteration in the course of textual transmission. The advantage of these terms is that they are polarised, that is, they indicate the direction of the change. For example, the phrase "anno autem domini CCCXXXI Saraceni Siciliam inuadentes" (Maggioni 2007, 926) [In the year of the Lord 331, after the Saracens had invaded Sicily] from the *Legenda aurea* contains an error: it is factually incorrect that Muslim Arabs took control of Sicily at that time – the Emirate of Sicily gained control of the entire island in 831. Nevertheless, the incorrect date seems to be a primary reading for this text, as it was incorporated from source material for the text. Later corrections (to 831) represent secondary readings (or independently arising secondary readings; see Maggioni 2016, 37).

Because it posits nothing about the correctness of a reading, the term "secondary reading" obviates the dispute and the distinction between variant and error. However, two important issues remain to be clarified: (*i*) how we polarise the reading (or how the textual critic decides the direction of readings), and (*ii*) what secondary readings are important for determining the relationships among witnesses. Both issues centre around probability. The analysis of witnesses will be concerned with determining which reading is primary as opposed to another. Moreover, one must assess the likelihood of a given secondary reading. Changes that arise independently, also known as p o l y g e n e s i s (see 2.2.5 above; Trovato 2017, 97), are of little use in devising a stemma. In other words:

> If a variant arose independently many times, distributed over changing groups of manuscripts, it can tell us little about the relationships among manuscripts because its distribution is unlikely to be simply related to the true stemma. On the other hand, a very improbable variant gives strong evidence that all the manuscripts in which it occurs are related by descent. (Spencer, Mooney, et al. 2004, 228)

Secondary readings that allow critics to construct a stemma can be called r e l a t i o n - s h i p - r e v e a l i n g (Salemans 2000). Maas (1960) labelled errors from which stemmatic inferences can be made as *errores significativi* (indicative/significant errors) or *Leitfehler* (guiding/indicative errors). Within this category of significant errors,

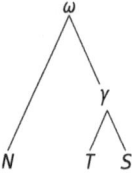

Fig. 4.3-1: The relationship of three manuscripts based on a conjunctive error. This simplified example is based on the manuscripts of Thomas Aquinas's *In librum Beati Dionysii De divinis nominibus expositio* 11.4 (Pera 1950).

traditional stemmatics (namely Maas) distinguished errors that grouped witnesses together and those that separated witnesses from others. Conjunctive errors (*errores coniunctivi, Bindefehler*) are errors that show that two or more witnesses can be grouped together against other witnesses. The following example illustrates a conjunctive error within a group of three manuscripts deriving from a single archetype. In this clause, two distinct readings are reported.
- N   causa quod omnia existentia sint
- T, S   causa quod divina existentia sint

N records the contextually required "omnia". T and S have the error "divina". If other readings in T and S provide separative errors that indicate that one does not derive from the other *and* T and S share errors that indicate they cannot be grouped with N, then the conjunctive error demonstrates that the two can be traced back to a common hyparchetype. The relationship between the three manuscripts can be illustrated accordingly (fig. 4.3-1).

Separative errors (*errores separativi, Trennfehler*), on the other hand, are errors that indicate that a witness is independent of another witness or of a group of witnesses. A more concrete example may illustrate the point. Two manuscripts, S and T, of a text share a significant number of conjunctive errors and are consequently postulated as deriving from the same hyparchetype. However, in the following sentence, the manuscripts report two different readings.
- S   At ille obiit viridis
- T   At ille obiit viribus

Here, T reports "viribus" where S correctly has "viridis", a separative error that indicates S is not derived from T, *provided that* the reading in S does not represent an independent scribal conjecture. In another reading, S records a variant that, while grammatical, is not contextually appropriate and T offers the preferred reading.
- S   Sed officia boni civis, boni amici, boni filii secutus est
- T   Sed officia boni civis, boni amici, boni filii executus est

In this case, in which S reports "secutus" where T has the contextually required "executus", the separative error shows T cannot be derived from S (provided that the reading in T does not arise from interposed scribal conjecture).

Fig. 4.3-2: The relationship of two manuscripts based on a separative error. This simplified and emended example is based on the manuscripts of Seneca's *Epistulae morales ad Lucilium* 93.4 (Reynolds 1965).

Because the identification of separative errors indicates that neither of the witnesses derives from the other, the relationship in the following illustration (fig. 4.3-2) can be posited.

Many scholars have noted the difficulty in determining the significance of a secondary reading (or error). As Michael Reeve points out: "Now in the phrase 'significant error' you will recognize two serious problems, namely how to decide what readings are errors and then which of these are significant errors" (1986, 68). Given the importance of determining the likelihood of a given secondary reading, it is not surprising that a number of scholars have developed a wide-ranging vocabulary to describe the types of innovations that can arise during the course of transmission (see 4.4.2). Moreover, recent stemmatological studies have explored the "weighting" of variants as a way of assessing significance (or potential for revealing relationships; Macé and Sanspeur 2000; Spencer, Mooney, et al. 2004; Macé, De Vos, and Geuten 2012). There have also been some attempts at partial automation of the procedures to measure the significance of variants (Roelli and Bachmann 2010; Camps and Cafiero 2014). Nevertheless, the evaluation of readings will remain largely a philological task.

4.3.2 Categories and types

As noted above with reference to Quintilian, four broad categories can be used to classify errors in transmission (and indeed secondary readings and innovations). An a d d i t i o n is any segment of text not present in the exemplar that a copyist introduces into the copied text. In the process of collating and editing, the term "addition" is a relative one which only indicates that a segment of text which is lacking in the base text is present in some witness(es), without making a judgement about whether the addition is secondary or not. An omission is any segment of text that a copyist does not reproduce in the copied text but that is present in the exemplar. Like "addition", "o m i s s i o n" is a relative term that does not assert whether an omission is secondary or not. T r a n s p o s i t i o n is an alteration in the order or a change in the position of letters, syllables, words, phrases, and/or passages between the exemplar and the copy. S u b s t i t u t i o n refers to letters, words, phrases, clauses, or passages present in an exemplar that are replaced by something else in a copy.

"Addition", "omission", "transposition", and "substitution" are relative and descriptive terms. These categories, however, provide little information about the context in which an error can arise. Similarly, objective descriptions of variants or errors – descriptions that do not rely on literary, historical, and geographical argu-

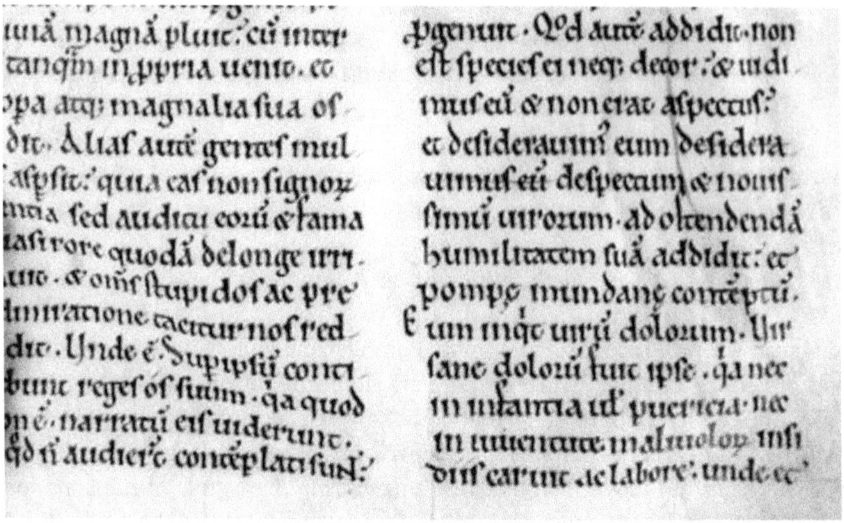

Fig. 4.3-3: An example of dittography: "desideravimus eum desideravimus eum despectum" (column B, lines 4–5). Source: Gallica, Bibliothèque nationale de France, gallica.bnf.fr/ark:/12148/btv1b9072445t/f215.image. Image: CC-BY-NC.

ments to judge the authenticity or trueness of a variant – may assign linguistic categories to classify changes (e.g. orthographical, phonological, morphological, and syntactic). The use of these broad categories, however, has not produced much success in terms of evaluating the significance of an error. Indeed, the categories used to classify errors (secondary readings) are an area that requires further refinement before weightings and likelihood can be properly assessed (Andrews and Macé 2013). For example, the model developed by Andrews and Macé employed a relationship graph but remained agnostic on the directionality of the graph (it could be cyclic, in other words). They noted that a semantic tagging scheme, which would provide information on changes in meaning in the text, might have given clearer results in their analysis.

Within the four broad categories discussed by Quintilian and used in many contemporary studies, there are differences of degree and type. In short, additions may share characteristics but may differ in execution and cause. Consequently, it may be useful to describe more specific types of errors within these broad categories, an undertaking which has a long tradition in textual criticism.

One prominent example is dittography (classified under "addition"): the writing of a word or part of a word twice, for example "renonown" for "renown". In figure 4.3-3, we can see that a scribe has written the same two words twice; subsequently, someone expunged the repetition.

The opposite of dittography is haplography (a type of omission): the writing of a segment of text once which appears twice (or more) in the exemplar, for example "defendum" instead of "defendendum".

Other examples of more specific types of errors include a n a s y l l a b i s m, or the reanalysis of the syllabification of a source word whereby the word is transformed into another word, such as "domo" for "modo". This reanalysis is a transposition, that is, an alteration in the order or a change in the position of letters, syllables, words, phrases, and/or passages between the exemplar and the copy. Two types of substitution are m i s r e a d i n g, the replacement of a letter in the exemplar with a similar-looking, but incorrect, letter, for example the writing of "c" for "e"; and i t a c i s m, the merger in pronunciation of vowel sounds that are characteristically distinguished in spelling. Similarly, m e t a t h e s i s is a type of substitution involving the transposition of sounds or letters in a word, commonly precipitated by a slip of the ear or of the pen. As a linguistic process, metathesis has changed the written form and pronunciation of many words. For example, *bird* is a metathesised form of Old English *bryd*. Usually, the phenomenon refers to contiguous sounds, and is then called adjacent metathesis. Metathesis can also describe the transposition of non-adjacent sounds and/or letters, as in Spanish *palabra* from Latin *parabola*.

Because errors frequently arise due to misreading on the part of the copyist – that is, errors in language processing that affect language production – textual scholars have also developed an elaborate vocabulary for the triggers or precipitators of errors. One important tenet in textual criticism is that scribes were more prone to error when working from an unfamiliar script. The process of copying from one script to another, t r a n s l i t e r a t i o n (or *transliteratio* in Latin) or *metacharakterismos* (Dain 1964, 124–135), can produce patterns of secondary readings in extant manuscripts which in turn can suggest the script type, and at times the layout, of a lost archetype. For example, by examining patterns of errors, Joseph Scaliger (1577) showed that the archetype of surviving Catullus manuscripts was written in a pre-Caroline minuscule (*langobardicae litterae* in Scaliger's terminology; see Grafton 1975). Lachmann famously argued that the tradition of Lucretius derived from an archetype in rustic capitals from the fourth or fifth century (Lachmann 1850, 2:3). Nevertheless, despite these well-known examples, Timpanaro, for instance, argues against conceiving of transliteration as an operation performed once and for all (Timpanaro 2005, 172n30).

Further examples of the types of phenomena that precipitate secondary readings include a n t i c i p a t i o n, which suggests a copyist who reads ahead (in the exemplar) of the text being written (in the copy) and therefore omits a section of the exemplar in the copy text; and a r r h y t h m i a, an irregularity in the reading activity of the copyist which can produce haplography, if the copyist skips ahead in the exemplar, or dittography, if he skips back and rereads part of the exemplar text. Generally, critics speak of e y e - s k i p, also known as a *saut du même au même* (literally "jump from the same to the same" in French), where similar words or phrases appear twice on the same page, inducing the copyist to skip unintentionally the passage between the first and the second occurrences of the phrase or, alternatively, to read (and copy) the passage twice. Less commonly, this procedure is referred to as parablepsis. More specifically, homoeoarcton suggests that the impetus for an omission or addition results from eye-skip to or from similar or identical beginnings of a word, whereas homoeoteleuton describes eye-skip to or from a similar or identical ending in two words which causes a copyist to produce an omission or an addition.

In some cases, the string of text need not be exactly the same to produce a *saut* or eye-skip. For example, the following sequence is found in a homily, *De Christi passione* (CPG 5526 = Geerard and Noret 1984–2018, 3:74), that describes Judas's betrayal of Jesus: "uenit Iudas ad eos et dedit eis signum" (Salzburg, Stiftsbibliothek St. Peter, a. VII. 5, f. 29v, s. ix²). In this scenario, Judas came to the chief priests (to whom he would betray Jesus) and then gave them a sign (that is, the kiss with which he betrays Jesus). Another manuscript, which represents the same scene in the homily, has "uenit Iudas ad eos et dixit eis, exsurgentes sequimini me et tradam eum uobis. Qui exsurgentes sequebantur eum cum gladiis et fustibus. Et dedit eis signum" (Rand 1904, 274–275) [Judas came to them [the chief priests] and said to them, "Get up and follow, and I will hand him over to you." After they rose, they followed him with swords and clubs. And he gave them a signal]. The shorter text from the Salzburg manuscript, which omits Judas's speech to the priests, seems to have arisen as the result of eye-skip from "et dixit eis" to "et dedit eis", in which case the skip (or *saut*) is not from/to the same string of words (*même au même*), but rather from one to another, very similar, string of text.

A number of terms encompass both the impetus for an innovation and the product of it, such as "assimilation" and "gloss-incorporation". Assimilation can refer to two distinct but similar processes. The first describes the way in which a scribe may write a word so that it resembles another nearby word. An illustration is "an excellent examplic of the rhetoric", in which "example" has been assimilated to the coming "rhetoric" (West 1973, 24).

The second process described as assimilation refers to the incorporation of wording from a parallel narrative, witness, or text into the copy text. This process is sometimes referred to as contamination, a term which is viewed as somewhat misleading in its pejorative connotations, or horizontal transmission (see 4.4). Gloss-incorporation is one way of introducing changes in a text transmitted through copying: a reading that was originally intended as a note or remark in an exemplar would be incorporated into the main text of a copy instead. As there were and are different types of *glossae* – like marginal and interlinear glosses – gloss-incorporation could happen in various intentional and unintentional ways. The marginal elements may be expository and/or provide commentary on the primary text, in which case the incorporation represents an example of an addition. Alternatively, glosses may provide a correction to a witness, in which case the subsequent incorporation of the gloss represents a case of assimilation or horizontal transmission. "Gloss-incorporation" is frequently used interchangeably with "interpolation" (see 3.2.4).

The range of nomenclature attests to the enduring interest and indeed delight in the complex processes and structures involved in the (re)production of handwritten texts (see further Magnani and Watt 2018). For the construction of a stemma, be it a computational model (4.2) or a historical tool (4.5), the student must not only identify innovations but also assess, as we have seen, their significance, that is, the extent to which a secondary reading is likely to be reproduced, reversed, or arise independently. For this reason, the concept of *lectio difficilior* ("the more difficult reading"; sometimes also expressed as *lectio difficilior potior*, "the more difficult reading is preferable") has and continues to hold important sway (see 2.1.2 on the early development of the concept and 6.2.3 for further examples). A similar principle is that of *lectio brevior*, or "the shorter reading [is preferable]", but this is generally regarded as a less valuable rule of thumb. The premise of *lectio difficilior* stipulates that a subsequent copyist is unlikely to restore a difficult reading and more likely to reproduce a simpler reading, or *lectio facilior*. The following example from the unedited and anonymous Latin homily *De Christi passione* illustrates the principle. Two manuscripts, O (Oxford, Bodleian Library, Bodley 343; s. xii²) and S (Salzburg, Stiftsbibliothek St. Peter, a. VII. 5; s. ix²), present the following readings.
- O   uidit me ignis rubens [the red fire saw me]
- S   uidit me ignea rumphea [the fiery sword saw me]

The second clause has the *lectio difficilior*, the relatively rare word *rumphea* (alternatively found as *rhomphaea* or *rumpia*), a double-edged sword. The more common *rubens*, "red, ruddy", likely represents the result of a process in which the more difficult and, over time, less familiar word became rewritten as a more familiar word. In this case, evidence that the Latin text is a translation of a Greek work (*CPG* 5526 = Geerard and Noret 1984–2018, 3:74), which has ῥομφαία, a long missile weapon associated with the Thracians in Antiquity, confirms the hypothesis.

The external confirmation is important because the principle of *lectio difficilior potior*, as explanatory as it seems, is not unequivocal. In some cases, the more difficult reading may well arise from a series of miscopyings, attempted corrections, and/or perceived improvements, meaning that the *lectio difficilior* may in fact be secondary rather than primary. To take a modern and well-known example, a Melville scholar defended the phrase "soiled fish of the sea" in the second edition of *White-Jacket* and lauded its *discordia concors*, "the unexpected linking of the medium of cleanliness with filth" (see Greetham 1999, 175). The true reading, found in the first edition, was simpler; the "coiled fish of the sea" was a description of eels. Such a misapprehension highlights the fact that the application of the principle of *lectio difficilior potior* is often based on the notion that the authorial text possesses literary qualities, such as the use of elevated rhetoric, learned vocabulary, and literary devices. In cases of simple, less elevated or marked texts, the simpler reading may well be preferred; the more difficult reading may represent attempts by subsequent users to improve a text, to add virtuosity where there was none.

4.3.3 The genesis of secondary readings

The exploration of types of errors and variants represents an effort to understand the dynamics leading to changes in texts, and consequently to present better tools for assessing the likelihood of a secondary reading. In other words, one aims to understand the extent to which a reading approaches irreversibility and non-reproducibility. This understanding is crucial for us to better evaluate the likelihood of any given innovation or secondary reading. There are two possible, yet relatively unexplored, fields that promise significant insights into the processes of textual reproduction which comprises language interpretation and language production. The first is a more in-depth analysis of copyists in contemporary contexts. Artificial traditions have been a positive step in this direction (Baret, Macé, and Robinson 2006; Roos and Heikkilä 2009), but they have not been set up to measure the contexts and triggers for the genesis of errors (they have rather been concerned with the outcomes and comparing them), and thus have not been so useful in considering the likelihood of a given error. As a result, scholars continue to struggle with ways to classify errors for the purposes of analysis. In a similar vein, research into reading and writing practices may offer further insight into the nature of errors. For example, more information might be gained from studying the effects of priming, that is, how one stimulus can influence a response to a subsequent stimulus, in reading and word recognition. Priming studies can test the time it takes to recognise a word after exposure to, that is priming from, another, often related word. Preliminary studies looking at how children are affected by priming in their first (L1) and second (L2) languages indicate that head-rhyme (or similar initial syllables in a word) is more likely to influence subsequent reading than is end-rhyme (Fitjar 2016). That said, studies to date (as far as I know) have not specifically addressed reading and writing processes during the copying of lengthier texts. Moreover, such studies cannot endeavour (or propose) to replicate the material conditions of premodern copyists who used different writing instruments and material. As such, their greatest promise resides in providing insights into the architecture of reading and writing, but not into the practice per se.

The second possible way to investigate copying phenomena is through the analysis of known exemplar–copy pairs. Palaeographers have emphasised the importance of these pairs (Ker 1972, 1979; Parkes 2008; Marchetti 2019) for philologists (both historical linguists and textual critics), but few in-depth studies have been carried out. One reason is that, unfortunately, few exemplar–copy pairs exist. Another reason is that, if a copy comes from a known exemplar, that copy is known within the common-errors method as a *codex descriptus*, irrelevant for *constitutio textus*, and so will usually have been discarded by the editor.

4.3.4 Variation of punctuation

Generally speaking, punctuation and word division have played a secondary role in determining innovations in the transmission of a text. Most mediaeval punctuation conventions differ from modern ones. Moreover, an editor dealing with a large number of witnesses may be confronted with a range of punctuation conventions and an individual witness may reflect the usage of the exemplar and/or the scribe in addition to a later corrector, whose hand may be difficult to determine when it comes to punctuation. Malcolm Parkes notes some of the difficulties:

> When considering copies as witnesses to the practices of a particular period in time, it is necessary to determine the status of the punctuation: for example, in a manuscript, whether it is that of the scribe in the same ink as the text, or has been added by a corrector or reader in ink of a different colour. (Parkes 1992, 5)

A detailed and substantive study of the development of punctuation in the Western European tradition is found in Malcolm Parkes, *Pause and Effect* (1992). The development of word division is charted in Paul Saenger's *Space between Words: The*

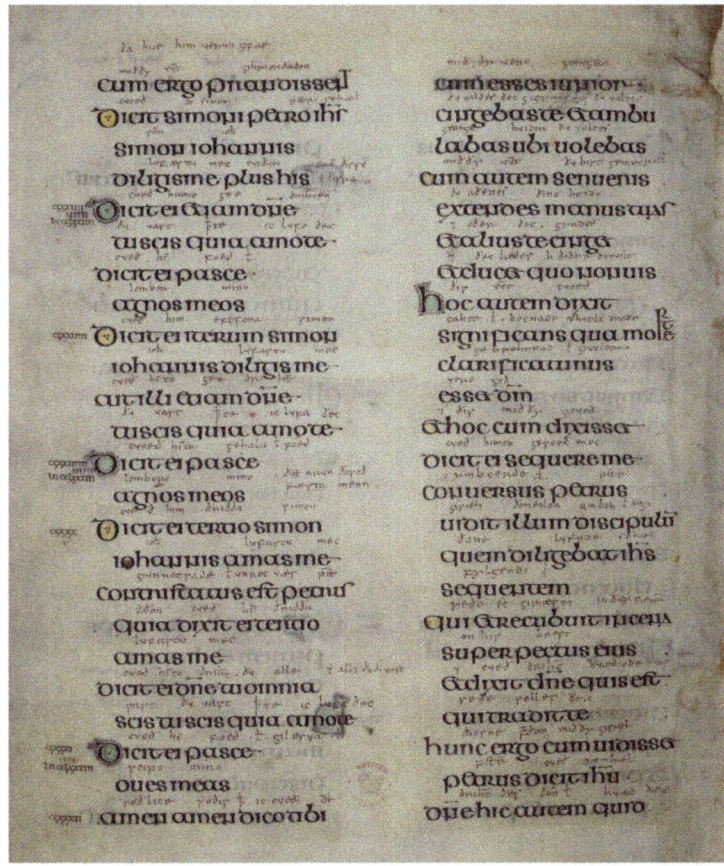

Fig. 4.3-4: *Per cola et commata* layout in the Lindesfarne Gospels (London, British Library, Cotton, Nero D. IV, f. 258v). Source: bl.uk/manuscripts/Viewer.aspx?ref=cotton_ms_nero_d_iv_fs001r. © The British Library Board.

Origins of Silent Reading (1997). Saenger's assertion that word division facilitated silent reading is, however, refuted by a range of classicists who have demonstrated that the ancients read silently in private even when public reading was oral (see Johnson 2010 for a summary of the debate).

In cases where a system of punctuation can be ascertained as authorial or archetypal, the edition will often reproduce the system. For example, Jerome in his preface to Isaiah describes a system of laying out text *per cola et commata* (by sense units) for the ease of reading, a system that is preserved in notable early biblical manuscripts, such as the Lindisfarne Gospels (London, British Library, Cotton, Nero D. IV; see fig. 4.3-4). The *per cola et commata* division is preserved in the present critical edition of the Vulgate (fig. 4.3-5).

Similarly, in the recent edition of Saxo Grammaticus' *Gesta Danorum*, the editor follows, as closely as possible, the system of division found in the *editio princeps*, whereby periods are separated by a full stop followed by a capital letter, which also reflects the tradition found in the mediaeval manuscript fragments (Friis-Jensen 2015, 1:lxxx). That said, the punctuation between full stops, such as the placing of commas and the introduction of quotation marks, was modified to facilitate readability for present-day users of the edition. In addition, whereas names are not regularly capitalised in the earlier tradition, the present edition consistently does so.

On the other hand, diplomatic editions which aim to reproduce as faithfully as possible a single witness (see 6.1.1) will reproduce the punctuation of the witness that serves as the basis of the edition.

Acknowledgement

The author would like to thank John Magee (University of Toronto) for his expertise and teaching in Latin textual criticism. The examples of separative and conjunctive errors were adapted from his teaching materials.

	1697	SECUNDUM IOHANNEM	Io 21,12–25	
Os 2,20!		scientes quia Dominus esset	te clarificaturus esset Deum	12,33; 18,32
6,11; Lc 24,30!		¹³ CCXXV̲ VIIII Et venit Iesus et accepit panem et dat eis et piscem similiter	et hoc cum dixisset dicit ei sequere me	
		¹⁴ CCXXVI̲ X Hoc iam tertio manifestatus est Iesus discipulis cum surrexisset a mortuis	²⁰conversus Petrus vidit illum discipulum quem diligebat Iesus sequentem	7; 19,26; 20,2
		¹⁵cum ergo prandissent dicit Simoni Petro Iesus	qui et recubuit in cena super pectus eius et dixit Domine quis est qui tradit te	13,23.25
1,42; Mt 16,17!		Simon Iohannis diligis me plus his dicit ei		
		etiam Domine tu scis quia amo te CCXXVII̲ VIIII Dicit ei	²¹hunc ergo cum vidisset Petrus dicit Iesu Domine hic autem quid	
I Pt 5,2!		pasce agnos meos	²²dicit ei Iesus	
		¹⁶ CCXXVIII̲ X Dicit ei iterum	si sic eum volo manere donec veniam	
Mt 16,17!		Simon Iohannis diligis me ait illi	quid ad te tu me sequere	
		etiam Domine tu scis quia amo te CCXXVIIII̲ VIIII Dicit ei	²³exivit ergo sermo iste in fratres quia discipulus ille non moritur	
I Pt 5,2! II Sm 5,2!		pasce agnos meos	et non dixit ei Iesus non moritur	
		¹⁷ CCXXX̲ X Dicit ei tertio	sed si sic eum volo manere donec venio quid ad te	
Mt 16,17!		Simon Iohannis amas me contristatus est Petrus quia dixit ei tertio amas me	²⁴hic est discipulus qui testimonium perhibet de his	15,27! 19,35; III Io 12
		et dicit ei Domine tu omnia scis tu scis quia amo te	et scripsit haec et scimus quia verum est testimonium eius	
		CCXXXI̲ VIIII Dicit ei	²⁵sunt autem et alia multa quae fecit Iesus	20,30!
I Pt 5,2!		pasce oves meas	quae si scribantur per singula	
		¹⁸ CCXXXII̲ X Amen amen dico tibi cum esses iunior cingebas te et ambulabas ubi volebas cum autem senueris extendes manus tuas et alius te cinget et ducet quo non vis	nec ipsum arbitror mundum capere eos qui scribendi sunt libros amen	
		¹⁹hoc autem dixit significans qua mor-	EXPLICIT EVANGELIUM SECUNDUM IOHANNEM	

12 esset] est sZCΦc | 13 accipit Dc | 14 discipulis + suis c | resurrexisset ADCcɔ | S(s)AM(Z)
15 *num.* 227/9 *ad* dicit simoni *pon.* Dɔ, *ad* simon *pon.* s, *ad* dicit ei etiam *pon.* AZFCΦ, *recte* (FG)DCΦ
ad dicit ei M, *cf. vv.* 16 *et* 17 | 17 et *om.* A | dicit²] dixit c. | ∼ omnia tu Z | scis¹] cɔ
nosti c. | dicit³] dixit c. | 18 ducit MD | quo + tu Gc | 19 ∼ cum hoc ZΦc | 20 conuersus + autem M | [*deest* Z *usque ad v.* 25] | tradit sAɔⓈ] tradidit F.; tradet *cet.* |
21 dixit c. | 22 si sic Fɔ] si M.; sic *cet.* | uenio s. | 23 in] inter sΦc | si sic MGɔ]
sic *cet.* | ueniam MCΦcɔ | 24 discipulus + ille c | 25 capere + posse c | amen *om.*
DCc ‖

Fig. 4.3-5: The end of the Gospel of John from the *Biblia Sacra Iuxta Vulgatam Versionem*, edited by Weber, Gryson, and Fischer (1994, 1697). Source: © 2007 Deutsche Bibelgesellschaft, Stuttgart. Used by permission.

4.4 Dealing with open textual traditions

Tuomas Heikkilä

"Contamination" sounds threatening in most fields of life. Even in textual criticism, in studying handwritten textual traditions and editing texts, the term bears an ominous tone: "contamination" is the term for the most serious and most frequent phenomenon endangering the reconstruction of the original reading and the understanding of the textual transmission and dissemination.

4.4.1 Challenges of contamination

In the world of texts and their transmission, c o n t a m i n a t i o n is understood as the copying of readings from more than one exemplar, resulting in complex and often hard-to-detect relationships between textual witnesses within the transmission of a text. The reconstruction of a stemma describing the relationships of all the textual witnesses of a text is traditionally based on the principle of common errors (see 2.2) – but contamination confuses this principle and distorts the stemma. In a contaminated tradition, it is hard for the *recensio* of textual criticism to reveal if an agreement in error is the result of common descent or of mixture between lines of descent. Moreover, it cannot reveal the direction of textual transmission (see M. W. Holmes 2011, 71–72). It has even been claimed that the presence of contamination is an insurmountable obstacle for shaping a stemma and thus for understanding the textual tradition altogether (West 1973, 14, 36).

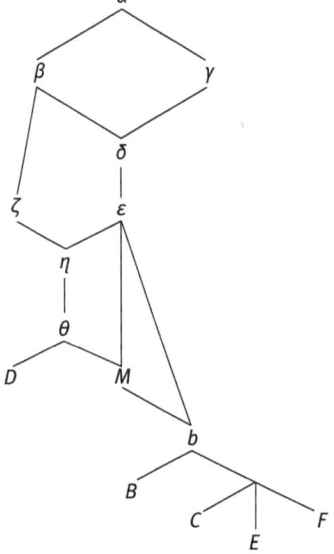

Fig. 4.4-1: Example of an open – i.e. contaminated – tradition. Several of the text versions are copied from more than one exemplar. Redrawn from West (1973, 40).

Let us elucidate the challenge with an example. Suppose we have a textual tradition in which the copyist of version *F* took readings from both *A* (now lost) and *B* (still extant). The true stemma is given (fig. 4.4-2) on the left-hand side. Based on the remaining manuscripts, *B*, *C*, *D*, *E*, and *F*, however, textual criticism would probably arrive at the stemma given on the right-hand side. We would observe that *F* sometimes does not have innovations common to the other witnesses and on the other hand contains its own peculiar readings. *B* would sometimes share *F* readings, sometimes *CDE* readings. We might easily view *F*, in fact a descendant of *B*, as its ancestor, and discard *B* as a contaminated witness offering nothing original (M. W. Holmes 2011, 72; example from West 1973, 35–36). Should we want to reconstruct the archetype *[a]*, we would do so on the basis of *F* and *[b]*, thus giving the text of *F* too much weight. This would result in a reconstruction of the archetype that would not be correct.

The possible consequences can be illustrated with an invented sentence; in real life, of course, innovations must not be so easily reversible if they are to be of any stemmatic value.

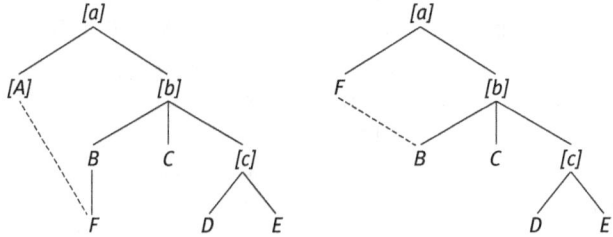

Fig. 4.4-2: Observe the difference between the correct (left) and reconstructed (right) stemmata. Source: West (1973, 35–36).

[a]	This is a fictitious example of contamination.
[A]	This was a fictitious example of contamination.
[b]	It is an example of contamination.
B	It is an example of contamination.
[c]	It is an instance of contamination.
C	It was an example on contamination.
D	It was an instance on contamination.
E	It is an instance on contamination.
F	It is a fictitious example of contamination.

4.4.2 Terminology

Emblematically of the frequency of this challenge in the study of textual traditions, contamination and its various forms have been identified with several, often pejorative terms by scholars. According to the traditional view, a textual tradition in which the content is transmitted by reproducing the text of just one exemplar at a time (i.e. without contamination) has been considered to be "normal", "pure", "unmixed", "virgin", or "mechanical". The prevailing idea has been that such a tradition is the norm, and any copy of the text resulting in transmission of two or more exemplars should be considered as suffering from "contamination", "conflation", "text bastardry", "hybridisation", or "cross-fertilisation" (on the terminology, see esp. M. W. Holmes 2011, 66–68).

However, it should be noted that the very basis of the idea of a "pure" and "non-contaminated" textual tradition as the norm is questionable. The concept is a product of nineteenth- and early twentieth-century scholars who did not know nearly as many ancient or mediaeval manuscripts as we do today. In the light of today's knowledge of textual traditions transmitted through copying by hand, it may well be that the use of two or more exemplars was far more usual than previously thought (see below). The prevailing terminology of the field and the earliest history of textual criticism, mainly interested in discovering the original readings of ancient texts by purifying them of the "falsifications" of later copyists (see Willis 1972), easily yields a very negative picture of contamination as a phenomenon. Still, it is important to keep in mind that it was normally a result of someone trying to correct rather than to spoil the text and its original readings (see e.g. Zink 2014, 3–7).

Whereas, for instance, the early German editor of Horace, Otto Keller (1838–1927), employed the colourful term "malady" (*Gebrechen*) when discussing the issue, the Italian textual scholar Giorgio Pasquali (1885–1952) introduced more unbiased and descriptive vocabulary. According to him, the textual transmission is **vertical** and **unidirectional** when the content is copied from one exemplar, and **horizontal** (or **transverse**) in cases in which more than one exemplar is involved (Keller 1879, viii; Pasquali 1934).

Contamination is closely tied to another terminological distinction, also coined by Pasquali: the difference between a **closed** and an **open recension** or tradition (Pasquali 1934, 126). According to Pasquali, the readings of a closed tradition can be mechanically reconstructed by the scholar, whereas this is impossible in an open tradition (see "1932–" in 2.4.3). The most typical reason for a textual tradition to be open is, in turn, the use of several exemplars in producing a copy (see Trovato 2017, 74–75; Timpanaro 2005, 137; Alberti 1979). In other words, a closed recension often corresponds to the vertical transmission of the text, an open recension in most cases to a contaminated tradition.

The biased term "contamination" is still widely in use even today, although a more descriptive *terminus technicus* like "horizontal", "transverse", or "lateral transmission" would be more accurate and less prejudiced. In fact, I would personally prefer to use the term "**mixture**" rather than "contamination" (like M. W. Holmes 2011, 67–68), but the two terms will be used interchangeably here. In future, it would be advantageous to strive towards as unbiased and descriptive a terminology as possible. In the following, I will follow the example of Giorgio Pasquali, Martin L. West, and Michael W. Holmes and use the term "open" for a "contaminated" textual tradition (M. W. Holmes 2011, 67–68; West 1973, 14; Pasquali 1934, 183).

4.4.3 Extent

The textual tradition of a hand-copied text of any importance or size is bound to be more or less open. It has even been suspected that open traditions were the norm, and purely vertical, closed transmissions the exception (Guglielmetti 2017; Tarrant 2016, 15; see also Guglielmetti and Orlandi 2014, 181–184, with examples from various genres). Perhaps the best example of an open tradition is that of the most popular work of the whole era of hand-copied texts, the Bible. Despite the efforts of the copyists to keep the sacred text as unaltered as possible – leaving aside, that is, the conscious editing of the text during the early centuries – the scribes introduced variants. (See e.g. M. W. Holmes 2002, 77–100; Mink 2004; Mink 2011, 141; Wachtel 2012b, 220–222; Guglielmetti and Orlandi 2014, 185; on the New Testament, see 7.1 below.)

Contamination is a very common phenomenon, probably much more so than most scholars realise. There have been some attempts to estimate the exact degree of mixture within textual traditions. For instance, Elisabetta Tonello and Paolo Trovato have hypothesised that around 14 % of the known manuscripts of Dante's *Divina Commedia* show signs of successive contamination (i.e. the successive use of different exemplars, the easiest sort of contamination to detect; see below). In addition, the two scholars give a list of known manuscripts with rather hard-to-detect simultaneous contamination. In all, their calculations point out that some 19 % of the *Divina Commedia* manuscripts suffer from some kind of contamination (Tonello and Trovato 2011, 19–31; Trovato 2017, 137). Still, such estimates are possibly considerably lower than the actual number, since contamination is not always easy to detect within a textual tradition.

The scholarly tendency, easy to understand from the viewpoint of work economy, to limit the study of the manuscripts and textual witnesses of a work to the ones considered most relevant by the scholar, has prevented us from seeing the big picture of entire textual traditions. One notable exception is John B. Hall's study on Claudian's *De raptu Proserpinae*, in which he collated 132 of the 134 known extant manuscripts and reached the convincing conclusion that the tradition was thoroughly open (Hall 1969, 61–64). The same applies to the *Navigatio Sancti Brendani*, an eighth-century travel account preserved in some 140 manuscripts and studied in detail: the tradition contains much contamination (Guglielmetti and Orlandi 2014). One of the examples used in this contribution, the *Vita et miracula Sancti Symeonis Treverensis*, is known to exist in nearly sixty manuscripts, and the collation of all of them reveals that the textual tradition contains contamination of versions and successive contamination, if not more. If we had more such comprehensive studies, we would surely understand better the real importance and prevalence of contamination within hand-copied textual traditions.

4.4.4 The mechanics of contamination

How did contamination come about in hand-copied textual traditions? It could take place in various ways. One should distinguish the contamination of readings/variants, resulting from a copyist using several exemplars, from the contamination of versions that occurred as a result of the author(s) editing and revising the text while it was already being disseminated (see Segre 1961, 71).

4.4.4.1 Simultaneous contamination

Simultaneous contamination is the trickiest form of horizontal transmission within a textual tradition to deal with. Paradoxically, it was typically a consequence of the copyists and scribes attempting to improve the content of the text. When a lengthy text is copied by hand, it almost inevitably changes. If the text was dictated, the scribe could mishear or misunderstand a word or a phrase. If it was copied from an exemplar, the copyist was bound to make mistakes. In addition, the copyist might feel the need to make changes in the text of his own accord. As a rule, copying errors in / alterations of the text can be classified in four general categories: addition, omission, transposition, and substitution (see 4.3 above for further descriptive vocabulary). The ancient and mediaeval copyists of a text were by no means naive, and they often had a far better command of the language of their text than many modern-day scholars. Thus, it is safe to assume that many of them recognised and were not indifferent to grammatically incorrect expressions or odd choices of words, and had an interest in improving the quality of the text in their copies. The results of such attempts are probably the most typical – as well as most challenging – form of contamination, called simultaneous (Vàrvaro 2010, 191; Trovato 2017, 132, 135; Segre 1961, 71; see also Wattel and van Mulken 1996, 105–106; den Hollander 2004, 99). The obvious tool to correct the text was consulting another exemplar (hence the Italian term *contaminazione di lezioni*). Such an activity, often resulting in deliberate simultaneous contamination, is known to have taken place even in the workshops of copyists in Antiquity. To ascertain the correctness of the newly made copy, the precaution was sometimes taken of checking it not only against its exemplar but also against another copy of the text. There are a number of famous ancient and mediaeval cases in which the copyist elucidates this process by specifying *expressis verbis* which manuscripts he used – for instance, Nicomachus Dexter copying and correcting Livy's first pentad, and Lupus of Ferrières copying Cicero's *Epistulae ad familiares* (see Tarrant 2016, 14; Reynolds and Wilson 2013, 105). If variants were noticed, they could be introduced into the text or the margins. This could, in fact, be done not only by the copyists but also – and very typically – by the readers (Trovato 2017, 131–132; Vàrvaro 2010, 191).

In most cases, the comparison of several copies could naturally provide the text with yet another layer of contamination (see e.g. Tarrant 2016, 14–15; Reynolds and Wilson 2013, 39–43). As the exemplars used for copying could already be contaminated, revisers of the copies probably spotted variation within the textual tradition, but it was exceedingly difficult for them to recover the original readings (Segre 1961, 72). In the case of very popular texts, like the Bible or other much-used ecclesiastical and liturgical works, copyists did not even need another copy to try to improve the content of the exemplar. They could cite the text from their own memory (m n e m o n i c c o n t a m i n a t i o n), often resulting in contamination that has nothing to do with a physical exemplar of the text and can thus be very misleading for the poor scholar trying to shape a stemma.

One should not envisage a scribe looking constantly at two or more exemplars while copying, but rather understand the birth of contamination within a text as a multilayered process. One set of readings was copied from one exemplar, and alterations were made or added to the text, or in the margins, from another manuscript by the same scribe or by someone deliberately correcting or just reading the text. This might have taken place almost immediately or after a considerable period of time, and it is important to keep in mind that all the variants of a text containing mixture need not derive from the same level of the tradition, neither in terms of time nor in relation to the original state of the text. In the latter respect, very complex c i r c u l a r c o n t a m i n a t i o n can even occur, at least in principle. This is possible since "usually a number of the variants of the ancestor in a contaminated tradition are posterior to the corresponding variants of the descendant, and a number of the variants of the descendant are prior to those of the ancestor" (Mink 2004, 50–51, 67–74, fig. 20).

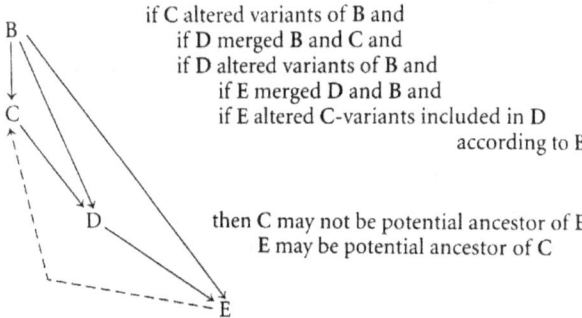

Fig. 4.4-3: The mechanics of an extreme case of contamination, a circular one.
Source: Mink (2004, 50, fig. 20).

It was only during the next phase of textual transmission – when the text was copied again – that these variant readings were really incorporated into the text so that they would no longer be palaeographically or codicologically distinguishable (for an example in the *Navigatio Sancti Brendani*, see P. Chiesa 2016, 56–59). The steps of contamination were normally small, as there was no underlying intention of a scribe to modify the text significantly. This also applies to the cases of seemingly more radical contamination: the steps just seem bigger because there are many links missing (see Mink 2004, 22–24, on New Testament material).

4.4.4.2 Successive contamination

Another frequent form of combining readings from multiple exemplars has been dubbed "consecutive", "block", or "successive" contamination. Here, the scribe used different exemplars to copy the content of different parts of the text (hence the Italian term *contaminazione di esemplari*). This mechanism is also called exemplar shift. The reasons behind such a procedure could be anything ranging from incomplete exemplars omitting a passage of the text to the copyist's zeal to use as high-quality exemplars as possible.

This kind of contamination did not occur only in individual copyists' work, but also – and apparently rather frequently – in proper *scriptoria*, universities, and professional workshops. We have already acquainted ourselves with the fact that the more popular the text, the more contaminated the tradition is bound to be. This is due to the simple fact that ancient and mediaeval libraries and workshops in which texts were copied may have contained more than one exemplar of a popular work. The *pecia* system (see 2.1.1), applied first at the University of Paris and then elsewhere, is an extreme example of how the assiduous copying of very popular texts resulted in thoroughly contaminated traditions. In order to answer the pressing need for certain works on the part of the general public or customers, it employed several exemplars of the same text, broken down into individual quires that, in turn, were copied gathering by gathering by several copyists. Such a way of working made it possible – or even probable – that the exemplar of the text would be shifted (see Vàrvaro 2010, 193; Tonello and Trovato 2011, 18–19). This procedure also explains the high degree of contamination of, for example, university texts but also many of the most popular works, such as the Bible. In New Testament textual criticism, this simplest and least problematic form of contamination has been labelled "block contamination".

Naturally, there are also cases that combine simultaneous and successive contamination, and it is no wonder that mixture causes headaches for modern scholars – just as it was problematic for contemporary scribes and readers.

4.4.4.3 Contamination of versions

Many texts were disseminated in various versions with slightly differing content. We already have a number of known examples of such a practice from Antiquity (see West 1973, 15–17). In the Middle Ages, the phenomenon was probably partly encouraged by the more ad-hoc nature of publishing new texts (Guglielmetti and Orlandi 2014, 179–180). In many cases, contamination of versions was closely related to successive contamination.

A good and typical example of a genre that was particularly prone to the mechanics of contamination of versions is that of hagiographical texts and miracle collections, to which new miracles could (and were expected to) be added, even after the first version had begun circulating. On the other hand, hagiographical texts were also often easily abridged to suit the needs of, for example, a collection of saints' lives.

4.4.5 Previous approaches towards contamination

Considering the fact that contamination is obviously a very common phenomenon posing great difficulties for scholars, it is hardly surprising that there have been continuous attempts to find remedies for it. Horizontal transmission was well known to the scribes producing copies of a text in Antiquity and the Middle Ages. With the rise of philology as a scholarly discipline, the phenomenon received new importance, and it was touched upon already by the early philologists, such as Gottlob Heyne (1729–1812) and Johann Jakob Griesbach (1745–1812; see Timpanaro 1961, 44). Paul Maas (1880–1964), who formalised a set of previously well-known practices dealing with a textual tradition into principles often known as the Lachmannian method, considered contamination to be one of the real challenges endangering the mechanical organisation of textual witnesses into a stemma and thus preventing the Lachmannian method from working. Whereas he seems to have been initially hopeful about solving the problem, he grew more pessimistic with time and concluded in the last edition of his influential *Textkritik*: "Gegen die Kontamination ist kein Kraut gewachsen" (Maas 1957, 31; in the first edition of the work, he wrote: "Gegen die Kontamination ist noch kein Kraut gewachsen"; Maas 1937, 294 [No specific has yet been discovered against contamination], trans. Flower 1958, 49). This is a sentiment shared by many modern-day scholars as well.

The exceedingly sceptical view of Paul Maas and others has not prevented scholars from trying to solve the challenge of contamination, for example Avalle (1961), in which very innovative methods were applied. In the 1960s, Jacques Froger proposed a robust method for calculating the relative frequencies of incompatible groups whose combination produces an irregularity in the stemma. Once the frequencies have been calculated, one should choose the most frequent explanation and forget the other ones (Froger 1968, 112–113; Froger 1965; see also 2.3.4.3 above). A contemporary of Froger, Gian Piero Zarri, developed early computational methods for studying complex textual traditions. He shared many of the ideas of Froger and relied heavily on the theories of Henri Quentin (e.g. Zarri 1971, 1973, 1976,

1977; compare Quentin 1926; see also 4.2.4 above). He did, in fact, have at least some success in unravelling very complex textual transmissions, including open traditions (Borsetta and Zarri 1981). For some reason, however, his contribution to the development of the use of computers in the service of textual criticism has largely been forgotten.

A more traditional textual scholar, Martin L. West, published an influential introduction to textual criticism in 1973. He introduced what are known as **West tables**, which aim to help recognise the proximity of textual versions by quantifying the shared features within the versions (West 1973, 37–47). These tables can also be used to try to track contamination within the tradition. Still, even this approach did not really solve the age-old problems that result in several exemplars. In essence, West tables are closely linked to Froger's previous ideas. In fact, the concept of quantifying the variants of contaminated traditions has been, and is, the prevailing idea of how to deal with contamination. Although this approach does not really tackle the problem, it provides a means to try to circumvent it. Recent textual criticism combines quantifying variants with understanding their emergence. For instance, Paolo Chiesa gives practical examples in the tradition of the *Navigatio Sancti Brendani* on how this helps choose between hypotheses. Here, the leading idea is that the most "economical" explanation is probably the correct one (P. Chiesa 2016, 59–61). This approach, in turn, shares the basic principle of computational approaches: the maximally parsimonious stemma is most probably the correct one.

On the other hand, there are ways to try to interpret the variants in order to decide if there is contamination within the tradition or not. For instance, both graphic traits and linguistic features (like dialects in vernacular texts) can be used to weigh up whether there is contamination or not, since they are more likely to follow vertical rather than horizontal transmission. Similarly, lacunae are normally transferred vertically within a tradition, but very seldom horizontally. In addition, external features such as geographical or other proximity, or otherwise known facts about the history of the tradition, can be useful indicators in its reconstruction (see 4.5).

Despite various attempts, a truly effective remedy against contamination has not been discovered by traditional textual critics. One potentially fruitful approach has scrutinised the few cases in which we can physically see the steps of contamination within extant manuscripts, in order to learn the general principles of how contamination takes place (P. Chiesa 2016, chap. 10). Still, even today, many leading scholars in the field have simply taken comfort in claiming that at least some parts of the stemma of an open tradition can still be reconstructed and original readings can probably be found (P. Chiesa 2016, 60; Trovato 2017, 130, 134; Huygens 2000, 10; West 1973, 38). Although this is a consolation for many philologists aiming to reconstruct the original content and not the whole tradition of the text, such scholars have simultaneously admitted being unable to cope with contamination. For anyone working with the tradition of a popular text, but especially for anyone interested in the tradition of a text in its entirety, this remains a huge problem.

The traditional "Lachmannian" approach quite obviously lacks the means to solve the challenge of mixture except in exceptional cases. The problem is very complicated, and the traditional method of limiting the variants by choosing the most "genealogically informative" ones may, in fact, be counterproductive when it comes to dealing with multiple exemplars. Therefore, answers must be sought elsewhere.

4.4.6 Current ways of dealing with contamination

As mentioned above, mixture is a common phenomenon but not always easy to notice at a glance. In fact, it can normally only be detected once the collation and thus classification of witnesses of a textual tradition is well under way.

4.4.6.1 There is a remedy – for successive contamination

Successive contamination, that is, the use of one exemplar for one part of the text, another for a second part, and so on, is the easiest case to detect. It also poses far fewer problems than simultaneous contamination for an editor of the text or a scholar studying it. In the easiest cases, successive contamination can instantly be seen in palaeographical or codicological traits of the manuscript containing the text: it may have been produced by two or more scribes using their own exemplars or put together from several codicological units. Such examples are numerous, but one should also keep in mind that a change of hand, ruling pattern, quality of parchment, or other feature of manuscript production often has other explanations that have nothing to do with exemplar shift. Even the seemingly obvious cases deserve to be studied thoroughly.

Let us take an example. Trier, Stadtbibliothek, Ms. 1353/132 is a hagiographical collection written in the monastery of Niederwerth in the mid-fifteenth century. It contains, among numerous other texts, the already mentioned eleventh-century hagiography of St Symeon of Trier on f. 27r–35v. A careful reader notices a discontinuity between f. 33v and 34r: one gathering ends on f. 33v and the next begins on the following f. 34r. In addition, the hand changes between the leaves. On top of everything else, the last sentence of f. 33v declares: "Explicit vita sancti Symeonis monachi" [The Life of St Symeon ends [here]]. After weighing up three different testimonies – one codicological, one palaeographical, and one of content – it becomes obvious that the life and miracle collection of Symeon in the manuscript has been put together from two codicological and palaeographical units (see fig. 4.4-4).

Since contamination always has to do with the relationships of the copied text (apograph) with the other witnesses of the textual tradition, any irregularities and changes in these relationships in different parts of the apograph may indicate a change of exemplar. In some cases, the important variants may point in one direction in one part of the text and somewhere else in others, and the successive contamination of the text becomes obvious. In most cases, however, a more thorough

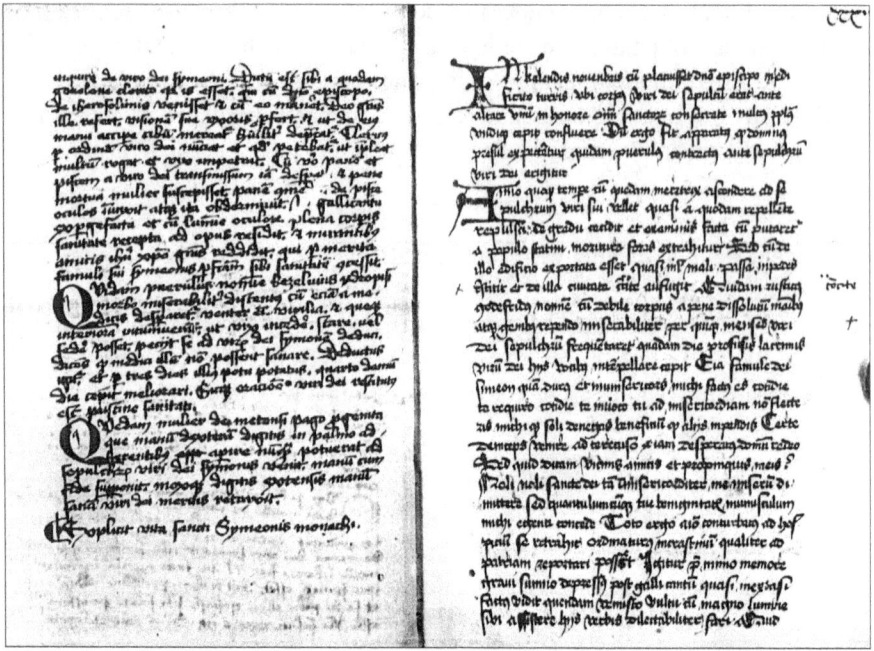

Fig. 4.4-4: Trier, Stadtbibliothek, Ms. 1353/132, f. 33v–34r. This shift in exemplar results in successive mixture in the apograph of the manuscript.

analysis is needed, and it is helpful to visualise the relationships between the witnesses to understand the changes within the textual tradition. One way of doing this is to divide the text into relatively short chunks and scrutinise them. For instance, West tables quantifying the variation between textual witnesses can be used for this. The underlying idea of finding changes in dependencies between textual witnesses is simple and has probably been applied *sub silentio* by an infinite number of scholars using traditional approaches.

While such "non-visual" approaches yield good results in studying successive contamination, drawing hypothetical stemmata of the individual passages of the text can be even more helpful. Today, various computational tools can be used to quickly and easily draw dozens of distance trees visualising the relationships of witnesses in various parts of the text. Should these relationships change significantly and consistently from one part of the text to another, successive contamination is one of the possible explanations that needs to be considered further. As a further advantage of drawing stemmata for various sections of the text, this method provides a scholar with hypotheses on where the exemplars of the apograph can be looked for in the stemma. To follow up on our previous example, let us draw the trees of the St Symeon text in Trier, Stadtbibliothek, Ms. 1353/132 before and after the exemplar shift hypothesised above on palaeographical, codicological, and content grounds (see fig. 4.4-5). The siglum of the Trier manuscript is *V*, both before

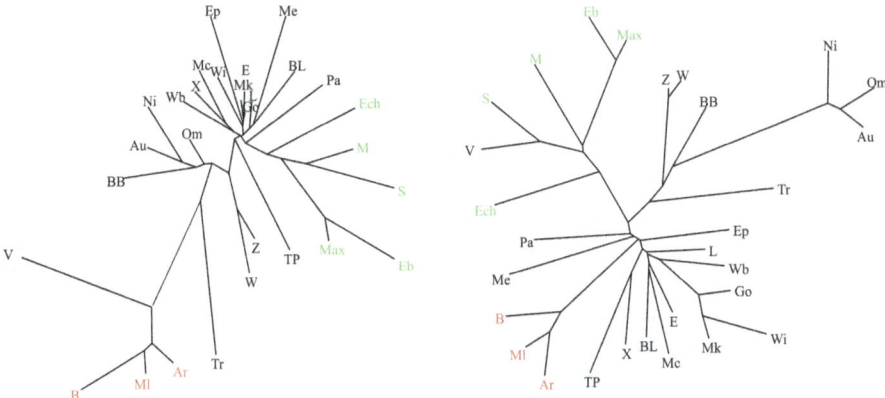

Fig. 4.4-5: Spotting successive contamination: witness V changes its location in the tree plots for the first and the second part of the text very conspicuously. (Unrooted trees, plotted with the "*Leitfehler*"-method script described in Roelli and Bachmann 2010, for a sample of twenty-eight witnesses.)

and after the exemplar shift. By comparing the two stemmata it is easy enough to conclude that we are indeed dealing with a case of successive contamination.

There are further methods that help a scholar trace a change of exemplar. In 1996, Evert Wattel and Margot van Mulken proposed a method for making part of the internal structure of the relationships within a textual tradition visible and thus helping to trace successive contamination: what they call a c a r d i o g r a m o f t h e t e x t t r a d i t i o n. By calculating a similarity graph for the witnesses of a given text, it is possible to pinpoint "shock waves", that is, locations within the text where the similarities/dissimilarities between witnesses change rapidly. This, in turn, may indicate an exemplar shift (Wattel and van Mulken 1996; den Hollander 2004).

A decade later, Heather Windram, Christopher Howe, and Matthew Spencer published an article with promising attempts to tackle successive contamination. They proposed the use of the maximum chi-squared method, a technique borrowed from molecular biology, to analyse the distribution of variants in various parts of *The Wife of Bath's Prologue* in the *Canterbury Tales* (Windram, Howe, and Spencer 2005; Windram, Spencer, and Howe 2006). Subsequently, the method has been used successfully to study the textual tradition of the Sanskrit *Dyūtaparvan* (Phillips-Rodriguez, Howe, and Windram 2009). The underlying idea is that an exemplar shift is analogous to DNA recombination. Applying the maximum chi-squared method allows a very concrete comparison between pairs of textual witnesses and clearly indicates if an exemplar shift took place. In the *Dyūtaparvan* tradition, the maximum chi-squared value is able to identify an exemplar shift when manuscripts *D5* and *D6* are compared; that is, the highest peak in the chart (fig. 4.4-6) pinpoints the greatest discrepancy between the observed and expected distribution of differences. This is where a change of exemplar is most likely to have occurred (at character 3735).

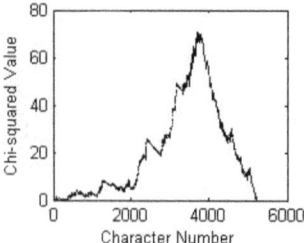

Fig. 4.4-6: Using the maximum chi-squared method to identify an exemplar shift when comparing manuscripts *D5* and *D6* of the *Dyūtaparvan* tradition. Source: Phillips-Rodriguez, Howe, and Windram (2009, 387).

4.4.6.2 How to deal with simultaneous contamination

While there are ways to tackle the consequences of exemplar shift, simultaneous contamination is harder to deal with. The experiments with artificial textual traditions have shown that the hypothesised relationships between the witnesses containing text with simultaneous mixture remain uncertain and often erroneous. This applies to both traditional and computer-assisted methods of textual criticism (Baret, Macé, and Robinson 2006, 264–265; Roos and Heikkilä 2009, 424–427). Still, in the best of cases there may be variants present that point with certitude to one exemplar or group of witnesses. Sometimes, albeit rarely, it is possible to find out all the exemplars used for the apograph in various stages simply due to the fortuitous presence of distinctive variants (see e.g. the methodologically excellent Guglielmetti 2007).

It is a clear indication of simultaneous contamination when the variants of the text point towards a connection with some witnesses here and with other witnesses there, without a clear pattern as in successive mixture. Often, the mere collating of a text reveals links to several other witnesses in such a way that simultaneous contamination can be suspected. If the text of witness *A* shows clear similarities to two or more other witnesses (*B*, *C*, and so on) that are not closely related with each other, it may well be that they were exemplars (or closely related to the exemplars) of *A*. In practice, the scholar tries to look for *Leitfehler* with direction and tries to shape a stemma based on them. The contradicting variants are probable candidates for simultaneous contamination. This is the traditional method in textual criticism for identifying simultaneous contamination in a textual witness.

The challenges do not end when a probably contaminated witness has been found. An open tradition obscures both the direct lines of descent and their direction. In order to put the witness in its proper place in the textual tradition and thus evaluate its significance, it is necessary to find out the direction of relationships between the witness suspected to be contaminated and its closest relatives. In many cases, a derivative witness can appear instead to be the exemplar because of contamination, which may have catastrophic implications for shaping a stemma (see fig. 4.4-2 above; M. W. Holmes 2011, 73–74).

The method of scrutinising the text and the relationships between its witnesses in short passages, so advantageous in finding exemplar shift, is helpful in studying simultaneous contamination, too. What distinguishes simultaneous from successive contamination in this respect is that in the former the links will be present every now and then throughout the text, whereas in the latter there will be distinct blocks of text linked to their respective exemplars. The above-mentioned "shock waves" or West tables can be used as tools to get an insight into the text. Windram, Spencer, and Howe (2006, 153) recommended applying the maximum chi-squared method to detect successive contamination and were sceptical whether the method could be used to trace simultaneous contamination. Still, just like with the "shock waves" or West tables, any further knowledge about the relationships between the witnesses of a textual tradition is welcome and can provide new understanding about contamination.

Previously, it was hoped that applying sophisticated network methods developed by mathematicians and evolutionary biologists to textual traditions could help tackle simultaneous contamination in a better way (Holland et al. 2004; Huson and Bryant 2006; Windram, Spencer, and Howe 2006, 153). Today, the most commonly used network methods include neighbour-joining and NeighborNet (Huson and Bryant 2006; Saitou and Nei 1987). While concretely showing various possible networks representing the relationships within a textual tradition, and thus giving food for thought concerning contamination, the use of network methods has unfortunately not led to a breakthrough (see e.g. Roos and Heikkilä 2009, 426).

One further example from the textual tradition of the life and miracle collection of St Symeon of Trier serves to elucidate the problems we still have. The nearly sixty extant manuscripts of the text can be divided into seven groups according to the variants. In terms of the variants, we can concentrate on just five very distinctive ones, of which every group has a slightly different combination. The writing history of the text makes it obvious that the *Life* and the *Miracles* were edited from very early on partly as separate entities. If we concentrate on just the *Life*, three of the five most distinctive variants are involved. And here comes the problem: of the seven groups, six give a different combination of those three variants, and in none of the variants is it possible to deduct the direction of the change. Consequently, there is no way of representing the groups as a neat tree; we can only assume that the origins of the groups represent various editorial versions that contain mixture with each other. In other words, we have to cope with the simultaneous contamination of versions.

4.4.7 New promises? Computer-assisted methods

As mentioned above, the idea of using computers for "automated textual criticism" stems from the 1960s and 1970s. In spite of some early and encouraging experiments, mainstream textual scholars remained distrustful, and there was an air of "hostility against the methods of automation which [was] based on rhetorical claims for the uniqueness of the 'human spirit'" (Timpanaro 2005, 89; see 5.5 below). Since the 1990s, computers have experienced a renaissance within textual scholarship, and various algorithms have been used to study textual traditions. The results have, again, been encouraging: many approaches of computer-assisted stemmatology have proven to be powerful tools not only for the task of reconstructing the archetypes and other early versions, as well as the development of the text, but also in providing insights into the way texts have been disseminated and altered during their history. At the same time, the computational capacity of modern computers has made it unnecessary to limit the number of variants under scrutiny and has thus allowed scholars to let go of the traditional – but inevitably subjective – selection of variants (on the status quo, see e.g. Heikkilä and Roos 2016, with articles by several scholars; the traditional caveats are summarised by e.g. Trovato 2017, 179–224).

There have been many promising attempts in the field of computer-assisted stemmatology, and computers are widely used when studying vast textual traditions (e.g. Barbrook et al. 1998; Spencer, Mooney, et al. 2004; Windram, Howe, and Spencer 2005; Huson and Bryant 2006). Still, even the best computerised methods share the traditional problems of good old-fashioned textual criticism. Most approaches only provide a scholar with bipartite, unrooted trees, that is, with oversimplifications that give a trustworthy hypothesis on the relationships between the witnesses but need to be elaborated further by traditional means. More importantly in the context of this contribution, there is still no computer-assisted method that reliably deals with contamination.

In 2009, Teemu Roos and Tuomas Heikkilä compared the performance of some twenty computer-assisted methods for stemmatology on three artificial datasets (Roos and Heikkilä 2009). Some of the methods were found to perform far better than others, but there were clearly two factors that affected the performance of all the approaches, even the best ones: the number of missing manuscripts (i.e. those withheld by the organisers of the experiment) and the degree of contamination. From a closer look, it becomes evident that the degree of mixture was – and still is – the most important single feature affecting the result of each method. All the methods got their best score on the dataset with no contamination at all (but with 24 % of the witnesses missing). Similarly, all the methods yielded their worst results on the artificial tradition that contained more contamination than the others (Roos and Heikkilä 2009, 420, 422–423).

At first glance, the results are disappointing when it comes to dealing with contamination. We started by analysing the best results of the artificial textual tradition *Notre besoin*, with only fourteen witnesses, of which one was held back and just one was a result of mixture. The most successful approaches – compression-based RHM and phylogeny-based PAUP* – did find out the overall structure of the tradition, but failed to put the only contaminated witness in the correct place (for a brief

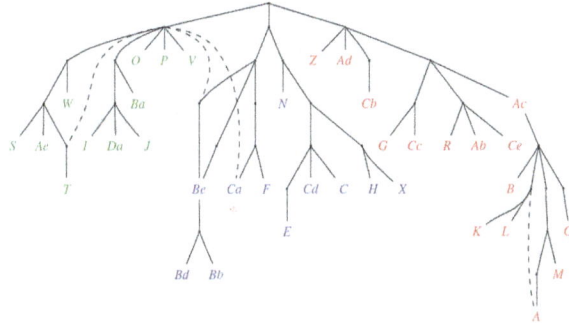

Fig. 4.4-7: The correct stemma of the artificial *Heinrichi* tradition. In the case of mixture, a dashed edge indicates the secondary exemplar.

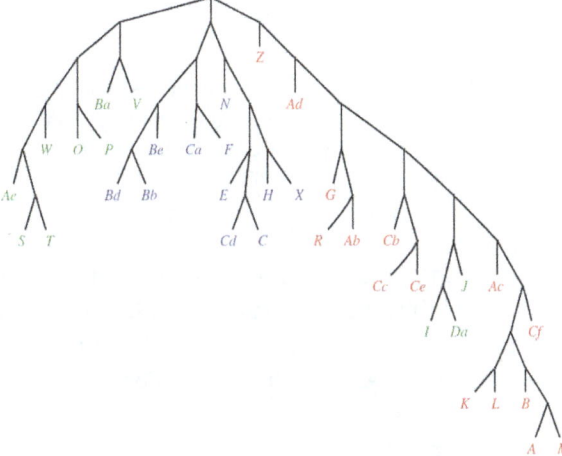

Fig. 4.4-8: The manually rooted stemma obtained by RHM for the artificial *Heinrichi* tradition.

explanation of the methods, see Roos and Heikkilä 2009, 432–433; Swofford 1998; see also 5.3 below) Still, the best results on the most difficult – and thus probably most realistic – textual tradition were not all that discouraging. Let us concentrate on the most complex (i.e. most contaminated and with missing witnesses) of the three artificial datasets, called *Heinrichi*, and compare the trees proposed by the highest-scoring RHM and PAUP* methods with the correct stemma (figs 4.4-7–9).

Our interest lies in the four witnesses that have more than one exemplar: *A, Be, Ca,* and *T*. It turns out that all of them are reasonably well located in their real context in the hypotheses of RHM and PAUP*. *A* is together with *B, K, L,* and *M*; *Be* together with *Bb, Bd,* and *Ca*; *Ca* with *Be, F,* and *N*; and *T* with *Ae* and *S*. The results are by no means perfect, but the relationships of the contaminated witnesses with the others are more or less correct (see also the encouraging results of Marmerola et al. 2016 on *Heinrichi* material). It should also be mentioned here that all four of them represent the more difficult variety of contamination, the continuous one.

In the 2010s, Jean-Baptiste Camps and Florian Cafiero approached contamination from another angle. Their idea is to distinguish genealogical (i.e. non-contaminated,

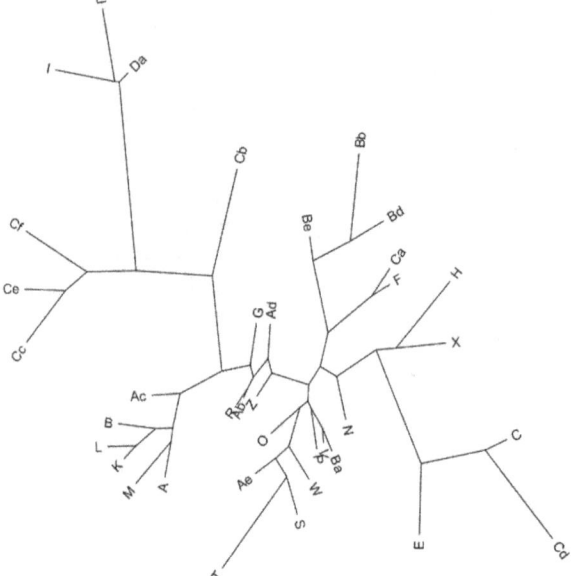

Fig. 4.4-9: The unrooted tree obtained by PAUP* (parsimony criterion) for the *Heinrichi* tradition.

according to them) and other (i.e. resulting from polygenesis or contamination of readings) variants from each other. To do this, they compare variant locations two by two. If the variants cannot be represented in a logical genealogical stemma, this points towards polygenesis or contamination. Despite their contribution to creating a new stemmatological algorithm, even Camps and Cafiero (2014, esp. 75–76, 90) do not really find a way to take mixture into account.

Marina Buzzoni et al. (2016) compared the hypotheses of several computer-assisted methods with the results of traditional textual criticism on open and closed real-life textual traditions. Despite their clear preference for traditional methods and some problems in interpreting the results of the algorithms, their conclusion was that the computerised methods yield better and more useful results on contaminated textual traditions.

4.4.8 Status quo and future prospects

One of the traditional weaknesses of textual criticism, be it traditional or computerised, is the unnecessary division of labour. Scholars of biblical exegesis, ancient texts, and mediaeval literature, for instance, work in surprising isolation from each other, even though they share many of the same scholarly challenges. Here, it is worth mentioning one example of a novel approach to reconstructing textual traditions including contamination, the Coherence-Based Genealogical Method, or CBGM (egora.uni-muenster.de/intf/service/downloads_en.shtml; see also 4.2.3.6, 7.1.2.2).

The recognition that the traditional "Lachmannian" method does not work on textual traditions with simultaneous contamination has led some scholars to question one of the core ideas of the discipline, the elimination of unnecessary witnesses, or *eliminatio codicum descriptorum*. This approach has been developed among scholars of the most commonly copied text (and probably the one with most thoroughly open tradition) of the Middle Ages, the New Testament. Here, it has been found impossible to strive directly towards a stemma of all witnesses. Instead, it has been judged useful to cut the text into a high number of very short passages consisting of single variants that are studied one by one to reconstruct a myriad of local stemmata of the readings. In principle, this should lead to several groups consisting of stemmata pointing in the same direction within the textual tradition, and it should thus be possible to identify the exemplars used in producing a copy. Furthermore, in the best of cases, it should be possible to combine the local stemmata of variants in a global stemma of witnesses. The novelty of the method lies in the fact that it reconstructs stemmata of the readings, based on which the stemma of the witnesses is inferred. In other words, the method applies to each passage individually the very same approach used by textual criticism for the whole tradition. The method builds heavily on Froger's previous work (see above), but employs a set of computer-based tools to deal with the stemmata (Mink 2004; M. W. Holmes 2011, 75; Wachtel 2012a, 123–138). In the context of this contribution, it is important to stress that the method seems promising in tackling contamination as well. In fact, the idea of building local stemmata based on single variants has many similarities with the use of "shock waves" or the maximum chi-squared method to detect contamination: a big scholarly challenge is divided into several smaller and thus more easily solved problems.

During the past few years, CBGM has been well received among the scholars of biblical exegesis (cf. Gurry 2017; Wasserman and Gurry 2017; Wasserman 2015). With regard to contamination, the method is said to solve the problem by forgoing the mechanical reconstruction of hyparchetypes and allowing multiple ancestors for each witness, and by using coherence to identify the likely ancestors of a witness. Some have even proclaimed that contamination is "a problem no longer" (Parker 2012, 84; Gurry 2017, 206). The most recent studies have shown, however, that even CBGM does not always succeed in tackling mixture, which thus does remain a problem (Gurry 2017, 206–207). Nevertheless, CBGM can be useful for gaining insights into vast and contaminated traditions where it would be virtually impossible to make a stemma using traditional methods. Curiously, the discussion about the applicability of CBGM has mostly been confined to biblical exegesis, and its core ideas have not been widely applied outside the study of the New Testament. This goes to show the importance of collaboration across the traditional boundaries of disciplines. CBGM approaches the challenge of contamination from a very different angle than traditional textual critics or the computer-assisted methods hitherto employed. It would be important to test the method on various artificial textual traditions to find out its performance in comparison to other approaches. The very same applies to all relevant computer-assisted methods: more tests on artificial datasets should be run before any hopefully watertight conclusions can be drawn.

In spite of the claims of success of some individual scholars in dealing with it in individual cases, contamination remains a challenge. The recent results of some computer-assisted methods and CBGM give reason for at least some optimism: progress has been made in two directions that complement each other. Still, one should not forget the traditional approach either. Computerised methods result only in hypotheses that need to be studied and refined by traditional means: using modern computational methods does not mean abandoning the traditional virtues of textual criticism. At the moment, this combination of traditional and novel approaches is the best way of dealing with mixture. One needs both deep understanding of the text and knowledge of the whole textual tradition.

Although these methods are not able to explain contamination on the level of individual readings yet, they are nevertheless often able to put a contaminated textual witness in its proper context. In other words, we may not yet have – to use Paul Maas's famous terminology – a "Kraut gegen Kontamination", but with our present tools, contamination does not make the part of textual tradition in which it occurs totally impossible to study or to reconstruct.

4.5 The stemma as a historical tool

Caroline Macé

The title of Giorgio Pasquali's book *Storia della tradizione e critica del testo* (1934) suggests a tension between the history of a tradition and textual criticism (see 2.4 above on neo-Lachmannian philology as a synthesis). Indeed, textual scholarship, even if not explicitly neo-Lachmannian, must combine a historical approach to manuscript traditions with a critical-philological approach to textual variation in order to be able to obtain a critical-historical general view of any textual tradition (Irigoin 1981). These two approaches, however, require different skills and methodologies, and there is no handbook explaining how this combination of approaches should work. This lack of a clear and simple recipe may be one of the reasons why several scholarly trends tend to keep both approaches separated, or even to make them oppose one another, like the so-called New Philology (see 2.3.4.4). De facto, it may prove methodologically sound to carry out either type of research – on the textual variation and on the history of the manuscripts – separately at first and then to combine and compare the results of both investigations, even though this comparison may lead, in an iterative process, to revising some of the results obtained in each of the two parts of the research. In text-critical practice, the very word "manuscript" is often ambiguous, as it may designate both the physical object carrying textual content and that content itself, that is, a text-state. The distinction between *traditio textus* and *traditio codicum* is somewhat artificial, since the history of the transmission of text-states and the history of the evolution and dissemination of text-carriers should ultimately correspond and be synthesised in one and the same *stemma codicum*. The concise expression "history of the text" is sometimes used in different languages (*histoire du texte, storia del testo, Textgeschichte*, and so on) to mean "history of the tradition of a work". The work (defined by its identification in repertories, histories of literature, and so on) exists through different textual states present in direct and indirect witnesses (see 3.1–2).

4.5.1 Types of evidence for the history of a manuscript tradition

In most cases, a tree-graph drawn using statistical or computational methods will represent only affinities (similarities) between the text-states contained in extant witnesses. If the tree can be oriented or rooted, the tree-graph will represent genealogical relationships between the text-states (see 4.1.3, 4.1.5, and in general 4.2). The situation is not so different when no computational methods are used, as the philologist will normally base his tree primarily on kinship-revealing (significant) secondary readings ("errors" in the text-critical sense; see 4.3.1). This tree will therefore also represent genealogical relationships between text-states, and not yet be a *stemma codicum* in the full sense (see 4.1.3). In all cases, the determination of the secondary readings or of the root is the most difficult part of the work (see 4.5.3).

In order for the tree to become a *stemma codicum*, other types of information should be added. The *stemma codicum*, thus conceived, summarises the history of the manuscript tradition. This history will be explained in the introduction to the edition or even as a separate book (e.g. Irigoin 1952 on the history of the tradition of Pindar's work). The critical edition must be based on the history of the tradition, but this is not the only possible use of that history. Combined, histories of different traditions will contribute greatly to the intellectual history of a given period, especially those periods in which manuscripts and philology have played an eminent role, for example Alexandrian philology or the Renaissance (see 2.1.4, 2.1.5).

Amongst the types of evidence that can be taken into account to depict the history of a given tradition, the following ones are the most important:
(*i*) material evidence: date and place of copy, palaeographical analysis, codicological analysis, and so on (see 1.4 above; see also Irigoin 2000);
(*ii*) "environmental" evidence: history of the transmission of other works contained in the same manuscripts (see the collection of essays on "multiple-text manuscripts" in Friedrich and Schwarke 2016); arrangement of a "collection" or "corpus" of works or subworks (chapters, sermons, letters, and so on) in a book or in a collection of books;

(iii) **paratextual evidence**: titles, divisions of the text, marginalia, and so on;
(iv) **indirect tradition**: ancient and mediaeval translations, citations of the work in anthologies; and
(v) transmission of the work in another **material support** than manuscripts, like graffiti, papyri, and so on (see 3.2 above; see also Macé et al. 2015, 328–329).

In order to illustrate how these different types of evidence can be combined with philological insights to draw up the history of a textual tradition, a few case studies are examined in the remainder of this section. In the first one (4.5.2), the manuscript tradition is extremely fragmentary and the determination of "errors" is made very difficult by the existence of various layers of corrections and contaminations; nevertheless, it was possible to draw a stemma manually. In the second case study (4.5.3), the situation is rather different, as the work is preserved in a very large number of witnesses. However, as is almost always the case for ancient and early mediaeval works, no direct witnesses are preserved from the early stages of the transmission, and therefore the top of the tree is missing and rooting is very difficult. It was feasible to produce some statistical representations of the relative proximity of the witnesses, but orienting the tree was possible only thanks to the use of an "outgroup" (this concept will be explained below). In this case, as well, material evidence was of crucial importance in order to consolidate a philological hypothesis about the transmission of the texts. In the final case study (4.5.4), no attempt at drawing a stemma of the transmission of the work was made, because the work is not transmitted through direct witnesses (it has disappeared in its original language) but only through indirect witnesses (translations). It was possible to infer some elements in the history of the tradition of the work from the application of textual criticism to comparison of the versions of the work in other languages and from what is known about the literary contacts between the languages in question. A genealogical study of the variation between the versions is a preliminary to any study of the versions in their individual context.

4.5.2 Proclus' Commentary on Plato's *Parmenides*

This commentary was composed in the fifth century CE by Proclus Diadochus (the "Successor"), one of the last pagan philosophers active in Athens. As Platonist philosophy was not allowed in the Byzantine Empire, or only in disguise, like the work of Pseudo-Dionysius Areopagita (see Steel 1997), only a few works by Proclus have survived, in scarce and late manuscripts. Of all the commentaries on Plato that Proclus must have written, the following are preserved: those on the *Alcibiades* (mutilated at the end), on the *Parmenides* (mutilated at the end), on the *Republic*, on the *Timaeus* (with the largest manuscript tradition, from the beginning of the twelfth century onwards), and on the *Cratylus*. The commentary on the *Republic* is preserved in a single manuscript dated to the end of the ninth or the beginning of the tenth century, and in Renaissance copies of that manuscript. For the commentary on the *Alcibiades*, we also have only one manuscript, copied by George Pachymeres in the thirteenth century. The manuscripts preserving the commentary on the *Cratylus* are relatively numerous, but none is dated prior to the twelfth century. For Proclus' own works, the *Platonic Theology* and the *Elements of Theology*, no manuscript is older than the thirteenth century. The *Tria opuscula* are known only through the translation of William of Moerbeke in the thirteenth century and through a plagiarism by Isaac Sebastokrator in the second half of the eleventh century (see 4.5.2.3).

Thirteenth century
A   Paris, Bibliothèque nationale de France, gr. 1810

Fourteenth century
M   Milano, Biblioteca Ambrosiana, B 165 sup. (159) (ca. 1340)
L   Firenze, Biblioteca Medicea Laurenziana, Conv. Soppr. 103 (a. 1358)

Fifteenth century
F   Firenze, Biblioteca Medicea Laurenziana, Plut. 85.8 (a. 1489)
V   Venezia, Biblioteca Marciana, gr. Z 191

Sixteenth century
W   Wien, Österreichische Nationalbibliothek, phil. gr. 7 (a. 1561)
G   Escorial, Real Biblioteca de San Lorenzo, T. II. 8 (gr. 147)
P   München, Bayerische Staatsbibliothek, gr. 425
R   Città del Vaticano, Biblioteca Apostolica Vaticana, Ross. 962

Fig. 4.5-1: *Conspectus siglorum* of Proclus' Commentary on Plato's *Parmenides*.

Proclus' commentary on the *Parmenides* met a similar fate. Although it is preserved in several manuscripts, most of them were copied in Italy or in Spain during the Renaissance, and only three came into existence before the end of the Byzantine Empire (i.e. 1453). Before the work of Carlos Steel (Steel and Macé 2006), it was believed that this manuscript tradition was to be divided into two families: on the one hand, a late thirteenth-century manuscript, which received the siglum *A*, and its descendants; on the other hand, some fifteenth- and sixteenth-century descendants (*F, G, P, R, W*) of a lost manuscript *Σ*. The *conspectus siglorum* in figure 4.5-1 gives the names and sigla of the main manuscripts. For the stemma as it was traditionally conceived, see figure 4.5-2.

In addition to the Greek manuscripts, a very literal Latin translation was made by William of Moerbeke at the end of the thirteenth century (*g*). This indirect witness is precious because it must have been made on the basis of a lost Greek manuscript containing a longer text of the commentary (*Γ*); see the edition of the Latin text by Steel (1982–1985) and a back-translation into Greek of the missing part in Steel and van Campe (2009, 279–355). The Latin translation preserves some readings that are obviously better than those of A and of the descendants of Σ, so that we must conclude that A and Σ share some secondary readings (errors). The stemma in figure 4.5-2 is therefore to be corrected as shown in figure 4.5-3.

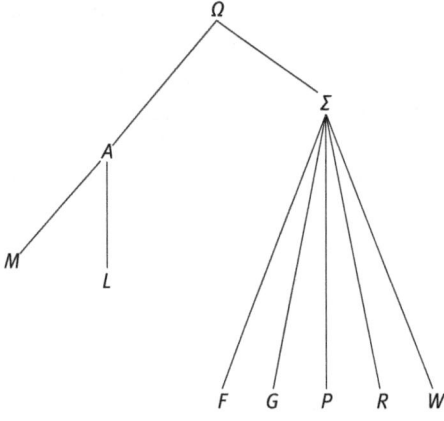

Fig. 4.5-2: Stemma 1 of the tradition of Proclus' *In Parmenidem*. The Greek letters represent lost manuscripts.

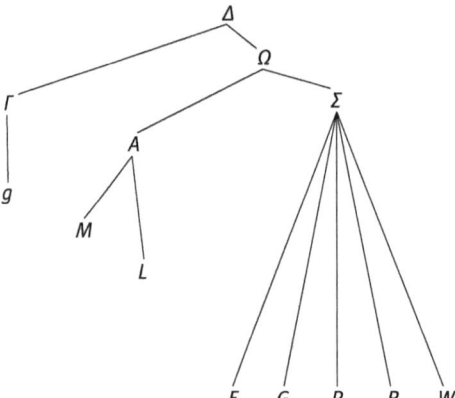

Fig. 4.5-3: Stemma 2 of the tradition of Proclus' *In Parmenidem*, with the translation of William of Moerbeke (*g*) and its lost Greek model (*Γ*).

Further, a philological comparison of the Latin translation with the Greek manuscripts allowed us to detect some apparent common mistakes of *g* and Σ against A – which is stemmatically impossible. In fact, those apparently better readings of A are not to be seen as primary readings but as c o r r e c t i o n s made by the copyist of A, George Pachymeres (1241–ca. 1310), himself a philosopher (see Golitsis 2010 on the activity of Pachymeres as philosopher, teacher, copyist, and philologist). Pachymeres not only thoroughly corrected the text he copied (not always successfully) but also adapted the text of Plato present as lemmata in the commentary (Steel 1999; see fig. 4.5-5 below: the lemmata are in red ink). Moreover, he wrote a sequel to the incomplete text of Proclus (Westerink et al. 1989). We were led to conclude that Pachymeres' model was actually Σ, the very same manuscript as the one used later by several copyists in Italy and Spain (*F, G, P, R, W*). The stemma must therefore be further modified as shown in figure 4.5-4. Obviously, Σ was still in a better state of conservation in the thirteenth century than it was in the fifteenth and sixteenth centuries, because in all those late copies there are lacunae, blank spaces, and obviously erroneous readings due to the difficulty of deciphering their exemplar; these lacunae and erroneous readings are not found in *A*. The fact that manuscripts evolve in the course of time must be taken into account when trying to understand the history of a textual tradition (for other cases, see Irigoin 1954).

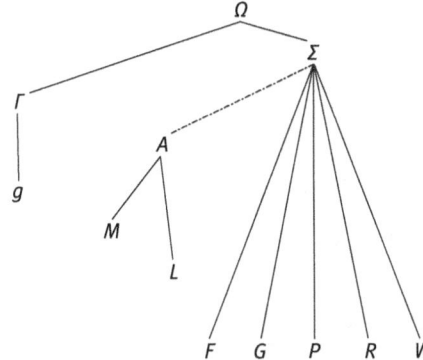

Fig. 4.5-4: Stemma 3 of the tradition of Proclus' *In Parmenidem*; the dot-dash line indicates that the copyist of *A* did not only copy the text of Σ but also heavily modified it.

Manuscript *A* was copied at least twice when it was still in Constantinople. The oldest copy, *M*, a fourteenth-century manuscript, was bought around 1445 by Cardinal Bessarion, a Greek intellectual converted to Catholicism, and entered his library in Italy. The second copy (*L*) was made not long after the first one (1358), but at that time manuscript *A* had suffered heavily from water damage and the upper external corner of most pages had become barely legible, especially towards the end of the book. In some cases, the copyist of *L* tried to restore the faded text in *A* (see fig. 4.5-5).

The text copied in *M* was of poor quality, full of mistakes and omissions, and its new owner, Bessarion, could not be satisfied with that. Therefore, he carefully corrected the text of his manuscript, and he even did so twice, as can be seen from the two different layers (made using different inks) of marginal and interlinear notes in his hand (see Macé, Steel, and d'Hoine 2009; fig. 4.5-6 below). At first, Bessarion corrected the text using his own excellent command of the Greek language and deep knowledge of Proclus' thought. But this was obviously not enough, because he looked for another manuscript containing Proclus' commentary to collate it against his own. There was indeed another manuscript of Proclus' *In Parmenidem* in Italy at that time, none other than manuscript Σ, which was then probably kept in Rome, where Bessarion, due to his work at the papal court, often resided. Indeed, the oldest known Italian copy of Σ was made by John Rhosos, a professional Greek copyist, in Rome in 1489, for Lorenzo de' Medici, as is known from the colophon of manuscript *F* (see fig. 4.5-7). Most of the changes made by Bessarion during the second phase of correction (at any event, before his death in 1472) were inspired by

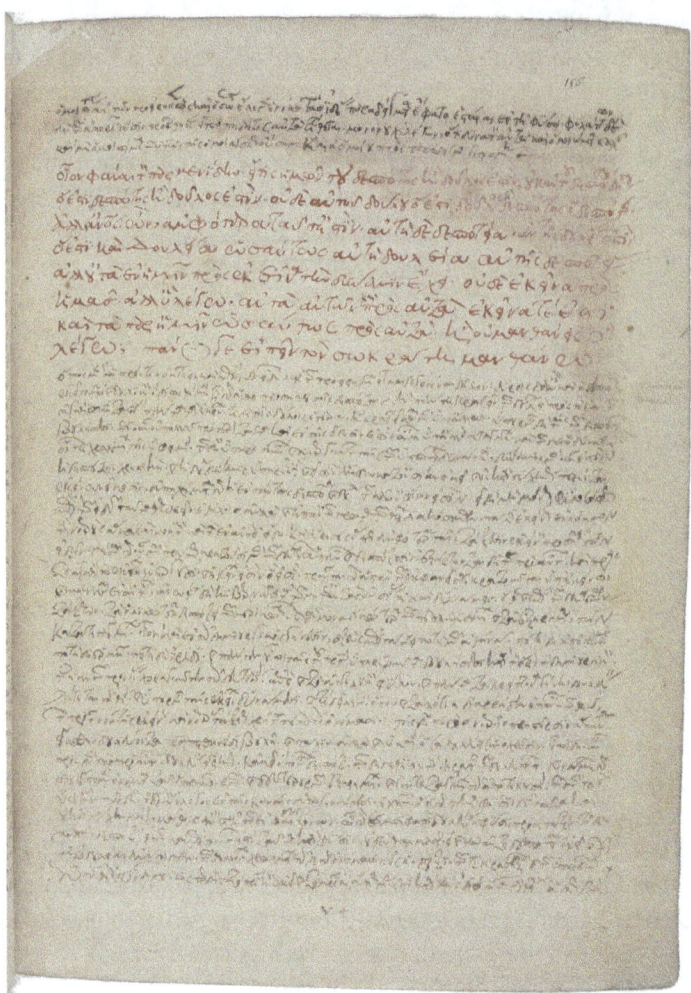

Fig. 4.5-5: Paris, Bibliothèque nationale de France, gr. 1810, f. 156r (*A*). Source: Gallica, Bibliothèque nationale de France, gallica.bnf.fr/ark:/12148/btv1b10507219n/f319.image. Image: CC-BY-NC.

Σ, to which Bessarion's marginal and interlinear notes are therefore the oldest preserved witness after *A* (before the copy by John Rhosos). Furthermore, professional copyists, such as Rhosos and the copyists of the other *recentiores*, were not always very accurate and, for financial reasons, speed sometimes prevailed over care, at the cost of several grave omissions. Most likely for the same pecuniary reasons, the margins of *F* are very large (and empty), presumably because Rhosos was paid by the page (see fig. 4.5-7; other reasons may be put forward, but in this context this seems the most obvious one). The way Bessarion made his corrections on the basis of Σ also tells us something about the form of that manuscript – so that, in this case, philology is an aid to codicology. Indeed, every time a new quire of Σ starts,

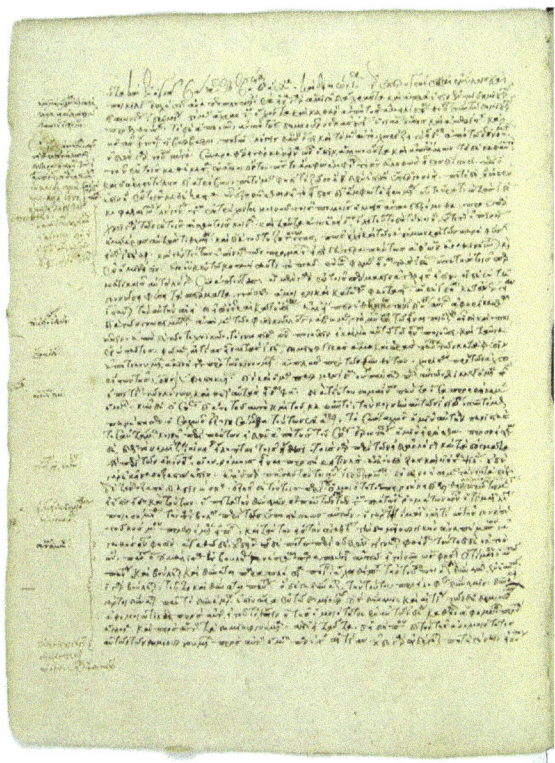

Fig. 4.5-6: Milano, Biblioteca Ambrosiana, B 165 sup. (159), f. 36v (*M*) – already published in Macé, Steel, and d'Hoine (2009). Apart from Bessarion, another, anonymous, reader left notes in the manuscript, sometimes discussing Bessarion's interpretations, as here.

Bessarion drew a line in the text of M and wrote "ἐνταῦθα" [here] in the margin. From that we can estimate the length of the quires in *Σ*.

Bessarion ordered a new copy to be made from *M*, incorporating his corrections into the text: this is manuscript *V*, now in the Biblioteca Marciana in Venice, like most of Bessarion's manuscripts. Manuscript *M*, however, was borrowed from the Marciana by Niccolò Leonico Tomeo (1456–1531), who also left a few notes in its margins. Tomeo never returned the manuscript to the library, and it was bought from his *Nachlass* in Padova by Vincenzo Pinelli (1535–1601), and then again by Federico Borromeo, who bequeathed it to the Biblioteca Ambrosiana in Milan (for all details concerning the manuscripts, see Luna and Segonds 2007–, vol. 1.1, and the introduction in Steel, Macé, and d'Hoine 2007). Had *M* not been preserved, it would have been very hard, perhaps impossible, to understand the position of *V* in the stemma (this is a very special case of contamination; see 4.4).

It was not only manuscript *M* that travelled quite a lot, first from Constantinople to Italy, then within Italy: manuscript *Σ*'s journeys can also be traced to some extent. We know it was in Constantinople at the end of the thirteenth century, because

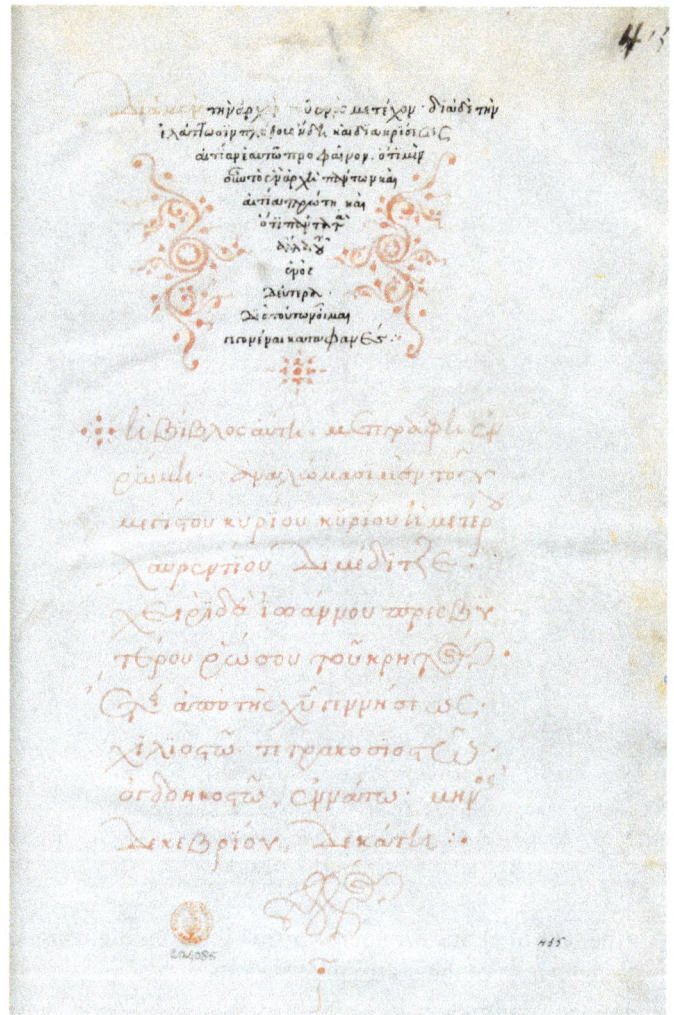

Fig. 4.5-7: Firenze, Biblioteca Medicea Laurenziana, Plut. 85.8, f. 435r, colophon (*F*).
Source: mss.bmlonline.it/Catalogo.aspx?Shelfmark=Plut.85.8.

Pachymeres copied it there. We know it was in Rome at the end of the fifteenth century, because John Rhosos completed his copy in that city in 1489 (and Bessarion used it some time before). Around the middle of the sixteenth century, it must have been in Venice, because manuscript *G* was copied before 1570 in Andreas Darmarios' workshop in that city. Philological analysis shows that two manuscripts were copied in their first part from *M*, or from its descendant *V*, and in their second part from *Σ*, or the other way around: *P* (books 1–3 from *M* and books 4–7 from *Σ*) and *W* (book 1 to the beginning of book 4 from *Σ*, and the end of book 4 to book 7 from *V*). This anomaly can be explained only if the first exemplar from which each copy was made suddenly became unavailable (or was defective, but we know this is not the case); otherwise, there is no reason why a copyist would change his model in the course of copying. P was copied in the workshop of Darmarios. W was copied in 1561 by Cornelius Murmuris of Nauplia (f. 359v, colophon), who was active in Venice. This is highly speculative, but one could imagine that Cornelius Murmuris used Σ as his model in Venice but could not finish his copy because Σ was taken away to another place (Spain), and that he had to look for another model available in Venice, V. One could also hypothesise that the copy of P was begun in Venice and completed in Spain, where Darmarios worked between 1571 and 1580 (Martínez Manzano 2008): for the first part of P, which was still copied in Venice, the copyists could use M, but for the second part they had to use another model, present in Spain – perhaps Σ was bought, like so many manuscripts, by the Spanish ambassador in Venice, Diego Hurtado de Mendoza (1503–1575), presumably before 1561. As mentioned previously, there is no trace left of Σ any more: it is not impossible that Σ disappeared, along with so many other manuscripts, in the great fire that destroyed the Escorial library in 1671.

The whole history of the tradition of Proclus' *In Parmenidem*, based on philological analysis, material and paratextual evidence, and the indirect tradition, is summarised in figure 4.5-8. I am very much indebted to Carlos Steel, with whom I have discussed the history of this tradition many times (see Steel 2010).

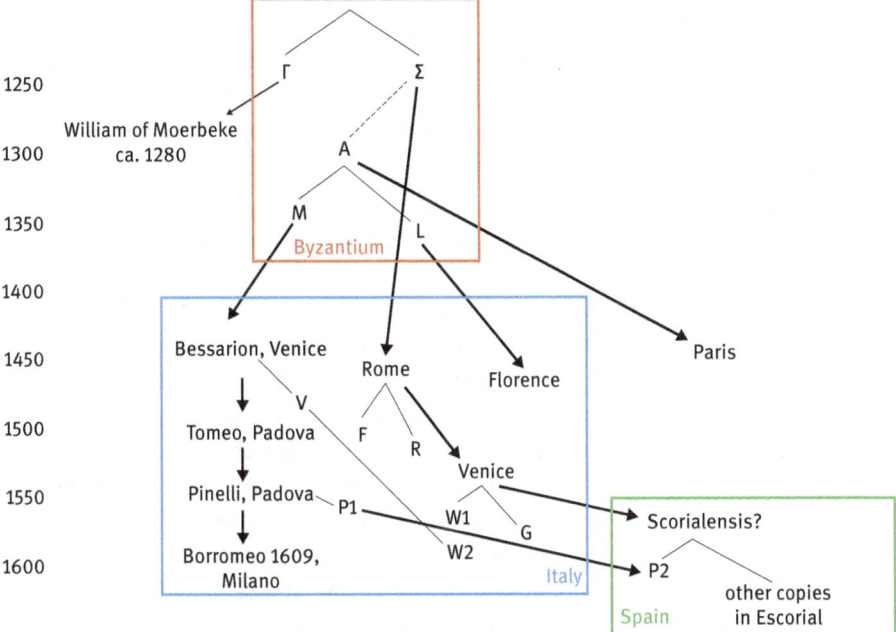

Fig. 4.5-8: Final stemma of the manuscript tradition of Proclus' *In Parmenidem* (previously unpublished). The arrows do not indicate filiations between text-states, but geographical relocations or changes of owners of manuscripts.

4.5.3 Gregory of Nazianzus' *Homilies*

The second example stands in many respects in contrast with the first one: Gregory of Nazianzus (ca. 330–390 CE), called "the Theologian", was a bishop and a Father of the Church; his homilies were therefore preserved in hundreds of manuscripts, translated into several languages at an early stage, and continuously quoted in many Byzantine works. This overabundance of witnesses poses methodological problems which are very different from those encountered in the first example (see Treu 1969; Amand de Mendieta 1987). In both cases, however, we are dealing with authorial works, even if the level of authority attributed to Gregory of Nazianzus was much higher. Copyists and scholars tended to preserve the text of Gregory untouched, *ne varietur*, as much as possible. In addition, the sociology of the copyists in the two cases under consideration is quite different. Gregory's manuscripts were mostly copied by monks, more or less educated, whereas Proclus' works were copied almost exclusively for, and often by, Byzantine intellectuals or Renaissance-era professional copyists. Gregory's homilies were found in every library, sometimes probably in several copies. The manuscripts containing his homilies are of very different types: poor manuscripts on bad parchment, written by not particularly skilled monks (sometimes in disastrous orthography); copies obviously made for the purpose of the study of the text, with copious explanations in the margins (see fig. 4.5-9); and luxuriously illustrated and perfectly executed copies meant to be displayed rather than read, such as the beautiful copy made for the imperial library, Paris, Bibliothèque nationale de France, gr. 510 (see fig. 4.5-10). This last manuscript, copied in a late uncial script around 880 CE, is one of the oldest preserved manuscripts of Gregory, but its text is of poor quality, with many omissions and traces of contamination.

I have presented elsewhere a sketch of the history of this very large tradition (see Macé et al. 2015, 424–429). I will not repeat it here, but only point out some possibly interesting elements.

As in several other traditions, scholars have tried to provide a first classification of the manuscripts based not on textual but on paratextual evidence, which is more readily apparent and less time-consuming to collect and analyse than the textual variants (see 3.3 on the transcription and collation of witnesses). In the present case, the main criterion used was the order of the homilies in the manuscripts (see 7.2.3 for an example of the same use of the order of works in Lucian manuscripts). In 1917, Tadeusz Sinko showed that two main sequences of the forty-five homilies (and some other texts) were found in the manuscripts he knew of that contained a "complete" collection of the homilies. Accordingly, he proposed to divide the tradition into two branches, which he called *M* and *N* (fig. 4.5-11).

This hypothesis held for about eighty years and served as a basis for the choice of the manuscripts to be used for the editions of the homilies in the *Sources Chrétiennes* collection. An exhaustive census, completed in 1998, revealed 1,500 manu-

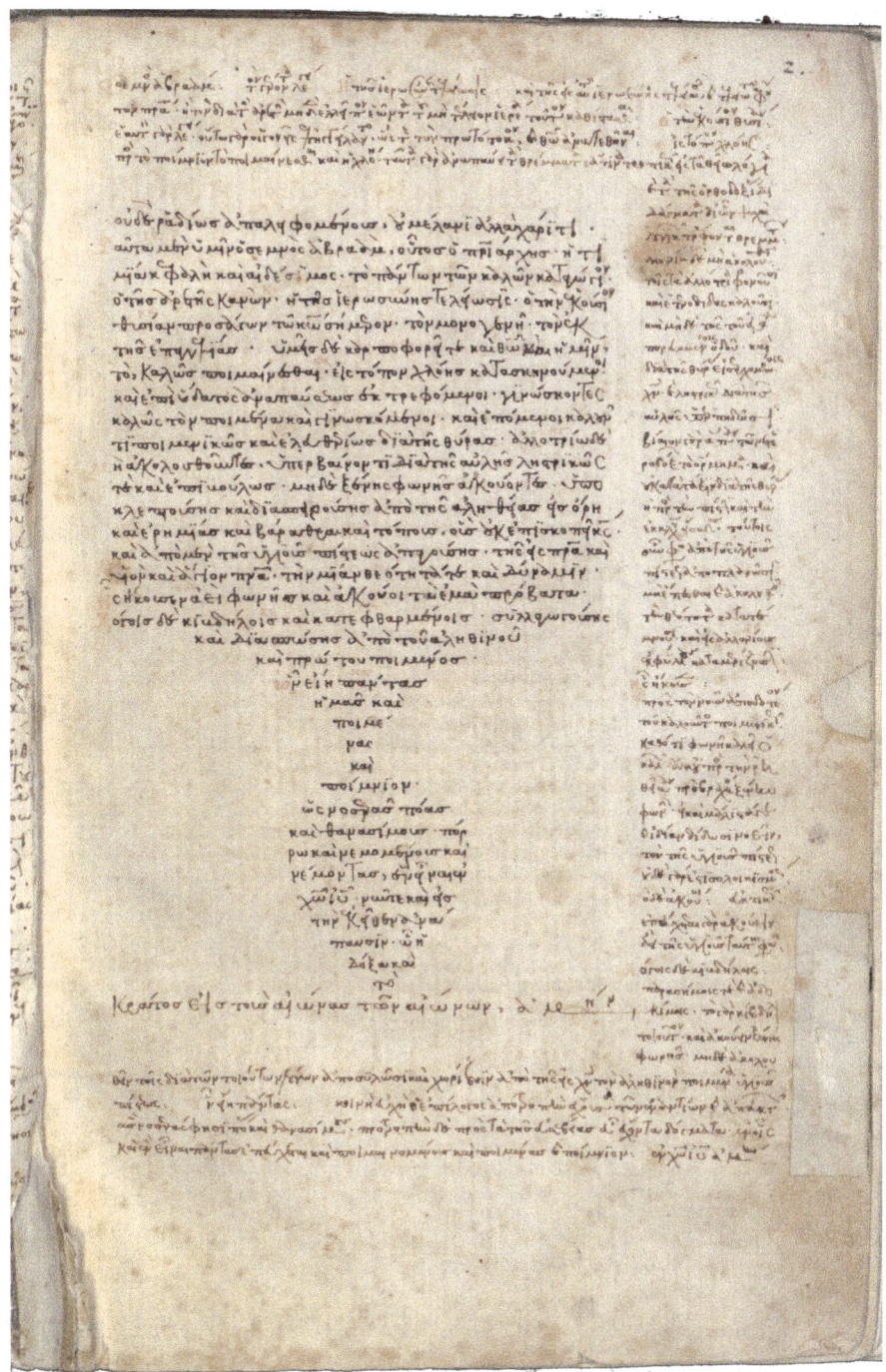

Fig. 4.5-9: München, Bayerische Staatsbibliothek, gr. 204, f. 2r. Source: digitale-sammlungen.de (urn:nbn:de:bvb:12-bsb00076037-2). Image: CC-BY-NC-SA 4.0.

Fig. 4.5-10: Paris, Bibliothèque nationale de France, gr. 510, f. 3r. Source: Gallica, Bibliothèque nationale de France, gallica.bnf.fr/ark:/12148/btv1b84522082/f19.image. Image: CC-BY-NC.

N (31 manuscripts) – 52 items
- vol. 1: Or. 1, 2, 3, 7, 8, 6, 23, 9, 10, 11, 12, 16, 18, 19, 17, 43, 14, 21, 24, 15, 25, 34, 20, 27, 28.
- vol. 2: Or. 29, 30, 31, 38, 39, 40, 45, 44, 41, 33, 22, 32, 26, 36, 42 – Ep. 101, 102, 202 – Or. 4, 5, 37, 13 – Vg. – Doxo. – Ep. 243 – Ez. – Eccl.

M (25 manuscripts) – 49 items
- vol. 1: Or. 2, 12, 9, 10, 11, 3, 19, 17, 16, 7, 8, 18, 6, 23, 22, 38, 39, 40, 1, 45, 44, 41, 32, 33, 27.
- vol. 2: Or. 29, 30, 31, 20, 28, 34, 14 – Ep. 101, 102 – Or. 36, 26, 25, 24, 21, 15, 42, 43, 4, 5, 37 – Ep. 202 – Or. 13 – Vg. – Doxo.

Fig. 4.5-11: Order of the homilies in the two main types of complete collection.

scripts containing one or more homilies of Gregory (pot-pourri.fltr.ucl.ac.be/manu scrits/nazianze/default.cfm), and a thorough examination of the complete collections amongst them – around a hundred – showed that about 50% did not follow any of the orders prevalent in the *M* or *N* manuscripts, but different ones peculiar to each manuscript (Somers 1997). This pointed to the necessity of revising the history of the tradition of the collections on the basis not only of paratextual elements, but also and primarily on the basis of a philological evaluation of the variant readings – a work which I have started, but so far completed only for one of the forty-five homilies, homily 27 (on theology). The phylogenetic tree shown below (fig. 4.5-12) is so far the best representation of the relationships between the 130 manuscripts containing homily 27 (Macé, Baret, and Lantin 2004).

This tree (fig. 4.5-12) shows only the relative textual proximity of the witnesses; it is not a stemma, and it cannot be used for any kind of *eliminatio codicum descriptorum* (see 2.2.8) or for the *constitutio textus* (see 6.2). Rooting the tree is not an easy task. Traditionally, as we have seen above, the tradition was divided into two main families: *M* and *N*. In the phylogenetic tree (fig. 4.5-12) a group of *M* manuscripts seems to emerge, with different sub-branches: *M1*, *M6*, *M10*, *M11*, *M12*, *M20*, *M21*; *M22*, *M23* with *V26*, *V35*; *M15*, *M16*, *M17*, *M17* with *V57*; and *M14*, *M24* with *V29*. But is this a "family" – that is, is it characterised by secondary significant variants? And what about the rest of the tree? The text of homily 27 is relatively short (2,000 words), and there is variation between the manuscripts (556 variant locations were defined, some of them with more than two variants), but significant variant locations are relatively rare and difficult to polarise, because the variants are often equally likely to be "original". As usual, the lowest parts of the stemma are easier to determine, since it is possible to find shared secondary readings in small groups of manuscripts that clearly identify them as separate branches. For example, in figure 4.5-12 (at the bottom of the tree), *N10* (thirteenth century) can be proved to be a descendant of *N6* (mid-eleventh century), and *N6* a descendant of *N17* (early eleventh century), from which *N13* (fourteenth century) also stems (the dating of the manuscripts is consistent with this hypothesis). The same could be done for other small groups, such as *V40*, *V40*, *V45* at the lower-left corner of the tree. But how can we then relate those small sub-trees to each other?

In the case of Gregory's homilies, it was possible to use what in biology is called an outgroup (see 5.2.1). This is rather unusual in philology, but it occasionally happens that an indirect witness (a translation or another recension of the work) can be proved to be independent from the archetype of the direct tradition and can therefore be used as an outgroup (see 3.2.8). In this instance, we observed that translations into Latin (ca. 400, made by Rufinus of Aquileia) and Armenian (ca. 500) had preserved shared readings that must be seen as primary and which are absent from all the Greek manuscripts (Macé 2011). This discovery has enormous consequences for the stemma and for the history of the tradition. It means that all Greek manuscripts (and the Syriac translation) share secondary readings and there-

286 — Caroline Macé

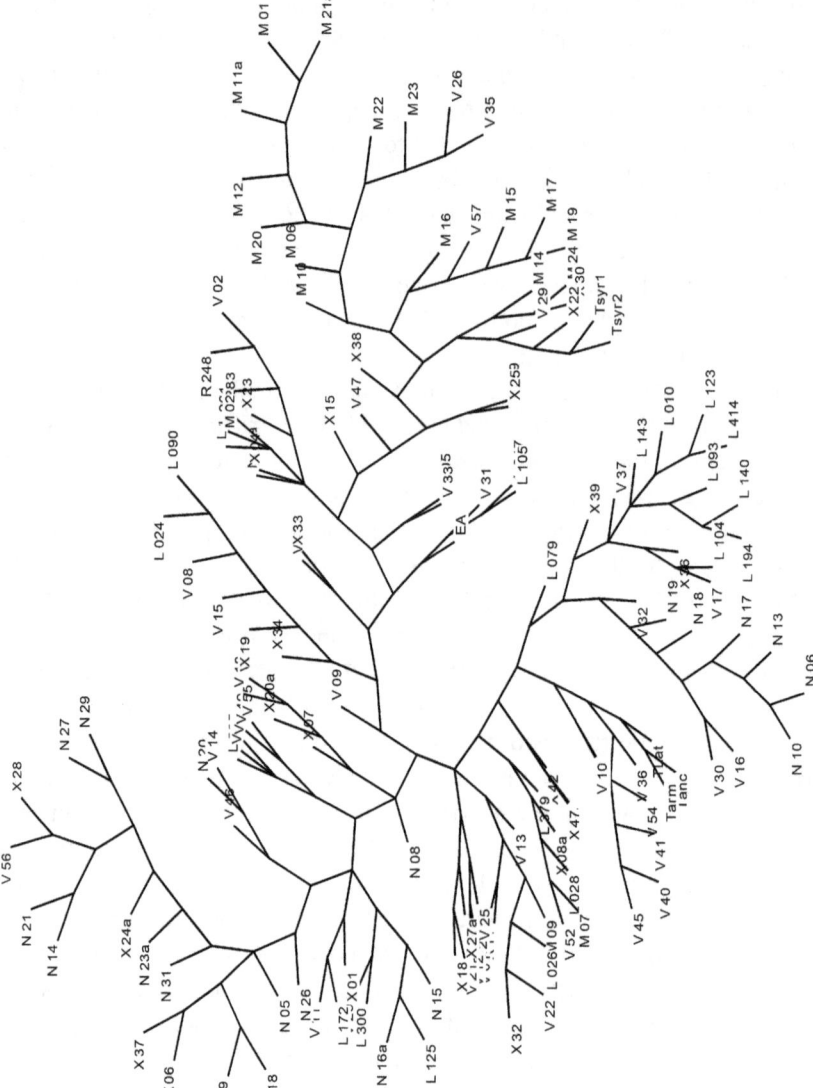

Fig. 4.5-12: Unrooted phylogenetic graph (maximum parsimony) of the 126 manuscripts and 4 ancient translations (*Tarm, Tlat, Tsyr1, Tsyr2*) of homily 27.

fore depend upon a hyparchetype φ (fig. 4.5-13). This hyparchetype must be dated before the Syriac translation, which was reworked and completed around 625 in Cyprus. However plentiful the direct manuscript tradition of Gregory's homilies may be, philological analysis shows that it ultimately goes back to one single point in time (φ). That point, φ, may itself have been preceded by a larger tradition, of which we have but indirect traces in the Latin and Armenian translations. The evolution of textual traditions can be seen as a succession of phases of extension and of reduction, thus following a bow-tie rather than a bottleneck model.

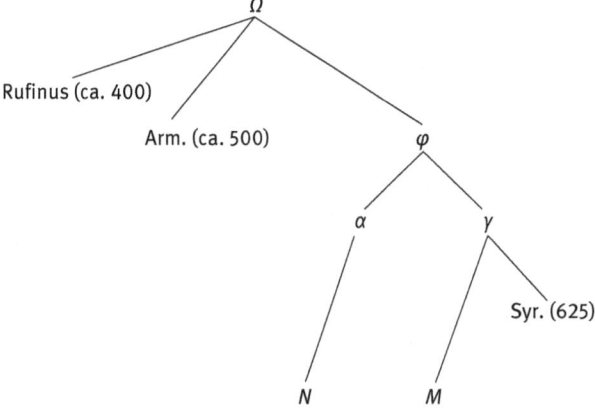

Fig. 4.5-13: Schema of the early history of the textual tradition of the homilies.

It was therefore possible to root the phylogenetic tree using *Tarm* and *Tlat* as the root (see fig. 4.5-14). The branches that are defined after the rooting are more solid candidates to become "families", and the agreement of *Tlat* and *Tarm* against one of the branches certainly points to the presence of secondary variants in that branch.

Material evidence and knowledge about the history of the Byzantine Empire allow for consolidation of some of the hypotheses made on the basis of the textual evidence alone. For example, it is clear in the different phylogenetic trees that the two Syriac translations (the oldest one, preserved only fragmentarily, and its revision in 625) are close to the *M* manuscripts. Some of these *M* manuscripts were copied in southern Italy in the tenth or eleventh century, or are at least related to southern Italy (*M1, M6, M10, M11, M12, M20, M21*). It is well known that southern Italy is a kind of "ecological niche" for Greek texts or text-states: as it was always at the periphery of the Empire, it sometimes preserved archaic or dissident types of texts. It is also known that there were cultural contacts between southern Italy and some Syriac-speaking regions of the Byzantine world (Macé 2004). The close textual relationship of the Syriac translations to a family of mostly southern Italian Greek manuscripts is therefore not surprising.

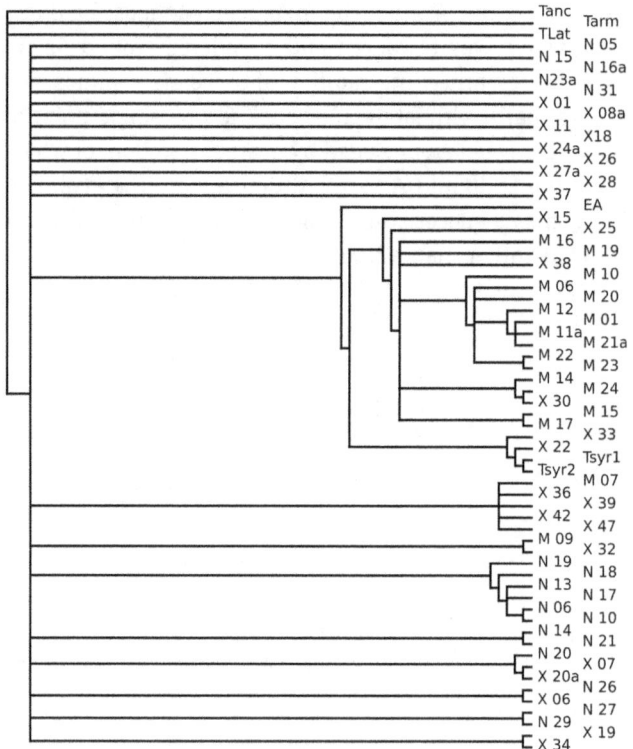

Fig. 4.5-14: Phylogenetic tree of manuscripts with a complete collection (fifty-nine manuscripts) containing homily 27 (branch length is not represented in the plot), rooted on *Tarm/Tlat*.

4.5.4 Pseudo-Dionysius the Areopagite's *Epistola de morte apostolorum*

The third case examined in this section deals with a work lost in its original language and preserved only through translations. In 1883, Jean-Baptiste Pitra and Paulin Martin edited the Syriac, Latin, and Armenian versions of a letter attributed to Dionysius, who was converted by Paul in Athens, and which was addressed to Timothy, Paul's disciple. The letter narrates the death of Paul and Peter, who were martyred together in Rome under Nero, and the miracles which the author witnessed on that occasion (Pitra 1883, 241–276). No trace of that letter could be found in Greek, either in the *Corpus Dionysiacum* (Suchla 2008, 55–61), or in hagiographical or apocryphal collections. The attribution to Pseudo-Dionysius the Areopagite, although attested by all witnesses, is to be rejected: the text has nothing to do with the *Corpus Dionysiacum* (a Neo-Platonist forgery from the end of the fifth century).

In the framework of an ongoing edition project at the Göttingen Academy of Sciences and Humanities, carried out by Ekkehard Mühlenberg, Michael Muthreich, and me, new critical editions of the known versions of the work are in preparation. Pitra almost exclusively used manuscripts from Paris, whereas we have been able to find more witnesses in other libraries. Other translations of what appears to be the same work exist in Arabic, Ethiopic, and Georgian. The Ethiopic translation was made from the Arabic, which was in turn based upon the Syriac (Muthreich 2013), but the Georgian version is related neither to the Armenian nor to the Arabic (late antique and mediaeval Georgian literary works, when not original, were mostly translated from Greek, Armenian, or Arabic). In fact, the Georgian and Latin versions share redactional features which distinguish them from the Armenian and Syriac versions: after the address to Timothy, they add a list of Paul's and Timothy's sufferings in the service of Christ, and at the end of the letter, they add a miraculous account of the discovery of Paul's skull some centuries later (the *inventio capitis Pauli*). In general, the Armenian and Syriac versions prove to be relatively close to one another, whereas the Georgian and Latin texts are practically identical (Macé and Muthreich forthcoming).

Examination of the biblical quotations shows that the Armenian and Syriac versions were both independently translated from two slightly different Greek *Vorlagen* (source texts for the translation), because the form of the quotations normally reflects a Greek model, sometimes differing from the Septuagint translation, and not the biblical text as it is known in the Armenian or Syriac traditions (Macé and Muthreich 2019). The comparison of the Georgian and Latin texts did not lead to clear conclusions, but the two versions are so similar, even in their word order, that they must have been translated from the same source. There is some evidence that the Georgian text was translated from Greek: the use of the demonstrative pronoun to render the Greek definite article; and the use of Georgian words typical of translations from Greek, and also of newly created calques for words like φακεόλιον, "face-cloth, turban, towel", a borrowing from the Latin *faciale*, which the Latin translator of the *Epistola* rendered with "velum quo operitur caput tuum" [a veil by which your head is covered]; or φώσσατον, "trench", again a borrowing from Latin *fossatum*, again strangely rendered by the Latin translator as *vallis*, "valley". There are at least two lacunae in the Latin in comparison with the Georgian version, obviously due to a *saut du même au même*. Although the possibility cannot yet be totally ruled out that the Georgian version may have served as a *Vorlage* for the Latin text, the case would be so exceptional, in fact unparalleled, that the hypothesis that both versions were made from a Greek model remains far more likely.

Therefore, two different Greek recensions of the same letter about the death of Peter and Paul must have existed, and they must have both disappeared in their original language (see fig. 4.5-15). It is very difficult to date their appearance and the disappearance, because it is also very difficult to date the four translations. The oldest manuscript is Syriac and dated to the ninth century; the Georgian version is preserved in collections of sermons and saints' lives for the liturgical year which date from the tenth and eleventh centuries. The oldest Armenian manuscripts preserving the *Epistola* are from the beginning of the thirteenth century, a situation which is not unusual for Armenian manuscripts, which suffered several periods of mass destruction

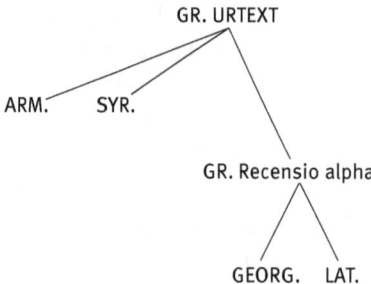

Fig. 4.5-15: Schema of the relationships between the four versions of the work.

throughout the tragic history of the Armenian people. As for Latin manuscripts, on the contrary, the absence of any trace of the text, in manuscript or in quotation, before the thirteenth century makes me suspect that the Latin text came into existence not so long before the time of the oldest preserved manuscripts, that is, the end of the twelfth century. The Latin text enjoyed some popularity: it was very frequently copied, and it was used by Jacobus de Voragine in his *Legenda aurea* before the end of the thirteenth century and, for example, by William Flete in the second half of the fourteenth century in his sermon on Catherine of Siena (Muessig 2012, 204–205).

It is also difficult to guess at the reasons for and circumstances of the disappearance of the *Epistola* in Greek. Obviously, its attribution to Pseudo-Dionysius the Areopagite did not protect it against censorship or accidents. Perhaps its emphasis on the religious pre-eminence of Rome, and its claim that Timothy was the true heir of Paul's religious charisma, made it unpopular in the Byzantine Empire. A closer look at the liturgical development of the common feast of Peter and Paul in the Middle Ages, and at the relationships between the *Epistola* and the apocryphal dossier of Paul's martyrdom which exists in several languages, may help us to better understand these questions.

In the meantime, the four texts in Armenian, Georgian, Latin, and Syriac will be critically edited, after a close examination of their manuscript traditions. It will not be possible to draw a stemma of the manuscripts for any of those four texts, because they are mostly preserved (except in the case of the Syriac) in liturgical manuscripts whose textual history is notoriously complicated (see Macé et al. 2015, 462–465). Nevertheless, the manuscript basis will be sufficient to establish reliable editions of the four versions. These editions will be a prerequisite for any comparison of the texts, and thus for assessing what their Greek models might have looked like – this has so far not been possible on the basis of Pitra's deficient editions.

4.5.5 The evolution of textual traditions

Textual traditions evolve under historical, ideological, and material conditions. They are subject to human interventions and also to chance. The passage of time has destroyed most of the early evidence concerning any textual tradition, even those with a large manuscript basis. Scholars can only reconstruct some snapshots from a complex history, by combining a philological analysis of the textual evidence and a historical analysis of the material and external evidence. Stemmata are, perforce, incomplete (see 4.1.3, 4.2.3.4, 4.2.3.5 for the difference between a stemma and the *arbre réel*) because they are based on fragmentary evidence. They are also by nature hypothetical – however, they become less and less hypothetical as more material, "environmental", paratextual, and "indirect" evidence is brought into the picture.

5 Computational methods and tools
Introductory remarks by the chapter editor, Joris van Zundert

This chapter may well be the hardest in the book for those that are not all that computationally, mathematically, or especially graph-theoretically inclined. Textual scholars often take to text almost naturally but have a harder time grasping, let alone liking, mathematics. A scholar of history or texts may well go through decades of a career without encountering any maths beyond the basic schooling in arithmetic, algebra, and probability calculation that comes with general education. But, as digital techniques and computational methods progressed and developed, it transpired that this field of maths and digital computation had some bearing on textual scholarship too. Armin Hoenen, in section 5.1, introduces us to the early history of computational stemmatology, depicting its early beginnings in the 1950s and pointing out some even earlier roots. The strong influence of phylogenetics and bioinformatics in the 1990s is recounted, and their most important concepts are introduced. At the same time, Hoenen warns us of the potential misunderstandings that may arise from the influx of these new methods into stemmatology. The historical overview ends with current and new developments, among them the creation of artificial traditions for validation purposes, which is actually a venture with surprisingly old roots.

Hoenen's history shows how a branch of computational stemmatics was added to the field of textual scholarship. Basically, both textual and phylogenetic theory showed that computation could be applied to the problems of genealogy of both textual traditions and biological evolution. The calculations involved, however, were tedious, error-prone, hard, and cumbersome. Thus, computational stemmatics would have remained a valid but irksome way of dealing with textual traditions if computers had not been invented. Computers solve the often millions of calculations needed to compute a hypothesis for a stemma without complaint. They do so with ferocious speed and daunting precision. But it remains useful to appreciate that this is indeed all they do: calculate. The computer – or algorithm – does not have any grasp of the concepts or problems that it is working on. Nowhere in the process leading from variant data to a stemmatic hypothesis does any software or hardware realise that it is working on a textual tradition or genetic material. It has no feelings about that work and – more saliently – is indifferent to the quality, correctness, or meaning of the result it calculates. It is especially for this last reason that textual scholars should take note of the methods and techniques involved in calculating stemmata, even if the maths may not always be palatable work. Computer code and chips process data and yield some result or other. None of the nouns in the previous sentence somehow becomes inherently neutral, objective, and correct by virtue of being digital or mathematical in nature. If an algorithm contains a calculation error, the computer will repeat that error faithfully a billion times at lightning speed. Thus, it follows that we can only trust digital tools and computational methods if we can trust their theoretical and mathematical underpinnings, if we can trust how they are implemented as software code, and if we understand how we are translating the computational concepts back into philological ones.

Providing a basic insight into the concepts, theory, and mathematical underpinnings of graph theory and computational tree construction is the aim of sections 5.2 and 5.3. These sections, where Staedler, Manafzadeh, and Roos try to explain the various methods and techniques that exist for the computational creation of stemmata, may make for challenging reading. Many new concepts are introduced – reticulation events, character-state matrices, and tree scores, to name but a few – some more relevant to stemmatology than others, but all important when it comes to understanding how the techniques of phylogenetics operate and what their relevance to stemmatology is. Aware of the dangers of overstretching the direct application of computational techniques from bioinformatics in the domain of stemmatology, Roos points out that the methods under discussion do not, in fact, produce stemmata; rather, they produce graphs, trees, or networks that can be regarded as hypotheses for stemmata. He then details the methods most commonly used to generate these stemma hypotheses. This handbook confines itself to providing a basic understanding of the computational methods that are involved with tree building and visualisation. Explaining all the fine-grained fundamental mathematical intricacies of parsimony tree scores, maximum likelihood, UPGMA, neighbour-joining, and so forth is beyond what will fit on its pages, and for this we refer to additional reading. The sections here aim to provide some intimations and a very basic but very necessary understanding about the calculations that are employed when inferring graphs and trees – accompanied by some warnings about the limitations of these methods.

Over the course of time, philologists, software engineers, and computer scientists have ventured to create tools that embrace the mathematical principles of phylogenetics and stemmatics to provide ready-to-use software tools for evolutionary biologists and textual scholars. These tools provide (somewhat) easier access to the calculations needed to create stemma hypotheses. Digital tool development unfortunately has its own problems of life-cycle management, sustainability, and compatibility. What worked five years ago may fail on the newest operating systems, tools sometimes get abandoned for economic and institutional policy reasons that have nothing to do with their actual usefulness or capabilities, and in general the digital landscape changes frighteningly quickly. Any author who has ever added a chapter or section on digital tools to a textbook knows that these efforts are at risk of becoming obsolete in part or in whole even when the copies are running off the press. Nevertheless, a chapter on computational methods and tools cannot be complete without such a list, even if it may become out of date with its very inception. Hoenen faithfully assembles a list of the tools (5.4) most visibly in use in the field of computational stemmatics (and some related work) today. Some tools, such as Phylip or PAUP*, have been around for years and may still be around for ages to come. Others may linger and die off. Some have been born very recently and still need to prove whether they will make it through their toddler years. All this aside, however, the list provides an impressively extensive overview of the tools that currently figure in the centre of computational stemmatics.

Finally, Jean-Baptiste Guillaumin directs our attention to the criticisms that computational approaches to stemmatology have met over time. The final section of this chapter (5.5) treats a number of well-known problems that are real problems from the perspective of both philologists (e.g. "How well does all this computation match the genealogical process of text descent?") and computationalists (e.g. "How do we model witnesses as internal nodes?"). Computational stemmatology is a young field, and its methods are still – and should be – in development, in flux, and under criticism. Some criticism pertains to basic concepts such as what we mean exactly by the distance between two (or more) texts: how such a distance is computed and what an appropriate measure for it could be. However, more advanced parts of the computational approach also meet with criticism. Computational methods to date tend to take all data as equally valuable. But philologists realise that some readings should be weighted more heavily than others; and, vice versa, what computational methods may regard as statistical noise may very well be pivotal readings that reveal genealogy to a philologist. And what about the prevalence of bifurcation in all computational approaches? As Guillaumin shows, both philologists and computationalists are taking these matters increasingly more seriously. The computational approach to stemmatology appears not to cut corners to a quick and dirty win. Rather, the particulars of textual genealogy prove a challenge to computer scientists that both computer scientists and philologists are engaging with deeply, and with mutual respect for the expertise on both sides.

5.1 History of computer-assisted stemmatology
Armin Hoenen

This section covers the history of the field, beginning roughly at a time when the first computers became commercially available and extending up to the present. Throughout this history, due to technological and epistemological developments, the umbrella term for the subject of this chapter has seen terminological variation: besides "computational stemmatology", a slightly more appropriate term is "stemmatology aided or assisted by computers". The computer cannot conduct certain tasks, such as digitising a manuscript text, on its own, and humans have to supervise the process of arriving at a stemma. "Digital stemmatology" is another synonym in use.

5.1.1 General remarks, early history, and consolidation (1950s–1990s)

There are many ways in which computers can be used for stemmatological purposes; a strict interpretation of the term implies the application of software where the input is a collection of digitised manuscript texts (or similar data) and the outcome a stemma. In a wider sense, the term may refer to all methods, processes, and approaches using the computer for any task connected with solving the question of how to reconstruct or display the history of a number of extant textual items related through processes of copying.

Shortly after the onset of publicly available computation, as early as 1957, John W. Ellison wrote a thesis at Harvard entitled "The Use of Electronic Computers in the Study of the Greek New Testament Text" (1957). He used the computer to group manuscripts and compare those groupings to established ones. Other early works, especially in French and English, theoretically elaborating calculations and ideas for algorithms and applying computer programs were, for instance, Griffith (1968) and Froger (1968). Glenisson et al. (1979) published the proceedings of a conference on the application of computers to the field of textual criticism. The application of the computer in those days seems to have been focused especially on variant and manuscript groupings and tables, although holistic approaches going as far as producing stemmata were already present too.

Poole (1974) wrote a program in Algol60 intended for stemma production, albeit without visual output of a stemma but with tabulation according to witness age instead. It was based on previous research (notably Froger 1968 and Griffith 1968) and tested on a real sample. Here, a u t o m a t i o n was presented as a holistic endeavour that included an algorithmic decision as to what variant was contained in what lost witness. Most publications up to this time were closely linked to manual philological practice (mathematically formalised to some extent), although not restricted to the Lachmannian genealogical method in terms of theory. For instance, the method of Quentin (1926) looks at all triples of extant manuscripts and determines their relationships (see 2.3.5). It was the basis for an implementation by Zarri (1976) which, for the first time, produced an unrooted tree. With the steady growth of processing capacity, in addition to a growing number of publications on automated stemma production, more subtasks became subject to experimental support by computers. Haigh (1970), for instance, invented a rooting algorithm. Improved collation and alignment algorithms were developed in computer science and bioinformatics. Robinson (1994) presented a program called Collate which supported philologically adapted, semi-automated collation. A descendant of Collate, CollateX (see Haentjens Dekker et al. 2015), now finally collates all by itself. The trend of more and more subtasks being delegated to the computer continues. Den Hollander (2004), for instance, demonstrated a successful method for detecting exemplar shift (see 4.4.6.1). Computers were employed to simulate the development in time of stemmata beginning in the 1980s, either by building up artificial genealogies simulating the concurrent texts or variant configurations (Flight 1992, 1994) or by simulating their growth abstractly (Weitzman 1982, 1987; Hoenen 2016).

5.1.2 Phylogenetic methods (1990s and beyond)

Because of the enormous influence and vast application of phylogenetic methods (see 8.1) in the preceding decades, sections 5.1.2.1–3 will present the historical transfer of methodology from bioinformatics to stemmatology, criticism which has arisen, and an outlook on the future.

5.1.2.1 Phylogenetic methods: Inner developments and parallels with stemmatology

Before describing the transfer of methods to stemmatology, we will briefly outline some developments within bioinformatics from the time when bioinformatics and stemmatology coexisted but had not been related much to each other yet. Prior to molecular methods (e.g. DNA sequencing), the dominant paradigm in phylogenetics was that of cladistics (see Hennig 1966). When applying cladistics, biologists ideally chose phenotypic traits of the group of species under scrutiny. For example, the diameter of nostrils can be classed in several groups, such as a "group 0" (up to 3 cm), "group 1" (3–5 cm), and "group 2" (larger than 5 cm). Additionally, the form of the cranium can be categorised binarily as "0" (rounded) or "1" (angular). Each species would then be characterised by an array of character states. In our fictitious two-character example, such sequences could be "00", "01", "10", "11", "20", or "21". These categories and choices, when devised and made reasonably, are in principle similar to the identification of significant errors common in philology. Indeed, both disciplines agreed on many things, for instance on using only shared innovations as a basis for classification. Nonetheless, there was little methodological exchange at this time. This "old" cladistics paradigm may have been more comparable to the methods used in stemmatology just before the bioinformatic influx.

Then, the paradigm in biology changed radically with cheap DNA sequencing. Cladistic choice-based methods were abandoned almost completely because molecular methods are less subjective and had become less work-intensive. Since DNA makes the underlying genotype explicit and because of the sheer amount of data in a DNA strand, the new approach is more informative and depends less on arbitrary (i.e. subjective) categorisation.

Unfortunately, we cannot assume that the superior effectiveness of molecular methods in biology – as compared to the earlier cladistics – carries over into stemmatology. The now well-established bioinformatic methods outperformed conventional cladistics because of the newly available molecular data. In other words, the superiority of molecular methods is primarily due to the amount and precision of the input data. The radical paradigm shift superseding cladistic methods was brought about in biology by a new source of input data: DNA, making the older character-data-based classification (choosing certain traits) obsolete. This new type of input data is not present in stemmatology. Of course, we do not suddenly get more or different data by assuming that a transformation of collations is a kind of pseudo-DNA.

If insufficiently recognised, these differences can lead to the risk of methodological misunderstanding. Biologists cannot expect stemmatologists to adopt their current methodologies as inherently better than cladistics or assume that the new methods will self-evidently supersede the "old" paradigms (which to stemmatology are not "old", since here no input-data revolution like the one replacing chosen character data by sequenced DNA has taken place, and it is unlikely that something similar will ever happen in stemmatology). Moreover, stemmatologists should, of course, not readily assume that the new methods are more objective or more adequate solutions for their problems of text genesis just because they work better in another field. Understanding the validity and quality of such new methods for another problem domain requires thorough testing and evaluation, and very possibly adaptation to the techniques involved. But, once these techniques have been mastered and are no longer merely "black boxes", the advantage may lie in the quick availability of results from phylogenetic programs, making it possible to test and contrast more stemmatic hypotheses.

To sum up: the application of phylogenetic methods should be exploited for text-critical purposes as they add the possibility of quickly producing many alternative hypotheses, but their biological provenance and prerequisites must be understood well and reflected on to avoid the dangers of a possibly misapplied model.

5.1.2.2 Transfer to stemmatology

In the early 1990s, the field of stemmatology began to change due to the introduction of phylogenetic methods from evolutionary biology, although similarities between the disciplines of biology and philology had been outlined earlier, for instance by Cameron (1987) on a theoretical level. Lee (1989) first introduced phylogenetic methods in practice to the field, using the software package Phylip (Felsenstein 1989) to generate a stemma automatically. In the years that followed, many methodologically similar publications ensued and eventually came to dominate the field in the early 2000s. Presumably the most famous contribution appeared in *Nature*: Barbrook et al. (1998). The most-often applied software packages were PAUP/PAUP* (Swofford 1998) and SplitsTree (Huson 1998); the most widely applied algorithms were parsimony, split decomposition, and neighbour-joining. Techniques such as bootstrapping and generating consensus trees were widely used. A comparable development took place in historical linguistics (see 8.2). Other useful insights or models stemming from analogies with biology have been discussed in and introduced to computational stemmatology – for instance the molecular clock, or error distribution patterns and models of errors (Spencer and Howe 2001) that exhibit similarities with mutation rates and places (see also Windram, Spencer, and Howe 2006). Investigations with a closer link to traditional methods used in textual criticism continued to exist but became rarer after the 1990s (cf. e.g. Salemans 2000).

Finally, the use of neighbour-nets is something that can be viewed as a genuine bioinformatic innovation transferred to stemmatology, and as such as an addition that complements the existing visualisation and analytical arsenal of stemmatologists. While in classical textual criticism such networks were not drawn and, technically, they are nowhere close to a tree, they have been adopted since they allow the testing of hypotheses involving contamination and are applicable to both open and closed traditions. For a visual rendering, see section 5.5.9. (On closed and open traditions respectively, see Spencer, Davidson, et al. 2004; Eagleton and Spencer 2006; see Bergel, Howe, and Windram 2016 for a discussion of this in the realm of print material.) Griffith (1984) already tried to depict visually how close manuscripts are to each other in a two-dimensional grid. A stemma is thus not the only way to display manuscript similarities, but if the goal is to approach the original text, it will still be the most effective tool.

5.1.2.3 Phylogenetic methods: Criticism, adaptation, adaptability

Stemma generation by phylogenetic software exhibits some graphical and some mathematical properties that render it incommensurate with previous methods used to produce graphs in textual criticism (see 5.5 for a fuller account). Most notable is the fact that phylogenetic software operates on DNA and protein code represented as pure string sequences. The software essentially understands DNA and proteins as merely linear sequences, even though there are non-linear dependencies between these natural phenomena which we do not understand very well. Likewise, language exhibits many layers of interdependence and structure, but phylogenetic software processes it as if it were a mere string sequence. Apart from this, the three most important different conceptual properties are the focus on leaves, bifurcativity, and unrootedness. Historically, these "alien" properties have been noted as technical challenges to be overcome. In the case of the focus on leaves, this has been achieved by Roos and Zou (2011); another bioinformatic method where the extant nodes can be non-leaves is described in Papamichail et al. (2017).

Bifurcativity in phylogenetic trees is the result of the most commonly applied concept of speciation (see, for more detail, Purves et al. 2004, 482; Hoelzer and Melnick 1994). Most algorithms of computational bioinformatics produce exclusively bifurcating trees; therefore, Bédier's debate (see 2.3.4) is largely irrelevant in phylogeny. Multifurcating trees can be generated automatically by collapsing some of the bifurcations. In this case, those bifurcations are collapsed which according to some statistical method appear the least probable/reliable. Therefore, computational procedures that introduce multifurcation come at the cost of introducing one more parameter, a threshold for reliability. Usually, these procedures prevent unifurcations (representing the filiation of only one new witness) arising from collapsing bifurcations. Unifurcations may result, however, from manual intervention by the philologist. Philological trees generated by Semstem, which supports multifurcation, can also contain unifurcations.

Finally, as for the aspect of unrootedness, some automatic rooting approaches have been developed (Haigh 1970, 1971; Marmerola et al. 2016; Hoenen 2019). These approaches have been successfully tested on the limited testbed of artificial traditions. But they are still far from being practically used (see 5.4 below). Furthermore, programs can be used for the automatic generation of an archetypal text (see Hoenen 2015b; Koppel, Michaely, and Tal 2016), whose importance in stemmatology is another point of difference to the biological field. However, such methods are still very experimental and remain as yet little tested.

5.1.3 Recent developments

Around the beginning of the twenty-first century, two important books were published with collections of articles that were mostly concerned with computer-assisted stemmatology: the two volumes of *Studies in Stemmatology* (van Reenen and van Mulken 1996; van Reenen, den Hollander, and van Mulken 2004). Roos, Heikkilä, and Myllymäki (2006) invented an algorithm to compute a stemma which was not a direct loan from phylogenetics but designed to meet needs specific to stemmatology. Other approaches than phylogenetic ones have become more numerous in recent times; see, for instance, Roelli and Bachmann (2010); Roos and Zou (2011); and Lai, Roos, and O'Sullivan (2010).

Another important innovation has occurred: the first digital artificial traditions have been made. Datasets were produced by volunteers copying texts while the true stemmatic relationships were recorded and are thus fully known. These traditions can serve as test data for computational methods (see Spencer, Davidson, et al. 2004; Baret, Macé, and Robinson 2006; Roos and Heikkilä 2009). The first attempts to produce artificial datasets for philology go back to long before the digital era, when Kantorowicz carried out experiments from 1914 onwards. He had students copy texts, calling this new field "experimental textual criticism" (Kantorowicz 1921, 47; see Kleinlogel 1979, 64). However, only some reflections on the process and no results were ever published. Kantorowicz mentions (1921, 49) that, when trying to reconstruct the archetypal text manually from his students' copies, he had judged roughly 10% of the words wrongly because copyists had independently made the same changes. Apparently, this strand of research then disappeared from academic memory for a long time. Recently, however, such traditions have become useful as benchmarks for evaluation. Such artificial traditions have been obtained by having volunteers copy an actual original text from one another in a fixed and recorded sequence, in several copy-rounds, and finally digitising all the manual copies. Evaluation now means the comparison of a stemma computed from the "witnesses" with the recorded true stemma. This allows for an estimate of how well a method works and for the quantitative comparison of different methods. In computer science, such validation is an essential and integral part of methodology, and therefore the availability of concrete test data invites more contributions from computer science. Roos and Heikkilä (2009) presented the results of a challenge that compared more than ten different algorithms in computing stemmata on the basis of three different datasets. This is, to date, the largest comparative study on algorithms for computer-assisted stemmatology. The reduced datasets for the traditions used there had almost no extant internal nodes, presumably in order to make the results more comparable – or comparable at all – with the output of bioinformatic programs. The evaluation was also designed in such a way that rooting or direction were not required.

Among the three disciplines producing "historical trees" (linguistics, biology, and stemmatology; O'Hara 1996), textual criticism is probably the domain that can attract contributions from computer science most easily, since, at least in case of closed traditions such as, for instance, the artificial *Parzival* tradition created by Spencer, Davidson, et. al. (2004), g o l d s t a n d a r d s (that is, datasets for which the truth is known) are more or less easily produced. However, it should be noted that computer science is not exclusively evaluation-driven, but it is certainly the case that studies involving numerical evaluation are numerous and important in the field.

The physiological root of miscopying is by and large the same today as in Antiquity or the Middle Ages in the sense that the cognitive apparatus of humans then and now is supposedly the same. However, many phenomena, such as *scriptio continua*, the widespread use of abbreviations, and writing being less standardised, have not yet been taken into account in the artificial datasets. Also, many historically relevant writing systems (e.g. ancient Greek, Hebrew), which may have different miscopying characteristics, have not been targeted yet. It is also rather questionable whether artificial traditions will be able to simulate a realistic time-depth, and with that the influence of language change that is exhibited in historical data. Finally, intentional change – which certainly occurred in the copying of many texts – may be hard to model, as well as the interactions between oral tradition and written tradition. These caveats were realised early on and are sometimes named as a reason to reject using artificial datasets, as Poole stated:

> To test the program [his Algol60 program] experimentally, it was first intended to run it with artificially constructed sets of data, incorporating deliberate contaminations. It soon became apparent, however, that these could hardly match the complexity of a real manuscript tradition, or put the program to a sufficiently rigorous test. (Poole 1974, 212)

Nevertheless, experiments on ever-new ways to produce artificial data or simulate text copying continue to be published (see e.g. Pompei, Loreto, and Tria 2018).

In summary, new digital artificial traditions are a new development in computational textual criticism that has parallels in the history of philology (Kantorowicz 1921). Although these artificial traditions certainly have limitations, they may make the field more attractive for computer science. Additionally, they may help to gain new insights into phenomena related to miscopying, their natural frequencies, and similar properties, since they are based on the same (or similar) human cognitive apparatus that brought forth historical traditions. Finally, artificial traditions may be able to help us understand where manual philological habits are most probable to misinterpret certain aspects of historical data (see Andrews 2014).

5.1.4 The Bible and other very large traditions

Using the aid of the computer for such a large and complex tradition as the Bible has seen the need for special approaches. The number of required witness comparisons grows rapidly with corpus size, and this puts limits on the size of traditions that can be processed computationally with standard methods in feasible computing time. Wachtel (2004) developed a method called the Coherence-Based Genealogical Method (CBGM), in which a "textual flow" based on variant stemmata (see 4.2.3.6) classifies witnesses in terms of relative age (i.e. age relative to the other texts). This pre-genealogical coherence that is thus established is then used to generate a final stemma in a less computationally intensive way. This method can be applied to any tradition but will be especially useful in dealing with larger bodies of manuscripts where a larger number of variant trees can be produced. Another way of coping with very large traditions is to produce partial stemmata. Partial stemmata have been produced for different parts of the Bible. Lin (2016) summarises to some degree the history and application of computer-assisted stemmatology (as a sub-branch of computer-assisted textual criticism) in relation to the New Testament and beyond. On Biblical textual criticism, see further section 7.1.

5.1.5 The digital age and its contributions

We are certainly still in a phase of transformation from the print age to a digital era. As soon as digital and print paradigms start to mutually influence each other, inspiring print publications modelled on natively digital output, parallel to discussions following McLuhan's (1962) famous *Gutenberg Galaxy*, we will be able to argue that we have moved into a "post-digital" paradigm. Some effects of the use of digital methods in stemmatology already point in this direction. The use of colour, for instance, is expensive in print, and mainstream stemmatic depictions in philology in the print age have rarely made use of this visual dimension. In contrast, since colour is cost-free (or at least cost-equal as compared to black and white) in the digital medium, stemmata and stemmatic software seem to have started to use colour in visualisations more widely. For instance, colour is used for group emphasis in C. J. Howe et al. (2001). Moreover, in the stemmata of Stemmaweb, colour is used in a variety of ways, such as showing which variants go with the stemma and which go against it. Another property of digital media is their dynamic nature. A stemma can, for instance, be built up step by step, node by node, or it can be made zoomable. Eventually, even the underlying transcription might be changed on the fly. Other visualisation forms that are more easily produced using digital media are, for instance, three-dimensional stemmata and heat-maps with cladograms on top. This dynamic nature also implies many further possibilities, such as linking entities in the stemma directly to their textual content and to facsimiles and vice versa, zooming in and out, giving additional information through mouse tooltips, generating a manipulatable 3D stemma, using a time series to show different states of the stemma (or *arbre réel*, or both), and so forth.

Thus, the digital environment enables philology to develop a much richer visual language than that possible within the constraints of print technology. It is, however, still unclear which devices and visualisations will ultimately form part of a stemmatic methodological canon. For the time being, conventions for a new digital visual language for stemmatology are still being sought, and in that process we may very well see some further emancipation from print-age constraints.

Another advantage of the dynamic nature of digital media is that it facilitates the application of various concurrent models to the same input with a simple button click. This enables the textual critic to investigate the effects of assumptions and of different models in much more detail and with a better overview. Examining in this way a multitude of underlying models allows a more holistic stemmatic analysis. We can point to teicat.huma-num.fr as an example of such dynamics. This software allows the user, by pointing and clicking, to change which witness text will be the base text for a comparative apparatus. But, of course, the user should be aware of the consequences of changing parameters and base versions; thus, with the advantage also comes a larger responsibility and demand for some kind of digital literacy.

The possibilities these dynamics create may be seen as both a blessing (for offering more solid insights) and a curse (they likely involve more effort). Realising these possibilities also entails that the way in which stemmatologists (will) work in the digital age may change considerably in comparison to earlier times. The technical development of software and online publications involves more teamwork. Indeed, there is already a marked difference noticeable insofar as many publications from digital stemmatology, in contrast to classical stemmatology, are multi-author works. Even if they may require more work, for the digitally literate user, digital tools and visualisations encompass more possibilities to analyse and compare different stemmata given the same underlying text data. Because some sensible defaults can also be implemented strictly, this freedom does not have to result in less guidance. Finally, the debate on philology initiated by Bédier need no longer be of an existential magnitude, since any electronic edition can offer both a stemmatological approach and a best-text approach and leave the choice (or comparison) between the two up to the user.

Printing costs always have to be covered by someone, but – contrary to some popular but misguided beliefs – digital tools and data, and the access to and availability of them, are certainly not free (or cheaper) either. Thus, economic dimensions and considerations in stemmatological research projects remain. The digital environment also introduces some new challenges: the problem of the long-term availability of vulnerable digital resources, graphical interfaces rampant with visual overcrowding and ambiguity, quotability and versioning, user-friendliness and usability problems, potential "black-boxing" of methods, and so forth. All of these (potential) problems will have to be dealt with and examined to find ways to circumvent, mitigate, or solve them.

For stemmatology, the digital age is not only an opportunity to apply novel methods to arrive at a stemma, but also a chance to develop a richer visual language, to allow more exploration and dynamic devices, to compare different approaches and their implications. For those who are able to use multiple stemmatological approaches, this may enable deeper reflections, and a higher quality and consistency of results. It also certainly increases the complexity of the stemmatological endeavour considerably.

5.2 Terminology and methods
Sara Manafzadeh and Yannick M. Staedler

This section serves to provide a conceptual understanding of the mathematical objects, concepts, and methods involved with visualising and computing phylogenetic stemmata. For those who want to investigate the mathematical underpinnings more fundamentally, suggestions for further reading are provided.

5.2.1 The basic building blocks of graph theory

In graph theory, a node or a vertex (plural "vertices") is the fundamental unit of which graphs are formed. An undirected graph is composed of a set of nodes and a set of edges (unordered pairs of nodes; see fig. 5.2-1a), whereas a directed graph is composed of a set of nodes and a set of directed edges (ordered pairs of nodes; see fig. 5.2-1b). Nodes are treated as featureless and indivisible objects, although they may have additional structure depending on the application. The two nodes forming an edge are said to be the endpoints of that edge. An edge connecting A to B is often written (A, B), in which case nodes A and B are said to be adjacent. The neighbourhood of node A is the subgraph formed by all nodes adjacent to A, in other words all the nodes in the direct vicinity of node A. The degree of a node is the number of edges connecting to it; in figure 5.2-1a, nodes B and C have degree 4; nodes A, E, F, and G have degree 2; and nodes D and H have degree 1. A leaf node is a node with degree 1 (nodes D and H in fig. 5.2-1b). A graph is said to be connected if there is a path between any two nodes. A cycle is a

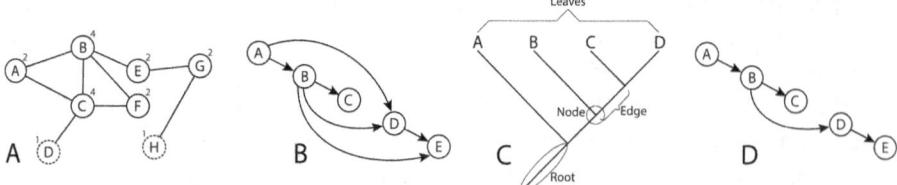

Fig. 5.2-1: Examples of graphs and trees.

path of nodes and edges in which a node can be reached again after setting out from it. More details about these mathematical entities can be found in Diestel (2005).

A directed acyclic graph (DAG) is a directed graph with no directed cycles (i.e. loops). It consists of a number of nodes and edges, with each edge directed from one node to another, in such a way that it is not possible to start at any node and follow a sequence of edges that loops back to the same node (fig. 5.2-1b). An undirected graph in which any two nodes are connected by one and only one path is called a tree. A polytree (or directed or oriented tree) is a DAG whose underlying undirected graph is a tree (fig. 5.2-1d is an example); stemmata representing the genealogy of a text without contamination usually take the shape of a polytree. In our contexts, trees are used to describe the genesis of related objects that evolve without interfering with one another. A phylogenetic tree represents the evolutionary ancestry of a set of tips. In biology, the tips (i.e. leaves; see fig. 5.2-1c) are usually extant species or groups of extant species (taxa, singular "taxon"), whereas in stemmatology tips represent extant witnesses of a text. Currently, almost all phylogenetic methods produce strictly bifurcating trees (also called binary trees) in which each node has at most two descendant nodes (see 5.1.2.1).

Looking more closely at the examples of graphs and trees may make things clearer. In figure 5.2-1a, an undirected graph is depicted. The circled letters in this graph are the nodes; the lines connecting the nodes are the edges. Here, the numbers above the nodes indicate the degree of each node, that is, the number of connections it has to other nodes. Letters encircled with dashed lines (nodes *D* and *H*) are leaf nodes, which like the leaves of a biological tree have only a single connection to the rest of the structure. Figure 5.2-1b is an example of a directed acyclic graph. In this type of graph, the relations between the nodes (i.e. the edges) have a direction (hence "directed"), indicated with arrows. Figure 5.2-1c shows the parts of a tree that are indicated with specifically phylogenetic terms.

A rooted tree is a tree in which one node has been designated as the root. Mathematically, this designation is arbitrary because the root can occur anywhere in the tree. People new to graph theory often have trouble with this concept. It helps to imagine the graph as a net, a set of beads connected with wires. If one were to lift the net by any randomly chosen bead, that bead (node) would become the root node, with all the other beads and wires hanging down from it. The edges of a

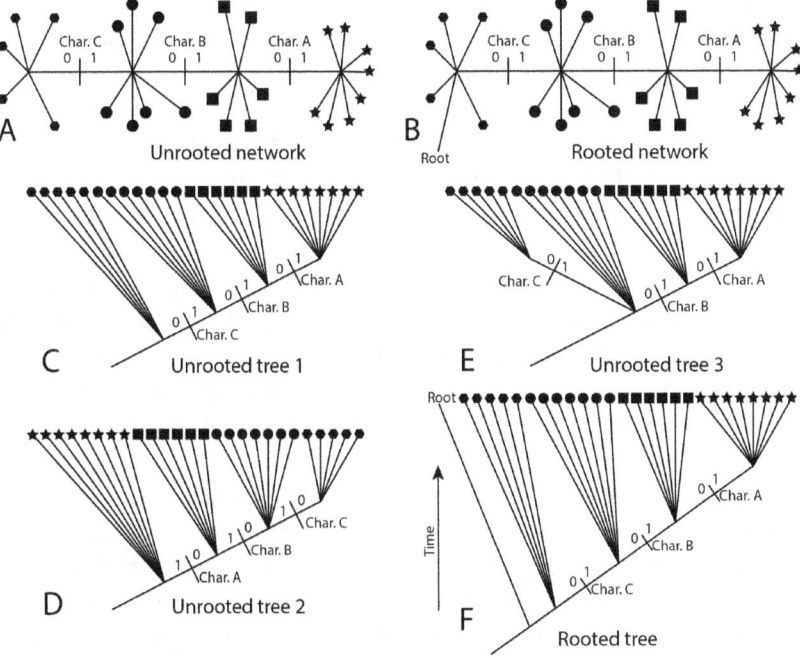

Fig. 5.2-2: Roots and their relevance for trees and networks. (*a*) is an unrooted graph (network). (*b*) is the same network as (*a*) but with a designated root. (*c*), (*d*), and (*e*) are simply different graphical representations of the same unrooted tree. (*f*) represents the same tree as (*c*), (*d*), and (*e*), but with a root.

rooted tree can be assigned an orientation, either all of them towards or all of them away from the root, in which case the structure becomes a directed rooted tree. If in a directed rooted tree there is one unique directed path to any node from the root, such a tree is called an arborescence. In phylogenetics, unrooted trees only display the relatedness of the leaves and do not represent a hypothesis of ancestry (cf. fig. 5.2-2a). Unrooted trees (see e.g. figs 5.2-2c–d) can always be generated from rooted trees (e.g. fig. 5.2-2f) simply by omitting the root. An unrooted tree is also called a network. Figures 5.2-2c–e show three different ways of recording and organising the same observations. Even though the network (fig. 5.2-2a) looks like a timeline, it is not: it could be read from left to right, from right to left, or from the middle outwards. To transform the network into a rooted tree, one must determine which changes are more recent than others; that is, the tree must be rooted.

A rooted phylogenetic tree is a directed tree with a unique node corresponding to the most recent common ancestor (MRCA) of all the entities at the leaves of the tree. In other words, that node represents a species from which all the other species in the tree eventually developed. Rooting polarises the character changes, giving them a direction. Again, if you imagine that the network is a piece of string, you can keep the connections exactly the same, even if you lift it up in different places. The network from figure 5.2-2a is redrawn in figure 5.2-2b with the addition of a root. Different placements of the root can change the order in which the character changes occur in the tree.

Rooting a phylogenetic tree is critical for interpreting how taxa evolved, that is, how the various groups of species, or "leaves", that are distinguished evolved. Different rootings suggest different patterns of change (i.e. different character polarisations). Of course, the pivotal issue is how the position of the root is to be determined.

The most common method for rooting trees in biology is by using an outgroup. An outgroup is a taxon that is a relative of the group under study. The key point of an outgroup is that, although related to the taxa under study, the outgroup taxon lacks some biological traits that are common to the group under study. Ideally, the outgroup should be close enough to allow inference from trait data or molecular sequencing, but distant enough to be a clear outgroup. For instance, the macaque can serve as outgroup for a group of apes under study. Clearly, macaques are related to apes, but apes, among other things, all lack a tail. On this basis, we can assume that macaques split off before any of the apes diverged as separate species. Thus, when selecting an outgroup, one must assume that all ingroup members (that is, the members of the group under study) are more closely related to one another than to the outgroup; in other words, the outgroup must have separated from the ingroup lineage before the ingroup diversified. Often, more than one outgroup is used to enhance the reliability of the hypothesis. If an outgroup is added to a network, the point at which it attaches is determined as the root of the tree. An analogue to biogenetic outgroups may be found in traditions that incorporate texts or parts of texts from other traditions – a text may have been included in a compendium or florilegium that has its own tradition, for example. Also, the existence of early translations (see the example in 4.5.3) can be seen as an analogue to outgroups. Usually, however, for stemmatologists no outgroups are available, and they have to turn to other methods to determine the roots in their trees (see 2.2), which are called archetypes (see 4.1.5).

Reticulation events are events that cause a new species to arise from the "merging" of two different parent species (note the difference to "normal" evolution, where traits of one species change over time until the species develops into a true new species of its own). An example of a reticulation event is hybridisation, where two species interbreed to produce a new (hybrid) species. Another example in biological evolution is horizontal gene transfer, where DNA migrates from one species to another. It happens, for instance, that bacterial DNA is moved from one bacterium species to another by a plasmid or a virus. Typically similar to reticulation events in stemmatology is contamination, as when a scribe used more than one exemplar to compile his copy (see 4.4). Such events are represented by phylogenetic networks. A phylogenetic network, or reticulation, is a graph used to visualise evolutionary relationships when reticulation events are believed to be

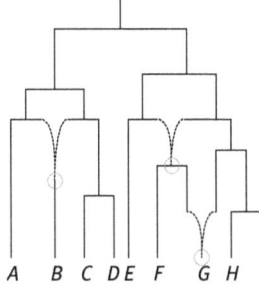

Fig. 5.2-3: A reticulated tree. Circled nodes represent nodes with two parents, also called hybrid nodes; dashed lines represent branches leading to a hybrid node.

involved (phylogenetic trees are a subset of phylogenetic networks). Whereas evolutionary trees usually only contain tree nodes, which are nodes with only one parent (see the continuous lines in fig. 5.2-3), reticulations contain additional **hybrid nodes**, which are nodes with two parents (marked with circles and dashed lines for lineage in fig. 5.2-3). An extension to the Newick format (see 3.4.8) is available for representing reticulations (see below; and Cardona, Rosselló, and Valiente 2008).

5.2.2 Phylogenetic inference

The data that is used to estimate the phylogeny of a set of leaves determines the characteristics of those leaves (taxa). The success of phylogenetic inference therefore depends largely on the choice of trait data and its accuracy and quantity. The first step in a phylogenetic analysis is to choose the taxa. The next step is to collect information on the traits of those taxa. These traits or properties are then stored in a data matrix. Two types of data matrices are mostly employed for carrying out phylogenetic analyses: **character-state matrices** or **distance matrices**. The character-state matrix can be viewed as a data sheet that has a list of taxa for the row headings. The columns represent properties or traits of species. Usually, each column is designated with a single character (with different possible character states). A character-state matrix has one specific entry for each character scored for each taxon (see fig. 5.2-4a). In this manner, a row with numbers becomes a very specific state description for a particular taxon.

In contrast, a distance matrix records for all pairs of taxa how dissimilar they are (or, more rarely, how similar). It therefore lists taxa both as row and column headers. The simplest way to compute a distance matrix from a character-state matrix is to calculate the proportion of characters for which two taxa differ in state in the character-state matrix. This value is then inserted into the appropriate cell in the distance matrix. It may be that a relative weight will be assigned to different characters, expressing the fact that we think (or have found) that certain traits or properties of species carry more information about genealogical relatedness than others. Returning to the macaques and apes example, we assume that having a tail is a very strong indicator that a species is not an ape. To express our very strong

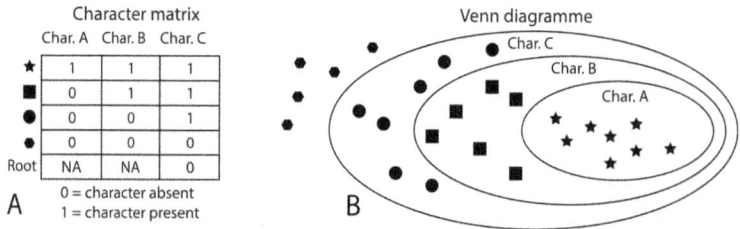

Fig. 5.2-4: Characters and trees. (*a*) character matrix; (*b*) Venn diagram derived from character matrix in (*a*).

suspicion, we can weight this trait by counting it more than once each time we find it in a species, and use this weighted value to calculate its distance from another species (thus setting it decisively further apart from species not having this trait). In stemmatology, the weighting of traits is connected to the issue of whether all "errors" in texts are equally revealing of genealogical relationships. Because opinions differ greatly about the relative weight of different variants, this has led to the study of significant errors (see 2.2.5).

Phylogenetic inference is based on the variable traits that have been scored for a set of taxa and that have been entered into one of the above-mentioned data matrices. A subsequent phylogenetic inference can be displayed in a number of different formats, for example tree diagrams (fig. 5.2-1c), hierarchical Venn diagrams (fig. 5.2-4b), indented classifications, Newick tree descriptions, or NEXUS tree descriptions. The two latter file formats are the most common formats for representing phylogenetic trees. The Newick format was created to represent trees in a computer-readable form. The development of the NEXUS format, which extended this format to encapsulate additional phylogenetic data, began in 1987 (Maddison, Swofford, and Maddison 1997). NEXUS files applying the Newick format are the most commonly used way of representing tree topologies through the use of characters (instead of visual lines, boxes, circles, and so forth). Monophyletic clades, that is, species or groups that share one common ancestor, are surrounded by parentheses, and sister clades are separated by commas. As an example, the tree in figure 5.2-1c can be written in Newick format as *(((C,D),B),A)*. The Newick format can also contain additional information about branch lengths (after colons) and node names (after closed parentheses). Each NEXUS file contains the following basic blocks: a data block containing the data matrix, a taxa block containing information about taxa, and a tree block presenting phylogenetic trees in Newick format (Archie et al. 1986). On this format and for an example, we refer the reader to figure 3.4-27 above.

5.2.3 On distance measures

In phylogenetic tree-construction methods, one will often encounter mentions of "distance" in connection to character sequences, matrix columns or rows, texts, and so forth. Such distance measures quantify how similar or dissimilar strings of characters are – note that character sequences, matrix columns, matrix rows, and texts can all essentially be understood as strings (or rows) of characters. The sheer number of different distance measures that have been developed defies any exhaustive listing; we will therefore, for the sake of clarity, present here only a few, basic approaches. Distance measures broadly fall into two categories: edit distance measures and vector distance measures. Edit distance measures express the difference between character sequences based on the minimum number of mutations that are needed to turn one sequence into another. "cat", for instance, is one edit distance away from "cot" (one substitution of "a" with "o" is required), and "cat" is two edits away from "cost" (one substitution of "a" with "o" and one addition of "s"). Many edit distance measures and related algorithms exist. Most notable and most frequently used are the Levenshtein distance and the Longest Common Subsequence (LCS). Levenshtein distance computes the minimal amount of insertions, deletions, and substitutions needed to morph one string into another. LCS, as its name suggests, calculates distances based on the longest coinciding substrings of characters it can find in the texts that are compared. For text distance measures in philological practice, it is advisable to apply a variant of Levenshtein, the Damerau–Levenshtein distance, which takes transpositions into account as a single edit. Vector-based distance measures express character or word sequences as paths in a high-dimensional space where each dimension represents the occurrence or frequency of individual words or characters in the sequence. The distance between sets of words or characters can then be computed as either the L1 distance (more colloquially known as Manhattan distance), which computes the number of steps that need to be travelled along every axis to reach another point in the high-dimensional space; or (more commonly) as the Euclidean distance; or as a cosine measure which computes the angle between two vectors. For a comprehensive overview of this topic, refer to Gomaa and Fahmy (2013).

5.2.4 Tree-reconstruction methods

Phylogenetic trees are usually inferred from genetic sequences or morphological data in biology, and from errors or variants in stemmatology (see 2.2). Phylogenetic reconstruction methods are based either on distance or on character data. In distance matrix methods, the distance between every pair of data sequences is calculated as explained in section 5.2.2. The distance matrix thus obtained is then used for tree reconstruction. Phylogenetic reconstruction methods based on character data include maximum parsimony, maximum likelihood, and Bayesian inference methods. Each method is introduced below and explained in more detail in section 5.3. For an in-depth treatment of the various concepts outlined here, we refer

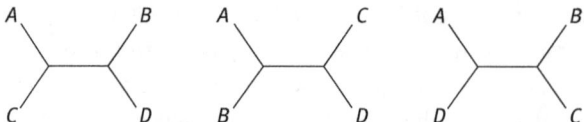

Fig. 5.2-5: All possible bifurcating unrooted trees when there are four taxa.

to Ziheng Yang and Bruce Rannala (2012). Here, we try to describe some common characteristics of these tree-construction methods and to provide some intimations about them.

The objective of any tree-reconstruction method is to infer the most likely tree given a number of taxa. It is theoretically possible to generate all possible trees for a given number of taxa. A possible way, therefore, to solve this problem is to simply draw all possible trees and subsequently compute which tree fits best according to some criterion. The problem with this approach is the enormous increase in possible trees as the number of taxa rises. For two taxa, there is really only one possible tree (two nodes and an edge). With four taxa, there are three possible unrooted bifurcating trees (see fig. 5.2-5). If we progress in this way, we can indeed draw all the possible trees for any number of taxa, but with five taxa the number of possible trees is 15, and with ten taxa it is already 2,027,025. With twenty taxa, the number of possible trees rises to some 222,000,000,000,000,000,000. Even for powerful modern computers, it is impossible to calculate that number of trees within a feasible time. Because the number of possible trees is so impossibly large, heuristic tree-search algorithms are used to bypass this problem. Heuristic approaches work by first generating a starting tree that fits the observed data using a rapid algorithm. After this, the algorithm tries to improve the score of the tree by making incremental changes to the tree based on heuristic data (hence "heuristic approach"). It should be noted that with heuristic methods there is always the possibility that the best tree may not be found because there may be many valid possibilities that are not computed.

The methods differ in the way they compute how well a tree fits the observed data, the tree score. In maximum parsimony-based methods, a tree score is considered better if fewer changes (mutations) are needed between taxa to realise the tree. In maximum likelihood methods, the tree score is based on the log-likelihood, which can be understood as a value that indicates how probable a tree is given the model for mutations the method uses. For Bayesian inference, the score is also a probability value, the posterior probability which is influenced by actual observed data. Maximum likelihood and Bayesian inference use a model for data change, that is, they assume in their calculations that mutations occur according to a certain given mechanism. They assume, for instance, that mutations are always DNA base substitutions or text modifications. Maximum parsimony does not have such an explicit model; it computes a score purely on the basis of the number of changes and does not adapt its approach based on the type of change.

In principle, all tree-building methods face the problem that it is only possible to generate all possible trees for a small number of taxa and that, for larger numbers of taxa, "short-cut" approaches need to be used. It is therefore always possible that the solution computed is actually not the real solution. To mitigate this problem to a certain extent, a technique called b o o t s t r a p p i n g is often applied. A bootstrap method consists of running the tree-building process a set number of times (e.g. 100 times), inputting the same data in a different (e.g. randomised) order or using different samples, or both. The consistency of the position of nodes and branch lengths can then be computed across all results as a ratio of how many times the same nodes and branch lengths appear in the calculated results. The larger this ratio, the more reliable the result is assumed to be.

5.2.4.1 Parsimony

> Pluralitas non est ponenda sine necessitate. (Ockham 1967, 74)

The principle of p a r s i m o n y, or "Ockham's Razor", named after Guillelmus de Ockham, OFM (1285–1349), states that when trying to explain a phenomenon, it is better to prefer the explanation involving fewer assumptions. In evolutionary biology and in stemmatology, the principle of parsimony is relevant because it is assumed that the probability of the same mutations (or text alterations) evolving independently is low. Empirical evidence strongly suggests that biological evolution is primarily based on random mutations in DNA. After a mutation, the altered DNA is propagated in a species through offspring. For this reason, it is assumed that if two species carry the same alteration in their DNA, it is highly unlikely that these alterations arose independently, and instead it is assumed that both species have a common ancestor species in which the change happened at some point. Similarly, in manuscript evolution it is assumed that if two witnesses have the same variant reading, the cause is much more likely to be that a common ancestor had that same reading, and not that the variant occurred twice independently. It should be noted, however, that this is only statistically true: in biology, because there are only four possible DNA bases, identical changes that happen independently do occur; they are just much less likely.

Parsimony tree score
The maximum parsimony tree is the tree for which the tree score is lowest. The way maximum parsimony minimises the number of changes in a tree is by assigning character states to the interior nodes of the tree in such a way that the changes in character states from node to node are minimal. The particular place of a character in a character state is called the s i t e of that character (roughly corresponding to the *loci critici* in textual criticism; see 3.3.4), and a mutation means that a site becomes occupied by a different character. Obviously, there is a minimum number of

changes that are required to progress from one character state to the next. This number is called the character length or site length. The tree score is the sum of the character lengths across all sites.

Some sites are not useful for parsimony-based tree comparison. Constant sites are sites for which the same nucleotide or text string occurs in all species or witnesses; they thus have a character length of zero in any tree, and are parsimony uninformative. Singleton sites are sites at which only one of the species or manuscripts has a distinct nucleotide or text string whereas all others are the same. These singleton sites can also be ignored because they do not allow a common ancestor to be inferred, which would require another species to also have that particular nucleotide or text string at that site. In stemmatology, these singleton sites are known as *Eigenfehler, Sonderfehler,* or *lectiones singulares.* The parsimony informative sites are those at which at least two distinct characters are observed, each at least twice.

A controversy arose in the 1990s as to whether maximum parsimony (without explicit assumptions) or maximum likelihood (with an explicit evolutionary model) was the better method for phylogenetic analysis. Today, the importance of model-based inference methods is broadly recognised. Parsimony, however, is still commonly used. Not because it is believed to be free of assumptions, but because it is computationally efficient and often produces acceptable results.

Strengths and weaknesses of parsimony

Parsimony's strength is its relative simplicity, which makes it easier to describe and understand. Moreover, it is amenable to rigorous mathematical analysis. Parsimony's primary weakness is its lack of explicit assumptions. This makes it almost impossible to include any knowledge about the process of sequence or text evolution to be applied during the tree-reconstruction process. Parsimony's failure to correct for multiple substitutions at the same site causes a problem known as long-branch attraction: if the correct tree has two long branches separated by a short branch, parsimony will tend to group the long branches together. In such cases, parsimony converges on a tree that is wrong. It should be noted that model-based methods (maximum likelihood and Bayesian methods) also suffer from long-branch attraction if the sequence or text evolution model is too simplistic and ignores, for instance, the rate of variation across sites.

5.2.4.2 Maximum likelihood methods

Maximum likelihood is a statistical method developed to estimate unknown parameters in a model. To understand what this means, we can, for instance, suppose that the monetary value of a painting is dependent on the surface area of its rectangular canvas – which may be less naive an assumption than one would think (see Renneboog and van Houtte 2002, 339). A model in that case may be $v = l \times b$, meaning that the value equals the length times the breadth of the canvas. But suppose also that we observe that this is not entirely correct: the larger the painting, the more the value estimated by our model falls short of the actual value. If that is the case, a better model would be $v = \alpha \times (l \times b)$. In that model, α is a parameter. The question in this case is: what is the value of that α? This is typically the sort of problem where maximum likelihood is applied. If we have prices and actual measurements of paintings, we can compute the likelihood of the observed data for any given value of the parameter α. The maximum likelihood estimate (MLE) of the parameter, then, is that value of the parameter which maximises the likelihood of observing the actual data in real life. In tree-reconstruction calculations, many such parameters may have to be estimated. Such unknown MLEs are usually assessed numerically via iterative optimisation algorithms.

Maximum likelihood tree reconstruction
Owing to increased computing power and advances in software implementation, and to the development of increasingly realistic models of sequence evolution, this method is now widely used. Maximum likelihood tree estimation involves two optimisation steps: (*i*) the optimisation of branch lengths to calculate the tree score for each tree, and (*ii*) a search in tree space for the tree with maximum likelihood. The tree (topology) is, from a statistical point of view, a model (see 4.2). Branch lengths in the given tree and substitution parameters, on the other hand, are parameters in the model. Maximum likelihood inference is therefore equivalent to a comparison of many statistical models with the same number of parameters. Most models used in molecular phylogenetics assume that the sites in the genetic sequence (or the text modifications) evolve independently: the likelihood is therefore a product of the probabilities for the different sites. The probability at any given site is an average over the unobserved character states at the ancestral nodes. Parsimony and likelihood analyses are similar in this aspect, although parsimony uses the optimal ancestral states only, whereas likelihood averages over all the possible states.

Strengths and weaknesses of the maximum likelihood method
The maximum likelihood method has two major advantages. The first is that all of its model assumptions are explicit and can therefore be evaluated and improved. Second, a broad range of sophisticated evolutionary models is available for likelihood-based methods. If the aim is to understand the process of witness or DNA sequence evolution, the maximum likelihood method has clear advantages over the minimal parsimony approach. The main disadvantage of maximum likelihood is that the likelihood calculation, and the tree search in particular, are computationally intensive. The other drawback of the method is that false or too simple models can be inaccurate about tree reliability, that is, they can suggest that the estimated tree is significantly supported when it actually is not (Z. Yang, Goldman, and Friday 1994).

5.2.4.3 Bayesian phylogenetics

The difference between Bayesian inference and maximum likelihood-based methods is that parameters in a Bayesian model are random variables with statistical distributions, whereas in maximum likelihood-based methods they are unknown constants. In other words, the Bayesian variant of our very simple $v = \alpha \times (l \times b)$ model for the value of paintings assumes that we should not compute the value of the parameter α as a fixed value (e.g. as exactly 5 or 0.4). Instead, the Bayesian variant of that model asserts that α may vary between certain values. The Bayesian model, in this manner, calculates what the likelihood of values for the parameter α is. In real-world situations, such parameters are assigned a "prior distribution" before the data analysis (i.e. the likelihood of the minimum and maximum values of the parameters is chosen or given, for instance based on earlier experience). This prior distribution is combined with actual data to generate a posterior distribution, and final parameter inferences are then based on this posterior distribution. Bayesian inference relies on Bayes's theorem:

$$P(T,\theta|D) = P(T,\theta) \times P(D|T,\theta) / P(D)$$

where

$P(T,\theta|D)$ is the posterior probability,
$P(T,\theta)$ is the prior probability for a tree T and a parameter θ,
$P(D|T,\theta)$ is the likelihood or probability of the data given the tree and parameter, and
$P(D)$ is a normalising constant to ensure that the sum over the trees and integration over the parameters of $P(T,\theta|D)$ is 1.

The theorem states that the posterior probability is proportional to the prior probability multiplied by the likelihood of the data given the parameters. Most often, the posterior probabilities of trees cannot be calculated directly, and calculating the normalising constant $P(D)$ is especially arduous. Bayesian inference therefore relies on Markov Chain Monte Carlo algorithms to create a sample from the posterior distribution.

Strengths and weaknesses of Bayesian inference

Both likelihood-based methods and Bayesian methods use a likelihood function. Advantages and drawbacks that apply to likelihood-based methods apply, therefore, equally to Bayesian methods. Bayesian statistics answers the biological or stemmatological questions in a relatively straightforward manner because a tree's posterior probability is simply the probability that the tree is correct, given the data and the model. In contrast, interpreting the confidence intervals in likelihood analyses is more complex: in phylogenetics, it has not been possible to define a confidence interval for trees, and the widely used bootstrap method is rather difficult to interpret.

On the other hand, Bayesian posterior probabilities for trees and clades calculated from real data often seem excessively high: in numerous analyses, most nodes have posterior probabilities of about 100 %. Posterior tree probabilities are sensitive to model violations, and the use of simplistic models may lead to inflated posterior probabilities. Moreover, although the prior probability allows for the incorporation of a priori information about the trees or parameters, such information is most often unavailable. Furthermore, high-dimensional priors are hard to specify, and they may influence the posterior probability in unexpected ways. Bayesian robustness analyses are therefore crucial for assessing the impact of the prior on the posterior estimates.

Despite these caveats, and thanks to advances in computational methods, Bayesian inference has increasingly gained in popularity in the past two decades.

5.3 Computational construction of trees

Teemu Roos

In this section, we outline the main approaches and methods for the automatic construction of hypotheses for genealogical trees. We caution the reader that these methods are to be applied as a part of a computer-*assisted* approach – instead of a "computerised" or fully automated approach – and that the results need to be subsequently critically examined and interpreted by the scholar. It is never a good idea to blindly accept whatever result these methods produce as the "correct" result. We avoid the use of the term "stemma" and use the term "tree" instead of it because, in our terminology, a stemma is a rooted diagram whereas the trees obtained by computer-assisted methods are almost invariably unrooted. Admittedly, the use of the term "tree" is also somewhat inaccurate, due to the fact that some of the methods actually produce networks rather than trees. Adopting the phylogenetic terminology, we refer to the objects whose relationships we are interested in as "taxa", instead of "witnesses" or "manuscripts", in this section.

5.3.1 Manual and computational construction

Traditionally, stemmata are constructed manually. They are based on a collation and careful scrutiny of the source material. It is noteworthy that manual, that is, non-computer-assisted stemma construction should follow a rigorous and strict procedure too. By this, we mean a procedure where each decision is based on sound principles applied to "internal" evidence in the collated material and possibly complemented by "external" evidence from other sources. Assuming that such a rigorous procedure exists, it follows that, in principle, the procedure can be formalised as a set of explicit rules for constructing a stemma – or, in other words, an algorithm. However, while all that is true in principle, in practice it is a simplification. In particular, external evidence, which can be made use of in order to, for instance, understand the historical context in which the source material was created, can be extremely hard to formalise with a set of clear-cut rules. This is why we use the term "computer-*assisted* stemmatology" rather than, say, "automatic stemmatology" or "artificial intelligence stemmatology".

In computer-assisted stemmatology, the working method often involves an iterative process where a hypothesis is constructed by an algorithm and scholars then reflect on the results by calling on their scholarly expertise (knowledge of the text, knowledge of the historical context, materiality, and so on). If the hypothesis is not entirely satisfactory, they may decide to adjust the method or the source material. This may lead to different encodings of the data, collating more material, removing some taxa (witnesses), splitting the material into multiple parts and analysing them separately, and so forth. Some methods may also include adjustable parameters or constraints that affect the outcome. Of course, it is pivotal to avoid the temptation to keep fiddling with the material or the method until a "desired" result is teased out of it. To this end, the iterative process should also follow clear and rigorous principles, and it should be documented carefully and disclosed together with the results obtained. We are not aware of a set of explicit principles of this kind, and we point this out here as a much-needed contribution to the field.

5.3.2 Classes of methods

In order to make it easier to get a grasp of the variety of approaches, we adopt the same categories or classes of methods as in section 5.2. Distance-based methods accept as input a set of pairwise distances between the taxa – that is, a list of distances according to some measure for each possible pair of taxa. The parsimony-based methods category mainly covers the maximum parsimony tree-construction method, where the objective is to minimise the number of "mutations" required to explain the variation in the data. Statistical methods are a large class of techniques based on statistical principles such as maximum likelihood. Bayesian methods are a subclass of statistical methods which we treat in a separate subsection. Finally, we describe methods that are specifically designed for stemmatological applications in their own subsection.

Of course, we can only ever provide an incomplete list of the existing methods in each subsection. The subsection categories or classes are also not mutually exclusive, and some methods might have been placed in one category just as well as in another. An example is the least-squares method, which we classify as a statistical method even though it is also a distance-based method.

For each of the described approaches or methods, we follow the same structure as far as possible:
- syntax and semantics of input data,
- key ideas,
- syntax and semantics of the output,
- underlying assumptions, and
- examples of application in the literature.

5.3.3 Distance-based methods

Distance-based methods operate on pairwise distances between the taxa. These can be obtained in different ways, which can obviously affect the outcome in significant ways. In stemmatology, a typical measure of distance is simply the number of words that are different. However, the treatment of changes in word order, gaps, non-words such as punctuation, annotations, colours, and other typographical elements needs to be decided. Section 2.2.5 describes how some changes are more relationship-revealing than others. Differences may therefore be weighted accordingly. This task is traditionally done on the basis of the expertise of a philologist. Nothing, however, hinders us from trying to define a model to handle this task automatically. Another potentially critical decision is whether to apply some sort of distance correction or not (see Spencer and Howe 2001).

5.3.3.1 Minimum spanning trees, arborescences, and Steiner trees

A minimum spanning tree is an undirected tree-shaped graph that connects a given set of nodes (taxa) by edges such that the total sum of the edge weights given by the pairwise distances between the corresponding nodes is minimised. Classical algorithms for constructing minimum spanning trees include Prim's algorithm and Kruskal's algorithms (see e.g. Cormen et al. 2009). The resulting tree diagram cannot usually be interpreted directly as a stemma because (a) it is unrooted and (b) it does not include any unobserved (missing) ancestral nodes at the branching points. Instead, each of the branching points is always occupied by a taxon corresponding to an extant version of the text. Related graph-theoretical concepts include arborescences (directed rooted trees) and Steiner trees (minimum spanning trees that allow additional nodes to be created to serve as branching points). However, these are rarely used in phylogenetics or stemmatology.

5.3.3.2 UPGMA

The Unweighted Pair Group Method with Arithmetic Mean (UPGMA) is a classical hierarchical clustering technique (Sokal and Michener 1958). The general idea is to start with separate "clusters" for each taxon, and iteratively merge the most similar pair of clusters in each step. When two clusters are merged, they are removed from the set of clusters and replaced by a single new cluster. Eventually, there will be only two clusters left, which are merged in the last step of the algorithm. The order in which the clusters are merged produces a tree structure such that in the bottom level of the tree, we have pairs of taxa, and the higher levels of the tree correspond to the steps where clusters consisting of multiple taxa have been merged.

Many hierarchical clustering techniques exist. They differ from each other in terms of how the distance between the newly created cluster and the other clusters is defined. Let $A, B, ..., E$ be taxa and the pairwise distances be denoted by $d(A, B)$, $d(A, C)$, $d(B, C)$, and so on. Let us now assume that it turns out that $d(D, E)$ – thus the distance between taxa D and E – is the smallest of all the pairwise distances. Because of this, the algorithm will begin by merging D and E. (Note that, in the beginning, each taxon is its own "cluster".) Then let us denote the new cluster by DE. We now need to define the distance between the new cluster and the other remaining clusters, A, B, C, and so forth. In UPGMA, this distance is defined as the arithmetic mean of the distances from the individual distances of A, B, C, and so on to the taxa *D and E*. So, for example, the distance $d(A, DE)$ is defined as $(d(A, D) + d(A, E)) / 2$. Moreover, when merging two clusters that consist of an unequal number of taxa, the two distances are weighted by the respective cluster sizes. So, for example, if we were to merge clusters A and DE, the distance $d(B, ADE)$ would be defined as $(1 \times d(B, A) + 2 \times d(B, DE)) / 3$, where the denominator 3 is the total number of taxa in the two merged clusters counted together. This process is now repeated until only one cluster remains.

The output of the algorithm is a rooted and directed tree structure. In addition to the topology of the tree, branch lengths are produced. The branch lengths are defined by the cluster-to-cluster distances when merging. We will not discuss the details of branch-length estimation, but, roughly speaking, short branch lengths indicate compact (more similar) clusters, while long branch lengths correspond to clearly separated clusters.

The UPGMA method can be shown to be consistent, that is, to produce the correct tree structure if one exists, under the assumption of a molecular clock. In technical terms, this is called the ultrametricity assumption. Intuitively, it means that all the lineages evolve at a constant rate and that the taxa are observed contemporaneously (at the same point of time). In terms of the tree structure, this implies that the leaf nodes (taxa) are at a constant distance from the root (most recent common ancestor, or archetype). This is usually not at all the case in text evolution. If (and when) this assumption is violated, the tree can be severely distorted. Another common problem scenario is the long-branch attraction phenomenon, where taxa that are very dissimilar to the others tend to cluster together even if they are also dissimilar to each other (Felsenstein 1978a).

5.3.3.3 Neighbour-joining

Neighbour-joining (NJ) is another commonly used distance-based method (Saitou and Nei 1987). Like UPGMA, it is also based on hierarchical clustering. There are two crucial differences related to the definition of pairwise distances. First, the pair of clusters to merge is selected by minimising an adjusted distance, Q, which is defined in a way that is designed to account for variable evolutionary rates. Intuitively, the long distances that are due to rapidly evolving lineages are discounted by subtracting the average distance between a taxon and the other taxa. Second, the definition of the cluster-to-cluster distances is adjusted in a similar fashion. The combined effect of these adjustments is that the method is not subject to long-branch attraction.

The input and the output of the method are similar in syntax and semantics to those of the UPGMA method, with the exception that the NJ tree is undirected. While the NJ method is not subject to long-branch attraction and does not require the ultrametricity assumption, it is still based on the assumption that the input distances faithfully reflect the genealogy. As with any distance-based methods, choices about the data encoding, treatment of gaps, and so on, as well as the use of distance correction, can make a significant difference to the outcome.

As tends to be the case with distance-based methods, NJ is relatively fast and scales up to hundreds of taxa. Furthermore, variants of the algorithm have been presented that can be applied to thousands of taxa (K. Howe, Bateman, and Durbin 2002).

5.3.4 Parsimony

Parsimony-based approaches are another classical category of phylogenetic methods. As opposed to distance-based methods, parsimony methods require a set of character sequences as input. The sequences must be aligned so that they can be easily compared character by character. The sequences are placed in the leaf nodes of a tree, where the internal (non-leaf) nodes correspond to ancestral taxa whose sequences are unobserved. If we attach hypothetical sequences to all the internal nodes, we can calculate for each edge in the tree a score which is simply the number of characters where the sequences at the opposite ends of the edge differ. The score of the whole tree, with the chosen hypothetical sequences, is then the sum of the scores of all the edges in it. The "small parsimony problem" is to find the set of hypothetical sequences that minimises this score for a given tree. The "large parsimony problem" is to find the tree *and* the hypothetical sequences at the internal nodes that minimise the score.

Computationally, the small parsimony problem is easy and can be solved in linear time with respect to the number of taxa by an elegant message-passing algorithm (Fitch 1971). This means that the calculation time increases linearly with the increase in taxa: if it takes four minutes to solve the problem for four taxa, it will take eight minutes for eight taxa. However, the large parsimony problem is, in computer science terms, "hard". The precise technical term is "NP-hard", and it implies that no scalable algorithm for solving it exactly is believed to be possible. In practice, therefore, the only possibility is to use a heuristics-based search that does not guarantee an exact solution except for a very small number of taxa (about a dozen).

The output of the method is a tree structure. The edge-specific scores mentioned above can be used to define branch lengths, which have a similar interpretation to that of the branch lengths in distance-based methods: small branch lengths indicate compact groups of taxa, while long branches indicate clearly separated groups. The logic is quite straightforward: if a set of taxa differ from each other in only a few characters, they tend to be grouped together with small branches separating them, whereas groups of taxa that differ by many characters will also be far apart in terms of the parsimony tree.

The maximum parsimony method has been criticised for producing misleading results due to long-branch attraction (see 5.3.3.2) and other scenarios where the number of differences is not directly proportional to the evolutionary distance between the taxa (see e.g. Felsenstein 1978a). However, in practice it is still widely applied, and often its performance is found to be relatively good.

Parsimony has been used several times in stemmatology – for instance, Robinson and O'Hara (1996); Baret, Macé, and Robinson (2006); Roos and Heikkilä (2009); and Tehrani (2013).

5.3.5 Statistical methods

From a statistical point of view, we can consider the tree model as a parameter to be estimated from data. There are various ways in which this can be done.

5.3.5.1 Least squares

Possibly the simplest scenario is one where the tree topology (the structure of the tree) is fixed and we only need to estimate the branch lengths. If the input data is in the form of pairwise distances, the "fit" of the model can be defined by comparing the input distances, $d(u, v)$, for all pairs of taxa u and v to the "tree distances". With "tree distance", we mean the length obtained by adding up the branch lengths on the path from u to v. This problem can be converted into a linear regression problem where the branch-length parameters correspond to coefficients which can be estimated using the standard least-squares method. The goodness of fit is given by the sum of squared errors in the distances (observed vs tree distances). This is analogous to the small parsimony problem discussed above. The corresponding large problem is to find the tree topology for which the goodness of fit is the best (minimum sum of squared errors; Cavalli-Sforza and Edvards 1967). Similar to the maximum parsimony method, the large problem is NP-hard, and no exact solution is guaranteed for more than about a dozen taxa.

Variants of the method exist where the distance errors are treated differently by, for example, weighting small distances more than large distances (see e.g. Fitch and Margoliash 1967).

The input data for the least-squares method is in the form of pairwise distances, so the method can also be categorised under distance-based methods. Consequently, all the considerations about the definition of distances, distance corrections, and so forth apply. The output is a tree with branch lengths. The interpretation of the branch lengths is also the same as in other distance-based methods.

The assumption underlying the least-squares method is – loosely speaking – that the distances reflect the evolutionary distance. Under this assumption, most variants of the method can be shown to be consistent (Rzhetsky and Nei 1992). In particular, least squares does *not* require the ultrametricity assumption (all lineages evolve at a constant rate), and it is not prone to the long-branch attraction problem.

5.3.5.2 Maximum likelihood

The statistical model underlying the least-squares method (see above) is not based on any concrete probabilistic model of sequence evolution: it simply assumes that the observed pairwise distances reflect evolutionary distances. Various explicit models of sequence evolution have been proposed in evolutionary biology. A sequence evolution model assigns a probability for a descendant sequence (e.g. CAGTA – A, C, G, and T denote the nucleotides in DNA sequences) to be produced from another, ancestral sequence (e.g. CAGAA). The model is typically parametrised by a branch-length parameter (or parameters) that corresponds to the time passed between the ancestral and the descendant sequences and an evolutionary rate at which mutations tend to occur per unit time.

Examples of sequence evolution models include the Jukes–Cantor model, often abbreviated as JC69 (Jukes and Cantor 1969), and the Kimura model (Kimura 1980), abbreviated as K80. The models have a varying number of parameters. For example, the JC69 model has only one parameter, which is the overall mutation rate. The K80 model, on the other hand, has two parameters to control the rate of change. One parameterises the A/G and C/T transitions. The other parameter pertains to the remaining mutations, A/C, A/T, G/C, and G/T. Similar sequence evolution models exist for protein sequences.

Again, we can separate the small phylogeny problem, which is estimating the parameters of the sequence evolution model for each branch under a given tree topology, and the large phylogeny problem, which is to find the tree topology as well as the parameters. In both cases, the maximum likelihood principle says that we should maximise the probability of the observed sequences under the model (tree and parameter values). In this case, even the small problem is computationally hard, and typically heuristic techniques based on the expectation maximisation (EM) algorithm are applied. The large problem is, again, harder still, and again heuristic search algorithms are commonly used to find a good, but possibly not the best, topology.

The sequence evolution model makes the assumptions of the maximum likelihood model explicit: the sequences are assumed to have evolved independently along the lineages in the tree according to the chosen sequence evolution model.

The input of the maximum likelihood method is a set of aligned sequences for the extant taxa. The output is a tree topology with branch-length parameters. Since the models may have multiple parameters, the branches do not necessarily have only a single branch-length parameter. However, in most cases, one is singled out in order to be able to draw the trees.

5.3.5.3 PhyloDAG

PhyloDAG is an extension of the maximum likelihood approach in order to handle non-tree-like relationships (Nguyen and Roos 2015). It is based on an evolutionary model proposed earlier by Strimmer and Moulton (2000) that allows a descendant sequence to have two parents rather than only one. This implies that the model topology is defined by a directed acyclic graph (DAG) instead of a tree.

The main challenge and drawback of adopting the more general DAG model instead of trees is the computational cost. Finding a good DAG is an extremely slow process and works reliably only for small datasets with up to 20–30 extant taxa. For larger datasets, the search time becomes prohibitive and the quality of the results degrades as the heuristic search fails to find good solutions.

As in the case of the maximum likelihood method, the input of the PhyloDAG method is a set of aligned sequences. The output is a DAG where nodes correspond either to unobserved ancestral taxa or observed extant taxa. The most interesting property of the output is often the arrangement of "reticulations" (the nodes with two parents), if any. Since the heuristic search method used in PhyloDAG is not deterministic, it is advisable to repeat the analysis multiple times to obtain a range of possible solutions. The method also outputs a log-likelihood score which measures the goodness of fit. However, since the models may have a variable number of parameters, direct comparison of the log-likelihoods is not meaningful, and an additional comparison stage, such as bootstrapping, is recommended.

Currently, the only sequence evolution model available in the PhyloDAG software package is the JC69 model (see above). The reticulation model of Strimmer and Moulton (2000) makes the assumption that each character in a reticulation node is inherited from a parent that is chosen independently of the choices made for the other characters. This assumption may be quite unrealistic since the sequences are often inherited as longer segments, each of which is inherited from a single parent, instead of randomly switching between the parents at each position along the sequence.

Tehrani, Nguyen, and Roos (2016) apply PhyloDAG to resolving the genealogy of the fairy tale *Little Red Riding Hood*. They recommend a parametric bootstrap procedure for comparing a number of output DAGs.

5.3.6 Bayesian methods

The defining property of Bayesian methods is that they assume that models also have prior probabilities which, together with the observed data, determine the outcome. For example, we can assume that the branch lengths are distributed according to some probability distribution. Given data, we can compute the posterior probabilities of the branch-length values. The posterior probability of a parameter value (e.g. branch length = 1.5 units) is proportional to its prior probability multiplied by the likelihood (i.e. probability) of the data given the value. Thus, the posterior probability is highest for parameters that have high prior probability and which explain the data well (high likelihood). The posterior probability is obtained from the prior probability and the likelihood by the Bayes rule (Bayes's theorem; see 5.2.3.3).

5.3.6.1 MrBayes

Perhaps the most popular Bayesian software package for constructing phylogenetic trees is MrBayes (Huelsenbeck and Ronquist 2001; Ronquist et al. 2012).

The MrBayes package provides implementations of the most common sequence evolution models, including the JC69 and K80 models mentioned above and many others. The default prior distribution for the tree topologies is uniform, which means that all possible bifurcating tree structures are considered equally probable a priori. The default prior distribution for the branch lengths is an exponentially decaying distribution that assigns less probability to longer branches. Both these choices can be changed in a number of ways.

Computationally, Bayesian methods are almost invariably as hard or harder than the corresponding "plain" (or frequentist, or classical) statistical methods. This is also true in the case of the method applied in MrBayes. The algorithm works by generating a large sample of different hypotheses, that is, tree topologies together with the associated parameter values, by a procedure known as Markov Chain Monte Carlo (MCMC). The default sample size (number of hypotheses) is one million. The sample is generated in such a way that the different hypotheses appear in it proportional to their posterior probabilities. In other words, the most probable hypotheses appear most often, and the very improbable hypotheses hardly ever appear. However, since the sample of hypotheses is finite, an element of chance is inevitable. Moreover, the whole procedure can be repeated multiple times in order to reduce the risk of unrepresentative outcomes. The default number of repetitions is two.

The input is in the format of aligned character sequences. The output is a sample of tree hypotheses (topologies with parameter values). MrBayes includes a number of techniques for summarising the sample, including a consensus tree similar to that often applied in bootstrap analysis. A benefit of the Bayesian approach is that the uncertainty in the outcome is always expressed clearly, and thus no additional sensitivity analysis such as bootstrapping is required.

The assumptions underlying the analysis are related to the adopted sequence evolution model. In addition, the chosen prior distribution should be considered an assumption as well. The prior distribution, however, is more flexible, and it is usually recommended that prior distributions are chosen to be so vague, or "flat", that the information in the data overrules them.

Tehrani (2013) applied MrBayes to analyse the oral tradition of the fairy tale *Little Red Riding Hood*.

5.3.6.2 BEAST

BEAST and BEAST2 are two comprehensive software packages for Bayesian phylogenetic inference (Drummond and Rambaut 2007; Bouckaert et al. 2014; Drummond and Bouckart 2015). They include the same kind of phylogenetic tree-sampling methods as MrBayes but also a large number of other phylogenetic models and methods. Like the algorithms in MrBayes, most of the algorithms in BEAST/BEAST2 are based on MCMC sampling, and they produce a set of possible results together with estimates of their posterior probabilities.

To mention an example of the alternative analyses available in BEAST/BEAST2, the multispecies coalescent model can be used to correct for misleading phylogenetic signals in cases where the underlying process involves a population of individuals rather than a single individual. Coalescent theory, developed in the 1980s by John Kingsman and others, describes such scenarios and motivates models that are somewhat more complicated than the traditional sequence evolution models discussed above (Kingman 1982).

Another type of analysis provided by BEAST/BEAST2 is phylogeographical analysis. In phylogeographical analysis, the phylogenetic tree models are combined with geographical migration models. Such an analysis can be used, for example, to trace epidemics or the migration of populations (Lemey et al. 2009).

5.3.7 Stemmatology-specific methods

The development of methods tailored for stemmatology is not common. This is probably in part because of the success in applying phylogenetic methods proper in the computer-assisted working mode discussed at the beginning of this section. Another part of the explanation for this is the fact that the field itself is relatively young – compared, for instance, to the more mature field of phylogenetics. Moreover, by modifying the data and the parameters of the methods, many possible deficiencies (see 5.5) of phylogenetic methods with respect to stemmatological applications can be alleviated to a degree that is often sufficient. It is reasonable, however, to expect that even better results can be achieved by designing methods for stemmatological needs from the outset.

5.3.7.1 RHM

The Roos–Heikkilä–Myllymäki (RHM) method resembles the maximum parsimony method (see above). In particular, its key idea is to minimise the amount of change along the branches of the tree. However, in contrast to parsimony, the RHM method measures the amount of change in terms of textual similarity instead of the number of different characters. The textual similarity comparison is done on a segment level rather than on a word-by-word level. The default length of a segment is ten words. To compare two segments, the RHM method applies a data compression measure (Roos, Heikkilä, and Myllymäki 2006). The higher the number of matching substrings (sequences of contiguous letters or other symbols), the higher the measured similarity.

A consequence of the segment-level compression measure is that RHM can automatically deal with changes in word order, since a segment where the order of two or more words is exchanged is still more similar (in terms of matching substrings) to the unmodified version than a segment where the words have been changed into some other words. Similarly, the compression measure assigns higher similarity scores to changes where a word is changed only slightly than to cases where a word is changed completely. A possibly problematic feature is that longer words are assigned higher importance since they contain more substrings, and changing them therefore leads to a greater decrease in the similarity score.

Since the RHM method operates directly on the text, the input is an aligned word table instead of the character table in, for example, maximum parsimony. The encoding of the words can still be adjusted by, for example, removing punctuation or word capitalisation if they are considered unimportant or even misleading from the genealogical point of view. The output of RHM is an undirected tree with no branch lengths.

The assumption underlying the RHM method is that the text evolves independently along the branches in a "compression-parsimonious" fashion. Loosely speaking, this means that changes that are smaller according to the compression measure are more likely than bigger changes. To measure the reliability of the resulting stemma, the bootstrap method can be used.

Roos and Heikkilä (2009) compared the RHM method and nine other methods on a suite of three artificial benchmark datasets where the correct stemmata are known. The results suggest that, especially for large and complex datasets, the RHM and maximum parsimony methods outperform the other methods, including neighbour-joining and least squares, but more comparisons would be needed to obtain more conclusive results.

5.3.7.2 Leitfehler

Philipp Roelli and Dieter Bachman (2010) proposed a method that encapsulates the principle that a stemma should be consistent with significant variants. The method automatically assigns a score between 0 and a fixed maximum (for example, 20 or 50) to each variant position based on how likely it is to be a *Leitfehler* (see 4.3.1). This score is used to weight the variants and to compute pairwise distances between each pair of witnesses. The weights are then used to construct a tree by a distance-based phylogenetic method.

The key idea in assigning the scores mentioned above is as follows. Let A denote a *locus* in the text, and A^1 and A^2 denote a pair of variant readings at *locus A*. Similarly, let B denote another *locus* with readings B^1 and B^2. If both A and B are *Leitfehler*, it holds that, no matter what the true stemma is, as long as there is no contamination, we can only expect to observe three of the four possible combinations (A^1, B^1), (A^1, B^2), (A^2, B^1), and (A^2, B^2). For example, if we let A^1 and B^1 denote the archetypal readings, and A^2 and B^2 denote the derived readings, then it should be virtually impossible that all three combinations (A^1, B^2), (A^2, B^1) and (A^2, B^2) are present in at least one witness each. This follows from the fact that the "mutations" A^2 and B^2 must have occurred either one after the other in the same branch or in seperate branches. We can observe variants (A^2, B^1) and (A^2, B^2) but not (A^1, B^2) in case A^2 emerged first followed by B^2, (A^1, B^2) and (A^2, B^2) but not (A^2, B^1) in case B^2 emerged first followed by A^2, or (A^2, B^1) and (A^1, B^2) but not (A^2, B^2) in case the variants emerged in separate branches. Thus, this approach treats occurrence only once in the tradition as the defining property of *Leitfehler*.

The algorithm of Roelli and Bachman uses as its input a variant table obtained after normalisation (see 3.3.2). Any readings with more than two variants are converted into absence–presence form to obtain only two-valued readings. Each candidate *Leitfehler* is then scored by counting the number of other candidates such that the above property, namely that at most three combinations appear, holds. So, for example, the score of *locus A* is determined by checking whether this is the case for *loci A* and *B*, *loci A* and *C*, and so forth. The candidate with the highest count is assigned the maximum score (e.g. 20 or 50), and the others are given scores in proportion to their counts. Roelli (2014) has also proposed more advanced means of weighting the obtained score.

The pairwise distances between the witnesses are calculated as sums of differences weighted by the *Leitfehler* scores of the *loci*. The distance matrix is used to construct an unrooted tree using the least-squares method of Fitch and Margoliash (see 5.3.5.1 above).

5.3.7.3 The Coherence-Based Genealogical Method

Partly heuristics-based, partly statistics-based, the Coherence-Based Genealogical Method (CBGM) could be called a hybrid approach (see also 7.1.2.2). It was developed starting in the 1980s by Gerd Mink at the Institut für Neutestamentliche Textforschung (INTF) in Münster. It was specifically developed for the editorial work on the major critical edition of the Greek New Testament, which presents a highly contaminated situation – the *Codex Sinaiticus*, for instance, has some 23,000 corrections in about eight hundred pages, or 30 per page on average (Wasserman and Gurry 2017, 21–22). In addressing this fundamental problem, CBGM allows witnesses to have multiple ancestors while also foregoing hypothetical intermediate ancestors known as hyparchetypes, which makes it easier to represent contamination. Furthermore it fundamentally relates texts rather than manuscripts. "Finally, and most importantly, the CBGM determines ancestry using a different principle. Rather than relating witnesses deductively based on shared errors, it relates them inductively using the relationship of their variants as determined by the editor" (Wasserman and Gurry 2017, 25). CBGM discerns two types of coherence. Pre-genealogical coherence is based on the percentage-wise agreement between two witnesses. This overall agreement is utilised to determine whether specific agreements are coincidental or not. Genealogical coherence is based on tracking editors' decisions: "At each such point where a variant is either prior or posterior to another variant, the computer tracks which witnesses attest each variant and then uses this to compile the information that constitutes genealogical coherence" (Wasserman and Gurry 2017, 28). The same decision-tracking process serves to support the consistency of editors' work. A full explanation is presented in Wasserman and Gurry (2017) and Mink (2009).

5.4 Software tools
Armin Hoenen

This section is meant to provide a rough overview of currently available tools for the creation of trees, their usage, and their dissemination. For a technical understanding of the algorithms implemented in these tools, see sections 5.2 and 5.3. Since software is part of a volatile digital ecosystem, it is subject to constant flux and change (updates, new developments, end of support or availability, operating system innovation and shift, and so on); the information provided here is almost by definition at risk of obsolescence once it is published. Readers and users should therefore always compare more recent information to what is given here. In addition, the information here is necessarily selective and the links provided in this section can thus be no more than a snapshot of what is available at the moment of writing.

5.4.1 Background

If digital stemmatology is understood as a whole domain, the physical manuscripts or fragments can be viewed as the initial input and the stemma as final output.

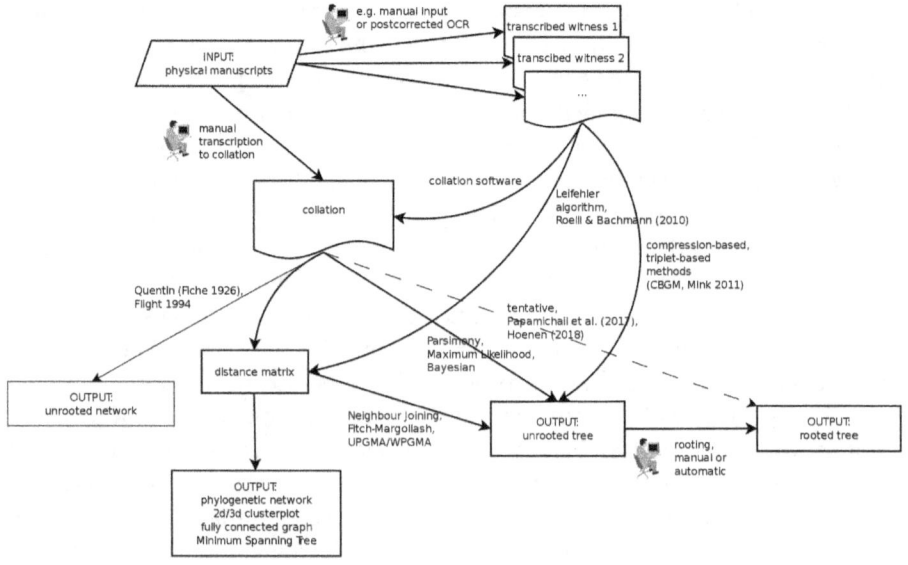

Fig. 5.4-1: Resources (nodes) and transformation processes for different ways to generate a stemma computationally (including processes that can be conducted "manually"). Terms that appear in the graphic are explained throughout the text of this section.

Between these two lie various transformations which can be achieved with the help of various tools. As can be seen in figure 5.4-1, there are many alternative ways to produce a stemma (how to arrive from ultimate input at ultimate output). Depending on which way (or technically, pipeline) one chooses, there will be different tools to use.

Tools in table 5.4-1 below are grouped by function (primarily) and then by the field they originated from (i.e. stemmatology, phylogeny, computer science, and so on). Functions proceed from collation (alignment) to tree creation. Tools may differ in aspects that apply to software in general and not to stemmatic principles alone. Are they designed for exclusively online or offline usage? Do they provide a special graphical interface? Are they accessed through a browser? Do they include well-documented functions and settings? Are there "simple" and "advanced" settings? Are they built for solving one or multiple problems (i.e. are they algorithms or suites of algorithms)? Are they a monolithic non-extendable block or are they modular (one main program with many libraries or packages)? And, finally, another important characteristic is whether they are freely available and modifiable ("free" or "open source licensed") or not (in which case, they are proprietary software). Since some tools are much more general and it is only some libraries for them that enable their use in stemmatology (such as the packages ape, phangorn, and others for R), they may be mentioned several times as a consequence of the order chosen for the list.

The general aim of this section is to enable the reader/user to produce a tree even from only the initial input. We start with tools for collating texts, the output of which can then be processed by the genuine tree-production tools, which come in three major flavours: distance matrices, cladistic methods (parsimony), and probability-based approaches (Bayesian), as was discussed above (5.3). There are also still other ways to produce trees (see 5.3.7), for which tools are rare. In conclusion, we wish to point out that knowing a general-purpose programming language (e.g. Python, Ruby, Java) well enough to customise or implement one's own model may by many be seen as the best tool for achieving tree construction. It is, however, not the aim of this book or this section to cover programming languages and their uses. Study books and sites on these languages abound.

5.4.2 Collation

A collation is an alignment of different versions of one work (see 3.3). Manuscript text digitisation (transcription) can be conducted primarily in two ways. The first is manually, where basically any software can be used that processes text. Some scholars, however, use software, such as the Classical Text Editor (CTE), where they create a base version of the text and then reuse this as the exemplar for a new transcription, just editing the differences in order to remain in one tool, which in this case serves its purpose since CTE can lay out critical editions afterwards. The other way of transcribing is the use of manually post-corrected OCR if the source's fonts are OCR-readable – which, unfortunately, for most historical texts dating before roughly 1750 is usually not the case. There are also tools that specifically facilitate transcription by hand from images of manuscripts, such as T-Pen (t-pen.org/TPEN), Transkribus (transkribus.eu), or TextGrid (textgrid.de/en). This section attempts to cover exhaustively those tools that have been applied in stemmatological research papers. Finally, some more general, widely used tools from computer science will be listed that can be employed to support stemmatology-related tasks (as in the phylogenetic case, this is a far from exhaustive selection). Collation tools specific to stemmatology are:
- Juxta (juxtasoftware.org) is described by the website as "an open-source tool for comparing and collating multiple witnesses to a single textual work". It is a stand-alone desktop application for input data in .txt or .xml formats.
- CollateX (collatex.net) is a multipurpose stand-alone application without a graphical interface which produces alignments of texts, offering a choice of different algorithms and output formats, including graphical output as a variant graph.

5.4.2.1 Bioinformatic and computer science tools for collation
Alignment software outside of stemmatology is widely available in bioinformatics or computer science. For instance, file difference analysers and editors can be used

to produce pairwise and sometimes multiple file alignments. The Unix command-line tool "diff" and the more text-oriented "wdiff" come natively with many Unix distributions. They identify the differences between two texts. ClustalW and ClustalX (clustal.org) are widely used tools for performing multiple sequence alignments in bioinformatics. Which of the many alignment tools from computer science and bioinformatics one prefers to use may depend on the specific tradition, the presence or absence of UTF-8 characters, and the algorithm one would prefer for alignment: whether gaps should be minimised, a weighting scheme should be possible, and so forth.

5.4.2.2 Manual collation

Of course, a collation can also be produced manually. The process then involves software, typically tabulation software such as (free and open) LibreOffice Calc or (non-free) Microsoft Excel, where texts of different witnesses can be entered side by side, each in one column or row. CTE has been used for manual collation as well. For manual vs automated collation, see section 3.3.3.

5.4.3 Distance matrix generation

A common way to produce a tree is from a distance matrix of pairwise witness distances (see 5.2.2, 5.3.3). In biology, such methods are the ones most commonly used to analyse DNA sequences, and many tools offer the possibility to produce a tree from a distance matrix as input. This is why we mention the tools appropriate to this end separately and first. Distance matrix generation requires as input data a collation and produces as output a pairwise distance matrix, that is, a table with one field for each possible pair of witnesses from the collation showing a value for that pair's distance (see fig. 5.5-2 in 5.5 for an example). Distance itself can be calculated simply as the (relative) number of agreements or disagreements (Hamming distance; Hamming 1950), but many other distance metrics exist, some more sophisticated than others, for example Damereau–Levenshtein (Damerau 1964; see 5.2.3 above) or phonetics-based distances (Downey, Sun, and Norquest 2017). If distance measures operate on strings, they are also called string distance measures, a subclass of edit distances. Apart from Stemmaweb, there seems to be no specifically stemmatological tool allowing scholars to convert their collation to a distance matrix or to pseudo-DNA, which would be required to easily produce distance matrices or trees with bioinformatic software. Some of the following tools produce distance matrices during computation and save them somewhere, while the overt output may just be the tree. Most of the programs, however, also allow uploading a distance matrix from which one then can test different tree-generating algorithms operating on distance matrices. The most widely used tree algorithms are neighbour-joining, UPGMA/WPGMA, and Fitch–Margoliash (see 5.3.3.2–3, 5.3.5.1, 8.1).

5.4.4 Tree generation

5.4.4.1 Tools for the generation of a tree from raw or pre-processed data: A theoretical overview

This overview discusses briefly the types of trees one can obtain from (mainstream) tools and standard post-processing procedures. As illustrated in figure 5.4-1, a tree can be generated in a number of ways: through a distance matrix, through statistical approaches such as maximum likelihood or Bayesian inference, or through cladistic approaches such as parsimony. Minimum spanning trees (5.3.3.1) can be retrieved from a pairwise distance matrix. Further ways to obtain tree structures are stepwise clustering approaches such as hierarchical clustering.

The kind of tree or, more generally, graph one produces may be of many kinds and should not be called a stemma unless it has certain properties such as an assigned root (see also 4.1). A classical stemma a priori for closed traditions is a rooted tree (rooted DAG) in graph-theoretical terms (see 4.2). Small amounts of contamination may be dealt with while maintaining the tree as the predominant visual structure, for instance in minimum hybridisation networks (see Huson and Scornavacca 2012). The most important kinds of graphs and trees that can be produced today using stemmatological, phylogenetic, and computer science software are (*a*) unrooted bifurcating trees with extant input data units (witnesses) at leaf positions and hypothetical ancestral nodes, and (*b*) unrooted multifurcating trees with extant units at internode positions but without hypothetical nodes; see figure 5.4-2.

Semstem (Roos and Zou 2011) and the approach in Hoenen (2018b) are the only stemmatological algorithms currently known to the author that produce trees which are both multifurcating and which have extant units at the internode positions. Rooted trees of this form would (apart from contamination) correspond to stemmata in philological practice. In order to turn other tree topologies (as shown in fig. 5.4-2) into formats closer to stemmata, tools may offer automatic post-processing methods. Alternatively, one can always modify the trees manually to achieve these results (rooting, conferring nodes on internode positions, collapsing bifurcations, and so on).

Unrooted trees can be made into rooted trees by applying rooting. Apart from outgroup rooting (see 5.2.1, 8.1) and midpoint rooting – which both hardly apply to

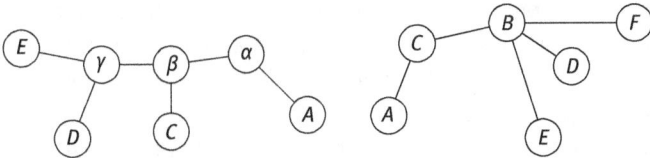

Fig. 5.4-2: Automatically producible (mainstream) tree types. (Left) unrooted bifurcating trees with extant texts (Latin letters) only at leaf positions and hypothetical nodes (Greek letters) are the output of many bioinformatic programs (although usually visually presented differently). (Right) an unrooted tree without hypothetical nodes, obtained as output of a Minimum Spanning Tree algorithm.

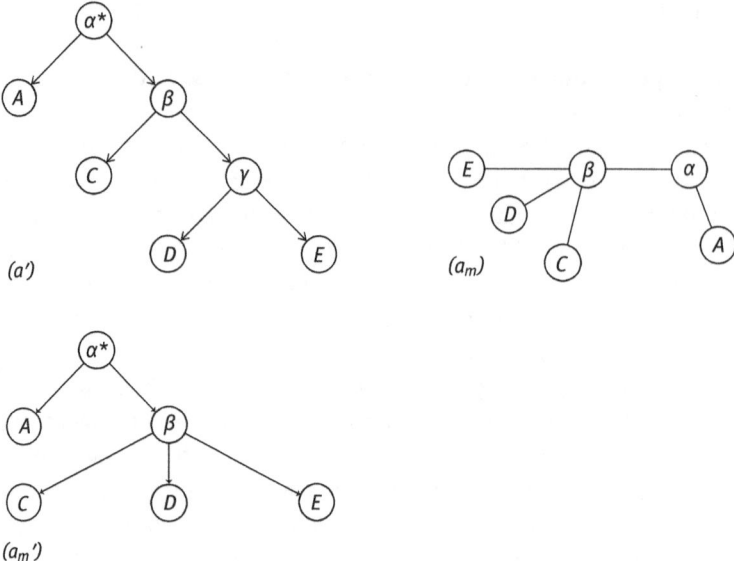

Fig. 5.4-3: Post-processed trees.

stemmatology – Marmerola et al. (2016) apply three rooting methods in the context of **multimedia phylogenies** (that is, phylogenies for digital media, mainly images and video; Marmerola et al. 2016, 2). One of these appoints any node in the unrooted tree as root, then counts the sum of sums of weights of all paths from the root to any other node, and finally chooses the minimum cost tree (MCT). Hoenen (2019) presents another method that attempts to detect directionality of changes. A statistical (and not strictly post-processing) method can transform bifurcating trees into trees that are multifurcating by collapsing splits below a certain level of reliability: bootstrapping consensus (see 5.2.4, 5.3.5.3; compare fig. 5.4-3). There are also approaches that turn minimum spanning trees into bifurcating trees with extant species at leaf positions (J. Yang et al. 2011).

In figure 5.4-3, a' represents is a bifurcating tree which has been rooted (root indicated by an asterisk; the tree is equivalent to the left-hand one in fig. 5.4-2); a_m shows a (hypothetical) bootstrap consensus tree for the same data: the method computed that the split at the y node was not significant and subsequently collapsed it. Note that, owing to the lack of unifurcations in a bifurcating tree, multifurcating trees obtained from a prior bifurcating tree will not contain unifurcations. Finally, a_m' shows a rooted multifurcating tree with extant texts only at leaf positions obtained from rooting a_m.

There is no general consensus as to which kind of method for tree generation is to be considered most appropriate. Some of them (e.g. minimum spanning trees) are very different from the others, and all may have features that are not very suitable for stemmatic analysis. For instance, a phenomenon called long-branch attraction is considered problematic for cladistic and maximum likelihood-based methods (see 5.2.4.1, 8.2.5). The literature on bioinformatic research features publications that analyse which methods imply what caveats and dangers; consider Felsenstein (2004) as a starting point for further reading.

5.4.4.2 Stemmatological tools

Stemmaweb (stemmaweb.net) is a platform that provides an online graphical interface for stemma generation. It is a suite of tools that also includes a remote service (Stemweb) offering algorithms that can be used to produce unrooted trees. The input is a collation (so the program does not collate by itself) and the output an unrooted tree. Apart from an unrooted tree as output, the user gets innovative visualisations such as a variant graph and a stemma visualisation which marks variants that go against a particular stemma (if a root has been assigned) and is useful for exploring the hypotheses implied by a certain stemma. Stemweb produces trees using the RHM (Roos and Heikkilä 2009), Semstem (Roos and Zou 2011), and neighbour-joining (Saitou and Nei 1987) algorithms. The first two of these algorithms are adapted to, and in part originated from, stemmatology. A manual for the offline installation of Stemmaweb and all dependencies is available.

Stam (cosco.hiit.fi/Projects/STAM) is another project providing an interface that can be used offline and that allows the inference of stemmata using one of the stemmatologically adapted algorithms such as RHM or Semstem. Users should be aware that both Stemmaweb (including its remote Stemweb service) and Stam are very much experimental projects and that indefinite maintenance or uninterrupted service thus cannot be guaranteed.

5.4.4.3 Phylogenetic tools

Both the stemmatological tools mentioned in section 5.4.4.2 are rather recent developments compared to phylogenetic programs. Because of the pivotal task of understanding the relationships between species, the detection of evolutionary relationships is an area of much interest in biology. It is thus unsurprising that this field has attracted much attention and research. The landscape of specifically stemmatological tools is not even close to that of phylogenetics in magnitude or specificity. Phylogenetic tools were readily available and applied to stemmatology before stemmatological ones could be developed, and the results have led to a number of publications (see 5.4.7). The tools listed below can be or have been applied to stemmatological data. It must be noted, however, that careful reflection on their internal workings and on the results they produce is necessary to establish their appropriateness for the stemmatological task at hand. Both input and output will necessarily have to be adapted in order to use these tools on text data. Computer programs are constantly subject to change (updates), new releases, and obsolescence. In the same vein, documentation, dissemination through manuals and tutorials, as well as blog posts by users experiencing and solving problems are dynamic and ephemeral. To underline this point, the first of the following tools started out as one for the computation of parsimonious trees, as the initial name "Phylogenetic Analysis Using Parsimony" (PAUP) suggests. But it has grown into an all-round tool allowing the application of various methods. Hence, a superscript asterisk has been added to its name, which signals "and other methods". The trend for tools is to incorporate more and more functionality. Keeping track of all phylogenetic software, functionality, and methods is a Sisyphean task that can only very partially be accomplished in a handbook. To mitigate this problem, we refer here also to quite extensive online resources which try to enumerate and reference all available software packages in phylogeny and which also list their characteristics. First, however, we will list the packages that have been used in stemmatology.

- PAUP* (paup.phylosolutions.com) has been the most widely applied phylogenetic program in stemmatology. It offers an easy-to-use graphical interface with many options, algorithms, and parameterisation options. It is very well documented and available on all major operating systems. It comes with a commercial license. For details, see the website. For an overview of the functionality of PAUP*, we refer to the links listed at evolution.genetics.washington.edu/phylip/software.html.
- Phylip (Felsenstein 1993; evolution.genetics.washington.edu/phylip.html). Similar to PAUP*, this is a stand-alone program with an interface that allows the user to input, for instance, a DNA alignment and to compute trees using different algorithms. The current version of Phylip is free.
- SplitsTree (Huson 1998; splitstree.org). One of the features of this program is an effective implementation of the split decomposition algorithm invented by Bandelt and Dress (1992). This algorithm produces networks instead of trees.
- MrBayes (nbisweden.github.io/MrBayes) is a suite of programs that offers a wide range of Bayesian (probabilistic) methods for producing trees.
- Phylogeny.fr (phylogeny.fr). While the above packages are stand-alone applications, this one is a collection of online tools for tree creation that incorporates some of those already mentioned, especially Phylip. It offers a wide range of input and output formats and of tree-generating algorithms. It does not require download or installation; data is processed through the phylogeny.fr servers.
- The R libraries phangorn, ape, and RPhylip. R is a general statistical programming language which is open source and available free of charge. The packages in question are provided by users to other users and offer a wide range of programming and visualisation functions in connection with bioinformatics. They can be used to compute virtually anything within phylogeny: trees from collations, roots, and so on. Many online tutorials for R are available.
- LisBeth (Bagils et al. 2012) is a program suite which allows the computation of a tree based on three-item analysis: infosyslab.fr/?q=en/resources/software/lisbeth/download.

- molbiol-tools.ca/Phylogeny.htm is an annotated list of tools from bioinformatics. Among its entries is T-Rex, a program that allows the inclusion of contamination-like structures.
- There is an extensive list of phylogenetic software currently documenting roughly 450 different sources as well as links to other lists at evolution.genetics.washington.edu/phylip/software.html.

Lastly, a word of caution about searching for tree-generating software on the Internet: the tree is a biological metaphor, and real physical trees obviously exist as well. There are programs which simulate the growth of natural trees, and these programs are naturally also "tree-generating programs" (see e.g. the list at vterrain.org/Plants/plantsw.html).

5.4.4.4 General computer science tools

Almost all major programming languages offer phylogenetics-oriented libraries (components and extensions in the same language that may come with the language but must often be installed separately). These libraries compute graphs and allow tree generation. They often include implementations of well-known tree-generating algorithms from bioinformatics or other origins. As a cursory example, a library for Java may be mentioned:
- jgraphT: a Java library including algorithms to produce trees, for instance, from pairwise distance matrices.

5.4.5 Tree visualisation

Apart from tools for generating trees, there are tools that specialise in visualising trees – for instance, visualising the non-graphical output of a phylogenetic program.
- DynStem (github.com/ArminHoenen/dynamicStemma; Hoenen 2016) describes how to dynamically generate a stemma from Newick input and mentions new visual tree formats such as circular tree maps, which depict trees as circles within circles (see fig. 5.4-4).
- FigTree (tree.bio.ed.ac.uk/software/figtree) is a phylogenetic tool mainly for visualising trees. For instance, it offers midpoint rooting of unrooted trees.
- Gephi (gephi.org) is a tool primarily used for graph visualisation, including, but not limited to trees. If one has, for instance, only a list of edges, Gephi offers many designs and patterns for rendering the implied graph and allows colouring and assigning labels. Additionally, some standard graph measures such as centrality can be automatically computed, thus providing some information about, for instance, how imbalanced texts are distributed in the stemma, whether there is one very large branch, and so on.

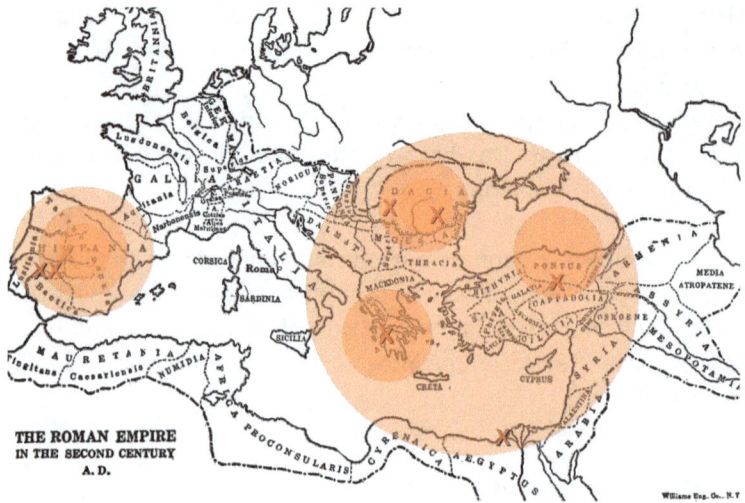

Fig. 5.4-4: A circular tree map overlaid on a geographical map. The circles stand for one witness text each, the crosses for the tentative origins of the witnesses. This is just one example of the many visualisations that can be achieved using visualisations of trees other than the usual node–edge ones. Source of geographical map: gutenberg.org/files/32624/32624-h/32624-h.html.

- Graphviz (graphviz.org), like TreeViz, provides a large number of highly customisable visualisations. Since trees are graphs, the software can be used to visualise stemmatic structures.
- igraph (igraph.org/r) is an R library with similar properties to Gephi.
- TreeDyn (treedyn.org) is stand-alone software for the post-processing of trees. One can link additional information to labels, compare different trees visually, or apply a wide range of other functions.
- TreeViz (randelshofer.ch/treeviz) is an interactive tool based on Java for the generation of visualisations of trees.

For an overview of phylogenetic tools for tree visualisation, consider Pavlopoulos et al. (2010). PhyloMap (Zhang et al. 2011) combines 2D plots with trees. Parks (2012) shows in his thesis various examples of combining trees with maps. Finally, Schulz (2011) presents a page (treevis.net) which tries to keep track of all the tree visualisation tools out there.

5.4.6 Urtext reconstruction

While at least four publications report attempts to automatically reconstruct urtexts (i.e. hypothetical archetypal texts), namely Nassourou (2013); Hoenen (2015b); Koppel, Michaely, and Tal (2016); and Hoenen (2018a), tools allowing this are currently available only in the realm of bioinformatics, mainly using Bayesian inference.

- PAML (abacus.gene.ucl.ac.uk/software/paml.html) is an open source tool allowing, among other things, the generation of ancestral sequences along given trees (or computed trees). It includes an option to input a custom-made substitution matrix.
- BEAST/BEAST2 (beast2.org). A program for Bayesian inference which also allows the generation of archetypal sequences.

A word of caution: although inferring stemma and archetype are related problems, mathematically one stemma may correspond to many archetypal texts, and one archetypal text can be consistent with different stemmata. That is, if one solves the problem of generating a stemma (automatically), one is still faced with the task of reconstructing the archetypal text. Given one and the same stemma, imagine a bifurcation with two texts. Imagine that, at position 0 of the collation, one has variant A and the other variant B, and at position 1, one has variant D and the other variant E. The reconstructed text may have any combination (AD, BE, AE, BD), or even lost variants, but the stemma remains the same. Inferring the stemma itself and reconstructing the text (deciding on significant variation and on original variants) are deeply intertwined in the classical, manual methods. For the computer, however, either task can be executed independently. Some of the tree-generating methods take into account variant configuration, for instance parsimony, others only operate on somehow variant-neutral distances. Devising a most likely archetypal text does also not necessarily determine genealogical relationships either. Koppel, Michaely, and Tal (2016) use an expectation maximisation-based approach for urtext reconstruction where no genealogical classification or stemma is involved.

5.4.7 A small empirical survey of tools used in stemmatology

Table 5.4-1 contains a non-exhaustive list of publications that have published stemmata generated by computational tools in the last few decades.

Tab. 5.4-1: A list of some publications that have published stemmata generated by computational tools in the last few decades.

Program	Publications that use it
PAUP/PAUP*	Lee (1989)
	Robinson and O'Hara (1992)
	Robinson and O'Hara (1996)
	Salemans (1996)
	Robinson (1996a)
	Salemans (2000)
	Spencer and Howe (2001)
	Spencer, Wachtel, and Howe (2002)

Tab. 5.4-1 (continued)

Program	Publications that use it
	Mooney et al. (2003)
	Spencer, Bordalejo, Robinson, et al. (2003)
	Spencer, Bordalejo, Wang, et al. (2003)
	Macé, Baret, and Lantin (2004)
	Lantin, Baret, and Macé (2004)
	Spencer, Mooney, et al. (2004)
	Spencer, Davidson, et al. (2004)
	Yorav, Dagan, and Graur (2005)
	Windram et al. (2008)
	Phillips-Rodriguez, Howe, and Windram (2009)
	Heikkilä (2014)
	Halonen (2015)
	Robinson (2015)
SplitsTree	Barbrook et al. (1998)
	Mooney et al. (2003)
	Stolz (2003)
	Spencer, Mooney, et al. (2004)
	Eagleton and Spencer (2006)
	Windram et al. (2008)
	Heikkilä (2014)
	Halonen (2015)
Phylip	Macé, Schmidt, and Weiler (2001)
	Woerther and Khonsari (2003)
	Roelli and Bachmann (2010)
	Heikkilä (2014)
	Roelli (2014)
others	Roos and Heikkilä (2009), own
	Le Pouliquen (2010), own
	Roos and Zou (2011), own
	Hoenen (2015b), PAML
	Papamichail et al. (2017), own
	Hoenen (2018a), own
	Lee (1989), MacClade

As one can see, PAUP/PAUP* has been used overwhelmingly most often. Apart from this, Phylip and SplitsTree are also commonly used, other programs only occasionally. With many other programs available, this may change in the future.

5.5 Criticisms of digital methods
Jean-Baptiste Guillaumin

Over the past few decades, digital methods of stemmatology have given birth to a new field of research at the interface between philology, biology, and computer science; a history of this approach can be found with a full bibliography in section 5.1 and in Trovato 2017 (chap. 3.2: "A Brief History of Computer-Assisted Stemmatics"). These methods, at first strictly based on bioinformatic algorithms (distance matrix-based methods, parsimony methods, maximum likelihood, and Bayesian inference), have been specifically adapted for stemmatology in some recent studies, for example with RHM or Semstem algorithms (see 5.2–3); more rarely, digital methods for stemmatology have also been developed within the field, without any reference to bioinformatics, for example by Camps and Cafiero (2014). All these approaches have also been tested on artificial traditions (Baret, Macé, and Robinson 2006; Roos and Heikkilä 2009; Roos and Zou 2011), and several software tools can now be used by philologists (see 5.4).

Generally speaking, these methods can be useful guides for philologists when representing a rich tradition, for they make it easy to visualise the clearest cases of kinship, even if they do not aim (nor claim) to produce proper stemmata taking into account all the historical features of a complex textual tradition. However, at the moment none of them is able to produce a proper stemma taking into account all the subtleties of such a tradition. Since the onset of these digital methods, philologists specialised in various fields using different linguistic corpora have highlighted some limits of these approaches, whether they have used them or not (see e.g. Hanna 2000; Cartlidge 2001; Love 2004; Bland 2005; Reeve 2011b, esp. 387–399); recently, Alexanderson (2018) radically criticised the application of phylogenetic methods to textual history. Moreover, other general studies on computer-assisted stemmatics have voiced some criticisms (see Robins 2007; Trovato 2017, chap. 4), and given rise to replies from specialists in this field (C. J. Howe, Connolly, and Windram 2012; Bordalejo 2016; Macé 2019). Some users of these methods have also taken advantage of their experience to highlight some unresolved issues (Roelli and Bachmann 2010, 329–331; Roelli 2014; Heikkilä 2014). The goal of this section is to summarise the most common of such criticisms, not in order to deny how useful the digital approach can be, but rather to assess for what issues a traditional philological approach cannot be relinquished at present. In such a topic requiring a high level of interdisciplinarity, it would be very difficult for a single person to fully understand all the approaches that have been developed and to evaluate their philological efficiency with real textual traditions: since the author of this contribution is not a computer scientist or a biologist, but a philologist who once tried a few of these methods for his own purposes, he does not claim to have a comprehensive view of all the algorithms presented above. Most of this section will therefore concern distance matrix-based methods, but when a specific kind of criticism is also valid for other methods (which is very often the case), this will be stressed.

5.5.1 Criticism of the phylogenetic paradigm and possible responses

A first type of criticism that can sometimes be found deals with the very possibility of an analogy between textual traditions and phylogenetics (Alexanderson 2018, 387–396). It is mainly based on the fact that the texts were copied by human hands which might induce changes either because of the copyist's negligence or, on the contrary, because of his clever interventions such as spontaneous corrections or search for better readings through contamination. From this point of view, the analogy with the natural evolution of species seems difficult to maintain.

Several answers to this kind of criticism are nevertheless possible. First, as has sometimes been emphasised, some ground for comparison can still be found between such interventions and the field of phylogenetics: contamination can be compared to recombination, which is also a difficult issue for phylogenetics; just like textual mistakes, some mutations in biology are reversible (see C. J. Howe, Conolly, and Windram 2012, 57–60). Caroline Macé, in her response to Bengt Alexanderson (Macé 2019), draws a parallel between "negligence" and "intention" on the one hand, and "hazard" and "necessity" on the other, following the terminology of the biologist Jacques Monod. More generally speaking, even if differences between the two fields are undeniable, drawing an analogy does not necessarily mean transposing exactly from the one to the other: using a metaphor sometimes enables a better understanding of complex issues. Besides, the notions of a stemma, a family of manuscripts, kinship between them, and so on are themselves metaphorical (see 2.2.2). It seems, then, legitimate to rely on this kind of analogy to explore a methodological convergence.

Of course, this methodological convergence does not mean that one can apply to texts, without critical thinking, the software developed to compare DNA sequences. It deals rather with a similar representation of the process of "descent with modification", as Darwin put it (as Macé 2019 recalls); it thus opens up the possibility of the same formal treatment. Intuitively speaking, the different stages of the copying process make the distance between witnesses grow: in the same way, the distance between two species appears as a result of changes through evolution, transmitted from common ancestors. According to this model (used by all the methods relying on distance matrices), the distance between two witnesses is inversely proportional to their degree of kinship. If one of the witnesses appears as very "distant" from its direct model due to the negligence or interventionism of the copyist, it will theoretically appear as more distant from other copies of the same model that were written by a meticulous copyist who conserved a text very close to the original. The intuitive notion of d i s t a n c e then leads to a mathematical problem, which is to find the tree structure able to represent in the most appropriate way the set of distances between the pairs of witnesses. This problem can be solved in a satisfactory way by the neighbour-joining algorithm (Saitou and Nei 1987, improved by Studier and Keppler 1988), as has been mathematically proved (see e.g. Mihaescu, Levy, and Pachter 2006). Thus, this approach aims less at importing some specifically phylogenetic methods into philology than at using a similar mathematical analysis in order to solve an analogous problem.

From our point of view, the analogy between phylogenetics and stemmatics is valid, but this kind of criticism encourages us to keep in mind this fundamental principle: when using these methods, the philologist must know exactly what he is doing and be able to check the different stages of the software process, which should never remain a "black box". He also needs to interpret the result, which is never exactly a stemma, as we shall see, but generally appears as an unrooted tree-like structure.

5.5.2 A brief invented example as an illustration

At this point, rather than examining abstract variant readings ("a", "b", "c", "d", and so on), we invent a very simple and brief artificial tradition in order to illustrate the different issues: all the witnesses quoted below will thus be fictitious, although their text may remind the reader of an allegorical *ekphrasis* by Martianus Capella (*De nuptiis Philologiae et Mercurii* 1.11), whose symbolism (trees, numbers, and harmony) is not inappropriate in the present context. Of course, the aim of this discussion is not to test the validity of the processes, which would require more extensive traditions; as Roelli and Bachmann (2010, 314) say, "the longer the excerpted text, the more reliable the result is going to be" (indeed, artificial text traditions already used for this purpose deal with hundreds or thousands of words; see the references in the introduction to 5.5). Our purpose is only to show practically how they work in order to comment on the graphs that are produced. As has been said above, most of the practical treatments will use distance-based methods. The constraints on section length pre-empt testing our artificial tradition with all the other existing methods. Of course, it would be a good exercise for the reader to undertake this kind of experimentation in order to obtain another illustration of the criticisms that have been developed.

Let us, then, consider nine (or ten) words in ten witnesses whose relationships are all assumed to be known (any resemblance to existing manuscripts being purely coincidental):

- A (ninth century): "Eminentiora prolixarum arborum culmina perindeque distenta acuto sonitu resultabant."
- B (eleventh century, copied from A): "Eminentiora prolixarum abietum cacumina perindeque distantia acuto sonitu resultabant."
- C (tenth century, copied from A): "Altiora prolixarum arborum culmina perindeque distenta acuto sonitu resonabant."
- D (eleventh century, copied from C): "Altiora promissarum arborum culmina perindeque distenta acutissimo sonitu resonabant."

- *E* (twelfth century, copied from *C*): "Altiora prolixarum arborum culmina perindeque distenta acuto sono resonabant."
- *F* (thirteenth century, copied from *C*): "Altiora prolixarum arborum fulmina perindeque et distenta acuto tinnitu resonabant."
- *G* (fourteenth century, copied from *E*): "Altiora arborum culmina perindeque discreta acuto sono resonabant."
- *H* (fifteenth century, copied from *E*): "Altiora prolixarum arborum culmina proptereaque distenta acuto sono resonabant."
- *I* (twelfth century, contaminated from *B* and *D*): "Eminentiora promissarum abietum culmina perindeque distenta acutissimo sonitu resultabant."
- *J* (twelfth century, copied from *B*): "Eminentiora prolixarum abietum cacumina per insignem distantiam acuto sonitu resultabant."

Of course, the rate and the nature of the modifications in this brief text are particularly improbable in the real world, in which there are few cases of substantive textual innovation; improbable is also the fact that all witnesses are extant. However, this simplistic example allows a practical description of some methods, and some modifications to it (e.g. the suppression of some witnesses) will be tested below. According to the list above, the correct stemma is the one in figure 5.5-1.

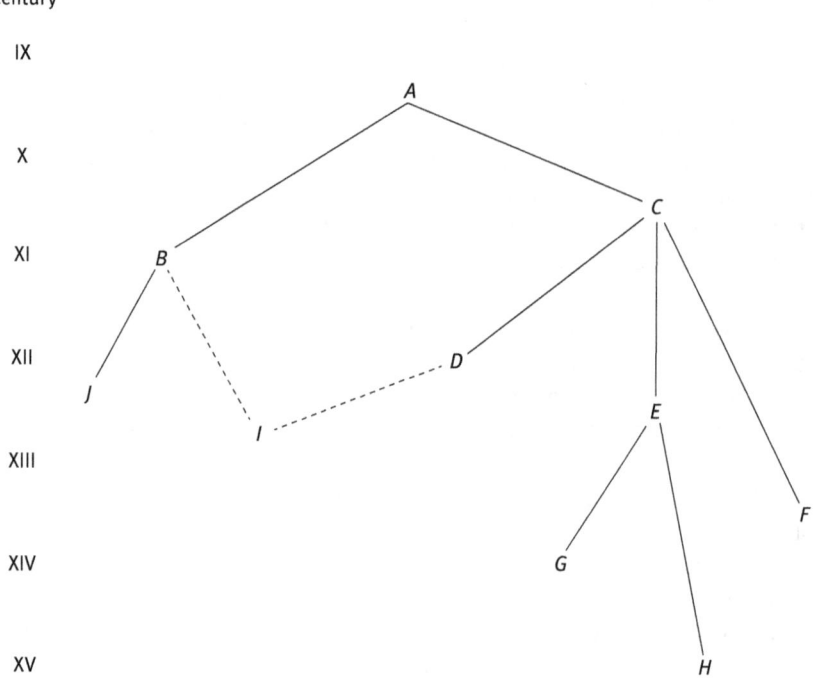

Fig. 5.5-1: Correct stemma for the artificial tradition.

5.5.3 How to calculate distances

Among all the digital methods, the most common ones are based on the calculation of a distance matrix, that is, a table which contains all the distances between each pair of items under consideration. It is then necessary to define as precisely as possible what is meant when one speaks about "distance" between two texts (see esp. Spencer and Howe 2001). Intuitively, it is possible to define distance as the number of modifications necessary to arrive from one to the other. But the proper counting of this distance can take various forms. Roughly speaking, a distance between two texts can be established by counting the number of characters or words that differ (an omission or addition being counted as one difference). With the example above, this method would yield the first matrix in figure 5.5-2 for a count based on the number of words differing between two texts, and the second matrix for a count based on the number of different characters (of course, since the distance calculation is commutative, each of these matrices is symmetrical and could be presented in a simpler way).

	A	B	C	D	E	F	G	H	I	J
A	0	3	2	4	3	5	5	4	3	5
B	3	0	5	7	6	7	7	7	4	3
C	2	5	0	2	1	3	3	2	5	6
D	4	7	2	0	3	5	4	4	3	8
E	3	6	1	3	0	3	2	1	6	7
F	5	7	3	5	3	0	5	4	8	8
G	5	7	3	4	2	5	0	3	7	7
H	4	7	2	4	1	4	3	0	7	6
I	3	4	5	3	6	8	7	7	0	6
J	5	3	6	8	7	8	7	6	0	0

	A	B	C	D	E	F	G	H	I	J
A	0	9	9	17	12	15	25	19	12	16
B	9	0	18	26	21	24	32	28	13	7
C	9	18	0	8	3	6	16	10	21	25
D	17	26	8	0	11	14	22	18	13	33
E	12	21	3	11	0	9	13	7	24	28
F	15	24	6	14	9	0	22	16	27	31
G	25	32	16	22	13	22	0	20	34	39
H	19	28	10	18	7	16	20	0	31	33
I	12	13	21	13	24	27	34	31	0	20
J	16	7	25	33	28	31	39	33	20	0

Fig. 5.5-2: Distance matrices for the example, based on different words (left) and characters (right).

Although there are some efficient algorithms for calculating this kind of edit distance (e.g. Levenshtein's algorithm or Unix's "diff"), both word- and character-based approaches present some theoretical inconveniences. In particular, one can intuitively see that not all the substitutions should have the same weight: graphical modifications (e.g. "i" instead of "y", "accidere" instead of "adcidere", and so on), or even substitutions of similar words (like "experimentum" instead of "experientia", to take an example quoted by Trovato 2017, 194), should not get a score as great as the substitution of a completely different word ("exemplum" instead of "experimentum"; on substantive and accidental variation, see 4.1.5). A count based on characters often allows us to introduce variation between these different cases, but only in an approximate and somewhat unpredictable manner ("experimentum"/"exemplum" would be counted as 6, "experimentum"/"periculum" as 6, and "experimentum"/"periclitatio" as 9). And what about mistakes caused by erroneous word breaks (like "experimentum"/"experti mentium"), which will be measured very differently depending on whether one chooses a word-based distance or a character-based one? Moreover, and more problematically, this kind of mechanical measure does not allow us to take into account the possible syntactic or semantic reasons for a replacement (modification affecting several consecutive words, replacement of a word with a synonym, or another kind of polygenetic modification).

Despite all these theoretical reproaches, which are legitimate, the naive measurement of character-based distance is often enough to give a good idea of the kinship between witnesses. For our illustrative purposes, we will simply use here the raw character-based distance matrix calculated above. With the neighbour-joining algorithm, for example, we get the following graph description (to make the presentation clearer, numbers are rounded, if necessary, to three decimal places):

(((((A:0.917,((B:0.125,J:6.875):6.143,I:6.857):3.083):7.05,D:5.95):1.708, (C:0,F:6):0.292):2.578,G:12.609):0.39,E:0.016,H:6.984).

This translates to the graphical representation in figure 5.5-3.

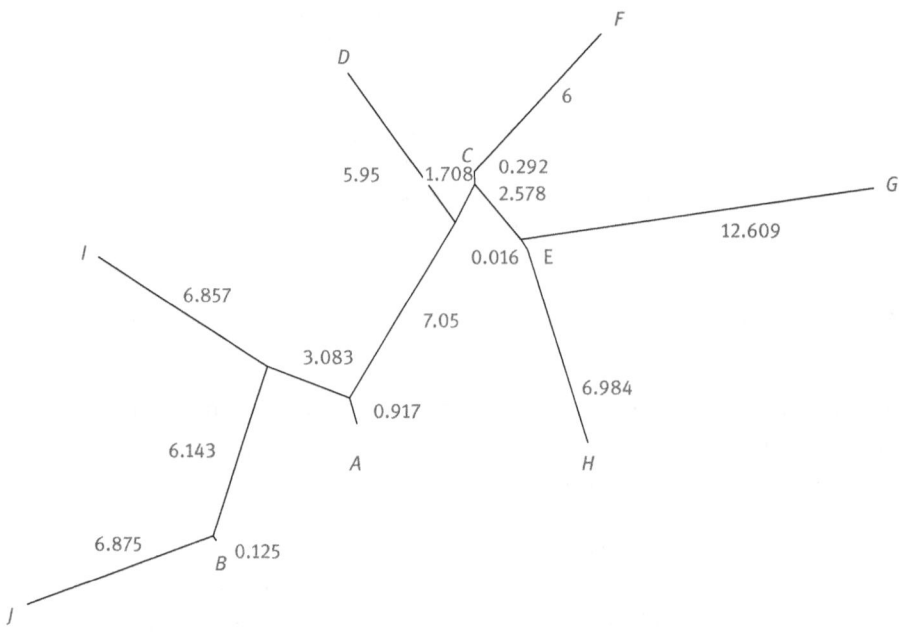

Fig. 5.5-3: Neighbour-joining graph from the distance matrix. The neighbour-joining calculation was done with purpose-made software written in Ocaml (which takes transcription text files as input, establishes a Levenshtein distance between them, and applies neighbour-joining); the graph was drawn with the "drawgram" software (part of Phylip package), and adapted for this paper; numbers were added manually to explain the link with the graph description above.

5.5.4 Noise and weighting of the readings

A comparison of figure 5.5-3 with the "real" stemma in figure 5.5-1 shows the general validity of this process, even using such a naive calculation of distances. However, beyond the points of criticism mentioned already, a fundamental question remains: is it legitimate to take all the variant readings into account without any hierarchy? This question is linked to the discussion of *Leitfehler* in (neo-)Lachmannian theory (see 2.2.5). Indeed, when one measures syntactic modifications or banal variant readings (which can be polygenetic) in the same way as mistakes introduced by a copyist at a precise moment in the transmission, "noise" risks interfering with the result, rendering the clustering less clear and less efficient.

In order to correct this problem, Roelli and Bachmann (2010, 317–318), after having chosen a word-based distance, propose an automated method to decrease the score of syntactic variants (with a parameter p between 0 and 1 applied on k consecutive edits) and weight the significant mistakes (i.e. the *Leitfehler*) by testing, for every pair of readings A and B, the distribution over the entire corpus between *(A, B)*, *(A, not B)*, *(not A, B)*, and *(not A, not B)* and picking out the variants for which one of these four categories does not occur: once found, these variants are weighted with a coefficient (see 5.3.7.2). In our artificial tradition, this would be the case, for example, for *("eminentiora", "arborum")* or *("culmina", "resultabant")*, but not for *("eminentiora", "prolixarum")* due to the contamination of *I* rather than polygenesis. Roelli (2014) proposed improvements on this method. The idea is to use several stages to improve the appearance of the tree: although the first is automated, the following ones require from the philologist the choice of hand-picked "good *Leitfehler*". The result seems very accurate, but one could object that this method requires a philological a priori intervention which aims not to interpret the result but rather to influence the process. Moreover, one could argue that the recurrence of banal variants may also give an idea of some kinship relations if they occur frequently at the same place in several manuscripts: if they do not, they make noise increase, apparently without a pernicious effect on the general structure. Although this point of view differs from the Lachmannian theory, taking into account all the variants, even the most trivial ones, may be justifiable; see Spencer, Davidson, et al. (2004), and Andrews and Macé (2013, 518): "even the most trivial changes, taken in aggregate, have some text-genealogical significance that should not be discounted". But, generally speaking, the discussion about weighting variants for a more accurate result remains open, as it is in the various methods used in phylogenetics.

5.5.5 Orientation and rooting of the tree

One of the recurrent points of criticism is based on the impossibility of rooting and orienting the tree with most of the digital methods. Indeed, the UPGMA method,

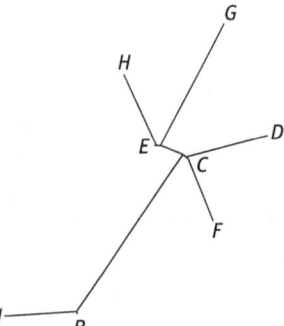

Fig. 5.5-4: The same plot without the archetype *A* and the contaminated manuscript *J*.

which produces a rooted and directed tree structure (see 5.3.3), is valid only for a constant evolutionary speed (the molecular clock in biology), but this case almost never occurs in stemmatics. As far as I know, other digital methods give neither a root nor an orientation, but an unrooted graph which the philologist has to interpret with his own methods (in particular, his knowledge of the historical background of each witness) to find the place of the root, that is, of the archetype.

One can say, using an image, that the result received from most of the digital methods looks like an articulated puppet which the philologist is to animate: an algorithm is thus successful if it gives the correct structure of this puppet (i.e. the place of the articulations for the different limbs), no matter how the philologist then decides to make it walk. Nevertheless, this limitation is not a really problematic issue; it is even useful, since the philologist himself keeps the responsibility of introducing into the graph the historical dimension of the studied textual tradition. In our example (fig. 5.5-3), the philologist should posit the archetype at A (or close by) because of the distribution of the variants considered as the best from a philological point of view (e.g. "eminentiora", "arborum", "resultabant") and because of its date. If A is unavailable (as is almost always the case for an archetype), and if we do not take into account the manuscript I because of the suspected contamination (which can change the topology of the tree; see 5.5.8), an analysis of the following graph, completed with a study of the distribution of variants, should correctly put the archetype somewhere on the segment between B and C (fig. 5.5-4).

In biology, one can root a graph produced with a phylogenetic method by introducing artificially into the calculation a remote species known to belong outside the studied group (outgroup rooting; see 5.2.1). In philology, this is practically impossible insofar as, by definition, the entire available tradition has to be taken into account in the stemma (the only comparable case would theoretically be an ancient rewriting, interpolation, or translation prior to the archetype, but this kind of example is uncommon and difficult to harmonise with the distance calculation; for an example, see 4.5.2). In the future, additional methods might be developed to "polarise" variant readings, for example by determining, for each of them, whether it is likely to be derived from another; for this purpose, a "categorisation system" could be useful (see Andrews and Macé 2013).

5.5.6 Prevalence of bifurcating trees

Another point of criticism, linked to a traditional discussion in stemmatics (see 5.1.2.1), deals with the prevalence of the bifurcating structure (i.e. structures in which each interior node has exactly three neighbours). Indeed, most of the methods presented above lead to bifurcating trees. This can sometimes be used on purpose in order to simplify the model: for example, Roos and Heikkilä (2009, 432), write that "for simplicity, and following the common practice in phylogenetics where it is perhaps better justified, we restrict the stemma to a bifurcating tree" (in their presentation of the RHM method). In other cases, this characteristic is the result of the algorithm used: thus, neighbour-joining most of the time produces a bifurcating tree because it groups taxa in pairs at each iteration – still, a multifurcating structure is theoretically not strictly impossible, since the calculation of distance between a group and a node can take a zero value: for example, with a tradition "a a a a" (*A*), "a b b b" (*B*), "a b c c" (*C*), "a b d d" (*D*), and the distance system $AB = 3$, $AC = 3$, $AD = 3$, $BC = 2$, $BD = 2$, $CD = 2$, one would get the tree ((*A*:2,*B*:1):0,*C*:1,*D*:1), corresponding to a trifurcation (fig. 5.5-5).

More precisely, it happens frequently that a distance between two nodes in a neighbour-joining tree appears very short: in this case, when interpreting the graph, the philologist can decide to remove this distance and to take only a single node into consideration instead of both. In the following graph (fig. 5.5-6), for example, the witnesses *C* and *E* have been removed from our sample to get a simpler structure without internal nodes (on this question, see 5.5.7) and to verify that the configuration is not fundamentally modified by such an absence (as a response to the possible objection about the unlikelihood of such a complete tradition; see 5.5.2). One could thus legitimately decide to link *D* and *F* to a unique common node; in this

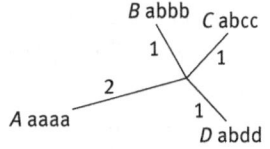

Fig. 5.5-5: A simple example of a trifurcation with neighbour-joining.

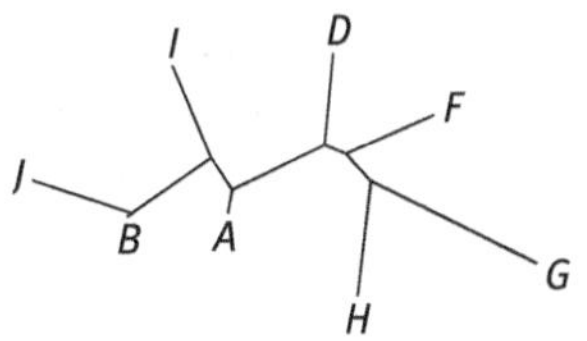

Fig. 5.5-6: The above example without the inner nodes *C* and *E*.

case, there would be a trifurcation from this common node (to *D*, *F*, and the common ancestor of *H* and *G*, namely *E*, not taken into account here).

Trifurcation is then an available option when two nodes appear very close to each other, but, as we have already pointed out previously for rooting, only the philologist has the competence to validate this kind of simplification.

5.5.7 Witnesses as internal nodes

Among the points of criticism dealing with the theoretical structure of the tree and the differences between phylogenetics and stemmatology, one can also mention the possibility that a witness appears as an internal node if it is proved to be the ancestor of one or several other(s) which are located as leaves on the tree. Indeed, this is even quite a frequent case, and it is fundamental to depict it in a stemma because it is the basis for the *eliminatio codicum descriptorum* (see 2.2.5). In phylogenetics, on the contrary, this case should not happen: the examined species are contemporaneous, and the internal nodes represent missing common ancestors. Most of the phylogenetic algorithms therefore do not offer the possibility of having a taxon as an internal node, except through manual intervention. With the distance matrix-based algorithms, it is very unusual (but not absolutely impossible, especially for a small set of data) to obtain internal nodes corresponding to witnesses still available: in the tree above (5.5.3), such a case can be observed with *C*, which is put at a zero distance from its common node with *F*. In the same tree, several internal distances are also close to zero – a far more common situation which would intuitively lead the philologist to assume a common node (observe the places of *E*, *C*, *B*). Even for a somewhat greater distance, for example between *C* and the origin of the branch of *D*, the philologist should assume a unique junction on *C* and seek to verify it with traditional methods (e.g. by picking out some *Leitfehler* and analysing their distribution): the distortion is here linked to the effects of contamination, as we shall see (5.5.8). Still in the tree above, the same hypothesis should be assumed for *A* as well.

But the fact remains that the standard bifurcating structure and the unlikelihood of getting witnesses exactly on internal nodes appear as obvious limitations for the distance-based methods, and more generally for all the bioinformatic methods, since they are a requirement of phylogenetics. This objection has been taken into account in some recent new methods specifically made for stemmatology, such as Semstem (Roos and Zou 2011). Indeed, this approach is based on the structural expectation maximisation (EM) algorithm used for phylogenetic trees (Friedman 1997; Friedman et al. 2002), but, whereas the algorithm, in phylogenetics, enables the detection and removal of non-bifurcating structures or observed interior nodes, its stemmatological use aims to confirm such features, which are quite frequent in textual criticism.

5.5.8 "Ist gegen Kontamination immer noch kein Kraut gewachsen?"

In the traditional conception of stemmatology, contamination is a serious difficulty. According to the famous adage of Paul Maas: "Gegen die Kontamination ist kein Kraut gewachsen" (1957, 31) [No specific has yet been discovered against contamination] (trans. Flower 1958, 49; on this point, see 2.2.7). This difficulty occurs also in the digital methods: for example, the tree-like approach does not allow the detection of conflation, that is, the use of two (or possibly more) ancestors in copying a unique new text. More problematically, whatever method is used, taking into account a contaminated text produces a distorting effect on the entire tree topology. Indeed, if we consider again the distance-based methods, we can see intuitively that a contaminated exemplar has quite a reduced distance from both its ancestors, even if these ancestors are distant from each other and close to other witnesses of their own families; due to the complex metric of the distance set, this distortion is even likely to produce a kind of artificial attraction between these ancestors. This is the case for I in the example above: since it takes more elements from B than from D, neighbour-joining introduces a common node between I and B; but, since I is more closely related to D (13) than to its ancestor C (21), D's branching is displaced, as can be shown with a comparison between the two graphs in figure 5.5-7 (without I in the first, with I in the second).

In the case of heavily contaminated traditions, such an approach produces a massive attraction towards a point near the graph's centre, which is absolutely not the place of the archetype (one should always keep in mind that neighbour-joining produces an unrooted tree). For example, in figure 5.5-8, a graph is plotted for a relatively brief passage (9.906–908; 245 words, containing both prose and verse) in the first hand of some manuscripts of Martianus Capella (Guillaumin 2008, 246–255), using a naive distance computation based on characters (see 5.5.3) and neighbour-joining with a dedicated piece of software (the branches of H and C have been shortened here for presentation purposes).

As one can see, there is a kind of convergence towards a point that appears as a sort of centre of gravity of contaminated witnesses; but, according to philological criteria, the place of the archetype should instead be close to the ancestor node of A, H, R, B, D. Very little can be said about the kinship of the branchings near the centre.

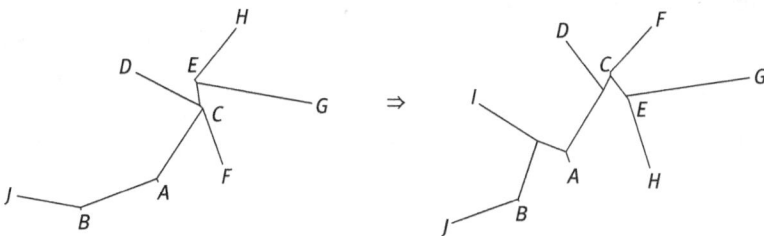

Fig. 5.5-7: The effect of the contaminated manuscript I on the entire tree.

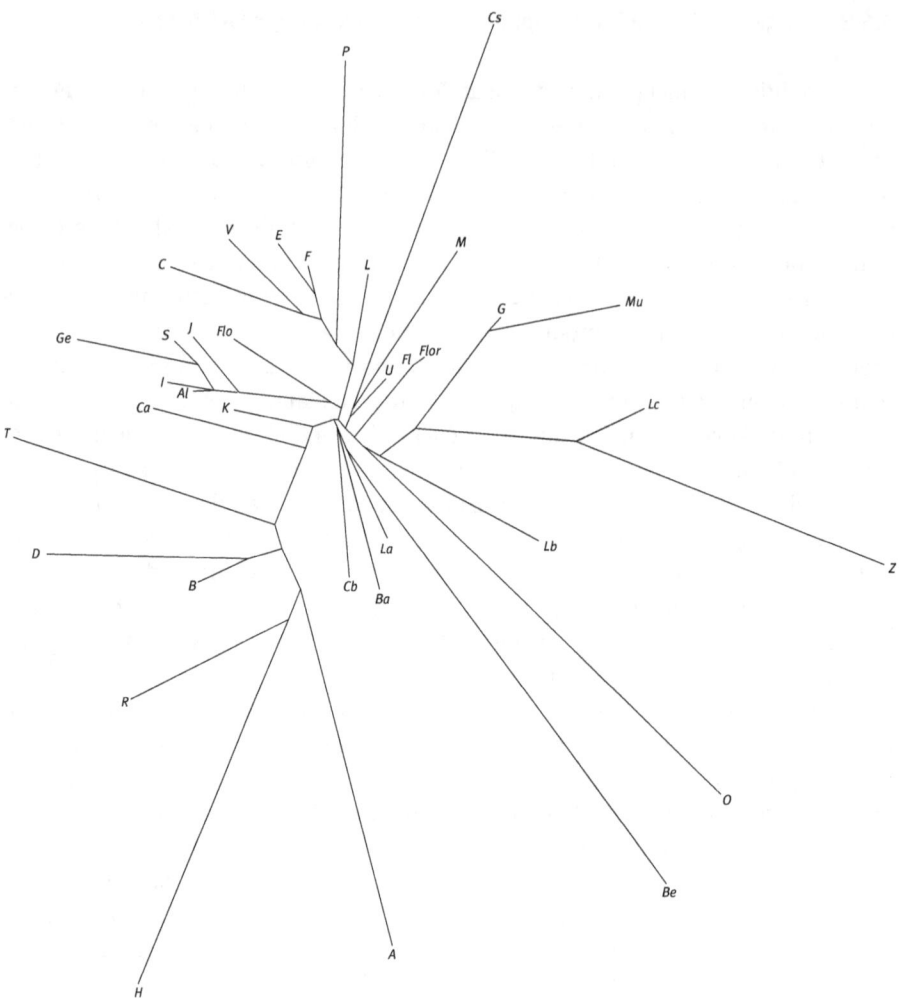

Fig. 5.5-8: Effect of contamination on a plot for Martianus Capella. The branches leading to H and C have been shortened.

For the shape of the stemma proposed for the *De nuptiis Philologiae et Mercurii* (quite unusual and probably questionable in some points), see figure 4.1-4 above.

However, there are some methods for detecting contamination: it is of course possible to test the manuscripts at different passages and look at the variations. If the copyist used sometimes one model, sometimes another, the tree topology will change from one passage to the other. Two objections are nevertheless possible: first, the delimitation of the tested sections is necessarily random, and generally unlikely to coincide with the model switch; on this point, see C. J. Howe, Connolly, and Windram (2012, 58), quoting Cartlidge (2001, 145). This method can be useful, *a contrario*, to prove the lack of contamination if the structure always remains the

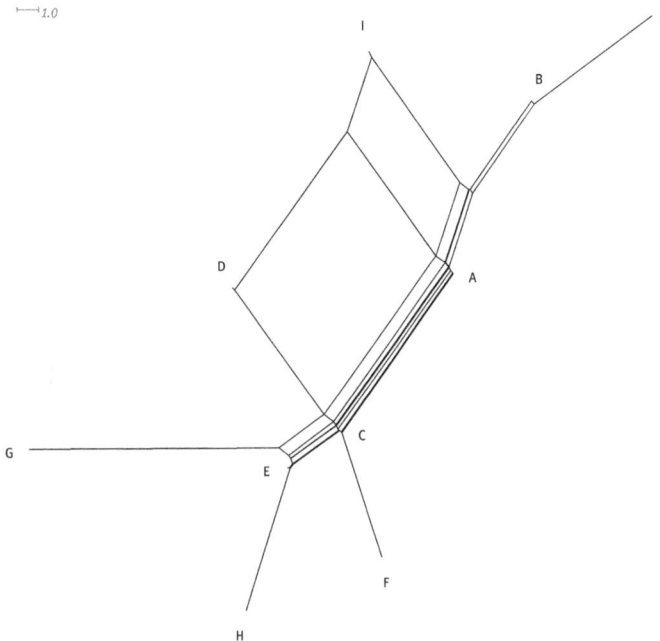

Fig. 5.5-9: Network graph edited with SplitsTree4 software, using the distance matrix presented in section 5.5.3 above.

same, no matter how many random tests are done. Second, and more fundamentally, contamination does not necessarily consist of a localisable model-switching: a copyist may have worked with two (or more) exemplars at the same time (this is the case for our artificial witness *I*). So, another solution is to use a network approach instead of a merely linear tree structure. It is possible to do this with the Neighbor-Net algorithm (D. Bryant and Moulton 2004), which has been tested in the field of stemmatology by Spencer, Davidson, et al. (2004). This algorithm takes a distance matrix as input and resorts to the same principle as neighbour-joining, but constructs a network rather than a tree, by agglomerating pairs of pairs which share one node in common. Topological irregularities thus appear like boxes, and, even if the interpretation of the graph tends to be more complex, it is then possible to detect phenomena such as contamination. In our previous example, the relation between *I* and *D* (due to contamination), complementary to the already detected proximity of *I* to *B* (quantitatively used a bit more than *D* by the imaginary copyist), can be shown as in figure 5.5-9.

However, in a strongly contaminated tradition, reading such a graph is not easy and may in the end not be very useful, except to encourage caution with regard to the interpretation of the relationships around the centre of the graph. For example, figure 5.5-10 displays the graph for the passage of Martianus mentioned above (based on the same distance matrix).

352 — Jean-Baptiste Guillaumin

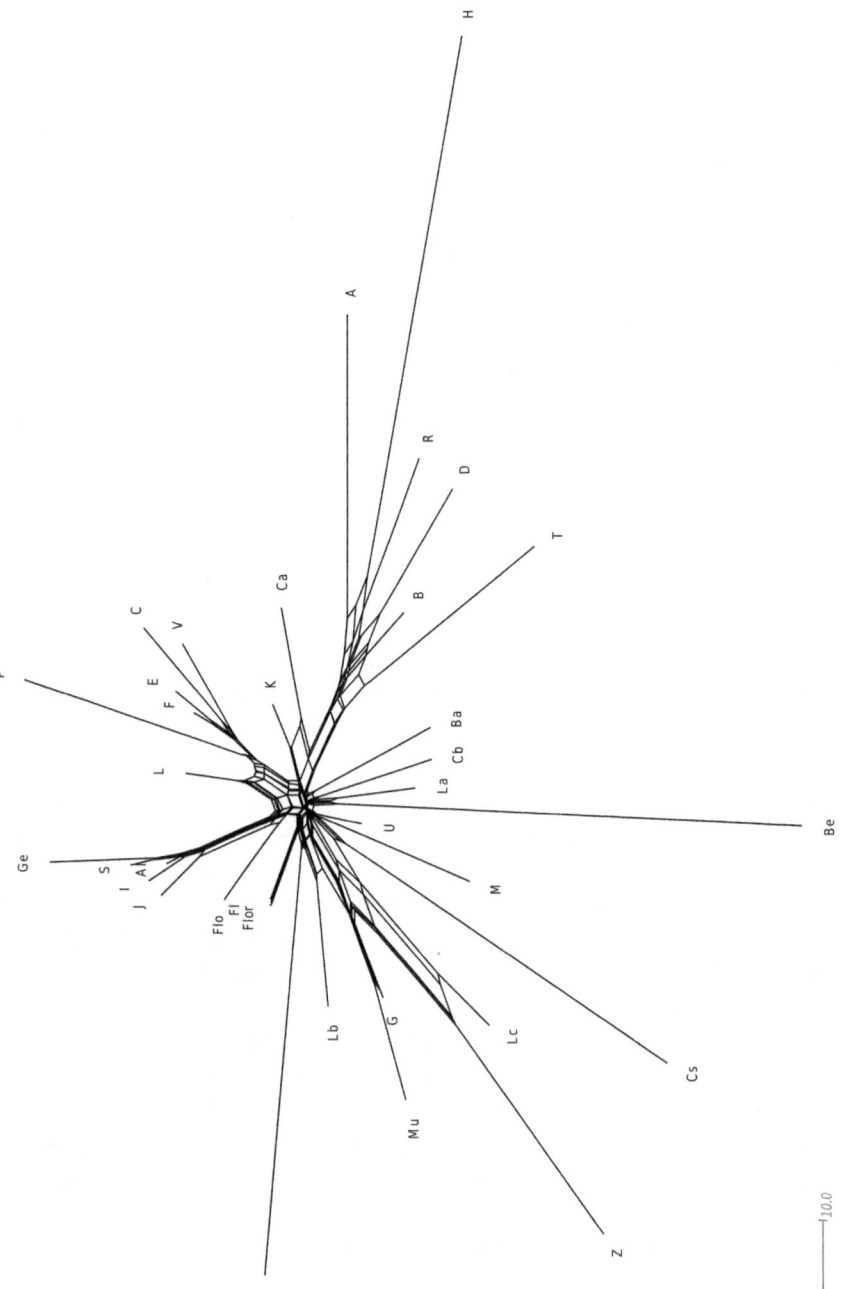

Fig. 5.5-10: Network graph for the passage from Martianus. The branch leading to H has been shortened.

5.5.9 Graphical habits, material issues and historical evolution of the manuscripts

Until now, we have considered manuscripts as if they were mere texts: this point of view is necessary for every automated approach, but it is of course simplistic, and the philologist who uses a digital method should always keep in mind that a manuscript is a material object liable to change over time.

This point concerns, for example, graphical habits, details of page layout, or even punctuation marks, all of which are likely to change over time and in different milieus: although these elements sometimes provide information that can be useful for a stemmatic approach (if they recur in the same places in several manuscripts), it seems difficult to include them in the available digital methods, for they are not real variant readings and can occur independently during the copying of a text. With the distance-based methods, it seems possible to encode this kind of detail by counting a small distance (e.g. if a manuscript has a capital letter and another a lower-case one, if one has a punctuation mark and another nothing, or if one has an abbreviation and another the full form). But the value of that distance should remain a lot smaller than that corresponding to a real variant reading, and the risk is that the noise will increase (on this point, see the discussion in 5.5.4). In most cases, due to the necessarily weak effect of these details, such a refinement would probably not change the result greatly.

However, an evolution of the material appearance of a manuscript is possible: some folios may have been damaged or even lost, and some terms may become unreadable when the parchment is worn out or scraped. In such cases, it is necessary to find a way to encode "missing data" which was not previously taken into account in the calculation, as is indeed possible with many kinds of bioinformatic software, whatever method is used. From a theoretical point of view, a first solution is to leave the *locus* out of the calculation for each manuscript, but this implies losing some information about the text of the readable manuscripts for the passage in question, which can be problematic if it contains an important variant reading. Another solution, with the distance-based methods, would be to consider that an unreadable word, unlike an omission, adds no distance, or a very small one, compared with all the readings found at the same place in other manuscripts, even if they are themselves different from one another (but this approach is also problematic if massively used, because it may contradict the "triangular inequality" that a metric by definition requires).

Moreover, the text itself will sometimes have evolved over the centuries: for example, it may have been corrected or completed with interlinear variants or glosses. Different copies of the same witness can thus be quite different depending on their dates. It is clear that this kind of textual history hardly conforms to a tree-like representation because of the cyclic graphs necessary to describe it (see Andrews and Macé 2013, 509–511). Furthermore, when a witness carries some corrections or variants, its offspring are necessarily characterised by a form of contamination that is very difficult to model, even with a traditional stemmatic approach, since this kind of paratext often has a tradition of its own: in this case, the very possibility of drawing a stemma can become doubtful. Such copying phenomena occur, for example, in the above-mentioned manuscript tradition of Martianus Capella, so that the neighbour-joining graph discussed above (5.5.8), based only on the text of the first hand, does not show all the complexity of this contaminated circulation: to do that, one could try to introduce as an independent witness the second hand (or even the third, fourth, and so on, where it is possible to distinguish them), but the multiplication of such contaminated texts would make the graph less readable. Moreover, when a manuscript has interlinear corrections or variants, it is hard to treat it as a linear text as if there were a unique way of reading and copying it: as in the case of contamination (see 5.5.8), phylogenetic methods do not work very well for this purpose. In such a case, one could try to introduce an artificial (and quite monstrous) witness containing a concatenation of all the parallel variants in order to treat it in a linear way.

In our artificial tradition, let us assume that B was corrected and glossed this way in the twelfth century:

> Eminentiora ^{altiora} prolixarum ^{altarum} abietum ^{sappinorum} cacumina $^{uel\ culmina\ uel\ uertices}$ perindeque dista ^{e}ntia acuto ^{claro} sonitu $^{sono\ uel\ tono}$ resultabant.

Let us also assume that it was copied in the thirteenth century into a new manuscript, K, as:

> Eminentiora altarum sappinorum culmina perindeque distenta claro sonitu et tono resultabant.

A raw neighbour-joining calculation taking into account only the first hand of B would produce the following graph (fig. 5.5-11).

Due to contamination, K appears near the centre. If we take into account the variants and corrections added in B, with a concatenation of all of them, and then use a NeighborNet treatment, we obtain figure 5.5-12.

The graph is not easy to read, and would probably become unreadable if one added other witnesses with such a complex history. This kind of treatment of complex and non-tree-like traditions is only a stopgap solution and should be replaced, in this case, by more complex descriptions such as those presented by Andrews and Macé (2013). In short, material and evolutionary aspects of the manuscripts constitute the most important difference from the phylogenetic model and probably the most difficult challenge in digital stemmatology.

5.5 Criticisms of digital methods — 355

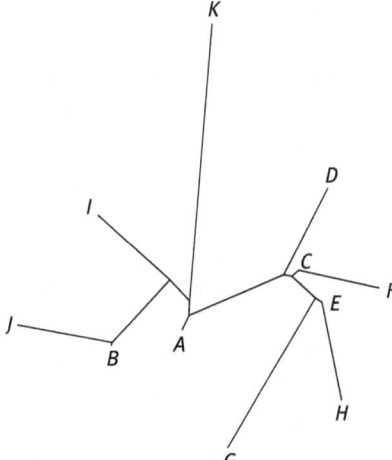

Fig. 5.5-11: Adding a new contaminated witness K to the above example.

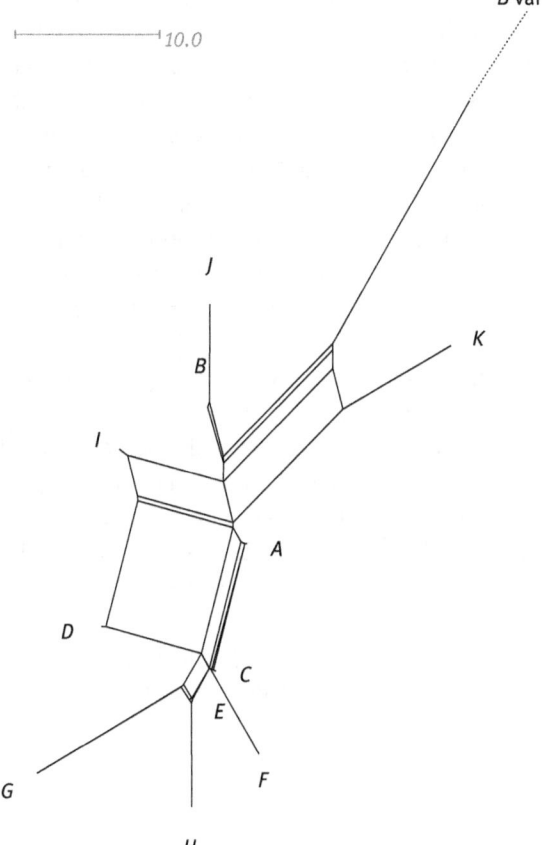

Fig. 5.5-12: NeighborNet graph for tradition with contaminated witness K. Plotted with SplitsTree4, with the branch length of *Bvar* reduced for presentation purposes.

5.5.10 Conclusion: For careful use guided by the philologist

To sum up this synthetic presentation of the different kinds of criticism that have sometimes been levelled against digital approaches in stemmatology, it is clear that algorithms in use for some twenty years have produced encouraging results, especially in allowing us to visualise quickly the most certain kinships in large textual traditions for which a traditional stemmatic approach would be much more tedious. However, intervention by the philologist still remains absolutely necessary to interpret the graphs produced by these methods: as has been said above, it would be absurd to consider them as stemmata. Indeed, the historical dimension of every textual tradition needs to be taken into account during the interpretation of the different graphs, even those obtained with methods specifically developed for stemmatology (such as RHM or Semstem). For every method, it thus remains necessary to apply a posteriori some transformations, especially concerning rooting, the polarisation of variants, or the detection of different forms of contamination.

Moreover, in order to become an efficient tool for philologists, digital stemmatology should allow philologists to work easily on raw data (e.g. semi-diplomatic transcriptions) without having to carry out long and tedious preparation (e.g. alignment tables). From this point of view, much has already be done on stemmaweb.net/stemmaweb, which provides the opportunity to try out several different tools. Finally, one could also expect the development of interaction between stemmatological software and digital editions: if all the variants of each witness of a tradition are encoded in a standard way (e.g. in TEI XML), it should be possible to adapt the available kinds of stemmatological software in order to make them work directly with this kind of base data. On the other hand, considering the improvements in character recognition (OCR), it could be exciting to envisage, in the medium term, a coupling of automatic transcription and stemmatic software in order to treat a larger amount of data.

As we have seen, digital stemmatology is still a very young discipline. Its main methods have been developed over the past twenty years. Despite its short history, and also despite the limitations presented above, this discipline should be regarded as a viable scientific auxiliary for textual criticism that embraces an interdisciplinary approach. In such cases, computer scientists, bioinformatic researchers, or digital humanities scholars and philologists should closely cooperate to ensure the validity and adequacy of their approaches. Obviously, such collaborative work should advance with respect for the expertise involved on all sides. And ultimately, as the domain experts, philologists need to decide on the historical plausibility and validity of the results. As careful interdisciplinary work, digital stemmatology in this way can contribute to the always necessary renewal of philology.

6 Editions

Introductory remarks by the chapter editor, Aidan Conti

Most readers and scholars encounter stemmatological practices when using an edition. While the detailed questions taken up in dedicated stemmatological studies and examinations occupy specialists, practically speaking stemmatology is employed in the service of producing a critical edition. The edition, however, is not a single, monolithic entity but a product that can be representative of a number of academic traditions and scholarly practices. Indeed, many editions are produced without using the stemmatological method. Consequently, it is not surprising that there is no shortage of books and essays that endeavour to set down how a text should be edited and what tools should be used. Recent handbooks espousing the genealogical tradition include Richard Tarrant's *Texts, Editors, and Readers* (2016) and Paolo Trovato's *Everything You Always Wanted to Know about Lachmann's Method* (2017). Ralph Hanna's *Editing Medieval Texts* (2015), on the other hand, espouses the principle of selecting a single manuscript while comparing known witnesses for variants (see Göransson 2018 for an account). While individual experience and academic orientation will necessarily shape and be apparent in individual contributions within this chapter, overall the chapter ventures to provide a practical survey of types of editions and editing tools, with a specific emphasis on the process of establishing a critical text through the common-errors method.

Given the variety of methods used to produce an edition, this chapter begins with Odd Einar Haugen's systematic description of various editorial practices (6.1), those that have tentatively employed stemmatology and those that have different theoretical bases for the presentation of edited text. Haugen usefully distinguishes reconstructive editing, which aims to present a hypothetical original or archetypal text, and non-reconstructive editing, which uses an extant witness as the basis for an edition. In the case of most editions, we see a link between the methodology used to establish the edited text and the presentation of the edited text. However, as Haugen shows, in some cases an editor may provide and argue for a stemma, but not use the stemma to present a reconstructed text.

In the subsequent section (6.2), Marina Buzzoni addresses the specific case in which the stemma is used to produce a critical text with the genealogical or common-errors method. The principles of the method and criticisms of it have been presented in earlier sections (see e.g. 2.2, 2.3). Buzzoni offers a number of examples from textual traditions that illustrate the principles of *recensio* (the establishment of the stemma and the classification of witnesses and readings), *emendatio* (the selection and emendation of readings), and *dispositio* (the final stage of laying out the edited text, apparatuses, and other material). The section also examines new perspectives that arise out of an increasing awareness of the prevalence of traditions that resist the clear lines and structures of a closed tradition, such as Wulfstan's

Sermo Lupi ad Anglos, Boiardo's *Amorum libri*, and *La Vie de Saint Alexis*, which will be familiar to readers of section 2.3.

Franz Fischer then (6.3) examines the presentation of the critical text. Of particular interest are the standards and conventions that have developed for print over the past two centuries and the ways in which the digital paradigm suggests changes and challenges to these conventions. Indeed, while new tools challenge conventions, the digital environment has implications and ramifications for the very idea of the edited text as well. As part of this survey, Fischer examines the question of what information should be included, and the capabilities and limitations of various formats. Of particular interest is the critical apparatus, which provides the evidence which supports and allows the reader to test the hypothesis of the edited text.

In the final section of this chapter (6.4), Tara Andrews continues the discussion of the digital paradigm, but shifts the focus to digital tools in the humanities and the current environment, that is support, or lack thereof, for them. This section surveys different forms of digital publication, from digital editions that require publication in print to those that are developed for online use. As Andrews indicates, despite the challenges facing those navigating digital publication – from the complexities of XML to the lack of infrastructure maintenance – the policies of funding bodies that mandate digital publication of supported editorial projects represent promising initiatives to ensure the availability of scholarly texts. Indeed, as availability becomes more widespread – at least for those with access to the Web – questions concerning increased public engagement and social relevance promise to represent critical concerns for all those engaged in producing and studying scholarly editing.

This chapter is structured so that the sections move from general considerations regarding types of critical editions to the specifics of developing a critical text using the common-errors method, from theoretical considerations regarding the presentation of a contemporary edition to the specific tools that can be used for digital publication. Some readers may find it more beneficial to read sections in a different order; in particular, the reader might find the material more approachable by reading about the specific tools that can be employed to develop a digital edition (6.4) before exploring the more theoretical concerns relevant to publication (6.3).

As this chapter addresses the forms and production of the scholarly edition, it becomes increasingly clear in the course of reading that the question of engaging users in the textual resources that scholars have developed is equally important. It is hoped that the examples and studies provided in this chapter present those curious about the development of scholarly editions with a more approachable vision of the field.

6.1 Types of editions

Odd Einar Haugen

The great majority of stemmata are to be found in introductions to editions, offering a graphical view of the interrelationship of the manuscripts and opening the door, as it were, to the edited text. In many editions, therefore, the stemma is actively used in the establishment of the text, the *constitutio textus*, as performed by the editor and shown in the apparatus to the text. However, many editions do not offer a stemma at all, and there are also examples of stemmatic analyses which are made outside any edition. After presenting a simple model of editions, this section will look at reconstructive and non-reconstructive editing, and the particular challenges posed by textual uniformity in reconstructive editions. A final discussion will address editions which, paradoxically, open with a full stemmatic *recensio* but do not implement it in the actual editing. In keeping with the author's background, the majority of examples will be taken from mediaeval vernacular philology.

6.1.1 Types of editions

For many textual critics, an edition is the end product of their editorial project. After going meticulously through the witnesses to the work, the editor has the opportunity of presenting the result in an edition which, in some cases, is refreshingly simple or, in other cases, a highly complex enterprise with multiple apparatuses and a host of editorial signs sprinkled over the pages. In the present introduction to stemmatology, the focus will be on editions that lay down and use a stemma for the actual establishment of the text, the *constitutio textus*, as explained in section 6.2.1 below. There are, however, many other types of editions, so a general overview will be helpful to put the complex, stemma-based editions in perspective. The very first question concerns the number of witnesses to the work that is going to be edited. This number can by anything from one, in the case of a *codex unicus*, to around five thousand (the Greek New Testament).

Assuming that there is more than one witness to the work, editors will, as a rule, try to base their editions on the whole tradition. In some cases, however, the editor may decide to look away from the broader transmission and follow a single manuscript, and only this manuscript, in what may be called a *monotypic* or *monoptic* edition (see Haugen 2013, 40; 2.1.3 above). If there is a generally accepted edition of the work based on the whole textual transmission, a monotypic edition may be seen as a supplementary type of edition, allowing users to focus on the orthography, style, or organisation of a single witness.

While the editors of some monotypic editions choose a close and faithful rendering of the source, often referred to as a *diplomatic* rendition, other editors prefer to regularise the orthography partially or completely. An example of both approaches is offered by the Old Norwegian translation of the Anglo-Norman *lais* of Marie de France, known as the *Strengleikar*, preserved in a single, partly fragmented manuscript, Uppsala, Universitetsbiblioteket, DG 4–7 fol, from ca. 1270. The *Strengleikar* can be studied in the diplomatic edition and translation into English by Mattias Tveitane and Robert Cook (1979), and in a fully regularised orthography by Aðalheiður Guðmundsdóttir (2006) – regularised, in fact, into modern Icelandic.

For the editor who would like to base an edition on more than one witness, there are basically two options available. One is to continue, as it were, the monotypic style, but offering two or more manuscripts at the same time. This is the *synoptic edition*, of which there are two major types. One is the juxtaposition of different versions, even in different languages, of essentially the same work, such as the famous *Hexapla* compiled by Origen of Alexandria in the third century AD. In this edition, preserved only in fragments, no fewer than six versions of the Old Testament are compared in parallel columns – two in Hebrew and four in Greek. Another example of this type is the display of closely related works, such as the 1776 synoptic edition of the Gospels of Matthew, Mark, and Luke by Johann Jakob Griesbach (see Greeven 1978). The other type is the juxtaposition of witnesses to the same work, thus, in principle the basis for a critical *recensio*. The four manuscripts displayed side by side in Jean Rychner's edition of *Lanval* (1958) in figure 6.1-6 below are one example; the two versions of *Þorláks saga helga* in the split-level edition by Jón Helgason (1978) in figure 6.1-7 are another. It should be noted, however, that the two types of synoptic editions may overlap, depending on the delimitation of the work and its witnesses.

As long as the synoptic editions of either type are confined to print, there is an upper limit to how many versions of the text can be displayed simultaneously. More than, say, six will not be practicable, unless the text is very short. In print, synoptic editions will organise the text in either vertical columns or horizontal blocks. As long as the texts to be compared synoptically are fairly close in form and content, the actual layout is not a huge challenge, apart from the fact that there may be a lot of white space if one text is considerably shorter than other texts. More challenging are *transpositions* in the text, which is why the Gospel of John, a Gospel differently organised compared to the other three, was not included in the earliest synoptic editions (it was included for the first time in the 1797 edition by Griesbach; see Greeven 1978).

The *eclectic edition* will, as a rule, be based on more than one witness and never rely exclusively on any one of them. The term "eclectic" has pejorative connotations for many scholars, implying a lack of rules or principles, but within editorial theory, it is generally used in a neutral sense, for example in the editing of the Bible (7.6.3), in the editing of mediaeval German texts (7.4.5), or in the editing of Anglo-American authors (see e.g. Bowers 1975b; Tanselle 1994). This neutrality also applies to the typology advocated here. Eclectic editing goes a long way back – the celebrated edition of the Greek New Testament by Erasmus of Rotterdam in 1516 is a type of eclectic editing, understandably so, given the overwhelming number of manuscripts and the practical difficulties in accessing them (see 2.1.3). Many eclectic editions were also made after the methodological advances of the nineteenth century, as exemplified by the edition of *Barlaams ok Josaphats saga* by Rudolf Keyser and Carl Richard Unger (1851), discussed in section 6.1.2.

Among the eclectic editions, the principal group (from the perspective of this book) is the strictly *critical edition*, which is an edition based on a genealogical *recensio* of the manuscripts and using this information in the establishment of the text. This has been, and remains, the preferred type of edition within classical scholarship, and it is the premier type of edition for any stemmatological *recensio*. As Richard Tarrant points out, almost any critical edition in the classical field has an eclectic basis (2016, 125), but he also underlines the importance of conjecture when dealing with textual difficulties – the *emendatio ope ingenii* has a long, though contested, tradition in textual scholarship (see 2.1, 6.2). Critical editions of the type favoured in classical scholarship are also found in other fields of editing, but possibly to a lesser extent due to the nature and distribution of the manuscript material. As argued in section 6.3.1, there are many editions which can be described as critical in the sense that they offer structured information on a number of aspects of the text, even if the actual establishment of the text is not as would be expected in a truly critical edition. The same applies to editions in the field of Old Norse, such as in the leading Editiones Arnamagnæanæ series, where the genealogical *recensio* is dutifully carried out in the introductions but the edited texts are established not on this basis, but more often than not in what might be called a critical synoptic edition, exemplified in figure 6.1-7 below. On this seemingly contradictory procedure of editing, see the historical and methodological overview by Louis-Jensen and Haugen (in press).

If the eclectic editions in figure 6.1-1 are thought of as occupying concentric circles, the strictly critical editions will populate the inner circle while the basically pre-Lachmannian editions will orbit in the outer circle. In between, there will be editions which are not strictly critical but which contain a methodological approach to the text which far exceeds that of the editions in the outer group. As in all typologies, there will be editions which can be placed in more than one group, and there are also examples of critical editions to the left of the dividing line in figure 6.1-1. A number of important texts have only been preserved in a single manuscript, such as, in Old High German, the short poem *Muspilli* in München, Bayerische Staatsbibliothek, Clm 14098 (ninth century) and the equally short *Hildebrandslied* in Kassel, Universitätsbibliothek, 2° Ms. theol. 54 (ninth century), or, in Old English, the extensive *Beowulf* in London, British Library, Cotton Vitellius A.xv (early eleventh century). These works may offer fertile ground for emendations to the text, an operation which is regarded as part and parcel of critical editing (see 6.2.3, esp. 6.2.3.1). As has been concisely put forward by Franz H. Bäuml:

> The editor of a unique manuscript has two possible courses of procedure open to him, depending on whether he is concerned with establishing the *Urtext* of his manuscript *per se*. If it is

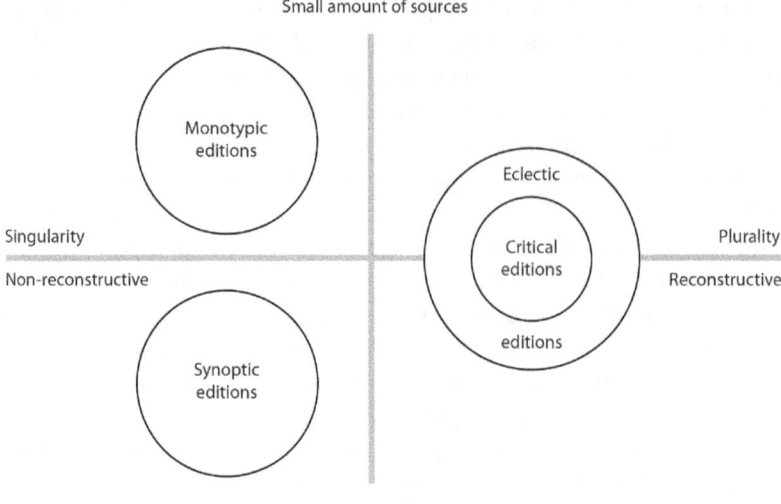

Fig. 6.1-1: A dichotomous view of editions (details in the main text). For another basically dichotomous model, see Göransson (2016, 421, fig. 2). The latter model charts the continuum between what the author calls "diplomatic" and "revisionist" approaches, a continuum which is comparable to the horizontal axis in the present model.

> his intention to establish the *Urtext*, he can avail himself of only one aspect of textual criticism, and that in isolation: since the techniques of heuristic, *collatio*, *recensio* are not applicable, he is limited to the *emendatio*. However, lexical emendation of all three types – with full, with partial, and with no palaeographical justification – is for the most part a comparative method and therefore also largely inapplicable, except in such cases where internal comparisons within a given text or type of text are possible. Where this is not the case, his emendations will be formed according to the principles of *Konjekturalkritik*. (Bäuml 1961, 27)

Since many early and, by that token, important works have been preserved in single and often fragmented manuscripts, much editorial zeal has been applied to them. An apt example is offered by the Old Norse Eddic poems; the majority of these have been handed down to us in a single manuscript, Reykjavík, Safn Árna Magnússonar, GKS 2365 4to (ca. 1270). Due to their literary and mythological value, the number of *Edda* editions is high and the secondary literature large. The *Kommentar zu den Liedern der Edda* in seven volumes (von See et al. 1997–2019) contains a full rendering of the Eddic poems, accompanied by a vast line-by-line commentary. The size of this commentary is in fact comparable to the apparatus that can be found in many critical editions.

In the simple and dichotomous view of editions discussed here, as displayed in figure 6.1-1, monotypic and synoptic editions are located to the left of the dividing line, distinguished by their singularity in the rendition of the sources, while the eclectic editions (and, within this group, the critical editions) are located to the right of the dividing line. While, from a stemmatological point of view, the editor of a monotypic edition may be envied for the ease of the undertaking, and the editor of a synoptic edition criticised for not standing up for a preferred version of the text, the editor of a critical edition has nowhere to hide. From the perspective of Karl Popper (1965), the critical edition delivers the most audacious hypothesis on the text and as such is continuously in danger of being refuted, but for this very reason it has the strongest explanatory power.

The critical edition is usually defined by virtue of its *recensio* and the implementation of its results in the text, in particular the selection of readings when the manuscript evidence is in conflict. This is, however, not the only challenge for the critical editor, especially not for editors of vernacular texts. In the introduction to the edition of the Old French *Alexis* legend, Gaston Paris draws a distinction between two major steps in the making of an edition, first the constitution of the readings (*constitution des leçons*) and second the constitution of the language (*constitution du langage*; Paris and Pannier 1872, 14). The first step is common to most texts discussed in this volume and is also examined in section 2.3.2 above. Referring to the simple model in figure 6.1-1, this step will be discussed below as a choice between r e c o n s t r u c t i v e and n o n - r e c o n s t r u c t i v e editing, or, as many would put it, between c r i t i c a l and n o n - c r i t i c a l editing. The second step is less acute for the editing of classical texts, where there is a long-standing tradition of regularising the orthography of the manuscripts and often scant interest among editors in this seemingly accidental variation. For vernacular texts, which have often been preserved in manuscripts of highly variable orthography, this is a question that the editor simply cannot avoid. It is perhaps not surprising that the greater part of the introduction to the *Alexis* legend is devoted to *la constitution du langage*. Below, this will be discussed under the heading of "textual unity" (6.1.5).

Ultimately, the choice of edition depends on the manuscript material. In the case of a *codex unicus*, there is little choice other than a monotypic edition. However, if the manuscripts contain a translation for which the source text has been identified, it is still possible to bring in an outside view of the text. A case in point is the above-mentioned *Strengleikar* manuscript (ca. 1270), which contains a rather free translation into Old Norwegian prose of the octosyllabic *lais* by Marie de France. Manuscript *H*, London, British Library, Harley 978 (thirteenth century), appears to be the closest to the translator's unknown exemplar. Even if the *Strengleikar* translation differs in many respects from its source, there are many readings which can be better understood after a comparison with the source, so that problematic readings can be emended with a high degree of certainty (for examples, see Budal 2009). There will also be cases where other versions of the manuscript text may shed light on its conceptions and readings, even if these versions cannot be used in a strict genealogical *recensio*.

When a work has been preserved in more than one manuscript, which probably is the case in the majority of instances, the type of edition to be chosen is still an open question. There are many considerations: the size and complexity of the manuscript material, the degree of horizontal transmission (or contamination), the degree of fragmentation, the existence of previous editions and their various strengths (or, indeed, weaknesses), and so on. In some cases, it will be possible to work towards an archetype, as in reconstructive editions. In other cases, it may be futile to do so, so the editor is left with the choice between a non-reconstructive edition, be it of a single, best, or most typical manuscript, and a selection of manuscripts in a synoptic approach.

Finally, it should be mentioned that a distinction may be drawn between, on the one hand, popular editions, intended for use in schools or for the general public, and, on the other hand, scholarly editions. The former type of edition is usually based on established scholarly editions, simplifying their often complicated interfaces and sometimes regularising the orthography. It goes without saying that it is the latter type which is discussed here, but that is not to say that popular editions should be disregarded. Many editors have offered both types of editions themselves, such as the two Old French editions by Jean Rychner discussed at the end of section 6.1.3.

There are numerous introductions to the art and science of editing texts, and several offer typologies. In spite of its modest title, "Some Types of Scholarly Edition", appendix 2 in Greetham (1994) is a good starting point, while later attempts can be found on a grand scale in Sahle (2013) and more briefly in Haugen (2014); see also 6.3 below.

6.1.2 Reconstructive editions

The editing of handwritten texts from the classical and mediaeval era has often taken the form of a reconstructive enterprise in which the editor tries to trace the text back to its original, removing errors and innovations in the manuscript transmission as he or she slowly sifts through the preserved material. It is commonly assumed that the original of all classical texts has been irrevocably lost:

> Eigenhändige Niederschriften (Autographa) der griechischen und lateinischen Klassiker besitzen wir nicht, auch keine Abschriften, die mit dem Original verglichen sind, sondern nur solche Abschriften, die durch Vermittlung einer unbekannten Zahl von Zwischenhandschriften aus dem Original abgeleitet, also von fragwürdiger Zuverlässigkeit sind. (Maas 1960, 5)

> [We have no autograph manuscripts of the Greek and Roman classical writers and no copies which have been collated with the originals; the manuscripts we possess derive from the originals through an unknown number of intermediate copies, and are consequentially of questionable trustworthiness.] (trans. Flower 1958, 1)

Also for mediaeval texts, preserved originals are indeed rare. Furthermore, for classical as well as mediaeval texts, the ensuing copies have also been lost to a very high extent. It is impossible to give an exact estimate of this loss of manuscripts,

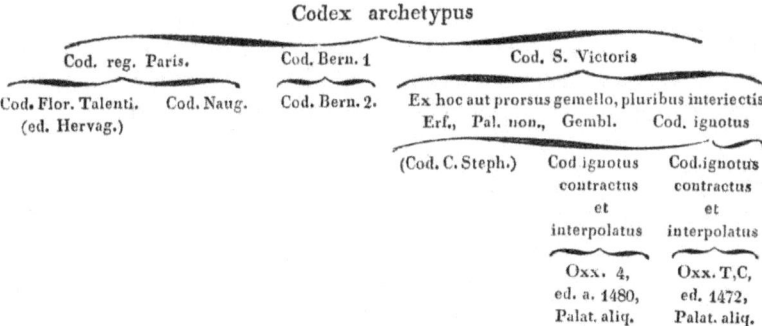

Fig. 6.1-2: The stemma for the manuscripts of two speeches by Cicero in Madvig (1833–1834, 1:9). Note the term "Codex archetypus", which probably should be taken to mean "original". In the treatise of Paul Maas (1st ed. 1927, 4th ed. 1960), "archetype" received a more technical meaning, as explained in section 4.1 above.

and it probably varied across genres and periods, but it is not uncommon to estimate that around 90 % of mediaeval manuscripts have been lost (Guidi and Trovato 2004; Åström 2005, 1071). As a consequence of this loss, an edited text can be no more than an approximation of the once-existing original. However, the edited text can claim to be the o p t i m a l t e x t, insofar as the point of the editorial exercise is to trace the history of the text as far back as possible. This program is what Karl Lachmann (1793–1851) succinctly formulated in 1817: "Wir sollen und wollen aus einer hinreichenden Menge von guten Handschriften einen allen diesen zum Grunde liegenden Text darstellen, der entweder der ursprüngliche selbst seyn, oder ihm doch sehr nahe kommen muss" (Lachmann 1876, 1:82) [On the basis of a sufficient number of good manuscripts, we should and want to build a text which reflects all of these, a text which either will be the original text or must come very close to it].

The approximation of the original was later termed the "archetype" (e.g. in Maas 1960, 6). Since the generation of Karl Lachmann (although not by Lachmann himself), the process of copying a text has been modelled as a tree turned upside down, a *stemma codicum* (see 4.1). The stemma has the original on top, the archetype directly beneath it, and the preserved manuscripts as leaves on the branches below. Stemmata can be drawn in different ways, but they are all basically tree models, depicting the copying process through one or more (usually many) generations of manuscripts.

The earliest full-scale stemma is found in the edition of the Westrogothic law, *Västgötalagen*, by the Swedish scholars Carl J. Schlyter and Hans S. Collin (1827), reproduced in figure 4.1-1 above. According to Britta Olrik Frederiksen (2009, 139–148), of the two editors, Schlyter should be regarded as the author of the stemma. Probably due to the fact that the *Västgötalagen* is a vernacular text, it remained isolated (see G. Holm 1972), also, perhaps, because of the modest location of the stemma on a small fold-out slip in an appendix to the edition. It is correct, as Sebastiano Timpanaro pointed out when he was made aware of this stemma, that it is not part of a genealogical *recensio* (Timpanaro 2004, 61–62; trans. Most 2005, 92), but it certainly comes across as a surprisingly modern tree.

A few years later, the Danish classical scholar Johan Nicolai Madvig published a stemma for the manuscripts of Cicero's *Oratio pro Publio Sestio* and *Oratio in Vatinium*, reproduced in figure 6.1-2 here. This was not part of a *recensio* for an edition, but since it was published by a leading classical scholar it had a much greater impact than Schlyter's stemma. When the stemma gradually made its way into editorial practice in Nordic philology, it was most likely through Madvig's teaching and example rather than the contribution by Schlyter. Like his colleague in Berlin, August Boeckh, Madvig was active in teaching for around five decades, and, like Boeckh, he frequently gave a course on the "Encyclopedia of Philology". Madvig was appointed professor in 1829 and kept teaching until he retired in 1880. In this long period, he influenced two generations of editors, of classical as well as of vernacular texts (see Ræder and Larsen 1981).

In the mid-nineteenth century, editions of texts in the vernaculars were on the whole eclectic, not only among Nordic scholars but also among other European editors. These editions were not critical in the strict sense defined above, since they did not offer a genealogical *recensio* of the manuscripts, nor did they build a text on the basis of a *recensio*. This does not mean that vernacular editing of the time should be discarded as unscholarly, only that editing in this field had not yet been informed by the later developments in the genealogical method. One example is the editing of the Latin *Barlaam* legend. When Rudolf Keyser and Carl Richard Unger edited the Old Norwegian translation of this legend, *Barlaams saga ok Josaphats* (1851), they were faced with a highly f r a g m e n t e d corpus of textual witnesses. Of the around fifteen preserved witnesses, many of which were small fragments, not a single one contained the entire text, and many manuscripts were much younger Icelandic specimens in a distinctively later orthography. Fortunately, one of the earliest manuscripts was fairly complete, preserving around 95 % of the text. This was an eastern Norwegian codex, Stockholm, Kungliga biblioteket, Holm perg 6 fol (ca. 1275), and it is the uncontested *codex optimus* of the saga. In their polished eclectic edition, Keyser and Unger followed this manuscript as far as possible, and supplied missing text from younger Icelandic manuscripts whenever necessary. Since the o r t h o g r a p h y of the main and the supplementary manuscripts was strikingly different, they decided to regularise the orthography of the younger manuscripts according to the thirteenth-century Norwegian orthography of the main manuscript. This meant that they, in a sense, back-dated the younger manuscripts more than two centuries. The result was a uniform edition, kept in a single, Old Norwegian orthography throughout. It was an edition of the *work*, not of its witnesses. It is still regarded as an eminent edition, and it remains the only edition offering a complete and unbroken rendition of the work.

Possibly the first stemmata which appeared as part of a truly genealogical *recensio* were published in the above-mentioned edition of the *Alexis* legend by Gas-

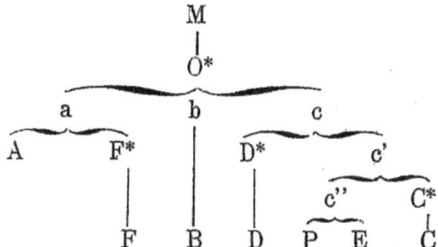

Fig. 6.1-3: The stemma for the latest, fourteenth-century version of the *Alexis* legend, drawn by Léopold Pannier. Source: Paris and Pannier (1872, 344).

ton Paris and Léopold Pannier (1872). The stemma for the manuscripts of the earliest, eleventh-century version of the legend was drawn by Paris and is reproduced in figure 7.3-1 below. Pannier drew the second stemma, for the latest, fourteenth-century version of the legend, reproduced here in figure 6.1-3. This is remarkable as an example of a tripartite stemma, which (as explained by Pannier) can be used to determine readings one by one:

> Voici maintenant comment je procède pour l'établissement du texte. Ayant d'abord la version de *a* (A confirmé par F), je considère si elle concorde avec *b* (B) et *c* (C D P E). Quand les trois groupes sont conformes, la leçon est assurée. Quand deux seulement le sont, ils condamnent le troisième. Mais lorsque les trois leçons diffèrent, j'examine, d'après le sens, la valeur de chacune d'elle. Si aucune ne s'impose, je préfère les manuscrits dans l'ordre suivant: A, puis B, puis D, qui est un bon manuscrit. (Paris and Pannier 1872, 344–345)

> [This is how I proceed for establishing the text. After having secured version *a* (A confirmed by F), I assess whether it agrees with *b* (B) and *c* (C D P E). When the three groups agree, their readings are confirmed. If only two groups agree, they exclude the third. If readings in three differ, I examine the value of each reading according to its sense. If no reading is stronger, I select the manuscripts in the following order: *A*, then *B*, then *D*, which is a good manuscript.]

The procedure described by Pannier turned a tripartite stemma into an automaton, since it could be used to select readings by a simple majority rule among the hyparchetypes, in this case *a*, *b*, and *c*, thus denying the editors the right to select for themselves. In fact, the majority rule will apply to any stemma with three or more hyparchetypes, as long as there is a majority among readings. Joseph Bédier's later criticism of the unyielding force of the tripartite stemma is discussed in section 2.3.4 above.

From the 1870s, a growing number of editions were based on a genealogical *recensio* of the manuscripts and embellished by one or more stemmata. This type of edition was applied to a great many literatures, classical as well as vernacular. In Old Norse editing, the earliest example of a genealogical *recensio* with a full *stemma codicum* is to be found in the edition of *Fljótsdøla saga*. This is a late mediaeval Icelandic saga which was edited by the Danish scholar Kristan Kålund (1883); the stemma is reproduced in figure 6.1-4.

Kålund argues explicitly on the basis of the distribution of "fælles fejl" [common errors] in the manuscripts, and claims that there are some errors in all the preserved manuscripts; in other words, there must have been a less faulty, but now-lost, manuscript *X* from which the preserved manuscripts are derived. Kålund con-

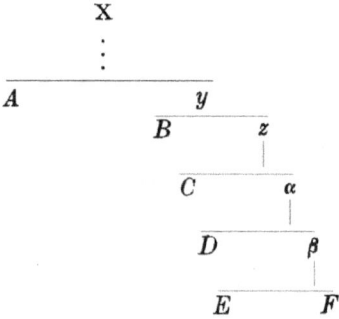

Fig. 6.1-4: The stemma for the six manuscripts A–F of *Fljótsdøla saga* by Kristian Kålund (1883, xvii). It is striking that this stemma has a high number of repeated bifurcations, a trait that Timpanaro, among others, found problematic (see the posthumous appendix, "Final Remarks on Bipartite Stemmas", in Timpanaro 2005, 214).

tinued his work with the more prominent *Laxdøla saga*, which he edited and published in two volumes (1889–1891). Worth mentioning is also the complex and highly reconstructive edition of *Þiðriks saga af Bern* (i.e. Verona) by another Dane, Henrik Bertelsen, published in two volumes (1905–1911). These editions offer a *recensio* of the manuscripts, a stemma, and a text which has been informed by the genealogical *recensio*.

When Jón Helgason, who later founded the definitive Editiones Arnamagnæanæ series (in 1958), edited a selection of Old Icelandic bishops' sagas, it was in a truly critical edition (1938). He explained his selection of readings, the *constitution des leçons* in the terms of Gaston Paris, with reference to the stemma he had arrived at, and he decided to render the text in regularised orthography. Figure 6.1-5 shows a typical page from this edition, in which the apparatus is divided into two levels: the upper level contains variation that is relevant for the establishment of the text, which might be called substantial variation, and the lower level covers accidental variation, which does not interfere with the establishment of the text. This is an edition of a vernacular text with a high degree of linguistic variability, but it was done in accordance with practice in classical editing and thus suppressing the linguistic variation in favour of reconstructing the work in its presumed original orthography of the early thirteenth century.

Among editors of classical texts, the genealogical method still holds sway. The stemma is the uncontested model, and the construction of the text is informed by *recensio*. However, it is a type of edition which seems best suited to prominent works, that is, works that have been preserved with a high degree of faithfulness to the chain of exemplars and a low degree of interference from other branches of the tradition – or simply, as Karl Stackmann concludes, it is preferable for classical texts that are seen as authoritative (1979, 252). For other types of editions and editorial traditions in various language areas, see the overviews in chapter 7 below, and also the typology in section 6.3.

> 59   1. Bækling þenna kalla ek Hungrvǫku, af því at svá mun mǫrgum
> mǫnnum ófróðum, ok þó [eigi] óvitrum, gefit vera, þeim er hann
> hafa yfir farit, at miklu* mundu gørr vilja vita upprás ok ævi ³
> þeira merkismanna er hér verðr fátt frá sagt á þessi skrá. En ek
> hefi þó nálega ǫllu við slegit, at rita þat sem ek hefi í minni fest.
> Hefi ek af því þenna bœkling saman settan, at eigi falli mér með ⁶
> ǫllu ór minni þat er ek heyrða af þessu máli segja hinn fróða mann
> Gizur Hallsson, ok enn nǫkkura menn aðra merkilega hafa í frá-
> sǫgn fœrt. Þat berr ok annat til þessa rits, at teygja til þess unga ⁹
> menn, at kynnisk várt mál at ráða, þat er á norrœnu er ritat, lǫg
> eða sǫgur eða mannfrœði. Set ek af því heldr þetta á skrá en annan
> fróðleik þann er áðr er á skrá settr, at mér sýnisk mínum bǫrnum ¹²

> *Overskrift:* Hungurvaka B^1, Hier Byriar Hungur wöku B^2, Eirn lytell Bæklingur
> af fäum Byskupum sem verid hafa ä Islande þeim fyrstu og huornenn Skalhollt
> var fyrst Bygtt og þar settur Byskups stöll og af huórium þad var tilsett og
> nær *(og nær)* ÷ C^2*)* $C^{1,2}$, Bæklíngur af nockrum Biskupum þeim firstu sem vered
> hafa ä Islande: og hvorninn Skälhollt var first biggt og af hvurium og hvenær
> þad var tilsett C^3. *Herefter ny overskrift til kapitlet:* Formälenn $C^{1,2}$, Formäle
> [incerti authoris] C^3.   2 eigi] ÷ BC *(og udgg.)*, indsat *(ved konjektur) i afskriften*
> 1B^{62} fol; enkelte hskrr. *(AM 373, 4to m. m.)* bøder paa fejlen ved at ændre óvitrum
> til vitrum *(saal. ogsaa OrIsl).*   3 miklu] + meir B.   4 verðr fátt] verid haffa
> og fatt verdur .C.   á] j B^2C^1.   5 þó] ÷ C.   8 nǫkkura] marga $C^{1,3}$.   9 -sǫgn
> *(saal. B^1, AM læser i AM 376, 4to med urette -saugu)* sǫgu $C^{1,2}$, -sǫgur B^2C^3.
> berr] bar C.   10 B^2 *interpungerer:* mál, at ráða þat er *(saal. Bps, Kahle)*,
> B^1 har intet skilletegn her. Af C-haandskrifterne, som har þá *(= þá er) for* þat er
> *(jfr. flg.),* har C^1 ingen interpunktion her, C^2 komma efter ráða og ritat, C^3 komma
> efter ritat *(det fjernes i afskriften AM 211 fol, hvor teksten saal. lyder: mäl, ad*
> *rada þa a Noræenu er ritad lǫg osv.).* þat er] þa C.   11 af] æ C.   á] ad C
> *(idet skrá opfattes som infinitiv).*   12 er(₂)] oprdl. er eigi?   á — settr] skräsettur
> C^1.   skrá] skrar $C^{2,3}$ *(og OrIsl).*

> *For kap. 1 har D:* I fyrstu vil eg nu segia fra því hversu bærinn hefur bygdzt
> j Skalhollti, og sidan fra þeim er hann hafa halldit.   2 vera] verda C^2.   3 vilja]
> efter vita $C^{2,3}$.   5 fest] sett C^2.   6 eigi] ecke C^3.   7 fróða] froma C^2.   10 kynnisk]
> kynnast B^2.   11 því] þa C^3.

Fig. 6.1-5: The Old Icelandic *Hungrvaka* in the edition by Jón Helgason (1938, 72).

6.1.3 Non-reconstructive editions

If there is just a single witness to a work, the editor is forced to rely on it, and there can be no reconstruction based on the evidence of lost manuscripts. At best, the editor can argue on the basis of presumably better readings and e m e n d the text, as Franz H. Bäuml pointed out in the quotation above (6.1.1). However, in the case of works preserved in more than one manuscript, an editor may also decide to focus on just one of the manuscripts, typically the one regarded as the best. While nobody would argue against selecting a supposedly best manuscript for a non-reconstructive edition, there are also manuscripts which are not regarded as the best but are still considered worthy of an edition for other reasons.

One example of a non-reconstructive edition is offered by the Old Norwegian *Barlaams saga ok Josaphats* (mid-thirteenth century). The eclectic edition by Keyser and Unger (1851), referred to above, was supplemented by a new, monotypic edition by Magnus Rindal (1981), based on the main manuscript, Stockholm, Kungliga biblioteket, Holm perg 6 fol. This manuscript is presented "as is", with all lacunae and errors. Since the first leaves of the manuscript have been lost, it opens *in medias res* with "oc mællte ekki fleiri orðum" [and did not utter any more words]. The text is rendered in a diplomatic manner, so that it is a faithful linguistic source, and this was indeed the main motivation for the edition. The work as such has not been highly regarded, at least not by earlier scholars, but it is beyond doubt an important source for the eastern Norwegian language of the thirteenth century. From this perspective, it is the *document* Holm perg 6 fol (covering approximately 95 % of the entire text) which is of scholarly interest. Supplying passages from later manuscripts for the remaining 5 % would simply be regarded as noise, distorting the linguistic data. *Barlaams saga ok Josaphats* in Holm perg 6 fol has since been published with full morphological annotation in the *Medieval Nordic Text Archive* (menota.org), which is a reminder that editions of some text traditions may be more suited to digital channels than other types (see 6.3 below).

Another example is the famous *Prose Edda* by the Icelander Snorri Sturluson (d. 1241), which illustrates and explains Old Norse mythology. This work has been preserved in four major manuscripts with varying degrees of fragmentation. København, Det Kongelige Bibliotek, GKS 2367 4to, dated to ca. 1325, is regarded as the *codex optimus* among them, and it has been edited and translated a number of times, recently in an edition with regularised orthography by Anthony Faulkes (1982) and in a translation into English also by Faulkes (1995). Another of the four manuscripts, Uppsala, Universitetsbiblioteket, DG 11 4to, has a somewhat earlier date, ca. 1300–1325, but it is regarded as a kind of *bête noir*, having a rather different and sometimes convoluted style. The relationship between the major manuscripts of the *Edda* has not been fully explained; for this reason, and because of the intrinsic qualities of the Uppsala *Edda*, this manuscript has been edited (and translated) on its own by Anthony Faulkes and Heimir Pálsson (2012).

In the case of an o p e n and perhaps inconsistent t e x t u a l   t r a d i t i o n, monotypic editions may seem the best route to follow. As long as the number of presumably good manuscripts is not too high, this is also a recommendable archive solution, in the sense that several monotypic editions of the same work offer a fuller view of the textual variation than an apparatus can. As such, monotypic editions can prove to be the first step towards a reconstructive edition, an edition that metaphorically hovers above the individual monotypic editions, drawing its readings from them.

There are examples of editions which combine the two opposing perspectives in figure 6.1-1, mediating between a non-reconstructive and reconstructive approach, as it were. The experimental edition of the Old French *Lanval* by Jean Rychner (1958), depicted in figure 6.1-6, is worth mentioning. Here, the text is synoptically presented, on facing pages, from the four manuscripts, *P, H, S, C*, each in its own

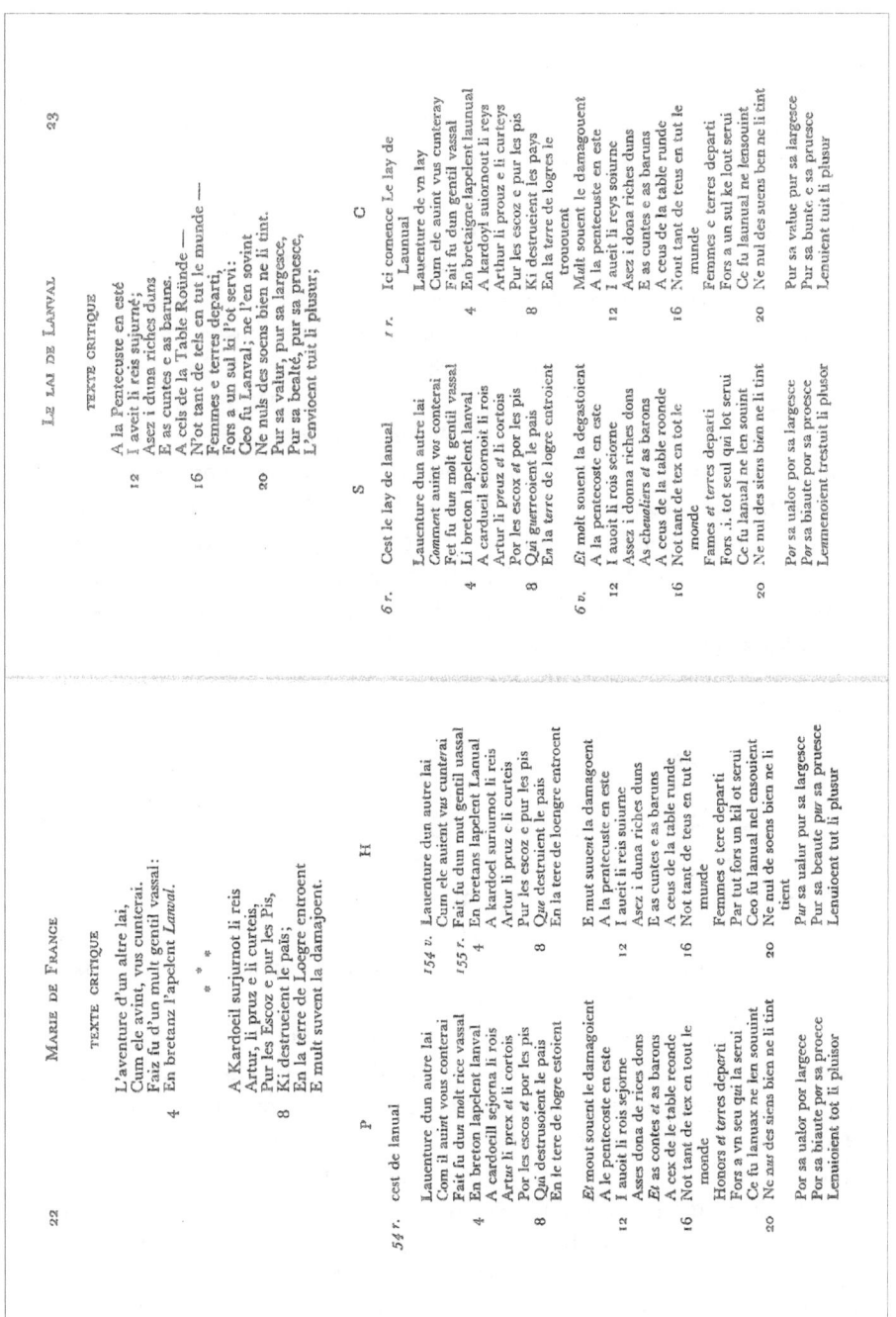

Fig. 6.1-6: The opening of *Lanval* in Jean Rychner's edition (1958). Manuscript *H*, regarded as the best, is London, British Library, Harley 978 (thirteenth century). For a full list of the other manuscripts, see the introduction (Rychner 1958, 7).

orthography. Above them is the critical text established by Rychner, based on these four manuscripts and rendered in a unified orthography. This is an instructive example, in which Rychner details the genealogical *recensio* of the four manuscripts and the orthographical choices made. It should be added that this type of editing is best suited for short texts in a limited number of manuscripts and preferably in verse (here, octosyllabic). Rychner (1968) later edited the entire corpus of *lais* by Marie de France, and in this edition *Lanval* occupies 21 out of a total of 191 pages. A similar consideration applies to the exploratory editions of the *Canterbury Tales* by Peter Robinson and colleagues. The edition of *The Wife of Bath's Prologue* contained diplomatic transcriptions of all manuscripts as well as digital images of them (Robinson 1996b). There was, however, at this stage of the project, no critical text. For the further development of the digital editions of the *Canterbury Tales*, see section 6.3.3.3 below.

For mediaeval text genres with complex text traditions, other types of editions may also be relevant, and they may in fact combine the two perspectives outlined here. The approach can be genetic (reconstructing different stages in the development of a text), synthetic (establishing a text that is representative of certain strands or selected groups), or representative (presenting a synthesis of a text tradition). For a discussion and examples of these types, primarily based on the editing of classical texts, see Göransson (2016).

6.1.4 Textual display

There are a few aesthetic considerations for editions which have practical implications. With reference to printed editions, some editors would ask for a "clean text", even to the point of relegating notes and apparatus to an appendix in the edition. In these editions, the text can be read without other distractions than those chosen by readers when they decide to check if there are any comments on or variants for a passage in the text. This presentation was advocated by the influential American scholar Fredson Bowers (see Tanselle 1972, 45–46). It probably makes sense for editions of post-mediaeval texts that are being read for their own sake, that is, for the literature studied by Bowers and Tanselle. Texts that are based on a stemmatological *recensio* seldom fall into this category. One can envisage a spectrum from scholarly, technical editions, often with multiple and large apparatuses, to smooth and clean-looking reading editions addressed at a broader audience. The experimental edition of *Lanval* by Jean Rychner (1958) sits at the scholarly end, even though it is designed with an intuitive layout, while his general edition of the entire collection of *lais* by Marie de France (1968) is at the other end. What most scholarly editions seem to agree on is the typographical principle that readings in the text should be linked to the apparatus by line numbers, not by footnotes (although there are some notable exceptions, such as the Monumenta Germaniae historica). Even if there are one or even more apparatuses at the bottom of the page and there are various refer-

Fig. 6.1-7: *Þorláks saga helga*, an Old Icelandic bishop's saga, in the edition by Jón Helgason (1978, 72). This was the second volume of his basically Lachmannian edition; see figure 6.1-5 above for an extract from the first.

ences in the margin, the text block, if nothing else, should look clean. The example page in figure 6.3-5 in section 6.3.2.2, below has abundant information in the margins and the apparatuses, but manages to keep the text clean – or at least fairly clean. It cannot be denied that there are some editorial signs that creep into an otherwise clean text, such as square brackets, angle brackets, asterisks, and obeli. The usage of these signs varies across editorial traditions and is not fully harmonised. While the Old Norse tradition of editing makes do with a limited set (see the overview in Haugen 2007, 118), there are more elaborate systems, perhaps most developed in the editing of epigraphical texts (see Dow 1969, with bibliography).

Jón Helgason's 1978 edition of bishops' sagas (see fig. 6.1-7) is an example of a scholarly edition in which the text is displayed synoptically on a split-level page, each version having its own apparatus. It is a far cry from the highly complex editions of, for example, the New Testament (as patiently explained in K. Aland and B. Aland 1989), but it is nonetheless located squarely at the scholarly end of the spectrum. For a reading edition of this selection of bishops' sagas, one has to turn to the recent edition of *Byskupa sögur* by Ásdís Egilsdóttir in the Íslenzk fornrit series (2002). This might be regarded as a kind of outreach edition, aimed at a broader audience, compared to the ascetic 1978 editor's edition by Jón Helgason.

6.1.5 Textual unity

Manuscripts usually show some internal variation in their orthography, even in the works of the most reliable scribes. This is especially so in the vernaculars, where the language in question sometimes developed considerably in the course of the textual transmission of a work. One should remember that the scribes did not have access to grammars or dictionaries, but had to rely on their internalised orthography, which from time to time was in conflict with the orthography of the exemplar. The external variation – that between manuscripts of the same work – was potentially even greater. This would almost always be the case when a sufficient amount of time had elapsed between the production of the manuscripts, perhaps several centuries, but it would also be the case for contemporaneous manuscripts from different regions.

Returning to Paris's dichotomy of the *constitution des leçons*, discussed at some length in section 2.3.2 above, and the *constitution du langage*, the latter approach deserves further discussion. It may be seen as a vernacular problem, but orthographical faithfulness is also debated among classical scholars; see, for example, the "vernacular" position of Hans Helander (2001, 5–44) and the critical comments by Heinz Hoffmann (2001, 51–58). No editor would claim that his or her edition is unfaithful to the sources, but there is a span from an extremely close rendering of a source to a fully regularised rendering, analogous to the span from narrow to broad transcriptions in phonology. Assuming that the edition is based on a single document, as in the editing of a complete *codex unicus*, for example, the editor still has to face two types of orthographical regularisation.

(i) Internal regularisation: introducing consistent use of graphemes to record the underlying phonological system as well as consistent morphological forms within the document. If an Old Norse scribe generally writes "lond" and "landum" (nom. and dat. pl. of *land*, nt., "land"), but occasionally slips to "londum" (with *u*-mutation of *a* > *o*), the editor might decide to regularise the latter "londum" to "landum" for the sake of orthographical consistency. This would be in keeping with the Old Norwegian provenance of the text, as witnessed by the distribution of *u*-mutation in it. Furthermore, if the source generally has the dative singular form "armi" (of *armr*, m., "arm") but offers an occasional "arm" (possibly reflecting a merger of dat. *armi* and acc. *arm*), the editor might want to reinstate the ending *-i*, thus correcting "arm" > "armi". Due to the widespread scribal variation in Old Norse, this type of inconsistency is common. It is not really a mark of scribal sloppiness, but rather a reflection of conflict between the linguistic norm of the exemplar and that of the scribe, as occurred when an Icelander copied a Norwegian exemplar. He might, for example, struggle with making the distinction between /æ:/ and /ø:/, which was kept in Norwegian but merged to /æ:/ in Icelandic, as in *bǿn*, f., "prayer" > *bæn* and *mǽla*, vb, "speak" > *mæla*. In other words, the scribal variation reflects linguistic developments in time and space, and it is for the editor to decide whether the edition should reflect this faithfully or whether he or she would like to present the text in a consistent orthography, true to the time and locale of its production, but cleansed of accidental variation.

(*ii*) E x t e r n a l   r e g u l a r i s a t i o n : introducing consistent orthography and morphology according to a norm outside of the document itself. Fortunately, at least for editors, the Old Norse language (i.e. Old Icelandic and Old Norwegian) has a well-defined and generally accepted orthography for mediaeval texts. This was established by scholars in the nineteenth century and it has been used ever since in a large number of editions, especially those aimed at beginners and a general audience, and also in grammars and dictionaries of the languages. Other vernacular literatures do not offer the same standard orthography, although dictionaries and grammars do have a normalising effect on the conception of the language. The creation of a standard orthography for Old Norse was greatly helped by the fact that Icelandic morphology has hardly changed between the earliest recorded documents in the twelfth century and today. There has been phonological development in Icelandic, to be sure, but this is not always reflected in the written forms; or, if it is, the changes can be inferred by simple rules, such as the addition of an epenthetic and easily identifiable vowel in words like *ungr*, adj., "young" > *ungur*. The closely related languages Swedish and Danish have seen comparatively dramatic changes in phonology and morphology, so no standard orthographies have been developed, and editions usually follow the source fairly closely, including internal variation. Norwegian has also seen similar changes to those of Swedish and Danish, but they metaphorically ride on the back of Icelandic; Norwegian can use the same standard orthography for its mediaeval sources, at least up to around 1400, as Icelandic.

In the introduction to the *Alexis* edition (Paris and Pannier 1872), Paris spends a considerable amount of energy on establishing an orthography suitable for the earliest of the four versions of the legend. The original, *O*, of this version was probably conceived in Normandy around 1040 and is preserved in several later manuscripts. The best of these is Hildesheim, Dombibliothek, St. God. Nr 1, named *L* by Paris after the abbey of Lambspringen near Hildesheim. It was written in England, though, and dates from around 1150, well after the Norman conquest. There is some orthographical vacillation in the manuscript, which Paris attributes to the fact that it was copied in England:

> Le scribe était assez intelligent et s'efforçait évidemment de reproduire avec fidélité le texte qu'il avait sous les yeux; mais il n'est arrivé, en ce qui concerne les formes des mots, qu'a une hésitation perpétuelle entre celles de son modèle et celles qui avaient prévalu de son temps et dans son pays. (Paris and Pannier 1872, 3)
>
> [The scribe was quite skilful, and evidently tried to faithfully reproduce the text before his eyes; however, regarding the forms of words, he could not get beyond a perpetual hesitation between those of his model and those which prevailed in his time and in his country.]

This is the crux of vernacular transmission everywhere: the conflict between the exemplar's linguistic norm and that of the scribe. When editing the *Alexis* legend, Paris was looking for no less than the nobility of the French language of the time, essentially true to Latin and reminiscent of contemporaneous architecture:

> Elle n'était pas encore embarrassée de cet insupportable attirail de particules oiseuses qui sont venues l'encombrer depuis; elle avait gardé du latin une ampleur de mouvements qui faisait ressortir encore la grâce qu'elle avait en propre. La langue de cette époque me rappelle ces belles églises romanes construites sur le sol de France et de la Normandie par les hommes même qui la parlaient. (Paris and Pannier 1872, 135)
>
> [The language had not yet been muddled by the unsupportable paraphernalia of idle particles which have since encumbered her; she had retained from Latin a breadth of movement which brought out the grace she had of her own. The language of that time reminds me of those beautiful Romanesque churches built on the soil of France and Normandy by the very men who spoke it.]

Other editors of a reconstructive inclination may have less ambitious aims, but they are faced with the same textual variation and the challenge of untangling it so that they can derive the earlier forms from the later ones. In the edition of the earliest version of the *Alexis* legend, Paris decided to follow manuscript *L* in most cases, after having performed an inductive analysis of the French language of the time. In his "Critique des formes", he detailed phonological and morphological properties over no fewer than 112 pages (Paris and Pannier 1872, 27–138).

For Latin, and particularly neo-Latin texts, there are similar considerations in the debate between Helander (2001) and Hofmann (2001), as pointed out above. Luc Deitz, who is a committed supporter of orthographical normalisation, cites neo-Latin examples such as *partius*, *moestus*, and *hyemps* for "classical" forms like *parcius*, *maestus*, and *hiems*, and believes that they are "likely to cause endless, and needless, trouble even to advanced students of Latin" (Deitz 2005, 351). It has to be said that, from a vernacular point of view, this variation is minute, but the need for normalisation from a didactic point of view is undeniable – it may, for example, not be immediately obvious that a form like *vuín* in an Old Icelandic manuscript is equivalent to *úvin*, m. acc., "un-friend, enemy", or that *þiuuær* in an Old Swedish manuscript would be *þjúfr*, m. nom., "thief", in some normalisations (see Haugen 2018b, 67–71). The willingness among many Latin scholars to normalise contrasts with the practice in the editing of Greek texts in the Corpus Christianorum series Graeca (CCSG) series, as pointed out by Caroline Macé:

Fig. 6.1-8: Lost leaves (indicated in red) in the eleven gatherings of the main manuscript of *Konungs skuggsjá*, AM 243 b α fol (ca. 1270). Of originally 86 leaves, 18 have been lost, or approximately 21% of the text. Even so, this is the *codex optimus* for the work. Illustration by Nina Stensaker, Bergen, for this volume.

> Jacques Noret, who was the reviser of the CCSG for about 25 years (1978–2004), expressed in several articles and in his editorial work the conviction that the only way to get a more accurate picture of Byzantine grammar, orthography, punctuation, etc. was to produce critical editions in which the practice of the manuscripts would be reproduced more adequately. (Macé 2016, 260)

In short, there is a general conflict between the didactic arguments for making texts easier to read and understand on the one hand, and the scholarly aspirations to faithfulness in the rendering of sources, even in critical editions, on the other.

A particular challenge concerns editions of texts which have a fragmented preservation such that no single manuscript can be used as the base manuscript for the entire edition, in contrast to the *L* manuscript of the *Alexis* legend discussed above. The mid-thirteenth century Old Norwegian *Konungs skuggsjá* provides an instructive example. It is widely accepted that the earliest Norwegian manuscript, København, Den Arnamagnæanske Samling, AM 243 b α fol (ca. 1270), is the *codex optimus*. Unfortunately, less than 80% of the once complete codex has been preserved, as shown in figure 6.1-8.

The latest edition of *Konungs skuggsjá* is the one by Ludvig Holm-Olsen (1st ed. 1945, 2nd ed. 1983), offering a strictly diplomatic approach. The full text of the work has to be supplied with the help of other manuscripts, in this case younger, Icelandic ones, as can be seen from the example in figure 6.1-9. Even for someone who does not understand the language, there is an obvious difference in the orthography of the first line, which follows AM 243 b α fol, and the second line, which is based on a fifteenth-century Icelandic manuscript. Since the Old Norwegian manuscript breaks off at the end of this line, the editor had to resort to the younger Icelandic manuscript.

First line in Norwegian of the 13th century, second line in Icelandic of the 15th century

en linklæðe þin þa skalltu lata gera afgoðo leræpti oc þo litil æfni í. geʀ stutta skyrtu ‖ þij*n*a *og* lij*n* klædi þij*n* oll. Lat *vel* ætla iafna*n* goda*n* mu*n* stutt*ari* skyrtu þij*n*a e*n* kyrtil.

Both lines in regularised Old Norse orthography of the 13th century

En línklǽði þín þá skalt þú láta gera af góðu lérefti ok þó lítil efni í. Ger stutta skyrtu ‖ þína ok línklǽði þín ǫll. Lát vel ætla jafnan góðum mun styttri skyrtu þína en kyrtil.

English Translation

(Your linen should be made of good linen stuff, but with little cloth used; make your shirt short, and all your linen rather light. Your shirt should be cut somewhat shorter than your coat.)

Fig. 6.1-9: Extracts from Ludvig Holm-Olsen's edition of *Konungs skuggsjá* (1983, 45). Expanded abbreviations are marked by italics.

For languages with an established and well-defined orthography, such as Latin, the editor may decide to regularise deviant orthography according to this standard as it has been established in grammars and dictionaries, in this case for classical as well as mediaeval Latin. Specific recommendations have been given by Klaus Sallmann in *Normae orthographicae et orthotypicae Latinae* (1990). As mentioned above, the same procedure is common in introductory and general editions of Old Icelandic and Old Norwegian texts (see Haugen et al. 2019, chap. 10, and, in greater detail, Berg 2014). For some scholars, regularisation is primarily an aesthetic consideration, since it looks rather strange to have an edition which skips from one orthography to another, perhaps in the middle of a sentence, and back again. For linguistic scholars, however, it is a question of accountability, since it would be highly misleading to use, for example, regularised fifteenth-century Icelandic orthography as a witness to Norwegian language two centuries earlier. Editions like the one exemplified in figure 6.1-9 are thus a compromise between textual reconstruction and linguistic accountability.

6.1.6 When Lachmann reigns in the introduction and Bédier in the text

In section 6.1.2 above, Kristian Kålund's editions of *Fljótsdǿla saga* (1883) and *Laxdǿla saga* (1889–1891), and Henrik Bertelsen's edition of *Þiðriks saga af Bern* (1905–1911), were put forward as examples of reconstructive editing in the field of Old Norse. They did not, however, set a precedent (see Haugen 2019). When looking back on Old Norse editing during the last century or so, it can safely be said that the ideal of a full and transparent *recensio* of the manuscripts of a work is uncontested, above all in the Editiones Arnamagnæanæ published in Copenhagen since 1958 (see Louis-Jensen and Haugen in press). The founding father of this series, Jón Helgason, was unequivocal in this respect, also underlining the fact that younger and often neglected paper manuscripts should not be ignored (Giorgio Pasquali would surely have endorsed this principle). At a seminar organised by the University of Copenhagen in 1979, he gave a concise expression of his editorial programme:

> The essential foundation for all close study of a text is a critical edition. One can demand of an edition that it presents, as far as is possible, an investigation of the whole manuscript tradition. The numerous young copies of older works must be examined because there is always the possibility that they derive from sources other than the surviving medieval texts. The result of such an examination is often that the younger copies prove to have no independent value, but this must nonetheless be demonstrated. The editor's aim must be to present as concisely as possible everything that the manuscripts themselves can tell us about a particular work's oldest form (that is to say, the oldest form we can establish which is not necessarily the original mould), while also giving an account of the work's history through the centuries. (Helgason 1979, 14)

This is a truly Lachmannian programme, if we allow ourselves to credit Lachmann with the later development of the genealogical method (see the important modifications in 2.3–4). There is hardly an edition in the Editiones Arnamagnæanæ which does not conclude with a stemma, and, even if the method as such is unnamed, it is the method of common errors which is the basis of *recensio*.

The surprising fact is that the stemma seems to be forgotten as soon as the editor moves from the introduction to the text itself. Rather than establishing the text with the help of the stemma, the edited text is more often than not a synoptic presentation, usually organised on split-level pages and with up to two apparatuses. When Jón Helgason returned to his edition of *Byskupa sögur* in a second volume, published in 1978, the reconstructive approach of the 1938 edition had become non-reconstructive, as shown in section 6.1.4 above. Bédier had, metaphorically speaking, suppressed Lachmann. On the page selected for figure 6.1-7 above, there are two manuscripts of widely different orthography – the upper one is in thirteenth-century orthography, the lower one in seventeenth-century orthography. No single, critical text is offered.

This synoptic approach might be understood as a solution to a particularly difficult manuscript tradition for the bishops' sagas and thus as a deviation from the Lachmannian programme defined by Jón Helgason himself. However, since the initiation of the Editiones Arnamagnæanæ series in 1958, non-reconstructive editing had become the norm. There is no explicit discussion of this *aporia* in the text editions themselves, so the explanation can only be a matter of hypothesis. At least three textual properties seem to line up against the construction of a single critical text.

(*i*) Textual dynamics. While certain texts were copied faithfully and thus with little textual variation over time, other texts were copied by scribes who also revised, added to, and subtracted from the text according to their tastes or to the text's presumed audience. When textual deviations become too plentiful, it is no longer practical to record them in an apparatus of variants, and one must rather accept that versions have to be presented on their own, synoptically or sequentially, or that one version has to be suppressed in favour of another, presumably better version. Trying to build a critical text would mean that the editor would offer a text that never was.

(*ii*) Linguistic diversity. Where texts were copied over time and space and thus acquired new and distinct orthographies, selecting a single linguistic form over others would skew the display of the texts. This is a particular challenge for vernacular texts where variation is a result not of deviation, conscious or not, but of the historical development of language over time and across regions. In this situation, the editor risks offering a text that should be, rather than the texts that actually were.

(*iii*) The ravages of time. As pointed out above, the majority of manuscripts from the classical and mediaeval periods have been lost. Some estimates put the number as high as at least 90 %. This degree of loss has been arrived at by extrapolating from the recorded loss of early printed books, for which we have good catalogues (see Neddermeyer 1996; Olrik Frederiksen 1999; Guido and Trovato 2004, discussed under "2004" in 2.4.3 above). One inevitable consequence is that one or more families will be irrevocably lost, and furthermore that the remaining manuscripts will be more prone to bifurcation, as argued by Guido and Trovato (2004), or members of once large families may be reduced to outliers in the tradition, carrying less weight than they should have carried. It goes without saying that, in such a situation, the editor will be driven towards the *codex optimus*, and that the edition will be of the text that was, rather than of the text that could have been.

If these considerations are relevant to the practice of editing, they may help to explain the limitations of reconstructive editing in the face of textual variability. It is not the failure of the reconstructive programme as such, but the realisation that the textual material may sometimes be too complex or too fragmented to be dealt with by reconstructive editing. Of particular interest, perhaps, is the fact that a stemma is no guarantee of a correct *constitutio textus* in the edition in which it appears. Nor is an edition a prerequisite for the stemma; there are a number of stemmata published outside editions. What stemmata have in common is the fact that they are the result of a *recensio* of the manuscripts, to be used, or not, in the establishment of the edited text.

6.2 Text-critical analysis

Marina Buzzoni

In section 2.2, the principles of the genealogical method were treated and the process of text restoration was critically assessed. As the main technical terms and procedures are of a rather abstract nature, this section will introduce them together with practical examples that illustrate them. Whenever possible, an inductive approach will be used, aimed at developing skills and knowledge by working on real examples from historically transmitted texts.

6.2.1 Definition and terminology

The expression "text-critical analysis" refers to the process of producing a critical text within the genealogical (or Lachmann's) method, also referred to as *constitutio textus* or *restitutio textus* (i.e. the restoration of the text as closely as possible to the original by the editor, see 2.2, 3.2 above; Tarrant 2016 speaks of "establishing the text"). In Paul Maas's handbook (1960, first ed. 1927), *constitutio textus* is not specifically defined, but it is associated with the overall editorial process: "Aufgabe der Textkritik ist Herstellung eines dem Autograph (Original) möglichst nahekommenden Textes (*constitutio textus*)" (Maas 1927, 1 = 1960, 5) [The business of textual criticism is to produce a text as close as possible to the original (*constitutio textus*)] (trans. Flower 1958, 1).

Consequently, the expression *constitutio textus* may be used in a broad sense to cover the whole process of textual criticism, which can be divided into the following phases:
- *recensio*, with *collatio*, followed by the establishment of a *stemma codicum* and *examinatio* of the variant readings;
- *emendatio*, that is, *selectio*, *combinatio*, and *divinatio*; and
- *dispositio*, the final stage of producing the critical edition, in which the text is laid out, apparatuses are created, and other complementary material such as an introduction, descriptions of manuscripts, and notes are incorporated.

On the other hand, other authors use *constitutio textus* in a stricter sense to refer to the phase of textual reconstruction which follows *recensio* (i.e. the comparison and evaluation of the witnesses) and includes *selectio* as well as *emendatio*, which, in this case, is synonymous with *divinatio* (see, among others, P. Chiesa 2002, 50–51, who is, however, well aware that these phases can be variously divided and labelled; see also Duval 2015, s. v. "emendatio", "établissement du texte"; Tarrant 2016, esp. 49–50, 65). The following table summarises the major terminological differences still in use (further differences will be accounted for, when relevant, in the pertinent

Tab. 6.2-1: A comparison of the usage of terminology for the phases of text-critical analysis.

Text-critical analysis = *constitutio textus* (whole process) (e.g. in Maas 1960)	Text-critical analysis (e.g. in P. Chiesa 2002)
	collatio

recensio
  collatio
  construction of the *stemma codicum*
  examinatio
	recensio
	  construction of the *stemma codicum*

emendatio
  selectio
  combinatio
  divinatio
	constitutio textus
	  selectio
	  emendatio = *divinatio*

subsections; see e.g. 6.2.3). It should be noted, however, that, despite these differences, the core of the method remains the same (see also Stussi 2006, 14, esp. n9).

In what follows, terminology equating *constitutio textus* with text-critical analysis as a whole will be used (the left-hand column in table 6.2-1). Among the reasons for this is that the author of this section considers the process of *recensio* an early stage in establishing the text (like Tarrant 2016, 49), and *selectio* a specific act of emendation by judgement (see also Luiselli Fadda 1994, 183–242; Duval 2015, "s. v. *selectio*", in particular the remark on meaning 1) rather than simply a phase that precedes it. We shall now take a look at the stages that have been mentioned separately.

6.2.2 *Recensio*

The first step in the establishment of a text entails the identification and the systematic comparison of the witnesses transmitting that text, taking into consideration both the direct tradition (i.e. either complete or partial copies of the text) and the indirect tradition (i.e. translations, quotations, summaries; see 3.2). This is commonly called *recensio*. Such a *recensio* includes the preliminary identification of the witnesses ("heuristics"; see 3.1) and *collatio* (i.e. the comparative examination of the witnesses in order to identify the places where the texts differ, as described under 3.3). Usually, only a subset of these variant readings (namely, only those readings that can be considered "significant errors" – *Leitfehler*, both conjunctive and disjunctive) are used to determine the genealogical relationship between the witnesses. The examination of shared errors is a crucial procedure of *recensio* whose purpose is at least threefold: eliminating derivative manuscripts (*codices descripti*; see 2.2, 2.4), reconstructing the lost ancestors (internal nodes) from which the surviving ones descend, and finally drawing up a *stemma codicum* (see 2.2, 4.1–2, 4.5) representing the genealogical connections among witnesses.

Example 1: The *Heliand*
Here is a relatively straightforward example taken from the ninth-century Old Saxon poem on the life of Christ entitled *Heliand* [The Saviour]. We will focus on lines 1306b–1308a (= Taeger 1996, 52; see xxi for text-critical details) from song 16, telling of the Chieftain's instructions on the mountain; note that the use of italics in the edited text signals the interventions of the editor, who chose *M* as his base manuscript.

Quað *that* ôc sâlige uuârin,
thie hîr *uuiopin* iro uuammun dâdi;   'thie môtun eft uuillion gebîdan,
frôfre *an iro frâhon rîkia*.'

1308a an iro frâhon rikea V; an iro rikia M; an them selbon rikie C

[He [Christ] said that those also were fortunate, who cried here over their evil deeds, "in return, they can expect the very consolation they desire in their Master's kingdom."] (trans. Murphy 1992, 46)

In line 1308, the sense requires the reading transmitted by manuscript *V*: "an iro frâhon rîkia" [in their Master's kingdom]; in fact, both the *M* ("an iro rikia" [in their kingdom]) and *C* ("an them selbon rikie" [in their own kingdom]) readings would attribute the "kingdom" to the repenting sinners rather than to God. We can therefore assume that *M* and *C* are in agreement in error – the error being basically the lack of *frâhon* (gen. sg. of the noun *frâho*, "master, lord"). We should recall here that only agreement in monogenetic errors is relevant from a genealogical perspective, since it offers clues for detecting innovation (secondary readings, or "errors") vs preservation (primary readings); and that, usually, only substantial readings (see 4.1.5) turn out to be useful, since formal readings (see 2.3.2) are more likely to be either accidental or polygenetic (on these topics, see also Stussi 2006, 9–16).

The assumption made about the *M* and *C* readings vs that of *V* for line 1308a leads to different stemmatic possibilities depending on the interpretation of the origin of the error. If we think that it is more likely that the change from the reading transmitted by *V* occurred only once, we are led to postulate a common ancestor of *M* and *C* (**CM*) that is not a source of *V*. That source could be either an independent one (fig. 6.2-1) or *V* itself (fig. 6.2-2).

Fig. 6.2-1: Bipartite stemma with *V* representing one independent branch and **CM* the other.

Fig. 6.2-2: Single-branch stemma with **CM* deriving from *V*.

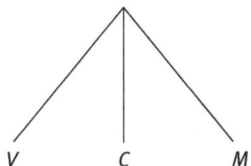

Fig. 6.2-3: Tripartite stemma with each witness representing an independent branch.

If, however, we think that it is more likely that the error was independently made twice in *M* and *C*, we would propose a representation where *M* and *C* are not affiliated, as in figure 6.2-3.

In order to decide between the possible options, we need more evidence: though relative probability favours the most economical hypothesis, that the error occurred only once, we require a number of instances in which *C* and *M* agree in error before concluding that they are stemmatically affiliated. In this case we are lucky, since a good number of such *Bindefehler* (conjunctive errors) – Taeger (1996, xxi) identifies twenty-three – support the first hypothesis, namely that *C* and *M* share a common ancestor against *V*.

We should now establish whether **CM* is (*i*) independent of *V* or (*ii*) derived from it. The required evidence will be an error present in *V* but not in **CM*, one that cannot be easily corrected (*Trennfehler*, or separative error). If we find such an error, it will be unlikely that **CM* derives from *V*; rather, it will be much more likely that **CM* represents a branch independent of *V*. A good candidate is line 1311a, where **CM* reads: "thie rincos, thie hîr rehto *adômiad*" [those fighting men who judged fairly here] and *V* reads: "thie rincos, thie hîr rehto duomeat". The reading of *V* is a clear mistake since it makes no sense and could not be easily restored by a scribe; on the contrary, the verb *adômian*, "to judge", transmitted by *C* and *M*, enhances the meaning of line 1309a: "rincos, that *sie* rehto adômien" [those fighting men who wanted to judge fairly]. In fact, the anaphorical use of the same verb produces a circular effect in this passage (lines 1308b–1311a = Taeger 1996, 52):

> Sâlige sind ôc, the sie hîr frumono *gilustid*,
> rincos, that *sie* rehto adômien.   Thes môtun sie uuerðan an them rîkia drohtines
> gifullit thurh iro ferhton dâdi: sulîcoro môtun sie frumono *bicnêgan*
> thie rincos, thie hîr rehto *adômiad*.

[Those too are fortunate who desired to do good things here, those fighting men who wanted to judge fairly. With good things they themselves will be filled to satisfaction in the Chieftain's kingdom for their wise actions; they will attain good things, those fighting men who judged fairly.] (trans. Murphy 1992, 46)

Although, in this example, the probability that *duomeat* is a trivial error is very high since the term makes no sense, it is not always easy to discriminate between an apparently wrong reading and a more difficult reading, that is, a *lectio difficilior* (see below). In fact, it is not uncommon that a scribal error creates a *lectio difficilior* or – conversely – that a *lectio difficilior* is taken as an error and therefore "corrected".

Returning to our question of whether **CM* is independent of *V* or derives from it, in the light of what has been discussed so far we are led to grant **CM* independence from *V*, and inclined to prefer hypothesis (*i*) over (*ii*). This conclusion is the result of judicious calculations of probabilities and close attention to all potentially relevant factors, including both form and substance of the variant readings – as shown by the *adômian* example – as well as elements of the whole manuscript tradition (for a comprehensive stemmatic hypothesis for the *Heliand* manuscript tradition, also including the *S* and *P* fragments, see Taeger 1996, xxiv, and Buzzoni

2011, 104, where the most recently recovered fragment from Leipzig in 2006 is also integrated into the stemma).

This leads to a further important consideration, particularly relevant in a reconstructive perspective: the presence or absence of an archetype distinct from the original in the tradition (see 4.1.5). The existence of such an archetype can, in fact, only be ascertained if one can detect at least one "error" common to the whole tradition, thus proving the existence of an already modified copy, the archetype, from which the entire extant tradition stems. (The main characteristic of such "errors" is that they could not have stood in the original, for whatever reason.) To continue with the *Heliand* example, this is a case of a tradition in which an archetype has been postulated between the two branches *V* and **CM* (see fig. 6.2-1) and the original due to some errors that these branches apparently share (Taeger 1996, xxiv). On the other hand, the tradition of the Old English *Sermo Lupi ad Anglos* (see example 13 below) lacks an archetype distinct from the original (see Luiselli Fadda 1994, 213), and so do a good deal of other mediaeval Germanic texts. The situation is very different for texts from Antiquity: due to the hiatus in time between the original and the oldest manuscripts, an archetype is usually present. Establishing whether an archetype or the original has to be posited at the basis of a tradition is fundamental, as it changes the scope of the editor's interventions: an editor is entitled to emend the text of the archetype in order to get as close as possible to the original, but if there was no archetype, the agreement of either all or the majority of branches in the stemma yields an original reading that the editor has to live with and should not emend (see e.g. P. Chiesa 2002, 81).

6.2.2.1 *Examinatio*

Recensio ends with *examinatio*, that is, the analysis of the complete set of variants (and not only of the indicative errors) in order to ascertain whether the readings to be attributed to the reconstructed text can be chosen solely on the basis of the stemma, or whether there still remain some corruptions that can be corrected only by *emendatio* (see 6.2.3).

Since a stemma, as shown in figures 6.2-1–3 above, is a working hypothesis in that it represents the best choice among a set of possible options, neither the process nor the results of *examinatio* are always straightforward. One should also consider the fact that stemmata can come in a wide variety of configurations (see 4.1), some of which are especially complex, in particular those shaped to represent contamination (see 4.4), a circumstance which renders the identification of original or archetypal readings extremely difficult. Some theoretical examples are provided here to illustrate some general principles of how to choose the readings most likely to be archetypal or original; these will be followed by real examples. The case of intra-stemmatic contamination was discussed *in extenso* in section 4.4, but is worth recalling here.

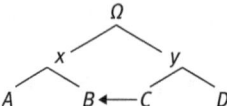

Fig. 6.2-4: A hypothetical stemma displaying intra-stemmatic contamination (Ω indicates the archetype).

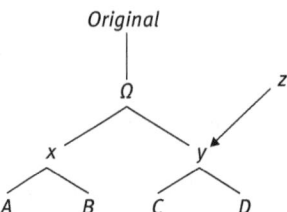

Fig. 6.2-5: A hypothetical stemma showing extra-stemmatic contamination (Ω indicates the archetype).

This stemma in figure 6.2-4 represents an instance of horizontal transmission, in that the copyist of B draws not only on the **antigraph** within the same branch of the stemma (i.e. the lost witness x) but also on an extant witness that belongs to another branch (i.e. C). Therefore, C is said to have contaminated B. Technically speaking, the readings that only B and C have in common against the other witnesses are *lectiones singulares* (see 5.2.3.1), which are unlikely to represent the readings of the archetype (for more complex situations, see, among others, 4.4 above; Avalle 1972a, 70–86; Timpanaro 1981, 143–144; Luiselli Fadda 1994, 220–222; Trovato 2017, 129–130).

Contamination may also be extra-stemmatic (already mentioned in 2.4.3 and shown in fig. 6.2-5). In this case, we assume that the copyist of y included in the text some readings (*Fremdlesungen*; Fränkel 1964, 78) taken from an external lost source – either a lost branch of the same textual tradition ("extra-archetypal contamination"; Trovato 2017, 134), or a different textual tradition altogether (Timpanaro 1981, 143; this second possibility, of which Timpanaro was well aware as early as the mid-twentieth century, is often overlooked by scholars, even though it is frequently present in real traditions, as shown in examples 2 and 3 below). The lost source is represented in the stemma by z. In this simple configuration, the unique readings shared by C and D cannot be ascribed with certainty to the text of y copied from the archetype Ω as they may also come from the external contaminating source (see Avalle 1972a, esp. 78, point 4; Luiselli Fadda 1994, esp. 221, point (*b*)). In other words, a reading which is shared by C and D alone may come from the archetype Ω, but it could also go back to z. In the latter case, that reading has no reconstructive value for the archetype Ω. In fact, in such a constellation, the readings with a reconstructive value are only those which x (A + B) and either C or D (or both) have in common, since only these readings are attested in both branches of the tradition and therefore ascribable with certainty to the archetype Ω. In some cases, the readings deriving from the external source might come from higher up in the stemma than those of the archetype itself and thus be potentially useful for reconstructing the original.

Example 2: The *Mahābhārata*
In real textual traditions, the situation can be even more complex, especially when oral tradition plays an important role in the transmission of a text. Vishwa Adluri and Joydeep Bagchee, in their work on the Old Indian epic poem *Mahābhārata* (Adluri and Bagchee 2018), claim that extra-stemmatic contamination can be of two types, namely contamination into an ancestor of the archetype, or "hyperarchetypal contamination", and contamination of an extant source from a no-longer-extant source, or "extra-stemmatic contamination in the proper sense". In the *Mahābhārata*, extra-stemmatic contamination is often present, especially due to the fact that an older oral epic tradition existed alongside the written one. Elements of this older oral epic have survived beyond its alleged Brahmanic redaction, and scholars have explained this fact in two ways: either the Brahmanic redaction was not complete, and thus episodes and narratives from the oral epic tradition present in the older "*kṣatriya* stage" were preserved, or the older epic tradition survived at the margins of Brahmanic society and occasionally caused the introduction of *kṣatriya* elements into the epic. The first view involves an instance of hyperarchetypal contamination (contamination of the original epic with a source prior to the formation of the archetype). The second view accounts for the occurrence of oral material in the *Mahābhārata* tradition by invoking extra-stemmatic contamination in the proper sense, and therefore the existence of a parallel tradition or transmission alongside the written one.

Example 3: The *Anglo-Saxon Chronicle*
The Old English text of the *Anglo-Saxon Chronicle* is transmitted in seven manuscripts labelled with the letters *A–G*: *G* is clearly a *codex descriptus* derived from *A*, and therefore can be left aside; *B* is very close to *C*, both having been copied from the same ancestor; and *F* is an epitome of *E*. The complex relationships between the extant witnesses, also including some Latin texts that have a version of the *Chronicle* among their sources – in particular Asser's *Life of Alfred*, Æthelweard's *Chronicon*, and the *Annals of St Neots* – have been variously interpreted and represented by scholars. However, two features in particular seem to point to the fact that the compiler of the Latin *Annals of St Neots* was using a copy which must have preceded all the other *Chronicle* witnesses: first, at lines 642 and 672, the form "koenuualch" for the name of a king is older than the "cenwalh" of all the vernacular texts; and second, the *Annals* lack the chronological dislocation between the years 756 and 842 shared by all the other manuscripts. Æthelweard's *Chronicon*,

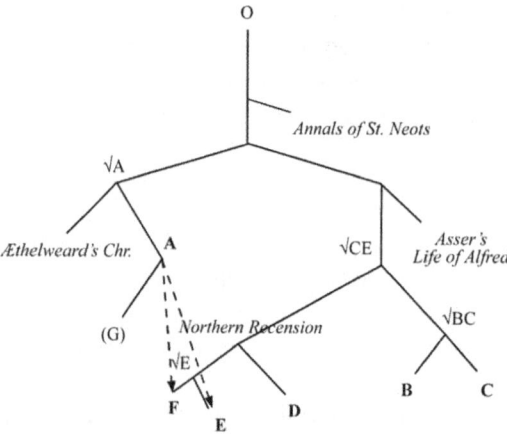

Fig. 6.2-6: Stemmatic proposal for the *Anglo-Saxon Chronicle* witnesses. Source: Buzzoni et al. (2016, 655).

contrary to all the surviving witnesses and Asser's *Life of Alfred*, has not lost a whole sentence from the annal for 885 by homoeoteleuton (or eye-skip; see 4.3.2) and does not have the additions also absent in *A*, which means that the *Chronicon* belongs to the same branch as *A*, though it is, in some respects, closer to the original. As for Asser's *Life of Alfred*, Dorothy Whitelock (1979, 118) claims that, since there are passages where Asser's text, Æthelweard's *Chronicon*, and *A* agree against *B*, *C*, *D*, and *E*, these four manuscripts of the *Chronicle* can be taken to descend from a common version which contained several new features (√CE). Due to their closeness (e.g. they agree in entering the portion called the "Mercian Register" as a whole block of annals, 902–924, and they share the annals for 957, 971, and 977, which do not occur anywhere else), it is generally assumed that *B* and *C* are copies of a common ancestor (√BC). Finally, *D* and *E* agree against all the other witnesses in their inclusion of an early set of annals known as the "Second Northern Group" (901–966), which contains material of northern interest drawn mainly from Bede's *Historia ecclesiastica gentis Anglorum* and from additional northern annals. It is generally assumed that they descend from a common ancestor, from which *E* seems to be at two removes (Cubbin 1996, liii). A stemmatic proposal (fig. 6.2-6) that captures the agreement of *B*, *C*, *D*, and *E* as opposed to *A*, as well as the strong contamination between the *A*-branch and the *E*-branch of the *Chronicle* tradition, has been put forward by Marina Buzzoni (Buzzoni 2001, 42; Buzzoni et al. 2016; in fig. 6.2-6, intra-stemmatic contamination is marked by dashed lines and the direction of contamination is represented by arrows). The stemma also captures the relationships with the above-mentioned Latin texts that have a version of the *Chronicle* among their sources.

Sometimes, computer-assisted stemmatology (see 5.1) can contribute to shedding new light on old problems. The graph obtained by applying NeighborNet (see 4.4.6.2, 5.5.8, 8.1) detects a further contamination path from *A* to the *BC*-branch,

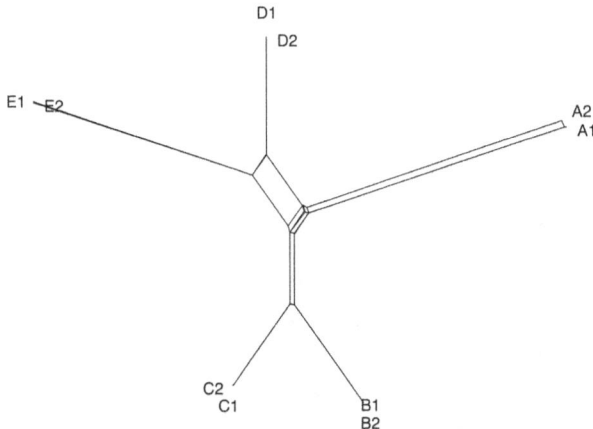

Fig. 6.2-7: NeighborNet graph of the *Anglo-Saxon Chronicle* witnesses (with the exception of the bilingual F, which bears entries in Old English and Latin). Source: Buzzoni et al. (2016, 662, fig. 6.2-7).

usually neglected in traditional stemmata, despite the fact that it is supported by textual data. *B* and *C*, in fact, share "a few supplementary notes" (Taylor 1983, xxxv) drawn from the ancestor of *A* specifically for the annals for 957, 959, 971, 976 (*C* only), and 977. The contamination between *A* and the *BC*-branch is clearly recognisable in figure 6.2-7, as the network linking the branches under inspection shows.

Example 4: The *Minnesänger*

Contamination can also move both ways. Such reciprocal contamination, represented below, leads to situations that can assume the shape of a ring, as shown in figure 6.2-8.

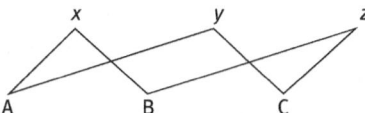

Fig. 6.2-8: A relationship between witnesses demonstrating reciprocal contamination.

In a case like this, where *A* and *B* draw on *x*, *A* and *C* draw on *y*, and *B* and *C* draw on *z* (reciprocal contamination), no genealogical reconstruction is, in fact, possible (Avalle 1972a, 104–105), and the relationship between the witnesses can perhaps be better represented as a ring, which, in contrast to a traditional stemma, lacks a temporal dimension. This is called a c o n f l a t i o n r i n g (Dearing 1967, 291; 1968, 553), as shown in figure 6.2-9.

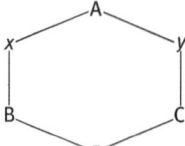

Fig. 6.2-9: A schema for a conflation ring.

Some scholars claim that this representation is suitable for illustrating the connections between three Middle High German manuscripts that transmit lyric compilations of *Minnesänger*, namely the *Kleine Heidelberger Liederhandschrift* (*A*; Heidelberg, Universitätsbibliothek, Pal. germ. 357, late thirteenth century), the *Weingartner Liederhandschrift* (*B*; Stuttgart, Württembergische Landesbibliothek, H.B. XIII, poet. germ. I, early fourteenth century), and the renowned *Codex Manesse*, or *Große Heidelberger Liederhandschrift* (*C*; Heidelberg, Universitätsbibliothek, Pal. germ. 848, made in Zurich in the first third of the fourteenth century, in all probability under the patronage of the Manesse family). The mutual relationships among these witnesses are still a matter of debate, but we are pretty sure that *B* and *C* share a common ancestor (*z*), and that *C* partially draws on a source of *A* (Frühmorgen-Voss 1975, 57–88), or perhaps on two different redactions of *A* (Sayce 1982, 56; Luiselli Fadda 1994, 222).

In addition to contaminated traditions, o v e r a b u n d a n t traditions can also be difficult to handle. In traditions that can hardly be assessed in their entirety due to the abundance of witnesses, philologists may decide to select a number of *loci critici* to establish the stemma. A *locus criticus* (or *selectus*) is a portion of the text in which the amount of significant errors between the various witnesses is particularly high (see also the notion of "variant location" in 3.3); the alternative adjective *selectus* alludes to the fact that the passage has been chosen for critical purposes. Although the expression seems to be first attested in the 1970s (Balduino 1979, 29: "il concentrarsi di errori significativi"), both Maas (1927, 13) and Pasquali (1934, 55–56) had already introduced the similar notion of "collation by samples" ("collazione per campioni"). Richard Tarrant similarly speaks of "selective collation" (2016, 56). The most important editions of Dante's *Divina Commedia* are based on the scrutiny of *loci critici*: 396 of them from 200 witnesses in Barbi's 1891 preparatory work (known as "Barbi's canon"), and 477 in Petrocchi's edition (1966–1967; for further information, see Brandoli 2007); in his 2001 edition of the *Commedia*, Federico Sanguineti goes back to Barbi's canon and extends the collation to more than 500 witnesses. There are, of course, some hurdles and risks in this procedure, especially when a new collation is entirely based on the results of previous collations assembled using samples (see, among others, Vàrvaro 1970, 574).

As stated before, once the stemmatic configuration has been determined, the process of *examinatio* goes on to ascertain whether it is possible to establish some either archetypal or original readings only on the basis of the stemma, using a simple calculus of shared readings, namely by applying the majority principle to independent branches (see esp. 2.2–3). Roughly speaking, this is more likely to happen, or is more easily recognisable, in a closed recension, and far less likely – if not completely impossible – in an open recension (Pasquali 1934, 126; the latter is also called a "non-mechanical recension" by Timpanaro 1981, 101; see esp. 2.4 above; see also 4.4 above). What follows are a few examples of selecting readings on the basis of the stemma.

Example 5: "mund" vs "mûð"
A simple example of choosing a reading according to the stemma can be found in the *Heliand*. At line 1293b (= Taeger 1996, 51), the reading "mund" [mouth], which is shared by *MV* against the *C*-reading "mûð" (the Ingvaeonic cognate form) has been preferred by scholars since it occurs in both branches of the stemma (see fig. 6.2-1 above):

> mildi an is môde,   endi thô *is mund* [C: mûð] antlôc.
>
> [mild in his heart;   and then he unlocked his mouth.] (my trans.)

Example 6: Jean Renart's *Lai de l'ombre*
Another interesting case study is offered by the manuscript tradition of Jean Renart's *Lai de l'ombre* (end of the twelfth or early thirteenth century). The text is transmitted in seven main witnesses mostly going back to the thirteenth century and labelled with letters from *A* to *G*. As a starting point for the stemmatic analysis, we can postulate the very well-known hypothesis put forth by Gaston Paris in 1890 (see Bédier 1928, 167; Trovato 2017, 290), who proposed the tripartite stemma reproduced in figure 6.2-10. This stemma has been discussed frequently (see Trovato 2017, 292–297), but this is not relevant for our purposes here.

At line 217 of the *Lai*, the **varia lectio** (the entirety of variation at this one *locus*) reads as follows.

> AB: en son penser et en sa voie
> DE: a son penser et a sa voie
> CG: celant son penser et sa voie
> F: a ses amours et a sa joie

F's reading is a unique reading (*lectio singularis*), isolated at the bottom of the stemma; therefore, it is highly unlikely to represent the reading of the original. *AB*'s reading can be traced back to their common ancestor, namely *x*. Similarly, *CG*'s reading can be taken to come from *y*. The only reading that is attested in two branches of the tradition is that transmitted by *D* and *E* ("a son penser et a sa voie"), which thus represents the best candidate with which to restore the line of the origi-

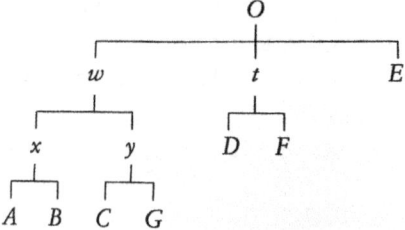

Fig 6.2-10: Gaston Paris's tripartite stemma for the *Lai de l'ombre*, as reshaped by Bédier (1928, 167).

nal – of course, this conclusion holds only if we give credence to the stemmatic configuration in figure 6.2-10.

6.2.2.2 The use of indirect traditions

On the use of indirect traditions to establish the readings as close as possible to the original, see sections 3.2 and 6.2.3 (example 7). On a more general level, it can be added here that the hazards of textual transmission may result in the indirect traditions having a central role compared to direct ones. For instance, the indirect tradition surviving in mediaeval manuscripts from what we might call "peripheral" European areas like England or the Nordic countries (see Pasquali 1952, 174–176) can be central to the retrieval of either completely lost texts or genuine readings of preserved traditions. For instance, many Latin codices reached England very early (i.e. the late sixth and seventh centuries), brought there by missionaries from Italy. Once in England, the texts contained in these codices were often translated or manipulated in various ways. The indirect tradition offered by these pre-Carolingian insular sources can be of great importance in establishing a number of readings of the original Latin texts that have otherwise been completely lost, as was convincingly demonstrated by Anna Maria Luiselli Fadda (1998) in her study of the indirect tradition of the *Vita Fursei*. A further paradigmatic example is offered by the Old Norwegian prose translation of *La Chanson de Roland* (usually labelled as *n*) which appears as the eighth chapter of a collection entitled *Karlamagnús saga* and is pretty close to the most authoritative witness of the *Chanson*, Oxford, Bodleian Library, Digby 23. As remarked by Paul Aebischer (1954) and Eyvind F. Halvorsen (1959), as well as by Cesare Segre in his 1971 groundbreaking edition of the text, *n* occupies a relevant position in the stemma and can therefore be used to determine a number of good variant readings of the β-branch (Segre 1971; see also Avalle 1972a, 23, and, on a similar topic, Willert Bortignon 1993).

When the tradition consists of three or more independent branches (as in fig. 6.2-3), the agreement of the majority of branches will usually give the archetypal or the original reading. However, especially in bipartite stemmata (see 4.1), difficulties may arise when the editor has to decide between readings that have equal stemmatic value (stemmatically undecidable variants, in Italian called *varian-*

ti adiafore). In such cases, the reading of the archetype or of the original can only be ascertained by judgement, that is, by weighing up the relative merits of the variants, as will be shown below in section 6.2.3.

6.2.3 Emendatio

In the broader perspective of *constitutio textus* adopted here, *emendatio* (see 2.2, 3.1, 4.1) is the second major step in textual restoration, whereby the editor tries to restore "archetypal" or "original" readings where no mechanical choice is possible (see 2.1), that is, in those cases where *examinatio* cannot yield an unambiguous result. This can be done by judgement, either according to internal criteria (*selectio*; see 2.2) or conjecturally (*divinatio*). As far as the actual text-critical procedure is concerned, *selectio* precedes *divinatio*: the latter is performed only when the results of the former are not decisive for establishing all the readings to be included in the critically assessed text which is potentially the original.

The most common internal criteria according to which the selection between readings of equal stemmatic value is carried out are *lectio difficilior* (*potior*), "the more difficult reading is the preferable reading" (see 2.1, 2.4); *usus scribendi*, "the practice of the author"; and other peculiarities ascribable to the potential author(s) of the work, for example the language variety they presumably used or the alleged period of composition of the work. Sometimes, the reconstructed reading can also be obtained by combining variants that are only partially correct, that is, by *combinatio*. Some scholars consider *combinatio* a subtype of *divinatio*; others see it as in between *selectio* and *divinatio*.

As for *divinatio*, two slightly different meanings of the term can be singled out. Following the terminology adopted in this section, *divinatio* is one of the three main operations which characterise *emendatio*, along with the already mentioned *selectio* and *combinatio*. It consists of correcting the allegedly corrupted textual passages only by conjecture, for example by providing additions or by deleting and substituting some readings (see, among others, Avalle 1972a, 111–112; Luiselli Fadda 1994, 236–237; McDonald 1970, 1048–1050). However, Paul Maas, in his *Textkritik* (1927, 6–8), gives *divinatio* a broader meaning, which is very close to the notion of *emendatio ope ingenii*. Maas, in fact, uses this term to designate the third and final stage of textual restoration.

Example 7: Cædmon's *Hymn*
When choosing between variants which have equal stemmatic value (*selectio*), the editor may take into account a variety of potentially relevant factors, for example grammar, diction, metrical patterns in verse or rhythm in prose, stylistic features, and so on. It goes perhaps without saying that, since these precepts are not rules but rather statements of relative probability, they have to be used with caution as

they have significant consequences for the text offered to the reader. The idea that the more difficult reading is also the preferable one seems to be logically robust (it encapsulates the assumption that scribes tend to simplify the text they are copying), but judging the difficulty of a reading can itself present challenges. The short Old English poem known as Cædmon's *Hymn* has come down to us in twenty-two Northumbrian and West Saxon witnesses, to which a Latin version should be added (Bede *Historia ecclesiastica* 4.22). Line 5b (O'Donnell 2005) of the *Hymn* contains a variant reading that identifies two recensions.

(a) hē ǣrist scōp   ylda/ælda b(e)arnum
(b) hē ǣrist scōp   eorðan/eordu/eorðe b(e)arnum

The first reading is that of the West Saxon *ylda* and Northumbrian *ælda* recensions, and would be translated "for the children of men": "He first created [the world] for the children of men". The West Saxon *eorðan*, Northumbrian *eordu*, and, with some corruption, West Saxon *eorðe* recensions would be translated "for the children of earth": "He first created [the world] for the children of earth". The indirect tradition (see 3.2) represented by the Latin text in Bede, *Historia ecclesiastica* 4.22, transmits the reading "filiis hominum", an image of biblical ascendancy and therefore preferred by many modern editors. Yet, as far back as 1946, Charles L. Wrenn interpreted "eorðan/eordu/eorðe b(e)arnum" as the *lectio difficilior* with respect to the later Christian formula "ylda/ælda b(e)arnum". The choice between the two readings has consequences for the meaning of the text: while the latter places the text within the context of Christian orthodoxy, the former adds a more archaic note.

It should be noted that the principle of *lectio difficilior*, which is indeed applicable to high-register literary texts, may not apply to low-register ones where copyists, when faced with clumsy original readings, are likely to adapt them to their own more refined register. This is the case for some mediaeval Latin texts, such as the *Itinerarium Antonini* (see the discussion in P. Chiesa 2002, 89) or the *Navigatio Sancti Brendani* (Guglielmetti 2017), which were sometimes improved by more learned Carolingian or humanist scribes. For this reason, Paolo Chiesa (2002, 88) suggests thinking in terms of u t r u m   i n   a l t e r u m   a b i t u r u m   e r a t, "the variant reading which is more likely to have passed into the other", by either corruption or improvement.

Example 8: *La Vie de Saint Alexis*
Connected with the notion of *lectio difficilior* is that of d i f f r a c t i o n (see "1955–" in 2.4.3), also called multiple innovations. The latter was first explored theoretically by Gianfranco Contini in 1955, and further clarified by the same scholar in a speech given in 1967 (Contini 1986, 135–148). Contini draws the term from physics and applies it to the field of textual criticism, where it refers to the substitution of a particularly difficult, infrequent, or rare original reading with several innovative (but trivial) readings or attempts at clarification by the copyists. Contini then distinguishes

the categories of diffraction *in praesentia*, where the reading that has caused diffraction is preserved in at least one witness, and diffraction *in absentia*, where the reading that has caused diffraction is lost. The following is an example of the second category, given by Contini himself (1986, 135–148) and taken from the tradition of the Old French *La Vie de Saint Alexis* (line 155; L, A, P, P2, and S are the manuscripts that transmit the diffracted readings). The previous line reads "Plainons ensemble le dol de nostre ami".

> *L*: tu de tun seinur, jo·l frai pur mun flz
> *A*: tu pur tun sire e je pur mun chier flz
> *P*: tu por tun seignor, je.l ferai por mun fz (*P2*: tu t. seigneur.)
> *S*: l'une son fil et l'autre son ami

None of the readings of the extant manuscripts (*L*: "tun seinur", *A*: "tun sire", *P*: "tun seignor", *S*: "son fil") are acceptable, for reasons of metre (*L P P2*), morphology (*A*), or meaning in context (*S*). It has been argued by Adolf Tobler (1872), in his review of Gaston Paris's *editio maior* of *Alexis*, that the lost original reading could be an unattested one, namely "ton per" [your spouse]: "tu por ton per, jol ferai por mon fil". Using Contini's terminology, one can assume that the rare meaning of *per*, "spouse" (a morphologically masculine form), has generated diffraction leading to the different trivial readings attested in the witnesses: "seinur"/"seignor" [lord, husband] (*L/P*), "sire", nom. [lord, husband] (*A*), "son fil" [his son] (*S*).

Example 9: Dante's *Divina Commedia*
The opposite of *lectio difficilior* is *lectio facilior*, "the easier reading", a form of trivialisation. In the *Divina Commedia*, *Inferno*, canto 14, Petrocchi's reading "marturi" [inflict pain] for line 48 (= Petrocchi 1966–1967, 2:230) seems clearly a *lectio facilior* if compared to the traditional "maturi" [ripen] (see Bosco 1968, esp. 59; Paratore 1968); the former, in fact, obscures a striking metaphor which produces sarcasm characteristic of Dante:

> chi è quel grande che non par che curi
> lo 'ncendio e giace dispettoso e torto,
> sì che la pioggia non par che 'l maturi? (lines 46–48)
>
> [Who is that mighty one who seems to heed not / The fire, and lieth lowering and disdainful, / So that the rain seems not to ripen him?] (trans. Longfellow 1867)

The verb *marturi* (vs *maturi*) would yield the easier reading "So that the rain seems not to torture him?", and therefore Petrocchi's choice seems, as some scholars have indeed argued, not to be the most appropriate in this context.

Another principle that can support the editor's judgement is that of *lectio brevior* (*potior*), according to which the shorter reading is the more probable one, on the grounds that the longer reading is more likely to be an attempt by copyists to clarify the meaning of the text (see 7.2.1). This notion seems to have been first used by Bengel (1734, 778): "plerumque, si non semper, genuina est lectio brevior, verbosior interpolata" [often, if not always, the shorter reading is authentic, the longer is interpolated]. The application of this general statement to real textual tradition is more problematic than that of *lectio difficilior*.

Example 10: Lucan's *Bellum civile*

The notion of *usus scribendi* is based on the assumption that authors have their own stylistic preferences, that is, their own preferred modes of expression. Therefore, the reading which is closer to these modes is to be chosen by the editor. In book 1 of Lucan's *Bellum civile*, the first word of line 381 appears in two variants in two different branches of the manuscript tradition, namely "castra" (Ω) and "signa" (Z). The former reading is usually preferred over the latter as it is thought to better reflect the *usus scribendi* of the Latin poet, who frequently uses the expression "castra ponere" in his works:

> castra super Tusci si ponere Thybridis undas
> Hesperios audax ueniam metator in agros. (lines 381–382 = Roche 2009, 78)
>
> [If you bid me set up camp above the waters of the Tuscan Tiber / I shall come, a bold planner, into Hesperian fields.] (trans. Leigh 2016)

Although it is unquestionable that this principle has general validity, it should also be used with caution in editorial practice. In fact, uniformity of style cannot necessarily be ascribed to the original text: it can also result from a process of stylistic levelling carried out by copyists once they have become aware of the stylistic preference of the authors whose works they transcribe (some examples are discussed in Tarrant 2016, 58–59). Thus, there will be cases where *usus scribendi* and *lectio difficilior* may be in conflict with one another.

Sometimes, the archetypal reading can be reconstructed by combining two partially wrong variants (*combinatio*). D'Arco Silvio Avalle (1972a, 116) reports that in Peire Vidal's song "Atressi co·l perilhans" [I Am Like a Shipwrecked Man], line 26 reads "Tornari l'ir'en conort" in manuscript *C* (Paris, Bibliothèque nationale de France, fr. 856) and "E tornara l'ir'en conort" in manuscript *R* (Paris, Bibliothèque nationale de France, fr. 22543). In both manuscripts, the verb ending (*C*: "Tornar-i", *R*: "tornar-a") is morphologically wrong; the correct future form can be reconstructed by combining *R* ("-a") and *C* ("-i"): "Tornarai l'ir'en conort" [I shall turn pain into joy] (see also Fraser 2006, 102). Furthermore, line 26 in *R* begins with an extrametrical "E" [And], which is a clear anticipation of the conjunction in the following line, line 27: "E vivarai m'en alhors" [And I shall turn elsewhere]. On the basis of this metrical evaluation, the archetypal reading of line 26 is assumed to lack the conjunction.

An emendation is called *ex fonte* (*emendatio ex fonte*) when the correction of a plainly wrong quotation in the text is based on the reading transmitted by the source of the quotation. For example, in the laudatory poem for St Catherine, "Or mi conforta, bella", contained in the *Laudario di Modena*, line 89 reads as follows: "cusí la te' a mostrare ch'eri sanctificata", while in the *Legenda aurea* one reads of her: "de eius corpore pro sanguine lac [= *la(t)te*, "milk"] emanauit" (Maggioni 2007, 1358). Therefore, line 89 should be emended accordingly as "ensí late a mostrare ch'eri sanctificata" [milk poured [from your body] to show that you were holy] (Del Popolo 2001, esp. 26).

When *selectio* is not enough to assess the readings that should be ascribed to the original, then *divinatio* may help. This is an extremely delicate operation, since the philologist relies only on conjecture. For this reason, it should be considered as a last-resort strategy and used with care. Nowadays, for example, editors tend not to emend heavily corrupted portions of texts, or extensive lacunae, since they are aware of the limits of this procedure. In critical editions, *loci* that are not emendable are usually marked with a *crux desperationis* (†). Even more so, grammatically acceptable readings should be treated with the highest care and emended with caution only when deemed absolutely necessary, in order not to produce erroneous conjectures, as exemplified in example 11 below. It is especially important to avoid anachronistic emendation that uses a form of language the author of the text may not have been familiar with.

Example 11: *The Battle of Brunanburh*
In his 1938 edition of a ninth-century Old English poem entitled the *Battle of Brunanburh*, Alistair Campbell found the readings of the witnesses for line 12b unsatisfactory, albeit grammatically correct: *A*: "feld dæn`n´ede" (the second *n* being written above the line) – *BC*: "feld dennade" – *D*: "feld dennode" [the battlefield resounded [with the blood of the warriors]]. Therefore, he emended the line by *divinatio* into "feld dunnade" [the battlefield was darkened [with the blood of the warriors]] on the assumption that the verb "to get dark" was semantically more appropriate. By doing this, however, Campbell ruled out the possibility of synaesthesia, which not only is completely acceptable in the context (the battlefield resounded with the blows of the warriors' swords that brought many of them to their death) but would also make the poetic diction more precious (see O'Brien O'Keeffe 1990, 115; Buzzoni 2001, 79–81). Further examples of overconfidence on the part of editors can be found in Tarrant (2016, esp. 282).

In open traditions (see 4.4), where stemmatic analysis plays a more limited role, the editor's judgement becomes much more important. In such traditions, the distinction between older manuscripts (*codices vetustiores*) and more recent ones (*codices recentiores*) can be so blurred as to be almost useless in discriminating between or among variants. *Codices vetustiores* are traditionally held to transmit better readings than the more corrupted *recentiores*, but this is clearly an overgeneralisation. As Pasquali (1952, 41–108) suggested, later witnesses are not necessarily inferior – *recentiores non deteriores* (see 2.2.4, 2.4 above) – since they may transmit *lectiones vetustiores* for which no older witness happens to survive. This may also apply to extremely late witnesses such as *editiones principes* (i.e. the first printed editions of a work; see 1.4): an excellent example is offered by the *editio princeps* of Jacopone da Todi's *Laudi* published in Florence in 1490 and based on manuscripts which were subsequently lost, thus transmitting a series of *lectiones vetustiores* despite its late date (Brambilla Ageno 1975, 18). With the exception of perspicuous instances, deciding when to accept a reading found in later witnesses is one of the most difficult choices an editor has to make.

6.2.3.1 Codices unici

Along with open traditions, another peculiar situation is represented by *codices unici* (singular: *codex unicus*; see 1.2.3), where judgement alone can be used to restore the text since the editor cannot rely on a stemma to choose between variants. Despite this, an interpretative critical process can be carried out: even in the absence of points of comparison, the editor should proceed from what is attested and known (the historical single witness) to what is unattested and therefore unknown (the original) following the emendation steps illustrated here. Many noteworthy Italian literary monuments are transmitted in single manuscripts, among them the anonymous *Il fiore* and *Il detto d'amore*, cleverly edited by Gianfranco Contini (1984) in a methodologically highly influential volume. Similarly, the majority of early Germanic texts are transmitted in single manuscripts. In these cases, in order to avoid the overuse of conjectural emendations, a thorough study of the unique witness and its transmission has to be performed (see, among others, Avalle 1972a, 25–27; Brambilla Ageno 1975, 26–37; Luiselli Fadda 1994, 190–191, 224–225; Stussi 2006, 19; on the potential offered by the digital environment, see Bleier et al. 2018).

Example 12: *Beowulf*

Line 2298 (= Fulk, Bjork, and Niles 2008, 79) of the Old English poem *Beowulf* reads as follows:

> on þ(*am*) westenne   hwæðre *wiges* gefeh.
> [in that wilderness,   however [he] looked forward to the battle.]

The unique manuscript which transmits the text (London, British Library, Cotton Vitellius A.xv) has the reading "hilde" instead of "wiges". The latter, included in the text by conjecture, is preferred by many editors (since Klaeber's 1922 edition) for metrical reasons: "wiges" in fact alliterates with "westenne" in 2298a, both beginning with the labio-velar semi-vowel [w].

6.2.4 Dispositio

Once critically established, the text has to be offered to the reader (see 6.3). The term *dispositio* refers to the final stage of editorial work, in which the critically established text is positioned on the page, together with the critical apparatus that records the evidence on which the text established by the editor rests. This is the main reason why the apparatus does not simply complement the edition; it is rather the result of editorial judgement and thus it is as essential to the critical edition as the text itself.

The various formats that an a p p a r a t u s can assume (in compliance with more minimalist or more maximalist approaches to it; see Tarrant 2016, 130), as well as the selection of information to be included, will be discussed in detail in section 6.3. Here, it will suffice to note that the main purpose of a critical apparatus is to account for the choices made by the editor by recording the pertinent textual evidence. Furthermore, by making the editor's acts of judgement visible, the critical apparatus allows the reader to either confirm or reject the readings accepted by the editor. The apparatus is therefore the core of the critical process, and perhaps even more. Back in 1974, Cesare Segre argued that the apparatus should be the location where the tension between respect for the antigraph and the innovative thrust of the copyist is brought to the fore:

> Occorre [...] capovolgere i rapporti gerarchici fra testo e apparato, dare la maggiore enfasi all'apparato e considerare il testo come una superficie neutra [...] su cui il filologo ha innestato le lezioni da lui considerate sicure, fra le tante considerate. Ma l'edizione si merita l'attributo di critica molto di più attraverso l'apparato, se discorsivamente problematico: perché esso sintetizza il diasistema della tradizione, e perché svolge un vaglio completo, anche se non sempre conclusivo, delle lezioni. (Segre 1978, 497)

> [There needs to be a turnaround [...] in the hierarchical relationships between the text and the apparatus, in order to give greater emphasis to the apparatus and consider the text as a neutral surface [...] onto which the philologist has grafted the readings which he deemed certain among the many considered. However, an edition deserves the attribute of being "critical" much more through the apparatus that ought to disclose a critical discourse: because it summarises the diasystem of the tradition, and because it carries out a full assessment of the readings, even if it is not always conclusive.]

It is precisely in the apparatus that the text emerges as a diasystem (see 2.4 above), a term first applied to textual criticism by Cesare Segre (1976) to express the idea that the text transmitted in a given manuscript represents the contact between the linguistic system of the author and those of the copyists who filter the exemplar through their own codes.

Usually, in print editions, the reconstructed text is placed on the upper part of the page, followed by two (or more) apparatus areas: an *apparatus fontium et locorum parallelorum* and a critical apparatus in the proper sense (either in its negative or positive version; see 6.3.2.2). An illustration of what a critical edition can look like is provided in figure 6.2-11, where the critically restored text of the *Heliand* is complemented by the critical apparatus as well as an *apparatus fontium*.

If different versions of the same work have been postulated by the editor, their texts are usually given in parallel columns, thus providing a synoptic edition (see 6.1).

| 24 | COTTON. 291—320. |

   endi mid hluttron treuuon. Uuarth thuo thie helago gest,
   that barn on iru buosme; endi siu an iro brioston *far*stuod
   iac an iro seƀon selƀo, sagda them siu uuelda
   that sea habda giocana thes alouualden craft
295 helag fan himila. Thuo uuarth hugi Iosepes,
   is muod giuuorrid, thie im er thia magat habda
   thia idis andhetia, aðalcnuosles uuiƀ
   giboht im ti brudi: hie afsuof that (12ᵇ) that siu
          haƀda barn under iru:
   ni uuanda thes mid uuihti [neua] that iru that uuiƀ haƀdi
300 giuuardot so uuarlico: ni uuisse hie uualdandes thuo noh
   blithi gibodscipi. Ni uualda sia im te brudi thuo
   halon im ti hiuuon, ac began im thuo an is hugie thenkean
   huo hie sia thuo* farlieti, so iru thar ni uurði lethes *uuiht*
   odan arƀedies. Ne uuelda sia after thiu
305 meldon for menigi: andried that sea manno barn
   liƀu binamin. So uuas *than* thero liudeo thau
   thuru then aldon eu, Ebreo folces,
   so huilik so thar an unreht idis gihiuuada,
   that siu simla thena bedscepi buggean scolda
310 fri mid iru ferahu. Ni uuas gio thiu fehmea so guod
   that siu gio mid them liudion leng libbean muosti,
   uuesan under them uuerode. Thuo bigan im the uuiso man,
   suitho guod gumo Ioseph an is muode
   thenkean thero thingo, huo hie thea thiornun tho
315 listion forlieti. Thuo ni uuas lang ti thiu
   that im thar an drome quam drohtines engil,
   hebancuninges bodo, (13ᵃ) endi hiet sia ina haldan uuel,
   minneon sia an is muode: 'Ni uuis thu' quathie,
          'Mariun uureth,
   thiornun thinero — siu is githungan uuiƀ —
320 ni forhugi thu sia ti hardo; thu scalt sea haldan uuel,

   91 brioston | stuod 300 giuᵘardot 11 mᵘosti *corr.* 2. *h.* 20 tiʰardo

  91—92. *Tat. V. Mt.* 1, 18 ... inventa est in utero habens de spiritu sancto. 95—305. *Mt.* 1, 19. Joseph autem vir eius, cum esset iustus et nollet eam tradere, voluit occulte dimittere eam. 12—25. *Mt.* 1, 20. Haec autem eo cogitante, ecce angelus domini apparuit ei

Fig. 6.2-11: Critically established text and apparatuses. Source: Sievers (1878, 24).

In this edition of the *Heliand* (Sievers 1878), the texts of the two major witnesses, C and M, are provided on facing pages as shown in figure 6.2-12.

A richer, multilayered apparatus is offered by Francesco Stella (2007) in his digital edition (see 6.4 below) of the Latin *Corpus rhythmorum musicum saec. IV–IX* (see fig. 6.2-13). This type of apparatus accommodates intertextual information such

24   COTTON. 291 — 320.

endi mid hluttron treuuon.   Uuarth thuo thie helago gest,
that barn on iru buosme;   endi siu an iro brioston *farstuod*
iac an iro sebon selbo,   sagda them siu uuelda
that sea habda giocana   thes alouualden craft
295 helag fan himila. Thuo uuarth hugi Ioseepes,
is muod giuuorrid,   thie im er thia magat habda
thia idis andhetta,   adalcnosles uuib
giboht im ti brudi: hie afsuof that (12ᵇ) that siu
                                habda barn under iru:
ni uuanda thes mid uuihti   [neua] that iru that uuif habdi
300 giuuardot so uuarlico: ni uuisse hie uualdandes thuo noh
blithi gibodscipi. Ni uualda sia im te brudi thuo
halon im ti hiunon,   ac began im thuo an is hugie thenkean
huo hie sia thuo* farlieti, so iru thar ni uurdi lethes uuiht
odan arbedies. Ne uuelda sia after thiu
305 meldon for menigi: antdred that sea manno barn
libu binamin. So uuas than thero liudeo thau
thuru then aldon eu,   Ebreo folces,
so huilik so thar an unreht   idis gihiuuada,
that siu simla thena bedscepi   buggean scolda
310 fri mid iru ferahu. Ni uuas gio thin fehmea so guod
that siu gio mid them liudion leng   libbean muosti,
uuesan under them uuerode. Thuo bigan im the uuiso man,
suitho guod gumo   Ioseph an is muode
thenkean thero thingo,   huo hie thea thiornun tho
315 listiun forlieti. Thuo ni uuas lang ti thiu
that im thar an drome quam   drohtines engil,
hebancuninges bodo,   (13ᵇ) endi hiet sia ina haldan uuel,
minneon sia an is muode: 'Ni uuis thu' quathie,
                                'Mariun uureth,
thiornun thinero   — siu is githuungan uuib —
320 ni forhugi thu sia ti hardo;   thu scalt sea haldan uuel,

91 brioston | stuod   300 giu°ardot   11 mᵒosti *corr.* 2. *h.*   20 tiᵖardo

91—92.   *Tat. V. Mt.* 1, 18 … inuenta est in utero habens de spiritu sancto.   95—305.   *Mt.* 1, 19.   Ioseph autem vir eius, cum esset
iustus et nollet eam tradere, voluit occulte dimittere eam.   12—25.
Mt. 1, 20.   Haec autem eo cogitante, ecce angelus domini apparuit ei

---

MONAC. 291—320 (9—10).   25

endi mid hluttrun treuun.   Uuard† the helago gest,
that barn an ira bosma;   endi siu an ira breostun forstod
iac an iro sebon selbo,   sagda them siu uuelda
that sie habde giocana   thes alouualdon craft
295 helag fon himile. Tho uuard hugi Ioseepes,
is mod gidrobid,   the im er thea magad habda
thea idis anthettea,   adalcnosles uuif
giboht im te brudiu: he afsof that siu habda barn
                                undar iru:
ni uuanda thes mid uuihti   that iru that uuif habdi
300 giuuardod so uuarlico: ni uuisse *he* uualdandes tho noh
blidi gibodskepi. Ni uuelde sie im te brudiu tho
halon im te hiunon,   ac bigan im tho an is hugi thenkean
huo he sie so forleti   so iru thar ni uurdi ledes uuiht
odan arbides. Ni uuelda sie aftar thiu
305 meldon for menigi: antdred that sie manno barn
libu binamin. So uuas than thero liudeo thau
thurh then aldon eu,   Ebreo folkes,
so huilik so thar an unreht   idis gihiuuida,
that siu simbla thana bedskepi   buggean scolda
310 fri mid ira ferhu. Ni uuas gio thin femea so god
that siu *io* mid them liudiun leng   libbien mosti,
uuesan undar them uueroda. †Bigan im the uuiso man,
suido god gumo   Ioseph an is moda
thenkean thero thingo,   huo he thea (5ᵇ) thiornun tho
315 listiun forleti. Tho ni uuas lang te thiu
that im thar an droma quam   drohtines engil,
hebancuninges bodo,   endi het sie ina haldan uuel,
minnion sie an is mode: 'Ni uuis thu' quad he,
                                'Mariun uuređ,
thiornun thinaro   —   siu is githuungan uuif —
320 ne forhugi thu sie te hardo;   thu scalt sie haldan uuel,

95 hugi Ioseepes, *das erste i auf rasur (für e?)*, *das zweite scheint
nachgetragen zu sein*   99 uuan¹³ 2. *hand*   uuar°lico 2. *hand*, 1 uuel¹³
siē imᵒ 2. *hand*   brudiu *auerudiert*   2 imᵒ 2. *hand*   12 mā 2. *hand* N

dicens: 'Ioseph fili David, noli timere accipere Mariam coniugem tuam;
quod enim in ea natum est, de spiritu sancto est.

Fig. 6.2-12: Synoptic edition. Source: Sievers (1878, 24–25).

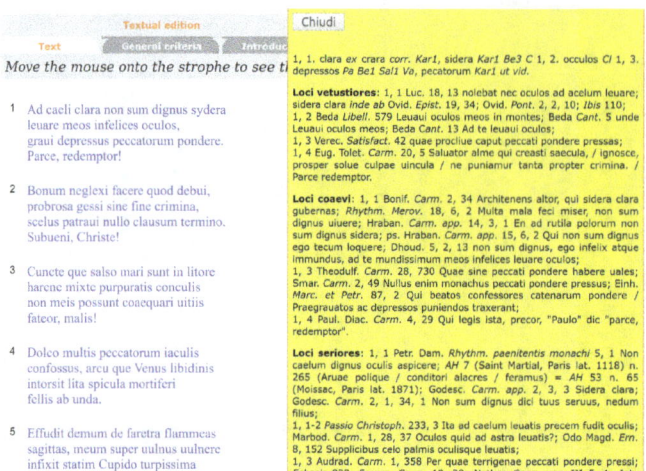

Fig. 6.2-13: Multilayered *apparatus fontium* along with *lectio variorum* (corimu.unisi.it).

as sources and antecedents (*loci vetustiores*), contemporary parallels (*loci coaevi*), and alleged later reuses (*loci seriores*), along with the variant readings found in the tradition of the *rhythmi* (*lectio variorum*) given in the upper right-hand part of the screen. It should be noted that, despite the digital environment, the construction of the apparatus follows the steps illustrated in the previous sections, and is therefore based on a thorough scrutiny of the manuscript tradition of every single poem.

An experimental kind of critical apparatus has been drafted by Burgio, Buzzoni, and Ghersetti (2015) in their hypertext edition of Giovanni Battista Ramusio's sixteenth-century version of Marco Polo's account of his travels in Asia. In this "Digital Ramusio", modal windows allow the user to visualise a chapter of the main text (*R*) in parallel with its major sources (*Z, V, VB, L, P* and *VA,* and *F*). Each chapter of *R* is accompanied by a philological commentary made accessible through pop-up windows and containing the identified sources along with their variant readings against *R*, analysis of their manipulation by Ramusio, as well as some informative notes. This more discursive apparatus (fig. 6.2-14) aims to filter the data provided by the editors after a thorough critical process by providing a narrative that explains and make sense of it (for the theoretical approach, see Lavagnino 2009, 63–76).

The layout of editions, as well as some other practical details, have changed over time. The format which is now standard for a critical print edition, with the apparatus of variants being placed below the text, is the result of a long development. It originated in the course of the eighteenth century from "earlier modes of presentation in which information about manuscript readings was usually embedded within a larger commentary surrounding the text on three or four sides" (Tarrant 2016, 125), a practice that can be traced back to thirteenth-century manuscripts transmitting texts along with their commentaries.

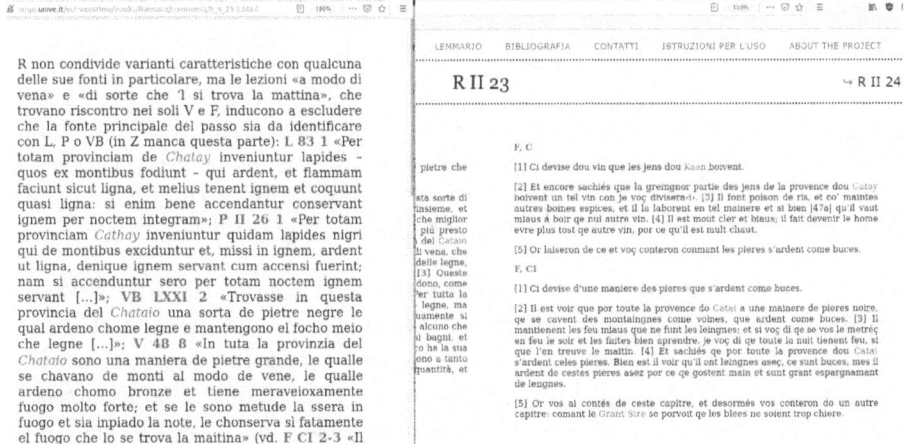

Fig. 6.2-14: A discursive scholarly apparatus.
Source: virgo.unive.it/ecf-workflow/books/Ramusio/commenti/R_II_23-main.html.

The habit of using s i g l a to denote manuscripts also developed over a long period of time. Only in the nineteenth century did it establish itself as a common procedure, superseding – though not completely eliminating – that of referring to manuscripts by Latin names, such as *Codex Monacensis* (= M) or *Codex Cottonianus* (= C) in the case of the *Heliand*.

6.2.5 Recent developments

Although the general principles of text-critical analysis discussed in the present section remain substantially valid today, new perspectives have arisen from the growing awareness that, especially in traditions that are likely to be highly unstable – such as many mediaeval ones – genealogical trees very rarely show a linear structure, and in some cases multiply rooted trees are perhaps more apt for representing the relationships between given groups of witnesses (see 2.2 above and example 13 below).

Furthermore, it is also possible that, in order to establish the older form of a reading, a philologist has to take into account textual traditions that are very different typologically, and sometimes also linguistically (see example 14), thus crossing the borders between texts.

Example 13: Wulfstan's *Sermo Lupi ad Anglos*
Contemporary scholars are becoming increasingly aware that the lack of significant errors in one or more witnesses, a very frequent case in real traditions, leaves a large number of trees possible. A paradigmatic example is represented by Wulf-

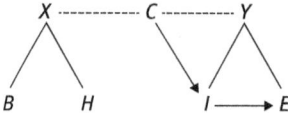

Fig. 6.2-15: Hypothesis of stemmatic configuration for the three different redactions of Wulfstan's *Sermo Lupi ad Anglos* (drawn on the basis of Bethurum 1971 and Whitelock 1980).

stan's *Sermo Lupi ad Anglos quando Dani maxime persecute sunt eos*, whose original composition is commonly assumed to go back to the year 1014 (Bethurum 1971, 22–24; Whitelock 1980). The text is transmitted in five manuscripts – usually labelled as *I, E, C, B, H* – and the lack of conjunctive errors between them blocks the reconstruction of a common archetype. There seem instead to be three different redactions of the *Sermo*, all of them traceable to Wulfstan himself, since his own interventions are visible in the witnesses: (*B H*) *C* (*I E*). The shortest redaction (*B H*) is usually taken to be the oldest (as shown, inter alia, by a clause referring to Æthelred's exile that is missing in *C, I*, and *E*); the *C*-text is a rewriting with deletion of political passages and incorporation of some additions, among which are the description of the Danish humiliations of the English in lines 97–126 in Bethurum's edition; *I E* is the most recent redaction, very close to *C* but with further interventions by the author himself, as the marginal additions in *I* demonstrate (Bethurum 1971, 23; Whitelock 1980, 5–6). The situation is made even more complex by intra-stemmatic contamination, as shown in figure 6.2-15. We are therefore confronted by at least three different forms of the sermon resulting from a process of rewriting primarily induced by a change in the political climate; in a stemmatic context, rewriting can produce multiply rooted trees like the one in figure 6.2-15.

The stemma tells us that the copyist of *I* had not only *Y*, but also *C* (or an ancestor of *C*) as a model, as demonstrated by a passage taken from *C* at line 85 in Bethurum's edition and later on expunged from the text (*I* was corrected by Wulfstan himself); furthermore, *E* used *I* as a source, since some of the corrections and authorial interventions in *I* are integrated into the text of *E*.

Example 14: Ecdotic stratigraphy
A further example of how intricate the relationship between texts can be is offered by Gianfranco Contini (quoted in Stussi 2006, 111), who performs a stratigraphic examination of a reading which appears in three different variant forms in the textual tradition of *La Vie de Saint Alexis*, namely "plorent si oil", "ploret de ses oilz", "ploret des oilz" [to cry the eyes out, to cry bitterly]. A comparison with the same variant forms as they occur in different textual traditions, in particular in the Old French *Chanson de Roland* and the Old Spanish *Cantar de mio Cid* allows Contini to postulate "plorent si oil" as the older form (attested only in *Alexis*), "ploret de ses oilz" as the intermediate form (attested in all three traditions), and "ploret des oilz" as the most recent one (widely

attested in *Roland* and only rarely in *Alexis*). Contini interprets such an example as an instance of *stratigrafia ecdotica*, "ecdotic stratigraphy", since from a reconstructive perspective it allows one to assess the older form of the reading.

The examples provided in this section are intended to provide some insight into how to practically handle textual data in order to figure out the most convincing stemmatic hypothesis among a set of theoretically possible stemmata, as well as how to determine the readings most likely to be original or archetypal. Although the application of the reconstructive method implies that the text to be restored is substantially unitary (*reductio ad unum*), a thorough scrutiny of real textual traditions shows that cases of texts that "live in variants", in that they are reshaped, for instance, by the authors themselves (see example 13 above) or by copyists who act as co-authors and editors, are not infrequent. Real case studies also help demonstrate that stemmata – as accurate as they may be – still remain working hypotheses, since they are based on the often partial data that has come down to us through the accidents of textual transmission. Given the evidence available, the goal of reconstructing the "original" version of a text is hardly ever achieved. As convincingly argued by Richard Tarrant, "one hallmark of the heroic mode of editing was the drive towards certainty, or even the confident assertion of certainty. Our time is one that finds such claims suspect" (2016, 29).

A further reflection induced by the treatment of real examples is that an approach which draws on multiple witnesses and tries to reconstruct a text that is identical to none of them does not undermine the importance of each single witness, provided that the editor offers the reader an apparatus where the diasystem of the tradition is summarised, as envisaged by Cesare Segre (see 6.2.4 above).

6.3 Representing the critical text
Franz Fischer

> Every scholarly edition has to be understood as an embodied argument about the textual transmission. (Eggert 2009, 177; quoted in Tarrant 2016, 124)

This section deals with the components and presentational features of critical texts which are essential to both print and digital editions. Standards and conventions for presenting the critical text in print have been developed over the past two centuries – and, as will be demonstrated in the following, are fundamentally challenged by the digital paradigm.

6.3.1 General considerations

The appearance of the critical text in print has not significantly changed since the publication of the first handbooks for the establishment of a critical text a century ago (for an account of the consolidation of the print format from a technological perspective, see Sahle's volume on the typographical legacy: Sahle 2013, vol. 1, here esp. 111–112). In 1909, detailed guidelines for the composition of critical editions were published by the German classicist Otto Stählin. Largely revised in 1914, these guidelines provide clear instructions regarding the content and design of the edition, from title page and preface, to text and margins, to apparatus and indexes (Stählin 1914, 45–108). In 1927, then, most influentially, Paul Maas proposed a small set of rules for the preparation of a critical edition (Maas 1927, § 23–24). First, a preface to the critical text should describe all witnesses, demonstrate the relationship between the witnesses (if possible with a stemma), and characterise the quality of the archetype; the handling of questions of orthography and (since Maas's revised edition of 1950) dialect, that is, linguistic regularisation, should be clarified. Second, in the critical text itself, all conjectures, supplements, and corruptions should be marked using special signs. Editorial interventions for reader-friendliness and elucidation such as word separation, punctuation, and capitalisation are desirable, but cannot be standardised in a set of rules of general applicability because the aims of interpretation change with changing times. Third, in a critical apparatus underneath the text, some deviations from the archetype should be noted: rejected variants (according to Maas, "variants" in this sense are only those readings where the top branches below the archetype differ and between which the editor has to use *iudicium*). Subvariants and groups of variants from lower down in the stemma may or may not be indicated; the same goes for uncertainties, changes of witness, and brief justifications of editorial decisions.

Subsequently, such manuals have been further refined and modified, especially with regard to mediaeval and vernacular texts in response to the criticisms of Bédier and, later, the proponents of a New Philology (see 2.3). *Conseils pour l'édition des textes médiévaux* by Pascale Bourgain and Françoise Vielliard (2002) is a more recent example of a highly instructive comprehensive guide on how to establish and lay out the critical text of a mediaeval Latin or vernacular work. The guide takes into account the different national traditions and practices regarding aspects of original and normalised orthography, abbreviations and punctuation, the selection and presentation of variants and sources in the respective apparatuses, and so on. However, the basic components and the general composition of a print edition remain stable and unchanged.

Influenced by the new technical possibilities and the prospect of unlimited space, Peter Robinson widened the aims of a critical edition in a digital format and at the same time loosened the requirement of providing an edited text. According to Robinson (2002, 51–54), a digital critical edition should (still) be anchored in a historical analysis of the material, present hypotheses about creation and change, and supply a record and classification of difference over time, in many dimensions and in appropriate detail. The final product of a single established critical text is not deemed necessary any more, even if Robinson concedes that, in most cases, a single text constructed by the editor is included among all the texts presented, such as transcripts and collations, as a starting point for explaining all the extant documents (Robinson 2002, 55–56; 2000, 5–14). But, more importantly, the edition should provide the space and tools for readers to develop their own hypotheses and ways of reading. And all this should be offered in a manner which enriches reading (Robinson 2002, 56–58).

In the light of the recent developments, extending the narrow definition of a critical edition – used in this handbook only if genealogical considerations in the sense of a traditional *recensio* are applied – the term "critical edition" may be understood in a wider sense in which it "refers to a whole spectrum of editions of texts, documents, and collections that offer well-defined and structured information relating to a clearly identified content" (Apollon and Bélisle 2014, 86). According to Daniel Apollon and Claire Bélisle, critical editions intend to make a record of the textual transmission "as faithfully, authentically, and completely as possible, including information about the processes that have made it possible to establish the selected and published text" (2014, 86). These intentions are combined with "efforts to establish (or restore) the possibility of interpreting a work as closely as possible to the intentions of the author (traditional version), to its immediate context (historicising version), or to its uses during the transmission through time and space" (86).

In more specific terms, Fischer (2017, 278–280) assembled various components of digital critical editions with reference to four basic manifestations of textual criticism. The first manifestation is critical annotation, that is, indispensably, the *apparatus criticus* or other means of recording textual variants and all justifications for the state of the edited text (established on the basis of various methods; see Göransson 2016, 407–415), but also an *apparatus fontium* or *testimoniorum*, an *apparatus biblicus*, and/or a commentary (see Giannouli 2015; more on these types of apparatuses below). The second manifestation is structural, linguistic and semantic markup – that is, the actual encoding of all textual and editorial components (see below). The third manifestation comprises all metadata, that is, all structured information on the author, the work, and the edition itself. Documentation, finally, comprises everything traditionally provided in the philological introduction (i.e. descriptions of the textual witnesses, a genealogical analysis, and a declaration of the editorial principles) but also, in a digital setting, facsimiles, transcriptions, source code, and raw data.

6.3.2 Print editions

6.3.2.1 The critical text

As described in the previous section (6.2.4), the disposition of the critical text on the page is a constituent part of the establishment of the text itself. In fact, critical editions are among the finest products of scholarly print culture. Both methodology and technology were decisive factors in the development of the sophisticated reference system linking the actual text and the critical annotation (Dahlström 2000; Sahle 2013, 1:272–275). The print format, with its preference for the one synthesised and definitive text, has undeniably been a factor in the success of the stemmatological method and promoted the idea of a reconstructed archetype over alternative, individualistic and pluralistic, textual concepts (see 6.1). Stemmatology is able to provide the methodological justification for a single text representation instead of multiple texts or any arbitrarily chosen individual copy. In addition, other justifications can also be taken into account, such as reader-friendliness and the convenience of a scholarly practice of reading and referring to one text only instead of many.

Even if divergent traditions are deemed equivalent with regard to their origin as authorial revisions (e.g. due to enforced or even self-imposed censorship) or to their impact on a subsequent readership, parallel views of two, sometimes three, and in very few cases even four versions remain the exception. A widely acclaimed edition of the *Nibelungenklage* pushed the print format to its limits and presented four critical text versions with four respective *apparatus critici* positioned on two facing pages (Bumke 1999). Even here, variation within a distinct tradition was condensed and represented in respective *apparatus critici* (fig. 6.3-1). Another exception is the monumental edition of Eriugena's *Periphyseon* in five volumes by Edouard Jeauneau (1996–2003), which establishes not only a critical text "of common type, easy to read and consult" (1:lxxxi), but also a synopsis of five variant versions as revised by the Irish author himself or contemporary scribes, displayed in four parallel columns (figs 6.3-2–3).

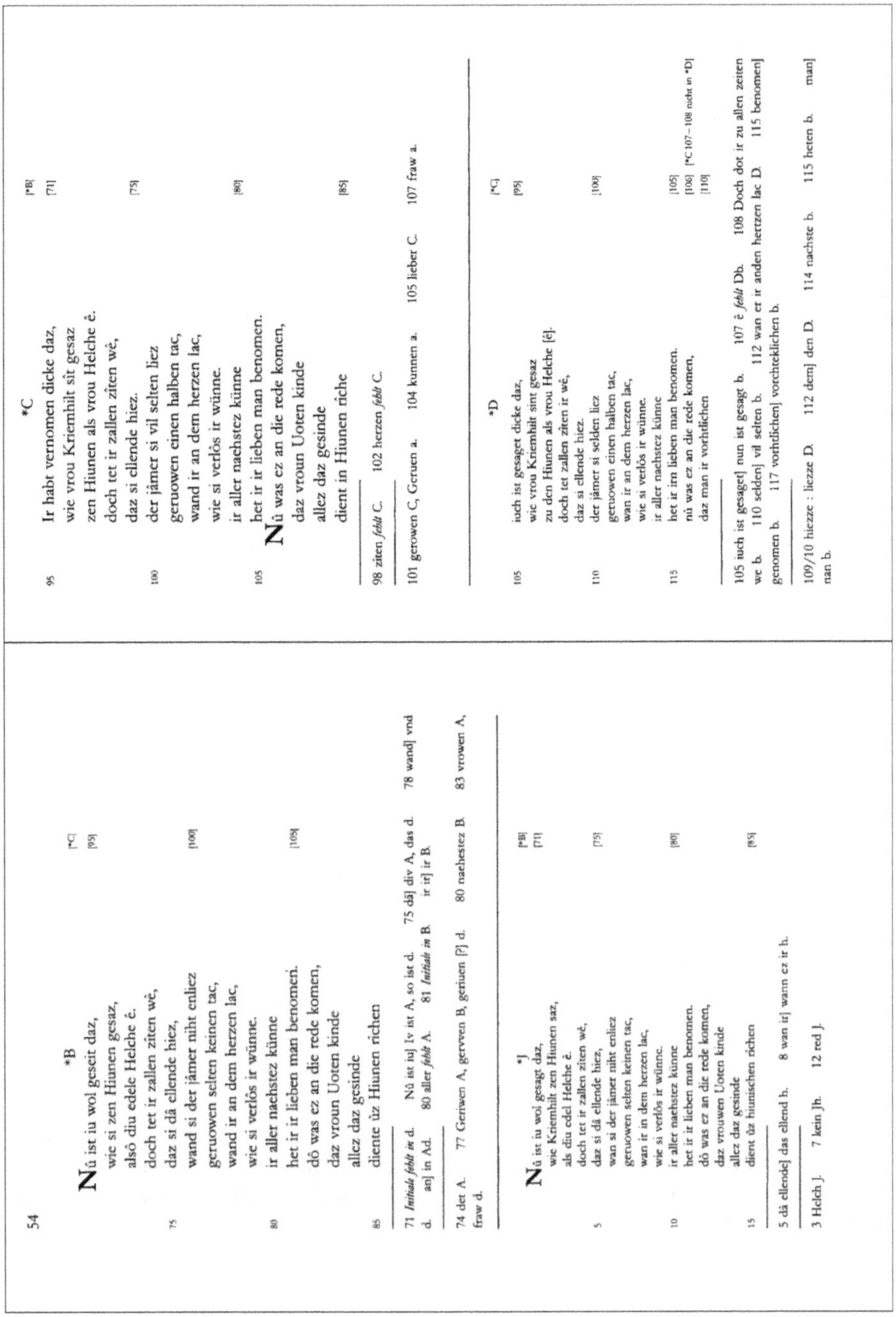

*B

54
Nū ist iu wol geseit daz,
wie si zen Hiunen gesaz,
alsô diu edele Helche ê.
75 doch tet ir zallen ziten wê,
daz si dâ ellende hiez,
wand si der jâmer niht enliez
geruowen selten keinen tac,
wand ir an dem herzen lac,
wie si verlôs ir wünne.
80 ir aller nachstez künne
het ir ir lieben man benomen.
dô was ez an die rede komen,
daz vrouwen Uoten kinde
allez daz gesinde
85 diente ûz Hiunen rîchen

71 *Initiale fehlt in* d.   Nû ist iu] Iv ist A, so ist d.   75 dâj] div A, das d.   78 wand] vnd
d.   an] in Ad.   80 aller *fehlt* A.   81 *Initiale in* B.   ir ir] ir B
74 det A.   77 Geriuwen A, gerwen B, geriuen [?] d.   80 nachestez B.   83 vrowen A, fraw d.

*J

Nū ist iu wol gesagt daz,
wie Kriemhilt zen Hiunen saz,
als diu edel Helche ê.
doch tet ir zallen ziten wê,
5 daz si dâ ellende hiez,   [*B]
wan si der jâmer niht enliez   [71]
geruowen selten keinen tac,
wan ir in dem herzen lac,   [75]
wie si verlôs ir wünne.
10 ir aller nachstez künne   [80]
het ir ir lieben man benomen.
dô was ez an die rede komen,
daz vrouwen Uoten kinde
15 dient ûz hiunischen rîchen   [85]

3 Helch J.   7 kein Jh.   12 red J.
5 dâ ellende] das ellend h.   8 wan ir] warin ez ir h.

*C

95 Ir habt vernomen dicke daz,
wie vrou Kriemhilt sit gesaz
zen Hiunen als vrou Helche ê.   [*B]
doch tet ir zallen ziten wê,   [71]
daz si ellende hiez.
100 der jâmer si vil selten liez
geruowen einen halben tac,   [75]
wand ir an dem herzen lac,
wie si verlôs ir wünne.
ir aller nachstez künne
105 het ir ir lieben man benomen.   [80]
Nû was ez an die rede komen,
daz vroun Uoten kinde
allez daz gesinde
dient in Hiunen rîche   [85]

98 ziten] *fehlt* C.   102 herzen *fehlt* C.
101 geruowen C, Geruen a.   104 kunnen a.   105 lieber C.   107 fraw a.

*D

105 iuch ist gesaget dicke daz,   [*C]
wie vrou Kriemhilt sint gesaz   [95]
zu den Hiunen als vrou Helche [ê].
doch tet zallen ziten ir wê,
daz si ellende hiez.
110 der jâmer si selten liez   [100]
wan ir an dem herzen lac,
wie si verlôs ir wünne.
ir aller nachstez künne
115 het ir irm lieben man benomen.   [105]
nû was ez an die rede komen,   [106]
daz man ir vorhtlîchen   [110]

105 iuch ist gesaget] nun ist gesagt b.   107 ê *fehlt* Db.   108 Doch dot ir zu allen zeiten
we b.   110 selden] vil selten b.   112 wan er ir anden hertzen lac D.   115 benomen]
genomen b.   117 vorhtlîchen] voerhteklichen b.
109/10 hiezze : liezze D.   112 dem] den D.   114 nachste b.   115 heten b.   man]
nan b.

Fig. 6.3-1: Joachim Bumke's synoptic print edition of four versions of the *Nibelungenklage*.

SIGLES DES MANUSCRITS

B = BAMBERG, *Staatsbibliothek*, Philos 2/1 (*olim* HJ IV 5)

B* = Texte primitif de B, avant toute correction ou addition
B¹ = Additions ou corrections dues à la main irlandaise i¹
B^c = Additions ou corrections introduites au IXe siècle par toute autre main que celle de i¹

M = CAMBRIDGE, *Trinity College*, O.5.20 (James 1301)

M* = Texte primitif de M, avant toute correction ou addition
M^c = Additions ou corrections introduites au XIIe siècle

P = PARIS, *Bibliothèque nationale de France*, Lat. 12964.

P* = Texte primitif de P, avant toute correction ou addition
P^c = Additions ou corrections introduites au IXe siècle

R = REIMS, *Bibliothèque municipale*, 875

R* = Texte primitif de R, avant toute correction ou addition
Ri¹ = Additions ou corrections dues à la main irlandaise i¹
Ri² = Additions ou corrections dues à la main irlandaise i²
R^c = Additions ou corrections introduites au IXe siècle par toute autre main que celles de i¹ ou i²

Les colonnes de l'édition de Heinrich Joseph Floss (PL 122, 441A-524B) sont mentionnées en marge, tant dans l'édition que dans la *Synopsis Versionum*.

441A DE PRIMA DIVISIONE OMNIUM IN EA QUAE SUNT ET QUAE NON SUNT

NVTRITOR. Saepe mihi cogitanti diligentiusque quantum uires suppetunt inquirenti rerum omnium quae uel animo percipi possunt uel intentionem eius superant primam summamque diuisionem esse in ea quae sunt et in ea quae non sunt horum omnium generale uocabulum occurrit quod graece ΦΥΣΙΣ, latine uero natura uocitatur. An tibi aliter uidetur?

ALVMNVS. Immo consentio. Nam et ego, dum ratiocinandi uiam ingredior, haec ita fieri reperio.

N. Est igitur natura generale nomen, ut diximus, omnium quae sunt et quae non sunt.

A. Est quidem. Nihil enim cogitationibus nostris potest occurrere quod tali uocabulo ualeat carere.

N. Quoniam igitur inter nos conuenit de hoc uocabulo generale esse, uelim dicas diuisionis eius per differentias in species ratiocinem; aut, si tibi libet, prius conabor diuidere, tuum uero erit recte iudicare.

A. Ingredere quaeso. Impatiens enim sum de hac re ueram rationem a te audire uolens.

N. Videtur mihi diuisio naturae per quattuor differentias quattuor species recipere, quarum prima est in eam quae creat et non creatur, secunda in eam quae et creatur et creat, tertia in eam   441B   DE DIVISIONE NATURAE

1/1 CICERO, *De oratore*, I, 1. In., *De diuinatione*, II, 1; *De amicitia*, VIII, 26. APULEIUS, *De mundo*, I (initio), ed. J. Beaujeu, Paris, 1973, p. 110. MINUCIUS FELIX, *Octauius*, I (PL 3 [1886], 240D-241A). LACTANTIUS, *Diuinae Institutiones*, IV, 1 (CSEL 19, p. 274, l. P. 6. 44BD-449A). Cf. P. d'Hérouville, "Une formule cicéronienne qui a fait fortune", in *Revue de philologie, de littérature et d'histoire anciennes*, 3 (1927), p. 81-83.

4 G. Piemonte, "L'expression *quae sunt et quae non sunt* chez Jean Scot et Marius Victorinus", in *Jean Scot Écrivain*, ed. G.H. Allard, Montréal, 1986, p. 81-113.

19/26 Hanc quadripartitam naturae diuisionem ab Augustino (*De ciuitate dei*, V, 9, 4; CCSL 47, p. 139; 138-144, PL 41, 151) deriuauit dixit H. Bett, *Johannes Scotus Erigena. A Study in Medieval Philosophy*, Cambridge, 1925, p. 21. Eandem tamen affiniorem esse discerim illi quadripartitae numerorum diuisioni cuius meminerunt Petro ALEXANDRINO, *De opificio mundi*, 99 (Cohn – Wendland editio minor, Berlin, 1886, p. 27, 28-30) et MARTIANUS CAPELLA, *De Nuptiis*, VII, 738 (ed. A. Dick, Leipzig, 1925, p. 372-373; ed. J. Willis, Leipzig, 1983, p. 266-267).

Fig. 6.3-2: An extract from the critical text of the first book of Eriugena's *Periphyseon* with *apparatus fontium* below and *index siglorum* on the left-hand page, edited by Edouard Jeauneau (1996–2003, 1:2–3). © Brepols Publishers.

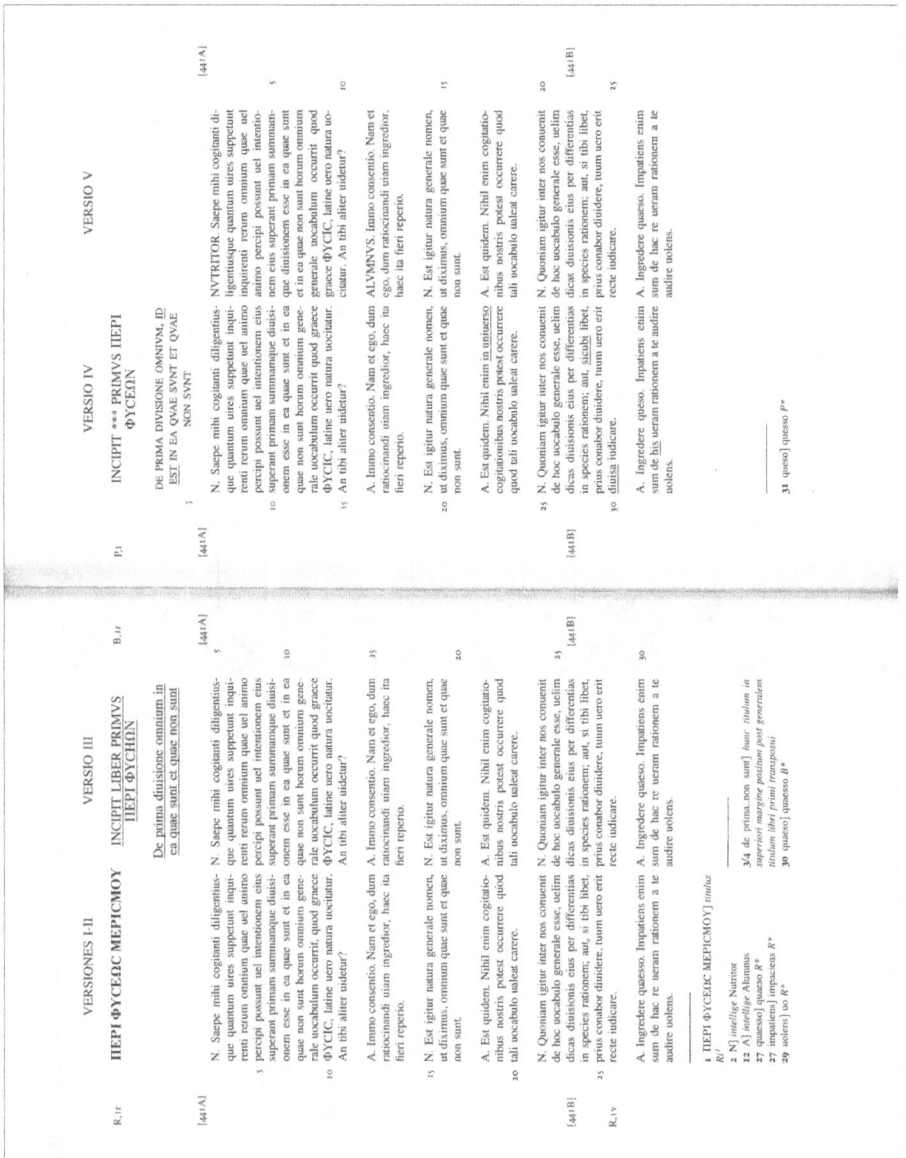

Fig. 6.3-3: Synopsis of the same book in five different versions presented in four columns with respective *apparatus critici* in the same edition. Source: Jeauneau (1996–2003, 1:114–115). © Brepols Publishers.

6.3.2.2 The critical apparatus

The design of the *apparatus criticus* is inherited from the print era. Maas already noted: "Daß der kritische Apparat unter den Text gesetzt wird, geschieht aus Rücksicht auf die Verhältnisse des Buchdruckes, besonders auf das Format unserer Bücher" (1960, 16) [The *apparatus criticus* is placed underneath the text simply on account of bookprinting conditions and in particular of the format of modern books] (trans. Flower, 1958, 23). The term itself, *apparatus criticus*, "may have been used for the first time in Bengel's book title *D. Io. Alberti Bengelii Apparatus criticus ad Novum Testamentum*, Tubingae 1763" (Conti and Roelli 2015; see also Timpanaro 1981, 35; 2005, 65). There, the elaborate apparatus was provided in a book printed separately from the edited text. Lachmann's edition of Lucretius' *De rerum natura libri sex* from 1850 presented a limited number of genealogically significant variants without further identification under the reconstructed text (fig. 6.3-4); a detailed philological explanation was provided in his commentary published in a separate volume.

The apparatus was to become the most distinctive feature of a critical text. Its aim is to ensure the reversibility and transparency of the editorial decisions. It pro-

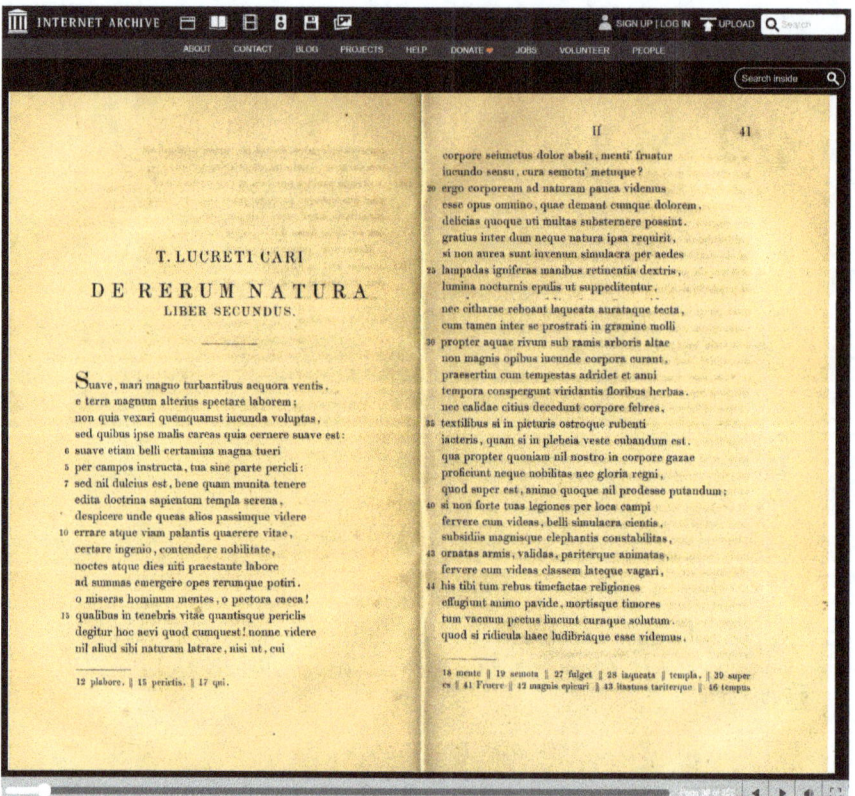

Fig. 6.3-4: PDF facsimile of Karl Lachmann's 1850 edition of Lucretius' *De rerum natura* from the Internet Archive (archive.org/details/dererumnaturali00lucr).

vides the evidentiary justification for the presentation of a specific text and allows the reader to test the hypothesis of the edited text. The reader should be able to follow the logic of the presentation of the text (and the selection of readings) and (re)trace the editor's work using the critical apparatus (P. Chiesa 2016, 228–236). A manifestation of textual criticism, the apparatus provides the mark of a scientific, scholarly, reliable, and authoritative text. It makes the text distinct from ordinary texts, randomly published or passed on. The apparatus distinguishes an edition that is critical (in the sense that it analyses data and presents a hypothesis) as opposed to those not based on scientific principles.

The critical apparatus is usually accompanied by an *apparatus fontium*, indicating the sources for passages in the edited text. References to similar passages in other works that have not been used as a source can either be included in the same apparatus, or they can be recorded in a dedicated *apparatus locorum parallelorum*. Relevant especially for theological and patristic texts, an *apparatus biblicus* may give references to biblical passages quoted or alluded to, while an *apparatus testimoniorum* may indicate the use of passages in later works. As proper complements to the critical apparatus, these various types of apparatuses should provide the essential justification for the established text and help to better understand and appreciate its composition technique and literary impact (Giannouli 2015). More extensive annotations such as historical, philological, and other commentaries are usually provided in separate sections of the book or accompanying publications.

In general, two types of critical apparatuses can be distinguished: a p o s i t i v e a p p a r a t u s indicates both those witnesses bearing variant readings that have been rejected and those witnesses attesting the reading accepted for the critical text; a n e g a t i v e a p p a r a t u s indicates only witnesses of discarded readings. For example, where the text below (fig. 6.3-5) reads "contemtibilissimus", the negative apparatus entry appears as "3 contemptibilissimus: contemptibilis sum D". A positive apparatus entry for the same scenario would appear as "3 contemptibilissimus Φ (=PVRFCG): contemptibilis sum D". The advantage of the positive apparatus is that it is explicit, which is especially helpful if the availability of witnesses is inconsistent, but it can get overcrowded and obstruct the reader's view of significant variation. For this, a middle path is often chosen: giving the full record of a positive apparatus only in those situations that seem to require more clarification.

Some conventional features and signs of a fully-fledged print edition are presented below using the example of Ludwig Bieler's edition of St Patrick's *Confessio* (fig. 6.3-5). References to individual manuscript witnesses are usually given by capital Latin letters (A, B, C, ...), references to early prints by minuscule Latin letters (d, e, f, ...), and references to manuscript families by Greek capital letters (Δ, Φ, Ψ, ...). Revisions in a witness by a second hand might be indicated with an apostrophe after the siglum (A'). Other typical editorial signs include angle brackets (<...>) for editorial insertions of text missing in the archetype (or, when a genealogical method

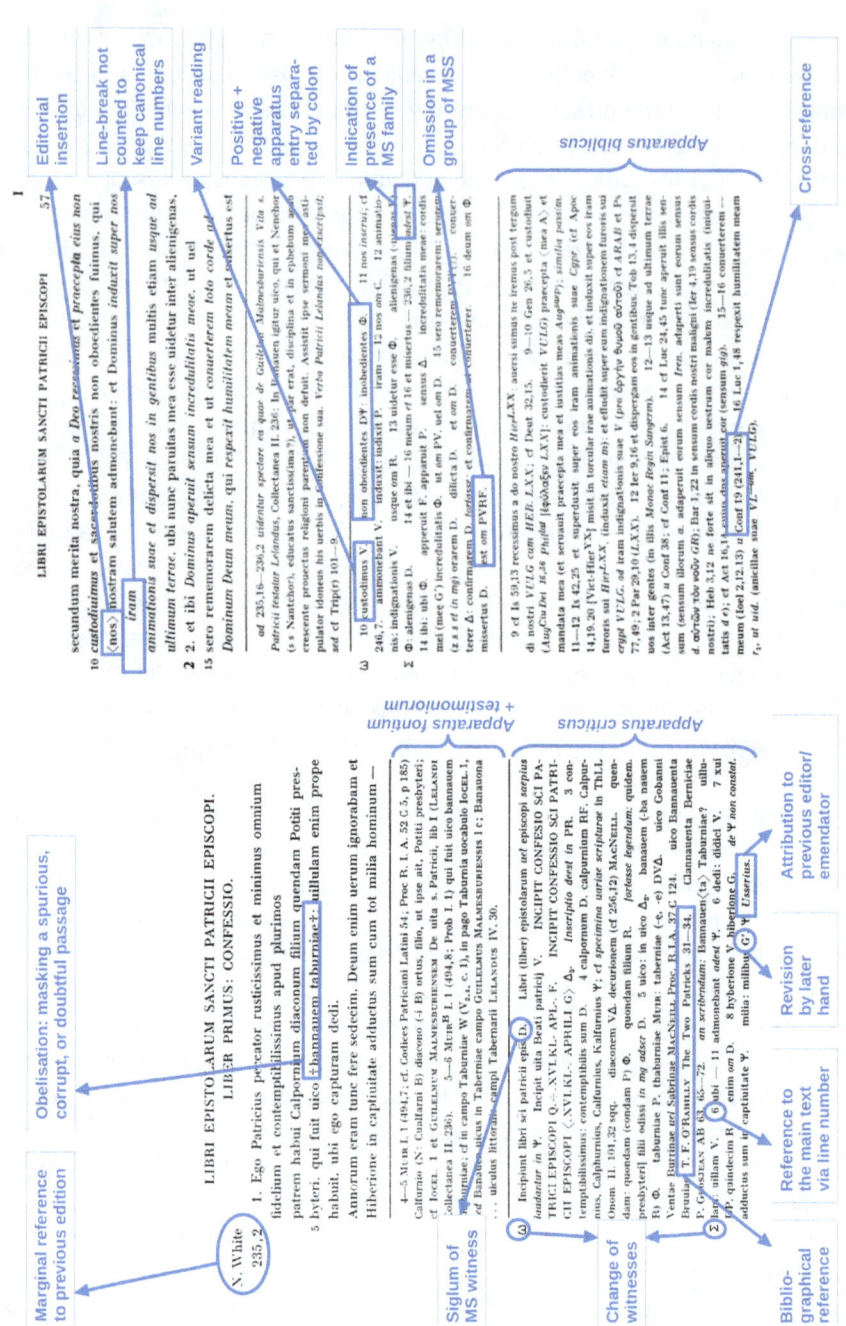

Fig. 6.3-5: Features of a critical text: the beginning of St Patrick's *Confessio* with a threefold apparatus (Bieler 1950, 56–57). "MS(S)" stands for "manuscript(s)" in the figure. © 1993 the Royal Irish Academy, reproduced by permission.

is not chosen, in the base text or chosen "best text") and *obeli*, or *cruces* (†...†), to mark a word or passage that is corrupted or spurious; a list of commonly used abbreviations and editorial signs along with short explanations is provided in the *PLS* (Roelli and Macé 2015, under "Abbreviations and Editorial Signs"; more signs and abbreviations can be found in e.g. Bernabé and Hernández Muñoz 2010, appendix 1; Tarrant 2016, 164–166; Bourgain and Vielliard 2002, 86–87; Dondaine 1960).

6.3.2.3 Unity of content and form
The way the critical text is presented is inseparable from its very nature. Content and form constitute the unity of the critical text. The essence of the critical text is realised with a clearly designed page layout for the actual text and its critical framework of apparatus(es) and marginal references, set in print. Usability and readability depend on its static presentation. Where a canonical work structure (such as chapters and verses of biblical books or classical works) is missing, contingent page breaks and line numbers are canonised in order to serve as stable reference points both for internal and external references as well as for citation.

6.3.3 Digital editions

6.3.3.1 The digital paradigm
Digital editions are "guided by a digital paradigm in their theory, method and practice" (Sahle 2016, 28). What is this digital paradigm? It can be defined by a number of differences and innovations compared to its predecessor, the print paradigm. The static text in print can be contrasted with the f l u i d i t y   o f   t e x t s in the ever-changing formats of software and devices, apparently with dramatic consequences for established practices and scholarly conventions of referencing and citation. Published online, they can be accessed by anyone at any time in any place connected to the World Wide Web. Overcoming the limits of space and the medial restrictions of the book, large amounts of textual material, digital images, and even audio and video content can be included. In fact, the provision of digital facsimiles, descriptions, and transcriptions of the textual witnesses has become a common feature of digital editions. H y p e r t e x t u a l i t y allows for interlinking and instant browsing between different textual layers and components both internal and external to the edition or resource. M a r k u p enables enrichment of transcripts with palaeographical details and codicological information; structural markup of paragraphs, lines, and other kinds of textual sections or segments supports precision in addressing, accessing, presenting, and extracting textual data at any degree of granularity, that is, at any level of detail, from words or even characters to any semantic, grammatical, or other structural unit of a text. Linguistic and semantic markup allows statistical analysis and evaluation of the grammatical and stylistic characteristics of a particular author, work, or genre. In the print era, scholarly editing was concerned with

the creation of a final and definite product – even if most textual editors were and are conscious that their texts are a scholarly hypothesis about a text, and that their print editions will not remain satisfactory for ever but will be outdated after "one or two generations, with fifty years an especially long life" (Tarrant 2016, 145–146). In the digital era, however, pre-publications of beta versions can be updated with corrections and additions of further material, transcriptions, variant readings, comments, enriched metadata, and textual markup, again regardless of the consequences concerning practices and conventions of quotation and referencing. Accordingly, the nature of a digital edition can be described as a p r o c e s s, not a product. O p e n   f o r m a t s ensure that research data such as digital images and texts can be used independently from proprietary platforms and shared via common software environments facilitating various ways of efficient collaboration between individual textual scholars, research teams, and wider communities. However, the most fundamental difference between printed and digital editions can be described in terms of the representation of content as data and its presentation in various and alternative publication formats.

6.3.3.2 Representation vs presentation

The current transformation of textual scholarship and scholarly editing is not primarily a change in publication format, from print to the Web, but a change for which the term "transmedialisation" has been coined (Sahle 2010, 31). As mentioned above (6.3.2.3), the unity of content and form is characteristic of textual scholarship and the scholarly edition of the print era. In contrast, digital scholarly editions are going beyond single medial realisations. Characteristic of textual scholarship and scholarly editions of the digital age is the s e p a r a t i o n   o f   c o n t e n t a n d   f o r m. Content is stored as data and metadata, that is, in the form of images, encoded text, markup, and annotation, and represented in the way the data is modelled in data formats and data models (see 3.4). This content is represented (stored) in a format that is clearly distinct from its form and appearance – the way it is presented on screen, in print, or in other formats of presentation such as variant graphs or tables (see 3.3), networks, lists or statistical charts, the search interface of a database, a hypertext or, in fact, a book. Transmedialisation is the representation of information, documents, and texts without determining a publication format. With regard to the critical text of a digital edition, this might mean that all critical annotations, lemmata, variant readings, sigla, and references are encoded in order to create sets of data on the representational level that are machine-readable, processable, and, ideally, interoperable and interchangeable. Ideally, one would follow the guidelines of the Text Encoding Initiative (tei-c.org), which are generally regarded as the de facto standard for text encoding. In fact, chapter 12 of the TEI guidelines defines a module for use in encoding an *apparatus criticus*. But to encode an *apparatus criticus* is to encode a phenomenon inherited from the print era, whereas digital textual scholars seek to go beyond what is seen as merely one possible physical embodiment of the editorial arguments and decisions about the textual tradition. For this, further revisions and refinements of the encoding method and data model seem necessary in order to create an even more coherent abstraction of textual criticism itself.

6.3.3.3 Digital approaches towards the critical text

The field of digital critical editions is still in an experimental state, and it may always remain this way owning to the dynamic and ever-changing nature of digital technology. Still, the advantages of digital data-representation formats for the analytical potential of scholarly editions are obvious: access, space, functionality, revisability and progressive enrichment, and linkage to, inclusions of, and integration into other knowledge resources on the one hand, and searchability, processability, and quantitative evaluation of data on the other. Even if the development of stemmatology and the production of critical texts is closely connected to and shaped by the technology of print culture, an insistence on or return to the book as the decisive or even exclusive publication format seems to be out of the question. Hybrid publication models, on the other hand, providing an edition in both formats, digital and print, each of which compensates for the shortcomings of the other, may seem desirable for some texts and attractive to textual scholars and publishers alike, at least for a transitional period of time while new scholarly practices need to be adopted (e.g. for the q u o t a t i o n of revisable digital resources) and technical, or rather, institutional solutions (including to serious problems such as l o n g - t e r m a v a i l - a b i l i t y) need to be implemented.

Textual scholars, scholars in the digital humanities, and software developers have produced a wide range of digital methods, tools, and formats for representing historical texts and textual transmission (see the overviews on the theories and practices of digital scholarly editing by Sahle 2013, esp. vols 2–3; Apollon, Bélisle, and Régnier 2014; Pierazzo 2015). Various strategies have been applied for transferring and enhancing scholarly standards and conventions of critical editing into a digital setting. Some of the most significant approaches will be presented in the following. It should be noted, however, that the practical realisations of digital scholarly editions usually implement and combine aspects of several approaches.

Reproduction

First of all, plain digital reproduction of an existing print edition is a common part of larger r e t r o - d i g i t i s a t i o n campaigns such as the Internet Archive (archive.org), the Open Library (openlibrary.org), or even the commercial Google Books (books.google.com). If provided with accurate metadata and OCR-generated electronic text versions, these digitised editions can already prove very useful, especially with regard to accessibility and searchability (figs 6.3-1 and 6.3-4 above are a case in point).

Imitation

Second, digital editions have been imitating the print paradigm regarding the selection and presentation of their content. Nowadays, the creation of critical editions adhering to the presentation standards and requirements of print editions can be realised with the free software package LaTeX – more precisely, with the reledmac package for typesetting scholarly critical editions (ctan.org/pkg/reledmac; see 6.4.1), which supports the creation of multiple apparatuses by indexing page and line numbers (see 6.4.1). Realised as static and printable PDF documents, such editions also exploit a number of beneficial functionalities in digital documents. They are fully searchable, cross-references and external references can be realised as hyperlinks, and they can be shared and published independently from application software, hardware, and operating systems (for alternative software packages, see wiki.contextgarden.net and tustep.uni-tuebingen.de; see also 6.3).

Often, digital publications of critical texts do not significantly exceed print formats in terms of content and functions. While editions such as the meritorious edition of Euripides *Scholia* by Donald J. Mastronarde (euripidesscholia.org) are critically annotated and digitally presented, the established texts are plain and one-dimensional from a technological point of view. Even if based on TEI XML-encoded source files, the semantic value of the markup does not allow for more advanced functionalities, visualisations, or in-depth analysis of the critical annotations. Still, even relatively flat data files offer an opportunity for further enrichment. Other digital editions are based on the layout-oriented XML output of the Classical Text Editor (CTE; see 6.4.1), such as the *Kleine und fragmentarische Historiker der Spätantike* [Fragments and Testimonies of Historians from Late Antiquity] edition (2016–), which was originally conceived as a print edition.

The renunciation of a single established critical text: Multi-witness editions

A far more innovative approach has been taken by one of the founding fathers of digital critical editing, namely Peter Robinson, with the edition of *The Wife of Bath's Prologue* from Geoffrey Chaucer's *Canterbury Tales*, a Middle English work from the end of the fourteenth century. Published on CD-ROM in 1996, this multi-witness edition aimed to create a comprehensive record of the textual transmission by transcribing and collating fifty-eight of the eighty-eight pre-1500 manuscripts and incunabula. Closely interlinked and fully searchable, all witnesses were presented as digital facsimiles and TEI-encoded transcriptions in both regularised and unregularised spelling; information on the parts of speech of individual words was given. However, instead of critically reconstructing an archetype version, "a very lightly edited" (Robinson 1996b, CD-ROM Manual, 30) version of the oldest manuscript witness, the Hengwrt manuscript (*Hg*) served as a "base text" which could be read against any of the other fifty-seven witnesses by means of automated word-by-word collations (fig. 6.3-6). Accordingly, Robinson refrained from creating a *stemma codicum* to trace the witnesses back to some original version or archetype, and created

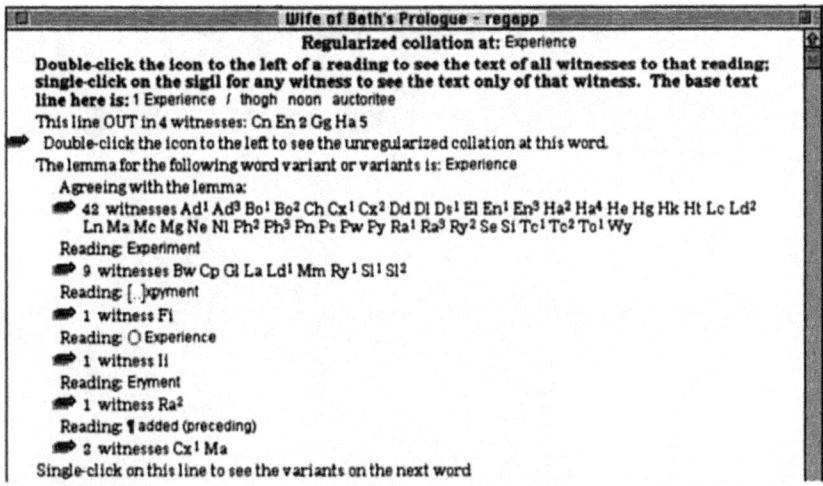

Fig. 6.3-6: The digital edition of *The Wife of Bath's Prologue*: apparatus entry resulting from the regularised collation for the word "Experience". Source: Robinson (1996b, CD-ROM Manual, 30).

a phylogenetic tree instead in collaboration with evolutionary biologists. The phylogenetic analysis limits itself to drawing conclusions about the genealogical closeness and distance of witnesses and witness families (Barbrook et al. 1998).

The digital edition of *The Wife of Bath's Prologue* set new standards for the representation of multi-witness works, especially as regards the amount of textual information and the accuracy of details. Several later editors would follow this paradigm, especially those of iconic vernacular mediaeval or early modern works of some national interest, providing facsimiles and transcriptions of the witnesses to be aligned and automatically collated, and critically annotated, but deliberately not providing a critically reconstructed version. Therefore, according to the definition used in this handbook, Robinson's edition of *The Wife of Bath's Prologue* cannot be called "critical" in a strict sense, that is, if a critical edition by definition is supposed to provide a critically reconstructed text by applying a genealogical methodology (see 6.3.1). If, however, the term "critical" is used in a wider sense, meaning that the base text (e.g. the transcript of a principal manuscript witness) is critically annotated (i.e. in a scholarly, rigorous manner) with information on variation, sources, and historical and philological details and explanations, enabling (at least in principle) any reader to critically assess any established version, then it definitely is.

Another multi-witness edition, created in collaboration with Peter Robinson and his team, is Prue Shaw's digital edition of Dante's *Divina Commedia*, providing electronic versions of the most important previous editions as well as facsimiles and transcripts of some of the most relevant manuscript witnesses, enriched with markup on metre. A sophisticated collation tool called VBase, along with stemmatic visualisations, enables the reader or user to critically assess any established and published critical text version (Shaw 2010; see also Spadini 2015).

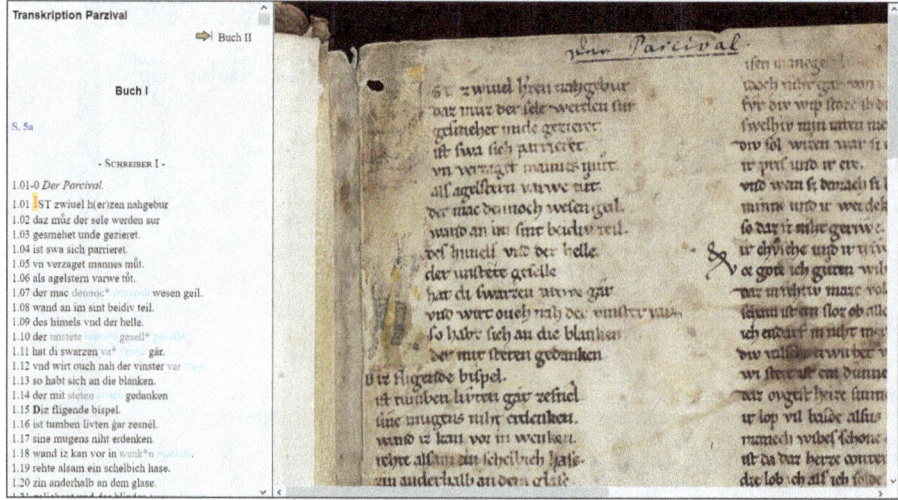

Fig. 6.3-7: *Parzival-Projekt* (2018): facsimile and transcription of the principal witness, *D* (St. Gallen, Stiftsbibliothek, Cod. Sang. 857, thirteenth century). Manuscript page: e-codices.unifr.ch/en/csg/0857/5; font size and colour indicate palaeographical features. CC-BY-NC. © Parzival-Projekt Universität Bern.

Yet another example is Michael Stolz's digital edition of Wolfram von Eschenbach's *Parzival* (fig. 6.3-7), again emphasising the variety of this work's transmission. In the spirit of the so-called "new" or "material" philology, the project began with detailed transcriptions of the important witnesses (fig. 6.3-8). However, in an attempt to reconcile Bédier's schism (Trovato 2017, 77–108), the edition aims to synthesise opposing philological perspectives, establishing a single critical text (fig. 6.3-9) as well as a synoptic edition of four versions, following the concept of *Fassungen* developed by Joachim Bumke.

The *Parzival* project has experienced a development from archive to edition similar to that of another pioneering project, the *Piers Plowman Electronic Archive* (*PPEA*, piers.chass.ncsu.edu). As early as 1994, the *PPEA* was conceived as a complex digital collection of the full textual tradition of *Piers Plowman*, a fourteenth-century allegorical dream vision attributed to William Langland, witnessed by more than fifty manuscripts. The electronic archive would:

> eventually consist of hypertextually linked documentary editions of every manuscript; edited texts of hyparchetypes and archetypes; critical texts of versions A, B, and C; facsimiles of all witnesses; and an *apparatus criticus* for each text to include codicological, palaeographic, linguistic, lexical, and textual annotations. (Duggan and Lyman 2005, § 5)

After initial publications of documentary editions and facsimiles on CD-ROM, the archive grew, and is still growing, into a critical online edition reconstructing three distinct archetypal versions of the poem (figs 6.3-10–11).

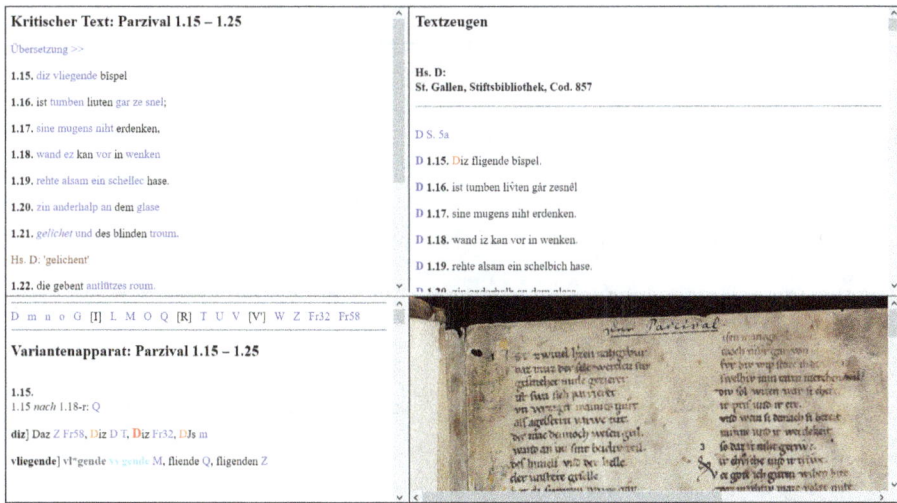

Fig. 6.3-8: *Parzival-Projekt* (parzival.unibe.ch): critical single text following the main manuscript, *D*. In the upper left-hand window is a normalised text, in the lower left-hand window is the apparatus of variant readings, and on the right are transcriptions and facsimiles of the various manuscript witnesses. © Parzival-Projekt Universität Bern.

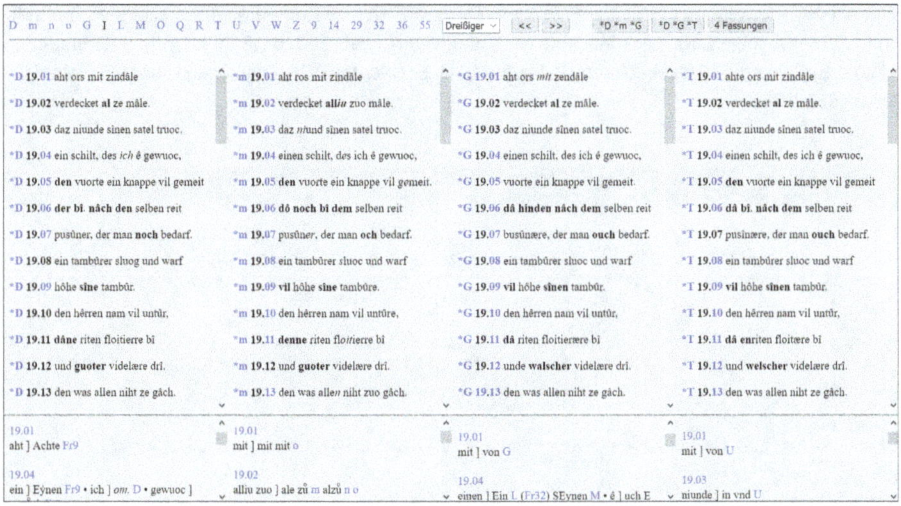

Fig. 6.3-9: *Parzival-Projekt* (parzival.unibe.ch): synoptic view of **D*, **m*, **G*, and **T*, the four versions of *Parzival*, along with critical apparatus. Clicking on a siglum opens a window displaying the transcription and facsimile of the respective manuscript witness. © Parzival-Projekt Universität Bern.

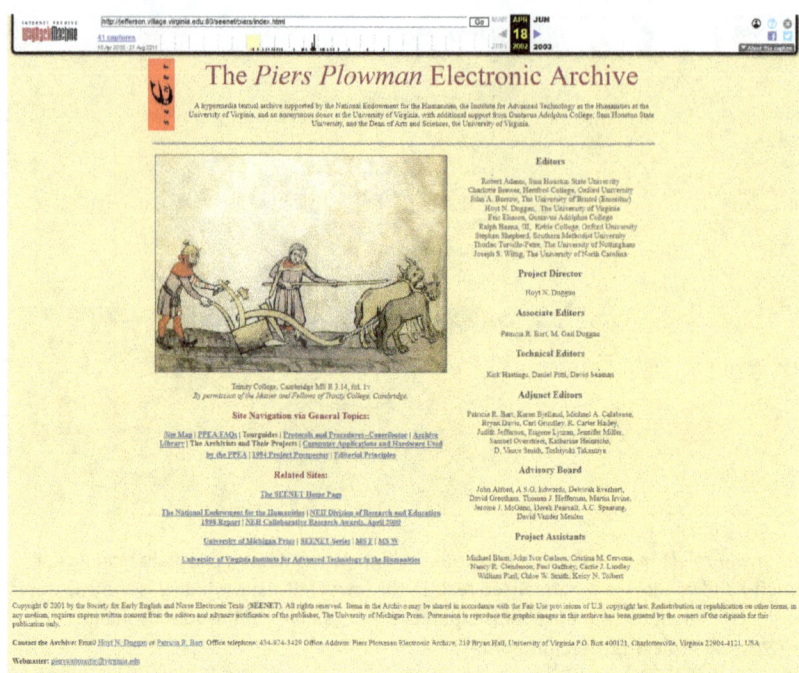

Fig. 6.3-10: The website of the *Piers Plowman Electronic Archive* from April 2002, accessed through the Internet Archive's Wayback Machine (web.archive.org/web/20020418175917/http://jefferson.village.virginia.edu:80/seenet/piers/index.html). © Society for Early English and Norse Electronic Texts (SEENET).

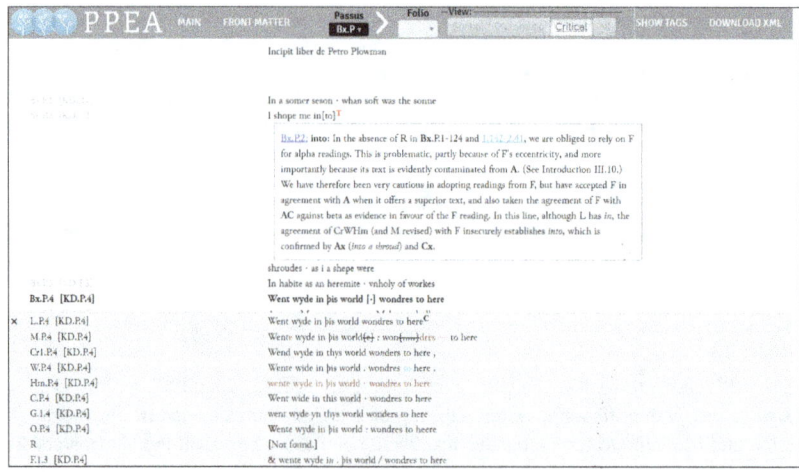

Fig. 6.3-11: Critical text of the *B*-version archetype of *Piers Plowman* in the electronic archive (as of 2017), with the option to display critical apparatus notes and synoptic views of diplomatic transcriptions of variant verses (linked to full transcriptions and facsimiles). © Society for Early English and Norse Electronic Texts (SEENET).

Amplification

Similarly, following a pluralistic notion of text (Fischer 2008, §27–38), the digital edition of St Patrick's *Confessio* presents a variety of textual layers by amplifying the canonical print edition by Ludwig Bieler from 1950 (see fig. 6.3-5 above). By hovering over an apparatus entry, the referenced lemma is highlighted in the base text (fig. 6.3-12). In the apparatus, all sigla of individual witnesses are linked to the digital facsimile of the relevant folio (fig. 6.3-13); abbreviations and sigla of witness families are expanded by hovering the cursor over them; other signs, symbols, and abbreviations are linked to a key with definitions and descriptions; bibliographical references are linked to a comprehensive bibliography, biblical references to external online versions of biblical books; and *testimonia* are linked to the texts of Patrick's two earliest biographers, Muirchú and Tírechán, which are also included in the edition. Through the further inclusion of facsimiles of all relevant editions that have been printed since the publication of the *editio princeps* from 1656 (among them a diplomatic and a facsimile edition of the oldest manuscript witness, the early ninth-century *Book of Armagh*), the critical text becomes just one, albeit the central, textual layer in a virtual stack of closely interlinked textual layers representing all aspects of the work's transmission (Fischer 2013).

Fig. 6.3-12: The digital critical text of St Patrick's *Confessio* with a threefold apparatus and commentary closely interlinked with facsimiles and further resources included in the edition based on the critical text of Ludwig Bieler's print edition from 1950 (see fig. 6.3-5 above). Source: Anthony Harvey and Franz Fischer (eds.), The St Patrick's *Confessio* Hypertext Stack (www.confessio.ie). Dublin: Royal Irish Academy, online since September 2011.

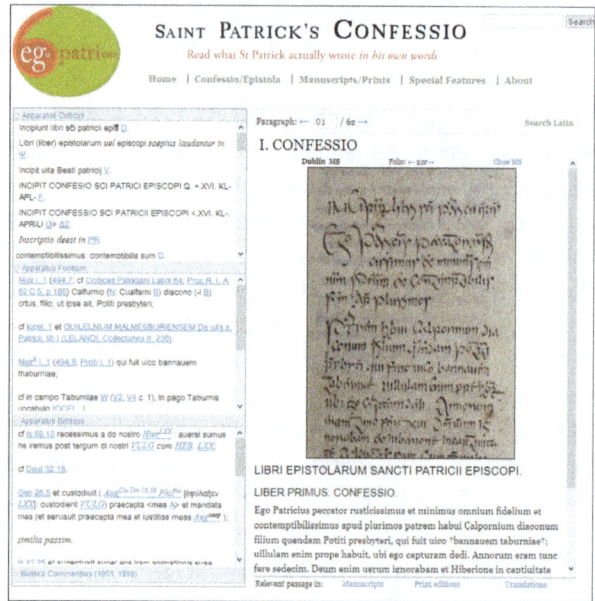

Fig. 6.3-13: The critical text of St Patrick's *Confessio* along with the facsimile of *D* (*Book of Armagh*, 808/809). Source: confessio.ie/etexts/confessio_latin#01.

Collaborative, peer-sourced, and progressive editing

The mantra of software developers, "release early, release often" (Raymond 1999), has been adopted by Jeffrey C. Witt in his critical edition of the lectures on Peter Lombard's *Sentences* by Peter Plaoul (1353–1415) – a p r o g r e s s i v e   e d i t i o n publishing a draft version of the critical text (or rather critical text to be) even before establishing a *stemma codicum* (fig. 6.3-14). Both the editor and the registered reader (or rather collaborator, or even co-editor) are able to leave comments on particular sections and to suggest additions or corrections of variant readings from relevant witnesses for the critical apparatus. Depending on the availability of transcripts, automated collations of paragraphs can be executed at any time (Witt 2011; see also Vasold 2014; Dunning 2015).

In connection with the *Canterbury Tales Project 2* (wiki.usask.ca/display/CTP2/Canterbury+Tales+Project+2+Home, a follow-up to the edition of Chaucer's *The Wife of Bath's Prologue* mentioned above), a software environment for the collaborative online creation of scholarly editions called *Textual Communities* (textualcommunities.org) has recently (2018) been launched, aiming at completing transcriptions of all remaining pre-fifteenth-century witnesses, a laborious task to be accomplished through the joint efforts of an open community of Chaucer scholars and interested students and citizens (Robinson 2017).

A third example of collaborative and progressive editing is the Nestle–Aland edition of the Greek New Testament (*Novum Testamentum Graece*), which has func-

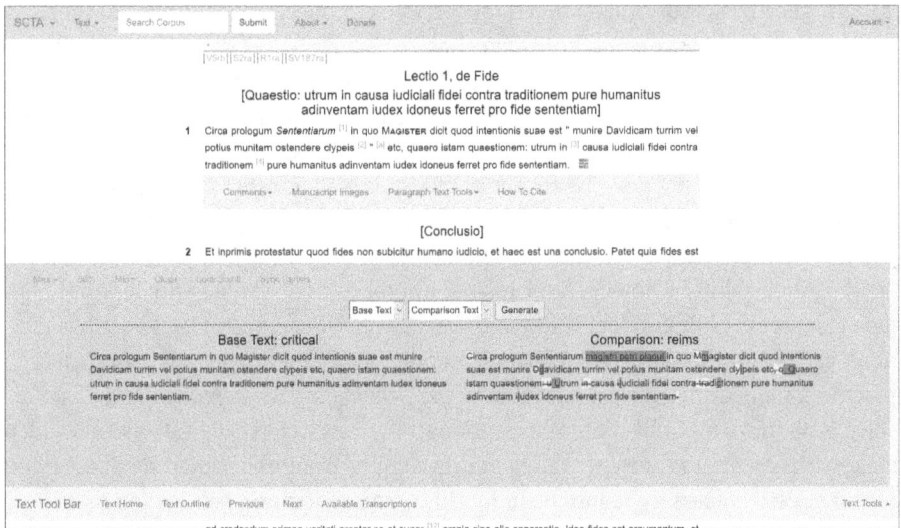

Fig. 6.3-14: Jeffrey C. Witt's edition of Petrus Plaoul's commentary on the *Sentences*. For each paragraph, comments, images, and a series of text tools can be opened (here, an integrated collation tool comparing the critical text with a witness from Reims). A disclaimer at the top of the page (not shown here) reads: "Please remember: the status of this text is draft. [...] Please use the comments to help make suggestions or corrections." Source: scta.lombardpress.org (*Scholastic Commentaries and Texts Archive*; *SCTA*). CC-BY-SA.

tioned as a catalyst for the development of textual criticism in a scholarly tradition beginning with the edition of Erasmus in 1516. The authoritative Nestle–Aland edition published in print by the Institut für Neutestamentliche Textforschung saw its twenty-eighth revision in 2012. The editorial work is ongoing, extended by the *Novum Testamentum Graecum – Editio critica maior* (*ECM*), listing a more complete set of variants and nowadays mainly supporting two digital projects: (*a*) the application of the Coherence-Based Genealogical Method (CGBM; see 5.3.7.3) to calculate the relations of each witness at any given place, with the final goal of a global stemma, as part, in principle, of an endless hermeneutical process of improving the genealogical hypothesis about the initial text and its history (Wachtel 2012a, 223–224; Mink 2012; see 7.1.2 below); and (*b*) the open digital editing environment of the *New Testament Virtual Manuscript Room* (ntvmr.uni-muenster.de), which provides a growing repository of images of more than five thousand Greek manuscripts and an open workspace for the preparation of transcriptions to be integrated into the editorial workflow and, ultimately, into the digital edition (to complement the definitive printed version of the *ECM*).

Distributed architecture for digital editions

More recent concepts and technological innovations point in the direction of a distributed architecture for the digital edition. Joris van Zundert (2018; see also Witt

2018) argues in favour of networked resources as opposed to resources that tend to subsist as isolated and monolithic data silos. An example of this is the new software application called Mirador, designed to operate on a community-driven reference standard/protocol, the International Image Interoperability Framework (IIIF). Adopted by a growing number of research libraries with manuscript collections, IIIF makes it possible to query images of manuscript folios, as well as other visual media, directly from library servers across the world. This approach, as exemplified most expediently by the Mirador viewer, plays a pivotal role in what may be seen as yet another "paradigmatic shift in how we understand, approach and interact with cultural heritage resources" (van Zundert 2018), and thereby how we conceive digital critical editions in the future. Again, the above-mentioned critical edition by Jeffrey C. Witt is playing a pioneering role by introducing the *Scholastic Commentaries and Texts Archive* (scta.info), a publication framework and Web service for digital editions which makes it possible to query text files and facsimiles from distributed databases and repositories. A necessary requirement for this organisation and publication of content is the development of field-standard data models that can make all textual and image data accessible in predictable ways to data-consuming applications (Witt 2018). It is for this very reason that the primacy of the data model is also advocated in the context of the *Digital Latin Library* project (digitallatin.org) as a prerequisite for the creation of intuitive and powerful interfaces for reading digital critical editions online (Cayless 2018).

6.3.4 Future perspectives

Digital philology has developed a wide range of models for scholarly editions and the critical representation of textual transmission. Further development of digital presentation and publication formats for critical texts (as a result of genealogical and stemmatological methods) will largely depend on the establishment of editor- and user-friendly work environments and publication frameworks. Through the integration of interactive tools that are especially designed for the analysis and visualisation of textual variation – e.g. as graphs, heat maps, or collation tables – such as CollateX, Juxta, Stemmaweb, CATview, and so on (see 5.4 above; see also Barabucci 2016), usability and attractiveness might increase even for more traditional, that is, print product-oriented editors. However, such advancements should be accompanied by an extension of the traditional skill set of critical editors and textual scholars, at least regarding text encoding and the formalisation of editorial practices.

The successful and advantageous use of digital tools and presentation formats, then, also depends on whether editors following genealogical or stemmatological methodologies are interested, intrinsically or extrinsically, in widening their research agenda to include other textual aspects (Monella 2012). Digital editions are particularly strong when it comes to the integration and interlinking of large amounts of textual material, including digital facsimiles and transcripts of relevant documents, as well as multiple versions of one particular text following different degrees of normalisation and regularisation. This may also include, among other things, having a synthetic or critical text version as the final aim of the editorial process. The data underlying these textual layers can be enriched with palaeographical, structural, linguistic, semantic, or metrical information, each of which supports different research questions and allows for alternative perspectives on the same text. But an increase in textual complexities, in turn, affects usability, especially as regards one of the most basic requirements for scholarly editions, namely addressability and citability. Either way, the scope of editorial decisions to be made has widened significantly. The decision about the optimal type of edition will always be determined by various and different factors such as, most importantly, the textual material at hand and its transmission, but also the time and financial resources available, skills, technical support, and not least the editor's individual understanding of textual criticism and how to make sense of textual transmission – all against the background of the technical conditions and intellectual paradigms in any given time and place.

The future of digital editions depends, finally, on technical and institutional solutions that address sustainability and long-term preservation concerning the curation of both data and applications. Whereas we seem to be relatively safe when it comes to archiving and preserving data in standardised models and formats, crucial issues remain problematic when it comes to software and technical infrastructure for keeping digital editions alive and accessible. Only a very few humanities research institutions, if any, are capable of what has been labelled Research Software Engineering (RSE) and to continuously maintain complex digital resources. Different approaches are being implemented, combined, and discussed, from dedicated portals and repository solutions, to formalised documentation and testing procedures, to the promotion of modularised technical architectures (Bleier et al. 2018; Dängeli 2019). Coordinated efforts on the organisational level between research institutions across local, regional, or national borders might open the way to a more sustainable infrastructure for digital critical editions.

6.4 Publication of digitally prepared editions

Tara Andrews

It will have become clear to the reader by now that the digital world has a great deal to offer not only for methods of stemmatic analysis of texts, but also for their editing and presentation. That said, digital tools in the humanities require a relatively high level of technical understanding and engagement, and the online publication of critically edited texts is no exception to this. At first glance, there would appear to be great demand among textual scholars for a software package or a suite of tools, akin to WordPress for websites, that would allow easy and straightforward publication of scholarly editions. When software developers in the humanities attempt to address this demand, however, we very quickly find that the seemingly unanimous demand is, in fact, a cacophony of individual demands, each different in its details.

This section will not be a survey of individual publication tools. Such a section would be unrepresentative, given the large number of online editions whose publication was the result of a custom development effort. It would also immediately be incomplete, and very quickly obsolete. Rather, we will survey here the different forms of digital publication that are possible, discuss the technologies behind them and the sort of institutional support that would be required to adopt them, and – where appropriate – give examples of tools where they exist for each category.

6.4.1 Print-ready solutions

In many circumstances, an edition that has been created digitally must be published in print – perhaps as the appendix to a thesis or dissertation, a journal article, or a submission to an edited series. In this case, the editor will prefer a tool that can handle typesetting or conversion to a document format that will be accepted by a publisher.

Perhaps the best-known software package for critical edition preparation and publication is the Classical Text Editor program (also known as CTE), which functions as a sort of word processor for editions (Hagel 2007). CTE has been under active development since 1997, and is widely used by textual scholars, although it only runs on the Windows operating system and its use requires purchase of a license. Its focus is very much on the preparation of critical edition text for print publication, with output available as PDF, TEI XML, or static HTML. Recent versions of CTE provide the possibility to import individual text transcriptions for automated pairwise collation with a given base text, and to produce data on textual variation in a format suitable for use with many cladistic analysis programs.

Another option for print publication, and one that is accepted by many academic and commercial publishers, is to use the LaTeX typesetting system. LaTeX was developed in the early 1980s as a document-focused variant of TeX, itself developed in the 1970s. The user creates a plain text file and uses a form of markup to indicate typesetting instructions – for example, to specify fonts or footnotes. The marked-up file can then be sent to a publisher as is, or passed to the TeX program for conversion to one of a number of formats, including, but not limited to, PDF (Portable Document Format). Although LaTeX does not by default use Unicode, this can be enabled either by use of the package inputenc or by use of the LaTeX variants XeLaTeX (for MacOS, using Apple's font system) or LuaTeX (for all operating systems).

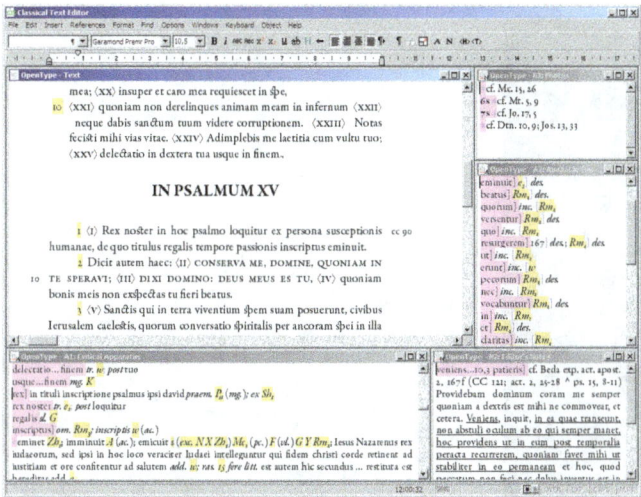

Fig. 6.4-1: The Classical Text Editor. Screenshot from cte.oeaw.ac.at.

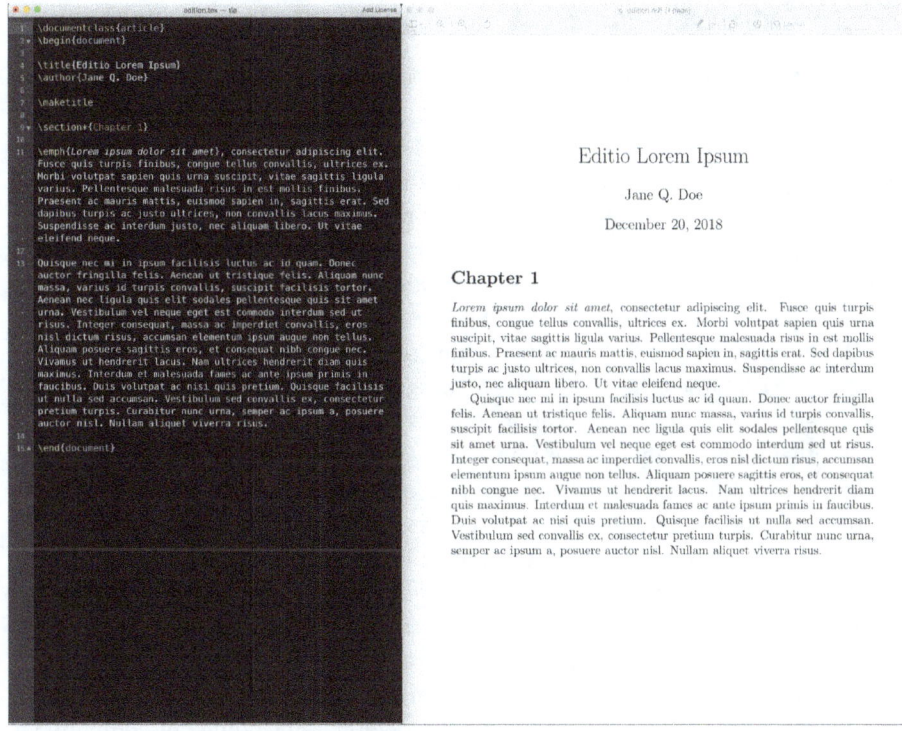

Fig. 6.4-2: A basic LaTeX example and the rendered result.

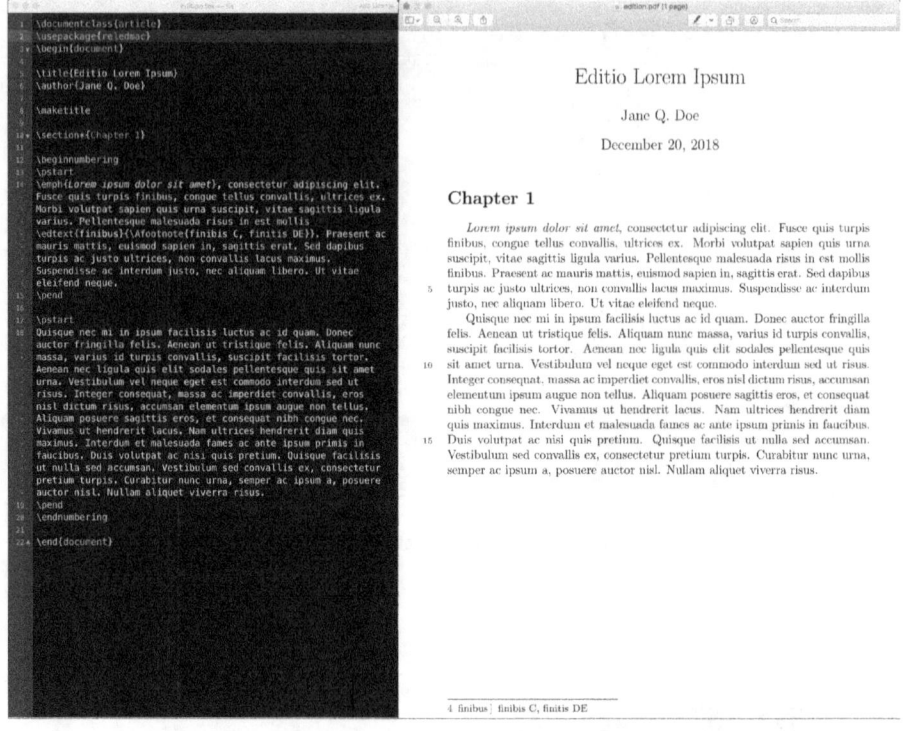

Fig. 6.4-3: Adding critical footnotes to the LaTeX example with the reledmac package.

Since LaTeX is free software, and is widely used in the scientific and scholarly community, a great many packages have been made available that extend its functionality. Two of these are reledmac and its sister package reledpar, developed by Peter Wilson and Maïeul Rouquette specifically for typesetting critical apparatus blocks and parallel text editions respectively (Rouquette 2018). These packages are based on an earlier package for TeX itself known as edmac (Lavagnino and Wujastyk 1996). The editor uses LaTeX markup to indicate lemma readings and provide apparatus entries for those readings; the package can support up to five apparatus blocks, either as footnotes or as endnotes.

Another increasingly popular format for writing texts, also based on a plain text format, is Markdown. Markdown, as its name implies, was created to provide as simple and intuitive a form of text markup as possible, one that is intelligible to a person who is looking directly at the source text. It is not a program or a piece of software, but rather a lightweight markup format that is used by an increasing number of software and Web platforms.

In combination with a program such as Pandoc (a "Swiss army knife" for conversion of document formats), Markdown can be a simple yet powerful strategy for producing a printed document in any necessary format, including but not limited to Microsoft Word, OpenOffice.org, EPUB, DocBook, HTML, LaTeX, PDF, and TEI XML.

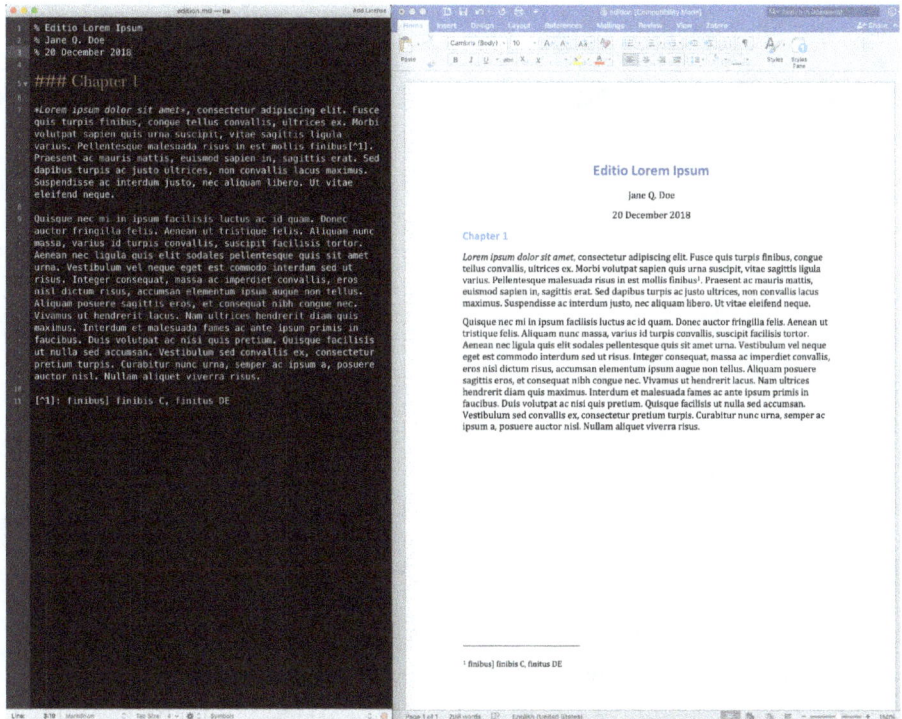

Fig. 6.4-4: Example of Markdown file and Pandoc output to MS Word.

6.4.2 XML-based solutions

But perhaps the editor intends that his or her edition be published not only to a print-ready format but fully electronically as a website. This will entail a set of decisions about what that website ought to look like, how the text itself is to be presented, and what sorts of interaction will be possible for its viewers. All of these decisions are heavily bound up with the editor's concept of the relevance and significance of the text and of his or her own editorial work on it (Andrews and van Zundert 2018); given the wide range of possibilities provided by the digital medium and the fact that these possibilities are not, so far, meaningfully restricted by widespread convention, it is much more common for an editor to be dissatisfied with existing software solutions for the digital publication of editions than it is for the same editor to be dissatisfied with the standard typesetting rules of well-known print-series editions.

Any editor who has online publication in mind will very likely have been encouraged to prepare the text in a TEI XML format (see 3.4.5). TEI is not, strictly speaking, a technical standard; rather, it provides an array of tools for defining one's own encoding scheme, and a set of prescriptive guidelines for the use of these tools, intended to ensure as far as possible a common vocabulary and structure. A

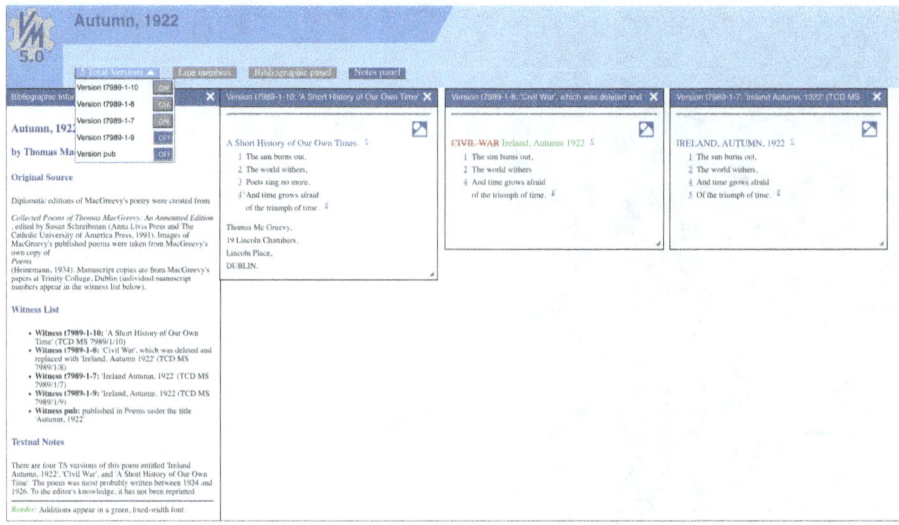

Fig. 6.4-5: Example of the Versioning Machine interface. Source: v-machine.org.

critical edition can therefore be encoded in a TEI XML format. The critical apparatus can be handled in a few different ways. TEI exported from the Classical Text Editor will use a system known as double-endpoint attachment, which relies on the use of a base text and attaches apparatus entries directly to that text, in a similar way to the example of the LaTeX reledmac package discussed above. The other system in common use is known as parallel segmentation. This does not rely on the use of a base text, although one can be specified; as such, it can easily be used to express a text collation as well as an eventual edition. Due to the syntax limitations of XML, however, editions encoded using the parallel segmentation system cannot have overlapping apparatus entries (see 3.3.4 for situations when these might arise).

One of the primary advantages of XML is that it can be parsed by computer programs and transformed into other formats relatively easily. A common way to do this is to write a stylesheet in a language known as XSLT (eXtensible Stylesheet Language Transformation), which specifies which elements of your XML document should be used for what purpose in the resulting document. These stylesheets are most commonly used to render a TEI-encoded edition into HTML for Web display, although they can also be used to transform it into LaTeX for print publication.

In theory, then, it would be possible to write a single XSLT stylesheet that could be used for any number of TEI XML-encoded editions so as to transform them into HTML. This is the idea underlying the *Menota Handbook* (Haugen et al. 2019), developed specifically for editions of mediaeval Norse manuscripts. The handbook provides a set of guidelines based on TEI, as well as a set of XSLT stylesheets that, when the published guidelines are followed, will render the XML-encoded edition into HTML for display in a Web page. An advantage of XSLT is that, as long as the

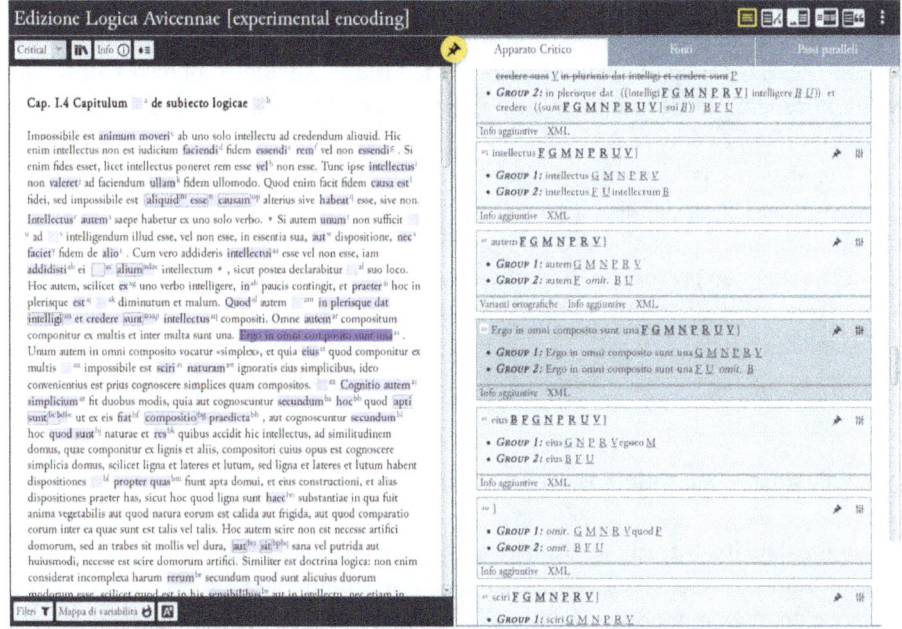

Fig. 6.4-6: Example of the EVT interface. Source: visualizationtechnology.wordpress.com.

user has a modern Web browser, there is no need to install and run additional software – the browser itself will read the XML file and the XSLT stylesheet provided that they are linked correctly, and perform the transformation automatically. Even without such a browser feature, an editor would be able to use the same software (e.g. Oxygen, a well-known XML editor) for writing the XML file and for performing the XSLT transformation. A similar piece of software, this one intended for editions of texts based on multiple witnesses, is the Versioning Machine (Schreibman, Kumar, and McDonald 2003), which uses a combination of XSLT and JavaScript to produce HTML suitable for direct publication to the Web.

Use of XML is not limited to XSLT, however; XML parsers exist for every major programming language. A software tool for the production of text editions that focuses primarily on letter collections is the ediarum program developed by the Berlin-Brandenburgische Akademie der Wissenschaften (Dumont and Fechner 2014). This program integrates multiple technologies for its use: Oxygen for creating and editing TEI XML documents; an XML database for storage of the documents; and a combination of XQuery, XSLT, and the Java programming language for Web display. Print publication is also offered through a tool based on the TeX typesetting system.

An example of a tool that avoids XSLT altogether in favour of a more general-purpose programming language is EVT (Edition Visualization Technology; Rosselli Del Turco et al., 2014). Like the Versioning Machine, the version of EVT currently under development expects text editions to be encoded in TEI XML using the parallel segmentation system, and is intended to be a reasonably self-contained system into which editors can simply drop their files and view the result in a browser. Unlike the Versioning Machine, EVT is written in the Angular framework of the JavaScript programming language, and manipulation of the XML is handled directly in the JavaScript code.

The biggest challenge of any TEI-based out-of-the-box solution is the sheer complexity of the TEI guidelines; it is next to impossible for any software tool to support the entire range of possible encoding practices that might be adopted by edition projects. The common practice of TEI schema customisation exacerbates this even further: even if the author of a software tool devised a way to anticipate all possible usages of the elements specified in the TEI guidelines, an editor would still be free to redefine those usages, or even to add new elements, and so exceed the scope of the tool.

6.4.3 Custom HTML solutions

Given the paucity of ready-made specialist software packages for the publication of critical editions, and given the difficulty of developing such a package that will satisfy more than a minority of editors, perhaps the most common publication solution remains the most complex: development of a custom-coded site using the core Web technologies of HTML, CSS, and JavaScript. Although these languages require a significant investment of time to learn well, they are well within reach of scholars/editors who have that time, as well as the interest to develop their skills.

HTML, or HyperText Markup Language, is the standard for describing the content of Web pages. It belongs to the same family of markup syntax as XML and has, consequently, some similarities to TEI, but is simultaneously more flexible and more restricted in scope. A user of HTML can define a basic text structure including titles, paragraphs, sections, and captions; can mark out selected spans of text; can include audiovisual media; and can give all of these elements arbitrary designations using the "class" attribute. A Web page in its most basic form consists of an HTML document viewed in a browser. In the early days of the Web, all content was published solely in HTML. As the platform matured, two additional languages with their own scopes of functionality were developed in order to separate more cleanly the burgeoning dynamic functionality of websites. The first is known as CSS, or Cascading Style Sheets. These provide the means to make systematic style and aesthetic decisions for a Web document. Using a CSS stylesheet, a Web content author can control such features as fonts, colours, margins, background graphics, and much more. Completing the triumvirate of Web technologies is the programming language JavaScript. Roughly speaking, where HTML defines the content of a page and CSS defines its look and feel, JavaScript defines how the reader/user can interact with a Web page. With a very few exceptions (such as navigation from page to page via hyperlinks), any action or dynamism that occurs on a Web page is controlled by a JavaScript function working on the page.

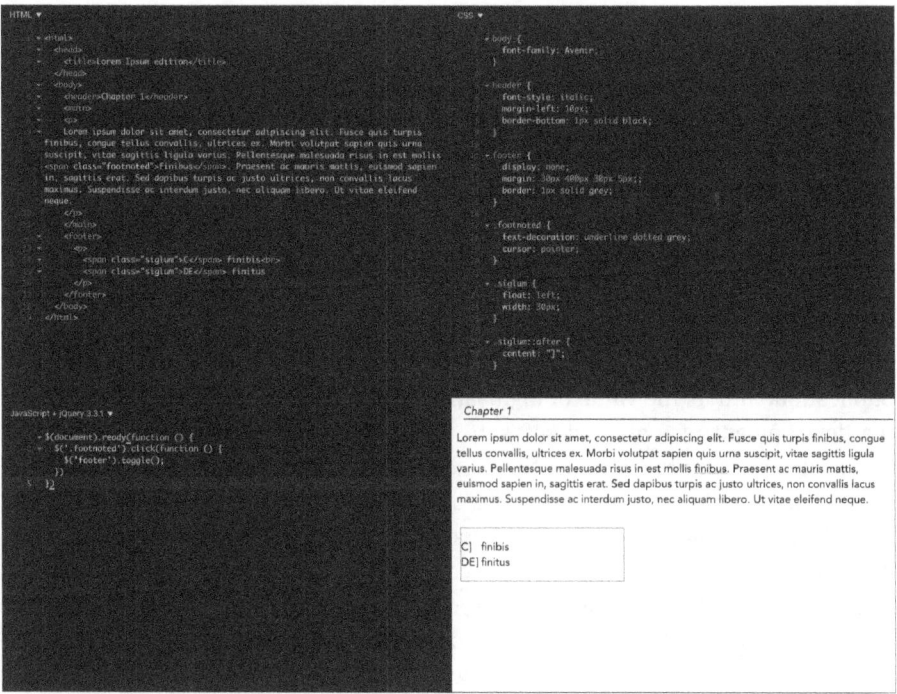

Fig. 6.4-7: An example of HTML (top left), CSS (top right), JavaScript (bottom left), and the rendered result (bottom right).

Atop these three technologies exists a vast and ever-growing ecosystem of publishing tools, frameworks, and libraries to speed up the task of Web development; by making use of these tools, or indeed by making direct and unadorned use of HTML, CSS, and JavaScript, a Web developer can publish an edition according to more or less any specification. The text may be divided arbitrarily into pages and retain a print-style critical apparatus; alternatively, it may be grouped into logical sections, with the variants displayed via JavaScript pop-ups and the sigla linked to manuscript transcriptions. Variants can be highlighted to indicate the position of their respective manuscripts in the stemma proposed by the editor, or a list of variants can be generated to allow other scholars the possibility to propose a different stemma hypothesis. Annotations to the text can be displayed as marginal notes, as hyperlinked endnotes, or hidden away entirely until the reader has a need to consult them. Editors can choose to make the manuscript transcriptions available as TEI XML downloads, or display them using normal HTML markup. The edition may include images of some or all manuscript pages, or may provide a link to the online collection of a library where a given manuscript can be viewed.

Since Web technologies themselves remain under steady and active development, the particular set of tools and frameworks employed will depend on the prior experience and existing skill set of the editor or Web developer, and will vary from edition to edition and from year to year. This makes standardisation around any particular tool or framework all but impossible, which remains perhaps the greatest challenge for the sustainability of digital scholarship. At the same time, custom Web development remains the only feasible option that allows editors to explore new ideas for how to present a text, and how to allow readers to engage with it.

6.4.4 Adoption of digital solutions

As academic institutions and funding bodies are won over to the merits of digital publication, and as the value of digitisation of source data is increasingly realised, the development of tools and software for handling the data and producing the publications is sure to continue. Nevertheless, digital publication is a difficult subject for many editors to navigate. The difficulties stem from a number of issues: first, the sheer complexity of existing standards such as TEI XML; second, the fact that Web technologies themselves are constantly maturing and changing even as archivists and textual scholars demand reliable standards; third, the relatively high level of technical skill that is necessary to develop and maintain a Web publication; fourth, the lack of incentives for those with Web development skills to apply their skills to the problem of critical edition publication; and fifth, the lack of a robust infrastructure for the maintenance of those applications that have been developed.

These are known difficulties, shared by many research domains, and are of ongoing concern to policymakers in research and higher education. In some countries, such as Switzerland and Austria, funding has been made available for initiatives to try to get to grips with the problem of sustainability for digital editions. This is particularly critical for Switzerland, for example, where, in a parallel policy move, the Swiss National Science Foundation has mandated digital publication of any edition project that it supports (Schweizerischer Nationalfonds 2014). This, along with similar de facto policies of other major research funding bodies, is an acknowledgment that digital publication, for all its challenges and pitfalls, has very quickly become an indispensable way to ensure that scholarly texts are made available, engaged with by the public, and acknowledged as relevant to our societies.

7 Philological practices
Introductory remarks by the chapter editor, Caroline Macé

Although the stemmatological methodology is not per se restricted to any specific language or period in the history of literature, it has not penetrated every field of textual studies in the same way, and its application has led to various interpretations and evaluations. In the present chapter, examples of the historical development of the stemmatic method, taken from different fields, will be presented. It is, of course, impossible to cover every aspect of textual scholarship, but we hope to provide here a representative sample.

The first section, authored by Christian Amphoux, is devoted to the development of textual criticism in Greek New Testament studies (7.1). Historically, the rejection of the *textus receptus* of the New Testament may be considered the starting point of a text-critical awareness (Reynolds and Wilson 2013, 209). The difficulties inherent in the very large number of direct and indirect witnesses, and in the high degree of contamination, led to the early development of a specific methodology and of computer tools. The study of the New Testament was a field in which Karl Lachmann, the emblematic historical figure of the stemmatic method, was very active, as much as in classical philology (7.2) and mediaeval German philology (7.4). The two sections devoted to these latter disciplines largely discuss the heritage of Lachmann and the way it was challenged and adapted in the following two centuries. After sketching the history of the Lachmannian method in classical philology, Heinz-Günther Nesselrath shows, referring to a new edition of Lucian of Samosata's work (a Greek-speaking sophist and writer active in the second century CE), the difficulties of understanding the history of this large and complex tradition, represented mostly by late manuscripts (7.2).

As Frédéric Duval shows, mediaeval Romance philology, a domain in which Lachmann did not work himself, was a battlefield between proponents of the Lachmannian method – indeed, the first truly Lachmannian edition was produced by Gaston Paris in 1872 – and its fiercest opponents, such as Joseph Bédier (7.3). Ralf Plate uses editions of mediaeval German courtly epics as an example with which to follow the development of the method and editing techniques in Germanic philology from Lachmann to the present day (7.4).

As an example of philological work on oriental Christian manuscript traditions, Alessandro Bausi shows how philology developed in the field of Ethiopic studies, influenced by classical philology and biblical studies, but also by Romance philology (7.5). Chaim Milikowsky illustrates the different tendencies in editing rabbinic literature since the beginning of the twentieth century, from "best-text" editions to "radical eclecticism"; examples of application of the stemmatic method are very rare (7.6). Christopher Nugent pinpoints some distinctive aspects of the transmission of classical Chinese literature which make it very different from any Western or

Near-Eastern mediaeval literary tradition (see 1.3), and therefore call for specific editorial responses (7.7).

The gradual introduction of printing technology in Western Europe marks a change of paradigm in the transmission of works. Taking a few Latin examples, Iolanda Ventura shows the methodological uncertainties arising when editing early modern printed texts, whose transmission is still partly conditioned by manuscript culture, but already partly resorts to the field of authorial philology (*filologia d'autore*), which focuses on authorial variants (7.8). Confronting textual criticism and "genetic criticism", Dirk van Hulle questions the very concept of authorship and of "purity" or "integrity" in contemporary textual scholarship. In doing so, he underlines the differences between several "national" schools within modern textual scholarship (reflecting partly the same "national" schools in mediaeval philology): the Anglo-American, the German, and the French schools, not to mention the Italian *variantistica* (see 6.2.5). Dirk van Hulle invites textual scholars to distinguish between different possible "orientations to text", which can be combined rather than opposed to one another, and to define different types of editorial strategies (7.9).

It was beyond the scope of this chapter to deal with all languages, periods, or literary genres. Classical Latin is not represented as such, but the situation is relatively similar to that of classical Greek, and several other sections in the book focus on the Graeco-Roman world or on mediaeval or Renaissance Latin. On mediaeval Latin, see, for example, C. Leonardi (1994) and P. Chiesa (2016, 2019). Equally partial is our treatment of the biblical corpus (or corpora), represented only by the Greek New Testament (its many translations into Latin and oriental Christian languages are alluded to), whereas the problems posed by the Hebrew Bible and its numerous translations are different and have not been solved in the same ways (see Tov 1992; B. Chiesa 2000, 2002; for an assessment of the impact of the discovery of the "Dead Sea Scrolls" on textual criticism of the Hebrew Bible, see e.g. Debel 2010). A very large portion of literature in many languages, be it parabiblical or apocryphal, is also neglected. As has been said above, Ethiopic literature is but one example, albeit a significant one, of the very rich and interesting oriental Christian traditions (in Armenian, Christian Arabic, Georgian, and Syriac – to name only some of the most important languages; see 7.5) which developed since late Antiquity (see Bausi et al. 2015). The Byzantine world and the vast continent of the Eastern European Middle Ages have merely been alluded to in other chapters (3.2, 4.5). Amongst the Western mediaeval literary cultures, only Romance philology is well represented (also in 2.3–4), although not so much is said about the Iberian literatures. Early German is dealt with in the present chapter, and alluded to in sections 3.1 and 6.3, whereas languages such as Old English (see 1.5, 6.3), Old Norse (see 6.1), or Old Saxon (see 6.2) are not fully treated. Many other languages are almost totally missing, such as Sanskrit and the vast universe of Indology (see Witzel 2014; see also 6.2.2 above).

A section on textual scholarship in the field of Arabic (Islamic) literature authored by Lucia Raggetti had been anticipated and would have been very welcome in the present chapter, but it was withdrawn at the very last moment by its author for unclear reasons and despite all editorial efforts. It would have been interesting to see the turn taken by textual scholarship in Arabic studies, especially after influential voices were raised against the Lachmannian method in that field (see Witkam 1988, 2013). Unfortunately, since this section had to be removed after the book had already been sent to the publisher, it was far too late to find a replacement.

Albeit incomplete, this survey of the impact of the genealogical method in different fields of textual scholarship is important in order to understand how the method has been reshaped differently to respond to different needs. It is also interesting to see how permeable the boundaries between the different disciplines are, and to what extent they have influenced one another in various manners and in different directions, definitely not only from classical philology towards the others, but also in many other ways. An often-mentioned principle should be remembered here: the only criterion for selecting a method is that it should be best suited to its object and to the aim that scholars have set for their work (this aim being shaped by several, sometimes contradictory, needs and constrains). The object varies very much indeed, and that in multiple respects:

- the language can be more or less actively known by the copyists (and even the writer), it may be more or less regulated, more or less artificial, and so on;
- the topic and the literary genre in which the transmitted work is written are of no little importance for the conditions under which it will be transmitted (poetry is not dealt with very much in this book, and nor – at the other end of the literary spectrum, as it were – are technical treatises and so on);
- the type of authorship can vary greatly, as can the involvement of other "textual actors" (see e.g. Schnell 1998 for a discussion of the concept of "author" in the Middle Ages, and P. Chiesa 2012, 381–382, for contrasting antique and mediaeval concepts of authorship); and
- the time gap between the composition of the work and its earliest witnesses is a determining factor in the choice of a suitable methodology, as is the more or less fragmentary character of the remaining tradition.

This list of factors that shape the object of textual criticism is far from being complete. Several publications gather case studies that can fill some of the gaps left by our survey, such as Dummer (1987), Hamesse (1992), Macé et al. (2015), and Göransson et al. (2016).

7.1 The New Testament

Christian-Bernard Amphoux

The New Testament (NT) is a special case among the transmission of texts from (late) Antiquity because its textual tradition includes thousands of manuscripts and innumerable patristic quotations. Moreover, the Greek text varied a lot from the second to the fourth centuries; it has never been unified, and specialists are today divided on the interpretation of variants: are they "deformations" of a primitive text restored well by the current editors or, in some cases, milestones in a history of the text so complex that current editions are but a temporary solution that can still evolve further? This section provides some information with which to understand what textual criticism of the NT is all about.

The NT was written in Greek, although some of its sources might have been written in Aramaic. It was transmitted in its original language, as well as in about ten other ancient languages into which it was translated. From the beginning of the second to the end of the fourth century AD, the text was unstable, until the time when – from the fifth century onwards – the text established in Antioch became the most widespread, without, however, the previous types of texts disappearing: they remained alive on the periphery of the Byzantine Empire. In the West, the printing press initially favoured the Byzantine text, which was replaced in the nineteenth century by the Alexandrian text. Neither of those texts, however, is "original"; they can both be proved to be the result of revisions undertaken at the beginning of the fourth century. So far, there has been no agreement amongst scholars regarding the details of this history, regarding how to distinguish between the different types of texts, and regarding the chronology.

This section is divided into two parts. First, I would like to present some insights concerning the history of the text, because this reveals much about the history of textual scholarship in modern times. Then, I will explain some of the methods developed over the last century to deal with such a complex textual history and the wealth of variant readings attested by the NT.

7.1.1 History of the text of the NT

7.1.1.1 A short survey of the manuscripts of the Greek NT

The NT has come down to us through an exceptionally high number of manuscripts copied from the middle of the second century to the end of the fifteenth century and beyond (see Vagany and Amphoux 1986, 21–84; trans. Heimerdinger 1991, 5–51; Amphoux 2014, 9–193; Ehrman and Holmes 2013, 1–113). The most important ones can be divided into four chronological categories: (*i*) papyri copied before 300; (*ii*) the first Greek Bibles from the fourth/fifth century; (*iii*) bilingual Greek and Latin manuscripts from the fifth/sixth century; and (*iv*) mediaeval manuscripts which are erratic witnesses to older variants. For a list of manuscripts of the NT and their sigla, see Kurt Aland (1994).

Papyri copied before 300
These are mainly fragments of books found during excavations in Egypt in the twentieth century. They attest an early form of the Alexandrian text. The most complete are P^{75} (third century, containing Luke and John) and P^{46} (end of the second century, containing the Pauline Epistles).

Greek Bibles from the fourth century
The first two Greek Bibles (Septuagint + NT), which are also the most important, are the *Codex Sinaiticus* (ℵ.*01*), copied in Caesarea around 330, reproducing the recension of Pamphilus of Caesarea, Origen's successor, and the *Codex Vaticanus* (*B.03*), copied around 340, reproducing the Alexandrian recension of Hesychius of Alexandria. These two recensions are different but related, and constitute the Alexandrian text of the fourth century.

Bilingual Greek–Latin manuscripts of the fifth/sixth century
Two bilingual manuscripts witness an old text, in use in the second century, before the other text types: the *Codex Bezae* (*D.05/VL 5*), copied around 400, containing the Gospels and Acts, and the *Codex Claromontanus* (*D.06/VL 75*), copied in the fifth or sixth century, containing the Epistles of Paul.

Mediaeval witnesses to older variants
Most mediaeval manuscripts attest the Byzantine text, which is derived from a recension dating from the beginning of the fourth century, that of Lucianus of Antioch. A few of them, however, contain variants that pertain to a more ancient text type, attested by Origen (around 230); amongst them are an uncial manuscript copied in Georgia, the *Codex Koridethi* (Θ.*038*) and families 1 and 13.

As there is no agreement on the genealogy of those text types, I offer here the opinion I have formed on the basis of my own research: the Western text, attested by the bilingual manuscripts, is at the origin of the other text types; the Alexandrian text is derived from it by means of several recensions from the end of the second century; the Byzantine text is the most recent and is derived from a revision of the Caesarean text type, of which many variants are preserved in mediaeval manuscripts, originating with Origen; and the Caesarean text type is itself derived from the Western text through a process of recension.

7.1.1.2 The printed editions
As is well known, the very first book to be printed was Gutenberg's Latin Bible in 1455. It is only half a century later that the first printed edition of the Greek NT was produced (see Elliott 2014).

The reign of the *textus receptus*

The first two editions were produced concurrently in Spain and in Switzerland. Xavier de Cisneros completed the printing of a polyglot Bible in Hebrew, Greek, and Latin in 1514 in Alcalá, although publication proper would occur only in 1522. The edition of the Greek NT prepared by Erasmus in Basle was first published in 1516, and was very well received in the reformed churches, where people would learn Greek in order to access the "original" text of the NT, confidence in the Vulgate having become weak. As early as 1517, Luther's sermons contained a doxology at the end of the Lord's Prayer ("For thine is the kingdom, the power, and the glory, for ever and ever") absent from the Vulgate but present in the Byzantine text which is the basis of Erasmus' edition. By 1535, Erasmus had produced five editions, which were reproduced by other publishers in – among other places – Venice, Hagenau, and Strasbourg (Reuss 1872, 28–31).

In 1534, in Paris, the edition of Simon de Coline was published and served as a basis for the French Bible translation by Pierre Robert Olivétan. This Bible was subsequently revised several times by Calvin in Geneva. Between 1546 and 1550, the editions of Robert Estienne, the printer of the king of France, were published, the last one in Geneva, to which he was forced to flee. In this fourth edition, the text is divided into verses for the first time (the division into chapters had been made for the Latin Bible at the beginning of the thirteenth century by the circle of Stephen Langton in Paris). After Estienne, Theodore Beza, Calvin's successor, published several editions in Geneva between 1565 and 1609, while Plantin printed a new polyglot Bible in Antwerp in 1572. In the introduction to the second edition, published in 1633 in Amsterdam by Elzevir, the expression *textus receptus* was used for the first time, and became the label for the type of text (Byzantine) printed since Erasmus. As more editions appeared and new manuscripts were consulted, the awareness that the text contained a great number of variants became more and more acute. The first systematic collations of Greek manuscripts of the NT were published in the polyglot Bible of London prepared by Brian Walton (1654–1657). It is not until the eighteenth century, however, that one sees a distinction being made between several recensions (Bengel 1734) and a first ordering of the manuscripts being proposed (Griesbach 1775–1807).

The evidence that eighteenth-century scholars had at their disposal was much scarcer than what we have today: in particular, all the papyri were lacking, since they were discovered in the twentieth century; the *Codex Sinaiticus* was not found until 1844, and most of the witnesses to the Caesarean type were still unknown; even the *Codex Vaticanus*, whose existence was known, was unavailable on account of Vatican policy. Although the attempts at classifying the witnesses were flawed by the shortcomings of this documentation, the outline of today's classification was nevertheless already in existence. The outcome of all this was that, until the beginning of the nineteenth century, the *textus receptus* was considered as the original text of the NT.

The triumph of the Alexandrian text

In 1809, consultation of the *Codex Vaticanus* was made possible in Paris, and the examination of its writing allowed Johann Leonhard Hug to conclude that it was copied before Jerome's revision of the Latin version of the Gospels (Hug 1810). Because of some agreements between the codex and Jerome's revision against the *textus receptus*, noted by Lucas of Bruges and published in the polyglot Bible of London (1654–1657), the codex had hitherto been suspected of having been influenced by the Vulgate. Hug's conclusions rehabilitated it, and it became the oldest known manuscript of the NT, having already been used in Rome for the edition of the Septuagint (1586). An era of glory began for the manuscript, as from now on it represented the main witness to the Alexandrian text.

In 1831, Lachmann applied to the NT the method used for editing classical texts (Lachmann 1831; see Timpanaro 1981, 53–58). As the principal manuscripts of the earliest times, he chose the following: *Alexandrinus* (A); *Vaticanus* (B); *Ephraemi rescriptus* (C), an incomplete Bible from the fifth century, whose text had been erased and overwritten in the twelfth century with patristic works; *Codex Bezae* (D for the Gospels and Acts); *Claromontanus* (D for the Pauline corpus); and the Vulgate. The text published by Lachmann was a sensation: it was full of new variants, mainly Alexandrian but also Western, thus highlighting that the *textus receptus* was not the original text but a relatively late revision. This opened up a new question: how can we reach the oldest form of the NT?

The discovery of the *Codex Sinaiticus* by Constantin Tischendorf in 1844 sanctioned the importance of the Alexandrian text: this manuscript often agrees with *Vaticanus*, they are both equally old, and its NT is complete. Some people suspected that the manuscript was a forgery; others believed that it had been revealed by divine intervention so that the faithful could finally know the original text of the NT! Tischendorf's critical edition (1869–1872) contains an Alexandrian text very heavily influenced by this manuscript.

But the "edition of reference" was still to come: this was the one published by Brook Foss Westcott and John Anthony Hort (Westcott and Hort 1881), without a critical apparatus but accompanied by a volume of introduction in which a theory was developed which is still today regarded as valid in the Anglo-Saxon world: the *Vaticanus* and the *Sinaiticus* manuscripts represent a "neutral text" dating from the time before the existence of recensions, whereas the other manuscripts depend on three main recensions, detected in the eighteenth century, called "Alexandrian", "Syrian", and "Western". A revision of the official English translation, the King James Version dating from the beginning of the seventeenth century, appeared in the same year, based on the new text and moving away from the *textus receptus* – this revision is the Authorised Revised Version. Conservatives did not accept it, and two different texts of the NT therefore coexist in English: the *textus receptus*, favoured by the evangelical churches, and the Alexandrian text, of which the new model is very close to the *Codex Vaticanus*.

In 1913, the edition by Hermann von Soden cast doubt on the idea of a "neutral text". Again, three main types of texts were put forward: the Egyptian text, called *H* after Hesychius, for which *Vaticanus* and *Sinaiticus* were the main witnesses; the Byzantine text, called *K* after the Greek word *koine*, that is, the common text, the one attested by the majority of manuscripts; and a text called *I* after the initial of "Jerusalem", a very diverse text that gathers together everything from before the fourth century, that is, material that is now, after the discovery of many papyri, distinguished into the Western and the Caesarean types of texts. In parallel, Caspar René Gregory published a volume of *Prolegomena* (1894^2) to Tischendorf's edition, then *Textkritik des Neuen Testaments* (1900–1909), which continued the search for NT manuscripts, giving one unique identification number to each manuscript. This directory would be completed by Kurt Aland (1994^2) following the same principles. The preparatory works of von Soden were also published (1902–1910), but he adopted another system of numbering the manuscripts which makes it difficult to use his edition today. Von Soden's merits must be acknowledged, however, since he made many fresh collations of manuscripts and recognised the existence of a multiform text prior to the text of the *Codex Vaticanus* and the *Codex Sinaiticus*.

This, however, could not change the powerful trend of editing the Alexandrian text, and editors would simply ignore other works and continue favouring the *Vaticanus* and *Sinaiticus* text as the basis for editions of the NT. It was in vain that several scholars highlighted the anteriority of the Western text to the Egyptian one, and also questioned the position of the Caesarean type. The new critical editions that were undertaken – those by Stanley Charles Edmund Legg (1935, 1940; Mark and Matthew respectively) and then by the Institut für neutestamentliche Textforschung in Münster (Catholic Epistles: B. Aland 1997–2005), but also that by Reuben Swanson (1995–2005; Matthew to Galatians) – all of them partial, favoured the Alexandrian text. The only exception is the International Greek NT Project (1984–1987; Luke), which chose to edit the *textus receptus* again. In actual fact, the making of a critical edition of the NT is rendered difficult because of the tension between the critical examination of the variant readings, on the one hand, which leads to priority for the Western text, and, on the other hand, the older age of the witnesses to the Alexandrian text, reinforced by the discovery of papyri copied around 200. The Western text, even though it is older, is not attested in its entirety and, more importantly, it is not suitable for use in churches: it is an old scholarly text which has been in decline since the end of the second century; it was not read or commented on in Antiquity, and had almost completely disappeared by the Middle Ages – it would make no sense to give it priority today in church use. On the other hand, the Caesarean type of text is not completely known either, because its witnesses are late and all contaminated by the Byzantine text, which was initially a revision of it. In comparison, the Alexandrian text, with its two main witnesses, the *Codex Vaticanus* and the *Codex Sinaiticus*, is complete, even though these two witnesses reflect an attempt, which would be abandoned and replaced by the Byzantine text, to construct a model for copying the Greek Bible.

7.1.2 How to deal with the variant readings

Because of the number of manuscripts and of variants and the even higher number of lost intermediaries, but also because of the nature of the transmission of the text, which occurred through a series of successive revisions, the Lachmannian method today seems impracticable for NT textual criticism, especially because of the contamination from the Byzantine text. Only for small groups of manuscripts is it possible to propose a *stemma codicum*, as, for example, in the case of family 13, which includes a dozen manuscripts of the Gospels all copied in southern Italy (Lafleur 2013, 158–241). The possibility of using statistical, and later automated, methods may change this situation, but so far the results obtained by those methods have not proved to be any better than a philological examination of the variants one by one. In what follows, we will present first the philological method applied to the NT, and then several attempts at using automated means to treat the variants of the NT.

7.1.2.1 Philological examination of the variant readings one by one
For the NT, the method that has been used and refined over time to deal with variant readings is divided into three successive steps.

Verbal criticism
The first step consists of looking for mistakes arising from the copying process, with the aim of eliminating them from the text. In practice, these mistakes have been removed in the standard editions (Nestle–Aland, *Novum Testamentum Graece*, 28th ed. 2012; B. Aland et al., *The Greek New Testament*, 5th ed. 2015) but are not fully documented in the critical apparatuses, which are incomplete; in more advanced editions (von Soden 1913; Legg 1935, 1940; Swanson 1995–2005), on the other hand, the documentary basis is greater but much still needs to be done as far as verbal criticism is concerned.

Some types of variant readings can be quite easily eliminated.
- Orthographical errors (deviating from the established rules for standardisation of written Hellenistic Greek).
- Haplographies or dittographies (i.e. omitting or repeating a syllable or a word). Example: "αποκρεις" instead of "αποκριθεις" (Matthew 21:21, in *Codex Bezae*, f. 70v, line 1; cudl.lib.cam.ac.uk/view/MS-NN-00002-00041/126).
Example: "ιερουερουσαλημ" instead of "ιερουσαλημ" (Luke 23:28, in *Codex Bezae*, f. 278v, line 17; cudl.lib.cam.ac.uk/view/MS-NN-00002-00041/537).
- Homoeoteleuton or homoeoarcton (i.e. omission of a group of words because of the similarity of letters at its beginning and end, causing the eye to jump; see 4.3.2).
Example: this type of mistake is found very often in the *Codex Sinaiticus* (codexsinaiticus.org/en/manuscript.aspx), where omitted passages are supplied in the margins.

- "Harmonising" variants, especially in the Gospels: a passage in one Gospel is made closer to the parallel passage in another Gospel.
  Example: in Mark 6:3, Jesus is called "ο τεκτων" [the carpenter], but in a few manuscripts (P^{45vid}, f^{13}, 565 700, and 33 579), he is called "ο του τεκτονος (ο) υιος" [the carpenter's son], in accordance with Matthew 13:55.

All these variants, because they are unintentional, can be left out of the apparatus, whereas those that are intentional should be noted in the apparatus. In practice however, except for obvious writing mistakes, it is generally hard to say whether a variant is intentional or not, and most cases will need to be carefully examined.

External criticism
This analysis consists of gathering all existing information concerning manuscripts and text types, in particular their dates and locations. It is important to bear in mind that the time when a manuscript was copied and the date of the text it contains are not necessarily the same. For example, patristic quotations allow the Western text contained in the *Codex Bezae* (*D.05*), which was copied around 400, to be dated at least to the second century. On the other hand, the Alexandrian text of the first papyri, copied between 180 and 230, is not attested before 175. Therefore, for the text of Luke, for instance, the *Codex Bezae* offers an older text than papyrus P^{75} and is very close to the *Vaticanus* text (Duplacy 1973, 111–128).

This external criticism leads to the following conclusion: the Western text, attested essentially by the *Codex Bezae* but also by second-century citations, and to a lesser extent by the Old Latin and Syriac translations, existed before the Alexandrian text, which in turn predates the Byzantine text that took shape during the fourth century. On the other hand, since the Western text is attested in regions that are far away from each other, it has been considered "universal" (Vaganay and Amphoux 1986, 160–161; trans. Heimerdinger 1991, 110), whereas the Alexandrian text is present mainly in Egypt, and the Byzantine text, as its name suggests, in the Byzantine Empire. But these conclusions remain hypothetical because the fact that a text is attested in an older witness does not mean that the text is genealogically older. To settle the question, it is necessary to carry out an internal analysis of the variants.

Internal criticism
This type of criticism is divided into two aspects: (*i*) a search for the variant-source (or primary variant) by comparing all variants found at one *locus*, and (*ii*) an examination of how those variants fit into their context.

(*i*) Searching for the source-variant
The central issue is to determine, if several variants occur in one place, in what order they came into existence. Some of the criteria developed to answer this ques-

tion go back to Gerardus de Trajecto Mosae (Gerard of Maastricht) in his 1711 edition of the NT (Vaganay and Amphoux 1986, 121–122; trans. Heimerdinger 1991, 79–80), the most important ones being *brevior lectio probabilior* (the shortest reading is the most probable) and *difficilior lectio potior* (the most difficult reading is preferable). In other words, experience shows that copyists tend to expand the text rather than shorten it, and to make it simpler rather than complicate it. Here are two examples of those principles.

- Mark 1:41: a leper asked Jesus to cure him, and in some manuscripts Jesus got angry ("οργισθεις"), whereas in others he felt compassionate ("σπλαγχνισθεις"). Regardless of the manuscripts in which it appears, the first variant seems more difficult to understand in the context, and it must therefore be the primary reading.
- Luke 11:2–4: some manuscripts offer a "complete" *Pater noster* with seven requests, whereas others attest a shortened prayer with a shorter address and only five requests. According to the principles stated above, the shorter version must be primary.

But these principles alone are inadequate, and the choice of the primary variant should always be justified by stronger arguments. In Mark 1:41, one has to interpret Jesus's anger: it is possible to read the passage in such a way that Jesus is not angry at the leper as a sick person, but at a group of people whom the leper represents and of whom Jesus disapproves. As for Luke 11:2–4, Tertullian states that the shorter version of the *Pater noster* in Luke was revised by Marcion (Tertullian *Adversus Marcionem* 4.26.1–4; Harnack 1924, 207*; Amphoux 1987, 106, 110). Marcion published his revision of Luke around 140, and he suppressed many passages. Is it therefore possible that he shortened the *Pater noster*, too? And if so, what did he want to suppress from the original prayer?

In the Gospels, many variants are "serious" in the sense that they present difficulties such as those in the two variants presented above. Many more variants are "slighter", however, as they have less impact on the meaning of the text and are therefore less interesting. Those "minor" variants have to do with grammar and literary style, and most of them are due to the copying process, in which the copy is never completely identical to the model (Dain 1964, 30–37; Amphoux 2014, 12–15). In all cases, the point of comparing the variants found at any one place is to determine the source-variant, that is, not the variant attested by the oldest witnesses but the variant from which all the others can be explained.

(ii) Appropriateness to the context

The search for the source-variant leads to one or more possible solutions, and it is necessary to verify the hypotheses by testing them against the context of the variants, this context being immediate or wider.

To provide just one example: in Mark 1:41, which we examined above, Jesus's anger occurs in an immediate context, where Jesus "blames" the leper (verse 43) and shows hostility towards him, which is not found in the parallel passages. But this still does not explain what the leper represents in the passage. To understand this, one must look at Leviticus 13–14, where leprosy is considered the sickness of impure priests. So, the leper in Mark 1:41 represents a category of employees of the Temple with whom Jesus is angry. This metaphorical meaning of the leper, being too complicated, was abandoned in some manuscripts by changing the word for "angry" into that for "compassionate".

This example, and many others which we could mention, reveal a new issue in the history of the NT text, an issue that is often ignored by exegesis: the NT text may have had other meanings in the course of time than that which has been transmitted. This also shows the complexity and the importance of applying textual criticism to the NT.

Given this complexity, is it possible to treat the variants automatically?

7.1.2.2 Towards an automated treatment of the variant readings (Pastorelli 2014)

In 1742, Johann Albrecht Bengel was the first to try to classify the manuscripts of the NT according to their variants and to establish significant groups of manuscripts, which would later become the witnesses of the various "recensions".

Quentin's method

In the 1920s, Henri Quentin (see 2.3.4) applied to the manuscripts of the Vulgate a new method, in which the number of common variants between manuscripts is compared using groups of three manuscripts: if two manuscripts have no (zero) agreement against a third one (what Quentin called the "zéro caractéristique"), then this third manuscript must be either an intermediary between the two or their common ancestor. This method, based on numbers and not requiring any philological analysis of the variants, was a first step towards systematisation and, ultimately, automation of the processing of variants.

Multiple Readings Method (Colwell)

In 1947, Ernest Cadman Colwell rejected the use of the genealogical method for the NT, using tables of variants to group manuscripts instead, and especially seeking to add other manuscripts to already existing groups as defined by previous research. This method has been applied with success by several scholars, among whom are William L. Richards (1977), Larry Hurtado (1981), and Eldon J. Epp and Gordon D. Fee (1993). See also Jean Duplacy (1975).

Claremont Profile Method (CPM)

With the arrival of computers, the Multiple Readings Method (Colwell 1969) gave birth to the International Greek NT Project, aimed at providing a critical edition of

Luke (1984–1987) based on 1,666 Greek manuscripts. Starting from base manuscripts that had already been classified, a number of characteristic variants for each group were selected, and each new manuscript was classified on the basis of these variants. This method is useful for rapidly grouping the Byzantine manuscripts, but it does not allow us to see if, among the variants, some manuscripts shift from one group to another.

Comprehensive Profile Method (Ehrman)

In 1986, Bart Ehrman refined the Claremont Profile Method and distinguished several categories of variants: (*i*) distinctive readings, attested by most witnesses of one group and only by them; (*ii*) exclusive readings, attested by at least two witnesses of one group and only by them; and (*iii*) primary readings, attested by witnesses of several groups. This method was applied successfully to the Gospel quotations of Didymus the Blind; then by Darrell Hannah (1997) to the quotations of the First Epistle to the Corinthians in Origen; by Roderic Mullen (1997) to the Gospel quotations in Cyril of Jerusalem; by Jean-François Racine (2004) to the quotations of Matthew in Basil of Caesarea; by Carroll D. Osburn (2004) to the quotations of Acts and the Pauline and Catholic Epistles in Epiphanius of Salamis; by Carl Cosaert (2008) to the Gospel quotations in Clement of Alexandria; and so on. It is apparent that this method is used to classify quotations rather than manuscripts.

Index of variation (weighting variants)

To take account of the relative importance of textual variations, I proposed an "index of variation" which I applied comparatively to the method of Quentin and to data analysis by computer (Amphoux 1988). This index gives more weight to lexical substitutions than to transpositions, and to substitutions of verbs or substantives than to those of prepositions or conjunctions. The results were promising, allowing a better classification of the manuscripts, but a huge amount of interpretation remains to be done by scholars, and this index should be further developed and fine-tuned.

Coherence-Based Genealogical Method (Mink)

Finally, in 1993, Gerd Mink set out to adapt the method of the *stemma codicum* to the Gospel manuscripts by establishing one sub-stemma for each variation unit, and then automatically gathering all sub-stemmata into a "textual stream" (see 5.3.7.3 above). This idea is very appealing, because, as I have shown above, the processing of variants in the NT is complicated by several phenomena. But the results are disappointing: used in Münster for the *Editio critica maior* of the Catholic Epistles, it led to the reproduction, with very few differences, of the edition of Nestle.

In short, all those formal approaches have as their point of departure the premise that the evolution of a text can be reduced to formal questions. Indeed, to a large extent, minor variations can be dealt with in such a way, and for them formal approaches may prove useful. As for major variants, however, it is necessary to approach them with the type of philological examination that I have elucidated above.

7.1.3 Implications

Scholars working on the NT face a contradictory situation: on the one hand, the NT, as a reference for Christian faith, needs to be edited as a fixed, non-fluctuating text; on the other hand, the history of this text is such that it has in reality changed considerably over the course of time, precisely because it was a reference text at the centre of ecclesiastical, liturgical, and dogmatic rivalries. It is therefore impossible, in view of the documentation that we have, to offer at the same time a unified text and its oldest possible state. As a result, the edited text can only be a compromise, and several solutions are possible. Most scholars nowadays tend to give preference to the text of the Greek Bibles from the beginning of the fourth century. Other scholars would rather go back to the Byzantine text, which was the most widely read in the Greek world in the Middle Ages – a solution close to that proposed by the supporters of the *textus receptus*. Personally, I am in favour of an edition that would show several – at least three – states of the text synoptically: the Western text above, and the Alexandrian and Byzantine texts in two columns below, with a critical apparatus gathering the main variants at the bottom of the page.

Acknowledgements

The author would like to thank Caroline Macé and Jenny Read Heimerdinger (University of Wales Trinity Saint David) for their help in translating this text into English, as well as David Pastorelli (Université d'Aix-Marseille) for suggesting additional bibliographical references.

Further reading

To learn more about the classification of the NT manuscripts and about the specific problems caused by the overabundance of documentation, see Duplacy (1975) and Pastorelli (2014). Interesting recent contributions are, for example, van Reenen, den Hollander, and van Mulken (2004); Carlson (2015); Gurry (2017); and Wasserman and Gurry (2017).

7.2 Classical Greek
Heinz-Günther Nesselrath

Until recently, in the field of classical philology, the Lachmannian method had been almost unchallenged, at least in theory, since its invention. After a historical introduction to the development of the Lachmannian method, and some considerations about the challenges faced when applying this method to real cases, I will focus on a specific example, that of the edition of Lucian of Samosata's work, which poses particular problems in Greek philology.

7.2.1 The development of stemmatology in Greek and Latin classical philology

In the field of Greek and Latin classical philology, stemmatology is closely associated with (if not in fact identified by) what is commonly called "Lachmann's method" (on the emergence of the term, see below). It is therefore all the more remarkable that Karl Lachmann (1793–1851) – who was not only a classicist but also an editor of mediaeval and modern German texts – was, in many of his editions (of Propertius, 1816 and 1829; of Tibullus, 1829), not "Lachmannian" at all (see Timpanaro 2005, 76–79; Trovato 2017, 83), and that his edition of Catullus of 1829 was based on a mathematical reconstruction of the archetype that was, even quite recently, severely criticised by Fiesoli (2000, 61–85). In other editions, however, like those of the New Testament (*editio minor*, 1831; *editio maior*, together with Philipp Buttmann, 1842–1850), Lucretius (1850), the *Nibelungenlied* (1826), and other Middle High German poems (1820s–1840s), he at least came close to the methodological approach which later received his name. His New Testament edition is not to be noted so much for its improvements to the text as for being the first to abandon the old *textus receptus* (established by Erasmus in the early sixteenth century; Fiesoli 2000, 147; see also 7.1 above). Even his highly acclaimed edition of Lucretius ("an dem wir alle die kritische Methode gelernt haben" [using which we all have learned the critical method]; von Wilamowitz-Moellendorff 1921, 59) exhibits errors in methods of judgement (Fiesoli 2000, 257), and in his editions of Middle High German texts he more than once proceeds with a "Bédieriste" (see below) preference for just one manuscript (Fiesoli 2000, 289, 295, 302, 329).

Timpanaro has pointed out that Lachmann had important predecessors – in the fifteenth century the Italian humanist Angelo Poliziano, in the eighteenth century the New Testament editor Johann Albrecht Bengel (the discoverer of the principle of *lectio difficilior*) – and that Lachmann's contemporaries, among them the Danish classicist Johan Nicolai Madvig and the Jewish German classicist Jakob Bernays (who published his own Lucretius edition in 1852), did fundamental work with regard to establishing *stemmata codicum* and reconstructing archetypes (Timpanaro 2005, 46–74, 97–98, 104–106; see also Kenney 1974, 103–105).

The most basic principle of the "method of Lachmann" – that, for establishing the relationships between manuscripts (as a precondition for the construction of a stemma), "what is significant [...] is not agreement in true readings [...], but agreement in readings of secondary origin, namely corruptions and emendations, provided that they are not such as might have been produced by two scribes independently" (West 1973, 32; see now Trovato 2017, 54–56, 109–117, insisting on the importance of distinguishing between "mere" variants and significant or indicative errors) – was not formulated (or even consciously applied) by Lachmann but by textual critics in the second half of the nineteenth century. According to Michael Reeve (1998, 68), Gaston Paris deserves the "title of the first scholar to have applied systematically the principle that only shared errors establish families of textual witnesses; and the first explicit formulation remains Paul Lejay's in 1888" (see also 2.3 above). However basic this principle is, even in recent times there have still been editors who (though claiming to use the stemmatological method) have not applied it consistently enough (see Reeve 2000, 201–202).

All in all, it is quite ironic that the "method of Lachmann" received its name from the anti-Lachmannian Bédier (see P. L. Schmidt 1988) and from others who criticised the method (Quentin, Greg, Pasquali; see Fiesoli 2000, 355–452).

7.2.2 Challenges of the method: Contamination, interpolation, Bédier's *optimus codex*

If the transmission of texts proceeded only in single "vertical" lines (producing new copies of a text by using just one older manuscript as exemplar), the stemmatic method would work perfectly well; however, the phenomenon of "contamination" (i.e. using more than one source of textual information, be it another manuscript or additional variants recorded in the margins or above the lines of the exemplar manuscript) can all too easily blur the picture and obscure relationships between manuscripts (see 4.4). Already in 1926, Paul Maas concluded: "Gegen die Kontamination ist kein Kraut gewachsen" (Maas 1960, 30) [No specific has yet been discovered against contamination] (trans. Flower 1958, 49). And contamination seems to be a more widespread phenomenon than stemmatologists would like. On the other hand, as Michael Reeve (1986, 39) pointed out, stemmatology is the one method that helps us detect contamination, and thus it should still be possible to discover "basic" relationships between manuscripts, even if contamination has caused some disturbances. In any case, the presence of contamination is a major obstacle "for the automatic generation of stemmata used in computer-assisted philology" (Trovato 2017, 136; see also below).

In the early twentieth century, Joseph Bédier (1864–1938; see 7.3), after initially following the stemmatic method (in his first edition of the *Lai de l'ombre* in 1890), became its most vehement critic and began to champion a radically different approach, that is, the privileging of the *optimus codex*. First in his new edition of the *Lai de l'ombre* in 1913, and then in a substantial article, "La Tradition manuscrite du Lai de l'ombre: Réflexions sur l'art d'éditer les anciens textes" (1928), he pointed out what is still known as Bédier's paradox: the fact that, of all the stemmata editors have drawn up following Lachmann's method, a suspiciously high percentage are made up of bipartite stemmata (i.e. ones consisting of only two main branches), resulting in an unnatural forest of only bifid trees. From this, Bédier inferred that "Lachmannian" scholars somehow – perhaps unconsciously, perhaps also because something is wrong with the method – interpreted the evidence of their stemmatological research always (or almost always) in such a way as to arrive at bipartite stemmata, which then would give them a choice between two variants found in the two branches (while, with more branches, the variant found in the majority would always have to be chosen as representing the archetype).

In the course of the twentieth century, a number of scholars have tried to grapple with Bédier's paradox. Giorgio Pasquali downplayed the high number of bipartite stemmata and confidently asserted that any number of "three-, four-, five-branched stemmas" (1934, 130–131) could be found; he did not, however, repeat this argument in later publications because, even among editions of classical texts, bipartite stemmata represent a clear majority, as Arrigo Castellani also had to admit in 1957 (see Timpanaro 2005, 159–160). In 1986, Michael Reeve expressed his continuing confidence in the stemmatic method:

> I believe that pluripartite stemmata are commoner among classical Latin texts than he [Timpanaro] allows; that Greg's hypothesis of decimation has not been refuted, though it will never be confirmed (or for that matter refuted) by purely mathematical calculations; that many bipartite stemmata are both textually and historically as certain as one can hope; that [...] interpolation is a more frequent cause of false bipartite stemmata than contamination; and that stemmatic method remains valid. (Reeve 1986, 69)

Recently, Paolo Trovato (2017, 85–93) has drawn attention to a solution to Bédier's paradox provided by Weitzman (1987), whose mathematical model "indicates a 77 % probability for two-branched trees for Greek texts, and 71 % for Latin texts" (Trovato 2017, 89). Trovato sees this confirmed by his own research. He also very pertinently points out that reconstructed stemmata are of course not "accurate depictions of the historical vicissitudes of transmission" (Trovato 2017, 144), because they can only take account of witnesses of a text that still exist (and not of the possibly many more lost ones, which, if still extant, might significantly alter a stemma). A quarter of a century earlier, James Grier had, in fact, already found some advantages in the possible over-representation of bipartite stemmata as a result of the stemmatological method:

> The key issue [...] is the question of reasonable competing readings [...] If the bipartite stemma is preferred in each case, this category is enlarged considerably and so too the number of readings on which critics must exercise their judgement and decide on the basis of their interpretation [...]. This is the procedure Lachmann hoped to avoid. The alternative, however, is

> even less attractive: that is to elevate some of those readings [...] to the level of certainty by eliminating their competitors and there can be no doubt that, among those so elevated to the archetype, some will be false. (Grier 1989, 274)

And he goes even further:

> My conviction is that, if the stemma is determined on textual grounds alone, no multipartite divisions and no *codices descripti* should be accepted at any level. My guidelines will thus result in a more responsible application of Lachmann's method. Even if the proposed bipartite relationships are false, they do not eliminate good readings, only those that would have been eliminated in any event by a true multipartite stemma. (Grier 1989, 277)

In this way, Bédier's argument – that editors proceeding according to Lachmann's method subconsciously (?) want to preserve their freedom to choose between readings – is actually turned on its head.

There is yet another challenge to the stemmatological method. In recent decades, attempts have increasingly been made to involve computer programs in the critical editing of texts; preliminary stages to these attempts can be seen in the work of two Benedictine monks, Henri Quentin in the 1920s and Jacques Froger in the 1960s (see 2.3). Like Bédier, Quentin impugned the common-errors method and chose to speak only of "variants"; Froger built on this idea and tried to pave the way to automated coverage of all variants. Within the field of Greek and Latin classical philology, such approaches still face major scepticism and, it seems, justifiably so. Michael Reeve (2000, 345) has cited an example of an edition of a Latin text which used the computer for collating thirty-seven manuscripts, but took more than twenty years to do so and still left more than fifty manuscripts out of the picture. In many cases, the texts of classical authors are transmitted by considerably fewer manuscripts, and in such cases computers may not really seem necessary to do the required collating. It is, however, not to be denied that digitisation can nowadays make excellent reproductions of manuscripts available (they can – thanks to the possibilities of magnification – even be clearer to read than the originals); I have myself greatly benefited from this technology for the production of a new critical edition of the Emperor Julian's writings from the time of his sole reign. In any case, Trovato (2017, 246) has well pointed out the limitations of computers for editorial work: "there are stages in editorial work that are not mechanical or serial, and hence cannot be delegated to machines", and even the distinction between what are "good" or "corrupt" readings can only be made by human minds, which will only change when an artificial intelligence of such capacity is developed that it will probably replace human dominance on this planet.

7.2.3 A concrete example of a stemmatological challenge: (Re)constructing a stemma for a new critical edition of the works of Lucian of Samosata

In my current project of re-editing the works of Lucian of Samosata for the Oxford Classical Texts series (OCT), I myself face the limitations of the stemmatological method discussed above (the possibility of an "open recension", a not fully satisfactory bipartite stemma, the presence of "contamination").

The last OCT critical edition of Lucian (by Matthew D. Macleod, 1972–1987) is based mainly on the results of an enquiry by Karl Mras (1911) into the transmission and manuscripts of Lucian that, at the time of Macleod's edition, was already more than sixty years old. Mras had based his findings primarily on ἀκολουθίαι, that is, the sequence of Lucianic works in the manuscripts, which he used to establish lines of kinship between them, as a result of which he posited two families (thus, we have a bipartite stemma again), β and y – which, however, were not coextensive (i.e. family β comprised considerably fewer works than family y) – as well as a class of *codices mixti*. Even very soon after Mras, however, Bruno Keil (1913, 512n1) pointed out that certain lines of dependence can only be established by the comparison of textual readings and variants. More recent editions of single Lucianic works (Coenen 1977; Itzkowitz 1986, 1992) have collated afresh all possibly relevant manuscripts and thus come to results that are at least partially different from Mras's findings. Moreover, shortly after Mras, another scholar, Hermann Wingels (1913), came to some rather different conclusions regarding the way the Lucianic *œuvre* came together: Wingels believed that the two main manuscript traditions observable in the transmission of Lucian came about not by the purposeful work of individual redactors (as Mras believed), but by the gradual accumulation or fusion of smaller editions of single or a few works.

In the case of a number of Lucian's works, these different perspectives have led to some disagreement over whether the transmission really took place in two distinct families or not. Thus, Mras and Macleod believed that for works 32 (*Somnium*) and 53–54 (*Tyrannicida, Abdicatus*) – the numbers are given here according to the sequence in one of the main Lucian manuscripts, Città del Vaticano, Biblioteca Apostolica Vaticana, Vat. Gr. 90 (Γ), which has become the basis for the arrangement of Lucian editions since the early twentieth century – a double tradition exists. According to Wingels, however, there is only a single tradition for these works. In the case of works 36 (*De mercede conductis*) and 39 (*Asinus*), Mras himself was unsure whether there were two traditions or just one, while Macleod posited one. Coenen (1977, cix–cx) pointed out that in works 15–19 (*De calumnia, Lis consonantium, Symposium, Soloecista, Cataplus*) and 25 (*Timon*), the differences between the two manuscript families (β and y) are much smaller than elsewhere; in works 52–54 (*Deorum concilium, Tyrannicida, Abdicatus*), he sees so little difference between them that it becomes unclear whether their manuscripts can be divided into two different families at all.

All these results tend to favour Wingels's thesis that the two corpora (which then became two families) grew only slowly over time and that their earliest parts probably exhibit the biggest differences. Furthermore, in those cases where only a single family seems to be extant, it is not always clear to which of the two mentioned families the works in question belong: works 1–12 are found in the namesake of the β tradition, B (Wien, Österreichische Nationalbibliothek, phil. gr. 123), which is a composite manuscript assembled (it seems) from groups belonging to the two families; but where did the switch occur, before works 1–12 or after them? This is not an idle question, because the two traditions – where they can be found in one and the same work and are clearly distinguished by *variae lectiones* – exhibit some remarkably different features: β seems more prone to "editing" or tampering with the text than γ; thus, the question of whether a given work belongs to the β or the γ tradition may be important for deciding whether a reading is a faithful witness to an original tradition or might have been subsequently changed by an editor.

There also remain further questions about the internal "set-up" of the two families which cannot be treated in detail here, but which suggest that relations between manuscripts may really vary from work to work and thus make it difficult to come to more general conclusions covering the whole corpus (or even large parts of it).

As one can see, the open questions regarding the tradition and textual history of Lucian's works are still considerable; but I am fairly confident that patient and consistent application of the stemmatological ("Lachmann's") method should help to obtain answers.

Further reading

Apart from West (1973), which is a good introduction to textual criticism in the field of classical philology, Bernabé and Hernández Muñoz (2010) deal specifically, and in a more practical way, with Greek classical and mediaeval texts. A new *Oxford Handbook of Greek and Latin Textual Criticism* should appear soon (de Melo and Scullion forthcoming).

7.3 Mediaeval Romance Philology
Frédéric Duval

Mediaeval Romance philology occupies a central place in the debates that have left their mark on the history of textual editing from ca. 1870 until the present. This can be explained by the richness of literature from mediaeval France (both in *langues d'oïl, R.* and Occitan), which is an inevitable meeting point for mediaevalists, not only from French-speaking countries. Through them, Romance philology has exerted some theoretical and methodological influences on other linguistic and cultural areas and, in turn, has received elements from other traditions. The stemmatic method has been at the core of these debates since the edition of the *Vie de Saint Alexis* by Gaston Paris (Paris and Pannier 1872).

The present section follows a chronological order, but without any teleological implications, since new approaches have never fully replaced previous trends. Romance philology has not undergone anything akin to a homogeneous evolution, due to national traditions and linguistic barriers that have temporarily hindered or isolated new trends. Italian neo-Lachmannian philology (see 2.4), for example, was largely neglected by Anglo-American "New Philology", even though the latter was largely supported by Romanists (and Germanists), and it was only in the last quarter of the twentieth century that neo-Lachmannian philology started to become widespread in Spanish philology.

7.3.1 Gaston Paris and the application of textual criticism to Romance literature

Romance philology established itself as an autonomous discipline very slowly from ca. 1830, first in Germany, where its development accelerated from ca. 1860 onwards. In the beginning, chairs of modern philology (comprising Romance and Germanic philology) were created as distinct from traditional chairs of classical philology. In the last decades of the nineteenth century, Romance philology began to differentiate itself from Germanic philology at the university level.

German influence on Gaston Paris (1839–1903), who was educated in Bonn and in Göttingen, was decisive when, in 1872, he published his edition of the *Vie de Saint Alexis*, which is considered to be the first application of textual criticism to any Romance text (see 2.3). Paul Meyer (1840–1917), who together with Paris promoted textual criticism, noted that, in his *Saint Alexis*, Paris was influenced by Karl Bartsch's edition of the *Nibelungenlied* (P. Meyer 1911, 632). Before this, textual criticism had actually been applied to a Romance text – in Gustav Gröber's dissertation on the manuscript tradition of *Fierabras* (1869) – but not to the extent of producing an edition.

Paris's *Saint Alexis* is distinguished by its methodological aspects and description of innovative concepts. In the introduction, one finds the seeds of many key concepts that would continue to be discussed or refined thereafter. Paris's goal was clear: he wanted to break with previous editing methods that either adhered to a *codex optimus* or that presented a composite text combining the readings of several manuscripts according to the taste and skill of the editor. Paris was conscious of his innovative work: "Les principes de la critique des textes n'ont guère été appliqués jusqu'à présent à l'ancienne littérature française, et particulièrement à la poésie épique" (Paris and Pannier 1872, 7) [The principles of textual criticism have hitherto hardly been applied to ancient French literature, especially not to epic poetry].

He wanted to impose a rigorous editing method which, through a reasoned comparison of manuscripts, would eliminate the subjectivity of the editor. Paris refused to accept that the scientific standards of the edition of a Romance text should be inferior than those of a text from antiquity, since the "exigences [de la critique], on ne saurait trop le dire, sont absolument les mêmes pour les productions du moyen-âge que pour celles de l'antiquité" (Paris and Pannier 1872, 7) [critical exigencies, it cannot be repeated often enough, are absolutely the same for the products of the Middle Ages as for Antiquity].

He was fully aware, however, that the conditions of transmission of these texts differed greatly from one another. In particular, he highlighted that mediaeval texts were subject to more significant alterations, due both to the actions of "innovaters" ("renouveleurs") and to the degradation inherent to the copying process. These ideas contain the germ of the later distinction between innovation and error. Paris did not draw any methodological conclusions from the specificity of mediaeval vernacular traditions, apart from the fundamental distinction between the analysis of readings ("critique des leçons") and analysis of forms ("critique des formes"). Forms, themselves highly unstable, are continuously "renewed" in the course of the copying process. This variation renders the genealogical method ineffective for the analysis of forms.

For Paris, these renewals could only damage the text. He kept to the idea that textual traditions were subject to progressive "degeneration": "l'éloignement de l'original conduit toujours à une version inférieure, car moins originale justement" [moving away from the original always leads to an inferior version, precisely because it is less original]. The aim of his edition was therefore to print a text that was as close as possible to the original:

> La critique des textes a pour but de retrouver, autant que possible, la forme que l'ouvrage auquel elle s'applique avait en sortant des mains de l'auteur. Ce but, elle ne l'atteint jamais complètement: elle s'en rapproche plus ou moins suivant que les conditions où elle s'exerce sont plus ou moins favorables. (Paris and Pannier 1872, 8)
>
> [Textual criticism's goal is to reconstruct as far as possible the form the work under study had when it left the author's hands. It can never reach this goal completely; it approaches it more or less closely depending on whether its working conditions are more or less favourable.]

From the outset, Paris excluded the possibility of recovering the original in all respects and considered the result he obtained as something to be perfected and, when necessary, questioned.

One of Paris's major contributions was to apply the analysis of common errors and innovations as a basis for establishing the readings of a text:

> la critique des textes, ou du moins l'une de ses parties les plus essentielles, repose en effet sur cette idée que des scribes différents, copiant un même texte, ne font pas les mêmes fautes; pour les œuvres du moyen-âge qui ont subi des renouvellements, il faut compléter cette formule par celle-ci: des 'renouveleurs' différents, travaillant sur un même poème, ne font pas les mêmes modifications. (Paris and Pannier 1872, 10)
>
> [textual criticism, or at least one of its most essential parts, rests in reality on the idea that different scribes copying the same text do not commit the same mistakes. For mediaeval works which have been subjected to innovations, this formula has to be extended by the following one: different innovators working on the same text do not make the same modifications.]

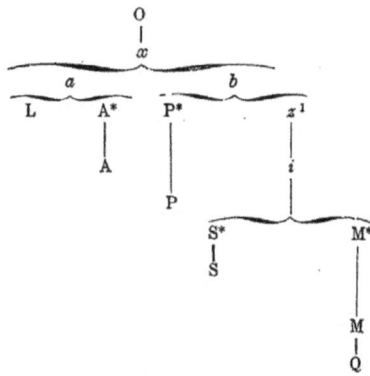

Fig. 7.3-1: Gaston Paris's stemma of the manuscripts containing the *Vie de Saint Alexis* (Paris and Pannier 1872, 27). Source: Gallica, Bibliothèque nationale de France, gallica.bnf.fr/ark:/12148/bpt6k33044x/f43.item). Image: CC-BY-NC.

Paris thus promoted the common-errors method, which was not an invention of Lachmann, but was instead formulated in Romanist circles (see also Gröber 1869). He went on to distinguish between classical philology, which can rely solely on common errors, and mediaeval philology, which must also take common innovations into account.

7.3.2 Joseph Bédier: The solution of the "good manuscript"

The efforts of Gaston Paris and Paul Meyer to introduce textual criticism in France were effective. At the same time, German scholars continued their work of publishing Romance texts by applying the stemmatic method. Among their great achievements, one should mention the edition of Bernart de Vantadorn by Carl Appel (1915) and that of Chrétien de Troyes by Wendelin Förster, completed by Alfons Hilka (Foerster and Hilka 1884–1932). On both sides of the Rhine, reconstructive editions appeared, which were based on the comparison of witnesses and on their genealogical classification.

This method gradually became established until Joseph Bédier, a former pupil of Gaston Paris, became aware of its limitations and recommended it be abandoned for the establishment of the text. A debate took shape around Bédier's edition of Jean Renart's *Lai de l'ombre*. In 1890, Bédier published a first edition which was consistent with Paris's teaching. However, Bédier's examination of the tradition led to a bifid stemma, which Paris contested in a review: "il résulte de ces remarques que bien probablement le *Lai de l'Ombre* nous est conservé non par deux, mais par trois familles, *y*, *v*, *E*, et que par conséquent l'original commun se reconstitue, à coup sûr, par l'accord de *y* ou de *v* ensemble ou avec *E*" (Paris 1890, 611) [it follows from these remarks that it is rather probable the *Lai de l'ombre* is extant not in two but in three families, *y*, *v*, *E*, and that therefore the common original is reconstructed with certainty by the agreement of *y* and *v* with each other or with *E*].

Questioning the stemma undermined the logic leading to the establishment of the text, especially since Paris had already pointed out in his *Saint Alexis* the methodological implications of a stemma with two vs three branches.

Bédier resumed his work and, in 1913, republished the *Lai de l'ombre* following a single manuscript, which he had chosen as the "base" of his edition. He thus abandoned the reconstruction of a textual state that was supposedly closer to the original on the basis of the whole of its manuscript tradition, and only corrected the text of his manuscript when absolutely necessary. After a debate with Quentin, who proposed reviewing the principles of *recensio* by first rejecting the notion of the common mistake (Quentin 1926), Bédier (1928) provided a long argumentation in support of his theory. He noted the significant fact that the stemmata of editions are almost always bifid (in seventy-eight out of eighty cases he examined; for the term, see 4.1.4 above). In addition, several competing stemmata could, in many cases, be offered for the same text. The application of the stemmatic method is therefore problematic, since, depending on the stemma one selects, one ends up with a different critical text; in the case of a bifid stemma, the editor's choice is decisive, leading to a discordant collaboration between the editor and the mediaeval author. Finally, Bédier recommended

> un extrême 'conservatisme', un extrême vouloir, porté, jusqu'au parti pris, d'ouvrir aux scribes le plus large crédit et de ne toucher au texte d'un manuscrit que l'on imprime qu'en cas d'extrême et presque évidente nécessité: toutes les corrections conjecturales devraient être reléguées dans quelque appendice. (Bédier 1928, 356)
>
> [an extreme "conservatism", an extreme wish carried out, to the point of partisanism, to afford the scribes as much as possible faith and not to touch a manuscript to be printed except in extreme and obviously necessary cases: all conjectural corrections should be delegated to some kind of appendix.]

Bédier was the first to associate the common-errors method with the name of the Berlin scholar Karl Lachmann (1793–1851). Since then, the opposition between the "method of Lachmann" and the "method of Bédier" has remained a necessary element in any introduction to the edition of texts in the field of Romance philology and beyond. These terms should, however, be considered with some circumspection, since, on the one hand, Bédier's criticism touches upon Paris's method much more than upon Lachmann's and, on the other, Bédier himself did not propose any method *stricto sensu*, but rather a set of editorial principles.

Abandoning the reconstructionist edition in favour of a conservative one led to the edition of a good manuscript. The choice of the latter depends on multiple criteria, sometimes contradictory, of which Bédier gave no systematic presentation. Let us simply note that the relationship to the original is only one criterion among others. This manuscript, called the "base manuscript" (Bédier 1913, xlii), is corrected only in the case of an obvious mistake, a concept that again is very vague and leaves the editor a considerable degree of latitude. The aim of such an edition is to present, as far as possible, a text that is as close as possible to what had been read by the mediaeval reader – in other words, a text that was used ("texte usagé"), rather than a hypothetical reconstruction. Bédier did not condemn *recensio*, since the stemma can be useful for the choice of the base manuscript and for discussing the probability that a reading is authentic or not. On the other hand, he contested the use of the stemma for the establishment of the text, because at this stage of the edition, especially in the case of a bifid tradition, the stemmatic method, far from producing an objective and firm result, leads to the construction of a largely subjective text that was never read as it is.

Bédier's "method" prevailed in France, to some extent in Belgium, in Great Britain, and the United States. In France, it continues to be applied, but with varying degrees of editorial interventionism. In the introductions to editions, one observes a tendency towards the declaration of principles, especially about faithfulness to the base manuscript, which are far from corresponding to the actual practices of the editors.

The interwar period brought some improvements to Bédier's principles. In order to regulate the editor's interventions in the edited manuscript, Eugene Vinaver (1939) proposed that a dubious reading cannot be considered erroneous if it is not possible to explain the origin of the error with a reasonable degree of probability. This approach leads the editor to rely naturally on *recensio*, since the analysis of variants often sheds light on the aetiology of mistakes. However, Vinaver takes this a bit too far, as some obvious mistakes remain inexplicable, especially in the absence of their immediate model.

At the same time, a shared desire emerged to find a middle ground between Bédier's conservatism and "Lachmannian" interventionism. Alexandre Micha (1939) proposed a compromise solution that consists of choosing a good manuscript which is then "controlled" using a suitable representative of each of the families of manuscripts discovered through the analysis of the tradition. At the theoretical level, this solution does not hold, because the degree of intervention by the editor is not specified: between the correction of an obvious error and the wish to get closer to the original, the editor has a very wide margin of freedom, in which personal taste and subjectivity may play a large role. Consequently, the edition delivers neither the text of a specific manuscript nor the most authentic readings. While the method of "control manuscripts", which experienced relatively large success in France, does not deserve to be applied generally, it offers an acceptable pragmatic solution for certain texts such as long romances transmitted by a large tradition, as has been shown by the edition of the *Tristan en prose* directed by Philippe Ménard (1987–1997).

7.3.3 Neo-Lachmannism: Refining and adapting *Textkritik*

While Bédier rejected the use of the genealogy of manuscripts for establishing the text, others sought to amend the genealogical method (see also 2.4). This was the case with Henry Quentin, who proposed a new computational method which did not rely on the subjective concept of common errors to classify manuscripts (1926). His method, reviewed by Jacques Froger (1968), inspired stemmatologists, but, although it was applied to the *Lai de l'ombre*, it had little effect on the work of Romanist scholars.

In Italy, Romanists were at the forefront of introducing textual criticism of German and French origin. In spite of the edition of Arnaut Daniel by Ugo Angelo Canello (1883), which relied on conjunctive and separative errors, and the methodological openness of Pio Rajna (1847–1930), it was not until the edition of Dante's *Vita Nuova* by Michele Barbi in 1907 that one saw the first rigorous application of the common-errors method to an Italian text endowed with a rich tradition (Barbi 1907).

The systematic treatise on textual criticism by Paul Maas (1927) was decisive in the development of Italian n e o - L a c h m a n n i s m (see 2.4). Outlined in a review of Maas's booklet (Pasquali 1929), the reflections of the Hellenist and Latinist Giorgio Pasquali (1885–1952) later resulted in a masterwork, *Storia della tradizione e critica del testo* (1934). The title is methodologically indicative: the history of textual traditions and their individual specificities must be taken into account in the application of the stemmatic method. Pasquali therefore encouraged a more flexible practice adapted to each tradition, emphasising especially the difficulties of stemmatic criticism by developing concepts such as horizontal tradition, contamination, authorial variant, and open recension.

The influence of Pasquali is reflected in the now-classic essay by Barbi, *La nuova filologia e l'edizione dei nostri scrittori da Dante a Manzoni* (1938). A critical and constructive revision of the Lachmannian method, adapted to the tradition of vernacular, mediaeval, and modern texts, was thereby encouraged. In line with Pasquali, the "nuova filologia" aimed at combining stemmatic rigour and attention to the textual tradition by considering witnesses individually as the products of a specific cultural context rather than as mere reservoirs of variants. Gianfranco Contini (1912–1990) pursued the renewal of editorial methods advanced by this school, now known as neo-Lachmannism (Contini 1986). Contini emphasised in particular the limits of a mechanical application of the stemma and insisted that the status of the critical edition cannot be presented as definitive but always remains a working hypothesis. This last point is a clever answer to Bédier's scepticism. Contini deepened, reformulated, and applied some concepts already used by Pasquali to Romance texts. He also proposed other concepts, such as diffraction (the process by which a *lectio difficilior* is modified by substitutions that differ from one copyist to another, resulting in a diffuse scattering of variants) or the diachrony of the text, which one can only perceive through a genealogical approach. The next generation further pursued these theoretical reflections, developing, for example, the concept of the text as a diasystem (Segre 1979) or the idea of active or quiescent traditions (Vàrvaro 1970; see, in more detail, 2.4.3 above).

The attention given to the history of textual traditions by the neo-Lachmannians encouraged them to claim a partial autonomy from classical philology: the temporal and cultural gap between original text and copy differs between antique and mediaeval texts, as does the authority they enjoyed; and classical languages display a degree of standardisation unknown to mediaeval vernacular languages. It is important that Romance philologists take these differences into consideration.

This moderate Lachmannism, which has become a trademark of the Italian school, spread particularly in Hispanic philology in the last quarter of the twentieth century, following the publication by Giorgio Chiarini of the *Libro de buen amor* (1964) and the teachings of two neo-Lachmannian scholars, Alberto Blecua (1983) in Barcelona and Germán Orduna (2000) in Buenos Aires. For linguistic reasons, the intense methodological reflection of the neo-Lachmannians did not find the audience it deserved: the "New Philology" (see 2.3.7) ignored their work, and the French tradition, largely atheoretical after Bédier, did not know it well. Efforts, with a hint of proselytism, have been made in recent years to win over French- (e.g. L. Leonardi 2003), English- (e.g. Trovato 2017), and Portuguese-speaking (Spaggiari and Perugi 2004) audiences.

7.3.4 Textual scholarship emancipated from author and original

Getting closer to the lost original was the goal of Gaston Paris, and it is still shared by the neo-Lachmannians, even though their approach is more cautious, adapting itself to each textual tradition. So-called Bédierist editions have a more ambiguous position. According to Bédier, the chosen good manuscript did not need to be the closest to the original. But one of his most influential disciples, Félix Lecoy (1978), spoke of the possibility of evaluating the authenticity of the readings printed in the apparatus. In fact, the criterion of proximity to the original often prevails. "Bédierist" editions are thus de facto oriented towards the mediaeval author, just like their Lachmannian cousins. Both are based, at least initially, on a conception of the text as an individual creation.

A third editorial trend has developed, which does not operate in terms of originals. Its origins are manifold and in some cases completely independent in their development: Spanish neo-traditionalism, advanced by Menéndez Pidal and the literary criticism of lyric texts, considers mediaeval texts not as fixed individual creations but as the result of a collective enterprise, always capable of evolving. The logical consequence of this, in editorial terms, is the publication of each manuscript or a representative of each family or group of manuscripts. Castilian neo-traditionalism anticipated the concept of *mouvance* formulated by Paul Zumthor (1972), and even that of variance promoted by Bernard Cerquiglini (1989, 111) and the "New Philology". It also joins the sociology of texts put forth by McGann, who, with respect to the modern period, postulates that "literary works are fundamentally social rather than personal or psychological products" (1983, 43). Finally, Avalle, at first an orthodox neo-Lachmannian, concludes that there is a double truth: that of the authoritative text sought in the reconstructionist edition, and that of the document. For Avalle, "Bédier's method makes sense only if it is applied on the basis of the mediaeval book and not of the original" (1972b, 554). The correction of the manuscripts by Bédier's followers does not make sense from this perspective. Avalle in turn emphasises the complexity of the manuscript, a crystallisation of several actors whose exact role is difficult to determine. In order to reach the truth of the document, it is necessary to multiply the editions of manuscripts. Avalle thus echoes the concerns of material philology.

The "New Philology", which places the manuscript (and no longer the text) at the heart of its thinking, appeared in the United States in the late 1980s and early 1990s, before its influence expanded; it first developed in the milieu of mediaevalists. In many respects, it converged with the views of Menéndez Pidal or Avalle, although it was independent of them. Cerquiglini's essay, *Eloge de la variante: Histoire critique de la philologie* (1989), which was quickly translated into English, contributed to its growth. In editorial terms, the "New Philology" could be considered as a radicalised form of Bédierism, which explains its lack of success in Italy. On the other hand, Spanish philologists familiar with Menéndez Pidal's work welcomed it warmly, especially following the publication of John Dagenais's *The Ethics of Reading in Manuscript Culture: Glossing the Libro de Buen Amor* (1994).

The stemmatic method, which assumes an orientated and orderly ranking of witnesses and an evaluation of readings (possibly authentic readings vs erroneous readings), has been rejected, sometimes violently, by the "New Philology", which adopts an undirected point of view. The latter has enjoyed support from technological developments, in particular in photography and computer science. The digitisation of manuscripts was the most radical proposal that the "realistic" "New Philologists" could make in order to distance themselves from the old "idealist" philology. As for computer science, thanks to "multi-fenestration" (Cerquiglini 1989) and hypertext, it is possible to simultaneously and conveniently display several transcriptions or reproductions of manuscripts of the same work.

The concurrent development of new theories of the text, of which the "New Philology" is an emanation, and progress in computer science led to the realisation of documentary digital editions which do not rely on a stemma, often also in the choice of the manuscripts to be transcribed. In terms of electronic publishing, a focus on the document largely dominates, and critical editions are being abandoned for the sake of digital archives or libraries, as in the project of the *Roman de la rose* led by Nichols (2014).

The importance of Romance philology in editorial practice is due to the now age-old debate initiated by Joseph Bédier. In each of the editorial approaches that have ensued, the fate of the stemmatic method differs: whereas neo-Lachmannians still utilise it for the establishment of the text, the Bédierist tradition stops using it after the initial *recensio*, which is useful both for choosing the base manuscript and analysing variants. The "New Philology" is more radical, because it envisions the manuscript as both its point of departure and its point of arrival.

One of the last articles by Cesare Segre, a great figure of Italian neo-Lachmannism, celebrates the end of the war between Lachmann and Bédier (Segre 2016). Segre admits the plurality of approaches: it is legitimate to look for the authentic reading, but also to examine as such the reading of a given manuscript, regardless of the genealogy of the witnesses. Digital technology today makes it possible to combine the two approaches within the same project (for examples, see 6.3.3). At a time when digital documentary editions and archives dominate, it is possible to imagine that integral transcriptions of the witnesses of a work will lead to a re-elaboration of stemmata thanks to the progress of stemmatology. For the moment, the application of stemmatology to mediaeval Romance texts is still at an early stage because it requires not only the encoding of all the witnesses but also their lemmatisation. Experiments are sporadically attempted, but a large-scale application has not yet been envisioned. In addition to the Amsterdam school initiated by Anthonij Dees (see van Reenen and Schøsler 2000, 31–32, 53–54, for a first assessment; see also de Visser-van Terwisga 1999, 200–211), there have been a few other, relatively isolated, initiatives (Trovato 2017, 179–227; Camps and Cafiero 2014). Stemmatology is dependent on progress in the automated lemmatisation of highly variable language states, like Old French, even though the rise of machine learning opens up new possibilities. In the meantime, the stemma can already serve as a gateway to the textual and codicological data of digital libraries. In the field of Romance philology, much of the work in this respect still remains to be undertaken.

Acknowledgement

The text was translated from the French by Caroline Macé and Laura Endress.

Further reading

An overview of philological practices in Europe can be found in Duval (2006). Montanari (2003) provides an Italian translation of Maas (1927) with a commentary situating the importance of Maas's method in Italian philology. Stussi (2006) is influential on the methodology of textual criticism in Romance philology. Readers interested in knowing more about the practice of philology in the study of mediaeval Spanish could refer to Altschul (2015).

7.4 Mediaeval German
Ralf Plate

Scarcely less extensive than the variation in the mediaeval German textual tradition of the manuscript era is the multiplicity of types of editions which, from their beginnings in the early nineteenth century, have been grappling with these texts. Between the extremes of diplomatic documentation and reconstruction by means of arbitrary conjectural criticism lies the domain of stemmatics. In this context, there is, right from the start, a wide range of goals, methods, and forms of realisation that have survived even the "iconoclasm of the 'New Philology'" (Heinzle 2003, 1; "der Bildersturm der 'New Philology'"). The following short historical survey can only outline, by means of examples, the main stages and aspects, concentrating on the way in which variation is handled and the role that is assigned, or alternatively denied, to stemmatics. It focuses on the stemmatics of the courtly epic around AD 1200, since it is here that the great controversies have flared up, right up to the present day.

7.4.1. Lachmann's *recensio* of the courtly epic ca. AD 1200

Lachmann, as is well known, never provided a stemma in his editions and was altogether sparing with the details he provided of the manuscript relationships – this applies not only to Lachmann the classical philologist (Timpanaro 2005) but also to Lachmann the Germanist (Sparnaay 1948; Ganz 1968; Fiesoli 2000, 269–358). In the case of Middle High German poetry, the reason for this was not so much Lachmann's oracular style (Timpanaro 2005, 96, 117) but the result of his *recensio*. It was always directed at the oldest attainable text in the manuscript tradition; Lachmann was interested in the history of a textual tradition not in its own right but only insofar as it was necessary for the establishment of the critical text, just as in the case of classical texts (Timpanaro 2005, 72). Three texts with an extensive manuscript tradition may serve as examples.

In the case of the *Nibelungenlied* (1st ed. 1826, notes (with full variants) 1836, 2nd ed. 1841), the main problem with any assessment of the manuscript tradition is the transition from oral tradition to the book epic and its written tradition, which took place in various stages at the beginning of the thirteenth century (for an overview of the subject from a modern perspective, see Heinzle 2013, 998–1006). The complex problems cannot be explored here in detail. According to Lachmann's *recensio*, the oldest stage of the text is represented by only one manuscript (*A*); all others go back to an adaptation, **B*, which appears in a subgroup in a further comprehensive adaptation, **C*. For the establishment of the text of **A*, the textual tradition of **B* and **C* is – because of their character as adaptations – only of limited value, that is to say, significant only when it allows the reading of *A* to be supported or, in the case of deviations from it, allows corruptions of the archetype *A to be established: "every word that is not in A is of no greater importance than a conjecture. All other manuscripts are teeming with obvious conjectures" (Lachmann 1841, x; "jedes wort das nicht in A steht, [hat] keine größere beglaubigung als eine conjectur. alle anderen handschriften wimmeln von augenscheinlichen conjecturen"). By this, Lachmann meant that emendations had been made to passages in the older text, *A, "where readers and scribes of the thirteenth century took offence" (Lachmann 1841, x; "woran leser und schreiber des dreizehnten jahrhunderts anstoß nahmen"). Lachmann's edition offers the reconstructed text of *A. The apparatus contains the variant readings of adaptation *B, as far as they could be reconstructed; otherwise, it gives the readings of individual manuscripts which could help establish the text of *B. Whereas *A is transmitted directly in only one manuscript, Lachmann had at his disposal eleven manuscripts for *B and six for *C (Lachmann 1841, x). Since Lachmann attempted to reconstruct the places where adaptation *B varied from *A, one might expect him to have provided details of the manuscript relationships in this group. However, we find only the conclusion that the manuscripts of *B in part diverge substantially and then do not permit the reconstruction of *B. Lachmann's edition offers no more specific explanation of his findings regarding the manuscript tradition, probably because he assumed this to be obvious. As we learn from Lachmann's 1817 review of von der Hagen's edition of the *Nibelungenlied*, based on manuscript B (1816), he posited in the case of *B (and, by analogy, probably also of *C) an unstable archetype: at the beginning of the manuscript tradition of the adaptation *B, there existed a manuscript with the text of *A, in which the *B adapter had noted his changes and additions in the margin; in part the copies of *B took over the changes and additions, in part they ignored them, and in part they introduced their own (Lachmann 1876, 1:87).

The basic picture of the manuscript tradition in the case of *Iwein* presents itself to Lachmann in a scarcely more favourable light (the establishment of the text and the variants in this edition are by Lachmann; see Lutz-Hensel 1975, 337–342). He states:

> The oldest manuscript, A, does not show a closer relationship to any of the others: changes that are clearly intentional are never shared with another manuscript. Thus, the critical rule of following this manuscript where it is not found to be in isolation established itself automatically, since it is nearest to the original source of the manuscript tradition. Each of the manuscripts used [...] has, through agreement with A, contributed something to our decisions. (Benecke and Lachmann 1877 [= 2nd ed. 1843], 362)

> (Die älteste handschrift A ist mit keiner der andern näher verwandt: veränderungen die erkennbar absichtlich sind, hat sie niemahls gemein mit einer andern. so ergab sich von selbst die kritische regel, ihr, da sie der ersten quelle der überlieferung am nächsten ist, zu folgen, wo sie nicht allein steht. jede der gebrauchten handschriften [...] hat durch übereinstimmung mit A etwas zur entscheidung beigetragen.)

In his introductory remarks on the variants, Lachmann provides no further information about the genealogy of the manuscript tradition (he did, however, mention some of his findings in his discussion of the variants; see Ganz 1968, 22–23, with a tentative stemma). The reason for this may be similar to that in the case of *Nibelungenlied* *B, for, as Lachmann already knew (Ganz 1968, 23) and Henrici's study later showed (see 7.4.3), the manuscript tradition of *Iwein* eludes genealogical description.

Concerning Wolfram von Eschenbach's *Parzival*, Lachmann in 1833 states: "The numerous manuscripts of Parzival fall [...] into two classes, which consistently display a different text" (in Schirok 1999, xiv; "die zahlreichen handschriften des Parzivals [...] zerfallen [...] in zwei klassen, die durchgängig einen verschiedenen text haben"), so that "in most cases, the reading of one class is of equal value to that of the other" (Schirok 1999, xvii; "in den allermeisten fällen [ist] die lesart der einen klasse mit der andern von gleichem werth"). Lachmann consistently compared the principal manuscripts of both classes (*D* and *G*); he compared others only in the case of disagreement between these two manuscripts. The constitution of the text rests largely on *D* – "admittedly a weakness of my text" (in Schirok 1999, xvii; "freilich eine schwäche meines textes") –, and the equally acceptable readings (presumptive variants) of *G are emphasised, where appropriate, in the apparatus by placing the sign "=" before them. Lachmann gives no information about the internal division of both classes, most noticeably in the case of the considerably larger *G* class; indeed, he specifically rejects the suggestion: "to what end should one pursue the investigation in the minutest detail" ("wozu sollte man die untersuchung ins kleinliche führen") when the equally acceptable readings that both classes demonstrate display nothing but "negligence, arbitrariness, and a craving for improvement, without any particular skill" ("nur nachlässigkeit, willkür und verbesserungssucht ohne sonderliches geschick") – when, that is, they are innovations of the manuscript tradition, not authorial variants ("no difference going back to the poet"; in Schirok 1999, xvi; "keine von dem dichter selbst ausgehende verschiedenheit")?

According to Timpanaro, the typically "Lachmannian" procedure in works of classical philology is characterised by an aversion against the eclectic selection of variants according to internal criteria and a consequent preference for mechanical *recensio* (Timpanaro 2005, 88–89, 116). French philologists have understood "Lachmann's method" in this sense since Bédier (see 7.3.2), Italian philologists likewise since Timpanaro's teacher Pasquali (Trovato 2017, 70–75), and Germanists have understood it thus since Stackmann (1964; see 7.4.4 below) at the latest. As we have seen, this is at any rate not accurate with regard to Lachmann's actual procedure when editing Middle High German literature (see also Fiesoli 2000, 269–358): Lachmann's *recensio* led in all three cases to a preference for one manuscript as the basis for the reconstruction of the text (*Nibelungenlied A, Iwein A, Parzival D*); his assessment of the three manuscript traditions and his editorial goals did not permit a mechanical selection of variants by the elimination of singular readings (*eliminatio lectionum singularium*) using a stemma as guide. In the case of *Iwein*, where the possibility of using a mechanical selection procedure seemed most likely (according to Lachmann's rule, where *A* was in agreement with any other manuscript), internal criteria (especially metre, grammar, and stylistics) in many cases break the rule of *recensio*, as the study of Lutz-Hensel (1975, 337–432) has demonstrated. The application of "Lachmann's method" to the Middle High German classics remained the preserve of those who opposed Lachmann's ideas and tried to refute his often acerbically and provocatively formulated findings about the textual tradition – by means of stemmatics.

7.4.2 Karl Bartsch's *recensio* and stemma of the *Nibelungenlied* (1865, 1870)

The first printed graphical displays of manuscript relationships in a *stemma codicum* are thought to have appeared around 1830 and then to have spread rapidly in the field of classical philology (see 4.1.2). The device was even used by Lachmann's pupils during his lifetime, whereas Lachmann himself did not make use of it, even in his last editions of Latin authors (Timpanaro 2005, 96). The technique of genealogical *recensio* had most likely been transferred from classical philology to that of the vernacular literatures. *Saint Alexis* by Gaston Paris (Paris and Pannier 1872) counts as the first edition of the new type in the field of Romance studies (see 7.3). It is known that Paris was influenced by Karl Bartsch's works on the *Nibelungenlied* (see 7.3.1 above; Trovato 2017, 50): the *Untersuchungen* [Studies] (Bartsch 1865); the *editio minor* of 1866 (this edition, in the revised version by Helmut de Boor, is by far the most frequently used to this day, Bartsch and de Boor 1979; see 7.4.5); and the *editio maior* (Bartsch 1870–1880), which appeared in three volumes: 1870 (introduction and text), 1876 (variants), and 1880 (glossary). Bartsch distinguishes between two adaptations of an older text which cannot be reconstructed: *AB (his siglum X) und *C (his siglum Y), where the adaptation *AB, best represented by manuscript B, remains closer to the lost "original", whereas *C is more distant from it. A is considered by Bartsch as an abbreviated adaptation of *AB. In the text volume of the *editio maior*, as also in the *editio minor*, X = *AB is reconstructed; the critical apparatus notes in comparison the variant readings of Y = *C. Bartsch does not yet provide a complete genealogy and rules for a mechanical selection of variants based upon it, nor does he give a graphical depiction of the manuscript relationships in the *Untersuchungen*; only in the *editio maior* does he sum up his remarks about this in a simplified diagram of his findings, which he calls a "table" ("Tabelle"; Bartsch 1870–1880, 1:xviii; see fig. 7.4-1 below). But Bartsch does differentiate subgroups of the manuscripts of a version; he argues using indicative (monogenetic) common errors, which he is able to distinguish from random agreements in secondary readings (polygenetic errors), and he discerns groups of manuscripts which alternately follow one version or another, or in some other way present "mixed texts" (Bartsch 1870–1880, 1:xviii–xxix; "gemischte Texte").

Folgende Tabelle stellt das Verhältniss der Handschriften übersichtlich dar.

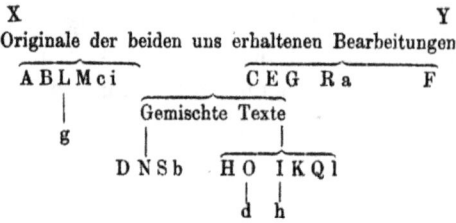

Fig. 7.4-1: Stemma for the *Nibelungenlied*. Source: Bartsch (1870–1880, 1:xviii).

7.4.3 Neogrammarian genealogical reconstruction of the courtly epic between caution and mechanics (Paul and Braune, 1873–1901)

It is perhaps no accident that the most prominent representatives of what counts today as "Lachmann's method" are two neogrammarians who were expressly opposed to the Lachmannian school, namely Hermann Paul and Wilhelm Braune. After having presented his own critical edition of the *Gregorius* of Hartmann von Aue in 1873 (replacing Lachmann's edition from 1838, partly due to new finds), in 1874 Paul launched, in the first volume of the neogrammarian periodical (*Beiträge zur Geschichte der deutschen Sprache und Literatur*), a general attack on Lachmann's text of Hartmann's *Iwein* in its second edition (1843), which until then had counted as "the exemplary critical edition, having had the greatest influence on the development of editorial technique as an unrivalled role model" (Sparnaay 1948, 79; "das Muster einer kritischen Ausgabe, das als unerreichtes Vorbild auf die Entwicklung der Editionstechnik den allergrößten Einfluss gehabt hat"). Paul accuses Lachmann of "arbitrariness and violence" (Paul 1874, 289; "willkür und gewalttätigkeit") in the establishment of the text. He claimed that Lachmann had failed "to employ an in-depth study of the mutual relationship of the manuscripts, which must be regarded as an essential prerequisite for the edition of a work that is contained in numerous manuscripts" (Paul 1874, 290; "eine eingehende untersuchung über das gegenseitige verhältnis des hss. anzustellen, was als notwendige vorbedingung für die herausgabe eines in zahlreichen hss. erhaltenen werkes angesehen werden muss"), and had instead evaluated the textual tradition on the basis of a system of metrical rules which totally lacked an adequate foundation but "according to which he constructed everything, leaving all other considerations aside" (289; "wonach er alles construierte mit hintansetzung jeder anderen rücksicht"). Paul's study, which is dependent almost entirely on Lachmann's critical apparatus, arrives in two steps initially "with tolerable accuracy" ("mit leidlicher bestimmtheit") at a stemma for the second, longer part of *Iwein* (Paul 1874, 336; see fig. 7.4-2 below). In this, nine textual witnesses are traced back over three reconstructed intermediate stages to two hyparchetypes of an archetype; the positing of one of the hyparchetypes is,

Ich denke also, dass es gelungen ist für den von uns bezeichneten abschnitt mit leidlicher bestimmtheit das abstammungsverhältnis der hss. zu ermitteln, welches sich etwa in folgender figur darstellen würde, in der die griechischen buchstaben die nur erschlossenen mittelglieder bezeichnen:

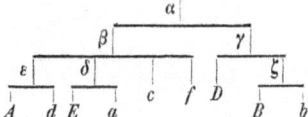

Fig. 7.4-2: Stemma for *Iwein*. Source: Paul (1874, 336).

however, designated as "dubious" ("zweifelhaft"), and further uncertainties are raised (Paul 1874, 337). For the first part of *Iwein*, an additional stemma is provided for the subsidiary sources of two of the manuscripts (*B* and *d*) which show contaminated readings (Paul 1874, 351). After formulating some critical key rules which he derives from this, Paul discusses, over more than forty pages, in detail and with reference to the constellations of the variant readings, the changes to Lachmann's text which his *recensio* indicates (Paul 1874, 359–401).

Paul's emphatic opposition to Lachmann's "arbitrariness" does not lead in the opposite direction, that is, towards the dogmatism of a mechanical *recensio*; the restricted ability of the stemma to help when evaluating variant readings in individual cases, as well as its hypothetical nature and potential for falsification, are clearly emphasised. Matters were different with Braune, whose studies of the manuscript relationships of the *Nibelungenlied* (1900) fill an entire year's volume of the *Beiträge*. Braune arrives at a stemma of the complete manuscript tradition without gaps, "right down to the individual manuscripts and fragments" (Braune 1900, 192; "bis zu den einzelnen hss. und fragmenten hinab"). Lachmann's *A* is thereby reduced still further than with Bartsch to a secondary position, as a member of a subfamily of the hyparchetype which is best represented by *B*. The application of the stemma to the critical establishment of the text (Braune 1900, 212–215) as a rule permits the reading of the archetype to be recognised with pleasing accuracy; for the most part, the agreement of two manuscripts (*B* and *d*), which are not related and which each reproduce the text of one of the two assumed hyparchetypes *x* and *y* in a fairly conservative way, fully suffices for this purpose. When they stand together with a common reading, in opposition to a common reading of unrelated groups of the remaining manuscript tradition, a chance "secondary coincidence" (Braune 1900, 212; "secundäres zusammentreffen") is only seldom the case with these two manuscripts, whereas it occurs "in the majority of cases" ("in der mehrzahl der fälle") with the others (213–214). Braune's detailed complete stemma has to be assembled from the partial stemmata which occur throughout his work (as in Brackert 1963, 174; see fig. 7.4-3 below). It represents the pinnacle of unbridled faith in genealogical reconstruction (in the field of the manuscript tradition of the courtly

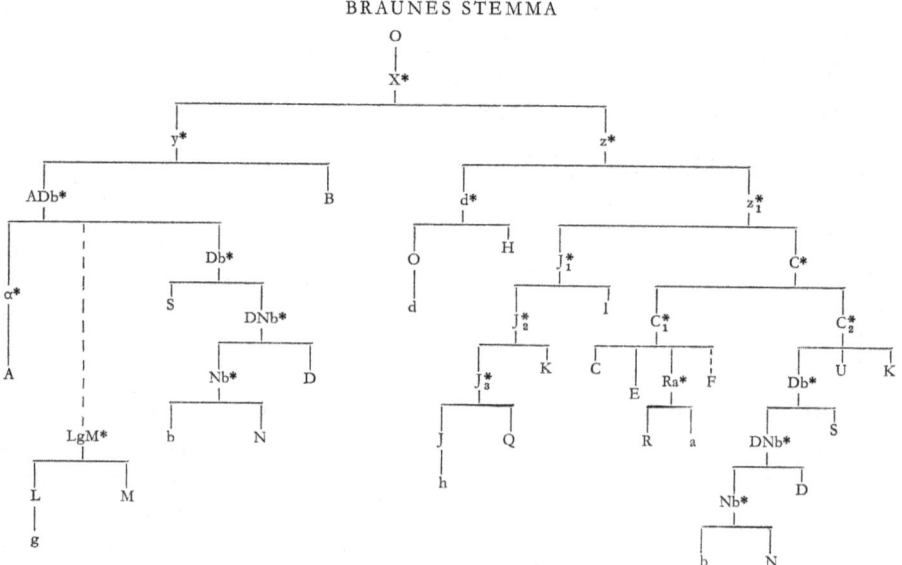

Fig. 7.4-3: Detailed complete stemma for the *Nibelungenlied* according to Braune (1900). Source: Brackert (1963, 174). © De Gruyter.

epic around AD 1200) that will then later, ironically, provoke fundamental criticism of "Lachmann's method" (see 7.4.5). Braune himself did not produce an edition, but the results of his study had an effect on the revision of the *editio minor* of Bartsch by Helmut de Boor (from the 10th ed., 1940, onwards; see 7.4.5 below).

However, Braune is not representative for stemmatics at the end of the century. Henrici, in his *Iwein* edition (text 1891, notes and variants 1893), was the first person to compare independently the entire known manuscript tradition. As a result, he rejects not only Lachmann's and Paul's *recensio*, but any possibility of a genealogy: contamination is rife, not only in the first part, as Paul assumed; it also occurs throughout the entire text and manuscript tradition, including *A*, even where Henrici confirms its relatively conservative unique position. Henrici considers it to be possible that there were several authorial versions, "several genuine *Iweins*" (Henrici 1891–1893, 2:xxxii; "mehrere echte Iweine") that are mixed together in the manuscript tradition.

Paul's handbook article on textual criticism, or more precisely, a short section in it about the determination of manuscript relationships (Paul 1901, 192–194) remains decidedly reserved about the possibilities of a genealogical *recensio*. He warns sternly against an unthinking mechanical approach: "the process must [...] not become a mechanical one" (Paul 1901, 193; "das Verfahren darf [...] kein mechanisches werden"). Paul stresses the need to determine genealogical relationships on the basis of "particular shared deviations from the original" (1901, 192; "besonderer gemeinsamer Abweichungen von dem Original"), that is, significant common errors/innovations, which indeed must "already be recognised on the basis of internal criteria" (193; "bereits auf Grund innerer Kriterien erkannt sein"). He points several times to the possibility of chance agreements in secondary readings (polygenetic errors/innovations), which can be assessed only according to probability ("to assess how much leeway may be attributed to chance is not an easy task", Paul 1901, 193; "abzuschätzen, wieviel Spielraum man dem Zufall zuweisen darf, ist keine so einfache Aufgabe"). He mentions the need to bear in mind the possibility of contamination ("the use by the same scribe of several source manuscripts", Paul 1901, 193; "Benutzung mehrerer Vorlagen durch den gleichen Schreiber"). He also determines that, all things considered, "there are enough cases where a decisive result is not reached" (Paul 1901, 193; "es Fälle genug gibt, in denen man zu einem entscheidenden Resultat nicht gelangt") – where the genealogical method, then, cannot be used. If a positive result is achieved and the method can be applied, however, the difficulties that were already encountered when the manuscript relationships were established recur in the selection of readings. Here, again, it is a case of using internal criteria and assessing the possibility of chance common secondary features; these uncertainties are multiplied when lost connecting links from manuscripts dependent on them have "to be constructed" (Paul 1901, 193; "zu konstruieren"), as Paul demonstrates with different constellations (194). Paul's reservations about the possibilities of a mechanical *recensio* are demonstrated by his own editions (first and foremost that of Hartmann von Aue's *Gregorius*; see 7.4.5 below), and also by some of the critical editions by others in the Altdeutsche Textbibliothek series, founded by Paul and still in existence today (on the diverse programme of the series, see Kiening 2016).

A similar attitude with regard to Paul's reservations was later adopted by the Middle Latin scholar Hermann Kantorowicz in his introductory monograph to textual criticism (1921). After the appearance of Maas's account in 1927, which quickly achieved canonicity, both works, Paul (1901) as well as Kantorowicz (1921), unfortunately hardly enjoyed any further reception at all in the field of German philology.

7.4.4 Editing post-classical and late mediaeval literature by printing "as good and as old a manuscript as possible": The Deutsche Texte des Mittelalters (1904–)

When Joseph Bédier, in his second edition of Jean Renart's *Lai de l'ombre* in 1913, made a programmatic plea for the rejection of the genealogically reconstructive edition in favour of printing the "best manuscript" and accomplished this himself with an example (see 7.3.2 above), twenty-four volumes of the Deutsche Texte des Mittelalters (DTM) series of the Königlich Preußische Akademie der Wissenschaften, founded in 1904 and still in existence today, had already appeared. The DTM programme corresponded fairly exactly to Bédier's demands (or the other way round): "As good and old a manuscript as possible should consistently be reproduced" (Roethe 1904, vi; "Es soll durchweg eine möglichst gute und alte Handschrift wiedergegeben werden"). The programme represented "a deep incision in the methodology" (Fromm 1995, 77; "einen tiefen Einschnitt in der Methodengeschichte") of mediaeval German literary editions, by rehabilitating the principle of the base manuscript. But, unlike in the case of Bédier, the programme was not principally directed against the genealogically reconstructive edition. That type of edition would not have been suitable anyway for some of the texts that were edited in the DTM series (because of traditions with a narrow or unique manuscript basis, or because they represented late mediaeval utilitarian prose texts). In the other cases, where it would appear to have been fundamentally possible, pragmatic considerations meant that the initial priority was instead a rapid supply of textual editions for the still largely unresearched areas of post-classical and late mediaeval literature (Roethe 1904, v; see also the assessment in Roethe 1913, 55–58). At any rate, this meant, in Roethe's opinion, "only a partial abandonment" ("nur teilweise einen Verzicht"), because the prints of the manuscripts "at the same time maintained their lasting independent value, inasmuch as they exemplify approximately the form in which the works of the Middle Ages were actually read" ("haben [...] zugleich ihren dauernden selbständigen Wert, insofern sie annähernd die Gestalt veranschaulichen, in der die Werke des Mittelalters wirklich gelesen worden sind"); in this function, they perform "services that could never be supplanted by critical editions" (Roethe 1904, vi; "Dienste, die durch kritische Ausgaben nie ersetzt werden können"). The print of a manuscript should show editorial interventions as little as possible (minor normalisations and sparing punctuation, insofar as this appeared essential for readability), and only obvious errors should be corrected. The use of corrective manuscripts was allowed as necessary; "a complete collation" ("eine vollständige Kollation"), on the other hand, "was not in accordance with the Academy's intentions" (Roethe 1904, vii; "entspräche [...] nicht den Absichten der Akademie"). This "one-manuscript rule" was often abandoned, even in the first phase of the DTM under Roethe's direction, because it would not have produced a satisfactory text, and even more often later, but it was adhered to in principle (overviews: Fromm 1995, 77–79; Stackmann 2005, 12–17). Though intended merely as a provisional solution, in some cases it has promoted the manuscript text chosen for print to become the *textus receptus* for all ensuing literary-historical research, despite the fact that its status within the manuscript tradition has never been clarified. A spectacular case in point is the world chronicle in verse of Rudolf von Ems (Ehrismann 1915 = DTM 20), a text with an extraordinarily broad transmission from the 13th through the 15th centuries (see Plate 2020).

7.4.5 Missing prerequisites of "Lachmann's method", vote for a renewal of the eclectic critical edition (Stackmann 1964)

Works of the classical courtly period and later texts in this tradition remained, even after the establishment of the DTM, the domain of the critical edition, partly because the DTM series of texts scarcely ventured into this field, and partly because when, contrary to the original plan, it did, critical editions were sometimes the result (Fromm 1995, 78–79; Stackmann 2005, 14–16), but first and foremost because people saw no reason to replace the old editions. Not until Stackmann in 1964 was their legitimacy discussed in depth, in what is today still one of the most frequently quoted essays about methods and problems of editing medieval German texts, albeit cited selectively by those who are opposed to critical editions in principle. The essay is dedicated to the question of the appropriate contemporary continuation of the critical edition. Stackmann seeks to connect with the methodological discussion that Bédier had initiated, principally concerning Romance and classical philology (Pasquali, Timpanaro), and takes from this discussion the picture of the "Lachmannian method" as that of mechanical stemmatic reconstruction as it was described by Maas (1927, 4th ed. 1960); he does not cite Paul (1901) or Kantorowicz (1921). Stackmann confronts this with a reference to its unquestioned prerequisites which, however, he maintains, are in reality rarely present. He states that the method rests on a "theory about a very special case" which is present only when the following criteria are satisfied (Stackmann 1964, 246–247): (*i*) the source of the manuscript tradition must be a single, clear-cut archetype; (*ii*) the manuscript tradition must follow an exclusively vertical path without contamination; (*iii*) the manuscript relationships must be recognisable on the basis of properly detected errors; and (*iv*) the manuscript tradition must be exclusively the work of copyists, and there must not be any unpredictable jumps between source and copy.

For confirmation that these conditions – at any rate in the tradition of the courtly epic – are rarely to be found, Stackmann could have appealed to Lachmann himself, as we have seen (7.4.1). In fact, Stackmann does not argue in terms of individual examples of unsuccessful genealogically reconstructive editions, so it remains unclear at what editorial practice the objection to the "Lachmannian method" is levelled; it is likely that Braune's stemma for the *Nibelungenlied* (see 7.4.3) lies behind it, as the spectacular dissertation by Brackert (co-supervised by Stackmann and published in 1963) had shortly before shown it to be fundamentally lacking and inadequate in all its details.

The conclusion that a genealogical *recensio* could not feasibly be employed presented various possibilities for editorial practice: either, with Bédier (and an eye to the DTM series) to give up resignedly the reconstruction of a text that is better than the manuscript tradition, that is, restricting editing to a cleaned-up print of the "best manuscript" – or alternatively deciding in favour of an eclectic critical edition (in the positive sense of the term), that is to say, one that is based on a profound knowledge of the manuscript tradition and critically reflective in method. Stackmann (1964) votes decisively in favour of the second option; the greater part of his essay is devoted to the fundamentals of an appropriately modern eclectic critical edition. The main points are orientation towards a base manuscript where linguistic form is concerned; acceptance of recurring variants (relatively small variations in linguistic usage that are insignificant for the sense of the text); elimination of obvious errors; in the case of competing variants, application of the criterion of *lectio difficilior*; in the case of equally acceptable variants, clear indication of the variants that do not appear in the reconstructed text by appropriate typographical means; and avoidance, as far as possible, of conjectural criticism, about which the most severe misgivings are voiced (Stackmann 1964, 256–265).

The eclectic critical type of edition favoured by Stackmann continues to be cultivated in the field of classical epics up until the present day, albeit with significantly decreasing popularity. Prominent examples of various kinds are Wolff's revision of Benecke and Lachmann's *Iwein* edition (1968), Brackert's edition of the *Nibelungenlied* (1970–1971), de Boor's revision of Bartsch's *editio minor* of the *Nibelungenlied* (most recently, 21st ed. 1979), and Schröder's edition of Wolfram von Eschenbach's *Willehalm* (1978). Werner Schröder has been a continually present figure in the recent history of mediaeval German editions, also as a reviewer, and has supported the position of the eclectic critical edition in some sharp exchanges; a series of reviews, which are worth reading, and review-essays from the 1990s, are reprinted in the anthology Schröder (1999). In addition, the formulation of decisive opposition to the now-common editorial resignation of Grubmüller (1993) must be mentioned and – as an example of further revisions of older editions in the Altdeutsche Textbibliothek – Wachinger's adaptation of Paul's *editio minor* (1st ed. 1882) of Hartmann von Aue's *Gregorius* (most recently, 15th ed. 2004). Wachinger, who was also the head editor of the series for many years, notes, with regard to *Gregorius*,

> that the combinations of manuscript readings that contradict the stemma, whether they occurred through mixing, through independent, but parallel, alterations, or through correct scribal conjectures, are so numerous and so weighty that the stemma on no account can be regarded as a secure basis for individual text-critical decisions. (Wachinger 2004, xix)

> (daß die dem Stemma widersprechenden Lesartenkombinationen, mögen sie nun durch Kreuzung, durch unabhängige aber gleichgerichtete Veränderung oder durch richtige Schreiberkonjekturen zustandegekommen sein, so zahlreich und so gewichtig sind, daß das Stemma keinesfalls als gesicherte Grundlage textkritischer Einzelentscheidungen angesehen werden darf.)

Wachinger then evaluates the advantages and disadvantages resulting from both the alternatives faced by the editor in view of these findings: to edit from a base manuscript or to opt for an eclectic critical edition. He concludes: "Both procedures, when performed competently, seem to me equally legitimate" (Wachinger 2004, xx; "Beide Verfahren, kompetent durchgeführt, scheinen mir gleich legitim"). Wachinger himself stays with Paul's cautious, eclectic critical procedure.

7.4.6 The history of textual tradition and the edition of late mediaeval utilitarian prose in the Texte und Textgeschichte series (1980–)

The genealogically reconstructive edition, which has been banished since Stackmann's article in 1964 from the field of the courtly epic (in which, however, it was hardly ever realised in its pure form), found its most comprehensive application in a Würzburg research group, begun in 1973, and its research into the history of the textual tradition of prose works (according to the title of the group's volume on methodology, *Textgeschichtliche Prosaforschung*; Ruh 1985). Its results are published in the series Texte und Textgeschichte, in which fifty-six volumes of studies and editions have appeared since 1980, including extensive multivolume editions of texts with extraordinarily broad and variable manuscript traditions in the late Middle Ages and beyond. An example can perhaps best illustrate the methodology and results achieved. The manuscript tradition of the *Rechtssumme* (a summa of ecclesiastical law and Christian life) by an otherwise unknown Dominican Friar Berthold, probably from the second half of the fourteenth century, begins at the end of the fourteenth century and is extant in approximately eighty-nine manuscripts and twelve early prints. The edition (Steer and Hamm 1987–2006) is based on a complete *recensio* of the entire manuscript and print tradition and a computerised collation. It leads to the assumption of four main versions (three redactions *A*, *B*, *C* and an adaptation of the third redaction, *Cy*), which have taken shape in the manuscript tradition and in turn appear in numerous post-redactional stages of the text. These stages are genealogically reconstructed in the traditional way (using significant common errors/innovations), as lost links between the versions and the surviving textual witnesses. The complete stemma is shown on a five-page pull-out (vol. 1, preceding p. 219*); only a few textual witnesses are to be classified as pre-redactional (preceding the redactions B and *C*). The edition does not aim at the archetype of an authorial text that lies at the heart of the versions, but at the four versions themselves. They are, admittedly, not directly preserved in the manuscripts, but are reconstructed from the post-redactional stages of the text (Steer 1985, 48–49); the edition offers the texts of the reconstructed versions synoptically on double pages in four columns, and the four apparatuses document the variant readings of the versions' textual traditions.

7.4.7 Stemmatics of equivalent parallel versions of the courtly epic (Bumke 1996): New aporias, digital perspectives

After Stackmann's article in 1964, there appeared to be, for editions of courtly epics, only two alternatives: the base manuscript or the eclectic critical method. In 1996, in a surprising turnaround, Bumke seemed to rehabilitate reconstructive stemmatics in this area – albeit under completely different conditions. Bumke draws the conclusion, from the critical study of the manuscript tradition since Lachmann, that the courtly epics of the period around AD 1200 existed from the very beginning in (critically) equivalent parallel versions that can neither have arisen from each other as adaptations nor are capable of being traced back to a fixed authorial text. He considers that the manuscript tradition, at least approximately for the first half of the thirteenth century, is fundamentally unstable. Not until the increase in vernacular literacy towards the end of the century did it stabilise and thus achieve the quality that makes it accessible to the genealogically reconstructive method.

Instead of the genealogy of the tradition of the authorial text, therefore, there appears, in Bumke's case, the genealogy of the tradition of the various versions. However, in this way, the authorial text creeps in again through the back door: this occurs where the manuscript tradition of a version diverges and comparison with the other versions tips the balance in favour of a particular reading (Bumke 1996, 605–608), for in this way it is acknowledged that a common source for the versions can be reconstructed (see Schröder 1998, 295–296). Admittedly, Bumke did not draw this conclusion in his editorial work. Instead, in the edition of the four versions of the *Nibelungenklage* that he had ascertained, he decided to edit according to the base-manuscript principle; he deviates from the base manuscripts only in the case of obviously erroneous text (Bumke 1996, 608; 1999, 19–28, with detailed discussion of variants in the tradition of version *B). In this, he was followed by Mertens (2004) in his base-manuscript edition of *Iwein* (after *B*) and Heinzle (2013) in his base-manuscript edition of the *Nibelungenlied* and *Klage* (after *B*).

The goal of limiting the genealogically reconstructive edition to a certain early stage in the history of the textual tradition (not necessarily with the quality of a version in Bumke's terms) has been realised without fundamentally departing from the idea of a fixed authorial text. The new edition of Stricker's *Karl der Große* by Singer (2016) can be mentioned as a recent example. Singer's *recensio* of the manuscript tradition led to five genealogically defined groups of manuscripts, beyond which it is not possible to penetrate further back in order to reach an archetype (Singer 2016, lxiv). From these five families, the text of the best one, relatively speaking, is edited, based on four manuscripts, for which a serviceable "recension formula" ("Rezensionsformel") can be derived from the "stemmatic structure" ("stemmatische Struktur") of the group; in the cases where the *recensio* leads to equally acceptable readings, "decisions are based on editorial judgement" ("entscheidet das editorische Urteil"), not least on the basis of the readings of the other groups ("die Konsultation der Lesartenverhältnsse der übrigen Gruppen"; Singer 2016, xxiv).

New methods of presentation are offered by digital editions. A salient example, with which we conclude, is the *Parzival* project by Michael Stolz (see the project website, parzival.unibe.ch/home.html). The project relates directly to the intensive efforts of twentieth-century research on the internal classification of Lachmann's manuscript classes *D and *G. They are viewed as versions in Bumke's terms and have, in the two studies of the manuscript tradition emanating from the project (Schöller 2009; Viehhauser 2009), been supplemented by two further manuscript groups suspected of representing versions (see, in agreement, but with implied reservations, Schirok 2011, 313–314; Chlench and Viehhauser 2014). The aim, which has already been realised to a considerable extent, is a comprehensive documentation of the manuscript tradition with digital facsimiles, manuscript transcriptions, and synoptic readings of individual lines, which are linked together; the synoptic edition of the four versions according to the base-manuscript principle with apparatuses for each version; and, finally, still at an experimental stage (Stolz 2016), a reading text of version *D (which Lachmann had already favoured) according to the base-manuscript principle, with variant readings of the other versions in the margin and a multilevel apparatus below the text.

Whereas in the early presentations of the project, attempts to elucidate manuscript relationships by means of tools which apply bioinformatic methods of cladistics/phylogenetics to textual relationships (see 5.1.3) were strongly emphasised (Stolz 2003), they are now more likely to be introduced in support of the results of research "according to strictly philological yardsticks" (Stolz 2016, 355; "nach streng philologischen Maßstäben"), in other words, stemmatics. Apart from the methodological problem of the transformation of an unrooted phylogenetic graph into an archetype-directed stemma (discussed in the case of *Parzival* by Chlench and Viehhauser 2014; in general, see Trovato 2017, 185–216; 5.5 above), which is indispensable (see the two illustrations in Stolz 2016, 356–357), the application of cladistics comes up first and foremost against practical limits, since it assumes the graphic normalisation of the manuscript texts that are to be compared (Chlench and Viehhauser 2014, 70–71) – an effort that can probably be made only in the case of smaller sections of text (in the case of Stolz 2016, 210 lines in twenty-one textual witnesses); compare the experiences in Romance studies (7.3.4).

Acknowledgement

The text was translated from the German by David Yeandle (King's College London).

Further reading

The following publications offer further insights into the questions dealt with above: Bumke (1996, 1–88; on the tradition history and textual criticism of the courtly epic in the thirteenth century), Schröder (1998; opposing Bumke 1996 from the point of view of reconstructive editing), Heinzle (2003; basic questions in the edition of mediaeval German texts between reproduction and reconstruction), and Chlench and Viehhauser (2014; relationship between stemmatics and cladistics as exemplified by *Parzival*).

7.5 Ethiopic
Alessandro Bausi

The scholarly edition of Ethiopic (Gəʿəz) texts can be taken in many respects as a paradigmatic example of practices common in other linguistic and cultural areas of

Christian oriental studies as they have developed in the West since the Renaissance, particularly since the eighteenth century. It is a fact that, while the field of Christian Arabic and especially Syriac studies has, if not a longer, then definitely a richer tradition, Christian oriental studies shares some common basic features and has become a relatively coherent field at an academic level as well. For textual criticism and editing, the two main series, both established at the very beginning of the twentieth century and still active, the Corpus scriptorum Christianorum Orientalium (since 1903) and the Patrologia Orientalis (since 1904), emblematically represent – albeit with some interruptions – a large part of the scholarly editorial activity carried out for the previous hundred years and longer. It is, however, important to stress a fundamental difference as far as ancient and late antique texts are concerned. Some traditions of the Christian Orient (Syriac, Coptic, and Armenian, to name the main ones) are important for the number and variety of transmitted texts (and the age of the relevant manuscripts), which are not limited to translations but also include many original texts. With only very few exceptions, however, most of the ancient (late antique) Ethiopic texts are translations from Greek, and therefore the philology of these ancient texts falls into the general typological class of editing translations (on which, see the several case studies in Macé et al. 2015 and some examples in 4.5 above).

7.5.1 Ethiopic philology within Christian oriental philologies

7.5.1.1 Ethiopic philology and manuscript studies

Despite the explosion of manuscript studies in recent decades, the issue of editorial practice – and particularly the utilisation of the stemmatic method in order to analyse or to edit and/or reconstruct texts – has not enjoyed much consideration in Christian oriental studies (an exception is *Comparative Oriental Manuscript Studies: An Introduction*; Bausi et al. 2015). Some contributions from Ethiopian studies in the last three decades are an exception, as I will show below. The accentuation of the archaeological and material aspects of manuscript research has, to an extent, been a disadvantage for the critical approach towards texts. Moreover, while many Ethiopic texts were and still are edited without any clearly determined or declared methodological approach, this practice is better understood in terms of a pre-Lachmannian state of the art of editing rather than in terms of a critical rethinking of stemmatic and reconstructive practices. On the other hand, focusing on single documents, or on the statistical evaluation of the average text circulating at a particular time, has substantially shifted the target of philological research towards single cases or the definition of successive stages in a tradition. This can be seen as a complementary task to that of determining the earliest textual phase (it is, in fact, a history of the tradition), but in practice it is usually meant as an a priori rejection of text-critical analysis. This line of action has, in my view, not replaced the stemmatic approach. Methodological considerations are further complicated by implications of political correctness in evaluating texts which, aside from their history and original form, have become accepted in a certain recension (*vulgata*) by institutions (typically, the national churches) which, in the opinion of some scholars, should be credited with a special status. This is, for example, the approach of the "Textual History of the Ethiopic Old Testament" (THEOT) project led by Steve Delamarter and Curt Niccum (see Jost 2015).

7.5.1.2 Main features of the transmission of Ethiopic texts

The first editorial methods applied to Ethiopic texts can be securely traced back to the environment of the Christian kingdom of Ethiopia, which was dominated by the cultural hegemony of the Church. A crucial role in the complex transmission of Ethiopic texts was played by the mediaeval adaptations of late antique written knowledge inherited from Greek-speaking Egypt and translated into Ethiopic early in the Aksumite period (ca. fourth to sixth century AD; for exemplary cases, see Bausi 2006a, 2015a, 2017a, 2018; Bausi and Camplani 2016). A decisive factor in prompting this mediaeval adaptation and revision was the presence of a new layer of Arabic-based texts, at times overlapping with and/or substituting the older ones. Also important was the fact that the literary language (Ethiopic, or Gəʿəz) remained the language of education and writing, but had no longer been a spoken language since the tenth century at the latest. This had implications for orthography (several phonemes merged in the course of time and orthographical interchanges occurred, also posing questions of standardisation and normalisation; see Bausi 2016a). Nonetheless, the methods of dealing with texts in premodern Ethiopia have not to date been studied sufficiently to be the subject of even a cursory presentation (for some first attempts, see Bausi 2017b; Brita 2014; Lusini 2004; Mersha Alehegne 2011a). Yet this phase cannot be ignored, since it is an important component in the history of the tradition of Ethiopic texts. Despite the presence of a substantial corpus of older Ethiopic translations from Greek models going back to late Antiquity, all Ethiopic texts are transmitted by mediaeval manuscripts (starting from the twelfth/thirteenth century) with the sole exception of the New Testament, which is also attested by two late antique manuscripts. Manuscripts from before the fourteenth century are still extremely rare. For texts dating back to the Aksumite period, the typology of transmission is not so different from that of Greek and Latin classical texts, which, aside from epigraphical and papyrological witnesses, are mainly attested by much later manuscripts. A different case is that of texts which were created later in mediaeval times and that may be much closer to their earliest manuscript witnesses. Yet there are extremely few, if any, cases of preserved a u t o g r a p h s, and textual witnesses (manuscripts) rather distant in time from the creation of the texts are the norm.

7.5.1.3 The earliest phases of editing Ethiopic texts in context

Although they were vaguely known already in mediaeval times, the first close encounters of Western scholars with Ethiopic texts date from the Renaissance, when representatives of Eastern Christian communities travelled to and dwelt in Rome under the protection of the pope. In the case of Ethiopians, the ecumenical councils which saw the participation of oriental delegations, such as the Council of Basle–Ferrara–Florence of 1431–1445, and the eventual establishment of a permanent Ethiopian community in Rome, played a decisive role in promoting the development of Ethiopian studies. The challenges of editing and printing Ethiopic texts started relatively early in time compared with other Christian oriental traditions. The first printed Ethiopic text (not by accident the psalter, the most commonly read Christian Ethiopic book) dates from 1513, with a second four-language edition in 1518, both edited by Potken in Rome (1513) and Cologne (1518). As early as 1548 and 1549, a two-volume edition of the New Testament was printed in Rome by the Ethiopian Tasfā Ṣǝyon with help of Italian scholars. A few Ethiopic texts were also printed in the seventeenth century, but it was only with Hiob Ludolf (1624–1704) that text editing was carried out in such a way that it can be methodologically evaluated. Ludolf's edition of the psalter (Ludolf 1701) still stands out as an advanced example of method in some respects: Ludolf based his edition on three manuscripts and the two available prints, and was well aware of questions of normalisation and standardisation. He did not hesitate to reintegrate *ex nihilo* missing verses or hemistichs when they were attested by the Greek and Hebrew text and missing in the Ethiopic version, where he explained their absence as due to the inaccuracy of the copyist, so that, ultimately, he fundamentally based his edition on his own *iudicium* (Ludolf 1701, 2v–3v). Nonetheless, this edition of the psalter, also furnished with a commentary, is still of great importance because of the critical comparison with the Greek and Hebrew texts on which it is based. Ludolf's works represent the high point in Ethiopian studies within the context of oriental studies in the modern age, as cultivated by humanists like Josephus Justus Scaliger (1540–1609) or Nicolas-Claude Fabri de Peiresc (1580–1637) and others, who had a strong interest in oriental cultures. This situation did not change with the Protestant and Catholic Reformations, after which the study of the Bible became even more important and had to be done in the original language in Protestant churches; this was a continuous source of impetus to oriental studies. The sixteenth and seventeenth centuries are also the period of the polyglot Bibles (from 1514 to 1657; see Wilkinson 2007), the last of which, edited by Brian Walton (1654–1657) in London, also includes an Ethiopic version of the psalter and of the Song of Songs along with a reprint of the New Testament from the Roman *editio princeps*.

7.5.1.4 Christian oriental studies in their connection with classical studies

The institutionalisation of oriental studies at European universities in the last decades of the eighteenth century (for example, in Germany at Göttingen) was undertaken in close connection with the extraordinary development of classical philology and still within the framework of biblical criticism. Theology still kept its central importance for oriental studies, and theologians in the Protestant tradition had to learn Greek and Hebrew. Besides the interest in the biblical text, the interest in ancient Judaism played a major role in keeping this ultimately humanistic tradition of Christian oriental studies alive. The overwhelmingly strictly religious character of Christian oriental texts determined a unification of Christian oriental texts under the umbrella of *philologia sacra* – a largely neglected aspect of Saidian orientalism (cf. Said 1978). Within this framework, the German theologian (theology was one of the main sites of Semitic studies) August Dillmann (1823–1894) refounded Ethiopian studies in the nineteenth century. He carried out substantial editorial work, not limited to but certainly focused on biblical and apocryphal texts dating from Aksumite times and typologically characterised by large gaps between the time of creation (presumably from the fourth to sixth centuries AD) and the date of the earliest extant manuscript witnesses (fourteenth century at the earliest). In doing so, whenever possible Dillmann carried out a *recensio* and oriented his editorial practice, as Ludolf had done, towards the available text of the *Vorlage* that he identified for a work, for example the Septuagint in the case of the Ethiopic Bible, without any prejudicial preference for a given manuscript (either *codex optimus* or *codex vetustissimus*). Ethiopic texts as edited by Dillmann, as well as by theologians and scholars in biblical studies in the decades immediately after his period – at least Robert Henry Charles (1855–1931) should be mentioned, since he dedicated much of his efforts to Ethiopic texts (see Bausi 2016a, 54–64) – were considered in terms of contemporary practice in biblical textual scholarship, particularly Septuagint studies (Erho and Stuckenbruck 2013 offer an overview of the manuscripts used for editing major Ethiopic apocryphal texts, but much less on the methods used, for which see still Piovanelli 1987, 1988).

7.5.1.5 A splitting of traditions
Dillmann's activity was deeply rooted in the long history of oriental and biblical studies and *philologia sacra* (see 7.1), and we can say that, up to the end of the eighteenth century, most of the editors of oriental texts had substantially shared the same methods and approaches as were used in classical philology: orientalists and classicists belonged to the same academic milieu and their attitudes largely overlapped. Yet the new method applied by Karl Lachmann (1793–1851; see 7.2) developed in a way that would eventually create a profound gap between *philologia sacra* on the one hand and classical philology (i.e. the disciplines using the stemmatic method conventionally placed under the name of Lachmann) on the other. In this respect, the non-adoption of Lachmann's method by oriental (non-classical) studies is a real landmark: it is at this point that classical studies (including Septuagint and Greek New Testament studies, and patristics to a large extent; see Castelli 2011) and oriental studies started to diverge more and more. While in the nineteenth century classical philology became more and more elaborate, oriental studies tended to become weaker and gradually less up to date and less methodologically oriented, since the mainstream was dictated now by classical and particularly Greek studies.

As stated by Marchand: "In the early modern period, oriental philologists had pioneered many of these text-critical skills, but nineteenth-century orientalists almost by definition could not concentrate on one language; nor could they secularize their field with equal alacrity" (2009, 73).

If the development and secularisation of oriental studies at the end of the eighteenth century also marked the moment when oriental studies ceased to follow the development of the mainstream humanistic disciplines, one cannot disregard the fact that this was also due to some intrinsic features of the respective fields. Besides, the needs and starting point of oriental studies were completely different, since the majority of texts remained unpublished (somewhat similarly to mediaeval Latin and Byzantine studies) and only an absolute minority could be considered. It is not a surprise that, for a long time, publishing one manuscript (the most accessible but not necessarily the best, or "the best" if more were accessible, and so on), rather than editing a text, was the normal approach, and this trend has in many cases survived to the present day. In oriental studies, the content of a single manuscript – understood exclusively as a text-carrier – has remained for much longer than in other fields a self-justified and sufficient object of study and research.

It is impossible to provide here even a draft history of Christian oriental text editing from a proper methodological perspective (a very short, slightly more detailed overview can be found in Bausi et al. 2015, 4–9, from which most of the following examples are taken). One must limit oneself to quoting a few examples, among many possible others, of orientalists who were familiar with the questions being discussed in their time. One case in point is that of one of the fathers of modern Coptology, as well as an outstanding classicist, Georg Zoëga (1755–1809). Zoëga applied principles that were very similar to those proposed by Friedrich August Wolf (1759–1824) but which he developed independently and in parallel. In his case, however, the specifically fragmented character of Coptic documentation, usually represented by dismembered codices, oriented his research in a decisive way, but it did not confront him with principles of philological reconstruction starting from multiple witnesses. It is important to point out that Zoëga did not feel the need to go beyond *philologia sacra* – probably he could not and did not want to do so, for various reasons, some of them being obvious (he worked at the papal court). Rather, he understood the potential interest of the almost virgin field of oriental Christian apocrypha, which he started to explore as far as Coptic texts were concerned (see Bausi 2015b).

7.5.2 The base-manuscript edition, or "the normal way"

In the course of the second half of the nineteenth century, philological discourse and methodologies were mainly developed within the field of classical and Romance studies (see 7.3). It is a fact that, with a very few exceptions – usually due to a stronger connection to biblical scholarship or classical studies – Christian oriental studies, even at the beginning of the twentieth century and later, by and large practised the base-manuscript method.

7.5.2.1 The base-manuscript method

As already mentioned, the practice of using a base manuscript was partly due to the particular kind of documentation being dealt with – very partially known and without the centuries-long research background of classical studies – but also reflected something akin to an acquired habit. All in all, it had little to do with the reasons put forward by Joseph Bédier (1864–1938) and his rethinking of the reconstructive Lachmannian method, and had much more to do with the continuation of a previous practice current in oriental studies, corresponding to what might be termed the "simple, normal way". In pre-Lachmannian classical studies, the editor normally started from the *textus receptus* and an existing edition which he emended, and recourse to codices was occasional and optional. In oriental studies, however, the editor normally started from one manuscript, since most of the time the text in question was to be published for the first time and was available in that manuscript only.

Exceptions to this trend can probably be found in every subfield, but they have never become the norm. An interesting early example is that of the Syriacist Arthur Amiaud (1849–1889). In the year of his death, 1889, following in the footsteps of Gaston Paris (see 7.3) both in content and method, he published an edition of the Syriac *Alexis* legends with an attempt at reconstructing the earliest text, stating in his introduction (with an explicit reference to Paris and Pannier 1872 in Amiaud 1889, x n1):

> Nous n'avons pas affaire [...] à des compositions personnelles [...]. Si l'on entreprenait de publier une famille de telles œuvres, où chaque auteur respectant seulement les grandes lignes de la légende l'a traitée pour tout le reste avec une liberté presque absolue [...], tout ce qu'on pourrait faire serait de donner chacune entièrement et séparément. Mais ici où nous n'avons [...] que des copies plus ou moins exactes mais toujours sincères d'un même texte, le devoir de l'éditeur est de chercher à retrouver l'original ou à le restituer au moins dans la mesure du possible, et c'est là le but que nous allons poursuivre maintenant au moyen de la comparaison et de la classification de nos manuscrits. (Amiaud 1889, ix)

> [We have not to deal [...] with personal compositions [...]. If one undertook the publication of a family of such works, where every author respecting only the general features of the legend has dealt with all other features with absolute freedom [...], all that one could do would be to present each one entirely and separately. But here, where we have only more or less precise copies of the same text, the duty of the editor is to try to trace the original or to restore it as far as possible, and this is the target we are aiming at now through the comparison and the classification of our manuscripts.]

Later, in 1922, Albrecht Götze (1897–1971), later a great Hittitologist, examined the manuscript tradition of the Syriac *Cave of Treasures*, and on the basis of the extant manuscripts he supposed the existence of an archetype, reconstructing its physical structure (columns and number of lines) as well as that of a hyparchetype. He also established subgroups on the basis of mechanical errors (loss of folia), and corroborated all this evidence with that of "verschiedene Lesungen und gemeinsame Neuerungen" [various readings and shared innovations], giving also a complex but clear stemma codicum (Götze 1922, 5–12).

In the second half of the twentieth century, Bernard Botte (1893–1980), the student of canonical oriental Christian liturgical texts, clearly advocated the consideration of versions as textual witnesses when undertaking the search for an original (see also Botte 1966, 177–179):

> Les principes que je viens d'exposer ne sont pas neufs [...]. Je ne crois pas qu'on puisse procéder autrement sous peine de tomber dans la fantaisie. Il ne faut se fier aveuglément à aucune version. La question n'est pas de trouver "la bonne version", pas plus que dans une édition critique d'un texte grec on ne doit chercher "le bon manuscrit". Le tout est de faire un bon usage de tous les témoins. (Botte 1955, 168)

> [The principles I have set out are not new [...]. I do not think one can proceed in any other way, without risking falling into fantasy. One cannot blindly trust any version. The question is not that of finding "the right version", any more than in a critical edition of a Greek text one must look for "the right manuscript". What is important is to make good use of all the witnesses.]

Hans Ferdinand Fuhs (Fuhs 1968, 31; see fig. 7.5-1 below, and later also Fuhs 1971, 25) has been credited with the first proposal of a *stemma codicum* for the edition of an Ethiopic text (Lusini 1988, 212n3), but the very first one was probably proposed by Louis Guerrier and Sylvain Grébaut in their edition of the *Testament of Our Lord in Galilee* in 1912 (Guerrier and Grébaut 1912, 173 [33]). Another early *stemma codicum* was proposed by Adolf Grohmann in his 1913 edition of several versions of the *Vision of Shenute*, particularly in the section dedicated to the Ethiopic tradition (Grohmann 1913, 198). Grohmann's contribution contains several interesting observations on the relationship of the manuscript witnesses (gained from applying a reconstructive method in order to determine the mutual relationships between them), as well as other observations concerning the establishment of the text, and presupposes reflection on the role of the introduction in a critical edition.

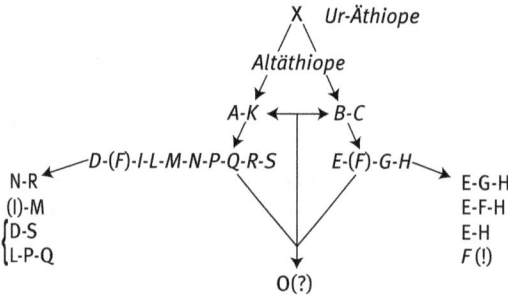

Fig. 7.5-1: *Stemma codicum* of the Ethiopic version of Micah. Source: Fuhs (1968, 31).

7.5.2.2 The purported reasons behind the base-manuscript method

Returning to the main series of text editions mentioned above, it is obvious that the base-manuscript method has largely been applied in them, with only very few exceptions. In the case of Christian oriental studies in particular, René Draguet's (1896–1980) credo of the base-manuscript method long dominated the Corpus scriptorum Christianorum Orientalium (CSCO), which Draguet directed from the late forties (1948) until his death (see Mengozzi 2015). Draguet himself canonised his suggested method for Syriac texts in a controversial contribution (Draguet 1977), a major part of which was dedicated to technical concerns of layout and printing and very little to proper text-critical methodology. It recommended a simple reproduction of the best manuscript's text – taking into consideration its age and legibility – with all its errors included. Draguet's "best manuscript" is thus simply the most suitable for the representation of the form; it is not even the best manuscript a posteriori, that is, the manuscript most similar to the critically established text that emerges from a *recensio*. It is therefore different – one might say worse – than the codex optimus (or codex vetustissimus, and so on) of pre-Lachmannian philology, which was a base manuscript whose errors could be corrected ope codicum and ope ingenii.

Ethiopic texts were no exception to this trend. If one browses through the introductions to editions published in the CSCO and Patrologia Orientalis series looking for explanations of why this method was applied, one will be soon disappointed. I have carried out this task in two contributions where more details are provided (Bausi 2006b, 2008), and I will not repeat the predominantly discouraging results here. The consideration of later editions does not change this picture (see e.g. Bausi 2009, 2010a, 2015c). As an advisor for the CSCO series, I have myself experienced the difficulty of ensuring respect for minimal standards such as, for example, consideration of all known available manuscripts (all the more so when digital reproductions are easily accessible). Almost all editions in these series are introduced by the same formulaic considerations, in a few cases by additional short comments, often with hardly more than a couple of words; just one representative example is: "Vulgatur textus codicis A notatis variantibus in B" (Arras 1986, v) [The text of codex *A* is published, the variants from *B* being noted].

7.5.3 Ethiopic philology in the past thirty years

Little more interest has generally been displayed in using the so-called neo-Lachmannian approach (see 2.4) in oriental studies (see Witkam 1988, 2013). Among the exceptions, one should mention the edition of the Ethiopic version of the *Life of Saint Alexis* by the renowned orientalist Enrico Cerulli (1898–1988; see at least Bausi 2016b, 191–194, with further references), where different recensions as well as individual authorial variations were distinguished, particularly in the more recent manuscripts, which Cerulli attributed to specific characteristics of this very widespread hagiographical text:

> Les observations qui précèdent font voir que les mss de la Vie d'Alexis se prêtent peu à l'établissement d'un *stemma codicum* rigide; ils ne diffèrent pas en cela de ceux des compositions hagiographiques du moyen âge et en particulier du moyen âge oriental. Une critique prudente doit avoir égard à la fantaisie des scribes, aux préoccupations des monastères où furent copiés les mss, et aux habitudes mêmes des scriptoria. En ce qui concerne particulièrement l'Éthiopie, il faut tenir compte que les Actes étaient destinés à la lecture dans les monastères, où on les divisait en sept sections égales pour les sept jours de la semaine, ou encore entièrement, dans une séance unique, dans certains couvents ou églises à l'occasion de la fête du Saint. Toutes ces circonstances pouvaient aisément conduire à des additions, ou à des suppressions. (Cerulli 1969, xv)

> [The preceding observations show that the manuscripts of the *Life of Alexis* lend themselves little to the establishment of a rigid *stemma codicum*. They do not differ in this from those of the hagiographical compositions of the Middle Ages and especially of the Eastern Middle Ages. Prudent criticism must have regard to the fantasy of the scribes, the preoccupations of the monasteries where the manuscripts were copied, and the very habits of the scriptoria. Concerning Ethiopia in particular, it must be borne in mind that the Acts were intended for reading in the monasteries, where they were divided into seven equal sections for the seven days of the week, or entirely in a single sitting, in certain convents or churches on the occasion of the feast of the saint. All these circumstances could easily lead to additions or deletions.]

Even in this case, however, Cerulli did not use a base-manuscript method. Although he distinguished three groups (ancient, intermediate, and modern) among the fifteen manuscript witnesses he used, he did not adopt any base manuscript for each of them. He edited what he thought was the most ancient version based upon the three manuscripts of the ancient group and provided the variants of all other manuscripts deviating from the older text form (fig. 7.5-2 below). Cerulli observes a tendency that is well known in hagiographical texts (for further references, see Bausi 2014a, 57n6), but it cannot be treated as a universal truth. But it is true in particular for texts which have a very rich manuscript tradition and enjoyed good fortunes and wide dissemination. This condition must be verified for each single case, and there is no getting around this.

In recent decades, remarkable achievements have, indeed, been reached in studies on the text of the Bible and apocrypha (e.g. the editions of the Gospels of Mark and Matthew by Zuurmond 1989, 2001, and of the Gospel of John by Wechsler 2005; the best overview is in Zuurmond and Niccum 2013), although even in this field the state of the art is very far from being uniform (cf. e.g. the editions by Tedros Abraha 2001, 2004, 2014; see also the general remarks in Bausi 2016a, 73–80). A scholar like Ernst Hammerschmidt (1928–1993), and even someone of the calibre of Edward Ullendorff (1920–2011), one of the editors of the Book of Enoch (Knibb and Ullendorff 1978), still justified the use of photographic reproductions for editing Ethiopic texts (for details and references, see Bausi 2016a, 53n28). Obsessed by the

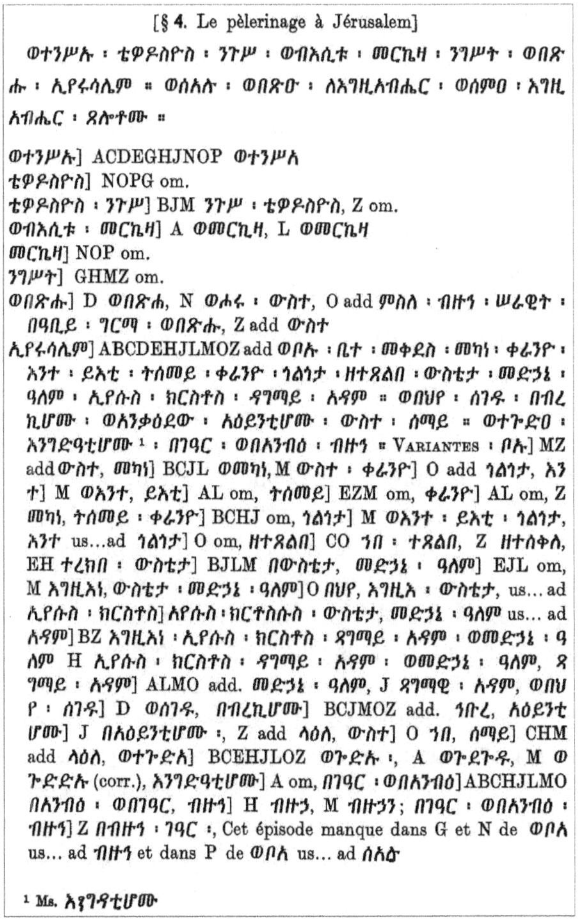

[§ 4. Le pèlerinage à Jérusalem]

ወተንሥኡ ፡ ቴዎዶስዮስ ፡ ንጉሥ ፡ ወብእሲቱ ፡ መርኬዛ ፡ ንግሥት ፡ ወበጽሑ ፡ ኢየሩሳሌም ። ወሰአሉ ፡ ወበጽሁ ፡ ለእግዚአብሔር ፡ ወሰምዐ ፡ እግዚአብሔር ፡ ጸሎቶሙ ።

ወተንሥኡ] ACDEGHJNOP ወተንሥአ
ቴዎዶስዮስ] NOPG om.
ቴዎዶስዮስ ፡ ንጉሥ] BJM ንጉሥ ፡ ቴዎዶስዮስ, Z om.
ወብእሲቱ ፡ መርኬዛ] A ወመርኪዛ, L ወመርኬዛ
መርኬዛ] NOP om.
ንግሥት] GHMZ om.
ወበጽሑ] D ወበጽሐ, N ወሖሩ ፡ ውስተ, O add ምስለ ፡ ብዙኅ ፡ ሠራዊት ፡ በዓቢይ ፡ ግርማ ፡ ወበጽሑ, Z add ውስተ
ኢየሩሳሌም] ABCDEHJLMOZ add ወቦኡ ፡ ቤተ ፡ መቅደስ ፡ መካነ ፡ ቀራንዮ ፡ እንተ ፡ ይእቲ ፡ ትሰመይ ፡ ቀራንዮ ፡ ጎልጎታ ፡ ዘተጸልበ ፡ ውስቴታ ፡ መድኀኔ ፡ ዓለም ፡ ኢየሱስ ፡ ክርስቶስ ፡ ዳግማይ ፡ አዳም ። ወበህየ ፡ ሰገዱ ፡ በብረኪሆሙ ፡ ወአንቃዕደው ፡ አዕይንቲሆሙ ፡ ውስተ ፡ ሰማይ ። ወተጉድዐ ፡ እንግድዓቲሆሙ [1] ፡ በገዓር ፡ ወበአንብዕ ፡ ብዙኅ ። VARIANTES ፡ ቦኡ] MZ add ውስተ, መካነ] BCJL ወመካነ, M ውስተ ፡ ቀራንዮ] O add ጎልጎታ, እንተ] M ወእንተ, ይእቲ] AL om, ትሰመይ] EZM om, ቀራንዮ] AL om, Z መካነ, ትሰመይ ፡ ቀራንዮ] BCHJ om, ጎልጎታ] M ወእንተ ፡ ይእቲ ፡ ጎልጎታ, እንተ us...ad ጎልጎታ] O om, ዘተጸልበ] CO ኀበ ፡ ተጸልበ, Z ዘተሰቅለ, EH ተረክበ ፡ ውስቴታ] BJLM በውስቴታ, መድኀኔ ፡ ዓለም] EJL om, M እግዚእነ, ውስቴታ ፡ መድኀኔ ፡ ዓለም] O በህየ, እግዚእ ፡ ውስቴታ, us... ad ኢየሱስ ፡ ክርስቶስ] አየሱስ ፡ ክርቶስሱስ ፡ ውስቴታ, መድኀኔ ፡ ዓለም us... ad አዳም] BZ እግዚእነ ፡ ኢየሱስ ፡ ክርስቶስ ፡ ዳግማይ ፡ አዳም ፡ ወመድኀኔ ፡ ዓለም H ኢየሱስ ፡ ክርስቶስ ፡ ዳግማይ ፡ አዳም ፡ ወመድኀኔ ፡ ዓለም, ዳግማይ ፡ አዳም] ALMO add. መድኀኔ ፡ ዓለም, J ዳግማዊ ፡ አዳም, ወበህየ ፡ ሰገዱ] D ወሰገዱ, በብረኪሆሙ] BCJMOZ add. ኀቡረ, አዕይንቲሆሙ] J በአዕይንቲሆሙ ፡, Z add ላዕለ, ውስተ] O ኀበ, ሰማይ] CHM add ላዕለ, ወተጉድአ] BCEHJLOZ ወጉድኡ ፡, A ወጉደጉዱ, M ወጉድድኡ (corr.), እንግድዓቲሆሙ] A om, በገዓር ፡ ወበአንብዕ] ABCHJLMO በአንብዕ ፡ ወበገዓር, ብዙኅ] H ብዙኃ, M ብዙኃን; በገዓር ፡ ወበአንብዕ ፡ ብዙኅ] Z በብዙኅ ፡ ገዓር ፡, Cet épisode manque dans G et N de ወቦአ us... ad ብዙኅ et dans P de ወቦአ us... ad ሰአሉ

[1] Ms. እኇግዳቲሆሙ

Fig. 7.5-2: Edition of the Ethiopic version of the *Gadla Gabra Krəstos* [Life of St Alexis].
Source: Cerulli (1969, 6).

importance of documenting the evidence, these editors advised reducing editing to the making of facsimiles, and apparently attached much less importance to critical editing as a specific task of its own.

In 2015, almost forty years after the publication of the edition of the Book of Enoch, the former main editor, Michael A. Knibb, who had worked in consultation with Ullendorff, published an edition that marks a decisive change of trend. Knibb's edition of Ezekiel (Knibb 2014, 2015; see also Knibb 2017) has a long exemplary introduction that culminates in a *stemma codicum* where the main aspects of the manuscript tradition are tentatively represented (Knibb 2015, 37). Most of all, Knibb's edition does not apply any base-manuscript method and attempts instead to reconstruct the oldest attainable layer of the text. This decisive change is the result of the debate and criticism of the base-manuscript method that have, to some extent, animated the past thirty years of Ethiopic text editing.

7.5.3.1 Paolo Marrassini and the application of a neo-Lachmannian approach

An important novelty for editing Ethiopic texts was represented by the work of Paolo Marrassini (1942–2013), one of the most outstanding scholars in Ethiopian studies of the past forty years (on him, see the introductory papers to his *Gedenkschrift*, Bausi, Gori, and Lusini 2014; Lusini 2014). Marrassini used with full awareness a neo-Lachmannian approach in a number of critical editions of Ethiopic texts, both original (hagiographical and historiographical) and translated ones (apocryphal writings, for example the Ethiopic version of the Apocalypse of Peter). Marrassini started with the edition of a hagiographical text in 1981 attested by four manuscripts (Marrassini 1981), for which he proposed a *stemma codicum* according to which he reconstructed a critical text (fig. 7.5-3). His work had the honour of being mentioned in the *Breviario di Ecdotica* by Gianfranco Contini as a first example of the stemmatic method in Semitic studies (Contini 1986, 66, in a section added to the first edition and entitled "Postilla 1985"). Moreover, besides producing a series of critical editions (at least Marrassini 1981, 1993, 1995, 2000, 2003), Marrassini defended his method in a series of methodological contributions where he approached, among other things, questions of c r i t i c i s m   o f   f o r m   a n d   s u b s t a n c e and of the relationship between l i n g u i s t i c s   a n d   p h i l o l o g y, and addressed the question of the role of the introduction in a critical edition, and what to do with p u n c t u a t i o n in manuscripts (Marrassini 1987, 1992, 1996, 2008a, 2008b, 2009). Even in Marrassini's work, there are obviously points to be revised. It is, for example, apparent, in light of further research and when considering more manuscripts, that the manuscript tradition of the *Life of Kiros* (a very widespread hagiographical text) is much more complex than he had thought (Marrassini 2004; see Krzyżanowska 2015).

One specific aspect of Marrassini's work is that of having established a school, both in Europe (pupils of his are philologists with chairs in Copenhagen, Hamburg, Naples, and Paris) and in Ethiopia. In fact, in Addis Ababa an MA and a PhD programme in philology were established and have started to yield encouraging results. More editions and studies based on the stemmatic method have been produced, and a few of them are also starting to be published, some of them in international series

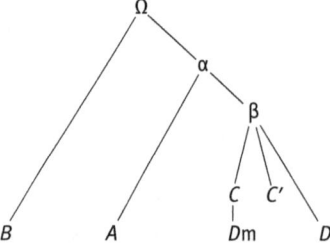

Fig. 7.5-3: *Stemma codicum* of the *Gadla Yoḥannəs Maśrāqāwi* [Life of John the Oriental]. Source: Marrassini (1981, xxvi; revised according to the *errata corrige*).

(Amsalu Tefera 2015; Hagos Abrha 2011). Pupils of Marrassini's pupils are doing the same (Brita 2007; Pisani 2013, 2015; Solomon Gebreyes 2019; Villa 2019), and more such editions are underway (cf. e.g. Hummel 2015, 2016; cf. also Mersha Alehegne 2011b; Yosef Demissie 2015). A few still-unpublished critical editions have also been produced as MA theses. The case of one thesis is remarkable: an MA thesis consisting of a new critical edition of the *Gadla Qawsṭos* (a hagiographical text already published by Raineri 2004), was published under the auspices of the national Orthodox Church of Ethiopia (Ḥəruya 'Ermyās 2014, 2014–2015). This is the first stemmatically reconstructed text ever published by the Ethiopian Orthodox Tawāḥədo Church. In comparison with what was said at the beginning concerning the standards of traditional text editing (consider the case of a recent edition for which it was possible to determine the ancestor of the manuscript on which the editor produced his own personal redaction; Bausi 2017b), this definitely marks a new trend. The stemmatic method proves, even in these cases, invariably effective.

7.5.3.2 The past decade

Notwithstanding the many texts that have been published in recent decades, there have been very few contributions explicitly dedicated to questions of critical editing. In July 2003, a plenary session of the Fifteenth International Conference of Ethiopian Studies in Hamburg was dedicated for the first time to "Current Trends in Ethiopian Studies: Philology". To my knowledge, the most relevant – but also the only – contributions of methodological character on Ethiopic philology remain, with very few exceptions, those by Marrassini or his pupils (Marrassini 1987, 1992, 1996, 2008a, 2008b, 2009; Lusini 2005, 2017; Bausi 2006b, 2008, 2010b, 2014b, 2015a; as far as reflexes in Ethiopia are concerned, cf. Baye Yimam 2008; Hussein Ahmad 2008; Shiferaw Bekele 2008; Moges Yigezu et al. 2006).

If Marrassini's school has adopted and applied, where possible – it should be taken for granted that everyone is aware of the complexity of editing – a neo-Lachmannian approach (for one of the most recent examples, see Bausi 2017c and fig. 7.5-4 below), there are also different views. A scholar who has clearly expressed a different view on editing Ethiopic texts is Manfred Kropp. He has devoted extensive work and an important monograph to disentangling the manuscript tradition of the Ethiopic royal chronicles and related texts (Kropp 1989), and has published several text editions (Kropp 1988a, 1988b, 1994, 2016), preparatory essays (Kropp 1985, 2011), and focused reviews (among the recent ones where methodological remarks are clearly expressed, see Kropp 2015a, 2015b). In his footsteps, to name some other authors, Anaïs Wion has, for example, rightly criticised the standardisation carried out by Carlo Conti Rossini (1872–1949) in editing documentary texts (Wion and Bertrand 2011, on Conti Rossini 1909), although one may strongly disagree that this is a good example of the adoption of Lachmann as a model by scholars in Ethiopian studies (see Bausi 2017–2018). Finally, a contribution by Reinhard Meßner

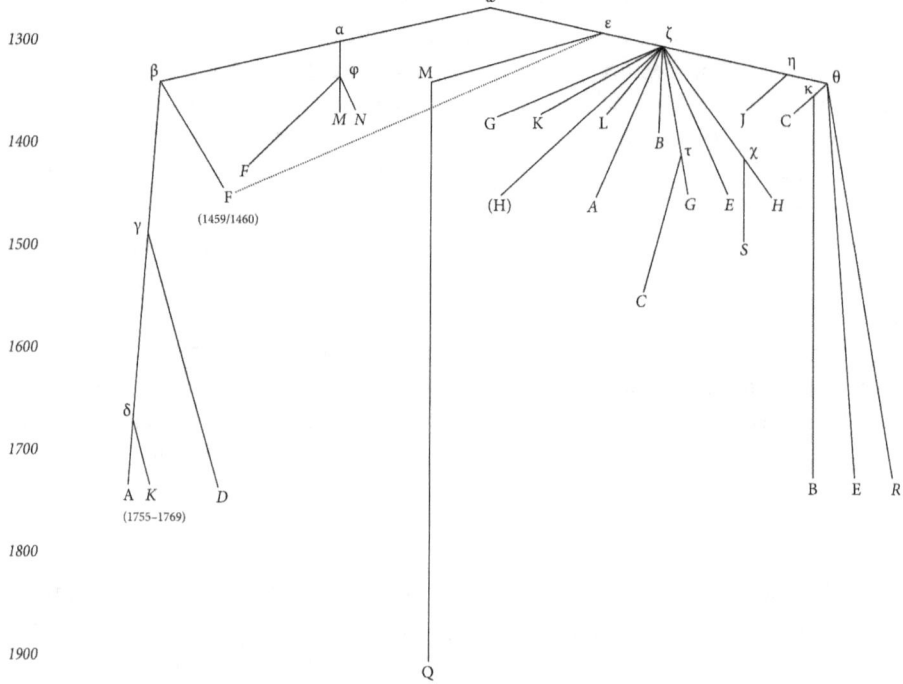

Fig. 7.5-4: *Stemma codicum* of the *Gadla 'Azqir* [Acts of Azqir]. Source: Bausi (2017c, 351).

(2007) on editing liturgical texts from the point of view of the researcher interested in "living texts" of liturgical use can also be mentioned.

Kropp, on the other hand, has expressed on several occasions a radically sceptical view of stemmatic and neo-Lachmannian approaches. He has noted, on the one hand, that, in his opinion, the practical results are in the end not far from what would result if a base-manuscript method were accepted; but, on the other hand, he has not clearly proposed a soundly based alternative method or even precisely motivated why the stemmatic method should not in principle be accepted, given all that it can offer. He also, even less correctly in my opinion, regards the solution of editing several distinct redactions to be contradictory to the stemmatic and reconstructive approach, something that was proposed for some portions of the *Gadla Libānos* (Kropp 2015a) where more authorial redactions clearly appear, each of them already attested by more witnesses. This is, by the way, a fortunate case where a conjectural emendation to the *editio princeps* (published by Conti Rossini 1903), which I could not have in the text as I would have wished due to the fierce opposition of the series advisor, eventually appeared to be the actually transmitted text when new manuscripts of the redaction in question were discovered (see Bausi 2003, 2014a).

All in all, the impression remains that some aspects of criticism of the use of the stemmatic method are rooted in a lack of familiarity with the method itself. We can be confident that what Paolo Trovato has undertaken with his remarkable book, now already in a second edition (Trovato 2017), will also profit the textual criticism of Ethiopic and Christian oriental texts. All those who criticise the inanity of the effort required by the stemmatic approach without clearly adopting a position of their own, do not, in my view, touch upon the core of the problem: that without a stemmatic approach, when this method allows clear results (and there are definitely cases where it does), it is simply impossible to provide any sound assessment of the value of the individual witnesses. It should probably suffice to repeat here the words of Alphonse Dain: "Le concept de manuscrit de base, qui rencontre tant de faveur, est un concept antiphilologique" (Dain 1964, 171) [The concept of the base manuscript, which meets with so much favour, is an anti-philological concept].

In Dain's usage – in case it is necessary to recall this – *le manuscrit de base* is really the base text methodologically speaking, and not the *manuscrit de surface*, that is, the "reference manuscript for the linguistic surface", the "surface manuscript", as in the neo-Lachmannian tradition (Trovato 2017, 346).

Further reading

A useful selection of further reading material and a general bibliographical orientation on Christian oriental philologies can be found in the chapter on textual criticism and text editing in *Comparative Oriental Manuscript Studies: An Introduction* (Bausi et al. 2015, esp. 324–327). The broadest, most systematic and updated information on the manuscript traditions of single Ethiopic texts and works is offered by the relevant articles in the five-volume *Encyclopaedia Aethiopica* (Uhlig 2003–2014), albeit with quite uneven approaches. Further information and bibliography on single texts can be found on the portal of the long-term project "Beta maṣāḥǝft: Manuscripts of Ethiopia and Eritrea", funded by the Union of the German Academies of Sciences and Humanities through the Academy of Hamburg. Within the traditions of the Christian Orient, the Syriac domain is largely covered by the international project syriaca.org (*The Syriac Reference Portal*), and Coptic by the recently launched European Research Council project "PAThs: An Archaeological Atlas of Coptic Literature" at the Sapienza University of Rome, which has integrated data from previous projects. Caucasian traditions (Armenian and Georgian) are largely represented on the TITUS portal of the University of Frankfurt (titus.uni-frankfurt.de). For the delicate linguistic questions posed by Christian Arabic texts, see the contributions by Paolo La Spisa (2012, 2015).

7.6 Hebrew
Chaim Milikowsky

The major group of texts in Hebrew which will be discussed in this section is the rabbinic corpus, a collection of texts, each of which is related to one or more other texts in the collection, which are generally dated to the second through sixth centuries CE. None of these texts are attributed in any manuscripts or in any *testimonia* to an author or editor. Most of them, in fact, should not be attributed to an author, but were generated by the accretion of textual matter, its collection together and subsequent redaction. Some have argued that no one moment and/or process of textual formation should be presumed for any of these texts, and that they were constantly in a state of becoming, but the extant evidence does not support such a position.

7.6.1 Language and boundaries of the corpus

Some of these texts are written solely in Hebrew, while others contain a mixture of Hebrew and Aramaic. The texts commonly assigned to this corpus are traditionally divided into two sets of two groups. One element of differentiation focuses upon date and the other upon subject matter. The earlier group of texts is ascribed to the Tannaitic period and the later one to the Amoraic period. In terms of subject matter, there are texts which are primarily legal – *halakhic* – in nature and there are those which are not legal but contain biblical exegesis, narratives and anecdotes, riddles and apophthegms, and ideas and beliefs, and are termed *aggadic*. Many texts exhibit a combination of both *halakhah* and *aggadah*.

Two texts within this corpus, the Mishnah and the Babylonian Talmud, have had a special status within Jewish tradition for the last two millennia or so. The Babylonian Talmud is a sort of expanded commentary on the Mishnah, and since the high Middle Ages most manuscript and printed versions of the Talmud have included the Mishnah within it. This entity has been the basis of Jewish law and practice since its formation, and therefore has been copied thousands of times, although for a variety of reasons, only a small number of manuscript copies survive; for most tractates (as each individual unit of the Talmud is generally called), it is less than ten. It should be pointed out that the Babylonian Talmud is a large composition, consisting of approximately nine and a half million characters (including spaces), and consequently was only very rarely copied in its entirety. It is divided by subject into orders and tractates, and generally one, two, or three tractates were copied at a time, although a small number of manuscripts contain more. This historical context means that the textual history of these two works is radically different from that of all other works in the rabbinic corpus and requires a separate discussion.

The puzzles regarding the transmission process of the Babylonian Talmud are much greater than those of other rabbinic compositions. The recensional variation found in some tractates suggests the possibility that at an early stage of the – oral (?) – transmission there was no urtext, or that passages not stemming from the urtext entered into the text at this time. Furthermore, there is no doubt that contamination between the various branches of the textual tradition was rampant throughout its transmission history. Clearly, then, textual analysis of any sort can be of only limited help for the textual critic of the Babylonian Talmud (see Sussman 1990, 92n160; Milikowsky 1988).

7.6.2 A very condensed history of philological practice in rabbinic studies

Relatively few rabbinic works have had the privilege of being the focus of extended textual analysis (of any sort). For many of the classic works of rabbinic literature, there exists no scholarly edition of the entire text, nor even lists of its *variae lectiones*. A comparison with Greek and Latin literature or with the New Testament (see 7.2 and 7.1 respectively) indicates how embarrassing the situation is. Instead of the sanguine possibility of various editors arguing over correct readings – only two foundational rabbinic compositions, the *Mekhilta* on Exodus and the *Sifre* on Numbers, have been edited critically twice. Scholars of rabbinics consider themselves fortunate when manuscript material has been made available, even if the citations are haphazard and the method non-critical.

Some sort of limited critical editing in rabbinics began in the eighteenth century, about a hundred years after the beginnings of the critical editing of classical literature (see 2.1.4). Similarly to the situation with Greek and Latin texts, editors initially combined together in one section at the bottom of the page textual notes and commentary. In most of these semi-critical texts, no attempt was made to delineate the textual history of the work, other than of the most basic, elementary kind.

The first rabbinic text which was edited in what became the standard format of critical editions was Zuckermandel's edition of the *Tosefta* (Zuckermandel 1877–1881). As was common then, often the lemma is omitted; as was common then and now (in classics), only a small fraction of the variants are cited. All other critical editions of rabbinic texts have both an apparatus of variants and either annotations or a commentary. By my count, eighteen critical editions of various compositions in rabbinic literature have been produced from Zuckermandel's edition until today. None of these editions is of the Mishnah, and only one is of a tractate of the Babylonian Talmud. In addition to these critical editions, and to the semi-critical editions mentioned above, a number of orders of the Mishnah and tractates of the Babylonian Talmud have been published in different types of variorum editions.

Within the past decade, the situation has progressed considerably, both with regard to the print publication of critical editions with concomitant textual analysis and with regard to the digital dissemination of manuscript images and collated transcriptions of variant versions of rabbinic compositions.

7.6.3 Editorial methodology

For heuristic purposes, I will schematically (and somewhat simplistically) divide critical editorial methodology into three groups. This scheme is roughly based upon Greetham (1987; see 6.1 above for a typology of editions in general).

One method is that of the best-text edition, as it is referred to by mediaevalists, or of the *codex optimus*, the term often used by classicists. The proponents of this method maintain that the editor should use one manuscript as the base for the entire text of the work, changing its readings only when they are "impossible", that is, clear scribal errors, and not when they are simply "improbable", to quote Vinaver (1939, 369).

Another method of editing texts is grounded in the stemmatic analysis (or genealogical analysis) of the textual witnesses. In this type of analysis, the scholar determines the relationships among the various manuscripts by locating the errors common to two or more manuscripts. After determining which manuscripts join together to form families, that is, derive from a common exemplar, the editor can use this information in order to conclude which variants are attested by more than one independent branch of the tradition, and thereby reconstruct the most original text that the extant documents allow (see 2.2).

Ideally, the establishment of the relationships among the manuscripts allows the editor to evaluate the importance and cogency of the variant readings for each and every passage. In practice, the situation is often more complicated, and textual analysis is insufficient in and of itself to establish the "best" reading. Nonetheless, at the very least, when the relationships among the manuscripts have been clarified, many readings which cannot be disallowed on the basis of the internal criteria of cogency can be firmly and unhesitatingly rejected.

The last method of editing we will mention here is that of radical eclecticism. An editor using this method will decide which is the preferable reading for each and every word in the work. He is deferential neither to the text of any document nor to any systemic analysis; all textual decisions are entirely dependent upon the editor's insight and judgement. This method is the only viable one when stemmatic analysis is not feasible – generally because of heavy contamination between the various branches of the stemmatic tree – and the editor is not willing to use the best-text method.

It is essential to note that all three editions are eclectic editions: any text presented by an editor who does not purport to give his readership an exact transcription of one document and presents a text of the work including at least one deviation from the text of the document serving as his base – such a text must be termed an eclectic text (see 6.1.1). What distinguishes the radical eclectic mode of editing from the other modes is the prior decision of the editor to use only his critical judgment – or possibly, his critical delusions – for the generation of his edition.

For some unfathomable reason, it is the general practice among philologists of rabbinic literature to distinguish between only two types of critical editions, the "diplomatic" and the "eclectic". The first term is used to denote the product of what was called above the best-text method of editing, and the second for every other type of critical edition. This nomenclature is faulty, and should not be used. As already noted, the meaning of the term "diplomatic edition" among textual scholars is precise and unambiguous. It can be used only when the editor means to present the text of a document, and not that of a work; such an editor makes no corrections to the text of the document, or, at most, if a correction is made, both the incorrect reading and the correct reading are included in the base text.

7.6.4 The editorial methodology used in editions of rabbinic literature

The three types of critical editions described above are ideal types, but nonetheless serve well to delineate the options available to the prospective editor. With regard to rabbinic literature, the prevalent mode has been that of best-text editing; indeed, many editors pride themselves on how little they have changed the manuscript upon which they based their text, though of course not every editor uses the same criteria to decide which readings of the base manuscript are corrected (see Lieberman 1955–1988, 2:5–6).

In this manner, Julius Theodor and Chanoch Albeck (1965) edited *Bereshit Rabba*, H. Saul Horovitz (1966) edited the *Sifre* on Numbers, Horovitz and Israel Abraham Rabin (1960) edited *Mekhilta d'Rabbi Yishmael*, Saul Lieberman (1955–1988) edited the *Tosefta*, Mordecai Margulies (1972) edited *Vayyiqra Rabba*, Bernard Mandelbaum (1962) edited *Pesiqta de-Rav Kahana*, Avigdor Shinan (1984) edited *Shemot Rabba I*, and Menachem I. Kahana (2011–2015) edited the *Sifre* on Numbers, to name just some examples.

The radical eclectic method was used by Henry Malter (1930) in his edition of the *Ta'anit* tractate of the Babylonian Talmud and by Jacob Lauterbach (1933–1935) in his edition of *Mekhilta d'Rabbi Yishmael*. In addition, in those chapters of *Vayyiqra Rabba* absent from London, British Library, Add. 27169 – the base manuscript for the greater part of the text – Mordecai Margulies leaned towards this method.

7.6.5 Louis Finkelstein's edition of *Sifre Devarim* – and its consequences

It is often thought that Louis Finkelstein used a radical eclectic mode of editing to produce his edition of *Sifre Devarim* (1939, 1969). This is not the case. Prior to the appearance of this edition, Finkelstein had published a stemmatic analysis of the textual tradition of *Sifre Devarim* (1931–1932), and it was on the basis of that analysis that he made many decisions in his presentation of the text. It should be noted that Finkelstein's edition originally appeared in 1939, approximately a month after the outbreak of World War II. Because of the need to publish in a hurry, Finkelstein could not finish his introduction, in which he would have outlined his method, and only included a page-long preface (see the prefaces to the first and second editions, both in Finkelstein 1969, n.p.).

In fact, Finkelstein's edition was the only edition of a rabbinic composition whose editor used the principles of stemmatic analysis in the presentation of the text until the second decade of the twenty-first century. The reasons for this are several and varied. One contributing factor is the fact that, in the Germany of the late nineteenth and early twentieth centuries – the time when many of the scholars who established the field of rabbinic philology received their training in German universities – a very conservative tendency prevailed in many of the centres of classical scholarship (see Kenney 1974, 126–127; Tarrant 1989, 122). Another point to consider is that, prior to World War II, the two centres of rabbinic philology were Germany and Palestine, while Finkelstein, who was born, trained, and taught in the United States, was an outlier.

Most important, however, were the two reviews of Finkelstein's edition (which appeared as separate fascicles prior to its final publication in 1939) written by Jacob Nahum Epstein (1936–1937) and Saul Lieberman (1937–1938), the two doyens of rabbinic philology in the middle years of the twentieth century. Both were negative.

The crucial point here is that any editor who decides not to use the best-text mode of editing – it is immediately obvious that this mode demands of the editor the least amount of textual acumen – takes upon himself a tremendous responsibility, and offers up his acumen and his critical judgement to the acclamation or, alternatively, the disparagement of all. It was this critical judgement of Finkelstein which was put to the test and found lacking, and that is why his edition was criticised extensively by Jacob Epstein, and, somewhat more moderately, by Saul Lieberman in their reviews.

Epstein opposed in principle the introduction of variants from other witnesses into the text without clear indication of this fact (unless the manuscript used as the base is clearly corrupt). This is especially ill-advised with Tannaitic literature, which had a long history in both oral and written form, and whose variants may be based upon ancient traditions. He continues with a long list of passages where Finkelstein's emendations of the text are unjustified. Epstein explicitly states in his review that Finkelstein's eclectic editorial method "is intrinsically dubious" (1936–1937, 375).

These comments by Epstein should be compared to what he published eight years earlier in a programmatic article on desiderata in the field of Talmudic studies: "We are lacking a scientific edition of the *Mishnah*, critical and precise, an edition which adjudicates and determines readings [...] by means of the use of manuscript versions" (Epstein 1925, 5).

Lieberman, though less critical of Finkelstein, also objects to his proclivity towards precipitate changes in his text. His objections are similar to those of Epstein, but he elaborates on the theoretical basis for his opposition. He quotes a sentence from his review of a different rabbinic text: "It is necessary to distinguish between a scribal error which has been introduced into a group of manuscripts and a tradition (either correct or incorrect) which was accepted in specific lands" (Lieberman 1937–1938, 324). Lieberman asserts that the editor should not mix together readings of different manuscripts of the same work, for at times we are dealing not with scribal errors but with scribal corrections, corrections which were made consciously and on purpose in accordance with the views prevalent in the country of the scribe. He expresses no opposition to the theoretical applicability of stemmatic theory to rabbinic texts, only to the practical application of that theory to the editing of the texts, that is, presenting to the reader a heavily eclectic text.

In his review of Lauterbach's edition of the *Mekhilta*, Lieberman acclaims Finkelstein's (1934–1935) stemmatic analysis of the manuscripts of the *Mekhilta* and says that such analysis is necessary for a "correct evaluation of the Mekhilta text" (Lieberman 1935–1936, 57). See also what Lieberman wrote about eclectic editions in his edition of the *Tosefta* (1955–1988, 1:12).

7.6.6 Beyond the consequences of Finkelstein's edition

The pronouncements of Epstein and Lieberman were considered definitive, and, as a consequence, no editions of rabbinic texts subsequent to the 1930s used any but the best-text method of editing – until 2013, when I published a critical edition of the rabbinic chronography *Seder Olam* (Milikowsky 2013). In this edition, a base textual witness was used for each section of the text, but it was changed hundreds of times during the course of the edition, not only when the base witness had what we, following Vinaver, earlier called "impossible" readings, but also whenever the stemmatic analysis indicated that the reading of the base witness was secondary (see fig. 7.6-1).

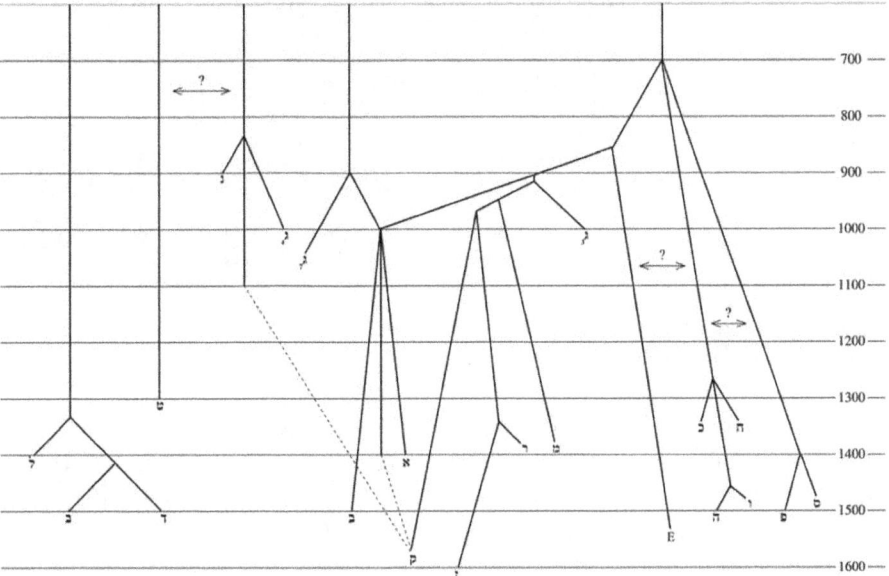

Fig. 7.6-1: Stemma of *Seder Olam* from Milikowsky (2013, 1:189). All the lines stem from one original; it was simply too difficult graphically to connect all the lines to one point at the top of the stemma.

Fig. 7.6-2: *Vayyiqra Rabba* fragment, with extensive interlinear emendations, ninth–tenth-century hand. Source: Oxford, Bodleian Library, heb. c.18,17.

Subsequently, two of my colleagues at Bar Ilan University, Joseph Tabory and Arnon Atzmon, critically edited *Midrash Esther Rabbah* (Tabory and Atzmon 2014), also extensively following stemmatic principles. In addition, my ongoing research on the textual history of the early midrashic text *Vayyiqra Rabba* (see fig. 7.6-2) very much focuses upon stemmatic analysis to delineate the lines of filiation among the various textual witnesses.

Further reading

From the above discussion, we can note that two related but distinct critical questions face the textual scholar of rabbinic literature. (*i*) Is it valid and proper to speak of an urtext with regard to the various compositions in the rabbinic corpus? (*ii*) What editorial methodology should be used to edit these compositions? The first question was debated in print by Schäfer (1986) and Milikowsky (1988), a debate revisited some twenty years later (Milikowsky and Schäfer 2010). Schäfer's conceptualisations form the theoretical underpinning of the work produced by his student Hans-Jürgen Becker (1999), which should be read with the review-essay by Milikowsky (2002). See also the somewhat similar perspective of Beit-Arié (2000), and Barth (1999). For the second question, there is a dearth of literature (in any language); most textual scholars in rabbinics barely touch upon the crucial methodological questions involved in producing a critical edition. See the relevant comments in Milikowsky (1996, 1999, 2006).

7.7 Chinese
Christopher Nugent

China has a continuous textual history that stretches back at least three thousand years; concerns with textual change over the course of both oral and written transmission appear in the early stages of that history. Confucius (551–479 BC) himself is portrayed in the *Analects* as lamenting lax editorial standards of his day, saying "I still recall when scribes would leave blanks in texts [...] today this is no more" (*Analects* 15.26). The dominant traditional interpretation of this line is that the Master believed scribes should not guess at the correct version of a missing or seemingly incorrect character when transcribing a text, but instead leave a blank. Numerous other texts from a few centuries later include examples of one character transforming into a completely different one over the course of multiple transcriptions, often with humorous results. Throughout this long history, scholars, and even ordinary readers, have developed a range of strategies for dealing with textual change that both overlap with and substantially diverge from those developed in Europe and elsewhere. Debates over textual criticism were often tied to contemporaneous political debates, in part because political arguments were typically grounded in specific readings of texts, classical texts in particular, but also because the scholars who undertook textual criticism as a specific pursuit were often powerful political actors themselves.

7.7.1 Textual criticism in China

The contemporary scholar William Boltz (1995, 394) has argued that, although Chinese textual critics have almost always sought to restore texts to some earlier state that they felt to be closer to the authors' original intentions, they typically saw textual change over time as an "inherent aspect of the life of the text itself", rather than a fundamental injury or defilement visited upon the text. Correcting a text was thus, in many contexts and periods, simply one of the tasks any serious reader would undertake as part of the full act of reading and understanding it. Boltz speculates that this attitude may have grown out of the nature of textual variation in the primarily logographic script used to write in China. Because all graphic variants are also potential lexical variants, they were not necessarily seen as errors; they were instead alternatives that the conscientious reader would always have to compare and judge for himself (Boltz 1995, 400).

There are a number of terms that have considerable overlap with the English "textual criticism" (though there are no traditional words for "stemmatology"). The earliest is *choujiao* 讎校 (or *jiaochou* 校讎), which was traditionally interpreted as including two kinds of collation: analysing a text based on internal cohesion and consistency, and comparing a text with one or more other versions (Cherniack 1994, 82). The earliest explanation of this term dates back to Liu Xiang 劉向 (79–8 BC), to whom a variety of later texts attribute the statement: "When one person reads a text and comparing what is above and below finds an error, this is called *jiao*. When one person holds a text and another person reads it as enemies facing each other, this is called *chou*." Beginning in the Northern and Southern dynasties period (420–589), the term *jiaokan* 校勘 began to be used for such scholarship and continues to be used as a general term up to the present. As Susan Cherniack notes, *jiaokan* (or the contemporary near-synonym *jiaokan xue* 校勘學) is typically taken to include not only collation, correction, and analysis of texts, but also *banben xue* 版本學 (the study of the physical characteristics and history of editions) and *mulu xue* 目錄學 (the study of bibliographical catalogues and classifications; Cherniack 1994, 82). The first full monograph on collation dates to the twelfth century AD. As described by modern scholars beginning with Chen Yuan (1880–1971), traditional collation practices with both single and multiple exemplars took four basic forms: (*i*) comparison of multiple editions to note differences, (*ii*) examining a single text to identify internal discrepancies, (*iii*) comparing a text with other sources on similar subjects, and (*iv*) using one's own judgment to correct perceived textual problems in a single witness (summed up in Cherniack 1994, 85; see also Cheng and Xu 1998).

Versions of all of these practices have been in use for over two thousand years in China. Covering such a vast span of time and texts in a brief account is near-impossible, and this contribution can only identify and explicate a few key issues and important stages in the evolution of Chinese textual criticism. After a brief account of material matters, I will discuss three historical periods in which crucial changes in textual practices took place.

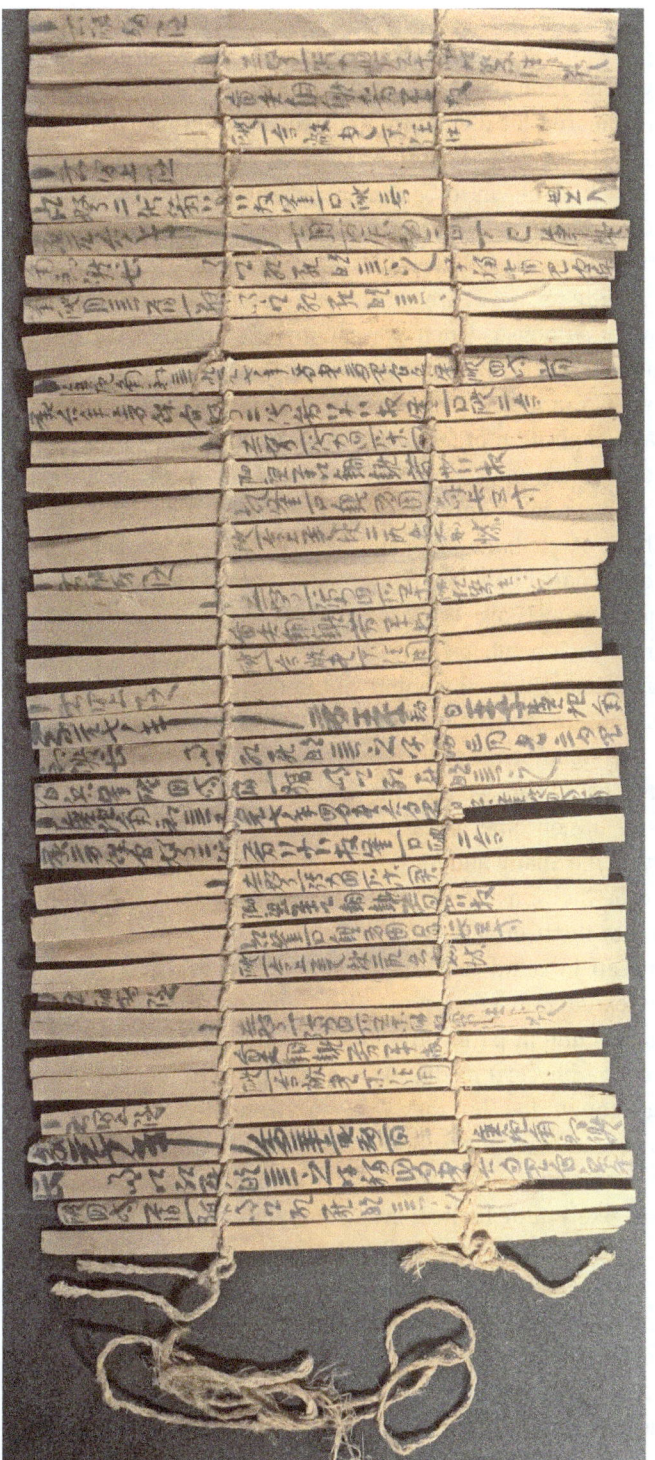

Fig. 7.7-1: Han-period military text written on bamboo slips. Held at Academia Sinica, Taiwan.
Source: wikimedia, commons.wikimedia.org/wiki/File:Military_documents_on_bamboo_slips_scroll_in_Han_Dynasty_09.jpg.

7.7.2 Textual media

The earliest surviving writing from China is found inscribed on cattle scapula and tortoise plastrons used primarily for divinatory practices by the royal court of the Shang 商 dynasty (ca. 1300–1046 BC). The written texts on these objects (known in English as oracle bones), which began to be discovered and recognised as written text only at the end of the nineteenth century, do not appear to have been transmitted or to have entered the historical textual record, and thus do not directly concern us here. The earliest surviving texts that are considered part of the literary tradition are found on vessels and other objects (such as weapons) cast in bronze during the Western Zhou 周 period (ca. 1045–771 BC). Many of these texts did enter the tradition and were later circulated in a range of formats. Bronzes were ritualistic objects, not a medium for the initial composition of texts or for more quotidian writing, which would have been done on more perishable surfaces, such as bamboo. Although direct archaeological evidence dates only to the end of the Warring States period 战国时代 (481–221 BC), both oracle-bone texts and bronzes include a word that appears to refer to strips of prepared bamboo, bound together by a string (most likely of either leather or hemp): *ce* 冊 (Boltz 1999, 107–108). Finds from Warring-States-period tombs indicate that such bamboo strips (and, less frequently, strips of other kinds of wood) were the primary textual medium of the time, one that many argue is the source of China's traditional vertical textual format. Silk was used for writing in some contexts, but the significant expense it entailed limited such use. Finds from the Warring States have also yielded the earliest examples of hair-tipped brushes, though traces of ink on other objects give indications that brushes were used for writing as early as the Shang and for precursors of writing centuries earlier. They would continue to be the primary writing tool, with ink based on lampblack or pine soot, until well into the twentieth century.

It is important to keep in mind that memorisation and oral recitation also played a primary role in textual transmission as late as the Western Han 漢 (206 BC–8 AD), if not later. This was due in part to traditional modes of instruction and in part to the limitations of the physical media. Bamboo strips were inexpensive and relatively easy to prepare for writing, but they were bulky and difficult to transport in large quantities. It is thus unlikely that full written versions of longer works regularly circulated as full texts as opposed to excerpts and individual chapters. Ownership of physical texts was likely quite limited, even among the elite. Moreover, excavated texts from the pre-Han period in particular demonstrate substantial graphic variation while often maintaining a high degree of lexical stability. This is a strong indication of memorisation and oral transmission: works were set to memory as sounds, but a range of different graphs could still be used to represent those sounds in writing (Kern 2002, 2010). Standardisation of the writing system would be a later development (see further discussion of these particular aspects of the written script below).

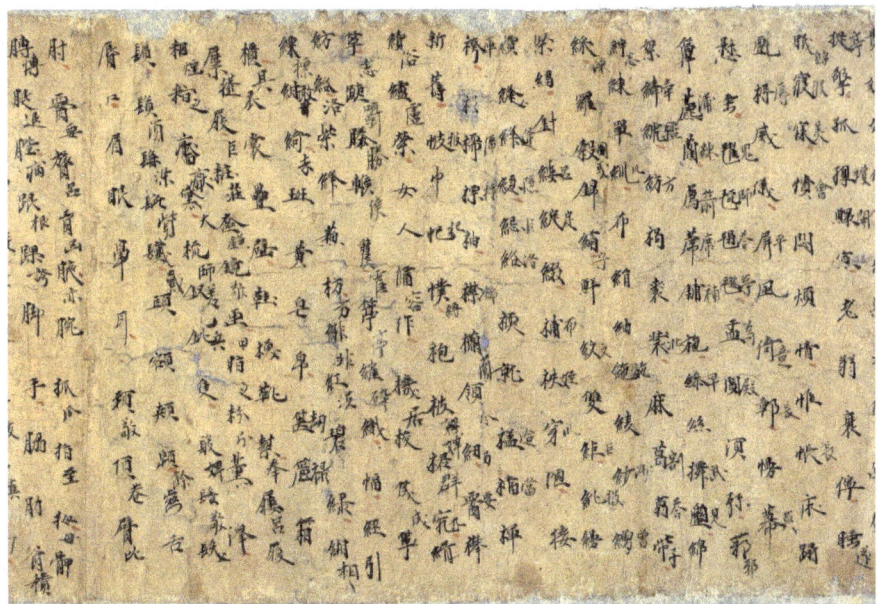

Fig. 7.7-2: Tenth-century AD paper manuscript from Dunhuang, China, containing the vocabulary primer *Kaimeng yaoxun* 开蒙要训 [Important Instructions for Beginners]. Source: Gallica, Bibliothèque nationale de France, gallica.bnf.fr/ark:/12148/btv1b8302088s/f2.image.

The dominant textual media for most of Chinese history has been paper, a material for which the earliest examples, excavated from tombs, date back to the early years of the second century BC (Tsien 2004, 146–147). These examples included limited writing, such as the name of the medicine the paper was presumably wrapped around, and even a drawn map, though there are no indications that paper was used for more extensive writing at that point. Refinements in quality resulted in a paper more suitable for writing by the second century AD, and by a century later it was likely the most common textual medium, though bamboo continued to be used, especially in more isolated regions. The development of xylographic printing began in the Tang 唐 dynasty (618–907), and was used by both the state and religious organisations by the end of that period. By the end of the eleventh century, there was a flourishing printing industry that would grow substantially in later centuries.

The widespread use of paper made textual production and reproduction more inexpensive than it had ever been. An educated person in the Tang would likely have owned hundreds of scrolls (the primary format of written texts before printing). Printing made large-scale reproduction much more efficient, with the result that the amount of written material and its accessibility increased rapidly and dramatically. At the same time, manuscripts continued to be used in a range of contexts. At one end of the economic spectrum, a fine manuscript would continue to be valued more than a fine printing for many centuries. At the other, copying out

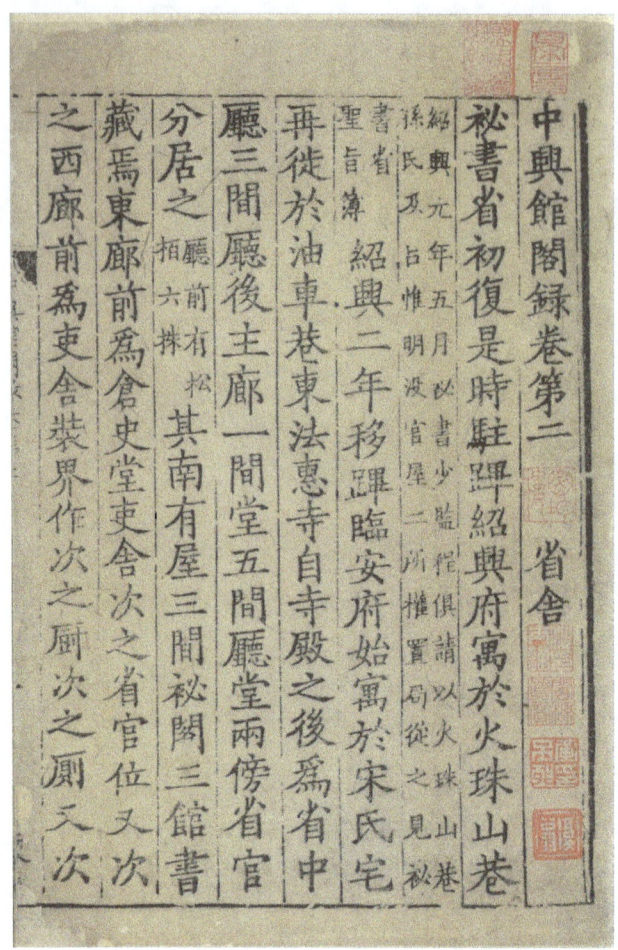

Fig. 7.7-3: Thirteenth-century AD paper woodblock print of an account of the Song dynasty imperial library. Held at the National Central Library, Taiwan. Source: wikimedia, commons.wikimedia.org/wiki/File:Records_of_the_Southern_Song_Imperial_Library_WDL7099.jpg.

books by hand was still often cheaper than buying a printed edition (and was also seen as an effective way to learn their contents). This textual abundance, however, did not fully eclipse the lively oral and memory-based aspects of literary culture. Poetry, in particular, remained an intensely oral endeavour, even though its products were frequently set down in writing. Texts would often be copied out from memory, and even printed texts would be recited and memorised (though by the thirteenth century, important thinkers had begun to lament that printing had resulted in a more superficial relationship with classical texts, as the wide accessibility of written material made memorisation a choice rather than a necessity; Gardner 1990, 139).

While all these media have contributed to textual survival, they have done so in different ways. Widespread memorisation and recitation of certain texts allowed them to survive times of large-scale social disruption, whether from the violence of war or from natural disasters, and the destruction of such material textual depositories as imperial libraries or private collections that inevitably resulted. Many texts inscribed on bronze vessels survived unchanged over centuries or even millennia, though they most often did so in the solitude of the tomb, unseen by human eyes. Paper has always been a fragile medium, susceptible to fire, water, insects, and simple neglect. Yet because it is light and inexpensive to produce, it allowed rapid and wide-ranging textual transmission on an unprecedented scale, with the constant textual alteration that always accompanied it. Printing meant that multiple copies of written works were far easier to produce and obtain, but rapid (and often careless) production massively increased textual instability.

7.7.3 Textual collation and creation in the Han

The first key period in the history of textual criticism is the later years of the Western Han, especially in the last part of the first century BC. The Han faced a chaotic textual inheritance: natural disasters and the widespread warfare that accompanied the fall of the Qin government in 221 resulted in massive textual loss and dispersal, as government archives were burned and personal libraries, such as there were, faced similarly dire fates. Recent scholarship has suggested that the infamous Qin bibliocaust, in which the First Emperor is said to have demanded the confiscation and burning of all books (and the scholars who taught them) that did not accord with his favoured political philosophy, is likely more an invention of Han-period historians anxious to establish the relative virtue of their own dynasty in comparison to their predecessor than an accurate account of events; yet there is no question that the years of chaos took their toll on the written word.

In 26 BC, Emperor Cheng 成帝 (r. 32–7 BC) assigned his Palace Superintendent, Liu Xiang, the task of organising and categorising the chaotic mass of bamboo scrolls (and, no doubt, scattered unbound strips) contained in the imperial library. He was, additionally, to fill any important gaps that he perceived in the collection by gathering texts, whether in written or oral form, wherever he could find them. Liu Xiang and his staff transformed these scattered materials into separate texts for which, in each case, they eventually provided a detailed account of the content, information about the author, descriptions of the sources, an account of the collation process, and a general discussion of the text. Liu Xiang himself combined and edited these accounts into a catalogue entitled *Divisional Records* (*Bielu* 別錄). After his death, his son, Liu Xin 劉歆 (d. 23 AD), continued the father's work and produced a further summarised version known as the *Seven Summaries* (*Qilüe* 七略).

The Lius and their staff thus undertook China's first great bibliographical project, and in fulfilling their charge they went far beyond simple collection, organisation, and description. It was, in fact, a full-scale transformation of the textual inheritance into something that, while carefully organised, in many ways bore little resemblance to the textual environment that preceded it. This transformation operated on multiple levels. In terms of script, Liu and his colleagues transcribed all of the materials, which had previously been in a diverse set of regional and archaic scripts, into the more standardised script then current at the Han court. In the process of transcription, they also radically reorganised their material, bringing together textual portions that may have originally circulated separately and changing the structure and order even of texts that were received in a seemingly more coherent form. They heavily redacted works as they organised them, excising often substantial amounts of text that they judged to be redundant. In some cases, as much as 90 % of the original material was discarded in the name of bringing organisation and coherence to a text, with smaller-scale redactions being common (Nylan 2014).

This process was intended to turn disparate materials into organised "books"; yet, as a number of scholars have recently argued, when we have excavated near-counterparts to the received works that passed through Liu's process, the received text often reads more awkwardly and seems more disjointed than its excavated counterpart (Kern 2010; Richter 2013; D. Meyer 2012). As Martin Kern has written, "Liu Xiang's editorial choices were meaningful and appropriate to the imperial environment of official learning but not necessarily the best reconstructions of ancient texts that originally functioned in a very different cultural context" (Kern 2010, 63). That "different cultural context" was a more intensely oral one, in which written texts would typically be used in conjunction with the oral instruction and argumentation that played an important part in conveying the texts' meanings (D. Meyer 2012). Such texts would often include structures that emphasised mnemonic efficiencies no longer deemed necessary or appropriate when the texts were transcribed in an archival context.

In short, the imperial bibliographical project created standardised versions of texts that differed sufficiently from their precursor material to justify considering them to be new works. They were given new organisational structures and scripts that distanced them from their original context. They were given authors where previously they had none. Liu Xiang and his staff were clearly engaged in an early form of textual criticism (and indeed, the four main categories described in the introduction above can likely be traced back to them), but their work also often obscured the textual past as it created the texts that would be the focus of centuries of scholars who followed.

7.7.4 Transitions to print

Some thousand years after the Lius completed their work for the Han imperial library, textual criticism in China entered a new stage with the increasingly widespread use of xylographic printing and the gradual shift from a manuscript culture to one in which print played a more dominant role. Needless to say, the millennium between these periods saw many important changes and innovations as well, from the spread of paper as the primary writing medium to new scholarly work on classical texts, but the impact of printing stands alone.

There are striking similarities here with the late Western Han. As in that earlier period, readers and bibliographers in the early Song 宋 (960–1279) faced a fragmented and confused textual situation due to the chaos of rebellions and war that brought about and followed the end of the preceding dynasty. Paper was, if anything, more fragile than bamboo, and the large-scale destruction of the holdings of imperial, private, and religious interests took a massive toll. Stephen Owen uses the evocative term "flotsam and jetsam" to describe what survived, noting that it refers, appropriately, to the remains of a shipwreck (Owen 2007, 296; see also Barenghi 2014). Like Emperor Cheng, the first Song emperors sought to restore the imperial collection from those remains, building from a limited base of 12,000 scrolls in the early years of the dynasty to reach over 46,000 just few years later; these additions came from a range of sources, including surviving collections of provincial and regional libraries and private collections (Dudbridge 2000, 2).

Perhaps the most important aspect of bibliography and textual criticism in the Song was the extent to which it was carried out not only by the government but by private individuals as well. The larger project of textual criticism had become far more diffuse than it was in the Han. Different actors had overlapping but often divergent goals for the work they did. The government sought to create model texts, especially of the classics, that could serve as the basis of everything from the exam system to imperial proclamations. As Cherniack argues, "the [governmental] editor's job was to present the single correct text, selected from a set of mistaken alternatives. To record and weigh the excluded alternatives in the form of scholarly annotations was irrelevant and even contrary to this purpose" (1994, 72).

Private scholars, on the other hand, would often emphasise the differing alternatives presented by multiple exemplars. This would allow them to put their own scholarly process on display and thus demonstrate their erudition in order to establish their authority (Cherniack 1994, 72). Again, even as central governments sought to establish model texts, individual readers had always seen correction and collation as one of the basic duties of any good reader. It was never the sole purview of specialists, and would not be until well into the modern period. Of course, scholars often lamented that those of lesser abilities ruined texts in the process because of their lack of sufficient learning, but they accepted that readers would take a critical attitude towards texts.

Printing was clearly not the sole cause of widespread awareness of textual variability, but it was an important one. The likelihood that an individual reader would encounter multiple editions of the same text increased dramatically with the spread of print, and many of the most famous writers in the Song describe collating different editions of texts for both edification and entertainment. Indeed, though printing is often described as having a stabilising effect on texts by "fixing" them, Song readers were well aware that this was not necessarily the case. Printing instead seemed to cause a massive proliferation of textual variation that required constant correction and collation to manage.

In addition to being influenced by increasing awareness of textual variation due to printing, textual criticism in the Song was connected to a scholarly orientation that encouraged a sceptical attitude towards large portions of the literary inheritance, including the texts of the classics. In a very broad sense, this grew out of philosophical notions that emphasised the ability of an individual to personally grasp the underlying patterns and order of all things in the universe, from the natural world to the moral and textual one. Song work on texts thus often focused not on hard textual, linguistic, and historical evidence, but rather on the individual reader's own grasp of fundamental truths that allowed him to understand what any given text *should* say and correct it to bring it in line with that deeper meaning if it appeared to have diverged from it. This was still an act of restoration, but it was a deeply subjective one (albeit undergirded by the belief that all sufficiently cultivated subjectivities will, as they are grounded in objective orders, come to the same conclusions), and would later come under intense criticism for this very quality.

Because of their long-standing cultural and institutional importance, the texts of the classics remained relatively stable through the transition to print during the Song. They were never at risk of falling out of circulation during the chaos at the end of the Tang. The same cannot be said of the vast quantities of literature produced during that latter period. Tang poetry, widely regarded as a high point of literary production in China, comes to us only through the very selective filter of what survived into the Song and what Song printers chose to print. As Stephen Owen and others have demonstrated, different collections that circulated during the Tang provide vastly different impressions of the output of individual poets. Only a very small subset of those collections made it into the Song and were reproduced in print, meaning that our understanding of any given poet is likely based on only a small portion of his works. The judgements of his contemporaries might have been quite different, being based on different material. Song collectors and editors shaped our own understanding of Tang literature in ways we are only beginning to fully understand (Owen 2007).

7.7.5 Evidence-based textual criticism in the Qing and later

Scholars in the Qing period 清 (1644–1911) shared their Song predecessors' sceptical orientation towards the received textual tradition. However, they believed that a significant portion of the problems with received texts could be traced to the sloppy emendations introduced by those very Song scholars and readers on the basis of their philosophical ideas. Qing textual critics famously turned away from philosophy as the foundation for their work, grounding it instead on rigorous evidence-based philology. The new orientation of textual scholarship became broadly labelled with the term *kaozheng* 考證 (evidential research). The term itself had been used in the later part of the Song period, but it gained new prominence and importance in the Qing as a way to describe a focus on verifiable evidence rather than philosophical speculation. The factors that led to this shift in orientation were many, ranging from the increasing interest in book collecting by literati in the preceding Ming 明 period (1368–1644) to new exposure to scientific ideas from the West (Elman 1985, 143).

Kaozheng scholarship was characterised by a focus on phonology and palaeography as the most effective ways to restore the texts of the classics to what they must have been in the time of their initial creation. Although their critiques of earlier scholarship were multifaceted, *kaozheng* scholars took particular issue with the basis of Song scholars' methodology and their lack of understanding of historical phonological shifts. Song-period textual criticism, they argued, was rarely based on observable evidence but instead grew out of much vaguer philosophical notions. Moreover, because these philosophical ideas had been heavily influenced by Buddhism and Daoism, the textual alterations based on them inevitably pulled texts away from their proper Confucian origins.

In terms of phonological issues, earlier readers had long observed that classical texts rhymed (or failed to rhyme) in unexpected ways. Their solution was sometimes to alter the texts so as to bring them in line with their expectations (Elman 1985, 213). Due to their meticulous research into phonology and etymology, *kaozheng*-based textual critics understood that these unexpected rhyming schemes were often the result of changes in pronunciation of the characters over the centuries since the classics were composed, rather than later mistakes that had crept into the texts. The later emendations to "force" the rhyme were thus themselves errors that the Qing textual critic would have to correct in order to return the texts to their original state.

Contemporary textual criticism as conducted in both China and elsewhere (especially Japan, Korea, Europe, and the United States) is diverse, but much of it ultimately grows out of earlier practices, especially the methodological advances made by *kaozheng* scholars. The vast majority of pre-Song-period works come to us through the received tradition consisting of printed texts. Collation of those texts, especially as practised by scholars producing critical editions for major academic presses in China, typically follows some combination of the long-standing methods described in the introductory section above, with particular emphasis on comparing multiple editions. In many cases, the earliest exemplar will be a Song imprint, but there are also numerous examples where our earliest exemplar dates from much later.

Recent decades have seen exciting new scholarship on excavated texts as the pace of archaeological discoveries in China has increased. These fall into two major groups: manuscripts on paper dating to approximately 400–1000 AD discovered in and around the oasis town of Dunhuang in Gansu province at the end of the nineteenth century; and documents on bamboo, silk, wood, and other materials dating to the Han and earlier that have been unearthed more recently. These very different sets of documents have been the subject of a range of scholarly approaches. The Dunhuang manuscripts consist primarily of previously known Buddhist works, although other types of writings found there are strikingly diverse in terms of genre, language, and degree of representation in the received tradition. When creating a critical text of works with multiple exemplars from Dunhuang but not part of the received tradition, scholars in China will often use a version of the Bédier "best-text" method, though they typically make more changes to their "best text" than one would expect. The situation with Han and pre-Han excavated texts is more complex. Because of the massive bibliographical project undertaken in the Han described above, even excavated texts that appear to have counterparts transmitted by copying differ from those later collations dramatically. Indeed, it is these discoveries that have revealed the extent of the impact of Liu Xiang's work. Some scholars in the West, such as Boltz (1995), have utilised a Lachmannian stemmatological approach to create an assumed semblance of an "original" text. Others, such as Kern (2002), have criticised such an approach, arguing that lengthy periods of oral and mixed oral/written transmission make attempts to create a true "original" misguided.

Regardless of the particular approach, recent theoretical and practical work on mediaeval European manuscript culture has been particularly influential for scholars working in the West (Boltz, Tian, Kern, Owen, Nugent, Richter, Meyer). The combination of traditional Chinese approaches and newer theoretical ideas coming from scholars working on European traditions looks to be a fruitful one, and many new avenues of scholarly exchange are sure to open up in coming years.

Further reading

Readers interested in exploring textual issues in the early and pre-imperial period would gain much from Kern (2002). For a fuller treatment, Richter (2013) is excellent as well. For the Song period, Lianbin Dai (2016) looks closely at the important case of Zhu Xi. For the Qing period, Sela's new work (2018) is recommended. For those who can read Chinese, see Hu (1931), Wang (1972), and Guan (2013).

7.8 Early modern printed texts
Iolanda Ventura

This section deals with examples of methodologies used when editing Renaissance printed works from the nineteenth to the twenty-first centuries (see 1.4 for an assessment of the technical and cultural revolution induced by the introduction of the printing press). These works can be divided into two main categories: works that circulated directly in printed form (and for which no manuscripts survive) and works preserved both as manuscripts and printed copies. Types of modern editions (see 6.1) include facsimile editions (7.8.1), diplomatic or critical editions based on one single printed copy or on several (7.8.2), and critical editions based on both printed books and manuscripts (7.8.3).

7.8.1 New life for old celebrities: The facsimile edition

A facsimile edition is an exact photostatic reproduction of one copy of a printed work. In contrast to a diplomatic edition (see 6.1.3), it does not offer a faithful and accurate transcription of the text but reproduces visually all external features of the text. Several reasons may be advanced to justify the choice of this technique. A first, obvious one is if the length of a work would make the transcription too long to complete in a reasonable amount of time (the possibility of OCRing early printed books, albeit not yet perfectly, will change this situation considerably). A second, no less important reason can be found *ex negativo* in the lack of interest in reproducing a text that is already clear and correct in its printed form (although an image of a text is, of course, less usable than a transcription).

The main contribution offered by the editor consists of an introduction providing readers with basic information about the author, the edited work, and its characteristics, and about the role it played in the history of the literary genres to which it belongs and/or in the history of its contemporary culture. The most important functions performed by facsimile editions are as follows. (*i*) They put works that are necessary for research at the disposal of scholars in a form closer to what could be accessed when those works were created and used. (*ii*) They compensate, although incompletely, for the lack of a critical edition, which may never be published. This is the case, for instance, with Avicenna's *Liber canonis* in the Latin translation made by Gerard of Cremona around 1150, which is still used and quoted, if not with the help of the printed versions scholars can find in a library, then according to the facsimile edition printed in Brussels in 1971 (Avicenna 1527, repr. 1971). This reprint presents the Latin version as published in a 1527 edition, which had corrections and improvements by one of the most illustrious Renaissance Arabists, Andrea Alpago (on Alpago, see Levi dalla Vida 1960). (*iii*) They allow readers to consult a precious old printed copy displaying relatively sophisticated production techniques. This is the case, for example, with Hartmann Schedel's *Chronik*. This universal chronicle, authored by the famous Nuremberg physician, humanist, and book collector Hartmann Schedel (1440–1514), was published in 1493 by Anton Koberger both in Latin and German. It was accompanied by a lavish corpus of illustrations consisting of some 1,800 coloured xylographs, which makes the work extremely valuable for experts both in the history of humanist historiography and of book illustration. The work was published as a facsimile in 2001 (Schedel 2001), in a version that reproduces the work and the illustrations exactly and can therefore be used as a substitute for the precious original.

Digital facsimile editions have now enhanced the accessibility of these early printed books. They are made available either in the framework of digitisation programmes for both manuscripts and early printed works run by single libraries, such as the Bayerische Staatsbibliothek, the Biblioteca Apostolica Vaticana, the Bibliothèque nationale de France, or the British Library, or in the framework of research projects that combine the study of a work or a group of works with the availability of digital editions on the Web. Digital reproductions offer several advantages compared to non-digital facsimile editions: (*i*) several printed copies of the same work can be displayed at the same time, allowing a comparison of form and content; (*ii*) digital facsimiles are searchable via library catalogues or search engines; (*iii*) most of them are accessible for free, whereas non-digital facsimiles are very expensive; and (*iv*) further material and tools for accessing, analysing, and understanding the work can be added. Among numerous projects, we can mention the website *Welt und Wissen auf der Bühne: Theatrum-Literatur der Frühen Neuzeit* (theatra.de), which allows the reader to access and download for free some two hundred works that use the metaphor of the theatre or of the garden as a model to represent encyclopedic knowledge, and to study them with the help of a large body of literature (albeit not updated since 2012).

7.8.2 Old wine in new barrels: Modern editions of Renaissance printed works

Renaissance works preserved only in print may differ greatly with respect to their connection to the author's original, to the number of editions, and, last but not least, to the versions of the text that were published. If, to name but one example, Johann Heinrich Alsted's *Encyclopaedia in septem tomos divisa* was printed only once in 1630 (Alsted 1989–1990), other works were printed several times, sometimes after being revised by their authors. Erasmus of Rotterdam's *Adagia*, for example, was printed thirteen times between 1508 (*editio princeps*, Venice: Aldus Manutius) and 1536 (Basle edition, printed by Hieronymus Frobenius). If, in the case of Alsted, a facsimile of the sole existing printed copy may suffice, in the case of Erasmus' bestseller or other relatively unstable texts, other editorial strategies will be called for.

When dealing with several different printed copies of the same early modern work, editors will need to select and collate these different copies, and to prepare an edition according to one or more printed witnesses. There are, again, several possibilities for an edition. (*i*) If based on one single printed copy, the edition corresponds, *mutatis mutandis*, to the monotypic edition of a *codex unicus* (see 6.1.3). (*ii*) The editor may use one printed copy as a base text, using one or more other printed copies to correct and improve the quality of the text, and including their variant readings in a critical apparatus. This corresponds to a best-manuscript edition (see 6.1.3). (*iii*) Several, if not all, printed copies may be collated to produce a critical (reconstructive) edition (see 6.1.2).

All types of editions aim at facilitating the consultation and use of these early modern works by contemporary readers. Consequently, in the editions, a normalised orthography will usually be adopted, abbreviations will be expanded, punctuation (4.3.4) will be adapted, and the text will often be translated into a modern language. Commentaries and apparatuses of sources are valuable features of these editions, allowing the reconstruction of the author's library and of his authorities and references. All these elements represent a decisive step forwards compared to a mere facsimile edition, and provide a more reliable basis for the study of an author's culture. On the other hand, editorial emendations or conjectures (see 6.2.3) are reduced to a minimum and are basically meant to correct obvious misprints. As for the criteria used for the reconstruction of the text, they are relatively different from those used in editing texts preserved in manuscripts, as the paths of transmission of printed copies are obviously very different for several reasons. First of all, the author's work did not undergo a long process of changes and deterioration due to manual copying. His final original text is easier to detect, especially if the *editio princeps* was published during his lifetime or even under his supervision. Even if the author reworked his text and published it again, the collation of the different versions does not have to wrestle with variant readings caused by later, non-authorial innovations, but only with deliberate changes that are valuable for research and have to be documented and highlighted. This generally leads to a reduced number, and less problematic nature, of variant readings, and to a general tendency towards philological work that is descriptive rather than invasive.

Furthermore, if we do not have to struggle with authorial versions, the texts we deal with are more stable and, as soon as they reach a fixed form, obtain an authoritative status. As a consequence of this, if the text does not contain evident misprints, it is not necessary to correct it. It is also normally possible to detect easily the (mostly chronological) connections between the different printed copies, and our evidence is rarely lacunose (only rarely is a complete set of printed copies lost in its entirety), and the *editio princeps* acquires a central position around which later printed copies are clustered.

A practical consequence of this stability of the tradition and centrality of the oldest printed edition is the small size of the critical apparatus. Generally speaking, the apparatus is only used to record variant readings shown by other printed editions, or to record the presence of marginalia. In fact, editions relying on a single printed copy without being a facsimile are quite rare. One important exception is represented by the two modern editions of the 1543 print (published in Basle by Johann Oporinus) of Vesalius' *De humani corporis fabrica*, each with a French translation. The first modern edition was published completely in the print medium

Fig. 7.8-1: Anatomical illustration from Vesalius (1543, 47).

(Bakelants 1961); the second modern edition is still ongoing as an online project (www3.biusante.parisdescartes.fr/vesale/debut.htm). The reason for ignoring the second, updated, print edition of the *Fabrica* published in 1555 by the same Johann Oporinus, and for concentrating on the *editio princeps*, is that the 1543 edition has attracted more attention because of the revolutionary character of its anatomical illustrations (see fig. 7.8-1), even though the 1555 edition is more advanced from an epistemological and scientific perspective.

The majority of the editions based on several printed copies take as a starting point either the entire printed tradition or a relevant part of it, and use them to provide a complete overview of the transmission and a critical text. Usually, the evidence used by editors consists of the *editio princeps* in combination either with a wide chronological range of secondary printed copies, or with those that are chronologically close to the *editio princeps* or relevant for scholarship. Normally, *editiones descriptae*, that is, printed copies that, after a precise examination, turn out to be pure reprints of a previous print, are left aside. As for the establishment of the text, the general rule is to select either the *editio princeps* or the last edition supervised by the author as a base text, and to use the others to correct the first one, or, more often, just to record the differences, possible errors, and innovations featured in them. These general principles can be adapted to the specific situation of the edited text. The following three examples are ordered in an increasing level of complexity.

7.8.2.1 Iacopo Zabarella, *De virtutibus naturalibus*

A first, linear, example of a new edition of a printed work following the principles I have just listed, and taking into account some necessary adaptations, can be found in the recent publication of Iacopo Zabarella's (1532–1589) *De virtutibus naturalibus* (Valverde 2016: for the editorial criteria, see 1:46–48). The editor, Juan Valverde, relied on the two independent copies printed in the same year (1590) in Venice (by Paolo Meietti) and in Cologne (by Giovanni Battista Ciotti). He collated them against the edition which had been the most famous up to that point, namely the one published in Frankfurt by Lazarus Zetzner in 1607, which scholars had long used thanks to a facsimile reprint (see 7.8.1) issued in Frankfurt in 1966; the facsimile should not be discarded, but nevertheless needed to be improved on.

As for the decision to collate the two earliest printed copies, the editor's choice is motivated by the fact that, whereas the Venetian print is closer to the author and its text is more correct, the Cologne edition features some elements that cannot be neglected when we attempt to understand the development of the text in print. The two editions resulted from two independent projects, and their opening sections show significant differences: the Cologne edition includes a dedicatory letter addressed by Zabarella to Pope Sixtus V, whereas the Venetian edition includes a prologue by the author that had already been published in his *De naturalis scientiae constitutione* (Zabarella 1586, printed in Venice by Paolo Meietti). The Cologne edition contains the same mistakes that are found in the text of the Venetian one, but has been emended in a list of errata published as a separate sheet in the Venetian print. All in all, we can conclude that the Venetian and the Cologne prints were based on the same urtext but developed differently. As for the Frankfurt edition, the modern editor notes that it keeps almost all errors that were corrected in the Venetian errata list but at the same time introduces some others.

From the approach followed by the editor, we can conclude that he selected his material by considering two *editiones principes* exhibiting substantial differences but nonetheless possibly relying on the same urtext, and chose to follow the more correct text; and that he did not dismiss an edition that might now be considered superfluous but nonetheless deserves attention because it was – in a well-known facsimile – the basis on which scholarship had relied for several decades.

7.8.2.2 Erasmus, *Opera omnia*

The project of a critical edition of Desiderius Erasmus' (1466–1536) *Opera omnia* began in the early sixties, and has been run by the Dutch Royal Academy for Sciences and Arts since its inception (description on huygens.knaw.nl/erasmi-opera-omnia/?lang=en; see also brill.com/view/serial/ASD). Following Erasmus' choices, as well as the structure of the editions published in Basle between 1538 and 1540 and in Leiden between 1703 and 1706, the arrangement of the edition reproduces the canon (*ordo*) that divides his *œuvre* into nine classes dealing respectively with (*i*) philology and pedagogy; (*ii*) proverbs (the *Adagia*); (*iii*) correspondence; (*iv*) morals and ethics; (*v*) religious instruction; (*vi*) the Greek text, annotations, and Latin translation of the New Testament; (*vii*) paraphrases of the New Testament; (*viii*) editions of or commentaries on patristic authors; and (*ix*) *apologiae*. According to the guidelines included in the general introduction in Erasmus (1969), the modern edition is to furnish a critical text based on prints and taking into account, whenever available, manuscripts. However, pre-eminence will be given, still according to the guidelines, to "the first edition authorized by Erasmus [which] will be the basis for the establishment of the text" (xviii); variant readings attested in "authoritative" editions will be recorded, whereas those derived from "reprints published without Erasmus' knowledge" will be left out (xix–xx). Each print is to determine the orthography chosen for the edition, thus explaining the eventual inconsistencies. All in all, the general plan acknowledges Erasmus' authority and control over the editions he could supervise. On the other hand, this plan does not intend to reduce the editorial work to the choice of one, fixed, stable edition for all works, nor to focus on the one print that constitutes the basis for the edition of each work. Rather, the goal of the editorial choices is to reconstruct in the edition the path followed by the writings before reaching a definitive printed form, and to show changes and updates made by Erasmus while reworking them. This concept of an e v o l u t i v e e d i t i o n, which places manuscripts and editions in a flow reflecting both Erasmus' activity and the circulation of the texts before and after the appearance of the authorised versions, leads to some important consequences. (*i*) In principle, even when the Basle *editio princeps* of the *Opera omnia* plays an important role, the stages of development that preceded it have to be taken into account, if not in the edited text, then at least in the introduction to the work. (*ii*) The same goes for each authorised version selected as the basis for the edition, which implies that, although it remains the basis, earlier stages of the work cannot be neglected. (*iii*) If an earlier version is preserved, entirely or in part, that clearly differs from the one represented in the printed editions, it is included in the edition, albeit in a separate place. For example, the first redaction of the *Antibarbarorum liber* comprises the "original version" written by Erasmus and witnessed only in a manuscript preserved in Gouda. (*iv*) Later versions are recorded insofar as they still belong to Erasmus' activity. The analysis of editions that do not belong to the horizon of Erasmus' life and activity, as well as contaminations between "authentic" and non-authentic prints are outside the scope of the edition. (*v*) According to these principles, each editor establishes, after a careful analysis of the circumstances of the redaction and the phases and main features of circulation, his own array of printed versions and, if still available and relevant, manuscripts. This array constitutes the basis of the edition in terms of selected text and sources of variant readings; it, and the stages of the history of the text, are to be described in the introduction.

A concrete example is the edition of the well-known *Encomium moriae* (Erasmus 1979), a work whose history stretches between 1511, the probable date of the first (unauthorised) edition, and 1532, the date of publication of the final version in Basle by Hieronymus Frobenius and Nicolaus Episcopius. It went through several revisions and additions of commentaries, partly by Gerardus Listrius and partly by Erasmus himself. Its editor, Clarence H. Miller, prepared it on the basis of the edition published in 1532. Seven other editions "in which Erasmus had a hand" (in Erasmus 1979, 39) are included (see also the *conspectus siglorum* on p. 66). They are selected with the main purpose of illustrating Erasmus' activity in reworking the text, and to exemplify all kinds of additions and revisions he made to the original text.

On the other hand, the rather problematic case of the *Iulius exclusus*, edited in 2013 by Silvia Seidel Menchi (Erasmus 2013; see the introduction, 5–222), a work whose attribution to Erasmus has long been denied, and that circulated in manuscripts before and after the publication of the *editio princeps* in 1517 (Mainz: Peter Schöffel the Younger), led to different choices. The edition is, in fact, based on Basel, Universitätsbibliothek, A IX 64, namely the manuscript written by Bonifacius Amerbach and completed in 1516. Further witnesses are Basel, Universitätsbibliothek, A IX 64a, written by the same Amerbach, and the *editio princeps*. The witnesses are chosen according to their closeness to the archetype and to their contribution to the establishment of a fixed, authoritative text that was diffused through print and became the *vulgata*.

7.8.2.3 Girolamo Fracastoro, *De sympathia et antipathia liber I*

The critical edition of Girolamo Fracastoro's *De sympathia et antipathia rerum liber I* published by Concetta Pennuto (2008) is remarkable in several respects. In order to understand this situation better, and to explain the methodology followed by the modern editor, a few words of explanation about the history of the text are necessary (see Pennuto 2008, xiii–xlvii). Girolamo Fracastoro (1478–1553) published the text for the first time in Venice in 1546 (printers: Tommaso and Giovan Maria Giunti). This edition is accompanied, in an appendix, by a list of *errata ita corrigenda* which did not enter the textual tradition immediately, and consequently did not influence the second and third prints (Lyon, 1550 and 1554; printers: Guillaume Gazeau and Jean de Tournes), but were integrated into the text only in 1555, when a new Venetian edition was brought out by the same Tommaso and Giovan Maria Giunti. This edition did not only, however, include Fracastoro's corrections, but was also marred by several interventions (or, better, by deliberate linguistic manipulation) on the part of its editor, Paolo Ramusio (1532–1600; son of the Arabist Giovan Battista Ramusio). Despite this, the 1555 edition became the reference text, practically erasing the memory of the *editio princeps* from all other editions (all in all, there are twelve, stretching from 1546 to 1671). Only the Nuremberg edition, published in 1662 as a part of the *Theatrum sympatheticum*, does not include any changes (i.e. neither the errata nor Ramusio's "improvements") and seems to go back to an "original" without any changes. Thus, the development of the text shows changes, updates, and innovations from several sides: the author, an editor, and the printed texts with

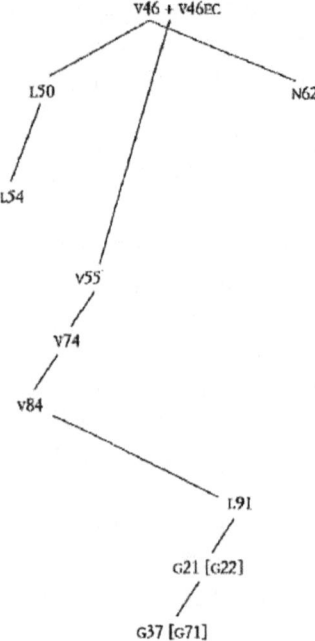

Fig. 7.8-2: Pennuto (2008, lxx).

their own errors and deviations. The consequences of such a state of the tradition for the modern editor can be summarised as follows. (*i*) She could not limit her work to the reconstruction of the author's original text, for this would be an artificial conflation formed by the text of the *editio princeps* and the insertion into it of the errata originally included in the appendix. (*ii*) She could not simply dismiss Ramusio's linguistic manipulations of the text as later interventions and, consequently, leave them out of the edition, for it is not certain whether they were the result of his own work or were inspired by written or oral contact and exchange between him and Fracastoro. Whatever their origin, they are part of the dynamic development of the text; therefore, they must be recorded, at least in the critical apparatus. (*iii*) As almost every printed copy showed variant readings of its own or, as we have seen in case of the one printed in Nuremberg, a distinctive connection to the *editio princeps*, the *editiones descriptae*, or those that could be considered as such, are almost non-existent. Therefore, all editions have to be taken into account. (*iv*) She could not limit her work to the establishment of a correct text according to one or more selected prints, including in the apparatus only errors and misprints from single editions that undermine the content, but had to put together two different, non-selective critical apparatuses, the first recording the "varianti d'autore" [author's variants] (i.e. the changes made by Fracastoro himself), and the second reflecting the historical development of the text: "un apparato storico evolutivo con le varianti chiaramente non d'autore" [an evolutive critical apparatus with the variants clearly not from the author] (Pennuto 2008, xviii). (*v*) Last but not least, she had to produce a *stemma editionum* representing the textual development graphically (see fig. 7.8-2).

7.8.3 Editing printed texts beyond prints: Some examples of interaction between prints and manuscripts

For some editorial projects of Renaissance works, resorting only to printed copies is not enough. For the preparation of such editions, which I call "mixed", the printed version of the work cannot constitute a reliable basis for an edition, because it does not deliver a complete text of the work or comprises one redaction of a work existing in several versions, or because the tradition of the work is also partially made up of manuscripts. In the following examples, I will simply sketch the methods followed by three scholars for integrating both printed copies and manuscripts in a single editorial project.

7.8.3.1 Bernardino Telesio, *Varii de naturalibus rebus libelli*

The first example is the edition of some minor works written by Bernardino Telesio (1509–1588) on subjects of natural philosophy (especially Aristotelian meteorology and biology), such as comets, the sea, lightning, colours, tastes, and respiration, published by Luigi de Franco (1981). These works (*De cometis et lacteo circulo, De mari, De fulmine, Quod animal universum ab unica substantia gubernatur, Contra Galenum, De usu respirationis, De coloribus, De saporibus*, and some others) were not unknown, as most of them had already been included in the 1590 printed edition supervised by Antonius Persius. Some others, neglected by Persius, had been made available as appendices in Francesco Fiorentino's book on Telesio's conception of nature (Fiorentino 1872–1874). Finally, the *De colorum generatione* had been published independently by Telesius (1570).

Almost all the works are preserved both in manuscripts (some of which are autographs) and in prints. In addition, they exhibit various stages of composition: *minutae* and sketches – which were sometimes later revised, with corrections introduced in the printed copy presented to the *revisore ecclesiastico* in order to obtain the *imprimatur* (de Franco 1981, xxi) – as well as final prints (de Franco 1981, xxxix–lvii).

In this distinctive case, the editor's task was twofold: to establish a critical text and to represent the genesis and the development of the work from scratch to its final shape (de Franco 1981, xliii). I cannot discuss all the texts edited by de Franco and their methodologies here, and point only to two specific cases, those of the *De mari* and the *Quod animal universum*. The former work is preserved in five manuscripts and in two printed editions, both published in 1570, one including it in the anthology supervised by Persius, the other containing it independently. Of the five manuscript witnesses, the most relevant ones are the two drafts preserved in Napoli,

Biblioteca Nazionale, VIII.C.29. The first draft is the autograph submitted to the *revisore ecclesiastico*; it preserves a first redaction with some corrections. The second draft is, in fact, the final version, and corresponds to the text printed independently in 1570. The printed text edited by Persius adds three chapters compared to the previous version, which also figure as sketches (*minutae*) in the autograph copy. This situation led the modern editor to choose the independent print of 1570 as the basis for the edition and the Persius edition as the basis for the three added chapters, and to edit the text of the first draft as an appendix.

The second case, the *Quod animal universum*, is apparently simpler, but by no means less interesting (de Franco 1981, 1–li). The work is preserved in print only thanks to Persius' edition. It might have circulated in manuscript form, but no copy of the complete text has survived. The printed text, however, cannot be considered a reliable basis, for it is disfigured by errors and unclear formulations as well as by further mistakes added either by mechanical factors or by unfortunate conjectures made by Persius in an attempt to improve the quality of the edition. Facing such a situation, the modern editor had to turn to the *minutae* preserved in two manuscripts (Città del Vaticano, Biblioteca Apostolica Vaticana, Ottob. Lat. 1929 and Città del Vaticano, Biblioteca Apostolica Vaticana, Ottob. Lat. 1306) to restore the disfigured passages and reconstruct a reliable text.

7.8.3.2 Anonymous, *Cinq-cent rondeaux d'amour*

In 2011, Françoise Féry-Hue published a new edition of an anonymous work sometimes attributed to Pierre Gringore (1475–1538/39), the *Cinq-cent rondeaux d'amour*, written during the first decades of the sixteenth century, whose origin can perhaps be placed at the court of Angoulême, as the dedicatory letter addressed to Francis I of France shows (Féry-Hue 2011). By using the metrical form of the *rondeau* and the fashion of short versified letters, the author tells a tragic love story that ends with the death of the lady and the retirement of her lover to a monastery. The purpose of the work was possibly to provide members of the court with material for private reading and spiritual cultivation; the destiny of the work was, however, different, for the print probably helped to widen its reception and to enlarge its audience. The *Cinq-cent rondeaux* is handed down by five sixteenth-century manuscripts (*C*: location unknown, Collection Particulière; *F*: Paris, Bibliothèque nationale de France, fr. 19183; *R*: Paris, Bibliothèque nationale de France, Rothschild 2855; *L*: Den Haag, Koninklijke Bibliotheek, 129.G.20; *S*: Soissons, Bibliothèque Municipale, 204), and was printed ten times between 1527 and 1550. The edition of the work is based on the Soissons manuscript, used as base text. But all other manuscripts were collated and used to improve the text, and their variant readings were recorded in the apparatus. Moreover, the editor offers, synoptically, a transcription of the text of the *editio princeps* published in Paris in 1527 (printer: Alain Lotrain). This editorial decision can be explained by the complicated tradition of the text, which did not allow the editor to draw a convincing stemma. Moreover, the editor wished to emphasise the development of the text and its dynamics, to show how it moved from a limited courtly readership in manuscripts towards a larger audience in print, and how both external and internal features of the two forms of dissemination contributed to shaping this dynamics. In this context, the printed text, as represented by the *editio princeps*, does not simply represent the end of the manuscript tradition and the beginning of a new way of disseminating the text, but is also one of the main steps in the dynamics leading towards the transformation of that text and of its perception.

7.8.3.3 Iacopo Ammannati Piccolomini, *Lettere*
The case study represented by the edition of Iacopo Ammannati Piccolomini's *Lettere* (Cherubini 1997) describes a more complex form of interaction between manuscripts and prints, and, above all, a different perception of printed version(s) compared to the codices. More specifically, it shows that the inclusion of manuscripts and prints in the same editorial enterprise is necessary for reconstructing the complete corpus of writings of the author, and that the perception of a printed text in such a project does not always correspond to our impression that the print represents a moment of fixation and consolidation of a tradition. Again, in order to make readers aware of the reasons determining the editor's choices and methodologies, some further information about the text and the edition should be provided. Iacopo Ammannati Piccolomini (1422–1479) had intended to commission and publish a collection of his own letters, but was prevented from doing so by his death. His friend and secretary Iacopo Gherardi took up the task of collecting, ordering, revising, and publishing the letters in a collection, but the *editio princeps* he managed to publish in 1506 in Milan (Piccolomini 1506), was incomplete and not satisfactory. This edition (Cherubini 1997, 1:25) was later used as a basis for further printed editions (the last of which was printed in Frankfurt in 1614; on the prints, see Cherubini 1997, 1:58–76), each of which was incomplete compared to the *editio princeps*, containing only parts of the epistolary production of Piccolomini. On the other hand, groups of letters handed down in the form of *minutae* and copies had already started to circulate independently in small manuscript collections (Cherubini 1997, 1:26–58). Facing such a situation, Paolo Cherubini, who published an edition of all the letters written between 1444 and 1479 found to date, not only had to gather together a complete corpus of the letters (found in different stages of composition) but also had to catalogue prints and manuscripts and to understand their relationships. Consequently, he edited, according to chronological principles, letters preserved either in single copies or in various copies in different forms and stages of completion.

One example is *Epistula* 17 (Cherubini 1997, 1:363–368), a moral treatise written in the form of a letter sent by Piccolomini to himself on December 18, 1461, after he had been made cardinal by Pius II. This letter is witnessed both by Salamanca, Biblioteca de la Universidad, ms. 2109, and by the printed editions published in 1506 (namely the *editio princeps*) and in 1614 in Frankfurt (in officina Aubriana). In this case, the modern editor reproduces the text according to the printed copies, and records the variant readings of the Salamanca codex in the critical apparatus.

The interaction between manuscripts and prints, between different forms of collection, and between different compositional stages of the individual letters influenced, together with variant readings, the stemmatological representation of their mutual relationships. Clearly, it was not possible to draw a single *stemma codicum*, nor does it seem that the editor intended to have one. Rather, he structured the numerous manuscript collections into groups or clusters according to the common elements they shared and the innovations they showed in comparison to what could be considered their models.

The situation that the editor of Ammannati Piccolomini's letters had to face is not an exceptional one. Other editors of collections of letters have had to develop similarly flexible strategies for representing the relationships between manuscripts and printed witnesses, and for editing the texts. The recently completed edition of Joseph Justus Scaliger's *Epistulae* (Botley and van Miert 2012; see also the Web version, emlo-portal.bodleian.ox.ac.uk/collections/?catalogue=joseph-justus-scaliger) clearly shows that its editors, Paul Botley and Dirk van Miert, had to edit different kinds of material, sometimes overlapping. The same letters were often transmitted through multiple copies, both as manuscript and in printed form, with different statuses: autograph letters, authorial drafts and copies, and so on.

Further reading

For a general assessment of the cultural importance of early printed editions, see Feld (1978) and Pettegree (2011). The following two handbooks of textual criticism offer insights into the methodology of editing early printed books: Stoppelli (2008) and Stussi (2015); see also Trovato (2017).

7.9 Genetic maps in modern philology
Dirk van Hulle

The notion of the stemma is a metaphor (see 2.2.2). Like all the "metaphors we live by" (Lakoff and Johnson 1980), this metaphor of the family tree is indicative of a particular way of thinking – in this case, of an ideology that inherits the fixation on "purity" of the textual "bloodline". In this sense, the genealogical method sometimes seems to reflect an ancient or mediaeval obsession with pedigree, combined with a nineteenth-century preoccupation with origins. In modern times, however, the problem is usually not the lack of an original autograph, but rather the abundance thereof. And among this abundance, the problem the early twentieth-century textual critics were faced with was choosing the most authoritative text. This section therefore starts with a brief historical background, discussing the tensions between two schools of scholarly editing that have determined much of the debate in modern-day textual scholarship, the German and the Anglo-American traditions. This historical background is followed by a discussion of two notable trends. First, a development from schools or traditions to "orientations to text" suggests a less prescriptive and less biased understanding of the discipline. A second notable trend is the development from a focus on (final) authorial intention to an openness to multiple intentions, which becomes especially manifest in sister-disciplines such as genetic criticism. This openness to multiple intentions implies an increased awareness of other agents of textual change. The section's central question relates to the suitability of the notion of the stemma when it comes to mapping the genesis of a text.

7.9.1 The tensions between Anglo-American and German editorial traditions

The British bibliographer Ronald B. McKerrow (1939, 7–8) defined the most authoritative text as "that one of the early texts which, on a consideration of their genetic relationship, appears likely to have deviated to the smallest extent in all respects of wording, spelling, and punctuation from the author's manuscript". It is interesting to note that McKerrow used the adjective "genetic" long before the emergence of "genetic criticism" in France in the second half of the 1960s (see below). McKerrow worked with the notion of an "ideal text", which "should approach as closely as the extant material allows to a fair copy, made by the author himself, of his plays in the form which he intended finally to give them" (McKerrow 1939, 6). F i n a l a u t h o r i a l i n t e n t i o n was the governing principle, and it remained so for several decades. In 1951, Walter Wilson Greg (1951, x) defined his first rule as an editor as follows: "The aim of a critical edition should be to present the text, so far as the available evidence permits, in the form in which we may suppose that it would have stood in a fair copy, made by the author himself, of the work as he finally intended it." In his second rule, he defined the c o p y t e x t as the most authoritative text of the early prints (Greg 1951, xii). In addition to final authorial intention as a guideline, giving the editor the freedom to make an educated guess as to what this intention was, the fixation on p u r i t y persisted.

When, building on McKerrow and Greg, Fredson Bowers further developed the "copy-text theory", he defined "the aim of textual criticism" as "the recovery of the initial *purity* of an author's text and of any revision (insofar as this is possible from the preserved documents), and the preservation of this *purity* despite the usual *corrupting* process of reprint transmission" (Bowers 1970, 30; my emphasis). The notion of purity in Bowers's definition is symptomatic of the then-dominant view, which almost automatically regarded textual agents other than the author as introducers of textual "corruption" in the sense of an intrusion into the text as the author wanted it to be, and thus as impeding realisation of the author's intention.

Because the notion of purity was linked to the author's final intention, this created a tension with Wimsatt and Beardsley's influential essay "The Intentional Fallacy" (1946). The growing sentiment against intentionalism in literary studies led to counter-narratives such as Eric Donald Hirsch's *Validity in Interpretation* (1967). But the debate itself seemed to suggest that there was an underlying assumption in both camps that the text is what the author wanted to write. As G. Thomas Tanselle noted in "The Editorial Problem of Final Authorial Intention" (1976, 171–172), "the question of the bearing of authorial intention on interpretation would hardly arise unless the text is assumed to be what its author wished". From the perspective of textual scholarship, this assumption is not self-evident. The copy-text theory allows the editor to choose readings from different versions in order to establish a text that reflects the author's final intention.

From the perspective of German editorial theory, the copy-text approach resulted in what was critically dubbed "an eclectic (contaminated) text" (Zeller 1975, 237). This criticism was voiced by the Swiss editorial theorist Hans Zeller, one of the most eminent representatives of the historical-critical edition and the German school of scholarly editing. Although his criticism opposed Bowers's eclectic approach, Zeller's notion of contamination again suggested a form of corruption, an impediment to purity, albeit a different kind of corruption and a different kind of purity. For what Zeller referred to was the "contamination" of the integrity of the text in a historical document. Criticising the assumption that "the sum of authoritative readings yields an authoritative text" (Zeller 1975, 137), he argued that an "eclectic editor contaminatingly synchronizes that which occurred diachronically", thus creating a text that has never existed before, "in the name of authorial intention" (Zeller 1995, 106). One of the most remarkable (post)modern editions of a modernist text that epitomised this debate was the 1984 edition of James Joyce's *Ulysses* by Hans Walter Gabler, Claus Melchior, and Wolfhard Steppe. This edition combined elements from both the German and the Anglo-American traditions of scholarly editing, and gave rise to a long controversy, partly because it confronted both these editorial traditions with their respective orientations to text. Because it tried to reconcile the reality of the historical documents with the ideality of the author's intention, it has been called "the climax of the traditional method" (Sahle 2013, 129).

7.9.2 From schools or traditions to orientations to text

The notion of purity gradually lost currency. This trend was, to some extent, facilitated by authors themselves. To illustrate this phenomenon, the Irish writer Samuel Beckett is a good example. Like many authors, Samuel Beckett was sensitive to changes in transmission and unsolicited modifications to his texts. This sensitivity, however, did not relate to purity but to integrity, in the etymological sense of "entirety" (from Latin *integer*, "whole"), that is, including all the impurities as well.

With reference to the play *Endgame*, Beckett actually tried to protect his text "in all its *im*purity" (to Alan Schneider, February 6, 1958, Beckett 2014, 103; my emphasis). This was his reaction against the attempts by the British censor, the Lord Chamberlain, to remove the line referring to God with "The bastard, he doesn't exist." A similar form of censorship had been applied to *Waiting for Godot*. The first British edition (Faber and Faber, 1956) had been expurgated by the Lord Chamberlain. Almost ten years later, in 1965, Faber and Faber decided to bring their version "closer to the original", and Beckett hoped the "integral" text would now be treated less "puritanically" (to Charles Monteith, November 15, 1963; Beckett 2014, 580).

Obviously, the recovery of a text's integrity is just as vague as what Bowers called "the recovery of the initial purity of an author's text". To provide more clarity, it is important to distinguish between the elemental material and forces involved in the production, revision, and dissemination of literary works. These elements are material, causal, temporal, genetic, commercial/aesthetic, and performance-related. The relative importance one attaches to these elements determines one's orientation to text. Peter Shillingsburg originally defined five orientations (documentary, sociological, authorial, bibliographical, and aesthetic) in *Scholarly Editing in the Computer Age* (1996). They were recently revised to add a "genetic orientation" and fine-tune the other orientations (van Hulle and Shillingsburg 2015). These orientations relate to the different ways of framing the narrative of the genesis, revision history, and publication of a text. They are conceived as a descriptive, not a prescriptive framework. There are no "right" or "wrong" orientations. The central issue is simply consistency: the framework helps determine one's orientation and, no matter which orientation one chooses at the start of a project, the trick is to apply it consistently.

(*i*) If one's focus is on the documentary evidence, the orientation is material, because, from this perspective, textual authority resides in the extant documentary material evidence. This material orientation can be subdivided into a bibliographical and a lexical approach. The bibliographical approach considers the visual, tactile, physical, or iconic aspects of the material document so important that it becomes logically impossible to replicate or emend it. The lexical approach does allow the text of a document to be replicated, but emendation is logically not allowed since the document is regarded as the ultimate textual evidence. The German model of the historical-critical edition sometimes does emend obvious errors (*Textfehler*), but that is, strictly speaking, a non-materialist intervention.

(*ii*) If an editor focuses on the involvement of every agent of textual change (not only the author but also any other agent involved in the composition, revision, and production of texts), the orientation is causal. This causal orientation is a continuum between an authorial and a social approach. The question is whether the interventions by all agents of textual change are to be valued equally. The authorial approach focuses on the text created and/or desired by the author; the social approach concentrates on the text created in concert with all the production staff involved. In the latter case, authority resides in the institutional unit of author *and* publisher.

(*iii*) If the moment when a text was produced is the central concern, the orientation is t e m p o r a l. If there are elements in the text that do not fit the period of its production, this will be a criterion for emendation. From this perspective, authority resides in periods of inscription or reinscription. This orientation can be divided into a production-oriented and a diachronic approach. The p r o d u c t i o n - o r i e n t e d a p p r o a c h views the work as a series of snapshots, each fixed more or less well in a document, whereas the d i a c h r o n i c a p p r o a c h regards the work as a creative development. For this orientation, the central issue is not the document but either the "moment in time" or the "sequence of development". The record of these two forms of temporality (captured in a document) can be faulty, so the logic of this approach allows the editor to emend the text.

(*iv*) If one is mainly interested in the dynamics of the composition as implied by the extant versions, their chronology, and the changes within (deletions, additions, substitutions) and between them (variants or rewritings), the orientation is g e n e t - i c. Its focus is on the actions and trajectories of creative invention as implied by the chronological succession of textual changes, which is different from material orientation (for which authority resides in the document) and from temporal orientation (for which authority resides in periods of inscription or reinscription). The genetic orientation not only investigates e n d o g e n e s i s (the succession of draft versions) and e p i g e n e s i s (the continuation of the creative process after publication), but also e x o g e n e s i s (the interaction with external source texts), which may result in editions that include the reconstruction of an author's personal library.

(*v*) If the editor wishes to pay special attention to the tension between a play's stage directions and its actual performance, this focus on p e r f o r m a n c e constitutes a separate orientation, which becomes all the more important in the case of postdramatic theatre.

(*vi*) If editors choose to modernise or revamp a text based on their subjective aesthetic preferences, or if they try to respect the known aesthetic principles of an author or of a historical publisher, the orientation is a e s t h e t i c.

For a more elaborate discussion of these orientations, see van Hulle and Shillingsburg (2015).

7.9.3 Stemmata and genetic maps

Given this variety of orientations, the notion of textual purity becomes increasingly problematic. And, whether one wishes to speak of textual "purity" or "impurity", the question is whether the stemmatological method works for modern texts in the way it does for older texts. One of the defining elements of philological practices in modern times is the relative abundance of autograph manuscripts or other (also digital) documents pertaining to the genesis (rather than the transmission) of texts. Still, this abundance is only relative, for manuscripts are "poor" material, according to Hans Magnus Enzensberger. In *Die Entstehung eines Gedichts* (1962), he distinguishes two approaches to a poem's genesis: from the inside and from the outside. The former can only be applied by the author, who has the advantage but also the disadvantage of hindsight, for memory tends to distort the past. The latter approach can only work with what Enzensberger calls "unequivocal" (*eindeutig*) but "poor" material, because no memories are attached to it. This was the case with the manuscripts of Heinrich Heine when they were acquired by the Bibliothèque nationale de France and Louis Hay was charged with their examination. This was the start of g e n e t i c c r i t i c i s m. Although the term was coined in the 1970s, the idea behind it was formulated by Louis Hay (1967) in the French newspaper *Le Monde*. Hay speaks of two ways of reading, vertical (across versions) and horizontal (following the narrative sequence). These two forms of reading should not be confused, he suggests, but their results might be mutually enriching and elucidating. This vision was developed in the subsequent decades. The research object of genetic criticism is the creative process. In spite of its abstract nature, this objective requires the examination of concrete documents. And, in spite of what Enzensberger claims, these material traces are not always unequivocal and involve quite a bit of interpretation. From this material, genetic critics infer the d y n a m i c s of the writing process.

Given the importance of m a t e r i a l t r a c e s as a starting point of genetic criticism, Pierre-Marc de Biasi conceived his basic model of the average writing process as a typology of documents (de Biasi 1996). Central in this model is the "pass for press" moment (*bon à tirer*, i.e. the moment the author decides that all is set for printing). In general, de Biasi distinguishes three different phases of the writing process: pre-composition (exploration, documentation, reading, note-taking, conceptualisation), composition (textualisation, drafts, typescripts, revisions), and post-composition (publication history, performance history, self-translations).

The notion of the s t e m m a is not (or very rarely) used in genetic criticism. Some scholars, however, do apply it to the genesis of literary works. A good example is Ruby Cohn's (2001, 220) "stemma" of the genesis of Samuel Beckett's *Fin de partie/ Endgame*. Cohn disagrees with other Beckett scholars, such as Giuseppina Restivo, about the "origin of the stemma". In "The Genesis of Beckett's *Endgame*", Restivo (1994, 85, 88) had suggested that a few early sketches in the Sam Francis Notebook were the "core" and the "basis" of the play. The notebook contains two dialogues between "A" and "B" (University of Reading, MS 2926, f. 6r–10r, 11r–20r) and one dialogue between "X" and his factotum "F" (f. 23v–48r). Restivo's thesis is that the A–B dialogues and the X–F dialogue in the Sam Francis Notebook together form the "two different starts" (Restivo 1994, 85). Ruby Cohn's alternative "stemma" for *Fin de partie/Endgame* differs from Restivo's "line of development" (Restivo 1994, 93), and deviates from the descriptions in the catalogue at the University of Reading, in that not all fragments that are catalogued as early versions of *Fin de partie* are included in the "stemma".

Genetic Map of *Fin de partie*

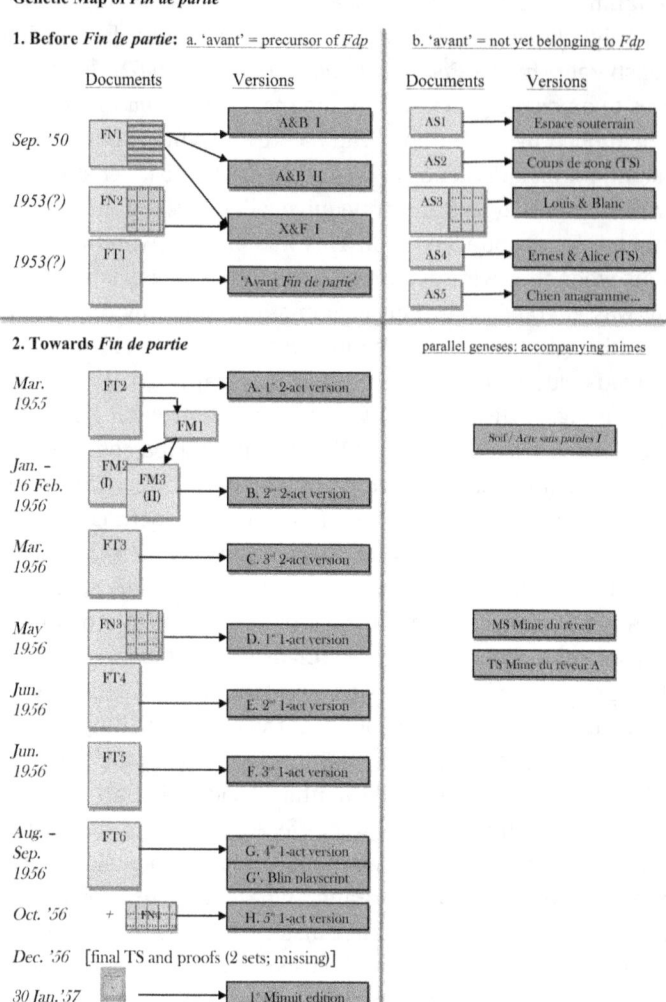

Fig. 7.9-1: Genetic map of Samuel Beckett's *Fin de partie*. Source: Beckett Digital Manuscript Project (beckettarchive.org/findepartie/about/chronology).

The question is whether this arboreal model is suitable for reconstructing a work's genesis. To begin with, an arboreal model suggests a "seed" as the beginning of the writing process. This metaphor is often used in literary criticism, but, as Restivo's idea of "two different starts" suggests, the reality of actual writing processes suggests that literary geneses seldom grow from one single "seed". Creativity is often sparked by a combination of numerous sources of inspiration, including a writer's personal library. But, even if one leaves exogenesis out of the equation, endogenesis does not always start in one single draft. Moreover, the arboreal model would imply two directions of growth from the seed, with not only a stem and branches, but also roots reaching down underground.

It might therefore be wise to work with less organic metaphors and to reconstruct the trajectory of the creative process by means of a map (fig. 7.9-1). The "genetic map" of *Fin de partie* in the Beckett Digital Manuscript Project works with Samuel Beckett's own notion of "Avant *Fin de partie*". This is the name Beckett gave to one of the typescripts (*FT1*), which he donated to the University of Reading (MS 1227/7/16/7). The notion of "avant" [before] points to a crucial question of genetic criticism: where the *avant-texte* of a particular work starts. Between the completion of the antecedent play, *En attendant Godot*, and *Fin de partie*, Beckett wrote several dramatic fragments that can all be called "before *Fin de partie*"; but then we have to make a distinction between "before" in the sense of a precursor of *Fin de partie* and "before" in the sense of "not yet belonging to *Fin de partie*" (because some of the dramatic fragments do not contain any significant characteristics of the published version of the play). Nonetheless, even in the latter case, the trials and errors that did not lead directly to a successful publication did indirectly contribute to the creative process. They would not belong to a "stemma", but they do have a place on a "map".

The genetic map also makes a distinction between d o c u m e n t s (which have material substance) and v e r s i o n s (which are a conceptual abstraction). One notebook (e.g. French notebook 1, *FN1*) can contain two early versions of the play and, vice versa, one version (e.g. the second two-act version) can be so long that it was written in two documents (*FM2* and *FM3*, which were separately sold and ended up on two sides of the Atlantic, at Ohio State University and Trinity College Dublin respectively).

7.9.4 From final authorial intention to multiple intentions

What genetic maps show, above all, is that authors' intentions can be highly changeable, to the extent that several genetic critics no longer see the writer as a monolithic "self" but as a succession of selves. The writer who cancels a word is already different from the one who wrote it. This interval opens up the space in which genetic criticism operates, according to Nicholas Donin and Daniel Ferrer (2015, 24). It is not only genetic critics who stress the f l u i d i t y of the text in modern times. When John Bryant developed his "fluid text" theory, he no longer referred simply to (final) authorial intention but to "an announced notion of intentionality" in defining the critical edition as

> a genre of scholarly editing in which a text is constructed usually after the inspection, and sometimes the conflation, of significant versions of the work; it is also a text that is invariably emended along certain principles so as to bring it closer to an announced notion of intentionality. (J. Bryant 2002, 20)

In the twentieth century, the notion of "intention" became such a taboo that critics increasingly eschewed the term. But, in scholarly editing, the notion cannot be avoided. Instead of steering clear of the term, textual scholars have sought to define it more clearly and suggested a distinction between what authors intended the text to *mean* and what they intended the text to *do* (i.e. what character or punctuation mark was intended to be inscribed; Shillingsburg 1996, 36–37). The latter type of intention is what textual scholarship usually has to deal with, and therefore the subjectivity involved in the critical act of determining an author's intention is "hedged in at every point by whatever can be ascertained or inferred about the history of the work's writing and early production", as Paul Eggert notes (2013, 104). In this sense, it may also have been one of the author's intentions to leave all matters of spelling and punctuation to the copy-editor at the publishing house. A famous example is Jane Austen, who relied on her publisher to correct her spelling mistakes, as Kathryn Sutherland pointed out (see Garner 2010). The help of a copy-editor can take on such proportions that a writer's "typical" style eventually turns out to be the work of someone else, as in the case of Raymond Carver and Gordon Lish. The author of the short-story collection *What We Talk About When We Talk About Love* is famous for his minimalistic writing style. But this style is actually, to a large extent, the work of his editor, Gordon Lish, who was fiction editor of the magazine *Esquire* from 1969 to 1977. Lish's papers (in the Lilly Library at Indiana University in Bloomington) show how drastically he pruned as an editor, sometimes even rewriting some of Carver's stories. For instance, the story "If It Please You" was so thoroughly rewritten that, according to Stephen King (2009), it is "a total rewrite, and it's a cheat". But others see Lish as a crucial agent of textual change who was instrumental in creating the Carver style in the first place. In 1971, he edited Carver's story "Neighbors" for publication in *Esquire*, making so many cuts that it resulted in the minimalist effect for which Carver is famous. For the *Collected Stories*, published in 2009, Carver's widow printed some of the stories in both the author's version and the version edited by Lish (see Lorentzen 2015). This practice does not represent two "schools" or "traditions" of editing. Instead, it shows two orientations to text at work. Within the causal orientation, Stephen King's attitude as a creative writer understandably belongs to the authorial approach; the edited version represents the social approach.

In conclusion, philological practices and editorial theory in modern times show a development from "purity" to "fluidity" and an increased awareness of other agents of textual change. These agents often play a role in the multiplicity of changing authorial intentions and thus in the creative process, which continues even after a text's first publication. This field of epigenetics is the common ground where traditional schools of scholarly editing and genetic criticism can meet and mutually benefit from each other's perspectives. What this mutual exchange of ideas could yield is a re-evaluation of the notion of the stemma when it comes to mapping a text's (endo- and epi-)genesis.

Further reading

Readers who would like to know more about the development of *critique génétique*, especially in France, can be referred to Grésillon (1994), de Biasi (2000), Ferrer (2011), and van Hulle (2014). A useful collection of articles on the topic is to be found in de Biasi and Herschberg Pierrot (2017). Ferrer (2002, 2016) offers insights about the relationships between genetic criticism and textual criticism in general. Van Hulle and Shillingsburg (2015), already cited above, is an introduction to what is meant by "orientations to text".

8 Evolutionary models in other disciplines
Introductory remarks by the chapter editor, Armin Hoenen

"Stemmatology usually works with texts that change during their copying history." If we conduct a small experiment of metaphorically zooming out and replacing the nouns in this sentence with nouns from a higher, more general category, we could say: "Genealogical science usually works with sequences that change during their transmission." Some sciences for which this statement is applicable – though not all of them – will be the focus of this chapter.

The formulation "sequences that change during transmission" hints at e v o l u - t i o n a r y theory, although the concept of evolution more specifically entails mutation and selection as agents of change, and therefore carries strong biological connotations. Nonetheless, it has been used to convey different notions of processes of change which lead to hierarchical or temporally successive structures in various disciplines; thus, we can speak of biological evolution, text evolution, language evolution, the evolution of writing materials, and so on. The main visual metaphor for such structures, and the only figure in Darwin's *On the Origin of Species* (1859), is the t r e e. The tree as a mathematical, analytical structure has been used, in turn, for a huge number of purposes, be it in one of its first attested usages, as a family tree for aristocratic families (see Lima 2014, 29); as a *stemma codicum*; or as a way of displaying folder and file structures on a computer. As Lima (2011, 43) points out, the tree has been appreciated on the one hand and attacked on the other (and not only in stemmatology). Yet it has survived criticism and continues to be widely used.

So far, in this book we have looked at many kinds of stemmatic trees. In this chapter, we will focus on fellow trees from other disciplines, which together form the forest of "trees of history", as O'Hara (1996) proposed to call some of them. The application of the tree model in science as an analytical tool is – as already stated – very broad and has had a special role as a "tool of thought" in Europe (Klapisch-Zuber 2007, 293). The habitat of our forest is indeed vast. In fact, it is so large that we will not be able to cover all the applications of trees (for which Lima 2014, among others, could be consulted); instead, we limit ourselves to some of the disciplines most intimately related to stemmatology: linguistics, cultural evolution, musicology, and biology. What are the parallels, what are the differences, what can we learn from each other, what can we borrow or incorporate, and what are the interfaces stemmatology shares with these sciences? These are some of the leading questions to keep in mind when reading this chapter.

Phylogenetics (8.1) has functioned as a donor of many computational tools (see 5.2, 5.4) to stemmatology. Linguistics (8.2) makes complex genealogical judgements just as stemmatology does, albeit with a focus on language as a whole, not on a single work. Anthropological phylomemetics (8.3; an umbrella term proposed by C. J. Howe and Windram 2011) is, on the one hand, concerned with trees of cultural artefacts (e.g. material relevant to codicology, book binding types) and, on the other, with the analysis of textual evolution, for instance story patterns. Finally, music (8.4) has been transmitted as musical notation, often along with texts, and musicology is a discipline which has looked to stemmatology to develop methods and models. The similarities and interdependencies between these disciplines (or some of them) were noted at an early date. Famous scientists such as Darwin, Schleicher, or Haeckel were aware of our forest, as has been outlined in publications on the similarities of these disciplines, but also on their differences. Some of the most relevant ones for stemmatology may be Platnick and Cameron (1977), Cameron (1987), and O'Hara (1996). They specifically highlight differences, such as a special focus on the survivors at the tips/leaves of the tree (the living species) in biology, and on the (presumably lost) root of the tree in stemmatology, but also similarities, such as the consensus of using shared innovations in morphological classification in both early biological cladistics and stemmatology.

Christopher Howe and Heather Windram (8.1) explain phylogeny, where trees are used to display and systematise, for instance, the relationships between species, but also between proteins or individuals. Phylogenetic trees are today usually generated from molecular data such as DNA, the universal vehicle transmitting genetic information. Its universality entails that there can be a tree of life including all living beings (and the entire fossil record); compare the site tolweb.org. In palaeontology, however, molecular data is usually not available, which is why other paradigms have to be followed here (such as selecting certain traits of the fossil – not unlike selecting certain variants as genealogically informative), and this biological subdiscipline is presumably the closest biological relative of stemmatology. Additionally, in botany, hybridisation, or the mixing of DNA of different species, is common among certain plants as well as in bacteria, which is why accommodating large amounts of "contamination" may be of great interest to botanists, bacteriologists, and stemmatologists alike. Howe and Windram walk the reader step by step through the construction of a phylogenetic tree and outline the history of the field, rooting, contamination, and other relevant phenomena.

Just as for organisms in biology, some scholars have assumed one common origin of all languages (e.g. Bengtson and Ruhlen 1994), implying one giant language tree. In section 8.2, problems similar to those in stemmatology for the genealogy of languages are discussed. They have led scholars to existential criticism: language contact on all levels of a language (Thomason 2001) calls tree models into question. Pidgins (reduced, mixed languages used as a lingua franca) and creoles (pidgins which have become mother tongues) are vivid witnesses to a problematic entity when it comes to accommodating it in a tree of languages. Another issue is the choice of the base data for tree generation. What is the DNA of a language? A list of carefully chosen words considered to withstand borrowing; or some grammatical, syntactic, morphological, phonological features; or a weighted ensemble of all of them? While in textual criticism, the basis is the usually relatively clearly delimited single work, for linguistics, it is much harder to determine the basis of tree generation. An exciting interface can be found in sound shifts that lead to trees for single lexemes similar to variant stemmata. Dieter Bachmann illustrates the answers and methods linguists have developed for these challenges. He focuses mainly on the history of Indo-European, the largest and presumably best-understood language family. He recalls the development of genealogical approaches in the field and outlines important currently discussed questions, such as understanding the time-depth of certain splits or the localisation of the *Urheimat* of the Indo-Europeans. He summarises the recent influx and perception of computation in the field and the mixed reactions it has received.

Section 8.3 has a broad scope. It deals with many phenomena to which a tree model can be applied from the sphere of anthropology and of human artefacts in general. Tomasello (1999) speaks of the "ratchet effect" when humans refine tools in subsequent generations (at some point in time, the hand axe became a true axe). This implies a model of evolution for anthropology where "descent with modification" applies. The basic data on which phylomemetics operates are (manually chosen) character states of artefacts such as cross-bows or of story patterns. This choice parallels the selection of significant errors in stemmatology and that of traits in cladistics and palaeontology. Jamshid Tehrani explains why, in this field, a certain class of algorithms has superseded prior approaches. His examples from the pre-literary transmission and admixture of story patterns across cultural borders may be especially relevant to stemmatology, which also analyses literary texts.

Section 8.4 provides a view of another related field which has inherited methodology from stemmatology proper: musicology. Reading text, we might say that we literally "hear" internally the words we read, but, reading musical notation, can we really "hear" the piece inside our heads? Even if we can, must the difference between experiencing a real musical performance and reading musical notation not necessarily be much larger than that between spoken and written text? Consequently, many more factors than the mere notation may interest the musicologist in determining the transmission history of a piece. Cristina Urchueguía introduces the reader to this field, maintaining a special focus on the transmission of notation and on stemmatological questions and methods.

When reading across these disciplines, their terminologies can be tricky, as each discipline has coined its own terms more or less independently: some of the terms or elements of models in one field may exactly map onto other terms in another field (e.g. "witness", "language", "taxon"), while others may not be exactly congruent ("contamination" vs "loaning", and "calquing" vs "hybridisation" and "lateral gene transfer").

8.1 Phylogenetics
Heather Windram and Christopher Howe

Darwin and Lamarck both saw species as evolving from their ancestors by a process of descent with modification, according to which mutations in a parent organism are inherited by their offspring. The "history of [...] the evolutionary development of an organism or groups of organisms" by descent with modification is referred to as phylogenetics (Allen 1990, 897). Phylogenetic studies often attempt to infer the relationships by descent between groups of organisms, such as which were descended from common ancestors. Today, we typically use data that are directly genetically determined (DNA or protein sequences) for this (see e.g. www.ebi.ac.uk/training/online/course/introduction-phylogenetics/what-phylogenetics), but the use of genetic data does not necessarily follow from the definition, and the term "phylogenetic(s)" predates the popularisation of the term "gene" by the influential early geneticist Bateson in the early twentieth century. The use of computers to infer trees showing phylogenetic relationships from genetic data (which we would recognise today as phylogenetics, or phylogenetic inference) really began in the early 1960s with work by Edwards and Cavalli-Sforza to infer the evolutionary relationship among different human populations based on data from blood groups (reviewed by Edwards 2009), which are, of course, genetically determined.

8.1.1 History

8.1.1.1 Development of phylogenetic and related methods

Edwards and Cavalli-Sforza developed three methods for phylogenetic inference (Edwards 2009), which have remained fundamental to the field. These were (*i*) the method of least-squares estimation on an additive tree (in effect, the distance matrix method); (*ii*) the method of minimum evolution (in effect, maximum parsimony); and (*iii*) the method of maximum likelihood. The methods are discussed in more detail below. A number of other scientists developed approaches to classification and/or phylogenetic inference around the same time, with varying degrees of similarity to those of Edwards and Cavalli-Sforza. The German entomologist Willi Hennig developed the approach he referred to as "phylogenetic systematics" (the title of his classic book in its translation into English, 1966), which later became known as "cladistics". This grouped organisms based on their sharing derived characters (synapomorphies) that others did not have, as a result of their sharing a common ancestor. Groups would therefore reflect evolutionary relationships. The use of characters shared by one or more taxa to the exclusion of others is, in effect, a maximum parsimony criterion (see below). This use of synapomorphies in preference to other characters differentiated cladistics (and maximum parsimony) from the "numerical taxonomy" advanced by Sneath and Sokal (1962). The latter method classified organisms based on a number of characters that were all weighted equally rather than used selectively, with the organisms grouped in a cluster analysis. It was described as a "phenetic" classification, and Sneath and Sokal (1962, 856) noted that it "practises the strict separation of phylogenetic speculation from taxonomic procedure". Nevertheless, Camin and Sokal (1965) employed the data matrices used for numerical taxonomy for a parsimony-based process of phylogenetic inference.

8.1.1.2 Application of molecular sequence data

Probably the biggest driver for the application of methods for phylogenetic inference in biology was the development of techniques for the rapid determination of DNA sequence data in the 1970s. DNA is composed of chains of units called nucleotides. There are four forms of these, referred to as adenosine (A), cytidine (C), guanosine (G), and thymidine (T) nucleotides. The order in which particular nucleotides come in a chain comprises the information carried by DNA. This information is used by the cell to build proteins, the molecules responsible for many of the functions of cells. Just as DNA molecules are chains of nucleotides, proteins are chains of units called amino acids. There are twenty different amino acids that occur in proteins (although in some instances individual amino acids may be chemically modified). The order of individual amino acids is determined by the order of nucleotides in the DNA. The region of DNA containing the information for the order of amino acids in a given protein is termed the "gene" for that protein. (The order of amino acids in a protein determines the shape of the protein and its function in an organism.) As there are twenty amino acids to be specified, but only four varieties of nucleotide to specify them, organisms use groups of three nucleotides to specify each amino acid. These groups are referred to as codons. Some amino acids can be specified by many different codons; others are specified by a single codon.

In 1977, two landmark papers were published that described simple methods for determining the sequence of nucleotides in defined pieces of DNA – referred to as DNA sequencing. These methods were developed by Maxam and Gilbert (1977) at Harvard, and Sanger, Nicklen, and Coulson (1977) at Cambridge, UK. The Sanger method became the more widely adopted, although it in turn has been largely superseded by so-called "high-throughput" methods capable of generating even larger amounts of data. These methods, and especially the Sanger method, led to an explosion in DNA sequencing (and protein sequencing by inference from DNA sequences), and the resulting data became widely used for phylogenetic analysis. Phylogenetic inference is used throughout biology. It can be used to study evolutionary events ranging from the very ancient, such as the origin of the main groups of organisms (Bacteria, Archaea, and Eukaryota) billions of years ago, to the very recent, such as the seasonal origin of different strains of influenza (T. A. Williams et al. 2013; Nelson et al. 2007).

8.1.1.3 Sequence-based phylogenetic methods

The principle underlying phylogenetic analysis based on sequence data is that, as cells in an organism divide, their DNA is first copied (replicated) so that each of the resulting cells inherits a full set of DNA from the parental cell. Errors may occur during the copying process. These are referred to as mutations, and each time the DNA carrying the mutation is copied the mutation is propagated. If a mutation occurs in cells that will ultimately give rise to egg or sperm cells, the mutation will be passed to the next generation. When species or other taxonomic groups of organisms (which we refer to here as taxa, but are sometimes also referred to as operational taxonomic units, or OTUs) become separated during evolution, different mutations occur in different taxa. In general, the more closely related two taxa are (i.e. the more recently they shared a common ancestor), the more similar their DNA sequences will be. Methods for phylogenetic tree building exploit these differences. Some methods assume that there is a constant rate of mutation over time, which is referred to as a molecular clock. However, not all methods require this. For example, cladistic methods, which assume that organisms sharing a particular mutation to the exclusion of others share common ancestry, do not need to presuppose a molecular clock.

8.1.1.4 Application of phylogenetic methods to textual scholarship

The process of copying of DNA with the incorporation of changes clearly shows many attractive similarities to the copying of manuscripts by scribes. Platnick and Cameron (1977) commented on the similarities between stemmatology and phylogenetic reconstruction – although Griffith (1969) had previously applied principles from numerical taxonomy to a range of classical and biblical texts. Platnick and Cameron noted that textual criticism (and linguistics) resembled "phylogenetic systematics in being primarily concerned with constructing and testing hypotheses about the interrelationships of taxa connected by ancestor-descendant sequences" (1977, 380). They pointed out that both fields of study used similar data ("The cladist need only substitute 'taxa' for 'witnesses,' 'derived character' for 'error'"; 381) – although they argued that chronological data might be available and applicable in the field of textual criticism, but not in cladistics. Lee (1989) applied computer programs from phylogenetic analysis to St Augustine's *Quaestiones in Heptateuchum*, and Peter Robinson and Robert O'Hara (1996) described the application of phylogenetic programs to a Norse narrative, discussing in detail the similarities between textual analysis and cladistics (see 5.1.2.1). The phylogenetic approach received much attention with the publication of an analysis of the prologue to Chaucer's *The Wife of Bath's Tale* (Barbrook et al. 1998), and a number of authors have commented on the similarities of the fields and the applicability of different methods (e.g. C. J. Howe et al. 2001; Macé and Baret 2006). Since these initial studies, phylogenetic methods have been applied to a range of textual traditions (reviewed by C. J. Howe and Windram 2011), including a set of music manuscripts (Windram, Charlston, and

Howe 2014). Adopting the term "meme" used by Dawkins as a "unit of cultural transmission", the term "phylomemetics" has been proposed to refer to the phylogenetic analysis of non-biological data (Dawkins 1976, 206; see C. J. Howe and Windram 2011). This includes not only texts but also data from other disciplines, such as languages and folk tales (see 8.3).

8.1.2 Methods

It is important to recognise that phylogenetic methods depend on a model of how the data is evolving. If the data has not really been generated in accordance with that model (model misspecification), the phylogenetic tree generated may be erroneous. The phylogenetic methods commonly applied to textual traditions represent a subset of those usually used with sequence data. We focus here on the methods most widely used with texts. We give a brief summary here, although more detailed descriptions are available elsewhere (see e.g. Lemey, Salemi, and Vandamme 2009; 5.3 above). Many of these have been tested for their accuracy in stemmatology, alongside other programs developed specifically for textual analysis (see e.g. Roos and Heikkilä 2009; 5.3.7 above).

The maximum parsimony method aims to find a tree structure (topology) that requires the smallest number of character changes to give rise to the DNA or protein sequences seen at the ends of the branches of the tree (referred to as terminal nodes). The total number of possible trees increases more than exponentially as the number of taxa increases (Felsenstein 1978b), so computer algorithms employ a variety of methods to reduce the number of trees that have to be considered, for example excluding further consideration of partially constructed trees that already require more character changes than the best trees (most parsimonious) recovered so far. Distance matrix methods aim to identify the tree that gives the best fit (in terms of numbers of changes along the branches of the tree) to a matrix of distances between the DNA or protein sequences of the taxa. Neighbour-joining builds up the tree in stages, and is therefore referred to as an agglomerative clustering method. NeighborNet and the related split decomposition are also distance matrix methods (more details in 5.3.3).

A family of probability-based methods are often used with sequence data. Maximum likelihood methods calculate the probability of each tree giving the observed data under a specific evolutionary model. The tree with the highest probability is the preferred solution. These methods are computationally demanding. Bayesian methods in effect start with a standard set of prior assumptions, and then consider the effects of randomly changing those parameters. If the new set of parameters is worse than before (in terms of the probability of generating the observed data), they are rejected.

When phylogenetic methods are used to determine the copying history of a textual tradition, the DNA or protein sequences are replaced by the words in texts.

This requires the conversion of the texts into datasets resembling DNA or protein sequences, and in a format that the phylogenetic programs can use. This conversion has been described elsewhere (e.g. C. J. Howe and Windram 2011). Essentially, each text is converted into a string of characters. At any one position in the string, a character may show different states in different texts (e.g. changes of a word, or mutations in the case of DNA sequences; see 3.3.1), with any one position in the string corresponding to the same feature of the text in different witnesses. Once the texts have been converted into a dataset analogous to biological sequence datasets, the phylogenetic programs can be used essentially unchanged to analyse them.

The methods most widely used for analysis of textual traditions are arguably maximum parsimony, and distance matrix methods such as neighbour-joining and NeighborNet. Maximum likelihood methods are not widely used with texts because of the difficulty of formulating a plausible underlying evolutionary model. Bayesian methods have been used with non-biological data (e.g. the analysis of the *Little Red Riding Hood* folk tale in Tehrani 2013; see 8.3 below). It will be interesting to look at the application of these methods to texts in more detail (for more on Bayesian methods, see 5.3.6).

8.1.3 Tree structure

8.1.3.1 Topology

In their simplest format, the programs generate a tree with each of the texts at the end of a branch in the tree. Trees can be considered equivalent if they can be interconverted without the need to break and rejoin any of the branches. They are said to have the same topology. The distance along the branches between any two texts is a measure of the amount of difference between them. However, it is not always easy to interpret these distances. A large distance might indicate that multiple rounds of copying separate two witnesses, or that there were a few rounds of inaccurate copying.

8.1.3.2 Multifurcation

The trees generated by software are usually bifurcating; that is to say, internal branches (often referred to as edges) divide into two. That is not surprising, as it is typically an inevitable consequence of the algorithm used, making the tree reconstruction more tractable. Some methods allow for trees to be represented as multifurcating, that is, with a particular branch giving rise to several others. A multifurcation, or polytomy, might be an appropriate representation when a taxon radiates simultaneously into several others or when the method is unable to resolve the branching order (fig. 8.1-1).

A polytomy that arises from radiation of a taxon into several others is often referred to as a hard polytomy. One that arises when the branching order cannot

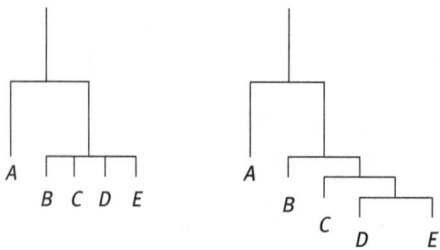

Fig. 8.1-1: A polytomy (left) can arise when a taxon simultaneously diverges into several others, or when a method is unable to resolve the branching order of a number of closely related taxa that are in principle resolvable (right).

be resolved is similarly a soft polytomy. The biological relevance of hard polytomies has been questioned (Lemey, Saelmi, and Vandamme 2009), but a hard polytomy could exist in the case of divergence of viral strains, for example where infection of an individual cell or organism could generate multiple progeny viruses by DNA replication using the same template. In the case of texts, it is clearly possible for the same text to be copied multiple times, in which case a hard polytomy would be appropriate. The question of how to allow for polytomies in textual traditions has been discussed by Phillips-Rodriguez, Howe, and Windram (2010).

8.1.3.3 Networks

Where evolutionary relationships among taxa are conflicting – e.g. if some characters in taxon *A* indicate a most recent common ancestry with *B*, whereas others indicate a most recent common ancestry with *C* – it is not possible to depict them all in a two-dimensional branching tree. In a biological context, this might arise if a taxon was derived by hybridisation between two others, or by transfer of a limited number of genes between separate taxa. In the context of textual analysis, this would occur as a result of contamination. In these cases, depicting relationships as a network may be appropriate. This is discussed in more detail below.

8.1.3.4 The root and outgroups

Many tree-building programs do not initially indicate the earliest part of the tree, referred to as the root. Care needs to be taken to avoid making an unjustified assumption about where the root lies, as shown in figure 8.1-2.

Outgroups (see 5.2.1) are used in order to allow the rooting of a phylogenetic tree in biological analysis. The outgroup is a taxon, or group of taxa, that is evolutionarily distinct from the group of species (or other taxa) that are being studied. The latter are termed the ingroup and have a close evolutionary relatedness. The outgroup must be evolutionarily related to the ingroup, but must be known to have diverged from the ingroup before the members of the ingroup diverged from one

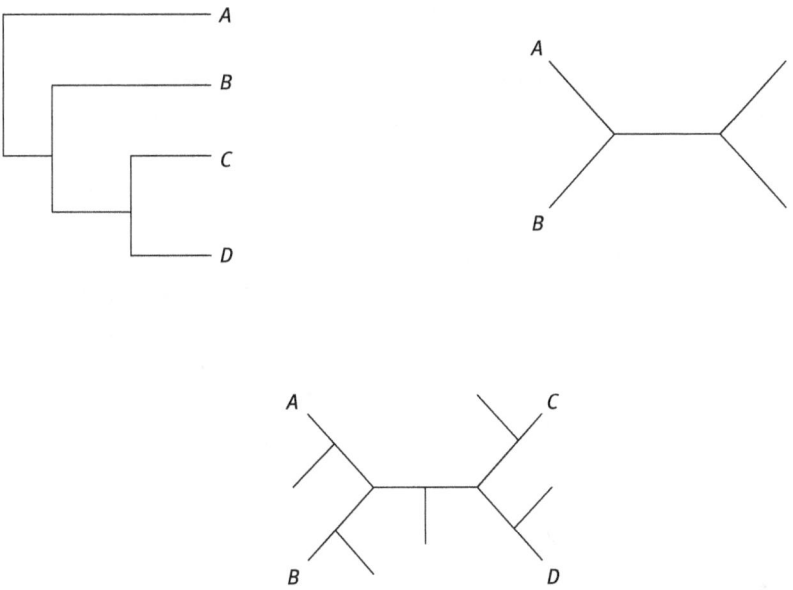

Fig. 8.1-2: Rooting a tree. Although the tree on the top left might be taken to imply that A was the earliest-diverged taxon, the tree is topologically identical to that on the top right, which makes no implication as to which taxon diverged earliest. This could be resolved by locating the root of the tree, which could go in any of five places, marked in the lower panel.

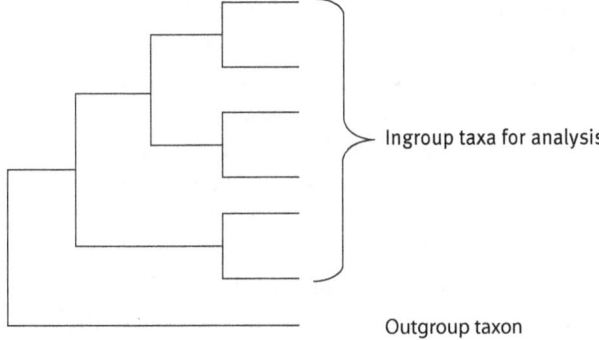

Fig. 8.1-3: Relationship of an outgroup to the ingroup.

another. Nevertheless, it must be sufficiently related that its molecular sequences (either DNA or amino acid) can be aligned unambiguously with those of the ingroup. The resultant phylogenetic tree can be rooted by the outgroup, as this is already known to represent the earliest branch on the tree (fig. 8.1-3).

It is generally not possible to use outgroups for the study of textual traditions. All witnesses to a particular text would be included in the ingroup, and there is no suitably related outgroup to include in the analysis. Other texts by the same author, or even other sections of the text under analysis, would clearly not align with the text being studied. However, in certain circumstances – e.g. if the identity of the earliest source is known from external (non-textual) evidence – it may be possible to root a textual phylogenetic tree (for an example, see 4.5.3). Rooting a tree is, in effect, indicating the direction of change along the edges within the tree. It may also be possible to do this based on an understanding of the changes involved (i.e. if change X to Y is much more likely than Y to X).

Some methods root the tree by finding the longest path separating two taxa on the tree, and placing the root half-way along that branch. This is known as midpoint rooting. This method is valid if the rate of change across the tree is constant; for sequence data, that means they are evolving according to a molecular clock (see above). This is not generally applicable to texts where the rate of change is not constant and depends on the frequency of copying, the exemplar used for making a new copy, and the number of alterations introduced into the text in a round of copying.

8.1.3.5 Reliability

A computer program for phylogenetic inference will always produce a tree. However, that does not mean that the tree is reliable. Many scholars find it helpful to use a range of different methods for phylogenetic reconstruction, and place more reliance on groupings that are consistently recovered with different methods. However, it should be realised that this is not infallible!

The technique of bootstrapping is often used to estimate the statistical reliability of particular groups. The method takes the original dataset, notes the number of sites in it, and picks the same number of sites randomly from within the dataset. That is to say, for a dataset of 200 sites, 200 sites would be picked at random from it, and the character states recorded; some sites would not be sampled, and others would be sampled once or more than once. This is described as sampling with replacement, and generates a subsidiary dataset. The process is repeated using the original dataset to generate a large number of subsidiary datasets (perhaps 100 or 1,000). They are all different from each other, but also all derived from the original. The chosen phylogenetic inference method is then applied to each of the datasets. Bootstrapping then considers the original tree and asks in what percentage of the trees derived from the subsidiary datasets a particular grouping from the original tree is seen. These percentages are then displayed on the original tree, adjacent to the nodes that define the groups. In effect, this method gives an indication of whether a particular grouping is independent (thus with a high bootstrap value) of the particular sites used to calculate the tree. Using each dataset to calculate a tree takes the same amount of time as calculating the initial tree, so for large datasets or computationally demanding methods, bootstrapping may take a large amount of time. Bayesian analysis automatically generates values indicating support for particular groupings shown in the tree, so bootstrapping is unnecessary.

It should be noted that these methods provide an estimate of how robust groupings are to the consequences of stochastic effects (e.g. whether a particular feature was included in the data). They do not provide a protection against systematic errors, for example in cases of model misspecification (see above).

8.1.3.6 Extant ancestors
Typical interpretations of phylogenetic trees with biological data assume that ancestors of extant species (which would be placed on internal nodes) no longer exist, and place all taxa at the ends (terminal nodes) of edges in the tree. Clearly, the assumption that ancestors no longer exist need not be valid for trees based on texts. Experiments with "artificial" manuscript traditions (i.e. where the copying history is known a priori) indicate that these extant ancestors are placed at the terminal nodes of very short branches emerging from their "true" position in the tree (Spencer, Davidson, et al. 2004, 507). This needs to be kept in mind when interpreting outputs.

8.1.3.7 Horizontal gene transfer and recombination
The construction of phylogenetic trees representing evolutionary relationships is underpinned by the assumption that genetic information passes down through the generations, with accumulated mutations allowing the evolution of new species. However, this vertical transmission of information is not the sole means of inheritance. It is estimated that some 20–30 % of the genome of bacteria is acquired by horizontal gene transfer (HGT), also known as lateral gene transfer (LGT). This process can be mediated by transmissible DNA molecules (plasmids, responsible, for example, for the spread of antibiotic resistance between bacterial strains), viruses, or the acquisition of naked DNA from the environment. The result of this lateral transfer is a molecule that has two or more different ancestors, rather than the single ancestor implied by a tree-like propagation. Other processes may generate products with two ancestors, including hybridisation between different taxa (which is especially significant in plant evolution), or recombination between individuals within the same taxon. Depending on the details of the process, the resulting molecule may show a single distinct break-point, with material from different ancestors on either side, or may be a patchwork (fig. 8.1-4). Recombination increases the amount of variation generated as a result of sexual reproduction.

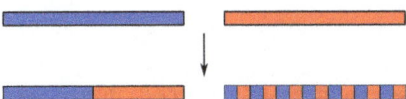

Fig. 8.1-4: Consequences of horizontal gene transfer, hybridisation, or recombination. The parental DNA sequences (red and blue) may undergo one or more recombination events to generate molecules that are composed either of two sections or of a patchwork.

These processes in biological systems are broadly analogous to contamination (see 4.4) in a textual tradition where a scribe used multiple exemplars, switching from one exemplar to another either at a single location (s u c c e s s i v e c o n t a m i - n a t i o n) or at multiple locations throughout a text (s i m u l t a n e o u s c o n t a m i - n a t i o n). Computational methods have been developed in the biological sciences that allow the representation of multiple affiliations between species. These methods show the relationships between taxa as networks rather than as simple branching trees. One such method is NeighborNet (D. Bryant and Moulton 2004).

The most likely location of a recombination event between two DNA strands (or texts) can be determined by statistical methods such as m a x i m u m c h i - s q u a r e d analysis (Maynard Smith 1992). Although this is not strictly a phylogenetic method, we nevertheless discuss it here. In this method, a putative break- (or hybridisation) point is moved stepwise along the two sequences selected for comparison, and at each point the number of differences between the two sequences on either side of the putative break-point is determined and compared with the number of differences that would be expected if the two sequences were equally related along their lengths. The chi-squared value for the deviation from the expectation is then calculated. If there is an instance of recombination or change of exemplar, it can be expected that the sequences will become more (or less) closely related after the break-point, and the site at which there is the greatest discrepancy between the observed and expected number of differences (and thus the maximum chi-squared value) is indicated as the most likely break-point. The chi-squared values at each location may be plotted, in which case the peak of the graph represents the most likely break-point. A statistical measure can be used to determine if the chi-squared value is significant, taking into account the number of taxa in the dataset, with a significant result indicating that the distribution of differences arose by recombination or exemplar change rather than simply by chance variation, at the specified level of statistical significance. Chi-squared analysis is not directly applicable where there is a mosaic of recombinant DNA or where there is more than one exemplar used throughout the generation of a given text, with multiple break-points throughout the sequence. In the context of textual analysis, the maximum chi-squared method was first applied to the prologue to *The Wife of Bath's Tale*, and gave results that were consistent with those obtained by conventional scholarship (Windram, Howe, and Spencer 2005, 202).

8.1.4 Ancestral state reconstruction

The aim of phylogenetic inference using sequence data is frequently to understand more of the evolutionary history of the taxa under consideration, rather than to reconstruct the DNA or protein sequence(s) of the ancestor of all the taxa. In some circumstances, however, reconstructing ancestral states may be useful. For example, it has been suggested that vaccines based on ancestors of present-day viral strains may be more useful than vaccines based on specific strains. A number of programs are available for ancestral state reconstruction using sequence data. They are typically based on principles of maximum parsimony, maximum likelihood, and Bayesian analysis, that is, methods dealing with individual character states rather than distance matrices. These methods have not been widely used for ancestral state reconstruction with textual data, although some examples have been described (e.g. Hoenen 2015b; 5.4.6 above). Instead, scholars have typically focused on consideration of variant readings at particular sites in a text.

8.1.5 Appropriateness of application of phylogenetic methods

Some scholars have expressed reservations over the application of phylogenetic methods to textual analysis. These reservations have been discussed elsewhere (Howe, Connolly, and Windram 2012) including in this book (see 5.5), so we will not consider them in detail here. Some of them are due to misunderstandings of the methods. Some of them are well founded, but usually they are equally applicable to conventional textual analysis as well – for example, the problem of dealing with contamination in traditions or with convergent changes (the same change occurring independently in different sequences or witnesses). It should be remembered, though, that when carrying out phylogenetic analysis in biology it is important to assess whether the methods and (often implicit) assumptions about how the data have evolved are correct. Otherwise, an incorrect phylogenetic tree may be inferred, and may even have a high statistical robustness. Similarly, analysis of texts should not be an exercise in using computer-based methods blindly to produce the single "correct" tree of relationships. Rather, it should be seen as a useful tool that allows textual scholars to focus attention most usefully on particular groups of witnesses or particular sections of a text. The process of encoding witnesses for phylogenetic analysis can be time-consuming. However, once that has been done, the ability to answer "what if" questions (What if we just look at this set of witnesses? What if we compare the copying history of this chapter with the following chapter?) may be very helpful indeed. Throughout, though, it is essential for textual scholars to use their experience in interpreting the results of phylogenetic analysis.

Further reading

Lemey, Salemi, and Vandamme (2009). Online resource: www.ebi.ac.uk/training/online/course/introduction-phylogenetics/what-phylogenetics.

8.2 Linguistics

Dieter Bachmann

This section discusses the history of the genetic, or phylogenetic, perspective in the study of the history of languages. An overview of the use of computational phylogenetic methods in the field of historical linguistics since the early 2000s is given.

8.2.1 Origins of historical linguistics

In the history of ideas, the discovery of language change is surprisingly recent. It may even be argued that the notion is an entirely modern one, made explicit only in scholarship of the seventeenth to eighteenth centuries. In the grammatical traditions of Antiquity, both in the Graeco-Roman West and in India, there certainly was an awareness of differences between languages and registers, such as Pāṇini's recognition of grammatical rules that apply only *chandasi* (i.e. in the Vedic hymns), but this does not amount to the hypothesis that such differences are due to a process of historical evolution. Such recognition of linguistic change as we find in the Greek classics (e.g. Plato *Cratylus* 432; Aristotle *Poetics* 1457) is concerned with the introduction of error, without the suggestion that the accumulation of such errors over sufficiently long timespans may result in entirely new languages. As noted by Gippert (forthcoming, citing Lentz 1870, 791), some grammarians of the first century BC do, however, seem to assume that Latin was derived from Greek; according to the testimony of Herodianus (second century AD), the grammarian Philoxenus notes the lack of a dual among Aeolians and among Romans, arguing that the Romans are descended from the Aeolians.

Indeed, the main reference to the idea of language change in ancient literature is Genesis 11, the confusion of tongues at Babel, which is also immediately paired with the idea of migration in the form of the "scattering over the face of the whole earth" of the speakers of the individual languages now "confused". The Babel story provides an explanation for language change implicit in the assumption that (*i*) all nations are descended from one common ancestor (the biblical Noah) and that (*ii*) each nation is characterised by its own language. Early Christian literature specified the number of nations as seventy-two (based on the number of grandsons of Noah; cf. Augustine *De civitate Dei* 16.3), and in mediaeval literature this occasionally appears as the number of languages created in the confusion of tongues (e.g. in the Irish *Auraicept na n-Éces*, which holds that the Irish language was created by combining what was best in each of the seventy-two languages).

The study of language change can thus be considered a strictly modern, and strictly Western, innovation. Observations regarding the similarity of words in different languages were made as early as the sixteenth century; notably, Filippo Sassetti, a Florentine traveller to India, noted the striking similarity of certain words in Sanskrit and Italian in a letter dated 1585. More systematic comparisons postulating the derivation of modern languages from a common source were published in the seventeenth century, notably by Marcus Zuerius Boxhornius (1647), without receiving widespread recognition (Muller 1986). The first exposition of the idea of a genealogical relationship of the world's languages paralleling the history of the world's peoples is probably a short essay by Leibniz published in 1710 (entitled "Brevis designatio mediationum de originibus gentium, ductis potissimum ex indicio linguarum"). Leibniz here aimed at what we would today call Proto-World, surveying most known languages of Europe, Asia, and Africa, and suggesting that the linguistic changes accumulating over time might be so extreme as to render the relationship unrecognisable. William Jones, in 1786, noted the similarity of Sanskrit to Greek and Latin, postulating their derivation from "a common source, which, perhaps, no longer exists" (quoted in e.g. Meier-Brügger 2003, 173–174).

8.2.2 Comparative Indo-European linguistics

The systematic comparative study of Indo-European languages developed in the early decades of the nineteenth century, as documented in the *Vergleichende Grammatik* of Franz Bopp (1833–1852). The first graphical representation of a family tree (*Stammbaum*) of Indo-European language families was published by August Schleicher (fig. 8.2-1).

The choice of representation by Schleicher was directly inspired by Darwin's *Origin of Species*, published only two years earlier in 1859. Schleicher would go on to make this explicit in a communication entitled "Die Darwinsche Theorie und die Sprachwissenschaft" to his friend, the evolutionary biologist Ernst Haeckel, in 1863.

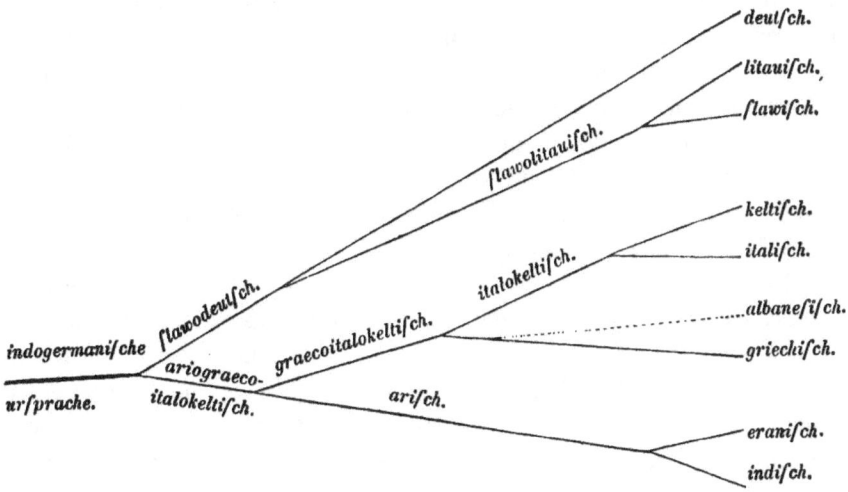

Fig. 8.2-1: Schleicher's genealogical tree. Source: Schleicher (1861, 1:7).

Schleicher's 1861 phylogenetic diagram depicts the genealogy of nine contemporary Indo-European language families with eight binary nodes (Armenian was recognised as an independent branch later, by Heinrich Hübschmann in 1875; the two eccentric branches of Tocharian and Anatolian were discovered still later, in 1908 and 1915 respectively). Branch length in Schleicher's diagram indicates relative time-depth: of his eight intermediate nodes, only the two most recent ones remain generally accepted, Balto-Slavic ("slawolitauisch") and Indo-Iranian ("arisch"); the others, including Italo-Celtic and Germano-Balto-Slavic ("slawodeutsch"), find at best very limited support today.

Schleicher postulated the phylogenetic relationship of Indo-European languages forcefully, to the point of being considered the originator of the *Stammbaum-theorie* (the stemmatological approach to relationships between languages). But Darwin (1859, 422) himself had already adduced the phylogeny of languages as an example. Like Leibniz (1710), he identifies the genealogy of languages and that of mankind as going back to Proto-World, saying that "a genealogical arrangement of the races of man would afford the best classification of the various languages now spoken throughout the world" and that "the various degrees of difference in the languages from the same stock, would have to be expressed by groups subordinate to groups; but the proper or even only possible arrangement would still be genealogical".

Nevertheless, as had been clear to historical linguists since before Schleicher's publication, the comparative evidence did not naturally result in a picture that favoured a genealogical or tree-like (phylogenetic) representation. Evidence considered in comparative linguistics is of at least three types: phonology (sound laws), lexicon (cognate vocabulary), and morphology (word formation), and, where possible, syntax. The study of these aspects in isolation will immediately result in relationships that are mutually exclusive in naive phylogenetic terms. An important example from the field of phonology is the centum–satem division, which bisects the Indo-European phylum (with the exception of the marginal branches of Anatolian and Tocharian, and possibly of Albanian and Armenian). At first glance, this is a major division of the Indo-European family of languages, neatly producing an eastern and a western group, Balto-Slavic and Indo-Iranian in the east (satem), and Greek, Italic, Celtic, and Germanic in the west (centum). But nothing else about the languages thus grouped necessarily suggests any closer relationship within each group; indeed, Balto-Slavic and Indo-Iranian end up at opposite ends of Schleicher's diagram. Schleicher's fashionable "linguistic Darwinism" was therefore harshly criticised from the outset. Its main opponent was Johannes Schmidt, who, in the assessment of Delbrück (1919, 118), had "done away for good with [endgültig beseitigt] Schleicher's theory" in 1872. Schmidt's *Wellentheorie* replaced the phylogenetic model of language change with the notion of waves of innovation which could travel across linguistic boundaries. It goes without saying that Schmidt's work by no means spelled the final end of attempts to describe the Indo-European family in phylogenetic terms, but the recognition of ubiquitous waves of linguistic innovation (in stemmatological terms, contamination; see 4.4) in the late nineteenth century had the beneficial effect of liberating historical linguistics from worrying over phylogenetic paradoxes, and instead allowed it to be led where the data pointed. Rather than by a phylogenetic structure, linguistic relationships in general are more naturally represented by means of a map of isoglosses. The more crossing of isoglosses is present, the less the situation will be amenable to a phylogenetic representation. Anttila (1989, 305) provides an exemplary isogloss map of the Indo-European phylum, including twenty-four isoglosses in which the centum–satem isogloss crosses eight others.

With the discovery of the Anatolian and Tocharian branches in the early twentieth century, the phylogeny of Indo-European began to look a little more articulated, or tree-like. The hypothesis that the Anatolian branch can serve as an archaic outgroup for the remaining phylum has become known under the somewhat misleading name of the "Indo-Hittite hypothesis", coined in the 1930s. This proposal long remained controversial, and was contrasted with the *Schwund-Hypothese*, which claimed that the absence from Anatolian of many features which appeared to be common elsewhere in the Indo-European phylum was due to loss rather than representing the archaic stage of the language family. While the question has not been resolved completely, progress in the reconstruction of Anatolian in the 1990s seems to bear out the early separation of Anatolian, albeit perhaps not as far removed from the breakup of non-Anatolian Indo-European as originally envisaged in the Indo-Hittite hypothesis (Melchert 1998, forthcoming). It is also commonly assumed that the Tocharian branch was the next to diverge from Common Indo-European after Anatolian (Watkins 2001). By contrast, a phylogenetic tree of Indo-European published by Hamp (1990), based on a combination of morphology, phonology, and lexicon, placed Tocharian under "Northwest-IE" alongside a number of poorly attested Palaeo-Balkan languages. If we wanted to represent the consensus in the field as to the phylogenetics of the Indo-European phylum, little more than three nodes, Anatolian–"Late PIE", Balto-Slavic, and Indo-Iranian, could be argued to be uncontroversial, at least for the most part, with a large "bush-like" node of nine branches not amenable to phylogenetic resolution. Figure 8.2-4 contrasts the minimal, or bush-like, phylogeny that can be said to be widely accepted with the more speculative but still fairly mainstream articulation distinguishing "early" (Proto-Indo-Hittite), "middle", and "late" stages of Proto-Indo-European (PIE).

With the addition of nodes at least widely held to be somewhat plausible – the early divergence of Tocharian, and the Italo-Celtic and Palaeo-Balkan (Graeco-Armenian) groupings – the bush-like node still unites at least five branches. Here, the question arises of what exactly should be understood as a genetic relationship between languages: languages thus grouped together may or may not reflect prolonged linguistic contact between already articulated groups, in the sense of a *Sprachbund*, at a time in prehistory when these languages had not yet diverged very widely.

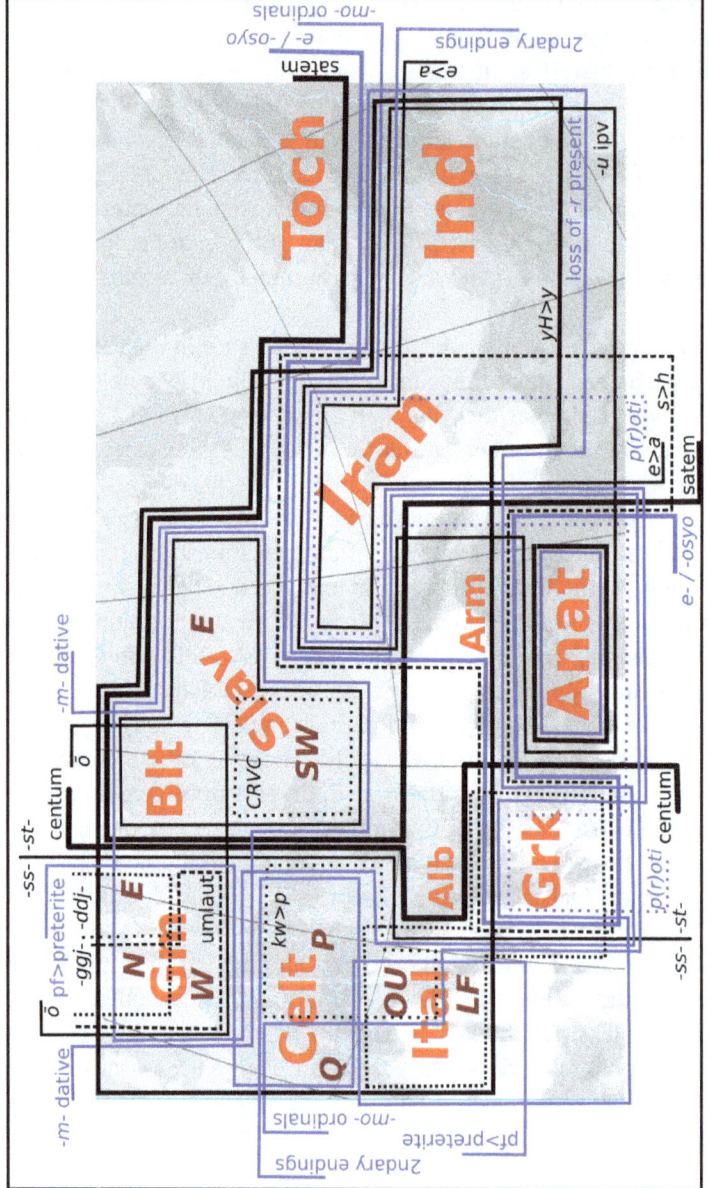

Fig. 8.2-2: A map of major isoglosses separating the twelve main Indo-European language families, after Anttila (1989, 305). All isoglosses shown are morphological (blue) or phonological (black), not lexical. Language families are shown in the approximate geographical location they (or their ancestral dialects) would have had around the late Bronze Age (although some of the later isoglosses may not have developed before the Iron Age). The isoglosses selected in Anttila (1989) divide some of the main families into subgroups: North, East, and West Germanic; East Slavic vs South and West Slavic; Q-Celtic vs P-Celtic; and Osco-Umbrian vs Latino-Faliscan within Italic.

The contrast between *Stammbaumtheorie* and *Wellentheorie* is illustrated in figures 8.2-2–3. The map in figure 8.2-2 shows a selection of major isoglosses separating the twelve main Indo-European language families (after Anttila 1989, 305). Isoglosses were selected for grouping families; each named family has numerous isoglosses unique to itself that are not shown. All isoglosses shown are morphological (in blue) or phonological (in black), not lexical. Any crossing isoglosses indicate the presence

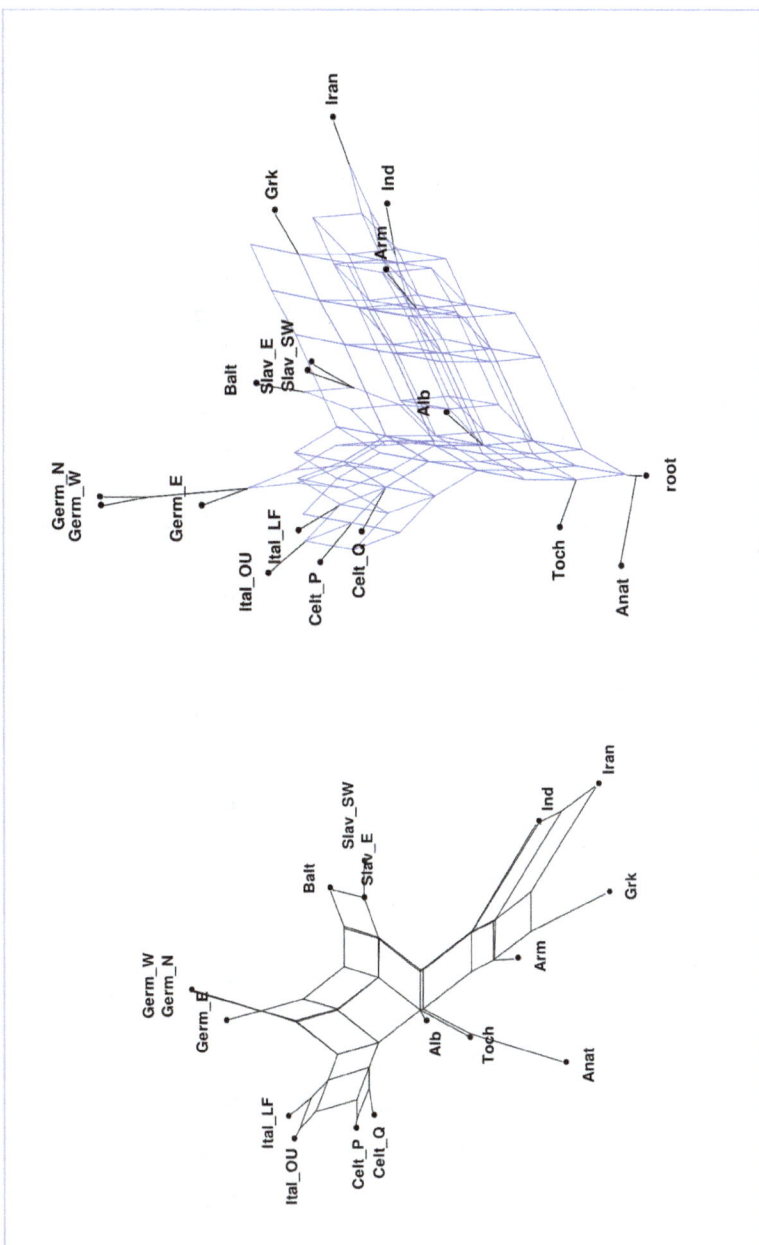

Fig. 8.2-3: Visualisation of the isogloss topology shown in figure 8.2-2 as phylogenetic networks, illustrating the significantly non-tree-like structure of Indo-European. Left: an unrooted network generated using the NeighborNet algorithm (D. Bryant and Moulton 2004); right: a rooted hybridisation network (Huson and Klöpper 2007) with Anatolian as outgroup, calculated using SplitsTree4 (Huson and Bryant 2006). A similar analysis has been published by Heggarty, Maguire, and McMahon (2010).

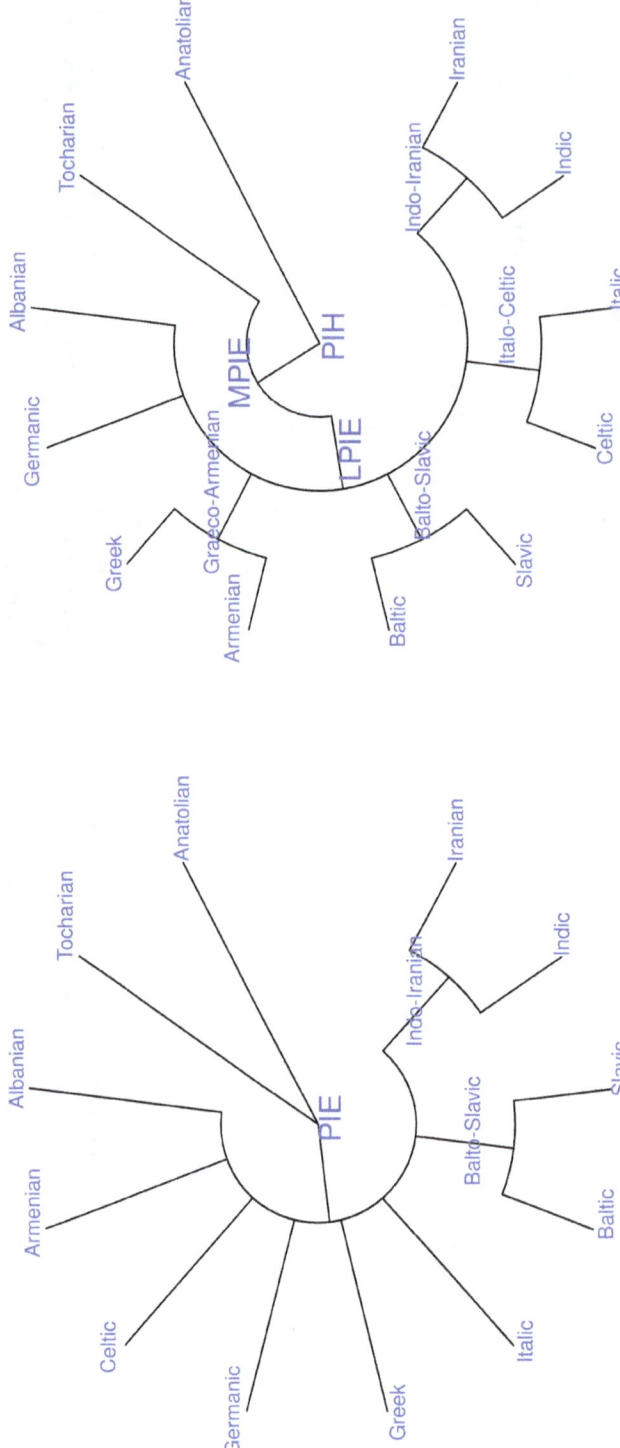

Fig. 8.2-4: Comparison of the unarticulated, high-consensus and the more articulated, low-consensus phylogenetic diagrams of Indo-European language families drawn as rooted phylogenetic trees. The more articulated variant distinguishes "early" (Proto-Indo-Hittite, PIH), "middle" (MPIE), and "late" (LPIE) stages of Proto-Indo-European.

of non-tree-like signals. Figure 8.2-3 uses these isoglosses to construct two phylogenetic networks. This can be taken as a rough visualisation of the significantly non-tree-like structure of Indo-European, evident even from a very limited (albeit not randomly selected) dataset based on phonology and morphology only. By contrast, figure 8.2-5 illustrates the use of purely lexical data typical of the lexico-statistical approach. A separate phylogeny can in principle be derived for each lexeme independently – in the case shown here, the lexeme for "sun". The task of calculating a phylogeny for entire language families would then amount to the search for a "consensus tree" for the phylogenies assumed for the individual lexemes.

It may be important to remind ourselves, focusing on the question of phylogenetics as we are here, that this inconclusiveness does not by any means represent a failure of the two-centuries-long project of Indo-European reconstruction: Indo-European studies is primarily a philological field tasked with studying the historical development of the recorded languages and with reconstructing their common proto-language. There is no compelling reason for the philologist to assume that any given subset of linguistic history can necessarily be represented by a genealogical tree with any degree of accuracy. The burden is on the phylogeneticists (that is to say, on such historical linguists as advocate phylogenetic methods) to show that their methods are of any use in the field. This point will become important presently in understanding the cool reception which the more recent attempts at introducing methods of computational phylogenetics into historical linguistics have tended to be met with.

8.2.3 Other phyla and proposed macro-families

Indo-European has been something of an ideal case for the development of historical linguistics and the comparative method: its numerous branches, its great time-depth, and the antiquity of the written record of several of its member families were all conducive to a bountiful picking of low-hanging fruit in the early phase of the field's history. While the phylum does not, as we have seen, present itself as overwhelmingly tree-like, it is still sufficiently "bush-like" to suggest genealogy rather than a history of random or purely areal wave-like exchange of linguistic features.

There are only a handful of candidates for linguistic phyla with similar properties among the world's languages. First, there are Afro-Asiatic and Sino-Tibetan, perhaps both, or at least the former, likely of an age comparable to that of Indo-European. Austronesian is of more recent attestation, but of no lesser attractiveness in this context, making up for its limited time-depth by the remarkably tree-like structure resulting from the literal isolation of its (island-dwelling) communities of speakers. Several others, such as Uralic, Niger–Congo, Mon–Khmer, Uto-Aztecan, or Tupi, may be of considerable antiquity, but reconstruction is fraught with difficulties due to very late attestation. Most other proposed large phyla are even more difficult to tackle, and often their very existence as a phylogenetic unit is disputed (Altaic, Nilo-Saharan). Other families are less diversified, comparable perhaps to the divisions within some of the branches of Indo-European (e.g. Dravidian, Tungusic, Eskimo–Aleut). In summary, there are perhaps in the order of half a dozen major linguistic phyla which can reasonably be hoped to yield information on proto-languages spoken in deep prehistory, that is, before around six thousand years ago (the Old World Neolithic or Chalcolithic). The scholarly effort poured into the comparative study of these families is, of course, far beyond the capacity of a single scholar, which may have led to a fragmentation of the field (Kortlandt 1995).

Beyond the reconstruction of the deep history of non-Indo-European phyla, there are proposals which combine already reconstructed phyla into super-phyla, which might then reach down to late Palaeolithic times, ten thousand years ago or earlier. The most notable proposal in this context is Nostratic (named thus by Holger Pedersen in 1903), which would combine at least Indo-European, Altaic, and Uralic into a large Eurasian super-phylum, besides various proposed subgroupings such as Indo-Uralic. The main proponent of this type of reconstruction during the second half of the twentieth century was Joseph Greenberg, who went against the linguistic mainstream in proposing that genealogical relationships can, after all, be extricated for very remote phyla if enough data is available (a notion which became known and criticised under the name of "mass comparison" in historical linguistics). While such proposals have gained somewhat wider popularity since the 1990s, it must be emphasised that they are much more speculative by their nature than conventional linguistic reconstruction, and not based on evidence of comparable reliability to that gained by the philologist's careful search for archaisms. As pointed out by Kortlandt (1995), comparative linguistics prides itself more in basing its conclusions on a small body of unassailable evidence than trusting in statistics. For this reason, Greenberg's mass comparison approach never achieved recognition in the mainstream of historical linguistics (Campbell 2003).

Greenberg can still be considered a pioneer of a data-driven, algorithmic approach reminiscent of the phylogenetic methods used in biology. His approach is also the only viable one in the case of large language families without a literary tradition, as in the case of African or New World languages. It is certainly meaningful to use mass comparison to group the hundreds of languages in the Niger–Congo group, quite regardless of whether this group is considered a phylum in the phylogenetic sense; the interpretation of such a grouping as a genetic classification goes to the heart of the question of what exactly we mean when we talk of the genetic relationship of languages. The main worry is essentially that the method is underdetermined, so that an algorithmic approach of this kind will always result in the "discovery" of ever larger "genetic" macro-families regardless of the data, without any objective criteria to judge the reliability of such proposals. For the macro-families discovered in this way, it is intractable whether their shared features (even assuming that pure chance, or onomatopoeia, has been duly ruled out) are in fact genetic in nature rather than merely areal and the result of prolonged language contact. The case of the Indo-Pacific family proposed by Greenberg himself in 1971, claimed by supporters to be at least forty thousand years old (Ruhlen 1994, 144), is just one example.

A level even more remote from the classical comparative method is represented by theories of m o n o g e n e s i s or g l o t t o g o n y, that is, the derivation of all known human languages from a common origin spoken in the middle Palaeolithic (the time of phylogenetic unity of *Homo sapiens* itself, or at least prior to the long-lasting division of humanity by its dispersal across continents). This debate can no longer pretend to be based on comparative evidence, however sparse. Instead, the argument is one of plausibility: since language is a human universal, it stands to reason that its genealogy goes back to the original dispersal of anatomically modern humans, represented by the split of the hunter-gatherers of southern Africa from the remaining populations of early *Homo sapiens*, at least 150,000, or possibly as early as 300,000 years ago (Schlebusch et al. 2017). The topic of glottogony has long been a taboo in linguistics, for the very good reason that it attracts boundless speculation: when Darwinism was freshly *en vogue* in the 1860s, linguistic debate was inundated with such proposals to the point where, in 1866, the Linguistic Society of Paris banned the entire topic as a hopeless exercise, a prohibition that had a lasting influence in the field of historical linguistics. The question of the first development of the human language faculty is of course a valid topic in contemporary evolutionary anthropology, but it is hardly amenable to the methods of historical linguistics. It may still be worth mentioning in this context that a 2012 study arrived at a plausible middle Palaeolithic estimate for the age of Proto-World based on a simple model of gradual increase of phonemic diversity over time (Perreault, Mathew, and Petraglia 2012).

8.2.4 Time-depth and *Urheimat*

A genealogical view of language is necessarily concerned with the history and prehistory of human migration. The parallelism of the genealogy of languages and the genealogy of the "races of man" were made explicit in the absolute in the statements by Leibniz (1710) and Darwin (1859) discussed above. And, even though the phenomenon of wave-like innovations through language contact is of course real, any postulate of a language family in the genealogical sense implies the geographical separation of a population of speakers of a proto-language over a period of time sufficient for language change beyond mutual comprehensibility.

The question of the original home or *U r h e i m a t*, or homeland, of the Indo-European phylum has received considerable attention ever since the existence of the phylum was recognised. The question does, however, go beyond the field of historical linguistics proper, and requires the evaluation of evidence from archaeology and anthropology. The early history of the preferred scholarly hypotheses regarding the Indo-European homeland does not inspire confidence. Opinion has fluctuated based on intellectual fashion in the best case, and based on political ideology in the worst. In the early nineteenth century, enthusiasm for the recent discovery of the surprisingly archaic nature of Sanskrit – combined with the equally recent infatuation of Western romanticism with Buddhism and Hinduism – produced the "Indomania" of which Friedrich Schlegel was the primary proponent. In the mid-nineteenth century, based on more systematic studies of the vocabulary for plants and animals, central Asia became the leading hypothesis, favoured by Max Müller, Franz Bopp, Jacob Grimm, and others (Sasse 2017, 334). During the second half of the nineteenth century, the central Asian hypothesis stood opposed to a northern European one. Northern Europe was strongly preferred by British scholars – such as Robert Latham, Canon Isaac Taylor, and John Rhys – in particular, and the idea was well received in the Scandinavian Romantic nationalism of the time. In the early twentieth century, northern Europe also tended to become favoured among German scholars such as Matthäus Much and Hermann Hirt (Hirt 1905–1907, 1:334). This is the origin of the unhappy association of the term "Aryan" (at the time used as a name for the entire Indo-European phylum) with northern European ethnography, even though Max Müller had warned, already in the 1880s, against the rash conflation of linguistic and anthropological features ("an ethnologist who speaks of Aryan race, Aryan blood, Aryan eyes and hair, is as great a sinner as a linguist who speaks of a dolichocephalic dictionary or a brachycephalic grammar"; Müller 1888, 120).

The question of geographical origin of a language family is of course closely tied to that of its temporal depth. The term "glottochronology" was coined for methods to estimate the age of reconstructed prehistoric languages – the "molecular clock" (see 8.1.1.3), as it were, of language change – by Morris Swadesh in the early 1950s (Jenset and McGillivray 2017, 62). Comparative linguists in the later twentieth century have tended to balk at participating in glottochronology or *Urheimat* debates, emphasising that comparative reconstruction has validity in its own right, but is by its nature capable of reconstructing linguistic features only, not of attaching an absolute time or place to the reconstructions. Indeed, arguments for both geographical and temporal estimates on the basis of reconstructed vocabulary can carry weight only in aggregate: semantic shift prevents the preservation of the type of compelling archaism favoured in purely linguistic reconstruction. For example, the reconstruction of a PIE word **laks* for "salmon" was used to argue for an area of origin in northern Europe where Atlantic salmon is found, first proposed by Otto Schrader (1883). This argument, in isolation, carries no weight, as the word in question could well have referred to trout in the proto-language and might have been independently transferred to salmon by such Indo-European groups as happened to settle near the North Sea (Thieme 1953). Similarly, the reconstruction of a PIE word **hrotha* for "wheel" or "wagon" would necessarily require a date for the proto-language later than the invention of the wheel about six thousand years ago. But the word might be a derivation from a verbal root meaning "to roll" and thus indicate any "rolling thing" without necessarily implying the presence of an axle and wheel, and, similarly to the "salmon" case, could easily have been independently used as a name for the wheel or chariot once they became available.

In the late twentieth century, a wide-ranging consensus nevertheless emerged, which favours the placement of the Indo-European proto-language on the Pontic–Caspian steppe roughly 6,500 to 5,000 years ago, that is, at the boundary between eastern Europe and central Asia geographically, and between the late Neolithic and the early Bronze Age temporally. This steppe-origin model is also known as the Kurgan hypothesis, advocated by archaeologist Marija Gimbutas, beginning in the 1950s. It was to a large extent predicated on the progress made by Soviet archaeology in the early to mid-twentieth century, and centres on the Pit Grave, or Yamnaya, cultural horizon and its immediate predecessors (*kurgan* being the Tatar and Russian word for the burial mounds associated with this and later cultures of the area). The Kurgan hypothesis was widely popularised by Mallory (1989). Kortlandt (1990) discusses the hypothesis in terms of a series of waves of expansion from the steppe area; an Indo-Hittite separation as early as 6,500 years ago; and the Yamnaya context of about 5,000 years ago, which he identifies with those groups affected by satem, that is, the proto-languages of Balto-Slavic and Indo-Iranian.

While the Kurgan hypothesis, among such Indo-Europeanists who do not prefer to remain agnostic as a matter of principle, has eclipsed the early theories of a northern European or Indian homeland, there are two competing hypotheses proposed in the 1980s that may be worth mentioning, both favouring a homeland in Asia Minor. The Armenian hypothesis proposed by Gamkrelidze and Ivanov (1984) proposes a late date (fourth millennium BC), and hinges on an idiosyncratic reconstruction of PIE phonology by these authors which has found little mainstream interest. The Anatolian hypothesis proposed by Renfrew (1987), on the other hand, proposes an extremely early date (seventh millennium BC), and equates the Indo-European expansion with the Neolithic expansion from Asia Minor to Europe. This suggestion has likewise found little support among Indo-Europeanists, but it has become notable in the context of the computational modelling of Indo-European phylogeny in the 2000s (see 8.2.6).

There is no shortage of treatments of the conflation of the Indo-European homeland question with nationalist ideology, which has indeed occurred, not exclusively but most notoriously in Germany. It is less common to point out that the history of the now most widely accepted scenario likewise has an ideological component, one of "eco-feminism" (Gimbutas, at least in her later years, painted a picture of the Indo-Europeans as patriarchal warriors invading peaceful matristic cultures of Neolithic Europe). As noted by Anthony (1996), such "interpretive abuse" of prehistoric migration in the light of present-day ideological preferences has caused many archaeologists to view the project of comparing linguistic and archaeological evidence with suspicion.

Urheimat debates for other linguistic families are plagued by similar uncertainty. For Afro-Asiatic, the debate is divided between the hypotheses of an African (most likely in or close to the Horn of Africa) and an Asiatic (Levantine) hypothesis (Blench 2006, 144). For Austronesian, the homeland question is tied to the speed of expansion, the "slow boat" hypothesis suggesting a deep prehistory in Melanesia as opposed to the "express train to Polynesia" hypothesis suggesting more recent origin in Taiwan. This latter question of Austronesian origins, at least, has a reasonable chance of being amenable to conclusive resolution based on population genetics (Oppenheimer and Richards 2001).

Kortlandt (1990, 1) states the following caveat on the difficulty of aligning archaeology and language: "Speculations about the linguistic affinity of a prehistoric culture are futile because it is reasonable to assume that the vast majority of prehistoric linguistic groups have vanished without leaving a trace." There is, that is to say, an asymmetry between archaeology and linguistics because the archaeological record is potentially far more complete than the linguistic one. This is a sentiment often expressed in comparative linguistics: since most of the history of languages is lost without trace, such vestiges as we have are due to the accidents of preservation and cannot be regarded as a representative sample of anything. The same view is expressed from the point of view of archaeology by Blench (2008). It is certainly well advised to avoid the rash conflation of archaeology, ethnography, and linguistics. Nevertheless, there is no reason to disregard independent evidence that may increase or decrease the plausibility of a hypothesis. And, in any case, speculation is necessary if progress is to be made, as in the case of the Kurgan hypothesis, which was originally proposed as an archaeological hypothesis and gained its mainstream status later due to cumulative evidence which happened to favour it quite independently of a possible ideological backdrop to its original formulation.

Unfortunately, during the 1960s to 1980s, scepticism towards such proposals was extended beyond the reasonable by an ideological fashion which rejected "migrationism" as nationalistic or imperialistic in favour of a "diffusionism" based on Marxist archaeology. The 1970s adage of "pots are not people" is trivially true, of course, but it entailed the prohibition of any attempt to link the two as politically irresponsible. This ideological reluctance to view material and linguistic prehistory in combination most strongly affected the English-speaking world, where it reached its apex in the fully postmodernist "post-processual archaeology" of the 1980s before it began to wane during the 1990s (Härke 1998).

It is partly for such reasons that progress regarding the age and phylogenetics of linguistic phyla, primarily of Indo-European, was not revived, and did not attract mainstream interest, until the 1990s. Other, more pragmatic reasons lie in technological advances that only then became available: the rapid progress in DNA sequencing (8.2.6) and the availability of computational methods capable of tackling complex phylogenetics (8.2.5).

8.2.5 Computational estimates

Comparative linguistics is traditionally concerned with the reconstruction of a proto-language without necessarily opining on the phylogenetic relationship between daughter languages, let alone on absolute time-depth. To this end, the most valuable information comes from archaisms, for example in the form of grammatical irregularities. A famous example is the exact equation of Sanskrit *vṛkīs* and Old Norse *ylgr*, "she-wolf", discovered by Karl Verner in 1877. This not only establishes the existence of a word for "she-wolf" in the parent language of Germanic and Indic, right down to its accentuation and inflection; it also establishes the presence of a grammatical feminine, or at least a morphological derivation for the female of an animal species. In contrast to stemmatology, perhaps, the ubiquitous possibility of language contact (or stemmatological contamination) reduces the value of what look like common innovations (or stemmatological *Leitfehler*). For these reasons, computational phylogenetic methods have so far played a limited role in comparative linguistics. Attempts to generate phylogenetic trees of language families have, of course, been made since the 1960s, but these have always been of limited or no use in adding information to what has already been worked out by the experts: the quality of the results achieved by the new method has been judged based on what was already known rather than in terms of previous knowledge being evaluated or verified in light of the new results. The main difficulty in such approaches lies in the choice of what type of information to use as input data. Most of the time, such material will already implicitly contain the judgement of the philologists who, for example, provided the etymological dictionaries used to produce a table of cognates used as the input to be analysed by the phylogenetic algorithm. In his overview of the history of phylogenetic methods applied to language history, Dunn (2014, 192) emphasises that "correct cognate classification is no trivial matter".

By far the most popular approach is the use of Swadesh lists, the comparison of languages based on the number of cognates they share in a short list of core vocabulary. As an example, let us consider a single lexeme of the Indo-European Swadesh-100 list in Dyen, Kruskal, and Black (1992). The word for "sun" in Indo-European, reconstructed as nom. **sahwl*, gen. **shwens* (a heteroclitic stem with alternating -*l*- and -*n*- suffix), can be traced throughout most of the branches of Indo-European, and in some cases undergoes characteristic evolution which is not only phonological but also morphological (see fig. 8.2-5). A Swadesh list-based phylogenetic study of the type of Gray and Atkinson (2003) will retain from this complex reconstruction only the binary information that the original lexeme is present in all branches other than Anatolian, Tocharian, Armenian, and Albanian (and is further absent in Gorkhali, an Indic language which appears to have adopted the same non-Indo-European lexeme found in Tocharian, and in Irish, which has retained as the unmarked word for "sun" what seems to be an epithet derived from the Indo-European word for "warm").

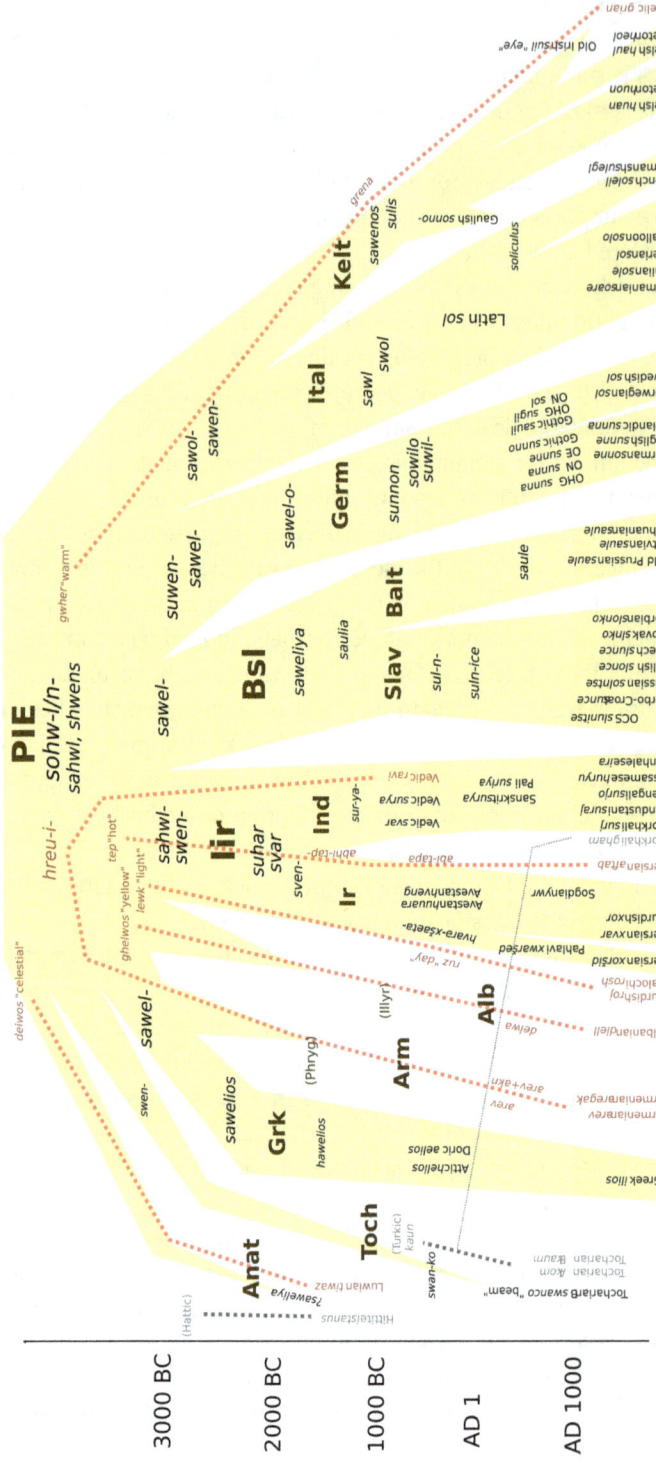

Fig 8.2-5: This figure shows a simplified phylogeny for the lexeme for "sun" in Indo-European. The forms given in attested languages are based on the *Indo-European Lexical Cognacy Database* (*IELex*; ielex.mpi.nl; originally from Dyen, Kruskal, and Black 1992), with simplified orthography. The time scale on the left is intended as a rough approximation only. The phylogenetic diagram shown in outline traces derivations from the PIE word for "sun", nom. **sahwl*, gen. **shwens* (a recent publication on the Indo-European lexeme is Simms 2017). Dotted lines trace cases where the word for "sun" was replaced with a different lexeme. A lexico-statistical analysis of this word in a Swadesh list will treat all words derived from the **sahwl*, **shwens* paradigm as etymologically identical.

Considering the extreme simplicity of the Swadesh list approach, it is capable of producing surprisingly solid results. But the method is abused if it has to carry epistemic weight of the kind of "English and Russian share 34 percent of lexemes in the Swadesh-100, which would imply that their common ancestor split [...] approximately 4000 years ago" (Pereltsvaig and Lewis 2015, 94). On the other hand, it is very difficult to go beyond the Swadesh list approach, as the more parameters are introduced, the more subjective the decision about which to include and how to weight them against one another becomes.

In the early 2000s, a series of publications presented reconstructions of language phylogenies calculated on the basis of Swadesh lists. Dunn (2014, 206) dates the beginning of the "modern phylogenetic era in linguistics" to the publication of Gray and Jordan (2000), who argued for the rapid model of Austronesian expansion based on a phylogenetic tree constructed from vocabulary lists.

An early such study dedicated to Indo-European, published in 2002, was a collaboration of two historical linguists and a computer scientist. Marked as "work in progress", the paper discusses methodology and presents a number of best trees based on a database including phonological, morphological, and lexical features. The paper's main takeaway is that "we need to devise appropriate methods for inferring non-treelike networks of linguistic diversification", echoing the conclusions drawn from the original *Stammbaumtheorie* approach in the 1870s (Ringe, Warnow, and Taylor 2002, 112).

The publication by Gray and Atkinson (2003) was less modest in its conclusions, and much more widely received. Published in *Nature*, this paper announced that "language-tree divergence times support the Anatolian theory of Indo-European origin". Based purely on Swadesh lists of modern Indo-European languages (with the addition of Hittite and Tocharian lists), the authors used a phylogenetic method which allowed for variable "molecular clocks" to estimate divergence times in their consensus tree. The claimed support for the Anatolian theory (Renfrew 1987) was derived from an estimated age of the tree root of close to nine thousand years, which, the authors concluded, favoured the theory of a spread of Indo-European in the course of the Neolithic revolution over the Chalcolithic steppe origin proposed by the Kurgan hypothesis. The main criticism that has to be raised against the 2003 paper is clearly that it was overselling itself with sensationalist PR. The strength of the study was the presentation of a surprisingly credible phylogeny with branch lengths, and its use of a variable clock genuinely addressed the most prevalent criticism of the failings of naive glottochronology. It was not concerned with Anatolia in any way, and the estimated age of the root was just one feature, and indeed the least reliable one in the reconstructed tree (because, at the root of the tree, there is no longer any data to suggest variation of clock speed). This result may serve as an illustration of the observation made more than a decade earlier by Kortlandt (1990, 2), who diagnosed "a general tendency to date proto-languages farther back in time than is warranted by the linguistic evidence". The problem addressed by Kortlandt is at least partly a terminological one: should, for example, "proto-Romance" refer to the time of the breakup of the varieties of Latin spoken in the late Roman Empire, or should it refer to a – possibly ahistorical – complete unity of the Latin language in early Rome about a millennium earlier? And, by analogy, should "PIE" refer to the period of Indo-European expansion and breakup, or should it refer to a theoretical dialect-free complete unity of Indo-Hittite? It is this exaggerated postulate of complete linguistic unity in a proto-language, never observed in any living language, that causes the excessive age estimates. In addition, the absence of any "methods for inferring non-treelike networks" forces the algorithm to assign temporal depth to what were likely wave-like or areal innovations across the early phase of IE expansion.

In 2012, Gray and Atkinson along with a larger author collective (Bouckaert et al. 2012) doubled down, this time with a publication in *Science*, repeating their result of an age for PIE of close to nine thousand years, but the phylogeny based on Swadesh lists had now been augmented by a Bayesian phylogeographical framework developed in 2010 to locate the origin of virus outbreaks. The authors did simulate the shape of the Eurasian landmass, but no topographical features, and determined Anatolia as the most likely geographical origin of the tree. The result is highly interesting but ultimately unconvincing. All topographical features are ignored, yet, as the historical record tells us, the steppes are vastly favoured as an invasion route. In addition, the random walk algorithm at the core of the method had little incentive ever to "set foot" near the Pontic steppe, as the language families (other than Anatolian and Tocharian) were given their mediaeval ranges as priors, with the entire steppe area, which we know was once Scythia, and populated by East Iranian-speakers, being treated as non-Indo-European. In effect, the historical circumstance of the Turkic expansion of the first millennium thus affected the likelihood estimate for a Pontic homeland several millennia before. On top of this, the exaggerated age estimate of proto-Anatolian discussed above might also have favoured Anatolian origin, as suggested by the reported loss of confidence for the Anatolian homeland by an order of magnitude once only living languages were taken into account (Bouckaert et al. 2012, 959, report a Bayes factor for "Anatolian vs. steppe II" reduced from 159.3 for "all languages" to 11.4 for "contemporary languages only").

For better or worse, the two papers (Gray and Atkinson 2003; Bouckaert et al. 2012) were widely advertised in the popular press as establishing the Anatolian origin of the Indo-Europeans, and caused substantial comment. Phylogenetic studies of numerous language families other than Indo-European have been performed since the early 2000s, and several conferences on the topic have been held since 2010 (summarised in Pereltsvaig and Lewis 2015, 55–57), but the Indo-European case has continued to attract the most attention and controversy.

Pereltsvaig and Lewis (2015, 3), a monograph mostly inspired by the Gray and Atkinson papers, is emphatic in pointing out the "spectacular failure" of the computational approach from the point of view of historical linguists. Unfortunately, the past decade appears to have deepened the chasm between historical linguists and computational phylogeny, as linguists accuse the phylogeneticists of lack of respect for their field and "unjustified and unjustifiable simplification" (Pereltsvaig and Lewis 2015, 127), while often lacking an understanding of the strengths of the methods proposed. On the other side of the divide, Atkinson and Gray (2006) and Greenhill and Gray (2009) attempt to explain their methodology with palpable frustration. The blame for this decade of unease in interdisciplinary exchange is most likely shared. On the one hand, the phylogeneticists, at least in their early publications, have been over-confident. On the other hand, critics have largely failed to engage with understanding the methods used and their genuine strengths. In an ideal world, Gray and Atkinson would have presented their approach as a preliminary study showing the promising potential of Bayesian phylogeny, to be revised in future studies with better linguistic data and better models of migration. Instead, the debate was immediately reduced to the Anatolian hypothesis. The complaint by Greenhill and Gray (2009, 390) regarding the "vexing misconception about phylogenetic linguistics: 'this method is not giving anything new'" may be instructive: it is true that phylogenetic methods may bring new, rigorously objective tools for assessing the degree of relationship between languages. On the other hand, it is quite obvious to the historical linguists that the quality of the results produced so far is not comparable to what has long been achieved by traditional philology: the credibility of the trees produced by the phylogeneticists is still judged by their congruence with traditional results, not vice versa (Greenhill, Drummond, and Gray 2010).

Many more examples of computational phylogenetics applied to historical linguistics were published from the 2000s to the early 2010s. Dunn et al. (2005) attempted to compare Papuan languages in the complete absence of etymology, purely based on typological similarity. Dunn (2009) is a similar study of Melanesian languages, notable as an early use of likelihood (Bayesian) algorithms rather than simple distance-based methods. These are examples of computational methods being used to arrive at an assessment of the phylogeny in groups of languages in the complete absence of any historical record or any etymologies. While it is not inconceivable that a phylogenetic signal may be detected using such brute-force methods, it is very difficult to quantify the confidence that should be placed in the results. The main problem of phylogenetic algorithms is, of course, that they will *always* result in a best-estimate tree, regardless of whether any actual phylogenetic signal was present in the data. Careful statistical analysis is especially important here in order to be able to quantify the probability that the signal discovered by the algorithm might be due to chance alone. Perhaps an instructive example of this effect is Fortunato (2011), a study which attempts to reconstruct PIE monogamy using phylogenetic methods (applied to languages) in combination with sociological data from an ethnographic atlas. The result presented is that polygyny was a Proto-Indo-Iranian innovation. While proper caveats are included in the article text, the result was nevertheless cast in terms of "evidence in support of PIE monogamy; this pattern likely extended back to PIH" (Fortunato 2011, 99). Without wishing to embark on too much of a tangent, this appears to be quite a *bold* conclusion from the mere distribution of modern-day polygyny in Iran and India without considering other, areal effects, such as the spread of Islam, which may have contributed to it, and in the complete absence of any knowledge as to the age, cultural stage, or economic situation of Proto-Indo-Hittite.

Unfortunately, the use of more advanced classes of algorithm, such as maximum parsimony or Bayesian inference, has not resulted in a noticeable improvement of the quality of results achieved in language phylogenies compared to what is quite easily derivable using distance-based methods. Dunn (2014, 197) names as one possible reason for this the phenomenon of long-branch attraction, where the parsimony algorithm tends to unduly combine areas of the phylogeny with a lot of change (long branches), fulfilling, as it were, the requirement of being maximally parsimonious by reducing the total number of mutation-heavy areas in the phylogeny.

Use of computational methods has also been attempted in the quite different context of dialectometry. In this case, the close historical relationship of the species under consideration is taken as a given, and the algorithm serves as an aid in giving a visualisation of the structure of the dialect group, for example in the form of network graphs (Dunn 2014, 195). Manni, Guérard, and Heyer (2004) used a boundary-detecting algorithm (Monmonier's algorithm) to automatically detect language barriers in dialect data.

Phylogenetics software has become more readily available and more sophisticated since the early 2000s. BEAST, in particular, is software developed in part for the purpose of modelling linguistic phylogenies (Drummond et al. 2012). It is unclear, however, whether increased sophistication in method will be able to substantially improve on current possibilities. Ultimately, the entire comparative method of historical linguistics can be seen as a single vast exercise in phylogenetics. An automated method approximating this programme would need to fully combine lexical, phonological, and morphological information into a single model. While this is perfectly possible in principle (Dunn 2014, 204), it is a formidable task, which can perhaps only be envisaged once fully machine-readable historical grammars and morphologically analysed text corpora become available for the languages in question, and even then it is questionable whether the computational power required to successfully run a Bayesian tree search on such an amount of data is within the realm of the possible, even in the longer term of technological progress.

8.2.6 Evidence from human genetics

With the rapid development of technological possibilities in genetics during the 2010s, many long-standing intractable questions related to the correlation of changes in material culture or language and migration now seem amenable to objective, quantitative analysis. Human population genetics has the potential of serving as arbiter in the old "pots vs people" debate. Genetic studies of the 2000s were mostly not autosomal, limiting themselves to patrilineal and matrilineal descent, leading to inconclusive results. Since the 2010s, both autosomal sequencing technology and ancient DNA have become much more readily available, in many cases leading to surprisingly detailed insights into prehistoric migrations.

For the historical period, in cases where a linguistic shift is a matter of record, it has become possible to estimate the extent of population movement associated with it. A prominent example of this kind is the question of the Anglo-Saxon settlement of Great Britain, a long-standing controversy of the "migrationist vs diffusionist" type. The gradual influx of West Germanic-speaking settlers in the fifth and sixth centuries was sufficient to replace the Celtic British language with the Germanic Anglo-Saxon one in what is now England. In the mediaeval period, the arrival of a comparatively small Norman-French elite was not quite sufficient to displace Anglo-Saxon, although a substantial impression from the French superstratum has been left on the English language. In the case of Anglo-Saxon migration, a 2016 study found evidence of early intermarriage between Anglo-Saxons and Britons (rather than a "genocidal" or "apartheid" scenario), with a genetic contribution in the order of 40% from the Anglo-Saxon settlers to the modern population of eastern England (Schiffels et al. 2016). The accumulation of this and similar examples of migration and linguistic change during the historical period may potentially serve to inform the study of prehistoric migration and language change.

Studies focused on the period of European prehistory relevant for the Indo-European question are bound to shed further light on the Anatolian vs Kurgan scenarios. Haak et al. (2015) is a study of the DNA of sixty-nine European individuals of the Neolithic and Bronze Age. The study was able to determine that the Neolithic farming population arrived from the Near East about 8,000 years ago, and that there was a gradual intermixture with people of local hunter-gatherer ancestry, followed by the sudden appearance of high amounts of "steppe ancestry" on the German plains at 4,500 years ago. This corresponds almost exactly to the classical scenario connecting the Beaker people with the Kurgan expansion and early Indo-European presence in western Europe. This is, obviously, by no means a linguistic result, and it cannot be ruled out, for example, that early forms of Indo-European were present in Europe before this (and Haak et al., abstract, are careful enough to postulate "a steppe origin" only for "at least some of the Indo-European languages of Europe"), but it does allows us for the first time to estimate the population movements associated with shifts in prehistoric culture such as the arrival of the Bronze Age in western Europe. Olalde et al. (2018) is a more extensive analysis of individuals associated with the Beaker culture, finding that the expansion of the Beaker complex was mostly, but not always, paired with substantial migration: in Britain, there was a substantial demographic transformation due to the influx of steppe-related ancestry, while the Beaker culture appears in Iberia with only limited presence of steppe ancestry. Reich (2018) summarises the recent confirmation of the appearance of "steppe" or "Yamnaya" genetic markers in European ancient DNA at 4,500 years ago, precisely as would be expected from the hypothesis of Indo-European expansion from the steppe at that time. The harsh impact of the new arrivals on genetic lineage, even to the point of extinction or near-extinction of the indigenous male line in the case of the Iberian peninsula, goes some way towards vindicating Gimbutas's views of the arrival of the Indo-Europeans as a warlike invasion of a small patriarchal elite (which resulted in a bottleneck in paternal lineages, while maternal lineages remained more diverse).

Even if these results are subject to further revision, their availability presents an entirely new foundation for the old "pots vs people" debate: instead of an ultimately ideological dispute over the relative importance of cultural transmission and human migration, we are now beginning to gather quantitative information on the balance between these two modes depending on time and geographical region. It might be a promising avenue for future Bayesian language phylogeny studies to include in their models such quantitative information about prehistoric population movements as a guide.

8.3 Anthropology
Jamshid Tehrani

Phylogenetic methods were originally developed to study the evolutionary relationships among biological species, but in recent years they have been adopted by a growing number of researchers in the humanities and social sciences to investigate the historical development of cultural traditions. As Howe and Windram point out in an influential review of this literature,

> in principle, phylogenetic methods can be applied to model the history of any system in which (i) elements can be replicated with the incorporation of changes and (ii) any change between a progeny element and its parent is stably transmitted in subsequent generations. (C. J. Howe and Windram 2011)

Following the convention of referring to elements of cultural transmission as "memes", Howe and Windram propose the term "phylomemetics" to describe cultural applications of phylogenetic analysis. While the phylomemetic approach in stemmatology has been covered elsewhere in this volume, this section will discuss the development of phylomemetics in other disciplines, focusing in particular on anthropology.

8.3.1 Historical precedents

As in stemmatology, the philosophical roots of phylomemetics run deep in anthropology, linguistics, folklore, and other disciplines. Indeed, the fundamental idea that "descent with modification" is a general evolutionary process that applies as much to cultural diversity as the natural world is explicit in Darwin's own works. In *The Descent of Man*, Darwin suggests that "the formation of different languages and of distinct species, and the proofs that both have been developed through a gradual process, are curiously the same" (Darwin 1871, 1:59).

This idea was taken up – or possibly even anticipated – by August Schleicher (1861), the founder of modern historical linguistics. Schleicher hypothesised that relationships among the Indo-European languages could be directly modelled with the kind of tree diagrams used by Darwin to depict the phylogeny of biological species (fig. 8.3-1). Thus, he suggested that they were all derived from a single common ancestral language that gradually differentiated into separate branches such as Romance, Germanic, and so on.

Many contemporaries of Darwin and Schleicher believed that the analogy between organisms and languages could be extended to other cultural domains. For instance, one of the pioneers of material culture studies in anthropology, Henry Augustus Pitt Rivers (1875, 1906), collected and organised artefacts from all over the world with the express intention of demonstrating how the principles of evolution are borne out in tools, weapons, and craft objects. As he explained,

> human ideas, as represented by the various products of human industry, are capable of classification into genera, species, and varieties, in the same manner as the products of the vegetable and animal kingdoms, and in their development from the homogeneous to the heterogeneous they obey the same laws. (Pitt Rivers 1875, 307)

As with species and languages, Pitt Rivers believed that it was possible to trace the development of artefacts that were widely distributed throughout the globe to their original "root forms". For example, he argued that similarities among crossbows made in different societies across Europe and Asia suggested that these traditions were all derived from a single proto-crossbow. His theory was tested by Henry Balfour (1889), who produced the first phylogeny of a material culture tradition that was explicitly based on the branching family-tree models employed by biologists and historical linguists (fig. 8.3-1).

In folklore studies, there is similarly a long and rich tradition of evolutionary theory that stretches from Julius Krohn, who founded the historio-geographical school of comparative folklore in the nineteenth century, through to the work of Carl von Sydow and Stith Thompson (1977) in the mid- and late twentieth century. These writers believed that folk tales shared among different cultures could be traced back to an original "archetype" tale, developing into locally distinct forms in each location as they adapted to culturally specific norms and preferences. Such theories often drew directly on biological models – as encapsulated by Stith Thompson's observation that "biologists have long since labelled their flora and fauna by a universal system", and that "the need for such an arrangement of narrative has been realized for a long time" (1977, 413, 414).

In all these fields, reconstructing lineages of cultural "descent with modification" presents the same kind of methodological challenges confronted by biologists.

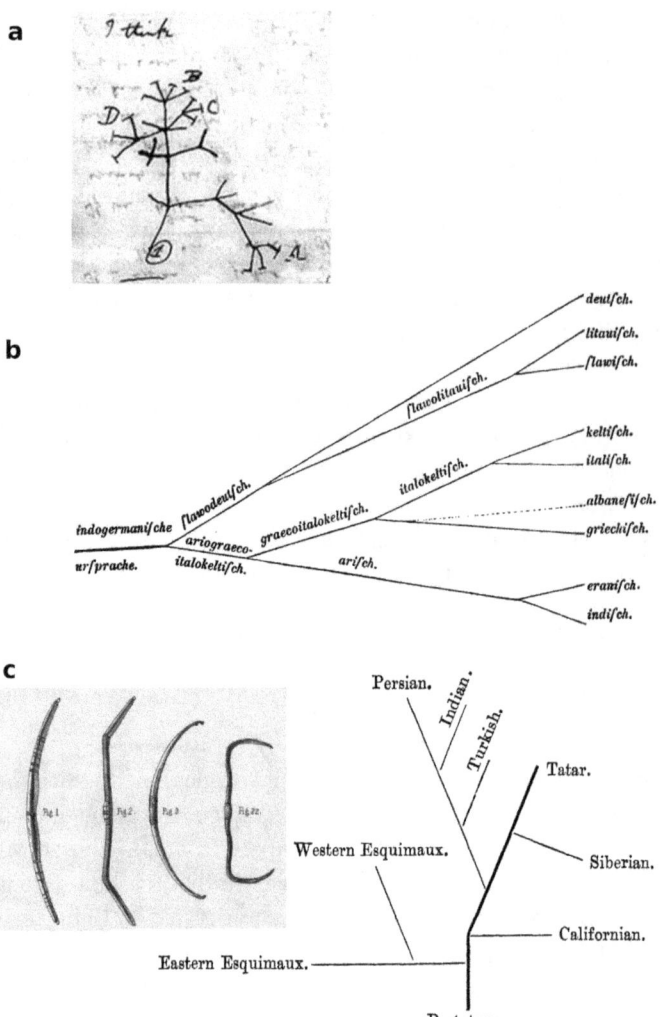

Fig. 8.3-1: Branching lineages drawn (a) by Darwin (1837, 36) for species, (b) by Schleicher (1861, 1:7; discussed in 8.2 above) for Indo-European languages, and (c) by Balfour (1889, 244) for crossbows.

Foremost among them is the problem of **missing links**, that is, the lack of direct physical evidence to trace relations of common ancestry back through time. Just as the fossil record bears witness to a tiny percentage of extinct ancestral species, data on ancient languages, material culture, and narratives is extremely scarce. The origins of most language families predate the invention of writing, and the archaeological record is very patchy and subject to numerous biases (not least the poor preservation of most material), while folk narratives have mainly been transmitted orally and rarely written down. Given these limitations, the characteristics of missing links can only be inferred from the traits exhibited by their (presumed) descendants. This brings us to another problem that anthropologists, linguists, and folklorists share with biologists, which is how to distinguish true family resemblances that are the result of hereditary transmission from similarities that arise through other kinds of processes. For example, similar morphological adaptations can be observed in species that almost certainly evolved independently (e.g. wings in bats and birds), just as similar cultural traits can arise in completely unrelated cultural contexts (e.g. writing in the Middle East, China, and Meso-America; or pyramids in ancient Egypt and Mexico). In evolutionary terms, this process is known as convergence. Another confounding factor is the transmission of traits across separate lineages, sometimes known as lateral transfer or horizontal transmission in biology and anthropology, or contamination in stemmatology. Horizontal transmission results in similarities among taxa that are only distantly related to one another. This can occur in many biological species, particularly in plants and microbes, and is likely to be even more common in cultural evolution, where trade and other forms of exchange can potentially lead to the widespread borrowing and blending of cultural traits (see e.g. Terrell 1988; Moore 1994).

In the past, anthropologists, linguists, and others had to rely on their own (often highly subjective) judgements to try and solve the problems of missing links and family resemblances. Below, we will see how phylomemetics provides a more rigorous and systematic means to address them.

8.3.2 Phylomemetic analysis

The first step in a phylogenetic/phylomemetic analysis is to define a set of characters, that is, the basic units of information that are transmitted from ancestral taxa to descendant taxa. In biology, these may be gene sequences or morphological traits. In linguistics, they may be lexical items or syntactic features. In material culture, they may be specific designs, craft techniques, and so on. In the case of traditional narratives, phylogenetic characters can be derived from narrative motifs – characters, objects, and episodes that withstand repeated transmission and which folklorists use to identify related versions of the same story (S. Thompson 1977). Once the characters have been defined, the state of every character in each variant of a tale is recorded in a matrix. Characters can be coded as either binary characters that take only two states – 0 (absent) or 1 (present) – or as multistate characters that take a variety of expressions.

While there are numerous types of phylomemetic analysis, here I will focus on two of the most widely used in anthropology and linguistics, one of which is fairly well established in stemmatology, and one of which is not (but in which, in the spirit of cross-fertilisation between disciplines, this section hopes to encourage greater interest). They are, respectively, cladistic analysis and Bayesian inference.

Cladistic analysis clusters entities (e.g. species, languages, or variants of a tale) into hierarchically nested branches known as clades. A clade represents a group of entities that share evolutionarily novel traits (known as derived character states) inherited from an exclusive common ancestor (and which are therefore lacking in other, more distant relatives). If the evolution of a cultural tradition conformed exactly to the accumulation of innovations within branching lineages of descent, the task of sorting the variants into clades would be straightforward. However, for the reasons explained above, evolution is rarely straightforward, and not all similarities among entities are true family resemblances (known in phylogenetic jargon as homologies). In most cases, we would expect the neat hierarchical pattern of inheritance to be disrupted by independent evolution and/or borrowing (similarities due to these processes are classed as homoplasies). Cladistic analysis deals with conflicting patterns in a dataset by searching for the tree (or trees) that minimise the number of evolutionary changes that are required to explain shared character states among the taxa. This approach invokes the philosophical principle of parsimony, which states that scientific explanations should never be more complicated than necessary.

Although cladistic analysis is logically appealing, there are some important limitations to the approach. In particular, the assumption of parsimony may be overly simplistic in many cases, such as when there is considerable variance in rates of evolution in different traits and/or different lineages. For example, folklorists (e.g. S. Thompson 1977) have suggested that motifs related to events in a story are more stable than motifs related to characterisation (e.g. the gender or species of the protagonists), and that storytellers are more likely to alter the beginning and end of a tale than the core middle section of a narrative. In these instances, a less parsimonious reconstruction that allows some motifs (e.g. characterisation, episodes that occur in the beginning or end of a story) to switch between states more freely might be more accurate than one which minimises the overall number of character changes.

For these reasons, cladistic methods have in recent years been largely superseded in anthropological phylomemetics by an alternative approach, known as Bayesian phylogenetic inference (P. O. Lewis 2001), which is better able to deal with these issues (A. M. Wright and Hillis 2014; see fig. 8.3-2 below). Bayesian inference proceeds by calculating the likelihood of the data (i.e. the chance of obtaining the observed distribution of character states) given an initial, randomly chosen tree topology, a set of branch lengths, and a model of character evolution (i.e. the substitution rates for character states). The state of each parameter is then modified (i.e. clades are re-sorted, branches get lengthened/shortened, variance in rates of character change is increased/decreased), and the likelihood of the data is recalculated. This process is then repeated hundreds of thousands of times using a Markov Chain Monte Carlo (MCMC) algorithm. In this analysis, moves that improve the likelihood of the data are always accepted, while those that do not are usually rejected – although some may occasionally be accepted within a certain threshold. This is

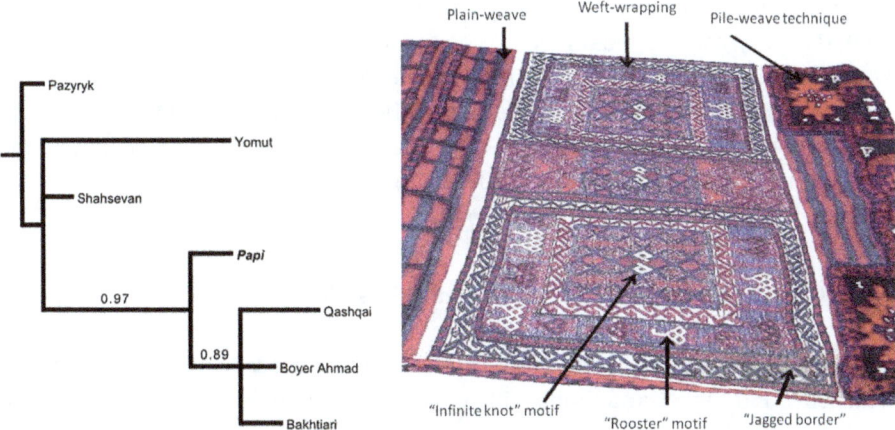

Fig. 8.3-2: Example of a Bayesian consensus tree based on analyses of Iranian textile traits (such as the example illustrated on the right). The values beside the nodes represent posterior probabilities for the corresponding clades. Source: Matthews et al. (2011).

because the search for the best parameter states (i.e. the most likely trees) is similar to walking through a mountain range to find the highest peak: sometimes one needs to go down in order to get higher up. However, in this case, the ground is constantly shifting below one's feet as each parameter gets adjusted simultaneously. Thus, the tree that seems to be the best one (i.e. that maximises the likelihood of the distribution of character states) under one set of conditions may turn out to be suboptimal when the branch lengths or variance in rates of character change are adjusted slightly (while, at the same time, the best values for these parameters will vary with different tree topologies). Bayesian phylogenetic inference integrates the uncertainty associated with alternative evolutionary scenarios by sampling trees at regular intervals in the MCMC chain to compile a posterior distribution of trees. Since the analysis usually favours moves that increase the likelihood of the data, it revisits higher peaks in the likelihood landscape more frequently than lower peaks, meaning that trees with higher probabilities get sampled more often than ones with lower probabilities.

Once the posterior distribution of trees has been compiled, phylogenetic relationships among tale variants can be represented by a consensus tree that shows the posterior probabilities of individual clades, which correspond to the percentage of posterior trees in which they occurred (fig. 8.3-2). The latter provides a useful indication of the robustness of these relationships under a range of plausible evolutionary models, rather than just a single optimality criterion such as parsimony. Moreover, since rates of change and branch lengths are also explicitly modelled, Bayesian inference has other useful features besides estimating phylogenetic relationships. For example, if the analysis includes taxa sampled from different historical periods (e.g. ancient languages in a linguistic analysis, archaeological artefacts in a material culture analysis, or early literary versions of folk tales in a folklore analysis), they can serve as reference points for calibrating an evolutionary clock which calculates the average number of character-state changes that would be expected over fixed intervals of time (e.g. centuries, millennia). The clock model can then be used to estimate the root age of the tradition under study, as well as all the internal nodes (ancestors) postulated in the tree.

8.3.3 Current applications of phylomemetics in anthropology

Cladistic and Bayesian methods provide modern-day academic descendants of Schleicher, Pitt Rivers, and Krohn with a powerful set of tools for testing long-standing hypotheses concerning the origins and taxonomic relationships among various cultural traditions, from prehistoric stone tools (e.g. O'Brien, Darwent, and Lyman 2001; Lycett 2009) and languages to textiles (Tehrani and Collard 2002, 2013; Matthews et al. 2011; Buckley and Boudot 2017), musical instruments (Tëmkin 2004), and folk tales (Tehrani 2013; Tehrani, Nguyen, and Roos 2016). For example, Tehrani (2013) investigated whether traditional classifications of similar folk tales from different cultures can be classified into distinct international types based on common origins. He carried out a cross-cultural phylomemetic analysis of a famous but controversial tale: *Little Red Riding Hood*. Tehrani's results established that, while European versions of *Little Red Riding Hood* form a phylogenetically distinct group, versions from Africa are actually more closely related to another international folktale type, *The Wolf and the Kids*, while East Asian versions are a hybrid of motifs from both types. In a follow-up study (Tehrani, Nguyen, and Roos 2016), Tehrani and colleagues used cladistics, Bayesian analysis, and phylogenetic networks to explore the origins of *Little Red Riding Hood* in Europe. Their analyses found strong evidence that the literary tradition, which dates back to the seventeenth century, is descended from an older oral tradition that probably goes back to at least mediaeval times and not to a literary tradition, as was assumed by some (e.g. Husing 1989).

In addition to reconstructing origins of cultural traditions, applications of phylomemetics in anthropology have also been used to draw wider inferences about population histories. For example, Gray, Drummond, and Greenhill (2009) carried out a Bayesian phylomemetic analysis of Austronesian languages to test the two major hypotheses about the peopling of the Pacific. The "pulse–pause" hypothesis suggests that Austronesians spread from their ancestral homeland in Taiwan in a series of rapid expansions interspersed with longer, more settled periods (see 8.2.3). The "slow boat" hypothesis proposes instead a more gradual and consistent process of diffusion from Wallacea. Gray, Drummond, and Greenhill (2009) found that the pattern and tempo of lexical evolution in their Bayesian Austronesian language trees was more consistent with the "pulse–pause" model than the "slow boat" model. Similar kinds of study have been carried out with material culture data, for

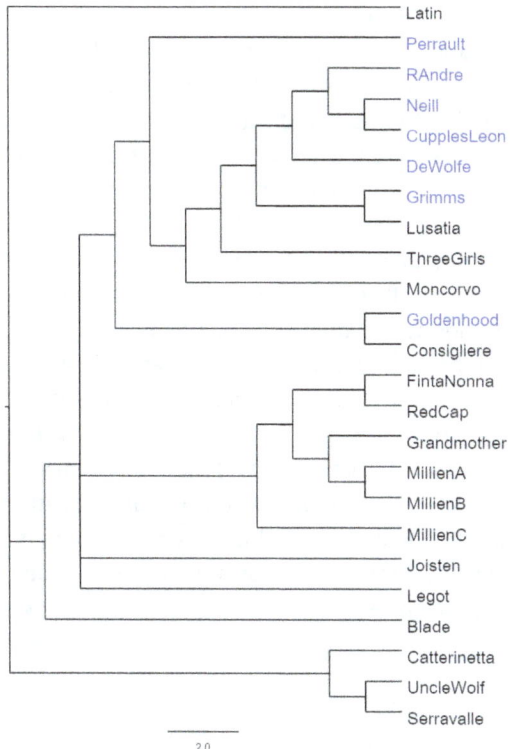

Fig. 8.3-3: Maximum parsimony tree of *Little Red Riding Hood* tales. Oral versions are labelled in black, literary versions in blue. The results suggest that the literary tradition is rooted in the oral one. Source: Tehrani, Nguyen, and Roos (2016, 615).

instance by using phylogenies of early stone tool assemblages to infer patterns of human migration out of Africa (Lycett 2009) and into the Americas (Buchanan and Collard 2007).

Finally, phylomemetic analysis has been used to address more general theoretical debates in anthropology about the genesis and diversification of cultures. Whereas Darwin, Schleicher, Pitt Rivers, and so on believed cultural evolution and biological evolution followed fundamentally similar principles, in the twentieth century many anthropologists came to reject this view. Among the most influential of them was Franz Boas, who argued:

> Animal forms develop in divergent directions, and an intermingling of species that have once become distinct is negligible in the whole developmental history. It is otherwise in the domain of culture. Human thoughts, institutions, activities may spread from one social unit to another. As soon as two groups come into close contact their cultural traits will be disseminated from one to the other. (Boas 1940, 251)

To test these claims, a number of studies have used phylomemetic techniques to assess the roles of branching vs blending evolution in the generation of cultural traditions (e.g. Tehrani and Collard 2002, 2013; Jordan and Shennan 2003; Collard, Shennan, and Tehrani 2006; Cochrane and Lipo 2010; Gray, Bryant, and Greenhill 2010). This involves estimating how well patterns of diversity in languages and material culture assemblages fit a tree model, that is, measuring the extent to which the distributions of shared character states among a set of cultural entities are homologous (similarities that are due to common descent, which are compatible with a tree-like model of descent) or homoplastic (similarities with are due to processes other than descent, and are thus incompatible with a tree model). These studies show that cultural evolutionary processes are strongly shaped by ethnic boundaries, patterns of conflict and marriage, migration rates, linguistic and ecological barriers, as well as a number of other factors (Tehrani and Collard 2013). Overall, however, these studies suggest that branching descent with modification plays a vitally important role in generating cultural diversity, and may even be as significant as it is in biological evolution (Collard, Shennan, and Tehrani 2006). These findings go some way to justifying Howe and Windram's claim that the "process of replication with the incorporation of changes is a fundamental one in human cultural activity" (C. J. Howe and Windram 2011), and highlight the wide scope and potential of phylomemetics in the humanities and social sciences.

8.4 Musicology
Cristina Urchueguía

The first striking fact about the relationship between stemmatology and musicology is how late the two disciplines met. First encounters cannot be traced before the end of the 1960s; eventually, musicologists became aware of stemmatological methods, discussed them, and tried using them for different purposes. From the beginning, "filiation" was the most popular term for referring to this philological discourse among German-speaking and Anglo-American musical editors and musicological scholars. Following an enthusiastic reception of stemmatology applied to music from the twelfth to seventeenth centuries, the 1970s and 1980s critically examined its capacity to find the "original" text, but this resulted in a certain degree of disenchantment. Today, the use of stemmatological methods continues to be taught and discussed, but its functionality has been reformulated. Editors of music from the eighteenth to twentieth centuries seldom adopt stemmatology as the principal method; instead, various versions of a best-text method are the norm. In this context, it was the very problematic term "urtext-edition" that functioned as catalyst in the general discussion.

The second specific element concerning this relationship is the attitude of some – sometimes even overt – scepticism that musicologists have shown towards stemmatology. The fact that musicology itself was accepted as an academic discipline rather late is one, but not the most important, reason for this attitude. It is true that musicology was not established in academia before the end of the nineteenth century, but musical editing based on some kind of rational principles can be traced back to as early as the beginning of the nineteenth century. The most important fields of editorial work on historical texts were the recuperation of vocal polyphony from the sixteenth century and the collected works of Johann Sebastian Bach, both begun in the middle of the eighteenth century. Even before the establishment of the discipline, there had been an awareness of the importance of defining methodological frameworks for editorial tasks.

The main objection scholarly music editors have raised against stemmatology is based on the conviction that the transmission of musical texts followed patterns completely different in nature from the transmission of literary texts, even in special cases such as historical chronicles (which were also often updated and recontextualised throughout the centuries). These differences have their roots in the structure of the musical works, their hybrid semiotic composition and the historical development of musical notation, the methods of compiling sources, and, last but not least, the inherently performative essence of music as a human activity. The methods developed for letter-based texts had to undergo a thorough adaptation in order to cope with the semiotic environment of music. Orality and performativity challenged musicological stemmatology from the beginning. The second reason for the misgivings of musicologists regarding stemmatology is the lack of relevant musical sources dating from before the ninth century. The few extant fragments of ancient Greek notation (Pöhlmann and West 2001) do not constitute a corpus comparable in size and relevance to the corpus of texts that were targeted by classical and biblical philologists to develop their methods and prestige. What musical scholars could infer from the scattered, fragmentary bits of clay or stone with ancient notation was so primitive in style and structure that any comparison with classical literature was pointless. These fragments were not perceived as being paradigmatic for musical repertoires in any sense, and had absolutely no impact on the development of musicological stemmatology. Thus, musicology could not rely on the arguments and goals that classical and modern philological disciplines had adopted to establish their editorial principles and textual traditions.

8.4.1 Stemmatology for music editors

Notwithstanding the common perception of music as a phenomenon of an aural nature, scholarly editorial work on music did not initially determine the sonic reconstruction of music as one of its main tasks. On the contrary, the basic material used by editors was the written text, and their first objective the constitution of an edited text. Nonetheless, performance practice and orality were not completely excluded from the critical discussion about the principles to be used in the constitution of musical editions when it came to *recensio* of the transmitted text; in fact, they became one of the main obstacles to an implementation of stemmatology in analogy to classical philology. The tension between music's various forms of medial representation and their contradictory implications for editions constituted a substantial methodological issue (Bent 1990, 1995).

The notation of Western music began as n e u m a t i c n o t a t i o n (see fig. 8.4-1), which served as a political tool in order to document and canonise Gregorian chant and further the hegemonic ambitions of the new rulers during the Carolingian period. Although descriptions of ancient Greek notation were rediscovered at the same time, the neumatic notation of the Middle Ages was not derived from the ancient principles but was created from scratch. This rupture in the written tradition of music is essential to understanding some of the characteristics of musical editing mentioned above. Musical philology was a latecomer within the philological family, lacking roots in a humanistic tradition of its own.

What we call Western music – and this has been almost the only style considered relevant to scholarly musical editions – was a changing, fashionable musical repertoire used first in church and court between the middle of the seventeenth and the end of the nineteenth century that entered the concert repertoire from the beginning of the nineteenth century. In this timeframe, musical styles changed with amazing speed: until the beginning of the nineteenth century, Catholic church music still used the corpus of Gregorian chant together with modern styles, whereas court musicians were always seeking fashionable novelties. A consciousness of the importance of the music of the preceding generation, and even of earlier periods, did not arise until the nineteenth century, together with the awareness of national cultural values. This is the moment this music became an object of scholarly and performative interest. The present contribution is not the place to outline these discourses in detail, but the essential facts are (*i*) the lack of humanistic roots for music editing, and (*ii*) the contextualisation of music editing within modern national states and the construction of their cultural identities. The most prominent examples of these historical origins are the importance of the edition of Johann Sebastian Bach's works for Germany, and the focus on Franco-Flemish polyphony for the Netherlands. It is worth mentioning that musicological stemmatology usually ignored the music of the Middle Ages. At the end of the nineteenth and the beginning of the twentieth century, it was rather the idea of the infinite multiplicity of versions due to the performative situation that inspired editors like Pierre Aubry in his collaboration with Bédier (see 2.3.4.1). In their edition of the *Chansons de Croisade* (1909), they reject the possibility of reconstructing an original melody from different versions, and thus also the applicability of textual criticism to music:

> La méthode critique, suivie par les éditeurs de textes littéraires, ne nous semble point d'une application possible, en raison de la différence qui existe entre la matière philologique, où tout est stable, et la matière musicale, où tout est fortuit et changeant. (Bédier 1909, xxxiii)

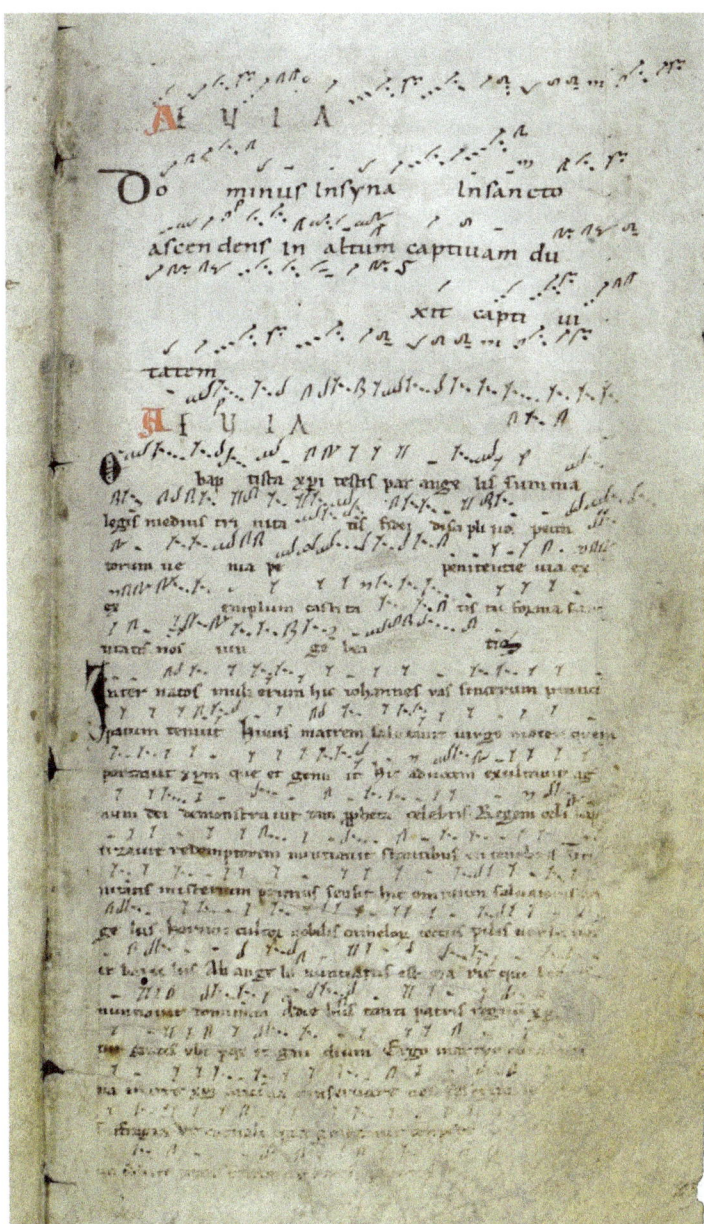

Fig. 8.4-1: Neumatic notation was used as a means to document the general shape of a melody, but it lacks information about the exact pitch, the intervals, and the rhythm. St. Gallen, Stiftsbibliothek, Cod. Sang. 359, p. 7. Source: e-codices.unifr.ch/de/searchresult/list/one/csg/0359. Image: CC-BY-NC.

> [The text-critical method, pursued by the editors of literary texts, does not at all seem applicable to us, because of the difference that exists between the philological material, where all is stable, and the musical material, where all is casual and changing.]

The editorial expression of this view is a synoptic reproduction of variant melodies. This radical embrace of variation was abandoned in the case other repertoires that could be used to support nationalistic arguments.

The complete edition of Bach's œuvre (1851–1899) initiated the series of large-scale editions of complete works that constitute the paramount achievements of German-language musicology (von Dadelsen 1967; Georgiades 1971; Bennwitz et al. 1975; B. R. Appel and Veit 2000; Emans and Krämer 2015). Focusing on repertoires from the late seventeenth to the beginning of the twentieth century – with only few exceptions predating this period – editors often had access to autographs and authorial witnesses that made any stemmatological analysis of their transmitted texts secondary or even unnecessary. The most common approach was (and continues to be) a case-by-case best-text method, aiming at producing a version intended by the authors, authorised by them, or legitimated by witnesses of reception sanctioned by the author. This method first reached prominence under the label "urtext" at the end of the nineteenth century, becoming the only editorial concept to transcend the scholarly realm and become popularised as a marketing feature (Feder and Unverricht 1959; Dahlhaus 1973; Badura-Skoda 1986). Today, however, scholarly music editors have questioned this highly problematic concept in response to the charges of eclecticism made against it. Strikingly, the most recent handbook on the topic issued in Germany – *Musikphilologie: Grundlagen, Methoden, Praxis* (B. R. Appel and Emans 2017) – does not address the concept of the urtext, or even include the term itself in the glossary.

Stemmatology was, thus, not the first choice in this editorial context, although editors did take note of it and discussed its potential capacity, marginalising it as a tool supplementary to their day-to-day business (Feder 1983; Wade 1988; Strohm 1995). The above-mentioned handbook deals with stemmatology in a rather shallow and pro forma subchapter of no more than five pages (Scheideler 2017).

The natural nurturing ground for stemmatology was the musicological and editorial work on early music, beginning with Franco-Flemish polyphony. Josquin des Prez became the paradigmatic composer because of the richness of his output, the complexity of its transmission patterns, and the fact that the transmission of his works crossed the threshold between manuscript and print (van Benthem 1969–1970; Porter 1976; Blackburn 1976; Hoffmann-Erbrecht 1976; Just 1983; Frobenius 2001). Thus, Josquin's *opera omnia* became a privileged object of study that combined the history of music and the history of music printing. The *New Josquin Edition*, a collaborative international project realised by the most prominent scholars in the field, set path-breaking standards based on filiation (Josquin 1987–2016). The use of stemmatic methods caused a real paradigm change in the perception of the music of Josquin's lifetime, as it provided evidence about the pre-eminence of some manuscript copies over printed copies, thus turning the scholarly consensus on its head. The bibliographical analysis of early music printing was another fruitful field for stemmatology in a less text-oriented medium (Boorman 1977, 1981b; Noblitt 1981; Hamm 1983; Staehelin 1998; Drake 1999; Mouser 2003, 2004). The scholarly debate about stemmatology largely focused on these two interrelated fields, which were considered alongside one another in special journal issues devoted to the music of Josquin and his time that established the state of the art as we find it in handbooks and monograph publications on musical editing today (Noblitt 1983; Just 1983; Noblitt 1995; for handbooks, cf. Caraci Vela 1995, 2005–2013; Grier 1996).

Although stemmatology proved to be helpful in this context, its results were not conclusive. The emphasis of scholarship has consequently shifted to the transmission process, scribal habits, cultures of compilation, and musical style. Taking into account the hypothesis that scribes of music themselves had to be proficient musicians, if not composers, led to a radical questioning of the validity of the written text with respect to the entity to be edited, the "music itself". It is needless to point out the lack of consensus about the ultimate aim of music editors, ranging from a religious attitude to the extant notation to the search for a modern transcription in order to represent a hypothetical, lost sound. Musicological editors have always faced diachronic changes in the way notation represents performance practice and historical sound, assuming the role of translators between trained musicological scholars and musicians used to deciphering only conventional modern notation. As the specificities of historical musical notation, scribal competence, and the perception of mutual influence between sound and writing became a central matter of scrutiny and debate, the written text itself began to be perceived as an early stage within the editorial process and not as the final goal. Transcriptions of historical notation into the editor's standard notation imply a high degree of speculation about the difference between the capabilities of the original and target notations to represent performance habits and sound quality. Stemmatology failed to fill the gap between the visible notation and the hypotheses about the represented sound, and was thus subject to criticism or rejection by musicologists.

From an aural point of view, editorial work on music of the past meant groping in the dark because the dynamics of the evolution of notation, historical instruments, and performance practice had veiled these elements of the musical work in all but absolute obscurity. Editors thus focused on the possibilities textual criticism offered for establishing an authentic written representation of the musical entity.

Even among the group of editors devoted to early music, the enthusiasm of having discovered stemmatology as a powerful tool to cope with the written text (Grier 1995, 1996) soon subsided, and a certain disillusionment took hold (Boorman 1981a, 1981c; Bent 1981; Brett 1988; Grier 1995; Boorman 1995). The *locus classicus* summarising the standard caveats is Stanley Boorman's unsurpassed discussions about filiation for musical editors (Boorman 1981a, 1981c). He enumerates three aspects characteristic of music that together constitute the main obstacles for an adaptation to music of the practice of stemmatology as developed by classical philology (Boorman 1981a, 320–321): (*i*) "the small size of most individual pieces [...], resulting in relatively little evidence", (*ii*) "the fact that most surviving sources were probably copied from more than one exemplar", and (*iii*) "the possible confusion between editorial and accidental changes to both substantive and non-substantive elements of the text". These problems may, sporadically and occasionally, appear also in some sources transmitting literature or other texts, and trouble their editors, but in musical texts they constitute the rule, not the exception, and they always appear together. Boorman's first issue concerns quantity, while the others have methodological and semiotic implications. Last but not least, musical works of large-scale dimensions that present a rich layer of variants, such as the Romantic symphonies, normally do not require a stemmatological approach because editors can use authorial witnesses.

Boorman's rather pessimistic affirmation that the "pursuit of an 'authentic' text for music is almost that of seeking the chimera, and it is also [...] essentially irrelevant" (Boorman 1981b, 168) should be contextualised within this semiotic frame. Music editors have not only been concerned about the period notation they edit but also about the sound these signs inspire when read by non-contemporary musicians who lack the knowledge and the training to read them properly. Reconstructing the original notation does not guarantee that musicians will understand the original musical text, and even when it comes to the reconstruction of a written text, stemmatology can offer only partial help.

8.4.2 Stemmatology for musicologists

This does not mean that stemmatology is useless. Musicologists have used stemmatological methods in various contexts: notated music, literary texts (mainly the lyrics of musical works), theoretical treatises (Bernhard 1979; Solomon 1983, 1986), the relationship of different versions of a work (see fig. 8.4-2), and even reconstructing the transmission of iconographic elements in music-related sources (Teviotdale 1988). Yet these cases do not require methods that differ from those applied by an editor of language-based material. Moreover, the most uncontested and fruitful contributions of stemmatology to musicology have occurred when scholars focused on a by-product of the process, namely its capacity to trace patterns of transmission within musical repertoires and unique, complex sources. If the combinatory, or, to use the terminology of philology, the contaminated nature of musical sources was an obstacle to the reconstruction of every single piece in a compilation, it proved to be a blessing for mapping the cultural context and origin of the collection as a distinct entity.

Many repertoires have been studied using stemmatological methods: mediaeval plainchant repertoires, Gregorian chant, Aquitanian and French tropes and versaria

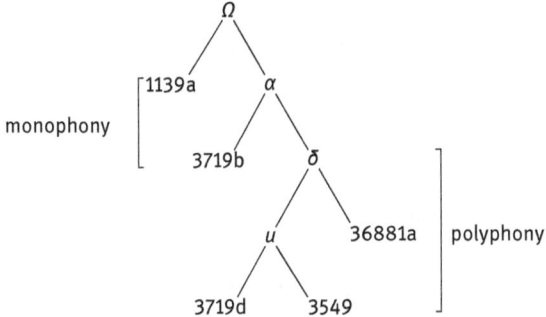

Fig. 8.4-2: This stemma shows the relationship between a monophonic and a polyphonic transmission of the same melody, thus conveying the emergence of polyphony from monophonic repertoires. Source: Grier (1995, 82).

(G. Weiss 1964; Hughes 1969; Grier 1988; Levy 2003; Procter 2006); vernacular monophony of the trouvère, troubadour, cantiga, and *Minnesang* traditions (Karp 1964; van der Werf 1972; Räkel 1973; Schaffer 2000; Wulstan 2000; Räkel 1977); and polyphony of the thirteenth to sixteenth centuries (Atlas 1977; Cook 1978; Atlas 1981; Bent 1981; Frobenius 1987; d'Alvarenga 2011). Even the very complex transmission of instrumental music has been tackled with stemmatological zeal (Memelsdorff 2010). Josquin was not the only composer whose works were scrutinised by stemmatological studies: the scholarly work on Machaut (Dömling 1969), and the editions of Jacob Obrecht (Hudson 1988) and other composers of the fifteenth and sixteenth centuries, included this method in its toolboxes but insisted upon its limitations rather than its accomplishments.

Although stemmatology did not achieve the results editors had envisaged as a result of the method's importance in other disciplines, its combination with theories about the transmission and compilation of music (Hamm 1962; Just 1981) in the period between the fourteenth and sixteenth centuries enabled stemmatology to contribute substantially to reaching new and promising insights. This was achieved by linking repertoires and compilation strategies to political relationships and knowledge of cultural exchange. This approach rendered the seemingly random content of sources historically consistent and plausible. A pattern of research was established by the pioneering work of Allan Atlas on the Capella Giulia *Chansonnier* (Atlas 1975–1976), a composite Renaissance source. This edition did not use stemmatology as a means of constituting an archetypal text; instead, assembling the scattered stemmatological evidence, Atlas succeeded in tracing the origin of the different chansons and the cultural contexts and intercultural relationships that made the formation of this collection possible. Atlas's approach inspired other colleagues, and a series of single-source studies appeared in the following decades (Just 1991b; Ros-Fabrégas 1992; Noblitt 1987–1996), all of which focus on the history of the manuscripts involved and the fascinating entanglement between Renaissance sources.

Other musicologists used stemmatological approaches to face problems that had been troubling the discipline for a long time, such as the phenomenon of reworking and contrafacture (Blackburn 1976; Schmid 1999), style (Kirsch 1981; Bent 1987), and scribal habits (Hortschansky 1981; Boorman 1983; H. M. Brown 1983; Bent 1990). Stemmatology featured as one of many tools, but its basic effect was to establish a methodological link with textual studies in other disciplines, thus preventing the complete detachment of musicological speculation from the written evidence. Another important achievement of stemmatology concerns its use as a method to establish hard criteria for the assessment of authenticity, authorial intentionality, and the textual status of musical transmission (Staehelin 1983; Brett 1988; Just 1991a). Having abandoned the aspiration of creating an archetype, the assessment of authenticity still served as a means of containment for pure speculation.

8.4.3 Stemmatology for performing artists

The importance of stemmatology for performing artists is twofold. On the one hand, performers often express a sense of belonging to a genealogy of preceding musicians. Their musical training relies heavily on a "master–disciple" relationship and oral transmission, due to the fact that many aspects of musical interpretation have not been or cannot be recorded as written instructions. Considering oneself the "grandson" of Franz Liszt is not only a metaphor, but also means having inherited a style, a pedigree, a responsibility, and a sense of mission. Yet this understanding of a stemma lies beyond the scope of the present volume.

Central to our concern is the preoccupation of musicologists with rendering the findings of conventional stemmatology fruitful for performing musicians (Boorman 1995; Göller and Mazzola 2002). The crucial element in these considerations is that performing artists should also focus on those elements of the notation which are unprofitable or useless to the music editor. While the differentiation between substantial and accidental aspects of notation has always been suspicious to editors because editorial practices obliged them to make decisions, musicians can use the ephemeral space of performance as a place for experimentation. This might be considered one methodological supplement that musicology has contributed to the stemmatological tradition.

8.4.4 Stemmatology for music ethnographers

Music ethnography, a discipline that frequently deals with orally transmitted music, has interpreted stemmatology in a completely different way than historical musicology. I mention here only two related lines of research in which stemmatology, understood in a broader sense, can be found as a methodological tool. The first is

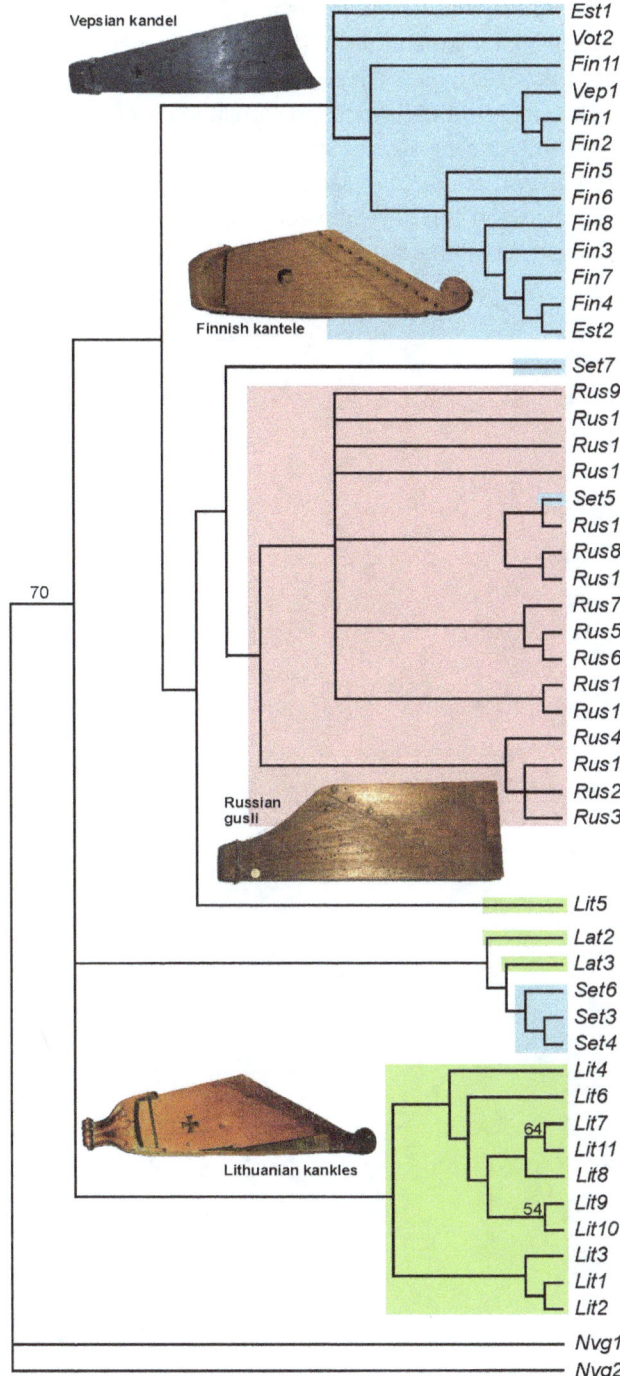

Fig. 8.4-3: Cladogram of the Baltic psaltery. Majority-rule consensus tree.
Source: Tëmkin and Eldredge (2007, 147).

the structural analysis of folkloric melodies (Steingrímsson 1975; Zamfir 1972). The hypothesis behind this method is that a structural similarity between melodies mirrors their ethnological relationship. This hypothesis has been strengthened in recent decades by biological research. Some studies have found correlations between DNA and the structural analysis of folkloric music, its structure, and its instruments (Tëmkin and Eldredge 2007; S. Brown et al. 2014); see figure 8.4-3. Moreover, some results establish a parallelism between the development of musical patterns and phylogenetics, claiming that musical patterns seem to match DNA more closely than linguistic relationships.

Terminology in other languages

This appendix lists important terminology in the four most important languages used in the field. In some cases, a (Graeco-)Latin term is still universally in use, displayed in a fifth column. This table serves a practical purpose and cannot, of course, replace comprehensive dictionary approaches (e.g. Beccaria 2004; Gomez Gane 2013; Duval 2015); rather, it is meant to provide an overview of key terminology in these four languages (the context of the terms can be found in the book via the index). It may, nonetheless, also help readers looking for the usual translation of English terms in French, German, or Italian. A few comments are added in parentheses.

English	German	French	Italian	(Graeco-)Latin
addition	Hinzufügung	addition	aggiunta	
alignment	Alignment	alignement	allineamento	
analysis of forms	Analyse der Formen	analyse des formes	analisi delle forme	
ancestor	Vorfahre	ancêtre	antenato	
anticipation	Antizipation	anticipation	anticipazione	
apograph	Abschrift	apographe	apografo	
apomorphic	apomorph	apomorphique	apomorfo	
apparatus, critical apparatus	Apparat, kritischer Apparat	apparat, apparat critique	apparato, apparato critico	
archetype	Archetyp	archétype	archetipo	(codex) archetypus
				arrhythmia
assimilation	Assimilation	assimilation	assimilazione	
autograph	Autograph	autographe	autografo	autographum
bifid, binary, bifurcating, bipartite	zweigespalten (Maas), binär/zweigliedrig, Bifurkations-, bipartit/zweiteilig (usage is not fixed)	bifide, binaire, bifurqué, bipartite (usage as in English)	bifido, binario, biforcato, bipartito	
branch	Zweig	branche	ramo	
character	Zeichen	caractère, signe graphique	carattere, segno grafico	
cladistics	Kladistik	cladistique	cladistica	
cladogram	Kladogramm	cladogramme	cladogramma	

English	German	French	Italian	(Graeco-)Latin
codex	Codex/Kodex	codex	codice	codex
				codex descriptus
				codex interpositus
				codex optimus
				codex unicus
collation	Kollationierung	collation	collazione (the Latin term collatio is often also used)	collatio
colophon	Kolophon	colophon	colophon	
common errors (method)	gemeinsame Fehler, Methode der Fehlergemeinschaften	(méthode des) erreurs communes	(metodo) degli errori (comuni)	combinatio
computer-assisted stemmatology	computergestützte Stemmatologie	stemmatologie assistée par ordinateur	stemmatologia digitale	
conjecture	Konjektur	conjecture	congettura	coniectura
consensus tree	Konsensusbaum, Consensus-Baum	arbre consensus	albero di consenso	
contamination	Kontamination	contamination	contaminazione	constitutio textus
contamination, extra-stemmatic	extrastemmatische Kontamination	contamination extrastemmatique	contaminazione extrastemmatica	
contamination, simultaneous	simultane Kontamination	contamination simultanée	contaminazione simultanea	
contamination, successive	sukzessive Kontamination	contamination successive	contaminazione successiva	
copy	Kopie, Abschrift	copie	copia	
copy text	Leithandschrift	texte de base, manuscrit de base	manoscritto guida, manoscritto base, copy text	
copying of texts	abschreiben, kopieren	copier des textes	copiatura di testi	
copyist	Kopist, Abschreiber	copiste	copista	
corruption	Korruptel(e)	corruption	corruttela	corruptēla
degree (of a node in a tree)	Grad	degré	grado	
descendant	Nachkomme	descendant	discendente	

diasystem	Diasystem	diasystème	diasistema	
diffraction	Diffraktion	diffraction	diffrazione	
directed acyclic graph (DAG)	gerichteter azyklischer Graph, DAG	graphe orienté acyclique, DAG	grafo aciclico orientato, DAG	
				dispositio
distance matrix	Distanzmatrix	matrice de distance	matrice di distanza	
dittography	Dittographie	dittographie	dittografia	
				divinatio
document	Dokument	document	documento	
duplication	Verdoppelung	duplication	duplicazione	
ecdotics	Ekdotik	ecdotique	ecdotica	
edge	Kante	arête	lato, spigolo, arco	
edition, best manuscript	(Text)Ausgabe, Edition nach der besten Handschrift	édition du meilleur manuscrit	edizione, codice migliore/ottimo	
edition, critical	kritische Edition/(Text)Ausgabe	édition critique	edizione critica	
edition, digital	digitale Edition/(Text)Ausgabe	édition électronique/numérique	edizione elettronica/digitale	
edition, diplomatic	diplomatische Edition/(Text)Ausgabe	édition diplomatique	edizione diplomatica	
edition, documentary	vergleichende Edition/(Text)Ausgabe, occasionally also Dokumentationsausgabe	édition documentaire	edizione documentaria	
edition, eclectic	eklektische Edition/(Text)Ausgabe	édition éclectique	edizione eclettica	
edition, monotypic				
edition, synoptic	synoptische Edition/(Text)Ausgabe	édition synoptique	edizione sinottica	
				eliminatio codicum descriptorum
				eliminatio lectionum singularium
				emendatio (the whole process)

English	German	French	Italian	(Graeco-)Latin
emendatio ex fonte	emendatio ex fonte	émendation à partir de la source	correzione ex fonte	emendatio ex fonte
emendation (single case)	Emendation	émendation, correction	emendamento (per congettura)	
error	Fehler	erreur	errore	
error, conjunctive	Bindefehler	erreur conjonctive	errore congiuntivo	
error, indicative/significant	Leitfehler	erreur significative	errore guida/significativo	
error, separative	Trennfehler	erreur séparative	errore separativo	examinatio
exemplar	Vorlage, Exemplar	exemplaire	esemplare	
exemplar shift	Vorlagenwechsel	changement d'exemplaire	cambio d'esemplare	
eye-skip	Augensprung	saut du même au même	salto da pari a pari, omissione ex homoeoteleuto	
facsimile (edition)	Faksimile (Faksimileausgabe)	(édition) fac similé	(edizione in) facsimile	
family (of witnesses)	Familie, Klasse (von Zeugen)	famille, classe (de témoins)	famiglia, classe (di testimoni)	
fragment	Fragment	fragment	frammento	
gloss	Glosse (pronounced with a long ō)	glose	glossa	
gloss-incorporation	Einfügung von Glossen im Text	incorporation de gloses	incorporazione di glosse	
glyph	Glyphe	glyphe	glifo	
graph	Graph	graphe	grafo	
group (of witnesses)	Gruppe (von Zeugen)	groupe (de témoins)	gruppo (di testimoni)	
haplography	Haplographie	haplographie	aplografia	
			om(e)oarcto (or the Latin)	homoeoarcton
			om(e)oteleuto (or the Latin)	homoeoteleuton
homoplasy	Homoplasie	homoplasie	om(e)oplasia	
hyparchetype (subarchetype)	Hyparchetyp (Subarchetyp)	hyparchétype (subarchétype)	iparchetipo (subarchetipo)	
innovation	Neuerung	innovation	innovazione	
interpolation	Interpolation	interpolation	interpolazione	
Lachmann's method	Lachmanns Methode	méthode de Lachmann	metodo del Lachmann	

English	German	French	Italian	
lacuna	Lacuna	lacune	lacuna	
leaf (of a tree)	Blatt	feuille	foglia	
				lectio brevior, lectio potior
				lectio difficilior, lectio potior
				lectio facilior
lectio singularis	Eigenfehler, Sonderfehler	leçon propre	lezione singolare	lectio singularis
				locus criticus
				locus desperatus
loss rate (of witnesses)	Verlustrate	taux de perte	tasso di perdita	
manuscript	Handschrift, Manuskript (usually in the sense of a typescript)	manuscrit	manoscritto	
material accident	physische/materielle Beschädigung	accident matériel	danno materiale	
media transmitting texts	textüberliefernde Medien	supports matériels	supporti scrittori/media	
metathesis	Metathese	métathèse	metatesi	
method, maximum likelihood	Methode der maximalen Wahrscheinlichkeit	méthode de maximum de vraisemblance	metodo della massima verosimiglianza	
method, maximum parsimony	Methode der maximalen Parsimonie, or English term	méthode du maximum de parcimonie	metodo della massima parsimonia	
methods, distance-based	distanzbasierte Methoden	méthodes basées sur les distances	metodi basati sulla distanza	
misreading	Fehllesung	mélecture, faute graphique	lettura sbagliata (rarely used), errore di lettura, errore paleografico	
mouvance (French term)	mouvance	mouvance	mouvance	
neo-Lachmannian philology	neolachmannsche Philologie (rare)	philologie néo-lachmannienne (rare)	neo-lachmannismo	
networks, evolutionary	evolutionäre Netzwerke	réseaux évolutifs	reti evolutive	

English	German	French	Italian	(Graeco-)Latin
New Philology	new philology, neue Philologie	nouvelle philologie	new philology (≠ Michele Barbi's "nuova filologia")	
node, internal	innerer Knoten, innere Ecke	nœud interne	nodo interno, vertice interno	
node/vertex	Knoten/Ecke	nœud/sommet	nodo/vertice	
normalisation	Normalisierung	normalisation	normalizzazione	
omission	Auslassung	omission	omissione	
origin	Ursprung	origine	origine	
original	Original	original	originale	
outgroup	Außengruppe, outgroup	outgroup	outgroup	
palaeography	Paläografie	paléographie	paleografia	palaeographia parablepsis
parsimoniously informative	parsimonisch informativ (or the English term)	parcimonieusement informatif	parsimoniosamente informativo	
parsimony	Sparsamkeit, Parsimonie	parcimonie	parsimonia	
path (in a graph)	Weg	chemin	percorso	
phylogenetic networks	phylogenetische Netzwerke	réseaux phylogénétiques	reti filogenetiche	
phylogenetic tree	phylogenetischer Baum	arbre phylogénétique	albero filogenetico	
phylogenetics	Phylogenetik, Phylogenese, Phylogenie	phylogénétique, phylogenèse, phylogénie	filogenetica, filogenesi, filogenia	
phylogram	Phylogramm	phylogramme	filogramma	
phylomemetics	Phylomemetik (rare)	phylomémétique (rare)	filomemetica (rare)	
plesiomorphic	plesiomorph (adj.), Plesiomorphismus (noun)	plésiomorphique (adj.), plésiomorphisme (noun)	plesiomorfo (adj.), plesiomorfismo (noun), plesiomorfia (noun)	
polarisation	Polarisation	polarisation	polarizzazione	
polygenesis	Polygenese	polygenèse	poligenesi	
reading	Lesart	leçon	lezione	lectio
reading, primary	primäre Lesart	leçon primaire	lezione primaria	
reading, secondary	sekundäre Lesart	leçon secondaire	lezione secondaria	
reading, variant	alternative Lesart, Variante	(leçon) variante	lezione alternativa, variante	varia lectio recensio

recension	*Rezension*	*recension*	*recensione*	
recension, closed/open	*geschlossene/offene Rezension*	*recension fermée/ouverte*	*recensione chiusa/aperta*	
				recentiores non deteriores
reconstruction	*Rekonstruktion*	*reconstruction*	*ricostruzione*	
redaction	*Redaktion*	*rédaction*	*redazione*	
redactor	*Redaktor*	*rédacteur*	*redattore*	
reference text	*Kollationsexemplar*	*exemplaire de collation, texte de référence, texte de base*	*esemplare di collazione*	
regularisation	*Regularisierung*	*régularisation*	*regolarizzazione*	
reticulation	*Netzstruktur, Retikulation*	*réticulation (rare)*	*reticolazione*	
reticulogram	*Retikulogramm*	*réticulogramme*	*reticologramma*	
revision	*Überarbeitung*	*révision*	*revisione*	
root	*Wurzel*	*racine*	*radice*	
scribal conjecture	*Kopistenkonjektur, Konjektur eines Kopisten*	*conjecture de copiste*	*congettura del copista, congettura scribale*	
scribe	*Schreiber*	*scribe*	*scriba/copista scuola storica*	
				selectio
separative error	*Trennfehler*	*erreur séparative*	*errore separativo/disgiuntivo (less frequent)*	
set, subset, set union, set intersection, empty set, disjoint set, complement of a set	*Menge, Untermenge, Vereinigungsmenge, Schnittmenge, leere Menge, disjunkte Mengen, komplementäre Mengen*	*ensemble, sous-ensemble, union d'ensembles, intersection d'ensembles, ensemble vide, ensembles disjoints, ensembles complémentaires*	*insieme, sottoinsieme, unione d'insiemi, intersezione d'insiemi, insieme vuoto, insiemi disgiunti, insieme complementare/complemento (di un insieme)*	

English	German	French	Italian	(Graeco-)Latin
siglum	Sigle	sigle	siglum	
standardisation	Standardisierung	standardisation	standardizzazione	
stemma	Stemma (also, less technically: Stammbaum)	stemma	stemma (pl. stemmi)	
stemmatics	Stemmatik	stemmatique	stemmatica	
stemmatology	Stemmatologie	stemmatologie	stemmatologia	
substitution	Ersetzung	substitution	sostituzione	
subtree	Teilbaum	sous-arbre	sottoalbero	
symplesiomorphic	symplesiomorph (adj.), Symplesiomorphie (noun)	symplésiomorphique (adj.), symplésiomorphie (noun)	simplesiomorfo (adj.), simplesiomorfismo (noun), simplesiomorfia (noun)	
taxon	Taxon	taxon	taxon	taxon (pl. taxa)
text	Text	texte	testo	
textual criticism	Textkritik	critique textuelle	critica testuale	
textual scholarship	Textforschung	étude des textes	scienze del testo, studio del testo	
tradition	Tradition	tradition	tradizione	
tradition, artificial	künstliche Texttradition	tradition textuelle artificielle	tradizione testuale artificiale	
tradition, indirect	indirekte Tradition	tradition indirecte	tradizione indiretta	
transmission	Überlieferung	transmission	trasmissione	
transposition	Umstellung, Transposition	transposition	trasposizione	
tree	Baum	arbre	albero	
tree, unrooted	ungewurzelter/unverwurzelter/wurzelloser Baum	arbre non enraciné	albero non radicato	
(stemmatically) undecidable (variant)	(stemmatisch) unentschiedbar	adiaphore, neutre	adiaforo, neutro	
urtext	Urtext	Urtext, texte original, texte primitif	Urtext	
				usus scribendi

variant graph	Variantengraph	graphe des variantes	grafo delle varianti, grafico varianti (rarer)
variant location	variierende Stelle (rare)	lieu variant	luogo variante (rare)
version	Fassung	version	versione
vertex, see node			
vulgarisation	Vulgarisierung	vulgarisation	volgarizzazione
vulgate	Vulgata	vulgate	vulgata
witness	Zeuge	témoin	testimone
work	Werk	œuvre	opera

References

Family names with prefixes (de, van, von, and so on) are listed under the prefix. Diacritics are ignored for the purposes of alphabetisation.

Adluri, Vishwa, and Joydeep Bagchee. 2018. *Philology and Criticism: A Guide to Mahābhārata Textual Criticism*. London: Anthem Press.
Aebischer, Paul. 1954. *Rolandiana borealia: La Saga af Runzivals bardaga et ses dérivés scandinaves comparés à la Chanson de Roland; Essai de restauration du manuscrit français utilisé par le traducteur norrois*. Lausanne: Publications de la Faculté des Lettres.
Aland, Barbara, ed. 1997–2005. *Novum Testamentum Graecum: Editio critica maior*. 4 vols. Stuttgart: Deutsche Bibelgesellschaft.
Aland, Barbara, Johannes Karavidopoulos, Carlos M. Martini, and Bruce M. Metzger, eds. 2015. *The Greek New Testament*. 5th ed. Stuttgart: Deutsche Bibelgesellschaft.
Aland, Kurt. 1994. *Kurzgefasste Liste der griechischen Handschriften des Neuen Testaments*. 2nd ed. Berlin: De Gruyter.
Aland, Kurt, and Barbara Aland. 1989. *Der Text des Neuen Testaments: Eine Einführung in die wissenschaftlichen Ausgaben sowie in Theorie und Praxis der modernen Textkritik*. 2nd ed. Stuttgart: Deutsche Bibelgesellschaft.
Alberti, Giovan Battista. 1979. *Problemi di critica testuale*. Florence: La Nuova Italia.
Alexanderson, Bengt. 2018. "Why Phylogenetic Methods Do Not Work Very Well in Textual Transmission". *Revue d'histoire des textes*, n.s., 13: 383–410.
Allen, Robert E., ed. 1990. *Concise Oxford Dictionary*. 8th ed. Oxford: Oxford University Press.
Alsted, Johann Heinrich. 1989–1990. *Encyclopaedia*. 4 vols. Stuttgart-Bad Cannstatt: Frommann-Holzboog.
Altschul, Nadia R. 2006. "The Genealogy of Scribal Versions: A Fourth Way". *Textual Cultures: Texts, Contexts, Interpretation* 1: 114–136.
Altschul, Nadia R. 2015. "L'Espagnol castillan médiéval et la critique textuelle". In *Manuel de la philologie de l'édition*, edited by David Trotter, 81–94. Berlin: De Gruyter.
Amand de Mendieta, Emmanuel. 1987. "Un problème d'ecdotique: Comment manier la tradition manuscrite surabondante d'un ouvrage patristique". In *Texte und Textkritik: Eine Aufsatzsammlung*, edited by Jürgen Dummer, 29–42. Berlin: Akademie-Verlag.
Amiaud, Arthur, ed. 1889. *La Légende syriaque de Saint Alexis l'homme de Dieu*. Paris: Bouillon.
Amphoux, Christian-Bernard. 1987. "La Révision marcionite du 'Notre Père' de Luc (11,2–4) et sa place dans l'histoire du texte". *Cahiers de la Revue théologique de Louvain* 19: 105–121.
Amphoux, Christian-Bernard. 1988. "Un indice de variation pour le classement des états d'un texte". *Revue d'histoire des textes* 18: 279–299.
Amphoux, Christian-Bernard. 2014. "Les Manuscrits grecs". In *Manuel de critique textuelle du Nouveau Testament*, edited by Christain-Bernard Amphoux, 9–74. Brussels: Safran.
Amsalu Tefera, ed. and trans. 2015. *The Ethiopian Homily on the Ark of the Covenant: Critical Edition and Annotated Translation of Dərsanä Ṣəyon*. Leiden: Brill.
Andrews, Tara L. 2009. "Prolegomena to a Critical Edition of the Chronicle of Matthew of Edessa, with a Discussion of Computer-Aided Methods Used to Edit the Text". PhD thesis, University of Oxford.
Andrews, Tara L. 2013. "The Third Way: Philology and Critical Edition in the Digital Age". *Variants* 10: 61–76.
Andrews, Tara L. 2014. "Analysis of Variation Significance in Artificial Traditions Using Stemmaweb". *Digital Scholarship in the Humanities* 31 (3): 523–539. doi.org/10.1093/llc/fqu072.

Andrews, Tara L., and Caroline Macé. 2012. "Trees of Texts – Models and Methods for an Updated Theory of Medieval Text Stemmatology". In *Digital Humanities 2012: Conference Abstracts*, 85–88. Hamburg: Hamburg University Press. dh2012.uni-hamburg.de/conference/programme/abstracts/trees-of-texts-models-and-methods-for-an-updated-theory-of-medieval-text-stemmatology.1.html.

Andrews, Tara L., and Caroline Macé. 2013. "Beyond the Tree of Texts: Building an Empirical Model of Scribal Variation through Graph Analysis of Texts and Stemmata". *Literary and Linguistic Computing* 28 (4): 504–521. doi.org/10.1093/llc/fqt032.

Andrews, Tara L., and Joris J. van Zundert. 2018. "What Are You Trying to Say? The Interface as an Integral Element of Argument". In *Digital Scholarly Editions as Interfaces*, edited by Roman Bleier, Martina Bürgermeister, Helmut W. Klug, Frederike Neuber, and Gerlinde Schneider, Schriftenreihe des Instituts für Dokumentologie und Editorik 12, 3–33. Norderstedt: BoD. kups.ub.uni-koeln.de/9118.

Andrist, Patrick, Paul Canart, and Marilena Maniaci. 2013. *La Syntaxe du codex: Essai de codicologie structurale*. Turnhout: Brepols.

Anthony, David W. 1996. "Nazi and Eco-Feminist Prehistories: Ideology and Empiricism in Indo-European Archaeology". In *Nationalism, Politics and the Practice of Archaeology*, edited by Philip L. Kohl and Clare Fawcett, 82–96. Cambridge: Cambridge University Press.

Anttila, Raimo. 1989. *Historical and Comparative Linguistics*. Philadelphia, PA: Benjamins.

Apollon, Daniel, and Claire Bélisle. 2014. "The Digital Fate of the Critical Apparatus". In *Digital Critical Editions*, edited by Daniel Apollon, Claire Bélisle, and Philippe Régnier, 81–113. Urbana: University of Illinois Press.

Apollon, Daniel, Claire Bélisle, and Philippe Régnier, eds. 2014. *Digital Critical Editions*. Urbana: University of Illinois Press.

Appel, Bernhard R., and Reinmar Emans, eds. 2017. *Musikphilologie: Grundlagen, Methoden, Praxis*. Kompendium Musik 3. Laaber: Laaber.

Appel, Bernhard R., and Joachim Veit, eds. 2000. *Editionsrichtlinien Musik*. Kassel: Bärenreiter.

Appel, Carl, ed. 1915. *Bernart von Ventadorn, seine Lieder, mit Einleitung und Glossar*. Halle an der Saale: Niemeyer.

Aquilon, Pierre. 2013. "La Réception du 'Manipulus curatorum' dans le monde germanique (1474–1500)". In *Le Cabinet du curieux: Culture, savoirs, religion de l'Antiquité à l'Ancien Régime*, edited by Witold Konstanty Pietrzak and Magdalena Kozluk, 197–220. Paris: Classiques Garnier.

Archie, James, William H. E. Day, Joseph Felsenstein, Wayne Maddison, Christopher Meacham, F. James Rohlf, and David Swofford. 1986. "The Newick Tree Format". evolution.genetics.washington.edu/phylip/newicktree.html.

Arras, Victor, trans. 1986. *Geronticon*. 2 vols. Leuven: Peeters.

Åström, Patrik. 2005. "Manuscripts and Bookprinting in Late Medieval Scandinavia and in Early Modern Times". In *The Nordic Languages: An International Handbook of the History of the North Germanic Languages*, edited by Oskar Bandle, Kurt Braunmüller, Lennart Elmevik, Ernst Håkon Jahr, Allan Karker, Hans-Peter Naumann, Ulf Teleman, and Gun Widmark, vol. 2, 1067–1075. Berlin: De Gruyter.

Atkinson, Quentin D., and Russell D. Gray. 2006. "How Old Is the Indo-European Language Family? Illumination or More Moths to the Flame?". In *Phylogenetic Methods and the Prehistory of Languages*, edited by Peter Forster and Colin Renfrew, 91–109. Cambridge: McDonald Institute for Archaeological Research.

Atlas, Allan Warren, ed. 1975–1976. *The Cappella Giulia Chansonnier, Rome, Bibl. Apostolica Vaticana d. G. XIII. 27*. 2 vols. New York, NY: Insitute of Medieval Music.

Atlas, Allan Warren. 1977. "On the Neapolitan Provenance of the Manuscript Perugia, Biblioteca Communale Augusta 431 (G20)". *Musica disciplina* 31: 45–106.

Atlas, Allan Warren. 1981. "Conflicting Attributions in Italian Sources of the Franco-Netherlandish Chanson, c. 1465–c. 1505: A Progress Report on a New Hypothesis". In *Music in Medieval and Early Modern Europe*, edited by Iain Fenlon, 249–293. Cambridge: Cambridge University Press.
Avalle, d'Arco Silvio, ed. 1960. *Peire Vidal: Poesie*. Milan: Ricciardi.
Avalle, d'Arco Silvio. 1961. *La letteratura medievale in lingua d'oc nella sua tradizione manoscritta: Problemi di critica testuale*. Turin: Einaudi.
Avalle, d'Arco Silvio. 1972a. *Princìpi di critica testuale*. Padua: Antenore.
Avalle, d'Arco Silvio. 1972b. "La critica testuale". In *Grundriss der romanischen Literaturen des Mittelalters*, vol. 1.1, edited by Maurice Delbouille, 538–558. Heidelberg: Winter.
Avalle, d'Arco Silvio. 1985. "I canzoneri: Definizione di genere e problemi di edizione". In *La critica del testo: Problemi di metodo ed esperienze di lavoro, Atti del Convegno di Lecce, 22–26 ottobre 1984*, edited by Enrico Malato and Andrea Mazzucchi, 363–382. Rome: Salerno editrice [repr. Avalle 2002, 155–173].
Avalle, d'Arco Silvio. 2002. *La doppia verità: Fenomenologia ecdotica e lingua letteraria del Medioevo Romanzo*. Florence: SISMEL.
Avicenna. 1527. *Liber canonis totius medicinae*. Venice: apud Iuntas [repr. Brussels, 1971].
Bach, Johann Sebastian. 1851–1899. *Werke*. Edited by Bach-Gesellschaft zu Leipzig. 46 vols. Leipzig: Breitkopf & Härtel.
Badura-Skoda, Paul. 1986. "Das Problem 'Urtext'". *Musica* 3: 222–228.
Baesecke, Georg, ed. 1945. *Das Hildebrandlied: Eine geschichtliche Einleitung für Laien, mit Lichtbildern der Handschrift, alt- und neuhochdeutschen Texten*. Halle an der Saale: Niemeyer.
Bagils, René Zaragüeta, Visotheary Ung, Anaïs Grand, Régine Vignes-Lebbe, Nathanaël Cao, and Jacques Ducasse. 2012. "LisBeth: New Cladistics for Phylogenetics and Biogeography". *Comptes Rendus Palevol* 11 (8): 563–566. doi.org/10.1016/j.crpv.2012.07.002.
Baierer, Konstantion, Evelyn Dröge, Kai Eckert, Doron Goldfarb, Julia Iwanowa, Christian Morbidoni, and Dominique Ritze. 2016. "DM2E: A Linked Data Source of Digitised Manuscripts for the Digital Humanities". *Semantic Web* 8 (5): 1–13.
Bakelants, Louis, ed. and trans. 1961. *Andreas Vesalius: La Fabrique du corps humain*. Brussels: Editions Arscia [repr. Arles: Actes Sud et Inserm, 1987].
Baker, Craig, Marcello Barbato, Mattia Cavagna, and Yan Greub, eds. 2018. *L'Ombre de Joseph Bédier*. Travaux de Littératures Romanes. Paris: Editions de linguistique et de philologie.
Baker, William, and Kenneth Womack. 2000. *Twentieth-Century Bibliography and Textual Criticism: An Annotated Bibliography*. Westport, CT: Greenwood.
Baldacchini, Lorenzo. 1996. "Ferrando, Tommaso". In *Dizionario Biografico degli Italiani*, vol. 46. Rome: Istituto della Enciclopedia Italiana. treccani.it/enciclopedia/tommaso-ferrando_ (Dizionario-Biografico).
Baldi, Philip. 2002. *The Foundations of Latin*. 2nd ed. Berlin: De Gruyter [1st ed. 1999].
Balduino, Armando. 1979. *Manuale di filologia italiana*. Florence: Sansoni.
Balfour, Henry. 1889. "On the Structure and Affinities of the Composite Bow". *Journal of the Anthropological Institute of Great Britain and Ireland* 19: 220–250.
Bandelt, Hans-Jürgen, and Andreas W. M. Dress. 1992. "Split Decomposition: A New and Useful Approach to Phylogenetic Analysis of Distance Data". *Molecular Phylogenetics and Evolution* 1 (3): 242–252. doi.org/10.1016/1055-7903(92)90021-8.
Bandini, Anton Maria. 1774–1777. *Catalogus codicum Latinorum Bibliothecae Mediceae Laurentianae*. 4 vols. Florence.
Bandini, Anton Maria. 1778. *Catalogus codicum Italicorum Bibliothecae Mediceae Laurentianae Gaddianae et Sanctae Crucis*. Florence.
Barabucci, Gioele. 2016. Review of CATview. *Digital Medievalist* 10. doi.org/10.16995/dm.57.

Barabucci, Gioele, Angelo Di Iorio, and Fabio Vitali. 2014. "Stemma codicum: Analisi e generazione semi-automatica". In *Digital Humanities: Progetti italiani ed esperienze di convergenza multidisciplinare*, edited by Fabio Ciotti, vol. 3, 129–145. Rome: Quaderni DigiLab. doi.org/10.13133/978-88-98533-27-5.

Barbaro, Ermolao. 1973–1979. *Castigationes plinianae*. Edited by Giovanni Pozzi. 4 vols. Padua: Antenore.

Barbi, Michele. 1891. *Per il testo della Divina Commedia*. Rome: Trevisini.

Barbi, Michele, ed. 1907. *Dante Alighieri: La vita nuova*. Florence: Società Dantesca Italiana.

Barbi, Michele. 1915. *Studi sul Canzoniere di Dante: Con nuove indagini sulle raccolte manoscritte e a stampa di antiche rime italiane*. Florence: Sansoni.

Barbi, Michele. 1938. *La nuova filologia e l'edizione dei nostri scrittori da Dante a Manzoni*. Florence: Sansoni [repr. 1973, 1994].

Barbier, Frédéric. 2006. *L'Europe de Gutenberg: Le Livre et l'invention de la modernité occidentale (XIIIe–XVIe siècle)*. Paris: Belin.

Barbier, Frédéric. 2017. *Gutenberg's Europe: The Book and the Invention of Western Modernity*. Translated by Jean Birrell. Cambridge: Polity Press [trans. of Barbier 2006].

Barbrook, Adrian C., Christopher J. Howe, Norman Blake, and Peter Robinson. 1998. "The Phylogeny of The Canterbury Tales". *Nature* 394 (August): 839. doi.org/10.1038/29667.

Barenghi, Maddalena. 2014. "Zheng Qiao (1104–1162), the *Jiaochou lüe* (Treatise on Collation), and the Retrieval of Lost Books". *Journal of Song-Yuan Studies* 44: 265–286.

Baret, Philippe V., Caroline Macé, and Peter Robinson. 2006. "Testing Methods on an Artificially Created Textual Tradition". In *The Evolution of Texts: Confronting Stemmatological and Genetical Methods: Proceedings of the International Workshop (Louvain la Neuve, sept. 2004)*, edited by Caroline Macé, Philippe V. Baret, Andrea Bozzi, and Laura Cignoni, 255–281. Pisa: Istituti editoriali e poligrafici internazionali.

Barth, Lewis. 1999. "Is Every Medieval Hebrew Manuscript a New Composition?". In *Agendas for the Study of Midrash in the Twenty-First Century*, edited by Marc Lee Raphael, 43–62. Williamsburg, VA: Department of Religion, College of William and Mary.

Bartsch, Karl. 1865. *Untersuchungen über das Nibelungenlied*. Vienna: Braunmüller.

Bartsch, Karl, ed. 1866. *Nibelungenlied*. 6th ed. Leipzig: Brockhaus.

Bartsch, Karl, ed. 1870–1880. *Der Nibelunge Nôt: Mit den Abweichungen von der Nibelunge Liet, den Lesarten sämmtlicher Handschriften und einem Wörterbuche*. 3 vols. Leipzig: Brockhaus.

Bartsch, Karl, and Helmut de Boor, eds. 1979. *Das Nibelungenlied: Nach der Ausgabe von Karl Bartsch herausgegeben von Helmut de Boor*. 21st ed. by Roswitha Wisniewski. Wiesbaden: Brockhaus.

Bäuml, Franz H. 1961. "Some Aspects of Editing the Unique Manuscript: A Criticism of Method". *Orbis litterarum* 16 (1–2): 27–33.

Bausi, Alessandro. 2003. "'Quando verrà …' (Mt 25,31): Su un passo del Gadla Libānos". *Aethiopica* 6: 168–176.

Bausi, Alessandro. 2006a. "The Aksumite Background of the Ethiopic 'Corpus canonum'". In *Proceedings of the XVth International Conference of Ethiopian Studies, Hamburg, July 20–25, 2003*, edited by Siegbert Uhlig, Maria Bulakh, Denis Nosnitsin, and Thomas Rave, 532–541. Wiesbaden: Harrassowitz.

Bausi, Alessandro. 2006b. "Current Trends in Ethiopian Studies: Philology". In *Proceedings of the XVth International Conference of Ethiopian Studies, Hamburg, July 20–25, 2003*, edited by Siegbert Uhlig, Maria Bulakh, Denis Nosnitsin, and Thomas Rave, 542–551. Wiesbaden: Harrassowitz.

Bausi, Alessandro. 2008. "Philology as Textual Criticism: 'Normalization' of Ethiopian Studies". *Bulletin of Philological Society of Ethiopia (Addis Ababa University, Department of Linguistics)* 1 (1): 13–46.

Bausi, Alessandro. 2009. Review of *Il Gädl di Abuna Demyanos santo eritreo (XIV/XV sec.): Edizione del testo etiopico e traduzione italiana*, edited by Tedros Abreha. *Scrinium: Revue de patrologie, d'hagiographie critique et d'histoire ecclésiastique* 5: 429–436.

Bausi, Alessandro. 2010a. Review of *I Gädl di Abunä Täwäldä-Mädehn e di Abunä Vittore: Edizione del testo etiopico e traduzione italiana*, edited by Tedros Abraha. *Aethiopica* 13: 244–253.

Bausi, Alessandro. 2010b. "Philology". In *Encyclopaedia Aethiopica*, edited by Siegbert Uhlig, vol. 4, *O–X*, 142a–144b. Wiesbaden: Harrassowitz.

Bausi, Alessandro. 2014a. "Filologi o 'falsari'? Ancora su un passo del Gadla Libānos". In *Linguistic, Oriental and Ethiopian Studies in Memory of Paolo Marrassini*, edited by Alessandro Bausi, Alessandro Gori, and Gianfrancesco Lusini, 55–70. Wiesbaden: Harrassowitz.

Bausi, Alessandro. 2014b. "Writing, Copying, Translating: Ethiopia as a Manuscript Culture". In *Manuscript Cultures: Mapping the Field*, edited by Jörg Quenzer, Dmitry Bondarev, and Jan-Ulrich Sobisch, Studies in Manuscript Cultures 1, 37–77. Berlin: De Gruyter.

Bausi, Alessandro. 2015a. "The Aksumite Collection: Ethiopic Multiple Text Manuscripts". In *Comparative Oriental Manuscript Studies: An Introduction*, by Alessandro Bausi, Pier Giorgio Borbone, Françoise Briquel Chatonnet, Paola Buzi, Jost Gippert, Caroline Macé, Marilena Maniaci, Zisis Melissakis, Laura E. Parodi, and Witold Witakowski, 367–372. Hamburg: Tredition.

Bausi, Alessandro. 2015b. "Zoëga e la filologia". In *The Forgotten Scholar: Georg Zoëga (1755–1809); At the Dawn of Egyptology and Coptic Studies*, edited by Karin Ascani, Paola Buzi, and Daniela Picchi, 57–66. Leiden: Brill.

Bausi, Alessandro. 2015c. Review of *Gädlä Abunä Yonas Zä-Bur: Eritrean Saint of the 15th Century*, edited and translated by Tedros Abraha. *Aethiopica* 18: 257–260.

Bausi, Alessandro. 2016a. "On Editing and Normalizing Ethiopic Texts". In *150 Years after Dillmann's Lexicon: Perspectives and Challenges of Gaʿəz Studies*, edited by Alessandro Bausi with Eugenia Sokolinsk, 43–102. Wiesbaden: Harrassowitz.

Bausi, Alessandro. 2016b. "The Encyclopaedia Aethiopica and Ethiopian Studies". *Aethiopica* 19: 188–206.

Bausi, Alessandro. 2017a. "The Earlier Ethiopic Textual Heritage". In *Scribal Practices and the Social Construction of Knowledge in Antiquity, Late Antiquity and Medieval Islam*, edited by Myriam Wissa, 215–235. Leuven: Peeters.

Bausi, Alessandro. 2017b. "The Ethiopic Book of Clement: The Case of a Recent Ethiopian Edition and a Few Additional Remarks". In *Studies in Ethiopian Languages, Literature, and History, Festschrift for Getatchew Haile presented by his Friends and Colleagues*, edited by Adam McCollum, 229–238. Wiesbaden: Harrassowitz.

Bausi, Alessandro. 2017c. "Il Gadla 'Azqir". *Adamantius* 23: 341–380.

Bausi, Alessandro. 2017–2018. "Documentary Manuscripts and Archives: The Ethiopian Evidence". In *Labor limae: Atti in onore di Carmela Baffioni*, edited by Antonella Straface, Carlo De Angelo, and Andrea Manzo, 63–80. Naples: Università degli Studi di Napoli.

Bausi, Alessandro. 2018. "Translations in Late Antique Ethiopia". In *Egitto crocevia di traduzioni*, edited by Franco Crevatin, 1, 69–99. Trieste: EUT Edizioni dell'Università di Trieste. hdl.handle.net/10077/21835.

Bausi, Alessandro, Pier Giorgio Borbone, Françoise Briquel-Chatonnet, Paola Buzi, Jost Gippert, Caroline Macé, Marilena Maniaci, Zisis Melissakis, Laura E. Parodi, and Witold Witakowsk. 2015. *Comparative Oriental Manuscript Studies: An Introduction*. Hamburg: Tredition.

Bausi, Alessandro, and Alberto Camplani. 2016. "The History of the Episcopate of Alexandria (HEpA): Editio Minor of the Fragments Preserved in the Aksumite Collection and in the Codex Veronensis LX (58)". *Adamantius* 22: 249–302.

Bausi, Alessandro, Alessandro Gori, and Gianfrancesco Lusini, eds. 2014. *Linguistic, Oriental and Ethiopian Studies in Memory of Paolo Marrassini*. Wiesbaden: Harrassowitz.

Baxter, Stephen. 2007. *The Earls of Mercia: Lordship and Power in Late Anglo-Saxon England*. Oxford: Oxford University Press.

Baye Yimam. 2008. "Rationale for PhD in Philology at AAU". *Bulletin of Philological Society of Ethiopia (Addis Ababa University, Department of Linguistics)* 1 (1): 60–64.

Bayet, Jean, ed. 1961. *Tite-Live: Histoire romaine*. Vol. 1. *Livre I*. Text by Jean Bayet. Translated by Gaston Baillet. Paris: Les Belles Lettres.

Beard, Mary, Alan K. Bowman, Mireille Corbier, Tim Cornell, James L. Franklin Jr, Ann Hanson, Keith Hopkins, and Nicholas Horsfall. 1991. *Literacy in the Roman World*. Ann Arbor: University of Michigan Press.

Beccaria, Augusto. 1956. *I codici di medicina del periodo presalernitano (Secoli IX, X e XI)*. Rome: Edizioni di Storia e Letteratura.

Beccaria, Gian Luigi, ed. 2004. *Dizionario di linguistica e di filologia, metrica, retorica*. Turin: Einaudi.

Becker, Hans-Jürgen. 1999. *Die großen rabbinischen Sammelwerke Palastinas: Zur literarischen Genese von Talmud Yerushalmi und Midrash Bereshit Rabba*. Tübingen: Mohr.

Beckett, Samuel. 2014. *The Letters of Samuel Beckett*. Vol. 2. *1957–1965*. Edited by George Craig, Martha Dow Fehsenfeld, Dan Gunn, and Lois Overbeck. Cambridge: Cambridge University Press.

Bédier, Joseph, ed. 1890. *Jean Renart: Le Lai de l'ombre*. Fribourg: Imprimerie et librairie de l'œuvre de Saint-Paul.

Bédier, Joseph. 1894. "La Société des Anciens Textes Français". *Revue des deux mondes* 121: 906–934.

Bédier, Joseph, ed. 1909. *Les Chansons de croisade*. Melodies published by Pierre Aubry. Paris: Champion.

Bédier, Joseph, ed. 1912. *Colin Muset: Chansons*. Melodies transcribed by Jean Beck. Les Classiques français du Moyen Age. Paris: Champion.

Bédier, Joseph, ed. 1913. *Jean Renart: Le Lai de l'ombre*. Paris: Société des anciens textes français.

Bédier, Joseph, ed. 1921. *La Chanson de Roland publiée d'après le manuscrit d'Oxford*. Paris: Piazza.

Bédier, Joseph, ed. 1927. *La Chanson de Roland commentée*. Paris: Piazza.

Bédier, Joseph. 1928. "La Tradition manuscrite du Lai de l'ombre: Réflexions sur l'art d'éditer les anciens textes". *Romania* 54: 161–196, 321–356 [repr. Paris: Champion, 1970. gallica.bnf.fr/ark:/12148/bpt6k8980].

Beer, Gillian. 2006. "Dame Gillian Beer's Speech on the Challenges of Interdisciplinarity". Speech at University of Durham, April 27. web.archive.org/web/20121025001957/http://www.dur.ac.uk/ias/news/annual_research_dinner/.

Bein, Thomas. 2010. "'schlechte handschriften', 'critische ausgaben', 'ausgezeichnete copisten': Über die Bedeutung der Materialität für Edition und Interpretation am Beispiel von Ton 36/36a Walthers von der Vogelweide". In *Materialität in der Editionswissenschaft*, edited by Martin Schubert, 267–274. Berlin: De Gruyter.

Beit-Arié, Malachi. 2000. "Publication and Reproduction of Literary Texts in Medieval Jewish Civilization: Jewish Scribality and Its Impact on the Texts Transmitted". In *Transmitting Jewish Traditions: Orality, Textuality, and Cultural Diffusion*, edited by Yaakov Elman and Israel Gershoni, 225–247. New Haven, CT: Yale University Press.

Bell, Alan. 2009. "Phillipps, Sir Thomas, Baronet (1792–1872)". In *Oxford Dictionary of National Biography*. oxforddnb.com/view/10.1093/ref:odnb/9780198614128.001.0001/odnb-9780198614128-e-22143.

Beltrami, Pietro. 2010. *A che serve un'edizione critica? Leggere i testi della letteratura romanza medievale*. Bologna: il Mulino.

Benecke, Georg F., and Karl Lachmann, eds. 1877. *Iwein, eine Erzählung von Hartmann von Aue: Mit Anmerkungen von G. F. Benecke und K. Lachmann*. 4th ed. Berlin: Reimer [= 2nd ed. 1843].
Benedictines of Bouveret, ed. 1965–1982. *Colophons de manuscrits occidentaux des origines au XVIe siècle*. 6 vols. Fribourg: Editions Universitaires.
Bengel, Johann Albrecht, ed. 1734. *Ἡ Καινὴ Διαθήκη: Novum Testamentum Graece*. Stuttgart: apud I. B. Metzlerum.
Bengel, Johann Albrecht. 1742. *Gnomon Novi Testamenti*. Tübingen: Io. Henri Philippi Schranii. mdz-nbn-resolving.de/urn:nbn:de:bvb:12-bsb10353422-5.
Bengel, Johann Albrecht. 1763. *Apparatus criticus ad Novum Testamentum […]*. Tübingen: sumptibus Ioh. Georgii Cottae. archive.org/details/dioalbertibengel00beng.
Bengtson, John D., and Merritt Ruhlen. 1994. "Global Etymologies". In *On the Origin of Languages: Studies in Linguistic Taxonomy*, edited by Merritt Ruhlen, 277–336. Stanford, CA: Stanford University Press.
Bennwitz, Hanspeter, Georg Feder, Ludwig Finscher, and Wolfgang Rehm, eds. 1975. *Musikalisches Erbe und Gegenwart: Musiker-Gesamtausgaben in der Bundesrepublik Deutschland*. Kassel: Bärenreiter.
Bent, Margaret. 1981. "Some Criteria for Establishing Relationships between Sources of Late-Medieval Polyphony". In *Music in Medieval and Early Modern Europe*, edited by Iain Fenlon, 295–317. Cambridge: Cambridge University Press.
Bent, Margaret. 1987. "A Contemporary Perception of Early Fifteenth Century Style: Bologna Q 15 as a Document of Scribal Editorial Initiative". *Musica disciplina* 41: 183–201.
Bent, Margaret. 1990. "Manuscripts as Repertories: Scribal Performance and Performing Scribe". In *Atti del XIV Congresso della Società Internazionale di Musicologia, Bologna, 27 agosto – 10 settembre 1987, Ferrara – Parma, 30 agosto 1987*, vol. 2, edited by Angelo Pompilio, Lorenzo Biaconi, Donatella Restani, and F. Alberto Gallo, 138–148. Turin: EDT.
Bent, Margaret. 1995. "The Limits of Notation in Defining the Musical Text". In *L'edizione critica tra testo musicale e testo letterario*, edited by Renato Borghi and Pietro Zappalà, Studi e testi, n.s., 3, 367–372. Lucca: Libreria Musicale Italiana.
Beretta, Marco, ed. 2016. *Lucretius: De rerum natura; Editio princeps (1472–73)*. Bologna: Bononia University Press.
Berg, Ivar. 2014. "Om normalisert norrønt". *Arkiv för nordisk filologi* 129: 21–54.
Bergel, Giles, Christopher J. Howe, and Heather F. Windram. 2016. "Lines of Succession in an English Ballad Tradition: The Publishing History and Textual Descent of The Wandering Jew's Chronicle". *Digital Scholarship in the Humanities* 31 (3): 540–562. doi.org/10.1093/llc/fqv003.
Bernabé Pajares, Alberto, and Felipe G. Hernández Muñoz. 2010. *Manual de crítica textual y edición de textos griegos*. 2nd ed. Madrid: Akal.
Bernhard, Michael. 1979. *Studien zur Epistola de armonica institutione des Regino von Prüm*. Bayerische Akademie der Wissenschaften: Veröffentlichungen der Musikhistorischen Kommission 5. Munich: Bayerische Akademie der Wissenschaften.
Bernheim, Ernst. 1889. *Lehrbuch der historischen Methode: Mit Nachweis der wichtigsten Quellen und Hülfsmittel zum Studium der Geschichte*. Leipzig: Duncker und Humblot.
Berté, Monica, and Marco Petoletti. 2017. *La filoogia medievale e umanistica*. Bologna: il Mulino.
Bertelsen, Henrik, ed. 1905–1911. *Þiðriks saga af Bern*. 2 vols. Samfund til udgivelse af gammel nordisk litteratur 34. Copenhagen: Møller.
Bethurum, Dorothy, ed. 1971. *The Homilies of Wulfstan*. 2nd ed. Oxford: Clarendon Press.
Bettarini Bruni, Anna, and Paolo Trovato. 2009. "Dittico per Antonio Pucci". *Filologia Italiana* 6: 81–128.

Bieler, Ludwig. 1950, ed. *Libri epistolarum Sancti Patricii Episcopi: Introduction, Text and Commentary*. Classica et Mediaevalia 11. Copenhagen: Librairie Gyldendal 1950 [reissued 1952, repr. 1993].

Binder, Vera. 2006. "Scriptorium". In *Brill's New Pauly*, edited by Hubert Cancik and Helmut Schneider. dx.doi.org/10.1163/1574-9347_bnp_e1106060.

Birnbaum, David J. 2014. "Collating the Rus' Primary Chronicle (Povest' Vremennyx Let)". In *Written Heritage and Information Technologies*, edited by Victor. A. Baranov, Veselka Zhelyazkova, and Alexey M. Lavrentiev, 20–24. Sofia: Izhevsk.

Bischoff, Bernhard. 1960. *Die südostdeutschen Schreibschulen und Bibliotheken in der Karolingerzeit*. Vol. 1. *Die Bayrischen Diözesen*. Wiesbaden: Harrassowitz.

Bischoff, Bernhard. 1961–1981. *Mittelalterliche Studien: Ausgewählte Aufsätze zur Schriftkunde und Literaturgeschichte*. 3 vols. Stuttgart: Hiersemann.

Bischoff, Bernhard. 1990. *Latin Palaeography: Antiquities and the Middle Ages*. Translated by Dáibhí Ó Cróinín and David Ganz. Cambridge: Cambridge University Press.

Bischoff, Bernhard. 1998–2017. *Katalog der festländischen Handschriften des neunten Jahrhunderts (mit Ausnahme der wisigotischen)*. 4 vols. Wiesbaden: Harrassowitz.

Bischoff, Bernhard. 2009. *Paläographie des römischen Altertums und des abendländischen Mittelalters*. 4th ed. Berlin: Schmidt [1st ed. 1979].

Blackburn, Bonnie. 1976. "Josquin's Chansons: Ignored and Lost Sources". *Journal of the American Musicological Society* 29: 30–76.

Bland, Mark. 2005. "Francis Beaumont's Verse Letters to Ben Jonson and the 'Mermaid Club'". *English Manuscript Studies 1100–1700* 12: 139–177.

Blecua, Alberto. 1983. *Manual de critica textual*. Madrid: Castalia [2nd ed. 1990].

Blecua, Alberto. 1995. "Medieval Castilian Texts and Their Editions". In *Scholarly Editing: A Guide to Research*, edited by David C. Greetham, 459–485. New York, NY: Modern Language Association.

Blecua, Alberto. 2012. *Estudios de critica textual*. Madrid: Gredos.

Bleier, Roman, Martina Bürgermeister, Helmut W. Klug, Frederike Neuber, and Gerlinde Schneider, eds. 2018. *Digital Scholarly Editions as Interfaces*. Schriftenreihe des Instituts für Dokumentologie und Editorik 12. Norderstedt: BoD. kups.ub.uni-koeln.de/9085.

Blench, Roger. 2006. *Archaeology, Language, and the African Past*. Lanham, MD: AltaMira Press.

Blench, Roger. 2008. "Archaeology and Language: Methods and Issues". In *A Companion to Archaeology*, edited by John Bintliff, 52–74. Malden, MA: Blackwell. doi.org/10.1002/9780470998618.ch4.

Boas, Franz. 1940. *Race, Language and Culture*. Chicago, IL: University of Chicago Press.

Böckmann, Aquinata. 2006. "Benedict of Nursia". In *Brill's New Pauly*, edited by Hubert Cancik and Helmut Schneider. dx.doi.org/10.1163/1574-9347_bnp_e215270.

Bolter, Jay David, and Richard Grusin. 2000. *Remediation: Understanding New Media*. Cambridge, MA: MIT Press.

Boltz, William G. 1995. "Textual Criticism More Sinico". *Early China* 20: 393–405.

Boltz, William G. 1999. "Language and Writing". In *The Cambridge History of Ancient China: From the Origins of Civilization to 221 BC*, edited by Michael Loewe and Edward L. Shaughnessy, 74–123. Cambridge: Cambridge University Press.

Bonath, Gesa. 1970. *Untersuchungen zur Überlieferung des Parzival Wolframs von Eschenbach*. Vol. 1. Lübeck: Matthiesen.

Boorman, Stanley H. 1977. "The 'First' Edition of the Odhecaton A". *Journal of the American Musicological Society* 30: 183–207.

Boorman, Stanley H. 1981a. "Limitation and Extension of Filiation Technique". In *Music in Medieval and Early Modern Europe: Patronage, Sources and Texts*, edited by Iain Fenlon, 319–346. Cambridge: Cambridge University Press.

Boorman, Stanley H. 1981b. "Petrucci's Type-Setters and the Process of Stemmatics". In *Quellenstudien zur Musik der Renaissance*, vol. 1, *Formen und Probleme der Überlieferung mehrstimmiger Musik im Zeitalter Josquin Desprez*, edited by Ludwig Finscher, 245–280. Munich: Kraus Int. Publications.

Boorman, Stanley H. 1981c. "The Uses of Filiation in Early Music". *Text: Transactions of the Society of Textual Scholarship* 1: 167–184.

Boorman, Stanley H. 1983. "Notational Spelling and Scribal Habit". In *Quellenstudien zur Musik der Renaissance*, vol. 2, *Datierung und Filiation von Musikhandschriften der Josquin-Zeit*, edited by Ludwig Finscher, 65–110. Wiesbaden: Harrassowitz.

Boorman, Stanley H. 1995. "Composition-Copying: Performance-Re-Creation – The Matrix of Stemmatic Problems for Early Music". In *L'edizione critica tra testo musicale e testo letterario*, edited by Renato Borghi und Pietro Zappalà, Studi e testi, n.s., 3, 45–55. Lucca: Libreria Musicale Italiana.

Booth, Joan, ed. and trans. 1991. *Ovid: The Second Book of Amores*. Warminster: Aris & Phillips.

Bopp, Franz. 1833–1852. *Vergleichende Grammatik des Sanskrit, Zend, Griechischen, Lateinischen, Litthauischen, Altslawischen, Gothischen und Deutschen*. Berlin: Dümmler.

Bordalejo, Barbara. 2016. "The Genealogy of Texts: Manuscript Traditions and Textual Traditions". *Digital Scholarship in the Humanities* 31 (3): 563–577. doi.org/10.1093/llc/fqv038.

Bordalejo, Barbara. 2018. "Digital versus Analogue Textual Scholarship; or, The Revolution Is Just in the Title". *Digital Philology: A Journal of Medieval Cultures* 7 (1): 7–28. doi.org/10.1353/dph.2018.0001.

Borgnet, Augustus, ed. 1890–1899. *Albertus Magnus: Opera omnia*. 38 vols. Paris: Vivès.

Borsetta, Pierfrancesco, and Gian Piero Zarri. 1981. "An Application of the Quentin/80 Software to the Study of the Manuscript Tradition of the Appendix Vergiliana (Semi-Automatic Construction of the Stemmata Codicum)". In *Actes du Congrès International Informatique et Sciences Humaines 1981*, edited by Mustapha Mojahid and Jerzy Karczmarczuk, 73–92. Liège: Université de Liège.

Bosco, Umberto. 1968. "Il XIV canto dell'Inferno". In *Nuove Letture dantesche*, vol. 2, 47–73. Florence: Le Monnier.

Botley, Paul, and Dierk van Miert, eds. 2012. *The Correspondence of Joseph Justus Scaliger: April 1561 to February 1609*. 8 vols. Geneva: Droz.

Botte, Bernard. 1955. "Le Texte de la 'Tradition apostolique'". *Recherches de théologie ancienne et médiévale* 22: 161–172.

Botte, Bernard. 1966. "A propos de la Tradition apostolique". *Recherches de théologie ancienne et médiévale* 33: 177–186.

Bouckaert, Remco, Joseph Heled, Denise Kühnert, Tim Vaughan, Chieh-Hsi Wu, Dong Xie, Marc A. Suchard, Andrew Rambaut, and Alexei J. Drummond. 2014. "BEAST 2: A Software Platform for Bayesian Evolutionary Analysis". *PLoS Computational Biology* 10 (4): e1003537. doi.org/10.1371/journal.pcbi.1003537.

Bouckaert, Remco, Philippe Lemey, Michael Dunn, Simon J. Greenhill, Alexander V. Alekseyenko, Alexei J. Drummond, and Russell D. Gray. 2012. "Mapping the Origins and Expansion of the Indo-European Language Family". *Science* 337 (6097): 957–960. doi.org/10.1126/science.1219669.

Bourgain, Pascale, and Françoise Vielliard. 2002. *Conseils pour l'édition des textes médiévaux*. Vol. 3. *Textes littéraires*. Paris: Ecole nationale des chartes.

Bowers, Fredson. 1970. "Textual Criticism". In *The Aims and Methods of Scholarship in Modern Languages and Literatures*, edited by James Thorpe, 23–42. New York, NY: Modern Language Association.

Bowers, Fredson. 1975a. *Essays in Bibliography, Text, and Editing*. Charlottesville: University Press of Virginia.

Bowers, Fredson. 1975b. "Remarks on Eclectic Texts". *Proof* 4: 31–76 [repr. Bowers 1975a, 488–528].
Bowman, Alan K. 1991. "Literacy in the Roman Empire: Mass and Mode". In *Literacy in the Roman World*, by Mary Beard, Alan K. Bowman, Mireille Corbier, Tim Cornell, James L. Franklin Jr, Ann Hanson, Keith Hopkins, and Nicholas Horsfall, 119–131. Ann Arbor: University of Michigan.
Bowman, Alan K. 2003. *Life and Letters on the Roman Frontier: Vindolanda and Its People*. 3rd ed. London: British Museum Press.
Bowman, Alan, and Greg Woolf, eds. 1994. *Literacy and Power in the Ancient World*. Cambridge: Cambridge University Press.
Boyle, Leonard. 1981. "The Nowell Codex and the Poem of Beowulf". In *The Dating of Beowulf*, edited by Colin Chase, 23–32. Toronto: University of Toronto Press.
Boyle, Leonard. 2001. *Integral Palaeography*. Turnhout: Brepols.
Bozzolo, Carla, and Ezio Ornato. 1980. *Pour une histoire du livre manuscrit au moyen âge*. Paris: Centre National de Recherche Scientifique.
Brackert, Helmut. 1963. *Beiträge zur Handschriftenkritik des Nibelungenliedes*. Berlin: De Gruyter.
Brackert, Helmut. 1970–1971. *Das Nibelungenlied: Mittelhochdeutscher Text und Übertragung*. 2 vols. Frankfurt am Main: Fischer.
Brambilla Ageno, Franca. 1975. *L'edizione critica dei testi volgari*. Padua: Anteriore.
Brambilla Ageno, Franca. 1986. "La funzione della fonti e dei luoghi paralleli nella fissazione del testo critico: Esperienze di un editore del Convivio". *Studi danteschi* 58: 239–273.
Brandoli, Caterina. 2007. "Due canoni a confronto: I luoghi di Barbi e lo scrutinio di Petrocchi". In *Nuove prospettive sulla tradizione della "Commedia": Una guida filologico-linguistica al poema dantesco*, edited by Paolo Trovato, 99–214. Florence: Cesati.
Braune, Wilhelm. 1900. "Die Handschriftenverhaeltnisse des Nibelungenliedes". *Beiträge zur Geschichte der deutschen Sprache und Literatur* 25: 1–222.
Brett, Philip. 1988. "Text, Context, and the Early Music Editor". In *Authenticity and Early Music: A Symposium*, edited by N. Kenyon, 83–114. Oxford: Oxford University Press.
Brita, Antonella. 2007. "I racconti tradizionali della cristianizzazione dell'Etiopia: Il 'Gadla Liqānos' e il 'Gadla Panṭalēwon'". PhD thesis, Università degli Studi di Napoli "L'Orientale".
Brita, Antonella. 2014. "'La gabira 'ab': Breve nota sul lessico filologico in etiopico". In *Linguistic, Oriental and Ethiopian Studies in Memory of Paolo Marrassini*, edited by Alessandro Bausi, Alessandro Gori, and Gianfrancesco Lusini, 169–175. Wiesbaden: Harrassowitz.
Brodersen, Kai. 2006. "Curiosum urbis Romae". In *Brill's New Pauly*, edited by Hubert Cancik and Helmut Schneider. dx.doi.org/10.1163/1574-9347_bnp_e308580.
Brown, Alison. 2010. *The Return of Lucretius to Renaissance Florence*. Cambridge, MA: Harvard University Press.
Brown, Howard Mayer. 1983. "In Alamire's Workshop: Notes on Scribal Practice in the Early Sixteenth Century". In *Quellenstudien zur Musik der Renaissance*, vol. 2, *Datierung und Filiation von Musikhandschriften der Josquin-Zeit*, edited by Ludwig Finscher, 15–63. Wiesbaden: Harrassowitz.
Brown, Steven, Patrick E. Savage, Albert Min-Shan Ko, Mark Stoneking, Ying-Chin Ko, Jun-Hun Loo, and Jean A. Trejaut. 2014. "Correlations in the Population Structure of Music, Genes and Language". *Proceedings of the Royal Society B: Biological Sciences* 281 (1774): 20132072. doi.org/10.1098/rspb.2013.2072.
Browning, Robert. 1960. "Recentiores non deteriores". *Bulletin of the Institute of Classical Studies of the University of London* 7: 11–21.
Brownrigg, Linda L., and Margaret M. Smith, eds. 2000. *Interpreting and Collecting Fragments of Medieval Books*. Los Altos Hills, CA: Red Gull Press.

Bryant, David, and Vincent Moulton. 2004. "Neighbor-Net: An Agglomerative Method for the Construction of Phylogenetic Networks". *Molecular Biology and Evolution* 21 (2): 255–265.

Bryant, John. 2002. *The Fluid Text: A Theory of Revision and Editing for Book and Screen*. Ann Arbor: University of Michigan Press.

Buchanan, Briggs, and Mark Collard. 2007. "Investigating the Peopling of North America through Cladistic Analyses of Early Paleoindian Projectile Points". *Journal of Anthropological Archaeology* 26: 366–393.

Büchner, Karl. 1961. "Überlieferungsgeschichte der lateinischen Literatur des Altertums". In *Geschichte der Textüberlieferung der antiken und mittelalterlichen Literatur*, by Herbert Hunger, Otto Stegmüller, Harmut Erbse, Max Imhof, Karl Büchner, Hans-Georg Beck, and Horst Rüdiger, vol. 1, 309–422. Zurich: Atlantis-Verlag.

Buchner, Rudolf, ed. 1955. *Gregorii episcopi Turonensis Historiarum libri decem*. Vol. 1. *Libri I–V*. Darmstadt: Wissenschaftliche Buchgesellschaft [8th ed. 2008].

Buckley, Christopher, and Eric Boudot. 2017. "The Evolution of an Ancient Technology". *Royal Society Open Science* 4 (5): 170208. doi.org/10.1098/rsos.170208.

Budal, Ingvil Brügger. 2009. "Strengleikar og Lais: Høviske noveller i omsetjing frå gammalfransk til gammalnorsk". 2 vols. PhD thesis, University of Bergen. bora.uib.no/handle/1956/3477.

Bullitta, Dario. 2017. *Niðrstigningar saga: Sources, Transmission, and Theology of the Old Norse "Descent into Hell"*. Toronto: University of Toronto Press.

Bumke, Joachim. 1996. *Die vier Fassungen der "Nibelungenklage": Untersuchungen zur Überlieferungsgeschichte und Textkritik der höfischen Epik im 13. Jahrhundert*. Berlin: De Gruyter.

Bumke, Joachim, ed. 1999. *Die "Nibelungenklage": Synoptische Ausgabe aller vier Fassungen*. Berlin: De Gruyter.

Burgio, Eugenio, Marina Buzzoni, and Antonella Ghersetti, eds. 2015. *Giovanni Battista Ramusio: Dei Viaggi di Messer Marco Polo, Gentilhuomo Venetiano*. virgo.unive.it/ecf-workflow/books/Ramusio/main/index.html.

Burkardt, John. 2016. "CSV Files: Personal Archiving Site". July 19. people.sc.fsu.edu/~jburkardt/data/csv/csv.html.

Burrows, Toby 2010. "Applying Semantic Web Technologies to Medieval Manuscript Research". In *Codicology and Palaeography in the Digital Age 2*, edited by Franz Fischer, Christiane Fritze, and Georg Vogeler, 117–131. Norderstedt: BoD.

Busby, Keith, ed. 1993. *Towards a Synthesis? Essays on the New Philology*. Amsterdam: Rodopi.

Butterfield, David James. 2013. *The Early Textual History of Lucretius' De rerum natura*. Cambridge: Cambridge University Press.

Buzzetti, Dino, and Jerome McGann. 2006. "Critical Editing in a Digital Horizon". In *Electronic Textual Editing*, edited by Lou Burnard, Katherine O'Brien O'Keeffe, and John Unsworth, 53–73. New York, NY: Modern Language Association.

Buzzoni, Marina, ed. 2001. *Le sezioni poetiche della Cronaca anglosassone: Edizione e studio tipologico*. Viareggio: Mauro Baroni Editore.

Buzzoni, Marina. 2011. "La *mouvance* nella tradizione manoscritta di *Hêliand*". In *Lettura di Heliand*, edited by Vittoria Dolcetti Corazza and Renato Gendre, 95–114. Alessandria: Edizioni dell'Orso.

Buzzoni, Marina, and Eugenio Burgio. 2014. "The Italian 'Third Way' of Editing between Globalization and Localization". In *Internationalität und Interdisziplinarität der Editionswissenschaft*, edited by Michael Stolz and Yen-Chun Chen, 171–180. Berlin: De Gruyter.

Buzzoni, Marina, Eugenio Burgio, Martina Modena, and Samuela Simion. 2016. "Open versus Closed Recensions (Pasquali): Pros and Cons of Some Methods for Computer-Assisted Stemmatology". *Digital Scholarship in the Humanities* 31 (3): 652–669.

Cadili, Luca. 2008. "Scholia and Authorial Identity: The Scholia Bernensia on Vergil's Georgics as Servius Auctus". In *Servio: Stratificazioni esegetiche e modelli culturali/Servius: Exegetical Stratifications and Cultural Models*, edited by Sergio Casali and Fabio Stok, 194–206. Brussels: Latomus.

Calzolari, Valentina, ed. 2017. *Apocrypha Armeniaca*. Vol. 1. *Acta Pauli et Theclae, Prodigia Theclae, Martyrium Pauli*. Turnhout: Brepols.

Cameron, Howard Don 1987. "The Upside-Down Cladogram: Problems in Manuscript Affiliation". In *Biological Metaphor and Cladistic Classification: An Interdisciplinary Approach*, edited by Henry M. Hoenigswald and Linda F. Wiener, 227–242. Philadelphia: University of Pennsylvania Press. jstor.org/stable/j.ctv4w3wb6.16.

Camin, Joseph H., and Robert R. Sokal. 1965. "A Method for Deducing Branching Sequences in Phylogeny". *Evolution* 19 (3): 311–326.

Campbell, Lyle. 2003. "Beyond the Comparative Method". In *Historical Linguistics: 15th International Conference on Historical Linguistics, Melbourne, 13–17 August 2001*, edited by Barry J. Blake, Kate Burridge, and Jo Taylor, 33–57. Amsterdam: Benjamins.

Camps, Jean-Baptiste, and Florian Cafiero. 2014. "Genealogical Variant Locations and Simplified Stemma: A Test Case". In *Analysis of Ancient and Medieval Texts and Manuscripts: Digital Approaches*, edited by Tara Andrews and Caroline Macé, Lectio 1, 69–93. Turnhout: Brepols.

Canello, Ugo Angelo, ed. 1883. *La Vita e le Opere del trovatore Arnaldo Daniello: Edizione critica, corredata delle varianti di tutti i manoscritti, d'un'introduzione storico-letteraria e di versione, note, rimario e glossario*. Halle an der Saale: Niemeyer.

Canfora, Luigi. 2002. *Il copista come autore*. Palermo: Sellerio.

Capron, Laurent. 2013. *Codex hagiographiques du Louvre sur papyrus (P. Louvre Hag.)*. Paris: Sorbonne.

Caraci Vela, Maria, ed. 1995. *La critica del testo musicale: Metodi e problemi della filologia musicale*. Lucca: Libreria musicale Italiana.

Caraci Vela, Maria. 2005–2013. *La filologia Musicale: Istituioni, storia, strumenti critici*. 3 vols. Lucca: Libreria Musicale Italiana.

Cardelle de Hartmann, Carmen, Darko Senekovic, and Thomas Ziegler, eds. 2019. *Petrus Alfonsi: Dialogus*. Vol. 1. Translated by Peter Stotz. Florence: Edizioni del Galluzzo.

Cardelle de Hartmann, Carmen, Darko Senekovic, and Thomas Ziegler. Forthcoming. *Petrus Alfonsi: Dialogus*. Vol. 2. *Prolegomena – Handschriftencensus – Kommentar – Edition der Schäftlarner Neufassung*. Florence: Edizioni del Galluzzo.

Cardona, Gabriel, Francesc Rosselló, and Gabriel Valiente. 2008. "Extended Newick: It Is Time for a Standard Representation of Phylogenetic Networks". *BMC Bioinformatics* 9 (1): 532. doi.org/10.1186/1471-2105-9-532.

Carlson, Stephen C. 2015. *The Text of Galatians and Its History*. Tübingen: Mohr Siebeck.

Carmody, Francis J. 1941. "Physiologus Latinus versio y". *University of California Publications in Classical Philology* 12 (7): 95–134.

Carter, Michael G. 1995. "Arabic Literature". In *Scholarly Editing: A Guide to Research*, edited by David C. Greetham, 546–574. New York, NY: Modern Language Association.

Cartlidge, Neil. 2001. "The Canterbury Tales and Cladistics". *Neuphilologische Mitteilungen* 102 (2): 135–150.

Cassin, Matthieu. 2018. "D'origène à l'édition de 1615: Sources et postérités des Homélies sur le Cantique de Grégoire de Nysse". In *Gregory of Nyssa: Canticum Canticorum; Analytical and Supporting Studies: Proceedings of the 13th International Colloquium on Gregory of Nyssa (Rome, 17–20 September 2014)*, edited by Giulio Maspero, Miguel Brugarola, and Ilaria Vigorelli, 53–76. Leiden: Brill.

Castellani, Arrigo. 1957. *Bédier avait-il raison? La Méthode de Lachmann dans les éditions de textes du Moyen Age: Leçon inaugurale donnée àl'université de Fribourg le 2 juin 1954*. Fribourg: Éditions universitaires [repr. Castellani 1980, 161–200].

Castellani, Arrigo. 1980. *Saggi di linguistica italiana e romanza (1946–1976)*. Vol. 3. Rome: Salerno Editrice.
Castelli, Emanuele. 2011. "L'edizione del testo patristico greco e latino: Sguardo alla ricerca del XX secolo". *Vetera Christianorum* 48: 81–98.
Cavalli-Sforza, Luigi L., and Anthony W. F. Edwards. 1967. "Phylogenetic Analysis: Models and Estimation Procedures". *American Journal of Human Genetics* 19 (3.1): 233–257. ncbi.nlm.nih.gov/pmc/articles/PMC1706274.
Cayless, Hugh. 2018. "Critical Editions and the Data Model as Interface". In *Digital Scholarly Editions as Interfaces*, edited by Roman Bleier, Martina Bürgermeister, Helmut W. Klug, Frederike Neuber, and Gerlinde Schneider, Schriftenreihe des Instituts für Dokumentologie und Editorik 12, 249–263. Norderstedt: BoD. kups.ub.uni-koeln.de/9119.
Cerquiglini, Bernard. 1989. *Eloge de la variante: Histoire critique de la philologie*. Paris: Seuil.
Cerquiglini, Bernard. 2007. "Une nouvelle philologie?". In *Vers une nouvelle philologie*, edited by Bernard Cerquiglini, Iván Horvát, and Levente Seláf, 2–6. Budapest: Hallgatói Információs Központ. tankonyvtar.hu/hu/tartalom/tkt/vers-une-nouvelle/adatok.html.
Cerulli, Enrico, ed. 1969. *Les Vies éthiopiennes de Saint Alexis l'homme de Dieu*. Leuven: Secrétariat du CorpusSCO.
Ceruzzi, Paul E. 2012. *Computing: A Concise History*. Cambridge, MA: MIT Press.
Chambert-Protat, Pierre. 2014. "Les Centons augustiniens de Florus de Lyon: Minutie, érudition et vulgarisation". *Revue d'etudes augustiniennes et patristiques* 60: 349–379.
Cheng Qianfan 程千帆 and Xu Youfu 徐有富. 1998. *Jiaochou guangyi: Jiaokan bian* 校讎廣義: 校勘編. Jinan: Qi-Lu.
Cherniack, Susan. 1995. "Book Culture and Textual Transmission in Sung China". *Harvard Journal of Asiatic Studies* 54: 5–125.
Cherubini, Paolo, ed. 1997. *Iacopo Ammannati Piccolomini: Lettere 1444–1479*. 3 vols. Rome: Ministero per i beni culturali e ambientali.
Chiarini, Giorgio, ed. 1964. *Juan Ruiz arcipreste de Hita: Libro de buen amor*. Milan: Ricciardi.
Chiesa, Bruno. 2000. *Filologia storica della Bibbia ebraica*. Vol 1. *Da Origene al Medioevo*. Brescia: Paideia.
Chiesa, Bruno. 2002. *Filologia storica della Bibbia ebraica*. Vol 2. *Dall'età moderna ai giorni nostri*. Brescia: Paideia.
Chiesa, Paolo. 1987. "Ad verbum o ad sensum? Modelli e coscienza metodologica della traduzione tra tarda antichità e alto medioevo". *Medioevo e Rinascimento: Annuario del Dipartimento di studi sul medioevo e il rinascimento dell'Università di Firenze* 1: 1–51.
Chiesa, Paolo. 2002. *Elementi di critica testuale*. Bologna: Patron.
Chiesa, Paolo. 2012. "Varianti d'autore nei testi letterari dell'alto medioevo: Qualche osservazione di metodo". In *Scrivere e leggere nell'alto medioevo*, vol. 1, 379–398. Spoleto: CISAM.
Chiesa, Paolo. 2016. *Venticinque lezioni di filologia mediolatina*. Florence: Edizioni del Galluzzo.
Chiesa, Paolo. 2019. *Medieval Latin Philology: An Overview through Case-Studies*. Florence: SISMEL.
Chlench, Kathrin, and Gabriel Viehhauser. 2014. "Phylogenese und Textkritik der 'Parzival'-Überlieferung: Bioinformatische Anregungen zur Lösung genealogischer Klassifizierungsprobleme in der Editionsphilologie". In *Internationalität und Interdisziplinarität der Editionswissenschaft*, edited by Michael Stolz und Yen-Chun Chen, 57–81. Berlin: De Gruyter.
Choi, Bernard C. K., and Anita W. P. Pak. 2006. "Multidisciplinarity, Interdisciplinarity and Transdisciplinarity in Health Research, Services, Education and Policy: 2. Promotors, Barriers, and Strategies of Enhancement". *Clinical and Investigative Medicine* 30 (December): E224–E232.
Clackson, James, and Geoffrey Horrocks. 2007. *The Blackwell History of the Latin Language*. Oxford: Blackwell.

Clark, Albert Curtis. 1899. "The Literary Discoveries of Poggio". *Classical Review* 13 (2): 119–30.
Clayman, Dee L. 2014. *Berenice II and the Golden Age of Ptolemaic Egypt*. Oxford: Oxford University Press.
CNRS. 1987. *Archéologie du livre médiéval: Cinquantenaire de l'Institut de Recherche et d'Historie des textes 1937–1987*. Paris: Presses du CNRS.
Cochrane, Ethan, and Carl Lipo. 2010. "Phylogenetic Analyses of Lapita Decoration Do Not Support Branching Evolution or Regional Population Structure during Colonization of Remote Oceania". *Philosophical Transactions of the Royal Society B* 365 (1559): 3889–3902.
Coenen, Jürgen. 1977. *Lukian Zeus Tragodos: Überlieferungsgeschichte, Text und Kommentar*. Meisenheim am Glan: Hain.
Cohn, Ruby. 2001. *A Beckett Canon*. Ann Arbor: University of Michigan Press.
Cole, John Young. 2018. *America's Greatest Library: An Illustrated History of the Library of Congress*. Washington, DC: Giles.
Coleman, Robert. 1999. "Vulgarism and Normalization in the Text of *Regula Sancti Benedicti*". In *Latin vulgaire – Latin tardif V: Actes du Ve Colloque International sur le latin vulgaire et tardif, Heidelberg, 5–8 septembre 1997*, edited by Hubert Petersmann and Rudolf Kettemann, 345–356. Heidelberg: Winter.
Collard, Mark, Steven Shennan, and Jamshid Tehrani. 2006. "Branching, Blending and the Evolution of Cultural Similarities and Differences among Human Populations". *Evolution and Human Behaviour* 27: 169–184.
Collomp, Paul. 1929. "L'Eclectisme des papyrus et la critique textuelle". *Revue des études grecques* 42: 255–287.
Colombi, Emanuela, ed. 2012. *La trasmissione dei testi patristici latini: Problemi e prospettive*. Turnhout: Brepols.
Colwell, Ernest C. 1969. *Studies in Methodology in Textual Criticism of the New Testament*. Leiden: Brill.
Colwell, Ernest C., and Ernest W. Tune. 1964. "Variant Readings: Classification and Use". *Journal of Biblical Literature* 83: 253–261.
Conte, Gian Biagio. 1993. *Letteratura latina: Manuale storico dalle origini alla fine dell'impero romano*. With Alessandro Barchiesi. Florence: Le Monnier.
Conte, Gian Biagio. 1994. *Latin Literature: A History*. Translated by Joseph B. Solodow. Revised by Don Fowler and Glenn W. Most. Baltimore, MD: Johns Hopkins University Press [trans. of Conte 1993].
Conti, Aidan, and Philipp Roelli. 2015. "Apparatus". In *Parvum lexicon stemmatologicum*, edited by Philipp Roelli and Caroline Macé. wiki.helsinki.fi/display/stemmatology/Apparatus
Conti Rossini, Carlo. 1903. *Ricordi di un soggiorno in Eritrea*. Vol. 1. Asmara: Tipografia della Missione Svedese.
Conti Rossini, Carlo, ed. 1909. *Documenta ad illustrandam historiam*. Vol. 1. Liber Axumae. Paris: Harrassowitz.
Contini, Gianfranco. 1937. "Come lavorava l'Ariosto". *Meridiano di Roma*, July 18 [repr. Contini 1939a, 247–257].
Contini, Gianfranco, 1939a. *Esercizî di lettura*. Florence: Parenti, 1939.
Contini, Gianfranco. 1939b. "Ricordo di Joseph Bédier". *Letteratura* 9: 145–152 [repr. Contini 1946, 114–132].
Contini, Gianfranco. 1946. *Un anno di letteratura*. Florence: Le Monnier, 1946.
Contini, Gianfranco. 1955. "Ancora sulla canzone 'S'eo trovasse Pietanza'". *Siculorum gymnasium* 8: 122–138.
Contini, Gianfranco. 1970. "La *Vita* francese di sant'Alessio e l'arte di pubblicare i testi antichi". In *Un augurio a Raffaele Mattioli*, 343–374. Florence: Sansoni [repr. Contini 2007, 2:957–985].

Contini, Gianfranco. 1977. "Filologia". In *Enciclopedia del Novecento*, vol. 2, 954–972. Rome: Istituto della Enciclopedia italiana [repr. *Filologia*. Edited by Lino Leonardi. Bologna: il Mulino, 2014].

Contini, Gianfranco, ed. 1984. *Il Fiore e Il Detto d'Amore attribuibili a Dante Alighieri*. Milan: Mondadori.

Contini, Gianfranco. 1986. *Breviario di ecdotica*. Milan: Ricciardi [2nd ed. Turin: Einaudi, 1992].

Contini, Gianfranco. 2007. *Frammenti di filologia romanza: Scritti di ecdotica e linguistica (1932–1989)*. Edited by Giancarlo Breschi. 2 vols. Florence: Edizioni del Galluzzo.

Cook, James Heustis. 1978. "Manuscript Transmission of the Thirteenth-Century Motets". PhD thesis, University of Texas.

Copeland, Rita. 2012. "Gloss and Commentary". In *The Oxford Handbook of Medieval Latin Literature*, edited by Ralph Hexter and David Townsend, 171–191. Oxford: Oxford University Press.

Coppens, Chris, Mark Derez, and Jan Roegiers. 2005. *Leuven University Library, 1425–2000*. Leuven: Leuven University Press.

Corbellari, Alain. 1997. *Joseph Bédier, écrivain et philologue*. Geneva: Droz.

Cormen, Thomas H., Charles E. Leierson, Ronald L. Rivest, and Clifford Stein. 2009. *Introduction to Algorithms*. 3rd ed. Cambridge, MA: MIT Press.

Cortesi, Mariarosa, ed. 2002. *I Padri sotto il torchio: Le edizioni dell'Antichità cristiana nei secoli XV–XVI; Atti del Convegno di Studi Certosa del Galluzzo, Firenze, 25–26 giugno 1999*. Florence: Edizioni del Galluzzo.

Cortesi, Mariarosa, ed. 2004. *Padri greci e latini a confronto (secoli XIII–XV): Atti del Convegno di studi della SISMEL, Firenze (Certosa del Galluzzo), 19. 10. 2001–20. 10. 2001*. Florence: Edizioni del Galluzzo.

Cortesi, Mariarosa, ed. 2006. *"Editiones principes" delle opere dei Padri Greci e Latini: Atti del Convegno di studi della SISMEL, Certosa del Galluzzo, Firenze, 24–25 ottobre 2003*. Florence: Edizioni del Galluzzo.

Cortesi, Mariarosa, ed. 2010. *Leggere i Padri tra passato e presente: Atti del Convegno Internazionale di Studi Cremona, 21–22 novembre 2008*. Florence: Edizioni del Galluzzo.

Cortesi, Mariarosa, and Claudio Leonardi, eds. 2000. *Tradizioni patristiche nell'Umanesimo: Atti del Convegno di Studi Promosso dalla Società Internazionale per lo Studio del Medioevo Latino (Firenze, 6–9 Febbraio 1997)*. Florence: Edizioni del Galluzzo.

Cosaert, Carl P. 2008. *The Text of the Gospels in Clement of Alexandria*. Atlanta, GA: Society of Biblical Literature.

Costamagna, Giorgio, Françoise Gasparri, Léon Gilissen, Francisco M. Gimeno Blay, Alessandro Pratesi, and Armando Petrucci. 1995–1998. "Commentare Bischoff". *Scrittura e Civiltà* 19: 325–348, 20: 401–407, 22: 395–417.

Coulie, Bernard. 1994, ed. *Gregorius Nazianzenus: Opera; Versio Armeniaca*. Vol. 1. *Orationes II, XII, IX*. Turnhout: Brepols.

Croenen, Godfried. 2010. "Stemmata, Philology and Textual History: A Response to Alberto Vàrvaro". *Medioevo Romanzo* 34: 422–426.

Crosley, Thomas W. 2015. "How Does a Signal to the CPU Look". electronics.stackexchange.com/a/156179.

Cubbin, George P., ed. 1996. *The Anglo-Saxon Chronicle: A Collaborative Edition*. Vol. 6. *MS. D: A Semi-Diplomatic Edition with Introduction and Indices*. Cambridge: Brewer.

Cummings, James. 2008. "The Text Encoding Initiative and the Study of Literature". In *A Companion to Digital Literary Studies*, edited by Ray Siemens and Susan Schreibman, 451–476. Oxford: Blackwell.

Dagenais, John. 1994. *The Ethics of Reading in Manuscript Culture: Glossing the Libro de Buen Amor*. Princeton, NJ: Princeton University Press.

Dain, Alphonse. 1964. *Les Manuscrits: Nouvelle édition revue*. Paris: Budé [repr. 1975].

Dalla Chiara, Maria Luisa, and Giuliano Toraldo di Francia. 1999. *Introduzione alla filosofia della scienza*. Rome: Laterza.

Dahlhaus, Carl. 1973. "Urtextausgaben". *Neue Zeitschrift für Musik* 134: 334.

Dahlström, Mats. 2000. "Drowning by Versions". *Human IT* 4 (4): 7–38. humanit.hb.se/article/view/174.

d'Alvarenga, João Pedro. 2011. "Manuscript Évora, Biblioteca Pública, CÓD. CLI/1–3: Its Origin and Contents, and the Stemmata of Late 16th- and Early 17th-Century Portuguese Sources". *Anuario musical* 66: 137–158.

Damerau, Fred J. 1964. "A Technique for Computer Detection and Correction of Spelling Errors". *Communications of the ACM* 7 (3): 171–176.

Dängeli, Peter. 2019. "Die Nachhaltigkeitsproblematik digitaler Editionen – Workshopbericht". February 9. dhd-blog.org/?p=11033.

Danti, Angiolo. 1993. *Fra Slavia orthodoxa e Slavia romana: Studi di ecdotica*. Edited by Alda Giambelluca Kossova. Palermo: Lombardi.

Darwin, Charles R. 1837. "*Notebook B:* Transmutation (1837–8)". Transcribed by Kees Rookmaaker. darwin-online.org.uk/EditorialIntroductions/vanWyhe_notebooks.html.

Darwin, Charles R. 1859. *On the Origin of Species by Means of Natural Selection; or, The Preservation of Favoured Races in the Struggle for Life*. London: Murray.

Darwin, Charles R. 1871. *The Descent of Man and Selection in Relation to Sex*. 2 vols. London: Murray.

Daston, Lorraine, and Peter Galison. 2007. *Objectivity*. New York, NY: Zone Books.

Davis, Tom. 2007. "The Practice of Handwriting Identification". *The Library*, 7th ser., 8: 251–276. doi.org/10.1093/library/8.3.251.

Dawkins, Richard. 1976. *The Selfish Gene*. New York: Oxford University Press.

de Angelis, Violetta, ed. 1974. *Papias: Elementarium*. Milan: Cisalpino-Goliardica.

de Angelis, Violetta. 2011. "Ansie ortografiche e censure umanistiche: Papia e Bonino Mombricio". In *Scritti di filologia medievale e umanistica*, edited by Filippo Bognini and Maria Patrizia Bologna, 73–92. Naples: D'Auria.

de Biasi, Pierre-Marc. 1996. "What Is a Literary Draft? Toward a Functional Typology of Genetic Documentation". *Yale French Studies* 89: 26–58.

de Biasi, Pierre-Marc. 2000. *La Génétique des textes*. Paris: Nathan.

de Biasi, Pierre-Marc, and Anne Herschberg Pierrot, eds. 2017. *L'Œuvre comme processus*. Paris: CNRS Editions.

de Franco, Luigi, ed. 1981. Bernardino Telesio, *Varii de naturalibus rebus libelli*. Florence: La Nuova Italia.

de Melo, Wolfgang, and Scott Scullion, eds. Forthcoming. *Oxford Handbook of Greek and Latin Textual Criticism*. Oxford: Clarendon Press.

De Robertis, Domenico. 1961. "Problemi di metodo nell'edizione dei cantari". In *Studi e problemi di critica testuale*, 119–138. Bologna: Commissione per i testi di lingua.

de Saussure, Ferdinand. 1972. *Cours de linguistique générale*. Edited by Charles Bally and Albert Sechehaye with Albert Riedlinger. 3rd ed. by Tullio de Mauro. Paris: Payot [1st ed. Lausanne: Librairie Payot, 1916].

De Simini, Florinda. 2016. "Śivadharma Manuscripts from Nepal and the Making of a Śaiva Corpus". In *One-Volume Libraries: Composite and Multiple-Text Manuscripts*, edited by Michael Friedrich and Cosima Schwarke, 233–286. Berlin: De Gruyter.

de Visser-van Terwisga, Marijke. 1999. *Histoire ancienne jusqu'à César (Estoires Rogier)*. Orleans: Paradigme.

De Vos, Ilse, Erika Gielen, Caroline Macé, and Peter van Deun. 2008. "L'Art de compiler à Byzance: La Lettre γ du Florilège Coislin". *Byzantion* 78: 159–223.

De Vos, Ilse, Erika Gielen, Caroline Macé, and Peter van Deun. 2010. "La Lettre B du Florilège Coislin: Editio princeps". *Byzantion* 80: 72–120.

Dearing, Vinton A. 1967. "Some Notes on Genealogical Methods in Textual Criticism". *Novum Testamentum* 9: 278–297.

Dearing, Vinton A. 1968. "Abaco-Textual Criticism". *Papers of the Bibliographical Society of America* 62: 547–578.

Debel, Hans. 2010. "Greek 'Variant Literary Editions' to the Hebrew Bible?". *Journal for the Study of Judaism* 41: 161–190.

Deegan, Marilyn, and Katheryn Sutherland, eds. 2008. *Text Editing, Print and the Digital World*. Aldershot: Ashgate.

Deitz, Luc. 2005. "The Tools of the Trade: A Few Remarks on Editing Renaissance Latin Texts". *Humanistica Lovaniensia* 54: 345–358.

Dekkers, Elegius, and Anselmus Hoste. 1980. "De la pénurie des manuscrits anciens des ouvrages le plus souvent copiés". In *"Sapientiae doctrina": Mélanges de théologie et de littérature médiévales offerts à Dom Hildebrand Bascour O.S.B.*, 24–37. Leuven: Recherches de Théologie Ancienne et Médiévale.

Del Popolo, Concetto. 2001. "Un paragrafo di critica testuale: 'Emendatio ex fonte'". *Studi e problemi di critica testuale* 63: 5–28.

Delbrück, Berthold. 1919. *Einleitung in das Studium der indogermanischen Sprachen: Ein Beitrag zur Geschichte und Methodik der vergleichenden Sprachforschung*. Leipzig: Breitkopf & Härtel.

Delisle, Léopold. 1868. *Cabinet des manuscrits de la Bibliothèque Impériale*. Vol. 2. Paris: Imprimerie Nationale.

den Hollander, August. 2004. "How Shock Waves Revealed Successive Contamination. A Cardiogram of Early Sixteenth-Century Printed Dutch Bibles". In *Studies in Stemmatology II*, edited by Pieter van Reenen, August den Hollander, and Margot van Mulken, 99–112. Philadelphia, PA: Benjamins.

Derolez, Albert. 2003. *The Palaeography of Gothic Manuscript Books: From the Twelfth to the Early Sixteenth Century*. Cambridge: Cambridge University Press.

DeRose, Steven J. 2004. "Markup Overlap: A Review and a Horse". In *Proceedings of Extreme Markup Languages*. Montreal: mulberrytech. conferences.idealliance.org/extreme/html/2004/DeRose01/EML2004DeRose01.html#t2.

DeRose, Steven J., David G. Durand, Elli Mylonas, and Allen H. Renear. 1990. "What Is Text, Really?". *Journal of Computing in Higher Education* 1 (2): 3–26.

Deufert, Marcus. 2017. *Kritischer Kommentar zu Lukrezens De rerum natura*. Berlin: De Gruyter.

Devreesse, Robert. 1954. *Introduction à l'étude des manuscrits grecs*. Paris: Imprimerie Nationale.

Dickey, Eleanor. 2007. *Ancient Greek Scholarship: A Guide to Finding, Reading and Understanding Scholia, Commentaries, Lexica, and Grammatical Treatises, from Their Beginnings to the Byzantine Period*. Oxford: Oxford University Press.

Diestel, Reinhard. 2005. *Graph Theory*. 3rd ed. Heidelberg: Springer.

Dinkova-Bruun, Greti, ed. 2014–2016. *Catalogus translationum et commentariorum: Mediaeval and Renaissance Latin Translations and Commentaries; Annotated Lists and Guides*. Vols 10–11. Toronto: Pontifical Institute of Mediaeval Studies.

Divizia, Paolo. 2009. "Appunti di stemmatica comparata". *Studi e problemi di critica testuale* 78: 29–48.

Divizia, Paolo. 2011. "Fenomenologia degli 'errori guida'". *Filologia e critica* 36 (1): 49–74.

Divizia, Paolo. 2017. "Texts and Transmission in Late Medieval and Early Renaissance Italian Multi-Text Codices". In *The Dynamics of the Medieval Manuscript: Text Collections from a European Perspective, Proceedings of the International Conference (Utrecht, 25–29 April*

2013), edited by Karen Pratt, Bart Besamusca, Ad Putter, and Matthias Meyer, 101–110. Göttingen: Vandenhoeck und Ruprecht.

Dolbeau, François. 1989. "Le Rôle des interprètes dans les traductions hagiographiques d'Italie du Sud". In *Traductions et traducteurs au Moyen Age: Actes du colloque international du CNRS organisé à Paris, IRHT, les 26–28 mai 1986*, edited by Geneviève Contamine, 145–162. Paris: CNRS.

Dömling, Wolfgang. 1969. "Zur Überlieferung der musikalischen Werke Guillaume de Machauts". *Die Musikforschung* 22: 189–195.

Dondaine, Antoine. 1960. "Abréviations latines et signes recommandés pour l'apparat critique des éditions de textes médiévaux". *Bulletin de la Societé Internationale pour l'Etude de la Philosophie Médiévale* 2: 142–149.

Dondi, Cristina. 2016. *Printed Books of Hours from 15th-Century Italy: The Texts, the Books, and the Survival of a Long-Lasting Genre*. Florence: Olschki.

Dondi, Cristina, Andreina Rita, Adalbert Roth, and Marina Venier, eds. 2016. *La stampa romana nella città dei Papi e in Europa*. Vatican City: Biblioteca Apostolica Vaticana.

Donin, Nicolas, and Daniel Ferrer. 2015. "Auteur(s) et acteurs de la genèse". *Genesis* 41: 7–26.

Dow, Sterling. 1969. *Conventions in Editing: A Suggested Reformulation of the Leiden System*. Durham, NC: Duke University Press.

Downey, Sean S., Guowei Sun, and Peter Norquest. 2017. "alineR: An R Package for Optimizing Feature-Weighted Alignments and Linguistic Distances". *R Journal* 9 (1): 138–152.

Draguet, René. 1977. "Une méthode d'édition des textes syriaques". In *A Tribute to Arthur Vööbus: Studies in Early Christian Literature and Its Environment, Primarily in the Syrian East*, edited by Robert H. Fischer, 13–18. Chicago: Lutheran School of Theology.

Drake, Warren J. 1999. "Textual Criticism, Its Usefulness and Limitations for Musicology: Petrucci's Motetti de passione (1503) – A Case Study". *Research Chronicle: New Zealand Musicological Society* 6: 6–20.

Driscoll, Matthew James, and Elena Pierazzo, eds. 2016. *Digital Scholarly Editing: Theories and Practices*. Cambridge: Open Book. openbookpublishers.com/reader/483.

Drummond, Alexei J., and Remco Bouckaert. 2015. *Bayesian Evolutionary Analysis with BEAST*. Cambridge: Cambridge University Press.

Drummond, Alexei J., and Andrew Rambaut. 2007. "BEAST: Bayesian Evolutionary Analysis by Sampling Trees". *BMC Evolutionary Biology* 7 (November): 214. doi.org/10.1186/1471-2148-7-214.

Drummond, Alexei J., Marc A. Suchard, Dong Xie, and Andrew Rambaut. 2012. "Bayesian Phylogenetics with BEAUti and the BEAST 1.7". *Molecular Biology and Evolution* 29 (8): 1969–1973.

Dubuisson, Marc, and Caroline Macé. 2003. "L'Apport des traductions anciennes à l'histoire du texte de Grégoire de Nazianze: Application *Discours* 2". *Orientalia Christiana periodica* 69: 287–340.

Dudbridge, Glen. 2000. *The Lost Books of Medieval China*. London: British Library.

Duggan, Hoyt N., and Eugene W. Lyman. 2005. "A Progress Report on *The Piers Plowman Electronic Archive*". *Digital Medievalist* 1. doi.org/10.16995/dm.5.

Dummer, Jürgen, ed. 1987. *Texte und Textkritik: Eine Aufsatzsammlung*. Berlin: Akademie-Verlag.

Dumont, Stefan, and Martin Fechner. 2014. "Bridging the Gap: Greater Usability for TEI Encoding". *Journal of the Text Encoding Initiative* 8 (December). doi.org/10.4000/jtei.1242.

Dumville, David N. 1988. "Beowulf Come Lately: Some Notes on the Palaeography of the Nowell Codex". *Archiv für das Studium der neueren Sprachen und Literaturen* 225: 49–63.

Dunn, Michael. 2009. "Contact and Phylogeny in Island Melanesia". *Lingua* 119 (11): 1664–1678.

Dunn, Michael. 2014. "Language Phylogenies". In *The Routledge Handbook of Historical Linguistics*, edited by Claire Bowern and Bethwyn Evans, 190–211. London: Routledge.

Dunn, Michael, Angela Terrill, Ger Reesink, Robert A. Foley, and Stephen C. Levinson. 2005. "Structural Phylogenetics and the Reconstruction of Ancient Language History". *Science* 309 (5743): 2072–2075.

Dunning, Andrew. 2015. "Rethinking the Publication of Premodern Sources: Petrus Plaoul on the *Sentences*". *RIDE: A Review Journal for Digital Editions and Resources* 3. doi.org/10.18716/ride.a.3.3.

Duplacy, Jean. 1973. "P75 et les formes les plus anciennes du texte de Luc". In *L'Evangile de Luc: problèmes littéraires et théologiques, Mémorial Lucien Cerfaux*, ed. by Frans Neirynck, 111–128. Gembloux: Duculot

Duplacy, Jean. 1975. "Classification des états d'un texte, mathématiques et informatique: Repères historiques et recherches méthodologiques". *Revue d'histoire des textes* 5: 249–309 [repr. Duplacy 1987, 193–257].

Duplacy, Jean. 1987. *Etudes de critique textuelle du Nouveau Testament*. Edited by Joël Delobel. Leuven: Leuven University Press, 1987.

Duval, Frédéric, ed. 2006. *Pratiques philologiques en Europe*. Paris: Ecole des chartes.

Duval, Frédéric. 2015. *Les Mots de l'édition de textes*. Paris: Ecole nationale des chartes.

Dyen, Isidore, Joseph B. Kruskal, and Paul Black. 1992. "An Indoeuropean Classification: A Lexicostatistical Experiment". *Transactions of the American Philosophical Society* 82 (5): 1–132.

Dykes, Lucinda, and Ed Tittel. 2005. *XML for Dummies*. 4th ed. Hoboken, NJ: Wiley.

Eagleton, Catherine, and Matthew Spencer. 2006. "Copying and Conflation in Geoffrey Chaucer's Treatise on the Astrolabe: A Stemmatic Analysis Using Phylogenetic Software". *Studies in History and Philosophy of Science Part A* 37 (2): 237–268. dx.doi.org/10.1016/j.shpsa.2005.08.020.

Eden, Paul T. 1979. "The Manuscript Tradition of Seneca's *Apocolocyntosis*". *Classical Quarterly* 29: 149–161.

Eden, Paul T., ed. 1984. *Seneca Apocolocyntosis*. Cambridge: Cambridge University Press.

Edwards, Anthony W. F. 2009. "Statistical Methods for Evolutionary Trees". *Genetics* 183 (1): 5–12.

Eggert, Paul. 2009. *Securing the Past: Conservation in Art, Architecture and Literature*. Cambridge: Cambridge University Press.

Eggert, Paul. 2013. "Apparatus, Text, Interface: How to Read a Printed Critical Edition". In *The Cambridge Companion to Textual Scholarship*, edited by Neil Fraistat and Julia Flanders, 97–118. Cambridge: Cambridge University Press.

Egilsdóttir, Ásdís, ed. 2002. *Biskupa sögur*. Vol. 2. Reykjavik: Hið íslenska fornritafélag.

Ehrismann, Gustav, ed. 1915. *Rudolfs von Ems Weltchronik: aus der Wernigeroder Handschrift*. Berlin: Weidmann.

Ehrman, Bart D. 1986. *Didymus the Blind and the Text of the Gospels*. Atlanta, GA: Society of Biblical Literature.

Ehrman, Bart D., and Michael W. Holmes, eds. 2013. *The Text of the New Testament in Contemporary Research*. 2nd ed. Leiden: Brill.

Eisenstein, Elizabeth L. 2000. *The Printing Revolution in Early Modern Europe*. Cambridge: Cambridge University Press.

Elliott, James Keith. 2014. "Histoire du texte grec imprimé". In *Manuel de critique textuelle du Nouveau Testament*, edited by Christian-Bernard Amphoux, 307–363. Brussels: Safran.

Ellison, John William. 1957. "The Use of Electronic Computers in the Study of the Greek New Testament Text". PhD thesis, Harvard University.

Elman, Benjamin. 1985. *From Philosophy to Philology: Intellectual and Social Aspects of Change in Late Imperial China*. Cambridge, MA: Harvard University Asia Center.

Emans, Reinmar, and Ulrich Krämer, eds. 2015. *Musikeditionen im Wandel der Geschichte*. Berlin: De Gruyter.

Enzensberger, Hans Magnus. 1962. *Gedichte: Die Entstehung eines Gedichts*. Frankfurt am Main: Suhrkamp.

Epp, Eldon J., and Gordon D. Fee, eds. 1993. *Studies in the Theory and Method of New Testament Textual Criticism*. Grand Rapids, MI: Eerdmans.

Epstein, Jacob Nahum. 1925. "Ha-mada' ha-talmudi u-zerakhav". *Yedi'ot ha-makhon le-mada'ei ha-yahadut* 2: 5–22 [repr. Epstein 1983–1991, 2.1:1–18].

Epstein, Jacob Nahum. 1936–1937. Review of *Siphre ad Deuteronomium*, edited by Louis Finkelstein. *Tarbiz* 8: 375–392.

Epstein, Jacob Nahum. 1983–1991. *Studies in Talmudic Literature and Semitic Languages*. Edited by Ezra Z. Melamed. 3 vols. Jerusalem: Magnes Press.

Erasmus, Desiderius. 1969. *Opera omnia: Ordo 1*. Vol. 1. Edited by Kazimierz Kumaniecki, Roger A. B. Mynors, Jan Hendrik Waszink, and Christopher Robinson. Amsterdam: North-Holland Publishing.

Erasmus, Desiderius. 1979. *Moriae encomium, id est stultitiae laus: Opera omnia; Ordo 4*. Vol. 3. Edited by Clarence H. Miller. Amsterdam: North-Holland Publishing.

Erasmus, Desiderius. 2013. *Opera omnia: Ordo 1*. Vol. 8. Edited by Silvia Seidel Menchi, Franz Bierlaire, and René Hoven. Leiden: Brill.

Erbse, Hartmut. 1961. "Überlieferungsgeschichte der griechischen klassischen und hellenistischen Literatur". In *Geschichte der Textüberlieferung der antiken und mittelalterlichen Literatur*, by Herbert Hunger, Otto Stegmüller, Harmut Erbse, Max Imhof, Karl Büchner, Hans-Georg Beck, and Horst Rüdiger, vol. 1, 207–283. Zurich: Atlantis-Verlag.

Erho, Ted M., and Loren T. Stuckenbruck. 2013. "A Manuscript History of Ethiopic Enoch". *Journal for the Study of the Pseudepigrapha* 23 (2): 87–133.

Ernout, Alfred, ed. 1948–1955. *Lucretius: De rerum natura libri sex*. 2 vols. Paris: Les Belles Lettres.

Faulkes, Anthony, ed. 1982. *Snorri Sturluson: Edda; Prologue and Gylfaginning*. Oxford: Clarendon Press [2nd ed. London: Viking Society for Northern Research, 2005. vsnrweb-publications.org.uk/Edda-1.pdf].

Faulkes, Anthony, trans. 1995. *Snorri Sturluson: Edda*. Everyman Library. London: Dent. vsnrweb-publications.org.uk/EDDArestr.pdf [frequently reprinted].

Faulkes, Anthony, trans., and Heimir Pálsson, ed. 2012. *Snorri Sturluson: The Uppsala Edda; DG 11 4to*. Edited by Heimir Pálsson. Translated by Anthony Faulkes. London: Viking Society for Northern Research. vsnrweb-publications.org.uk/Uppsala%20Edda.pdf.

Fava, Domenico. 1939. *La Biblioteca Nazionale Centrale di Firenze e le sue insigni raccolte*. Florence: Hoepli.

Feder, Georg. 1983. "Textkritische Methoden: Versuch eines Überblicks mit Bezug auf die Haydn-Gesamtausgabe". *Haydn-Studien* 5: 77–109.

Feder, Georg, and Hubert Unverricht. 1959. "Urtext und Urtextausgaben". *Die Musikforschung* 12: 432–454.

Feld, Maury D. 1978. "The Early Evolution of the Authoritative Text". *Harvard Library Bulletin* 26: 81–111.

Felsenstein, Joseph. 1978a. "Cases in Which Parsimony or Compatibility Methods Will Be Positively Misleading". *Systematic Zoology* 27 (4): 401–410. doi.org/10.2307/2412923.

Felsenstein, Joseph. 1978b. "The Number of Evolutionary Trees". *Systematic Zoology* 27 (1): 27–33.

Felsenstein, Joseph. 1989. "PHYLIP Phylogeny Inference Package (Version 3.2)". *Cladistics* 5 (2): 164–166. doi.org/10.1111/j.1096-0031.1989.tb00562.x.

Felsenstein, Joseph. 1993. *PHYLIP Phylogeny Inference Package Version 3.5c*. csbf.stanford.edu/phylip.

Felsenstein, Joseph. 2004. *Inferring Phylogenies*. Sunderland: Sinauer Associates.

Ferguson Smith, Martin, ed. 1975. *Lucretius: De rerum natura libri sex*. Cambridge, MA: Harvard University Press.

Fernández-Ordóñez, Inés. 2002. "Tras la *collatio* o cómo establecer correctamente el error textual". *La Corónica* 30 (2): 1051–1080.

Ferrer, Daniel. 2002. "Production, Invention, and Reproduction: Genetic vs. Textual Criticism". In *Reimagining Textuality: Textual Studies in the Late Age of Print*, edited by Elizabeth Bergmann Loizeaux and Neil Fraistat, 48–57. Madison: University of Wisconsin Press.

Ferrer, Daniel. 2011. *Logiques du brouillon: Modèles pour une critique génétique*. Paris: Seuil.

Ferrer, Daniel. 2016. "Genetic Criticism with Textual Criticism: From Variant to Variation". *Variants* 12–13: 57–64.

Féry-Hue, Françoise, ed. 2011. *Cent cinq rondeaux d'amour: Un roman dialogué pour l'édification du futur François Ier*. Turnhout: Brepols.

Fiesoli, Giovanni. 2000. *La genesi del lachmannismo*. Florence: Edizioni del Galluzzo.

Finkelstein, Louis. 1931–1932. "Prolegomena to an Edition of the Sifre on Deuteronomy". *Proceedings of the American Academy for Jewish Research* 3: 3–42.

Finkelstein, Louis. 1934–1935. "The Mekhilta and Its Text". *Proceedings of the American Academy for Jewish Research* 5: 3–54.

Finkelstein, Louis, ed. 1939. *Siphre ad Deuteronomium*. Berlin: Gesellschaft zur Förderung der Wissenschaft des Judentums.

Finkelstein, Louis, ed. 1969. *Sifre on Deuteronomy*. 2nd ed. New York, NY: Jewish Theological Seminary of America.

Fiorentino, Francesco. 1872–1874. *Bernardino Telesio ossia Studi Storici sulla Idea della Natura nel Risorgimento Italiano*. 2 vols. Florence: Successori Le Monnier [repr. Naples: La Scuola di Pitagora, 2008].

Fischer, Franz. 2008. "The Pluralistic Approach – The First Scholarly Edition of William of Auxerre's Treatise on Liturgy". *Jahrbuch für Computerphilologie* 10: 151–168. computerphilologie.digital-humanities.de/jg08/fischer.html.

Fischer, Franz. 2013. "All Texts Are Equal, but … Textual Plurality and the Critical Text in Digital Scholarly Editions". *Variants* 10: 77–92. kups.ub.uni-koeln.de/5056.

Fischer, Franz. 2017. "Digital Corpora and Scholarly Editions of Latin Texts: Features and Requirements of Textual Criticism". *Speculum* 92, no. S1 (October): S265–S287. doi.org/10.1086/693823.

Fischer, Franz, and Anthony Harvey, eds. 2011. *Saint Patrick's Confessio*. Dublin: Royal Irish Academy. confessio.ie.

Fitch, Walter M. 1971. "Toward Defining the Course of Evolution: Minimum Change for a Specified Tree Topology". *Systematic Zoology* 20 (4): 406–416. doi.org/10.2307/2412116.

Fitch, Walter M., and Emanuel Margoliash. 1967. "Construction of Phylogenetic Trees". *Science* 155 (3760): 279–284. doi.org/10.1126/science.155.3760.279.

Fitjar, Camilla. 2016. "Priming Effects in Early Readers: A Quantitative Study of Children's Response Times in Visual Lexical Decision-Making in Their First and Second Language". MA thesis, University of Stavanger.

Fleith, Barbara. 1991. *Studien zur Überlieferungsgeschichte der lateinischen Legenda aurea*. Brussels: Société des Bollandistes.

Flight, Colin. 1990. "How Many Stemmata?". *Manuscripta* 34 (2): 122–128. doi.org/10.1484/J.MSS.3.1335.

Flight, Colin. 1992. "Stemmatic Theory and the Analysis of Complicated Traditions". *Manuscripta* 36 (1): 37–52. doi.org/10.1484/J.MSS.3.1391.

Flight, Colin. 1994. "A Complete Theoretical Framework for Stemmatic Analysis". *Manuscripta* 38 (2): 95–115. doi.org/10.1484/J.MSS.3.1455.

Foerster, Wendelin, and Alfons Hilka, eds. 1884–1932. *Christian von Troyes: Sämtliche Werke*. 5 vols. Halle an der Saale: Niemeyer.

Fogelmark, Staffan. 2015. *The Kallierges Pindar: A Study in Renaissance Greek Scholarship and Printing*. 2 vols. Cologne: Dinter.

Forrai, Réka. 2012. "The Readership of Early Medieval Greek–Latin Translations". In *Scrivere e leggere nell'alto medioevo*, vol. 1, 293–311. Spoleto: CISAM.

Förtsch, Reinhard. 2006. "Atrium Libertatis". In *Brill's New Pauly*, edited by Hubert Cancik and Helmut Schneider. dx.doi.org/10.1163/1574-9347_bnp_e207180.

Fortunato, Laura. 2011. "Reconstructing the History of Marriage Strategies in Indo-European-Speaking Societies: Monogamy and Polygyny". *Human Biology* 83 (1): 87–105. doi.org/10.3378/027.083.0106.

Foulet, Alfred, and Mary B. Speer. 1979. *On Editing Old French Texts*. Lawrence: Regents Press of Kansas.

Fourquet, Jean. 1946. "Le Paradoxe de Bédier". In *Melanges 1945*, edited by Prosper Alfaric, vol. 2, *Etudes littéraires*, 1–16. Paris: Les Belles Lettres.

Fourquet, Jean. 1948–1949. "Fautes communes ou innovations communes?". *Romania* 70: 85–95.

Fracastoro, Girolamo. 1546. *De sympathia et antipathia rerum liber unus*. Venice: Hered. Lucae Juntae.

Frank, István. 1955. "De l'art d'éditer les textes lyriques". In *Recueil de travaux offerts à M. Clovis Brunel*, 463–475. Paris: Société de l'Ecole des Chartes.

Frank, István. 1976. "The Art of Editing Lyric Texts". In *Medieval Manuscripts and Textual Criticism*, edited by Christopher Kleinhenz, 123–138. Chapel Hill: University of North Carolina Press [trans. of Frank 1955].

Fränkel, Hermann. 1964. *Einleitung zur kritischen Ausgabe der Argonautika des Apollonios*. Göttingen: Vandenhoeck und Ruprecht.

Fraser, Veronica M. 2006. *The Songs of Peire Vidal: Translation and Commentary*. New York, NY: Lang.

Friedman, Nir. 1997. "Learning Belief Networks in the Presence of Missing Values and Hidden Variables". In *ICML '97: Proceedings of the Fourteenth International Conference on Machine Learning*, edited by Douglas H. Fisher, 125–133, San Francisco: Morgan Kaufmann.

Friedman, Nir, Matan Ninio, Istik Pe'er, and Tal Pupko. 2002. "A Structural EM Algorithm for Phylogenetic Inference". *Journal of Computational Biology* 9: 331–354.

Friedrich, Michael, and Cosima Schwarke, eds. 2016. *One-Volume Libraries: Composite and Multiple-Text Manuscripts*. Berlin: De Gruyter.

Friis-Jensen, Karsten, ed. 2015. *Saxo Grammaticus: Gesta Danorum, The History of the Danes*. Translated by Peter Fisher. 2 vols. Oxford: Oxford University Press.

Frobenius, Wolf. 1987. "Zum genetischen Verhältnis zwischen Notre-Dame-Klauseln und ihren Motetten". *Archiv für Musikwissenschaft* 44: 1–39.

Frobenius, Wolf. 2001. "Josquins Chanson Plus nulz regretz: Quellenkritik und Analyse". In *Musik und Szene: Festschrift für Werner Braun zum 75. Geburtstag*, edited by Bernhard Appel and Werner Braun, 431–453. Saarbrücken: Saarbrücker Druckerei.

Froger, Jacques. 1965. "The Electronic Machine at the Service of Humanities Studies". *Diogenes* 52: 104–142.

Froger, Jacques. 1968. *La Critique des textes et son automatisation*. Paris: Dunod.

Fromm, Hans. 1995. "Zur Geschichte der Textkritik und Edition mittelhochdeutscher Texte". In *Beiträge zur Methodengeschichte der neueren Philologien: Zum 125jährigen Bestehen des Max Niemeyer Verlags*, edited by Robert Harsch-Niemeyer, 63–90. Tübingen: Niemeyer.

Frühmorgen-Voss, Hella. 1975. *Text und Illustration im Mittelalter: Aufsätze zu den Wechselbeziehungen zwischen Literatur und bildender Kunst*. Munich: Beck.

Fuhs, Hans Ferdinand. 1968. *Die äthiopische Übersetzung des Propheten Micha: Edition und textkritischer Kommentar nach den Handschriften in Oxford, London, Paris, Cambridge, Wien und Frankfurt am Main.* Bonn: Hanstein.

Fuhs, Hans Ferdinand. 1971. *Die äthiopische Übersetzung des Propheten Hosea: Edition und textkritischer Kommentar nach den Handschriften in Berlin, Cambridge, Frankfurt am Main, London, München, Oxford, Paris und Wien.* Bonn: Hanstein.

Fulk, Robert D., Robert E. Bjork, and John D. Niles, eds. 2008. *Klaeber's Beowulf.* 4th ed. Toronto: University of Toronto Press.

Gabler, Hans Walter, Claus Melchior, and Wolfhard Steppe, eds. 1984. *James Joyce: Ulysses; A Critical and Synoptic Edition.* New York, NY: Garland.

Gamkrelidze, Tamaz V., and Vjačeslav Ivanov. 1984. *Индоевропейский язык и индоевропейцы.* 2 vols. Tbilisi: Издательство Тбилисского университета [English version: *Indo-European and the Indo-Europeans.* Translated by Johanna Nichols. 2 vols. Berlin: De Gruyter, 1995].

Gamper, Rudolf, Marina Bernasconi Reusser, Birigt Ebersperger, and Ernst Tremp, eds. 2015. *Scriptorium: Wesen – Funktion – Eigenheiten; Comité international de paléographie latine, XVIII. Kolloquium, St. Gallen 11.–14. September 2013.* Munich: Beck.

Ganz, Peter F. 1968. "Lachmann as an Editor of Middle High German Texts". In *Probleme mittalalterlicher Überlieferung und Textkritik: Oxforder Colloquium 1966,* edited by Werner Schröder and Peter F. Ganz, 12–30. Berlin: Schmidt.

Gardner, Daniel K., trans. 1990. *Chu Hsi, Learning to Be a Sage: Selections from the Conversations of Master Chu, Arranged Topically.* Berkeley: University of California Press.

Garner, William. 2010. "Jane Austen Could Write – But Her Spelling Was Awful". *The Independent,* October 22. independent.co.uk/arts-entertainment/books/news/jane-austen-could-write-ndash-but-her-spelling-was-awful-2114237.html.

Gastgeber, Christian. 2003. "Die Überlieferung der griechischen Literatur im Mittelalter". In *Einführung in die Überlieferungsgeschichte und die Textkritik der antiken Literatur,* edited by Egert Pöhlmann, vol. 2, *Mittelalter und Neuzeit,* 1–46. Darmstadt: Wissenschaftliche Buchgesellschaft.

Geerard, Maurits, and Jacques Noret. 1984–2018. *Clavis Patrum Graecorum.* 6 vols. Turnhout: Brepols.

Géhin, Paul. 2005. *Lire le manuscrit médiéval: Observer et décrire.* Paris: Colin.

Gentile, Sebastiano. 1997. "Umanesimo fiorentino e riscoperta dei Padri". In *Umanesimo e Padri della Chiesa: Manoscritti e incunaboli di testi patristici da Francesco Petrarca al primo Cinquecento,* edited by Sebastiano Gentile, 45–62. Rome: Rose.

Georgiades, Thrasybulos Georgios, ed. 1971. *Musikalische Edition im Wandel des historischen Bewußtseins.* Kassel: Bärenreiter.

Giannouli, Antonia. 2015. "Critical Editions and the Complementary Apparatuses to a Critical Apparatus". *Comparative Oriental Manuscript Studies Bulletin* 1 (1): 21–28. www.aai.uni-hamburg.de/en/comst/pdf/bulletin1/pp21-28.pdf.

Gilissen, Léon. 1977. *Prolégomènes à la codicologie: Recherches sur la construction des cahiers et la mise en page des manuscrits médiévaux.* Ghent: Story-Scientia.

Gippert, Jost. 2015. "Palimpsests of Caucasian Provenance: Reflections on Diplomatic Editing". In *Comparative Oriental Manuscript Studies: An Introduction,* by Alessandro Bausi, Pier Giorgio Borbone, Françoise Briquel Chatonnet, Paola Buzi, Jost Gippert, Caroline Macé, Marilena Maniaci, Zisis Melissakis, Laura E. Parodi, and Witold Witakowski, 403–410. Hamburg: Tredition.

Gippert, Jost. 2018. *Georgische Handschriften.* Wiesbaden: Reichert.

Gippert, Jost. Forthcoming. "Sprachwandel und Rekonstruktion – Perspektiven und Grenzen der Heuristik". In *Die Ausbreitung des Indogermanischen: Thesen aus Sprachwissenschaft und Archäologie: Akten der Tagung der Indogermanischen Gesellschaft vom 24. bis 26. September 2009 in Würzburg,* edited by Heinrich Hettrich and Sabine Ziegler.

Gjessing, Håkon K., and Richard H. Pierce. 1994. "A Stochastic Model for the Presence/Absence of Readings in Nirstigningar Saga". *World Archaeology* 26 (2): 268–294.

Glenisson, Jean, Jean Irigoin, Robert Marichal, Jaques Monfrin, and Gian Piero Zarri, eds. 1979. *"La Pratique des ordinateurs dans la critique des textes": Actes du Colloque international (Paris, 29–31 mars 1978)*. Paris: Editions du CNRS.

Glessgen, Martin-Dietrich, and Franz Lebsanft, eds. 1997. *Alte und neue Philologie*. Tübingen: Niemeyer.

Glock, Anne. 2006. "Mouseion: C". In *Brill's New Pauly*, edited by Hubert Cancik and Helmut Schneider. dx.doi.org/10.1163/1574-9347_bnp_e812620.

Goldfarb, Charles F. 1997. "SGML: The Reason Why and the First Published Hint". *Journal of the American Society for Information Science* 48 (7): 656–661. doi.org/10.1002/(SICI)1097-4571(199707)48:7<656::AID-ASI13>3.0.CO;2-T.

Golitsis, Pantelis. 2010. "Copistes, élèves et érudits: La Production de manuscrits philosophiques autour de Georges Pachymère". In *The Legacy of Bernard de Montfaucon: Three Hundred Years of Studies on Greek Handwriting*, edited by Antonio Bravo García, Inmaculada Pérez Martín, and Juan Signes Codoñer, 157–170, 757–768. Turnhout: Brepols.

Göller, Stefan, and Guerino Mazzola. 2002. "Performance and Interpretation". *Journal of New Music Research* 31: 221–232.

Gomaa, Wael H., and Aly A. Fahmy. 2013. "A Survey of Text Similarity Approaches". *International Journal of Computer Applications* 68 (13): 13–18. pdfs.semanticscholar.org/5b5c/a878c534aee3882a038ef9e82f46e102131b.pdf.

Gomez Gane, Yorick. 2013. *Dizionario della terminologia filologica, premessa di Leopoldo Gamberale*. Turin: Accademia University Press.

Göransson, Elisabet. 2016. "Connecting the Case Studies: Editorial Methods and the Editorial Circle Model". In *The Arts of Editing Medieval Greek and Latin: A Casebook*, edited by Elisabet Göransson, Gunilla Iversen, Barbara Crostini, Brian M. Jensen, Erika Kihlman, Eva Odelman, and Denis Searby, 400–429. Toronto: Pontifical Institute of Mediaeval Studies.

Göransson, Elisabet. 2018. Review of *Editing Medieval Texts: An Introduction, Using Exemplary Materials Derived from Richard Rolle, "Super canticum" 4*, by Ralph Hanna. *Speculum* 93:1: 224–225.

Göransson, Elisabet, Gunilla Iversen, Barbara Crostini, Brian M. Jensen, Erika Kihlman, Eva Odelman, and Denis Searby, eds. 2016. *The Arts of Editing Medieval Greek and Latin: A Casebook*. Toronto: Pontifical Institute of Mediaeval Studies.

Gottheil, Richard. 1899. "The Greek Physiologus and Its Oriental Translations". *American Journal of Semitic Languages and Literatures* 15 (2): 120–124.

Götze, Albrecht. 1922. *Die Schatzhöhle: Überlieferung und Quellen*. Heidelberg: Winter.

Graf, Georg. 1944. *Geschichte der christlichen arabischen Literatur*. Vol. 1. *Die Übersetzungen*. Vatican City: Biblioteca Apostolica Vaticana.

Grafton, Anthony Thomas. 1975. "Joseph Scaliger's Edition of Catullus (1577) and the Traditions of Textual Criticism in the Renaissance". *Journal of the Warburg and Courtauld Institutes* 38: 155–181.

Grafton, Anthony Thomas. 2011. *Humanists with Inky Fingers: The Culture of Correction in Renaissance Europe*. Florence: Olschki.

Grane, Leif, Alfred Schindler, and Markus Wriedt, eds. 1993–1998. *Auctoritas patrum: Zur Rezeption der Kirchenväter im 15. und 16. Jahrhundert*. 2 vols. Mainz: Philipp von Zabern.

Gray, Russel D., and Quentin D. Atkinson. 2003. "Language-Tree Divergence Times Support the Anatolian Theory of Indo-European Origin". *Nature* 426 (6965): 435–439. doi.org/10.1038/nature02029.

Gray, Russel D., David Bryant, and Simon Greenhill. 2010. "On the Shape and Fabric of Human History". *Philosophical Transactions of the Royal Society B* 365 (1559): 3923–3933.

Gray, Russel D., Alexei Drummond, and Simon Greenhill. 2009. "Language Phylogenies Reveal Expansion Pulses and Pauses in Pacific Settlement". *Science* 323: 479–483. doi.org/10.1126/science.1166858.
Gray, Russel D., and Fiona M. Jordan. 2000. "Language Trees Support the Express-Train Sequence of Austronesian Expansion". *Nature* 405 (6790): 1052–1055. doi.org/10.1038/35016575.
Graziosi, Barbara. 2002. *Inventing Homer: The Early Reception of Epic*. Cambridge: Cambridge University Press.
Greenhill, Simon J., Alexei J. Drummond, and Russell D. Gray. 2010. "How Accurate and Robust Are the Phylogenetic Estimates of Austronesian Language Relationships?". *PLoS One* 5 (3): e9573. doi.org/10.1371/journal.pone.0009573.
Greenhill, Simon J., and Russell D. Gray. 2009. "Austronesian Language Phylogenies: Myths and Misconceptions about Bayesian Computational Methods". In *Austronesian Historical Linguistics and Culture History: A Festschrift for Robert Blust*, edited by Andrew Pawley and Malcolm Ross, 375–397. Canberra: Pacific Linguistics.
Greetham, David C. 1987. "Challenges of Theory and Practice in the Editing of Hoccleve's Regement of Princes". In *Manuscripts and Texts: Editorial Problems in Later Middle English Literature*, edited by Derek Pearsall, 60–86. Cambridge, MA: Brewer.
Greetham, David C. 1994. *Textual Scholarship: An Introduction*. New York, NY: Garland [1st ed. 1992].
Greetham, David C., ed. 1995. *Scholarly Editing: A Guide to Research*. New York, NY: Modern Language Association.
Greetham, David C. 1996. "Phylum-Tree-Rhyzome". In *Readings from the Margins: Textual Studies, Chaucer, and Medieval Literature*, edited by Seth Lerer, 99–126. San Marino, CA: Huntington Library.
Greetham, David C. 1999. *Theories of the Text*. Oxford: Oxford University Press.
Greetham, David C. 2013. "A History of Textual Scholarship". In *The Cambridge Companion to Textual Scholarship*, edited by Neil Fraistat and Julia Flanders, 16–41. Cambridge: Cambridge University Press.
Greeven, Heinrich. 1978. "The Gospel Synopsis from 1776 to the Present Day". In *Johann J. Griesbach: Synoptic and Text-Critical Studies 1776–1976*, edited by Bernard Orchard and Thomas R. W. Longstaff, 22–49. Cambridge: Cambridge University Press [repr. 2005].
Greg, Walter Wilson. 1927. *The Calculus of Variants: An Essay on Textual Criticism*. Oxford: Clarendon Press.
Greg, Walter Wilson. 1950–1951. "The Rationale of Copy-Text". *Studies in Bibliography* 3: 19–36.
Greg, Walter Wilson. 1951. *The Editorial Problem in Shakespeare: A Survey of the Foundations of the Text*. Oxford: Clarendon Press.
Gregory, Caspar René. 1894. *Prolegomena scripsit Caspar Renatus Gregory*. Vol. 3 of *Novum Testamentum Graecum*. Edited by Constantinus Tischendorf. 8th ed. Leipzig: Hinrichs.
Gregory, Caspar René. 1900–1909. *Textkritik des Neuen Testaments*. 3 vols. Leipzig: Hinrichs.
Grésillon, Almuth. 1994. *Eléments de critique génétique: Lire les manuscrits modernes*. Paris: Presses Universitaires de Paris.
Grier, James. 1988. "The Stemma of the Aquitanian Versaria". *Journal of the American Musicological Society* 41: 250–288.
Grier, James. 1989. "Lachmann, Bédier and the Bipartite Stemma: Towards a Responsible Application of the Common-Error Method". *Revue d'histoire des textes* 18: 263–278.
Grier, James. 1995. "Musical Sources and Stemmatic Filiation: A Tool for Editing Music". *Journal of Musicology* 13: 73–102.
Grier, James. 1996. *The Critical Editing of Music: History, Method, and Practice*. Cambridge: Cambridge University Press.
Griesbach, Johann Jakob, ed. 1775–1807. *Novum Testamentum Graece*. 3 vols. Halle an der Saale: apud Curtii haeredes et Londini apud Petr. Elmsly, 1775–1777 [repr. 1796–1806, 1803–1807].

Griffith, John G. 1968. "A Taxonomic Study of the Manuscript Tradition of Juvenal". *Museum Helveticum* 25 (2): 101–138. jstor.org/stable/24813890.

Griffith, John G. 1969. "Numerical Taxonomy and Some Primary Manuscripts of the Gospels". *Journal of Theological Studies* 20 (2): 389–406.

Griffith, John G. 1984. "A Three-Dimensional Model for Classifying Arrays of Manuscripts by Cluster Analysis". *Studia patristica* 15 (1): 79–83.

Gröber, Gustav. 1869. *Die handschriftlichen Gestaltungen der Chanson de geste "Fierabras" und ihre Vorstufen*. Leipzig: Vogel.

Grohmann, Adolf. 1913. "Die im Äthiopischen, Arabischen und Koptischen erhaltenen Visionen Apa Schenute's von Atripe". *Zeitschrift der Deutschen Morgenländischen Gesellschaft* 67: 187–267.

Grotans, Anna. 2010. *Reading in Medieval St. Gall*. Cambridge: Cambridge University Press.

Gruber, John. 2004. "Daring Fireball: Markdown". December 17. daringfireball.net/projects/markdown.

Grubmüller, Klaus. 1993. "Wider die Resignation: Mären kritisch ediert; Einige Überlegungen am Beispiel der 'Halben Birne'". In *Methoden und Probleme der Edition mittelalterlicher Texte*, edited by Rolf Bergmann and Kurt Gärtner, 92–106. Tübingen: Niemeyer.

Guan Xihua 管錫華. 2013. *Jiaokanxue jiaocheng 校勘學教程*. Beijing: Beijing Daxue chubanshe.

Guðmundsdóttir, Aðalheiður, ed. 2006. *Strengleikar*. Reykjavik: Bókmenntafræðistofnun Háskóla Íslands.

Guerrier, Louis, and Sylvain Grébaut. 1912. *Le Testament en Galilée de Notre-Seigneur Jésus-Christ*. Paris: Firmin Didot et Cie.

Guglielmetti, Rossana E. 2007. "Riconoscimento delle linee verticali della tradizione presenza di contaminazioni sistematiche: L'esperienza del Policraticus di Giovanni di Salisbury". *Filologia mediolatina* 14: 107–127.

Guglielmetti, Rossana E., ed. 2017. *Navigatio sancti Brendani: Editio Maior a cura di Rossana E. Guglielmetti; Testo critico di Giovanni Orlandi e Rossana E. Guglielmetti*. Millennio Medievale 114, Testi 29. Florence: Edizioni del Galluzzo.

Guglielmetti, Rossana E., and Giovanni Orlandi, eds. 2014. *Navigatio sancti Brendani, alla scoperta dei segreti meravigliosi del mondo edizione critica*. Florence: Edizioni del Galluzzo.

Guidi, Vincenzo, and Paolo Trovato. 2004. "Sugli stemmi bipartiti: Decimazione, asimmetria e calcolo delle probabilità". *Filologia Italiana* 1: 9–48.

Guillaumin, Jean-Baptiste. 2008. "Aethera cantibus numerisque laetificans: La Musique dans l'œuvre de Martianus Capella; Edition, traduction et commentaire du livre IX des Noces de Philologie et de Mercure". PhD thesis, Université de Caen – Basse Normandie.

Guillaumin, Jean-Baptiste, ed. 2011. *Martianus Capella: Les Noces de Philologie et de Mercure; L'Harmonie, texte établi et traduit par Jean-Baptiste Guillaumin*. Paris: Les Belles Lettres.

Gumbert, J. Peter. 1998. "Commentare 'Commentare Bischoff'". *Scrittura e Civiltà* 22: 397–404.

Gurry, Peter J. 2017. *A Critical Examination of the Coherence-Based Genealogical Method in New Testament Textual Criticism*. Leiden: Brill.

Haak, Wolfgang, Iosif Lazaridis, Nick Patterson, Nadin Rohland, Swapan Mallick, Bastien Llamas, Guido Brandt, Susanne Nordenfelt, Eadaoin Harney, Kristin Stewardson, et al. 2015. "Massive Migration from the Steppe Was a Source for Indo-European Languages in Europe". *Nature* 522 (7555): 207–211. doi.org/10.1038/nature14317.

Haentjens Dekker, Ronald, and David J. Birnbaum. 2017. "It's More than Just Overlap: Text as Graph". *Balisage Series on Markup Technologies* 19 (= "Proceedings of Balisage: The Markup Conference 2017"). doi.org/10.4242/BalisageVol19.Dekker01.

Haentjens Dekker, Ronald, Dirk van Hulle, Gregor Middell, Vincent Neyt, and Joris van Zundert. 2015. "Computer Supported Collation of Modern Manuscripts: CollateX and the Beckett Digital Manuscript Project". *Literary and Linguistic Computing* 30 (3): 452–470. doi.org/10.1093/llc/fqu007.

Hagel, Stefan. 2007. "The Classical Text Editor: An Attempt to Provide for Both Printed and Digital Editions". In *Digital Philology and Medieval Texts*, edited by Arianna Ciula and Francesco Stella, 77–84. Ospedaletto: Pacini. pdfs.semanticscholar.org/b4d3/bbfb63657e71c1a023e0af028bae52604035.pdf.
Hägg, Tomas. 1983. *The Novel in Antiquity*. Oxford: Blackwell.
Hagos Abrha. 2011. "Philological Analysis of the Manuscripts of Gädlä Yəm'ata". *Ityopis* 1: 61–75.
Haigh, John. 1970. "The Recovery of the Root of a Tree". *Journal of Applied Probability* 7 (1): 79–88.
Haigh, John. 1971. "The Manuscript Linkage Problem". In *Mathematics in the Archaeological and Historical Sciences: Proceedings of the Anglo-Romanian Conference, Mamaia, 1970*, edited by Frank Roy Hodson, David George Kendall, and Petre Tăutu, 396–400. Edinburgh: Edinburgh University Press.
Hall, John Barry, ed. 1969. *Claudian: De raptu Proserpinae*. Cambridge: Cambridge University Press.
Halonen, Marko. 2015. "Computer-Assisted Stemmatology in Studying Paulus Juusten's 16th-Century Chronicle *Catalogus et ordinaria successio episcoporum Finlandensium*". *Digital Scholarship in the Humanities* 31 (3): 578–593. doi.org/10.1093/llc/fqv004.
Halvorsen, Eyvind F., ed. 1959. *The Norse Version of the Chanson de Roland*. Copenhagen: Munksgaard.
Hamesse, Jacqueline, ed. 1992. *Les Problèmes posés par l'édition critique des textes anciens et médiévaux*. Louvain-la-Neuve: Université catholique de Louvain.
Hamm, Charles. 1962. "Manuscript Structure in the Dufay Era". *Acta musicologica* 34: 166–184.
Hamm, Charles. 1983. "Interrelationships between Manuscript and Printed Sources of Polyphonic Music in the Early Sixteenth Century – An Overview". In *Quellenstudien zur Musik der Renaissance*, vol. 2, *Datierung und Filiation von Musik Handschriften der Josquin-Zeit*, edited by Ludwig Finscher, 1–13. Wiesbaden: Harrassowitz.
Hamming, Richard W. 1950. "Error Detecting and Error Correcting Codes". *Bell System Technical Journal* 29 (2): 147–160. doi.org/10.1002/j.1538-7305.1950.tb00463.x.
Hamp, Eric P. 1990. "The Pre-Indo-European Language of Northern (Central) Europe". In *When Worlds Collide: The Indo-Europeans and the Pre-Indo-Europeans*, edited by Thomas Lloyd Markey and John Aird Coutts Greppin, 291–309. Ann Arbor, MI: Karoma.
Han, Mira V., and Christian M. Zmasek. 2009. "PhyloXML: XML for Evolutionary Biology and Comparative Genomics". *BMC Bioinformatics* 10 (1): 356. doi.org/10.1186/1471-2105-10-356.
Hanna, Ralph. 2000. "The Application of Thought to Textual Criticism in All Modes – With Apologies to A. E. Housman". *Studies in Bibliography* 53: 163–172.
Hanna, Ralph. 2015. *Editing Medieval Texts: An Introduction, Using Exemplary Materials Derived from Richard Rolle, "Super Canticum" 4*. Liverpool: Liverpool University Press.
Hannah, Darrell. 1997. *The Text of I Corinthians in the Writings of Origen*. Atlanta, GA: Society of Biblical Literature.
Härke, Heinrich. 1998. "Archaeologists and Migrations". *Current Anthropology* 39 (1): 19–46.
Harlfinger, Dieter, ed. 1980. *Griechische Kodokologie und Textüberliefering*. Darmstadt: Wissenschaftliche Buchgesellschaft.
Harnack, Adolf von. 1924. *Marcion: Das Evangelium vom fremden Gott*. 2nd ed. Leipzig: Hinrichs.
Harris, William Vernon. 1989. *Ancient Literacy*. Cambridge, MA: Harvard University Press.
Hartl, Eduard. 1928. *Die Textgeschichte des Wolframschen Parzival: I. Teil; Die jüngeren *G-Handschriften: 1. Abteilung; Die Wiener Mischhandschriftengruppe *W ($G^nG^\delta G$ $^\mu G^\varphi$)*. Berlin: De Gruyter.
Hassner, Tal, Malte Rehbein, Peter A. Stokes, and Lior Wolf. 2012. "Computation and Palaeography: Potentials and Limits". *Dagstuhl Manifestos* 2: 14–35. doi.org/10.4230/DagMan.2.1.14.

Haugen, Odd Einar. 2007. "Textkritik und Textphilologie". In *Altnordische Philologie: Norwegen und Island*, edited by Odd Einar Haugen, 99–145. Berlin: De Gruyter.

Haugen, Odd Einar. 2010. "Stitching the Text Together: Documentary and Eclectic Editions in Old Norse Philology". In *Creating the Medieval Saga: Versions, Variability and Editorial Interpretations of Old Norse Saga Literature*, edited by Judy Quinn and Emily Lethbridge, 39–65. Odense: Syddansk Universitetsforlag.

Haugen, Odd Einar. 2013. "Editionen westnordischer Mittelaltertexte in Skandinavien – Ein historischer Überblick". In *Geschichte der Edition in Skandinavien*, edited by Paula Henrikson and Christian Janss, 13–47. Berlin: De Gruyter.

Haugen, Odd Einar. 2014. "The Making of an Edition: Three Crucial Dimensions". In *Digital Critical Editions*, edited by Daniel Apollon, Claire Bélisle, and Philippe Régnier, 203–245. Urbana: University of Illinois Press.

Haugen, Odd Einar. 2016. "The Silva Portentosa of Stemmatology: Bifurcation in the Recension of Old Norse Manuscripts". *Digital Scholarship in the Humanities* 31 (3): 594–610. doi.org/10.1093/llc/fqv002.

Haugen, Odd Einar. 2018a. "Høgmellomalderen (1050–1350)". In *Norsk språkhistorie*. Vol. 4. *Tidslinjer*, edited by Helge Sandøy and Agnete Nesse, 197–292. Oslo: Novus.

Haugen, Odd Einar, ed. 2018b. *Le lingue nordiche nel medioevo*. Vol. 1. *Testi*. Oslo: Novus Press. omp.novus.no/index.php/novus/catalog/book/2.

Haugen, Odd Einar. 2019. "The Critical Edition in Old Norse Philology: Its Demise and Redefinition". *Storie e linguaggi* 5 (1): 93–109.

Haugen, Odd Einar, Haraldur Bernharðsson, Marco Bianchi, Alex Speed Kjeldsen, Friederike Richter, Beeke Stegmann, Nina Stensaker, and Tarrin Wills. 2019. *The Menota Handbook*. Version 3.0. Bergen: Medieval Nordic Text Archive. menota.org/handbook.xml.

Haverling, Gerd V. M. 2003, "Sur le latin vulgaire dans la traduction 'ravennate' des *Aphorismes* d'Hippocrate". In *Latin vulgaire – Latin tardif VI: Actes du VIe Colloque International sur le latin vulgaire et tardif, Helsinki 28 août–2 septembre 2000*, edited by Heikki Solin, Martti Leiwo, and Hilla Halla-aho, 157–172. Hildesheim: Olms-Weidmann.

Haverling, Gerd V. M. 2008. "On Variation in Syntax and Morphology in Late Latin texts". In *Latin vulgaire – Latin tardif VIII: Actes du VIIIe Colloque International sur le latin vulgaire et tardif, Oxford, 6–9 septembre 2006*, edited by Roger Wright, 351–360. Hildesheim: Olms-Weidmann.

Haverling, Gerd V. M. 2014. "Il latino letterario della tarda antichità". In *Latin vulgaire – Latin tardif X: Actes du Xe colloque international sur le latin vulgaire et tardif, Bergamo 5–9 septembre 2012*, edited by Piera Molinelli, Pierluigi Cuzzolin, and Chiara Fedriani, 845–872. Bergamo: Bergamo University Press.

Haverling, Gerd V. M. 2019. "Some More Remarks on the Language of the Late Latin Translation of the Hippocratic Aphorisms". In *On Medical Latin in Late Antiquity: Acts of the 11th International Colloquium on Ancient Latin Medical Texts*, edited by Gerd V. M. Haverling, 89–107. Uppsala: Acta Universitatis Upsaliensis.

Havet, Louis. 1911. *Manuel de critique verbale appliquée aux textes latins*. Paris: Hachette.

Hay, Louis. 1967. "Des manuscrits, pour quoi faire?". *Le Monde*, "Le Monde des livres" supplement, February 8.

Haye, Thomas. 2016. *Verlorenes Mittelalter: Ursachen und Muster der Nichtüberlieferung mittellateinischer Literatur*. Leiden: Brill.

Hayes-Sheen, Josh. 2017. "GraphViz Pocket Reference". graphs.grevian.org.

Heggarty, Paul, Warren Maguire, and April McMahon. 2010. "Splits or Waves? Trees or Webs? How Divergence Measures and Network Analysis can Unravel Language". *Philosophical Transactions of the Royal Society B* 365 (1559): 3829–3843. doi.org/10.1098/rstb.2010.0099.

Heikkilä, Tuomas. 2014. "The Possibilities and Challenges of Computer-Assisted Stemmatology: The Example of Vita et Miracula s. Symeonis Treverensis". In *Analysis of Ancient and Medieval Texts and Manuscripts: Digital Approaches*, edited by Tara. L. Andrews and Caroline Macé, 19–42. Turnhout: Brepols.

Heikkilä, Tuomas, and Teemu Roos, eds. 2016. "Thematic Section on Studia Stemmatologica". *Digital Scholarship in the Humanities* 31 (3): 520–669.

Heinzelmann, Martin. 2001. *Gregory of Tours: History and Society in the Sixth Century*. Translated by Christopher Carroll. Cambridge: Cambridge University Press.

Heinzle, Joachim. 2003. "Zur Logik mediävistischer Editionen: Einige Grundbegriffe". *editio* 17: 1–15.

Heinzle, Joachim. 2013. *Das Nibelungenlied und die Klage: Nach der Handschrift 857 der Stiftsbibliothek St. Gallen; Mittelhochdeutscher Text, Übersetzung und Kommentar*. Frankfurt am Main: Deutscher Klassiker Verlag.

Helander, Hans. 2001. "*SO Debate:* Neo-Latin Studies; Significance and Prospects". *Symbolae Osloenses* 76: 5–44.

Heldmann, Georg. 2003. "Von der Wiederentdeckung der antiken Literatur zu den Anfängen methodischer Textkritik". In *Einführung in die Überlieferungsgeschichte und die Textkritik der antiken Literatur*, edited by Egert Pöhlmann, vol. 2, *Mittelalter und Neuzeit*, 97–135. Darmstadt: Wissenschaftliche Buchgesellschaft.

Helgason, Jón, ed. 1938. *Byskupa sögur*. Vol. 1. *Byskupa ættir*. Copenhagen: Munskgaard.

Helgason, Jón, ed. 1978. *Byskupa sögur*. Vol. 2. *Jartegnabók þórláks byskups en forna*. Copenhagen: Munskgaard.

Helgason, Jón. 1979. "Om udgivelse af islandske tekster". *Arnamagnæan Institute & Dictionary: Bulletin* 12: 14–15.

Hellinga-Querido, Lotte. 2014. *Texts in Transit: Manuscript to Proof and Print in the Fifteenth Century*. Leiden: Brill.

Hellinga-Querido, Lotte. 2018. *Incunabula in Transit: People and Trade*. Leiden: Brill.

Hendel, Roland. 2016. *Steps to a New Edition of the Hebrew Bible*. Atlanta, GA: Society of Biblical Literature.

Henkel, Nikolaus. 1976. *Studien zum Physiologus im Mittelalter*. Tübingen: Niemeyer.

Hennig, Willi, 1966. *Phylogenetic Systematics*, translated by D. Dwight Davis and Rainer Zanger. Urbana: University of Illinois Press [repr. 2000].

Henrici, Emil. 1891–1893. *Hartmann von Aue: Iwein, der Ritter mit dem Löwen*. 2 vols. Halle an der Saale: Buchhandlung des Waisenhauses.

Hering, Wolfgang. 1967. "Zweispaltige Stemmata". *Philologus* 111 (1–2): 170–185.

Herren, Michael W. 1999. "Literary and Glossarial Evidence for the Study of Classical Mythology in Ireland A.D. 600–800". In *Text and Gloss: Studies in Insular Learning and Literature Presented to Joseph Donovan Pheifer*, edited by Helen Conrad-O'Briain, Anne Marie D'Arcy, and John Scattergood, 49–67. Dublin: Four Courts Press.

Həruya 'Ermyās. 2014. "The Gädlä Qäwsṭos: A Fourteenth-Century Ethiopian Saint (A New Text-Critical Edition, Translation and Commentary)". MA thesis, University of Hamburg.

Həruya 'Ermyās, ed. 2014–2015. *Gadla Qawsṭos 1207–1335 'ā/m gə'əzənnā 'amāraññā tərgum bamaggābe məśṭir*. Addis Abäba: 'Asattāmi 'Ǝtisā Dabra Ṣəlāləš 'Abuna Takla Haymānot Gadām.

Hilchenbach, Kai Peter, ed. 2009. *Das vierte Buch der Historien von Gregor von Tours: Edition mit sprachwissenschaftlich-textkritischem und historischem Kommentar*. Vol. 1. Berne: Lang.

Hinge, George. 2006. *Die Sprache Alkmans*. Wiesbaden: Reichert.

Hirsch, Eric Donald. 1967. *Validity in Interpretation*. New Haven, CT: Yale University Press.

Hirt, Hermann. 1905–1907. *Die Indogermanen: Ihre Verbreitung, ihre Urheimat und ihre Kultur*. 2 vols. Strassburg: Trübner.

Hoelzer, Guy A., and Don J. Melnick. 1994. "Patterns of Speciation and Limits to Phylogenetic Resolution". *Trends in Ecology and Evolution* 9 (3): 104–107. doi.org/10.1016/0169-5347(94)90207-0.

Hoenen, Armin. 2015a. "Das Artifizielle Manuskriptkorpus TASCFE". In *DHd 2015: Von Daten zu Erkenntnissen: 23. bis 27. Februar 2015; Book of Abstracts*, 302–309. dhd2015.uni-graz.at/de/nachlese/book-of-abstracts.

Hoenen, Armin. 2015b. "Lachmannian Archetype Reconstruction for Ancient Manuscript Corpora". In *Proceedings of the 2015 Conference of the North American Chapter of the Association for Computational Linguistics: Human Language Technologies*, 1209–1214. doi.org/10.3115/v1/N15-1127.

Hoenen, Armin. 2016. "Silva Portentosissima – Computer-Assisted Reflections on Bifurcativity in Stemmas". In *Digital Humanities 2016: Conference Abstracts*, 557–560. dh2016.adho.org/abstracts/311.

Hoenen, Armin. 2018a. "From Manuscripts to Archetypes through Iterative Clustering". In *Proceedings of the Eleventh International Conference on Language Resources and Evaluation (LREC 2018)*, edited by European Language Resources Association, 712–718. aclweb.org/anthology/L18-1114.

Hoenen, Armin. 2018b. "Multi Modal Distance: An Approach to Stemma Generation with Weighting". In *Proceedings of the Eleventh International Conference on Language Resources and Evaluation (LREC 2018)*, edited by European Language Resources Association, 2105–2112. aclweb.org/anthology/L18-1332.

Hoenen, Armin. 2019a. "An open problem in computational stemmatology – a model for contamination". In *Umanistica Digitale*, 5: 35–57. umanisticadigitale.unibo.it/article/view/8555.

Hoenen, Armin. 2019. "Rooting through Direction – New and Old Approaches". In *DHd 2019: Digital Humanities; Multimedial & Multimodal: Konferenzabstracts*, edited by Patrick Sahle. zenodo.org/record/2596095#.XQICqXWg-vo.

Hoenen, Armin, and Gerrit Brüning. 2019. "Überlegungen zur Stemmatologie neuerer Überlieferungen". In *DARIAH-DE Working Papers 29*, edited by Mirjam Blümm, Thomas Kollatz, Stefan Schmunk, and Christof Schöch. urn:nbn:de:gbv:7-dariah-2019-1-3.

Hoenen, Armin, Steffen Eger, and Ralf Gehrke. 2017. "How Many Stemmata with Root Degree k?". In *Proceedings of the 15th Meeting on the Mathematics of Language*, 11–21. aclweb.org/anthology/W17-3402.

Hofmann, Heinz. 2001. "SO Debate: Neo-Latin Studies; Significance and Prospects" [comments on Helander 2001]. *Symbolae Osloenses* 76: 51–58.

Hoffmann-Erbrecht, Lothar. 1976. "Problems in the Interdependence of Josquin Sources". In *Josquin des Prez: Proceedings of the International Josquin Festival-Conference Held at the Juilliard School at Lincoln Center in New York City, 21–25 June 1971*, edited by Edward E. Lowinsky und Bonnie J. Blackburn, 285–293. Oxford: Oxford University Press.

Holland, Barbara R., Katharina T. Huber, Vincent Moulton, and Peter J. Lockhart. 2004. "Using Consensus Networks to Visualize Contradictory Evidence for Species Phylogeny". *Molecular Biology and Evolution* 21: 1459–1461.

Holm, Gösta. 1972. "Carl Johan Schlyter and Textual Scholarship". *Saga och Sed* 28–80.

Holm, Tawny L. 2005. "Literature". In *A Companion to the Ancient Near East*, edited by Daniel Snell, 253–265. Malden, MA: Blackwell.

Holm-Olsen, Ludvig, ed. 1983. *Konungs skuggsiá*. 2nd ed. Oslo: Norsk Historisk Kjeldeskrift-Institutt. [1st ed. 1945]

Holmes, David. 1998. "The Evolution of Stylometry in Humanities Scholarship". *Literary and Linguistic Computing* 13: 111–117.

Holmes, Michael W. 2002. "The Case for Reasoned Eclecticism". In *Rethinking New Testament Textual Criticism*, edited by David Alan Black, 77–100. Grand Rapids, MI: Baker Academic.

Holmes, Michael W. 2011. "Working with an Open Textual Tradition: Challenges in Theory and Practice". In *The Textual History of the Greek New Testament: Changing Views in*

Contemporary Research, edited by Klaus Wachtel and Michael W. Holmes. 65–78. Atlanta, GA: Society of Biblical Literature.

Hoppe, Henricus, ed. 1939. *Tertullianus: Apologeticum secundum utramque libri recensionem*. Vienna: Tempsky.

Horovitz, H. Saul, ed. 1966. *Siphre d'be Rab*. 2nd ed. Jerusalem: Wahrmann.

Horovitz, H. Saul, and Israel Abraham Rabin, eds. 1960. *Mechilta d'Rabbi Ismael*. 2nd ed. Jerusalem: Wahrmann.

Horrocks, Geoffrey. 2014. *Greek: A History of the Language and Its Speakers*. 2nd ed. Malden, MA: Wiley Blackwell [1st ed. London: Longman, 1997].

Hortschansky, Klaus. 1981. "Notationsgewohnheiten in den burgundischen Chansonniers des 15. Jahrhunderts". In *Quellenstudien zur Musik der Renaissance*, vol. 1, *Formen und Probleme der Überlieferung mehrstimmiger Musik im Zeitalter Josquin Desprez*, edited by Ludwig Finscher, 9–24. Munich: Kraus Int. Publications.

Howatson, Margaret C. 1989. *The Oxford Companion to Classical Literature*. 2nd ed. Oxford: Oxford University Press.

Howe, Christopher J., Adrian C. Barbrook, Matthew Spencer, Peter Robinson, Barbara Bordalejo, and Linne R. Mooney. 2001. "Manuscript Evolution". *Trends in Genetics* 17 (3): 147–152.

Howe, Christopher J., Ruth Connolly, and Heather F. Windram. 2012. "Responding to Criticism of Phylogenetic Methods in Stemmatology". *Studies in English Literature, 1500–1900* 52 (1): 51–67. jstor.org/stable/41349051.

Howe, Christopher J., and Heather F. Windram. 2011. "Phylomemetics – Evolutionary Analysis beyond the Gene". *PLoS Biology* 9 (5): e1001069. doi.org/10.1371/journal.pbio.1001069.

Howe, Kevin, Alex Bateman, and Richard Durbin. 2002. "QuickTree: Building Huge Neighbour-Joining Trees of Protein Sequences". *Bioinformatics* 18 (11): 1546–1547. doi.org/10.1093/bioinformatics/18.11.1546.

Hu Pu'an 胡樸安. 1931. *Jiaochouxue* 校讎学. Shanghai: Shangwu.

Hudson, Barton, ed. 1988. *Missa O lumen ecclesie, Missa Petrus Apostolus, Jacob Obrecht*. Utrecht: Koninklijke Vereniging voor Nederlandse Muziekgeschiedenis.

Huelsenbeck, John P., and Fredrik Ronquist. 2001. "MRBAYES: Bayesian Inference of Phylogenetic Trees". *Bioinformatics* 17 (18): 754–755. doi.org/10.1093/bioinformatics/17.8.754.

Hug, Johann Leonhard. 1810. *De antiquitate codicis Vaticani commentatio*. Freiburg im Breisgau: Typis Herderianis.

Hughes, David. 1969. "Further Notes on the Grouping of Aquitanian Tropes". *Journal of the American Musicological Society* 19: 3–12.

Huitfeldt, Claus. 1995. "Multi-Dimensional Texts in a One-Dimensional Medium". *Computers and the Humanities* 28 (4–5): 235–241.

Hummel, Susanne. 2015. "Searching for the Appropriate Editorial Technique: The Case of Gädlä Śärṣä P̣eṭros". *Aethiopica* 18: 128–144.

Hummel, Susanne. 2016. "The Disputed Life of the Saintly Ethiopian kings 'Abrəhā and 'Aṣbəḥa". *Scrinium: Journal of Patrology and Critical Hagiography* 12: 35–72.

Hunger, Herbert, Otto Stegmüller, Harmut Erbse, Max Imhof, Karl Büchner, Hans-Georg Beck, and Horst Rüdiger. 1961–1964. *Geschichte der Textüberlieferung der antiken und mittelalterlichen Literatur*. 2 vols. Zurich: Atlantis-Verlag.

Hurtado, Larry W. 1981. *Text-Critical Methodology and the Pre-Caesarean Text: Codex W in the Gospel of Mark*. Grand Rapids, MI: Eerdmans.

Husing, Georg. 1989. "Is Little Red Riding Hood a Myth?". In *Little Red Riding Hood: A Casebook*, edited by Dundes Alan, 64–71. Madison: University of Wisconsin Press.

Huson, Daniel H. 1998. "SplitsTree: Analyzing and Visualizing Evolutionary Data". *Bioinformatics* 14 (1): 68–73. doi.org/10.1093/bioinformatics/14.1.68.

Huson, Daniel. H., and David Bryant. 2006. "Application of Phylogenetic Networks in Evolutionary Studies". *Molecular Biology and Evolution* 23 (2): 254–267.

Huson, Daniel H., and Tobias Klöpper. 2007. "Beyond Galled Trees – Decomposition and Computation of Galled Networks". In *Annual International Conference on Research in Computational Molecular Biology (RECOMB 2007)*, 211–225. Berlin: Springer. doi.org/10.1007/978-3-540-71681-5_15.

Huson, Daniel H., Tobias Klöpper, Pete J. Lockhart, and Mike Steel. 2005. "Reconstruction of Reticulate Networks from Gene Trees". In *RECOMB 2005: Research in Computational Molecular Biology*, edited by Satoru Miyano, Jill Mesirov, Simon Kasif, Sorin Istrail, Pavel Pevzner, and Michael Waterman, 233–249. Heidelberg: Springer.

Huson, Daniel H., and Celine Scornavacca. 2012. "Dendroscope 3: An Interactive Tool for Rooted Phylogenetic Trees and Networks". *Systematic Biology* 61 (6): 1061–1067.

Hussein Ahmad. 2008. "Arabic Philology as a Source of Islamic History in Ethiopia". *Bulletin of Philological Society of Ethiopia (Addis Ababa University, Department of Linguistics)* 1 (1): 56–59.

Huygens, Robert B. C. 2000. *Ars Edendi: A Practical Introduction to Editing Medieval Latin Texts*. Turnhout: Brepols.

International Greek NT Project. 1984–1987. *The New Testament in Greek: The Gospel according to St. Luke*. 2 vols. Oxford: Clarendon Press.

Irigoin, Jean. 1952. *Histoire du texte de Pindare*. Paris: Klincksieck.

Irigoin, Jean. 1954. "Stemmas bifides et états de manuscrits". *Revue de philologie, de littérature et d'histoire anciennes*, 3rd ser., 28: 211–223 [repr. Irigoin 2003, 67–77].

Irigoin, Jean. 1968–1969. "Conférences (résumé)". *Annuaire de l'EPHE, IVe section*: 137–145.

Irigoin, Jean. 1977. "Quelques réflexions sur le concept d'archétype". *Revue d'histoire des textes* 7: 235–245 [repr. Irigoin 2003, 37–53].

Irigoin, Jean. 1981. "La Critique des textes doit être historique". In *La critica testuale greco-latina, oggi: Metodi e problemi*, edited by Enrico Flores, 27–43. Rome: Edizioni dell'Ateneo [repr. Irigoin 2003, 19–36].

Irigoin, Jean. 2000. "Deux servantes maîtresses en alternance: Paléographie et philologie". In *I manoscritti greci tra riflessione e dibattito: Atti del V Colloquio Internazionale di Paleografia Greca (Cremona, 4–10 ottobre 1998)*, edited by Giancarlo Prato, 589–600. Florence: Gonnelli.

Irigoin, Jean. 2003. *La Tradition des textes grecs: Pour une critique historique*. Paris: Les Belles Lettres.

Isaac, Daniel, ed. 1977. *Proclus: Trois études sur la providence*. Vol. 1. *Dix problèmes concernant la providence*. Collection des Universités de France. Paris: Les Belles Lettres.

Italia, Paola, and Giulia Raboni. 2010. *Che cos'è la filologia d'autore*. Rome: Carocci.

Itzkowitz, Joel B. 1986. *Prolegomena to a New Text of Lucian's Vitarum Auctio and Piscator*. Hildesheim: Olms.

Itzkowitz, Joel B., ed. 1992. *Luciani Vitarum Auctio et Piscator*. Stuttgart: Teubner.

Jammy, Petrus, ed. 1644–1651. *Albertus Magnus: Opera*. Lyon: sumptibus Claudii Prost, Petri & Claudii Rigaud, Hieronymi Delagarde, Ioannis Antonii Huguetan.

Jeauneau, Edouard, ed. 1996–2003. *Iohannes Scottus Eriugena: Periphyseon*. 5 vols. Turnhout: Brepols.

Jeauneau, Edouard, and Paul Edward Dutton. 1996. *The Autograph of Eriugena*. Turnhout: Brepols.

Jeffreys, Elizabeth 2012. "Tapestries of Quotation: The Challenges of Editing Byzantine Texts". In *Ars Edendi Lecture Series*, vol. 2, edited by Alessandra Bucossi and Erika Kihlman, 35–61. Stockholm: Stockholm University Library.

Jeffreys, Elizabeth, and Michael Jeffreys, eds. 2009. *Iacobus monachus: Epistulae*. Turnhout: Brepols.

Jenset, Gard Buen, and Barbara McGillivray. 2017. *Quantitative Historical Linguistics: A Corpus Framework*. Oxford: Oxford University Press.

Johnson, William A. 2010. *Readers and Reading Culture in the High Roman Empire: A Study of Elite Communities*. Oxford: Oxford University Press.

Johnson, William, and Holt Parker, eds. 2009. *Ancient Literacies: The Culture of Reading in Greece and Rome*. Oxford: University Press.

Jones, Steven E. 2016. *Roberto Busa, S.J., and the Emergence of Humanities Computing: The Priest and the Punched Cards*. New York, NY: Routledge.

Jordan, Peter, and Stephen Shennan. 2003. "Cultural Transmission, Language, and Basketry Traditions amongst the Californian Indians". *Journal of Anthropological Archaeology* 22: 42–74.

Josquin, Desprez. 1987–2016. *Josquin Des Prez: New Edition of the Collected Works*. 30 vols. Utrecht: Koninklijke Vereniging voor Nederlandse Muziekgeschiedenis.

Jost, Garry. 2015. "The Textual Criticism of Ethiopic Obadiah: Identification of Five Forms of the Text". In *Essays in Ethiopian Manuscript Studies: Proceedings of the International Conference Manuscripts and Texts, Languages and Contexts; The Transmission of Knowledge in the Horn of Africa, Hamburg, 17–19 July 2014*, edited by Alessandro Bausi, Alessandro Gori, Denis Nosnitsin, and Eugenia Sokolinski, 161–179. Wiesbaden: Harrassowitz.

Joyce, James. 1984. *Ulysses: A Critical and Synoptic Edition*. Edited by Hans Walter Gabler, Wolfhard Steppe, and Claus Melchior. New York, NY: Garland.

Jukes, Thomas H., and Charles R. Cantor. 1969. "Evolution of Protein Molecules". In *Mammalian Protein Metabolism*, vol. 3, edited by Hamish M. Munro, vol. 3, 21–132. New York, NY: Academic Press.

Juola, Patrick. 2013. "How a Computer Program Helped Show J. K. Rowling Write A Cuckoo's Calling: Author of the Harry Potter Books Has a Distinct Linguistic Signature". *Scientific American*, August 20. scientificamerican.com/article/how-a-computer-program-helped-show-jk-rowling-write-a-cuckoos-calling.

Just, Martin. 1981. "Bemerkungen zu den kleinen Folio-Handschriften deutscher Provenienz um 1500". In *Quellenstudien zur Musik der Renaissance*, vol. 1, *Formen und Probleme der Überlieferung mehrstimmiger Musik im Zeitalter Josquin Desprez*, edited by Ludwig Finscher, 25–43. Munich: Kraus Int. Publications.

Just, Martin. 1983. "Zur Examinatio von Varianten". In *Quellenstudien zur Musik der Renaissance*, vol. 2, *Datierung und Filiation von Musikhandschriften der Josquin-Zeit*, edited by Ludwig Finscher, 129–152. Wiesbaden: Harrassowitz.

Just, Martin. 1991a. "Zur Frage der Autorschaft in den Josquin des Prez zugeschriebenen Werken: Ein Überblick". In *Opera incerta: Echtheitsfragen als Problem musikwissenschaftlicher Gesamtausgaben, Kolloquium Mainz 1988*, edited by Hanspeter Bennwitz, Gabriele Buschmeier, Georg Feder, Klaus Hofmann, and Wolfgang Plath, 301–314. Suttgart: Steiner.

Just, Martin, ed. 1991b. *Der Kodex Berlin 40021: Staatsbibliothek Preußischer Kulturbesitz Berlin Mus. ms. 40021*. 4 vols. Kassel: Bärenreiter.

Kahana, Menachem I., ed. 2011–2015. *Sifre on Numbers: An Annotated Edition*. 5 vols. Jerusalem: Magnes Press.

Kålund, Kristian, ed. 1883. *Fljótsdœla hin meiri; eller, Den længere Droplaugarsona-saga* [*Fljótsdœla saga*]. Copenhagen: Møller.

Kålund, Kristian, ed. 1889–1891. *Laxdœla saga*. Copenhagen: Møller.

Kantorowicz, Hermann. 1921. *Einführung in die Textkritik: Systematische Darstellung der textkritischen Grundsätze für Philologen und Juristen; Mit 3 Stammtafeln*. Leipzig: Dieterich.

Karlsson, Lina, and Linda Malm. 2004. "Revolution or Remediation? A Study of Electronic Scholarly Editions on the Web". *HUMAN IT* 7 (1): 1–46.

Karp, Theodore. 1964. "The Trouvère MS Tradition". In *The Twenty-Fifth Anniversary Festschrift (1937–1962): Queens College of the City University of New York Department of Music*, edited by Albert Mell, 25–52. New York, NY: Queens College.

Katre, Sumitra, M. 1954. *Introduction to Indian Textual Criticism*. 2nd ed. Pune: Deccan College.
Keil, Bruno. 1913. "Über Lukians Phalarideen". *Hermes* 48: 494–521.
Keller, Otto. 1879. *Epilegomena zu Horaz*. Leipzig: Teubner.
Kenney, Edward J. 1974. *The Classical Text: Aspects of Editing in the Age of the Printed Book*. Berkeley: University of California Press.
Ker, Neil Ripley. 1972. "Eton College MS 44 and Its Exemplar". In *Varia codicologica: Essays Presented to Gerard I. Lieftinck*, edited by Peter J. Gumbert and Max J. M. de Haan, 77–89. Amsterdam: Gendt.
Ker, Neil Ripley. 1979. "Copying an Exemplar: Two Manuscripts of Jerome on Habbakuk". In *Miscellanea codicologica F. Masai dicata*, edited by Pierre Cockshaw, Monique-Cécile Garand, and Pierre Jodogne, 203–210. Gand: Story-Scientia.
Kern, Martin. 2002. "Methodological Reflections on the Analysis of Textual Variants and the Modes of Manuscript Production in Early China". *Journal of East Asian Archaeology* 4: 143–181.
Kern, Martin. 2010. "Early Chinese Literature: Beginnings through Western Han". In *The Cambridge History of Chinese Literature*, vol. 1, *To 1375*, edited by Stephen Owen, 1–115. Cambridge: Cambridge University Press.
Kerstens, Johan, Eddy Ruys, and Joost Zwarts. 1996. "Labeled Bracketing". In *Lexicon of Linguistics*. www2.let.uu.nl/UiL-OTS/Lexicon/zoek.pl?lemma=Labeled+bracketing&lemmacode=577.
Kestemont, Mike, Vincent Christlein, and Dominique Stutzmann. 2017. "Artificial Paleography: Computational Approaches to Identifying Script Types in Medieval Manuscripts". *Speculum* 92: 86–109. doi.org/10.1086/694112.
Keyser, Rudolf, and Carl Richard Unger, eds. 1851. *Barlaams ok Josaphats saga*. Christiania: Feilberg og Landmark.
Kiening, Christian. 2016. *Die Altdeutsche Textbibliothek (ATB): Materialien zur Geschichte der Reihe*. Berlin: De Gruyter.
Kiernan, Kevin. 1996. *Beowulf and the Beowulf Manuscript*. Rev. ed. Ann Arbor: University of Michigan Press.
Kihlman, Erika. 2006. *Expositiones sequentiarum: Medieval Sequence Commentaries and Prologues*. Stockholm: Stockholm University.
Kimura, Motoo. 1980. "A Simple Method for Estimating Evolutionary Rates of Base Substitutions through Comparative Studies of Nucleotide Sequences". *Journal of Molecular Evolution* 16 (2): 111–120. doi.org/10.1007/BF01731581.
King, Stephen. 2009. "Raymond Carver's Life and Stories". *The New York Times*, November 19, "Sunday Book Review". nytimes.com/2009/11/22/books/review/King-t.html?pagewanted=all.
Kingman, John F. C. 1982. "On the Genealogy of Large Populations". *Journal of Applied Probability* 19: 27–43. doi.org/10.2307/3213548.
Kirsch, Winfried. 1981. "Unterterz- und Leittonklauseln als quellentypische Varianten". In *Quellenstudien zur Musik der Renaissance*, vol. 1, *Formen und Probleme der Überlieferung mehrstimmiger Musik im Zeitalter Josquin Desprez*, edited by Ludwig Finscher, 167–178. Munich: Kraus Int. Publications.
Klaeber, Friedrich, ed. 1922. *Beowulf and the Fight at Finnsburg*. London: Heath.
Klapisch-Zuber, Christiane. 2007. "The Tree". In *Finding Europe: Discourses on Margins, Communities, Images ca. 13th–ca. 18th Centuries*, edited by Anthony Molho and Diogo R. Curto, 293–314. New York, NY: Berghahn.
Kleine und fragmentarische Historiker der Spätantike. 2016–. Paderborn: Schöningh.
Kleinhenz, Christopher, ed. 1976. *Medieval Manuscripts and Textual Criticism*. Chapel Hill: University of North Carolina Department of Romance Languages.

Kleinlogel, Alexander. 1968. "Das Stemmaproblem". *Zeitschrift für antike Literatur und ihre Rezeption* 112 (1–2): 63–82.
Kleinlogel, Alexander. 1979. "Archetypus und Stemma: Zur Problematik prognostisch-retrodiktiver Methoden der Textkritik". *Berichte zur Wissenschaftsgeschichte* 2 (1–2): 53–64. doi.org/10.1002/bewi.19790020108.
Klemm, Elisabeth. 1998. *Die illuminierten Handschriften des 13. Jahrhunderts deutscher Herkunft in der Bayerischen Staatsbibliothek, Text- und Tafelband*. Wiesbaden: Reichert.
Kline, Mary-Jo. 1998. *A Guide to Documentary Editing*. 2nd ed. Baltimore, MD: Johns Hopkins University Press.
Klopsch, Paul. 2003. "Die Überlieferung der lateinischen Literatur im Mittelalter". In *Einführung in die Überlieferungsgeschichte und die Textkritik der antiken Literatur*, edited by Egert Pöhlmann, vol. 2, *Mittelalter und Neuzeit*, 47–95. Darmstadt: Wissenschaftliche Buchgesellschaft.
Knibb, Michael A. 2014. "Reflections on an Edition of Ethiopic Ezekiel: Agenda for the Future". In *Linguistic, Oriental and Ethiopian Studies in Memory of Paolo Marrassini*, edited by Alessandro Bausi, Alessandro Gori, and Gianfrancesco Lusini, 503–509. Wiesbaden: Harrassowitz.
Knibb, Michael A., ed. 2015. *The Ethiopic Text of the Book of Ezekiel: A Critical Edition*. Oxford: Oxford University Press.
Knibb, Michael A. 2017. "Textual Commentary on the Ethiopic Text of Ezekiel 1–11". *Aethiopica* 20: 7–49.
Knibb, Michael A., and Edward Ullendorff, eds. 1978. *The Ethiopic Book of Enoch: A New Edition in the Light of the Aramaic Dead Sea Fragments*. 2 vols. Oxford: Clarendon Press.
König, Jason, Katerina Oikonomopoulou, and Greg Woolf. 2013. *Ancient Libraries*. Cambridge: Cambridge University Press.
Koppel, Moshe, Moty Michaely, and Alex Tal. 2016. "Reconstructing Ancient Literary Texts from Noisy Manuscripts". In *Proceedings of the Fifth Workshop on Computational Linguistics for Literature, NAACL–HLT 2016*, edited by Anna Feldman Anna Kazantseva, and Stan Szpakowicz, 40–46. San Diego: Association for Computational Linguistics. doi.org/10.18653/v1/W16-0205.
Kortlandt, Frederik. 1990. "The Spread of the Indo-Europeans". *Journal of Indo-European Studies* 18: 131–140.
Kortlandt, Frederik. 1995. "General Lnguistics and Indo-European Reconstruction". *Rask* 2: 91–109.
Krämer, Sigrid. 2007. *Latin Manuscript Books before 1600: A List of the Printed Catalogues and Unpublished Inventories of Extant Collections*. With Birgit Christine Arensmann. Hannover: Hahn.
Kristeller, Paul Oskar, ed. 1960–2003. *Catalogus translationum et commentariorum: Mediaeval and Renaissance Latin Translations and Commentaries; Annotated Lists and Guides*. Vols 1–9. Washington, DC: Catholic University of America.
Kristeller, Paul Oskar, and Sigrid Krämer. 1993. *Latin Manuscript Books before 1600: A List of the Printed Cataogues and Unpublished Inventories of Extant Collections*. 4th ed. by Sigrid Krämer. Munich: Monumenta Germaniae historica.
Kropp, Manfred. 1985. "La Réédition des chroniques éthiopiennes: Perspectives et premiers résultats". *Abbay* 12: 49–72.
Kropp, Manfred. 1988a. "The Sərʿatä gəbr: A Mirror View of Daily Life at the Ethiopian Royal Court in the Middle Ages". *Northeast African Studies* 10 (2–3): 51–87.
Kropp, Manfred, ed. 1988b. *Die Geschichte des Lebna-Dengel, Claudius und Mināi*. 2 vols. Leuven: Peeters.
Kropp, Manfred. 1989. *Die äthiopischen Königschroniken in der Sammlung des Däǧǧazmač Ḥaylu: Entstehung und handschriftliche Überlieferung des Werks*. Frankfurt am Main: Lang.

Kropp, Manfred. 1994. *Der siegreiche Feldzug des Königs ʿĀmda-Ṣeyon gegen die Muslime in Adal im Jahre 1332 n. Chr.* 2 vols. Leuven: Peeters.

Kropp, Manfred. 2011. "Notes on Preparing a Critical Edition of the Śərʿatä mängəśt". *Northeast African Studies* 11 (2): 111–140.

Kropp, Manfred. 2015a. Review of *La Vita e i Miracoli di Libānos*, by Alessandro Bausi. *Oriens Christianus* 97: 242–245.

Kropp, Manfred. 2015b. Review of *Tradizioni orientali del "Martirio di Areta": La Prima recensione araba e la Versione etiopica*, edited and translated by Alessandro Bausi and Alessandro Gori. *Oriens Christianus* 97: 245–249.

Kropp, Manfred, ed. 2016. *Zekra Nagar: Die universalhistorische Einleitung nach Giyorgis Walda-Amid in der Chronikensammlung des Haylu*. Speyer: Brodersen.

Kroymann, Emil, ed. 1906. *Tertullianus: Opera; Pars tertia*. Vienna: Tempsky.

Krzyżanowska, Magdalena. 2015. "The Gädlä Kiros in Ethiopian Religious Practices: A Study of Eighteen Manuscripts from Eastern Təgray". In *Veneration of Saints in Christian Ethiopia: Proceedings of the International Workshop Saints in Christian Ethiopia; Literary Sources and Veneration, Hamburg, April 28–29, 2012*, edited by Denis Nosnitsin, 95–136. Wiesbaden: Harrassowitz.

Kuhn, Thomas. 1962. *The Structure of Scientific Revolutions*. Chicago, IL: University of Chicago Press [50th anniversary edn. Chicago, IL: University of Chicago Press, 2012].

Kwakkel, Erik. 2018. *Books before Print: Medieval Manuscript Culture*. Kalamazoo, MI: Arc Humanities Press.

Kwakkel, Erik, and Rodney Thomson. 2018. *The European Book in the Twelfth Century*. Cambridge: Cambridge University Press.

La Spisa, Paolo. 2012. "Perspectives ecdotiques pour textes en moyen arabe: L'Exemple des traités théologiques de Sulaymān al-Ġazzī'". In *Middle Arabic and Mixed Arabic: Diachrony and Synchrony*, edited by Liesbeth Zack and Arie Schippers, 187–208. Leiden: Brill.

La Spisa, Paolo. 2015. "Middle Arabic Texts: How to Account for Linguistic Features".
In *Comparative Oriental Manuscript Studies: An Introduction*, by Alessandro Bausi, Pier Giorgio Borbone, Françoise Briquel Chatonnet, Paola Buzi, Jost Gippert, Caroline Macé, Marilena Maniaci, Zisis Melissakis, Laura E. Parodi, and Witold Witakowski, 415–418. Hamburg: Tredition.

Lai, Po-Hsiang, Teemu Roos, and Joseph O'Sullivan. 2010. "MDL Hierarchical Clustering for Stemmatology". In *2010 IEEE International Symposium on Information Theory*, 1403–1407. Austin, TX: IEEE. doi.org/10.1109/ISIT.2010.5513627.

Lachmann, Karl, ed. 1820. *Auswahl aus den Hochdeutschen Dichtern des dreizehnten Jahrhunderts: Für Vorlesungen und zum Schulgebrauch*. Berlin: Reimer.

Lachmann, Karl, ed. 1831. *Novum Testamentum Graece*. Berlin: Reimer.

Lachmann, Karl, ed. 1841. *Der Nibelunge Noth und die Klage: Nach der ältesten Überlieferung mit Bezeichnung des Unechten und mit den Abweichungen der gemeinen Lesart*. 2nd ed. Berlin: Reimer [repr. Berlin: De Gruyter, 1960].

Lachmann, Karl, ed. 1842–1850. *Novum Testamentum Graece et Latine, Carolus Lachmannus recensuit, Philippus Buttmannus Graecae lectionis auctoritates apposuit*. 2 vols. Berlin: Reimer.

Lachmann, Karl, ed. 1850. *T. Lucreti Cari De rerum natura libri sex*. 2 vols. Berlin: impensis G. Reimeri.

Lachmann, Karl. 1876. *Kleinere Schriften*. 2 vols. Edited by Karl Müllenhoff (vol. 1) and Johannes Vahlen (vol. 2). Berlin: Reimer [repr. Berlin: De Gruyter, 1969].

Lafleur, Didier. 2013. *La Famille 13 dans l'évangile de Marc*. Leiden: Brill.

Lakoff, George, and Mark Johnson. 1980. *Metaphors We Live By*. Chicago, IL: University of Chicago Press.

Lantin, Anne-Catherine, Philippe V. Baret, and Caroline Macé. 2004. "Phylogenetic Analysis of Gregory of Nazianzus' Homily 27". In *Le Poids des mots: Actes des 7es journées internationales d'analyse statistique des données textuelles*, edited by Gérald Purnelle, Cédrick Fairon, and Anne Dister, vol. 2, 700–707. Louvain-la-Neuve: Presses universitaires de Louvain.

Lauterbach, Jacob, ed. and trans. 1933–1935. *Mekilta de-Rabbi Ishmael*. 3 vols. Philadelphia, PA: Jewish Publication Society of America.

Lavagnino, John. 2009. "Access". *Literary and Linguistic Computing* 24: 63–76, doi.org/10.1093/llc/fqn038.

Lavagnino, John, and Dominik Wujastyk. 1996. *Critical Edition Typesetting: The EDMAC Format for Plain TEX*. Birmingham: TEX Users Group, the UK TEX Users Group.

Le Clerc, Jean. 1730. *Ars critica*. 5th ed. Amsterdam: Janssonio-Waesbergii [1st ed. 1697].

Le Pouliquen, Marc. 2010. "Filiation de manuscrits sanskrits et arbres phylogénétiques". *Mathématiques et sciences humaines/Mathematics and Social Sciences* 192 (4): 57–91. doi.org/10.4000/msh.11919.

Lecoy, Félix. 1978. "L'Edition critique des textes". In *Atti del xiv Congresso Internazionale di Linguistica e Filologia Romanza (Napoli, 15–20 aprile 1974)*, edited by Alberto Várvaro, vol. 1, 501–508. Naples: Macchiaroli.

Lee, Arthur R. 1989. "Numerical Taxonomy Revisited: John Griffith, Cladistic Analysis and St. Augustine's Quaestiones in Heptateuchum". In *Studia Patristica: Vol. XX – Critica, Classica, Orientalia, Ascetica, Liturgica*, edited by Elizabeth A. Livingstone, 24–32. Leuven: Peeters.

Legg, Stanley Charles Edmund. 1935. *Novum Testamentum Graecum: Euangelium secundum Marcum*. Oxford: Clarendon Press

Legg, Stanley Charles Edmund. 1940. *Euangelium secundum Matthaeum*. Oxford: Clarendon Press.

Leibniz, Gottfried W. 1710. "Brevis designatio mediationum de originibus gentium, ductis potissimum ex indicio linguarum". *Miscellanea Berolinensia* 1: 1–16.

Leigh, Matthew. 2016. "Lucan's Caesar and Laelius". In *Wordplay and Powerplay in Latin Poetry*, edited by Phillip Mitsis and Johannis Ziogas, 259–272. Berlin: De Gruyter.

Lejay, Paul. 1888. Review of *La Critica del testo del de Officiis di Cicerone e delle poesie Pseudo-Vergiliane secondo due nuovi codici*, by Remigio Sabbadini. *Revue critique d'histoire et de littérature* 26: 281–283.

Lejay, Paul. 1899. Review of *De Heroidum Ouidii Codice Planudeo*, edited by Alfredus Gudeman. *Revue critique d'histoire et de littérature* 23 (1) [= n.s., 27]: 143–144.

Lejay, Paul. 1903. Review of *Aeli Donati quod fertur Commentum Terenti*, edited by Paulus Wessner. *Revue critique d'histoire et de littérature* 38 (2) [= n.s., 56]: 168–172.

Lemaire, Jacques. 1989. *Introduction à la codicologie*. Louvain-la-Neuve: Université catholique de Louvain.

Lemey, Philippe, Andrew Rambaut, Alexei J. Drummond, and Marc A. Suchard. 2009. "Bayesian Phylogeography Finds Its Roots". *PLoS Computational Biology* 5 (9): e1000520. doi.org/10.1371/journal.pcbi.1000520.

Lemey, Philippe, Marco Salemi, and Anne-Mieke Vandamme. 2009. *The Phylogenetic Handbook: A Practical Approach to Phylogenetic Analysis and Hypothesis Testing*. 2nd ed. Cambridge: Cambridge University Press.

Lentz, August. 1870. *Grammatici graeci*. Vol. 3.2. Leipzig: Teubner.

Leo, Fridericus. 1881. *Venanti Honori Clementiani Fortunati presbyteri Italici opera poetica recensuit et emendavit Fridericus Leo*. Berlin: apud Weidmannos.

Leonardi, Claudio, ed. 1994. *La critica del testo mediolatino: Atti del Convegno (Firenze 6–8 dicembre 1990)*. Spoleto: CISAM.

Leonardi, Lino. 2003. "Le Texte critique de la *Mort le roi Artu*: Question ouverte". *Romania* 121: 133–163.

Leonardi, Lino. 2009a. "L'Art d'éditer les anciens textes (1872–1928): Les Stratégies d'un débat aux origines de la philologie romane". *Romania* 127: 273–302.

Leonardi, Lino. 2009b. Review of *Essays on the Lancelot of Yale 229* and *La Mort le Roi Artu (The Death of Arthur) from the Old French Lancelot of Yale 229*, edited by Elizabeth Moore Willingham. *Medioevo romanzo* 33: 437–440.

Leonardi, Lino. 2011. "Il testo come ipotesi (critica del manoscritto-base)". *Medioevo Romanzo* 35: 5–34.

Leonardi, Lino. 2014. "Filologia della ricezione: I copisti come attori della tradizione". *Medioevo Romanzo* 38: 5–27.

Leonardi, Lino. 2015. Review of *Everything You Always Wanted to Know about Lachmann's Method*, by Paolo Trovato. *Medioevo romanzo* 39: 194–196.

Leonardi, Lino. 2017. "Romance Philology between Anachronism and Historical Truth: On Editing Medieval Vernacular Texts". In *Philology Matters! Essays on the Art of Reading Slowly*, edited by Harry Lönnroth, 97–117. Leiden: Brill.

Lesky, Albin. 1971. *Geschichte der griechischen Literatur*. 3rd ed. Berne: Francke.

Lesky, Albin. 1996. *A History of Greek Literature*. Translated by Cornelis de Heer and James Willis. London: Duckworth and Hackett [trans. of Lesky 1971].

Levi dalla Vida, Giorgio. 1960. "Andrea Alpago". In *Dizionario Biografico degli Italiani*, vol. 2. Rome: Istituto della Enciclopedia Italiana. treccani.it/enciclopedia/andrea-alpago_ (Dizionario-Biografico).

Levy, Kenneth. 2003. "Gregorian Chant and the Romans". *Journal of the American Musicological Society* 56: 5–41.

Lewis, Charlton, and Charles Short. 1879. *A Latin Dictionary*. Oxford: Clarendon Press.

Lewis, Paul O. 2001. "Phylogenetic Systematics Turns Over a New Leaf". *Trends in Ecology and Evolution* 16: 30–37.

Lianbin Dai. 2016. "From Philology to Philosophy: Zhu Xi as a Reader-Annotator". In *Canonical Texts and Scholarly Practices: A Global Comparative Approach*, edited by Anthony Grafton and Glenn W. Most, 136–163. Cambridge: Cambridge University Press.

Libri, Gugliemo, and Félix Ravaisson, eds. 1849–. *Catalogue général des manuscrits des bibliothèques publiques des départements, publié sous les auspices du ministre de l'Instruction publique*. Paris: Imprimerie Nationale.

Lieberman, Saul. 1935–1936. Review of *Mekilta de-Rabbi Ishmael*, edited and translated by Jacob Lauterbach. *Kiryat Sefer* 12: 54–65.

Lieberman, Saul. 1937–1938. Review of *Siphre ad Deuteronomium*, edited by Louis Finkelstein. *Kiryat Sefer* 14: 323–336.

Lieberman, Saul, ed. 1955–1988. *Tosefta*. 5 vols. New York, NY: Jewish Theological Seminary.

Lima, Manuel. 2011. *Visual Complexity: Mapping Patterns of Information*. Princeton, NJ: Architectural Press.

Lima, Manuel. 2014. *The Book of Trees: Visualizing Branches of Knowledge*. Princeton, NJ: Architectural Press.

Lin, Yii-Jan. 2016. *The Erotic Life of Manuscripts: New Testament Textual Criticism and the Biological Sciences*. New York, NY: Oxford University Press.

Lindsay, William. 1914. "The New Palaeography". *Classical Review* 28: 209–210.

Little, Lester K. 2007. "Life and Afterlife of the First Plague Pandemic". In *Plague and the End of Antiquity: The Pandemic of 541–750*, edited by Lester K. Little, 3–32. Cambridge: Cambridge University Press.

Littré, Emile. 1839–1861, ed. and trans. *Œuvres complètes d'Hippocrate, traduction nouvelle avec le texte grec en regard, collationné sur les manuscrits et toutes les éditions, accompagnée*

d'une introduction, de commentaires médicaux, de variantes et de notes philologiques, suivie d'une table générale des matières. 10 vols. Paris: Baillière.
Longfellow, Henry W., trans. 1867. *The Divine Comedy of Dante Alighieri*. Boston, MA: Ticknor and Fields.
Lord, Albert B. 1960. *The Singer of Tales*. Cambridge, MA: Harvard University Press.
Lorentzen, Christian. 2015. "Gordon Lish, The Art of Editing No. 2". *Paris Review* 215 (winter). theparisreview.org/interviews/6423/gordon-lish-the-art-of-editing-no-2-gordon-lish.
Lorenz, Chris. 2002. "Heuristik". In *Lexikon Geschichtswissenschaft: Hundert Grundbegriffe*, edited by Stefan Jordan, 139–141. Stuttgart: Reclam.
Louis-Jensen, Jonna, and Odd Einar Haugen. In press. "Udgivelse af den vestnordiske middelalderlitteratur: Perioden fra 1936". In *Dansk editionshistorie*, vol. 2, *Udgivelse af vestnordisk og dansk middelalderlitteratur*, edited by Britta Olrik Frederiksen. Copenhagen: Museum Tusculanum Press.
Love, Harold. 2004. "The Work in Transmission and Its Recovery". *Shakespeare Studies* 32: 73–80.
Lowe, Elias Avery, ed. 1934–1971. *Codices Latini Antiquiores: A Palaeographical Guide to Latin Manuscripts prior to the Ninth Century*. 11 vols and supplement. Oxford: Clarendon Press.
Ludolf, Hiob, ed. 1701. መጽሐፈ፡ መዝሙራት፡ ዘዳዊት – *Psalterium Davidis Aethiopice et Latine cum duobus impressis & tribus MSStis codicibus diligenter collatum & emendatum, nec non variis lectionibus & notis philologicis illustratum, ut in præfatione pluribus dicetur*. Frankfurt am Main: prostat apud Johannem David Zunner et Nicolaum Wilhelmum Helwig.
Luiselli Fadda, Anna Maria. 1988. "Problemi di *recensio* e *restitutio textus*: La *Vita Fursei* e la sua interpretazione anglosassone". *Helion* 28: 183–201.
Luiselli Fadda, Anna Maria. 1994. *Tradizioni manoscritte e critica del testo nel Medioevo germanico*. Rome: Laterza.
Luna, Concetta, and Alain-Philippe Segonds, eds. 2007–. *Proclus: Commentaire sur le Parménide de Platon*. Paris: Les Belles Lettres.
Lusini, Gianfrancesco. 1988. "L'omelia etiopica 'Sui Sabati' di 'Retuʿa Haymanot'". *Egitto e Vicino Oriente* 11: 205–235.
Lusini, Gianfrancesco. 2004. "Copisti e filologi dell'Etiopia medievale: Lo Scriptorium di Dabra Māryām del Sarā'ē (Eritrea)". *La Parola del Passato* 59 (336): 230–237.
Lusini, Gianfrancesco. 2005. "Philology and the Reconstruction of the Ethiopian Past". In *Afrikas Horn: Akten der Ersten Internationalen Littmann-Konferenz 2. bis 5. Mai 2002 in München*, edited by Walter Raunig and Steffen Wenig, 91–106. Wiesbaden: Harrassowitz.
Lusini, Gianfrancesco. 2014. "Paolo Marrassini (1942–2013) e la filologia etiopica all'Orientale". *AION Annali: Università degli studi di Napoli "L'Orientale"* 74: 239–242.
Lusini, Gianfrancesco. 2017. "The Stemmatic Method and Ethiopian Philology". *Rassegna di Studi Etiopici, Serie terza* 1 (48): 75–86.
Lutz-Hensel, Magdalene. 1975. *Prinzipien der ersten textkritischen Editionen mittelhochdeutscher Dichtung: Brüder Grimm – Benecke – Lachmann; eine methodenkritische Analyse*. Berlin: Schmidt.
Lycett, Stephen J. 2009. "Understanding Ancient Hominin Dispersals Using Artefactual Data: A Phylogeographic Analysis of Acheulean Handaxes". *PLoS One* 4 (10): e7404. doi.org/10.1371/journal.pone.0007404.
Maas, Paul. 1927. "Textkritik". In *Einleitung in die Altertumswissenschaft*, edited by Alfred Gercke and Eduard Norden, vol. 1.2, 1–18. Leipzig: Teubner.
Maas, Paul. 1937. "Leitfehler und stemmatische Typen". *Byzantinische Zeitschrift* 37 (2): 289–294.
Maas, Paul. 1950. *Textkritik*. 2nd ed. Leipzig: Teubner.
Maas, Paul. 1957. *Textkritik*. 3rd ed. Leipzig: Teubner.
Maas, Paul. 1958. *Textual Criticism*. Translated by Barbara Flower. Oxford: Clarendon Press [trans. of Maas 1957].

Maas, Paul. 1960. *Textkritik*. 4th ed. Leipzig: Teubner.
Maas, Paul. 1994. "Krytyka textu". Translated by Katarzyna Sybilska. *Pamiętnik Literacki* 85: 184–206 [partial trans. of Maas 1960].
Maas, Paul. 2011. "Kritika texta". Translated by Dmitrij Olegovič Toršilov. *Aristej* 4: 136–173 [trans. of Maas 1960].
Maas, Paul. 2017. *La critica del testo*. Translated by Giorgio Ziffer. Rome: Edizioni di Storia e Letteratura [trans. of Maas 1960].
Macé, Caroline. 2004. "Note sur la tradition manuscrite d'un passage disputé du Discours 38 de Grégoire de Nazianze (BHG 1938)". *Analecta Bollandiana* 122: 51–68.
Macé, Caroline. 2011. "Latin and Armenian Translations and the Prehistory of the Homilies of St. Gregory of Nazianzus". *Comparative Oriental Manuscript Studies Newsletter* 1: 21–23.
Macé, Caroline. 2016. "Rules and Guidelines in Book Series and Their Impact on Scholarly Editions". In *The Arts of Editing Medieval Greek and Latin: A Casebook*, edited by Elisabet Göransson, Gunilla Iversen, Barbara Crostini, Brian M. Jensen, Erika Kihlman, Eva Odelman, and Denis Searby, 248–267. Toronto: Pontifical Institute of Mediaeval Studies.
Macé, Caroline. 2019. "Textual Criticism Is Not Only an Art: A Response to B. Alexanderson". *Revue d'histoire des textes* 14: 353–358.
Macé, Caroline. Forthcoming. "Animals in Pseudo-Eustathius of Antioch's Chronicle". In *Von der Historienbibel zur Weltchronik: Die byzantinisch-slavische Palaea/Paleja*, edited by Christfried Böttrich, Dieter Fahl, and Sabine Fahl. Leipzig: Evangelische Verlagsanstalt.
Macé, Caroline, and Philippe Baret. 2006. "Why Phylogenetic Methods Work: The Theory of Evolution and Textual Criticism". In *The Evolution of Texts: Confronting Stemmatological and Genetical Methods; Proceedings of the International Workshop (Louvain la Neuve, sept. 2004)*, edited by Caroline Macé, Philippe V. Baret, Andrea Bozzi, and Laura Cignoni, 89–108. Pisa: Istituti editoriali e poligrafici internazionali.
Macé, Caroline, Philippe V. Baret, and Anne-Catherine Lantin. 2004. "Philologie et phylogénétique: Regards croisés en vue d'une édition critique d'une homélie de Grégoire de Nazianze". In *Digital Technology and Philological Disciplines*, edited by Andrea Bozzi, Laura Cignoni, and Jean-Louis Lebrave, 305–341. Pisa: Istituti editoriali e poligrafici internazionali.
Macé, Caroline, Alessandro Bausi, Johannes Den Heijer, Jost Gippert, Paolo La Spisa, Alessandro Mengozzi, Sébastien Moureau, and Lara Sels. 2015. "Textual Criticism and Text Editing". In *Comparative Oriental Manuscript Studies: An Introduction*, by Alessandro Bausi, Pier Giorgio Borbone, Françoise Briquel Chatonnet, Paola Buzi, Jost Gippert, Caroline Macé, Marilena Maniaci, Zisis Melissakis, Laura E. Parodi, and Witold Witakowski, 321–465. Hamburg: Tredition.
Macé, Caroline, Ilse De Vos, and Koen Geuten. 2012. "Comparison of Stemmatological and Phylogenetic Methods to Understand the Copying History of the *Florilegium Coislinianum*". In *Ars Edendi Lecture Series*, vol. 2, edited by Alessandra Bucossi and Erika Kihlman, 107–129. Stockholm: Stockholm University Press.
Macé, Caroline, and Michael Muthreich. 2019. "Latin and Oriental Translations of the Epistola de morte apostolorum Attributed to Dionysius the Areopagite". In *Caught in Translation: Studies on Versions of Late-Antique Christian Literature*, edited by Dan Batovici and Madalina Toca, 9–34. Leiden: Brill.
Macé, Caroline, and Clotaire Sanspeur. 2000. "Nouvelles perspectives pour l'histoire du texte des Discours de Grégoire de Nazianze: Le Cas du *Discours* 6 en grec et en arménien". *Le Muséon* 113: 377–416.
Macé, Caroline, Thomas Schmidt, and Jean-François Weiler. 2001. "Le Classement des manuscrits par la statistique et la phylogénétique: Le Cas de Grégoire de Nazianze et de Basile le Minime". *Revue d'histoire des textes* 31: 243–273. doi.org/10.3406/rht.2003.1513.

Macé, Caroline, Carlos Steel, and Pieter d'Hoine. 2009. "Bessarion lecteur du commentaire de Proclus sur le *Parménide*, avec une édition de ses scholies aux livres II et III". *Byzantion* 79: 241–279.

Mackenzie, Charles E. 1980. *Coded Character Sets, History and Development*. Reading, MA: Addison-Wesley. textfiles.meulie.net/bitsaved/Books/Mackenzie_CodedCharSets.pdf.

Macleod, Matthew D., ed. 1972–1987. *Luciani opera*. 4 vols. Oxford: Clarendon Press.

Maddison, David R., David L. Swofford, and Wayne P. Maddison. 1997. "Nexus: An Extensible File Format for Systematic Information". *Systematic Biology* 46 (4): 590–621. doi.org/10.1093/sysbio/46.4.590.

Madvig, Johan Nicolai. 1833–1834. *De emendandis Ciceronis orationibus pro P. Sestio et in P. Vatinium disputationis*. 3 vols. Copenhagen: Schultz.

Maggioni, Giovanni Paolo. 1994. "L'uso delle fonti in sede di 'recensio' nella filologia mediolatina: Riflessioni su di un'esperienza". *Filologia mediolatina* 1: 37–44.

Maggioni, Giovanni Paolo. 1995. *Ricerche sulla composizione e sulla trasmissione della Legenda aurea*. Spoleto: CISAM.

Maggioni, Giovanni Paolo, ed. 2007. *Iacopo da Varazze: Legenda aurea; Con le miniature del codice Ambrosiano C 240 inf*. Florence: SISMEL.

Maggioni, Giovanni Paolo. 2016. "Editing Errors". In *Ars Edendi Lecture Series*, vol. 4, edited by Barbara Crostini, Gunilla Iversen, and Brian M. Jensen, 26–39. Stockholm: Stockholm University Press.

Magnani, Roberta, and Diane Watt. 2018. "Towards a Queer Philology". *postmedieval: a journal of medieval cultural studies* 9 (3): 252–268. doi.org/10.1057/s41280-018-0094-2.

Mallon, Jean. 1952. *Paléographie romaine (letters, planches)*. Madrid: Inst. Ant. de Nebrija de filología.

Mallory, James Patrick. 1989. *In Search of the Indo-Europeans: Language, Archaeology and Myth*. London: Thames and Hudson.

Mallory, James Patrick, and Douglas Q. Adams. 2006. *The Oxford Introduction to Proto-Indo-European and the Proto-Indo-European World*. Oxford: Oxford University Press.

Malter, Henry, ed. 1930. *The Treatise Ta'anit of the Babylonian Talmud*. New York, NY: American Academy for Jewish Research.

Mandelbaum, Bernard, ed. 1962. *Pesikta de rav Kahana*. 2 vols. New York, NY: Jewish Theological Seminary of America.

Manfredi, Antonio. 2010. "La nascita della Vaticana in età umanistica da Niccolò V a Sisto IV". In *Le origini della Biblioteca Vaticana tra umanesimo e rinascimento (1447–1534)*, edited by Antonio Manfredi, 147–236. Vatican City: Biblioteca Apostolica Vaticana.

Maniaci, Marilena. 2002. *Archeologia del manoscritto: Metodi, problemi, bibliografia recente*. Rome: Viella.

Manni, Franz, Etienne Guérard, and Evelyne Heyer. 2004. "Geographic Patterns of (Genetic, Morphologic, Linguistic) Variation". *Human Biology* 76: 173–190.

Marchand, Suzanne. 2009. *German Orientalism in the Age of Empire: Religion, Race, and Scholarship*. Cambridge: Cambridge University Press.

Marchetti, Federico. 2019. "'Scribal behaviour' e 'scribal habits': Un problema metodologico; Fenomenologia dei codices descripti". PhD thesis, University of Ferrara.

Margulies, Mordecai, ed. 1972. *Vayyiqra Rabba*. 2nd print. 3 vols. Jerusalem: Warhmann.

Marmerola, Guilherme D., Marina A. Oikawa, Zanoni Dias, Siome Goldenstein, and Anderson Rocha. 2016. "On the Reconstruction of Text Phylogeny Trees: Evaluation and Analysis of Textual Relationships". *PLoS One* 11 (12): e0167822. doi.org/10.1371/journal.pone.0167822.

Marrassini, Paolo, ed. and trans. 1981. *Gadla Yoḥannǝs Maṣraqawi: Vita di Yohannes l'Orientale*. Florence: Instituto di Linguistica e di Lingue Orientali.

Marrassini, Paolo. 1987. "L'edizione critica dei testi etiopici: Problemi di metodo e reperti linguistici". In *Linguistica e filologia: Atti del VII Convegno Internazionale di Linguisti tenuto* a Milano nei giorni 12–14 settembre 1984, edited by Giancarlo Bolognesi and Vittore Pisani, 347–356. Brescia: Paideia.

Marrassini, Paolo. 1992. "Interpunzione e fenomeni demarcativi nelle lingue semitiche". In *Storia e teoria dell'interpunzione: Atti del Convegno Internazionale di Studi, Firenze, 19–21 maggio 1988*, edited by Emanuela Cresti and Nicoletta Maraschio, 501–520. Rome: Bulzoni.

Marrassini, Paolo. 1993. *Lo scettro e la croce: La campagna di 'Amda Ṣeyon contro l'Ifāt (1332)*. Naples: Università degli Studi di Napoli "L'Orientale".

Marrassini, Paolo, ed. and trans. 1995. *Il Gadla Yemreḥanna Krestos: Introduzione, testo critico, traduzione*. Naples: Istituto Universitario Orientale.

Marrassini, Paolo. 1996. "Problems of Gə'əz Philology". In *Studies in Near Eastern Languages and Literatures: Memorial Volume of Karel Petráček*, edited by Petr Zemánek, 371–378. Prague: Academy of Sciences of the Czech Republic, Oriental Institute.

Marrassini, Paolo. 2000. "Some Philological Problems in the 'Miracles' of Gabra Manfas Qeddus". *Aethiopica* 3: 46–78.

Marrassini, Paolo, ed. and trans. 2003. *"Vita", "Omelia", "Miracoli" del santo Gabra Manfas Qeddus*. Leuven: Peeters.

Marrassini, Paolo. 2004. "Il Gadla Kiros". In *Studia Aethiopica in Honour of Siegbert Uhlig on the Occasion of His 65th Birthday*, edited by Verena Böll, Denis Nosnitsin, Thomas Rave, Wolbert Smidt, and Evgenia Sokolinskaia, 79–90. Wiesbaden: Harrassowitz.

Marrassini, Paolo. 2008a. "Salient Features of Philology: The Science of Establishing Primary Sources". *Bulletin of Philological Society of Ethiopia (Addis Ababa University, Department of Linguistics)* 1 (1): 4–12.

Marrassini, Paolo. 2008b. Review of *Die äthiopischen Studien im 20. Jahrhundert/Ethiopian Studies in the 20th Century: Akten der internationalen äthiopischen Tagung Berlin 22. bis 24. Juli 2000*, edited by Rainer Vogt. *Bibliotheca Orientalis* 65 (1–2): 267–274.

Marrassini, Paolo. 2009. "Problems in Critical Edition and the State of Ethiopian Philology". *Journal of Ethiopian Studies* 42: 25–68.

Marrou, Henri-Irénée. 1948. *Histoire de l'éducation dans l'Antiquité*. Vol. 2. *Le Monde romain*. Paris: Editions du Seuil.

Martin, Josef, ed. 1963. *Lucretius: De rerum natura libri sex*. Leipzig: Teubner.

Martínez Manzano, Teresa. 2008. "Die Aufenthalte des Andreas Darmarios in Madrid und Salamanca und ihre Bedeutung für die 'Recensio' der Philostrat- und Oppianscholien". *Rheinisches Museum für Philologie*, n.s., 151: 400–424.

Matthews, Luke J., Jamshid Tehrani, Fiona M. Jordan, Mark Collard, and Charles L. Nunn. 2011. "Testing for Divergent Transmission Histories among Cultural Characters: A Study Using Bayesian Phylogenetic Methods and Iranian Tribal Textile Data". *PLoS One* 6 (4): e14810. doi.org/10.1371/journal.pone.0014810.

Maxam, Allan M., and Walter Gilbert. 1977. "A New Method for Sequencing DNA". *Proceedings of the National Academy of Sciences* 74 (2): 560–564.

Maynard Smith, John. 1992. "Analyzing the Mosaic Structure of Genes". *Journal of Molecular Evolution* 34 (2): 126–129.

Mazzatinti, Giuseppe, ed. 1890–2013. *Inventari dei manoscritti delle biblioteche d'Italia*. 113 vols. Florence: Olschki.

McCarty, Willard. 2014. *Humanities Computing*. London: Palgrave Macmillan.

McCulloh, Marc R. 1983. "Myller's Parcival and Lachmann's Critical Method: The 'Wolfram-Reise' Revisited". *Modern Language Notes* 98: 484–491.

McDonald, Alexander H. 1970. "Textual Criticism". In *The Oxford Classical Dictionary*, edited by Howard Hayes Scullard and Nicholas G. L. Hammond, 1048–1050. Oxford: Clarendon Press.

McGann, Jerome. 1983. *A Critique of Modern Textual Criticism*. Chicago, IL: University of Chicago Press.

McGann, Jerome. 1991. *The Textual Condition*. Princeton, NJ: Princeton University Press.

McKerrow, Ronald B. 1939. *Prolegomena for the Oxford Shakespeare: A Study in Editorial Method*. Oxford: Clarendon Press.

McLuhan, Marshall. 1962. *The Gutenberg Galaxy: The Making of Typographic Man*. London: Routledge.

Meier-Brügger, Michael. 2000. *Indogermanische Sprachwissenschaft*. 7th ed. with Matthias Fritz und Manfred Mayrhofer. Berlin: De Gruyter.

Meier-Brügger, Michael. 2003. *Indo-European Linguistics*. Translated by Charles Gertmenian. Berlin: De Gruyter [trans. of Meier-Brügger 2000].

Melchert, Craig H. 1998. "The Dialectal Position of Anatolian within Indo-European". In *Proceedings of the Twenty-Fourth Annual Meeting of the Berkeley Linguistics Society: Special Session on Indo-European Subgrouping and Internal Relations*, edited by Benjamin K. Bergen, Madelaine C. Plauché, and Ashlee C. Bailey, 24–31. Berkeley, CA: Berkeley Linguistics Society.

Melchert, Craig H. Forthcoming. "The Position of Anatolian". In *Handbook of Indo-European Studies*, edited by Michael Weiss and Andrew Garrett. Oxford: Oxford University Press. linguistics.ucla.edu/people/Melchert/The%20Position%20of%20AnatolianRevised3.pdf.

Memelsdorff, Pedro. 2010. "The Filiation and Transmission of Instrumental Polyphony in Late Medieval Italy: The Codex Faenza 117". PhD thesis, University of Utrecht.

Ménard, Philippe, ed. 1987–1997. *Le Roman de Tristan en prose*. 9 vols. Geneva: Droz.

Mengozzi, Alessandro. 2015. "Past and Present Trends in the Edition of Classical Syriac Texts". In *Comparative Oriental Manuscript Studies: An Introduction*, by Alessandro Bausi, Pier Giorgio Borbone, Françoise Briquel Chatonnet, Paola Buzi, Jost Gippert, Caroline Macé, Marilena Maniaci, Zisis Melissakis, Laura E. Parodi, and Witold Witakowski, 435–439. Hamburg: Tredition.

Mening, Robert. 2018. "HTML Tutorial (for Beginners) – Learn HTML, Step-by-Step". websitesetup.org/html-tutorial-beginners.

Merisalo, Outi. 2012. "The Early Tradition of the Pseudo-Galenic De spermate". *Scripta* 5: 99–109.

Merisalo, Outi. 2016. "*Liber Hartmanni Schedel Nurembergensis artium utriusque medicine doctoris*: Histoire de quelques textes de la bibliothèque de Hartmann Schedel de Nuremberg (1440–1514)". In *La Rigueur et la passion: Mélanges en l'honneur de Pascale Bourgain*, edited by Dominique Poirel and Cédric Girard, 821–830. Turnhout: Brepols.

Merisalo, Outi. 2017. "Ludwig Traube and Philology". In *Philology Matters! Essays on the Art of Reading Slowly*, edited by Harry Lönnroth, 182–196. Leiden: Brill.

Merivuori, Toni, and Teemu Roos. 2009. "Some Observations on the Applicability of Normalized Compression Distance to Stemmatology". In *2009 Workshop on Information Theoretic Methods in Science and Engineering*. sp.cs.tut.fi/WITMSE09/Proceedings/WITMSE2009_papers/Merivuori_Roos.pdf.

Mersha Alehegne. 2011a. "Towards a Glossary of Ethiopian Manuscript Culture and Practice". *Aethiopica* 14: 145–162.

Mersha Alehegne. 2011b, ed. and trans. *The Ethiopian Commentary on the Book of Genesis: Critical Edition and Translation*. Wiesbaden: Harrassowitz.

Mertens, Volker, ed. 2004. *Hartmann von Aue: Gregorius, Der Arme Heinrich, Iwein*. Frankfurt am Main: Deutscher Klassiker Verlag.

Mertens, Volker. 2011. "Die Wiederentdeckung Wolframs und die Anfänge der Forschung". In *Wolfram von Eschenbach: Ein Handbuch*, edited by Joachim Heinzle, vol. 1, 705–741. Berlin: De Gruyter.

Meßner, Reinhard. 2007. "Probleme und Aufgaben bei der Edition, historischen Erforschung und theologischen Interpretation orientalischer Anaphoren". *Bollettino della Badia Greca di Grottaferrata*, 3rd ser., 4: 145–175.

Meyer, Dirk. 2012. *Philosophy on Bamboo: Text and the Production of Meaning in Early China*. Leiden: Brill.

Meyer, Paul. 1870. "Etudes sur la Chanson de Girart de Roussillon: I. Les Manuscrits". *Jahrbuch für romanische und englische Literatur* 11: 121–142.

Meyer, Paul. 1911. "Chronique". *Romania* 40 (160): 631–635.

Micaeli, Claudio. 2014. "L'exordium del De pudicitia di Tertulliano: Fortuna letteraria e questioni esegetiche e critiche nei secoli XVI/XVII". In *Edition und Erforschung lateinischer patristischer Texte: 150 Jahre CSEL*, edited by Victoria Zimmer-Panagl, Lukas J. Dorfbauer, and Clemens Weidmann, 1–16. Berlin: De Gruyter.

Micha, Alexandre. 1939. *La Tradition manuscrite des romans de Chrétien de Troyes*. Paris: Droz.

Mihaescu, Radu, Dan Levy, and Lior Pachter. 2006. "Why Neighbor-Joining Works" [abstract]. arxiv.org/abs/cs/0602041.

Miles, Brent. 2011. *Heroic Saga and Classical Epic in Medieval Ireland*. Cambridge: Brewer.

Milikowsky, Chaim. 1988. "The Status Quaestionis of Research in Rabbinic Literature". *Journal of Jewish Studies* 39: 201–211.

Milikowsky, Chaim. 1996. "On Editing Rabbinic Texts: A Review-Essay of *Baraita de-Melekhet ha-Mishkan: A Critical Edition with Introduction and Translation* by Robert Kirschner". *Jewish Quarterly Review* 86: 409–418.

Milikowsky, Chaim. 1999. "Further on Editing Rabbinic Texts: A Review-Essay of *A Synoptic Edition of Pesiqta Rabbati Based Upon All Extant Manuscripts and the Editio Princeps* by Rivka Ulmer". *Jewish Quarterly Review* 90: 137–149.

Milikowsky, Chaim. 2002. "On the Formation and Transmission of Bereshit Rabba and the Yerushalmi: Questions of Redaction, Text-Criticism and Literary Relationships; A Review-Essay of *Die großen rabbinischen Sammelwerke Palästinas: Zur literarischen Genese von Talmud Yerushalmi und Midrash Bereshit Rabba* by Hans-Jürgen Becker". *Jewish Quarterly Review* 92: 521–567.

Milikowsky, Chaim. 2006. "Reflections on the Practice of Textual Criticism in the Study of Midrash Aggada: The Legitimacy, the Indispensability and the Feasibility of Recovering and Presenting the (Most) Original Text". In *Current Trends in the Study of Midrash*, edited by Carol Bakhos, Supplements to the Journal for the Study of Judaism 106, 79–109. Leiden: Brill.

Milikowsky, Chaim, ed. 2013. *Seder Olam*. 2 vols. Jerusalem: Yad Ben-Zvi Press.

Milikowsky, Chaim, and Peter Schäfer. 2010. "Current Views on the Editing of the Rabbinic Texts of Late Antiquity: Reflections on a Debate after Twenty Years". In *Rabbinic Texts and the History of Late-Roman Palestine*, edited by Martin Goodman and Philip Alexander, 79–88. Oxford: Oxford University Press.

Miller, Matthias, and Karin Zimmermann. 2007. *Die Codices Palatini germanici in der Universitätsbibliothek Heidelberg (Cod. Pal. germ. 304–495)*. Wiesbaden: Harrassowitz.

Miller, Steven J. 2011. *Metadata for Digital Collections: A How-to-Do-It Manual*. New York, NY: Neal-Schuman.

Mills, Chris, Rafey Iqbal Rahman, "Anawriter1", "Boyejay", and Richard Zacur. n. d. "Introduction to CSS". developer.mozilla.org/en-US/docs/Learn/CSS/Introduction_to_CSS.

Milnor, Kristina. 2019. "Epigrams in the Graffiti of Pompeii". In *A Companion to Ancient Epigram*, edited by Christer Henriksén, 491–503. Hoboken, NJ: Wiley Blackwell.

Mink, Gerd. 1993. "Eine umfassende Genealogie der neutestamentliche Überlieferung". *New Testament Studies* 39: 481–499.

Mink, Gerd. 2004. "Problems of a Highly Contaminated Tradition: The New Testament; Stemmata of Variants as a Source of Genealogy for Witnesses". In *Studies in Stemmatology II*, edited by Pieter van Reenen, August den Hollander, and Margot van Mulken, 127–43. Philadelphia, PA: Benjamins. benjamins.com/catalog/z.125.

Mink, Gerd. 2009. "The Coherence-Based Genealogical Method (CBGM) – Introductory Presentation by Gerd Mink". uni-muenster.de/INTF/cbgm_presentation.

Mink, Gerd. 2011. "Contamination, Coherence, and Coincidence in Textual Transmission: The Coherence-Based Genealogical Method (CBGM) as a Complement and Corrective to Existing Approaches". In *The Textual History of the Greek New Testament: Changing Views in Contemporary Research*, edited by Klaus Wachtel and Michael W. Holmes, Text-Critical Studies 8, 141–216. Atlanta, GA: Society of Biblical Literature.

Mink, Gerd. 2012. "The Coherence-Based Genealogical Method – What Is It About?". uni-muenster.de/INTF/Genealogical_method.html.

Minsky, Marvin. 1965. "Matter, Mind and Models". In *Information Processing: Proceedings of the International Federation of Information Processing*, edited by Wayne A. Kalenich, vol. 1, 45–49. Washington, DC: Spartan.

Moges Yigezu, Baye Yimam, Hirut Woldemariam, and Yonas Admassu, eds. 2006. *Proceedings of the First International Symposium on Ethiopian Philology, October 15–16, 2004, Ras Mekonnen Hall*. Addis Ababa: Department of Linguistics, Addis Ababa University.

Monella, Paolo. 2012. "Why Are There No Comprehensively Digital Scholarly Editions of Classical Texts?". In *Digital Philology: New Thoughts on Old Questions*, edited by Adele Cipolla, 141–159. Padua: Libreriauniversitaria.it. www1.unipa.it/paolo.monella/lincei/files/why/why_paper.pdf.

Montanari, Elio. 2003. *La critica del testo secondo Paul Maas: Testo e commento*. Florence: Edizioni del Galluzzo.

Montaner, Alberto. 2018. "The Poema de mio Cid as Text: Manuscript Transmission and Editorial Politics". In *A Companion to the Poema de mio Cid*, edited by Irene Zaderenko and Alberto Montaner, 44–88. Leiden: Brill.

Montfaucon, Bernard de. 1739. *Bibliotheca bibliothecarum manuscriptorum nova*. 2 vols. Paris: apud Briasson.

Montuschi, Claudia, ed. 2014. *La Vaticana nel Seicento (1590–1700): Una biblioteca di biblioteche*. Vatican City: Biblioteca Apostolica Vaticana.

Mooney, Linne R., Adrian C. Barbrook, Christopher J. Howe, and Matthew Spencer. 2003. "Stemmatic Analysis of Lydgate's 'Kings of England': A Test Case for the Application of Software Developed for Evolutionary Biology to Manuscript Stemmatics". *Revue d'histoire des textes* 31: 275–297. doi.org/10.3406/rht.2003.1514.

Moore, John H. 1994. "Putting Anthropology Back Together Again: The Ethnogenetic Critique of Cladistic Theory". *American Anthropologist* 96: 370–396.

Morrison, Michael. 1999. *XML Unleashed*. Indianapolis, IN: Sams.

Mouser, Marilee J. 2003. "Petrucci and His Shadow: A Study of the Filiation and Reception History of the Venetian Motet Anthologies, 1502–1508". PhD thesis, University of California, Santa Barbara.

Mouser, Marilee J. 2004. "Petrucci and His Shadow: A Case Study of Reception History". *Fontes artis musicae* 51: 19–52.

Mras, Karl. 1911. *Die Überlieferung Lucians*. Vienna: Hölder.

Muessig, Carolyn. 2012. "Catherine of Siena in Late Medieval Sermons". In *A Companion to Catherine of Siena*, edited by Caroline Muessig, George Ferzoco, and Beverly Kienzle, 203–226. Leiden: Brill.

Mullen, Roderic L. 1997. *The New Testament Text of Cyril of Jerusalem*. The New Testament in the Greek Fathers. Atlanta, GA: Society of Biblical Literature.

Müller, F. Max. 1888. *Biographies of Words and the Home of the Aryas*. London: Longman.

Muller, Jean-Claude. 1986. "Early Stages of Language Comparison from Sassetti to Sir William Jones (1786)". *Kratylos* 31: 1–31.

Munby, Alan Noel Latimer. 1951–1960. *Phillipps Studies*. 5 vols. Cambridge: Cambridge University Press.

Munk Olsen, Birger. 1985. *Catalogue des manuscrits classiques latins copiés du IXe au XIIe siècle.* Vol. 2. Paris: CNRS.

Munro, Hugh, A. J., ed. 1864. *Lucretius: De rerum natura libri sex.* 2 vols. Cambridge: Bell.

Muradyan, Gohar. 2005. *Physiologus: The Greek and Armenian Versions with a Study of Translation Technique.* Leuven: Peeters.

Murano, Giovanna. 2005. *Opere diffuse per exemplar e pecia.* Turnhout: Brepols.

Murphy, G. Ronald, trans. 1992. *The Heliand: The Saxon Gospel.* Oxford: Oxford University Press.

Muthreich, Michael. 2013. "Bemerkungen zur arabischen und äthiopischen Fassung der Epistola de morte apostolorum Petri et Pauli (zugeschrieben dem Dionysius Areopagita)". *Philotheos* 13: 166–175.

Mynors, Roger. 1963. *Catalogue of the Manuscripts of Balliol College Oxford.* Oxford: Clarendon Press.

Najock, Dietmar, and Christopher C. Heyde. 1982. "On the Number of Terminal Vertices in Certain Random Trees with an Application to Stemma Construction in Philology". *Journal of Applied Probability* 19 (3): 675–680.

Nassourou, Mohamadou. 2013. *Computer-Supported Textual Criticism: Theory, Automatic Reconstruction of an Archetype.* Norderstedt: BoD.

National Library of the Czech Republic. 2012. "From Klementinum's History". en.nkp.cz/about-us/about-nl/national-library-s-history/history-1.

National Library of Russia. 2018. "The History of the National Library of Russia". nlr.ru/eng/RA2081/history-of-library.

Nebbiai, Donatella. 2013. *Le Discours des livres: Bibliothèques et manuscrits en Europe, IXe–XVe siècle.* Rennes: Presses Universitaires de Rennes.

Nebbiai, Donatella, Claire Angotti, and Gilbert Fournier, eds. 2017. *Les Livres des maîtres de Sorbonne: Histoire et rayonnement du collège et de ses bibliothèques du XIIIe siècle à la Renaissance.* Paris: Editions de la Sorbonne.

NEDCC. 2007. "1 Microfilm and Microfiche". nedcc.org/free-resources/preservation-leaflets/6.-reformatting/6.1-microfilm-and-microfiche.

Neddermeyer, Uwe. 1996. "Möglichkeiten und Grenzen einer quantitativen Bestimmung der Buchproduktion im Spätmittelalter". *Gazette du livre médiéval* 28: 23–31.

Nelson, Martha I., Lone Simonsen, Cecile Viboud, Mark A. Miller, and Edward C. Holmes. 2007. "Phylogenetic Analysis Reveals the Global Migration of Seasonal Influenza A Viruses". *PLoS Pathogens* 3 (9): e131. doi.org/10.1371/journal.ppat.0030131.

Nestle–Aland, eds. 2012. *Novum Testamentum Graece.* Based on the work of Eberhard and Erwin Nestle. Edited by Barbara Aland, Kurt Aland, Johannes Karavidopoulos, Carlo M. Martini, and Bruce M. Metzger. 28th ed. Stuttgart: Deutsche Bibelgesellschaft.

Nguyen, Quan, and Teemu Roos. 2015. "Likelihood-Based Inference of Phylogenetic Networks from Sequence Data by PhyloDAG". In *Algorithms for Computational Biology* 9199: 126–140. doi.org/10.1007/978-3-319-21233-3_10.

Nichols, Stephen G., ed. 1990. "The New Philology", special issue, *Speculum* 65.

Nichols, Stephen G. 1997. "Why Material Philology? Some Thoughts". *Zeitschrift für Deutsche Philologie* 116: 10–30.

Nichols, Stephen G. 2014. "New Challenges for the New Medievalism". In *Rethinking the New Medievalism*, edited by R. Howard Bloch, Alison Calhoun, Jacqueline Cerquiglini-Toulet, Joachim Küpper, and Jeanette Patterson, 12–38. Baltimore, MD: Johns Hopkins University Press.

Nicolodi, Fiamma, and Paolo Trovato. 2003. "La tradizione primo ottocentesca dei libretti (1814–1830)". In *Gioachino Rossini: Il Turco in Italia*, edited by Fiamma Nicolodi, lxi–ci. Pesaro: Fondazione Rossini.

Nielsen, Inge. 2006. "Library: B". In *Brill's New Pauly*, edited by Hubert Cancik and Helmut Schneider. dx.doi.org/10.1163/1574-9347_bnp_e216740.

Noblitt, Thomas L. 1981. "Textual Criticism of Selected Works Published by Petrucci".
    In *Quellenstudien zur Musik der Renaissance*, vol. 1, *Formen und Probleme der Überlieferung mehrstimmiger Musik im Zeitalter Josquin Desprez*, edited by Ludwig Finscher, 201–244. Munich: Kraus Int. Publications.
Noblitt, Thomas L. 1983. "Filiation vis-à-vis Its Alternatives: Approaches to Textual Criticism".
    In *Quellenstudien zur Musik der Renaissance*, vol. 2, *Datierung und Filiation von Musikhandschriften der Josquin-Zeit*, edited by Ludwig Finscher, 111–127. Wiesbaden: Harrassowitz.
Noblitt, Thomas L., ed. 1987–1996. *Der Kodex des Magister Nicolaus Leopold, Staatsbibliothek München Mus. ms. 3154*. 4 vols. Kassel: Bärenreiter.
Noblitt, Thomas L. 1995. "Criteria for Choosing between Stemmatically Equivalent Texts".
    In *L'edizione critica tra testo musicale e testo letterario*, edited by Renato Borghi and Pietro Zappalà, 213–232. Lucca: Libreria Musicale Italiana.
Norbrook, David, Stephen Harrison, and Philip Hardie, eds. 2016. *Lucretius and the Early Modern*. Oxford: Oxford University Press.
Nordh, Arvast, ed. 1949. *Libellus de regionibus urbis Romae*. Lund: Gleerup.
Null, Linda, and Julia Lobur. 2003. *The Essentials of Computer Organization and Architecture*. Sudburry, MA: Jones and Bartlett.
Nuovo, Angela. 2013. *The Book Trade in the Italian Renaissance*. Leiden: Brill.
Nury, Elisa. 2018. "Automated Collation and Digital Editions: From Theory to Practice". PhD thesis, King's College London.
Nuvoloni, Laura. 2016. "Aldo Manuzio e l'oggetto libro: 2. Le vesti del libro di Aldo fra tradizione e innovazione". In *Aldo Manuzio: Il Rinascimento di Venezia,* edited by Guido Beltramini and Davide Gasparotto, 79–89. Venice: Marsilio.
Nyhan, Julianne, and Andrew Flinn. 2016. *Computation and the Humanities: Towards an Oral History of Digital Humanities*. Springer Series on Cultural Computing. Cham: Springer Open. springer.com/gp/book/9783319201696.
Nylan, Michael. 2014. "Manuscript Culture in Late Western Han and Authors' Authority". *Journal of Chinese Literature* 1: 155–185.
Nyström, Eva. 2009. *Containing Multitudes: Codex Upsaliensis Graecus 8 in Perspective*. Uppsala: Uppsala Universitet.
O'Brien, Michael J., John Darwent, and R. Lee Lyman. 2001. "Cladistics Is Useful for Reconstructing Archaeological Phylogenies: Palaeoindian Points from the Southeastern United States". *Journal of Archaeological Science* 28: 1115–1136.
O'Brien O'Keeffe, Katherine. 1990. *Visible Song: Transitional Literacy in Old English Verse*. Cambridge: Cambridge University Press.
Ockham, Guillelmus. 1967. *Guillelmi de Ockham opera philosophica et theologica ad fidem codicum manuscriptorum edita*. Vol. 1. St. Bonaventure, NY: Franciscan Institute of St. Bonaventure University.
O'Donnell, Daniel. 2005. *Cædmon's Hymn: A Multimedia Study, Edition and Archive*. caedmon. seenet.org/.
O'Hara, Robert J. 1996. "Trees of History in Systematics and Philology". *Memorie della Società Italiana di Scienze Naturali e del Museo Civico di Storia Naturale di Milano* 27 (1): 81–88.
Olalde, Iñigo, Selina Brace, Morten E. Allentoft, Ian Armit, Kristian Kristiansen, Thomas Booth, Nadin Rohland, Swapan Mallick, Anna Szécsényi-Nagy, Alissa Mittnik, et al. 2018. "The Beaker Phenomenon and the Genomic Transformation of Northwest Europe". *Nature* 555: 190–196. doi.org/10.1038/nature25738.
Olrik Frederiksen, Britta. 1999. "Dansksprogede bøger fra middelalderen – I tørre og mindre tørre tal". In *Levende ord & lysende billeder*, edited by Erik Petersen, 154–162. Copenhagen: Det Kongelige Bibliotek – Moesgård Museum.

Olrik Frederiksen, Britta. 2009. "Stemmaet fra 1827 over Västgötalagen – En videnskabshistorisk bedrift og dens mulig forudsætninger". *Arkiv för nordisk filologi* 124: 129–150.

Ommundsen, Åslaug, and Tuomas Heikkilä. 2017. "Piecing Together the Past: The Accidental Manuscript Collections of the North". In *Nordic Manuscript Fragments: The Destruction and Reconstruction of Medieval Books*, edited by Åslaug Ommundsen and Tuomas Heikkilä, 1–23. Oxford: Routledge.

Oppenheimer, Stephen, and Martin Richards. 2001. "Fast Trains, Slow Boats, and the Ancestry of the Polynesian Islanders". *Science Progress* 84 (3): 157–181.

Orduna, Germán. 1995. "Hispanic Textual Criticism and the Stemmatic Value of the History of the Text". In *Scholarly Editing: A Guide to Research*, edited by David C. Greetham, 486–503. New York, NY: Modern Language Association.

Orduna, Germán. 2000. *Ecdótica: Problemática de la edición de textos*. Kassel: Reichenberger.

Orlandi, Giovanni. 1981. "Problemi di ecdotica alto-medievale". In *La cultura in Italia fra Tardo Antico e Alto Medioevo: Atti del Convegno tenuto a Roma, Consiglio nazionale delle ricerche, dal 12 al 16 novembre 1979*, edited by Manlio Simonetti, Giuseppina Simonetti Abbolito, and Alessandro Fo, 333–356. Rome: Herder.

Orlandi, Giovanni. 1985. "La tradizione del Physiologus e i prodromi del bestiario latino". In *L'uomo di fronte al mondo animale nell'alto medioevo*, 1057–1106. Spoleto: Centro di studi sull'alto medioevo.

Orlandi, Giovanni. 1995. "Perché non possiamo non dirci lachmanniani". *Filologia mediolatina* 2: 1–42 [repr. Orlandi 2008, 95–130].

Orlandi, Giovanni. 2008. *Scritti di filologia mediolatina*. Edited by Paolo Chiesa, Anna Maria Fagnoni, Rossana E. Guglielmetti, and Giovanni Paolo Maggioni. Florence: Edizioni del Galluzzo.

Osburn, Carroll D. 2004. *The Text of the Apostolos in Epiphanius of Salamis*. Atlanta, GA: Society of Biblical Literature.

O'Sullivan, Sinéad. 2011. "Obscurity, Pagan Lore, and Secrecy in Glosses on Books I–II from the Oldest Gloss Tradition". In *Carolingian Scholarship and Martianus Capella: Ninth-Century Commentary Tradition on De nuptiis in Context*, edited by Mariken Teeuwen, 99–122. Turnhout: Brepols.

O'Sullivan, Sinéad. 2016. "Servius in the Carolingian Age: A Case Study of London, British Library, Harley 2782". *Journal of Medieval Latin* 26: 77–123.

O'Sullivan, Sinéad. 2017a. "Reading and the Lemma in Early Medieval Textual Culture". In *The Annotated Book in the Early Middle Ages: Practices of Reading and Writing*, edited by Mariken Teeuwen and Irene van Renswoude, 371–396. Turnhout: Brepols.

O'Sullivan, Sinéad. 2017b. "Text, Gloss and Tradition in the Early Medieval West: Expanding into a World of Learning". In *Teaching and Learning in Medieval Europe: Essays in Honour of Gernot R. Wieland*, ed. by Greti Dinkova-Bruun and Tristan Major. Turnhout: Brepols.

Ottaviano, Silvia. 2013. "Scholia non serviana nei manoscitti carolingi di Virgilio: prime notizie degli scavi". *Examplaria classica* 17: 221–244.

Owen, Stephen. 2007. "The Manuscript Legacy of the Tang: The Case of Literature". *Harvard Journal of Asiatic Studies* 67: 295–326.

Pabel, Hilmar M. 2002. "Reading Jerome in the Renaissance: Erasmus' Reception of the *Adversus Iovinianum*". *Renaissance Quarterly* 55: 470–497.

Pabel, Hilmar M. 2008. *Herculean Labors: Erasmus and the Editing of St. Jerome's Letters in the Renaissance*. Leiden: Brill.

Pakis, Valentine A. 2010. "Contextual Duplicity and Textual Variation: The Siren and Onocentaur in the Physiologus Tradition". *Mediaevistik* 23: 115–186.

Palmer, Ada. 2014. *Reading Lucretius in the Renaissance*. Cambridge, MA: Harvard University Press.

Palumbo, Giovanni. 2018. "L'Art d'éditer les anciens textes: Joseph Bédier philologue, entre théorie et pratique". In *L'Ombre de Joseph Bédier*, edited by Craig Baker, Marcello Barbato, Mattia Cavagna, and Yan Greub, Travaux de Littératures Romanes, 91–134. Strasbourg: Editions de linguistique et de philologie.

Palumbo, Giovanni, and Paolo Rinoldi. 2015. "Prolégomènes à l'édition du corpus français de la Chanson d'Aspremont". In *Epic Connections, Rencontres épiques: Proceedings of the Nineteenth International Conference of the Société Rencesvals, Oxford, 13–17 August 2012*, edited by Marianne J. Ailes, Philip E. Bennett, and Anne Elizabeth Cobby, vol. 2, 549–576. Edinburgh: Société Rencesvals British Branch.

Papamichail, Dimitris, Angela Huang, Edward Kennedy, Jan-Lucas Ott, Andrew Miller, and Georgios Papamichail. 2017. "Live Phylogeny with Polytomies: Finding the Most Compact Parsimonious Trees". *Computational Biology and Chemistry* 69 (August): 171–177. doi.org/10.1016/j.compbiolchem.2017.03.013.

Paratore, Ettore. 1968. *Tradizione e struttura in Dante*. Florence: Sansoni.

Paris, Gaston. 1890. Review of *Le Lai de l'ombre*, edited by Joseph Bédier. *Romania* 19: 609–615.

Paris, Gaston, and Léopold Pannier. 1872. *La Vie de Saint Alexis, poème du XIe siècle et renouvellements des XIIe, XIIIe et XIVe siècles*. Paris: Franck. gallica.bnf.fr/ark:/12148/bpt6k33044x/f3.image.textelmage [repr. Geneva: Slatkine, 1974].

Parker, David C. 2012. *Textual Scholarship and the Making of the New Testament: The Lyell Lectures*. Oxford: Oxford University Press.

Parkes, Malcolm B. 1992. *Pause and Effect: An Introduction to the History of Punctuation in the West*. Aldershot: Scolar Press.

Parkes, Malcolm B. 2008. *Their Hands before Our Eyes: A Closer Look at Scribes*. Oxford: Oxford University Press.

Parks, Donovan H. 2012. "Georeferenced Trees and the Phylogenetic Similarity of Biological Communities". PhD thesis, Dalhousie University.

Parry, Milman. 1930. "Studies in the Epic Technique of Oral Verse-Making: I. Homer and Homeric Style". *Harvard Studies in Classical Philology* 41: 73–148.

Pasquali, Giorgio. 1929. Review of "Textkritik", by Paul Maas. *Gnomon* 5: 417–435, 498–521.

Pasquali, Giorgio. 1932. "Edizione critica". In *Enciclopedia Italiana*, vol. 13, 477–480. Rome: Treccani.

Pasquali, Giorgio. 1934. *Storia della tradizione e critica del testo*. Florence: Le Monnier [2nd ed. 1952].

Pasquali, Giorgio. 1952. *Storia della tradizione e critica del testo*. Reprint with a new introduction and three appendices. Florence: Casa Editrice Le Lettere.

Passannante, Gerd. 2011. *The Lucretian Renaissance: Philology and the Afterlife of Tradition*. Chicago: University of Chicago Press.

Pastorelli, David. 2014. "Le Traitement des variantes". In *Manuel de critique textuelle du Nouveau Testament*, edited by Christian-Bernard Amphoux, 213–247. Brussels: Safran.

Paul, Hermann. 1873. *Gregorius von Hartmann von Aue*. Halle: Niemeyer. [editio maior].

Paul, Hermann. 1874. "Über das gegenseitige Verhältnis der Handschriften von Hartmanns Iwein". *Beiträge zur Geschichte der deutschen Sprache und Literatur* 1: 288–401.

Paul, Hermann. 1882. *Gregorius von Hartmann von Aue*. Halle: Niemeyer. [editio minor].

Paul, Hermann. 1901. "Textkritik". In *Grundriss der Germanischen Philologie*, 2nd ed., edited by Hermann Paul, vol. 1, 184–196. Strasbourg: Trübner.

Pavlopoulos, Georgios A., Theodoros G. Soldatos, Adriano Barbosa-Silva, and Reinhard Schneider. 2010. "A Reference Guide for Tree Analysis and Visualization". *BioData Mining* 3 (1): 1. doi.org/10.1186/1756-0381-3-1.

Peeters, Emil. 1898. *Der griechische Physiologus und seine orientalischen Übersetzungen*. Berlin: Calvary.

Pellegrin, Elisabeth. 1988. *Bibliothèques retrouvées: Manuscrits, bibliothèques et bibliophiles du Moyen Age et de la Renaissance; Recueil d'études publiées de 1938 à 1985*. Paris: CNRS.

Pennuto, Concetta, ed. 2008. *Girolamo Fracastoro: De sympathia et antipathia liber I*. Rome: Edizioni di Storia e Letteratura.

Pera, Ceslai, ed. 1950. *In librum Beati Dionysii de Divinis nominibus expositio*. Turin: Marietti.

Pereltsvaig, Asya, and Martin W. Lewis. 2015. *The Indo-European Controversy*. Cambridge: Cambridge University Press.

Peri, Vittorio. 1967. "Nicola Maniacutia: Un testimone della filologia romana del XII secolo". *Aevum* 41: 67–90.

Perreault, Charles, Sarah Mathew, and Michael D. Petraglia. 2012. "Dating the Origin of Language Using Phonemic Diversity". *PLoS One* 7 (4): e35289. doi.org/10.1371/journal.pone.0035289.

Petitmengin, Pierre. 2004. "Tertullien entre la fin du XIIe et le début du XVIe siècle". In *Padri greci e latini a confronto: Atti del Convegno di studi della SISMEL, Certosa del Galluzzo, Firenze, 19–20 ottobre 2001*, edited by Mariarosa Cortesi, 63–88. Florence: Edizioni del Galluzzo.

Petitmengin, Pierre. 2006. "Le Match Bâle-Paris au XVIe siècle: Editions princeps, éditions revues des Pères latins". In *"Editiones principes" delle opere dei Padri Greci e Latini: Atti del Convegno di studi della SISMEL, Certosa del Galluzzo, Firenze, 24–25 ottobre 2003*, edited by Mariarosa Cortesi, 3–39. Florence: Edizioni del Galluzzo.

Petrocchi, Giorgio, ed. 1966–1967. *Dante Alighieri: La commedia secondo l'antica vulgata*. 4 vols. Milan: Mondadori.

Petrucci, Armando. 1992. *Breve storia della scrittura latina*. 2nd ed. Rome: Bagatto Libri.

Pettegree, Andrew. 2011. *The Book in the Renaissance*. New York, NY: Yale University Press.

Petzold, Charles. 2000. *Code: The Hidden Language of Computer Hardware and Software*. Redmond, WA: Microsoft Press.

Phillips-Rodriguez, Wendy J., Christopher J. Howe, and Heather F. Windram. 2009. "Chi-Squares and the Phenomenon of 'Change of Exemplar' in the Dyūtaparvan". In *Sanskrit Computational Linguistics: First and Second International Symposia Rocquencourt, France, October 29–31, 2007 Providence, RI, USA, May 15–17, 2008*, edited by Gérard Huet, Amba Kulkarni, and Peter Scharf, 380–390. Berlin: Springer.

Phillips-Rodriguez, Wendy J., Christopher J. Howe, and Heather F. Windram. 2010. "Some Considerations about Bifurcation in Diagrams Representing the Written Transmission of the Mahābhārata". *Wiener Zeitschrift für die Kunde Südasiens/Vienna Journal of South Asian Studies* 52–53: 29–43.

Piccolomini, Giacomo Ammannati. 1506. *Epistolae et commentarii Jacobi Piccolomini Cardinalis Papiensis*. Milan: apud Alexandrum Minutianum.

Pierazzo, Elena. 2011. "A Rationale of Digital Documentary Editions". *Literary and Linguistic Computing* 26: 463–477. doi.org/10.1093/llc/fqr033.

Pierazzo, Elena. 2015. *Digital Scholarly Editing: Theories, Models and Method*. Farnham: Routledge.

Piez, Wendell. 2014. "Hierarchies within Range Space: From LMNL to OHCO". *Balisage Series on Markup Technologies* 13 (= "Proceedings of Balisage: The Markup Conference 2014"). doi.org/10.4242/BalisageVol13.Piez01.

Piovanelli, Pierluigi. 1987. "Sulla Vorlage aramaica dell'Enoch etiopico". *Studi Classici e Orientali* 37: 545–594.

Piovanelli, Pierluigi. 1988. "Il testo e le traduzioni dell'Enoch etiopico 1976–1987". *Henoch* 10: 85–95.

Pisani, Vitagrazia. 2013. "Il culto di san Qirqos nell'Etiopia storica: Analisi storico-filologica, con edizione critica della 'Passio' (Gädlä Qirqos)". PhD thesis, Università degli Studi di Napoli.

Pisani, Vitagrazia. 2015. "Pantaleone da Nicomedia in Etiopia: Il Gädl e la tradizione manoscritta". In *Aethiopia Fortitudo ejus: Studi in onore di Monsignor Osvaldo Raineri in occasione del suo 80° compleanno*, edited by Rafał Zarzeczny, 355–380. Rome: Pontificio Istituto Orientale.

Pitra, Jean-Baptiste. 1883. *Analecta sacra spicilegio solesmensi parata*. Vol. 4. Paris: Didot.

Pitt Rivers, Augustus H. Lane-Fox 1875. "On the Principles of Classification Adopted in the Arrangement of His Anthropological Collection Now Exhibited in the Bethnal Green Museum". *Journal of the Anthropological Institute* 4: 293–308.

Pitt Rivers, Augustus H. Lane-Fox. 1906. *The Evolution of Culture and Other Essays*. Oxford: Clarendon Press.

Plachta, Bodo. 1997. *Editionswissenschaft: Eine Einführung in Methode und Praxis der Edition neuerer Texte*. Stuttgart: Reclam.

Plachta, Bodo, and Hendricus T. M. van Vliet. 2000. "Überlieferung, Philologie und Repräsentation: Zum Verhältnis von Editionen und Institutionen". In *Text und Edition: Positionen und Perspektiven*, edited by Rüdiger Nutt-Kofoth, Bodo Plachta, Hendricus T. M. van Vliet, and Herman Zwerschina, 11–35. Berlin: Schmidt.

Plate, Ralf. 2020. "Zur Text- und Überlieferungsgeschichte der 'Weltchronik' Rudolfs von Ems." In *Rudolf von Ems. Beiträge zu Autor, Werk und Überlieferung*, edited by Elke Krotz, Norbert Kössinger, Henrike Manuwald, and Stephan Müller, 201–266. Stuttgart: S. Hirzel Verlag.

Platnick, Norman I., and Howard Don Cameron. 1977. "Cladistic Methods in Textual, Linguistic, and Phylogenetic Analysis". *Systematic Zoology* 26 (4): 380–385.

Poccetti, Paolo, and Carlo Santini. 1999. "Orale e scritto". In *Una storia della lingua latina: Formazione, usi, communicazione*, edited by Paolo Poccetti, Diego Poli, and Carlo Santini, 173–234. Rome: Carocci editore.

Pöhlmann, Egert. 1994. *Einführung in die Überlieferungsgeschichte und die Textkritik der antiken Literatur*. Vol. 1. *Altertum*. Darmstadt: Wissenschaftliche Buchgesellschaft.

Pöhlmann, Egert. 2003. "Textkritik und Texte im 19. und 20. Jh.". In *Einführung in die Überlieferungsgeschichte und die Textkritik der antiken Literatur*, edited by Egert Pöhlmann, vol. 2, *Mittelalter und Neuzeit*, 137–182. Darmstadt: Wissenschaftliche Buchgesellschaft.

Pöhlmann, Egert, and Martin West, eds. 2001. *Documents of Ancient Greek Music: The Extant Melodies and Fragments*. Oxford: Clarendon Press.

Poirel, Dominique. 2016. "Lachmann, Bédier, Froger: Quelle méthode d'édition donne les meilleurs résultats?". In *La Rigueur et la passion: Mélanges en l'honneur de Pascale Bourgain*, edited by Cédric Giraud and Dominique Poirel, 939–968. Turnhout: Brepols.

Poli, Diego. 1999. "Il latino tra formalizzazione e pluralità". In *Una storia della lingua latina: Formazione, usi, communicazione*, edited by Paolo Poccetti, Diego Poli, and Carlo Santini, 377–431. Rome: Carocci editore.

Poliziano, Angelo. 1567. *Miscellaneorum centuria I*. Antwerp: Nutius.

Pompei, Simone, Vittorio Loreto, and Francesca Tria. 2018. "Copystree". *Language Dynamics and Change* 8 (1): 55–77.

Poole, Eric. 1974. "The Computer in Determining Stemmatic Relationships". *Computers and the Humanities* 8 (4): 207–216. doi.org/10.1007/BF02402342.

Popper, Karl R. 1965. *Conjectures and Refutations: The Growth of Scentific Knowledge*. 2nd ed. London: Routledge.

Porter, A. 1976. "Problems in Editing the Music of Josquin des Prez: A Critique of the First Edition and Proposals for the Second Edition". In *Josquin des Prez: Proceedings of the International Josquin Festival-Conference held at the Juilliard School at Lincoln Center in New York City, 21–25 June 1971*, edited by Edward E. Lowinsky und Bonnie J. Blackburn, 721–754. Oxford: Oxford University Press.

Potken, Johannes. 1513. *Psalterium David et cantica aliqua*. Rome: Marcellus Silber.

Potken, Johannes. 1518. *Psalterium in quatuor linguis Hebraea Graeca Chaldaea Latina*. Cologne: Johannes Soter.

Procter, Michael. 2006. "*Alma redemptoris mater*: Notes toward a Filiation of the Chant". *Sacred Music* 133: 39–41.
Purves, William K., David Sadava, Gordon H. Orians, and H. Craig Heller. 2004. *Life: The Science of Biology*. 7th ed. Gordonsville, VA: Sinauer.
Quentin, Henri. 1908. *Les Martyrologes historiques du moyen âge: Etude sur la formation du martyrologe romain*. Etudes d'histoire des dogmes et d'ancienne littérature ecclésiastique. Paris: Gabalda.
Quentin, Henri. 1922. *Mémoire sur l'établissement du texte de la Vulgate*. Rome: Desclée.
Quentin, Henri. 1926. *Essais de critique textuelle (ecdotique)*. Paris: Picard.
Raben, Joseph. 1991. "Humanities Computing 25 Years Later". *Computers and the Humanities* 25 (6): 341–350. doi.org/10.1007/BF00141184.
Racine, Jean-François. 2004. *The Text of Matthew in the Writings of Basil of Caesarea*. The New Testament in the Greek Fathers 5. Atlanta, GA: Society of Biblical Literature.
Ræder, Hans, and Helge Larsen. 1981. "J. N. Madvig". In *Dansk Biografisk Leksikon*, 3rd ed., vol. 9, 344–348. Copenhagen: Gyldendal. denstoredanske.dk/index.php?sideId=294017.
Raineri, Osvaldo. 2004. *Gli Atti di Qawesṭos martire etiopico (Sec. XIV)*. Vatican City: Biblioteca Apostolica Vaticana.
Rajna, Pio. 1907. "Testi critici" [appendix]. In *Avviamento allo studio critico delle lettere italiane*, by Guido Mazzoni, 2nd ed., 207–217. Florence: Sansoni.
Rajna, Pio. 1929. "Un nuovo testo parziale del Saint Alexis primitivo". *Archivum Romanicum* 13: 1–86.
Räkel, Hans-Herbert. 1973. "Drei Lieder zum dritten Kreuzzug". *Deutsche Vierteljahrsschrift für Literaturwissenschaft und Geistesgeschichte* 47: 508–550.
Räkel, Hans-Herbert. 1977. *Die musikalische Erscheinungsform der Trouvèrepoesie*. Bonn: Haupt.
Ramsay, Stephen. 2004. "Databases". In *A Companion to Digital Humanities*, edited by Susan Schreibman, Ray Siemens, and John Unsworth, 177–197. Oxford: Blackwell.
Rand, Edward Kennard, ed. 1904. "Sermo de confusione diaboli". *Modern Philology* 2: 261–278.
Raymond, Eric S. 1999. *The Cathedral and the Bazaar: Musings on Linux and Open Source by an Accidental Revolutionary*. Cambridge, MA: O'Reilly. catb.org/~esr/writings/cathedral-bazaar.
Reeve, Michael D. 1980. "The Italian Tradition of Lucretius". *Italia Medievale e Umanistica* 23: 27–48.
Reeve, Michael D. 1985. "Archetypes". In *Studi in onore di Adelmo Barigazzi*, vol. 2, 193–201. Rome: Ed. dell'Ateneo.
Reeve, Michael D. 1986. "Stemmatic Method: 'Qualcosa che non funziona'?". In *The role of the Book in Medieval Culture: Proceedings of the Oxford International Symposium 26 September–1 October 1982*, edited by Peter Ganz, vol. 1, 57–69. Turnhout: Brepols [repr. Reeve 2011a, 28–44].
Reeve, Michael D. 1989. "Eliminatio codicum descriptorum: A Methodological Problem". In *Editing Greek and Latin Texts: Papers Given at the Twenty-Third Annual Conference on Editorial Problems, University of Toronto, 6–7 November 1987*, edited by John N. Grant, 1–35. New York, NY: AMS Press.
Reeve, Michael D. 1998. "Shared Innovations, Dichotomies, and Evolution". In *Filologia classica e filologia romanza: Esperienze ecdotiche a confronto; Atti del Convegno Roma 25–27 maggio 1995*, edited by Anna Ferrari, 445–505. Spoleto: CISAM [repr. Reeve 2011a, 55–103].
Reeve, Michael D. 2000. "Cuius in usum? Recent and Future Editing". *Journal of Roman Studies* 90: 196–206 [repr. Reeve 2011a, 339–359].
Reeve, Michael D. 2011a. *Manuscripts and Methods: Essays on Editing and Transmission*. Rome: Edizioni di Storia e Letteratura.
Reeve, Michael D. 2011b. "Editing Classical Texts with a Computer: Hyginus's *Astronomica*". In *Manuscripts and Methods: Essays on Editing and Transmission*, by Michael D. Reeve, 361–393. Rome: Edizioni di Storia e Letteratura.

Reich, David. 2018. "Social Inequality Leaves a Genetic Mark – When Genetic Structure Follows Social Structure". *Nautilus Magazine*, March 29. nautil.us/issue/58/self/social-inequality-leaves-a-genetic-mark.

Renear, Allen H. 2004. "Text Encoding". In *A Companion to Digital Humanities*, edited by Susan Schreibman, Ray Siemens, and John Unsworth, 218–239. Oxford: Blackwell.

Renear, Allen H., Elli Mylonas, and David G. Durand. 1996. "Refining Our Notion of What Text Really Is: The Problem of Overlapping Hierarchies". In *Research in Humanities Computing*, edited by Nancy Ide and Susan Hockey, 263–277. Oxford: Oxford University Press.

Renfrew, Colin. 1987. *Archaeology and Language: The Puzzle of Indo-European Origins*. London: Cape.

Renneboog, Luc, and Tom van Houtte. 2002. "The Monetary Appreciation of Paintings: From Realism to Magritte". *Cambridge Journal of Economics* 26 (3): 331–358. doi.org/10.1093/cje/26.3.331.

Restivo, Giuseppina. 1994. "The Genesis of Beckett's *Endgame* Traced in a 1950 Holograph". *Samuel Beckett Today/Aujourd'hui* 3: 85–96.

Reuss, Eduard. 1872. *Bibliotheca Novi Testamenti Graeci*. Brunswick: Schwetschke.

Reynolds, Leighton D., ed. 1965. *L. Annaei Senecae ad Lucilium Epistulae morales*. 2 vols. Oxford: Oxford University Press.

Reynolds, Leighton D. 1983. "Lucretius". In *Texts and Transmission: A Survey of the Latin Classics*, edited by Leighton D. Reynolds, 218–222. Oxford: Clarendon Press.

Reynolds, Leighton D. 2000. "Experiences of an Editor of Classical Latin Texts". *Revue d'histoire des textes* 30: 1–15.

Reynolds, Leighton D., and Nigel G. Wilson. 2013. *Scribes and Scholars: A Guide to the Transmission of Greek and Latin Literature*. 4th ed. Oxford: Clarendon Press [1st ed. 1968, 2nd ed. 1974, 3rd ed. 1991].

Rhoby, Andreas. 2014. *Byzantinische Epigramme in inschriftlicher Überlieferung*. Vol. 3. *Byzantinische Epigramme auf Stein*. Vienna: Österreichische Akademie der Wissenschaften.

Riccò, Laura. 1996. "Testo per la scena, testo per la stampa: Problemi di edizione". *Giornale storico della letteratura italiana* 173: 210–266.

Richards, William L. 1977. *The Classification of the Greek Manuscripts of the Johannine Epistles*. Missoula, MT: Scholars Press.

Richter, Matthias L. 2013. *The Embodied Text: Establishing Textual Identity in Early Chinese Manuscripts*. Leiden: Brill.

Rindal, Magnus, ed. 1981. *Barlaams ok Josaphats saga*. Oslo: Norsk Historisk Kjeldeskrift-Institutt.

Ringe, Don, Tandy Warnow, and Ann Taylor. 2002. "Indo-European and Computational Cladistics". *Transactions of the Philological Society* 100 (1): 59–129. doi.org/10.1111/1467-968X.00091.

Rizzo, Silvia. 1973. *Il lessico filologico degli umanisti*. Rome: Edizioni di Storia e Letteratura.

Robins, William. 2007. "Editing and Evolution". *Literature Compass* 4 (1): 89–120.

Robinson, Peter. 1989. "The Collation and Textual Criticism of Icelandic Manuscripts (1): Collation". *Literary and Linguistic Computing* 4: 99–105.

Robinson, Peter. 1994. "Collate: A Program for Interactive Collation of Large Textual Traditions". *Research in Humanities Computing* 3: 32–45.

Robinson, Peter. 1996a. "Computer-Assisted Stemmatic Analysis and 'Best-Text' Historical Editing". In *Studies in Stemmatology*, edited by Pieter van Reenen and Margot van Mulken, 71–104. Philadelphia: Benjamins.

Robinson, Peter, ed. 1996b. *Geoffrey Chaucer: The Wife of Bath's Prologue on CD-ROM*. The Canterbury Tales Project. Cambridge: Cambridge University Press.

Robinson, Peter. 2000. "The One Text and the Many Texts". *Literary and Linguistic Computing* 15 (1): 5–14.

Robinson, Peter. 2002. "What Is a Critical Digital Edition?". *Variants* 1: 43–62.
Robinson, Peter. 2013a. "Towards a Theory of Digital Editions". *Variants* 10: 105–131.
Robinson, Peter. 2013b. "Why Digital Humanists Should Get Out of Textual Scholarship". Presentation at Social, Digital, Scholarly Editing, University of Saskatchewan, Saskatoon, July 11–13. academia.edu/4124828/SDSE_2013_why_digital_humanists_should_get_out_of_textual_scholarship.
Robinson, Peter. 2015. "Four Rules for the Application of Phylogenetics in the Analysis of Textual Traditions". *Digital Scholarship in the Humanities* 31 (3): 637–651.
Robinson, Peter. 2017. "Some Principles for Making Collaborative Scholarly Editions in Digital Form". *Digital Humanities Quarterly* 11.2 digitalhumanities.org/dhq/vol/11/2/000293/000293.html.
Robinson, Peter, and Robert J. O'Hara. 1992. "Report on the Textual Criticism Challenge 1991". *Bryn Mawr Classical Review* 3 (4): 331–337.
Robinson, Peter, and Robert J. O'Hara. 1996. "Cladistic Analysis of an Old Norse Manuscript Tradition". *Research in Humanities Computing* 4: 115–137. rjohara.net/cv/1996-rhc.
Roche, Paul, ed. 2009. *Lucan: De bello civili; Book 1*. Oxford: Oxford University Press.
Rocher, Ludo. 1995. "Sanskrit Literature". In *Scholarly Editing: A Guide to Research*, edited by David C. Greetham, 575–599. New York, NY: Modern Language Association.
Roelli, Philipp. 2014. "Petrus Alfonsi; or, On the Mutual Benefit of Traditional and Computerised Stemmatology". In *Analysis of Ancient and Medieval Texts and Manuscripts: Digital Approaches*, edited by Tara Andrews and Caroline Macé, 43–64. Turnhout: Brepols.
Roelli, Philipp, and Dieter Bachmann. 2010. "Towards Generating a Stemma of Complicated Manuscript Traditions: Petrus Alfonsi's Dialogus". *Revue d'histoire des textes* 5 (2010): 307–331. doi.org/10.1484/J.RHT.5.101260.
Roelli, Philipp, and Caroline Macé, eds. 2015. *Parvum lexicon stemmatologicum*. wiki.helsinki.fi/display/stemmatology/Parvum+lexicon+stemmatologicum, doi.org/10.5167/uzh-121539.
Roethe, Gustav. 1904. [Untitled preliminary note on the DTM series]. In *Friedrich von Schwaben aus der Stuttgarter Handschrift*, edited by Max Hermann Jellinek, Deutsche Texte des Mittelalters 1, v–vii. Berlin: Weidmann.
Roethe, Gustav. 1913. "Die deutsche Kommission der Königlich Preussischen Akademie der Wissenschaften: Ihre Vorgeschichte, ihre Arbeiten und Ziele". *Neue Jahrbücher für das klassische Altertum, Geschichte und deutsche Literatur und für Pädagogik* 31: 37–74.
Roncali, Renata, ed. 1990. *L. Annaei Senecae Apokolokyntosis*. Leipzig: Teubner.
Ronquist, Frederik, Maxim Teslenko, Paul van der Mark, Daniel L. Ayres, Aaron Darling, Sebastian Höhna, Bret Larget, Liang Liu, Marc A. Suchard, and John P. Huelsenbeck. 2012. "MrBayes 3.2: Efficient Bayesian Phylogenetic Inference and Model Choice across a Large Model Space". *Systematic Biology* 61 (3): 539–542. doi.org/10.1093/sysbio/sys029.
Roos, Teemu, and Tuomas Heikkilä. 2009. "Evaluating Methods for Computer-Assisted Stemmatology Using Artificial Benchmark Data Sets". *Literary and Linguistic Computing* 24 (4): 417–433. doi.org/10.1093/llc/fqp002.
Roos, Teemu, Tuomas Heikkilä, and Petri Myllymäki. 2006. "A Compression-Based Method for Stemmatic Analysis". In *Proceedings ECAI 2006: 17th European Conference on Artificial Intelligence August 29–September 1, 2006, Riva Del Garda, Italy*, Frontiers in Artificial Intelligence and Applications, 805–806. Amsterdam: IOS Press. ebooks.iospress.nl/volume/ecai-2006.
Roos, Teemu, and Yuan Zou. 2011. "Analysis of Textual Variation by Latent Tree Structures". In *2011: IEEE 11th International Conference on Data Mining*, 567–576. Vancouver: IEEE. doi.org/10.1109/ICDM.2011.24.
Ros-Fábregas, Emilio. 1992. "The Manuscript Biblioteca de Catalunya, M. 454: Study and Edition in the Context of the Iberian and Continental Manuscript Traditions". 2 vols. PhD thesis, City University of New York.

Rosselli Del Turco, Roberto, Giancarlo Buomprisco, Chiara Di Pietro, Julia Kenny, Raffaele Masotti, and Jacopo Pugliese. 2014. "Edition Visualization Technology: A Simple Tool to Visualize TEI-Based Digital Editions". *Journal of the Text Encoding Initiative* 8. doi.org/10.4000/jtei.1077.

Rouquette, Maïeul. 2018. "Reledmac: Typeset Scholarly Editions with LaTeX". mirrors.ctan.org/macros/latex/contrib/reledmac/reledmac.pdf.

Ruh, Kurt, ed. 1985. *Überlieferungsgeschichtliche Prosaforschung: Beiträge der Würzburger Forschergruppe zur Methode und Auswertung*. Tübingen: Niemeyer.

Ruhlen, Merritt. 1994. *The Origin of Language: Tracing the Evolution of the Mother Tongue*. New York, NY: John Wiley & Sons.

Russell, Beth. 2001. "Cataloging in Medieval Libraries". *Encyclopedia of Library and Information Science* 69: 17–33.

Russo, Carlo Ferdinando, ed. 1942. *L. Annaei Senecae Divi Claudii Apokolokyntosis*. Florence: La Nuova Italia.

Rychner, Jean, ed. 1958. *Marie de France: Le Lai de Lanval*. Textes littéraires de français. Geneva: Droz; Paris: Minard.

Rychner, Jean, ed. 1968. *Les Lais de Marie de France*. Paris: Champion.

Rzhetsky, Andrey, and Masatoshi Nei. 1992. "Statistical Properties of the Ordinary Least-Squares, Generalized Least-Squares, and Minimum-Evolution Methods of Phylogenetic Inference". *Journal of Molecular Evolution* 35 (4): 367–375. doi.org/10.1007/BF00161174.

Sabbadini, Remigio. 1967. *Le scoperte dei codici latini e greci ne' secoli XIV e XV (ed. anastatica con nuove aggiunte e correzioni dell'autore a cura di Eugenio Garin)*. 2 vols. Florence: Sansoni.

Saenger, Paul. 1997. *Space between Words: The Origins of Silent Reading*. Stanford, CA: Stanford University Press.

Sahle, Patrick. 2010. "Zwischen Mediengebundenheit und Transmedialisierung: Anmerkungen zum Verhältnis von Edition und Medien". *editio* 24: 23–36.

Sahle, Patrick. 2013. *Digitale Editionsformen: Zum Umgang mit der Überlieferung unter den Bedingungen des Medienwandels – Befunde, Theorie und Methodik*. 3 vols. Norderstedt: BoD.

Sahle, Patrick. 2016. "What Is a Scholarly Digital Edition (SDE)?". In *Digital Scholarly Editing: Theory, Practice and Future Perspectives*, edited by Matthew Driscoll and Elena Pierazzo, 19–39. n.p.: Open Book. dx.doi.org/10.11647/OBP.0095.02.

Said, Edward W. 1978. *Orientalism*. London: Routledge & Kegan Paul.

Saitou, Naruya, and Masatoshi Nei. 1987. "The Neighbor-Joining Method: A New Method for Reconstructing Phylogenetic Trees". *Molecular Biology and Evolution* 4 (4): 406–425. doi.org/10.1093/oxfordjournals.molbev.a040454.

Salemans, Ben J. P. 1996. "Cladistics or the Resurrection of the Method of Lachmann: On Building the Stemma of Yvain". In *Studies in Stemmatology*, edited by Pieter van Reenen and Margot van Mulken, 3–55. Philadelphia, PA: Benjamins.

Salemans, Ben J. P. 2000. "Building Stemmas with the Computer in a Cladistic, Neo-Lachmannian, Way: The Case of Fourteen Text Versions of *Lanseloet van Denemerken*". PhD thesis, Katholieke Universiteit Nijmegen. dbnl.org/arch/sale003buil01_01/pag/sale003buil01_01.pdf.

Salles, Catherine. 2010. *Lire à Rome*. 3rd ed. Paris: Editions Payot [1st ed. Paris: Les Belles Lettres, 1992].

Sallmann, Klaus. 1990. *Normae orthographicae et orthotypicae Latinae: Regeln für die lateinische Rechtschreibung und den Drucksatz*. Rome: Academia Latinitati focendae.

Sanger, Frederick, Steven Nicklen, and Alan R. Coulson. 1977. "DNA Sequencing with Chain-Terminating Inhibitors". *Proceedings of the National Academy of Sciences* 74 (12): 5463–5467.

Sanguineti, Federico, ed. 2001. *Dantis Alagherii Comedìa: Edizione critica per cura di Federico Sanguineti*. Florence: Edizioni del Galluzzo.
Sargent, Michael G. 2013. "Organic and Cybernetic Metaphors for Manuscript Relations: Stemma – Cladogram – Rhizome – Cloud". In *The Pseudo-Bonaventuran Lives of Christ*, edited by Ian Johnson and Alan F. Westphall, 197–263. Turnhout: Brepols.
Sasse, Barbara. 2017. *Die ur- und frühgeschichtliche Archäologie 1630–1850*. Berlin: De Gruyter.
Sawyer, Peter. 1968. *Anglo-Saxon Charters: An Annotated List and Bibliography*. London: Royal Historical Society.
Sayce, Olive. 1982. *The Medieval German Lyric, 1150–1300: The Development of Its Themes and Forms in Their European Context*. Oxford: Oxford University Press.
Sbordone, Francesco, ed. 1936. *Physiologus*. Milan: in Aedibus Societatis Dante Alighieri.
Scaliger, Joseph. 1577. *Castigationes in Catullum, Tibullum, Propertium*. Paris: Mamert Patison.
Schäfer, Peter. 1986. "Research into Rabbinic Literature: An Attempt to Define the *Status Quaestionis*". *Journal of Jewish Studies* 37: 139–152.
Schaffer, Martha E. 2000. "The Evolution of the Cantigas de Santa Maria: The Relationships between T, F and E". In *Cobras e Son: Papers on the Text, Music and Manuscripts of the Cantigas de Santa Maria*, edited by Stephen Parkinson, 188–213. Oxford: Legenda.
Schedel, Hartmann. 1493. *Liber chronicarum*. Nuremberg: Anton Koberger. doi.org/10.11588/diglit.8305.
Schedel, Hartmann. 2001. *Weltchronik: Kolorierte Gesamtausgabe von 1493*. Cologne: Taschen.
Scheideler, Ulrich. 2017. "Filiation". In *Musikphilologie: Grundlagen, Methoden, Praxis*, edited by Bernhard Appel und Reinmar Emans, Kompendium Musik 3, 191–195. Laaber: Laaber.
Schiegg, Markus. 2016. "Scribes' Voices: The Relevance and Types of Early Medieval Colophons". *Studia neophilologica* 88 (2): 129–147.
Schiffels, Stephan, Wolfgang Haak, Pirita Paajanen, Bastien Llamas, Elizabeth Popescu, Louise Lou, Rachel Clarke, Alice Lyons, Richard Mortimer, Duncan Sayer, et al. 2016. "Iron Age and Anglo-Saxon Genomes from East England Reveal British Migration History". *Nature Communications* 7. doi.org/10.1038/ncomms10408.
Schirok, Bernd, ed. 1999. *Wolfram von Eschenbach: Parzival; Studienausgabe: Mittelhochdeutscher Text nach der sechsten Ausgabe von Karl Lachmann*. Berlin: De Gruyter.
Schirok, Bernd. 2011. "Die Handschriften und die Entwicklung des Textes". In *Wolfram von Eschenbach: Ein Handbuch*, edited by Joachim Heinzle, vol. 1, 308–334. Berlin: De Gruyter.
Schlebusch, Carina M., Helena Malmström, Torsten Günther, Per Sjödin, Alexandra Coutinho, Hanna Edlund, Arielle R. Munters, Mário Vicente, Maryna Steyn, Himla Soodyall, et al. 2017. "Southern African Ancient Genomes Estimate Modern Human Divergence to 350,000 to 260,000 Years Ago". *Science* 360 (6396): 652–655. doi.org/10.1126/science.aao6266.
Schleicher, August. 1861. *Compendium der vergleichenden Grammatik der indogermanischen Sprachen*. 2 vols. Weimar: Boehlau.
Schlyter, Carl Johan, and Hans Samuel Collin, eds. 1827. *Westgöta-Lagen*. Stockholm: Häggström.
Schmeidler, Bernhard, ed. 1917. *Adam von Bremen: Hamburgische Kirchengeschichte*. 3rd ed. Hanover: Hahnsche Buchhandlung.
Schmid, Bernhold. 1999. "Lassos Nunc gaudere licet: Zur Geschichte einer Kontrafaktur". In *Compositionswissenschaft: Festschrift Reinhold und Roswitha Schlötterer zum 70. Geburtstag*, edited by Bernd Edelmann and Sabine Kurth, 47–56. Augsburg: Wißner.
Schmidt, Desmond, and Robert Colomb. 2009. "A Data Structure for Representing Multi-Version Texts Online". *International Journal of Human-Computer Studies* 67: 497–514.
Schmidt, Peter Lebrecht. 1988. "Lachmann's Method: On the History of a Misunderstanding". In *The Uses of Greek and Latin*, edited by Anna Carlotta Dionisotti, Anthony Grafton, and Jill Kraye, 227–236. London: Warburg Institute, University of London.
Schmidt, Peter Lebrecht. 2006. "Asinius [IV.1] Pollio". In *Brill's New Pauly*, edited by Hubert Cancik and Helmut Schneider. dx.doi.org/10.1163/1574-9347_bnp_e203220.

Schneider, Thomas Franz. 2006. "Zwei Neufunde zu Wolframs von Eschenbach 'Parzival': Die beiden dreispaltigen Solothurner Fragmente F 31 (A) und F 69". In *Text und Text in lateinischer und volkssprachliger Überlieferung des Mittelalters*, edited by Eckart Conrad Lutz, Wolfram-Studien 19, 449–479. Berlin: Schmidt.

Schnell, Rüdiger. 1998. "'Autor' und 'Werk' im Deutschen Mittelalter: Forschungskritik und Forschungsperspektiven". In *Neue Wege der Mittelalter-Philologie: Landshuter Kolloquium 1996*, edited by Joachim Heinzle, L. Peter Johnson, and Gisela Vollmann-Profe, Wolfram-Studien 15, 12–73. Berlin: Schmidt.

Schöller, Robert. 2009. *Die Fassung *T des "Parzival" Wolframs von Eschenbach: Untersuchungen zur Überlieferung und zum Textprofil*. Berlin: De Gruyter.

Schrader, Otto. 1883. *Sprachvergleichung und Urgeschichte: Linguistisch-historische Beiträge zur Erforschung des indogermanischen Altertums*. Jena: Costenoble.

Schreibman, Susan. 2016. "Home". January 21. v-machine.org.

Schreibman, Susan, Amit Kumar, and Jarom McDonald. 2003. "The Versioning Machine". *Literary and Linguistic Computing* 18: 101–107.

Schröder, Werner, ed. 1978. *Wolfram von Eschenbach: Willehalm*. Berlin: De Gruyter.

Schröder, Werner. 1998. "Bumke contra Lachmann; oder, Wie die 'Neue Philologie' die mittelhochdeutschen Dichter enteignet". *Mittellateinisches Jahrbuch* 33 (1): 171–183 [repr. Schröder 1999, 284–296].

Schröder, Werner. 1999. *Critica Selecta: Zu neuen Ausgaben mittelhochdeutscher und frühneuhochdeutscher Texte*. Edited by Wolfgang Maaz and Fritz Wagner. Hildesheim: Weidmann.

Schulz, Hans-Jörg. 2011. "Treevis.net: A Tree Visualization Reference". *IEEE Computer Graphics and Applications* 31, no. 6 (November–December): 11–15. doi.org/10.1109/MCG.2011.103.

Schweizerischer Nationalfonds. 2014. "Call für Editionsprojekte mit Blick auf die Finanzierungsperiode 2017–2020". snf.ch/SiteCollectionDocuments/call_editionen_d.pdf.

Seeck, Otto, ed. 1883. *Q. Aurelii Symmachi quae supersunt*. Berlin: Weidmann [repr. 1961].

Segre, Cesare. 1961. "Appunti sul problema delle contaminazioni nei testi in prosa". In *Studi e problemi di critica testuale: Convegno di studi di filologia italiana nel centenario della Commissione per i testi di lingua, 7–9 aprile 1960*, 63–67. Bologna: Commissione per i testi di lingua [repr. Segre 1998, 71–74].

Segre, Cesare, ed. 1971. *La Chanson de Roland*. Milan: Riccardi.

Segre, Cesare. 1976. "Critique textuelle, théorie des ensembles et diasystème". *Bulletin de la classe des lettres et des sciences morales et politiques de l'Académie royale de Belgique* 62: 279–292.

Segre, Cesare. 1978. "La critica testuale". In *Atti di XIV Congresso internazionale di Linguistica e Filologia Romanza, Napoli, 15–20 aprile 1974*, vol. 1, *Sedute plenarie e tavole rotonde*, edited by Alberto Vàrvaro, 439–499. Naples: Macchiaroli.

Segre, Cesare. 1979. "Les Transcriptions en tant que diasystèmes". In *La Pratique des ordinateurs dans la critique des textes: Paris 29–31 mars 1978*, edited by Jean Irigoin and Gian Zarri, 45–49. Paris: Editions du CNRS.

Segre, Cesare. 1998. *Ecdotica e comparatistica romanze*. Milan: Ricciardi.

Segre, Cesare. 2001. Review of *Joseph Bédier, écrivain et philologue*, by Alain Corbellari. *Revue critique de philologie romane* 2: 82–91.

Segre, Cesare. 2016. "Lachmann et Bédier: La Guerre est finie". In *Actes du XXVIIe congrès international de linguistique et de philologie romanes*, edited by Eva Buchi, Jean-Paul Chauveau, and Jean-Marie Pierrel, 15–28. Strasbourg: Editions de linguistique et de philologie.

Sela, Ori. 2018. *China's Philological Turn: Scholars, Textualism, and the Dao in the Eighteenth Century*. New York, NY: Columbia University Press.

Shannon, Ross. 2019. "HTML Source: HTML Tutorials". yourhtmlsource.com/fullindex.
Shaw, Prue, ed. 2010. *Dante Alighieri: Commedia; A Digital Edition.* sd-editions.com/AnaAdditional/commediaonline/home.html.
Sheldon-Williams, Inglis Patrick, ed. 1968–. *Iohannis Scotti Eriugenae Periphyseon (De divisione naturae).* With Ludwig Bieler, Edouard A. Jeauneau, and John J. O'Meara. 4 vols. Dublin: Dublin Institute for Advanced Studies.
Shiferaw Bekele. 2008. "Interface between Philology and History: The Search for Medievalist Historians". *Bulletin of Philological Society of Ethiopia (Addis Ababa University, Department of Linguistics)* 1 (1): 47–55.
Shillingsburg, Peter. 1996. *Scholarly Editing in the Computer Age.* 3rd ed. Ann Arbor: University of Michigan Press.
Shinan, Avigdor, ed. 1984. *Midrash Shemot Rabba: Chapters I–XIV.* Jerusalem: Devir.
Siegmund, Albert. 1949. *Die Überlieferung der griechischen christlichen Literatur in der lateinischen Kirche bis zum zwölften Jahrhundert.* Munich: Filser.
Sievers, Eduard, ed. 1878. *Heliand.* Halle an der Saale: Verlag der Buchhandlung des Weisenhauses.
Signes Codoñer, Juan. 2014. "Towards a Vocabulary for Rewriting in Byzantium". In *Textual Transmission in Byzantium: Between Textual Criticism and Quellenforschung*, edited by Juan Signes Codoñer and Inmaculada Pérez Martín, 61–90. Turnhout: Brepols.
Simms, Douglas. 2017. "The Old English Name of the S-Rune and 'Sun' in Germanic". *Journal of Germanic Linguistics* 29 (1): 26–49.
Simonetti, Manlio. 2012, "L'edizione critica di un testo patristico: Caratteri e problemi". In *La trasmissione dei testi patristici latini: Problemi e prospettive*, edited by Emanuela Colombi, 33–49. Turnhout: Brepols.
Singer, Johannes, ed. 2016. *Strickers Karl der Große.* Berlin: De Gruyter.
Sinko, Taddeus. 1917. *De traditione orationum Gregorii Nazianzeni.* Cracow: Gebethner et Wolff.
Siponta De Salvia, Maria, ed. 1986. *Biblioteca Medicea Laurenziana.* Florence: Nardini.
Sirat, Colette. 2006. *Writing as Handwork: A History of Handwriting in Mediterranean and Western Culture.* Turnhout: Brepols.
Siri, Francesco. 2013. "*Lectio, disputatio, reportatio*: Note su alcune pratuiche didattiche nel XII secolo e sulla loro transmissione". In *Medioevo e filosofia per Alfonso Maierù*, edited by Massimiliano Lenzi, Cesare A. Musatti, and Luisa Valente, 109–128. Rome: Viella libreria editrice.
Skafte Jensen, Minna. 1980. *The Homeric Question and the Oral-Formulaic Theory.* Copenhagen: Museum Tusculanum Press.
Smith, Lesley. 1992. "Yet More on the Autograph of John the Scot: MS Bamberg Ph.2/2 and Its Place in Periphyseon Tradition". In *From Athens to Chartres: Neoplatonism and Medieval Thought; Studies in Honour of Edouard Jeauneau*, edited by Haijo J. Westra, 47–70. Leiden: Brill.
Smith, Marc. 2008. "Du manuscrit à la typographie numérique: Présent et avenir des écritures anciennes". *Gazette du livre médiéval* 52–53: 51–78.
Sneath, Peter H. A., and Robert R. Sokal. 1962. "Numerical Taxonomy". *Nature* 193 (4818): 855–860.
Sokal, Robert R., and Charles D. Michener. 1958. "A Statistical Method for Evaluating Systematic Relationships". *University of Kansas Science Bulletin* 38, part 2 (22): 1409–1438. archive.org/details/cbarchive_133648_astatisticalmethodforevaluatin1902/page/n1.
Solomon Gebreyes. 2019. *Chronicle of King Gälawdewos (1540–1559).* 2 vols. Leuven: Peeters.
Solomon, Jon D. 1983. "Vaticanus gr. 2338 and the Eisagoge harmonike". *Philologus* 127: 247–253.

Solomon, Jon D. 1986. "Venetus Marcianus gr. 322 and the Manuscripts of the Pseudo-Euclidean Eisagoge harmonike". *Classica et mediaevalia: Revue danoise de philologie et d'histoire* 37: 136–144.

Somers, Véronique. 1997. *Histoire des collections complètes des Discours de Grégoire de Nazianze*. Louvain-la-Neuve: Publications de l'Institut Orientaliste de Louvain.

Spadini, Elena. 2015. "Processing Dante's *Commedia*: From Sanguineti's Edition to Digital Tools". *RIDE: A Review Journal for Digital Editions and Resources* 3. doi.org/10.18716/ride.a.3.2.

Spadini, Elena, Magdalena Turska, and Misha Broughton. 2015. "TEI Standoff Markup – A Work in Progress". In *Text Encoding Initiative: Connect, Animate, Innovate; 2015 Annual Members' Meeting and Conference of the TEI Consortium*. Lyon: TEI. urn:nbn:nl:ui:17-f4d0afe1-5c62-4999-8271-7e8cadcd4805.

Spaggiari, Barbara, and Maurizio Perugi. 2004. *Fundamentos da crítica textual*. Rio de Janeiro: Lucerna.

Spanò Martinelli, Serena. 2011. "Mombrizio, Bonino". In *Dizionario Biografico degli Italiani*, vol. 75. Rome: Istituto della Enciclopedia Italiana. treccani.it/enciclopedia/bonino-mombrizio_(Dizionario-Biografico).

Sparnaay, Hendricus. 1948. *Karl Lachmann als Germanist*. Berne: Francke.

Speer, Mary B. 1995. "Old French Literature". In *Scholarly Editing: A Guide to Research*, edited by David C. Greetham, 382–416. New York, NY: Modern Language Association.

Spencer, Matthew, Barbara Bordalejo, Peter Robinson, and Christopher J. Howe. 2003. "How Reliable Is a Stemma? An Analysis of Chaucer's Miller's Tale". *Literary and Linguistic Computing* 18 (4): 407–422. doi.org/10.1093/llc/18.4.407.

Spencer, Matthew, Barbara Bordalejo, Li-San Wang, Adrian C. Barbrook, Linne R. Mooney, Peter Robinson, Tandy Warnow, and Christopher J. Howe. 2003. "Analyzing the Order of Items in Manuscripts of *The Canterbury Tales*". *Computers and the Humanities* 37 (1): 97–109. doi.org/10.1023/A:1021818600001.

Spencer, Matthew, Elizabeth A. Davidson, Adrian C. Barbrook, and Christopher J. Howe. 2004. "Phylogenetics of Artificial Manuscripts". *Journal of Theoretical Biology* 227 (4): 503–511. doi.org/10.1016/j.jtbi.2003.11.022.

Spencer, Matthew, and Christopher J. Howe. 2001. "Estimating Distances between Manuscripts Based on Copying Errors". *Literary and Linguistic Computing* 16 (4): 467–484. doi.org/10.1093/llc/16.4.467.

Spencer, Matthew, and Christopher J. Howe. 2002. "How Accurate Were Scribes? A Mathematical Model". *Literary and Linguistic Computing* 17 (3): 311–322. doi.org/10.1093/llc/17.3.311.

Spencer, Matthew, Linne Mooney, Adrian Barbrook, Barbara Bordalejo, Christopher Howe, and Peter Robinson. 2004. "The Effects of Weighting Kinds of Variants". In *Studies in Stemmatology II*, edited by Pieter van Reenen, August den Hollander, and Margot van Mulken, 227–240. Philadelphia, PA: Benjamins.

Spencer, Matthew, Klaus Wachtel, and Christopher J Howe. 2002. "The Greek Vorlage of the Syra Harclensis: A Comparative Study on Method in Exploring Textual Genealogy". *TC: A Journal of Biblical Textual Criticism* 7: 3. purl.org/TC/v07/SWH2002/index.html.

Sperberg-McQueen, Michael, and Claus Huitfeldt. 2018. "Interpreting Difference among Transcripts". In *Digital Humanities 2018: Book of Abstracts*, edited by Jonathan Girón Palau and Isabel Galina Russell, 287–291. Mexico City: Red de Humanidades Digitales A. C. dh2018.adho.org/interpreting-difference-among-transcripts.

Springhetti, Emilio. 1962. *Lexicon linguisticae et philologiae*. Rome: apud Pontificiam Universitatem Gregorianam.

Squillacioti, Paolo. 2011. "Sulla contaminazione nella tradizione manoscritta trobadorica: Varianti alternative, doppie lezioni ed effetti sulla pratica editoriale". In *La tradizione della lirica nel medioevo romanzo: Problemi di filologia formale; Atti del convegno internazionale, Firenze-Siena, 12–14 novembre 2009*, edited by Lino Leonardi, 23–41. Florence: Edizioni del Galluzzo.

Stäcker, Thomas. 2010. "Digitalisierung buchhistorischer Quellen, Fachportale und buchhistorische Forschung jenseits der Gutenberggalaxie". In *Buchwissenschaft in Deutschland: Ein Handbuch*, edited by Ursula Rautenberg, 711–733. Berlin: De Gruyter.

Stackmann, Karl. 1964. "Mittelalterliche Texte als Aufgabe". In *Festschrift für Jost Trier zum 70. Geburtstag*, edited by William Foerste and Karl Heinz Borck, 240–267. Cologne: Böhlau.

Stackmann, Karl. 1979. "Die Klassische Philologie und die Anfänge der Germanistik". In *Philologie und Hermeneutik im 19. Jahrhundert*, edited by Hellmut Flashar, Karlfried Gründer, and Axel Horstmann, 240–259. Göttingen: Vandenhoeck und Ruprecht.

Stackmann, Karl. 2005. "Der Takt, die besonderen Neigungen und Überlegungen des Herausgebers: Zur Erinnerung an Roethes Konzept für die 'Deutschen Texte des Mittelalters'". In *Deutsche Texte des Mittelalters zwischen Handschriftennähe und Rekonstruktion: Berliner Fachtagung 1.–3. April 2004*, edited by Martin J. Schubert, 7–20. Tübingen: Niemeyer.

Staehelin, Martin. 1983. "Bemerkungen zum Verhältnis von Werkcharakter und Filiation in der Musik der Renaissance". In *Quellenstudien zur Musik der Renaissance*, vol. 2, *Datierung und Filiation von Musikhandschriften der Josquin-Zeit*, edited by Ludwig Finscher, 199–215. Wiesbaden: Harrassowitz.

Staehelin, Martin. 1998. "Petruccis Canti B in deutschen Musikdrucken des 16. Jahrhunderts". In *Quellenstudien zur Musik der Renaissance*, vol. 3, *Gestalt und Entstehung musikalischer Quellen im 15. und 16. Jahrhundert*, edited by Martin Staehelin, 125–132. Wiesbaden: Harrassowitz.

Stählin, Otto. 1914. *Editionstechnik: Ratschläge für die Anlage textkritischer Ausgaben*. Leipzig: Teubner.

Stauber, Richard. 1908. *Die Schedelsche Bibliothek: Ein Beitrag zur Geschichte der Ausbreitung der italienischen Renaissance, des deutschen Humanismus und der medizinischen Literatur […]*. Freiburg im Breisgau: Herder.

Steel, Carlos, ed. 1982–1985. *Proclus: Commentaire sur le Parménide de Platon; Traduction de Guillaume de Moerbeke*. Leuven: Leuven University Press.

Steel, Carlos, ed. 1997. "Proclus et Denys: L'Existence du mal". In *Denys l'Aréopagite et sa postérité en Orient et en Occident*, edited by Ysabel de Andia, 89–116. Paris: Institut d'Etudes Augustiniennes.

Steel, Carlos. 1999. "Proclus comme témoin du texte du Parménide". In *Tradition et traduction: Les Textes philosophiques et scientifiques grecs au Moyen Age latin; Hommage à Fernand Bossier*, edited by Rita Beyers, Jozef Brams, Dirk Sacré, and Koenraad Verrycken, 281–303. Leuven: Leuven University Press.

Steel, Carlos. 2010. Review of *Proclus: Commentaire sur le Parménide de Platon*, edited by Concetta Luna and Alain Philippe Segonds. *Mnemosyne* 63: 120–142.

Steel, Carlos, and Caroline Macé. 2006. "Georges Pachymère philologue: Le Commentaire de Proclus au Parménide dans le manuscrit Parisinus gr. 1810". In *Philosophie et sciences à Byzance de 1204 à 1453: Les Textes, les doctrines et leur transmission; Actes de la Table Ronde organisée au XXe Congrès International d'Etudes Byzantines (Paris, 2001)*, edited by Michel Cacouros and Marie-Hélène Congourdeau, 77–99. Leuven: Peeters.

Steel, Carlos, Caroline Macé, and Pieter d'Hoine, eds. 2007. *Procli in Platonis Parmenidem commentaria*. Vol. 1. *Libri I–III*. Oxford: Oxford University Press.

Steel, Carlos, and Leen van Campe, eds. 2009. *Procli in Platonis Parmenidem commentaria*. Vol. 3. *Libri VI–VII*. Oxford: Oxford University Press.

Steer, Georg. 1985. "Textgeschichtliche Edition". In *Überlieferungsgeschichtliche Prosaforschung: Beiträge der Würzburger Forschergruppe zur Methode und Auswertung*, edited by Kurt Ruh, 37–52. Tübingen: Niemeyer.

Steer, Georg, and Marlies Hamm, eds. 1987–2006. *Die "Rechtssumme" Bruder Bertholds: Eine deutsche abecedarische Bearbeitung der "Summa confessorum" des Johannes von Freiburg.* 8 vols. Tübingen: Niemeyer.

Steingrímsson, Hreinn. 1975. "Problemer i forbindelse med klassifisering av rimurmelodier". *Swedish Journal of Musicology* 57: 11–14.

Steinova, Evina, 2013. "Carolingian Critters III: Munich, Bayerische Staatsbibliothek, Clm 6253". mittelalter.hypotheses.org/1316.

Stella, Francesco, ed. 2007. *Corpus rhythmorum musicum saec. IV–IX.* Florence: Edizioni del Galluzzo. www.corimu.unisi.it.

Stokes, Peter A. 2011. "The Vision of Leofric: Manuscript, Text and Context". *Review of English Studies* 63: 529–550. doi.org/10.1093/res/hgr052.

Stokes, Peter A. 2018a. "Modelling Multigraphism: The Digital Representation of Multiple Scripts and Alphabets". In *Digital Humanities 2018: Book of Abstracts*, edited by Jonathan Girón Palau and Isabel Galina Russell, 292–296. Mexico City: Red de Humanidades Digitales A. C. dh2018.adho.org/modelling-multigraphism-the-digital-representation-of-multiple-scripts-and-alphabets/.

Stokes, Peter A., ed. 2018b. *Exon: The Domesday Survey of South-West England.* exondomesday.ac.uk.

Stolz, Michael. 2002. "Wolframs 'Parzival' als unfester Text: Möglichkeiten einer überlieferungsgeschichtlichen Edition im Spannungsfeld traditioneller Textkritik und elektronischer Darstellung". In *Wolfram von Eschenbach – Bilanzen und Perspektiven: Eichstätter Colloquium 2000*, edited by Wolfgang Haubrichs, Eckart C. Lutz, and Klaus Ridder, Wolfram-Studien 17, 294–321. Berlin: Schmidt.

Stolz, Michael. 2003. "New Philology and New Phylogeny: Aspects of a Critical Electronic Edition of Wolfram's Parzival". *Literary and Linguistic Computing* 18 (2): 139–150. doi.org/10.1093/llc/18.2.139.

Stolz, Michael. 2016. "Von den Fassungen zur Eintextedition: Eine neue Leseausgabe von Wolframs 'Parzival'". In *Überlieferungsgeschichte transdisziplinär: Neue Perspektiven auf ein germanistisches Forschungsparadigma*, edited by Dorothea Klein, 353–388. Wiesbaden: Reichert.

Stoppelli, Pasquale. 2008. *Filologia dei testi a stampa.* 2nd ed. Cagliari: CUEC.

Strijbosch, Clara. 1995. *De bronnen van De reis van Sint Brandaan.* Hilversum: Verloren.

Strimmer, Korbinian, and Vincent Moulton. 2000. "Likelihood Analysis of Phylogenetic Networks Using Directed Graphical Models". *Molecular Biology and Evolution* 17 (6): 875–881. doi.org/10.1093/oxfordjournals.molbev.a026367.

Strohm, Reinhard. 1995. "Does Textual Criticism Have a Future?". In *L'edizione critica tra testo musicale e testo letterario*, edited by Renato Borghi und Pietro Zappalà, 193–211. Lucca: Libreria Musicale Italiana.

Studier, James A., and Karl J. Keppler. 1988. "A Note on the Neighbor-Joining Method of Saitou and Nei". *Molecular Biology and Evolution* 5: 729–731.

Stussi, Alfredo. 1994. *Introduzione agli studi di filologia italiana.* Bologna: il Mulino.

Stussi, Alfredo. 2006. *Fondamenti di critica testuale.* Bologna: il Mulino [1st ed. 1998].

Stussi, Alfredo. 2015. *Introduzione agli studi di filologia italiana.* 5th ed. Bologna: il Mulino [1st ed. *Avviamento agli studi di filologia italiana*. Bologna: il Mulino, 1983].

Suchla, Beate Regina. 2008. *Dionysius Areopagita: Leben – Werk – Wirkung.* Freiburg: Herder.

Sussman, Yaacov. 1990. "Veshuv le-yerushalmi neziqin". In *Mehqerei Talmud: Talmudic Studies*, vol. 1, edited by David Rosenthal and Yaacov Sussman, 55–133. Jerusalem: Magnes Press.

Swanson, Reuben. 1995–2005. *New Testament Greek Manuscripts.* Sheffield: Sheffield Academic Press; Pasadena, CA: William Carey International University Press.

Swofford, David L. 1998. PAUP* 4.0: Phylogenetic Analysis Using Parsimony (* and Other Methods). Version 4.0. CD-ROM. Newer versions available at paup.phylosolutions.com.

Tabory, Joseph, and Arnon Atzmon, eds. 2014. *Midrash Esther Rabbah*. Jerusalem: Schechter Institute of Jewish Studies.
Taeger, Burkhard, ed. 1996. *Heliand und Genesis*. Edited by Otto Behaghel. 10th ed. Tübingen: Niemeyer.
Tanselle, George Thomas. 1972. "Some Principles for Editorial Apparatus". *Studies in Bibliography* 25: 41–88.
Tanselle, George Thomas. 1976. "The Editorial Problem of Final Authorial Intention". *Studies in Bibliography* 29: 167–211.
Tanselle, George Thomas. 1994. "Editing without a Copy-Text". *Studies in Bibliography* 47: 1–22.
Tanselle, George Thomas. 1995. "The Varieties of Scholarly Editing". In *Scholarly Editing: A Guide to Research*, edited by David C. Greetham, 9–32. New York, NY: Modern Language Association.
Tarrant, Richard J. 1989. "The Reader as Author: Collaborative Interpolation in Latin Poetry". In *Editing Greek and Latin Texts*, edited by John N. Grant, 121–162. New York, NY: AMS Press.
Tarrant, Richard J. 2016. *Texts, Editors, and Readers: Methods and Problems in Latin Textual Criticism*. Cambridge: Cambridge University Press.
Taylor, Simon, ed. 1983. *The Anglo-Saxon Chronicle: A Collaborative Edition*. Vol. 4. MS. B: A Semi-Diplomatic Edition with Introduction and Indices. Cambridge: Brewer.
Tedros Abraha, ed. 2001. *La lettera ai Romani: Testo e commentari della versione Etiopica*. Wiesbaden: Harrassowitz.
Tedros Abraha, ed. 2004. *The Ethiopic Version of the Letter to the Hebrews*. Vatican City: Biblioteca Apostolica Vaticana.
Tedros Abraha, ed. and trans. 2014. *The Ethiopic Versions of 1 and 2 Corinthians*. Rome.
Teeuwen, Mariken. 2010. "Glossing in Close Co-operation: Examples from Ninth-Century Martianus Capella Manuscripts". In *Practice in Learning: The Transfer of Encyclopaedic Knowledge in the Early Middle Ages*, ed. by Rolf H. Bremmer Jr. and Kees Dekker, 85–100. Leuven: Peeters.
Tehrani, Jamshid J. 2013. "The Phylogeny of Little Red Riding Hood". *PLoS One* 8 (11): 78871. doi.org/10.1371/journal.pone.0078871.
Tehrani, Jamshid, and Mark Collard. 2002. "Investigating Cultural Evolution through Biological Phylogenetic Analyses of Turkmen Textiles". *Journal of Anthropological Archaeology* 21: 443–463.
Tehrani, Jamshid, and Mark Collard. 2013. "Do Transmission Isolating Mechanisms (TRIMS) Influence Cultural Evolution? Evidence from Patterns of Textile Diversity within and between Iranian Tribal Groups". In *Understanding Cultural Transmission in Anthropology: A Critical Synthesis*, edited by Roy Ellen, Stephen J. Lycett, and Sarah E. Johns, 148–164. New York, NY: Berghahn.
Tehrani, Jamshid, Quan Nguyen, and Teemu Roos. 2016. "Oral Fairy Tale or Literary Fake? Investigating the Origins of Little Red Riding Hood Using Phylogenetic Network Analysis". *Digital Scholarship in the Humanities* 31 (3): 611–636. doi.org/10.1093/llc/fqv016.
Telesius, Bernardinus. 1570. *Bernardini Telesii Consentini De colorum generatione opusculum*. Naples: Josephus Cacchius.
Telesius, Bernardinus. 1590. *Varii de naturalibus rebus libelli*. 8 vols. Venice: apud Felicem Valgrisium.
Tëmkin, Ilya. 2004. "The Evolution of the Baltic Psaltery: A Case for Phyloorganology". *Galpin Society Journal* 57: 219–230.
Tëmkin, Ilya, and Niles Eldredge. 2007. "Phylogenetics and Material Cultural Evolution". *Current Anthropology* 48: 146–154.
Terrell, John E. 1988. "History as a Family Tree, History as a Tangled Bank". *Antiquity* 62: 642–657.

Teviotdale, Elizabeth C. 1988. "The Filiation of Music Illustrations in a Boethius in Milan and in the Piacenza Codice magno". *Imago musicae: International Yearbook of Musical Iconography* 5: 7–22.

Thaller, Manfred. 2004. "Reproduktion, Erschließung, Edition, Interpretation: Ihre Beziehungen in einer digitalen Welt". In *Vom Nutzen des Edierens: Akten des internationalen Kongresses zum 150-jährigen Bestehen des Instiuts für Österreichische Geschichtsforschung*, edited by Brigitte Merta, Andrea Sommerlechner, and Herwig Weigl, 205–228. Vienna: Oldenbourg. doi.org/10.7767/boehlau.9783205160274.205.

Theodor, Julius, and Chanoch Albeck, eds. 1965. *Midrash Bereshit Rabba*. 2nd ed. 3 vols. Jerusalem: Wahrmann.

Thieme, Paul. 1953. *Die Heimat der indogermanischen Gemeinsprache*. Mainz: Akademie der Wissenschaften und der Literatur.

Thomason, Sarah G. 2001. *Language Contact*. Edinburgh: Edinburgh University Press.

Thompson, Edward Maunde, George Frederic Warner, Frederic George Kenyon, and Julius Parnell Gilson, eds. 1903–1912. *The New Palaeographical Society, Facsimiles of Ancient Manuscripts and Inscriptions*. 1st ser. 2 vols. London: Oxford University Press.

Thompson, Edward Maunde, George Frederic Warner, Frederic George Kenyon, Julius Parnell Gilson, John Alexander Herbert, and Harold Idris Bell, eds. 1913–1930. *The New Palaeographical Society, Facsimiles of Ancient Manuscripts and Inscriptions*. 2nd ser. 2 vols. London: Oxford University Press.

Thompson, Stith. 1977. *The Folktale*. Berkeley, CA: University of California Press.

Thomson, Robert. 1995. *A Bibliography of Classical Armenian Literature to 1500 AD*. Turnhout: Brepols.

Thum, Tobias, ed. 2018. *Iohannis monachi (VII saeculo ineunte) sacra, olim Iohanni Damasceno attributa*. 2 vols. Die Schriften des Johannes von Damaskos 8.4–5, Patristische Texte und Studien 74–75. Berlin: De Gruyter.

Timpanaro, Sebastiano. 1961. *La genesi del metodo del Lachmann*. Florence: Le Monnier.

Timpanaro, Sebastiano. 1965. "Ancora su stemmi bipartiti e contaminazione". *Maia* 17: 392–399.

Timpanaro, Sebastiano. 1971. *Die Entstehung der Lachmannschen Methode*. Translated by Dieter Irmer. 2nd ed. Hamburg: Buske.

Timpanaro, Sebastiano. 1981. *La genesi del metodo del Lachmann*. Rev. ed. Padua: Liviana.

Timpanaro, Sebastiano. 1985. *La genesi del metodo del Lachmann*. Rev. ed. Padua: Liviana [repr. with corrections of Timpanaro 1981].

Timpanaro, Sebastiano. 2004. *La genesi del metodo del Lachmann*. Introduction and postscript by Elio Montanari. Turin: Utet Libreria [repr. of Timpanaro 1985].

Timpanaro, Sebastiano. 2005. *The Genesis of Lachmann's Method*. Edited and translated by Glenn W. Most. Chicago: University of Chicago Press [trans. of Timpanaro 1985 with some additional material].

Tischendorf, Constantinus, ed. 1869–1872. *Novum Testamentum Graecum*. 8th ed. 2 vols. Leipzig: Hinrichs.

Tissoni Benvenuti, Antonia. 1986. *L'Orfeo del Poliziano con il testo critico dell' originale e delle successive forme teatrali*. Padua: Antenore.

Tobler, Adolf. 1872. "Compte rendu de l'édition du Saint Alexis par Gaston Paris". *Göttingen gelehrte Anzeigen*, June 5, 881–903.

Tomasello, Michael. 1999. *The Cultural Origins of Human Cognition*. Cambridge, MA: Harvard University Press.

Tonello, Elisabetta, and Paolo Trovato. 2011. "Contaminazione di lezioni e contaminazione per giustapposizione di esemplari nella tradizione della 'Commedia'". *Filologia Italiana* 8: 17–32.

Touwaide, Alain. 2010. "Codicology and Palaeography". In *Handbook of Medieval Studies: Terms – Methods – Trends*, edited by Albrecht Classen, 266–329. Berlin: De Gruyter.

Tov, Emanuel. 1982. "The Limitations of Textual Rules". *Harvard Theological Review* 75, no. 4 (October): 429–448.
Tov, Emanuel. 1992. *Textual Criticism of the Hebrew Bible*. Assen: van Gorcum.
Treu, Kurt. 1969. "Patristische Fragen". *Svensk exegetisk årsbok* 34: 186–200 [repr. Harlfinger 1980, 613–628].
Trisoglio, Francesco. 1965. "Sulle interpolazioni nella XLV orazione di S. Gregorio Nazianzeno". *Aevum* 39: 25–44.
Trovato, Paolo. 2005. "Archetipo, stemma codicum e albero reale". *Filologia Italiana* 2: 9–18.
Trovato, Paolo. 2014. "Bédier's Contribution to the Accomplishment of Stemmatic Method: An Italian Perspective". *Textual Cultures: Texts, Contexts, Interpretation* 9 (1): 160–176.
Trovato, Paolo. 2017. *Everything You Always Wanted to Know about Lachmann's Method: A Non-Standard Handbook of Genealogical Textual Criticism in the Age of Post-Structuralism, Cladistics, and Copy-Text*. Padua: Libreriauniversitaria.it [1st ed. 2014].
Truhlář, Josephus. 1905. *Catalogus codicum manu scriptorum latinorum qui in C. R. Bibliotheca publica atque Universitatis Pragensis asservantur*. Vol. 1. Prague: sumptibus Regiae Societatis Scientiarum Bohemicae.
Tsien, Tsuen-hsuin. 2004. *Written on Bamboo and Silk: The Beginnings of Chinese Books and Inscriptions*. Chicago, IL: University of Chicago Press.
Tuilier, André. 1987. "Remarques sur les fraudes des Apollinaristes et des Monophysites: Notes de critique textuelle". In *Texte und Textkritik: Eine Aufsatzsammlung*, edited by Jürgen Dummer, 581–590. Berlin: Akademie-Verlag.
Turcan-Verkerk, Anne-Marie. 2016. "La Diffusion du 'Waltharius' et son anonymat: Essai d'interprétation". *Filologia mediolatina* 23: 59–122.
Turner, Eric G. 1968. *Greek Papyri: An Introduction*. Oxford: Clarendon Press.
Tveitane, Mattias, and Robert Cook, eds. and trans. 1979. *Strengleikar: An Old Norse Translation of Twenty-One Old French Lais*. Oslo: Norsk Historisk Kjeldeskrift-Institutt.
Uhlig, Siegbert. 2003–2014. *Encyclopaedia Aethiopica*. 5 vols. Harrassowitz: Wiesbaden.
Ullman, Berthold Louis, and Philip A. Stadter. 1972. *The Public Library of Renaissance Florence: Niccolò Niccoli, Cosimo de' Medici and the Library of San Marco*. Padua: Antenore.
Vaganay, Léon, and Christian-Bernard Amphoux. 1986. *Initiation à la critique textuelle du Nouveau Testament*. 2nd ed. Paris: Les Editions du Cerf.
Vaganay, Léon, and Christian-Bernard Amphoux. 1991. *An Introduction to New Testament Textual Criticism*. Translated by Jenny Heimerdinger. Cambridge: Cambridge University Press [trans. of Vaganay and Amphoux 1986].
Valentinelli, Joseph. 1868. *Bibliotheca manuscripta ad S. Marci Venetiarum codices mss. Latini*. Vol. 1. Venice: ex Typographia Commercii.
Valverde, José Manuel García, ed. 2016. *Jacobus Zabarella: De rebus naturalibus*. 2 vols. Leiden: Brill.
Van Benthem, Jaap. 1969–1970. "Die chanson *Entré je suis* à 4 von Josquin des Prez und ihre Überlieferung". *Tijdschrift van de Vereiniging voor Nederlandse Muziekgeschiedenis* 21: 203–210.
Van der Werf, Hendrik. 1972. *The Chansons of the Troubadours and Trouvères*. Utrecht: Oosthoek.
Van Hulle, Dirk. 2014. *Modern Manuscripts: The Extended Mind and Creative Undoing from Darwin to Beckett and Beyond*. London: Bloomsbury.
Van Hulle, Dirk, and Peter Shillingsburg. 2015. "Orientations to Text, Revisited". *Studies in Bibliography* 59: 27–44.
Van Maerlant, Jacob. 1858. *Rymbybel van Jacob van Maerlant, met voorrede, varianten van hss., aenteekeningen en glossarium*. Edited by J. David. Vol. 1. Brussels: M. Hayez, Drukker der Koninklyke Akademie.
Van Reenen, Peter, August den Hollander, and Margot van Mulken, eds. 2004. *Studies in Stemmatology II*. Philadelphia, PA: Benjamins.

Van Reenen, Pieter, and Margot van Mulken, eds. 1996. *Studies in Stemmatology*. Philadelphia, PA: Benjamins.
Van Reenen, Pieter, and Lene Schøsler. 2000. "Corpus et stemma en ancien et en moyen français: Bilan, résultats et perspectives des recherches à l'Université libre Amsterdam et dans les institutions collaboratrices". In *Le Moyen Français: Le Traitement du texte (édition, apparat critique, glossaire, traitement électronique)*, edited by Claude Buridant, 25–54. Strasbourg: Presses universitaires de Strasbourg.
Van Strien, Daniel. 2016. "An Introduction to Version Control Using GitHub Desktop". June 17. programminghistorian.org/lessons/getting-started-with-github-desktop.
Van Zundert, Joris. 2018. "On Not Writing a Review about Mirador: Mirador, IIIF, and the Epistemological Gains of Distributed Digital Scholarly Resources". *Digital Medievalist* 11. doi.org/10.16995/dm.78.
Van Zundert, Joris J., and Tara L. Andrews. 2017. "Qu'est-ce qu'un texte numérique?". *Digital Scholarship in the Humanities* 32 (suppl_2): ii89–ii105. doi.org/10.1093/llc/fqx039.
Van Zundert, Joris J., Smiljana Antonijevic, Anne Beaulieu, Karina van Dalen-Oskam, Douwe Zeldenrust, and Tara L. Andrews. 2012. "Cultures of Formalisation: Towards an Encounter between Humanities and Computing". In *Understanding Digital Humanities*, edited by David M. Berry, 279–294. Basingstoke: Palgrave McMillan.
Vanhoutte, Edward. 2010. "Defining Electronic Editions: A Historical and Functional Perspective". In *Text and Genre in Reconstruction: Effects of Digitalization on Ideas, Behaviours, Products and Institutions*, edited by Willard McCarty, 119–144. Cambridge: Open Book.
Vàrvaro, Alberto. 1970. "Critica dei testi classica e romanza: Problemi comuni ed esperienze diverse". *Rendiconti dell'Accademia di Archeologia, Lettere e Belle Arti di Napoli* 45: 73–117 [repr. Vàrvaro 2004, 567–612].
Vàrvaro, Alberto. 1989. Review of *Eloge de la variante*, by Bernard Cerquiglini. *Medioevo romanzo* 14: 474–477.
Vàrvaro, Alberto. 2004. *Identità linguistiche e letterarie nell'Europa romanza*. Rome: Salerno Editrice.
Vàrvaro, Alberto. 2010. "Considerazioni sulla contaminazione, sulle varianti adiafore e sullo stemma codicum". In *Storia della lingua italiana e filologia: Atti del VII Convegno ASLI, Associazione per la Storia della Lingua Italiana (Pisa–Firenze, 18–20 dicembre 2008)*, edited by Claudio Ciociola, 191–196. Florence: Cesati.
Vàrvaro, Alberto. 2012. *Prima lezione di filologia*. Rome: Laterza.
Vasold, Gunter. 2014. "Progressive Editionen als multidimensionale Informationsräume". In *Digital Diplomatics: The Computer as a Tool for the Diplomatist?*, edited by Antonella Ambrosio, Sébastien Barret, and Georg Vogeler, 75–88. Cologne: Böhlau.
Vasoli, Cesare. 1997. "I fondamenti umanistici della ripresa dei Padri". In *Umanesimo e Padri della Chiesa: Manoscritti e incunaboli di testi patristici da Francesco Petrarca al primo Cinquecento*, edited by Sebastiano Gentile, 25–31. Rome: Rose.
Vázquez Buján, Manuel Enrique. 2010. "Eléments complémentaires en vue de l'édition critique de l'ancienne version latine des Aphorismes hippocratiques". In *Body, Disease and Treatment in a Changing World: Latin Texts and Contexts in Ancient and Medieval Medicine*, edited by David Langslow and Brigitte Maire, 119–130. Lausanne: Editions BHMS.
Vesalius, Andreas. 1543. *Andreae Vesalii Brvxellensis, scholae medicorum Patauinae professoris, de humani corporis fabrica libri septem*. Basle: Johann Oporinus. e-rara.ch/doi/10.3931/e-rara-20094.
Vesalius, Andreas. 1555. *Andreae Vesalii Bruxellensis, invictissimi Caroli V. Imperatoris medici, de humani corporis fabrica libri septem*. Basle: per Ioannem Oporinum.
Viehhauser, Gabriel. 2009. *Die "Parzival"-Überlieferung am Ausgang des Manuskriptzeitalters: Handschriften der Lauberwerkstatt und der Straßburger Druck*. Berlin: De Gruyter.

Vielliard, Françoise, and Gilles Désiré dit Gosset, eds. 2007. *Léopold Delisle: Actes Colloque de Cerisy-la-Salle, 8–10 octobre 2004*. Saint-Lô: Archives départementales de la Manche.

Villa, Massimo. 2019. *Filologia e linguistica dei testi gaʿaz di età aksumita: Il Pastore di Erma*. Naples: UniorPress.

Vinaver, Eugène. 1939. "Principles of Textual Emendation". In *Studies in French Language [...] Presented to M. K. Pope*, 351–369. Manchester: Manchester University Press [repr. Kleinhenz 1976, 139–159].

Vincentius Bellovacensis. 1624. *Speculum quadruplex; sive, Speculum maius*. 4 vols. Duaci: Beller [repr. Graz: Akademische Druck- und Verlagsanstalt, 1964–1965].

Vitali, Fabio. 2016. "The Expressive Power of Digital Formats: Criticizing the Manicure of the Wise Man Pointing at the Moon". Workshop lecture at DiXiT Convention 2, Cologne. dixit.uni-koeln.de/wp-content/uploads/Vitali_Digital-formats.pdf.

von Dadelsen, Georg, ed. 1967. *Editionsrichtlinien musikalischer Denkmäler und Gesamtausgaben*. Kassel: Bärenreiter.

von der Hagen, Friedrich Heinrich. 1816. *Der Nibelungen Lied, zum ersten Mal in der ältesten Gestalt aus der St. Galler Handschrift mit Vergleichung der übrigen Handschriften herausgegeben*. Breslau: Max.

von See, Klaus, Beatrice La Farge, Katja Schulz, Simone Horst, and Eve Picard. 1997–2019. *Kommentar zu den Liedern der Edda*. 7 vols. Heidelberg: Winter.

von Soden, Hermann. 1902–1910. *Die Schriften des Neuen Testaments*. Vol. 1. *Untersuchungen*, Berlin: Duncker.

von Soden, Hermann, ed. 1913. *Die Schriften des Neuen Testaments*. Vol. 2. *Text*. Göttingen: Vandenhoeck und Ruprecht.

von Wilamowitz-Moellendorff, Ulrich. 1921. *Geschichte der Philologie*. Leipzig: Teubner.

Vössing, Konrad. 2006. "Library: 2. History; a) α". In *Brill's New Pauly*, edited by Hubert Cancik and Helmut Schneider. dx.doi.org/10.1163/1574-9347_bnp_e216740.

Wachinger, Burghart, ed. 2004. *Gregorius von Hartmann von Aue*. Edited by Hermann Paul. Revised by Burghart Wachinger. 15th ed. Tübingen: Niemeyer.

Wachtel, Klaus. 2004. "Kinds of Variant in the Manuscript Tradition of the Greek New Testament". In *Studies in Stemmatology II*, edited by Pieter van Reenen, August den Hollander, and Margot van Mulken, 87–98. Philadelphia, PA: Benjamins.

Wachtel, Klaus. 2012a. "The Coherence-Based Genealogical Method: A New Way to Reconstruct the Text of the Greek New Testament". In *Editing the Bible: Assessing the Task Past and Present*, edited by John S. Kloppenborg and Judith H. Newman, 123–138. Leiden: Brill.

Wachtel, Klaus. 2012b. "Conclusions". In *The Textual History of the Greek New Testament: Changing Views in Contemporary Research*, edited by Klaus Wachtel and Michael W. Holmes, Text-Critical Studies 8, 217–226. Leiden: Brill.

Wade, Rachel W. 1988. "Filiation and the Editing of Revised and Alternate Versions: Implications for the C. P. E. Bach Edition". In *C. P. E. Bach Studies*, edited by Stephen L. Clark, 277–294. Oxford: Clarendon Press.

Wagner, Bettina, ed. 2014. *Welten des Wissens: Die Bibliothek und die Weltchronik des Nürnberger Arztes Hartmann Schedel (1440–1514)*. Munich: Bayerische Staatsbibliothek.

Wahlgren, Lena. 1993. *The Letter Collections of Peter of Blois: Studies in Manuscript Tradition*. Gothenburg: Acta Universitatis Gothoburgensis.

Walde, Otto. 1916–1920. "Storhetstidens litterära krigsbyten: En kulturhistorisk bibliografisk studie". 2 vols. PhD thesis, Uppsala University.

Walton, Brian, ed. 1654–1657. *Biblia Sacra Polyglotta, complectentia textus originales, Hebraicum, cum Pentateucho Samaritano, Chaldaicum, Graecum*. 6 vols. London: Roycroft.

Wang Shumin 王叔岷. 1972. *Jiaochouxue* 斠讎學. Taipei: Academia Sinica.

Ward-Perkins, Bryan. 2005. *The Fall of Rome and the End of Civilization*. Oxford: Oxford University Press.

Wasserman, Tommy. 2015. "The Coherence Based Genealogical Method as a Tool for Explaining Textual Changes in the Greek New Testament". *Novum Testamentum* 57 (2): 206–218.

Wasserman, Tommy, and Peter J. Gurry. 2017. *A New Approach to Textual Criticism: An Introduction to the Coherence-Based Genealogical Method*. Atlanta, GA: Society of Biblical Literature.

Watkins, Calvert. 2001. "An Indo-European Linguistic Area and Its Characteristics: Ancient Anatolia. Areal Diffusion as a Challenge to the Comparative Method? Problems in Comparative Linguistics". In *Areal Diffusion and Genetic Inheritance: Problems in Comparative Linguistics*, edited by Alexandra Y. Aikhenvald and Robert M. W. Dixon, 44–63. Oxford: Oxford University Press.

Wattel, Evert, and Margot van Mulken. 1996. "Shock Waves in Text Traditions: Cardiograms of the Medieval Literature". In *Studies in Stemmatology*, edited by Pieter van Reenen and Margot van Mulken, 105–121. Philadelphia, PA: Benjamins.

Weber, Robert, Roger Gryson, and Bonifatius Fischer, eds. 1994. *Biblia Sacra iuxta vulgatam versionem*. 4th ed. Stuttgart: Deutsche Bibelgesellschaft.

Wechsler, Michael G., ed. 2005. *Evangelium Iohannis Aethiopicum*. Leuven: Peeters.

Weiss, Günther. 1964. "Zum Problem der Gruppierung südfranzösischer Tropars". *Archiv für Musikwissenschaft* 12: 163–171.

Weiss, Michael. 2009. *Outline of the Historical and Comparative Grammar of Latin*. Ann Arbor, MI: Beech Stave Press.

Weitzman, Michael P. 1982. "Computer Simulation of the Development of Manuscript Traditions". *Bulletin of the Association for Literary and Linguistic Computing* 10: 55–59.

Weitzman, Michael P. 1985. "The Analysis of Open Traditions". *Studies in Bibliography* 38: 82–120.

Weitzman, Michael P. 1987. "The Evolution of Manuscript Traditions". *Journal of the Royal Statistical Society: Series A (General)* 150 (4): 287–308. doi.org/10.2307/2982040.

Werner, Shirley. 1998. *The Transmission and Scholia to Lucan's Bellum civile*. Hamburg: Lit.

West, Martin L. 1973. *Textual Criticism and Editorial Technique Applicable to Greek and Latin Texts*. Stuttgart: Teubner.

West, Martin L., ed. 1978. *Hesiod: Works and Days*. Oxford: Oxford University Press.

Westcott, Brooke Foss, and Fenton John Anthony Hort, eds. 1881. *The New Testament in the Original Greek*. Cambridge: Macmillan.

Westerink, Leendert G., Thomas A. Gadra, Sion M. Honea, Patricia M. Stinger, and Gretchen Umholtz, eds. 1989. *George Pachymeres: Commentary on Plato's Parmenides (Anonymous Sequel to Proclus' Commentary)*. Athens: Akadēmia Athēnōn.

Westra, J. Haijo. 2014. "What's in a Name: Old, New, and Material Philology, Textual Scholarship, and Ideology". In *Neo-Latin Philology: Old Tradition, New Approaches*, edited by Marc van der Poel, 7–24. Leuven: Leuven University Press.

Whitelock, Dorothy, ed. 1979. *English Historical Documents c. 500–1042*. 2nd ed. London: Eyre Methuen.

Whitelock, Dorothy, ed. 1980. *Sermo Lupi ad Anglos*. 2nd ed. Exeter: University of Exeter.

Wieland, Gernot Rudolf. 1983. *The Latin Glosses on Arator and Prudentius in Cambridge University Library, MS Gg.5.35*. Toronto: Pontifical Institute of Mediaeval Studies.

Wilkinson, Robert J. 2007. *The Kabbalistic Scholars of the Antwerp Polyglot Bible*. Leiden: Brill.

Willert Bortignon, Inger-Mari. 1993. "La versione danese della leggenda di Roncevaux e lo stemma della Chanson de Roland". *Medioevo Romanzo* 48: 403–422.

Williams, Gordon. 1982. "The Genesis of Poetry in Rome". In *The Cambridge History of Classical Literature*, vol. 2.1, *The Early Republic*, edited by E. J. Kenney and W. V. Clausen, 53–59. Cambridge: Cambridge University Press.

Williams, Tom A., Peter G. Foster, Cymon J. Cox, and T. Martin Embley. 2013. "An Archaeal Origin of Eukaryotes Supports Only Two Primary Domains of Life". *Nature* 504 (7479): 231–236.

Willingham, Elizabeth Moore, ed. 2007. *La Mort le Roi Artu (The Death of Arthur) from the Old French Lancelot of Yale 229*. Turnhout: Brepols.

Willingham, Elizabeth Moore, ed. 2012. *La Queste del Saint Graal (The Quest of the Holy Grail) from the Old French Lancelot of Yale 229*. Turnhout: Brepols.

Willis, James. 1972. *Latin Textual Criticism*. Urbana: University of Illinois Press.

Wimsatt, William K. Jr, and Monroe C. Beardsley. 1946. "The Intentional Fallacy". *Sewanee Review* 54 (3): 468–488.

Windram, Heather F., Terence Charlston, and Christopher J. Howe. 2014. "A Phylogenetic Analysis of Orlando Gibbons's Prelude in G". *Early Music* 42 (4): 515–528.

Windram, Heather F., Christopher J. Howe, and Matthew Spencer. 2005. "The Identification of Exemplar Change in the Wife of Bath's Prologue Using the Maximum Chi-Squared Method". *Literary and Linguistic Computing* 20 (2): 189–204.

Windram, Heather F., Prue Shaw, Peter Robinson, and Christopher J. Howe. 2008. "Dante's Monarchia as a Test Case for the Use of Phylogenetic Methods in Stemmatic Analysis". *Literary and Linguistic Computing* 23 (4): 443–463. doi.org/10.1093/llc/fqn023.

Windram, Heather F., Matthew Spencer, and Christopher J. Howe. 2006. "Phylogenetic Analysis of Manuscript Traditions, and the Problem of Contamination". In *The Evolution of Texts: Confronting Stemmatological and Genetical Methods; Proceedings of the International Workshop (Louvain la Neuve, sept. 2004)*, edited by Caroline Macé, Philippe V. Baret, Andrea Bozzi, and Laura Cignoni, 141–155. Pisa: Istituti editoriali e poligrafici internazionali.

Wingels, Hermannus. 1913. "De ordine libellorum Lucianeorum". *Philologus* 72: 125–148.

Winterbottom, Michael, ed. 1970. *M. Fabi Quintilliani Institutionis oratoriae libri duodecim*. 2 vols. Oxford: Oxford University Press.

Wion, Anaïs, and Paul Bertrand. 2011. "Production, Preservation, and Use of Ethiopian Archives (Fourteenth–Eighteenth Centuries)". *Northeast African Studies* 11 (2): vii–xvi.

Witkam, Jan Just. 1988. "Establishing the Stemma: Fact or Fiction?". *Manuscripts of the Middle East* 3: 88–101.

Witkam, Jan Just. 2013. "The Philologist's Stone: The Continuing Search for the Stemma". *Comparative Oriental Manuscript Studies Newsletter* 6: 34–38.

Witt, Jeffrey C., ed. 2011. *Petrus Plaoul: Commentarius in libros Sententiarum; Editiones electronicas*. petrusplaoul.org.

Witt, Jeffrey C. 2018. "Digital Scholarly Editions and API Consuming Applications". In *Digital Scholarly Editions as Interfaces*, edited by Roman Bleier, Martina Bürgermeister, Helmut W. Klug, Frederike Neuber, and Gerlinde Schneider, Schriftenreihe des Instituts für Dokumentologie und Editorik 12, 219–247. Norderstedt: BoD. kups.ub.uni-koeln.de/9118.

Witzel, Michael. 2014. "Textual Criticism in Indology and in European Philology during the 19th and 20th Centuries". *Electronic Journal of Vedic Studies* 21 (3): 9–91. doi.org/10.11588/ejvs.2014.3.258.

Woerther, Frédérique, and Hossein Khonsari. 2003. "L'Application des programmes de reconstruction phylogénétique sur ordinateur à l'étude de la traduction manuscrite d'un texte: L'Exemple du chapitre XI de l'Ars Rhetorica du Pseudo-Denys d'Halicarnasse". *Revue d'histoire des textes* 31: 227–240.

Wolf, Jürgen. 2007. "Hilfsmittel für die Editionspraxis: Das Handschriftenarchiv der Berlin-Brandenburgischen Akademie der Wissenschaften und der Handschriftencensus". *editio* 21: 151–163.

Wolff, Ludwig, ed. 1968. *Iwein: Eine Erzählung von Hartmann von Aue*. Edited by Georg Friedrich Benecke and Karl Lachmann. 2 vols. 7th ed. Berlin: De Gruyter.

Wrenn, Charles L. 1946. "The Poetry of Caedmon". *Proceedings of the British Academy* 32: 277–295.

Wright, April M., and David M. Hillis. 2014. "Bayesian Analysis Using a Simple Likelihood Model Outperforms Parsimony for Estimation of Phylogeny from Discrete Morphological Data". *PLoS One* 9 (10): e109210.

Wright, Roger. 2002. *A Sociophilological Study of Late Latin*. Turnhout: Brepols.

Wulstan, David. 2000. "The Compilation of the Cantigas of Alfonso el Sabio". In *Cobras e Son: Papers on the Text, Music and Manuscripts of the "Cantigas de Santa Maria"*, edited by Stephen Parkinson, 154–185. Oxford: Legenda.

Yang, Jie, Zhi Cao, Huanwen Chen, Kai Long, Gangcheng Li, and Li Zhao. 2011. "A Method for Constructing Phylogenetic Tree Based on the Minimum Spanning Tree of the Complete Graph". *MATCH Communications in Mathematical and in Computer Chemistry* 65 (2): 469–476. match.pmf.kg.ac.rs/electronic_versions/Match65/n2/match65n2_469-476.pdf.

Yang, Ziheng, Nick Goldman, and Adrian Friday. 1994. "Comparison of Models for Nucleotide Substitution Used in Maximum-Likelihood Phylogenetic Estimation". *Molecular Biology and Evolution* 11 (2): 316–324.

Yang, Ziheng, and Bruce Rannala. 2012. "Molecular Phylogenetics: Principles and Practice". *Nature Reviews Genetics* 13 (5): 303–314. doi.org/10.1038/nrg3186.

Yorav, Avishai, Tal Dagan, and Dan Graur. 2005. "An Exploratory Study on the Use of a Phylogenetic Algorithm in the Reconstruction of Stemmata of Halachic Texts". *Hebrew Union College Annual* 76: 273–288. jstor.org/stable/23508935.

Yosef Demissie. 2015. "Text Emendations in Ethiopic Manuscript NLM 27 (National Archives and Library Agency, Addis Abeba)". *Aethiopica* 18: 163–172.

Zabarella, Giacomo. 1586. *Liber de naturalis scientiae constitutione*. Venice: Meietus.

Zamfir, Constantin. 1972. "Despre obîrsia si filiatia unor melodii de doina". *Studii de muzicologie* 8: 263–295.

Zarri, Gian Piero. 1971. "L'automazione delle procedure di Critica Testuale: Problemi e prospettive". In *Problemes posés par la formalisation et l'automatisation des méthodes d'analyse de la transmission su discours, écrit ou oral*, edited by Alain Laurier and Jacques Virbel, 147–166. Paris: Centre d'analyse documentaire pour l'archeologie.

Zarri, Gian Piero. 1973. "Algorithms, Stemmata Codicum and the Theories of Dom H. Quentin". In *The Computer and Literary Studies*, edited by J. Aitken, R. W. Bailey, and N. Hamilton-Smith, 225–237. Edinburgh: Edinburgh University Press.

Zarri, Gian Piero. 1976. "A Computer Model for Textual Criticism?". In *The Computer in Literary and Linguistic Studies*, edited by Alan Jones and Robert F. Churchhouse, 133–155. Cardiff: University of Wales Press.

Zarri, Gian Piero. 1977. "Some Experiments of Automated Textual Criticism". *ALLC Bulletin* 5: 266–290.

Zeller, Hans. 1975. "A New Approach to the Critical Constitution of Literary Texts". *Studies in Bibliography* 28: 231–264.

Zeller, Hans. 1995. "Structure and Genesis in Editing: On German and Anglo-American Textual Editing". In *Contemporary German Editorial Theory*, edited by Hans Walter Gabler, George Bornstein, and Gillian Borland Pierce, 95–123. Ann Arbor: University of Michigan Press.

Zetzel, James E. G. 1975. "On the History of Latin Scholia". *Harvard Studies in Classical Philology* 79: 335–354.

Zetzel, James E. G. 2018. *Critics, Compilers and Commentators: An Introduction to Roman Philology, 200 BCE–800 CE*. New York, NY: Oxford University Press.

Zhang, Jiajie, Amir Madany Mamlouk, Thomas Martinetz, Suhua Chang, Jing Wang, and Rolf Hilgenfeld. 2011. "PhyloMap: An Algorithm for Visualizing Relationships of Large Sequence Data Sets and Its Application to the Influenza A Virus Genome". *BMC Bioinformatics* 12 (June): 248. doi.org/10.1186/1471-2105-12-248.

Zinelli, Fabio. 2018. "La Genèse de la méthode éditoriale de Bédier par la musique". In *L'Ombre de Joseph Bédier*, edited by Craig Baker, Marcello Barbato, Mattia Cavagna, and Yan Greub,

Travaux de Littératures Romanes, 227–254. Strasbourg: Editions de linguistique et de philologie.
Zink, Michel. 2014. "Contamination, influence et pureté". *Critica del testo* 17 (3): 3–8.
Zorzi, Marino. 1980. *La libreria di San Marco: Libri, lettori, società nella Venezia dei Dogi*. Milan: Mondadori.
Zuckermandel, Moses Samuel, ed. 1877–1881. *Tosefta, nach den Erfurter und Wiener Handschriften, mit Parallelstellen und Varianten*. Pasewalk: Zuckermandel.
Zumpt, Carl Gottlob. 1831. *M. Tullii Ciceronis Verrinarum libri septem, ad fidem codicum manu scriptorum recensuit et explicavit Carolus Timotheus Zumptius*. Berlin: Dümmler. archive.org/details/mtulliiciceroni05cicegoog.
Zumthor, Paul. 1972. *Essai de poétique médiévale*. Paris: Seuil.
Zuurmond, Rochus, ed. 1989. *Novum Testamentum Aethiopice: The Synoptic Gospels*. Stuttgart: Steiner.
Zuurmond, Rochus, ed. 2001. *Novum Testamentum Aethiopice: The Synoptic Gospels*. Part 3. *The Gospel of Matthew*. Aethiopistische Forschungen 55. Wiesbaden: Harrassowitz.
Zuurmond, Rochus, and Curt Niccum. 2013. "The Ethiopic Version of the New Testament". In *The Text of the New Testament in Contemporary Research: Essays on the Status Quaestionis*, edited by Bart D. Ehrman and Michael W. Holmes, 231–252. Leiden: Brill.

General Index

abbreviations (in manuscripts) 46, 62, 140, 174, 300, 353, 406, 515
abbreviations (used in textual criticism) 415, 423
active vs quiescent manuscript traditions 124, 462
ad sensum (translations) 151
ad verbum (translations) 151
Adam of Bremen 215
addition 173f, 209, 245–248, 404, 488, 509, 519, 528
adiafore, varianti 88, 90, 392f
adjacent (node) 303
aesthetic approach 529
Afro-Asiatic languages 555, 560
aggadic texts 494
Aksumite period 481
Albertus Magnus 44
Alexander the Great 25
Alexander Romance 63
Alexander's Letter to Aristotle 53, 64
Alexandria 6, 16, 25, 58, 49, 65, 141, 273
Alexandria, library of 25, 59, 65
Alexandrian text (NT) 441, 443–450
Alexis → *Vie de St Alexis*
alignment 168–170, 187, 189, 192–195, 295, 328
alignment table 161, 163, 191
Alpago, Andrea 513
alphabetic writing 8–11, 60
Alsted, Johann Heinrich 514
Altaic languages 556
Amerbach, Bonifacius 519
amino acids 538, 543
Amoraic period 494
Amsterdam school 465
analysis of forms vs analysis of readings 458, 490
anasyllabism 247
ancestral state reconstruction (also → Urtext) 546f
Andernach, Johannes Günther von 43
Anglo-Saxon Chronicle 387–389
Anglo-Saxon settlement in Great Britain 567
Annals of St Neots 387
anonymous texts 494
ante correctionem 271

anthology → florilegium
anthropology 568–576
anticipation 247
antigraph 386, 399
ape (R) 328, 334
apocrypha 483, 488, 490
apograph 10, 22
apostrophe (in apparatuses) 413
apparatus biblicus 407, 412
apparatus criticus 167, 173, 372, 399, 406f, 408, 412f (positive vs negative), 443, 495, 515, 522
apparatus fontium 399, 402, 407, 410, 412
apparatus locorum parallelorum 399, 412
apparatus testimoniorum 407, 412
Apuleius 130, 222
Arabic philology 138, 150, 289, 438f, 493
Aramaic language 494
arborescence 305, 317
arbre réel 119f, 213, 221, 232–235, 291, 302
archaeology 560
archetype 36, 72f, 77, 82, 100–104, 124, 127–129, 210, 212, 214, 221–225, 247, 255, 306, 346, 349, 364f, 385–387, 396, 486, 569, 584
archetype, extant 222
archetype, trivial 222
archetype, unstable 467
archives 27–29
Aristarchus of Samothrace 65
Aristophanes (comedian) 24
Aristophanes of Byzantium 16, 141
Aristotle 25f, 64, 548
Armenian philology 150–157, 288–290, 438, 480, 493
Arnaut Daniel 462
arrhythmia 247
art vs science 5, 50f, 99f
artificial traditions 129, 232–234, 250, 266–271, 299–301, 325, 339–342, 345f, 354, 545
ASCII 182
AsciiDown 186
Asinius Pollio 26
Asser 387
assimilation 248
Athenaeus 72

Atom (software) 186
Augustine 40, 42, 155, 539, 548
Augustus (emperor) 25f
Aulus Gellius 32
Auraicept na n-Éces 548
Austen, Jane 532
Austronesians languages 555, 560, 563, 574
author 97–99, 397, 463
authorial approach 527
authorial intention, final 525
authorial revisions 215, 404, 408, 462
authorial variants 85f, 115, 468
authority (of a text) 167, 282, 525, 528
autograph 22, 72, 89f, 124, 212, 215, 364, 481, 521f, 524
automation 176, 245, 258, 295, 465
auxiliary sciences 51, 54
Avicenna (Ibn Sina) 513

Babylonian Talmud 494–501
Bach, Johann Sebastian 580
Balliol College 28
Baltic psaltery 585
bamboo strips 503–505, 507, 512
banben xue 502
Barbaro, Ermolao 34
Barbi's canon 390
Barlaams saga ok Josaphats 361, 366, 369
base text 166f, 170–173, 184, 245, 302, 415, 418f, 432, 464, 485, 488, 493, 514, 516, 522
Basil of Caesarea 449
Battle of Brunanburh 397
Bayesian phylogenetics 239, 310, 314–316, 323f, 331, 336, 337, 339, 541, 544, 547, 565f, 571–574
Bayes' theorem 314
Beaker people 567
BEAST(2) (software) 324, 337, 566
Beatus Rhenanus 34f, 40, 42f
Beckett, Samuel 526–531
Bede the Venerable 388, 394
Benedictine Rule 27
Bengel, Johann Albrecht 73, 211, 396, 412, 448, 451
Bentley, Richard 38, 73
Beowulf 53f, 361, 398
Bereshit Rabba 497
Bernart de Vantadorn 459
Bessarion (cardinal) 40, 69f, 158, 277–279

best manuscript → *codex optimus*
Beza, Theodore 442
Bible (Ethiopic) 482
Bible (Latin) 68, 71f, 99, 252f, 442f
Bible philology 301, 440–450
bibliographical approach 527
Biblioteca Apostolica Vaticana 28f, 31f, 514
Biblioteca nazionale di Roma 30
Bibliothèque nationale de France 30, 514
bifid stemma 108, 217–219, 453, 459–461
bifurcating stemma 347, 368
bifurcation 217–219, 223, 240, 298, 368
bilingual manuscripts 440f
binary numbers 176f
binary stemma 217–219
binary tree 241, 304
Bindefehler → error, conjunctive
binio 17
biology 7, 105, 223, 239–241, 296f, 304, 340, 346, 534f, 537–547
bipartite (graph theory) 219
birth-death processes 234
Boeckh, August 366
Boiardo 358
bon manuscript 93, 96, 459–461
Bongars, Jacques 29
book illustrations 513f
Book of Armagh 423
bootstrapping 297, 311, 322, 324, 332, 544
Borromeo, Federico 279
Boxhornius, Marcus Zuerius 549
Bracciolini, Poggio 33, 36, 40
brackets (in apparatuses) 413
branching (in stemmata) 217–220
Brendan (Saint) → *Navigatio Sancti Brendani*
Byskupa sögur 379
Byzantine text (NT) 442–450
Bédier, Joseph (Bédierism) 94–97, 136, 379, 451–454, 459–464, 485, 512, 578
Bédier's paradox 118f, 130f, 451, 453

Caelius Aurelianus 33, 43
Caelius Sedulius 18
Caesar, Julius 14
Caesarean text type (NT) 442
Callimachus of Cyrene 69, 141
calque 536
canonical version of a text 16, 65, 67
Canonici, Luigi 30
cantari 115, 122

Canterbury Tales → Chaucer, Geoffrey
cantigas 583
cardiogram (of a text tradition) 265f
Carmen Arvale 12
Carmen Saliare 12
Carolingian minuscule 24, 27, 60f
Carver, Raymond 532
Casaubon, Isaac 72
Cassiodorus 14, 27
catalogues (of manuscripts) 30, 142–147, 514
Catalogus scriptorum ecclesiae 145
Catullus 69, 247, 451
CATview 426
Celsus 32
Celtic minuscule 22
censorship 527
cento 155
Centum vs Satem languages 550f
chandasi 548
change of exemplar 104, 263, 265
Chanson de Roland 95, 108, 392, 404
chansonniers 116f, 583
Chansons de croisade 93, 578
chansons de geste 115, 122
character state matrix 307
character states 296, 311–313, 544, 572f, 576
Charlemagne 14, 27, 33
Chaucer, Geoffrey 265, 372, 418f, 539
Cheng (emperor) 507, 509
choujiao 502
Christian Orient 150, 480–493
Chrétien de Troyes 459
Cicero 26, 32–34, 258, 365f
Cid, cantar de mio 19, 404
Ciotti, Giovanni Battista 517
circular tree maps 335
citations → quotations
cladistics 87, 105, 296, 537–539, 574
Claremont Profile Method 448f
Classical Text Editor (CTE) 329f, 418, 428
Claudian 257
clay tablets 9
clean text 372
Clement of Alexandria 449
closed recension (also → open recension) 115, 256
ClustalW / ClustalX 330
cluster philology 134
codex (book form) 16f
Codex Bezae (NT) 441

Codex Claromontanus (NT) 441
codex descriptus 22, 45, 78, 87, 89, 130, 135, 250, 382, 387
codex interpositus 233
Codex Koridethi (NT) 441
Codex Nitriensis 17f
codex optimus (also → bon manuscript) 122f, 366, 370, 377, 380, 452f, 457, 483, 487, 496
Codex Salmasianus 64
Codex Sinaiticus (NT) 441–450
codex unicus 19, 163, 222, 359, 363, 374, 398, 514
Codex Vaticanus (NT) 441–450
codex vetustissimus 483, 487
codicological unit 17, 263
codicology 46–56
codon 538
Coherence Based Genealogical Method (CBGM) 234, 270–272, 301, 326f, 449
COLLATE 168
CollateX 168, 295, 329, 426
collatio 160, 381f
collation 139, 158, 160–175, 329f, 502, 507, 511f
collation by samples 390
collation, selective 106
Coline, Simon de 442
colophon 19, 213, 277
combinatio 381, 393, 396
commentary 18–20, 65, 71, 155f, 158, 274–281, 362, 407, 412, 423–425, 494f, 515
common errors method → Lachmann's method
Comprehensive Profile Method 449
computer-assisted stemmatology 267–270, 294–303 (history), 388
computers 5, 49, 102, 175–178, 310
conflation ring 389f
Confucius 501
conjectures 37, 67, 69–71, 73, 82, 102, 361, 393, 397f
consensus tree 297, 573
conspectus siglorum 275
Constantinople, Fall of 15, 69
constitutio textus 75, 85, 149, 285, 359, 381–405
constitution des leçons 89, 363, 368f, 374
constitution du langage 89, 363, 374
contamination 23, 62, 84–86, 102, 104, 106f, 121f, 212, 225, 248, 254–272, 349, 364,

386, 452, 455, 462, 471, 475, 518, 536, 561
contamination, block → contamination, successive
contamination, circular 259
contamination, consecutive → contamination, successive
contamination, extra-archetypal → contamination, extra-stemmatic
contamination, extra-stemmatic 123, 386 (vs intra-stemmatic), 387
contamination, hyperarchetypal 387
contamination, mnemonic 259
contamination of exemplars → contamination, successive
contamination of readings → contamination, simultaneous
contamination of versions 260
contamination, reciprocal 389f
contamination, simultaneous 122, 258–260, 546
contamination, successive 122, 260, 546
context 447
control manuscript 461
convergence (evolution) 547, 571
coptology 484
copy-text (theory) 525
copyist 22f, 134f, 282, 399
Corbie (monastery) 27
Corpus Christianorum 376
Corpus rhythmorum musicum 400
Corpus Scriptorum Christianorum Orientalium (CSCO) 480, 487
correction 20, 34, 106, 158, 171, 236, 274, 276, 327, 498, 519, 521f
corruption of texts 65, 385, 452, 525f
cosine distance 309
Cotton library fire 18
Council of Basle–Ferrara–Florence 482
courtly epic 465–479
coïncidence habituelle (Paris) 90
creole 535
critica delle varianti 115
critical apparatus → *apparatus criticus*
criticism (of digital stemmatology) 339–356
critique génétique 115, 533
crossbow 569
crux (desperationis) 82, 397, 415
CSS 206, 434f
CSV format 180, 187, 193, 195, 198

cycle (graph theory) 303
cyclicity (graph theory) 229
Cyril of Jerusalem 449
Cædmon 393f

Damerau-Levenshtein distance 309, 330
Dante Alighieri 122, 135, 170, 225, 257, 390, 395, 419, 462
Darmarios, Andreas 280f
Darwin, Charles 7, 340, 534f, 549f, 557, 569f, 575
data formats 179–206
decimation rates → loss (of manuscripts)
degree (of a node) 303
Delisle, Léopold 30
Demetrius of Phaleron 25
descent with modification (Darwin) 7, 536, 537, 568–570, 576
Deutsche Texte des Mittelalters 473–474
diachronic approach 528
dialectometry 566
diasystem (Segre) 126, 399, 462
dictation 16, 23, 26, 62
Didymus the Blind 449
diff algorithm 343
diffraction (Contini) 120f, 394f (*in praesentia* vs *in absentia*), 462
digital data 176–178, 207, 417
digital libraries 465, 487
digital manuscript catalogues 147
digital transcription 164
digitisation (of manuscripts) 31f, 436
Diogenes Laertius 72
directed acyclic graph (DAG) 228f, 241, 304, 322
directed, error → error, significant
direction (graph theory) 230
dispositio 357, 381, 398–403
distance 101, 241, 294, 308f, 340, 343–351
distance based methods 309, 317–319, 339, 353, 565f
distance matrix 307, 330f, 343, 537, 540f
disturbing factors (in producing a stemma) 114
dittography 23, 246, 445
divinatio 381, 393, 397
DNA 296–298, 535, 537–547, 586
DNA sequencing 538
doc(x) format 180, 186
document vs work 464, 497, 531
documentary edition 159, 420, 465

documentary evidence 527
DOT language 195–200
double endpoint attachment 432
Dravidian languages 556
Dunhuang manuscripts 512
DynStem 335
Dyūtaparvan 265f

e-codices 32
ecdotic stratigraphy (Contini) 404f
eclecticism of papyri 159
eclecticism, radical 496
eco-feminism 559
Edda 155, 362, 370
edge → vertices
edge-weighted graph 230
edit distance 309, 330
editio descripta 516, 520
editio princeps 37f, 40, 42, 423, 492, 515–523
edition, critical 361, 363, 379, 407
edition, digital 55, 145, 164, 204, 207, 356–358, 400, 405, 415–427, 436, 464, 478, 514
edition, diplomatic 252, 359–362, 377, 496, 513
edition, eclectic 89, 360–362, 366, 496, 526
edition, evolutive 520
edition, interventionist 97
edition, monotypic (monoptic) 70, 359–363, 514
edition, non-reconstructive 363, 369–372
edition, optimal text 365
edition, outreach 374
edition, progressive 424
edition, reading 374
edition, reconstructive 363–369
edition, reference 443
edition, scholarly 373
edition, synoptic 360–364, 373, 379, 399, 401, 409, 420–422, 479, 522
Editiones Arnamagnæanæ 361, 368, 378f
editorial signs 359, 373, 413–415
editors (conservative, interventionist, reconstructive) 97
Egnatius, Johannes Baptista 43
Egypt, ancient 9
Eigenfehler → *lectio singularis*
eliminatio codicum descriptorum 69, 77, 118, 130, 134, 222, 271, 285, 348
eliminatio lectionum singularium 468

Emacs 186
emendatio 357, 381, 385, 393–398
emendatio ex fonte 126f, 396
emendation 67, 158, 361, 369
enchaînement (Quentin) 100f, 104f, 452
endogenesis 528
Ennius, Quintus 26
Enoch, Book of 488f
environmental evidence 273
Epictetus 63
epigenesis 529
epigraphy 47
Epiphanius of Salamis 449
Episcopius, Nicolaus 519
epitome 64, 149, 157, 387
EPUB format 204
Erasmus of Rotterdam 34, 40, 71, 73, 360, 425, 442, 451, 514, 517–519
error 23, 62, 79, 81 (analysis of), 82, 102, 245–250 (typology), 527
error, conjunctive 37, 118, 123, 125, 132f, 144, 218, 244, 384
error, direction revealing → error, significant
error, indicative → error, significant
error, separative 37, 118, 133, 208, 244f, 384, 462
error, significant 79, 103, 117f, 132f, 167, 243, 266, 296, 345, 382, 403, 452, 561
Eskimo-Aleut languages 556
Estienne, Robert 442
Ethiopic philology 137, 289, 479–493
ethnography (music) 584–586
Euclid 17
Euclidean distance 309
Euclides (politician) 25
Europeana regia 32
evolution → Darwin, Charles
EVT (Edition Visualisation Technology) 433f
examinatio 381, 385, 390, 393
Excel (Microsoft) 330
excerpt 155f
exemplar 23
exemplar shift 23, 62, 104, 260
external criticism 446
exogenesis 529
expectation–maximisation (EM) algorithm 348
eye-skip 225, 247f, 289, 388

Fabri de Peiresc, Nicolas-Claude 482
facsimile (edition) 48f, 489, 513f

672 — General Index

facsimile, digital 139, 145, 147, 514, 412, 415, 418–427, 478, 513–517
family tree 75, 83–85, 524, 549
Fierabras 89, 457
FigTree 335
filologia d'autore 438
First Vatican Mythographer 21
Fitch and Margoliash (algorithm) 326, 330
Flete, William
Fleury (monastery) 27
Fljótsdǿla saga 367f, 378
florilegium 64, 156, 274, 306
Florus of Lyon 155
fluid texts 23, 212f, 415, 531f
folklore 568, 586
forest (graph theory) 241
formalisation 179f, 184–187, 227, 236f, 241, 426
Fracastoro, Girolamo 519f
fragment, fragmentation 18f, 29, 61, 102, 126, 141–148, 159, 221, 360, 364, 366, 370, 484, 500, 509, 531, 577
Fredegar 63
Fremdlesung 386
French Revolution 30
French language, nobility of 376
Friar Bertold → *Rechtssumme*
Frobenius, Hieronymus 34, 514, 519
Froger, Jacques 101–103, 121, 261f, 271, 454, 462
Froissart, Jean 157

Gadla Libānos 492
Gadla Qawsṭos 491
Galen 66
Gallica 32
gaps 483
gathering → quire
Gazeau, Guillaume 519
Gebrauchsliteratur 159
Gelenius, Sigismundus 70
gene (also → DNA) 537f
genealogical tree → tree
genealogical method → method of common errors
genetic criticism 524–533
genetic map 528–533
geographical criterion 120
Georgian philology 150, 152, 289f, 438, 493
Gephi 335f

Gerard of Cremona 513
Gherardi, Iacopo 523
Giunti, Giovan Maria 519
Giunti, Tommaso 519
gloss-incorporation 156, 248
Glossa ordinaria 24
glosses 20f, 67, 139, 156, 159, 248
glottochronology 558, 563
glottogony 557
good manuscript → *bon manuscript*
Gothenburg model 168
graffiti 159, 275
graph theory 228–236, 303–307
graph, undirected vs directed 303
GraphViz 197, 335
Greg graph, notation, tree 230f, 232, 237f
Gregorian chant 578, 582
Gregory of Nazianzus 40, 150, 155, 158, 282–288
Gregory of Nyssa 155
Gregory of Tours 14, 63
Gringore, Pierre 522
Gronovius, Friedrich 73
Guido de Monte Rocherii 44
Gutenberg Bible 34, 441
Gǝʽǝz → Ethiopic philology

Haeckel, Ernst 534, 549
hagiography 263, 488, 490f
halakhic texts 494
Handschriftenzensus 147f
haplography 23, 246, 445
harmonising variants 446
Hartmann von Aue 467–471
Hebrew philology 493–501
Heine, Heinrich 529
Heinrichi (artificial tradition) 269f
Heinsius, Nicolaus 73
Heliand 382–385, 391, 400, 403
Hemming (monk at Worcester) 53
Herodianus 548
Hesiod 12
Hesychius of Alexandria 444
Hesychius of Sinai 444
Hieronymus → Jerome
Hildebrandslied 174, 361
Hippocrates (Hippocratic corpus) 48, 71
historical-critical edition → critical edition
history of manuscripts 353
history of the text 272–291, 480

Homeric poems 12, 15, 18, 65, 67, 141, 156
Homo sapiens 557
homoeoarcton 248, 445
homoeoteleuton (also → eye-skip) 248, 445
homologies 571
homoplasies 571
Horace 72, 256
horizontal gene transfer 306, 536, 545, 571
HTML format 187, 203f, 206, 434–436
Hungrvaka 369
Hurtado de Mendoza, Diego 281
Hutton, James 7
hybridisation 306, 536, 542
hyparchetype 221f, 367, 486
hyperedges 241
hypertextuality 415

Iacobus de Voragine 46, 290
Icelandic → Old Norse
ideal text 525
idiographic writing 9
igraph (R) 336
Il detto d'amore 398
Il fiore 398
Iliad 12, 17
imperial library (Rome) 27
imprimatur 521
incunabula 35
index of variation 449
indirect tradition 148–160
Indo-European languages 549–567
Indo-Hittite hypothesis 551
ingroup → outgroup
innovation (also → error) 76f, 79, 82f, 106, 243, 250, 383, 468
innovation, shared → method of common errors
inscriptions 11f, 60, 62, 160
integrity (text ideal) 526
intentional vs unintentional changes 446
intentionalism 526
interlinear notes 20f, 248, 277f, 353f
intermediate witness 100f, 213, 364, 445, 448, 470
internal criticism 446
International Image Interoperability Framework (IIIF) 49
interpolation 45, 149, 156f, 248, 346, 452f
introduction (of editions) 38, 88f, 92, 94, 156, 359–364, 457, 485, 489f, 497, 513, 518f

inventio capitis Pauli 289
inversion 172
Irene (sebastokratorissa) 155
IRHT microfilm collection 31
Isaac (sebastokrator) 275
Isidore of Seville 66
isoglosses 551–555
itacism 247
Italian school 109–138, 463
iudicium 74, 78, 90, 116, 132, 406, 482
Iwein → Hartmann von Aue

Jacobus de Voragine → Iacobus de Voragine
Jacopone da Todi 398
JavaScript 206, 433–435
Jerome 40, 252
jgraphT 335
jiaochou 502
jiaokan 502
John of Damascus 156
Josquin des Prez 580–583
Joyce, James 526
JSON format 167, 180f, 195, 197–199, 203, 206
Judith (Old English Text) 53
Jukes-Cantor model (JC 69) 321f
Justinian plague 14
Juvenal 26
Juvencus 18
Juxta 329, 426

Kallierges, Zacharias 70
kaozheng 511
Kimura model (K80) 321
King James Bible 443
kinship-revealing variants → error, indicative
Koberger, Anton 513
Kokkinobaphos, Jacob 155
Komnenos, Isaac 149
Konungs skuggsjá 377f
Kurgan hypothesis 559f, 567

L1 distance 309
labelling (graph theory) 230
Lachmann, Karl 2–4, 36, 50, 57, 73, 74, 88, 120, 132, 141–148, 247, 412, 365, 378, 443, 451f, 460, 465–479, 483, 491
Lachmann's method (term; otherwise → method of common errors) 88
lacuna 19, 23, 71, 123, 132, 219, 262, 276f, 289, 370, 397

Lai de l'ombre → Renart, Jean
LangScape 51
Langton, Stephen 442
Lanval 360, 370–372
Laxdøla saga 368
lateral gene transfer → horizontal gene transfer
latest common ancestor → MRCA
LaTeX 205, 418, 428–430, 432
Laudario di Modena 397
layout 142, 165, 213, 247, 251, 353, 360, 402, 415, 418, 487
leaf (tree) 298, 304, 318f, 331f
least squares method 320f
lectio brevior 249, 395, 447
lectio difficilior 66, 107, 121, 223, 249, 384, 393–395, 447, 451, 462, 476
lectio facilior → *lectio difficilior*
lectio singularis 312, 386, 391
Leibniz, Gottfried Wilhelm 549f, 557
Leitfehler method 326
Leitfehler → error, indicative
lemma (apparatus) 171
lemma (in commentaries) 156, 276, 495
lemmatisation 465
Leofric (earl of Mercia) 52
Levenshtein distance (also → Damerau-Levenshtein) 309
lexical approach 527
lexical variants 502
Liber glossarum 21
libraries 10, 16, 24–27 (antiquity), 28–33, 47f, 62, 145–148, 260, 426, 507, 514
libraries (digital) 32, 204, 465
Library of Congress 30
library of the kings of France 28
LibreOffice 186, 189, 330
librettos (opera) 122f
Libro de buen amor 463f
Lindisfarne Gospel 20, 252
linear regression 320
linguistic diversity → vernaculars
linguistics 490, 548–568
Lipsius, Justus 72
LisBeth 334
Listrius, Gerardus 519
Liszt, Franz 584
literary languages 14f, 481
Little Red Riding Hood fairy tale 574f
liturgical texts → living texts
Liu Xiang 502, 507

Liu Xin 502, 507f
living texts 91, 99, 104, 492
Livius Andronicus 26
Livy (Titus Livius) 67, 69, 258
LMNL 165
locus criticus (or *locus selectus*) 160, 170f, 213, 311, 390
logographic writing 9
loi d'airain (Bédier) 92f
long-branch attraction 312, 318, 332f, 566
long-term availability → sustainability
longest common subsequence (LCS) distance 309
Lorsch fragment (*Waltharius*) 19
loss (of manuscripts) 90, 106, 128, 130f, 132, 213, 364, 380, 453
Lotrain, Alain 522
LUCA (last universal common ancestor) 223
Lucan 396
Lucian of Antioch 451
Lucian of Samosata 454–456
Lucretius 32–39, 42, 74, 247, 412, 451
Ludolf, Hiob 482
Lupus of Ferrière 32, 68, 258
Luther, Martin 442
Lyceum (Aristotle's school) 25

Maas, Paul 3f, 50, 58, 74, 84–88, 91, 103, 105–107, 111f, 114–121, 126, 136, 211, 222, 231, 244, 261, 272, 349, 364f, 390, 393, 406, 452, 462, 465, 473, 475
Mabillon, Jean 47
MacClade 337
machine learning 465
Madvig, Johan Nicolai 57, 365f, 451
Maffei, Scipione 48
Mahābhārata 387
majority principle 38, 78, 390
majuscule writing 60
Malthus, Thomas Robert 7
Manhattan distance 309
manuscript → witness
manuscript, lost 19, 15, 36, 70, 75, 77, 94, 127, 239, 275f, 369
manuscript, old (also → *codex vetustissimus*) 66, 71, 73, 78, 155
manuscript pseudo-DNA 240
Manuscripta mediaevalia 32
Manutius, Aldus 34, 70, 514
Marcion 447

marginalia 17, 21, 23, 139, 149, 156, 158, 161, 221, 236, 248, 274, 277f, 404, 415, 435, 515
Marie de France 360, 363, 372
Markdown 185f, 430f
Markov Chain Monte Carlo (MCMC) algorithm 314, 323, 572f
markup languages 140, 164f, 178f, 184–187, 203, 415f, 430, 434
Martial 26
Martianus Capella 21, 24, 216, 341, 349–352
Material Philology 98–99, 273, 464
materiality 142, 316, 527
maximum chi-squared method 265, 267, 271, 546
maximum likelihood methods 309–313, 321f, 339, 541
maximum parsimony → parsimony
mechanical loss 486
media (transmitting texts) 16–20
Medici, Lorenzo de' 29, 277
Meietti, Paolo 517
Mekhilta d'Rabbi Yishmael 497
Mekhilta on Exodus 495
Merovingian spelling 14
metacharakterismos 247
metaphors (in textual criticism) 87
metathesis 247
method of common errors 4, 90, 91–108 (criticism), 111, 135, 379
microfilms 31
mid-point rooting 544
Middle High German poetry 465–479
Midrash Esther Rabba 500
Migne, Jacques-Paul 41, 48
Ming dynasty 511
Minimum spanning trees 317, 331f
Minnesänger 389f, 583
minuscule writing 60
Mishnah 494
misreading 23, 52, 247
missing links 570
mistake → error
mixture → contamination
model misspecification 540
models (stemma) 226–241
molecular clock 297, 318, 346, 539, 558, 563
Mombrizio, Bonino 45
Mon-Khmer languages 555
monastic scriptorium 27

Monmonier's algorithm 566
monogenesis (of errors) 80f, 89, 117, 133, 469
monogenesis (of language) 557
monoptic edition → edition, monotypic
Montfaucon, Bernard de 30, 47
Monumenta Germaniae Historica (MGH) 372
Morelli, Giacomo 30
Mouseion (library) 25f
mouvance (Zumthor) 463
MrBayes 323f, 334
MRCA (most recent common ancestor) 223, 237, 305
multi-text codices 134
multi-version document 161
multiedges 241
multifurcation 298, 541
Multiple Readings Method 448
multitrees 241
mulu xue 502
Murmuris, Cornelius 281
musicology 93, 576–586
Muspilli 361
Musuro, Marco 34
mutation 239, 297, 534
mutation rate → molecular clock
mysql 189
Münchner Digitalisierungszentrum 32

narrative motifs 571
National Libraries 31
national schools (of philology) 2
nationalist ideology 559
Navagero, Andrea 34
Navigatio Sancti Brendani 257, 260, 262
neighbour-joining 267, 293, 297, 319, 330, 341, 344, 347, 349, 351, 354, 540
neighbour-nets (NeighborNet) 267, 298, 354f, 388f, 540f, 546
neighbourhood (of a node) 303
neo-Lachmannism 108–139, 457, 461–463, 487–493
neogrammarians 470
network, phylogenetic 241, 306f, 542, 546, 574,
neums 578f
neutral text-form (NT) 443
New Philology 59, 97–99, 134, 138, 272, 406, 457, 463f, 465
New Testament (Greek) 69, 71, 73, 137, 271, 295, 360, 424f, 440–450

Newick format 199f, 237, 307f, 335
Nexus files 190, 193, 199f, 308
Nibelungenklage 408f, 478
Nibelungenlied 451, 457, 466–470, 475, 478
Niccoli, Niccolò 29, 37
Niger-Congo languages 555
Nilo-Saharan languages 555f
Niðrstigningar saga 127
node, hypothetical 331
node, internal 300, 348, 382, 545, 574
node, terminal → leaf
nodes 195, 212, 218f, 228, 230–233, 237–241, 303–307, 322
noise 294, 345f, 353, 370
non-reproductibility (of errors) 250
normalisation (collation) 174f
normalisation (orthography) 14, 140 169, 174, 376, 427, 474, 481
normalisation (transcription) 165–169
Nostratic language 556
notation (music) 577
Notepad++ 186
Nowell Codex 53
nucleotides 312, 321, 538
nuova filologia (Barbi) 462

obelus 82, 415
obscuring of the archetype 124
Ockham's razor 311
OCR 329, 356, 417, 513
odt format 186
Odyssey 12, 26
Öffentliche k. k. Universitätsbibliothek 31
OHCO model 164f
Old Norse philology 361f, 367, 375, 378, 438
Old Roman cursive 61
Old Slavonic 150
Olivétan, Pierre Robert 442
omission 23, 45, 82, 157, 172, 209, 225, 242, 245–248, 258, 277f, 282, 343, 353, 445
ope codicum, emendatio 71, 73, 487
ope ingenii, emendatio 34, 37, 42, 71, 73, 361, 393, 487
open formats 180, 204, 416
open recension 116, 256, 370, 391, 455, 462
open-source software 329
operational taxonomic units (OTUs) → taxon
Oporinus, Johann 515f
oracle bones 504
orality 494, 577

Oribasius 71
orientation (Quentin) 100f, 104f
orientation to text 527f
Origen 360, 441, 449
original 44f, 63, 65, 75f, 97, 144, 167, 214, 218, 221, 223, 364f, 375, 381, 385, 442, 458, 463, 469
original readings, agreement in 102
originals, multiple 117
orthography (also → normalisation) 168, 366, 374f, 406, 445, 481, 515
outgroup (rooting) 306, 346, 542f
overabundance (of witnesses) 42, 120, 170, 282, 301, 390
Ovid 63
Oxygen (software) 186

Pachymeres, Georges 276, 280
Palaeographical Society 48
palaeography 46–56, 273
Palatine library 30
palimpsest 17, 159
PAML (software) 336f
Pandoc 430
Pāṇini 548
Papal Curia 28
paper 17
Papias (lexicographer) 43–46
papyrus 24, 159, 274, 440
parablepsis 248
parallel segmentation 432
paraphrase 157
paratextual elements 149, 158, 209, 274, 281f, 285, 291
parchment 17
Paris, Gaston 2, 57f, 88–91, 106, 110, 210, 219, 367, 369, 374f, 391f, 452, 456–458, 463, 469, 485
parsimony 105, 297, 311f, 319f, 540, 572
parsimony-based methods 310, 312, 316, 538
parsimony problem 319f
partial stemmata 301, 471
Parvum Lexicon Stemmatologicum (PLS) 1, 3–6
Parzival (artificial tradition) 300
Parzival project 144
Pasquali, Giorgio 3, 91, 105, 108, 111, 115–117, 120, 137, 256f, 272, 378, 390, 453, 462
Pater noster 447
path 221, 292, 303, 305, 320, 388, 544
Patristic literature 39–43, 150, 156, 440

Patrologia Latina, Graeca → Migne, Jacques-Paul
Patrologia Orientalis 480
Paul's martyrdom 290
PAUP(*) 190, 268–270, 293, 297, 334, 337f
PDF format 180, 204, 207, 418, 428
peciae 28, 62
per cola et commata 251f
performativity 577
peripheral areas, criterion of 287
Perseus (king of Persia, his library) 26
Persius 26, 72
Persius, Antonius 521f
Pesiqta de-Rav Kahana 497
Petrarca, Francesco 33, 40
Petronius 26, 63
Petrus Alfonsi 219, 224
Petrus Blesensis 63
Petrus Comestor 191f
Petrus Plaoul 424f
Petrus Riga 24
phangor (R) 328, 334
Phillips, Thomas Sir (library of) 30
philologia sacra 483
Philoxenus 548
Photian renaissance 14
photography 30, 32, 464
Phylip 293, 297, 334, 338, 344
PhyloDAG 322f
phylogenetics 105, 298–301 (in stemmatology), 537–547, 556–568 (in linguistics)
phylogeny.fr 334
PhyloMap 336
phylomemetics 540, 568
PhyloXML 199–201
Physiologus 152, 154f, 157
Physiologus Bernensis 152
Piccolomini, Iacopo Ammannati 523f
pictograms 9
pidgins 534
Piers Plowman 420, 422
Pindar 48, 70, 273
Pinelli, Vincenzo 279
Pius II (pope) 523
Pius X (pope) 99
Plantin, Christoph 442
Plato 24, 274–281, 548
Pliny the Younger (rediscovery) 32f
polarisation (of a tree) 305

Poliziano, Angelo 34, 69, 451
Polo, Marco 402
polygenesis (of errors) 106, 117, 133, 270, 383, 469
polyglot Bible 442f, 482
polygyny 566
polytomy 541f
polytree 304
Pompeii 159
Popper, Karl 59, 135
popular texts 116, 122, 259f, 262
post correctionem 215
posterior probability 323
pots are not people maxim 560, 567f
printing technology 17, 29, 33f, 70, 438, 440
prints, early modern 512–524
prints (texts for which no manuscripts survive) 32, 43, 513
prior probability 323
Probus (grammarian) 66
Proclus 149, 156, 158, 274–281
production-oriented approach 528
Propertius 451
Proto-World language 557
Pseudo-Dionysius Areopagita 274–281, 288–290
punch cards 177
punctuation 175, 223, 250–252, 317, 353, 406, 490, 515
purity (text ideal) 525f
Pydna, battle of 26

Qin bibliocaust 507
Qing dynasty 510
quantitative analysis of errors 102, 104
quaternio 17
Quentin, Henry 3, 58f, 91, 99–105, 108, 110–112, 119, 295, 448f, 454, 460, 462
quiescent manuscript traditions → active vs quiescent manuscript traditions
quire 17, 19, 52f, 260, 278f
Qumran 137
quotations 2, 22, 65, 75, 137, 155f, 289, 382, 417, 440, 446, 449

R (software) 328, 334
Rabanus Maurus 22
rabbinic literature 493–501
Ramusio, Giovanni Battista 402
Ramusio, Paolo 519

ratchet effect 436
Ratherius of Verona 44
re-mediation 202
reading, accidental 135, 223, 343, 368, 375, 383, 582
reading, authentic vs "good" 100
reading, confirmatory 125
reading, distinctive 449
reading, exclusive 449
reading, formal 383
reading, primary 150, 243, 276, 383, 449
reading, variant 38, 43, 97, 167f, 189–193, 233, 381f, 413, 416, 445, 515
reading, substantial 88, 223, 383
readings 74, 170
real tree → *arbre réel*
recensio 24, 34, 58, 75, 79, 91, 99, 105, 132, 210, 357, 359, 363, 366, 372, 379, 381f, 385, 407, 460, 464, 468f, 471, 483, 578
recensio brevior vs *fusior* 157
recensio, ex parte subiecti vs *obiecti* 106
recension → redaction
recentiores non deteriores 116, 397
Rechtssumme (Friar Bertold) 477
redaction 44, 46, 123, 157, 235, 387, 390, 404, 443, 445, 477, 492, 518, 521f
reductio ad unum 405
Registrum librorum Angliae 145
regularisation 359, 374 (internal), 375f (external), 378, 406, 427
Reis van Sente Brandane 199
Renaissance scholars 32, 212
Renart, Jean 91, 391, 452, 459–462, 473,
reportatio 64
reprint 41, 48, 71, 513, 516–518
restitutio textus → *constitutio textus*
reticulation 306f
retro-digitisation 417
reversible vs irreversible errors 133, 250
revision 16, 20, 22, 408, 443–445
RHM (Roos-Heikkilä-Myllymäki) method 269, 325, 332, 347
Rhosos, John 277–280
Robortello, Francesco 72
roll → rotulus
Roman de la rose 464
root (rooted tree) 101, 213, 223, 227–232, 285, 287, 304f, 331–335, 345f, 403, 535, 542–544
roots, several 213, 223, 403

rotulus 16, 24
rtf format 186
Rufinus of Aquileia 285, 287
Rustaveli, Shota 159
rustica Romana lingua 14
règle de fer (Quentin) 100

Sacra parallela (Ps-Damascenus) 156
Saidian orientalism 483
Saints' Lives 159
Salutati, Coluccio 33, 40
Sanskrit philology 11, 137, 160, 265, 387, 548f, 558, 561
Sassetti, Filippo 548
Saussure, Ferdinand de 64
saut du même au même → eye-skip
Saxo Grammaticus 252
Scaliger, Joseph Justus 72, 247, 482, 524
Schedel, Hartmann 29, 513f
Schlegel, Friedrich 558
Schleicher, August 7, 535, 549f, 569f, 574f
Schlyter, Carl J. 57, 211, 365f
scholia 65, 70, 156, 418
Schwund-Hypothese 551
Schöffel, Peter 519
Scottus Eriugena, Johannes 22, 217, 221, 408, 410f
scribal habits 134, 581, 584
scribe 22, 99, 374, 376
scriptio continua 62, 300
scriptoria 6–28, 62, 260, 488
scroll → rotulus
Scythia 564
secondary reading → innovation
Seder Olam 499
selectio 82, 381f, 393, 397
selection (natural) 534
self-loops 230
Semantic Web 187
Semstem 331
Seneca 26, 72f, 80f, 245
separation of content and form (digital editions) 416
Septuagint 25, 150, 289, 441, 443, 483
sequence (of works) 455
sequence evolution model 321
Serapeum (library) 25
Sermo Lupi ad Anglos 385
Servius 18
set theory 87, 102

Seven summaries (Qilüe 七略)
SfarData 49
SGML language 178
Shang dynasty 504
Shemot Rabba 497
shock waves → West tables
Sifre Devarim 497–499
Sifre on Numbers 495, 497
sigla 68, 73, 122, 215, 238, 275, 416, 423, 435, 441
significant errors → error, significant
silent reading 13
Silius Italicus 26
site (phylogenetics) 311
site, constant 312
site, singleton 312
Śivadharmaśāstra 160
Śivadharmottara 160
Sixtus IV (pope) 29
Sixtus V (pope) 517
Snorri Sturluson 155, 370
social approach 527
Sonderfehler → *lectio singularis*
Song dynasty 509
Sophists 24
Sorbonne, Collège 28
sound law 550
Southern Italy (Greek) 287, 445
split decomposition 241, 297, 540
SplitsTree 297, 334, 338, 351, 355
Sprachbund 551
spreadsheets 161, 167, 180, 187, 191, 193, 195
SSDs 177
St Emmeram (monastery) 22
St Gall (monastery) 27
St Patrick's confessio 413f, 423f
Stammbaumtheorie 550–552, 563
standardisation 16, 436, 445, 463, 481
Statilius Maximus (scribe) 20
Steiner tree 317
stemma (codicum) 34, 37, 46, 67, 75, 78, 83, 85, 88, 105, 119, 209–220 (definition), 273, 365, 381, 390, 418, 445, 469, 486, 489f, 524, 524f (metaphor)
stemma editionum 211, 521
stemma variantium 234
stemma, bipartite (also → bifurcation) 91, 217, 453
stemma, tripartite → trifurcation
stemma, true (relation to *arbre réel*) 232

stemmatology 1, 4
Stemmaweb 234, 301, 330, 333, 356, 426
Strabo 72
strenge Stemmatik (Maas) 84, 86f
stylometry 176
sub-stemma 449
substitution 245
substitution matrix 239f
surface text 493
sustainability (digital resources) 147, 179, 205–207, 293, 303, 417, 427, 436
Swadesh lists 561–563
Symeon, Saint of Trier → *Vita et miracula Sancti Symeonis*
Symmachus 70
synoptic Gospel edition 360
Syriac philology 150, 287–290, 438, 446, 480, 485, 487, 493

T-Pen 329
tags (tagging) 179, 182, 246
Tang dynasty 505
Tannaitic period 494
Tasfā Ṣəyon 482
Tassin, René Prosper 48
taxon, pl. taxa 304, 306, 307, 536, 538, 541–543
TEI XML format 181f, 186f, 189f, 236, 356, 428, 431–434
Telesio, Bernardino 521
Terence 67
ternio 17
Tertullian 40f, 43, 447
Testament of Our Lord in Galilee 486
testimonia 423, 494
Text Encoding Initiative (TEI) 55
text evolution 312, 534
TextGrid 329
textile traits 573
textual dynamics 379
textus receptus 71, 73, 74, 442f, 451, 474, 485
theatre plays 123
Theodulf of Orléans 32, 68
Thucydides 69
Tibullus 451
Tironian notes 20
tokenisation 168–170
Tomeo, Niccolò Leonico 279
Tosefta 495, 499
Tournes, Jean de 519

Tours (monastery) 27
Toustain, Charles François 48
traditio textus vs *traditio codicum* 273
tradition (of a work) 75
tradition, indirect 75, 141, 148–160, 274, 281, 382, 392
Trajan 27
transcription 50f, 54, 98, 160–173, 185–189, 329, 415f, 420f, 435, 465, 478, 501, 513
transcription, narrow vs broad 374
transition from roll to codex 16
Transkribus 329
translations (indirect tradition) 22, 68, 127, 149–155, 159f, 274–280, 285–289, 438, 480f, 490, 529
transliteration 62, 247
translocation 172
transmission, horizontal 58, 84, 87, 229, 248, 258, 261f, 364, 386, 462
transmission, oral and written 15f
transmission, unidirectional → transmission, vertical
transmission, vertical 106, 256
transposition 172f, 192, 209, 242, 245, 247, 258, 309, 360, 449
Traube, Ludwig 30, 48
Traversari, Ambrogio 40
tree (graph theory) 273, 304, 534
tree generation, automatic 331–335
tree, phylogenetic 298, 304–309, 324, 419, 535, 539–547, 551, 561, 563
tree score 293, 310–313
tree, unrooted 299, 305
tree visualisation software 335
TreeDyn 336
treeViz 336
Trennfehler → error, separative
trifurcation 91, 348, 367
Tristan en prose 461
trivialisation 395
tropes (Aquitanian and French) 582
troubadours 583
trouvères 583
Tungusic languages 556
Tupi languages 555
TXT format 181, 185

ultrametricity 318–321
uncial writing 60–62, 158, 282, 441
Unicode 182, 428

unifurcation 298, 332
units of production vs units of circulation 52
universities (mediaeval) 28
unstable texts 478
Unweighted Pair Group Method with Arithmetic Mean (UPGMA) 317f, 330, 345
Uralic languages 555
Urheimat 557–560
Urtext (also → ancestral state reconstruction) 336f, 501
usus scribendi 107, 393, 396
UTF-8 182, 186
Uto-Aztecan languages 555
utrum in alterum abiturum erat 394

Valerius Flaccus 69
Valla, Giorgio 34
Valla, Lorenzo 69
Vardzia 159
varia lectio 139
variance (New Philology) 98, 463
variant location 139, 160f, 170–173, 240, 270, 285, 390
variant stemma 213, 217, 233f, 536
variant reading → reading
variant, stemmatically undecidable 392, 468
variant-carriers 168, 222
variante inutile 38
variantistica 438
Varro 221
Västgötalagan 57, 211, 365
Vayyiqra Rabba 497, 500
VBase 419
vector-based distance measures 309
Vedic texts 11
vellum → parchment
Venantius Fortunatus 214
verbal criticism 445
vernaculars 20, 35, 68, 89, 92, 124, 141, 262, 363–368, 374–376, 380, 406, 463
version management 189
versions (of a text) 46, 531
vertex 228, 303
Vesalius, Andreas 515
Vidal, Peire 107, 396
Vie de St Alexis 363, 366f, 375–377, 394f, 404, 456f, 485 (Syriac)
VIM 186
Vincent de Beauvais 175
Vindolanda tablets 13

Virgil 16–22, 66f, 214
Vision of Leofric 52
Vision of Shenute 486
visualisation (collation) 169
Vita et miracula Sancti Symeonis 257
vocabulary, cognate 550
volumen → rotulus
Vorlage → exemplar
vulgarisation 14
vulgate reading 225
vulgate text 215, 225, 481, 519
Vulgate → Bible (Latin)

Waltharius 19
Walton, Brian 442
Wanley, Humfrey 47
Warring States period 504
Wattenbach, Wilhelm 30
Wellentheorie 550–552
West tables 262, 267, 271
Western Han 504
Western text (NT) 450
Western Zhou
William of Moerbeke 275f, 281
Winter, Johannes of Andernach 71
witnesses (of texts) 22, 75, 536
Wolf and the Kids fairy tale 574

Wolf, Friedrich August 484
Wolfram von Eschenbach 142–148, 420f, 468
wooden tablets 17
word formation 550
World War I 31
Wulfstan 357, 403f
Wunderkammern 29

XML format 178–184, 195, 197, 199, 205f, 431–434
XSLT stylesheet 183, 205, 432f
xylograph 505, 513

Yule Furry linear birth process 234

Zabarella, Iacopo 517
Zenodotus of Ephesus 16, 25
zéro caractéristique (Quentin) 100, 448
Zetzner, Lazarus 517
Zipf's law 176
Zoëga, Georg 484
Zumpt, Carl Gottlob 211

Æthelweard 387f
Þiðriks saga af Bern 368, 378
Þorláks saga helga 360, 373
ἀκολουθίαι → sequence (of works)

Index of Manuscripts

Basel, Universitätsbibliothek, A IX 64   519
Basel, Universitätsbibliothek, A IX 64a   519
Cambridge, Corpus Christi College, MS 367   53
Città del Vaticano, Biblioteca Apostolica Vaticana, Ottob. lat. 25   41
Città del Vaticano, Biblioteca Apostolica Vaticana, Ottob. lat. 1306   522
Città del Vaticano, Biblioteca Apostolica Vaticana, Ottob. lat. 1929   522
Città del Vaticano, Biblioteca Apostolica Vaticana, Reg. lat. 1625 (III)   18
Città del Vaticano, Biblioteca Apostolica Vaticana, Ross. 962   275
Città del Vaticano, Biblioteca Apostolica Vaticana, Vat. gr. 90   445
Città del Vaticano, Biblioteca Apostolica Vaticana, Vat. lat. 11458   20
Den Haag, Koninklijke Bibliotheek, 129.G.20   522
Escorial, Real Biblioteca de San Lorenzo, T. II. 8 (gr. 147)   275
Firenze, Biblioteca Medicea Laurenziana, Ii.10   221
Firenze, Biblioteca Medicea Laurenziana, Conv. Soppr. J.VI.9   41
Firenze, Biblioteca Medicea Laurenziana, Conv. Soppr. 103   275
Firenze, Biblioteca Medicea Laurenziana, Plut. 35.30   36
Firenze, Biblioteca Medicea Laurenziana, Plut. 85, 8   275, 280
Hamburg, Staats- und Universitätsbibliothek, Cod. 17 in scrin.   19
Heidelberg, Universitätsbibliothek, Pal. germ. 357   390
Heidelberg, Universitätsbibliothek, Pal. germ. 848   390
Hildesheim, Dombibliothek, St. God. Nr 1   375
Kassel, Universitätsbibliothek, 2° Ms. theol. 54   361
København, Den Arnamagnæanske Samling, AM 243 b α fol.   377
København, Det Kongelige Bibliotek, GKS 211 fol.   36
København, Det Kongelige Bibliotek, GKS 2367 4to   370
Leiden, Universiteitsbibliotheek, Voss. Lat. F. 30   36
Leiden, Universiteitsbibliotheek, Voss. Lat. Q. 94   36
London, British Library, Add. 11983   80
London, British Library, Add. 17210   17
London, British Library, Add. 17211   17
London, British Library, Add. 27169   497
London, British Library, Cotton, Nero D. IV   252
London, British Library, Cotton, Vitellius A.xv   53, 361
London, British Library, Harley 978   363, 371
London, British Library, Harley 2782   17
London, National Archives, C66/308   51
Madrid, Biblioteca Nacional, Ms. Sig. v. 7–17   19
Milano, Ambrosiana, A 45 sup.   152
Milano, Ambrosiana, B 165 sup. (159)   275, 279
Milano, Ambrosiana, E 50 inf.   158
Montpellier, Bibliothèque interuniversitaire, Section Médecine, H 253   21
Moskva, Gosudarstvennyj Istoričeskij Muzej, Sinod. Gr. 467   154
München, Archäologische Staatssammlung, Bernhard Starks Collectaneen, his. Ver. 18, VIII   19
München, Bayerische Staatsbibliothek, clm 14098   361
München, Bayerische Staatsbibliothek, gr. 425   275
Oxford, Bodleian Library, Auct. F. 2. 8
Oxford, Bodleian Library, Digby   23
Oxford, Bodleian Library, Huntington   600
Paris, Bibliothèque nationale de France, fr. 19183   522
Paris, Bibliothèque nationale de France, gr. 510   282
Paris, Bibliothèque nationale de France, gr. 515   158
Paris, Bibliothèque nationale de France, gr. 923   156
Paris, Bibliothèque nationale de France, gr. 1810   275
Paris, Bibliothèque nationale de France, lat. 10307   18

Paris, Bibliothèque nationale de France, lat. 10318 64
Paris, Bibliothèque nationale de France, Rothschild 2855 522
Reims, Bibliothèque municipale, 875 22, 215
Reykjavík, Safn Árna Magnússonar, GKS 2365 4o 155, 362
Salamanca, Biblioteca de la Universidad, ms. 2109 523
Salzburg, Stiftsbibliothek St. Peter, a. VII. 5 248
Sélestat, Bibliothèque humaniste, MS 88 41
Sinai, St Catherine's Monastery, gr. 399 158
Soissons, Bibliothèque Municipale, 204 522
St. Gallen, Stiftsbibliothek, Cod. Sang. 189 51
St. Gallen, Stiftsbibliothek, Cod. Sang. 231 66
St. Gallen, Stiftsbibliothek, Cod. Sang. 359 579
St. Gallen, Stiftsbibliothek, Cod. Sang. 569 80
St. Gallen, Stiftsbibliothek, Cod. Sang. 857 143, 420
St. Emmeram, fragmentary manuscript 22
Stockholm, Kungliga biblioteket, Holm perg 6 fol. 366
Stuttgart, Württembergische Landesbibliothek, H.B. XIII, poet. germ. I 390
Trier, Bibliothek des Priesterseminars, Ms 100 21
Trier, Stadtbibliothek, Ms. 1353/132 264
Uppsala, Universitetsbiblioteket, DG 4–7 360
Uppsala, Universitetsbiblioteket, DG 11 370
Valenciennes, Bibliothèque municipale, 411 80
Venezia, Biblioteca Marciana, gr. Z 191 275
Wien, Österreichische Nationalbibliothek, Cod. 107 36
Wien, Österreichische Nationalbibliothek, Phil. gr. 7 275
Wien, Österreichische Nationalbibliothek, Phil. gr. 123 456
Zürich, Zentralbibliothek, 2.103 143

List of authors

Christian-Bernard Amphoux was a researcher at the CNRS from 1974 to 2008 studying Greek Bible manuscripts, especially the Septuagint's relation to the Hebrew original as well as the Greek NT text used in the second century AD.

Tara Andrews is a historian of the mediaeval Christian Near East, an Armenian philologist, and a software engineer. She is responsible for teaching and research in digital humanities at the University of Vienna.

Dieter Bachmann has a background in experimental physics, computational linguistics, and comparative Indo-European philology. He has pursued projects in computational stemmatology since 2009 alongside his main occupation of teaching physics in Zurich.

Alessandro Bausi is a philologist at the Universität Hamburg heading several projects in Ethiopic and Eritrean philology, manuscript studies, linguistics, and corpus linguistics. He is a member of the Cluster of Excellence "Understanding Written Artefacts", and has published extensively as an author and served as a journal and series editor.

Marina Buzzoni teaches Germanic philology and historical linguistics at Ca' Foscari University of Venice, Italy. Her major academic interests include textual criticism, digital philology, diachronic linguistics, and translation theory and practice. She is an editor and co-editor of mediaeval Germanic texts, as well as a coordinator of scholarly editorial projects.

Paolo Chiesa teaches mediaeval Latin Philology at the University of Milan. His research mainly focuses both on mediaeval manuscript traditions and on theoretical textual criticism; he has provided several scholarly editions of Latin works of the Middle Ages.

Aidan Conti teaches classical and mediaeval Latin at the University of Bergen, Norway. His research interests include early mediaeval homiletics and related manuscripts and textual traditions, as well as mediaevalism.

Frédéric Duval teaches Romance philology at the Ecole nationale des chartes (Paris). His research concerns mediaeval French, especially diachronic linguistics, lexicography, and translation theory. It also covers edition philology.

Franz Fischer is a mediaeval Latinist and digital humanities specialist who works and teaches at the Ca' Foscari University of Venice. His research interests include digital philology, scholarly editing, and mediaeval studies.

Elisabet Göransson is a Latinist at Lund University, Sweden. Her research interests concern methods and tools for investigating, analysing, editing, and visualising textual traditions in different genres and across languages.

Jean-Baptiste Guillaumin teaches Latin literature and philology at the Sorbonne Université (Paris); he is a junior member of the Institut universitaire de France (since 2015). His main research fields include late antique encyclopedism, the history of the transmission of Latin texts, and textual criticism, especially on Martianus Capella's work.

Open Access. © 2020 Philipp Roelli, published by De Gruyter.
This work is licensed under the Creative Commons Attribution 4.0 Public License.
https://doi.org/10.1515/9783110684384-014

Odd Einar Haugen is an Old Norse scholar who works and teaches at the University of Bergen, Norway. His research interests include textual criticism, text encoding, language history, palaeography, and font development, and his didactic interests include grammars and textbooks for Old Norse.

Gerd V. M. Haverling received her PhD in Latin from Gothenburg University (1988). She became a lecturer for classical philology at the University of Aarhus in 2001, and since 2007 she has held the chair of Latin at Uppsala University. Her research interests mainly cover the history of the Latin language, especially late Latin and textual criticism.

Tuomas Heikkilä is a historian concentrating on mediaeval history. His fields of expertise include hagiography, mediaeval book history, and stemmatology. Previously the director of the Finnish Institute in Rome, Heikkilä currently works at the University of Helsinki.

Armin Hoenen is a researcher and digital humanist at the Goethe University Frankfurt, where he teaches digital methods to humanities students. His research interests also include visualisation, phylogenetics, computational stylistics, lexicography, minority languages, language typology, digital Japanese studies, and the history and effects of medial transformations.

Christopher Howe is a biochemist at the University of Cambridge. His biochemical research interests concentrate on the biochemistry and evolution of photosynthesis, but with Heather Windram and others he has worked for many years on the application of phylogenetic methods from evolutionary biology to non-biological data.

Caroline Macé is a researcher at the Academy of Sciences and the Humanities in Göttingen. After a PhD in classics at the Oriental Institute in Louvain-la-Neuve, she worked at the universities of Leuven, Frankfurt, and Lausanne. Her main research fields include textual criticism, translation studies (Greek, Latin, Armenian, Georgian), and the *Physiologus*.

Sara Manafzadeh is an evolutionary biologist at the ETH Zurich. Her main research interests are the evolutionary and ecological processes that have shaped biodiversity across the planet, especially in the Irano-Turanian bioregion. She uses various tools, such as phylogenetics and niche modelling, to address her questions.

Outi Merisalo teaches Romance philology at the University of Jyväskylä and has published extensively on manuscript studies, Old French documents, Old and Middle French translations from Latin, Italian Renaissance texts, Scandinavian book history from the sixteenth to the eighteenth century, and medical manuscripts of the late Middle Ages.

Chaim Milikowsky teaches in the Talmud Department at Bar Ilan University, and has been Visiting Professor at Yale University and Yeshiva University, and also Visiting Fellow at All Souls' College, Oxford. He has published an 1,100-page edition of, introduction to, and commentary on *Seder Olam* (2013), a rabbinic chronography of the world, and is presently involved in projects focusing upon textual criticism and midrashic literature.

Heinz-Günther Nesselrath teaches classics at the Georg-August-Universität in Göttingen, Germany. His research interests are Greek literature of Roman imperial times and late Antiquity, Greek comedy, and Greek historiography (classical and Christian). Major recent publications include *Libanios, Zeuge einer schwindenden Welt* (2012), *Iulianus Augustus Opera* (2015), and *Herodot, Historien* (2017).

Christopher Nugent teaches Chinese language and literature at Williams College in Massachusetts, United States. His research interests include mediaeval Chinese manuscript culture, Dunhuang educational texts, and mediaeval mnemonic technologies.

Sinéad O'Sullivan is a mediaevalist at Queen's University, Belfast. She specialises in the reception of classical and late Antique texts in the early Middle Ages. Her main focus is on early mediaeval glosses and their importance.

Giovanni Palumbo teaches Romance philology at the University of Namur. He is a member of the Académie royale de Belgique. His research focuses mainly on mediaeval manuscript traditions and on textual criticism. He has provided scholarly editions of French and Italian texts of the Middle Ages and Renaissance.

Ralf Plate is a philologist of medieval German. He is a long-time contributor to the new Middle High German dictionary and heads its workgroup at Trier University. He teaches medieval German language at the Goethe University, Frankfurt, and publishes regularly on topics in the field of the manuscript traditions and textual criticism of medieval German.

Philipp Roelli is a Hellenist and mediaeval Latinist who works and teaches at the University of Zurich. His research interests include edition philology, corpus linguistics, monasticism, and Latin as language of scientific communication.

Teemu Roos is a computer scientist working on machine learning and its multidisciplinary applications at the University of Helsinki.

Yannick M. Staedler is an evolutionary biologist at the University of Vienna. His main research interests lie in the evolution of plant shape and function, and biological imaging.

Peter Stokes works and teaches at the Ecole pratique des hautes études, Université PSL. His main research interests include the palaeography of eleventh-century England and digital and computational approaches to palaeography, including especially the modelling and analysis of writing in manuscript books and charters.

Jamshid Tehrani is an anthropologist at Durham University, UK. He specialises in cultural evolution, with a particular interest in the application of phylogenetic methods to the study of narrative and material culture.

Paolo Trovato, after working at the universities of Leiden, Venice, and Salerno, now teaches the history of the Italian language at Ferrara. He has also served as visiting professor in Aix-en-Provence and Jerusalem. His main research fields include, inter alia, textual criticism. Since 2002, he has been working on a critical edition of Dante's *Commedia* (forthcoming).

Cristina Urchueguía teaches musicology at the University of Berne, Switzerland. She has been active as an editor of music and opera libretti. Reflection about editorial methods from an interdisciplinary and transnational perspective is one of her main research fields.

Dirk van Hulle teaches English literature at the University of Antwerp, where he directs the Centre for Manuscript Genetics. He has edited several works by Samuel Beckett in the Beckett Digital Manuscript Project and the Beckett Digital Library.

Joris J. van Zundert is a senior researcher in computational and digital humanities at the Huygens Institute for the History of the Netherlands in Amsterdam. His research interests include computational algorithms for the analysis of literary and historical texts, and the nature and properties of humanities data, information, and text modelling.

Iolanda Ventura teaches mediaeval Latin at the University of Bologna. Her research interests include the history of medical and pharmacological texts during the Middle Ages, and of encyclopedic literature. She is currently preparing a critical edition of the Salernitan pharmacological collection *Circa instans* (ca. 1150).

Gabriel Viehhauser is professor for digital humanities at the University of Stuttgart. His research interests include digital editions and digital text analysis. He is currently preparing an edition of a Nuremberg redaction of the *Heiligen Leben*, a collection of legends from the fifteenth century, that focuses on the comparison of variants.

Heather Windram is a researcher in the Department of Biochemistry at the University of Cambridge. With Christopher Howe, she has published widely on the application of phylogenetic methods from evolutionary biology to non-biological data, including both literary and musical textual traditions.

www.ingramcontent.com/pod-product-compliance
Lightning Source LLC
Chambersburg PA
CBHW081201240426
43669CB00040B/2898